Other Great Guides for Your Trip:

Frommer's Greek Islands

Frommer's Turkey

Frommer's Italy

Frommer's Europe

Frommer's Gay & Lesbian Europe

Frommer's European Cruises & Ports of Call

Here's what the critics say about Frommer's:

"Amazingly easy to use. Very portable, very complete."
—*Booklist*

◆

"The only mainstream guide to list specific prices. The Walter Cronkite of guidebooks—with all that implies."
—*Travel & Leisure*

◆

"Complete, concise, and filled with useful information."
—*New York Daily News*

◆

"Hotel information is close to encyclopedic."
—*Des Moines Sunday Register*

Greece

3rd Edition

by John S. Bowman,
Fran Wenograd Golden,
Sherry Marker, Mark Meagher
& Robert E. Meagher

HUNGRY MINDS, INC.

New York, NY • Cleveland, OH • Indianapolis, IN

PUBLISHED BY:

HUNGRY MINDS, INC.

909 Third Ave.
New York, NY 10022
www.frommers.com

ISBN 0-7645-6267-3
ISSN 1089-6007

Editor: Leslie Shen
With thanks to Vanessa Rosen, Olga Stavropoulos, Lorraine Festa, and Matt Hannafin
Production Editor: Tammy Ahrens
Photo Editor: Richard Fox
Design by Michele Laseau
Cartographers: Roberta Stockwell and Nick Trotter
Production by Hungry Minds Indianapolis Production Services

SPECIAL SALES

For general information on Hungry Minds' products and services please contact our Customer Care department; within the U.S. at 800-762-2974, outside the U.S. at 317-572-3993 or fax 317-572-4002. For sales inquiries and reseller information, including discounts, bulk sales, customized editions, and premium sales, please contact our Customer Care department at 800-434-3422.

Manufactured in the United States of America

5 4 3 2 1

Contents

List of Maps

ABOUT THE AUTHORS

John S. Bowman has been a freelance writer and editor for more than 35 years. He specializes in nonfiction ranging from archaeology to zoology, baseball to biography. He first visited Greece in 1956 and has traveled and lived there over the years. He is the author of numerous guides to regions of Greece and is best known for his *Traveller's Guide to Greece.* He currently resides in Northampton, Massachusetts.

Fran Wenograd Golden is author of *Cruise Vacations for Dummies* and writes about cruises and travel for the *Boston Herald,* Concierge.com, and Cruisemates.com. She is also the author of *Frommer's European Cruises & Ports of Call* and *TVacations: A Fun Guide to the Sites, the Stars, and the Inside Stories Behind Your Favorite TV Shows* (Pocket Books, 1996), and coauthor of *Frommer's Alaska Cruises & Ports of Call.* She lives north of Boston with her husband and two teenagers.

Sherry Marker majored in classical Greek at Harvard, studied archaeology at the American School of Classical Studies in Athens, and did graduate work in ancient history at the University of California at Berkeley. The author of a number of guides to Greece, she has also written for the *New York Times, Travel & Leisure,* and *Hampshire Life.* When not in Greece she lives in Massachusetts, where she teaches a writing seminar at Smith College.

Mark Meagher has passed many fine days exploring the Greek islands in search of the perfect beach, the most venerable ruin, and the ideal supper. A resident of Boston, he is currently pursuing graduate studies in architecture. Mark also contributes to *Frommer's Ireland, Frommer's Ireland from $60 a Day, Frommer's Portable Dublin,* and *Frommer's Europe from $60 a Day.*

Robert E. Meagher is Professor of Humanities at Hampshire College, Amherst, Massachusetts, where he teaches ancient East Mediterranean history, literature, and religion. He is the author of more than a dozen books, plays, and translations.

AN INVITATION TO THE READER

In researching this book, we discovered many wonderful places—hotels, restaurants, shops, and more. We're sure you'll find others. Please tell us about them, so we can share the information with your fellow travelers in upcoming editions. If you were disappointed with a recommendation, we'd love to know that, too. Please write to:

Frommer's Greece, 3rd Edition
Hungry Minds, Inc.
909 Third Ave.
New York, NY 10022

AN ADDITIONAL NOTE

Please be advised that travel information is subject to change at any time—and this is especially true of prices. We therefore suggest that you write or call ahead for confirmation when making your travel plans. The authors, editors, and publisher cannot be held responsible for the experiences of readers while traveling. Your safety is important to us, however, so we encourage you to stay alert and be aware of your surroundings. Keep a close eye on cameras, purses, and wallets, all favorite targets of thieves and pickpockets.

WHAT THE SYMBOLS MEAN

✪ Frommer's Favorites

Our favorite places and experiences—outstanding for quality, value, or both.

The following abbreviations are used for credit cards:

AE	American Express	ER	EnRoute
CB	Carte Blanche	JCB	Japan Credit Bank
DC	Diners Club	MC	MasterCard
DISC	Discover	V	Visa
EC	Eurocard		

FIND FROMMER'S ONLINE

www.frommers.com offers up-to-the-minute listings on almost 200 cities around the globe—including the latest bargains and candid, personal articles updated daily by Arthur Frommer himself. No other Web site offers such comprehensive and timely coverage of the world of travel.

The Best of Greece

Greece is, of course, the land of ancient sites and architectural treasures—the Acropolis in Athens, the amphitheater of Epidaurus, and the reconstructed palace at Knossos being among the best known. But Greece is much more: it offers age-old spectacular natural sights, for instance—from Santorini's caldera to the gray pinnacles of rock of the Meteora—and modern diversions ranging from elegant museums to luxury resorts. It can be bewildering to plan your trip with so many options vying for your attention. Take us along and we'll do the work for you. We've traveled the country extensively and chosen the very best that Greece has to offer. We've explored the archaeological sites, visited the museums, inspected the hotels, reviewed the tavernas and ouzeries, and scoped out the beaches. Here's what we consider to be the best of the best.

1 The Best Travel Experiences

- **Making Haste Slowly:** Give yourself time to sit in a seaside taverna and watch the fishing boats come and go. If you're visiting Greece in the spring, take the time to smell the flowers: The fields are covered with poppies and daisies. Even in Athens, you'll see hardy species growing through the cracks in concrete sidewalks— or better yet, visit Athens's ancient agora, which will be carpeted in a dazzling variety of wildflowers. See chapter 5.
- **Island-Hopping in the Cyclades:** Though the Cyclades are bound by unmistakable family resemblance, each island has its own unique personality. Distances between islands are small, making travel by ferry pleasant and logistically straightforward (at least in principle). The element of uncertainty inherent to ferry timetables and all island events is part of the experience, and your vacation will be much less stressful if you don't plan too much in advance and allow yourself to "go with the flow." See chapter 9.
- **Leaving the Beaten Path:** Persist against your body's and mind's signals that "this may be pushing too far," leave the main routes and major attractions behind, and make your own discoveries of landscape, villages, or activities. For instance, seek out some obscure church or monastery such as Moni Ayios Nikolaos outside Metsovo—to be rewarded by a moving encounter with the church and its caretaker. Such experiences can still happen—but you must overrule common sense! See chapter 13.

- **Exploring the Naturalists' Greece:** There is a Greece beyond the columns and cafes—a land of rugged terrain and wildflowers and birds and other natural forms and phenomena. Sign up to join a special tour (see chapter 2) or go it alone with one of the several beautifully illustrated handbooks available, such as George Sfikas's *Wildflowers of Greece* (Efstathiadis Books) or *Birds of Europe* (McGraw-Hill), by Bertel Bruun and Arthur Singer. And don't forget your binoculars!

2 The Best of Ancient Greece

- **The Acropolis** (Athens): No matter how many photographs you've seen, nothing can prepare you for watching the light turn the marble of the buildings, still standing after thousands of years, from honey to rose to deep red to stark white. If the crowds get you down, remember how crowded the Acropolis was during religious festivals in antiquity. See chapter 5.
- **Nemea** (Peloponnese): This gem of a site has it all: a beautifully restored stadium, a handsome museum, and picnic tables with a view of the romantic Doric temple with its three long-standing columns. If you're lucky, you may see Nemea's archaeologists lovingly reconstructing and re-erecting columns from the temple's north facade in an ambitious restoration project. See chapter 7.
- **Olympia** (Peloponnese) **& Delphi** (Central Greece): Try to visit both Olympia, where the Olympic Games began, and Delphi, home of the Delphic Oracle. That's the only way you'll be able to decide whether you think Olympia, with its massive temples and shady groves of trees, or Delphi, perched on mountain slopes overlooking olive trees and the sea, is the most beautiful ancient site in Greece. See chapters 7 and 11.
- **Palace of Knossos** (Crete): A seemingly unending maze of rooms and levels and stairways and corridors and frescoed walls—the Minoan Palace of Knossos. It can be packed at peak hours, but it still exerts its power if you enter into the spirit of the labyrinth, where King Minos ruled over the richest and most powerful of Minoan cities and, according to legend, his daughter Ariadne helped Theseus kill the Minotaur and escape. See chapter 8.
- **Delos** (Cyclades): This temple city, on a tiny isle just 2 miles offshore of Mykonos, was considered by the ancient Greeks to be the spiritual center of the Cyclades and its holiest sanctuary. Although in ruins, much of this remarkable site still remains in testament to its former grandeur. From Mount Kinthos (really just a hill, but the island's highest point), you can see the whole archipelago on a clear day. The 3 hours allotted by excursion boats from Mykonos or Tinos are hardly sufficient to explore this vast archaeological treasure. See chapter 9.
- **Vergina** (Northern Greece): In the brilliantly designed museum here, you can peek into what may have been the tomb of Alexander the Great's father, Philip of Macedon, and see the more than 300 burial mounds that stretch for miles across the Macedonian plain. See chapter 15.

3 The Best of Byzantine Greece

- **Mistra** (Peloponnese): This Byzantine ghost town has streets lined with the remains of homes both humble and palatial, as well as some of the most beautiful churches in all Greece. If you have the energy, climb to the top of the defense walls for the superb view over the plain of Sparta. Try to visit in the spring, when Mistra is carpeted with wildflowers. See chapter 7.

- **Church of Panayia Kera** (Kritsa, Crete): If Byzantine art sometimes seems a bit stilted and remote, this striking chapel in the foothills of eastern Crete will reward you with its unexpected intimacy. The 14th- and 15th-century frescoes not only are stunning, but also depict all the familiar Biblical stories. See chapter 8.
- **The Churches of Thessaloniki** (Northern Greece): Thessaloniki's Byzantine churches are the finest not just in Greece, but in the entire world. From the tiny Osios David to the towering Ayios Dimitrios, these churches boast mosaics and frescoes that give you an astonishing glimpse of the artistic grandeur of the mighty Byzantine empire. See chapter 15.
- **Nea Moni** (Hios, Northeastern Aegean): Once home to 1,000 monks, this 12th-century monastery high in the interior mountains of Hios is now quietly inhabited by one elderly but sprightly nun and two friendly monks—try to catch one of the excellent tours sometimes offered by the monks. The mosaics in the cathedral dome are works of extraordinary power and beauty; even in the half-obscurity of the nave they radiate a brilliant gold. Check out the small museum, and take some time to explore the extensive monastery grounds. See chapter 16.

4 The Best Beaches

- **Nafplion** (Peloponnese): After a vigorous and tiring day of sightseeing, this small municipal beach can seem like the best in Greece. Handy changing rooms and showers make this a great place for a quick break between exploring the ruins at Mycenae and heading off to take in a play at Epidaurus. See chapter 7.
- **Plaka** (Naxos, Cyclades): Naxos has the longest stretches of sea sand in the Cyclades, and Plaka is the most beautiful and pristine beach on the island. A 3-mile stretch of mostly undeveloped shoreline, you could easily imagine yourself here as Robinson Crusoe in his island isolation (bending the plot somewhat to include a few sunbathing Fridays). If you need abundant amenities and a more active social scene, you can always head north to Ayia Anna or Ayios Prokopios. See chapter 9.
- **Paradise** (Mykonos, Cyclades): Paradise is the quintessential party beach, known for wild revelry that continues through the night. An extensive complex built on the beach includes a bar, taverna, changing rooms, and souvenir shops. This is a place to see and be seen, a place to show off muscles laboriously acquired during the long winter months. Don't miss the opportunity to experience the pure, unrestrained hedonism on which Mykonos has built its international reputation. See chapter 9.
- **Grammata** (Siros, Cyclades): Grammata possesses all the elements of a vision of paradise. The small beach is enclosed by a lush oasis of palm trees at the outlet of a natural spring, sheltered and hidden by a rocky promontory extending into the bay. The beach is only accessible on foot or by boat, so it's rarely crowded. See chapter 9.
- **Lalaria Beach** (Skiathos, Sporades): This gleaming white pebble beach boasts vivid aquamarine water and white limestone cliffs, with natural arches cut into them by the elements. Lalaria is not nearly as popular nor accessible as Skiathos's famous Koukounaries, which is one of the reasons why it's still gorgeous and pristine. See chapter 12.
- **Megalo Seitani** (Samos, Northeastern Aegean): Megalo Seitani and its neighbor, Micro Seitani, are situated on the mountainous and remote northwest coast of Samos. There aren't any roads to this part of the island, so the only way to reach

the beaches is a short boat ride or a rather long (and beautiful) hike. You won't regret taking the trouble, since both beaches are superb: Micro Seitani's crescent of pebbles in a rocky cove, and Megalo Seitani's expanse of pristine sand. See chapter 16.

- **Vroulidia** (Hios, Northeastern Aegean): White sand, a cliff-rimmed cove, and a remote location at the southern tip of the island of Hios combine to make this one of the most exquisite small beaches in the Northeastern Aegean. The rocky coast conceals many cove beaches similar to this one, and it's rare for them to become crowded. See chapter 16.

5 The Best Scenic Villages & Towns

- **Monemvassia & Nafplion** (Peloponnese): Everyone says it, and for once, everyone is right: Nafplion is the loveliest town in the Peloponnese, and Monemvassia is the region's most spectacular village. Thanks to the speedy hydrofoils (Flying Dolphins), you can visit both spots and decide for yourself which has the best cafes, castles, and sunsets. See chapter 7.
- **Chania** (Crete): Radiating from its handsome harbor and backdropped by the White Mountains, Chania has managed to hold on to much of its Venetian-Renaissance and later Turkish heritage. This allows you to wander the old town's narrow lanes, filled with a heady mix of colorful local culture, yet still enjoy its charming hotels, excellent restaurants, interesting shops, and swinging nightspots. See chapter 8.
- **Hora** (Folegandros, Cyclades): In this town huddled at the edge of a cliff, one square spills into the next, its green and blue paving slates outlined in brilliant white. On a steep hill overlooking the town is the looming form of Panayia, the church that holds an icon of the Virgin which is paraded through the streets of Hora with great ceremony and revelry each Easter Sunday. Mercifully free of vehicular traffic, Hora is one of the most beautiful and least spoiled villages in the Cyclades. See chapter 9.
- **Yialos** (Simi, Dodecanese): The entirety of Yialos, the main port of the tiny, rugged island of Simi, has been declared a protected architectural treasure, and for good reason. This pristine port with its extraordinary array of neoclassical mansions is a large part of why Simi is known as "the jewel of the Dodecanese." See chapter 10.
- **Skopelos Town** (Skopelos, Sporades): The amazingly well-preserved Skopelos, a traditional whitewashed island port town, is adorned everywhere with pots of flowering plants. It offers some fairly sophisticated diversions, several excellent restaurants, some good hotels, and lots of shopping. See chapter 12.
- **Metsovo** (Western Greece): Steep slopes, ever-green conifers, stone houses with slate and slanted roofs, stolid villagers in traditional clothing speaking a Latin-based language—if this is Thursday, you must be in Switzerland. But no, it's Metsovo, in Epirus. Occasionally jammed with excursionists, this mountain town still comes through as an authentic locale, refreshing in the summer and invigorating in the winter ski season. See chapter 13.
- **Corfu Town** (Corfu, Ionian Islands): With its Esplanade framed by a 19th-century palace and the arcaded Liston, its old town a Venice-like warren of structures practically untouched for several centuries, its massive Venetian fortresses, and all this enclosing a lively population and constant visitors, here is urban Greece at its most appealing. See chapter 14.

- **Piryi & Mesta** (Hios, Northeastern Aegean): These two small towns, in the pastoral southern hills of Hios, are marvelous creations of the medieval imagination. Connected by their physical proximity and a shared history, each is quirkily unique and a delight to explore. In Piryi, every available surface is covered with elaborate geometric black-and-white decorations known as *Ksisti*, a technique that reaches extraordinary levels of virtuosity in the town square. Mesta has preserved its medieval urban fabric, and conceals two fine churches within its maze of narrow streets. See chapter 16.

6 The Best Islands

- **Hydra** (Saronic Gulf Islands): Old-timers keep waiting for Hydra, with its handsome stone mansions overlooking a picture-postcard harbor, to be "spoiled." After all, even before Mykonos and Santorini, Hydra was one of the first Greek islands to be "discovered." So far, so good: donkeys still outnumber motorcycles, and the day-trippers who blitz the appealing harborside shops leave at twilight. That means you can almost always find the table you want at one of Hydra's pleasant small restaurants. See chapter 6.
- **Crete:** Whether for its rugged mountains or its countless beaches, its ancient remains or its ultramodern hotels, its layered history or its intense people, Crete cannot be denied. It is not just a distinctive Greek island—it is a world unto itself. See chapter 8.
- **Santorini** (Cyclades): This is undoubtedly one of the most spectacular islands in the world. The streets of Fira and Ia are carved into the face of a high cliff, overlooking the circular caldera left by an ancient volcanic eruption and now filled with the deep blue waters of the Aegean. The site of Akrotiri offers a unique glimpse into life in a Minoan city, frozen in time by the eruption 3,600 years ago. Add to this the Fira nightlife scene, and you'll see why this is one of the most popular (and overcrowded) summer vacation spots in the Aegean. See chapter 9.
- **Siros** (Cyclades): This tiny island has it all: a vivacious, cosmopolitan capital town; thriving beach resorts; and a starkly beautiful region of farming communities, archaeological remains, and remote beaches to the north. Siros is also one of the centers of *rembetika*, a form of Greek traditional music with roots in Asia Minor; the *Fragosiriani,* a classic known throughout Greece, was composed by the Siriot Markos Vamvakaris, and you're sure to hear its simple and infectious rhythms many times during your stay here. See chapter 9.
- **Rhodes** (Dodecanese): The island of Rhodes has everything a visitor could want—dazzling ancient and medieval ruins, great food, spectacular beaches, and the hottest nightlife outside of Athens—the one drawback being that everyone knows it. See chapter 10.
- **Skyros** (Sporades): Winding roads and remote beaches, one main town and a few minor villages, some ancient legends and 20th-century tales: Skyros's charms remain perhaps the most elusive of the four Northern Sporades. But though the island remains a bit difficult to access and still not overstocked with touristy amenities, Skyros also offers both a living local culture and some natural wildness. See chapter 12.
- **Corfu** (Ionian Islands): Lush vegetation, some still undeveloped interior and unspoiled coast, ancient sites and a 19th-century presence, a dash of Italy and a dose of the cosmopolitan, Corfu is a Greek island like no other. Tourism may be rampant, but Corfu's attractions have survived worse. See chapter 14.

- **Hios** (Northeastern Aegean): You'd think that an island with such gorgeous beaches, exquisite medieval towns, and remarkable scenery wouldn't remain a secret for long. Despite the qualities that attract a small group of devotees year after year, Hios remains surprisingly quiet. If you like the idea of getting away from the tour buses, being alone on a beach to rival any in the Cyclades, and exploring towns that preserve the contours of medieval life, Hios is for you. Another benefit: the local hospitality hasn't worn thin here, as it has on many of the more heavily toured islands. See chapter 16.

7 The Best Places to Get Away from It All

- **National Garden** (Athens): It's all too easy to overlook this oasis of calm and cool in the heart of Athens. If you explore, you'll discover shady benches, a small cafe, and lots of opportunities to enjoy watching Greek families out for a stroll. See chapter 5.
- **Folegandros** (Cyclades): Many visitors have passed the formidable Folegandros cliffs from the Santorini-Paros ferry, and glimpsed whitewashed Kastro walls perched 300 meters above the sea. The austere beauty of Hora, the fine beaches, and the great walking trails are no longer a secret, but if you arrive off-season, Folegandros still offers a restful retreat. Completely free from the commercialism that has engulfed so many Aegean isles, the only shopping here seems to involve milk, bread, and eggs. There's still no bank; a recent addition is a taxi that travels up and down the island's only paved road. See chapter 9.
- **Sifnos** (Cyclades): Sifnos is an island of ravines, mountaintops, and pristine beaches. Despite its small size (a hardy walker can explore the entire island on foot), Sifnos has numerous attractive small towns which can be used as bases for your explorations. Apollonia, in the central hills, offers elegant small-town civility, with the added benefit of being the hub of an excellent public transportation system. Kastro, on its seaside rock, is the medieval locus of the island, while Platis Yialos is a quiet beach resort. Don't visit in August, when the island is mobbed with vacationing Athenians. See chapter 9.
- **Zagori & the Vikos Gorge** (Western Greece): If the 40-some tiny villages linked by roads lined with spectacular terrain are not enough, you can venture into at least a section of one of the most spectacular gorges in Europe. Greeks and some Europeans have long appreciated this undeveloped corner of northwestern Greece known as the Zagoria. See chapter 13.

8 The Best Museums

- **National Archaeological Museum** (Athens): This stunning collection has it all: superb red and black figured vases, bronze statues, Mycenaean gold, marble reliefs of gods and goddesses, and the hauntingly beautiful frescoes from Akrotiri, the Minoan site on the island of Santorini. See chapter 5.
- **Museum of Greek Popular Musical Instruments** (Athens): Life-size photos of musicians beside their actual instruments and recordings of traditional Greek music make this one of the country's most charming museums to visit. On our last visit, an elderly Greek gentleman listened to some music, transcribed it, stepped out into the courtyard, and played it on his own violin! See chapter 5.
- **Archaeological Museum of Iraklion** (Crete): Few museums in the world can boast of holding virtually all the important remains of a major culture. This museum's Minoan collection is just that, including superb frescoes from

Knossos, elegant bronze and stone figurines, and exquisite gold jewelry. The museum also contains Neolithic, Archaic Greek, and Roman finds from throughout Crete. See chapter 8.

- **Archaeological Museum of Chania** (Crete): Let's hear it for a truly engaging provincial museum, not one full of masterworks but rather of representative works from thousands of years, a collection that lets us see how most people probably experienced their worlds. All this in a former Italian-Renaissance church that makes you feel you're in a special place. See chapter 8.
- **Archaeological Museum of Thessaloniki** (Northern Greece): This is the place to go to see the gold star of Vergina, a profusion of delicate gold wreaths, and the gold box that may have held the bones of Philip of Macedon, father of Alexander the Great—all found in the royal tombs at and around Vergina. These Macedonian treasures tend to draw the crowds, so you may find that you have the rest of the collection—including fascinating exhibits on the early history of Thessaloniki—almost to yourself. See chapter 15.

9 The Best of Greece's Religious Treasures

- **Panayia Evanyelistria** (Tinos, Cyclades): The most revered Eastern Orthodox shrine in Greece, Evanyelistria is a neoclassical gem, filled to the gills with treasures. It's above the pleasant port of Tinos town, on one of the friendliest, most hospitable islands in Greece. See chapter 9.
- **Patmos** (Dodecanese): For 2 millennia, this small island of more than 300 churches has been hallowed ground, a place of pilgrimage. The Monastery of St. John the Divine and the Cave of the Apocalypse, where St. John is said to have dictated the Book of Revelation, are among the most revered and wondrous Byzantine treasures in the world. See chapter 10.
- **The Monasteries of the Meteora** (Central Greece): Even from a distance, the monasteries perched atop the weird rock formations and mini-mountains of the Meteora are one of the most awesome sights in Greece. Inside, the monasteries are equally impressive, with fine collections of manuscripts, frescoed chapels, shy monks, and chatty nuns. See chapter 11.
- **The Aslan Pasha Mosque & Cami at Ioannina** (Western Greece): Little of Greece's Turkish-Muslim phase has survived beyond the odd minaret, but here on the promontory of the walled quarter of Ioannina are the still-solid fine old mosque (now a museum), minaret, and school. Picturesque from afar, they speak up close of Ioannina's—and Greece's—diverse past. See chapter 13.
- **Mount Athos** (Northern Greece): Only men can visit the Holy Mountain, where monks still live in isolation in some of the most isolated—and beautiful—monasteries in all Greece. If you can't go to Athos itself, take heart: The boats from Ouranopolis that cruise around the peninsula offer excellent views of the rugged, pine-clad promontory and some of the monasteries. See chapter 15.

10 The Best Resorts & Hotels

- **Andromeda Hotel** (Athens; ☎ 01/643-7302): The city's only real "boutique" hotel, located on a wonderfully quiet side street, the classy Andromeda offers charm, comfort, and a reassuringly helpful staff. See chapter 4.
- **Malvasia** (Monemvassia, Peloponnese; ☎ 0732/62-223): Each room in the Malvasia is different, with some of the nicest overlooking the sea; all are tastefully furnished with hand-loomed rugs and antiques. A visit here gives the illusion of

staying in the home of wealthy Greek friends of enormous taste—who just happen to be away, but have left the staff behind to tend to your needs. See chapter 7.

- **Atlantis Hotel** (Iraklion, Crete; ☎ **081/229-103**): There are many more luxurious hotels in Greece, but few can beat the Atlantis's urban attractions: a central location, modern facilities, and views over a busy harbor. You can swim in the pool, work out in the fitness center, send e-mail via your laptop, and then within minutes be enjoying a fine meal or visiting a museum. See chapter 8.
- **Doma** (Chania, Crete; ☎ **0821/51-772**): A former neoclassical mansion east of downtown, the Doma has been converted into a comfortable and charming hotel, furnished with the proprietor's family heirlooms. Although not for those seeking the most luxurious amenities, its atmosphere appeals to many. See chapter 8.
- **Astra Apartments** (Santorini, Cyclades; ☎ **0286/23-641**): This small hotel with handsomely appointed apartments looks like a miniature whitewashed village—and has spectacular views over Santorini's famous caldera. The sunsets here are not to be believed, the staff is incredibly helpful, and the village of Imerovigli itself offers an escape from the touristic madness that overwhelms the island each summer. See chapter 9.
- **Chelidonia** (Santorini, Cyclades; ☎ **0286/71-287**): These traditional houses occupy a sheltered furrow in the Ia cliff-face known locally as *Chelidonia,* the place where the swallows roost. Triandafyllos Pitsikalis began by renovating his childhood home, and has since built several other houses in the vicinity, each with its own unique curvilinear geometry. The fresh herbs on the terraces and comfortably functional furnishings make these houses feel like home. Add the quiet location in an appealing village and the intoxicating caldera view, and you have one of the finest places in the Aegean for a restful getaway. See chapter 9.
- **Castro Hotel** (Folegandros, Cyclades; ☎ **0286/41-230**): With some rooms perched directly over a 250-meter sea cliff, the simple Castro has one of the best locations in the Cyclades. Situated in a 12th-century Venetian castle, the hotel has lots of character, and a 1993 renovation added the necessary modern comforts. The Danassi family are gracious hosts, and Despo Danassi prepares a delicious breakfast. Come during the off-season to assure yourself one of the remarkable seaside rooms. See chapter 9.
- **Rodos Palace** (Rhodes, Dodecanese; ☎ **0241/25-222**): The largest five-star hotel in Greece and possibly in the entire Mediterranean, this is truly a palace, decorated, in fact, by the famed designer of *Ben Hur* and *Quo Vadis.* Located in Iksia, just outside Rhodes city, it offers all the amenities imaginable—the latest addition is a new family center, a resort within a resort designed to provide the ultimate holiday for families with children. See chapter 10.
- **Hotel Nireus** (Simi, Dodecanese; ☎ **0241/72-400**): Perfect island, perfect location, unpretentious, and tasteful—we nearly had to be pried loose from here. The views from the sea-facing rooms, framed by the fluid swirls of the wrought-iron balcony, define the spell of this little gem of an island. You'll never regret one more night on Simi, and here's the place to spend it. See chapter 10.
- **White Rocks Hotel & Bungalows** (Kefalonia, Ionian Islands; ☎ **0671/28-332**): For those who appreciate understated elegance, a shady retreat from all that sunshine, a private beach, and quiet but attentive service, this hotel, located a couple of miles outside Argostoli, can be paradise. See chapter 14.

11 The Best Restaurants

- **Vlassis** (Athens; ☎ **01/646-3060**): This small restaurant with a very loyal following, ranging from prominent ambassadors to struggling artists, serves traditional (*paradisiako*) Greek cooking at its very best. A tempting choice if you have only one night in Athens—but be sure to make a reservation. See chapter 4.
- **Varoulko** (Piraeus; ☎ **01/411-2043**): Everything here is seafood, and everything here is so good that many Athenians believe chef/owner Lefteris Lazarou has created not just the finest restaurant serving only seafood, but the finest restaurant in the greater Athens area. See chapter 4.
- **Taverna Klimataria** (Methoni, Peloponnese; ☎ **0723/31-544**): If there's a better restaurant in the Peloponnese, we haven't found it. The Klimataria takes old familiar dishes like fried zucchini and eggplant salad and makes them taste fresh and new—and offers delicacies such as chicken in puff pastry that are unheard of in rural regional restaurants. The staff is congenial, the wine delicious, and eating under the stars in the vine-hung garden is everything that dining out in Greece should be. See chapter 7.
- **Nykterida** (Chania, Crete; ☎ **0821/64-215**): We're not denying that the location may influence your taste buds here, but the spectacular views from this restaurant high above Chania and Soudha Bay can definitely make you feel you're eating a meal like few others in Greece. See chapter 8.
- **To Koutouki Tou Liberi** (Siros, Cyclades; ☎ **0281/85-580**): Open only 2 days a week and devilishly difficult to find (even the local taxi drivers have a hard time), this restaurant is so popular that you may need to book a table several days in advance. Amazingly, it's worth the trouble—the food is excellent, the view is stunning, and you might even catch an impromptu traditional music session if you're willing to stay around until the early hours of the morning. See chapter 9.
- **Papadakis** (Paros, Cyclades; ☎ **0284/51047**): Argyro Barbarigou has made a name for herself as one of the most creative cooks on Paros, an island known for good food. Her appetizers conjure subtle variations on traditional Greek fare, with results that elicit superlatives from the most laconic diners. The fresh fish, grilled by her husband, Manolis, is also a delight. See chapter 9.
- **Petrino** (Kos, Dodecanese; ☎ **0242/27-251**): When royalty come to Kos, this is where they dine. Housed in an exquisitely restored, two-story, century-old stone (*petrino*) private residence, this is hands-down the most elegant taverna in Kos, with cuisine to match. This is what Greek home cooking would be if your mother were part divine. See chapter 10.
- **Venetian Well** (Corfu, Ionian Islands; ☎ **0661/44-761**): A bit severe in its setting at the edge of a small enclosed square in Corfu town, with no attempt at the picturesque, this restaurant gets by on its more esoteric, international, and delicate menu. It's for those seeking a break from the standard Greek scene. See chapter 14.

12 The Best Nightlife

- **Theater Under the Stars** (Athens and Epidaurus, Peloponnese): If you can, take in a performance of whatever is on at the Herodes Atticus Theater in Athens, the theater at Epidaurus, or the theater at Dodona. You'll be sitting where people have sat for thousands of years to enjoy a play under Greece's magical night sky. See chapters 5 and 7.

- **Mykonos** (Cyclades): Mykonos isn't the only island town in Greece with nightlife that continues through the morning, but it was the first and still offers the most abundant, varied scene in the Aegean. Year-round, the town's narrow, labyrinthine streets play host to a remarkably diverse crowd—Mykonos's unlimited ability to reinvent itself has assured it of continuous popularity. The spring and fall tend to be more sober and sophisticated, while the 3 months of summer are reserved for unrestrained revelry. See chapter 9.
- **Rhodes** (Dodecanese): From cafes to casinos, Rhodes has not only the reputation, but also the stuff to back it up. A good nightlife scene is ultimately a matter of who shows up—and this, too, is where Rhodes stands out. It's the place to be seen, and, if nobody seems to be looking, you can always watch. See chapter 10.
- **Skiathos** (Sporades): With as many as 50,000 foreigners packing this tiny island during the high season, the many nightspots in Skiathos town are often jammed with a mostly younger set. If you don't like the music at one club, just move across the street. See chapter 12.
- **Corfu** (Ionian Islands): If often-raucous nightspots are what you look for on a holiday, Corfu offers probably the largest concentration in all Greece. Most of these are at beach resorts frequented by younger foreigners. Corfu town, however, also offers more sedate locales. Put simply, Corfu hosts a variety of music and dancing and "socializing" opportunities. See chapter 14.

13 The Best Natural Wonders

- **The Caves of Dirou** (Peloponnese): No one knows just how far these caves run into the seaside cliffs of Dirou in the Peloponnese's Mani peninsula. You can get some idea of how vast they are by taking a tour on one of the boats that explore this underground labyrinth. See chapter 7.
- **Samaria Gorge** (Crete): At 18 kilometers (11 miles) long, the Samaria is the longest gorge in Europe. But although its walls reach up to 500 meters and at one point are only 2 meters apart, it's not the physical dimensions that attract thousands each year. For that, you can credit the wildflowers, the cold stream, and the whole experience of making your way from the heart of Crete to its coast. See chapter 8.
- **The Santorini Caldera** (Cyclades): As you approach Santorini by ferry, the whitewashed clifftop villages of Ia and Fira resemble at first a new dusting of mountain snow. Then the ferry enters the caldera, the cliff walls rise steeply on either side, and you're suddenly enclosed in a fantastic bowl whose sides are formed of red, yellow, and ochre rock, and whose surface is the shimmering blue Aegean. Some 3,600 years ago, the center of the island was blown away in a colossal volcanic eruption, leaving behind a roughly circular depression in the sea floor and the crescent-shaped sliver of rock known as Santorini. The best places to view the caldera are the walking path between Fira and Ia, or the clifftop streets in either of these two towns. See chapter 9.
- **Vikos Gorge** (Western Greece): With its wooded slopes, often taxing terrain, and rugged riverbed, the Vikos Gorge in Epirus is in many ways at least as impressive as the far better known Samaria Gorge of Crete. Its remoteness means that it is also far less frequented—and that much more of a wilderness challenge. See chapter 13.

Planning a Trip to Greece

by John S. Bowman

Before any trip, most of us like to do a bit of advance planning. When should I go? What is this trip going to cost me? Will there be a special holiday when I visit? What special bits of practical advice might I appreciate? We'll answer these and other questions for you in this chapter.

1 The Regions in Brief

by Robert E. Meagher

Greece is a land of sea and mountains. Over a fifth of the Greek land mass is comprised of islands, numbering several thousand if you count every floating crag—and nowhere in Greece will you find yourself more than 96 kilometers (60 miles) from the sea. It should come as no surprise that the sea molds the Greek imagination, as well as its history.

Mainland Greece, meanwhile, is a great vertebrate, with the Pindos range reaching from north to south, and continuing, like a tail, through the Peloponnese. The highest of its peaks is Mount Olympus, the seat of the gods, nearly 10,000 feet above sea level. Eighty percent of the Greek mainland is mountainous, which you will rapidly discover whether you make your way on foot or on wheels.

ATHENS Whether you're arriving by sea or air, chances are you'll be debarking in Athens. The city is not always pleasant and is sometimes exhausting, yet it's simply invaluable. Its **archaeological sites** and its **museums** alone warrant a couple of days of exploration. Between visits to the sites, a stroll in the **National Garden** will prove reviving. Then, after dark as the city cools, the old city streets of the **Plaka** provide atmospheric strolling, shopping, and informal dining, while the square and lanes of **Kolonaki** provide an upscale version of the same. **Piraeus,** as in antiquity, serves as the port of Athens and the jumping-off point to most of the islands.

Athens is also a great base for day trips, whether to the temple of Poseidon at **Cape Sounion,** the forested slopes of **Mount Hymettus (Imittos),** the monastery of **Kaisariani (Kessariani),** the sanctuary of Artemis at **Brauron (Vravrona),** the Byzantine monastery of **Daphni,** the legendary plains of **Marathon,** or the ruins of **Eleusis,** place of ancient mysteries.

THE SARONIC GULF ISLANDS Cupped between Attica and the Peloponnese, in the sheltering Saronic Gulf, these islands offer both proximity and retreat for the nearly four million Athenians who, like

Greece

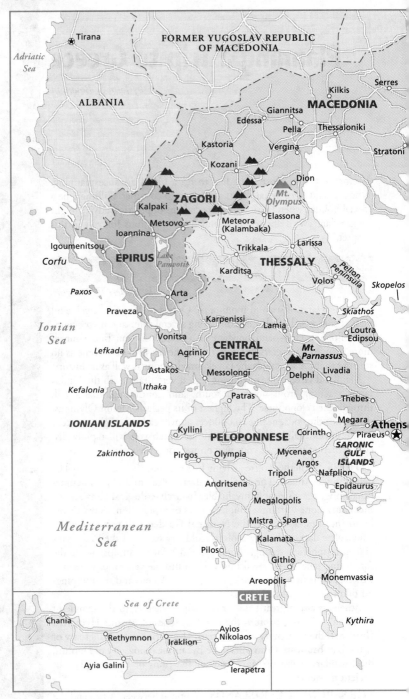

BULGARIA

Drama Xanthi **THRACE**

Kavala Komotini TURKEY

Alexandroupolis *Sea of Marmara*

Black Sea

Thasos

Samothraki

▲ **Mt. Athos**

Limnos

Aegean Sea

Alonissos

SPORADES

Skyros

Lesvos

NORTHEASTERN AEGEAN ISLANDS

TURKEY

Kimi

EVVIA

Karystos

Hios

Andros

Sounion *Samos*

Kea *Tinos*

Siros *Mykonos*

Delos *Patmos*

Serifos *Paros* *Naxos* *Donoussa* *Kalimnos*

Antiparos

Sifnos *Kos*

CYCLADES

Ios *Amorgos*

Milos *Folegandros*

Simi

Anafi

DODECANESE

Santorini

Rhodes

0   25 mi
0   25 km   N   Mountain ▲▲

Karpathos

Izmir

13

their visitors, long for calming waters and cooler breezes. The accessibility of these islands, on any given day or especially weekend in high season, can be their downfall. Choose carefully your day and island, or you may be part of the crowd you're trying to avoid.

Aegina, so near to Athens as to be a daily commute, is the most besieged and yet possesses its own character and charm. The main port town of Aegina is picturesque and pleasant, while across the island to the east, set atop a pine-crested hill, stands the remarkably preserved temple of Aphaia, a Doric gem. **Poros,** next in line proceeding south, is convenient both to Athens and to the Peloponnese. Its beaches and lively port are a real draw, and there's an ancient temple thrown in, scenically situated but mostly in a heap.

Still further to the south lies car-less **Hydra,** remarkable for its natural beauty and Italianate architecture. The port of Hydra has a lot to offer and knows it, all of which is reflected in the prices. It's a great place for pleasant strolls, views, and a swim. **Spetses,** the farthest of these islands from Athens, wins the getaway prize, with its exceptional beaches, comparatively lush interior, and lineup of noteworthy restaurants.

THE PELOPONNESE   Crossing the narrow isthmus—less than 4 miles across at its narrowest point—into the southern peninsula of Greece is a move you will never regret. Once an island, the Peloponnese retains a sense of remove from the north and from the rest of Greece. Its often barren landscape is virtually forested with stunning archaeological remains, each with a richly evocative past: **Mycenae,** the mountain citadel of Agamemnon; **Olympia,** birthplace of the Olympic Games; **Sparta,** home of Helen and Menelaus; the palace of Nestor at **Pylos;** the magnificent and active theater of **Epidaurus;** and the Bema at **Corinth,** where Paul addressed the Corinthians. The small but stately port of **Nafplion** provides a comfortable, convenient base from which to explore the surrounding sites.

At least two drives are worth going out of your way for. One is the spectacular coastal stretch from **Areopoli to Kalamata;** the other is the vertiginous climb and descent of the **Taygetos** mountains en route from Sparta to the monastic ghost city of **Mistra** and on to the western coastal town of Pylos. In fact, the entire three-fingered southern tip of the peninsula is unspoiled and splendid, with first-class destinations at **Monemvassia,** the **Mani,** the caves of **Dirou,** and the Venetian castles of **Koroni** and **Methoni.**

CRETE   The largest of the Greek islands, birthplace of the painter El Greco, possesses a landscape so diverse, concentrated, and enchanting that no description is likely to do it justice. Especially if you rent a car and do your own exploring, a week will pass like a day. More or less circling the island on the national highway (don't imagine an interstate) will take you to a ring of inviting ports like **Rethymnon, Chania, Ayios Nikolaos,** and **Iraklion,** the capital.

Venturing into the heartland of Crete—not far, since Crete's width ranges from 12 to 56 kilometers (7.5 to 35 miles)—you'll find the legendary palaces of the Minoans just as they once were, with a little imagination: **Knossos, Phaestos,** and **Ayia Triadha,** to mention only a few. This is not to say that Crete is without monasteries and Venetian ruins. It's Greece, after all. For the energetic, the **Gorge of Samaria** calls out, as does the sea.

When night falls, remember that Crete has been known for thousands of years for its wines, which complement nicely the fresh goat cheese and olives, all local and all part of Crete's spell.

THE CYCLADES   The "Cyclades"—the "encirclers" or "circling islands"—have at their center the ancient spiritual, cultural, and commercial hub of the Aegean, the

Greece on the Web

Anyone with access to the World Wide Web can obtain a fair amount of information about Greece. Sites are constantly being changed and added, but among the most useful for broad-based searches are:

- www.gtpnet.com
- www.greekembassy.org
- www.phantis.com
- www.perseus.tufts.edu

There is also a very helpful free service provided by Matt Barrett of North Carolina: **www.greektravel.com**.

Remember that none of these sources can necessarily be counted on for the most up-to-date, definitive, or complete information. We advise that you use all such computer searches as *supplements only*, then check out specific "facts" if you are going to base your travel plans on the information.

vibrant island of **Delos.** Declared a sanctuary, where both birth and death were prohibited, Delos was well on its way to becoming uninhabited in ancient times. At the moment it's a very interesting pile of ruins, well worth a detour. At the other extreme is **Mykonos,** whose reputation as a sacred place is yet to be built, unless worship of beaches, clubs, and the sun counts.

Paros is the transport hub of the Cyclades, the to-and-from-place with its own reputation for windsurfing. From here you can get to **Tinos,** a modern holy place, home to perhaps the most revered of all Orthodox churches; **Naxos,** whose unspoiled forests and mountains lure hikers and campers; **Folegandros,** whose principal port is a beautiful haven for anyone craving a brief respite; and the Cycladic pièce de résistance, magical **Santorini,** to some the lost-and-found Atlantis, to others the here-and-now hot spot of the southern Aegean. Whether you prefer to scamper among ruins or bake on a beach, Santorini does not disappoint.

THE DODECANESE This string of islands, named "the 12" despite the fact that they number more than that, nearly embrace the Turkish shoreline. Except for Rhodes and Kos, all of the Dodecanese are deforested, bare bones exposed to sun and sea. But what bones! Far to the north lies **Patmos,** already in the 5th century nicknamed "the Jerusalem of the Aegean," a holy island where the Book of Revelation is said to have been penned and where the Monastery of St. John still dominates the island. Far to the south basks **Rhodes,** "the city of the Sun," with more than 300 days of sunshine per year. It's the most touristed of the islands, and for obvious reasons. Rhodes has it all: history and hysteria, ruins and resorts, knights and nightlife. There's even peace and quiet—we'll tell you where to find it.

In between these two lie an array of possibilities: from the uncompromised traditional charm of tiny **Simi** to the ruins and well-known beaches of **Kos.** The truth is that part of the popularity of the southern Dodecanese comes from its proximity to Rhodes—a simple matter of overflow for those who can't fit on or afford the most popular package-tour destination in Greece. Just remember that while "close" counts in horseshoes and hand grenades, it often doesn't when planning a holiday. *One other tip:* With Turkey so near, you may want to consider a side trip, quite easy to arrange.

CENTRAL GREECE Central Greece, for our purposes, stretches from the Corinth Canal to Mount Olympus. Its landscape is vastly diverse, from the fertile Boetian plains to the snowy peaks of **Parnassus** and **Olympus.** Enshrined here are the legendary battlegrounds of **Thermopylae** and **Chaironeia.**

Far from the chaos of battle, there is an ineffable stillness that has deep roots in Central Greece. The sanctuary of **Delphi,** especially at either sunset or sunrise, retains its mystery to this day. Then there are the otherworldly heights of **Meteora,** where anyone with vertigo, spiritual or otherwise, best not ascend. If you have a less austere retreat in mind, the lush, gentle slopes of **Pelion,** once roamed by centaurs, may suit. If, confronted with all of these choices, you can't decide what to do, it's best to start with Delphi, where authoritative advice has long been available.

THE SPORADES   Whether by ferry or hydrofoil, the Sporades, strewn north and east of the island of Evvia (Euboea), are readily accessible from the mainland and offer verdant forest landscapes, golden-sand beaches, and crystalline waters. That's the good news. The bad news is that they are no secret. **Skiathos** is the most in demand with all that that implies. **Skopelos,** whose lovely port is one of the most striking in Greece, is more rugged and remote than Skiathos, with more trails and fewer nightclubs. Relatively far-off **Skyros** is well worth a visit, offering underwater fishing and diving, sandy beaches, and luminously clear waters. On top of that, it's almost a secret and, for the time being, a bargain.

WESTERN GREECE   Northwestern Greece, or **Epirus,** is predominantly mountainous and mostly cut off by those mountains from the sea. You won't likely encounter many tourists here. Much of its appeal is to nature lovers and trekkers, for whom the **Vikos Gorge** and **Perama Cave** pose engaging challenges. Epirus is not, however, without its amenities and attractions.

Ioannina, on the shores of Lake Pamvotis, is the largest and most appealing city in the region; it is one of the few places in Greece where the long Muslim occupation is still manifestly visible. The traditional mountain village of **Metsovo,** perched several thousand feet up in the Pindos mountains, offers a number of local attractions and vista-ridden hiking.

Only 20 miles from Ioannina lie the ruins of one of the most famous of ancient shrines, the Oracle of Zeus at **Dodona,** where the voice of the great lord of Olympus was believed to speak through the rustling leaves of a sacred oak tree, though not the one currently planted there.

THE IONIAN ISLANDS   Across centuries, these islands have been the apple of more than one empire's eye. Lush, temperate, blessed with ample rain and sun, and tended like an architectural garden, they are quite splendid. **Corfu,** the most noted and ornamented, is a gem, and is priced accordingly. **Ithaka** is as yet somewhat out of the tourist loop, but needs no introduction for readers of the *Odyssey.* With certain adjustments for the nearly three millennia that have elapsed, Homer's descriptions of the island still hold their own. If you can do without name recognition, **Kefalonia,** still relatively inconspicuous and unspoiled, has a lot to offer: picturesque traditional villages, steep rocks plunging into the sea, fine beaches, and excellent local wine.

THESSALONIKI & NORTHERN GREECE   Just as it once was the urban understudy of Constantinople, **Thessaloniki** is modern Greece's second city. With less than 20% of Athens's population, however, it is not a close second. Even so, among Greece's major cities, it may be second to none in visual appeal and international flair. Among the city's many attractions are the legendary White Tower and its archaeological and Byzantine museums. As a home base, it offers comfortable proximity to many of Macedonia's major sites.

Macedonia is Greece's largest geographical region—rich in natural beauty, soaked in history, and mostly removed from the epicenters of the tourist explosion that, in places, has almost leveled the diverse traditions and cultures of Greece. Besides Thessaloniki, Macedon is also home to three major archaeological sites associated with Alexander and his father—**Pella, Vergina,** and **Dion**—as well as to the independent religious state of **Mount Athos.** This mountaintop theocracy, off-limits to women since the year 1060, may be viewed from cruise ships (departing from Thessaloniki) or visited with special permission.

THE NORTHEASTERN AEGEAN ISLANDS   The four major islands comprising this group form Europe's sea border with the east. Beyond their strategic and thus richly historic location, they offer a taste of Greece that is less compromised by tourism and more deeply influenced by nearby Asia Minor and modern Turkey. **Samos,** unique among the islands in the extent to which it is covered with trees, also produces from its vineyards some excellent local wine. Its important archaeological sites and opportunities for outdoor activities make it a congenial and interesting destination, and it is an ideal point from which to enter and explore the northwestern Turkish coast. **Hios** is unspoiled and welcoming, offering isolated and quite spectacular beaches, as well as the stunning monastery of Nea Moni, and some of Greece's most striking village architecture. The remaining islands of **Lesvos** and **Limnos,** for various reasons not major tourist destinations, each have their ways of inviting and rewarding those who explore them.

2 Visitor Information & Entry Requirements

VISITOR INFORMATION

The **Greek National Tourism Organization** (GNTO, or EOT in Greece—but increasingly referred to as the Hellenic Tourism Organization) has offices throughout the world that can provide you with information concerning all aspects of travel to and in Greece. Look for them at **www.gnto.gr** or contact one of the following GNTO offices:

UNITED STATES   Olympic Tower, 645 Fifth Ave., 5th Floor, New York, NY 10022 (☎ **212/421-5777;** fax 212/826-6940); 168 N. Michigan Ave., Suite 600, Chicago, IL 60601 (☎ **312/782-1084;** fax 312/782-1091); 611 W. Sixth St., Suite 2198, Los Angeles, CA 90017 (☎ **213/626-6696;** fax 213/489-9744).

In the U.S., you can call, fax, or send a self-addressed, stamped envelope to the **Overseas Citizens Emergency Center,** Department of State, Room 4811, Washington, DC 20520 (☎ **202/647-5225;** fax 202/647-3000), for Consular Information Sheets—travel advisories that include security problems and health risks. You can also get the latest information by contacting any U.S. embassy, consulate, or passport office.

AUSTRALIA & NEW ZEALAND   51 Pitt St., Sydney, NSW 2000 (☎ **02/ 241-1663;** fax 02/235-2174).

CANADA   1300 Bay St., Toronto, ON M5R 3K8 (☎ **416/968-2220;** fax 416/968-6533); 1170 Place du Frères André, Montréal, H3B 3C6 (☎ **514/ 871-1535;** fax 514/871-1498).

UNITED KINGDOM & IRELAND   4 Conduit St., London W1R ODJ (☎ **0171/734-5997;** fax 0171/287-1369).

ENTRY REQUIREMENTS

Citizens of Australia, Canada, New Zealand, South Africa, the United States, and almost all other countries are required to have a **valid passport,** which is stamped upon entry and exit, for stays up to 90 days. All U.S. citizens, even infants, must have a valid passport, but Canadian children under 16 may travel without a passport if accompanied by either parent. Longer stays must be arranged with the **Bureau of Aliens,** Leoforos Alexandras 173, 11522 Athens (☎ **01/770-5711**).

Citizens of the United Kingdom and other members of the European Union are required to have only a valid passport for entry into Greece, and it is no longer stamped upon entry; they may stay an unlimited period (although they should inquire at a Greek consulate or their embassy in Greece if they intend to stay for an extended period). Children under 16 from EU countries may travel without a passport if accompanied by either parent. But all EU citizens should check to see what requirements are for non-EU countries they may be traveling through to get to Greece!

3 Money

The unit of currency in Greece is the **drachma** (*drachmi* in Greek), abbreviated "Dr." The exchange rate with other currencies varies, but we have chosen here to go with a rate of Dr350 (*drachmas*) per U.S. dollar and Dr530 per British pound. Coins come in denominations of Dr5, Dr10, Dr20, Dr50, and Dr100 (with old Dr1 and Dr2 coins still occasionally surfacing). Bills come in denominations of Dr200 (orange), Dr500 (green), Dr1,000 (brown), Dr5,000 (gray-green), and Dr10,000 (pinkish). The old blue Dr50 and Dr100 bills still come up occasionally, and be especially careful not to confuse the Dr500 and Dr5,000 bills!

ATM NETWORKS   Automated teller machines are now almost as abundant in Greece as they are in all economically advanced countries.

But while singing the praises of Greek ATMs, *we must emphasize:* It is always possible that the one or two machines in your immediate locale may not be able to provide cash (due to incompatibility with your card, a mechanical malfunction, a labor strike, lack of cash due to a long holiday), so you are strongly advised to always have some "fallback" source of cash (traveler's checks or your national currency).

If your bank credit or debit card is affiliated with one of the major international credit cards (such as **MasterCard** or **Visa**), you should not have any trouble getting money in Greece; if in doubt, ask your bank or credit-card company if your card will be acceptable in Greece. For one thing, Greek ATMs usually allow for only a four-digit password; you must get advice from your bank as to how to deal with this if your regular password has more than four. Also note that the punch keys on Greek ATMs do not use letters, so you must convert your password to numbers. The machines, in case you're wondering, all have some method of allowing you to conduct its operations in English.

Transaction fees are usually built into the exchange rate you get; in any case, exchange rates are usually based on the wholesale rates of the major banks, so you may actually save money by withdrawing larger sums and paying your bills in cash. However, just as at home, there is usually some limit on how much you can withdraw in one day. Note, too, that the sums withdrawn are designated on the ATM screen in drachmas, not other currencies.

In commercial centers, airports, all cites and larger towns, and most tourist centers, you will find at least a couple of machines accepting a wide range of cards; smaller towns will often have only one ATM—and it may not accept your card. The **Commercial Bank** (Emboriki Trapeza) services PLUS and Visa, **Credit Bank** (Trapeza Pisteos) accepts Visa and American Express, **National Bank** (Ethiniki Trapeza) takes Cirrus and MasterCard/Access. To check if your destination has ATMs for Visa holders, use the ATM locator function at **www.visa.com**; for MasterCard, go to **www.mastercard.com**.

The Greek Drachma, the U.S. Dollar & the British Pound

At this writing, $1 = about Dr350; this was the rate of exchange used to calculate the dollar values given in the table below and throughout this book. The £1 at this same time was about Dr530; we give the exchange for that as another aid.

Note: International exchange rates fluctuate from time to time and may not be the same when you travel to Greece. Furthermore, there can be considerable variation in the rate depending on where you make the exchange. Therefore, this table should be used as a guide for approximate values only.

Dr	U.S.$	U.K.£	Dr	U.S.$	U.K.£
5	0.015	0.01	5,000	14	9.44
10	0.03	0.02	7,500	22	14.15
25	0.07	0.07	10,000	29	18.87
50	0.15	0.10	12,500	36	23.59
75	0.22	0.14	15,000	43	28.30
100	0.30	0.19	17,500	50	33.02
125	0.36	0.24	20,000	57	37.74
250	0.72	0.47	22,500	64	42.45
1,250	3.57	2.36	25,000	72	47.17
2,500	7.14	4.72	30,000	86	56.60

One final reminder: If you use your card as a credit card, you are borrowing money and presumably going to pay very high interest; it's better to use it as a debit card, which means you are simply taking cash out of your account.

CURRENCY-EXCHANGE OFFICES & MACHINES   Commercial foreign-exchange offices are found in major cities, larger towns, and centers of tourism. Their rates vary, so shop around if you must use one.

In these same locales, some banks also have currency-exchange machines, on the exterior of buildings and open 24 hours a day. You put in your own national currency, press the proper buttons, and get drachmas in exchange. However, they hold back a Dr500 ($1.45) fee for this service, no matter what the denomination of the bill.

TRAVELER'S CHECKS   Traveler's checks are still probably the safest means of carrying money while traveling, and in Greece they are accepted by most hotels, some restaurants, and some shops—although often with a small commission charged. Do not expect most Greek operations to cash your traveler's checks, however, unless you are paying for their services or goods. Most banks sell traveler's checks with a charge of 1% to 3%. If your bank charges more, you can call the check issuers about more competitive rates. Some organizations sell traveler's checks at reduced rates; the Automobile Association of America, for example, sells American Express checks in several currencies without commission.

American Express (☎ **800/221-7282** in the U.S. and Canada) is one of the largest and best known issuers of traveler's checks. American Express cardholders and members of AAA can obtain checks without paying a commission.

Citicorp (☎ **800/645-6556** in the U.S. and Canada; elsewhere, contact the local operator and ask to place a collect call to 813/623-1709 in the U.S.) also issues traveler's checks.

MasterCard/Thomas Cook (☎ **800/223-9920** in the U.S.; elsewhere, contact the local operator and ask to place a collect call to 33/318-550 in the U.K. or 609/987-7300 in the U.S.) traveler's checks are among the better known in Greece.

What Things Cost in Athens	U.K. £	U.S. $
Taxi from airport to the city's center	4.70–6.60	7.00–10.00
Local telephone call	.04	.06
Double room at a B-class hotel	57.00	86.00
Double room, without private bathroom, in a pension	20.00	30.00
Lunch for one at a taverna	6.00	9.00
Dinner for one, with wine, at a restaurant	9.00	14.00
Bottle of beer	1.10	1.70
Soda	.67	1.00
Cup of Greek coffee	.38–1.15	.58–$1.75
Roll of ASA 100 Kodacolor film, 36 exp.	4.25	6.45
Admission to National Archaeological Museum	3.75	5.72

Visa/Interpayment Services (☎ 800/221-2426 in the U.S. or Canada; 800/453-4284 from most other countries) sells Visa checks issued by Barclays Bank and Bank of America.

Most British banks can issue their account holders a **Eurocheque** card and checkbook, which can be used at most cash machines and at Greek banks for an annual fee and a 2% charge.

CREDIT & CHARGE CARDS Credit cards are accepted in the better hotels and shops, and they are effectively required for renting a car, but most restaurants and smaller hotels still do not accept them. (Indeed, be warned: Even many of the better restaurants in major cities do *not* accept credit cards. Also, some hotels that require credit cards when making advance reservations will demand payment in cash; inquire beforehand if this might be a problem.) Visa is the most widely accepted, and MasterCard is usually accepted where you see signs for Access or Eurocard. Diners Club is also increasingly recognized. American Express is less frequently accepted because it charges a higher commission and is more protective of the cardholder in disagreements.

Even when credit cards are accepted, most smaller restaurants and shops are reluctant to accept payment in plastic unless the bill is above a certain amount. Many small establishments will accept them only if you agree to pay their commission (usually about 6%); this seems fair enough, especially in some of the more out-of-the-way destinations where negotiating and receiving payment remains difficult and time-consuming for the proprietors.

EMERGENCY CASH In an emergency, you can arrange to send money from home to a Greek bank. Telex transfers from the United Kingdom usually take at least 3 days and sometimes up to a week, with a charge of about 3%. Bank drafts are more expensive but potentially faster if you are in Athens. From Canada and the United States, money can be wired by **Western Union** (☎ 800/325-6000) or **MoneyGram** (☎ 800/543-4080). In Greece, call Western Union in the United States (☎ 001-314/298-2313) to learn the location of an office. For MoneyGram, call the head office in Athens (☎ 01/322-0005). For a fee (usually from 4% to 10%, depending on the sum involved), money can be available in minutes at an agent for Western Union or Moneygram. And, of course, you can always borrow cash on your credit card from an ATM machine (so long as you're prepared to pay the high interest rate).

What Things Cost in Corfu	U.K. £	U.S. $
Taxi from airport to the city's center	2.85–4.75	4.30–7.15
Local telephone call	.04	.06
Double room at a B-class hotel	53.00	80.00
Double room, without private bathroom, in a pension	19.00	29.00
Lunch for one at a taverna	6.00	9.00
Dinner for one, with wine, at a restaurant	9.00	14.00
Bottle of beer	1.10	1.70
Soda	.67	1.00
Cup of Greek coffee	.38–1.15	.58–1.75
Roll of ASA 100 Kodacolor film, 36 exp.	4.25	6.45
Admission to Archaeological Museum	1.90	2.86

4 When to Go

THE WEATHER   Greece has a generally mild climate, though in the mountainous northern interior the winters are rather harsh and summers brief. Southern Greece enjoys a relatively mild winter, with temperatures averaging around 55°F to 60°F (13°C to 16°C) in Athens. Summers are generally hot and dry, with daytime temperatures rising to 85°F to 95°F (30° to 35°C), usually cooled by prevailing north winds (the *meltemi*), especially on the islands, which often cool appreciably in the evenings. And at some point in most summers, usually July, the temperature will rise to over 100°F (38°C).

The best time to visit is **late April to mid-June,** when the wildflowers are blooming and before summer arrives in force with hordes of tourists, higher prices, overbooked facilities, and strained services. **Orthodox Easter**—close to but usually not exactly concurrent with Western Easter—is a particularly delightful time to visit, though reservations are necessary and service is not the best, as so many Greeks living abroad return for the holiday. After Easter, most of the island resorts crank up for the season.

Average Monthly Temperature & Precipitation

Month	Athens			Crete		
	ADT		RF	ADT		RF
	F°	C°	Inches	F°	C°	Inches
January	52	12	2.4	54	13	3.7
February	54	13	2.0	54	13	3.0
March	58	15	1.3	57	14	1.6
April	65	19	0.9	62	17	0.9
May	74	24	0.8	68	20	0.7
June	86	30	0.2	74	24	0.1
July	92	33	0.1	78	26	0.0
August	92	33	0.2	78	26	0.1
September	82	28	1.1	75	24	0.7
October	72	23	2.0	69	21	1.7
November	63	18	2.9	63	18	2.7
December	56	14	4.1	58	15	4.0

ADT = Average Daytime Temperature, RF = Rainfall

If you possibly can, avoid traveling in **July and August** (and especially on or around August 15)—the crowds from Europe overwhelm facilities. In overcrowded southern Greece and the islands, midday temperatures are too high for much but beach and water activities. We strongly recommend you not go unless you have firm reservations and enjoy close encounters with masses of fellow tourists and footloose students. The higher elevations remain cooler and less crowded, a plus for hikers, bikers, and those who don't demand sophisticated pleasures.

By **mid-September,** temperatures begin to fall and crowds thin, but it can still be hot. The weather remains generally calm and balmy well into October. If you can't get to Greece in the spring, and beaches are not your primary goal, this is a fine time to visit.

By **late October,** ferry service is reduced and most facilities on the islands begin to close for the winter, but the cooler fall atmosphere makes Athens and the mainland all the more pleasant. If you have the time, visit the islands first, then return for a tour of the mainland archaeological sites.

Winter (say, November through March) is no time for fun in the sun, unless you want to join the Greeks for skiing and winter sports in the mountains—but some hotels and many good tavernas are open still, prices are at their lowest, and the southern mainland and Crete remain inviting, especially for those interested in archaeology and authentic local culture.

HOLIDAYS   The legal national holidays of Greece are: **New Year's Day,** January 1; **Epiphany** (Baptism of Christ), January 6; **Clean Monday** (Kathari Deftera), day before Shrove Tuesday, 41 days before Easter (which in Greece may come in late March to late April; every few years it coincides with Easter Sunday in Western Christian lands); **Independence Day,** March 25; **Good Friday to Easter,** including the Monday after Easter Sunday; **May Day** (Labor Day), May 1; **Whitmonday** (Holy Spirit Monday), day after Whitsunday (Pentecost), the 7th Sunday after Easter; **Assumption of the Virgin,** August 15; **Ochi Day,** October 28; **Christmas,** December 25 and 26.

On these holidays, government offices, banks, post offices, most stores, and many restaurants are closed; a few museums and attractions may remain open on several of the lesser holidays. Meanwhile, visitors are often included in the celebration. Consult the "Greece Calendar of Events," below, if you are in the planning stage. If you are already in Greece, ask at your hotel or find one of the current English-language publications, such as the *Athens News,* the *Kathimerini* insert in the *International Herald Tribune,* the weekly brochure *Athens Today,* or the *Athenscope* section of the weekly *Hellenic Times.*

Greece Calendar of Events

January

- **Feast of St. Basil** (Ayios Vassilios). St. Basil is the Greek equivalent of Santa Claus. The holiday is marked by the exchange of gifts and a special cake, *vassilopita,* made with a coin in it; the person who gets the piece with the coin will have good luck. January 1.
- **Epiphany** (Baptism of Christ) is celebrated with the blessing of baptismal fonts and water. A priest may throw a cross into the harbor and young men will try to recover it; the finder wins a special blessing. Children, who have been kept good during Christmas with threats of the *kalikantzari* (goblins), are allowed on the 12th day to help chase them away. January 6.

- **Gynecocracy** (Gynaikokratia, Rule of Women). Some villages in Thrace celebrate with the women taking over the cafes while the men stay home and do the housework. January 8.

February

○ **Carnival (Karnavali)** is celebrated with parades, marching bands, costumes, drinking, dancing, and more or less loosening of inhibition, depending on the locale. Some scholars say the name comes from the Latin for "farewell meat," while others hold that it comes from "car naval," the chariots celebrating the ancient sea god Poseidon (Saturn, to the Romans). The city of Patras shows its support of the latter theory with its famous chariot parade and wild Saturnalia, private parties and public celebrations. Masked revels are also widely held in Macedonia. On the island of Skyros, the pagan "Goat Dance" is performed, reminding us of the primitive Dionysiac nature of the festivities. Crete has its own colorful versions, while in the Ionian islands, festivities are more Italian. In Athens, people bop each other on the head with plastic hammers. Celebrations last the 3 weeks before the beginning of Lent.

March

- **Independence Day and the Feast of the Annunciation** are celebrated simultaneously with military parades, especially in Athens. The religious celebration is particularly important on the islands of Tinos and Hydra and in churches or monasteries named *Evanyelismos* ("Bringer of Good News") or *Evanyelistria* (the feminine form of the name). March 25.

April

- **Sound-and-light performances** begin on the Acropolis in Athens and the Old Town on Rhodes. Nightly to October.
- ○ **Procession of St. Spyridon (Ayios Spyridon)** is held in Corfu town on Palm Sunday. (St. Spyridon's remains are also paraded through the streets of Corfu town on Holy Saturday, August 1, and the first Sunday in November.)
- **Feast of St. George** (Ayios Yioryios), the patron saint of shepherds, is an important rural celebration with dancing and feasting. Arachova, near Delphi, is famous for its festivities. The island of Skyros also gives its patron saint a big party. April 23. (If the 23rd comes before Easter, the celebration is postponed until the Monday after Easter.)

Holy Week Celebrations

Orthodox Easter, a time of extraordinary festivities in Greece, usually falls one or more weeks after Easter in the West—inquire ahead! The Good Friday exodus from Athens is truly amazing, and you can remain and enjoy the deserted city or, if you're fortunate—and have made reservations, because Greeks take up most travel facilities—you can be among the celebrants in any town or village. Holy Week is usually marked by impressive solemn services and processions; serious feasting on roasted lamb, the traditional margaritsa soup, and homemade wine; and dancing, often in traditional costumes. One unique celebration occurs on Patmos, where the Last Supper is reenacted at the monastery of St. John the Divine. *Tip:* Tourists should remember to dress appropriately, especially at this Easter time (shorts, miniskirts, and sleeveless shirts will all cause offense).

May

- **May Day.** On this important urban holiday, families have picnics in the country and pick wildflowers, which are woven into wreaths and hung from balconies and over doorways. May Day is still celebrated by Greek Communists and socialists as a working-class holiday. May 1.
- **Folk-dance performances** begin in the amphitheater on Filopappos Hill in Athens and continue to September. Among the most regular and popular groups is the Dora Stratou Dance Troupe.
- ✪ **Hippocratic Oath.** Ritual recitations of the oath by the citizens of Kos honor their favorite son Hippocrates. Young girls in ancient dress, playing flutes, accompany a young boy in procession until he stands and recites in Greek the timeless oath of physicians everywhere. May through September.
- **Sound-and-light shows** begin in Corfu town and continue to the end of September.
- **Feast of St. Constantine** (Ayios Konstandinos), the first Orthodox emperor, and his mother, **St. Helen** (Ayia Eleni), is celebrated, most interestingly, by fire-walking rituals (*anastenaria*) in four villages in Macedonian Greece: Ayia Eleni, Ayios Petros, Langada, and Meliki. It's a big party night for everyone named Costa and Eleni. (Name-days, rather than birthdays, are celebrated in Greece.) The anniversary of the Ionian reunion with Greece is also celebrated, mainly in Corfu. May 21.

June

- **Athens Festival** features superb productions of ancient drama, opera, orchestra performances, ballet, modern dance, and popular entertainers in the handsome Odeum of Herodes Atticus, on the southwest side of the Acropolis. June to early October.
- **Folk-dance performances** are given in the theater in the Old Town of Rhodes.
- **Wine Festival** is held annually at Daphni, about 10 kilometers (7 miles) west of Athens; other wine festivals are held on Rhodes and elsewhere.
- The **Simi Festival** is a 4-month feast of concerts, theater, storytelling, and dance, featuring acclaimed Greek and international artists. With its epicenter on the tiny island of Simi, the events spill over into seven other neighboring islands: Astypalea, Halki, Kastellorizo, Karpathos, Kassos, Nissiros, and Tilos. June through September.
- **Lycabettus Theater** presents a variety of performances at the amphitheater on Mount Likavitos (Lycabettus) overlooking Athens, from mid-June to late August.
- The **Miaoulia,** celebrated on a mid-June weekend on Hydra, honors Hydriot Admiral Miaoulis, who set much of the Turkish fleet on fire by ramming them with explosives-filled fireboats.
- **Aegean Festival** on Skiathos presents ancient drama, modern dance, folk music and dance, concerts, and art exhibits in the Bourtzi Cultural Center in the harbor of Skiathos town. June through September.
- **International Classical Musical Festival** is held annually for one week in June or July at Nafplion, in the Peloponnese.
- **Midsummer Eve** (June 23 to 24) is celebrated by burning the dry wreaths picked on May Day to drive away witches, a remnant of pagan ceremonies now associated with the birth of John the Baptist on Midsummer Day, June 24.

- **The Feast of the Holy Apostles** (Ayii Apostoli, Petros, and Pavlos) is another important name-day. June 29.
- **Navy Week** is celebrated throughout Greece. In Volos, the voyage of the Argonauts is reenacted. On Hydra, the exploits of Adm. Andreas Miaoulis, naval hero of the War of Independence, are celebrated. Fishermen at Plomari on Lesvos stage a festival. End of June and beginning of July.

July

- Hydra's annual **puppet festival** has drawn puppeteers from countries as far away as Togo and Brazil. Early July.
- **Dodoni Festival** presents classical dramas at the ancient theater of Dodoni, south of Ioannina. For information, call ☎ **0651/20-090.** July through September.
- **Epidaurus Festival** of classical Greek drama begins in the famous amphitheater and continues to early September. For information, contact the **Greek Festival Office,** Odos Stadiou 4 (☎ **01/322-1459** or 01/322-3111 to 3119, ext. 137).
- **International Folklore Festival** at Naoussa, in northern Greece, features both amateur and professional dance companies from all over the world. For information, call ☎ **0332/20211** or e-mail cioff@nao.forthnet.gr.
- The **Northern Greece National Theater** performs classical drama in the amphitheaters in Phillipi and on the island of Thasos. Here's a way to see these productions free of the hassles of Athens. For information, call ☎ **051/223-504.** July and August.
- **Hippokrateia Festival** brings art, music, and theater to the medieval castle of the Knights of St. John, in the main harbor of Kos. July and August.
- **Kalamata International Dance Festival** is held each summer in Kalamata, in the southern Peloponnesos, with performances by prestigious dance companies from all over the world.
- **Dionysia Wine Festival** is held on the island of Naxos. Not a major event, but fun if you're there. For information, call ☎ **0285/22-923.** Mid-July.
- ✪ **Wine Festival** at Rethymnon, Crete, continues through the middle weeks of July. Rethymnon also hosts a **Renaissance Festival** starting in July and running into early September. There are now wine festivals and arts festivals all over Greece, but among the more engaging are those held in Rethymnon. Sample the wines, then sample something of the Renaissance theatrical and musical performances.
- **Feast of Ayia Marina,** protector of crops, is widely celebrated in rural areas. July 17.
- **Feast of the Prophet Elijah** (Profitis Elias) is celebrated in the hilltop shrines formerly sacred to the sun god Helios, the most famous of which is on Mount Taygetos, near Sparta. July 18 to 20.
- **Feast of Ayia Paraskevi** continues the succession of Saint Days celebrated at the height of summer, when agricultural work is put on hold. July 26.

August

- **Feast of the Transfiguration** (Metamorphosi) is celebrated in the numerous churches and monasteries of that name, though it isn't much for name-day parties. August 6.
- **Aeschylia festival** of ancient drama stages classical dramas at the archaeological site of Eleusis, home of the ancient Mysteries and birthplace of Aeschylus, west of Athens. August to mid-September.

✪ **Feast of the Assumption of the Virgin** (Apokimisis tis Panayias) is an important day of religious pilgrimage. Many take the opportunity to go home for a visit, so rooms are particularly hard to find. The holiday reaches monumental proportions in Tinos; thousands of people descend on the small port town to participate in an all-night vigil at the cathedral of Panayia Evanyelistria, in the procession of the town's miraculous icon, and in the requiem for the soldiers who died aboard the Greek battleship *Elli* on this day in 1940. August 15.

• **Epirotika Festival** in Ioannina presents theatrical performances, concerts, and exhibitions. August to early September.

• **Olympus Festival** presents cultural events in the Frankish Castle of Platamonas, near Mount Olympus. August.

• **Santorini festival of classical music** features international musicians and singers in outdoor performances for 2 weeks beginning at the end of the month.

September

• **Feast of the Birth of the Virgin** (Yenisis tis Panayias) is another major festival, especially on Spetses, where the anniversary of the Battle of the Straits of Spetses is celebrated with a re-enactment in the harbor, fireworks, and an all-night bash. September 8.

• **Feast of the Exaltation of the Cross** (Ipsosi to Stavrou) marks the end of the summer stretch of feasts, and even Stavros has had enough for a while. September 14.

• **Thessaloniki International Trade Fair.** This is one of the world's major trade fairs. Rooms are scarce in the city, so if the fair's not your destination, try to come to Thessaloniki at another time. For information, call ☎ **031/271-888.** Mid-September.

• **Thessaloniki Film Festival and Festival of Popular Song.** That lively and sophisticated city continues to live it up. End of September.

October

• **Feast of St. Demetrius** (Ayios Dimitrios) is particularly important in Thessaloniki, where he is the patron saint, and the Demetrius Festival features music, opera, and ballet. New wine is traditionally untapped. October 26.

• **Ochi Day,** when General Metaxa's negative reply (*ochi* is Greek for "no") to Mussolini's demands in 1940 gives a convenient excuse for continuing the party with patriotic outpourings, including parades, folk music and dancing, and general festivity. October 28.

November

• **Feast of the Archangels Gabriel and Michael** (Gavriel and Mihail), with ceremonies in the many churches named for them. November 8.

• **Feast of St. Andrew** (Ayios Andreas), patron saint of Patras, is another excuse for a party in that swinging city. November 30.

December

• **Feast of St. Nikolaos** (Ayios Nikolaos). This St. Nick is the patron saint of sailors. Numerous processions head down to the sea and the many chapels dedicated to him. December 6.

• **Christmas.** The day after Christmas honors the Gathering Around the Holy Family (Synaksis tis Panayias). December 25 and 26.

• **New Year's Eve,** when children go out singing Christmas carols (*kalanda*) while their elders play cards, talk, smoke, eat, and imbibe. December 31.

5 The Active Vacation Planner

BICYCLING   Increasing numbers of foreigners are choosing to travel in Greece by bicycle, and those interested in the possibility can get more information from the **Greek Cycling Federation,** Odos Bouboulinas 28, 11742 Athens (☎ **01/883-1414**).

Trekking Hellas, Odos Filellinon 7, 10557 Athens (☎ **01/331-0323;** fax 01/323-4548; www.trekking.gr; e-mail: t.laskaratos@trekking.gr), can also assist you in arranging mountain-biking trips. But Greece is not the place to start learning how to tour on a bicycle; Greek drivers have little experience in accommodating bicyclists, road shoulders in Greece are often nonexistent and even at best are not generous, and roads are not especially well maintained.

In the United States, **Classic Adventures,** Box 143, Hamlin, NY 14464 (☎ **800/777-8090** or 716/964-8488) has been around since 1979 and has a fine reputation for its bicycle tours, such as a 12-day excursion that follows the coast and includes Corinth, Epidaurus, Mycenae, Olympia, and the island of Zakinthos, or a 13-day tour of Crete.

Mountain bikes are better suited for Greek terrain, and you can even bring your own along by train (for a small fee) or plane (free, though not easy). You can take them along on Greek ferries and trains usually at no extra cost. You should also bring along spare parts, as they are rarely available outside the major cities.

If you insist on trying a bicycle in Greece, you can rent an old bike for very little in most major resorts, and good mountain bikes are increasingly available. On Crete, mountain bikes are available for rent in Iraklion at **Creta Travel Bureau,** Odos Epimenidou 20–22 (☎ **081/227-002**), which also has offices in Rethymnon and Ayios Nikolaos. In Chania, try **Athanasakis Tours,** Odos Halidon 25 (☎ **0821/24-965**). On Paros, the **Mountain Bike Club,** near the post office in Parikia (☎ and fax **0284/23-778**), rents good mountain bikes. On Rhodes, they are available at **Mike's Motor Club,** Odos Kazouli 23 (☎ **0241/37-420**). Kos is also well suited to cycling, and bicycles are widely available for rent there.

CAMPING   Greece offers a wide variety of camping facilities throughout the country. Rough or freelance camping—setting up your camp on some apparently unoccupied land—is forbidden by law but may be overlooked by some local authorities. The **Greek National Tourism Organization** should have further information on its many licensed facilities, as well as a very informative booklet, *Camping in Greece,* published by the **Greek Camping Association,** Odos Solonos 102, 10680 Athens (☎ **01/362-1560;** fax 01/346-5262).

DIVING   Scuba diving is currently restricted throughout most of Greece because of potential harm to sunken antiquities and the environment. That said, there are now many locales where diving is allowed under supervision by accredited "schools." On the mainland, these may be found along the coast of Attica, off the Peloponnese peninsula, and off Halkidiki and a few other places in the north. There is also limited diving off the islands of Corfu, Crete, Hydra, Kalimnos, Kefalonia, Mykonos, Paros, Rhodes, Santorini, Skiathos, and Zakinthos.

Just to single out a few at the more popular locales, on Corfu there is **Calypso Scuba Divers,** Ayios Gordis (☎ **0661/53-101;** fax 0661/34-319); on Rhodes, the **Dive Med Center,** Odos Dragoumi 5, Rhodes town (☎ **0241/33-654**); on Crete, the **Paradise Dive Center,** Odos Giamboudaki 51, Rethymnon (☎ and fax **0831/53-258**); and on Mykonos, **Lucky Scuba Divers,** Ornos Beach (☎ **0289/22-813;** fax **0289/23-764**). Even if you are qualified, you must dive under supervision. And above all, you are forbidden to even photograph, let alone remove, anything that might possibly be regarded as an antiquity.

For more information, contact the **Organization of Underwater Activities** (☎ **01/982-3840**) or the **Union of Greek Diving Centers** (☎ **02/922-9532**). If you're a serious underwater explorer, contact the **Department of Underwater Archaeology,** Odos Kalisperi 30, 11741 Athens (☎ **01/924-7249**).

Snorkeling, however, is permitted, and the unusually clear water makes it a special pleasure. Simple equipment is widely available for rent or sale.

FISHING   Opportunities for fishing abound. Contact the **Amateur Anglers and Maritime Sports Club,** Akti Moutsopoulou, 18537 Piraeus (☎ **01/451-5731**).

GOLF   There are relatively few golf courses in Greece, although several more are in the planning stages. Those now in existence are in Glifada (along the coast outside of Athens), Halkidiki, Corfu, Crete (Elounda), and Rhodes. Any travel agent can supply the details.

HIKING   Greece offers endless opportunities for hiking, trekking, and walking. Greeks themselves are now showing interest in walking for pleasure, and there are a number of well-mapped and even signed routes.

Probably the best and most up-to-date source for information on nature-oriented tours or groups are the ads in magazines geared toward people with these interests— *Audubon Magazine,* for instance, for birders. But it is important to realize that one need not sign up for special (and expensive!) tours to enjoy the wildlife of Greece. Bring your own binoculars, and buy one of the many illustrated handbooks such as *Wildflowers of Greece,* by George Sfikas (Efstathiadis Books, Athens), or *Birds of Europe,* by Bertel Brun (McGraw-Hill).

In Greece, we recommend **Trekking Hellas,** in Athens at Odos Filellinon 7 (☎ **01/331-0323;** fax 01/323-4548), and in Thessaloniki at Odos Tsimiski 71 (☎ **031/222-128;** fax 031/222-129), for both guided tours and help in planning your own private trek. Other Greek travel agencies specializing in nature tours include: **Adrenaline Team,** Odos Kornarou 2 and Odos Hermou 28, 10563 Athens (☎ **01/331-1777;** fax 01/331-1778); **Athenogenes,** Plateia Kolonaki 18, 10673 Athens (☎ **01/361-4829**); and **Ey-Zhn,** Leoforos Syngrou 132, 17671 Athens (☎ **01/921-6285**). In the Sporades, try **Ikos Travel,** Patitiri, 37005 Alonissos (☎ **0424/65-320**).

In the United States, the **Appalachian Mountain Club,** 5 Joy St., Boston, MA 02108 (☎ **617/523-0636**), often organizes hiking tours in Greece. **Classic Adventures,** Box 143, Hamlin, NY 14464 (☎ **800/777-8090** or 716/964-8488), offers hiking tours of Crete and the Zagori region of Epirus. **Mountain Travel-Sobek,** 6420 Fairmount Ave., El Cerrito, CA 94530 (☎ **800/227-2384;** www. mtsobek.com), sometimes conducts summer hikes and kayaking trips in the Greek mountains. **Country Walkers,** P.O. Box 180, Waterbury VT 05676 (☎ **800/ 464-9255;** www.countrywalkers.com), is another company that conducts occasional walking tours through regions of Greece.

Birders and nature lovers should contact the **Hellenic Ornithological Society,** Odos Emmanouil Benaki 53, 10681 Athens (☎ **01/381-1271**). **Questers World-wide Nature Tours,** 381 Park Ave. S., Suite 1201, New York, NY 10016 (☎ **800/468-8668** or 212/251-0444), sometimes offers nature tours in Greece. Also specializing in walking tours is **Alternative Travel Group,** 69–71 Banbury Rd., Oxford, OX2 6PE England (☎ **44/1865-315678,** or 800/527-5997 in the U.S.).

HORSEBACK RIDING   There are a fair number of opportunities for horseback riding in Greece. Near Athens you'll find the **Athletic Riding Club** of Ekali

(☎ 01/813-5576), the **Hellenic Riding Club** in Maroussi (☎ **01/682-6128**), and the **Riding Club of Parnitha** (☎ **01/240-2413**); call for directions and reservations. Good facilities are also located near Thessaloniki and on the islands of Corfu, Crete, Rhodes, and Skiathos, with smaller stables elsewhere (inquire at local travel agencies).

In the United States, **Equitour,** Box 807, Dubois, WY 82513 (☎ **800/545-0019** or 307/455-3363), offers an 8-day riding tour of the beautiful Mount Pelion coast.

MOUNTAINEERING   Those interested in more strenuous trekking and mountain climbing should contact the **Hellenic Federation of Mountaineering & Climbing,** Odos Milioni 5, 10673 Athens (☎ **01/364-5904;** fax 01/364-4687).

SKIING   There are a number of attractive skiing centers in Greece. They can't compare to those further north in deep snow and posh facilities, but they don't approach them in steep prices either, and there is much charm in their little hotels and lively après-ski life. The season generally begins after Christmas and continues until the end of April, depending on the weather.

The best developed is the **Parnassos Ski Center,** near Arachova, on Mount Parnassus (☎ **0234/22-689;** fax 0234/22-695), with 20 runs, chairlifts, tow bars, classes, equipment rental, snack bars and restaurants, and even child care. There is also skiing on the gentler slopes of Mount Pelion and at charming Metsovo, in Epirus northeast of Ioannina, where the season is somewhat shorter. Other centers are found on the Peloponnese at Helmos, near Kalavrita; in central Greece at Velouhi, near Karpenissi; and in Macedonia, at Pisoderi, near Florina, and Vermion, near Naoussa. For more information, contact the **Greek Skiers Organization,** P.O. Box 8037, Athens 10010 (☎ **01/524-0057;** fax 01/524/8821).

SPELUNKING   If you don't know what the word refers to, then you won't be wanting to do it. It refers to cave exploring, and there are numerous caves in Greece and numerous individuals who are skilled in exploring them. For details, contact the **Hellenic Speleological Society,** Odos Mantzarou 8 (☎ **01/361-7824**).

WATER SPORTS   Water sports of various kinds are available at most major resort areas, and we mention the more important facilities in the relevant chapters that follow. Parasailing is possible at the larger resorts in summer. Although some of these facilities are limited to patrons of the hotels and resorts, in many places they are available to anyone willing to pay.

River rafting and kayaking are definite possibilities, especially in Epirus, with more limited opportunities on the Peloponnese peninsula. Contact the **Alpine Club,** Plateia Kapnikareas 2, 11743 Athens (☎ **01/321-2355**). One quite special opportunity is the kayaking trip occasionally conducted by the American agency **Mountain Travel-Sobek,** 6420 Fairmount Ave., El Cerrito, CA 94530 (☎ **800/227-2384** or 510/527-8105).

Waterskiing facilities are widely available; there are several schools at Vouliagmeni, south of Athens, and usually at least one on each of the major islands. Contact the **Hellenic Water-Ski Federation,** Leoforos Poseidonos, 16777 Glyfada (☎ **01/894-7413**).

Windsurfing has become increasingly popular in Greece, and boards are widely available for rent. The many coves and small bays along Greece's convoluted coastline are ideal for beginners, and instruction is usually available at reasonable prices. The best conditions and facilities are found on the islands of Corfu, Crete, Lefkada, Lesvos, Naxos, Paros, Samos, and Zakinthos. There are a number of excellent schools. Contact the **Hellenic Wind-Surfing Association,** Odos Filellinon 7, 10557 Athens (☎ **01/323-0330**), for details.

6 Special-Interest Vacations

ARCHAEOLOGICAL DIGS   The **American School of Classical Studies at Athens,** 6–8 Charlton St., Princeton, NJ 08540 (☎ **609/683-0800**), often sponsors tours in Greece and adjacent Mediterranean lands guided by archaeologists and historians. **Archaeological Tours,** 271 Madison Avenue, Suite 904, New York, NY 10016 (☎ **212/986-3054;** e-mail: archtours@aol.com), offers tours led by expert guides; typical tours might be to classical Greek sites or to Cyprus/Crete/Santorini. **FreeGate Tourism,** 585 Stewart Ave., Suite 310, Garden City, NY 11530 (☎ **800/223-0304** or 516/222-0855; fax 516/222-0848), also specializes in guided trips in Greece.

ART   International Study Tours, 225 W. 34th St., No. 1020, New York, NY 10122 (☎ **800/833-2111** or 212/563-1202; fax 212/594-6953), offers studies in the architecture, art, and culture of Greece, led by professionals. Especially attractive are the **Aegean Workshops** run by Harry Danos, a Greek-American architect and watercolorist; in the spring and autumn, he leads groups to various regions of Greece, where he provides instruction in drawing and watercolors (and also ends up teaching some of the language). To learn more, call ☎ **860/739-0378** from mid-May through October, or ☎ **941/455-2623** from November to mid-May.

The **Athens Center for the Creative Arts,** Odos Archimidou 48, Pangrati, 11636 Athens (☎ **01/701-2268**), offers summer programs. The **Hellas Art Club** on the island of Hydra, at the Leto Hotel, 18040 Hydra (☎ **0298/53-385;** fax 01/361-2223 in Athens), offers classes in painting, ceramics, music, theater, photography, Greek dancing, and cooking.

MODERN GREEK   There are numerous courses offered at both formal educational institutions and private language institutes throughout the English-speaking world; there are also several quite decent courses on tape for self-study. Just be sure that it is modern Greek that you want to study—and not classical Greek! If you are already in Greece, the **Athens Center for the Creative Arts,** Odos Archimidou 48, Pangrati, 11636 Athens (☎ **01/701-2268**), is highly recommended. The **School of Modern Greek Language of Aristotle University in Thessaloniki** also offers summer courses.

PERSONAL GROWTH   The **Skyros Center,** which can be contacted in the United Kingdom at 92 Prince of Wales Rd., London NW5 3NE (☎ **020/ 7284-3065;** fax 020/7284-3063; www.skyros.com; e-mail: connect@skyros.com), offers "personal growth" vacations on the island of Skyros, with courses in fitness, holistic health, creative writing, and handicrafts.

7 Health & Insurance

STAYING HEALTHY   There are no immunization requirements for getting into the country, though it's always a good idea to have polio, tetanus, and typhoid covered when traveling anywhere.

Diarrhea can be a minor problem with all travelers everywhere, so it's wise to take along some of your preferred remedy. In practice, though, Greece's natural water is excellent; meanwhile, you will usually be served bottled water. Cola soft drinks are said to be helpful for those having digestive difficulties stemming from too much olive oil in their food. Milk is pasteurized, though refrigeration is sometimes not the best, especially in out-of-the-way places. Allergy sufferers should carry along some antihistamines, especially in the spring. And everyone should be aware that overexposure to the much-lauded Greek sun can cause sun poisoning or sunstroke.

Health services are good, if not as noticeable as they are in most English-speaking countries. The hospitals in the large cities are excellent. Virtually all doctors in Greece can speak English or some other European language. For minor health problems, go first to the nearest **pharmacy** (*pharmakio*), which will be marked with a green cross. (In the larger cities, if it is closed, there should be a sign in the window directing you to the nearest open one. Newspapers also list the pharmacies that are open late or all night.) Pharmacists are well trained and usually speak English quite well, and many medications are available without prescription. You should bring along a sufficient quantity of any prescription medication you are taking, and keep it in your carry-on luggage. Just in case, ask your doctor to write you new prescriptions, using the generic—not the brand—name.

For more serious medical problems, your embassy or consulate or hotel can recommend an English-speaking doctor. In an emergency, call a **first-aid center** (☎ **166**), the nearest **hospital** (☎ **106**), or the **tourist police** (☎ **171**).

If you have special concerns, before heading abroad you might check out **www.cdc.gov/travel** or **www.istm.org** for advice on health and medical situations in foreign lands. One of the best sources for travelers with medical problems is the **International Association for Medical Assistance for Travelers (IAMAT).** It not only has a list of English-speaking doctors (who agree to reasonable fees) in some 120 cities abroad, but also puts out specialized publications on diseases such as malaria. It can be reached in the United States at 417 Center St., Lewiston, NY 14092 (☎ **716/ 754-4883**), and in Canada at 40 Regal Rd., Guelph, ON N1K 1B5 (☎ **519/ 836-1002**); you can also write the office at 57 Voirets, 1212 Grand-Lancy, Geneva, Switzerland, or browse **www.sentex.net/~iamat**.

Those with chronic illnesses should discuss their travel plans with their physician. Those with epilepsy, diabetes, or significant cardiovascular disease should wear a Medic Alert identification tag or bracelet, which will alert a health-care provider to the condition and provide the telephone number of the 24-hour hot line from which your medical record can be obtained. Before setting off, contact the **Medic Alert Foundation** (☎ **800/432-5378**).

Emergency treatment is usually given free of charge in state hospitals, but be warned that only basic needs are met. (Citizens of EU nations should inquire before leaving, but their policies will probably cover treatment in Greece.) The care in out-patient clinics, which are usually open in the mornings (from 8am to noon), is often somewhat better; you can find them next to most major hospitals, on some islands, and occasionally in rural areas, usually indicated by prominent signs.

INSURANCE   Before you purchase any additional insurance, check your current medical, automobile, and homeowner's policies as well as any insurance provided by credit-card companies and auto and travel clubs. You may already have adequate off-premises theft coverage, and your credit-card company may provide cancellation coverage on tickets paid for with their card. If you are prepaying for your trip or taking a flight that has cancellation penalties, consider cancellation insurance.

Four of many companies that can provide insurance and further information are: **Travel Guard International,** 1145 Clark St., Stevens Point, WI 54481 (☎ **800/ 782-5151**); **Travel Insurance International,** P.O. Box 280568, East Hartford, CT 06128 (☎ **800/243-31740**); **International Medical Group,** 475 N. Fulton St., Indianapolis IN 46202 (☎ **800/628-4664;** e-mail: insurance@imglobal.com); and **Wallach and Co.,** 107 W. Federal St., P.O. Box 480, Middleburg, VA 22117 (☎ **800/237-6615;** fax 540/687-3172).

8   Tips for Travelers with Special Needs

FOR TRAVELERS WITH DISABILITIES   Few concessions exist for the disabled in Greece. Steep steps, uneven pavement, almost no cuts at curbstones, narrow walks, slick stone, and traffic congestion can cause problems. Archaeological sites by their very nature are usually difficult to navigate, and crowded public transportation can be all but impossible. More modern and private facilities are only now beginning to provide ramps, but little else has been done. (That said, foreigners in wheelchairs—accompanied by companions—are becoming a more common sight in Greece, and we have read a first-person account of a wheelchair-using individual who found a cruise ship well designed to service her needs.) The **Greek National Tourism Organization** can provide you with a short list of hotels that may be suitable, and in the following chapters we mention the special facilities in those few hotels that have them. In Greece, the **Hermes Association,** Odos Patriarchou 13, Argiroupoli, 16542 Athens (☎ **01/996-1887**), also offers advice.

One of the best sources of free travel information for the disabled is **Access-Able Travel Source,** P.O. Box 1796, Wheat Ridge, CO 80034 (☎ **303/232-2979;** www. access-able.com; e-mail: bill@access-able.com), which issues occasional informative sheets and refers you to travel agencies that handle arrangements for the disabled. Another excellent source for information is the nonprofit **Society for the Advancement of Travel for the Handicapped,** 347 Fifth Ave., Suite 619, New York, NY 10016 (☎ **212/447-7284;** fax 212/725-8253; www.sath.org), which also publishes the quarterly *Open World* ($18 a year), with lots of useful information on travel. Philadelphia's **Moss Rehabilitation Hospital** maintains a Web site that offers help and references for people with disabilities: **www.mossresourcenet.org**. The **American Foundation for the Blind,** 11 Penn Plaza, Suite 300, New York, NY 10001 (☎ **800/ 232-5463;** www.afb.org), is the best source of information for those with visual impairment. **New Directions,** 5276 Hollister Ave., Suite 207, Santa Barbara, CA 93111 (☎ **805/967-2841;** fax 805/964-7344), arranges tours for people with disabilities.

FOR GAY & LESBIAN TRAVELERS   A most helpful source is *Our World,* a magazine designed specifically for gay and lesbian travelers (10 issues a year, $35), at 1104 N. Nova Rd., Suite 251, Daytona Beach, FL 32117 (☎ **904/441-5367;** www.ourworldmagazine.com); it not only is full of ads for travel agencies and facilities that accommodate gays and lesbians, but also carries firsthand accounts of visits to locales all around the world. (Its May 1997 and March 2001 issues are devoted to Greece; each can be purchased for $4.99.) The **International Gay Travel Association,** 4331 North Federal Hwy., Suite 304, Fort Lauderdale, FL 33308 (☎ **800/ 448-8550**), can advise you about travel opportunities, agents, and tour operators. The monthly newsletter *Out and About* also has information for gay and lesbian travelers (☎ **800/929-2268**). *Frommer's Gay & Lesbian Europe* provides immense amounts of information for gay-, lesbian-, and bisexual-friendly destinations in Greece and eight other countries.

In Athens, information about the **Hellenic Homosexual Liberation Movement (EOK)** can be found at Odos Apostolou Pavlou 31, Thisio/Athens (☎ **094/ 771/9291**). The **Autonomous Group of Gay Women** can be contacted through the Women's House, Odos Romanou Melodou 4, Likavitos, 10022 Athens (☎ **01/ 281-4823**). The *Greek Gay Guide,* published by Kraximo Press, P.O. Box 4228, 10210 Athens (☎ **01/362-5249**), can be purchased at some kiosks.

FOR SENIORS   There are not that many "senior-citizen discounts" available in Greece. Some museums and archaeological sites offer discounts for those 60 and over, but the practice seems unpredictable; for example, some places limit such a discount to citizens of an EU nation.

For general information before you go, Americans can acquire *Travel Tips for Older Americans,* available for $1.25 from the Superintendent of Documents, U.S. Government Printing Office, Washington, DC 20402 (☎ **202/512-1800**).

Another booklet, *101 Tips for Mature Travelers,* is available free from **Grand Circle Travel,** 347 Congress St., Boston, MA 02210 (☎ **800/248-3737**), which specializes in travel for seniors. **Vantage Travel,** 90 Canal St., Boston MA 02114 (☎ **800/ 322-6677;** www.vantagetravel.com), which also arranges for tours for seniors, offers a free booklet, *99 Travel Tips for Mature Travelers.* The monthly newsletter *The Mature Traveler* is available for $29.95 a year by contacting P.O. Box 50400, Reno, NV 89513 (☎ **800/460-6676**).

The **American Association of Retired Persons (AARP),** 1909 K St. NW, Washington, DC 20049 (☎ **800/424-3410;** www.aarp.org), offers its members information on airfare, car-rental, and hotel discounts. **Saga International Holidays,** 222 Berkeley St., Boston, MA 02116 (☎ **800/921-9291;** www.sagaholidays.com), specializes in all-inclusive tours in Greece for those ages 50 and older.

Elderhostel, 75 Federal St., Boston, MA 02110 (☎ **617/426-7788;** www.elderhostel.org), offers study programs in Greece for people over 55.

Interhostel, University of New Hampshire, 6 Garrison Ave., Durham, NH 03824 (☎ **800/733-9753** or 603/862-1147), offers 2-week programs in more than three dozen countries for people over 50. In Greece, groups typically settle in one area for a week or so, with excursions that focus on getting to know the history and culture.

FOR STUDENTS   In the United States, one of the major organizations for arranging overseas study for college-age students is the **Council on International Education Exchange,** or **CIEE** (☎ **800/407-8839;** www.ciee.org). Its travel arrangements are handled by **Council Travel** (☎ **800/2-COUNCIL**), which maintains offices in most major US cities and many college towns. Council Travel assists with such matters as budget travel and work permits; sells special student medical insurance as well as ISIC, Go 25, and ITIC cards; and publishes the free *Student Travels* magazine. Another agency that specializes in students' travel needs is **STA Travel,** with over 150 offices around the world; in the United States, call ☎ **800/777-0112** for the nearest location.

In Greece, students with proper identification (ISIC and IYC cards) are given reduced entrance fees to archaeological sites and museums, as well as discounts on admission to most artistic events, theatrical performances, and festivals. The ISIC card can also gain students various reductions in phone calls, faxes, e-mail, and related services; contact **ISIConnect** (☎ **732/365-5000;** www.usitmail.com).

A Hostelling International membership can save students money in some 5,000 hostels in 70 countries, where sex-segregated, dormitory-style sleeping quarters cost about $10 to $25 a night. In the United States, membership is available through **Hostelling International–American Youth Hostels,** 733 15th St. NW, Suite 840, Washington, DC 20005 (☎ **202/783-6161;** www.hiayh.org). One-year membership is free for ages 17 and under, $25 for ages 18 to 54, and $15 for ages 55 and over.

In Greece, an International Guest Card can be obtained at the **Greek Association of Youth Hostels (OESE),** in Athens at Odos Botassi 11 near Kaningos Square, behind Omonia (☎ **01/330-2340**). You can also get information on various student arrangements in Greece from the **International Student and Youth Travel Service,** Odos Nikis 11, 10557 Athens (☎ **01/322-1276**).

9 Getting There

The vast majority of travelers reach Greece by plane. Many also come by car or train, often taking the ferry from Italy. There is still bus service from Europe, but few except the young are interested in the arduous journey; if you are so inclined, contact the London-based outfit **Eurolines** (☎ **0990/143219**).

BY PLANE
FROM NORTH AMERICA

UNITED STATES   At press time, only two regularly scheduled airlines offer direct, nonstop flights from the States to Athens—Olympic and Delta. Some travelers find the planes a bit shabby, the personnel inattentive, and the occasional delays aggravating, but **Olympic Airways** (☎ **800/223-1226**; www.olympic-airways.gr) has long offered nonstop service daily from New York, twice weekly from Boston, and twice weekly from Chicago via New York. **Delta Air Lines** (☎ **800/241-4141**; www.delta.com) offers satisfactory service from throughout the United States, with all flights connecting to their nonstop Athens flights at JFK in New York (and in Atlanta during the summer).

All the other airlines make stops at some major European airport, where they usually require a change of planes. **Alitalia** (☎ **800/223-5730**; www.alitalia.com) offers flights from JFK that go to Greece via Rome. **British Airways** (☎ **800/247-9297**; www.british-airways.com) has service to Athens from a number of major U.S. cities, all stopping in London (most at Heathrow, but some at Gatwick). **Lufthansa** (☎ **800/645-3880**; www.lufthansa.com) provides superior service to Athens, Thessaloniki, and Crete from 10 U.S. cities, via Frankfurt. **Northwest/KLM Royal Dutch Airlines** (☎ **800/374-7747**; www.klm.nl) has superior service from 10 major cities in the United States to Athens, with all flights stopping in Amsterdam. **Sabena** (☎ **800/955-2000**; www.sabena.com) has good service to Athens from Atlanta, Boston, Chicago, and New York, with all flights stopping in Brussels. **Virgin Atlantic Airways** (☎ **800/862-8621**; www.fly.virgin.com) offers excellent service via London, with daily flights from Los Angeles and the New York area, and less frequent service from several other cities.

CANADA   In addition to the various airlines flying out of the United States, Canadians have a number of other choices. **Olympic Airways** (☎ **800/223-1226**; www.olympic-airways.gr) offers the only direct flights from Canada to Athens—two flights a week from Montreal and Toronto. **Air Canada** (☎ **888/247-2262**; www.aircanada.ca) flies from Calgary, Montréal, Toronto, and Vancouver to various airports in Europe, with connections on Olympic to Athens. **Air France** (☎ **800/237-2747**; www.airfrance.com), **British Airways** (☎ **800/247-9297**; www.british-airways.com), **CSA Czech Airlines** (☎ **800/223-2365**; www.csa.cz), **Iberia** (☎ **800/772-4642**; www.iberia.com), **KLM Royal Dutch Airlines** (☎ **800/361-5073**; www.klm.nl), **Lufthansa** (☎ **800/645-3880**; www.lufthansa.com), **Sabena** (☎ **800/955-2000**; www.sabena.com), **Swissair** (☎ **800/221-4750**; www.swissair.com), and **TAP Air Portugal** (☎ **800/221-7370**; www.tap-airportugal.pt) all have at least one flight per week from Calgary, Montréal, Toronto, or Vancouver via other European cities to Athens.

FROM EUROPE

IRELAND   **Aer Lingus** (☎ **01/844-4777** in Dublin; www.aerlingus.ie) and **British Airways** (☎ **0345/222-111** in Belfast; www.british-airways.com) both fly to Athens via London's Heathrow. Less-expensive charters operate in the summer from

Belfast and Dublin to Athens, less frequently to Corfu, Crete, Mykonos, and Rhodes. Contact any major travel agency for details. Students should contact **USIT,** at Aston Quay, O'Connell Bridge, Dublin 2 (☎ **01/679-8833**), or at Fountain Centre, College Street, Belfast (☎ **1232/324-073**).

UNITED KINGDOM British Airways (☎ 0345/222-111; www.british-airways.com), **Olympic Airways** (☎ 0870/6060-460; www.olympic-airways.gr), and **Virgin Atlantic** (☎ 01293/747-747; www.fly.virgin.com) have several flights daily from London's Heathrow Airport. For the smaller companies that offer no-frill flights, contact **EasyJet** (www.easyjet.com) or **Cronus Airlines** (☎ 020/7580-3500; www.cronus.gr). Eastern European airlines, such as **CSA Czech Airlines** (☎ 0171/255-1898; www.csa.cz), **Balkan Bulgarian Airlines** (☎ 0171/637-7637; www.balkan.com), and **Malev Hungarian Airlines** (☎ 0171/439-0577; www.malev-airlines.com), offer service to Athens via their capitals at good prices, but with frequent delays. There are also connecting flights to Athens and to Thessaloniki from Aberdeen, Belfast, Birmingham, Bristol, Edinburgh, Glasgow, Leeds, Liverpool, Newcastle, and Southampton; as well as flights to Athens and the major islands from Birmingham, Cardiff, Gatwick, Glasgow, Luton, and Manchester.

FROM AUSTRALIA & NEW ZEALAND

AUSTRALIA   Service to Athens is offered daily from Perth and Sydney and several times weekly from Brisbane and Melbourne by **Alitalia** (☎ 02/247-1308 in Sydney; www.alitalia.com), via Bangkok and Rome; **KLM Royal Dutch Airlines** (☎ 800/505-747 throughout Australia; www.klm.nl), via Singapore and Amsterdam; **Lufthansa** (☎ 02/367-3800 in Sydney; www.lufthansa.com), via Frankfurt; and **Olympic Airways** (☎ 02/251-2204 in Sydney; www.olympic-airways.gr), via Bangkok.

Generally, the lowest fares are offered by **Aeroflot** (☎ 02/233-7148 in Sydney; www.aeroflot.org), which provides weekly service from Sydney via Moscow; and by **Thai Airways** (☎ 02/844-0900 in Sydney; www.thaiair.com), which flies from Brisbane, Melbourne, Perth, and Sydney to Greece, via Bangkok. **British Airways** (☎ 02/258-3000 in Sydney; www.british-airways.com) and **Qantas Airways** (☎ 02/957-0111 in Sydney; www.qantas.com) have regular service to London; the "Global Explorer Pass" allows you to make up to six stopovers wherever the two airlines fly, except to South America.

NEW ZEALAND   The cheapest fares at press time were offered by **Singapore Airlines** (☎ 09/303-2506 in Auckland; www.singaporeair.com), with service via Singapore, and **Thai Airways** (☎ 09/377-3886 in Auckland; www.thaiair.com), with service via Bangkok. **Air New Zealand** (☎ 09/309-6171 in Auckland; www.airnz.co.nz) and **Qantas Airways** (☎ 09/303-3209 in Auckland; www.qantas.com) offer connections through **Lufthansa** (☎ 09/303-1529 in Auckland) to Athens. **British Airways** (☎ 09/367-7500 in Auckland; www.british-airways.com) and **Qantas** can get you to Europe; ask about the "Global Explorer Pass," with up to six stopovers. **Alitalia** (☎ 09/379-4457; www.alitalia.com) also flies to Athens, via Rome.

FROM SOUTH AFRICA

Olympic Airways (☎ 11/880-1614; www.olympic-airways.gr) offers the only direct flights from Johannesburg to Athens—about three times a week, each way. **Air France** (☎ 01/880-8040; www.airfrance.com), **Alitalia** (☎ 01/880-9254; www.alitalia.com), **British Airways** (☎ 01/975-3931; www.british-airways.com), and **Ethiopian Airlines** (☎ 01/616-7624; www.ethiopianairlines.com) also offer occasional flights to and from Johannesburg, with connections via other foreign cities.

FINDING THE BEST AIRFARE

BUCKET SHOPS & CONSOLIDATORS   Bucket shops—those companies you see advertising the very low prices—buy unused seats in bulk from the various airlines and sell them at a profit. You must usually be prepared to leave on short notice. A few are not entirely trustworthy, changes can be difficult, and most will not make refunds, so take precautions: Pay for tickets with a credit card, consider taking out cancellation insurance, and always confirm the reservation with the airline itself. Some frequently recommended consolidators that seem to stay in business are **Travac** (☎ **800/872-8800;** www.thetravelsite.com) and **greeceflights.com**. Another one that has gained boosters in recent years is **Europe By Air,** which has been offering a $99 flight pass between any two European cities; check its Web site (**www.europebyair.com**) or call ☎ **888/387/2479.**

CHARTER FLIGHTS   Most charter flights to Greece involve package groups originating in European cities; this is such a major business in Europe that we can only advise you to deal with travel agents who can provide all necessary details. There are a number of companies that charter less-expensive flights to Athens from the United States and that do not require package tours; generally you must book through a travel agent, and at least a month in advance to get on a flight in summer. Flights are less expensive in spring and fall, least expensive in winter, and slightly less expensive during the week. One company we continue to recommend is **Homeric Tours** (☎ **800/223-5570** or 212/753-1100), which at press time charged about $570 for a round-trip from New York in winter, about $700 in spring, and from about $500 to $700 in summer. It may have several flights a week between June and September, only one flight a week during the rest of the year. **Tourlite International** (☎ **800/272-7600** or 212/599-2727) charges similar fares for its flights between New York and Athens. Both companies also offer low-cost tours, car rentals, cruises, and hotel accommodations at considerable savings.

Note: Greece prohibits visitors on charter flights from leaving and reentering the country on their own—to prevent visitors from taking advantage of subsidized landing fees only to spend their time and money in, say, Turkey—and you should determine if this rule is being enforced before you break it.

INTERNET TRAVEL SITES   Increasingly more travel services are being offered on the Internet. Not everyone will feel comfortable ordering their tickets this way—it may seem complicated, impersonal, and even risky. Tickets bought from such agencies usually do not allow for changes or refunds. But some travelers might like to look to see what is offered. Among the better known and more useful Web sites are **expedia.msn.com**, **www.travelocity.com**, and **www.cheaptickets.com**.

BY TRAIN

In the late 1990s, train service from Western Europe was disrupted by the trouble in the Balkans. Even when running, the trains tend to be slow, and uncomfortable in the summer. But a Eurail Pass is valid for connections all the way to Athens or Istanbul and includes the ferry service from Italy. Note that North Americans must purchase their Eurail Passes before arriving in Europe. For information, see **www.raileurope. com**, or in the U.S. call ☎ **800/438-7245.**

BY BOAT

Most people who travel by ship to Greece from foreign ports come from Italy, although there is occasional service from Cyprus, Egypt, Israel, and Turkey. Brindisi to Patras is the most common ferry crossing, about a 10-hour voyage, with as many as seven departures a day in summer. There is also regular service, twice a day in

Street Names

The Greek word for "street" is *odos* and the word for "avenue" is *leoforos,* often abbreviated *Leof.,* usually applied to major thoroughfares. Numbers are written after rather than before the street name.

Plateia—think "place" or "plaza"—is Greek for square, and usually means a large public square, such as Syntagma (Constitution) Square in Athens, though sometimes a *plateia* may be little more than a wide area where important streets meet.

summer, from Ancona and Bari, once daily from Otranto, and two or three times a week from Trieste or Venice. Most ferries stop at Corfu or Igoumenitsou, often at both; in summer, occasionally a ship will also stop at Kefalonia.

If you want to learn more about the various ferry services between Greece and foreign ports, try the London-based agency **Viamare Travel,** Graphic House, 2 Sumatra Rd., London NW6 1PU (☎ **020/7431-4560;** fax 0171/431-5456; www. viamare.com; e-mail: ferries@viamare.com). There is also the new **Superfast Ferries Line,** Leoforos Alkyonidon 157, 16673 Athens (☎ **01/969-1100;** fax 01/969-1190; www.superfast.com; e-mail: superfast@superfast.com), which offers service between Ancona and Patras (17 hrs.) or Ancona and Igoumenitsa (15 hrs.); also between Bari and Patras (12 hrs.) or Bari and Igoumenitsa (8 hrs.). Not all these so-called superfast ferries actually save that much time if you take into consideration the time required to board and disembark from any ship, and they cost almost twice as much as regular ferries.

On the regular ferries, one-way fares during high season from Brindisi to Patras at press time cost from about Dr12,000 ($34) for a tourist-class deck chair to about Dr35,000 ($100) for an inside double cabin. Vehicles cost at least another Dr15,000 ($43). (*Note:* The lines usually offer considerable discounts on round-trip/return tickets.) Fares to Igoumenitsou are considerably cheaper, but by no means a better value unless your destination is nearby. Because of the number of shipping lines involved and the variations in schedules, we're not able to provide more concrete details. Consult a travel agent about the possibilities, book well ahead of time in summer, and reconfirm with the shipping line on the day of departure.

10 Getting Around

BY CAR

Driving in Greece is a bit of an adventure, but it's the best way to see the country at your own pace. Greece has one of the highest accident rates in Europe, probably due somewhat to treacherous roads, mountain terrain, and poor maintenance of older cars as much as to reckless driving—although Greeks are certainly aggressive drivers. Athens is a particularly intimidating place to drive in at first, and parking spaces are practically nonexistent in the center of town. Several of the major cities are linked by modern expressways with tolls: Athens to Thessaloniki, for instance, is expected to go up to Dr7,740 ($22). Accidents must be reported to the police for insurance claims.

The **Greek Automobile Touring Club (ELPA),** Odos Mesoyion 2, Athens (☎ **01/779-1615**), with offices in most cities, can help you with all matters relating to your car, issue international driver's licenses, and provide maps and information (☎ **174,** 24 hours daily). The emergency road service number is ☎ **104,** and the service provided by the able ELPA mechanics is free for light repairs, but you should definitely give a generous tip.

CAR RENTALS   There is an abundance of rental cars, with considerable variation in prices. However, many cars have a standard shift; if you must have an automatic, you are strongly advised to make your reservation before leaving home and well in advance. Always ask if the quoted price includes insurance; many credit cards make the collision-damage waiver unnecessary, but you will find that most rental agencies simply include this in their rates. You can usually save by booking at home before you leave, and this is especially advisable in summer. When shopping around for a bargain, be sure to carry along and display a number of brochures from competitors.

Most companies require that the renter be at least 21 years old (25 for some models, and sometimes no older than 70 to 75: Inquire!); possess a valid Australian, Canadian, EU-nation, U.S., or international driver's license; and have a major credit card or leave a large cash deposit.

The major rental companies in Athens are **Avis** (☎ **01/322-4951**), **Budget** (☎ **01/921-4771**), **Hertz** (☎ **01/922-0102**), and **National** (☎ **01/459-6381**), all with additional offices in major cities, at most airports, and on most islands. Smaller local companies usually have lower rates, but their vehicles are often older and not as well maintained. If you prefer to combine your car rental with your other travel arrangements, we recommend **Galaxy Travel,** Odos Voulis 35, near Syntagma Square (☎ **01/322-5960;** fax 01/322-9538; www.galaxytravel.gr; e-mail: info@galaxytravel. gr). It's open Monday through Saturday.

Daily rates for cars during the high season start at about Dr6,000 ($17), plus Dr100 (30¢) per kilometer, or Dr114,000 ($328) a week with unlimited mileage for the smallest cars such as a Fiat or Suzuki; for larger models, comparable rates are Dr17,000 ($49) and Dr160 (50¢), or Dr320,000 ($921). In low season, rates are often negotiable. And be prepared to have about 18% in VAT taxes plus 2% in municipal taxes added to the quoted price! (There's also a hefty surcharge for pickup and drop-off at airports.) *Note:* You must have written permission from the car-rental agency to take your car on a ferry or into a foreign country.

DRIVING YOUR OWN VEHICLE   To drive your own vehicle, valid registration papers, an international third-party insurance certificate, and a driver's license are required. Valid American and EU licenses are accepted in Greece. A free entry card allows you to keep your car in the country up to 4 months, after which another 8 months can be arranged without having to pay import duty.

DRIVING RULES   You drive on the right in Greece, pass on the left, and yield right-of-way to vehicles approaching from the right except where otherwise posted. Greece has adopted international road signs, though many Greeks apparently haven't learned what they mean yet. The maximum speed limit is 100 kilometers per hour (65 m.p.h.) on open roads, and 50 kilometers per hour (30 m.p.h.) in town, unless otherwise posted. Seat belts are required. The police have become increasingly strict in recent years, especially with foreigners in rental cars; alcohol tests can be given and fines imposed on the spot. (If you feel you have been stopped or treated unfairly, get the officer's name and report him at the nearest tourist police station.) Honking is illegal in Athens, but you can hear that law broken by tarrying at a traffic signal.

PARKING   Parking a car has become a serious challenge in the cities and towns of Greece. The better hotels probably provide parking, either on their premises or by some arrangement with a nearby lot. There are few parking garages or lots in Greece. Follow the blue signs with their white *"P"* and you may be lucky enough to find an available space. Most Greek city streets have restricted parking of one kind or another. But in some cities, signs—usually yellow, and with the directions in English as well as Greek—will indicate that you can park along the street but must purchase a ticket from the nearest kiosk. Otherwise, be prepared to park fairly far from your base or destination. If you lock your car and remove all obvious valuables from sight, you should not have to worry about it being broken into.

CAR FERRIES   Car ferry service is available on most larger ferries, and there's regular service from Piraeus to Aegina and Poros in the Saronic Gulf, most of the Cyclades, Chania and Iraklion on Crete, Hios, Kos, Lesvos, Rhodes, and Samos. For the Cyclades, crossing is shorter and less expensive from Rafina, an hour east of Athens. From Patras, there's daily service to Corfu, Ithaka, and Kefalonia. In the summer, there are four car ferries daily from Kyllini to Zakinthos. The Sporades have service from Ayios Konstandinos, Kimi, and Volos (and then among the several islands). The short car ferry across the Gulf of Corinth from Rio to Antirio can save a lot of driving for those traveling between the northwest and the Peloponnese or Athens. There's also service between many of the islands, even between Crete and Rhodes, as well as car crossing to and from Turkey between Hios and Çesme, Lesvos and Dikeli, and Samos and Kusadasi. (If you intend to continue on with your vehicle into either country coming from the other, you better inquire long before setting off for either country and make sure that you have all the necessary paperwork.)

BY PLANE

Compared to the cheaper classes on ships and ferries, air travel within Greece can be expensive, but we recommend it for those pressed for time and/or heading for the more distant destinations (even if the planes don't always hold strictly to schedule). Until the late 1990s, **Olympic Airways** (☎ **01/966-6666;** fax 01/921-9933) maintained a monopoly on domestic air travel and thus had little incentive to improve service; in fact, it effectively became bankrupt and was placed under new management, which has been steadily improving service. Better computerized booking has reduced the possibility of finding out at the last minute that you don't actually have a seat, but delayed flights are still common; although the quality of the service is criticized by some, Olympic actually has one of the best safety records of any major airline. (Their domestic flight attendants tend to be more pleasant than their international counterparts.) Book as far ahead of time as possible (especially in the summer), reconfirm your booking before leaving for the airport, and try to arrive at the airport at least an hour before departure; the scene at a check-in counter can become quite hectic.

Olympic Airways has a number of offices in Athens, though most travel agents sell tickets as well. It offers service on the **mainland** to Aktaion Preveza, Alexandroupolis, Ioannina, Kalamata, Kavala, Kastoria, Kozani, and Thessaloniki; and for **islands,** to Astipalea, Corfu (Kerkira), Crete (Iraklion, Chania, Sitia), Chios, Ikaria, Karpathos, Kassos, Kastellorizo, Kefalonia, Kos, Kithira, Leros, Limnos, Milos, Mykonos, Mitilini (Lesvos), Naxos, Paros, Rhodes, Samos, Santorini (Thira), Skiathos, Skyros, Siros, Sitia, and Zakinthos. All of Olympic's domestic flights leave from Athens's West Terminal, often called Olympiki. Most flights are to or from Athens, though there is some inter-island service. The baggage allowance is 15 kilos (33 lb.) per passenger, except with a connecting international flight; even the domestic flights generally ignore the weight limit unless you are way over. Smoking is prohibited on all domestic flights.

Round-trip tickets cost simply double the one-way fare. Some sample one-way fares (including taxes) at this writing are: Athens to Corfu, Ioannina, Mykonos, Rhodes, or Thessaloniki, Dr15,700 to Dr20,000 ($45 to $57)); Athens to Iraklion, Chania, or Skiathos, Dr14,000 to 18,000($40 to $52); Athens to Rhodes or Santorini, Dr18,500 ($53). As you can see, the shorter trips, such as to Mykonos or Santorini, are not especially cheap, but there's no denying that for those with limited time, air travel is

Greece by Plane

the best way to go. Ask about Olympic's new offer of reduced fares for trips between Monday and Thursday and trips that include a Saturday-night stay.

Meanwhile, several small private airlines have sprung up, the two survivors at press time being **Aegean Airlines** and **Cronus Airlines.** They offer limited service at somewhat reduced prices between Athens and a few major destinations such as Alexandropoulis, Corfu, Crete, Ioannina, Kavala, Mitiline, Patras, Rhodes, Santorini, and Thessaloniki. As schedules and fares remain in flux, ask a travel agent to check these out. People who are using these flights report they are reliable, safe, cheaper, and generally satisfactory.

Note: Most of these Greek domestic tickets are nonrefundable, and changing your flight can cost you up to 30% within 24 hours of departure and 50% within 12 hours.

BY TRAIN

Greek trains are generally slow, but inexpensive and fairly pleasant. The **Hellenic State Railway (OSE)** also operates some bus service from stations adjacent to major terminals. (Bus service is faster, but second-class train fare is nearly 50% cheaper, and trains offer a more comfortable and scenic ride.) If you are interested in some of the special arrangements involving rail passes for Greece (sometimes in combination with Olympic flights within Greece), check out **www.raileurope.com** or call ☎ **888/382-7245** (in the U.S. only).

For information and tickets in Athens, visit the **OSE office** at Odos Karolou 1–3 (☎ **01/522-4563**), or Odos Sina 6 (☎ **01/362-4402**), both near Omonia Square.

Information is also available at Odos Filellinon 17 (☎ 01/323-6747), near Syntagma Square.

Purchase your ticket and reserve a seat ahead of time, as a 50% surcharge is added to tickets purchased on the train and some lines are packed, especially in summer. A first-class ticket may be worth the extra cost, as seats are more comfortable and less crowded. There is sleeper service (costly, but a good value if you can sleep on a train; you must be prepared to share a compartment with three to five others) on the Athens–Thessaloniki run, and express service (6 hrs.) twice a day, at 7am and 1pm.

Trains to northern Greece (Alexandroupolis, Florina, Kalambaka, Lamia, Larissa, Thessaloniki, Volos, etc.) leave from the Larissa Station (Stathmos Larissis). **Trains to the Peloponnese** (Argos, Corinth, Patras) leave from the nearby Peloponnese Station (Stathmos Peloponnisou). Take trolley no. 1 or 5 from Syntagma Square to both stations.

The Peloponnese circuit from Corinth to Patras, Pirgos (near Olympia), Tripolis, and Argos is one way to experience this scenic region, though the Athens–Patras stretch is often crowded. The spectacular spur between Diakofto and Kalavrita is particularly recommended for train enthusiasts.

BY BUS

Public buses are inexpensive but often overcrowded. Local buses vary from place to place, but on most islands the bus stop is usually fairly central with a posted schedule; destinations are (usually—so ask!) displayed on the front of the bus. Fare is collected after departure by a conductor. In Athens and other large cities, a ticket must be purchased before boarding—kiosks usually offer them, as well as schedule information—and validated after boarding. *Note:* Save your ticket in case an "inspector" comes aboard!

Greece has an extensive **long-distance bus service (KTEL),** an association of regional operators with green-and-yellow buses that usually leave from convenient central stations. For information about the long-distance offices, contact the KTEL office in Athens (☎ 01/512-5954).

In Athens, **most buses head to destinations within Attica** leave from the Mavromate terminal, north of the National Archaeological Museum; **most buses to central Greece** leave from Odos Liossion 60, 5 kilometers (3.1 miles) north of Omonia Square (take local bus no. 024 from Leoforos Amalias in front of the entrance to the National Garden and tell the driver your destination); **most buses to the Peloponnese, Western, and Northern Greece** leave from the terminal at Odos Kifissou 100, 4 kilometers (2.5 miles) northeast of Omonia Square (take local bus No. 051 from 2 blocks west of Omonia, near the big church of Ayios Konstandinos, at Zinonos and Menandrou).

Express buses between major cities, usually air-conditioned, can be booked through travel agencies. Make sure you're pronouncing your destination properly, or at least are being understood—you wouldn't be the first to see a bit more of Greece than bargained for—and determine the bus's schedule and comforts before purchasing your ticket. Many buses are not air-conditioned, take torturous routes, and make frequent stops. (NO SMOKING signs are generally disregarded by drivers and conductors, as well as by many older male passengers.)

Organized and guided **bus tours** are widely available; some of them will pick you up at your hotel. Ask at your hotel or almost any travel agent in Athens. One that is especially recommended is **CHAT Tours,** the oldest and probably most experienced in providing a wide selection of bus tours led by highly articulate guides. Almost any travel agent can book its tours, but if you want to deal with the organization directly, contact its office at 214 Bedford Rd., Toronto, Ontario M5R 2K9 (☎ 800/ 268-1180). And of course there is always the longtime favorite, **American Express,** with offices all over North America and Europe; the Athens office is located prominently on Syntagma Square. *Note:* Readers have complained that some bus groups are so large that they feel removed from the leader; inquire about group size if this concerns you.

BY BOAT

BY FERRY   Ferries are the most common, cheapest, and generally the most "authentic" way to visit the islands, though the slow roll of a ferry can be authentically stomach-churning. A wide variety of vessels sail Greek waters—some huge, sleek, and new, with comfortable TV lounges, discos, and good restaurants; some old and ill-kept, but pleasant enough if you stay outside. Now, too, there are the "flying dolphins," or hydrofoils, that service all the major islands. These are undoubtedly faster, but they cost almost twice as much as regular ferries and their schedules are often interrupted by weather conditions. (Never rely on a tight connection between a hydrofoil and, say, an airplane flight.) Ferries, too, often don't hold exactly to their schedules, but they can be fun if you enjoy opportunities to meet people. Drinks and snacks are almost always sold, but the prices and selection are never that good, so you may want to bring along your own.

The map of Greece offered by the Greek Tourist Organization (EOT), which has the common routes indicated, is very useful in planning your sea travels. Once you've learned what is possible, you can turn your attention to what is available. Remember that the summer schedule is the fullest, spring and fall have reduced service, and winter schedules are skeletal.

There are dozens of shipping companies, each with its own schedule—which, by the way, are regulated by the government. Your travel agent might have a copy of *Hellenic Travelling,* a monthly travel guide published by GNTO, or another similar summary of schedules, *Greek Travel Pages.* But it's best to go straight to an official information office, a travel agency, or the port authority as soon as you arrive at the place that you intend to leave via ferry.

Photos can give you some idea of the ships, but remember any photo displayed was probably taken when the ship was new, no matter when it was reproduced, and it is unlikely that anyone will be able (or willing) to tell you its actual age. The bigger ferries offer greater stability during rough weather. Except in the summer, you can usually depend on getting aboard a ferry by showing up about an hour before scheduled departure—inter-island boats sometimes depart before their scheduled time—and purchasing a ticket from a dockside agent or aboard the ship itself, though this is often more expensive.

Your best bet is to buy a ticket from an agent ahead of time. In Athens we recommend **Galaxy Travel,** Odos Voulis 35, near Syntagma Square (☎ 01/322-5960; fax 01/322-9538), and **Alkyon Travel,** Akademias 97, near Kanigos Square (☎ 01/ 383-2545; fax 01/383-03948). During the high season, both keep long hours from

> ### Early-Season Ferries
>
> In the early weeks of the tourist season, from April to early May, the boat services are altogether unpredictable. Boat schedules, at the best of times, are tentative—but during this time, they are wish lists, nothing more. Our best advice is to wait until you get to Greece, and then go to a major travel agency and ask for help.

Greek Ferry Routes

Monday through Saturday. But be aware: Different travel agencies sell tickets to different lines—this is usually the policy of the line itself—and one agent might not know or bother to find out what else is being offered (although we believe that if you press reputable agencies like those above, they will at least tell you of the other possibilities). The port authority is the most reliable source of information, and the shipping company itself or its agents usually offer better prices and may have tickets when other agents have exhausted their allotment. It often pays to shop around a little to compare vessels and prices.

First class usually has roomy air-conditioned cabins and its own lounge and on some routes costs almost as much as flying; but consider that on longer overnight hauls, you're essentially on a comfortable floating hotel and thus save that cost. Second class has smaller cabins (which you will probably have to share with strangers) and its own lounge. The tourist-class fare entitles you to a seat on the deck or in a lounge. (Tourists usually head for the deck, while the Greeks stay inside, watch TV, and smoke copiously.) Hold on to your ticket; crews usually conduct ticket-control sweeps.

Note: Those taking a ferry to Turkey from one of the Dodecanese islands must submit their passport and payment to an agent the day before departure.

We include more details on service and schedules in the relevant chapters that follow, as well as suggested travel agencies and sources of local information. But just to give some sense of the fares, here are examples for first-class travel from Piraeus at press time: to Crete (Iraklion), Dr19,000 ($54); Kos, Dr26,000 ($74); Mitilini (Lesvos),

Dr19,000 ($54); Mykonos, Dr11,000 ($32); Naxos, Dr12,000 ($34); Rhodes, Dr28,900 ($83); Santorini, Dr14,000 ($40). The value-added tax (VAT) of 8% and a small embarkation tax will be added.

BY HYDROFOIL Hydrofoils (often referred to by the principal line's trade name, **Flying Dolphins,** or by Greeks as *to flying*) are nearly twice as fast as ferries, and have comfortable airline-style seats. Their stops are much shorter, and they are less likely to cause seasickness. Although they cost nearly twice as much as ferries, are frequently fully booked in summer, can be quite bumpy during rough weather, and give little or no view of the passing scenery, they're the best choice for those with limited time, and everyone should try one of these sleek little craft at least once. There is presently regular hydrofoil service to nearly all the major islands, with new service appearing every year. Longer trips over open sea, such as between Santorini and Iraklion, Crete, may make them well worth the extra expense. (Smoking is prohibited, and actually less likely to be indulged in, possibly because the cabins seem so much like those of an aircraft.) The forward compartment offers better views, but is also bumpy.

The Flying Dolphins are now operated by **Minoan Flying Dolphins,** Leoforos Vassilios Constantinou 2, 11635 Athens (☎ **01/428-0001;** e-mail: booking@mfd.gr). The service from Zea Marina in Piraeus to the Saronic Gulf islands and the Peloponnese is especially good. (The fare to Spetses is about Dr7,000/$20, as compared to about Dr3,500/$10 for tourist-class ferry service.) Flying Dolphin service in the Sporades is also recommended for its speed and regularity. There is also service from Rafina, on the east coast of Attika, to several of the Cyclades islands.

BY SAILBOAT & YACHT Increasing numbers of people are choosing to explore Greece by sailboat or yacht. Sailing and yachting require such specialized skills and equipment that it is unlikely that anyone wanting to undertake either of these activities in Greece will depend on a general guide such as this. But clearly there are numerous facilities and possibilities for both. Experienced sailors interested in renting a boat in Greece can contact the **Hellenic Professional and Bareboat Yacht Owners' Association,** Zea Marina, 18536 Piraeus (☎ **01/452-6335**). One possibility is to sign up for one of the flotillas—a group of around 12 or more sailboats that sail about as a group led by a boat crewed by experienced sailors; the largest of such organizations is **Sunsail,** 980 Awald Rd., Annapolis, MD 21403 (☎ **800/327-2276**), but travel agencies should be able to put you in touch with one of these organizations.

At the other extreme, those who want to charter a yacht with anything from a basic skipper to a full crew should probably first contact the **Hellenic Professional Yacht Owners' Association** (listed above) or **Ghiolman Yachts,** Odos Filellinon 7, 10557 Athens (☎ **01/323-0330;** fax 01/322-3251; www.ghiolman.com). If you feel competent to make your own arrangements, contact **Valef Yachts Ltd.,** P.O. Box 391, Ambler, PA 19002 (☎ **215/641-1624;** www.valefyachts.com; e-mail: valef@ix. netcom.com). In Greece, you can either contact one of these associations or a private agency such as **Alpha Yachting,** Leoforos Vasileos Yioryios 67, 16674 Glyfada (☎ **01/968-0486**); **Aris Drivas Yachting,** Odos Neorion 147, Piraeus (☎ **01/ 411-3194**); or **Thalassa Charter and Yacht Brokers,** Odos Grypari 72, Kallithea, Athens (☎ **01/956-6866**). Just to give some idea of the prices, in 2000 Ghiolman Yachts offered a 1-week sail around the Cyclades for $675—quite reasonable when you consider what airfares and hotels might cost.

BY TAXI

Taxis are one of the most convenient means of getting about in Greece. They can also be the most exasperating, although there have been improvements in recent years. For

Taxi Tips

- Check that the meter's turned on—sometimes the driver hopes you won't notice it's been left off, and then tries to extort a much larger fare from you. Even if you don't speak a word of Greek besides "taxi," point at the meter and say "meter."
- The little window next to the Drachma display on the meter will be set on "2" for late-night/early-morning or outside-the-city-limits rates. If that's not the case, reach over and indicate that you notice.
- With a group of tourists, a driver may insist that each person pay the full metered fare. Pay one fare only. (In pairs or groups, have a designated arguer; the others can write down names and numbers, stick with the luggage, or look for help—from a policeman, maitre d', or desk clerk.)
- Late at night, especially at airports, ferry stops, and bus and railroad stations, a driver may refuse to use his meter and demand an exorbitant fare. Smile, shake your head, and look for another cab; if none are available, begin to write down the license number of the first driver and he will probably relent.
- Legal surcharges include Dr300 (90¢) for pickup from an airport; Dr150 (45¢) for pickup from bus, train, or seaport terminals; and Dr50 (15¢) per piece of luggage over 10 kilos (22 lbs).
- A driver may say that your hotel is full, but he knows a better and cheaper one. Laugh, and insist you'll take your chances at your hotel.
- A driver may want to let you off where it's most convenient for him. Be cooperative if it's easier and quicker for you to cross a busy avenue than for him to get you to the other side, but you don't have to get out of the cab until you're ready.

If things are obviously not going well for you, conspicuously write down the driver's name and number and by all means report him to the **tourist police** (☎ 171) if he has the nerve to call your bluff. One of the best countertactics is to simply reach for the door latch and open the door slightly; he won't want to risk damaging it. (Two of you can each open a door.)

Our final advice: Don't sweat the small change. So the driver is charging you Dr2,300 ($7) for a ride you have been told should be about Dr2,000 ($6); are you prepared to go to court for $1? But any difference from Dr500 ($1.45) up probably should be questioned. Most cabbies are honest—we don't want to make you paranoid, just aware of the possibilities. And please be sure to reward good service with a tip.

instance, you no longer have to fight for a cab at most airports; just find the line. Cabs are considerably less expensive in Athens than they are in London, New York, or Toronto. There are probably no greater percentage of cheats among the drivers than in all major cities around the world—and many Greek taxi drivers are good-natured, helpful, and informative. Language and cultural difficulties, however, can make it easier for them to gouge you, and some drivers take advantage of the opportunity. The converse, though, is sometimes true: Language gaps often lead to genuine misunderstandings. There are some legitimate surcharges—for heavy luggage, from midnight to 5am (almost twice the regular rate!), on holidays, from and to airports, etc. Ask to see the official rate sheet that the driver is required to carry.

Get your hotel desk to help you in hailing or booking a taxi. Radio cabs cost Dr600 ($1.75) extra, but you'll have some leverage. Restaurants and businesses can also help in calling or hailing a cab, negotiating a fare, and making sure your destination is understood. Take a card from your hotel, have your destination written down, or learn to pronounce it at least semi-correctly. Be willing to share a cab with other passengers picked up on the way, especially during rush hour; think of it as your contribution to better efficiency and less pollution (and you are not supposed to pay more than your proportion of the shared fare). Always have some vague idea of where you're going on the map, so you don't end up going to Plaka from Syntagma by way of Kolonaki. (There are, however, several ways of getting to Plaka from Syntagma.) Don't be bothered by bullying or bluster; try to find it amusing and counter with your own bluff, showing your superiority by keeping your cool. See also "Taxi Tips," above.

BY MOPED, MOTORBIKE & MOTORCYCLE

There seems to be no end to the number of mopeds, motorbikes, motorcycles, and related vehicles available for rent in Greece. They can be an inexpensive way to get around, especially in the islands, but they are not recommended for everyone: Greek hospitals admit scores of tourists injured on mopeds or motorbikes every summer, and there are a number of fatalities. Roads are often poorly paved and shoulderless; loose gravel or stones are another common problem. Meanwhile, as of 2000, Greek law requires that all renters of mopeds and motorcycles be licensed to operate such vehicles; it remains to be seen how this will be enforced. In any case, make sure you have insurance and that the machine is in good working condition before you take it. Helmets are required by law and strongly recommended, although you will rarely see Greeks wearing them.

Some of us wish the larger motorbikes and motorcycles were forbidden on all the islands, as Greek youths seem to delight in punching holes in the muffler and tearing around all hours of the day and night. (Some islands are wisely banning them from certain areas and restricting the hours of use, as they are the single most common cause of complaint from tourists and residents alike.) The motorcycles rented to tourists are usually a bit quieter, but they are more expensive and at least as dangerous; strictly speaking, a special license is required to rent one.

BY BICYCLE

Bicycles are not nearly as common in Greece as they are throughout most of Europe, as they are not well suited to Greek terrain or temperament and would be downright dangerous in traffic. In less hectic towns and countryside, however, a bicycle might be a fine way to get about short distances. Older bikes are usually available for rent at modest prices in most resort areas, and good mountain bikes are increasingly available. (See "The Active Vacation Planner," above, for more information.)

Warning

Although mopeds are the vehicle of choice in Greece, especially on the islands, be aware that there is a Greek law (prompted by a huge number of accidents) requiring a motorcycle license for anyone driving a moped. Agencies offering moped rentals rarely tell tourists this because very few tourists have motorcycle licenses. This makes for a whirlwind of troubles if an accident occurs and the rider is found to not have been licensed. The rider will not be covered by insurance and will have broken the law. Better check with your own driver's and/or medical insurance plan to see if you are covered for such an eventuality.

Fast Facts: Greece

Area Code   The international telephone country code for Greece is **30.** To call Greece from abroad, dial the international access code from your base country plus 30 (Greece's code) plus the Greek area (or city) code *minus* the first zero, then the number. The international access code from Australia is **0011;** from Ireland, New Zealand, and the United Kingdom, **00;** from the United States and Canada, **011.** See also "Telephone," below.

ATMs   See "Money," earlier in this chapter.

Banks   Banks are open to the public Monday through Thursday from 8am to 2pm, Friday from 8am to 1:30pm. Some banks have additional hours for foreign currency exchange. All banks are closed on the long list of Greek holidays (see "When to Go," earlier in this chapter).

Business Hours   Greek business and office hours take some getting used to, especially in the afternoon, when most English-speaking people are accustomed to getting things done in high gear. Compounding the problem is that it is virtually impossible to pin down the precise hours of opening. We can start by saying that almost all stores and services are still closed on Sunday—except, of course, tourist-oriented shops and services. On Monday, Wednesday, and Saturday, hours are usually 9am to 3pm; Tuesday, Thursday, and Friday, 9am to 2pm and 5 to 7pm. The afternoon siesta is still generally observed from 3 to 5pm, though many tourist-oriented businesses have a minimal crew during nap time and may keep extended hours, often from 8am to 10pm. (In fact, in tourist centers, shops may be open at all kinds of hours.) Most government offices are open Monday through Friday only, from 8am to 3pm. We suggest you call ahead to check the hours of businesses you *must* deal with and that you not disturb Greek friends during siesta hours. Final advice: Anything you really need to accomplish in a government office, business, or store should be done on weekdays between about 9am and 1pm.

Car Rentals   See "Getting Around," earlier in this chapter.

Climate   See "When to Go," earlier in this chapter.

Climate Control   Almost all Greek hotels in the categories patronized by most users of this guide now promise air-conditioning in the hot season and heating in the colder months. The equipment is indeed there, but you should be aware that—except in the most expensive hotels—neither will necessarily be as adequate as you might like.

Crime   Crimes against tourists are not a significant concern in Greece. Athens is probably the safest capital in Europe. Pocket-picking and purse-snatching may be slightly on the rise, especially in heavily touristed areas, but breaking into cars remains rare. Tourists, however, are conspicuous and much more likely to be carrying valuables, so take normal precautions—lock the car, don't leave cameras and such gear visible, etc. Young women should observe the obvious precautions in dealing with males in isolated locales.

Currency   See "Money," earlier in this chapter.

Customs   You are allowed to bring into Greece duty-free personal belongings including clothes, camping gear, and most sports equipment. (Certain water-sports equipment, such as Windsurfers, can be brought in only if a Greek citizen residing in Greece guarantees they will be re-exported. Scuba diving is presently

Booking a Room

Try to make reservations by fax so that you have a written record of what room and price were agreed upon. Also, a double room in Greece usually does not mean a room with a double bed, but a room with two twin beds. Double beds in Greece are called "matrimonial beds," and rooms with such beds are often designated "honeymoon rooms." This can lead to misunderstandings.

Note that in a few instances—usually at the most expensive hotels—the prices quoted are per person. Note, too, that room prices, no matter what people say officially, are often negotiable, especially at the edges of the season. Because of Greek law and OTE regulations, hotel keepers are often reluctant to provide rates far in advance and often quote prices higher than their actual rates. When you bargain, don't cite our prices, which may be too high, but ask instead for the best current rate. Actual off-season prices may be as much as 25% lower than the lowest rate given to us for the book.

---

restricted to special areas, and divers may have difficulty bringing in equipment.) You may bring two cameras with 10 rolls of film each, a movie or video camera, a portable radio, a phonograph or tape recorder, a typewriter, a laptop computer, and new articles (including electronic equipment) worth up to Dr10,000 ($29) or Dr40,000 ($115) for EU members, provided they are not for resale.

Visitors from outside the European Union are allowed up to 10 kilos of food and beverage, 200 cigarettes (300 for EU members), 50 cigars (75, EU), 250 grams of tobacco (400, EU), 1 liter of distilled alcohol or 2 liters of wine (1¹/₂ liters of alcohol or 5 liters of wine, EU), 50 grams of perfume (75 grams, EU), 500 grams of coffee (1 kilo, EU), and 100 grams of tea (400 grams, EU).

There are presently no restrictions on the amount of traveler's checks either arriving or departing, though amounts over $1,000 should technically be declared. If you plan to leave the country with more than $500 in bank notes (or its equivalent in other currency), technically you must declare at least that sum on entry. No Greek money more than Dr10,000 per traveler may be imported or exported.

Explosives, weapons, and narcotics are prohibited; violations are subject to severe punishment. Medication, except for amounts properly prescribed for your own use, and plants with soil are prohibited. Passengers from North America arriving in Athens aboard international flights are generally not searched, and if they have nothing to declare, continue through a green lane. (Because of the continuing threat of terrorism, baggage is x-rayed before boarding domestic flights.)

Dogs and cats may be brought in with proper health documentation, including rabies inoculation, not newer than 6 days before arrival nor older than 12 months for dogs and 6 months for cats.

Greek antiquities are strictly protected by law, and no genuine antiquities may be taken out of Greece without prior special permission from the **Archaeological Service,** Odos Polignotou 3, Athens. Also, you should expect to explain how you acquired any genuinely old objects—in particular, icons or religious articles. A dealer or shopkeeper should provide you with an export certificate for any object dating from before 1830.

Remember to keep receipts for at least all major purchases for clearing customs on your return home.

Dentists & Doctors   Ask your embassy or consulate in a major city or your hotel's management to direct you to a dentist or doctor who speaks either English or some other common European language.

Driving Rules   See "Getting Around," earlier in this chapter.

Drugs   Greek authorities and laws are reputed to be extremely tough when it comes to finding foreigners with drugs—starting with marijuana. Do not attempt to bring any illicit drugs into or out of Greece.

Drugstores   See "Pharmacies," below.

Electricity   Electric current in Greece is 220 volts AC, alternating at 50 cycles. (Some larger hotels have 110-volt low-wattage outlets for electric shavers, but they aren't good for hair dryers and most other appliances.) Electrical outlets require Continental-type plugs with two round prongs. U.S. travelers will need an adapter plug *and* a transformer/converter, unless their appliances are dual-voltage. (Such transformers can be bought in stores like Radio Shack.) Laptop-computer users will want to check their requirements; a transformer may be necessary, and surge protectors are recommended.

Embassies & Consulates   See "Fast Facts: Athens" in chapter 5 for a list of embassies and consulates. United Kingdom citizens can get emergency aid by calling ☎ **01/723-6211** during the day; at night, try ☎ **01/723-7727** or 01/724-1331. United States citizens can get emergency aid by calling ☎ **01/721-2951** during the day; at night, try ☎ **01/729-4301** or 01/729-4444.

Emergencies   These numbers can be used throughout Greece. For the regular **police,** dial ☎ **100;** for **tourist police,** dial ☎ **171.** For **fire,** dial ☎ **199.** For **medical emergencies** and/or first aid and/or an ambulance, dial ☎ **166.** For **hospitals,** dial ☎ **106.** For **automobile emergencies,** put out a triangular danger sign and telephone ☎ **104** or **174.**

Faxes   Almost all hotels in the higher categories, many telephone offices, some post offices, and some travel agencies will send and receive faxes locally and internationally for you at set fees. But don't forget: Sending a fax is the equivalent of making a phone call, so you must be prepared to pay for that plus the extra service of the fax machine (about Dr1,500/$4.30 per page to the U.S.).

Guides   Some individuals may prefer to employ local guides to take them and/or a small circle of fellow travelers to visit sites or cities. Professional guides in Greece are thoroughly trained, and the fees they charge are well regulated. Most reputable travel agencies can arrange for such guides. You can also contact the **Union of Official Guides,** Odos Apollonos 9A, 10557 Athens (☎ **01/322-9705;** fax 01/323-9200). We might only caution that as good as these official guides are, they are trained to produce a stream of facts, not make small talk.

Holidays   See "When to Go," earlier in this chapter.

Information   See "Visitor Information," earlier in this chapter.

Internet Access   Now immensely popular throughout the world, **Internet cafes,** or cafes-with-computers (sometimes known as cybercafes), are springing up in most of Greece's cities and resort towns. For a set fee—usually about Dr1,500 ($4.30) an hour, with a Dr500 ($1.45) minimum—you get access to the Internet. (It is not required that you buy a drink while using the computer, but why not enjoy the experience?) It should be said, though, that most Greek computers and Internet-access services are considerably slower than what North Americans are accustomed to.

In the destination chapters that follow, we indicate the location of such Internet cafes wherever they are known. If you want to be prepared before you leave for Greece, visit one of the Web sites dedicated to listing Internet cafes worldwide. At press time, two of the better ones are **www.cybercafe.com** and **www.netcafeguide.com**. But be warned: Although such listings might be more up-to-date than our text, we also find these listings are by no means complete.

Once you're seated in an Internet cafe, there are several ways you might access to your e-mail. If your provider is AOL, you should be able to easily access your e-mail on the Web. Numerous **free e-mail services** are available: Try **www.excite.com** or **www.hotmail.com**. Any traveler with this kind of account can access e-mail from any computer worldwide that has Internet access. Simply enter your ID and password, and hope for (relatively) rapid and reliable access.

There is yet another way to get e-mail: Sign up with one of the free services that allows you to get access to your e-mail on your home computer, no matter what provider you subscribe to. One of the best is **www.webmail.com**; make sure you register for the service before leaving home.

If you're trying to access e-mail through your own laptop, note that it's not all that easy, at least as of this writing. For one thing, many Greek hotel rooms do not have the proper data or fax lines, so even if you find a phone jack, your computer cannot connect. (Digital lines do not work and some say can damage your modem. In any case, they require an expensive ISDN modem.) Assuming you can get a connection, unless you have arranged for some special service before leaving home, you will be charged heavily for a long-distance phone call along with any fees that your own service provider may charge. That said, increasing numbers of Greek hotels and conference centers are promoting Internet access as an amenity, so if it matters to you, make specific inquiries before reserving. We recommend that you not plan to use your laptop for modem-based operations unless you are very sure of what you are doing. (For details, see **www. roadnews.com**.)

Language   Language is usually not a problem for English speakers in Greece, as so much of the population has lived abroad, where English is the primary language; meanwhile, young people learn it in school, from Anglo-American–dominated pop culture, and in special classes meant to prepare them for the contemporary world of business. Many television programs are also broadcast in their original language, and American prime-time soaps are very popular, nearly inescapable. Even advertisements have an increasingly high English content.

Don't let all this keep you from trying to pick up at least a few words of Greek; your effort will be rewarded by your hosts, who realize how difficult their language is for foreigners and will patiently help you improve your pronunciation and usage. There are various taped programs, including **Berlitz's Greek for Travelers** and **Passport's Conversational Greek in 7 Days,** which can be very helpful.

Our appendix B, "The Greek Language," will teach you the basics.

Laptops   Increasing numbers of travelers are choosing to take their laptops along, whether to keep up with work assignments, write personal notes, or stay in touch with the outside world via the Internet. Since Greece operates on 220 volts, you must make sure that your computer has a built-in capacity to handle this voltage or else travel with a transformer and probably a surge protector

(See "Electricity," above). That will take care of the computer for all non-modem functions, but if you want to use it to gain access to the Internet, considerably more is involved. For this, see "Internet Access," above.

Laundry & Dry Cleaning   All cities and towns of any size will have both laundry and dry-cleaning establishments. Many travelers will prefer to make arrangements through their hotel desks; this is fine, but be prepared to pay heavily for even the smallest bundle. (Then again, everything including socks will have been ironed!) If you are more ambitious (or frugal), you can seek out one of the laundries that we try to mention in later chapters wherever available. In most instances, these are attended; you can leave your laundry to be picked up later (be sure you are in agreement as to the time it will be ready, especially if you must leave town!). A medium-size bag of laundry may cost about Dr2,500 ($7), washed, dried, and neatly folded.

Mail   You can receive mail addressed to you c/o Poste Restante, General Post Office, City (or Town), Island (or Province), Greece. You will need your passport to collect this mail. Many hotels will accept, hold, and even forward mail for you also; ask first. American Express clients can receive mail at any Amex office in Athens, Corfu, Iraklion, Mykonos, Patras, Rhodes, Santorini, Skiathos, and Thessaloniki, for a nominal fee and with proper identification.

Newspapers & Magazines   All cities, large towns, and major tourist centers now have at least one shop or kiosk that carries a selection of foreign-language publications; most of these are flown or shipped in on the very day of publication. English-language readers have a wide selection, including most of the British papers (*Daily Telegraph, Financial Times, Guardian, Independent, Times*), the *International Herald Tribune* (with its inserted English-language version of the well-known Athens newspaper, *Kathimerini*), and *USA Today.* A decent (and cheaper!) alternative is the English-language paper published in Athens, *Athens News,* widely available throughout Greece.

Pets   See "Customs," above.

Pharmacies   The *pharmakio,* identified by a green cross, is the first place to go with minor medical problems, as pharmacists usually speak English well and many medications can be dispensed without prescription. Ask for directions at your hotel. In larger cities, if the one you find is closed, look in the window for a sign giving the address of one that might be open.

Photographic Needs   Cameras, film, accessories, and photo developing (including express service) are widely available, though slightly more expensive, in Greece.

Police   To report a crime or medical emergency, or for information or other assistance, first contact the local tourist police (telephone numbers will be found under "Essentials" in the particular destination chapters that follow), where an English-speaking officer is more likely to be found. If there is no tourist police officer available (☎ 171), contact the local police. The telephone number for emergencies throughout Greece is ☎ **100.**

Radio & Television   The Greek ERT 1 radio station has weather and news in English at 7:40am. The BBC World Service can be picked up on short-wave frequencies, often at 9.140, 15.07, and 12.09 Mhz; on FM it is usually at 107.1. Antenna TV, CNN, Eurochannel, and other cable networks are widely available. Many better hotels offer cable television.

A Word on Hotel Bathrooms

The bathrooms in all the newer and higher-grade Greek hotels are now practically "state of the art," but there are a few things travelers might appreciate knowing in advance. Few hotels ever provide washcloths, and the soap is often the old-fashioned minibar. Many hotels still don't offer generous-sized towels, and even many mid-priced hotels provide only cramped showers. As it happens, the one thing the Greeks are generous with is slippery marble: Be very careful getting in and out of tubs or showers.

Rentals (Apartments & Houses)   An increasingly popular way to experience Greece is to rent an apartment or house; the advantages include freedom from the formalities of a hotel, often a more desirable location, and a kitchen that allows you to avoid the costs and occasional crush of restaurants. Such rentals do not come cheap, but if you calculate what two or more people might pay for a decent hotel, not to mention all the meals eaten out, it can turn out to be a good deal. (Costs per person per day in really nice apartments run about $85; the fancier villas might cost about $250 a day for two bedrooms.) Any full-service travel agency in your home country or in Greece should be able to put you in touch with an agency specializing in such rentals.

Among those in the United States are **Greek Island Connection,** 38-01 23rd Ave., Long Island City, NY 11105 (☎ **800/241-2417;** fax 718/204-8055; e-mail: grislcon@gte.net), and **Villas International,** 950 Northgate Dr., San Rafael, CA 94903 (☎ **800/221-2260;** fax 415/499-9491; www.villasintl.com). In Canada, try **CTI Carriers,** 65 Overlea Blvd., Toronto, Ontario M4H 1P1 (☎ **800/363-8181;** fax 416/429-7159), or **Grecian Holidays,** 75 The Donaway West, Don Mills, Ontario M3C 2E9 (☎ **800/268-6786;** fax 416/510-1509). In the United Kingdom, try **Simply Travel Ltd.,** 598–608 Chiswick High Rd., London W4 5XY (☎ **020/8541-2203**), or **Pure Crete,** 79 George St., Croydon, Surrey CRO 1LD (☎ **020/8760-0879**). For those interested in investigating such possibilities on the Web, try **www.crete.tournet.gr**, **www.vacationhomes.com**, **www.vacationspot.com**, or **www.villavacations.com**.

Another possibility is to rent a traditional house in one of about 12 relatively rural or remote villages or settlements throughout Greece. These small traditional houses have been restored by the Greek National Tourist Organization (GNTO); to learn more about this possibility, contact the GNTO office nearest you. (See "Visitor Information," earlier in this chapter, or go to **www.gnto.gr**.)

Rest Rooms   Public rest rooms are generally available in any good-sized Greek town, and though they are sometimes rather crude, they usually do work. (Old-fashioned stand-up/squat facilities are still found.) Carry some type of tissue or toilet paper with you at all times. In some places—even quite modern restaurants and hotels—you are still told not to flush it down the toilet; use the receptacles provided. In an emergency, you can ask to use the facilities of a restaurant or shop, though near major attractions they have to be denied to all but customers because the traffic is simply too heavy. If you use any such facilities, respect its sponsor and leave at least a small tip to any attendant.

Smoking   Greeks continue to be among the most persistent smokers. Smoking is prohibited on all domestic flights and in certain areas or types of ships, but elsewhere, Greeks—and foreigners—feel free to puff away at will. (The airport in Athens is virtually a cancer culture lab.) Hotels are only beginning to claim that they have set aside rooms or even floors for nonsmokers, so ask if it matters to you. If you are really bothered by smoke while eating, about all you can do is position yourself as best as possible—and then be prepared to move if it gets really bad.

Taxes & Service Charges   Unless otherwise noted, all hotel prices include a service charge, usually 12%, a 6% value-added tax (VAT), and a 4½% community tax. In most restaurants, a 13% service charge, an 8% VAT, and some kind of municipal tax (in Athens it is 5%) are also included in the prices and final bill. (By the way, don't confuse any of these charges with a standard "cover charge" that may be Dr100 to Dr300 (30¢ to 90¢) per setting. Also see "Tipping," below.) A VAT of 18% is added to rental-car rates.

All purchases also include a VAT tax of anywhere from 4% to 18%. If you have purchased an item that costs Dr40,000 ($115) or more and are a citizen of a non–European Union nation, you can get at least most of this refunded (provided you are exporting it within 90 days of time of purchase). The easiest thing to do is to shop at stores that display the sign TAX-FREE FOR TOURISTS. But any store should be able to provide you with a Tax-Free Check Form, which you complete in the store. As you are leaving the country, you present a copy of this to the refund desk (usually with the Customs office); be prepared to show both the goods and the receipt as proof of purchase, and be prepared to spend a fair amount of time before you get the refund.

Telephone   In the cities and larger towns, many kiosks have telephones from which you can make local calls for Dr20 (6¢). (In remote areas, they will let you make long-distance calls from these phones.) Older public telephones require a Dr20 coin—which are in short supply, so hold onto several if they come your way. Deposit the coin and listen for a dial tone, an irregular beep. A regular beep indicates the line is busy.

In the old days, most foreigners went to the offices of the **Telecommunications Organization of Greece** (*Organismos Tilepikinonion tis Ellados*), **OTE**— pronounced *oh*-tay—to place most of their phone calls, especially overseas calls. But because card phones are now so widespread throughout Greece, this is no longer necessary, once you get the hang of using them. You must first purchase a phone card at an OTE office or at most kiosks. (If you expect to make any phone calls while in Greece, you should buy one at the OTE office at the airport on first arriving.) These come in three denominations: Dr1,000 ($2.90) for 100 units, Dr1,900 ($5.45) for 200 units, and Dr4,200 ($12) for 500 units; there are plans to introduce a 1,000–unit card for Dr8,200 ($24). Note that the more costly the card, the cheaper the units.

A local call of up to 3 minutes costs Dr20 or two units off a phone card; for each minute beyond that, it costs another Dr20 or two units off the card (so that a 10-minute local call costs 16 units).

Long-distance calls, both domestic and international, can be quite expensive in Greece, especially at hotels, which may add a surcharge up to 100%, unless you have a telephone credit card from a major long-distance provider such as AT&T, MCI, or Sprint.

If you still prefer to make your call from an OTE office, these are usually centrally and conveniently located. (Local offices are given under "Essentials" for the destinations in the chapters that follow.) At OTE offices, you first go to one of the clerks, who will assign you a booth with a metered phone. You can make collect calls, but this can take much longer, so it's easier to pay cash, unless you have a phone card or intend to use your own international credit card.

To call Greece from abroad, follow your long-distance provider's directions for making a long-distance call. For AT&T, for instance, to reach Greece, this means dialing 011 + 30 + the city code + telephone number. We provide the Greek city codes and local numbers throughout our text. Note, however, that when calling from abroad, you *drop* the 0 that precedes the city code.

To make an international long-distance call from Greece, the easiest and cheapest way is to make use of your long-distance service provider; call your company before leaving home to determine the access number that you must dial in Greece. The principal access codes in Greece are: **AT&T,** ☎ **00800-1311; MCI,** ☎ **00800-1211;** and **Sprint,** ☎ **00800-1411.** Most companies also offer a recorded-message service in case the number you're calling at home is busy or doesn't answer.

To make a direct call abroad from Greece—whether placing the call from an OTE office, a card phone, or a coin phone—dial the country code plus the area code, omitting the initial zero (if any), then the number. Some country codes are: **Australia,** 0061; **Canada,** 001; **Ireland,** 00353; **New Zealand,** 0064; **United Kingdom,** 0044; and **United States,** 001. Note that if you are going to put all the charges on your phone card (that is, not on your long-distance provider), you will be charged at quite a high rate per minute (at least Dr1,000/$2.90 to North America), so you should not start a call unless your phone card has a fair number of drachmas still valid.

Increasing numbers of travelers are considering using **cell phones** while traveling abroad. The first thing to be said is that it is definitely possible; the second thing is that the situation is changing so rapidly that no account here can anticipate all developments speeding down the line. For starters, though, most cell phones that work in North America will not work in Europe, including Greece. Although it is possible to buy a cell phone that can be converted to European technology, make sure about this before you go. Two companies that do offer such phones are **Nextel** (www.nextel.com/worldwide) and **VoiceStream** (☎ **877/666-4246**). Meanwhile, it might be simpler to rent a phone that works in Europe; contact a company such as **International Mobile Communications** (☎ **888/967-5323**) or **VoiceStream** (☎ **877/666-4246**).

Another possibility is to buy a cheaper cell phone in Greece; OTE (Greece's national telecommunications company) offers a selection of phones and will gladly explain the various services. (These phones will work in many other countries as well.) If you do this and are to be in Greece for a relatively brief period, the best plan is to purchase a special phone card (that is, different from the phone card used for wired phones) with a certain number of prepaid units. But don't imagine that any of these cell phones provide cheap service; rates per minute can vary from $2 to $5. Also, you will not be able to get a connection in the more remote parts of Greece.

Time   The European system of a 24-hour clock is used officially, and on schedules you'll usually see noon written as 1200, 3:30pm as 1530, and 11pm as 2300. In informal conversation, however, Greeks express time much as we do—though noon may mean anywhere from noon to 3pm, afternoon is 3 to 7pm, and evening is 7pm to midnight.

Time Zone   Greece is 2 hours ahead of Greenwich mean time. With reference to North American time zones, it's 7 hours ahead of eastern standard time, 8 hours ahead of central standard time, 9 hours ahead of mountain standard time, and 10 hours ahead of Pacific standard time.

Tipping   A 10% to 15% service charge is included in virtually all restaurant bills. (It is no longer shown in a second column of prices next to the menu item.) Nevertheless, it's customary to leave an additional 5% to 10% for the waiter, especially if there has been some special service. Certainly round off on larger bills; even on small bills, change up to the nearest Dr100 is left. Good taxi service merits a tip of 10% or so. (Greeks rarely tip taxi drivers, but tourists are expected to.) Hotel chambermaids should be left about Dr500 ($1.45) per night per couple. Bellhops and doormen should be tipped Dr200 to Dr500 (60¢ to $1.45), depending on the services provided.

Water   The public drinking water in Greece is safe to drink, though it can be slightly brackish in some locales near the sea. Many people prefer the bottled water commonly available at restaurants, hotels, cafes, food stores, and kiosks, but don't expect all brands to be especially "lively." The days when Greek restaurants automatically served glasses of cold fresh water are gone; you are now usually made to feel that you must order bottled water, at which point you will have to choose between natural or carbonated (*metalliko*), and domestic or imported. Cafes, however, still tend to provide a glass of natural water.

3 Cruising the Greek Islands

by Fran Wenograd Golden

A cruise around the Greek islands affords travelers an easy and convenient way to enjoy the region's spectacular scenery and ancient historic sites without the hassle of deciphering ferry schedules and changing hotel rooms—you get on the ship, you unpack once, and you're transported to a world of whitewashed villages, volcanic shorelines, and lost cities surrounded by very blue sea. The ship—your floating hotel—goes with you, providing accommodations and food, attentive service, and a familiar retreat to return to after a day of touring or just kicking back in the Greek sun.

The Greek islands are one of the best cruise destinations in the world. The seas are relatively calm and the islands individual in character, offering travelers a satisfying mix of local culture, gorgeous scenery, and ancient and medieval ruins to explore.

Most Greek island itineraries highlight the region's history with optional guided **shore excursions** that take in the major sights, spicing up the vacation brew with other, less history-minded excursions such as visits to beaches, meals at local restaurants, and fishing or sailing excursions.

Of course, you can also choose to get off the ship at each port of call and head off on your own to explore the sights, hit the beach, or check out the local color at the nearest taverna. It's entirely up to you.

1 Choosing the Right Cruise for You

In choosing your cruise, you need to think about what you want to see and in what level of comfort you want to see it.

We recommend you first decide **what you want to see.** Are you looking to visit the most popular islands—Mykonos, Santorini, and Rhodes—or are you interested in places off the beaten path? Whichever it is, you'll want to make sure the itinerary you choose allows enough time for you to experience the place or places that really take your fancy. Some ships visit a port and spend the full day, while others visit two ports in one day, which limits your sightseeing time in each.

In the past, Greek law was designed so that only Greek-flagged ships could cruise between Greek ports, meaning that foreign-flagged vessels had to visit en route between other European ports, usually in Italy or Turkey. This law officially changed in 1999, but many Greek islands cruises still maintain a similar routing, either beginning or ending their itineraries elsewhere. You'll have to consider embarkation and disembarkation points in making your decision. Do you mind flying to Venice or Istanbul to catch your ship?

Greece is also visited by ships as part of European itineraries where Greece is not the sole focus, but only one of several countries visited. If you're looking for a trip that includes several countries, that's fine. But if you're looking to spend most of your time in Greece, make sure you choose an appropriate itinerary.

Next, consider **how long you want to spend cruising the islands**—3 days, a week, 2 weeks? If you have the time, you may want to consider a **cruisetour,** which combines a cruise to the islands with a guided tour of important sights on the mainland. This is made easy in Greece by the fact that some lines offer cruises of only 3 or 4 days, which you can combine with a land tour into a 1-week vacation, and 1-week cruises you can combine with a land tour to make a 2-week vacation.

Also consider **when you want to cruise.** While Greece has traditionally been a summer destination, the season has been stretched in recent years, and some lines now offer cruises here year-round. While most of the action on the islands still takes place in the warmer months, from late April through October, traveling at other times has its own special charms, including the fact it allows you to avoid the tourist crush (although some visitor facilities may be closed in the off-season) and the months of highest temperatures (in July and August, temperatures can reach 100°F). For the record, August is the month the islands are most crowded with European vacationers (expect beaches, bars, and discos to be packed) and April and November are the rainiest months. May and October are relatively problem-free, making them particularly nice times to sail in Greece.

You'll also want to think about **what you want out of the cruise experience.** Is the purpose of your cruise to see as much as you can of the islands, or to relax by the ship's pool? And what level of comfort, entertainment, onboard activities, and so forth do you require? Some ships spend a day or more at sea, meaning they don't visit a port at all that day, and while some experienced cruisers enjoy those days the most, treasuring the opportunity they offer for real relaxation, they won't do you much good if your goal is seeing as much of Greece as you can.

CHOOSING YOUR SHIP

Ships cruising the Greek islands range from small yacht-type vessels carrying fewer than 50 passengers to traditional midsize ships to resortlike, 2,000-plus-passenger megaships. Which you choose has a lot to do with your personality and vacation goals.

MEGASHIPS & LARGE SHIPS   Cruises aboard these vessels focus as much on onboard activities as they do on the destination they're visiting. The ships are floating resorts—sometimes of the glitzy variety—offering American-style luxury and amenities and attentive service. In a recent brochure, Holland America Line unabashedly said that "When asked which European city he liked best, one guest replied 'My Holland America ship—that was my favorite city.'" We think that kind of says it all.

These ships, which tend to be newer, feature Las Vegas–style shows, lavish casinos, big spas and gyms, plenty of bars, extravagant meals, lots of daytime activities (such as games, contests, cooking lessons, wine tastings, and sport tournaments), and generally few ethnic Greek offerings.

CLASSIC & MIDSIZE SHIPS   Ships in this category include older, classic vessels as well as some newer ships. Destination is more a focus than on the bigger ships, and itineraries may be very busy, with the ship visiting an island a day, or sometimes two. This leaves little time for onboard daytime activities, although some will be offered. In the Greek market, some of these ships feature Greek crews and cuisine, and service tends to be a big area of focus. Because these ships are popular with Europeans, you'll likely hear many languages spoken on board. The ships offer a variety of bars and lounges, at least one swimming pool and a small casino, a spa and gym, and plenty of open deck space, and have entertainment generally in a main show lounge, with some also having cinemas that show recent-release films. Accommodations are generally good-sized, and range from rather plain to quite lavish.

SMALL SHIPS & YACHTS   Small ships and yachts tend to offer more of a relaxed pace and may seek itineraries that focus on smaller, alternative ports, which they can get into because of their smaller size and shallow draft (the amount of ship that rides beneath the waterline). They may offer a "soft adventure" cruise experience, with nature- and outdoor-oriented activities as a big focus, or they may offer more of a luxury yacht experience. Some of the ships feature Greek crews and Greek cuisine. There will typically be more interaction with fellow passengers than on larger ships—partially because there will be less entertainment, and there may or may not be a swimming pool, casino, spa, or gym. Both cabins and public rooms range from small and serviceable to large and luxurious, depending on which ship you choose. Some are fully engine-powered while others are sailing vessels (though even on these the sails are typically more for show than for power).

2 Calculating the Cost

Cruises in the Greek islands range from 3 days (for the purpose of this book, we calculate days as nights on board) to 2 weeks, with brochure prices per day ranging from around $150 to over $1,500 per person, double occupancy. To determine the real value of the cruise, though, you have to examine what you get for your money.

The prices include three meals a day (with a couple of exceptions, which we've noted in the ship reviews below), accommodations, onboard activities and entertainment, and, if you book your airfare through the cruise line, a transfer from the airport to the ship. Some rates even include airfare (the inclusion of airfare is more common on European cruises than Caribbean cruises), and in rare cases the fare may also include tips, shore excursions, and/or pre- and/or postcruise hotel stays. Some cruises are packaged as cruisetours, meaning they include both hotel stays and land tours. Rarely included in the price are alcoholic beverages or spa and beauty treatments. Port charges, taxes, and other fees are usually, but not always, included in the cruise fare. We've noted exceptions below.

Don't be scared by the **brochure prices** (which are the prices we quote in this chapter). Brochures typically state the highest rate the line will charge for the cruise, but cruises rarely actually sell for that rate. Think of the brochure rates as the equivalent of new-car sticker prices. Various discounts and deals are calculated off this price, including early-booking savings (typically ranging from 10% to 40%), group deals, and last-minute deals including two-for-one and free airfare or free hotel stays.

Cruise prices are based on two people sharing a cabin. Most lines have special **single supplement** prices for solo passengers wishing to have a cabin to themselves, usually ranging from 150% to 200% of the per-person rate. The "supplement," in this case, goes to the cruise line as their compensation for not getting two passenger fares for the cabin. At the opposite end, most lines offer highly discounted rates for a third or fourth person sharing a cabin with two full-fare passengers.

Senior citizens may be able to get extra savings on their cruise. Some lines will take 5% off the top for those 55 and over, and the senior rate applies even if the second person in the cabin is younger. Membership in groups such as AARP is not required, but such membership may bring additional savings.

Cruising the Web

The Internet is a good tool for researching your cruise, and in our cruise reviews (see below) we include the addresses of the cruise lines' Web sites, most of which feature photos of the ships and their cabins, and some of which even offer virtual tours. A few allow you to actually book your cruise on the spot, but keep in mind that if you book this way, and goof up your reservation, you have no one to blame but yourself. For first-time cruisers especially, we recommend you use the Web as an information-gathering venue, then take what you've learned to a travel agent to make the final reservations.

In addition to the cruise lines' sites, several independent sites are excellent sources for cruise information, ship reviews, chats, links to special deals, and industry news. Among the best (and one that this author contributes to) is **www.cruisemates.com**. Other sites worth taking a look at are **www.cruisecritic.com** (or AOL keyword Cruise Critic) and **www.cruise-news.com**.

You can also use the Web to find a good, experienced, cruise-savvy travel agent. At the following sites you can find listings of agents by ZIP code, telephone area code, and special areas of expertise.

- **Cruise Lines International Association (CLIA):** www.cruising.org (☎ 212/921-0066)
- **National Association of Cruise Oriented Agents (NACOA):** www.nacoa.com (☎ 305/663-5626)
- **American Society of Travel Agents (ASTA):** www.astanet.com (☎ 800/275-2782)

Some of the more upscale lines will reward customers willing to pay their full fare in advance (thus giving the cruise line cash in hand), with savings of as much as 10%.

If your package does not include **airfare,** you should consider booking air transportation through the cruise line. The rates offered by the lines tend to be competitive, and booking through the line allows the cruise company to keep track of you if, for instance, your flight is delayed. The cruise lines also negotiate special deals with hotels at port cities if you want to come in a few days before your flight or stay after.

3 Booking Your Cruise

There are a lot of nuances to booking a cruise vacation, and the best way to assure you get what you paid for is to work with an experienced travel agent. The agent can help you find the best deal on the cruise itself as well as airfare, and can clue you in on the latest discounts to help you decide whether, for instance, you want to combine your cruise with a land tour.

To find an agent, ask friends for advice, or contact one of the organizations listed above. Try to find someone who is experienced in selling cruises and who has cruised before, preferably in Greece. Work with a cruise-only agency (an agency that specializes in cruises) or a cruise specialist (an agent that specializes in cruises).

Cruise specialists are in frequent contact with the cruise lines and are kept informed by the lines about the latest and greatest deals and special offers. Some agencies even buy blocks of space that they sell at a special price.

Be wary of high-volume operators who advertise with really low pricing in the Sunday newspaper and on the Internet. You may get a decent price, but will probably not get a high level of service and expertise. And, since these operators are typically selling either last-minute space or space they've pre-blocked on a ship, they may not have many options available in terms of cabin types (see below) and sailing dates—you'll be conforming to their schedules rather than them conforming to yours.

CHOOSING A CABIN

One of your biggest decisions once you choose the ship you want to sail on is what type of cabin you need. Will you be happy with a slightly cramped space without a window (the most budget-minded choice) or do you require a suite with a private veranda?

Obviously, price will be a determinant here. If you aren't planning to spend time in your cabin except to sleep, shower, and change clothes, an **inside cabin** (that is, one without a porthole or window) might do just fine. If you get claustrophobic, however, or insist on sunshine first thing in the morning, or intend to hole up in your cabin for extended periods, pay a bit more and take an **outside cabin** (one with a window).

When you book your cabin, you generally will not be choosing a specific cabin number but rather a cabin category, within which all units have the same amenities. With this in mind, one concern if you do go the window route is **obstructed views.** Check to make sure none of the cabins in the category you've selected have windows that directly face lifeboats or other objects that may stand between you and your view of the clear blue sea. You can determine this by looking at a diagram of the ship (included in the cruise brochure) or consulting with your travel agent.

Most ships offer cabins for two with private bathrooms and showers (bathtubs are considered a luxury on most ships, and are usually offered only in the most expensive cabins) and twin beds that may be convertible to a queen. There are other variations, of course. For instance, a number of ships have some cabins with bunk beds (referred to in the brochures as "upper and lower berths"), many ships have cabins designed for three or four people, and some have connecting cabins for families.

Cabin amenities vary by line, and might include TVs (with a closed system of programmed movies and features), VCRs, hair dryers, safes, and mini-refrigerators. If any of these are must-haves, let your agent know.

Usually the higher on the ship the cabin is located, the more expensive it is. But upper decks also tend to be rockier in rough seas than the middle or lower parts of the ship, a factor to consider if you're prone to seasickness.

Size of cabin is determined in terms of square feet. As a rough guide, 120 square feet is low-end and cramped, 180 square feet is midrange (and the minimum for people with claustrophobia), and 250 square feet and larger is suite-sized and roomy.

A popular innovation over the past decade or so is **private verandas** or balconies, where you can step right from your cabin to enjoy the sea breezes in your own lounge chair—but you pay for the privilege.

If noise bothers you, try to pick a cabin far from the engine room and nowhere near the disco.

CHOOSING A MEALTIME

Because most ship dining rooms are not large enough to accommodate all passengers at one dinner seating, times and tables are assigned. When you book your trip, you will have to indicate your preferred mealtime. Early, or "main," seating is usually 6 or 6:30pm, late seating at 8 or 8:30pm.

There are advantages to both times. **Early seating** is usually less crowded, and the preferred time for families and older passengers who want to get to bed early. Food items are fresher (they don't have to sit in warmers), but the waiters know that the second wave is coming in a couple hours, and so may be rushed. Early diners get first dibs on nighttime entertainment venues, and might be hungry enough in a few hours to take advantage of the midnight buffet. **Late seating** allows time for a nap or late spa appointment before dinner. Service is slower paced, and you can linger with after-dinner drinks, then catch the late show at 10pm.

When choosing a mealtime, you also need to consider **table size** (on most ships, you can request to be at a table for 2, 4, 8, 10, or 12) and whether you want to sit at a **smoking or nonsmoking table**—a particularly important factor in Europe, where smoking is still quite popular.

On most ships, **breakfast** and **lunch** are open seating, but you may be requested to eat at an assigned time. (Early means breakfast at 7 or 8am, lunch at noon; late, breakfast at 8:30 or 9am, lunch at 1:30pm.) On ships with buffet restaurants, you can also choose to have both meals there, at any time during their open hours.

You should inform the cruise line at the time you make your reservations if you have any **special dietary requests.** Some lines offer kosher menus; all will have vegetarian, low-fat, low-salt, and sugar-free options available.

DEPOSITS, CANCELLATIONS & EXTRAS

After you've made your decision as to which ship you will vacation on, you will be required to put down a deposit, with the remaining fare usually paid no later than 2 months in advance of your departure date.

Cruise lines have varying policies regarding cancellations, and it's important to look at the fine print in the line's brochure to make sure you understand the policy. Most lines allow you to cancel for a full refund on your deposit and payment any time up to 76 days before the sailing, after which you have to pay a penalty. If you cancel at the last minute, you will typically be refunded only 75% of what you've paid.

Your agent will discuss with you optional **airfare programs** offered by the lines, **transfers** from the airport to the pier, and any pre- or postcruise **hotel or tour programs.** Some lines also let you purchase **shore excursions** in advance (for more on shore excursions, see below). And there may also be packages of onboard spa services available for prebooking.

If you are not booking airfare through the cruise line, make sure to allow several hours between the plane's arrival and when you need to get on the ship. It may be best, in terms of reducing anxiety, to come in a day before and spend the night in a hotel.

4 Cruise Preparation Practicalities

About 1 month before your cruise and no later than 1 week before, you should receive your **cruise documents,** including your airline tickets (if you purchased them from the cruise line), a boarding document with your cabin number and sometimes dining choices on it, boarding forms to fill out, luggage tags, and your prearranged bus transfer vouchers and hotel vouchers (if applicable).

There will also be information about **shore excursions** and additional material detailing things you need to know before you sail. In some cases, you may be able to book shore excursions in advance of your sailing, which will give you first dibs at popular offerings that may sell out later.

Read all of this pre-trip information carefully. Make sure your cabin category and dining preferences are as you requested and that your airline flight and arrival times are what you were told. If there are problems, call your agent immediately. Make sure there is enough time so you can arrive at the port no later than an hour before departure time.

You will be required to have a passport for your trip (see chapter 2 for more on this). If you are flying into Istanbul, you will also be required to have a Turkish visa.

We recommend you confirm your flight 3 days before departure. Also, before you leave for the airport, tie the tags provided by the cruise line onto your luggage and fill in your boarding cards. This will save you time when you arrive at the ship.

CASH MATTERS

You already paid the lion's share of your vacation when you paid for your cruise, but you will need a credit card or traveler's checks to handle your **onboard expenses** (such as bar drinks, dry cleaning and laundry, phone calls, massage and other spa services, beauty-parlor services, photos taken by the ship's photographer, baby-sitting, wine at dinner, and souvenirs) as well as **shore excursions** and **tips** (see below for tips on tipping).

Some ships (but not all) will take a personal check for onboard expenses. If you want to pay in cash or by traveler's check, you will be asked to leave a deposit, usually $250 for a 1-week sailing. Some ships have ATMs if you need to get cash while aboard, and some (but not all) offer currency-exchange services.

We suggest you keep careful track of your onboard expenses to avoid an unpleasant surprise at the end of your cruise. Some ships make this particularly easy by offering interactive TVs in cabins: by pushing the right buttons, you can check your account from the comfort of your own stateroom. On other ships, you can get this information at the purser's office or guest-relations desk.

You will want to have some cash in hand when going ashore for expenses such as taxis, snacks or meals, drinks, small purchases, and tips for guides.

PACKING

Generally, ships describe their **daily recommended attire** as casual, informal, and formal, prompting many people to think they'll have to bring a steamer trunk full of clothes just to get through their trip. Not true; you can probably get along with about half of what you think you need. Also, almost all ships offer laundry and dry-cleaning services, and some have coin-operated self-serve laundries aboard, so you have the option of packing less and just having your clothes cleaned midway through your trip.

During the day, the onboard style is casual, but keep in mind some ships do not allow swimsuits or tank tops in the dining room. For dinner, there are usually two formal nights and two informal nights during a 5- to 7-day cruise, with the rest casual. There will usually be proportionally more formal nights on longer cruises.

The daily bulletin delivered to your cabin each day will advise you of the proper dress code for the evening. **Formal** means a tux or dark suit with tie for men and a nice cocktail dress, long dress, gown, or dressy pantsuit for women. **Informal** is a jacket, tie, and dress slacks or a light suit for men (jeans are frowned upon) and a dress, skirt and blouse, or pants outfit for women. **Casual** means a sports shirt or open dress shirt with slacks for men (some men will also wear a jacket); women can wear a dress, pants outfit, or skirt and blouse.

Check your cruise documents to determine the number of formal nights (if any) during your cruise. Men who don't own a tuxedo might be able to rent one in advance through the cruise line's preferred supplier (who delivers the tux right to the ship). Information on this service often is sent with your cruise documents. Also, some cruises offer **theme nights,** so you may want to check your cruise documents to see if there are any you'll want to bring special clothes for. (For instance, Greek night means everyone wears blue and white—the Greek national colors.)

We recommend you bring costume jewelry instead of the real stuff, but if you must bring the crown jewels, be careful. If you're not wearing them, leave them either in your in-room safe (if there is one) or with the purser.

In general, for Greece you're best off packing loose and comfortable cotton or other lightweight fabrics. You'll also want to pack a swimsuit, a sun hat, sunglasses, and plenty of sunscreen—the Greek sun can be intense. Obviously, you should adjust your wardrobe depending on when you plan to travel (summer is hotter than spring and fall). Even if you're traveling in August, though, you should bring a sweater, as you'll be in and out of air-conditioning. And don't forget an umbrella.

For shore excursions, comfortable walking shoes are a must, as some involve walking on stone or marble. Also, some tours may visit religious sites that have a "no shorts or bare shoulders" policy, so it's best to bring something to cover up with. (If you're taking the tour through the cruise line, you'll be advised of this before you go.)

If you plan on bringing your own hair dryer, electric razor, curling iron, or other electrical device, you will want to check out the electric current available on the ship in advance. An adapter may be required.

5 Embarkation

Check-in is usually 2 to 3 hours before sailing. You will not be able to board the ship before the scheduled embarkation time. You have up until a half hour (on some ships it's 1 hour) before departure to board.

At check-in, your boarding documents will be checked and your passport will likely be taken for immigration processing. You will get it back sometime during the cruise (you might want to carry a photocopy as backup). Depending on the cruise line, you may establish your **onboard credit account** at this point by presenting a major credit card or making a deposit in cash or traveler's checks (usually $250). On other ships you need to go to the purser's office on board to establish your account.

You may be given your **dining-room table assignment** in advance of your sailing (on your tickets) or as you check in, or find a card with your table number waiting for you in your stateroom. If you do not receive an assignment by the time you get to your stateroom, you will be directed to a maitre d's desk. This is also the place to go to make any changes if your assignment does not meet with your approval.

Once aboard you'll be shown to your cabin by a crew member, who will probably offer to help carry your hand luggage. No tip is required for this service.

In your cabin you will find a **daily program** detailing the day's events, mealtimes, and so forth, as well as important information on the ship's **safety procedures** and possibly a **deck plan** of the ship. There are also deck plans and directional signs posted around the ship, generally at main stairways and elevators.

If you are planning to use the ship's **spa services,** it's best to stop by early to make appointments so you can get your preferred times (the best times go fast, and some popular treatments sell out).

Note the ship's casino and shops are always closed when the ship is in port, and the swimming pool(s) will also likely be tarped. They will be filled with either fresh or saltwater after the ship sets sail.

Some lines offer **escorted tours** of the public rooms to get you acquainted with the ship. Check the daily program in your cabin for details.

Dealing with Seasickness

If you suffer from seasickness, plan on packing some **Bonine** or **Dramamine** in case your ship encounters rough seas. Keep in mind that with both these medications it is recommended you not drink alcohol; Dramamine in particular can make you drowsy. Both can be bought over the counter, and ships also stock supplies onboard, available at either the purser's office or the medical center (in both cases it's usually free).

Another option is the **Transderm patch,** available by prescription only, which goes behind your ear and time-releases medication. The patch can be worn for up to 3 days, but comes with all sorts of side-effect warnings. Some people have also had success in curbing seasickness with **ginger capsules** available at health-food stores. If you prefer not to ingest anything, you might try the **acupressure wristbands** available at most pharmacies. When set in the proper spot on the wrist, they effectively ease seasickness, although if the seas are particularly rough they may have to be supplemented with some medication.

LIFEBOAT/SAFETY DRILL

Ships are required by law to conduct safety drills the first day out. Most do this either right before the ship sails or shortly thereafter. Attendance is mandatory. A notice on the back of your cabin door will list the procedures and advise as to your assigned **muster station** and how to get there. You will also find directions to the muster station in the hallway. You will be alerted as to the time in both the daily program and in repeated public announcements (and probably by your cabin steward as well).

At the start of the drill, the ship will broadcast its emergency signal. At this time, you will be required to return to your cabin, grab your **life jacket** (which you're shown as soon as you arrive in your cabin), and report to your assigned muster station—usually in a lounge, the casino, or other public room. If you're traveling with children, make sure your cabin is equipped with special children's life jackets. If not, alert your steward.

During the drill, crew members will review how to use the life jackets and explain the ship's safety procedures. Some drills last only a few minutes, while others are quite detailed. If you have any questions about safety procedures, you can address them to a crew member or officer at this time.

6 End-of-Cruise Procedures

Your shipboard account will close in the wee hours before departure, but prior to that time you will receive a preliminary bill in your cabin. If you are settling your account with your credit card, you don't have to do anything but make sure all the charges are correct. If there is a problem, you will have to report to the purser's office.

If you are paying by cash or traveler's check, you will be asked to settle your account either during the day or night before you leave the ship. This will require you to report to the purser's office. A final invoice will be delivered to your room before departure.

TIPS

You will typically find tipping suggestions in your cabin on the last day of your cruise. These are only suggestions, but, since service personnel make most of their salaries through tips, we don't recommend tipping less—unless, of course, bad service warrants it. (A few lines operate on a **no-tipping-required** basis, but the staff will still accept a tip if it's offered. On some very upscale lines, acceptance of tips is strictly forbidden.)

Each passenger should usually tip his or her cabin steward and waiter about $3.50 per day each, and the bus boy about $2 (the cruise line will provide suggested minimums). That totals up to a minimum of $63 for a 7-night cruise (you do not have to include disembarkation day). You are, of course, free to tip more. On some European ships, the suggested minimums are even less (on Costa ships, for instance, they total only $5 a day). The reason: Europeans aren't as used to tipping as Americans. On some ships you are also encouraged to tip the maitre d' and head waiter (don't feel you have to give either more than $5 per person, unless they have given you particularly great service). You may also encounter cases where tips are pooled: you hand over a suggested amount and it's up to the crew to divide it among themselves. Some smaller ships recommend you tip a percentage of your cruise fare, usually 5%. Some luxury lines, including Radisson and Silversea, include tips in the cruise fare.

You may have to pay tips in cash (U.S. dollars are okay), although some lines let you put the tips on your charge account.

Bar bills automatically include a 15% tip, but if the wine steward, for instance, has served you exceptionally well, you can slip him or her a bill, too. If you have spa or beauty treatments, you can tip that person at the time of the service (you can even do it on your shipboard charge account).

Don't tip the captain or other officers. They're professional, salaried employees.

The porters who carry your bags at the pier will likely expect a tip.

PACKING UP

Because of the number of bags being handled, big ships require guests to pack the night before departure and leave their bags in the hallway, usually by midnight. (Be sure they're tagged with the cruise line's luggage tags, which are color-coded to indicate deck number and disembarkation order.) The bags will be picked up overnight and removed from the ship before passengers are allowed to disembark. You'll see them again in the cruise terminal, where they'll most likely be arranged by deck number.

Pack all the purchases you made during the trip in one suitcase. This way you can easily retrieve them if you're stopped at customs.

7 The Cruise Lines & Their Ships

In this section, we describe the ships offering Greek islands cruises. Later in the chapter, we describe ships that visit Greece as part of longer itineraries.

The lines are listed alphabetically. Rates are 2001 **brochure prices.** As stated earlier, various discounts and deals are calculated off this price, including early-bird savings, group deals, and last-minute deals. Most lines also offer special savings for third and fourth passengers sharing a cabin, and some have special rates for children (as noted below). Prices given are per person, per day, based on double occupancy. To get an estimate of the per-person cruise price, you can multiply the listed **per diem rate** by the number of nights you'll be on the ship.

Since cruise lines have various ways of expressing the number of days or nights of the itinerary, we've come up with a standard formula, eliminating the disembarkation day (since you usually get off the ship first thing in the morning). So when we describe an itinerary as 7-day, that means you spend 7 nights on the ship.

The **itineraries** we list are also for the 2001 season. Both prices and itineraries are subject to change.

We've listed the **sizes of ships** in two ways: **passenger capacity** and **gross registered tons (GRTs).** Rather than describing actual tonnage, the latter is a measure of interior space used to produce revenue on a vessel. One GRT = 100 cubic feet of enclosed, revenue-generating space.

Please also note that Piraeus, mentioned frequently below as an embarkation and disembarkation point, is the port city for Athens.

AIRTOURS
Wavell House, Holcombe Rd., Helmshore, Rossendale, Lancashire BB4 4NB, United Kingdom. ☎ **44/8702412567.** www.airtours.co.uk.

This large British tour firm has big U.S. connections. Carnival Corporation, parent company of Carnival Cruise Line, Costa, Holland America, Windstar, Cunard, and Seabourn, owns 26% of the firm. The ship the line operates in the Greek market, the *Seawing* (built in 1971; 727 passengers, 16,607 GRTs), also has U.S. connections— it used to operate in North America as Norwegian Cruise Line's *Southward.* Today the ship offers an informal experience with a decidedly British appeal and mostly British passengers, many of whom are first-timers attracted by the line's affordable prices. Cabins have radios and phones; some have picture windows and sitting areas.

Entertainment and dancing are offered at the ship's lounge and nightclub. There's also a casino, an outdoor pool, two saunas, a gym, a spa, and a library. Special activities are offered for teens.

ITINERARIES & RATES
SEAWING   Two different itineraries from Limmasol, Cyprus: (1) visits Athens, Santorini, Kos, and Marmaris (Turkey); (2) visits Volos, Lesvos, and Rhodes, as well as Istanbul and Kusadasi (Turkey). Both offered May through October, alternating with Holy Lands itineraries that do not visit Greece. Per diem rates: $185–$220 inside, $195–$230 outside, $257–$293 suite.

CLASSICAL CRUISES
c/o Travel Dynamics, 132 E. 70th St., New York, NY 10021. ☎ **800/252-7745.** www.classicalcruises.com.

This operator of small yachts offers a number of interesting itineraries that include Greek ports. The journeys are tailored to be unique, visiting some of the smaller and less known ports, and are complemented by high-quality onboard educational programs.

The *Clelia II* (built in 1990; 84 passengers, 4,077 GRTs) is a luxury all-suite yacht that was purchased in 1996 for private use by one of Greece's most prominent shipping families (the ship is named for owner Clelia Hadjiioannou) and is chartered by Classical. The owners put $3 million into the vessel, creating clublike interiors and a full-size gym, and outfitting the deluxe cabins and public rooms with designer fabrics and original art. All cabins are spacious and comfortable, and offer ocean views, a sitting area or separate living room, TV/VCR, and minibar. The penthouse boasts 520 square feet of space. The ship's facilities also include a swimming pool, steam bath, and beauty salon.

The *Callisto* (built in 1964; 34 passengers, 435 GRTs) and *Harmony* (built in 2000; 44 passengers, GRTs not available) are both Greek-flagged ships and new to the Classical fleet. Cabins offer outside views from either panoramic windows or portholes. Public areas are nicely outfitted and, on the *Callisto,* include a gym. You can swim off a platform on either yacht's stern.

ITINERARIES & RATES

CALLISTO 7-day **Lavrion to Samos** cruisetour visits Delos, Mykonos, Tinos, and Lavrion, and includes two hotel nights in Athens. May through September. The ship also does a 9-day itinerary in April and May that explores Crete. **Per diem rates:** $428–$614 outside (no inside or suite). Rates include hotel stays and shore excursions.

CLELIA II 13-day **Istanbul-to-Piraeus** cruise traces places recounted in Homer's epic *Odyssey*. Ports in Greece include Corfu, Ithaka, and Nafplion; the itinerary also includes Italy, Tunisia, Malta, and Turkey. April and September. **Per diem rates:** $607–$1,146 suite (no standard cabins). Rates include hotel stays and shore excursions.

HARMONY 10-day **Nafplion to Corinth cruisetour** visits Monemvassia, Githio, Kalamata, Koroni, Pylos, Katakolon, Nafpaktos, and Itea, and includes three hotel nights in Athens. October and November. **Per diem rates:** $399–$489 outside (no inside or suite). Rates include hotel stays and shore excursions.

COSTA CRUISE LINES

World Trade Center, 80 SW 8th St., Miami, FL 33130-3097. ☎ **800/462-6782.** www.costacruises.com

This Italian line traces its origins back to 1860 and the Italian olive-oil business. Today, Carnival Corporation, parent of Carnival Cruise Lines, is the owner. Onboard, Italy shows through in nearly everything Costa offers, from the food to the Italian design of the vessels to the Italian-speaking crew (although they are not all from Italy) to the mostly Italian entertainers. The Italian experience is presented in casual elegance, in a warm and humorous manner. You'll feel like you're a part of one big Italian family.

The line's six ships represent one of the newest fleets in the industry, sporting blue-and-yellow smokestacks emblazoned with a huge letter *C*. They are popular in the U.S./Caribbean market but are not designed strictly for a North American audience, and therein lies their charm. In Europe, the ships attract a good share of Italian and French passengers.

Entertainment includes puppet and marionette shows, mimes, and acrobats. Opera singers sometimes come aboard to entertain. The line also offers an activities program for kids and teens.

The *CostaClassica* (built in 1991; 1,300 passengers, 54,000 GRTs) offers spacious public rooms done up in contemporary Italian design, with Italian marble and original artwork, including sculptures, paintings, murals, wall hangings, and handcrafted furnishings. The ship's 446 cabins average almost 200 square feet each (that's big by industry standards). There are also 10 spacious suites with verandas.

The *CostaAtlantica* (built in 2000; 2,112-passengers, 84,000 GRTs) is the line's new flagship, and boasts a large number of cabins with private verandas (nearly 65% of the ship's outside cabins have them). Other neat features include Caffe Florian, a replica of the landmark 18th-century cafe of the same name in Venice.

In addition to these vessels, The *CostaAllegra* (built in 1992; 800 passengers, 30,000 GRTs) also does a 10-day Holy Lands itinerary from Genoa that includes port calls in Rhodes and Kithera, April through October. The *CostaRomantica* (built in 1993; 1,356 passengers, 54,000 GRTs) does an 11-day Holy Lands itinerary from Genoa that stops in Rhodes, Santorini, and Katakolon (late September and October) and an 11-day Black Sea cruise that calls at Santorini, Mykonos, and Kithera (May and September).

ITINERARIES & RATES

COSTACLASSICA   7-day round-trip from Venice visits Katakolon, Santorini, and Mykonos, plus Rhodes and Bari (Italy) and Dubrovnik (Croatia). Late April to early November. **Per diem rates:** $347–$489 inside, $400–$550 outside, $479–$686 suite. Rates include round-trip airfare from New York, Newark, and selected other U.S. gateways.

COSTAATLANTICA   7-day round-trip from Venice visits Katakolon and Piraeus, plus Kusadasi and Istanbul (Turkey) and Bari (Italy). May through October. **Per diem rates:** $354–$483 inside, $394–$564 outside, $493–$686 suite. Rates include round-trip airfare from New York, Newark, and selected other U.S. gateways.

FIRST EUROPEAN CRUISES

95 Madison Ave., Suite 1203, New York, NY 10016. ☎ **888/983-8767** or 212/779-7168. www.first-european.com.

First European is the name adopted by European line Festival Cruises for U.S. marketing purposes. The company was established in 1992 in Athens by Greek entrepreneur George Poulides, who has ambitious growth plans.

While the line was started with older, classic vessels, the company in 1999 introduced its first new ship, the *Mistral*. Another brand new ship, the *European Vision*, debuts this year. Two older ships, the *Bolero* and *Flamenco* (which do not cruise in Greece), complete the fleet. The vessels cater to a diverse European audience, with Americans a more recent addition to the passenger roster.

The *Mistral* (built in 1999; 1,200-passengers, 48,000 GRTs) was built in France at a cost of $240 million. It is staffed by Greek officers and an international crew and offers a contemporary interior design created by leading international architects and designers. Each deck is named after a European city: Paris, Rome, London, Berlin, Brussels, Athens, Cannes, and Madrid. The ship offers several dining options, a show lounge, a ballroom, and a disco, plus a full casino and numerous other public rooms and lounges, as well as a solarium, health spa, and outdoor thalasso-therapy center. Cabins include 80 large suites with private verandas.

Sister ship *European Vision* (built in 2001; 1,500 passengers, 58,600 GRTs) is a larger vessel and was built at the same shipyard in France. It debuts this year. The ship has 132 suites with balconies, and also adds a golf simulator and climbing wall, as well as an Internet cafe.

In addition to these vessels, one of First European's older ships, the *Azur* (built in 1971; 750 passengers, 15,000 GRTs) also visits Piraeus and sometimes Rhodes as well on 10- to 12-Holy Lands itineraries that include Egypt and Israel.

ITINERARIES & RATES

EUROPEAN VISION   7-day round-trip from Genoa visits Katakolon, Crete, and Mykonos, plus Kusadasi (Turkey) and Naples (Italy). July through November. **Per diem rates:** $130 $270 inside, $213 $320 outside, $281 $380 suite. Port charges are $90 additional. Children 2–17 pay $630 to $830 per cruise, plus port charges of $80. Book 120 days or more in advance and save 15% per person.

MISTRAL   7-day round-trip from Venice visits Santorini, Mykonos, Rhodes, Piraeus, and Corfu, plus Dubrovnik (Croatia). June to November. **Per diem rates:** $156–$261 inside, $256–$310 outside, $341–$369 suite. Port charges of $90 are extra. Children 2–17 pay $500 to $680 per cruise, plus port taxes of $80. Book 120 days or more prior to departure and save 15% per person.

MEDITERRANEAN SHIPPING CRUISES

420 Fifth Ave., New York, NY 10018-2702. ☎ **800/666-9333** or 212/764-4800. www.mscruise.com.

This Swiss/Italian line offers "classic Italian cruising" on older ships that aren't the fanciest afloat, but do offer good value for the money. The vessels are mid-sized and have been updated with modern decor that's more comfortable than plush. Most passengers are European. Itineraries are port-intensive, and the onboard experience friendly and fun.

The *Rhapsody* (built in 1974; 768 passengers, 16,852 GRTs) was once operated by Cunard as the *Cunard Princess* and still shows some signs of elegance, although the onboard atmosphere today is informal. Cabins are small, but the ship's public rooms are big, and there's a good deal of open deck space.

In addition to these itineraries, the line's *Monterey* (built in 1952; 576 passengers, 20,046 GRTs) also does an 11-day sailing in May, round-trip from Genoa, that calls in Santorini, Mykonos, Kalamata, and Katakolon, as well as ports in Italy, Malta, Tunisia, and France (Corsica). The *Monterey* also sails Holy Land cruises that include stops in Piraeus and Patmos.

ITINERARY & RATES

RHAPSODY   **7-day round-trip from Venice** visits Katakolon, Rhodes, and Patmos, plus Kusadasi (Turkey), Bari (Italy), and Dubrovnik (Croatia). Late May through September. **Per diem rates:** $178–$257 inside, $228–$314 outside, $278–$357 suite. Port charges are an additional $99.

ORIENT LINES

1510 SE 17th St., Suite 400, Fort Lauderdale, FL 33316. ☎ **800/333-7300.** www.orientlines. com.

Orient is a two-ship line that was owned by a British entrepreneur until he decided to sell to Norwegian Cruise Line in 1998. The line offers a good value on cruisetours, which combine a cruise and a land tour to create a more in-depth travel experience.

The line's original ship, the *Marco Polo* (formerly the *Alexandr Pushkin;* 800 passengers, 22,080 GRTs), built in East Germany in 1965 and completely refitted in 1993, offers classic style and is comfortable and slightly upscale, with art-deco interiors featuring Oriental art and antiques. Cabins are mostly average-sized, and the top categories have bathtubs.

The *Crown Odyssey* (built in 1988; 1,050 passengers, 34,272 GRTs), which Norwegian Cruise Line transferred into the fleet (the ship previously operated as the *Norwegian Crown*), is a larger and newer vessel that boasts a good range of public rooms done up with marble and glass. Cabins are larger than on the *Marco Polo,* and many have bathtubs. The top suite offer verandas, and some cabins have bay windows.

Cuisine aboard both ships is continental/American, and the passengers—who tend to be older, American, and experienced travelers—tend to dress up at night. The line's goal is to offer an enriching travel experience, and to that end puts a special emphasis on shore excursions and hires expert lecturers to join the sailings. Local entertainers are brought aboard at various ports of call to add to the experience of your destination.

ITINERARIES & RATES

CROWN ODYSSEY   **12-day Piraeus-to-Istanbul cruisetours** include 6 days on land (with hotel stays and tours in Athens and Istanbul) and a 6-day cruise with stops in Piraeus, Delos, Mykonos, Santorini, Iraklion, and Rhodes, plus Kusadasi (Turkey). A similar 12-day itinerary includes Delphi and Nafplion (with a hotel stay in

Nafplion). April through October. Also visits Greece as part of Italy and Mediterranean itineraries. **Per diem rates:** $151–$236 inside, $207–$300 outside, $280–$427 suite. Pre- and postcruise hotel stays, transfers, and sightseeing included. Port charges are an additional $195.

MARCO POLO   11-day Venice-to-Istanbul and Istanbul-to-Venice cruisetours include a hotel stay in Istanbul and a 7-day cruise that visits Santorini, Delos, and Mykonos, plus Kusadasi (Turkey) and Dubrovnik (Croatia). Late September and October. Also visits Greece as part of longer Mediterranean itineraries. **Per diem rates:** $222–$286 inside, $299–$422 outside, $464–$555 suite. Port charges are an additional $225.

RADISSON SEVEN SEAS CRUISES

600 Corporate Dr., Suite 410, Fort Lauderdale, FL 33334. ☎ **800/477-7500.** www.rssc.com.

In 1992, Radisson Hotels Worldwide decided to translate its hospitality experience to the cruise industry, offering to manage and market upscale ships for their international owners. The ships all offer itineraries geared towards affluent travelers, plus excellent cuisine, service, and amenities. A no-tipping policy is employed aboard all their ships, as is a no-tie-required policy.

The line assumes most of its passengers want to entertain themselves, so organized activities are limited, though they do include lectures by well-known authors, producers, and oceanographers, among others. There are also card and board games, shuffleboard, and dance lessons.

The *Radisson Diamond* (built in 1992; 350 passengers, 20,295 GRTs) is to the cruise industry what the DeLorean was to the car industry, sporting an unusual design concept: two side-by-side hulls, with the main passenger areas perched above and across them, creating a ship that is in essence a giant, very wide catamaran—only 420 feet long, she is nonetheless only 2 feet narrower (at 102 feet) than the QE2, which is more than twice as long at 963 feet.

Thanks to her design, the *Diamond* is quite roomy. The ship's cabins are all large and luxurious suites, and there are two VIP master suites that are even bigger and more luxurious. All the suites are outside, 121 offering balconies and 53 offering bay windows.

The smaller *Song of Flower* (built in 1986; 172 passengers, 8,292 GRTs) offers good-size cabins, all with outside views, bathtub or shower, TV/VCR, radio, phone, hair dryer, refrigerator, and fully stocked complimentary minibar. Some cabins offer sitting areas. There are also 20 suites, 10 with private verandas.

Both ships have a pool, gym, spa, and casino. The *Diamond* also has a free-floating retractable marina that provides easy access to water sports including sailing, windsurfing, and waterskiing.

The new *Seven Seas Navigator* (built in 1999; 490 passengers, 30,000 GRTs), introduced last year, is an all-suite luxury vessel. All the suites are large and boast ocean views, and 80 have private balconies. It's both larger and faster than the earlier Radisson ships.

ITINERARIES & RATES

RADISSON DIAMOND   7-day Piraeus-to-Istanbul and Istanbul-to-Piraeus cruises visit Santorini, Rhodes, Patmos, Samos, and Mykonos, plus Kusadasi and Dikili (Turkey). May, June, late September, and October. **Per diem rates:** $514–$1,070 suites (no standard cabins). Port charges are an additional $175.

SEVEN SEAS NAVIGATOR   7-day **Istanbul-to-Piraeus** visits Mykonos, Rhodes, Crete, Santorini, and Nafplion, plus Kusadasi (Turkey). Late September. **Per diem rates:** $556–$1,542 suites (no standard cabins). Port charges are an additional $175.

SONG OF FLOWER   7-day **Piraeus-to-Istanbul** visits Itea, Santorini, Rhodes, and Mykonos, plus Dikili and Kusadasi (Turkey). October. **Per diem rates:** $595–$842 outside, $1,056–$1,085 suites (no inside cabins). Prices include airfare.

The *Diamond, Seven Seas Navigator,* and *Song of Flower* also offer Greek ports of call on itineraries that include Italy, and the *Song of Flower* offers Greece as part of longer itineraries that include the Middle East.

ROYAL CARIBBEAN INTERNATIONAL
1050 Caribbean Way, Miami, FL 33132. ☎ **800/ALL-HERE.** www.rccl.com.

Royal Caribbean International is one of the most successful cruise companies in the world, selling a big-ship, American-style experience that's reasonably priced and designed to please everyone—except, perhaps, those turned off by crowds. The line's ships are well-run and offer a consistent product, overseen by a veritable army of service employees.

The line is known for offering a wealth of onboard activities, although in Europe the ports are more the focus than in, say, the Caribbean. Entertainment is varied and top-notch.

The company's vessel in Greece, the *Grandeur of the Seas* (built in 1996; 1,950 passengers, 73,817 GRTs), is a megaship with a multistory atrium, mall-like shopping complex, two-story dining room and show lounge, vast public spaces, and two pools (one outdoor and one indoor, with a retractable roof), but relatively small cabins.

In addition to the itineraries of the *Grandeur,* the *Legend of the Seas* (built in 1995; 1,804 passengers, 69,130 GRTs) does two 10-day cruises, one Piraeus-to-Barcelona and one Barcelona-to-Piraeus, that visit Rhodes, Santorini, and Crete, plus Kusadasi (Turkey) and ports in Italy; May and November. The *Splendour of the Seas* (built in 1996; 1,804 passengers, 69,130 GRTs) will also offer cruises in Greece in the summer of 2001, but they will be marketed strictly to Europeans.

GRANDEUR OF THE SEAS   7-day **round-trip from Rome** visits Katakolon, Rhodes, and Piraeus, plus Kusadasi (Turkey). June to August. **Per diem rates:** $321–$354 inside, $407–$493 outside, $600–$1,714 suite.

ROYAL OLYMPIC CRUISES
805 Third Ave., New York, NY 10022. ☎ **800/872-6400.** www.royalolympiccruises.com.

Royal Olympic is to Greece what Carnival Cruise Line is to the Caribbean: the dominant market giant. The line was formed in 1995 by the merger of top Greek lines Sun Line and Epirotiki, and in 2001 will have seven ships sailing the Greek islands, including some that also visit Egypt and Israel. The fleet includes two brand-new ships and a variety of older, classic vessels.

The Royal Olympic ships focus on destination as much as the shipboard experience (the line makes more onboard revenue on its shore excursions than on selling drinks) and passengers usually have a goal of seeing as much of the islands as is possible in 3, 4, or 7 days. Some of the itineraries are consequently quite loaded, visiting as many as two ports a day. The line offers special shore-excursion rates for kids, and packages all its excursions so you can book several and save.

The onboard atmosphere is relaxed. Passengers tend to go to bed pretty early, exhausted from busy days of sightseeing (although the ships do offer late-night discos for those who want to stay up late).

The Royal Olympic experience includes a friendly and accommodating Greek crew who offer a talent show complete with Greek music and Zorba-style dancing at least once during each cruise. Food on the ships is continental but with Greek specialties. On these ships, you won't forget you're in Greece.

The cruises are affordably priced and attract about 60% Americans, with the other 40% predominantly Europeans. Most tend to be seasoned travelers, but these ships, with their intimate atmosphere, are also suitable for first-timers and families. Children's and teens' activities are offered based on need—if there are enough kids booked, the line will put a youth counselor on board.

The **Olympic Voyager** and **Olympic Explorer** (built in 2000/2001; 840 passengers, 25,000 GRTs) are the new ships in the fleet, mid-sized sister vessels built in Germany, and among the fastest cruise ships afloat, able to cruise comfortably at upwards of 27 knots. Their speed allows them to do interesting itineraries like a Three Continents cruise that starts in Piraeus and includes port calls in Greece, Turkey, Israel, and Egypt, all in one week. The new vessels are fancier than their older peers, boasting modern and well-designed public rooms and a good number of suites, a few with verandas.

The other ships vary in style and design. The **Stella Solaris** (built in 1953; 620 passengers, 18,000 GRTs) and **Olympic Countess** (built in 1976; 840 passengers, 18,000 GRTs) are the fanciest of the older vessels; the *Countess* was formerly one of Cunard's lesser vessels. Along with the **Stella Oceanis** (built in 1965; 300 passengers, 5,500 GRTs), **Triton** (built in 1971; 620 passengers, 14,000 GRTs), and **World Renaissance** (built in 1966; 400 passengers, 12,000 GRTS), all the older ROC ships have classic features like teak decking, brass fittings, and expansive decks, and the line has been busy lately renovating and upgrading. Cabins are comfortably furnished but can be a bit cramped (they're bigger on the *Stella Solaris* than on the other old ships). Most cabins, except for some suites, do not come with TVs, though they do have radios. All the ships offer at least a few suites. Public rooms are comfortable, and there are plenty of quiet nooks to get away from it all.

ITINERARIES & RATES

OLYMPIC COUNTESS/WORLD RENAISSANCE **3- and 4-day round-trip from Piraeus** visit Mykonos, Rhodes, and Patmos, plus Kusadasi (Turkey), adding Crete and Santorini on 4-day. Both itineraries February through November. **Per diem rates:** $212–$280 inside, $252–$349 outside, $358–$549 suite.

OLYMPIC EXPLORER **7-day round-trip from Piraeus** visits Corfu, Nafplion, Mykonos, and Santorini, plus Venice (Italy) and Dubrovnik (Croatia). **7-day round-trip from Venice** visits Nafplion, Mykonos, Santorini, Piraeus, and Corfu, plus Istanbul (Turkey) and Dubrovnik (Croatia). May through October. **Per diem rates:** $321–$379 inside, $397–$455 outside, $550–$777 suite.

OLYMPIC VOYAGER **7-day round-trip from Piraeus** visits Santorini, Rhodes, and Mykonos, plus Kusadasi and Istanbul (Turkey), and ports in Egypt and Israel. May through November. **Per diem rates:** $321–$379 inside, $397–$455 outside, $550–$777 suite.

STELLA OCEANIS **3- and 4-day round-trip from Piraeus** (same as *Olympic Countess*, above). February through November. **7-day round-trip from Iraklion (Crete)**, visiting Delos, Mykonos, Patmos, Piraeus, Hydra, Rethymnon, Santorini, Amorgas, and Rhodes, plus Kusadasi and Marmais (Turkey). May to October. **Per diem rates:** $210–$241 inside, $257–$296 outside, $368–$370 suite.

STELLA SOLARIS   7-day round-trip from Piraeus visits Patmos, Mykonos, Rhodes, Crete, and Santorini, plus Istanbul and Kusadasi (Turkey). April through October. **Per diem rates:** $261–$299 inside, $320–$367 outside, $460–$585 suite.

TRITON   7-day round-trip from Civitavecchia (Rome) visits Katakolon, Santorini, Mykonos, Patmos, Piraeus, and Itea, does a Corinth Canal transit, and also visits Messina (Taormina, Italy) and Kusadasi (Turkey). May to October (the October 13 cruise disembarks in Venice). **10-day round-trip from Venice** visits Thessaloniki, Kavala, Crete, and Piraeus, transits the Corinth Canal twice, and also visits Istanbul and Kusadasi (Turkey). October and November. **11-day Holy Lands cruise from Venice** includes port calls in Piraeus, Itea, Patmos, and Corfu, plus Kusadasi (Turkey), a Corinth Canal transit, and port calls in Israel, Egypt, and Croatia. Late October. **Per diem rates:** $229–$264 inside, $282–$324 outside, $408–$465 suite.

SEABOURN CRUISE LINE
6100 Blue Lagoon Dr., Suite 400, Miami, FL 33126. ☎ **800/929-9391.** www.seabourn.com.

Seabourn really is what it was created to be: the best cruise line in the world in terms of food, service, ship design, itineraries, and refined environment. That said, the Seabourn cruise experience is not for everyone. These cruises are very pricey, and the customers who can afford them often very discriminating, even about who they choose to chat with on their vacation. Most passengers have household incomes that exceed $200,000.

Discretion is key on these ships, and the discreet environment and decor prove it. Like the passengers, the staff and crew are well mannered.

In Greece, the line's ships are the ultramodern, yachtlike *Seabourn Spirit* (built in 1989; 204 passengers, 10,000 GRTs) and the former Cunarders *Seabourn Goddess I* and *Seabourn Goddess II* (built in 1984/1985; 116 passengers, 4,250 GRTs).

The *Seabourn Spirit* is designed to allow passengers plenty of space to stretch out and feel at home (remembering that most of these people live in really big houses). The *Sea Goddess* vessels do not offer the same level of space but do offer a high level of service. The line brags that its waiters will wade through water to deliver guests a glass of champagne at the beach.

Cuisine is innovative, with French influences, and the dining rooms on all the vessels follow an open-seating policy, allowing passengers to sit with whomever they choose. The *Sea Goddess* ambiance is more casual. On the *Seabourn Spirit*, men wear jackets at dinner and everyone dresses up for formal nights.

The line enhances its cruises with guest lecturers, past examples of which have included celebrities like Walter Cronkite and Art Linkletter. Nighttime entertainment is very low-key, with the ship's soloist doubling as social host or hostess.

All the cabins on the *Seabourn Spirit* are outside suites, and each has a 5-foot-wide picture window and comes with a fully stocked complimentary bar. Owner's suites are very plush and offer private verandas; 36 cabins on the *Spirit* (and on each of the sister ships) recently got the added feature of French balconies with doors you can open to let in the ocean breezes (but which are too narrow to sit on).

The *Goddess* ships offer all outside cabins, each with sitting area, full bath with tub and shower, bar, refrigerator, and TV/VCR. While the standard cabins are much smaller than on the *Spirit*, the deluxe suites are generously proportioned. The *Goddess* ships are not suitable for kids (those under 16 are not even allowed).

The *Seabourn Spirit* carries a floating marina that, when lowered, provides a teak-decked platform for water sports (Sunfish, kayaks, snorkeling gear, high-speed banana boats, and water skis are available for passenger use). There's also a mesh net that becomes a saltwater swimming pool. The *Goddess* ships also have platforms in their sterns, but they are not as elaborate.

ITINERARIES & RATES

SEABOURN SPIRIT A number of itineraries visit smaller ports and some popular ones, too. **14-day Istanbul-to-Venice** visits Volos, Paros, Mykonos, Nafplion, Piraeus, and Katakolon, transits the Corinth Canal, and also calls at Kusadasi (Turkey) and ports in Croatia. Also available as a 7-day Istanbul-to-Piraeus or Piraeus-to-Venice itinerary. **14-day Venice-to-Piraeus** visits Corfu, Zakinthos, Nafplion, Monemvassia, and Santorini, plus Kusadasi (Turkey) and Hvar (Croatia), and transits the Corinth Canal. **12-day Piraeus-to-Istanbul** visits Crete, Rhodes, Patmos, Mykonos, Paros, and Volos, plus Fethiye, Bodrum, and Kusadasi (Turkey). **14-day Civitavecchia (Rome)-to-Istanbul** visits Katakolon, Corfu, Galaxidhi (Delphi), Piraeus, Monemvassia, Patmos, Skiathos, and Volos, transits the Corinth Canal, and also calls on Sorrento and Taormina (Sicily, Italy). Can also be taken as a 7-day Civitavecchia (Rome)-to-Piraeus or Piraeus-to-Istanbul itinerary. The ship visits Greece on Holy Land and Black Sea itineraries, as well as itineraries that combine Greece and Italy or Greece, Italy, and France. Late March to November. **Per diem rates:** 735–$2,018 suite (no standard cabins). Rates include tips, an in-cabin bar setup, and wine at lunch and dinner.

SEABOURN GODDESS I/SEABOURN GODDESS II **7-day Venice-to-Piraeus and Piraeus-to-Venice** visit Corfu, Kefalonia, Itea, and Hydra, transit the Corinth Canal, and also call at Ancona (Italy) and Korcula (Croatia). **7-day Piraeus-to-Istanbul** visits Nafplion, Monemvassia, Santorini, and Mykonos, plus Kusadasi (Turkey). **7-day Istanbul-to-Piraeus** visits Volos, Skiathos, Samos, Rhodes, and Patmos. **Per diem rates:** $674–$1,678 suite (no standard cabins). Rates include tips, an in-cabin bar setup, and wine at lunch and dinner.

SILVERSEA CRUISES

110 E. Broward Blvd., Fort Lauderdale, FL 33301. ☎ **800/722-9055.** www.silversea.com.

The luxurious sister ships **Silver Cloud** and **Silver Wind** (both built in 1994; 296 passengers, 16,800 GRTs) and new **Silver Shadow** (built in 2000; 388 passengers, 25,000 GRTs) carry their guests in true splendor, in an atmosphere that's elegant but low-key, and in a milieu that's sociable rather than stuffy. Passengers are generally experienced cruisers, not necessarily American, and certainly are well traveled. Most are in the over-50 group. These ships are not for kids.

On the *Silver Cloud* and *Silver Wind*, all accommodations are outside suites with picture windows, writing tables, sofas, walk-in closets, marble bathrooms, and all the amenities you'd expect of a top-of-the-line ship. Throughout, both vessels allot more space to each passenger than most other ships. There's also more crew, with the large staff at your service, ready to cater to your every desire on a 24-hour basis.

The newer *Silver Shadow* carries on the fine tradition on a slightly bigger ship. The all-suite vessel also adds features such as more suites with verandas, poolside dining venues, a larger spa facility, a computer center, a cigar lounge designed by noted cigar purveyor Davidoff, and a wine and champagne bar designed by Moët & Chandon.

The fine accoutrements that complement the luxurious experience aboard all three ships include Limoges china, Christofle silverware, Frette bed linens, and soft down pillows. Activities offerings include bridge and other games, aerobics, dance lessons, wine tastings, and lectures (including a *National Geographic Traveler* series), as well as such cruise staples as bingo and quiz shows. Nighttime entertainment venues include showrooms for resident musicians and local talent, a piano bar, a small casino, and rooms for dancing.

The ships offer five-star cuisine served in a single seating, with guests able to dine when, where, and with whom they choose.

The relatively small size and design of the ships allows them to dock in intimate harbors that are off-limits to large vessels.

ITINERARIES & RATES

SILVER CLOUD   **8-day Piraeus-to-Malta** visits Rhodes, Crete, and Kithira, plus Kusadasi and Marmaris (Turkey), and includes a hotel night in Athens. Can be combined with a Valletta (Malta)-to-Rome itinerary that calls in Italy and France, to make a 15-day cruisetour. **13-day Monte Carlo–to–Piraeus** visits Santorini and Rhodes as well as Marmaris and Kusadasi (Turkey), and ports in Italy and Malta. Also does a Greece and Black Sea itinerary. June and October. **Per diem rates:** $684–$1,487 suite (no standard cabins). Rates include tips, a shoreside cultural event (such as a local folk performance), airfare, hotel accommodations, transfers, wines and spirits, champagne, and more.

SILVER SHADOW   **11-day Piraeus-to-Istanbul** in April visits Crete and Rhodes, plus Limassol (Cyprus) and ports in Turkey, and includes one hotel night in Athens. **13-day Istanbul-to-Rome cruisetour** in May visits Piraeus, Katakolon, and Corfu, plus ports in Croatia and Italy. **12-day Nice (France)-to-Istanbul itinerary** in August visits Argostoli (Kefalonia), Kithira, Piraeus, and Crete, plus ports in Italy and Izmir (Turkey), and includes a pre-cruise hotel night in Nice. **7-day Istanbul-to-Piraeus** in August visits Thessaloniki, Volos, and Mykonos, includes a pre-cruise hotel night in Istanbul, and can be combined with a **7-day Piraeus-to-Rome** itinerary that visits Nafplion as well as ports in Italy and Malta. **8-day Genoa-to-Venice** visits Itea and Corfu, as well as ports in Italy and Dubrovnik (Croatia), includes a pre-cruise hotel stay in Genoa, and can be combined with an **8-day Venice-to-Piraeus** itinerary that calls at Monemvassia and Santorini, as well as Korcula (Croatia) and Marmaris (Turkey). April to September. **Per diem rates:** $715–$1,962 suite (no standard cabins). Rates include tips, a shoreside cultural event (such as a local folk performance), airfare, hotel accommodations, transfers, wines and spirits, champagne, and more.

SILVER WIND   A number of 8-day itineraries, all of which include a pre-cruise hotel night, visit Greece and can be combined with other itineraries to create longer sailings. For example, an **8-day Monte Carlo–to–Piraeus** in June visits Corfu and Katakolon, as well as Rome (Italy) and Dubrovnik (Croatia) and can be combined with an **8-day Piraeus-to-Istanbul** itinerary that includes Lesvos and Kusadasi (Turkey), as well as ports in the Ukraine. An **8-day Istanbul-to-Rome** itinerary in July visits Delos, the Peloponnese, Kithira, and Katakolon, and can be combined with an **8-day Rome–to–Monte Carlo** sailing that visits Italy, France, and Tunisia. **13-day Rome-to-Piraeus** in September visits Nafplion, Mykonos, and Rhodes, as well as ports in Italy, Turkey, and Israel. June to October. **Per diem rates.** $699–$1,562 suite (no standard cabins). Rates include tips, a shoreside cultural event (such as a local folk performance), airfare, hotel accommodations, transfers, wines and spirits, champagne, and more.

STAR CLIPPERS

4101 Salzedo St., Coral Gables, FL 33146. ☎ **800/442-0551.** www.starclippers.com.

The **Star Flyer** (built in 1991; 170 passengers, 3,025 GRTs), the vessel this three-ship line operates in Greece, is a replica of the big 19th-century clipper sailing ships (or barkentines) that once circled the globe. Its tall square rigs carry enormous sails and are glorious to look at, and a particular thrill for history buffs.

And on this ship, the sails are more than just window dressing. The *Star Flyer* was constructed using original drawings and the specifications of a leading 19th-century naval architect, but updated with modern touches so that today it is among the tallest and fastest clipper ships ever built—it has reached speeds of more than 19 knots.

The atmosphere onboard is akin to being on a private yacht rather than a mainstream cruise ship. It's casual in an L. L. Bean sort of way, and friendly. Passengers generally fall into the 30-to-60 age range.

Cabins are pleasant, and decorated with wood accents. There is one owner's suite. The public rooms include a writing room, an open-seating dining room, and an Edwardian-style library with a belle-époque fireplace and walls lined with bookshelves. There are two swimming pools.

Local entertainment is sometimes brought aboard, and there's also a resident pianist and a makeshift disco in the Tropical Bar. Movies are piped into passenger cabins.

Activities on the ship tend toward the nautical, such as visiting the bridge, observing the crew handle the sails, and participating in knot-tying classes.

It should be noted that despite stabilizers, movement on this vessel may be troublesome to those who get seasick.

ITINERARIES & RATES

STAR FLYER   **7-day Northern Cyclades itinerary round-trip from Piraeus** visits Delos/Mykonos, Patmos, and Kea, as well as Kusadasi and Gulluk (Turkey). **7-day Southern Cyclades itinerary round-trip from Piraeus** visits Rhodes, Santorini, and Hydra, as well as Bodrum and Dalyan River (Turkey). Both itineraries include a full day at sea. May through September. **Per diem rates:** $239 inside, $268–$399 outside, $542 suite. Port charges are an extra $175.

SWAN HELLENIC

U.S. Sales Agent: Kartagener Associates, 12 W. 37th St., New York, NY 10018. ☎ **877/ 219-4239.** www.swanhellenic.com.

This British firm is owned by Peninsular and Orient Steam Navigation Company (P&O), the company that also owns U.S.-based Princess Cruises.

With its one ship, *Minerva* (built in 1996; 300 passengers, 12,000 GRTs), Swan Hellenic offers a small-ship experience that is both high-quality and enriching, visiting ports off the beaten path. All the itineraries feature acclaimed guest lecturers who are authorities in their fields, and the passengers—a mix of British and Americans—tend to be experienced, inquisitive travelers.

Public rooms are spacious, and include two open-seating restaurants, a large library, and a variety of lounges and bars done up in understated, English-country decor, complete with cushy upholstered chairs. The ship does not have a casino. Every cabin has a TV, phone, and fax. All feature private bathrooms with showers, and some have full-size bathtubs. The ship's luxurious suites offer private verandas.

ITINERARIES & RATES

MINERVA   The ship visits Greece on a number of itineraries. A **14-day Istanbul-to-Piraeus** sailing in April is one of the most comprehensive Greek itineraries available, with port calls in Kavala, Thessaloniki, Hios, Patmos, Nafplion, Githio, Kithira, Kalamata, Katakolon, and Itea, and a Corinth Canal transit. **7-day Piraeus-to-Istanbul** sailing in August calls at Naxos, Delos, Tinos, Skyros, and Thessaloniki. The cruise can also be combined with a **7-day Venice-to-Piraeus** that visits Corfu, Ithaka, and the Corinth Canal, as well as ports in Croatia, to make a 14-day sailing. A **14-day Crete-to-Venice** itinerary in October visits Delos, Piraeus, Nafplion,

Githio, Kalamata, Katakolon, and Itea, as well as Albania and Croatia. **Per diem rates:** $314–$358 inside, $357–$566 outside, $600–$696 suite. Rates include shore excursions, tips, transfers, and airfare from London. Special half-price rates are available on some sailings for those up to the age 26 when traveling with a full-fare adult passenger.

WINDSTAR

300 Elliott Ave. W., Seattle, WA 98119. ☎ **800/258-7245.** www.windstarcruises.com.

While they look like sailing ships of yore, the *Wind Song* (built in 1987; 148 passengers, 5,350 GRTs) and *Wind Spirit* (built in 1988; 144 passengers, 5,350 GRTs) are more like luxury floating resorts, complete with top-notch service and extraordinary cuisine. Million-dollar computers operate the sails, and stabilizers allow for a smooth ride.

Casual, low-key elegance is the watchword on these vessels. There's no set regime, unless you consider pampering a regime. Most of the passengers are well heeled and range in age from 30 to 70.

Cabins are all outside and roomy (through not suite-sized) and boast teak-decked bathrooms and large portholes. The top-level owner's cabins are slightly bigger. Amenities include VCRs and CD players.

A water-sports platform at the stern allows for a variety of activities when the ships are docked. Daytime entertainment is low-key and sometimes includes local entertainers brought aboard at ports of call. The ships also have small casinos. Passengers can visit the bridge whenever they want.

The line is owned by Carnival Corporation, which is also the parent of Carnival, Holland America Line, Costa, Seabourn, and Cunard.

ITINERARIES & RATES

WIND SONG 7-day **Piraeus-to-Istanbul (and Istanbul-to-Piraeus)** visits Mykonos, Santorini, and Rhodes, plus Kusadasi and Bodrum (Turkey). May to October. An **8-day Rome-to-Piraeus** cruise in May visits Githio, Spetsai, and Aegina, as well as ports in Italy (and can be combined with an earlier Monte Carlo–to–Rome sailing to make a 14-day itinerary). **Per diem rates:** $701–$940 outside.

WIND SPIRIT 7-day **Piraeus-to-Istanbul and Istanbul-to-Piraeus** itineraries, as above. May to October. The ship also does an **8-day Piraeus-to-Rome** sailing in late October, visiting Aegina, Spetsai, Githio, and Siros, as well as ports in Italy (the cruise can be combined with a Rome–to–Monte Carlo sailing to make a 14-day itinerary). **Per diem rates:** $552–$940 outside.

ZEUS TOURS & YACHT CRUISES

551 Fifth Ave., Suite 1001, New York, NY 10176. ☎ **800/447-5667.** www.zeustours.com.

This 50-plus-year-old firm represents several lines, including its own fleet of yachts (known as Zeus Cruises), Galileo Cruises' sailing ship *Galileo Sun,* and two classic vessels operated by Golden Sun Cruises.

The yachts, the *Zeus I* and *Zeus II* (built in 1995; 40 passengers, GRTs unavailable), offer a casual, reasonably priced, soft-adventure cruise experience with an international group of passengers, visiting both popular and out-of-the-way ports. The *Zeus I* has sails, although it is also motor-powered. The *Zeus II* is a motorized yacht. The company chooses which ship you will sail aboard. Both ships feature outside cabins that are small but comfortable and fitted with picture windows. Some have upper and lower beds. There's also a dining room, bar, and lounge.

Two meals are served each day, breakfast and either lunch or dinner (passengers are in port for the third meal). Local wine, beer, ouzo, and soft drinks are free.

The crew is Greek and adds much to the ambience. An English-speaking cruise leader is also aboard each yacht. Each cruise features a Beach BBQ, a Greek day with Greek dancing, and a Captain's Dinner.

The *Galileo Sun* (built in 1994; 34 passengers, GRTs unavailable), on the other hand, provides a more upscale yacht experience. Cabins are all outside; some have double beds. A special emphasis is put on cuisine, which is served in a wood-paneled dining room. Public rooms also include a bar/lounge. Again, the crew is Greek, with an English-speaking cruise leader.

Zeus is also the preferred representative for Golden Sun's *Aegean I* (built in 1973; 570 passengers, 13,000 GRTs) and *Arcadia* (built in 1968; 278 passengers, 5,200 GRTs), cruises aboard which are also sold through other tour operators. Both ships are older vessels, with numerous public rooms and a casual ambience.

ITINERARIES & RATES

Zeus Tours offers 7-day cruises on the *Zeus* ships and *Galileo Sun* that can be purchased as cruise-only or with a 3-day hotel stay in Athens. Cruises on the *Aegean I* and *Arcadia* combine a 3-, 4-, or 7-day cruise with a 2- or 3-day hotel stay in Athens.

AEGEAN I/ARCADIA   3-, 4-, and 7-day round-trip from Piraeus. The **3-day cruises** visit Mykonos, Rhodes, and Patmos, plus Kusadasi (Turkey). The **4-day cruises** visit Mykonos, Kusadasi, Patmos, Rhodes, Crete, and Santorini. The **7-day cruises** visit Crete, Santorini, Rhodes, Patmos, Delos, and Mykonos, plus Kusadasi and Istanbul (Turkey). March through November. **Per diem rates:** From $153 inside, from $200 outside (no suites). Rates include round-trip air from New York and a hotel stay. Port charges and taxes are extra. (Rates are 2000; 2001 not available at press time.)

GALILEO SUN   7-day round-trip from Piraeus visits Santorini, Amorgos, Patmos, Samos, Delos, Rhinia, Mykonos, and Cape Sounion, plus Kusadasi (Turkey). May through October. **Per diem rates:** $253–$313 outside (no inside cabins or suite). Port charges are an additional $80. (Rates are for 2000; 2001 not available at press time.)

ZEUS I/ZEUS II   7-day round-trip from Piraeus visits Santorini, Ios, Paros, Delos, Mykonos, Tinos, Kea, and Cape Sounion (on the mainland). April through October. **7-day round-trip from Corfu** visits Paxi, Lefkada, Kefalonia, Ithaka, Zakinthos, and Parga (on the mainland). May through September. **7-day round-trip from Rhodes** visits Kalimnos, Kos, Patmos, Lipsi, Leros, and Simi, plus Marmaris (Turkey). May through October. **Per diem rates:** $151–$220 outside (no inside cabins or suites). Port charges of $30 to $50 are extra.

8 Ships Visiting Greece on Longer Mediterranean Itineraries

The following lines and ships visit Greece as part of longer itineraries.

Celebrity Cruises. 1050 Caribbean Way, Miami, FL 33132. ☎ **800/327-6700.** www.celebrity-cruises.com.

Celebrity, a decently priced yet upscale U.S. operator, offers Greece as part of Barcelona-to-Istanbul and Istanbul-to-Barcelona itineraries, June to September, aboard the new *Millennium* (built in 2000; 1,950 passengers, 91,000 GRTs). Port calls include Katakolon and Piraeus, plus Kusadasi (Turkey) and ports in Italy. The ship also stops by Piraeus on 12-day Holy Land itineraries that include Egypt and Israel.

Crystal Cruises. 2049 Century Park E., Suite 1400, Los Angeles, CA 90067. ☎ **310/785-9300.** www.crystalcruises.com.

This luxury operator offers Greece on the *Crystal Symphony* (built in 1997; 940 passengers, 51,004 GRTs) as part of 12-day cruises in August and September. Departures are from Rome, Venice, or Piraeus, with the itinerary including Italy and Croatia or Italy, France, and Malta. Greek stops are either Santorini and Mykonos, Corfu, or Mykonos and Rhodes, and three of the four itineraries also stop at Kusadasi (Turkey).

Peter Deilmann EuropAmerica Cruises. 1800 Diagonal Rd., Suite 170, Alexandria, VA 22314. ☎ **800/348-8287.** www.deilmann-cruises.com.

This German company, which operates river ships in Europe as well as two oceangoing vessels, offers Eastern Mediterranean sailings in April and September on its *Lili Marleen* (built in 1994; 50 passengers, 750 GRTs), a luxury sailing yacht that's a re-creation of a 19th-century tall ship. An 8-day sailing in April from Limassol (Cyprus) to Iraklion (Crete) includes port calls in Rhodes, Kos, and Santorini, as well as several ports in Turkey. A 12-day cruise from Iraklion (Crete) to Cantania (Italy), also in April, visits Santorini, Githio, Pylos, Katakolon, Zakinthos, Vathi, and Corfu.

In September, there's a 7-day cruise from Piraeus to Limassol (Cyprus) that visits Mykonos, Kos, Rhodes, and Megisti, as well as Kusadasi (Turkey); an 8-day cruise from Catania (Turkey) to Piraeus that calls at Katakolon and Itea and transits the Corinth Canal; and a 7-day cruise, round-trip from Piraeus, that visits Hydra, Crete, Santorini, and Milos.

Peter Deilmann also offers two cruises in October that include Greece on its elegant oceangoing flagship *Deutschland* (built in 1998; 505 passengers, 22,400 GRTs). An 11-day sailing from Venice to Limassol (Cyprus) visits Corfu, Katakolon, Nafplion, Piraeus, Crete, and Rhodes, and also calls at ports in Turkey, Croatia, and Lebanon. An 11-day itinerary from Limassol (Cyprus) to Venice includes port calls in Crete, Pylos, and Itea, and also visits Egypt, Israel, and Croatia.

EuroCruises/Fred Olsen Cruise Lines. 33 Little West 12th St., Suite 106, New York, NY 10014. ☎ **800/688-3876.** www.eurocruises.com.

EuroCruises offers two long, pan-Mediterranean itineraries, 20 nights and 23 nights, in April and October. Both are round-trip from Dover, England, on the line's *Black Prince* (built in 1966; 451-passengers, 11,209 GRTs), a small, upscale, European-style ship. The spring cruise includes Crete, Delos, Mykonos, a Corinth Canal transit, and Piraeus. The longer itinerary, in the fall, visits Itea, Piraeus, Santorini, Rhodes, and Crete, and does a Corinth Canal transit.

Holland America Line. 300 Elliott Ave. W., Seattle, WA 98119. ☎ **800/426-0327.** www.hollandamerica.com.

Holland America offers Greece on 12-day itineraries aboard the modern *Maasdam* (built in 1993; 1,266 passengers, 55,451 GRTs). In April, the ship sails round-trip from Venice, visiting Piraeus, Nafplion, and Katakolon in addition to Dubrovnik (Croatia) and Kusadasi and Istanbul (Turkey). In May and September, the ship sails from Venice to Istanbul, stopping in Piraeus and Kusadasi (Turkey) as well as ports in Croatia, Ukraine, Romania, and Bulgaria. In October, the ship stops in Piraeus and Kusadasi (Turkey) on an Istanbul-to-Venice cruise that also includes Egypt, Israel, and Croatia. Also in October, the ship visits Katakolon, Piraeus, and Kusadasi on a Venice-to-Barcelona itinerary that also includes port calls in Malta, Italy, and Monaco.

The line's flagship, the *Rotterdam* (built in 1997; 1,316 passengers, 62,000 GRTs), offers a 12-day itinerary in September and October from Piraeus to Rome, visiting Rhodes, Patmos, and Katakolon, plus ports in Egypt, Israel, Cyprus, and Malta. Another itinerary offered in September, from Rome to Istanbul or vice versa, includes Italy, Greece, Croatia, and Turkey, with Greek stops in Corfu, Katakolon, and Iraklion, plus Kusadasi (Turkey). A 12-day Rome-to-Piraeus itinerary in September has port calls in Greece, Turkey, Bulgaria, Romania, and Ukraine, with Greek stops in Nafplion and Patmos, plus Kusadasi (Turkey).

Lindblad Expeditions. 720 Fifth Ave., New York, NY 10019. ☎ **800/762-0003.** www.specialexpeditions.com.

Soft-adventure operator Lindblad Expeditions (formerly Special Expeditions) offers two sailings on its expedition ship *Caledonia Star* (built in 1966; 110 passengers, 3,905 GRTs) in September, between Valeta, Malta, and Izmir (near Kusadasi), Turkey, that include Italy, Greece, and Turkey. The Greek ports are Katakolon, Delphi, Skyros, Delos, and Santorini.

Norwegian Cruise Line. 7665 Corporate Center Dr., Miami, FL 33126. ☎ **800/ 327-7030.** www.ncl.com.

Norwegian, a midpriced American line, offers Greece aboard the *Norwegian Dream* (built in 1992; 1,726 passengers, 46,000 GRTs) as part of a 12-day Black Sea sailing between Piraeus and Istanbul, in October, and as part of a 12-day Holy Lands sailing between Istanbul and Piraeus, also in October. The Black Sea itinerary includes visits to Rhodes, Santorini, and Mykonos, plus Kusadasi (Turkey), Limassol (Cyprus), and ports in the Ukraine and Bulgaria. The Holy Lands itinerary visits Rhodes and Santorini, as well as Kusadasi (Turkey) and ports in Egypt and Israel.

P&O Cruises. 77 New Oxford St., London, WC1A 1PP England. ☎ **44-171-800-2345.** In the U.S., contact Princess Tours, 2815 Second Ave., Suite 400, Seattle, WA 98121-1299. ☎ **800/340-7074.** www.pocruises.com.

British operator P&O visits Greece on several sailings, most round-trip from Southampton (U.K.). The *Arcadia* (built in 1989; 1,500 passengers, 63,500 GRTs) does a 16-day sailing in August that includes Piraeus, Soudha Bay, and Zakinthos, plus Kusadasi (Turkey), Palma (Spain), and Gibraltar. The *Victoria* (built in 1965; 726 passengers, 27,670 GRTs) calls on Greek ports on a number of itineraries including a 14-day Black Sea cruise in October, round-trip from Venice, that includes port calls in Thessaloniki, Mykonos, and Ithaka; and a 14-day Mediterranean in November, also round-trip from Venice, that includes port calls in Hios, Piraeus, and Corfu.

The newer and larger *Aurora* (built in 2000; 1,870 passengers, 76,000) visits Corfu, Zakinthos, and Piraeus on a 16-day cruise in September that also includes Dubrovnik (Croatia) and ports in Spain. The ship also stops in Piraeus on a 17-day Holy Lands itinerary in October.

Princess Cruises. 10100 Santa Monica Blvd., Suite 1800, Los Angeles, CA 90067. ☎ **800/421-0522.** www.princesscruises.com.

Premium U.S. operator Princess, which is owned by P&O, offers several 12-day itineraries that include Greece. The brand new *Golden Princess* (built in 2001; 2,600 passengers, 109,000 GRTs), one of the world's largest ships, sails between Barcelona and Istanbul, June to September, with stops in Piraeus and Kusadasi (Turkey) as well as Monte Carlo and ports in Italy. The considerably smaller *Pacific Princess* (built in 1971; 610 passengers; 20,000 GRTs) offers a Christmas holiday Holy Land cruise from Piraeus that visits Rhodes, Santorini, and Crete, as well as ports in Israel and Egypt. The mid-sized *Royal Princess* (built in 1984; 1,200 passengers; 45,000 GRTs) also stops by Rhodes and Kusadasi (Turkey) in April and May, on Holy Land itineraries between Piraeus and Rome.

Renaissance Cruises. 350 East Las Olas Blvd., Fort Lauderdale, FL 33301. ☎ **800/ 525-5350.** www.renaissancecruises.com.

This upscale line offers several 10- to 15-day itineraries that include Greece. The line's vessels are all sleek, new, and almost completely identical luxury ships simply named *R1, R2,* and *R5* (built in 1998, 1999, 2000; 684 passengers, 30,200 GRTs). The vessels are all no-smoking, and kids under age 13 are not allowed onboard. The 10-day cruises include Rome-to-Piraeus sailings that call at Katakolon, Crete, and Rhodes, as well as several ports in Italy; the 15-day cruises include Piraeus-to-Venice Holy Lands itineraries, with port calls in Rhodes, Santorini, Mykonos, and Corfu, as well as ports in Israel, Egypt, and Croatia.

9 Best Shore Excursions in the Ports of Call: Greece

Shore excursions are designed to help you make the most of your limited time in port, taking you by various transport to sites of historical or cultural value or natural or artistic beauty. The tours are usually booked on the first day of your cruise, are sold on a first-come, first-served basis, and are nonrefundable. Some lines allow bookings in advance, and some include shore excursions in their cruise fares.

Generally, shore excursions that take you well beyond the port area are the ones most worth taking—you'll get professional commentary and avoid having to hassle with local transportation. In ports whose attractions are all within walking distance of the pier, however, you may be best off touring on your own.

Keep in mind that shore excursions are a revenue-generating area for the cruise lines, and the tours may be heavily promoted aboard the ship. They aren't always offered at bargain prices.

When touring in Greece, remember to wear comfortable walking shoes and bring a hat, sunscreen, and bottled water to ward off the effects of the hot sun. Most lines make bottled water available as you disembark, usually for a fee.

Remember, in some places such as churches and other religious sites, modest attire may be required, meaning shoulders and knees should be covered.

Below we highlight a selection of shore-excursion offerings at the major cruise ports. Keep in mind that not all the tours will be offered by every line. For more information on many of these ports, consult the relevant chapters in this book.

CORFU (KERKIRA)
See chapter 14 for complete sightseeing information.

ACHILLEION PALACE & PALEOKASTRITSA (4 hrs., $42): Visit Achilleion Palace and see the statues of Achilles. Continue on to Paleokastritsa to visit the 13th-century Monastery of the Virgin Mary. There's usually free time and an opportunity to swim in Paleokastritsa. Stop in Corfu town and visit St. Spyridon Church, named for the patron saint of Corfu, or stroll the narrow streets.

IRAKLION & AYIOS NIKOLAOS (CRETE)
See chapter 8 for complete sightseeing information.

THE PALACE OF KNOSSOS (3 hrs., $47): Travel by motor coach from Iraklion to Knossos, once the capital of the prehistoric Minoan civilization, and thought to be the basis for the original mythological Minotaur's labyrinth. Visit the excavation of the palace of King Minos. Return to Iraklion for a museum tour or free time. Similar tours are offered from Rethymnon (5 hrs., $53) and from Ayios Nikolaos, including lunch (7 hrs., $136).

EXPLORING CRETE (4 hrs., $47): Ride by bus to Ayios Nikolaos, stopping for photos outside the archaeological site of Mallia, home of King Radamanthys. Travel to the Greek Orthodox monastery of St. George Selinaris. Take photos at scenic Elounda Bay. Free time in Ayios Nikolaos.

ITEA (DELPHI)

See chapter 11 for complete sightseeing information.

DELPHI EXCURSION (4 hrs., $55): Delphi is located on the slope of Mount Parnassus. Visit the Sanctuary of Apollo to see the Temple of Apollo, the theater, the treasury buildings, and the Sacred Way. Visit the Archaeological Museum. There's usually a short stop at Castalian Spring.

KATAKOLON (OLYMPIA)

See chapter 7 for complete sightseeing information.

EXCURSION TO OLYMPIA (4 hrs., $52–$72): Visit the site of the original Olympic Games, held from 776 B.C. to A.D. 393. See the Temple of Hera, in front of which burns the Olympic Flame; the Temple of Zeus, which once housed the gold-and-ivory statue of Zeus that was one of the Seven Wonders of the Ancient World; and the original stadium and *bouleuterion*, where Olympic competitors swore an oath to conform to the rules of the games. Visit the famous Archaeological Museum of Olympia to see the marble statue of the Temple of Zeus and the statue of Hermes. Also included is a short stop in the town of Olympia.

MYKONOS (& DELOS)

See chapter 9 for complete sightseeing information.

DELOS APOLLO SANCTUARY (3–4½ hrs., $37–$63): Travel by small boat from Mykonos harbor to Delos for a 2-hour guided walking tour of the tiny island that was once the religious and commercial hub of the Aegean, but now is home only to ancient ruins and their caretakers. View the Agora; the Sacred Way, which leads to the Sanctuary of Apollo; and the Terrace of the Lions, where marble beasts from the 7th century B.C. guard the now-dry Sacred Lake. View the remains of the Maritime Quarter with its harbors, water houses, and villas (including the House of Cleopatra) and the renowned mosaic floors in the House of the Masks and the House of Dionysos. Also visit the Archaeological Museum (if it's open).

NAFPLION

See chapter 7 for complete sightseeing information.

PALAMIDI CASTLE & MYCENAE (4 hrs., $59–$72): Visit the area ruled by Agamemnon. Visit the Palamidi Castle, which was built by Venetians and seized by the Turks. The path up consists of nearly a thousand steps (motor coaches can drive up to the gate). At Mycenae, you walk through the Lion Gate to view the ruins, which will remind you of Homer's *Iliad*.

EPIDAURUS & PALAMIDI CASTLE (4 hrs., $56): See the countryside as you travel to Epidaurus, the town dedicated to Asklepios, god of healing. Visit the 4th-century B.C. theater with its remarkable acoustics. On the way back, stop by Palamidi Castle, located on a hill above Nafplion.

COMBO TOUR OF EPIDAURUS & MYCENAE (5–7 hrs., $76–$89): Includes lunch at a traditional restaurant.

ANCIENT CORINTH (4 hrs., $49): Visit the ancient city where the most impressive relic is the 6th-century B.C. Doric temple of Apollo. You can also view the canal from 200 feet up on the bridge that straddles the waterway.

PATMOS

See chapter 10 for complete sightseeing information.

THE MONASTERY OF ST. JOHN & CAVE OF THE APOCALYPSE (2½–4 hrs., $32–$68): Depart the port of Skala and travel by bus to the village of Hora and the 900-year-old Monastery of St. John. Visit the main church and view the ecclesiastical treasures in the museum. Continue on by bus to the nearby Cave of the Apocalypse to see the silver niches in the wall that mark the pillow and ledge used as a desk by the author of the Book of Revelation and the crack made by the Voice of God. Longer tours may include a visit to the 300-year-old Simandris House, which boasts a rich collection on antiques, and a stop for a wine tasting at a local taverna.

EXPLORATION OF HORA (3½ hrs., $42): Depart the port of Skala by bus to visit the Cave of the Apocalypse (see above). Walk uphill to Hora, where you will visit Plateia Xanthos, which houses the City Hall and the bust of Emmanuel Xanthos, one of the Greek independence leaders of 1821. Also visit Symantiri House, a typical Patmian Mansion, and the historical chapel and museum of the Monastery of St. John. The trip includes a visit to a local tavern to sample *mezedes* (Greek hors d'oeuvres) and *ouzo,* and to be entertained by local musicians.

AFTERNOON AT THE BEACH (2 hrs., $15): Depart the ship on tenders to Kambos beach, where you'll have 2 hours to swim and tan. Changing facilities are available and sun beds and umbrellas will be provided, along with soft drinks.

PIRAEUS/ATHENS

See chapter 5 for complete sightseeing information.

ATHENS CITY TOUR (3½–4 hrs., $38–$42): Includes a guided tour of the Acropolis, Athens's most prominent historical and architectural site; a drive past other Athens highlights, including Constitution Square, the Parliament, the Temple of Zeus, Hadrian's Arch, and Olympic Stadium; and time for souvenir shopping in the Plaka. A full-day city tour (8½–9 hrs., $90–$92) also includes a visit to the National Archeological Museum and sometimes a stop at the Temple of Poseidon, located high on a cliff overlooking the Aegean Sea.

ATHENS, THE ACROPOLIS & THE CORINTH CANAL (9 hrs., $91): Visit the Acropolis and, by bus, tour past other sights in Athens, then take the highway from Athens to the Corinth Canal (about 96km/60 miles) for views of the canal and to visit Ancient Corinth, once a grand city with a forum larger than that of Rome. Also visit the Corinth Museum.

A DAY TOUR OF DELPHI (9–10 hrs., $89–$109): If you've been to Athens before or just aren't into big cities and crowds, you may want to try this full-day trip to one of the great sights of antiquity. The tour visits the ruins of the Temple of Apollo, located in a stunning setting on the slope of Mount Parnassus. Lunch is included.

RHODES

See chapter 10 for complete sightseeing information.

RHODES & LINDOS COMBINED (4–4½ hrs., $40–$56): Travel by bus through the scenic countryside to Lindos, an important city in ancient times. At Lindos, view the medieval walls which were constructed by the Knights of St. John in the 14th century. Walk or take a donkey up to the ancient Acropolis, where there are ruins and great views—and, of course, souvenir shops on the way. The trip may include a walking tour of Old Town Rhodes (see description below), a stop at a workshop selling Rhodian ceramics, and/or a visit to Mount Smith to view the ruins of ancient Rhodes, the Temple of Apollo, and Diagoras Stadium.

LINDOS WITH LUNCH BY THE BEACH (7½–8 hrs., $65–$87): Drive to Lindos and explore the city (see above). Enjoy lunch at a beachfront restaurant or other scenic location. Return to Rhodes, driving along the walls of the medieval city and stopping at Port d'Amboise for a walk through Old Town. View the Palace of the Knights and the medieval houses, as well as the Hospital of the Knights of St. John. The tour may stop at a ceramics workshop to see how Rhodian ceramics are made.

SANTORINI (THIRA)

See chapter 9 for complete sightseeing information.

AKROTIRI EXCAVATIONS & FIRA TOWN (3 hrs., $48–$57): Visit Akrotiri, an excavation site that dates back to the 2nd millennium B.C. See pottery, two- and three-story houses, and a variety of rooms, all 3,600 years old. Visit Fira, perched on the caldera rim, and take a stroll through town. Take a cable car ride or mule back down the slope to your ship.

VOLOS

See chapter 11 for complete sightseeing information.

THE MONASTERIES OF THE METEORA (9 hrs., $99): Visit the Meteora, where incredible granite rocks soaring hundreds of feet in the air served as a refuge for medieval monks. Originally, the only way to get to the site was via net baskets operated by rope pulley, but now a road leads close to the base of the site, and many steps have been cut into the stone, leading to the top. You'll visit monastic buildings that contain Byzantine artifacts, icons, and wall paintings, and enjoy sweeping views of the low plains and neighboring monasteries. Shopping time is offered in Kalambaka, and lunch at a local hotel is included.

VOLOS & MAKRINITSA VILLAGE (3½ hr., $36–$53): Visit the Volos Archaeological Museum, which houses a collection of ancient treasures. Also visit Makrinitsa village, located on the slopes of Mount Pelion. The narrow cobblestone streets are filled with small shops selling candied fruit, herbs, spices, and the like. The village square offers a stunning view of the surrounding countryside. Free time to shop is also included. In addition, some tours visit Portoria, a resort village located high above sea level, and offering stunning views of the Aegean below.

10 Best Shore Excursions in the Ports of Call: Turkey

The following Turkish ports of call are commonly visited on Greek itineraries.

ISTANBUL

HIGHLIGHTS OF ISTANBUL (7–9 hr., $79–$97): Includes the Hippodrome, once the largest chariot race grounds of the Byzantine Empire; Sultan Ahmet Mosque, also known as the Blue Mosque for its 21,000 blue Iznik tiles; the famous St. Sophia, once the largest church of the Christian world; and Topkapi Palace, the official residence of the Ottoman Sultans and home to treasures that include Spoonmaker's Diamond, one of the biggest diamonds in the world. Also visit the Grand Bazaar, with its 4,000 shops. Some tours bring you back to the ship for lunch, while others include lunch in a first-class restaurant. Shorter tours are also available that include some, but not all, of the above.

BYZANTINE UNDERGROUND CISTERN & GRAND BAZAAR (3 hrs., $22): Visit the underground cistern (also known as "The Underground Palace"), which dates from the 6th century and is supported by 336 Corinthian columns. You reach the water-filled cavern by traveling with a guide down steep steps and along a raised walkway. Also visit the Grand Bazaar and view the outside of St. Sophia.

BEYLERBEYI PALACE (2½ hrs., $34): Visit Istanbul's grandest seaside mansion, built by Sultan Abdulaziz on the Asian side of the Bosporos in 1865. The tour includes the palace's harem, men's quarters, and grand central hall.

ISTANBUL NIGHTLIFE WITH DINNER (4 hrs., $55): Enjoy traditional Turkish cuisine and belly dancing in a city nightclub.

DOLMABAHCE PALACE & CHORA MUSEUM (8 hrs., $75): Visit the 285-room 19th-century palace, the principal imperial residence of the late years of the Ottoman Empire. Drive across the Bosporos Bridge to enjoy a panoramic view of Istanbul from the Asian side. Drive past gardens, old mansions, fortresses, and fishermen's villages. Return to the European side via Faith Bridge, arriving at the suburb of Tarabya for a Turkish seafood lunch. After lunch, drive to the modern part of Istanbul and across the Golden Horn to visit the Chora Museum and a Byzantine church that dates back to the 11th century. The tour ends at the Grand Bazaar. Some lines also offer a tour of Dolmabahce Palace as a half-day excursion (4 hrs., $46).

KUSADASI

EPHESUS (3–4 hrs., $30–$46): Visit one of the best-preserved ancient cities in the world. Your guide will take you down the city's actual marble streets to the baths, theater, and incredible library building, and along the way you'll pass columns, mosaics, monuments, and ruins. The tour may include a stop at a shop for a presentation of Turkish carpets (with an emphasis on getting you to buy).

EPHESUS & THE HOUSE OF THE VIRGIN MARY (3½–4½ hrs., $47–$52): This tour combines a visit to Ephesus with the House of the Virgin Mary, a humble chapel located in the valley of Bulbuldagi. Located here is the site where the Virgin Mary is believed to have spent her last days. The site was officially sanctioned for pilgrimage in 1892.

EPHESUS, ST. JOHN'S BASILICA & THE HOUSE OF THE VIRGIN MARY (4½ hrs., $52): This tour combines the above two with a visit to St. John's Basilica, another holy pilgrimage site. It is believed to be the site where St. John wrote the fourth book of the New Testament. A church at the site, which is now in ruins, was built by Justinian over a 2nd-century tomb believed to contain St. John the Apostle. This tour may also be offered as a full-day excursion, including lunch at a local restaurant and a visit to the museum of Ephesus (6½–7½ hr., $75–$89).

THREE ANCIENT CITIES (6–7 hrs., $69–$85): This tour takes in the ruins that surround the region of Ephesus, including Priene, known for its Athena Temple bankrolled by Alexander the Great; Didyma, known for the Temple of Apollo; and Miletus, which includes a stadium built by the Greeks and expanded by the Romans to hold 15,000 spectators. A light lunch at a restaurant in Didyma is included.

EPHESUS, PRIENE & DIDYMA (7½ hrs., $75): Includes the above plus Ephesus and a buffet lunch at a five-star hotel.

4 Settling into Athens

by Sherry Marker

Athens is the city that Greeks love to hate, complaining that it's too expensive, too crowded, too polluted. Some 40% of the country lives here, making the city burst at the seams with five million inhabitants, a rumored 15,000 taxis—but try to find one that's empty—and streets so congested that you'll suspect that each of the five million Athenians has a car. The new Metro (subway) station in Syntagma Square opened in January 2000, although work on the Metro elsewhere in Athens proceeds at a snail's pace, with the tunneling further complicating traffic in much of central Athens.

Knowing this, you may be wondering if Athens, with all its fabled glories, is the place for you. Don't despair: Quite soon, you'll almost certainly develop your own love-hate relationship with Athens, snarling at the traffic and gasping in wonder at the Acropolis, fuming at the taxi driver who tries to overcharge you—and marveling at the stranger who realizes that you're lost and walks several blocks out of his way to take you where you're going.

Even though you've probably come here to see the "glory that was Greece," perhaps best symbolized by the Parthenon and the superb statues and vases in the National Archaeological Museum, allow some time to make haste slowly in Athens. Your best moments may come sitting at a small cafe, sipping a tiny cup of the sweet sludge that the Greeks call coffee, or getting hopelessly lost in the Plaka—only to find yourself in the shady courtyard of an old church, or suddenly face to face with an ancient monument you never knew existed. With only a little advance planning, you can find a good hotel here, eat well in convivial restaurants, enjoy local customs such as the refreshing afternoon siesta and the leisurely evening *volta* (promenade or stroll)—and leave Athens planning to return, as the Greeks say, *tou chronou* (next year).

And if you do get caught in an Athenian gridlock, just remember what it was like when the Parthenon was built: Teams of mules dragged carts laden with 12-ton blocks of marble from Mount Pendeli along today's Queen Sophia Avenue to the Acropolis. If an axle broke, traffic stopped for several days until the damage was repaired.

If you take a look at "Suggested Itineraries for First-Time Visitors" in the beginning of chapter 5, you'll get some good ideas on how to approach the city. As far as when to go, from March through May it's almost always pleasant and mild in Athens, although Greeks say that the March wind can have "teeth." Between June and August, the temperature usually rises steadily, making August a good month to emulate Athenian practice and try to avoid the city. If you do come here in August, you'll find that Athens, like Paris, belongs to the tourists: 56% of all Athenians take their summer holiday between the first and fifteenth of August. September is usually balmy, with occasional light rain, although it's not unknown for August heat to spill over well into September. October usually offers beautiful summer/autumn weather, with rain and some high winds likely, and it might be intermittently chilly. Most rain falls between November and February, when Athens can be colder and windier than you might expect. Average daytime temperatures range from 52°F in January to 92°F in August. Stretches when it's well over 100°F are not uncommon in summer, when anyone with health problems such as asthma should be wary of Athens's *nefos* (smog). The city can be very hot and exhausting—be sure to give yourself time off for a coffee or a cold drink in a cafe. After all, you're on vacation!

1 Orientation

ARRIVING

BY PLANE

Athens's **Hellenikon International Airport** is only 11 kilometers (7 miles) south of central Athens, but traffic to and from the airport is often so heavy that you should allow an hour for the trip. The **East (*Anatoliko*) Air Terminal** on the eastern side of the airport runways handles non-Olympic Airways flights and some charters. The **West Airport (*Dhitiko*,** usually called ***Olympiakon*)** handles all Olympic flights. A third, smaller terminal handles most charter flights.

Both the East and West terminals have free luggage trolleys, exchange and banking facilities, ATMs, post offices and telephone offices, luggage storage, cafes, taxi and bus stands, tourist information offices, and hotel-booking agencies.

In the East Terminal, the **Greek National Tourism Organization** (abbreviated **GNTO** in English-speaking countries and **EOT** in Greece) information desk, slightly to the left as you exit customs, is officially open Monday through Friday from 9am to 7pm, Saturday from 9am to 2pm (but, as with everything in Greece, the official hours do not always reflect reality). This office usually has maps of Athens and a selection of pamphlets on various regions of Greece. **Pacific Travel,** located by the EOT desk, can help you book a hotel room. There's a poorly signposted **luggage storage facility** across from the parking lot near the East Terminal entrance.

Numbers for the East Air Terminal include **Switchboard** (☎ **01/969-4111**), **Arrival/Departure Information** (☎ **01/949-4466** or 01/949-4467), and **Tourist Information** (☎ **01/969-4500** or 01/961-2722).

If you arrive at the West Air Terminal, you will see the **GNTO office** after you clear customs; beside it is the **hotel reservations** office. The **luggage storage office** is (poorly) signposted on the sidewalk outside the terminal.

Numbers for the West Air Terminal include **Switchboard** (☎ **01/926-9111** or 01/936-9111), **Arrival/Departure Information** (☎ **01/936-3363**), and **Tourist Information** (☎ **01/969-4500** or 01/961-2722).

Flight information on Olympic flights is sometimes available at ☎ **01/966-6666** or 01/926-9111; both numbers are usually busy.

Many charter flights now use the **Charter Terminal,** the former U.S. military facility, to the south of the main terminals. There sometimes is, and sometimes is not, bus service directly from this terminal to Piraeus and Athens; sometimes, buses from the East and West terminals stop here to pick up passengers. The information numbers for the Charter Terminal are ☎ **01/997-2581** and 01/997-2686.

There is no shuttle bus between any of these terminals, but they are usually linked by bus nos. 091 and 91, which run into Athens and Piraeus.

A New Airport

In June 2000, a test flight touched down at Athens's new airport, **Eleftherios Venizelos International,** at Spata, 23 kilometers (14 miles) outside Athens. The airport is scheduled to open on March 1, 2001, well in advance of the 2004 Olympics. Check with your travel agent to see whether the airport has, in fact, opened. You'll also want to find out whether the projected access road and Metro from Athens to Spata have opened. At press time, road and Metro links were not yet in place.

GETTING TO ATHENS   Since buses run on erratic schedules, the easiest way into town is to take a **taxi** from immediately outside the terminal. This is not as simple as it sounds: Greeks regard waiting in line with amusement, and getting a cab is usually a fiercely competitive sport. A cab into the center (*kentro*) of town usually costs Dr2,000 to Dr3,000 ($6 to $9), double that between midnight and 5am. Depending on traffic, the cab ride can take under 30 minutes or well over an hour—something to remember when you return to the airport. At press time (with an increase in the works), the meter starts at (Dr250/75¢), with a surcharge (Dr50/15¢) for each piece of luggage and for airport pick-up (Dr300/90¢).

If you want to take a **bus** from the airport into central Athens, be prepared for what may be a substantial wait and a slow journey. Do *not* assume that the destination indicated on the front of the bus, or on the sign at the bus stop, is the actual destination of the bus. Ask the driver where the bus is going. In theory, bus no. 019 (and, confusingly, sometimes bus no. 091) runs to Syntagma and Omonia squares before continuing to Piraeus every half hour from 7am to 10pm (Dr300/90¢), and then every hour from about 10:15pm to 6:30am (Dr600/$1.75).

GETTING BETWEEN THE AIRPORT & PIRAEUS (PIREAS)   A taxi from the airport to Piraeus should cost Dr2,000 to Dr2,500 ($6 to $7). It's important to know that island boats leave from *several different Piraeus harbors.* Most ferryboats and hydrofoils (Flying Dolphins) for Aegina leave from the **Main Harbor.** Hydrofoils for other islands leave from **Marina Zea,** a vigorous half-hour walk from the Main Harbor. All this makes Piraeus a good place to take a taxi to and from the airport. If you do not know which harbor your boat is leaving from, tell your taxi driver your final destination and he can probably find out the harbor and even the pier you are leaving from.

In theory, **bus no. 019** runs from the East to the West Terminal and then to Piraeus every hour from 5am to midnight (Dr250/85¢), and every 2 hours from midnight to 5am (Dr600/$1.75). The bus will leave you in Karaiskaki Square, several blocks from the harbor.

AIRLINE OFFICES   Most international carriers have ticket offices in or near Syntagma Square. Try to find out the location of your airline's Athens office before you leave home, as these offices can move without warning. The **Air Canada** office is at Odos Othonos 10 (☎ 01/322-3206). The **American Airlines** office is located at Odos Panepistimiou 15 (☎ 01/331-1045 or 01/331-1046). The **British Airways** office is at Odos Themistokleous 1, at Leoforos Vouliagmenis 130, Glyfada (☎ 01/890-6666). The **Delta Air Lines** office is at Odos Othonos 4 (☎ 01/331-1660-8). The **Lufthansa Airlines** office is at Leoforos Vas. Sofias 11 (☎ 01/617-5200). The **Qantas Airways** office is at Odos Nikodimou 2 (☎ 01/323-9063). The **Swissair** office is at Odos Othonos 4 (☎ 01/323-5811). The **Turkish Airlines** office is at Odos Filellinon 19 (☎ 01/324-6024). The **Virgin Atlantic Airways** office is at Odos Tzireon 8–10 (☎ 01/924-9100-05).

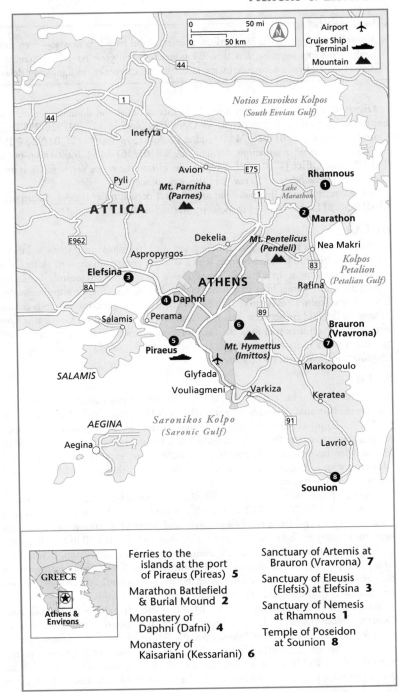

0   50 mi
0   50 km

Airport ✈
Cruise Ship Terminal
Mountain ▲

Notios Envoikos Kolpos
(South Evvian Gulf)

44

1

44

Inefyta

Avion   E75

Pyli

Mt. Parnitha
(Parnes) ▲

ATTICA

Rhamnous ❶

Lake
Marathon

1

❷ Marathon

Dekelia

Mt. Pentelicus
(Pendeli) ▲

Nea Makri

E962

Aspropyrgos

Elefsina ❸

8A

Salamis

Perama

Piraeus ❺

SALAMIS

ATHENS

Daphni ❹

Mt. Hymettus
(Imittos) ▲

❻

89

83

Rafina

Kolpos
Petalion
(Petalian Gulf)

Brauron
(Vravrona)
❼

Glyfada

Vouliagmeni   Varkiza

Markopoulo

Keratea

AEGINA

Aegina

Saronikos Kolpo
(Saronic Gulf)

91

Lavrio

Sounion ❽

GREECE

⭐

Athens &
Environs

Ferries to the
islands at the port
of Piraeus (Pireas) **5**

Marathon Battlefield
& Burial Mound **2**

Monastery of
Daphni (Dafni) **4**

Monastery of
Kaisariani (Kessariani) **6**

Sanctuary of Artemis at
Brauron (Vravrona) **7**

Sanctuary of Eleusis
(Elefsis) at Elefsina **3**

Sanctuary of Nemesis
at Rhamnous **1**

Temple of Poseidon
at Sounion **8**

A word about making air connections after an island trip: It is unwise—even fool-hardy—to allow anything less than 24 hours between your return to Piraeus by island boat and your departure by air, as rough seas can make for significant delays.

Olympic, the national carrier, offers both international and domestic service and has offices just off Syntagma Square at Odos Filellinon 15 (☎ **01/926-7555**), at Odos Othonos 6 (☎ **01/926-7444**), and at Leoforos Syngrou 96 (☎ **01/926-7251** to 7254). The main reservations numbers are ☎ **01/961-6161** and 01/966-6666. The **Olympic Office** (☎ **01/926-7445**) in the Hilton, Leoforos Vas. Sofias 6, is usually less crowded and easier to use than the main offices.

For information on Olympic flight arrivals and departures at the Athens airports, try **01/936-9111;** for all other carriers, try **01/969-4111.**

BY CAR

If you arrive by car **from Corinth** (to the southwest), the signs into Athens will direct you fairly clearly into Omonia Square, which you will enter from the west along Odos Ayiou Konstandinou. In Omonia, signs *should* direct you on towards Syntagma Square and other points in central Athens (signs in Omonia disappear mysteriously). If you arrive **from Thessaloniki** (to the north), the signs pointing you into central Athens are few and far between. It is not a good idea to attempt this for the first time after dark, as you may well miss the turn for Omonia Square. If this happens, your best bet is to try to spot the Acropolis and head toward it until you pick up signs for Omonia Square or Syntagma Square.

BY BUS

Before you start out on any bus trip, check with the **Tourist Police** (☎ **01/171**) or the **Greek National Tourism Organization (EOT)** office (☎ **01/331-9437** or 01/331-0561) for current schedules and fares. As the new Metro continues to open stations, bus routes and fares will change. It's best to double-check all routes and to be prepared for fare increases. If possible, get someone to write down the name and address of your bus station in Greek; this will be a great help to you when you take a taxi or bus to the station.

There are two principal stations for **KTEL,** the national bus company. **Terminal A,** Odos Kifissou 100 (☎ **01/512-9233**), off the road out of Athens toward Corinth, handles buses **to and from the Peloponnese and parts of Northern Greece.** A taxi here from Syntagma Square should cost Dr1,000 to Dr1,500 ($2.90 to $4.30); if traffic is light, the journey is less than 20 minutes, but it can take an hour. If you don't have much to carry, take public bus no. 51 to the terminal (Dr100/30¢). It leaves from the corner of Odos Zinonos and Odos Menandrou, several blocks off Omonia Square; you can catch the same bus at the terminal for the trip into town.

Terminal B, Odos Liossion 260 (☎ **01/831-7096**), handles buses **to and from Central Greece** (including Delphi, Thebes, Evvia, and Meteora) and some destinations **to the north and east of Athens.** Bus no. 24, which stops at Leoforos Amalias in front of the entrance to the National Garden (a block south of Syntagma Square), will take you to and from the terminal for Dr100 (30¢). If you take this bus, tell the driver you want to get off at the bus terminal and then head right onto Odos Yousiou to reach the terminal.

The **Mavromateon terminal** at Patission and Alexandras, a few hundred meters north of the Archaeological Museum, handles buses for most **destinations in Attica.**

BY TRAIN

Trains **from the south and west,** including Eurail connections via Patras, arrive at the **Peloponnese Station** (Stathmos Peloponnisou; ☎ **01/513-1601**), about a mile northwest of Omonia Square. Trains **from the north** arrive at **Larissa Station** (Stathmos Larissis; ☎ **01/529-8837**), just across the tracks from the Peloponnese Station. The Larissa Station has both an exchange office, usually open daily from 8am to 9:15pm, and luggage storage, usually open from 6:30am to 9pm.

To get to the train stations, a taxi from the center of town should cost no more than Dr1,000 ($2.90). Trolley 1 runs from Larissa Station to Omonia, Syntagma, and Koukaki for Dr100 (30¢). The most central place from which to catch it is the stop in front of the Parliament Building in Syntagma Square.

You can purchase train tickets just before your journey at the station (running the risk that all seats may be sold); at the Omonia Square ticket office, Odos Karolou 1 (☎ **01/524-0647**); at Odos Filellinon 17, off Syntagma Square (☎ **01/323-6747**); or at most travel agents. Information (in theory in English) on timetables is available by dialing ☎ **145** or 147.

BY BOAT

Piraeus, the main harbor of Athens's main seaport, 11 kilometers (7 miles) southwest of central Athens, is a 15-minute **Metro** (subway) ride from Monastiraki and Omonia squares. The subway runs from about 5am to midnight and costs Dr250 (75¢). The far-slower bus no. 040 runs from Piraeus to central Athens (with a stop at Odos Filellinon, off Syntagma Square) every 15 minutes between 5am and 1am and hourly from 1am to 5am for Dr200 (60¢).

You may prefer to take a **taxi** to avoid what can be a long hike from your boat to the bus stop or subway terminal. Be prepared for some serious bargaining. The normal fare on the meter from Piraeus to Syntagma should be about Dr1,800 to Dr2,000 ($5.15 to $6), but many drivers simply offer a flat fare, which can easily be as much as Dr5,000 ($14). Pay it if you're desperate, or walk to a nearby street, hail another taxi, and insist that the meter be turned on.

If you arrive at Piraeus by hydrofoil (Flying Dolphin), you'll probably arrive at the **Zea Marina** harbor, about a dozen blocks south across the peninsula from the main harbor. Even our Greek friends admit that getting a taxi from Zea Marina into Athens can involve a wait of an hour or more—and that drivers usually drive a hard (and exorbitant) bargain. To avoid both the wait and big fare, you can walk up the hill from the hydrofoil station and catch bus no. 905 for Dr100 (30¢), which connects Zea to the Piraeus subway station, where you can complete your journey into Athens. You must buy a ticket at the small stand near the bus stop or at a newsstand before boarding the bus. *Warning:* If you arrive late at night, you may not be able to do this, as both the newsstand and the ticket stand may be closed.

If you've landed at the port of **Rafina** (about an hour's bus ride east of Athens), you'll see a bus stop up the hill from the ferryboat pier. Inquire about the bus to Athens; it runs often and will return you within the hour to the **Areos Park Terminal,** Odos Mavromateon 29, near the junction of Leoforos Alexandras and Odos Patission (about 25 minutes by trolley from Syntagma Square or 1 block from the Victoria Square Metro stop). From the terminal, there are buses to Rafina every half hour.

In August 2000, the Greek government announced plans to expand the port of **Lavrion,** 52 kilometers (32 miles) southeast of Athens, by summer 2001. The hope is that this will take pressure off the very crowded ports of Piraeus and Rafina. You may want to check with the GNTO to see if Lavrion is operational when you visit Greece.

VISITOR INFORMATION

The **Greek National Tourism Organization** (EOT, also known as the Hellenic Tourism Organization), with no clearly visible sign or street number, is located behind the street-level plate-glass windows at Odos Amerikis 2 (☎ **01/331-0437** or 01/331-0561), 2 blocks west of Syntagma between Odos Stadiou and Odos Venizeliou. It's open Monday through Friday from 9am to 7pm and Saturday from 9:30am to 2pm. The GNTO Web site is **www.gnto.gr**; **www.greece.gr** is another government-sponsored site.

Information about Athens, free city maps, transportation schedules, hotel lists, and other booklets on many regions of Greece are available in Greek, English, French, and German—although whenever we stop by, many publications we ask for are described as "all gone"—even when we can see them on display just out of reach. The staff members often appear bored with their jobs and irritated by any questions; be persistent.

Information on Greece is also available on the Internet; see chapter 2 for details.

Available 24 hours a day, the **Tourist Police** (☎ **01/171**) speak English, as well as other languages, and will help with problems or emergencies.

CITY LAYOUT

As you begin to explore Athens, you may find it helpful to look up to the **Acropolis,** west of Syntagma Square, and **Mount Likavitos** (Lycabettus), to the northeast. You can see both Acropolis and Likavitos, whose marble lower slopes give way to pine trees and a summit crowned with a small white church, from most parts of the city.

Think of central Athens as an almost perfect equilateral triangle, with its points at **Syntagma (Constitution) Square, Omonia (Harmony) Square,** and **Monastiraki (Little Monastery) Square,** near the **Acropolis.** With luck, by the time you arrive in Athens, the construction cranes towering over Monastiraki and Omonia, like those in Syntagma, will be gone, and more of the new Athens Metro (subway) will be open. In government jargon, the area bounded by Syntagma, Omonia, and Monastiraki squares is defined as the commercial center, from which cars are banned (in theory, if not in practice) except for several cross streets. Most Greeks think of **Omonia Square**— Athens's commercial hub—as the city center, but most visitors take their bearings from **Syntagma Square**, site of the House of Parliament. The two squares are connected by the parallel **Odos Stadiou** and **Odos Panepistimiou.** (Panepistimiou is also known as Eleftheriou Venizelou.) Flanking the Parliament Building is Athens's largest park, the **National Garden.** West of Syntagma Square, **Odos Ermou** and **Odos Mitropoleos** lead slightly downhill to **Monastiraki Square,** home of the city's famous flea market. From Monastiraki Square, **Odos Athinas** leads north back to Omonia past the modern Central Market. The old warehouse district of **Psirri**—now the home of many chic galleries, cafes, and restaurants—is between Odos Athinas and Odos Ermou.

If you stand in Monastiraki Square and look south, you'll see the Acropolis. At its foot are the **Ancient Agora** (Market) and the **Plaka,** Athens's oldest neighborhood, many of whose street names honor Greek heroes from either classical antiquity or the Greek War of Independence. The twisting labyrinth of streets in the Plaka can challenge even the best navigators. Don't panic: The Plaka is small enough that you can't go far astray, and its side streets with small houses and neighborhood churches are so charming that you won't mind being lost. The excellent *Historical Map of Athens,* produced by the Greek Archaeological Service, may help; it costs about Dr1200 ($3.45) and is sold at many bookstores, museums, ancient sites, and newspaper kiosks. Many Athenians speak some English, and almost all are helpful to direction-seeking strangers.

FINDING AN ADDRESS   If possible, have the address you want to find written out in Greek so that you can show it to your taxi driver or ask for help from pedestrians. Most street signs are given both in Greek and a transliteration, which is a great help. Most taxi drivers carry a good Athens street guide in their glove compartment, and can usually find any destination, although a certain number of Athenian cabbies are newcomers to the capital, and may have trouble with out-of-the-way addresses.

STREET MAPS   As already mentioned, you can get a free map of central Athens from the **Greek National Tourism Office** at Odos Amerikis 2, off Syntagma Square. With its small print and poor-quality paper, this is not a great map, and you may prefer to stop at a newspaper kiosk or bookstore to pick up a copy of the *Historical Map of Athens* or another congenial city map (see "Books" under "Shopping A to Z," in chapter 5).

Neighborhoods in Brief

It's not easy to see that this sprawling city is divided into distinct districts and neighborhoods, each with its own character and associations, each with its favorite cafe and bakery. If you have the time to explore Athens, here are some of the neighborhoods that await you. Unless you have a specific goal and limited time, why not just stroll, get lost—and be pleasantly surprised when you discover that you're on a street where almost all the shops sell only icons or sugared almonds (an essential gift for guests at weddings and baptisms), or find a little park where you can sit on a bench and study your map.

CENTRAL ATHENS

THE COMMERCIAL CENTER   The commercial center (a name no one uses and that appears on no map) lies between **Omonia, Syntagma,** and **Monastiraki** squares, and includes the **Plaka** and **Psirri** districts. In theory, vehicles are mostly forbidden here; in practice, they're endemic. Nonetheless, certain streets are pedestrian, which makes parts of the area quite pleasant. Keep in mind that many motorists and virtually all motorcycle riders assume that pedestrian-only regulations do not apply to them.

   Omonia Square is the heart of the working city of Athens, a tumultuous square around a circular fountain that's currently but a memory, thanks to the ongoing subway construction. You'll probably pass through Omonia when you walk to the National Archaeological Museum or head out of Athens by car or bus. Take a look at the increasingly decrepit 19th-century building façades around Omonia. Once, many housed some of Athens nicest hotels, now abandoned or desultory at best. One thing that hasn't changed much: **Odos Athinas,** between Omonia and Monastiraki squares. This is where you'll find Athens's **Central Market,** where you can browse the fish and meat halls, buy vegetables and fruits from all over Greece, sample cheeses from distant islands—or buy a pair of shoes or sunglasses from a street vendor. By day, this is the best street in town to get a sense of Athens's nonstop bustle. By night, most of the Omonia area has something of the tacky ambiance of New York's Times Square in the mid-1980s, and is one of Athens's few high-crime areas, with a vigorous and often violent drug trade. Omonia attracts a good number of wanderers, including refugees from Albania and Eastern Europe, who will try to sell you pirated CDs, leather jackets, and, sometimes, themselves.

   Syntagma (Constitution) Square is, for most visitors, the heart of Athens. This is where you'll find the major banks, travel agencies, American Express and Thomas

Athens at a Glance

American Express
    Office **2**
EOT (Greek National
    Tourism Organization) **1**
Olympic Airways office **3**

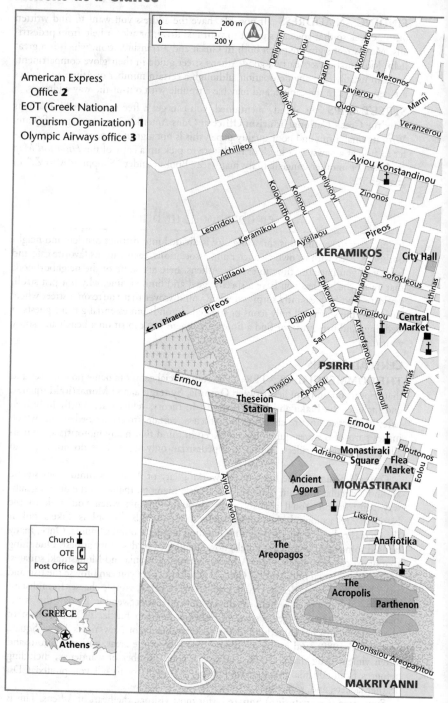

Church ✝
OTE 🄲
Post Office ✉

GREECE

Athens

0   200 m
0   200 y

Deliyanni
Chiou
Psaron
Akominatou
Mezonos
Favierou
Ougo
Marni
Veranzerou
Deliyoryi
Achilleos
Ayiou Konstandinou
Zinonos
Kolokynthous
Kolonou
Deliyoryi
Leonidou
Keramikou
Ayisilaou
Pireos
KERAMIKOS
City Hall
Ayisilaou
Sofokleous
Menandrou
Athinas
Epikourou
To Piraeus
Pireos
Dipilou
Evripidou
Central
Market
Sari
Aristofanous
Athinas
Ermou
PSIRRI
Miaouli
Thissiou
Apostoli
Ermou
Theseion
Station
Monastiraki
Ploutonos
Adrianou
Square
Flea
Market
Eolou
Ayiou Pavlou
Ancient
Agora
MONASTIRAKI
Lissiou
Anafiotika
The
Areopagos
The
Acropolis
Parthenon
Dionissiou Areopayitou
MAKRIYANNI

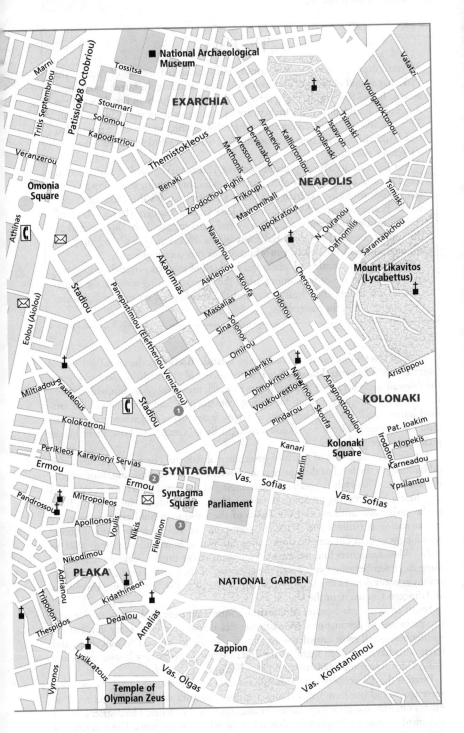

Marni
Tritis Septembriou
Patission (28 Octobriou)
Tossitsa
Stournari
Solomou
Kapodistriou
Veranzerou

■ National Archaeological
Museum

EXARCHIA

Themistokleous
Benaki
Zoodochou Pighis
Methonis
Aressou
Dervenakou
Arachevis
Kallidromiou
Trikoupi
Mavromihali
Ippokratous
Smolenski
Issavron
Tsimiski
Voulgaroktonou
Vatatzi

NEAPOLIS

N. Ouranou
Dafnomilis
Sarantapichou
Tsimiski

Omonia
Square

Athinas

Stadiou
Eolou (Aiolou)

Akadimias
Panepistimiou (Eleftheriou Venizelou)

Navarinou
Asklepiou
Massalias
Sina
Skoufa
Solonos
Omirou
Amerikis
Didotou
Chersonos

Mount Likavitos
(Lycabettus)

Aristippou

Miltiadou
Praxitelous
Kolokotroni
Stadiou

Dimokritou
Voukourestiou
Pindarou
Navarinou
Skoufa
Anagnostopoulou

KOLONAKI

Pat. Ioakim
Alopekis
Irodotou
Karneadou

Perikleos Karayioryi Servias
Ermou
Ermou

SYNTAGMA

Kanari
Merlin
Kolonaki
Square

Vas. Sofias
Vas. Sofias

Ypsilantou

Pandrossou
Mitropoleos
Apollonos
Voulis
Nikis
Filellinon
Nikodimou

Syntagma
Square
Parliament

PLAKA

Adrianou
Tripodon
Thespidos
Kidathineon
Dedalou
Amalias
Lysikratous
Vyronos

NATIONAL GARDEN

Zappion

Vas. Olgas
Vas. Konstandinou

Temple of
Olympian Zeus

The Plaka

As you'd expect from the oldest continuously inhabited section of Athens, the Plaka has a good number of archaeological sites, including the Greek and Roman agoras. It also has the charming district of Anafiotika, high on the slopes of the Acropolis, founded in the 19th century by emigrants from the island of Anafi. This is still a villagelike community where, on twisting streets like Epimenidou and Epikharmou, you could almost think you'd been whisked out of Athens to a Cycladic island.

But let's face it: This is probably not the Plaka you've heard of and come to see. That Plaka is the Plaka of restaurants, cafes, nightclubs, and nonstop souvenir shops on Odos Hadrian and Odos Kidathineon. It's the Plaka that's not unlike Boston's Quincy Market, or London's Covent Garden Market—both of which, until quite recently, actually were real markets. Similarly, shops aimed at the tourist market have displaced most of the Plaka's neighborhood shops—although, if you look closely, you'll find one or two corner groceries.

If you find the hustle and bustle and hard sell of the Plaka overwhelming, try to come back in the early morning, when the streets are being washed, the caged canaries are trilling their hearts out, and the shopkeepers have a smile, rather than a sales pitch, for passersby.

Cook, and several fine hotels, including the **Grande Bretagne,** the grand old lady of Greek hotels. The **central post office** is at the corner of Odos Mitropoleos. For years, the sidewalk cafes here were popular places to watch the world go by, but with the center of Syntagma Square torn up for subway construction, and a proliferation of fast-food joints, you'll probably not want to linger. Syntagma is also where many young (and not so young) Greek men, known colloquially as "spearmen," hone their skills at picking up foreign women.

Syntagma is the home of much of governmental Athens: The handsome neoclassical building at the head of the square is the **Greek Parliament building,** formerly the Royal Palace. That's where you'll see the changing of the guard several times a day and may hear a band playing on Sundays around 11am. The soldiers who march in front of the parliament building and the **Tomb of the Unknown Soldier** often wear the *evzone* uniforms (frilly white skirts and pom-pommed red shoes) of their ancestors who fought to gain Greece's freedom during the War of Independence (from 1821 to 1828). Most foreigners find the evzones' uniforms rather droll; Greeks do not, something to remember when you watch the changing of the guard. Laughing at this ceremony is equivalent to snickering when taps is played at the Tomb of the Unknowns at Arlington Cemetery in the United States.

South of Syntagma Square, **Monastiraki Square** and the **Plaka** area are Athens's two main tourist destinations. Monastiraki's flea markets are open every day, but are usually best—and most crowded—on Sundays. In the Plaka, wall-to-wall shops and restaurants have displaced many of the area's elegant 19th-century homes, especially along Odos Adrianou (Hadrian) and Odos Filellinon.

Psirri is the district between Odos Athinas and Odos Ermou which until only a few years ago would not have merited any mention. Now, it's where you'll find some of Athens's newest and most popular restaurants, cafes, and galleries. The district is being reclaimed by young entrepreneurs drawn here by relatively low rents. The area can still be rather deserted at night, but is usually perfectly safe—although walking alone at late hours is not a great idea, as Odos Athinas has a vigorous drug and prostitution trade. Near Psirri, two more districts are being revitalized: **Gazi,** formerly known only for its once noxious gasworks, but now the home of the Athens Municipal Technopolis Center gallery; and **Rouf,** site of the fruit and vegetable market.

KOLONAKI This is the posh area in town, on the slopes of **Mount Likavitos** (Lycabettus), a few blocks northwest of Syntagma Square, spreading out around a central square. The **square** is officially named Plateia Filikis Eterias (Square of the Friendly Society), but is usually called Kolonaki, after the fragmentary marble column in the square.

Although many Athenians have fled the city's smog and congestion for northern suburbs, Kolonaki remains one of *the* places to live—or at least see and be seen—in Athens. If you're here on a Friday, try to take in the **street market** snaking along Odos Xenokratous. You may be surprised at how many Asian women you see shopping here: Most of these young women, usually from the Philippines, work as maids and nannies in the homes of the Kolonaki elite.

If you're in Kolonaki on a Saturday, you can't miss seeing the beautiful people and the wannabes promenading up and down the streets, thronging in front of favorite boutiques to ogle the latest fashions before collapsing into street cafes to revive their spirits with cool drinks. There are more shoe stores per inch in Kolonaki than almost anywhere else in Greece, a nation that takes its footwear very seriously.

If you tire of window-shopping, you may want to take the funicular railway up Mount Likavitos to enjoy the panoramic view (smog permitting) of the entire metropolitan area and the sea and mountains beyond. If you walk down, you'll end up passing through some of central Athens's nicest and greenest streets, that wind around Likavitos's lower slopes.

THE UNIVERSITY AREA Kolonaki gradually merges to the northwest with the university area, spread loosely between the 19th-century university buildings on Panepistimiou and the Polytechnic some 10 blocks to the northwest. Lots of publishers have their offices in this area, and bibliophiles may enjoy the window displays of everything from children's books on Hercules to mathematical texts. A few blocks from the Polytechnic, **Exarchia Square,** with its many sandwich shops, cafes, and bars, is usually full of students. When there are demonstrations at any of Athens's institutions of higher learning, Exarchia Square is often where speeches are made.

KOUKAKI & MAKRIYANNI **Koukaki,** once the working-class counterpart to Kolonaki, has been increasingly gentrified. The district lies at the base of **Filopappos Hill** (Lofos Filopappou), also known as the Hill of the Muses (Lofos Mousseon). There are a number of pleasant paths leading from streets at the base of Filopappos up through its pine-clad slopes, some ending at the Dora Stratou Theater or the Observatory. The main road through Koukaki is Veïkou, along which buses and trolleys run, and where there are some unpretentious cafes and restaurants as well as reasonably priced hotels. This is a nice area to stay in if you want to be out of tourist Athens, enjoy shopping in neighborhood groceries and shops—and don't mind the walk back into tourist Athens.

Makriyanni, the neighborhood just north of Koukaki, at the southern base of the Acropolis, is more upscale, probably because it's that little bit closer to the city center. There are some quite luxurious hotels here, as well as some middle-of-the-road places and several good restaurants, including the popular **Socrates's Prison.** This is a good area to stay in if you want to be almost as centrally located as you would be in the Plaka or Syntagma, but a bit out of the tourist maelstrom.

Plaka Tram Rides

In spring 1998, a tram service leaving from and returning to Palia Agora Square in the Plaka was initiated. The tram does a loop through the Plaka, out onto Odos Dionissiou Areopayitou, past the Acropolis, and back into the Plaka. The ride lasts 30 to 40 minutes, costs Dr1,000 ($2.90), and is offered from 10am to 10pm in summer and sometimes on weekends the rest of the year.

Something to keep in mind if you're thinking of staying in Koukaki or Makriyanni: The pedestrianization of Odos Dionissiou Areopayitou has brought an unwelcome incursion of traffic into both areas.

PANGRATI & METS   Surrounding the reconstructed Athens Stadium known to the Greeks as **Kallimarmaro** (Beautiful Marble), **Pangrati** is popular with those who can't afford Kolonaki, and seems to have a high percentage of foreigners, including academics attached to various schools of archaeology in Athens. If you enjoy baroque funerary monuments, don't miss the sprawling **First Cemetery,** where luminaries such as the late Prime Minister Andreas Papandreou are buried. If you prefer your green spaces without tombs, explore Pangrati's lovely green **park,** almost a miniforest in the heart of Athens. There are lots of neighborhood restaurants and tavernas scattered in Pangrati, so you won't go hungry here.

Mets is southeast of Pangrati, on the other side of the Stadium, between the temple of Zeus and the First Cemetery. There are still some elegant private homes here, although most of Mets has Athens's typical low, concrete apartment buildings. Mets takes its name from a popular 19th-century cafe, the Metz, that once flourished here. Appropriately, the district still has some elegant bars and good restaurants—including the longtime favorite Manesis and the newcomer Bajazzo, the first Greek restaurant to be awarded a Michelin star.

THE EMBASSY DISTRICT   Leoforos Vas. Sofias (Queen Sophia Boulevard) runs from Syntagma Square toward Athens's fashionable northeastern suburb of Kifissia. If you walk along Vas. Sofias and explore the side streets that run uphill from it into Kolonaki, you'll notice the national flags of many countries on elegant office buildings and town houses. This is the Embassy District, which stretches as far as the Hilton, where many embassy workers head for a snack at the Byzantine Cafe.

THE NORTHEAST SUBURBS

Athens is growing every-which-way, but much of its expansion is to the northeast, in the valley between the mountains of Penteli to the east and Parnitha to the west. Two major roads—the **National Road** to the west and **Leoforos Kifissias** to the east—run north from Athens through wall-to-wall bedroom suburbs before reaching Kifissia, some 12 kilometers (8 miles) from the center of Athens.

Cooler than Athens, thanks to its elevation, **Kifissia** was fashionable enough for the Royal Family to have a villa here. Until recently, many wealthy Athenian mothers and children decamped to the elegant hotels in Kifissia for the summer, leaving the men behind to work (and, some said, play) in Athens. Now, Kifissia has a distinctly suburban feel, with large supermarkets and incipient malls, although its spreading plane trees still give many streets a rural feel. There are some good restaurants, but there's no reason to trek out here until you've spent a lot of time in central Athens.

PIRAEUS (PIREAS)

The main port of Athens, Piraeus is a city very much in its own right—although even locals have trouble telling precisely where Athens ends and Piraeus begins. Piraeus prides itself on being rough and tough—a stronghold of communism, the home of *rembetika* (street-slang songs of political protest), and the workplace of a profusion of prostitutes. Probably none of this will be particularly obvious when you come here to catch a boat to the islands from the **Main Harbor,** or Megas Limani (Great Harbor), or **Zea Marina,** also called Pasalimani. (For ferry information, see "Getting Around," below.) What will be obvious if you go to any of the many fish tavernas in the little harbor of **Mikrolimani** (Little Harbor), which is also still called by its former name of Turkolimani (Turkish Harbor), is the prices, which range from exorbitant to extortionate.

THE SOUTHERN SUBURBS

Heading southeast out of Athens along the coast are a string of once-pleasant suburbs, now virtually entirely absorbed by Athens. This used to be a good place for a swim, but now there are frequent pollution alerts for these, and virtually no other, beaches in Greece.

Paleo Faliro, a once-lovely coastal suburb, has become almost a city by the sea, full of apartment buildings in the occasionally deafening flight path to the airport. South of the large yacht harbor of Kalamaki along Leoforos Poseidonos, the coast road, there's a big, busy public beach at **Ayios Kosmas.** Farther south, **Glyfada,** Attica's largest resort, with a yacht harbor, has lots of restaurants, bars, discos, food and clothing stores—and an almost always crowded, but decent, public beach.

Voula, farther southeast, has another public beach. The major resort area of **Vouliagmeni,** 23 kilometers (14 miles) south of Athens, has two good public beaches and several hotels, notably the luxury Astir Palace.

2 Getting Around

BY PUBLIC TRANSPORTATION
BY METRO

The new Metro (subway), designed to allow travel in much of central Athens and beyond, is still under construction, although the central Syntagma Station opened in January 2000. Check there, or at the GNTO, to see what stations have opened by the time of your visit. To travel on the Metro, buy your ticket at the station, validate it in the machines as you enter, and hang on to your ticket until you get off. The fare at press time for tickets on the new Metro line was Dr250 (75¢); tickets on the old Metro cost Dr200 (60¢). Even if you do not use the Metro to get around Athens, you may take it from Omonia or Monastiraki to Piraeus to catch a boat to the islands. (Don't miss the spectacular view of the Acropolis as the subway comes above ground by the Agora). If you're not carrying much luggage, the harbor in Piraeus is a 5-minute walk (head left) from the station.

BY BUS & TROLLEY BUS

The public transportation system is cheap—and, if you use it, you may think deservedly so. Although you can get almost everywhere you want to in central Athens and the suburbs by bus or trolley, you would need more time than you will probably have to figure out which bus to take. This is especially so at present, when many bus

Athens's New Metro Finally Gets Moving

In January 2000, the long-awaited new branch of the Athens Metro opened after 8 years of construction and the expenditure of at least 700 billion drachmas. The new Metro, which adds 13 stations, is an extension of the existing 130-year-old Athens subway, which already carried 350,000 passengers a day. Try to pick up a map at the new hub at Syntagma Square.

At present, the Metro usually runs at least every 10 minutes from 5am to midnight from the Defense Ministry (known as the Pentagon) to Sepolia (individual tickets cost Dr250/75¢; from mid-July to early September, when Athenians leave town, service may stop at 10pm). Press releases trumpeted that pollution was cut by 70 metric tons on the first day that the new Metro ran, when 100,000 fewer vehicles entered central Athens. As this reduction in atmospheric pollution continues day by day, Athens's infamous *nefos* (smog) should diminish considerably. In addition, city buses now have a fighting chance of running on schedule, with fewer cars clogging the roads. (Keep in mind that the new Metro and on-going Metro construction leave many bus routes in a state of flux).

Plans call for the entire 21-station Metro system, carrying 450,000 additional passengers a day, to be up and running by 2002—certainly by 2004 when the Olympics are held in and around Athens. Now, if only someone could figure out how to build adequate parking lots near the new Metro stops so that commuters wouldn't leave their cars on every available inch of sidewalk!

routes are changing as new Metro stations open. Even if you know which bus to take, you will usually have to wait a long time until the bus appears—usually stuffed with passengers. The bus service does have an information number (☎ **01/185**), but it's usually busy.

If you find none of this daunting, tickets cost Dr150 (45¢) each and can be bought from the kiosks (*periptera*) scattered throughout the city. The tickets are sold individually and in packets of 10; there is also a monthly bus pass for Dr12,000 ($34). Tickets are good for a ride anywhere on the system. Be certain to validate yours when you get on, and keep it until you get off. Occasionally, inspectors board the bus and check to see that everybody has paid the fare.

If you're heading out of town and take a blue A-line bus for transferring to another blue A-line bus, your ticket will still be valid on the transfer bus. In central Athens, the minibuses numbered 60 and 150 serve the commercial area free of charge.

Buses heading out to farther points of Attica leave from **Odos Mavromateon** on the western edge of the Pedion tou Areos park at the western end of Leoforos Alexandras.

BY TAXI

It's rumored that there are more than 15,000 taxis in Athens, but finding one empty is almost never easy. Especially if you have travel connections to make, it's a good idea to reserve a radio taxi (see below). Fortunately, taxis are inexpensive in Athens, and most drivers are honest men trying to wrest a living by maneuvering through the city's endemic gridlock. However, some drivers, notably those working Piraeus, the airports, and popular tourist destinations, can't resist trying to overcharge obvious foreigners. When you get into a taxi, check to see that the meter is turned on and set on "1" rather than "2"; the meter should be set on "2" (double fare) only between midnight and 5am, or if you take a taxi outside the city limits (if you plan to do this, try to negotiate a flat rate in advance). Unless your cab is caught in very heavy traffic, a trip to the center of town from the airport between 5am and midnight should not cost more than Dr3,000 ($9). Don't be surprised if your driver picks up other passengers en route; the driver will work out everyone's fair share of the fare.

Keep in mind that your driver may have difficulty understanding your pronunciation of your destination: If you are taking a taxi from your hotel, a staff member can assist you by telling the driver your destination or writing down the address for you to show to the driver. If you carry a business card from your hotel with you, you can show it to the taxi driver for your return.

If you suspect that you have been overcharged, before you pay the fare, ask for help at your hotel or other destination.

At press time, the minimum fare is Dr200 (65¢), and the "1" meter rate is Dr62 (20¢) per kilometer, with a surcharge of Dr150 (45¢) for service from a port or rail or bus station, Dr300 (90¢) for service from the airport, and a luggage fee of Dr50 (15¢) for every bag over 10 kilograms (22 pounds). These prices will almost certainly be higher by the time you visit Greece, as increases were scheduled to go into effect at press time.

There are about 15 **radio taxi** companies in Athens; as their phone numbers often change, it's worth checking the daily listing in "Your Guide" in the *Athens News*. Some established companies include **Athina** (☎ 01/921-7942), **Express** (☎ 01/993-4812), **Parthenon** (☎ 01/581-4711), and **Piraeus** (☎ 01/418-2333-5). If you're trying to make travel connections or traveling during rush hour, a radio taxi is well worth the Dr300 (90¢) surcharge. Your hotel can make the call for you and make sure that the driver knows where you want to go. Most restaurants will call a taxi for you without charge.

The GNTO's pamphlet *Helpful Hints for Taxi Users* has information on taxi fares as well as a complaint form, which you can send to the **Ministry of Transport and Communication,** Xenophondos 13, 10191 Athens. Replies to complaints should be forwarded to the *Guinness Book of Records.* See also the "Taxi Tips" feature in chapter 2 of this book.

BY CAR

In Athens, a car is more trouble than convenience. The traffic is heavy and finding a parking place is so difficult that once, in desperation, we drove to the airport, left the car in the long-term parking lot there, and took a cab back into town.

If you want to drive outside Athens, there are plenty of rental agencies south of Syntagma Square. Some of the better agencies include: **Athens Cars,** Odos Filellinon 10 (☎ 01/323-3783 or 01/324-8870); **Autorental,** Leoforos Syngrou 11 (☎ 01/923-2514); **Avis,** Leoforos Amalias 46–48 (☎ 01/322-4951 to 4957); **Budget Rent a Car,** Leoforos Syngrou 8 (☎ 01/921-4771 to 4773); **Eurodollar Rent a Car,** Leoforos Syngrou 29 (☎ 01/922-9672 or 01/923-0548); **Hellascars,** Leoforos Syngrou 148 (☎ 01/923-5353 to 5359); **Hertz,** Leoforos Syngrou 12 (☎ 01/922-0102 to 0104) and Leoforos Vas. Sofias 71 (☎ 01/724-7071 or 01/722-7391); **Interrent-Europcar/Batek SA,** Leoforos Syngrou 4 (☎ 01/921-5789 or 01/921-5789); and **Thrifty Hellas Rent a Car,** Leoforos Syngrou 24 (☎ 01/922-1211 to 1213). Prices for rentals range from about Dr15,000 to Dr30,000 ($43 to $86) per day. *Warning:* Be sure to take full insurance and ask if the price you are quoted includes everything— taxes, drop-off fee, gasoline charges, etc.

ON FOOT

Since most of what you want to see and do in Athens is in the city center, it's easy to do most of your sightseeing on foot. Fortunately, Athens has created pedestrian zones in sections of the **Commercial Triangle** (the area bounded by Omonia, Syntagma, and Monastiraki squares), the **Plaka,** and **Kolonaki,** making strolling, window-shopping, and sightseeing infinitely more pleasant. In January 2000, Odos Dionissiou Areopay-itou, at the southern foot of the Acropolis, was also pedestrianized. Still, don't relax completely even on pedestrian streets: Athens's multitude of kamikaze motorcyclists seldom respects the rules, and you should remember that a red traffic light or stop sign is no guarantee that cars will stop for pedestrians.

Wheelchair users will find Athens a major challenge, although curbs on some streets are being redesigned. The government announced plans in 1998 to make the Acrop-olis more easily accessible for those in wheelchairs.

Fast Facts: Athens

American Express   The office at Odos Ermou 2, near the southwest corner of Syntagma Square (☎ **01/324-4975**), is open Monday through Friday from 8:30am to 4pm and Saturday from 8:30am to 1:30pm; it often closes earlier in winter. For lost or stolen credit cards and checks, you can call collect during off-hours to the American Express office in London (☎ **0044/273/675-975**).

ATMs   Automatic teller machines are increasingly common at banks through-out Athens, and the **National Bank of Greece** operates a 24-hour ATM in Syn-tagma Square.

Banks   Banks are generally open Monday through Thursday from 8am to 2pm and Friday from 8am to 1:30pm. In summer, the **National Bank of Greece,** in Syntagma Square (☎ **01/334-0015**) usually has an exchange office open Mon-day through Thursday from 3:30 to 6:30pm, Friday from 3 to 6:30pm, Saturday from 9am to 3pm, and Sunday from 9am to 1pm. Other centrally located banks include **Citibank,** in Syntagma Square (☎ **01/322-7471**); **Bank of America,** Odos Panepistimiou 39 (☎ **01/324-4975**); and **Barclays Bank,** Voukourestiou 15 (☎ **01/364-4311**). All banks are closed on the long list of Greek holidays (See "When to Go," in chapter 2). Most banks exchange currency at the rate set daily by the government. This rate is usually more favorable than that offered at unofficial exchange bureaus. Still, it's worth doing a little comparison shopping. Some hotels offer better-than-official rates, usually only for cash, as do some stores, usually only when you are making an expensive purchase.

Business Hours   Even Greeks get confused by their complicated and change-able business hours. In winter, Athens's shops are generally open Monday and Wednesday from 9am to 5pm; Tuesday, Thursday, and Friday from 10am to 7pm; and Saturday from 8:30am to 3:30pm. In summer, shops are generally

A Warning About ATMs

It is *not* a good idea to rely on using ATMs exclusively in Athens, since the machines here are often out of service when you need them most: on holidays or during bank strikes.

If your PIN number includes letters, be sure that you know their numerical equivalent, as Greek ATMs do not have letters.

open Monday, Wednesday, and Saturday from 8am to 3pm; and Tuesday, Thursday, and Friday from 8am to 2pm and 5:30 to 10pm.

Most food stores are open Monday and Wednesday from 9am to 4:30pm, Tuesday from 9am to 6pm, Thursday from 9:30am to 6:30pm, Friday from 9:30am to 7pm, and Saturday from 8:30am to 4:30pm.

Many shops geared to visitors stay open late into the night—but often only if the shop owner thinks that business will be good. In other words, the shop that was open late yesterday may close early today.

Dentists & Doctors   Embassies (see below) usually have a list of dentists and doctors; some English-speaking physicians advertise in the daily *Athens News*.

Drugstores   See "Pharmacies," below.

Embassies & Consulates   Australia, Leoforos Dimitriou Soutsou 37 (☎ 01/645-0404-5); **Canada,** Odos Ioannou Yenadiou 4 (☎ 01/727-3400 or 01/725-4011); **Ireland,** Vas. Konstantinou 7 (☎ 01/723-2771); **New Zealand,** Xenias 24, Ambelokipi (☎ 01/771-0112); **South Africa,** Kifissias 60, Maroussi (☎ 01/680-6645); **United Kingdom,** Odos Ploutarchou 1 (☎ 01/723-6211); **United States,** Leoforos Vas. Sofias 91 (☎ 01/721-2951; emergency number 01/729-4301). Be sure to phone ahead before you go to any embassy; most keep limited hours and are usually closed on their own as well as Greek holidays.

Emergencies   In an emergency, dial ☎ **100** for the **police** and ☎ **171** for the **tourist police.** Dial ☎ **199** to report a **fire** and ☎ **166** for an **ambulance** and the **hospital.** If you need an English-speaking doctor or dentist, call your embassy for advice or try **SOS Doctor** (☎ **01/331-0310** or 01/331-0311). There are two medical hotline numbers for foreigners: ☎ **01/721-2951** (day) and **01/729-4301** (night) for U.S. citizens and ☎ **01/723-6211** (day) and **01/723-7727** (night) for British subjects. The English-language daily *Athens News* lists some American- and British-trained doctors and hospitals offering emergency services. Most of the larger hotels have doctors whom they can call for you in an emergency, and embassies will sometimes recommend local doctors.

KAT, the emergency hospital in Kifissia (☎ **01/801-4411** to 4419), and **Asklepion Voulas,** the emergency hospital in Voula (☎ **01/895-3416** to 3418), both have emergency rooms open 24 hours a day. **Evangelismos,** a respected centrally located hospital below the Kolonaki district on Vas. Sophias 9 (☎01/722-0101), usually has English-speaking staff on duty. If you need medical attention fast, don't waste time trying to call these hospitals: Just go. Their doors are open and they will see to you as soon as you enter.

In addition, one of the major hospitals takes turns each day being on emergency duty. A recorded message in Greek at ☎ **01/106** tells which hospital is open for emergency services and gives the telephone number.

Eyeglasses   If anything happens to your glasses, **Optical,** Odos Patriarchou Ioakim 2 (☎ **01/724-3564**), has a wide range of designer shades and specs at designer prices, and can provide a fast replacement.

Hospitals   Except for emergencies, hospital admittance is gained through a physician. See "Dentists & Doctors," above.

Information   See "Visitor Information," earlier in this chapter.

Internet Access   Internet cafes, where you can check and send e-mail, are proliferating almost as fast as cellular telephones in Athens. For a current list of Athenian cybercafes, check out **www.netcafeguide.com.**

As a general rule, most cybercafes charge about Dr1,500 ($4.30) an hour. The very efficient ✪ **Sofokleous.com Internet C@fe,** Stadiou 5, a block off Syntagma Square (☎ and fax **01/324-8105;** e-mail: sofos1@ath.forthnet.gr or sofos1@telehouse.gr), is open daily from 10am to 10pm. The **Astor Internet Caféé,** Odos Patission 17, a block off Omonia Square (☎ **01/523-8546**), is open Monday through Saturday from 10am to 10pm and Sunday from 10am to 4pm. Across from the National Archaeological Museum is the **Central Music Coffee Shop,** Odos Octobriou 28, also called Odos Patission (☎ **01/883-3418**), open daily from 9am to 11pm.

Laundry & Dry Cleaning   The **self-service launderette** at Odos Angelou Yeronda 10, in Filomouson Square, off Odos Kidathineon, Plaka, is open daily from 8:30am to 7pm; it charges Dr2,000 ($6) per load, including wash, dry, and soap. The **National Dry Cleaners and Laundry Service,** Odos Apollonos 17 (☎ **01/323-2226**), next to the Hermes Hotel, is open Monday and Wednesday from 7am to 4pm and Tuesday, Thursday, and Friday from 7am to 8pm; laundry costs Dr1,500 ($4.30) per kilo (2.2 lb.). Hotel chambermaids will often do laundry as well. Dry cleaning in Athens is reasonable, about Dr1,000 ($2.90) for a pair of slacks, and next-day service is usually possible.

Lost & Found   If you lose something on the street or on public transport, contact the **police lost and found,** Leoforos Alexandras 173 (☎ **01/642-1616**), open Monday through Saturday from 9am to 3pm. Lost passports and other documents may be returned by the police to the appropriate embassy, so check there as well. It's a good idea to travel with a photocopy of all important documents.

Luggage Storage/Lockers   If you're coming back to stay, many hotels will store excess luggage while you travel. Just southwest of Syntagma Square, **Pacific Ltd.,** Odos Nikis 26 (☎ **01/324-1007** or 01/322-3213), has a per-piece charge of Dr500 ($1.45) per day, Dr1,000 ($2.90) per week, Dr3,000 ($9) per month; open Monday through Saturday from 8am to 8pm. **Bellair Travel and Tourism Inc.,** Odos Nikis 15 (☎ **01/323-9261** or 01/321-6136), is open Monday through Friday from 9am to 5pm and has similar charges. Although both Pacific and Bellair keep regular hours, you may want to phone ahead to make sure they are open before you lug your luggage over. There are storage facilities at the Metro station in Piraeus, at both train stations, and across from the entrance at the East Air Terminal.

Newspapers & Magazines   The *Athens News* is published Tuesday through Sunday in English, with a weekend section ("Scope") listing events of interest; it's available at kiosks everywhere for Dr300 (90¢). Most central Athens newsstands also carry the *International Herald Tribune,* which has an English-language insert of highlights from the Greek daily *Kathimerini,* and *USA Today.* Local weeklies include the *Hellenic Times,* with its entertainment listings, and *Athinorama* (in Greek), which has comprehensive listings of events. *Now in Athens,* published every other month, has information on restaurants, shopping, museums and galleries, and is usually available free in major hotels and sometimes from the Greek National Tourism Organization.

Pharmacies   *Pharmakia,* identified by green crosses, are scattered throughout Athens. Hours are usually Monday through Friday from 8am to 2pm. In the evening and on weekends most are closed, but usually post a notice listing the names and addresses of pharmacies that are open or will open in an emergency. Newspapers such as the *Athens News* list the pharmacies open outside regular hours.

Police   In an **emergency,** dial ☎ **100.** For help dealing with a troublesome taxi driver, hotel, restaurant, or shop owner, stand your ground and call the **tourist police** at ☎ **171.**

Post Offices   The main post offices in central Athens are at Odos Eolou 100, just south of Omonia Square, and in Syntagma Square at the corner of Odos Mitropoleos. These are open Monday through Friday from 7:30am to 8pm, Saturday from 7:30am to 2pm, and Sunday from 9am to 1pm. The two post offices at the East and West air terminals also keep these extended hours. Oddly, mail posted at the air terminals almost always takes longer to arrive than mail posted in Athens itself.

All the post offices can accept parcels, but the **parcel post office** is at Odos Stadiou 4, inside the arcade (☎ **01/322-8940**), open Monday through Friday from 7:30am to 8pm. It usually sells twine and cardboard shipping boxes in four sizes. Parcels must be open for inspection before you seal them at the post office.

You can receive correspondence in Athens in care of **American Express,** Odos Ermou 2, 10225 Athens, Greece (☎ **01/324-4975**), near the southwest corner of Syntagma Square, open Monday through Friday from 8:30am to 4pm and Saturday from 8:30am to 1:30pm. If you have an American Express card or traveler's checks, the service is free; otherwise, each article costs Dr600 ($1.75).

Radio & Television   Generally, English-language radio—BBC and Voice of America—is available only via shortwave radio. CNN and various European channels are available on cable TV. Most foreign-language films shown on Greek TV are not dubbed, but have the original soundtracks with Greek subtitles. All current-release foreign-language films shown in Greek cinemas have the original soundtracks with Greek subtitles.

Rest Rooms   There are public rest rooms in the underground station beneath Omonia Square and beneath Kolonaki Square, but you'll probably prefer a hotel or restaurant rest room. (Toilet paper is often not available, so carry some tissue with you. Do not flush paper down the commode; use the receptacle provided.)

Safety   Athens is among the safest capitals in Europe, and there are few reports of violent crimes. **Pickpocketing,** however, is not uncommon, especially in the Plaka and the Omonia Square area, on the Metro and buses, and in Piraeus. We advise travelers to avoid the side streets of Omonia and Piraeus at night. As always, leave your passport and valuables in a security box at the hotel. Carry a photocopy of your passport, not the original.

Taxes   A VAT (value-added tax) of between 4% and 18% is added onto everything you buy. Some shops will attempt to cheat you by quoting you one price and then, when you hand over your credit card, adding on a hefty VAT charge. Be wary. In theory, if you are not a member of a Common Market/EU country, you can get a refund on major purchases at Hellenikon airport when you leave Greece. In practice, you would virtually have to arrive at the airport a day before your flight to get to the head of the line, do the paperwork, get a refund, and catch your flight.

Telephone/Telegrams/Faxes   Many of the city's public phones now accept only phone cards, available at newsstands and **Telecommunications Organization of Greece (OTE)** offices in several denominations starting at Dr1,700 ($4.90). The card works for 100 short local calls (or fewer long-distance or international calls). Some kiosks still have metered phones; you pay what the meter records. Local phone calls cost Dr20 (6¢). North Americans can phone home directly by contacting **AT&T** (☎ **00/800-1311**), **MCI** (☎ **00/800-1211**), or **Sprint** (☎ **00/800-1411**); calls can be collect or billed to your phone charge card. You can send a telegram or fax from OTE offices. The OTE office at Stadiou 15, near Syntagma, is open 24 hours a day. The Omonia Square OTE, at Odos Athinas 50, and the Victoria Square OTE, at Odos Patission 85, are open Monday through Friday from 7am to 9pm, Saturday from 9am to 3pm, and Sunday from 9am to 2pm. Outside Athens, most OTEs are closed on weekends.

Tipping   Athenian restaurants include a service charge in the bill, but many visitors add a 10% tip. Most Greeks do not give a percentage tip to taxi drivers, but often round out the fare to Dr1,000, for example, on a fare of Dr950.

3 Accommodations

While virtually all Greek hotels are clean and acceptably comfortable, few are charming or cozy, and fewer still are elegant or distinctive. If shower and tub facilities are important to you, be sure to have a look at the bathroom of the room you are offered: Many Greek tubs are tiny, shower curtains are not invariably supplied, and the showers are often hand-held and capricious. Another warning: Decent reading lamps are virtually unknown—consider using one of the little traveler's nightlights that clip onto your book.

The **Syntagma Square** area and the **Plaka/Monastiraki** district are the most convenient locations for sightseeing. If you have only a few days in Athens, you should seriously consider staying here. There are also good choices in **Makriyanni** and the **Embassy District,** as well as some good budget choices near the National Archaeological Museum. We've enjoyed staying in **Kolonaki,** the upscale Athenian neighborhood on the slopes of Mount Likavitos, although there were times we didn't look forward to the uphill walk back to the hotel. We have friends who always stay in the **Koukaki** district, near Filopappos Hill and off the non-Acropolis side of Dionissiou Areopayitou. They love the quiet residential streets and the bonus of being out of the heart of tourist Athens in a real Greek neighborhood. If you do stay there, you'll be doing extra walking to get to almost everything you want to do. Sadly, the neighborhoods are not as quiet as they were before Odos Dionyssiou Areopayitou was pedestrianized in January 2000, forcing motorists to find new routes on the south side of the Acropolis.

In summer, we strongly advise that you reserve ahead of time. If you do arrive without a reservation, you can usually book a room at the **tourist information booth** in the West Air Terminal. It's run by a private agency and is open daily from 7am to 1am; the service costs a small fee.

Note: Although the rates below were accurate at press time, annual increases of 10% to 15% are common.

THE PLAKA
EXPENSIVE

Electra Palace. Odos Nikodimou 18, Plaka, 10557 Athens. ☎ **01/324-1401** or 01/324-1407. Fax 01/324-1875. 106 units. A/C MINIBAR TV TEL. Dr39,800–Dr49,400 ($114–$142) double. Rates include breakfast. AE, DC, MC, V.

The Electra, just a few blocks southwest of Syntagma Square on a relatively quiet side street, is the most modern and stylish Plaka hotel. Top-floor rooms are smaller, but they're where you want to be, both for the view of the Acropolis and to escape traffic noise. (Ask for a top-floor unit when you make your reservation. Your request will be

Bargaining for a Room

Room prices, no matter what people say officially, are negotiable, especially at the edges of the season. Because of Greek law and OTE regulations, hotel keepers are very reluctant to give out any rates in advance and often quote prices higher than their actual rates. When you bargain, don't cite our prices, but ask instead for the best current rate. Off-season and other special prices may well be 20% lower than the lowest rate given to us for the book.

honored "subject to availability.") Guest rooms here are hardly drop-dead elegant, but they are pleasant, decorated in soft pastels. Don't miss the rooftop pool with a terrific view of the Acropolis. If you're too tired to go out for dinner, the hotel restaurant is quite decent.

MODERATE

Acropolis House Hotel. Odos Kodrou 6–8, 10558 Athens. ☎ **01/322-2344.** Fax 01/324-4143. 25 units, 15 with bathroom. A/C TEL. Dr16,104 ($46) double without bathroom, Dr21,640 ($62) double with bathroom. Dr4,000 ($11) surcharge for A/C. Rates include continental breakfast. V.

This small hotel in a handsomely restored 150-year-old villa retains many of its original classical architectural details. It offers a central location—just off Odos Kidathineon in the heart of the Plaka, a 5-minute walk from Syntagma Square—and the charm of being on a quiet pedestrian side street. Rooms 401 and 402 have good views and can be requested (but not guaranteed) when making a reservation. The newer wing, only 60 years old, isn't architecturally special; each unit's spartan bathroom is across the hall. There's a book-swap spot and a washing machine, free after a 4-day stay.

If the Acropolis House is full, try the **Adonis Hotel,** on the same street at Odos Kodrou 3 (☎ **01/324-9737;** fax 01/323-1602); it's architecturally undistinguished, and somewhat haphazard, but does have an appealing location and a rooftop garden cafe with a view of the Acropolis. A few steps away, the **Kouros Hotel,** Odos Kodrou 11 (☎ **01/322-7431**), is very basic and can be noisy.

Byron Hotel. Odos Vyronos 19, 10558 Athens. ☎ **01/325-3554.** Fax 01/323-0327. 20 units. TEL. Dr25,000 ($72) double. Rates include breakfast. No credit cards.

Although the Byron has remodeled its bathrooms and installed much new furniture, the staff, alas, remains as curt as ever. Still, the Byron (pronounced Vyron in Greek) has a convenient Plaka location just off recently pedestrianized Odos Dionyssiou Areopayitou.

✪ **Hotel Plaka.** Mitropoleos and Odos Kapnikareas 7, 10556 Athens. ☎ **01/322-2096.** Fax 01/322-2412. E-mail: plaka@tourhotel.gr or rofos@athforthnet.gr. 67 units. A/C TV TEL. Dr34,000 ($98) double. Rates include breakfast. AE, EC, MC, V. Follow Mitropoleos out of Syntagma Square past cathedral and turn left onto Kapnikareas.

This hotel is popular with Greeks, who prefer its modern conveniences to the old-fashioned charms of most other hotels in the Plaka area. It has a terrific location just off Syntagma Square. Most guest rooms have balconies; those on the fifth and sixth floors in the rear (where it's usually quieter) have views of the Plaka and the Acropolis, also visible from the roof-garden snack bar. Friends who stayed here recently were not charmed by the service, but enjoyed the location.

Athens Accommodations

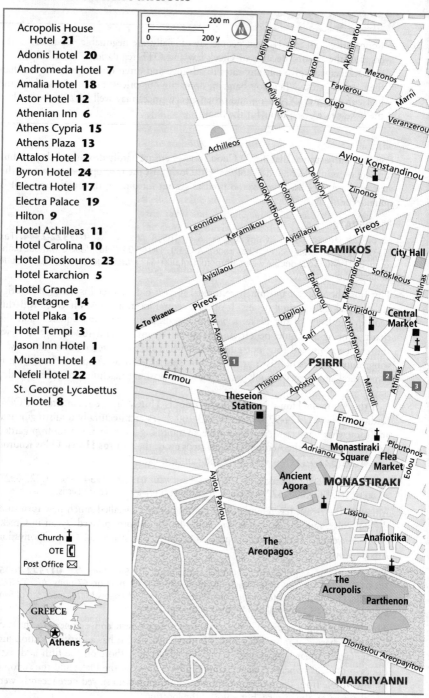

Acropolis House Hotel **21**
Adonis Hotel **20**
Andromeda Hotel **7**
Amalia Hotel **18**
Astor Hotel **12**
Athenian Inn **6**
Athens Cypria **15**
Athens Plaza **13**
Attalos Hotel **2**
Byron Hotel **24**
Electra Hotel **17**
Electra Palace **19**
Hilton **9**
Hotel Achilleas **11**
Hotel Carolina **10**
Hotel Dioskouros **23**
Hotel Exarchion **5**
Hotel Grande Bretagne **14**
Hotel Plaka **16**
Hotel Tempi **3**
Jason Inn Hotel **1**
Museum Hotel **4**
Nefeli Hotel **22**
St. George Lycabettus Hotel **8**

Church †
OTE C
Post Office ⊠

GREECE
★
Athens

0   200 m
0   200 y

Deliyanni
Chiou
Psaron
Akominatou
Mezonos
Favierou
Marni
Ougo
Veranzerou
Deliyoryi
Achilleos
Ayiou Konstandinou
Deliyoryi
Zinonos
Kolokynthous
Kolonou
Leonidou
Keramikou
Ayisilaou
Pireos
KERAMIKOS   **City Hall**
Ayisilaou
Sofokleous
Menandrou
Athinas
Epikourou
Pireos
← To Piraeus
Dipilou
Evripidou
Central Market
Safi
Aristofanous
Ay. Asomaton
1
PSIRRI
Ermou
Thissiou
Apostoli
Miaouli
Athinas
2
3
Theseion Station
Ermou
Adrianou
Monastiraki Square
Ploutonos
Flea Market
Eolou
Ancient Agora
MONASTIRAKI
Lissiou
Ayiou Pavlou
Anafiotika
The Areopagos
The Acropolis
Parthenon
Dionissiou Areopayitou
MAKRIYANNI

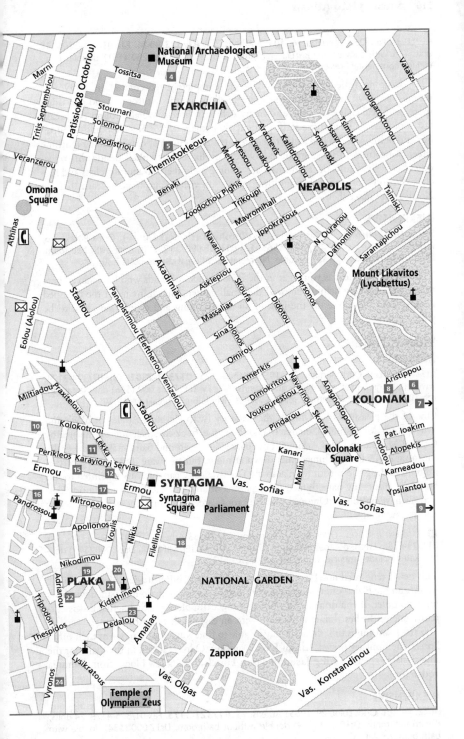

National Archaeological Museum

4

EXARCHIA

Tossitsa

Marni

Patission(28 Octobriou)

Tritis Septembriou

Stournari

Solomou

Kapodistriou

Veranzerou

5

Themistokleous

Benaki

Zoodochou Pighis

Arachevis

Dervenakou

Aressou

Methonis

Trikoupi

Mavromihali

Kallidromiou

Issavon

Tsimiski

Smolenski

NEAPOLIS

Voulgaroktonou

Vatatzi

Ippokratous

Omonia
Square

Athinas

Eolou (Aiolou)

Stadiou

Panepistimiou (Eleftheriou Venizelou)

Akadimias

Navarinou

Asklepiou

Skoufa

Massalias

Sina

Solonos

Omirou

Amerikis

Dimokritou

Voukourestiou

Pindarou

Didotou

Chersonos

N. Ouranou

Dafnomilis

Sarantapichou

Tsimiski

Mount Likavitos
(Lycabettus)

Aristippou

6

8

KOLONAKI

7 →

Miltiadou

Praxitelous

Stadiou

10

Kolokotroni

Lekka

Perikleos

Karayioryi Servias

Ermou

15

11

12

13

14

Ermou

SYNTAGMA

Vas. Sofias

Kanari

Merlin

Navarinou

Skoufa

Anagnostopoulou

Kolonaki
Square

Pat. Ioakim

Irodotou

Alopekis

Karneadou

Ypsilantou

9 →

Vas. Sofias

16

Pandrossou

Mitropoleos

17

Syntagma
Square

Parliament

Apollonos

Voulis

Nikis

Filellinon

18

Nikodimou

Adrianou

19

PLAKA

22

21

20

Kidathineon

23

Dedalou

Amalias

Tripodon

Thespidos

Lysikratous

Vyronos

24

Temple of
Olympian Zeus

NATIONAL GARDEN

Zappion

Vas. Olgas

Vas. Konstandinou

Nefeli Hotel. Odos Iperidou 16, 10558 Athens. ☎ **01/322-8044.** Fax 01/322-5800. 18 units (13 with shower only). TEL. Dr15,000 ($43) single; Dr21,200 ($61) double. Rates include continental breakfast. AE, V.

The charming little Nefeli ("Cloud") was completely redecorated in 1999; the rooms—most with air-conditioning—are small (as are the bathrooms) and pleasantly spare, with real character, unlike so many Athenian hotels. We also found the breakfast room congenial and the staff, particularly manager Tasos Kanellopoulos, courteous and helpful. We've had some recent reports from guests of considerable nighttime street noise from the pedestrianized Odos Angelikes Hatzimihali beside this once-quiet hotel. Evidently, the authorities are turning a blind eye to motorcyclists and revelers. We look forward to hearing from off-season visitors and hope to learn that the Nefeli is still quiet then.

INEXPENSIVE

Hotel Dioskouros (also known as the Dioskouros Guest House). Odos Pittakou 6, Plaka, 10558 Athens. ☎ **01/324-8165.** Fax 01/321-0907. 12 units, none with bathroom. Dr8,000–Dr10,000 ($23–$29) double. No credit cards. Breakfast Dr800 ($2.30).

This is as good a deal as you'll get in the Plaka. Student friends who have stayed here found the staff very helpful, enjoyed the small garden, and didn't mind the cramped rooms, the Plaka noise, or the lack of air-conditioning and ceiling fans. Ah, to be young again!

MONASTIRAKI
MODERATE

Attalos Hotel. Odos Athinas 29, 10554 Athens. ☎ **01/321-2801.** Fax 01/324-3124. www.attalos.gr. E-mail: atthot@hol.gr. 80 units. A/C TV TEL. Dr23,000 ($66) double (ask for the 10% discount for Frommer's readers). Rates include buffet breakfast. AE, V.

One of the pleasures of staying at the six-story (with elevator) Attalos, a block and a half from Monastiraki Square, is taking in the frenzied street life of the nearby Central Market on Odos Athinas. The market opens around 5am, making the early-morning hours lively. Things quiet down at night, but be aware that there's a certain amount of drug and prostitution activity. The Attalos's clean, recently repainted rooms are plain, but many have framed color photos of archaeological sites and antiquities, and 44 have balconies. One real plus: the roof garden, with its fine views of the city and the Acropolis.

✪ **Jason Inn Hotel.** Odos Ayion Assomaton 12, 10553 Athens. ☎ **01/325-1106.** Fax 01/523-4786. Email: douros@otenet.gr. 57 units. A/C TV TEL MINIBAR. Dr27,000 ($77) double. Rates include American buffet breakfast. DC, MC, V.

This newly renovated hotel (admittedly on a dull street, but just a few blocks from the Agora and the Plaka) offers attractive, comfortable rooms with double-paned windows for extra quiet. If you don't mind walking a few extra blocks to Syntagma, this is currently one of the best values in Athens, with an eager-to-help staff.

If the Jason Inn is full, the staff may be able to find you a room in one of their other hotels: the similarly priced **Adrian Hotel,** on busy Odos Hadrian in the Plaka, or the slightly less expensive **King Jason** or **Jason Hotels,** both a few blocks from Omonia Square.

INEXPENSIVE

Hotel Tempi. Odos Eolou 29, 10551 Athens. ☎ **01/321-3175.** Fax 01/325-4179. 24 units, 8 with bathroom. Dr10,000 ($29) double without bathroom, Dr12,000 ($34) double with bathroom. AE, MC, V.

If you believe that location is all for a hotel, consider the three-story Tempi, which faces the flower market by the church of Ayia Irini on a basically pedestrian-only street. The Tempi has very simply furnished rooms (bed, table, chair), the mattresses are overdue for replacement, and plumbing here can be a problem—hot water is intermittent, and the toilets sometimes smell. But 10 rooms have balconies from which (if you lean) you can see the Acropolis. This hotel is popular with students and other spartan travelers able to ignore the Tempi's drawbacks and focus on its location (and price).

SYNTAGMA
VERY EXPENSIVE

Athens Plaza. Syntagma Sq., 10564 Athens. ☎ **01/325-5301.** Fax 01/323-5856. 207 units. A/C MINIBAR TV TEL. Dr120,000 ($345) double. AE, DC, MC, V.

The Athens Plaza, managed by the Grecotel group, reopened its glitzy doors in March 1998 after a complete remodeling, and we were pretty excited to stay here shortly thereafter. There are acres of marble in the lobby, and almost as much in some bathrooms, which have their own phones and hair dryers. Many of the bedrooms are larger than our own living room, and many have balconies overlooking Syntagma Square. Hardly a place where you'd expect bare wires dangling from the ceiling in your bathroom, or a bedside table with a small hole cut out of its side and covered in aluminum foil. Mysterious. No doubt former senator Gary Hart, whom we saw lounging in the lobby, had no such problems in his room, but at these prices, should anyone?

Hotel Grande Bretagne. Syntagma Sq., 10563 Athens. ☎ **01/321-5555.** Fax 01/322-0211. In the U.S. you can make reservations through Sheraton Hotels at ☎ **800/325-3535**; in Greece, 01/321-5555. Fax 01/322-0211. www.hotelgrandebretagne-ath.gr. E-mail: gbhotel@otenet.gr. 398 units. A/C MINIBAR TV TEL. Dr52,500–Dr122,500 ($151–$352) double; from Dr228,000 ($657) suite. AE, CB, DC, MC, V.

Built in 1864 with an elegant beaux-arts decor, the Grande Bretagne has hosted everyone from Churchill to Sting. Although Greek political and social movers and shakers still pass through the lobby with its ornately carved wood paneling, soaring ceilings, and polished marble floors for power lunches at the popular GB Corner, so increasingly do the tour groups staying here. Although many bedrooms were renovated in 1992, too many inner-courtyard units look the worse for wear and utterly lack the elegance of the rooms fronting Syntagma Square with Acropolis views. Let's hope that rumored future renovations will restore this hotel to its former glory. For now, you may prefer to have a look at the lobby or a drink in the GB Corner, but stay elsewhere—although of late the Grande Bretagne has had some very good off-season prices.

EXPENSIVE

Electra Hotel. Odos Ermou 5, 10563 Athens. ☎ **01/322-3223.** Fax 01/322-0310. E-mail: electrahotels@ath.forthnet.gr. 110 units. A/C TV TEL. Dr48,400 ($139). Rates include buffet breakfast. DC, MC, V.

If Odos Ermou remains pedestrian, the Electra has a location that is both central (steps from Syntagma Square) and quiet. Most of the guest rooms have comfortable armchairs, large windows, and modern bathrooms with hair dryers. Be sure to have a look at your room before you accept it: Although most are large, some are quite tiny. The front desk is sometimes understaffed, but the service is generally acceptable, although it can be brusque when groups are checking in and out.

MODERATE

If the following choices are full, you might consider as a fall-back option the 98-unit **Amalia Hotel,** Leoforos Amalias 10 (☎ **01/323-7301** to 7309; fax 01/323-8792). Although it's overdue for a complete renovation, it has a convenient location and fair price (Dr44,000/$126 double) for the area.

Astor Hotel. Karayioryi Servias 16, 10562 Athens. ☎ **01/335-1000.** Fax 01/325-5115. www.astorhotel.gr. 131 units. A/C TV TEL Dr29,600 ($85) double. Rates include buffet breakfast. AE, V.

We've never been very impressed with this hotel, which does a heavy business in tour groups, and has service that is impersonal at best. That said, a well-traveled journalist tells me that he always stays here when in Athens because of the central location, bright rooms (some with Acropolis views), and efficient (if not pleasant) front desk staff. The journalist also says that he sometimes succeeds in bargaining down the room price.

Athens Cypria. Odos Diomias 5, 10562 Athens. ☎ **01/323-8034.** Fax 01/324-8792. 71 units. A/C TV TEL MINIBAR. Dr29,850 ($86) double. Rates include breakfast. AE, MC, V.

After extensive renovations, the former Diomia Hotel has been reborn as the spanking new Athens Cypria. Gone are the Diomia's gloomy lobby and bedrooms, but the convenient central location on a street with (usually) no traffic and the splendid Acropolis views from units 603 to 607 remain. The halls and rooms throughout have been painted bright white, the units have cheerful floral bedspreads and curtains, and the bathrooms (with hair dryers) are freshly tiled with all new fixtures. The breakfast buffet offers hot and cold dishes from 7 to 10am. In short, the Athens Cypria promises to be an excellent addition to the city's moderately priced hotels.

Hotel Achilleas. Odos Lekka 21, 10562 Athens. ☎ **01/323-3197.** Fax 01/322-2412. www.achilleashotel.gr. E-mail: achilleas@tourhotel.gr. 34 units. A/C TV TEL. Dr28,000 ($80) double. Rates include breakfast. AE, DC, EC, MC, V.

The Achilleas (Achilles), on a relatively quiet side street, steps from Syntagma Square, has just completed a total renovation. The good-sized bedrooms are now bright and cheerful and the beds have new mattresses; some rear rooms have small balconies. The Achilleas's very central location and fair prices make it a good choice.

INEXPENSIVE

Hotel Carolina. Odos Kolokotroni 55, 10560 Athens. ☎ **01/324-3551.** Fax 01/324-3350. 31 units, 15 with shower and toilet. TEL. Dr14,000 ($40) double without shower and toilet; Dr17,500–21,000 ($50–$60) double with shower and toilet. AE, EC, MC, V.

The Carolina, a 5-minute walk from Syntagma Square, has undertaken some badly needed renovations. It's an appealing choice for the young-at-heart who will appreciate the low prices and house-party atmosphere that make the place popular with students.

KOLONAKI
VERY EXPENSIVE

St. George Lycabettus Hotel. Odos Kleomenous 2, 10675 Athens. ☎ **01/729-0711.** Fax 01/721-0439. www.sglycabettus.gr. E-mail: info@sglycabettus.gr. 167 units. A/C TV TEL. Dr68,000–95,000 ($196–$274) double. Breakfast Dr5,500 ($16). AE, DC, MC, V.

The rooftop pool is a plus, there's often contemporary Greek art on view in the lobby, and the hotel is just steps from the chic Kolonaki restaurants and shops. The nicely appointed guest rooms look toward Mount Likavitos or a small park, although the surrounding street traffic keeps this from being a real oasis of calm. As yet, the St. George Lycabettus does not get many tour groups, which helps it to maintain its tranquil tone.

MODERATE

✪ **Athenian Inn.** Odos Haritos 22, Kolonaki, 10675 Athens. ☎ **01/723-8097.** Fax 01/724-2268. 28 units. A/C TEL. Dr38,000 ($109) double. Rates include breakfast. AE, DC, V.

The Athenian Inn's quiet location 3 blocks from Kolonaki Square is a blessing, as Hellenophile Lawrence Durrell indicated in the guest book: "At last the ideal Athens hotel, good and modest in scale but perfect in service and goodwill." Some of the balconies look out on Mount Likavitos. Breakfast is served in a small lounge with a fireplace, piano, and TV. Between stays, we tend to forget how small the rooms are, which suggests that the staff is doing a good job of making guests feel comfortable and at home.

EMBASSY DISTRICT

VERY EXPENSIVE

✪ **Andromeda Hotel.** Odos Timoleontos Vassou 22 (off Plateia Mavili), 11521 Athens. ☎ **01/643-7302.** Fax 01/646-6361. 42 units. A/C MINIBAR TV TEL. Dr91,000–Dr122,500 ($262–$352) double. Special rates sometimes available. AE, DC, EC, MC, V.

The city's only boutique hotel is easily the most charming in Athens, with a staff that makes you feel like this is your home away from home. Rooms are large and elegantly decorated, with furniture and paintings you'd be happy to live with (plus hair dryers to boot). This very quiet hotel overlooks the garden of the American ambassador's home, and serves marvelous breakfasts and snacks (at present there is no on-site restaurant). The only drawbacks: It's a serious hike (20 to 30 mins.) or 10-minute taxi ride to Syntagma, and there are few restaurants in this residential neighborhood, although the superb Vlassis is just around the corner. If you're planning a long stay in Athens, check out the Andromeda's new (and very lovely) service apartments just across the street.

Hilton. Leoforos Vas. Sofias 46, 11528 Athens. ☎ **800/445-8667** in the U.S., 01/728-1000. Fax 01/728-1111. www.hilton.com. E-mail: athens@hilton.com. 446 units. A/C MINIBAR TV TEL. Dr129,500–Dr156,000 ($373–$449) double. AE, DC, EC, MC, V.

Since its opening in 1963, the Hilton, near the U.S. Embassy, has been an Athenian institution, where businessmen and diplomats meet for a drink or a meal. In 2000, plans were announced for a major renovation to be completed in time for the 2004 Athens Olympics, so you might want to check to see if there's any noisy work scheduled for the time of your visit. If not, the Hilton, a 10-minute stroll from Syntagma Square, is an excellent choice. Small shops, a salon, and cafes and restaurants surround the glitzy lobby. The guest rooms (looking toward either the hills outside Athens or the Acropolis) have large marble bathrooms and are decorated in the generic (but comfortable) international Hilton style, with some Greek touches. The Plaza Executive floor of rooms and suites offers a separate business center and higher level of service. Facilities include a pool and health club. The Hilton often runs promotions, so ask about special rates before booking.

KOUKAKI & MAKRIYANNI (NEAR THE ACROPOLIS)

Keep in mind that with all the Makriyanni/Koukaki hotels, you'll be doing some extra walking to get to most places you want to visit.

VERY EXPENSIVE

✪ **Divani-Palace Acropolis.** Odos Parthenonos 19–25, Makriyanni, 11742 Athens. ☎ **01/922-2945.** Fax 01/921-4993. E-mail: acropol@otenet.gr. 253 units. A/C MINIBAR TV TEL. Dr70,000–Dr87,500 ($201–$245) double. AE, DC, MC, V.

Just 3 blocks south of the Acropolis, in a quiet residential neighborhood (there's a handy Veropoulos SPAR supermarket a block away at Odos Parthenos 4, as well as a shop at Odos Parthenos 7 that sells American and English newspapers), the Divani

Palace Acropolis does a brisk tour business, but is welcoming to independent travel-ers. The blandly decorated bedrooms are large and comfortable and the large bath-rooms have hair dryers (some even have two wash basins). The cavernous marble-and-glass lobby contains copies of classical sculpture, and other facilities include a small handsome pool, bar, restaurant, and lovely roof garden with the view you'd expect. A section of Athens's 5th century B.C defense wall is preserved behind glass in the basement, by the gift shop. The same hotel group operates the **Divani Caravel Hotel,** near the National Art Gallery and the Hilton at Leoforos Vas. Alexan-drou 2 (☎ **01/725-3725;** fax 01-725-3770).

MODERATE

✪ **Acropolis View Hotel.** Odos Webster 10, 11742 Athens. ☎ **01/921-7303.** Fax 01/923-0705. 32 units. A/C TV TEL. Dr40,000 ($115) double. Rates include generous breakfast. Substantial reductions Nov–Mar. AE, EC, MC, V.

This nicely maintained hotel with helpful staff is on a residential side street off Rover-tou Galli, not far from the Herodes Atticus theater. The usually quiet neighborhood, at the base of Filopappos Hill, is a 10- to 15-minute walk from the heart of the Plaka. The guest rooms (most freshly painted each year) are small but pleasant, with good bathrooms; 16 units have balconies. Some, like room 405, overlook Filopappos Hill, while others, like room 407, face the Acropolis. There's a congenial breakfast room and a bar in the lobby.

Art Gallery Hotel. Odos Erechthiou 5, Koukaki, 11742 Athens. ☎ **01/923-8376.** Fax 01/923-3025. E-mail: ecotec@atenet.gr. 22 units. A/C TV TEL. Dr31,500 ($91) double. Rates include generous breakfast. Substantial reductions Nov–Mar. AE, EC, MC, V. Breakfast Dr1,500 ($4.30).

As you might expect, this small hotel—in a half-century-old house that has been home to several artists—has an artistic flair (and a nice old-fashioned cage elevator). Rooms are small and plain, but comfortable, with polished hardwood floors and ceiling fans. There's a nice Victorian-style breakfast room on the fourth floor, with heavy marble-topped tables and old velvet-covered chairs. In early 2000, the manager was talking about "modernizing"—not too much, we hope.

Austria Hotel. Odos Mousson 7, Filopappou, 11742 Athens. ☎ **01/923-5151.** Fax 01/924-7350. www.austriahotel.com. E-mail: austria@topservice.com or austria@hol.gr. 37 units, 30 with bathroom. A/C TEL. Dr30,000 ($86) double with or without bathroom. Rates include breakfast. AE, DC, EC, MC, V.

This quiet, well-maintained hotel at the base of Filopappos Hill is operated by a Greek-Austrian family, who offer guests use of the hotel safe-deposit box and fax ser-vices, will exchange your foreign money into drachmas (which not all small hotels are prepared to do), and can point you to the convenient neighborhood Laundromat. Guest rooms are rather spartan (the linoleum floors are not enchanting), but tidy. There's a great view over Athens and out to sea (we could see the island of Aegina the day we visited) from the rooftop, where you can sun or sit under an awning in the shade.

Herodion Hotel. Odos Rovertou Galli 4, Makriyanni, 11742 Athens. ☎ **01/923-6832** or 01/923-6836. Fax 01/921-6150. www.vacation.net.gr/herodion. E-mail: herodion@otenet.gr. 90 units. A/C TV TEL. Dr49,000 ($140) double. Rates include breakfast. AE, DC, MC, V.

An archaeologist friend who always stays at this attractive hotel a block south of the Acropolis, near the Herodes Atticus theater, reports that there's considerably more traf-fic noise on Rovertou Galli since Odos Dionyssiou Areopayitou was pedestrianized. Still, the rooms here are good-sized, many with balconies. The lobby leads to a lounge

Accommodations & Dining South of the Acropolis

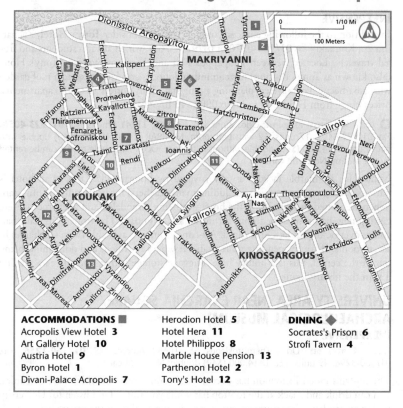

ACCOMMODATIONS ■	Herodion Hotel **5**	**DINING** ◆
Acropolis View Hotel **3**	Hotel Hera **11**	Socrates's Prison **6**
Art Gallery Hotel **10**	Hotel Philippos **8**	Strofi Tavern **4**
Austria Hotel **9**	Marble House Pension **13**	
Byron Hotel **1**	Parthenon Hotel **2**	
Divani-Palace Acropolis **7**	Tony's Hotel **12**	

and patio garden where you can have drinks and snacks under the trees. The same owners run the nearby **Hotel Philippos,** Mitseon 3, Makriyanni (☎ **01/922-3611;** fax 01/922-3615).

✪ **Hotel Hera.** Odos Falirou 9, Makriyanni, 11742 Athens. ☎ **01/923-6682.** Fax 01/924-7334. E-mail: hhera@hol.gr. 49 units. A/C TEL. Dr35,000 ($99) double. Rates include breakfast. AE, MC, V.

The Hera boasts a garden behind its breakfast room and great views of the Acropolis from the rooftop garden. That's a lot of greenery in Athens, and since the bland bedrooms have balconies with hanging plants and are perfectly comfortable, you may find that the location out of the heart of tourist Athens is just what you want. If you have a car, you'll appreciate the garage here.

Parthenon. Odos Makri 6, 11527 Athens. ☎ **01/923-4594.** Fax 01/644-1084. 79 units. TEL. Dr35,000 ($99) double. MC, V.

This modern, recently redecorated hotel has an excellent location just steps from the Plaka and the Acropolis. The carpeted bedrooms contain bright, cheerful bedspreads and decent-sized bathrooms, and some have TVs. Facilities include a bar, restaurant, and small garden. The Parthenon is one of a group of four hotels; if it's full, the management will try to get you a room at the **Christina,** a few blocks away, or at the **Riva** or **Alexandros,** near the Megaron (the Athens Concert Hall). One warning: On occasion we have found the desk staff at the Parthenon less than helpful and infuriatingly vague about room prices.

INEXPENSIVE

In addition to the following choices, you may want to consider **Tony's Hotel,** Zacharitsa 26, Koukaki (☎ **01/923-6370** or 01/923-5761), which attracts students and frugal travelers. Located between Filopappos Hill and Leoforos Syngrou, Tony's Hotel (also known as Tony's Pension) has communal lounges and kitchens and a roof garden with a barbecue. For travelers planning a long stay, Tony's offers 11 studio apartments; prices range from Dr14,000 to Dr16,000 ($40 to $46).

✪ **Marble House Pension.** Odos Zinni 35A, Koukaki, 11741 Athens. ☎ **01/923-4058.** Fax 01/922-6461. 17 units, 12 with bathroom. MINIBAR TEL. Dr15,600 ($45) double with bathroom; Dr14,000 ($40) double without bathroom. Oct–Mar double rooms can be rented by the month. No credit cards.

Named for its marble façade, usually covered by bougainvillea, this small hotel is famous among budget travelers (including many teachers) for its friendly, helpful staff. When we visited in early 2000, the hotel was being remodeled and guest rooms were getting new bathrooms, bedroom furniture, and minibars. The front units have balconies overlooking quiet Odos Zinni. Air-conditioning is available (with surcharge) in seven rooms. If you're spending more than a few days in Athens and don't mind being out of the center, this is a homey base. Luggage storage is free, and there's a satellite TV in the library/lounge.

UNIVERSITY AREA (NEAR EXARCHIA SQUARE/ ARCHAEOLOGICAL MUSEUM)
INEXPENSIVE

Hotel Exarchion. Odos Themistokleous 55, 10683 Athens. ☎ **01/360-1256.** Fax 01/360-3296. 49 units. TEL. Dr14,000 ($40) double. No credit cards.

The no-frills Hotel Exarchion has decent-sized rooms, most of which have balconies. You can drink and snack at the rooftop bar while you watch (and listen to) University of Athens students debating and sometimes demonstrating in the square below.

Museum Hotel. Odos Bouboulinas 16, 10682 Athens. ☎ **01/360-5611.** Fax 01/380-0057. 58 units. TEL. Dr13,500 ($39) double. Rates include breakfast. AE, DC, V.

This venerable hotel is so close to the Archaeological Museum that its balconies overlook the museum's relatively quiet, tree-filled park. The rooms are bland and could use a lot of sprucing up (especially the saggy mattresses). In short, this is a you-get-what-you-pay-for good-value place in a good location, although the traffic here is, as almost everywhere in Athens, pretty steady.

4 Dining

Since June 2000, Greek restaurants have had to display a menu with prices either in the window or another prominent place. Most restaurants have menus in Greek and English, but many don't keep their printed (or handwritten) menus up-to-date. If the menu is not in English, there's almost always someone working at the restaurant who will either translate or rattle off suggestions for you in English. Consequently, you may be offered some fairly repetitive suggestions, as restaurant staff tend to suggest what most tourists request. In Athens, that means *moussaka* (baked eggplant casserole, usually with ground meat), *souvlaki* (chunks of beef, chicken, pork, or lamb grilled on a skewer), *pastitsio* (baked pasta, usually with ground meat and a béchamel sauce), or *dolmadakia* (grape leaves stuffed usually with rice and ground meat). Although these dishes can be delicious—you may have eaten them outside of Greece and looked

You Paid What?

47,000 hotels, 700 airlines, 50 rental car companies. And a few million ways to save money.

Travelocity.com
A Sabre Company

Go Virtually Anywhere.

AOL Keyword: Travel

Will you have enough stories to tell your grandchildren?

Yahoo! Travel

A Note on Credit Cards

Many Athenian restaurants do not accept credit cards. Each year, some restaurants that formerly accepted credit cards stop accepting them. Be prepared to pay with cash or traveler's checks at even the finest establishments. If you want to pay with a credit card, double-check to make sure the restaurant will accept your credit card before going.

forward to enjoying the real thing here—you may end up cherishing your memories and regretting your meal. All too often, restaurants catering to tourists tend to serve profoundly dull moussaka and unpleasantly chewy souvlaki. We hope that the places we're suggesting do better.

In the last few years, a number of Athenian restaurants have begun to experiment with a "nouvelle Greek" cuisine. Usually, this involves aspects of *paradisiako* (traditional) cooking, but with a lighter hand on the olive oil and an adventurous combination of familiar ingredients. In our reviews, we draw attention to these restaurants.

THE PLAKA

Some of the most charming old restaurants in Athens are in the Plaka—as are some of the worst tourist traps. Here are a few things to keep in mind when you head off for a meal in the Plaka.

Some Plaka restaurants station waiters outside who don't just urge you to come in and sit down, but virtually pursue you down the street with an unrelenting sales pitch. The hard sell is almost always a giveaway that the place caters to tourists. (That said, remember that announcing what's for sale is not invariably a ploy reserved for tourists. If you visit the Central Market, you'll see and hear stall owners calling out the attractions of their meat, fish, and produce to passersby—and even waving particularly tempting fish and fowl in front of potential customers.)

In general, it's a good idea to avoid places with floor shows; many charge outrageous amounts (and levy surcharges not always openly stated on menus) for drinks and food. If you get burned, stand your ground, phone the **Tourist Police** (☎ **171**), and pay nothing before they arrive. Often the mere threat of calling the Tourist Police has the miraculous effect of causing a bill to be lowered.

EXPENSIVE

✪ **Daphne's.** Odos Lysikratous 4. ☎ and fax **01/322-7971.** Main courses Dr4,500–Dr8,500 ($13–$24), with some fish priced by the kilo. AE, DC, MC, V. Daily 7pm–1am. Closed Dec 20–Jan 15. ELEGANT GREEK/NOUVELLE.

There are frescoes on the walls of this neo-classical 1830s former home, a shady garden courtyard with bits of ancient marble found here when the restaurant was built, and sophisticated Athenians at many tables. The outside garden courtyard makes Daphne's a real oasis in Athens, especially when summer nights are hot. The cuisine here (recommended in the *New York Times* and *Travel and Leisure*) gives you all the old favorites with new distinction (try the zesty eggplant salad), and combines familiar ingredients in innovative ways (delicious hot pepper and feta cheese dip). We could cheerfully just eat the hors d'oeuvres all night, but have also enjoyed the *stifado* (stew) of rabbit in *mavrodaphne* (sweet wine) sauce and the tasty prawns with toasted almonds. Most nights, there's a pair of strolling musicians, whose repertoire ranges from Greek favorites to "My Darling Clementine."

Athens Dining

Church ✝
OTE Ⅽ
Post Office ✉

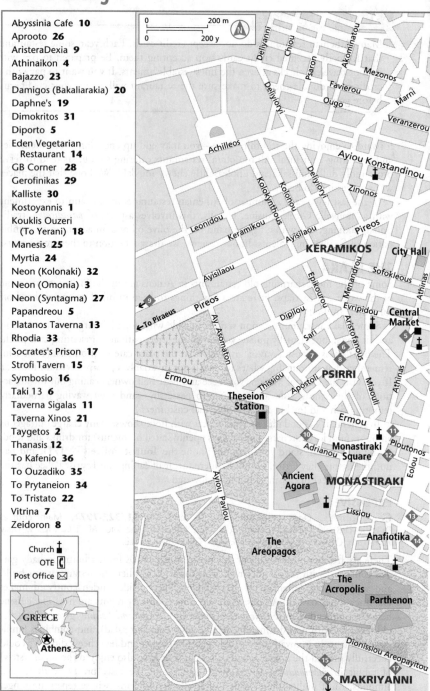

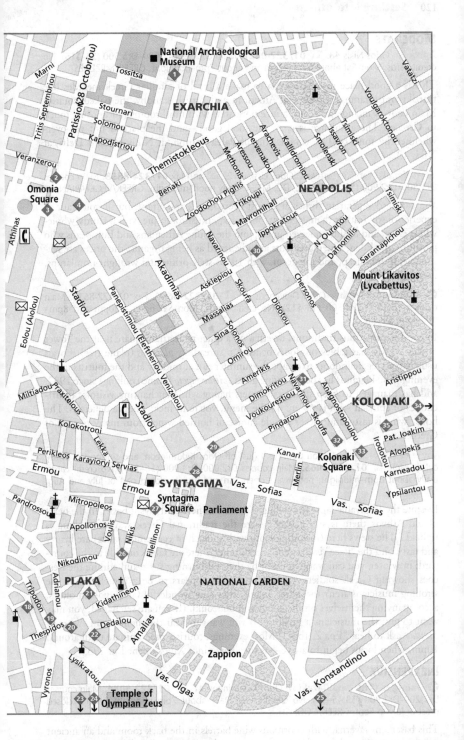

National Archaeological
Museum

Tossitsa

EXARCHIA

Marni

Tritis Septembriou

Patision(28 Octobriou)

Stournari

Solomou

Kapodistriou

Veranzerou

Omonia
Square

Athinas

Themistokleous

Benaki

Zoodochou Pighis

Methonis

Aressou

Dervenakion

Arachevis

Kallidromiou

Issavron

Tsimiski

Smolenski

Voulgaroktonou

Vatatzi

NEAPOLIS

Trikoupi

Mavromihali

Ippokratos

Navarinou

Akadimias

Chersonos

N. Ouranou

Dafnomilis

Tsimiski

Sarantapichou

Mount Likavitos
(Lycabettus)

Stadiou

Panepstimiou (Eleftheriou Venizelou)

Asklepiou

Skoufa

Didotou

Massalias

Sina

Solonos

Omirou

Amerikis

Dimokritou

Navarinou

Skoufa

Anagnostopoulou

Aristippou

Eolou (Aiolou)

Miltiadou

Praxitelous

Kolokotroni

Lekka

Perikleos

Karayioryi Servias

Ermou

Pandrossou

Mitropoleos

Apollonos

Voulis

Nikis

Filellinon

Nikodimou

PLAKA

Adrianou

Kidathineon

Tripodon

Thespidos

Dedalou

Amalias

Lysikratous

Vyronos

Temple of
Olympian Zeus

Stadiou

Voukourestiou

Pindarou

Kanari

Merlin

SYNTAGMA

Ermou

Syntagma
Square

Parliament

Vas. Sofias

Vas. Sofias

KOLONAKI

Pat. Ioakim

Irodotou

Alopekis

Karneadou

Ypsilantou

Kolonaki
Square

NATIONAL GARDEN

Zappion

Vas. Olgas

Vas. Konstandinou

MODERATE

Aprooto. Odos Nikis 48. ☎ **01/322-0521.** Main courses Dr2,000–Dr5,500 ($6–$16). No credit cards. Mon–Sat about 11am–2pm and about 7pm–midnight. GREEK/MEZEDES.

This is a good place near Syntagma to make a meal of familiar Greek mezedes like tzatziki and taramosalata (or that American and British standby, the baked potato). Main courses include grills and a nice pork stew with mushrooms (an unusual touch in Greece). The ambiance is cozy, the food good—and the place is not yet overwhelmed by tourists. The same is true of **Palea Athina,** at Nikis 46, and **Delfi,** at Nikis 13.

Eden Vegetarian Restaurant. Odos Lissiou 12. ☎ and fax **01/324-8858.** Main courses Dr1,800–Dr2,900 ($5.15–$8). AE, DC, MC, V. Daily noon–midnight. GREEK/VEGETARIAN.

You can find vegetarian dishes at almost every Greek restaurant, but if you want to experience soy (rather than eggplant) moussaka, mushroom pie with a sturdy wholewheat crust, and freshly squeezed juices, join the young Athenians and Europeans who patronize the Eden. The ingredients are advertised as being organic, the prices are reasonable, if not cheap, and the decor, with 1920s-style prints and wrought-iron lamps, is engaging.

✪ Platanos Taverna. Odos Dioyenous 4. ☎ **01/322-0666.** Fax 01/322-8624. Main courses Dr2,800–Dr4,300 ($8–$12). No credit cards. Mon–Sat noon–4:30pm and 8pm–midnight. GREEK.

In good weather, this traditional taverna, on a quiet pedestrian square near the Tower of the Winds, has tables outdoors beneath a spreading *platanos* (plane tree). Locals usually congregate indoors to escape the summer sun at midday and the tourists in the evening. The Platanos has been serving good *spitiko fageto* (home cooking) since 1932, and has managed to keep steady customers happy while enchanting visitors. If artichokes or spinach with lamb are on the menu, you're in luck: They're delicious. The house wine is tasty, and there's a wide choice of bottled wines from many regions of Greece.

Taverna Xinos. Odos Agelou Geronta 4 (just off Odos Kidathineon, and signposted in the cul-de-sac). ☎ **01/322-1065.** Main courses Dr2,000–Dr4,000 ($6–$11). No credit cards. Daily about 8pm–midnight; not always open Sun and usually closed part of July and Aug. GREEK.

Despite the forgivable lapse in spelling, Xinos's business card says it best: "In the heart of old Athens there is still a flace where the traditional Greek way of cooking is upheld." The stews here (including lamb with spinach in egg lemon sauce) are hearty and tasty, and the "flace" is charming. In summer, there are tables outside in the courtyard; in winter, you can warm yourself by the coal-burning stove and admire the frescoes showing Greek soldiers, gypsies, and what appears to be a camel. While the strolling musicians aren't the Three Tenors, they sing wonderful Greek golden oldies, accompanying themselves on the guitar and bouzouki. (If you are serenaded, you may want to give the musicians a small tip. If you want to hear the theme from *Never on Sunday,* ask to hear "Ena Zorbas.") Most evenings, tourists predominate until around 10pm, when locals begin to arrive—as they have since Xinos opened in 1935.

INEXPENSIVE

✪ Damigos (The Bakaliarakia). Odos Kidathineon 41. ☎ **01/322-5084.** Main courses Dr1,200–Dr2,900 ($3.45–$8). No credit cards. Daily about 7pm–midnight. Usually closed most of July to Sept. GREEK/CODFISH.

This basement taverna, with enormous wine barrels in the back room and an ancient column supporting the roof in the front room, has been serving delicious deep-fried codfish and eggplant, as well as chops and stews, since 1865. The wine comes from the family vineyards, and there are few pleasures greater than sipping retsina while you watch the cook turn out unending meals in his absurdly small kitchen. Don't miss the delicious *skordalia* (garlic sauce), which is equally good with the cod, eggplant, bread—well, you get the idea.

Kouklis Ouzeri (To Yerani). Odos Tripodon 14. ☎ **01/324-7605.** Appetizers Dr600–Dr1,800 ($1.75–$5.15). No credit cards. Daily 11am–2am. GREEK.

Besides Kouklis Ouzeri and To Yerani, Greeks also call this popular old favorite with its winding staircase the "Skolario" because of the nearby school. A waiter will present to you a large tray with about a dozen plates of *mezedes*—appetizer portions of fried fish, beans, grilled eggplant, taramosalata, cucumber-and-tomato salad, olives, fried cheese, sausages, and other seasonal specialties. Accept the ones that appeal. If you don't order all 12, you can enjoy a tasty and inexpensive meal, washed down with the house *krasi* (wine). (No prices are posted, but the waiter will tell you what everything costs if you ask.) Now, if only the staff here could be just a bit more patient when foreigners are trying to decide what to order....

MONASTIRAKI
INEXPENSIVE

⭐ **Abyssinia Cafe.** Plateia Abyssinia, Monastiraki. ☎ **01/321-7047.** Appetizers and main courses Dr1,000–Dr2,500 ($2.90–$7). No credit cards. Tues–Sun 10:30am–2pm; often open evenings as well. Usually closed for a week at Christmas and Easter, sometimes closed part of Jan and Feb. Abyssinia Square is just off Odos Ifaistou (Hephaistos) across from the entrance to the Ancient Agora on Adrianou. GREEK.

This small cafe in a ramshackle building has a nicely restored interior featuring lots of gleaming dark wood and polished copper. It faces lopsided Abyssinia Square off Odos Ifaistou, where furniture restorers ply their trade and antiques shops sell everything from gramophones to hubcaps. You can sit indoors or out and have just a coffee, but it's tempting to snack on Cheese Abyssinia (feta scrambled with spices and garlic), mussels and rice pilaf, or *keftedes* (meatballs).

Diporto. Central Market, Odos Athinas. No phone. Main courses Dr900–Dr2,500 ($2.60–$7). No credit cards. Mon–Sat 6am–6pm. GREEK.

This little place, sandwiched between olive shops, serves up salads, stews, and delicious *revithia* (chickpeas), a Greek winter dish popular among stall owners, shoppers, and Athenians who make their way to the market for cheap and delicious food.

Papandreou. Central Market, Odos Athinas. ☎ **01/321-4970.** Main courses about Dr1,800 ($5.15). No credit cards. Mon–Sat from about 8am–5pm. GREEK.

The butcher, the baker, and the office worker duck past the sides of beef hanging in the Meat Hall and head to this hole-in-the-wall for zesty tripe dishes. Don't like tripe? Don't worry: There's usually something on the menu that doesn't involve it. Papandreou has a virtually all-male clientele, but a woman alone need not hesitate to eat here.

Taverna Sigalas. Plateia Monastiraki 2. ☎ **01/321-3036.** Main courses Dr1,800–Dr3,000 ($5.15–$9). No credit cards. Daily 7am–2am. Sigalas is across Monastiraki Square from the Metro station. GREEK.

This longtime Plaka taverna, housed in a vintage 1879 commercial building with a newer outdoor pavilion, boasts that it is open 365 days a year. Its lively interior has huge old retsina kegs in the back and dozens of black-and-white photos of Greek movie stars on the walls. After 8pm nightly, there's Greek Muzak. At all hours, both Greeks and tourists wolf down large portions of stews, moussaka, grilled meatballs, baked tomatoes, gyros, and other hearty dishes, washed down with the house red and white retsinas.

✪ **Thanasis.** Odos Mitropoleos 69 (just off the northeast corner of Monastiraki Square). ☎ **01/324-4705.** Main courses Dr500–Dr3,000 ($1.45–$9). No credit cards. Daily 9am–2am. GREEK/SOUVLAKI.

Thanasis serves terrific souvlaki and pita—and exceptionally good french fries—both to go and at its outdoor and indoor tables; as always, prices are higher if you sit down to eat. On weekends, it often takes the strength and determination of an Olympic athlete to get through the door and place an order here. It's worth the effort: This is both a great budget choice and a great place to take in the local scene, which often includes a fair sprinkling of gypsies.

SYNTAGMA
EXPENSIVE

GB Corner. In the Grande Bretagne Hotel, Syntagma Sq. ☎ **01/323-0251.** Reservations required for lunch. Main courses from Dr6,000–Dr12,000 ($17–$34). AE, DC, EC, MC, V. Daily about 10am–1am. INTERNATIONAL.

We always envy the people whom we glimpse through the windows here. There we are, foot-weary and hot outside; there they are, lounging in the dark leather booths and toying with salads and shrimp while waiters hover nearby. When we have eaten here, it's been very pleasant—and very expensive. The menu has a full international/continental range, as well as breakfast, tea, and late-night offerings.

MODERATE

Gerofinikas. Odos Pindar 10. ☎ **01/363-6710.** Reservations strongly recommended. Main courses Dr3,000–Dr6,000 ($9–$17). Fixed-price menu Dr8,500 ($24), not including beverage. AE, DC, MC, V. Daily usually noon–2pm and 7pm–midnight. GREEK/INTERNATIONAL.

For years, this was *the* place to go for a special lunch or dinner. The food is still very good—which is why tour groups have, alas, discovered it. Still, it's always pleasant to walk down the passageway into Gerofinikas ("the old palm tree"), look at the long display cases of tempting dishes and try to decide between the shrimp with feta cheese, the rabbit stew with onions, and the tasty eggplant dishes—all the while saving room for one of Gerofinikas's rich desserts. The fixed-price menu is good value—but this is a place where choosing what to order is half the fun.

INEXPENSIVE

Neon. Odos Mitropoleos 3 (on the southwest corner of Syntagma Sq.). ☎ **01/322-8155.** Snacks Dr200–Dr650 (60¢–$1.90); sandwiches Dr700–Dr1,400 ($2–$4); main courses Dr1,000–Dr4,200 ($2.90–$12). No credit cards. Daily 9am–midnight. GREEK/INTERNATIONAL.

This new addition to the Neon chain is convenient, although not as charming as the original on Omonia Square. You're sure to find something to your taste—maybe a Mexican omelet, spaghetti Bolognese, the salad bar, or sweets ranging from Black Forest cake to tiramisu. If you're tired of practicing your restaurant Greek, this is a good place to eat, since most things are self-service.

KOLONAKI
MODERATE

Dimokritos. Odos Dimokritou 23 and Tsakalof. ☎ **01/361-3588.** Fax 01/361-9293. Main courses Dr4,700–Dr5,500 ($14–$16). No credit cards. Mon–Sat 1–5pm and 8pm–1am. GREEK.

Quick Bites in Syntagma

In general, Syntagma Square is not known for good food, but there are a number of places in the area to get a snack. The **Apollonion Bakery,** Odos Nikis 10, and the **Elleniki Gonia,** Odos Karayioryi Servias 10, make sandwiches to order and sell croissants, both stuffed and plain. **Ariston** is a small chain of *zaharoplastia* (confectioners) with a branch at the corner of Karayioryi Servias and Voulis (just off Syntagma Square) selling snacks as well as pastries. **Floca** is another excellent pastry-shop chain; look in the arcade on Panepistimiou near Syntagma Square. As always, you pay extra to be served at one of the tables.

For the quintessentially Greek *loukoumades* (round donut-center-like pastries that are deep-fried, then drenched with honey and topped with powdered sugar and cinnamon), nothing beats **Doris,** Odos Praxitelous 30, a continuation of Odos Lekka, a few blocks from Syntagma Square. If you're still hungry, Doris serves hearty stews and pasta dishes for absurdly low prices Monday through Saturday until 3:30pm. **Everest** is another chain worth trying; there's one a block north of Kolonaki Square at Tsakalof and Iraklitou. Also in Kolonaki Square, **To Kotopolo** serves succulent grilled chicken to take out or eat in. In the Plaka, the **K. Kotsolis Pastry Shop,** Odos Adrianou 112, serving excellent coffee and sweets, is an oasis of old-fashioned charm in the midst of the souvenir shops. The **Oraia Ellada** ("Beautiful Greece") cafe at the Center of Hellenic Tradition, opening onto both Odos Pandrossou 36 and Odos Mitropoleos 59 near the flea market, has a spectacular view of the Acropolis. You can revive yourself here with a cappuccino and a few pastries.

Overlooking the Church of Ayios Dionysios, this cozy taverna—only the word TAVERNA on the door tells you this is a restaurant—serves good food to lots of steady customers. The large menu features grilled veal and veal with *hilopites* (a tiny pasta), rabbit, fish, and lamb, and often excellent swordfish souvlaki. A variety of Greek salads and hors d'oeuvres are usually on display in a case by the entrance, and you can usually point out what you want for starters on your way to your table.

✪ **To Kafeneio.** Odos Loukianou 26. ☎ **01/722-9056.** Main courses Dr2,000–Dr7,000 ($6–$20). No credit cards. Mon–Sat 11am–midnight or later. From Kolonaki Sq., follow Odos Patriarkou Ioakim several blocks uphill to Loukianou and turn right. GREEK/INTERNATIONAL.

This is hardly a typical rough-and-ready Kafeneio (coffeeshop/cafe): There are pictures on the walls, pink tablecloths on the tables, and a clientele of ladies who lunch, as well as staff from the many embassies located in Kolonaki. In short, it's a great people-watching place, where you can easily run up a substantial tab, but where you will also eat elegantly. Try the artichokes à la polita (tender artichokes flanked by carrots and potatoes in an egg-lemon sauce) or leeks in crème fraîche, washed down with draft beer or the house wine—and save room for the delectable profiteroles. We've always found this an especially congenial spot when dining alone (perhaps because we love people-watching and profiteroles).

To Ouzadiko. Odos Karneadou 25–29 (in the Lemos International Shopping Center). ☎ **01/729/5484.** Mezedes and main courses Dr2,300–Dr5,000 ($7–$14). No credit cards. Mon–Sat 9pm–12:30am. GREEK.

This trendy ouzo bar has at least 40 kinds of ouzo and as many mezedes, including fluffy *keftedes* (meatballs) that make all others taste leaden. If you can find a seat here, this is a great place for a snack or a full meal, but not a tête-à-tête: The tables are close together and intimate conversation is not easy. A serious foodie friend of mine comes here especially for the wide variety of *horta* (greens), which she says are the best she's ever tasted.

To Prytaneion. Milioni 7. ☎ **01/364-3353-4.** Mezedes and snacks Dr2,000–Dr7,000 ($6–$20). No credit cards. Mon–Sat 10am–3am. GREEK/INTERNATIONAL.

The trendy bare stone walls here are decorated with movie posters and illuminated by baby spotlights. Waiters dressed mostly in black serve customers glued to cellular phones some of Athens's most expensive and eclectic mezedes, including beef carpaccio, smoked salmon, bruschetta, and shrimps in fresh cream, as well as Greek olives and that international favorite, the hamburger.

Rhodia. Odos Aristipou 44. ☎ **01/722-9883.** Main courses Dr2,000–Dr4,200 ($6–$12). No credit cards. Mon–Sat 8pm–2am. GREEK.

This long-time taverna in a handsome old Kolonaki house has tables in its small garden in good weather—although the interior, with its tile floor and old prints, is so charming that you might be tempted to eat indoors. The Rodia is a favorite of visiting archaeologists from the nearby British and American Schools of Classical Studies, as well as of Kolonaki residents. It may not sound like just what you'd always hoped to have for dinner, but the octopus in mustard sauce is terrific, as are the veal and *dolmades* (stuffed grape leaves) in egg-lemon sauce. The house wine is excellent, as is the halva, which manages to be both creamy and crunchy.

INEXPENSIVE

Neon. Odos Tsakalof 6, Kolonaki Sq. ☎ **01/364-6873.** Snacks Dr200–Dr650 (60¢–$1.90); sandwiches Dr700–Dr1,400 ($2–$4); main courses Dr1,000–Dr4,200 ($2.90–$12). No credit cards. Daily 9am–midnight. GREEK/INTERNATIONAL.

The Kolonaki Neon serves the same food as the Syntagma and Omonia branches, but the reasonable prices are especially welcome in this pricey neighborhood. Tsakalof is a shady pedestrian arcade, and the Neon has tables inside and outdoors.

OMONIA SQUARE & UNIVERSITY AREA (NEAR EXARCHIA SQUARE/ARCHAEOLOGICAL MUSEUM)
EXPENSIVE

✪ **Kostoyannis.** Odos Zaimi 37 (2 blocks behind the Archaeological Museum). ☎ **01/822-0624.** Main courses Dr2,500–Dr8,000 ($7–$23). No credit cards. Mon–Sat 8pm–2am. GREEK.

It's not easy to simply walk into Kostoyannis and sit down: Just inside the entrance is a show-stopping display of shrimp, mussels, fresh fish, seemingly endless appetizers, tempting stews in ceramic pots, and yards of chops. Choose the items you'd like to sample—you may decide to make an entire meal just from the mezedes, which we think are even better than the entrees. Don't be put off by this restaurant's slightly out-of-the-way location on a rather uninteresting street: It's well worth the trip.

MODERATE

✪ **Athinaikon.** Themistokleous 2, Omonia. ☎ **01/383-8485.** Main courses Dr1,000–Dr4,500 ($2.90–$13). No credit cards. Mon–Sat 11am–midnight. Closed Aug. GREEK.

This is a favorite haunt of lawyers and businesspeople working in the Omonia Square area. You can have just some appetizers (technically, this is an *ouzeri*) or a full meal. Obviously, the way to have a reasonably priced snack is to stick to the appetizers, including delicious *loukanika* (sausages) and *keftedes* (meatballs) and pass on the more pricy grilled shrimp or seafood casserole. Whatever you have, you'll enjoy taking in the old photos on the walls, the handsome tiled floor, and the marble topped tables and bentwood chairs.

INEXPENSIVE

Neon. Dorou 1, Omonia Sq. ☎ **01/522-9939.** Snacks Dr200–Dr650 (60¢–$1.90); sandwiches Dr700–Dr1,400 ($2–$4); main courses Dr1,000–Dr4,200 ($2.90–$12). No credit cards. Daily 9am–midnight. GREEK/INTERNATIONAL.

In a handsome 1920s building, the Neon serves up cafeteria-style food, including cooked-to-order pasta, omelets, and grills, as well as salads and sweets. Equally good for a meal or a snack, the Neon proves that fast food doesn't have to be junk food.

Taygetos. Odos Satovriandou 4. ☎ **01/523-5352.** Main courses Dr1,500–Dr3,000 ($4.30–$9). No credit cards. Mon–Sat 9am–1am. GREEK/SOUVLAKI.

This is a great place to stop on your way to or from the museum. Service is swift, and the souvlaki and fried potatoes are excellent, as are the grilled lamb and chicken (priced by the kilo). The menu has sometimes included delicious *kokoretsi* (grilled entrails), but Common Market regulations threaten to make this a thing of the past. The **Ellinikon Restaurant** next door is also a good value.

METS
VERY EXPENSIVE

✪ **Bajazzo.** At Odos Tyrteou 1 and Odos Anapafseos 14. ☎ and fax **01/921-3013.** Reservations required Fri–Sat, and always a good idea. Dinner for 2 from Dr52,500 ($151). AE, DC, MC, V. Mon–Sat 8pm–1am. INTERNATIONAL.

Bajazzo put Greek cuisine on the map when it won its Michelin star in 1998. Chef Klaus Feuerbach's specialties include a feta tart, langostino souvlaki, kid with Peloponnesian herbs, and sea bass with mustard sauce—perhaps not all to be eaten at one sitting. The menu changes from night to night, so part of the fun is finding out what's being prepared on any given evening.

Myrtia. Odos Trivonianou 32–34. ☎ **01/924-7175.** Reservations recommended. Fixed-price menu Dr15,000–Dr22,500 ($43–$64). AE, DC, EC, MC, V. Mon–Sat 8:30pm–2am. Closed Aug. GREEK.

The Myrtia is a bit too kitschy for our taste, but lots of visitors love this famous fixed-menu taverna, up the hill behind the Olympic Stadium in Mets. The atmosphere, with strolling musicians, is either charmingly bucolic or a bit artificial, depending on your frame of mind. You'll be served a full array of mezedes, tender roast chicken, delicious lamb, fruit, sweets, various wines, and much more—all you can eat (and all you can drink of the house wine)—although there are rumors that this may change.

MODERATE

Manesis. Markou Mouzourou 3. ☎ **01/922-7684.** Main courses Dr2,500–Dr5,200 ($7–$15). No credit cards. Daily about 7pm–midnight. GREEK.

This longtime favorite, with a pleasant garden and wide range of delicious mezedes, continues to be popular with locals, and increasingly attracts visitors (including the occasional tour group). The swordfish souvlaki here is usually excellent, the *loukanika* (sausage) tasty, and the stews nicely seasoned with dill and lemon. The basic menu hasn't changed in years, although more nonmeat dishes have been added, including an excellent, creamy hummus.

KOUKAKI & MAKRIYANNI (NEAR THE ACROPOLIS)

See the "Accommodations & Dining South of the Acropolis" map on p. 115 to locate these restaurants.

MODERATE

✪ **Socrates's Prison.** Odos Mitseon 20. ☎ **01/922-3434.** Main courses Dr3,000–Dr4,500 ($9–$13). MC, V. Mon–Sat 11am-4pm; 7pm–1am. Closed Aug. GREEK.

This is a favorite with both Greeks and American and European expatriates living in Athens, who lounge at tables outdoors in good weather and in the pleasant indoor rooms year-round. Some long tables are communal, and there are also tables for four. The food here is noticeably more imaginative than average Greek taverna fare (try the veggie croquettes), and includes continental dishes such as salade niçoise and pork roll stuffed with vegetables. The retsina is excellent, and there's a wide choice of bottled wines and beers. This is a good place to head if you don't want to eat in the Plaka, but enjoy strolling through it on your way to or from dinner.

Strofi Tavern. Odos Rovertou Galli 25, Makriyanni. ☎ **01/921-4130.** Reservations recommended. Main courses Dr3,500–Dr4,500 ($10–$13). DC, MC, V. Mon–Sat 8pm–2am. Located 2 blocks south of Acropolis. GREEK.

The Strofi serves standard Greek taverna fare (although the *mezedes* are especially good here), but the view of the Acropolis is so terrific that everything tastes particularly good. Keep this place in mind if you're staying south of the Acropolis, an area that is not packed with restaurants. Strofi is popular with the after-theater crowd that pours out of the nearby Herodes Atticus theater during the Athens Festival.

Symbosio. Odos Erechthiou 46. ☎ **01/922-5321.** Fax 01/923-2780. Main courses Dr2,500–Dr8,000 ($7–$23). AE, MC, V. Mon–Sat about 8pm–midnight. Usually closed second half of Aug; sometimes closed in Jan. ELEGANT GREEK/CONTINENTAL.

This is a very pretty place to eat: a lovingly cared for 1920s Makriyanni town house with its own garden. The food, although delicious, can be fussy, with a bit too much lily gilding and use of sauces. That said, friends of ours make a point of eating here every time they get to Athens, and swear by the mezedes, the quality of the fish, the delicate seasonings used in meat dishes, the fresh veggies, and the excellent wine list.

HERE & THERE—AND WORTH THE JOURNEY

Archeon Gefsis. Odos Kodratou 22, Karaiskaki Square. ☎ **01/523-9661.** Main courses Dr3,000–Dr7,000 ($9–$20). AE, DC, MC, V. Mon–Sat 8pm–midnight. ANCIENT GREEK.

This restaurant, which attempts to recreate ancient Greek cooking, seems to be a place people either love or hate. If you think you'd like to be served piglet stuffed with game, eggs, cheese, fried liver, chestnuts, apples, and pine nuts by waiters in togas (wasn't that what the Romans wore?), then this is the place for you. You can recline while eating, as at a symposium, and use a spoon instead of an anachronistic fork. If you enjoy the experience, you can seek out others in this chain—the first modern ancient food chain—on Mykonos and Cyprus.

AristeraDexia. Andronkou 3, Gazi. ☎ **01/342-2380.** Reservations recommended. Main courses Dr4,000–Dr10,000 ($11–$29). AE, V. Mon–Sat 9pm–1am.

Gazi, the district best known as the home of Athens's gasworks, is following in Psirri's fashionable footsteps. Certainly, AristeraDexia was all the rage in 2000, with its glass catwalk over the wine cellar, open kitchen, and endless small tables packed with hipsters with cell phones. As for the food, it draws on traditional Greek flavors and ingredients, but combines them in unusual ways. The menu is always changing, but has

Rising Stars in the Psirri District

It's hard to keep up with the cafes, bars, restaurants, and galleries opening in the newly fashionable Psirri district, between Odos Ermou and Odos Athinas. Until about 5 years ago, this was a neighborhood with derelict warehouses and tumbledown houses. The low rents prompted young would-be restaurateurs and gallery owners to renovate neglected buildings. You'll see lots of bare brick walls, minimalist decor, and *tons* of yuppies here, especially after dark.

The drop-dead fashionable **Vitrina,** Odos Navarchou Apostoli 7 (☎ **01/ 321-1200**), was one of the first to open its doors in Psirri. The walls are pale gold, the tablecloths and chairs are pale gray, and many of the pale young waiters and waitresses are aspiring actors and writers. The kitchen seems to try too hard (shrimp in muscatel and lavender sauce, for example), but the nouvelle Greek food is usually both delicious and beautifully presented, and there's a serious wine list. The early birds arrive around 10pm, with most of the crowd showing up considerably later. Definitely make reservations.

Other eateries include **Taki 13,** Odos Taki 13 (☎ **01/325-4707**), where the food is less the thing than the bar, the music, and the stylish young Athenians who gather here; and **Zeidoron,** Odos Taki 10 and Ayios Anaryiron (☎ **01/ 321-5368**), which is basically a *mezedopolio* (hors d'oeuvres place) although it also serves entrees. The *mezedes* are also delicious at **To Krasopoulio tou Kokkora,** Karaiskaki and Aisopou 4 (☎ **01/321-1565**), where you can dine indoors or out. At **Couzina Cine-Psyrri,** Odos Sarri 40 (☎ **01/321-5534**), you can eat and (in summer) watch a movie on an outdoor screen.

As for Psirri's galleries, many stay open late, which means that you can eat and browse—or browse and eat. **Epistrofi,** Odos Taki 6–8 (☎ **01/321-8640;** www.epistrofi.gr), is worth a visit just to see the handsomely restored early-19th-century town house it occupies—and it sometimes hosts concerts as well as art exhibitions. **Stigma,** Odos Agios Anargyros 20–22 (☎ **01/322-1675**), features frequent shows of local artists.

---

recently included crayfish dressed with lavender, sweet moschato wine, and squid in egg lemon sauce.

Kalliste. Odos Asklepiou 137, off Odos Akadimias above the University of Athens. ☎ **01/645-3179.** Reservations recommended. Main courses Dr3,300–Dr6,500 ($10–$19). No credit cards. Mon–Sat about noon–2pm and 8pm–midnight. ELEGANT GREEK.

In a beautifully restored 19th-century house with polished wooden floors and ornamental plaster ceilings, Kalliste manages to be both cozy and elegant. The menu features traditional dishes with a distinctive flair, such as lentil soup with pomegranate, and chicken with hazelnuts and celery purée. Even that old standby crème caramel is enlivened by the addition of rose liqueur.

✪ **Varoulko.** Deligeorgi 14, Piraeus. ☎ **01/411-2043.** Fax 01/422-1283. Reservations necessary (arrange several days in advance). Dinner for 2 from Dr35,000 ($99); fish priced by the kilo. No credit cards. Mon–Sat about 8pm–midnight. SEAFOOD/NOUVELLE.

In a most unlikely location on a side street in Piraeus, chef/owner Lefteris Lazarou has created what many consider not just the finest restaurant serving only seafood, but the finest restaurant in the greater Athens area. We had one of the best meals of our lives here, tasting smoked eel, artichokes with fish roe, crayfish with sun-dried tomatoes, monkfish livers with soy sauce, honey, and basalmic vinegar—and the best sea bass and monkfish we have ever eaten. Everything is beautifully presented, but nothing is fussy—and it's all delicious. We liked the austere brick walls enlivened by paintings of the old warehouse that Varoulko inhabits, although some find the style a bit too understated.

✪ **Vlassis.** Odos Paster 8 (off Plateia Mavili in the Ilissia district). ☎ **01/646-3060** or 01/642-5337. Reservations necessary. Main courses Dr2,000–Dr5,000 ($6–$14). No credit cards. Mon–Sat about 7pm–midnight. Closed much of June–Sept. TRADITIONAL GREEK.

Greeks call this kind of food *paradisiako* (traditional), but paradisiacal is just as good a description. This is traditional food fit for the gods: delicious fluffy vegetable croquettes, eggplant salad that tastes like no other eggplant salad you've had, hauntingly tender lamb in egg lemon sauce. It's a sign of Vlassis's popularity with Athenians—the last time we ate there, we were the only obvious foreigners in the place—that there's not even a discreet sign announcing its presence in a small apartment building on hard-to-find Odos Paster. Take a taxi; you may feel so giddy with delight after eating that you won't mind the half-hour walk back to Syntagma Square.

Exploring Athens

5

by Sherry Marker

It's quite likely that you'll arrive in Athens in the late afternoon, groggy and disoriented after a seriously long flight. The ride into town from the airport is unlikely to help your spirits: You'll creep through Athens's ferocious traffic along an outstandingly ugly road lined with garish furniture and chandelier shops. Somewhere, you know, not far away, must be the blue Aegean and the lofty Acropolis. But where? Surrounded by cars that are either stuck in gridlock or maniacally racing along a three-lane highway with no observable (or observed) lanes, deafened by the explosions of hordes of mufflerless kamikaze motorcycles, you'll almost certainly be considering asking your cab driver to make a U-turn and take you back to the airport.

Don't despair. When you get to your hotel, jump in the shower, take a nap, and then set off for an evening stroll through **Syntagma (Constitution) Square** past the House of Parliament (now with its own Web site, www.parliament.gr). Take a few minutes to explore Syntagma's handsome new marble Metro station, with its display of finds from the excavations here. If it's warm out, escape into the shade of the **National Garden,** and join the Athenians feeding pigeons. Then head into the **Plaka,** the old neighborhood on the slopes of the Acropolis that has more restaurants, cafes, and souvenir shops than private homes. If you get off the Plaka's main drags, Kidathineon and Adrianou, and follow one of the streets such as Thespidos that run up the slope of the Acropolis, you'll find yourself in **Anafiotika.** This Plaka district, built in the 19th century by immigrants from the Cycladic island of Anafi, retains much of its old village character. From time to time as you stroll, look up: You're bound to see the Acropolis, probably floodlit, and the best possible reminder of why you came.

After you have your first Greek meal, perhaps washed down with some astringent retsina wine, head back to your hotel and get a good night's sleep so that you'll be ready for your first real day in Athens.

Suggested Itineraries for First-Time Visitors

If You Have 1 Day

Something to check as soon as you arrive: For the last several years, most major attractions have remained open in the summer until 7pm. If this plan remains in effect, you'll have a lot of extra opportunities to see the sites and museums that otherwise close in mid-afternoon.

Athens Attractions

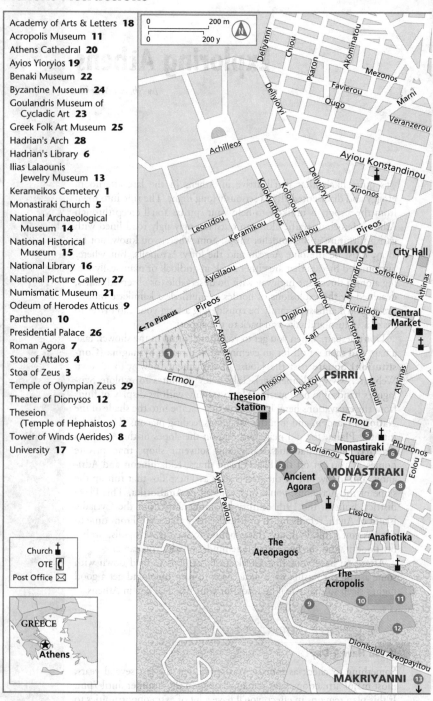

Church †
OTE **C**
Post Office ✉

GREECE
★ Athens

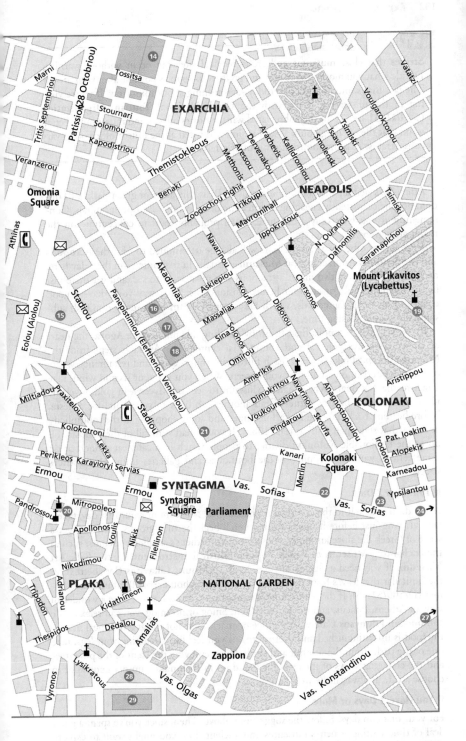

EXARCHIA

Tossitsa

Marni
Tritis Septembriou
Patission(28 Octobriou)
Stournari
Solomou
Kapodistriou
Themistokleous
Veranzerou
Benaki
Omonia
Square
Zoodochou Pighis
Trikoupi
Mavromihali
Ippokratous

Arachevis
Dervenakou
Aressou
Methonis
Kallidromiou
Tsimiski
Isavron
Smolenski
Voulgaroktonou
Vatatzi

NEAPOLIS

N. Ouranou
Dafnomilis
Tsimiski
Sarantapichou

Athinas
Akadimias
Navarinou
Asklepiou
Skoufa
Massalias
Solonos
Sina
Omirou
Amerikis
Panepistimiou (Eleftheriou Venizelou)
Stadiou
Didotou
Chersonos

Eolou (Aiolou)
Stadiou
Miltiadou Praxitelous
Kolokotroni
Lekka
Perikleos Karayioryi Servias
Ermou

Mount Likavitos
(Lycabettus)

Aristippou

KOLONAKI

Dimokritou
Navarinou
Voukourestiou
Skoufa
Pindarou
Anagnostopoulou

Pat. Ioakim
Irodotou
Alopekis
Karneadou
Ypsilantou

Kanari
Merlin
Kolonaki
Square

SYNTAGMA
Ermou
Syntagma
Square
Parliament
Vas. Sofias
Vas. Sofias

Pandrossou
Mitropoleos
Apollonos
Voulis
Nikis
Filellinon
Nikodimou

PLAKA

Kidathineon
Adrianou
Tripodon
Thespidos
Dedalou
Amalias
Vyronos
Lysikratous

NATIONAL GARDEN

Zappion

Vas. Olgas
Vas. Konstandinou

14
15
16
17
18
19
20
21
22
23
24
25
26
27
28
29

An Important Warning

Strikes that close museums and archaeological sites can occur without warning. Decide what you most want to see, and go there as soon as possible after your arrival. The fact that something is open today says nothing about tomorrow. If you're visiting in the off-season, check with the **Greek National Tourism Organization** (☎ 01/331-0437) for the abbreviated **winter hours** of sites and museums. Keep in mind that the opening hours posted at sites and listed at the tourist office often vary considerably. Alas, no information is utterly reliable.

Athens has neither the grand boulevards of Paris, the acres of green parks of London, nor the consistently engaging architecture of most other European capitals. Consequently, if you have only a day here, you'll probably want to concentrate on the major attractions.

Since lots of other first-time visitors will also be determined to "do" the **Acropolis** and the **National Archaeological Museum**—usually in that order—in their day here, decide which of these two major attractions you most want to see, and get there just before opening time, or an hour before closing time. That way you'll have a good chance of escaping the crowds, which take over by 10am but usually diminish substantially toward closing time.

If you visit the Acropolis first, finish by strolling downhill to the **Agora,** the heart of ancient Athens's political and commercial center. The Agora is steps from the **Monastiraki** and **Plaka** districts, each filled with shops, cafes, and restaurants, where over lunch you can digest all that you've seen. When you get your second wind, take a taxi to the National Archaeological Museum to see the Mycenaean gold, Cycladic idols, and classical bronze statues. Grab another cab back to your hotel for a siesta, before heading back into the Plaka for dinner and some shopping at the multiplicity of stores that stay open until at least 10pm. If you've had your fill of the Plaka, stroll up to the fashionable **Kolonaki** district to people-watch in a cafe, eat dinner, or do some serious window-shopping at the boutiques and galleries lining the district's streets.

If You Have 2 Days

If you didn't make it to the National Archaeological Museum on your first day, take a taxi, arriving just before it opens so that you'll beat the tour groups. Then, to get a sense of Greek life since antiquity, take in some of Athens's smaller museums, such as the enchanting **Museum of Greek Popular Musical Instruments** or the **Folk Art Museum.** If you need a change of pace, head up **Mount Likavitos** (Lycabettus) on the funicular that leaves from the top of Odos Ploutarchou every 20 minutes in summer (Dr500/$1.45). If the habitual *nefos* (smog) isn't too bad, you'll have a wonderful view of Athens, Piraeus, and the Saronic Gulf. Smog or no smog, you can relax at the summit-top **Dionysos Café** with a coffee or snack (best not to eat a full meal here—the food is undistinguished and overpriced). If you feel like stretching your legs, take one of the paths from the summit and stroll down, enjoying the scent of the pine trees and the changing views of the city. You'll end up in **Kolonaki**, another good spot to choose a cafe and watch the world go by.

If You Have 3 Days or More

For your first two days, follow the suggestions above. Then, since you've spent a good deal of time visiting Athens's museums and ancient sites, you might want to explore the city. If you want to see how Athens is fed, head to the **Central Market,** on Odos

Athinas, and wander through the fish and meat halls before having a coffee and (if you're in the mood) a bowl of tripe stew at **Papandreou,** a hole-in-the-wall restaurant where the butcher, the baker, and the office worker all meet to eat (see p. 121). If tripe stew isn't your snack of choice, you may prefer to head to **Zonar's,** the venerable sweet shop and restaurant on Odos Panepistimiou, where you can spy on elegant matrons reviving themselves with cups of tea after the exertions of their shopping expeditions. Then you can wander through the **National Garden,** watching Greek toddlers watching the ducks and peacocks in the small zoo. If your conscience begins to bother you at this point, head back into the Plaka and visit the **Roman Agora** or ancient Athens's cemetery, the **Kerameikos,** with its handsome marble funerary monuments.

If a day wandering Athens is too unstructured for your tastes, consider taking a day trip to one of the great sites of antiquity, such as **Delphi** (see p. 411) or **Sounion** (see p. 149). You can even go on a dawn-to-dusk whirlwind day trip to **Corinth, Mycenae,** and **Epidaurus** (best done on a bus tour). If you've had your fill of ancient monuments, visit the Byzantine monasteries of **Daphni** (see p. 169) or **Kaisariani** (see p. 165).

If you don't want to leave Athens without seeing one of the "isles of Greece," you can take a day trip by boat from Piraeus to one or more of the islands of the Saronic Gulf. **Aegina** (Egina), **Poros,** and **Hydra** (Idra) are all feasible day trips—all covered in chapter 6—but best not done the day before you leave Athens, lest bad weather strand you on an island. Whatever you do, be sure to give yourself time to sit in cafes and watch the world go by.

1 The Top Attractions

✪ The Acropolis. ☎ 01/321-0219. Admission Dr2,000 ($6) adults, or Dr4,000 ($11) with combined admission to National Archaeological Museum. Free on Sun. Admission includes entrance to the Acropolis Museum, which sometimes closes earlier than the site. Summer Mon–Fri 8am–6pm; Sat–Sun and holidays 8:30am–3pm (sometimes to 6pm). You can reach the path up to the ticket booth and thence to the entrance for the Acropolis by following Dionissiou Areopayitou or Odos Theorias, or the path up through the Ancient Agora.

The Acropolis is one of a handful of places in the world that are so well known it's hard not to be nervous when you finally get here. Will it be as beautiful as its photographs? Will it be, ever so slightly, a disappointment? Rest assured: The Acropolis does not disappoint—but it usually *is* infuriatingly crowded. What you want here is some time—time to watch as the columns of the Parthenon appear first beige, then golden, then rose, then stark white in changing light; time to stand on the Belvedere and take in the view over Athens (and listen for the muted sounds of conversations floating up from the Plaka); time to think of all those who have been here before you.

When you climb up the Acropolis—the heights above the city—you know that you're on your way to see Greece's most famous temple, the **Parthenon**. What you may not know is that people lived on the Acropolis as early as 5,000 B.C. The Acropolis's sheer sides made a superb natural defense, just the place to avoid enemies and be able to see any invaders coming across the sea or the plains of Attica. And, of course, it helped that in antiquity there was a spring here.

In classical times, when Athens's population had grown to around 250,000, people moved down from the Acropolis, which had become the city's most important religious center. The city's **civic and business center**—the **Agora**—and its **cultural center,** with several theaters and concert halls, bracketed the Acropolis. When you peer over the sides of the Acropolis at the houses in the Plaka, and the remains of the ancient Agora and the theater of Dionysos, you'll see the layout of the ancient city. Syntagma and Omonia squares, the heart of today's Athens, were well out of the ancient city center.

Even the Acropolis's superb heights couldn't protect it from the Persian invasion of 480 B.C., when most of its monuments were burned and destroyed. You may notice some immense column drums built into the Acropolis's walls. When the great Athenian statesman Pericles ordered the monuments of the Acropolis rebuilt, he had these drums from the destroyed Parthenon built into the walls lest Athenians forget what had happened—and so they would remember that they had rebuilt what they had lost. Pericles's rebuilding program began about 448 B.C.; the new Parthenon was dedicated 10 years later, but work on other monuments continued for a century.

As you enter the Acropolis, you'll first go through the **Beulé Gate,** built by the Romans, and named for the French archaeologist who discovered it in 1852. After that, you'll pass through the **Propylaia,** the monumental 5th-century B.C. entranceway. It's characteristic of the Roman mania for building that they found it necessary to build an entranceway to an entranceway!

Just above the Propylaia is the little temple of **Athena Nike** (Athena of Victory); this beautifully proportioned Ionic temple was built in 424 B.C.and heavily restored in the 1930s. To the left of the Parthenon is the **Erechtheion,** which the Athenians honored as the tomb of Erechtheus, a legendary king of Athens. A hole in the ceiling and floor of the northern porch indicates the spot where Poseidon's trident struck to make a spring gush forth during his contest with Athena to have the city named in his honor. Athena countered with an olive tree; the olive tree planted beside the Erechtheion reminds visitors of her victory—as, of course, does Athens's name.

Give yourself a little time to enjoy the delicate carving on the Erechtheion, and be sure to see the original **Caryatids** in the Acropolis Museum. The Caryatids presently holding up the porch of the Erechtheion are the casts put there when the originals were moved to prevent further erosion by Athens's acid *nefos* (smog).

However charmed you are by these elegant little temples, you're probably still heading resolutely toward the **Parthenon,** dedicated to Athena Parthenos (Athena the Virgin), patron goddess of Athens, and, of course, the most important religious shrine here. You may be disappointed to realize that visitors are not allowed inside, both to protect the monument and to allow restoration work to proceed safely. If you find this frustrating, keep in mind that in antiquity only priests and honored visitors were allowed in to see the monumental—some 36 feet tall—statue of Athena designed by the great Phidias, who supervised Pericles's building program. Nothing of the huge gold-and-ivory statue remains, but there's a small Roman copy in the National Archaeological Museum—and horrific renditions on souvenirs ranging from T-shirts to ouzo bottles. Admittedly, the gold-and-ivory statue was not understated; the 2nd-century A.D. traveler Pausanias, one of the first guidebook writers, recorded that the statue stood "upright in an ankle-length tunic with a head of Medusa carved in ivory on her breast. She has a Victory about 8 feet high, and a spear in her hand and a shield at her feet, with a snake beside the shield, possibly representing Erechtheus."

If you look over the edge of the Acropolis toward the **Temple of Hephaistos** (now called the **Theseion**) in the ancient Agora, and then at the Parthenon, you can't help but be struck by how much lighter and more graceful the Parthenon is. Scholars tell us that this is because Ictinus, the architect of the Parthenon, was something of a

For the past couple of years, 55 ancient sites throughout Greece—including, of course, the Acropolis—were open to the public on the night of the August full moon. The Culture Ministry plans to do this every August—and even stage free concerts at some of the moonlit sites.

magician of optical illusions. The columns and stairs—the very floor—of the Parthenon all appear straight because all are minutely curved. The exterior columns are slightly thicker in the middle (a device known as *entasis*), which makes the entire column appear straight. That's why the Parthenon, with 17 columns on each side and eight at each end (creating an exterior colonnade of 46 relatively slender columns), looks so graceful, while the Temple of Hephaistos, with only six columns at each end and 13 along each side, seems so squat and stolid.

Of course, one reason the Parthenon looks so airy is that it is, quite literally, open to the air. The Parthenon's entire roof and much of its interior were blown to smithereens in 1687, when the Venetians attempted to capture the Acropolis from the Turks. A shell fired from nearby Mouseion Hill struck the Parthenon—where the Turks were storing gunpowder and munitions—and caused appalling damage to the building and its sculptures. Most of the remaining sculptures were carted off to London by Lord Elgin in the early 19th century. Those surviving sculptures—known as the **Elgin Marbles**—are on display in the British Museum, causing ongoing pain to generations of Greeks, who continue to press for their return. Things heated up again in the summer of 1988, when English historian William St. Clair's book *Lord Elgin and the Marbles* received a lot of publicity. According to St. Clair, the British Museum "over-cleaned" the marbles in the 1930s, removing not only the outer patina, but also many sculptural details. The museum countered by saying that the damage wasn't all that bad—and that the marbles would remain in London.

The Parthenon originally had sculpture on both of its pediments, as well as a frieze running around the entire temple. The frieze was made up of alternating **triglyphs** (panels with three incised grooves) and **metopes** (sculptured panels). The east pediment showed scenes from the birth of Athena, while the west pediment showed Athena and Poseidon's contest for possession of Athens. The long frieze showed the battle of the Athenians against the Amazons, scenes from the Trojan war, and the struggles of the Olympian gods against giants and centaurs. The message of most of this sculpture was the triumph of knowledge and civilization—that is, Athens—over the forces of darkness and barbarians. An interior frieze showed scenes from the Panathenaic Festival each August, when citizens processed through the streets, bringing a new tunic for the statue of Athena. Only a few fragments of any of these sculptures remain in place, and visitors will have to decide for themselves whether it's a good or a bad thing that Lord Elgin removed so much before the smog became endemic in Athens and ate away much of what he left here.

If you're lucky enough to visit the Acropolis on a smog-free and sunny day, you'll see the gold and cream tones of the Parthenon's handsome Pentelic marble at their most subtle. It may come as something of a shock to realize that in antiquity, the Parthenon—like most other monuments here—was painted in gay colors that have since faded, revealing the natural marble. If it's a clear day, you'll also get a superb view of Athens from the Belvedere at the east end of the Acropolis.

Near the Belvedere, the **Acropolis Archaeological Museum** hugs the ground to detract as little as possible from the ancient monuments. Inside, you'll see the four original Caryatids from the Erechtheion still in Athens (one disappeared during the Ottoman occupation and one is in the British Museum). Other delights statues of smiling *korai* (maidens) and *kouroi* (young men). You'll have to decide whether you find their smiles insufferably smug or becomingly modest. While you're deciding, don't miss the graceful 5th-century relief called the **Mourning Athena,** the athletic **Calfbearer,** and the three-headed figure of the **Tryphon,** whose tripartite body ends in a snaky tail. You can see clear traces of the ancient paint that decorated much ancient sculpture on the Tryphon.

As you leave the Acropolis, you'll probably feel that you've seen a great many monuments. In fact, almost all of what you've seen comes from Athens's heyday in the mid-5th-century B.C., when Pericles rebuilt what the Persians destroyed. In the following centuries, every invader who came built monuments, most of which were resolutely destroyed by the next wave of invaders. If you had been here a century ago, you could have seen the remains of mosques and churches, plus a Frankish bell tower. The great archaeologist Schliemann, the discoverer of Troy and excavator of Mycenae, was so offended by the bell tower that he paid to have it torn down.

If you'd like to know more about the Acropolis and its history, as well as the Elgin Marbles controversy, you can check to see whether the **Center for Acropolis Studies,** on Odos Makriyanni just southeast of the Acropolis (☎ **01/923-9381**), is open (usually from 9am to 2:30pm; admission is free). The center has been shut intermittently since excavations in 1998 for the adjacent new **museum** unearthed important Byzantine antiquities. The center houses artifacts, reconstructions, photographs, drawings, and plaster casts of the Elgin Marbles.

If you find the Acropolis too crowded, you can usually get a peaceful view of its monuments from one of three nearby hills (all signposted from the Acropolis): the **Hill of the Pnyx,** where the Athenian assembly met; the **Hill of the Areopagus,** where the Athenian upper house met; and the **Hill of Filopappos** (also known as the Hill of the Muses), named after the 2nd-century A.D. philhellene Filopappos, whose funeral monument tops the hill.

✪ **Ancient Agora.** Below the Acropolis on the edge of Monastiraki (entrance on Odos Adrianou, near Ayiou Philippou Sq., east of Monastiraki Sq.). ☎ **01/321-0185.** Admission Dr1,200 ($3.45) adults, Dr900 ($2.60) seniors, Dr600 ($1.75) students. Tues–Sun 8:30am–3pm.

The Agora was Athens's commercial and civic center. Its buildings were used for a wide range of political, educational, philosophical, theatrical, and athletic purposes—which may be why it now seems such a jumble of ancient buildings, inscriptions, and fragments of sculpture. This is a nice place to wander, to enjoy the views up toward the Acropolis, and to take in the herb garden and flowers planted around the 5th-century B.C. Temple of Hephaistos and Athena (the Theseion).

Find a shady spot by the temple, sit a while, and imagine the Agora teeming with merchants, legislators, and philosophers—but very few women, who didn't often go into public places. Athens's best-known philosopher, **Socrates,** often strolled here with his disciples, including **Plato,** in the shade of the Stoa of Zeus Eleutherios, asking questions that alternately infuriated and delighted his friends. In 399 B.C., Socrates was accused of "introducing strange gods and corrupting youth," and sentenced to death. He drank his cup of hemlock in a prison in the southwest corner of the Agora—where excavators centuries later found small, clay cups, just the right size for a fatal drink. Another figure who spoke in the Agora and irritated most Athenians was **St. Paul,** who rebuked them as superstitious when he saw an inscription here to the "Unknown God."

The one monument you can't miss in the Agora is the 2nd-century B.C. **Stoa of Attalos,** built by King Attalos of Pergamon, in Asia Minor, and totally reconstructed by American archaeologists in the 1950s. (You may be grateful that they chose to include an excellent modern toilet in the stoa.) The museum in the stoa's ground floor has finds from 5,000 years of Athenian history, including sculpture and pottery, a voting machine, and a child's potty seat, all with labels in English. The stoa is open Tuesday through Sunday from 8:30am to 2:45pm.

The Acropolis & Monastiraki Square

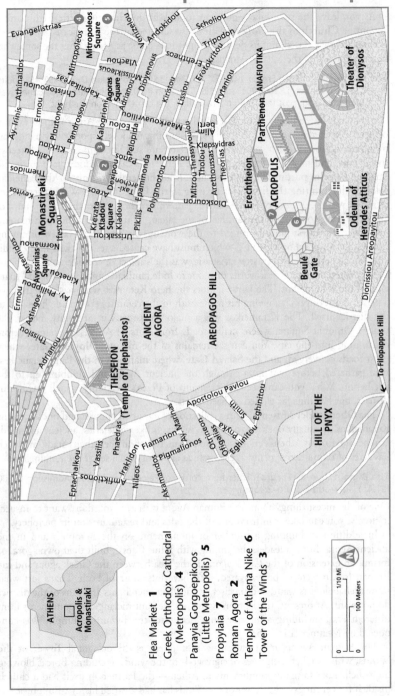

ATHENS

Acropolis & Monastiraki

Flea Market **1**
Greek Orthodox Cathedral (Metropolis) **4**
Panayia Gorgoepikoos (Little Metropolis) **5**
Propylaia **7**
Roman Agora **2**
Temple of Athena Nike **6**
Tower of the Winds **3**

0   1/10 Mi
0   100 Meters

As you leave the stoa, take a moment to look at the charming little 11th-century Byzantine **Church of the Holy Apostles,** also restored by the Americans. The church is almost always closed, but its delicate proportions come as a relief after the somewhat heartless façade of the Stoa of Attalos.

The Kerameikos. Odos Ermou 148. ☎ **01/346-3552.** Admission Dr500 ($1.45) adults, Dr400 ($1.15) seniors, Dr300 (90¢) students. Tues–Sun 8:30am–3pm. Take Odos Ermou west from Monastiraki Sq. past the Thisio metro station; the cemetery is on the right.

You may not immediately think that you'd want to visit ancient Athens's most famous cemetery, located just outside the city walls—but this is a lovely spot. Many handsome monuments from the 4th century B.C. and later are still lined up along the Street of the Tombs, and relatively few visitors come here. This can be a nice place to sit and imagine **Pericles** putting the final touches on his **Funeral Oration** for the Athenian soldiers killed during the first year's fighting in the Peloponnesian War. Athens, Pericles said, was the "school of Hellas" and a "pattern to others rather than an imitator of any." Offering comfort to the families of the fallen, he urged the widows to remember that the greatest glory belonged to the woman who was "least talked of among men either for good or for bad"—which must have caused a few snickers in the audience, since Pericles's own mistress, Aspasia, was the subject of considerable gossip.

Very often ancient Greek words turn out to hide familiar English words, and that's true of the Kerameikos. The name honors the hero Keramos, who was something of a patron saint of potters, giving his name both to the ceramics they made here and to the district itself. The Kerameikos was a major crossroads in antiquity, rather like today's Omonia Square, where major roads from outside Athens converged before continuing into the city. You can see remains of the massive **Dipylon Gate,** where most roads converged, and the **Sacred Gate,** where marchers in the Panathenaic Festival gathered before marching through the ancient Agora and climbing up to the Parthenon. What you can't see is the remains of **Plato's Academy,** which was in this district, but has thus far eluded archaeologists.

The **Oberlaender Museum,** with a collection of terra-cotta figures and finds from the Kerameikos, is usually open when the site is. If you like cemeteries, ancient and modern, be sure to visit Athens's enormous **First Cemetery,** near the Athens Stadium, which has acres of monuments, many as elaborate as anything you'll see at the Kerameikos.

The Roman Agora (Forum). Enter from corner of Pelopida and Eolou. Admission Dr500 ($1.45). Tues–Sun 8:30am–2:45pm.

One of the nicest things about the Roman Agora is that, if you don't want to inspect it closely, you can take it in from one of the cafes and restaurants on its periphery.

In addition to building a number of monuments on the Acropolis and in the ancient Agora, Roman leaders, beginning with Julius Caesar, built their own agora, or forum, an extension of the Greek agora. If the area between the Greek agora and the Roman forum were to be excavated, we'd have lots more of both. That's just what some archaeologists want, and precisely what Plaka merchants and fans of the district do not want. At present, the Roman Agora is a pleasant mélange of monuments from different eras, including a mosque built here after the Byzantine Empire was conquered by Mehmet II in 1453.

The Roman Agora's most endearing monument is the octagonal **Tower of the Winds,** with its relief sculptures of eight gods of the winds, including Boreas blowing on a shell. Like so many monuments in Athens—the Parthenon itself had a church inside it for centuries—the Tower of the Winds has had a varied history. Built by a 1st-century B.C. astronomer as a combination sundial and water-powered clock, it became a home for whirling dervishes in the 18th century. When Lord Byron visited Athens, he lodged near the tower, spending much of his time writing lovesick poetry to the beautiful "Maid of Athens."

You can usually find the remains of the Roman latrine near the Tower of the Winds by following the sound of giggles and seeing people taking pictures of each other in the seated position. The less-well-preserved remains of the enormous and once-famous **library of Emperor Hadrian** go largely unnoticed. Draw your own conclusions.

The Theater of Dionysos. Odos Dionissiou Areopayitou, on the south slope of the Acropolis. ☎ **01/322-4625.** Admission Dr500 ($1.45). Daily 8:30am–2:30pm.

This theater was built in the 4th century B.C. to replace and enlarge the earlier theater in which the plays of the great Athenian dramatists were first performed. The new theater seated some 17,000 spectators in 64 rows of seats, 20 of which survive. Most spectators sat on limestone seats—and probably envied the 67 grandees who got to sit in the handsome Pentelic marble thronelike seats in the front row. The most elegant throne belonged to the priest of Dionysos, the god of wine, revels, and theater; appropriately, carved satyrs and bunches of grapes ornament the priest's throne.

The Odeum (Odeion; also known as the Irodio) of Herodes Atticus. Odos Dionissiou Areopayitou, on the south slope of the Acropolis.

This Odeum (Music Hall) was one of an astonishing number of monuments built in Greece by the wealthy 2nd-century A.D. philhellene Herodes Atticus. If you think it looks suspiciously well preserved, you're right: It was reconstructed in the 19th century. Since the Odeum is usually closed, the best way to see it is either looking down from the Acropolis or, better yet, during one of the performances staged here during the Athens Festival each summer. If you attend a performance, bring a cushion: marble seats are as hard as you'd expect, and the cushions provided are lousy.

Hadrian's Arch. On Leoforos Amalias, near the Temple of Olympian Zeus, and easily seen from the street.

The Roman emperor Hadrian built a number of monuments in Athens, including this enormous triumphal arch with its robust, highly ornamental Corinthian columns. Although Hadrian was a philhellene, he didn't hesitate to use his arch to let the Athenians know who was boss: An inscription facing the Acropolis side reads THIS IS ATHENS, THE ANCIENT CITY OF THESEUS. On the other side it states THIS IS THE CITY OF HADRIAN, NOT OF THESEUS. Ironically, much more of ancient Athens is visible today than of Hadrian's Athens, and much of Roman Athens lies unexcavated under modern Athens.

Hadrian's Arch is still a symbolic entrance to Athens: A number of times when demonstrations blocked traffic from the airport into central Athens, our taxi driver told us that he could get us as far as Hadrian's Gate, and that we'd have to walk into town from there.

The Temple of Olympian Zeus (the Olympieion, also known as the Kolonnes [the columns]). At Leoforos Vas. Olgas and Amalias and easily seen from the street. ☎ **01/922-6330.** Admission Dr500 ($1.45). Tues–Sun 8:30am–3pm.

Hadrian also built this massive temple—or, rather, he finished the construction that had begun in the 6th century B.C. and continued on and off (more off than on) for 700 years. At 360 feet long and 143 feet wide (110m by 44m), this was one of the largest temples in the ancient world. The 13 56-foot-high Pentelic marble columns that remain standing, as well as the one sprawled on the ground, give a good idea of how impressive this forest of columns must have been—although we have a sneaking suspicion that it may be more appealing as a ruin than it ever was as a contender for the title "mother of all temples."

✪ **National Archaeological Museum.** Odos Patission 44. ☎ **01/821-7724.** Fax 01/821-3573. E-mail: protocol@eam.culture.gr. Admission Dr2,000 ($6) adults, or Dr4,000 ($12) with combined admission to the Acropolis. Mon 12:30–5pm; Tues–Fri 8am–5pm; Sat–Sun and holidays 8:30am–3pm. (The museum is sometimes open to 7pm, but you cannot count on this.) The museum is a third of a mile (10 mins. on foot) north of Omonia Sq. on the road named Leoforos 28 Octobriou but usually called Patission.

This is an enormous and enormously popular museum; try to be at the door when it opens so that you can see the exhibits, and not just the backs of other visitors. Early arrival, except in high summer, should give you at least an hour before most tour groups arrive; alternatively, get here an hour before closing or at lunchtime, when the tour groups may not be as dense. If possible, come more than once, so that your experience here is a pleasure rather than an endurance contest.

Immediately ahead of you as you enter is the **Mycenaean Hall,** with gold masks, cups, dishes, and jewelry unearthed from the site of Mycenae by Heinrich Schliemann in 1876. Many of these objects are small and delicate, and very hard to see when the gallery is crowded. Don't miss the stunning **burial mask** that Schliemann misnamed the "Mask of Agamemnon." Alas, Schliemann was wrong: Spoilsport archaeologists are sure that the mask is not Agamemnon's, but belonged to an earlier, unknown monarch. In the same gallery are the stunning **Vaphio cups,** showing mighty bulls, unearthed in a tomb at a seemingly insignificant site in the Peloponnese. If little Vaphio could produce these riches, what else remains to be found in future excavations?

Just off the Mycenaean Gallery, **Cycladic figurines,** named after the island chain, are on display. Although these figurines are among the earliest known Greek sculpture (about 2,000 B.C.), almost everyone is struck by how modern they look, often comparing the idols' faces to those wrought by Modigliani. One figure, a musician with a lyre, seems to be concentrating on his music, cheerfully oblivious to his onlookers.

The museum's staggeringly large sculpture collection spreads through much of the rest of the ground floor. You may want to simply wander along, stopping when something catches your fancy. Almost everyone's fancy is captured by the **bronzes,** from the tiny jockey to the monumental figure variously identified as Zeus or Poseidon. Much ink has been spilt trying to prove that the god was holding either a thunderbolt (which would make him Zeus) or a trident (which would mean that he was Poseidon). And who could resist the bronze figures of the staggeringly handsome young men, perhaps athletes, seemingly about to step forward and sprint away through the crowds?

The second floor is expected to remain closed until at least 2002. There are plans to move some of the museum's vast collection of vases onto the ground floor in the meantime. It is possible, but not probable, that the **frescoes** from the site of Akrotiri on the island of Santorini (Thira) may also be displayed on the ground floor. Around 1450 B.C., the volcanic island exploded, destroying not just most of the island itself but also, some say, the Minoan civilization of Crete. Could Santorini's virtual disappearance have given rise to the legend of the lost civilization of Atlantis? Perhaps. Fortunately, these beautiful frescoes survived and were brought to Athens for safekeeping and display. Just as Athens wants the Elgin Marbles back, the present-day inhabitants of Santorini want their frescoes back, hoping that the crowds who come to see them in Athens will come instead to Santorini. There are as many theories on what these frescoes show as there are tourists in the museum on any given day. Who were the boxing boys? Were there monkeys on Santorini, or does the scene show another land? Are the ships sailing off to war, or returning home? No one knows, but it's impossible to see these lilting frescoes and not envy the people of Akrotiri who looked at such beauty every day.

Museum Update

The second floor of the National Archaeological Museum, which housed the beautiful frescoes from the island of Santorini (Thira), was closed after the earthquake that shook Athens in November 1999. In July 2000, the Culture Ministry announced that the second floor would remain closed for at least two more years. There are plans, not definite, to move the frescoes back to Santorini. In addition, a number of splendid marble statues on the ground floor remained under protective wraps at press time. One other change at the museum: Many guards are strictly enforcing long-ignored rules regulating the size of bags, briefcases, and knapsacks allowed inside. Don't be surprised if you are told to check your bag at the cloakroom—and be sure to remove any valuables. Finally, in 2000, the National Archaeological Museum remained open until 7pm in summer. You may wish to check with the GNTO to see if this is still the case when you visit.

✪ **N. P. Goulandris Foundation Museum of Cycladic Art.** Odos Neofytou Douka 4. ☎ **01/722-8321.** www.cycladic-m.gr. E-mail: info@Cycladic-m.gr. Admission Dr800 ($2.30) adults, Dr400 ($1.15) students. Mon and Wed–Fri 10am–4pm; Sat 10am–3pm.

This handsome museum opened its doors in 1986 and houses the astonishing collection of Nicolas and Aikaterini Goulandris, the largest collection of Cycladic art outside the National Archaeological Museum. There are some 230 stone and pottery vessels and figurines from the 3rd millennium B.C. on view, and if you didn't make up your mind at the National Museum that the faces of the idols remind you of the work of Modigliani, here's your chance. Despite the impressive number of displays, this museum is as congenial as the National Museum is overwhelming. It helps that the Goulandris does not usually get the same huge crowds, and it also helps that the galleries here are small and well lit, with labels throughout in Greek and English. The collection of Greek vases is both small and exquisite—the ideal place to find out if you prefer black or red figure vases. The museum's elegant little shop, which takes most major credit cards, has reproductions of a number of items from the collection, including a pert Cycladic pig.

When you've seen all you want to here (and perhaps refreshed yourself with something in the basement snack bar), be sure to walk through the courtyard into the museum's newest acquisition: the elegant 19th-century **Stathatos Mansion,** with some of the original furnishings, providing a glimpse of how wealthy Athenians lived a hundred years ago.

✪ **Greek Folk Art Museum.** Odos Kidathineon 17, Plaka. ☎ **01/322-9031.** Admission Dr500 ($1.45) adults, Dr400 ($1.15) seniors, Dr300 (90¢) students. Tues–Sun 10am–2pm.

This endearing small museum has dazzling embroideries and costumes from all over the country, and a small room with zany frescoes of gods and heroes done by the eccentric artist Theofilos Hadjimichael, who painted in the early part of the 20th century. We stop by here every time we're in Athens, always finding something new, always looking forward to our next visit—and always glad we weren't born Greek women 100 years ago, when we would have spent endless hours embroidering, crocheting, and weaving. Much of what is on display was made by young women for their *proikas* (dowries) in the days when a bride was supposed to arrive at the altar with enough embroidered linen, rugs, and blankets to last a lifetime.

○ **Museum of Greek Popular Musical Instruments.** Odos Dioyenous 1–3 (around the corner from the Tower of the Winds). ☎ **01-325-0198.** Free admission. Tues and Thurs–Sun 10am–2pm; Wed noon–6pm.

Photographs show the musicians, while recordings let you listen to the tambourines, Cretan lyres, lutes, pottery drums, and clarinets on display. Not only that, but this museum is steps from the excellent Platanos taverna, so you can alternate the pleasures of food, drink, and music. The last time we were here, an elderly Greek gentleman listened to some music, transcribed it, stepped out into the courtyard, and played it on his own violin! The shop has a wide selection of CDs and cassettes.

2 More Museums & Galleries

MORE MUSEUMS

The Athens City Museum. Paparigopoulou 7 (Klathmonos Sq., off Odos Stadiou). ☎ **01/ 323-0168.** Fax 01/322-0765. www.athenscitymuseum.gr. E-mail: info@athenscitymuseum.gr. Admission Dr500 ($1.45). Mon, Wed, and Fri–Sat 9am–1:30pm. Possible Sun openings.

This handsomely restored 19th-century Athenian town house is where modern Greece's first king, young King Otho, and his bride, Amalia, lived while a more spacious royal palace (now the Parliament) was built. Poor Otho attempted to ingratiate himself with his Greek subjects by wearing the *foustanella* (short pleated skirt); most thought him dotty. He and Amalia were sent packing in 1862 and Greece imported a new king, George I, from Denmark.

The museum has a wonderful collection of watercolors of 19th-century Athens, including many by the English painter—and author of *The Owl and the Pussy-Cat*—Edward Lear. Amalia's piano is still here, along with some nice portraits of the royal couple. There's even a mini–throne room where the royal couple received important visitors—and a wonderful model of the amazingly small town of Athens in 1842.

○ **Benaki Museum.** Odos Koumbari 1 (at Leoforos Vas. Sofias, Kolonaki, 5 blocks east of Syntagma Sq.). ☎ **01/367-1000.** Admission Dr2,000 ($6); free on Thurs. Mon, Wed, and Fri–Sat 9am–5pm; Thurs 9am–midnight; Sun 9am–3pm.

In early 2000, after 10 years of restoration and expansion, the much-missed Benaki Museum reopened. An entire new wing doubles the exhibition space of the original 20th-century neoclassical Benaki town house. This stunning private collection—nothing here is second rate—includes treasures from the Neolithic era to the 20th century. The collection of folk art (including magnificent costumes and icons) is superb, as are the two entire rooms from 18th-century northern Greek mansions, the ancient Greek bronzes, gold cups, Fayum portraits, and rare early Christian textiles. The museum shop is excellent, the cafe has a spectacular view over Athens, and new galleries house special exhibitions.

Byzantine Museum. Leoforos Vas. Sofias 22 (at Leoforos Vas. Konstandinou, 12 long blocks east of Syntagma Sq.). ☎ **01/723-1570** or 01/721-1027. Admission Dr500 ($1.45) adults, Dr250 (75¢) students. Tues–Sun 8:30am–3pm.

This museum in a 19th-century Florentine-style villa is devoted to the art and history of the Byzantine era, and contains Greece's most important collection of icons and religious art, along with sculptures, altars, mosaics, religious vestments, and bibles. Early, middle, and late Byzantine chapels have been recreated in three rooms on the ground floor. The museum hopes to reopen all its galleries by 2004.

The Jewish Museum. Odos Nikis 39 (on the left side of Nikis as you walk away from Syntagma Sq.). ☎ **01/322-5582.** Fax 01/323-1577. www.jewishmuseum.gr. E-mail: jmg@otenet.gr. Admission Dr500 ($1.45) adults, Dr250 (75¢) students and children. Mon–Fri 9am–2:30pm; Sun 10am–2pm.

Greece's Jewish community, a strong presence throughout the country, and a dominant force in Thessaloniki, was essentially obliterated in the Holocaust. Heartrending exhibits here include the wedding photograph of Yosef Levy and Dona Habif, who married in April 1944 and a month later were sent to Auschwitz, where they were killed. Articles of daily life and religious ceremony include children's toys and special Passover china. Perhaps the most impressive exhibit is the handsome reconstruction of the Patras synagogue. Most exhibits have English labels. If you contact museum curator Zanet Battinou in advance of your visit, she will try to have a staff member take you through the collection.

The Kanellopoulos Museum. Odos Theorias and Odos Panos, Plaka. ☎ **01/321-2313.** Admission Dr500 ($1.45). Tues–Sun 8:30am–3pm.

The Kanellopoulos, in a former private home with a wonderful position high on the slopes of the Acropolis, is another nice place to visit when you've had your fill of big museums. This private collection has some superb red and black figure vases, stunning Byzantine and post-Byzantine icons, and even some Mycenaean pottery baby bottles. The house itself, with some fine painted ceilings, is a delight.

Ilias Lalaounis Jewelry Museum. Odos Kalisperi 12 (at Karyatidon). ☎ **01/922-1044.** Fax 01/923-7358. www.lalaounis-jewelrymuseum.gr. E-mail: jewelrymuseum@ath.forthnet.gr. Admission 1,000Dr ($2.90) adults; 500Dr ($1.45) students, seniors, and children. Mon and Thurs–Sat 9am–4pm, Wed 9am–9pm (free after 3pm), Sun 10am–4pm. Walk 1 block south of the Acropolis between the Theater of Dionysos and the Odeum of Herodes Atticus.

The 3,000 pieces of jewelry on display here are so spectacular that even those with no special interest in baubles will enjoy this glitzy new museum, founded by one of Greece's most successful jewelry designers. The first floor contains a boutique and small workshop. The second and third floors display pieces honoring ancient, Byzantine, and Cycladic designs, as well as plants, animals, and insects. The shop carries copies of some of the displays, and jewelers in the museum's workshop take orders, in case you want your own gold necklace inspired by insect vertebrae.

The National Gallery. Vasileos Konstantinou 50. ☎ **01/723-5857.** Admission Dr2,000 ($6). Mon and Wed–Sat 9am–3pm; Sun 10am–2pm. Sometimes open Mon and Wed 6–9pm during special exhibits.

The core collection here is small, and of that, little is on display. Still, it's well worth finding out if there's a special exhibit on: The El Greco exhibit in 1999 and 2000 was a blockbuster.

The Numismatic Museum. Odos Panepistimiou 12. ☎ **01/364-3774.** Admission Dr800 ($2.30); free Sun. Tues–Sun 8am–2:30pm.

Many Greek coins were works of art, and it's nice to see them handsomely displayed in the magnificent 19th-century town house of the great archaeologist Henrich Schliemann. Until this museum opened in 1999, visitors could only imagine the decor behind the ornate arcaded façade of Schliemann's mansion. Lest anyone forget that he had discovered Troy, Schliemann emblazoned the inscription *Iliou Melathron* ("Palace of Troy") across the façade. The interior is equally impressive, as are the more than 60,000 ancient bronze, silver, and gold coins on view (many displayed with helpful magnifying lenses).

GALLERIES

One of the great pleasures of visiting Athens is browsing in its small art galleries. This is a wonderful way to get a sense of the contemporary Greek art scene—and possibly buy something to take home. Openings are usually open to the public, so if you see a notice of one, feel free to stop by. Here are some galleries to keep an eye out for.

In trendy Psirri, the **Epistrofi Gallery,** Odos Taki 6–8 (☎ **01/321-8640;** www.epistrofi.gr), has occasional concerts as well as shows. The **Epikentro Gallery,** Armodiou 10 (☎ **01/331-2187**), stages frequent exhibits in its improbable location in the Athens Central Market, while not far away is one of the city's best known galleries, the **Rebecca Kamhi Gallery,** Sophokleous 23 (☎ **01/321-0448**), open by appointment only in August. **Bernier/Eliades Gallery,** Eptachalkou 11, Theseion (☎ **01/341-3935**), stages group exhibitions, as does **Kappatos,** Agias Irenes 6 (☎ **01/321-7931**). There are also frequent shows at the **Melina Mercouri Cultural Center,** Iraklidon and Thessalonikis 66 (☎ **01/345-2150**), near the Theseion, and at the **Melina Mercouri Foundation,** Polygnotou 9–11 (☎ **01/331-5601**), in Plaka.

The fashionable Kolonaki district is chock-a-block with galleries: The **Athens Art Center,** Glyconos 4, Dexameni (☎ **01/721-3938**), **Photohoros,** Tsakalof 44 (☎ **01/321-0448**), and **Medussa,** Xenokratous 7 (☎ **01/724-4552**), are three to look for. The **Athens Arts and Technology School** (☎ **01/381-3700**) usually stages shows around town in July and August, when many galleries close or move out of town. One just-out-of-town suburban gallery that's open year-round and well worth a visit (in part for its great cafe and shop) is the **Deste Foundation for Contemporary Art,** Omirou 8, Nea Psychico (☎ **01/672-9460;** www.deste.gr), a 20-minute cab ride from Syntagma.

3 Ancient Monuments

One small, graceful monument that you might easily miss is the 4th-century B.C. **Choregic Monument of Lysikrates,** on Odos Lysikratous in the Plaka, handily located just a few steps from the excellent **Daphne's** restaurant (see p. 156). This circular monument with Corinthian columns and a domed roof bears an inscription stating that Lysikrates erected it when he won the award in 334 B.C. for the best musical performance with a "chorus of boys." There's a lovely frieze showing Dionysos busily trying to turn evil pirates into friendly dolphins.

Three hills near the Acropolis deserve at least a respectful glance: the **Areopagus,** the **Pnyx,** and **Filopappos.** The **Areopagus** is the bald marble hill across from the entrance to the Acropolis; it is so slippery, despite its marble steps, that it is never an easy climb, and is positively treacherous in the rain. This makes it hard to imagine the distinguished Athenians who served on the Council and Court making their way up here to try homicide cases. Still harder to imagine is St. Paul thundering out criticisms of the Athenians for their superstitious devotion to the Unknown God from this slippery perch.

From the Areopagus and Acropolis, you can see two nearby wooded hills. The one with the monument visible on its summit is **Filopappos** (also known as the Hill of the Muses), and the monument is the funeral stele of the Roman consul after whom the hill is named. There are some nice walks on the wooded slopes of this hill; one nice Byzantine church, **Ayios Demetrios;** and the **Dora Stratou Theater,** where folk dances take place (see p. 156). If you climb to the summit (don't try this, or any wanderings here or on the Pnyx, alone at night) and face the Acropolis, you can imagine the wretched moment in 1687 when the Venetian commander Morosini shouted "Fire!"—and his cannon shells struck the Parthenon.

The **Pnyx,** crowned by the Athens Observatory, is where Athens's citizen assembly met. The Pnyx, as much as any spot in Athens—which is to say, any place in the world—is the "birthplace of democracy." Here, for the first time in history, every citizen could vote on every matter of common importance. True, citizens did not include women, and there were far more slaves than citizens in Athens—but that was the case in most of the world for a very long time after democracy was born in Athens.

4 Historic Buildings

Athens was a small village well into the mid–19th century, and did not begin to grow until it became capital of Independent Greece in 1834. It's hard to believe in today's traffic-clogged Athens, but the **Byzantine Museum,** at Vas. Sofias 22, occupies the Renaissance-style villa that the Duchess of Plaisance built—imagine this, in today's Athens—as her country retreat in the 1840s. Several other buildings from the same period, including the **Parliament House** (the former royal palace), the **Grande Bretagne Hotel** (a former mansion), and Schliemann's house, the **Iliou Melathron** (see the Numismatic Museum, above) are still standing in Syntagma Square. Unfortunately, all too many of the neoclassical buildings built in the 19th century were torn down in Athens's rapid expansion after World War II. Here are a few suggestions of some buildings you may pass on your explorations of central Athens.

In the Plaka, several 19th-century buildings have survived, tucked between the T-shirt shops and restaurants on busy Odos Adrianou (Hadrian) and Odos Kidathineon. **Adrianou 96** is thought to be one of the oldest surviving prerevolutionary houses in Athens, dating from the Turkish occupation, and the nearby 19th-century **Demotic School** has a pleasant neoclassical façade. Over on Kidathineon is the house in which mad **King Ludwig** of Bavaria stayed when he visited Athens in 1835 (there's no number on the house, but a small plaque identifies it), and several other buildings here are former houses from the same period.

Finally, if you climb up through the Plaka to the **Anafiotika district** on the slopes of the Acropolis, you'll find yourself in a delightful neighborhood with many small 19th-century homes. This district is often compared to an island village, and small wonder: Most of the homes were built by stonemasons from the Cycladic island of Anafi, who came to Athens to work on the buildings of the new capital of independent Greece.

5 Churches & Synagogues

As you stroll through Athens, you'll discover scores of charming churches. Many date from the Byzantine era of A.D. 330 to A.D. 1453—although virtually nothing survives from the early centuries of that Christian empire. Alas, vandals and thieves have forced many churches to lock their doors, so you may not be able to go inside unless a caretaker is present. If you do go inside, **remember to dress suitably:** Shorts, miniskirts, and sleeveless shirts cause offense. If you wish, you can leave a donation in the collection boxes. Below we list a few churches to keep an eye out for.

Athens's 19th-century **Greek Orthodox Cathedral (Metropolis)** on Odos Mitropoleos gets almost universally bad press: too big, too new, too…well, ugly. It also suffers terribly in comparison with the adjacent 12th-century **Little Metropolis,** with the wonderful name of the **Panayia Gorgoepikoos** ("the Virgin Who Answers Prayers Quickly"). The little church has a number of fragments of classical masonry, including inscriptions, built into its walls that create a delightful crazy-quilt effect.

The square in front of the cathedral is a great place to people-watch on summer weekends, when nonstop weddings often take place, usually in the evening. As one bride leaves the church, the next one (and her flowers, attendants, and guests) are poised to enter. It's a very Greek assembly line, with limousines pulling up, horns blaring, and everyone having a fantastic time.

Also on Mitropoleos, crouched on the sidewalk below an ugly modern building, is the minuscule chapel of **Ayia Dynamis,** a good place for women to light a candle if they want to become pregnant.

If you like spying (from a respectful distance) on weddings and baptisms, continue on to the 12th-century **Church of Ayia Aikaterini,** in the little square off Odos Frinihou. The church sits well below ground level, an indication of just how Athens has grown over the centuries. You'll notice some ancient columns strewn around the courtyard, and may even decide to sit on one while you watch the comings and goings.

If you walk from Syntagma to Monastiraki Square, you can take in a few more churches. A few blocks from Syntagma Square, on Odos Skouleniou, the little 11th-century **Church of St. Theodore** is also below street level, another reminder of how the ground level has risen over the centuries. Over on Odos Hrissopileotissis, the small **Church of the Virgin** is a good place to stop and buy some incense from one of the street vendors usually here. At the **Square of St. Irene,** off Odos Eolou, there's a very nice flower market in front of the church, and on Monastiraki Square, the **Church of the Pantanassa** is all that remains of a convent on this spot. A short walk away on busy Odos Ermou, the 11th-century **Kapnikarea Church** sits right in the middle of the road.

If you're walking along busy Leoforos Vas. Sofias, you may want to sit for a bit and rest in the courtyard of the **Church of Ayios Nikolaos.** A few blocks further along on Odos Gennadius, the 12th-century **Church of the Taxarchi** is set in a small park.

Beth Shalom, the Athens synagogue, on Odos Melidoni, stands in what was, before World War II, a vibrant Jewish neighborhood. Across the street from Beth Shalom is the old synagogue, which Beth Shalom, with its marble façade, replaced. You can get information on visiting the synagogue and on services from the **Jewish Museum,** Odos Nikis 39 (☎ 01/322-5582; fax 01/323-1577).

6 Parks & Gardens

In addition to the parks and gardens listed here, see "Especially for Kids," below.

The **National Garden,** between Leoforos Amalias and Irodou Attikou, south of Vas. Sofias, was once the royal family's palace garden. Now a public park, the area combines a park, a garden, and a small, rather sad zoo with shady trees, benches, and small lakes and ponds with ducks, swans, and a few peacocks. There are several cafes tucked away in the garden, and you can also picnic here. In summer 2000, the elegant **Aigli** cafe/restaurant reopened—after being closed for more than a decade—and staged a number of musical evenings. The large neoclassical exhibition/reception hall in the garden was built by the brothers Zappas and so is known as the **Zappion.** The garden is open daily from 7am to 10pm. *Note:* This is not a good place to loiter alone at night.

Mount Likavitos (Lycabettus), which dominates the northeast of the city, is a favorite retreat for Athenians and a great place to get a bird's-eye view of Athens and its environs—if the *nefos* (smog) isn't too bad. Even when the nefos is bad, sunsets can be spectacular here. On top, there's a small **Chapel of Ayios Yioryios** (St. George), whose name-day is celebrated on April 23. Each summer, there are performances at

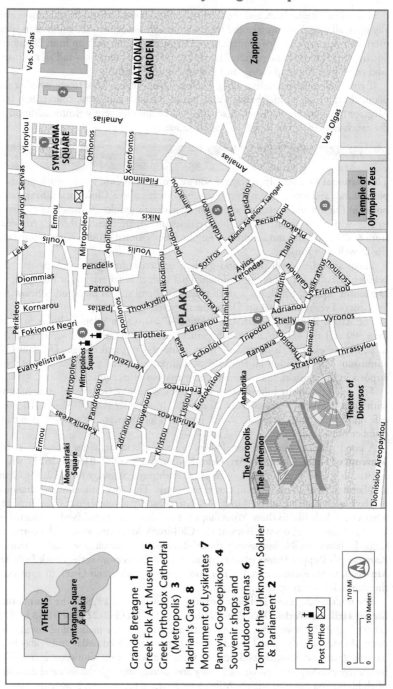

the Lykavitos Theater here, and the (expensive) **Dionysos Café** on the summit is usually open all year. You can take the funicular (which leaves every 20 minutes in summer) from the top of Odos Ploutarchou (Dr500/$1.45), or walk up from Dexameni Square, which is the route preferred by young lovers, the energetic—and all too many who come here to dump kittens and garbage, and to use drugs.

If you find yourself heading along Leoforos Vas. Sofias, check to see whether the planned expansion of **Eleftherias Park,** beside Athens's handsome concert hall (the Megaron), has been completed. If so, this will be another very welcome addition to the much-needed "green lungs" of central Athens.

7 Especially for Kids

The **National Garden** off Syntagma Square has a small **zoo,** several duck ponds, a playground, and lots of room to run around. There's also a **Children's Library** with books in English and some toys and coloring materials (adults are usually not allowed to stay with their children). The library is usually open Tuesday through Saturday from 8:30am to 3pm, and is closed in August. The National Garden is open from sunrise to well after sunset.

There are other small parks and gardens scattered throughout Athens, but the National Garden is the best for children. That said, if you're staying in Kolonaki, try **Dexamini Square,** which has a small playground and several cafes and is below the St. George Lycabettos hotel off Odos Kleomenous.

The **Attica Zoological Park** (☎ 01/663-4724), Odos Yalou, is home to more than 300 varieties of birds, a butterfly garden, and a small farm; the zoo, which plans to add more exhibits, is open daily from 10am to 7pm and charges Dr2,500 ($7) admission. The zoo is not far from the new airport at Spata; given the state of most airports in the summer, the zoo might seem an oasis of tranquility.

The ride up **Mount Likavitos** on the cable-car railway (*teleferique*) is often a hit with kids. It usually operates every 20 minutes in summer (Dr500/$1.45). There's a cafe on top that sells ice cream, and children can let off steam by running along any number of paths downhill.

A good place to check to see if there are any special activities going on is the **Museum of Greek Children's Art,** Odos Kodrou 9, Plaka (☎ 01/331-2621), where admission is Dr500 ($1.45). It's open Tuesday through Saturday from 10am to 2pm and Sunday from 11am to 2pm; closed in August. This small museum has changing displays of children's art from throughout Greece, and your children may enjoy seeing what Greek kids like to draw. Workshops for children are offered (and conducted in Greek). There are also workshops at the **Children's Museum,** around the corner at Odos Kidathineon 14, but usually no exhibitions. In addition, there are sometimes **Karaghiozis Puppet Shows** (shadow theater) a few doors away at the **Greek Folk Art Museum,** Odos Kidathineon 17. You don't need to understand Greek to appreciate the slapstick comedy of Karaghiozis.

The multimedia center **Hellenic Cosmos** was founded in 1998 by the **Foundation for the Hellenic World,** Odos Pireos 254, Tavros (☎ 01/342-2292 or 01/483-5300; fax 01/342-2272; www.fhw.gr or www.hellenic-cosmos.gr; e-mail: info@fhw.gr). It's open Monday, Tuesday, and Thursday from 9am to 6pm, Wednesday and Friday from 9am to 9pm, and Saturday and Sunday from 11am to 3pm; admission is free. The interactive exhibits focus on Greek history and culture through the ages and draw lots of children. You can visit ancient Miletus on a virtual reality tour, browse the Web in the Internet cafe, and, more traditionally, see a collection of Greek costumes. Kalithea is the nearest Metro stop (a 10-minute walk away), but if you're bringing small children, you might want to take a taxi to avoid the walk.

There are usually lots of new-release American **movies** showing in central Athens, and a couple of hours in an air-conditioned theater is not a bad way to pass a hot afternoon. Check the English-language daily *Athens News* (www.ana.gr or http://athensnews.dolnet.gr) or the daily *Kathimerini* insert in the *International Herald Tribune* for listings.

The "Scope" section in the weekly *Hellenic Times* lists activities of interest to children in Athens, including Girl Scout meetings, hiking excursions, and day camps, in its "Kids Corner."

The beaches nearest to Athens are a fair trek—and crowded and often polluted. Consider buying a day pass for the **Hilton pool.** The cost is Dr10,000 ($29) Monday through Friday, Dr12,500 ($36) Saturday and Sunday; information on any price changes is available at ☎ **01/725-0201.**

8 Organized Tours

Many independent travelers (ourselves included) tend to turn up their noses at organized tours. Nonetheless, this can be an efficient and easy way to get an overview of an unfamiliar city. We're impressed by how many people we know who have confessed that they were very glad they had taken one of these tours, which helped them orient themselves and find out what they wanted to go back and see thoroughly. Almost all the tour guides have passed stiff tests to get their licenses.

The best-known Athens-based tour groups are **CHAT Tours,** Odos Stadiou 4 (☎ **01/322-3137** or 01/322-3886); **GO Tours,** Odos Voulis 31–33 (☎ **01/322-5951**); and **Key Tours,** Odos Kaliroïs 4 (☎ **01/923-3166**). Each offers half- and full-day tours of the city, Athens by Night tours, and day excursions from Athens. Expect to pay about $40 for a half-day tour, $60 for a full-day tour, and at least $60 for Athens by Night (including dinner, and sometimes a folk-dance performance at the Dora Stratou Theater). With all these tours, you must book, and usually pay, in advance. At that time, you will be told when you will be picked up at your hotel, or where you should meet the tour.

Each company also offers excursions from Athens. A visit to the very popular **Temple of Poseidon at Sounion** costs about $40 for a half-day trip, including swimming and a meal. A trip to **Delphi** usually costs about $80 for a full day, which often includes a stop at the Monastery of Osios Loukas and the village of Arachova. If you want to spend the night in Delphi (hotel, site and museum admissions, dinner, breakfast and sometimes lunch included), the price goes up about $40 to $120. (We've heard high praise for the GO excursion to Delphi.) Rates for excursions to the **Peloponnese,** taking in Corinth, Mycenae, and Epidaurus, are similar to those for Delphi. If your time in Greece is limited, you may find one of these day trips considerably less stressful than renting a car for the day and driving yourself.

Other companies include **Educational Tours & Cruises,** Odos Artemidos 1, Glyfada (☎ **01/898-1741**), which can arrange tours in Athens and throughout Greece, including individual tours; and **Amphitriton Holidays,** Karayioryi Servias 2 (☎ **01/322-8884**), which places an emphasis on history and education. If you want to hire a private guide, you can speak to the concierge at your hotel or contact the **Association of Guides,** Apollonas 91 (☎ **01/322-9705**). Expect to pay from $100 for a 5-hour tour.

9 Spectator Sports

The Greeks are passionately devoted to soccer and basketball, and betting (legal and nationwide) on sports events is heavy. All sports events are listed in the Greek press and sometimes in the English-language daily *Athens News*. You can also try to get information by stopping by the office of the **Greek National Tourism Organization,** Odos Amerikis 2, and asking if anyone is playing (unless you speak Greek, do not try this by phone). The best-known soccer teams are the fierce rivals **Olympiakos** (Piraeus) and **Panathanaikos** (Athens).

The Greek national basketball team endeared itself to the nation when it won the European Championship by defeating Russia in 1987. Celebrations went on all night. (We should know: We were among the few people in Greece trying to sleep that night.) The championships take place in July or August at different venues in Europe. You may also be able to catch a game between Greek teams in Athens.

If you're in Greece when major international sports events in the world of football or basketball take place, you probably will be able to see them on Greek television or CNN. If you're in Greece during Wimbledon and not staying in a hotel with CNN or STAR cable service, you may have to settle for listening to the live radio coverage on the BBC.

10 Shopping

THE SHOPPING SCENE

You may find a copy of the monthly magazines *Athens Today* and *Now in Athens,* both of which have a shopping section, in your hotel room; sometimes copies are also available at the **Greek National Tourism Organization,** Odos Amerikis 2. Keep in mind that most of the restaurants and shops featured pay for the privilege.

You're in luck shopping in Athens, because almost everything you'll probably want to buy can be found in the central city, bounded by Omonia, Syntagma, and Monastiraki squares. This is where you'll find most of the shops frequented by Athenians, including a number of large **department stores.**

Monastiraki has its famous **flea market,** which is especially lively on Sundays. Although there's a vast amount of ticky-tacky stuff for sale here, there are still some real finds, including retro clothes and old copper. Many Athenians furnishing new homes head here to try to pick up old treasures.

The **Plaka** has pretty much cornered the market on souvenir shops, with enough T-shirts, reproductions of antiquities (including obscene playing cards, drink coasters, bottle openers, and more), fishermen's sweaters (increasingly made in the Far East), and jewelry (often not real gold) to circle the globe.

In the Plaka-Monastiraki area, several shops worth seeking out amidst the endlessly repetitive souvenir shops include **Stavros Melissinos,** the Poet-Sandalmaker of Athens, Odos Pandrossou 89 (☎ 01/321-9247); **Iphanta,** the weaving workshop, Odos Selleu 6 (☎ 01/322-3628); **Emanuel Masmanidis' Gold Rose Jewelry Shop,** Odos Pandrossou 85 (☎ 01/321-5662); the **Center of Hellenic Tradition,** Odos Mitropoleos 59 and Odos Pandrossou 36 (☎ 01/321-3023), which sells arts and crafts; and the **National Welfare Organization,** Odos Ipatias 6 and Apollonos, Plaka (☎ 01/325-0524), where a portion of the proceeds from everything sold (including handsome woven and embroidered carpets) goes to the National Welfare Organization, which encourages traditional crafts. Two shops in Monastiraki have impressive selections of traditional Greek musical instruments, including bouzoukis,

Museum Shops

Keep in mind that most museums have shops. Especially good are those at the National Archaeological Museum, the Goulandris Foundation Museum of Cycladic Art, and the Museum of Greek Popular Musical Instruments.

tambourines, and lyres: **Vasilios Kevorkian,** Ifestou 6 (☎ **01/321-0024**), and **Xannis Samouelian's Musical Instruments,** Ifestou 36 (☎ **01/321-2433**).

Kolonaki, up on the slopes of Mount Likavitos, is boutique heaven—but a better place to window-shop than to buy, since much of what you see here is imported and heavily taxed. If you're here during the January or August sales, you may find some bargains. If not, it's still a lot of fun to work your way up pedestrian Odos Voukourestiou, along Odos Tsakalof and Odos Anagnostopoulou (with perhaps the most expensive boutiques in Athens), before collapsing at a cafe by one of the pedestrian shopping streets in Kolonaki Square—perhaps the very fashionable Odos Milioni. Then you can engage in the other really serious business of Kolonaki: people watching. Give yourself about 15 minutes to figure out the season's must-have accessory. Since it was skin-tight capri pants, navel-revealing halters, and miniscule handkerchief skirts at press time, it's bound to be something else soon.

SHOPPING A TO Z
ANTIQUES

Warning: If you're hoping to take home an antique—perhaps an icon or a wood carving—keep in mind that not everything sold as an antique is genuine, and that it's illegal to take antiquities and icons more than 100 years old out of Greece without a hard-to-obtain export license.

If you're looking for first editions, prints showing 19th-century Athens, a silver sword, or amber worry beads, try **Antiqua,** Leoforos Vas. Sofias 2–4, off Syntagma Square (☎ **01/323-2220**). This is one of Athens's oldest antiques stores, and perhaps the best, with handsome ancient coins and old icons—but take heed of the warning above.

Also near Syntagma Square, **Giannoukos,** Vas. Amalias 4 (☎ **01/324-1700**), has a sound reputation, and the small but tempting **Mati,** Odos Voukourestiou 20 (☎ **01/362-6238**), has some antiques as well as icons, plus a range of items in blue glass to ward off the evil eye. If you're near Syntagma and looking for antiquarian books, maps, and prints, try **Salaminia,** with branches at Panepistimiou 47 (☎ **01/321-8155**), and Odos Stadiou 22 (☎ **01/331-3944**).

Over in Monastiraki on Odos Pandrossou, there are any number of pseudo-antiques shops, and one or two good ones. **Martinos,** Odos Pandrossou 50 (☎ **01/321-3110**), has Venetian and ancient glass, embroidery and kilims, swords and side tables. **Anita Patrikiadon,** Odos Pandrossou 58 (☎ **01/324-6325**), also has a good selection of weavings and wood carvings. If you're more interested in reproductions than the real thing, **Orpheus,** Odos Pandrossou 28B (☎ **01/324-5034**), has museum copies of classical and Byzantine art.

Up in Kolonaki, the eponymous proprietor of **Argyriadis,** Patriarchou Ioakim 42 (☎ **01/725-1727**), specializes in 18th-century furniture and also has a variety of more transportable bibelots. **Mihalarias Art,** Odos Alopekis 1–3 (☎ **01/721-3079**), in a gorgeous neoclassical Kolonaki mansion, has museum-quality furniture, paintings, and just about anything else you can imagine.

BOOKS

✪ **Eleftheroudakis,** with its old quarters still open at Odos Nikis 4 (☎ 01/322-2255), has a new eight-story headquarters at Leoforos Panepistimiou 17 (☎ 01/331-4480), with Athens's widest selection of English-language books and a good range of CDs, including much Greek music. There's also a cafe (with some free newspapers and journals to read) and clean rest rooms. The staff seems amazingly tolerant of tourists who stop by to read, but not buy, the wide selection of books on Greece. Check the bulletin board by the cafe to see if there are any readings by local authors (sometimes in English) or upcoming concerts.

Compendium, Odos Nikis 28 (☎ 01/322-1248), on the edge of the Plaka near Syntagma Square, is a small but fine English-language bookstore, selling both new and used fiction and nonfiction, plus magazines and maps. Local writers sometimes hold readings here. Just off Panepistimiou and steps from Syntagma Square, **Reymondos,** Voukourestiou 18 (☎ 01/364-8189), has a good selection in English (including some dazzling photography books on Greece), stocks English-language magazines and newspapers, and is often open after usual shop hours. In the stoa, one floor up, **Folia tou Bibliou** (The Book Nest), Panepistimiou 25–29 (☎ 01/323-1703), has lots of English fiction and a wide selection of maps and books on Greece, as does **Pantelis,** Amerikis 11, up from Panepistimiou (☎ 01/362-3673).

In Kolonaki, try **Rombos,** Kapsali 6, off Kolonaki Square (☎ 01/724-2082), for English-language books, including books on Greece.

CRAFTS

There are lots of mass-produced "crafts" for sale in Athens, which is why it's good to know about some shops that have quality work. The **Center of Hellenic Tradition,** Mitropoleos 3 and Pandrossou 36 in the Plaka (☎ 01/321-3023), is a wonderful place for quality traditional Greek art, including icons, pottery, wood carvings, embroideries, and prints. Best of all, you can take a break from shopping and look at the Acropolis while you have coffee and a snack at the cafe here.

Also in the Plaka, **Anoyi,** Sotiros 1 (☎ 01/322-6487), is an absolute delight, with old prints, furniture, reproduced icons, and fabrics. On the fringes of the Plaka, the **National Welfare Organization** (Ethnikos Organismos Pronias), Ypatias 6 and Apollonos, just east of the Cathedral (☎ 01/325-0524), has gorgeous embroideries, rugs, pottery, icons, and, usually, very bored and unhelpful salespeople. The **Greek Women's Institution,** Kolokotroni 3 (☎ 01/325-0524), specializes in embroidery from the islands and copies of embroideries from the Benaki Museum.

DEPARTMENT STORES

Head toward Omonia Square to see the city's best-known department stores: **Lambropoulos,** Eolou 99 (☎ 01/324-5811); **Minion,** Veranzerou 17 at Patission (☎ 01/523-8901); and **British Home Stores (BHS)** and **Klaudatos,** Kratinou 3–5 at Odos Athinas (☎ 01/324-1915). BHS occupies the first two floors including mezzanine, Klaudatos all the upper floors. The building faces north on Kotzia Square 3 blocks south of Omonia on Athinas, and isn't easy to see until you're right at one of the two entrances. The self-service restaurant on the eighth floor is just a bit lower than the Acropolis and treats the startling view casually.

FASHION

If you do any window-shopping in Athens, you'll soon see how expensive most things are, except during the January and August sales. Not surprisingly, Athens's poshest

Pack & Send

Pallis, Odos Ermou 8 (☎ **01/324-2115**), has a good selection of envelopes, tape, wrapping paper, and pens and pencils—everything you might need to wrap and send a package home.

---

clothing stores are in **Kolonaki**. Much of what you'll see is American or European and carries a hefty import duty; most of the rest is Greek designer wear. Good streets to browse include Voukourestiou, Kanari, Milioni, Tsakalof, Patriarchou Ioakim, and the most expensive street in town, Anagnostopoulou—where Versace, Ferre, Lagerfeld, and Guy Laroche have boutiques, as do well-known Athenian designers such as Aslanis, Nikos, Filemon, and Sofos. If shoes are your thing, head for Tsakalof, with a heavy concentration of the shoe stores that most Athenians find irresistible.

Here are a few individual shops near Kolonaki Square: **Artisti Italiani,** Kanari 5 (☎ **01/363-9085**), has Italian-designed clothes for men and women. The well-known French firm **Lacoste** has men's and women's sportswear at Solonos 5 (☎ **01/361-8030**). **Jade,** Anagnostopoulou 3 (☎ **01/364-5922**), **Ritsi,** Tsakalof 13 (☎ **01/363-8677**), and **Sofos,** Anagnostopoulou 5 (☎ **01/361-8713**), all sell designer women's clothing. **Elina Lembessi,** Irakleitou 13 (☎ **01/363-1731**), has elegantly casual tops, bottoms, and accessories. **Desmina,** Koubare 5 (☎ **01/364-1010**), offers sportier women's clothing, with lots of pantsuits and casual wear. **New Man,** Solonos 25 at Voukourestiou (☎ **01/360-8876**), has casual men's clothes, while nearby **Berto Lucci,** Solonos 8 (☎ **01/360-3775**), has more trendy attire. See also "Shoes" and "Sweaters," below.

JEWELRY

All that glitters most definitely is not gold in Athens's myriad jewelry shops. Unless you know your gold very well, you'll want to exercise caution in shopping here, especially in the Plaka and Monastiraki stores that cater to tourists.

We've been pleased with the quality and prices at Emanuel Masmanidis's small **Gold Rose Jewelry shop,** Odos Pandrossou 85 (☎ **01/321-5662**). Others report satisfaction in dealings with **Stathis,** Pa. Venizelou 2, Mitropoleos Square (☎ **01/322-4691**).

Greece's best-known jewelry stores are **Zolotas,** Odos Panepistimiou 10 (☎ **01/361-3782**), and **Lalaounis,** Odos Panepistimiou 6 (☎ **01/362-1371**), both at the foot of pedestrian Odos Voukourestiou. Both shops have gorgeous reproductions of ancient and Byzantine jewelry, as well as their own designs. You can see more of the Lalaounis designs at the Lalaounis museum (see "More Museums & Galleries," above).

Up on Voukourestiou, there are at least five excellent jewelers, of which we prefer **Mati,** Voukourestiou 20 (see "Antiques," above). A bit further along, **Ioannidis,** Valaoritou 9 (☎ **01/361-0677**), is the place to head if you want a Faberge egg or Piaget watch.

One of the best shops for silver is **Nisiotis,** Lekka 23, just off Syntagma Square (☎ **01/324-4183**). Off Syntagma, but toward Plaka, **Pantelis Mountis,** Odos Apollonos 27 (☎ and fax **01/324-4574**), has reproductions of Byzantine icons and religious medals.

MARKETS & GROCERIES

The ✪ **Central Market** (fish, meat, vegetables, and more) on Odos Athinas is open Monday through Saturday from about 8am to 6pm. You may not want to take advantage of all of the bargain prices (two sheeps' heads for the price of one is our all-time favorite), but this is a great place to buy Greek spices and herbs, cheeses, and sweets—and to see how Athens is fed.

Every Friday from about 8am until 2pm, **Odos Xenokratous** in Kolonaki turns into a street market selling flowers, fruits, and vegetables. This is a very different scene from the rowdy turmoil of the Central Market, although it's lively enough. Many Kolonaki matrons come here with their Filipino servants, then let the servants lug their purchases home while they head off for some shopping and light lunch (perhaps at the fashionable **To Kafenio**).

MUSIC

You won't have trouble finding **Metropolis,** Odos Panepistimiou 66 and Odos Tsakalof 15 (☎ 01/361-1463), Athens's largest music store: Just follow the booming vibrations. At **Slammin',** Odos Asklepiou 22 (☎ 01/361-3611), you can buy CDs and clothes. The excellent bookstore **Eleftheroudakis** (see above) has a wide selection of CDs, as does the **Virgin Megastore,** Stadiou 7 (☎ 01/361-8080).

SHOES

If you walk along Odos Tsakalof or Odos Patriarchou Ioakim in Kolonaki, or almost any street in central Athens, you'll begin to get an idea of how serious Greeks are about their footwear. Sometimes the biggest crowds in town on a Saturday night are the window-shoppers eyeing the shoes on Odos Ermou off Syntagma Square. Some good-quality stores include **Kaloyirou,** at Pandrossou 12, Plaka (☎ 01/331-0727), and Patriarchou Ioakim 4, Kolonaki (☎ 01/722-8804); **Mouriadis,** Odos Stadiou 4 (☎ 01/322-1229); and **Moschoutis,** Voulis 12 at Ermou (☎ 01/324-6504).

SWEATERS

Several travelers recommend **Nick's Corner,** Pandrossou 48, Monastiraki (☎ 01/321-2990), for the heavy-knit sweaters that are usually bargains in Greece. Look downstairs. You'll see many more sweaters along Odos Adrianou in the Plaka and, if you don't mind that many of these "authentic" Greek sweaters are made by machines and imported from third-world countries, you can find decent prices almost everywhere.

SWEETS

You'll have no problem satisfying your sweet tooth in Athens. If anything, you'll come up gasping for air as you eat the seriously sweet sweets that most Greeks adore.

The long-established **Aristokratikon,** Karayioryi Servias 9, just off Syntagma Square (☎ 01/322-0546), has excellent chocolates, glazed pistachio nuts, and *loukoumia* (Turkish delight). Beware—even chocoholics may find the truffles coated with white chocolate too sweet. Next, head over to **Karavan,** the hole-in-the-wall at Voukourestiou 11 (no phone), with the best Levantine delights in town. Serving excellent coffee and sweets, **K. Kotsolis Pastry Shop,** Odos Adrianou 112, is an oasis of old-fashioned charm in the midst of the Plaka souvenir shops.

Loukoumades are the Greek donut with a difference—they are about the size of an American donut hole, served hot, drenched in honey, and covered with cinnamon. Delicious. If you're near Syntagma Square, try **Doris,** Praxitelous 30 (☎ 01/323-2671), and if you're nearer Omonia Square, try **Aigina,** Panepistimiou 46 (☎ 01/381-4621). Better yet, try both.

11 Athens After Dark

Greeks enjoy their nightlife so much that they take an an afternoon nap to rest up for it. The evening often begins with a leisurely *volta* (stroll); you'll see this in most neighborhoods, including the main drags through the Plaka and Kolonaki Square. Most Greeks don't think of dinner until at least 9pm in winter, 10pm in summer. Around midnight, the party may move on to a club for music and dancing.

Check the daily *Athens News* or the daily *Kathimerini* insert in the *International Herald Tribune* for current cultural and entertainment events, including films, lectures, theater, music, and dance. The weekly *Hellenic Times* and monthly *Now in Athens* list nightspots, restaurants, movies, theater, and much more.

FESTIVALS

New festivals spring up every year in Athens and throughout Greece. You may want to check with the Greek National Tourism Organization to see what's new where you're going. You can also check **www.greekfestival.gr** for information.

THE ATHENS FESTIVAL   From early June through September, the Athens Festival (also known as the **Greek** or **Hellenic Festival**) features famous Greek and foreign artists (including Elton John and Placido Domingo in the summer of 2000) performing on the slopes of the Acropolis. You may catch an opera, concert, drama, or ballet here—and, usually, see the Acropolis illuminated over your shoulder at the same time. To enjoy the performance to the fullest, bring some kind of cushion to sit on (the cushions available are often minimal). Schedules are usually available at the **Athens Festival Office,** Odos Stadiou 4 (☎ **01/322-1459,** 01/331-2400, 01/322-3111, or 01/322-3110, ext. 137). The office, in the Spiromilios Arcade, is open Monday through Saturday from 8:30am to 2pm and 5 to 7pm, Sunday from 10am to 1pm; you will have better luck coming here in person than trying to reach the office by phone. If available—and that's a big if—tickets can also be purchased at the **Odeon of Herodes Atticus** (☎ 01/323-2771 or 01/323-5582) several hours before the performance. Shows usually begin at 9pm.

THE LYCABETTUS (LIKAVITOS) FESTIVAL   There are usually pop-music concerts (the Pet Shop Boys and the Buena Vista Social Club appreared in 2000) and other special events at the outdoor amphitheater near the top of Likavitos during the summer. For information, check with the **Athens Festival Office** (see above) or the **Likavitos Theater** (☎ 01/722-7209). Tickets are sometimes also available at the **Ticket House,** Panepistimiou 42 (☎ **01/618-9300** or 01/360-8366).

THE EPIDAURUS FESTIVAL   From late June to late August, performances of ancient Greek tragedies and comedies (usually given in modern Greek translations) take place at Epidaurus, in Greece's most beautiful ancient theater. This makes for a long evening, but a memorable one. If you take advantage of the bus service that you can purchase with your ticket (about 2 hrs. each way), the evening doesn't have to be exhausting. For information, check with the **Athens Festival Office** (see above) or the **Rex Theater** box office (☎ **01/330-1881**), on Panepistimiou just outside Spiromilios Arcade. You can also sometimes get tickets at Epidaurus (☎ **0753/ 22-026**) just before a performance.

THE ROCKWAVE FESTIVAL   What started as a one-time event in 1996 has taken place every summer since then, with concerts at various venues in and around Athens. Groups performing in 2000 included Oasis and Supergrass, although a number of last-minute cancellations disappointed fans. For information on what's taking place during your visit, check with the Greek National Tourism Organization or Ticket House (see above).

THE PERFORMING ARTS

The acoustically marvelous new **Megaron Mousikis Concert Hall,** Leoforos Vas. Sofias 89 (☎ **01/729-0391** or 01/728-2333), hosts a wide range of classical-music programs that include quartets, operas in concert, symphonies, and recitals. On performance nights, the box office is open Monday through Friday from 10am to 6pm, Saturday from 10am to 2pm, and Sunday from 6 to 10:30pm. Tickets are also sold Monday through Friday from 10am to 5pm in the Megaron's convenient downtown kiosk in the Spiromillios Arcade, Odos Stadiou 4. Ticket prices run from Dr1,000 to Dr20,000 ($2.90 to $57), depending on the performance. The Megaron has a limited summer season, but is in full swing the rest of the year.

The **Greek National Opera** performs at the **Olympia Theater,** Odos Akadimias 59, at Mavromihali (☎ **01/361-2461**). The summer months are usually off-season.

The **Pallas Theater,** Odos Voukourestiou 1 (☎ **01/322-8275**), hosts many jazz and rock concerts, as well as some classical performances. Prices vary from performance to performance, but you can usually get a cheap ticket for about Dr3,000 ($9).

The **Hellenic American Union,** Odos Massalias 22 between Kolonaki and Omonia squares (☎ **01/362-9886**), often hosts performances of English-language theater and American-style music (tickets are usually about Dr3,500/$10). If you arrive early, check out the art shows or photo exhibitions in the adjacent gallery.

The **Athens Center,** Odos Archimidous 48 (☎ **01/701-8603**), often stages free performances of ancient Greek and contemporary international plays in June and July.

Since 1953, the **Dora Stratou Folk Dance Theater** has been giving performances of traditional Greek folk dances on Filopappos Hill. At present, performances take place May through September, Tuesday through Sunday at 10:15pm, with additional performances at 8:15pm on Wednesday and Sunday. There are no performances on Monday. You can buy tickets at the **box office,** Odos Scholio 8, Plaka, from 8am to 2pm (☎ **01/924-4395,** or 01/921-4650 after 5:30pm). Prices range from Dr3,500 to Dr5,000 ($10 to $14). Tickets are also usually available at the theater before performances.

Seen from the Pnyx, **Sound-and-Light** shows illuminate (sorry) Athens's history by telling the story of the Acropolis. As lights pick out monuments on the Acropolis and the music swells, the narrator tells of the Persian attack, the Periclean days of glory, the invidious Turkish occupation—you get the idea. Shows are held April through October. The 45-minute performances in English are given at 9pm on Monday, Wednesday, Thursday, Saturday, and Sunday. Tickets can be purchased at the **Athens Festival Office,** Odos Stadiou 4 (☎ **01/322-7944**), or at the entrance to the Sound-and-Light (☎ **01/922-6210**). Tickets are Dr2,000 ($6) for adults and Dr600 ($1.75) for students. You'll hear the narrative best if you do not sit too close to the very loud public address system.

THE CLUB, MUSIC & BAR SCENE

Your best bet here is to have a local friend; failing that, try asking someone at your hotel. The listings in the weekly *Hellenic Times* can be very helpful. If you ask a taxi driver, he's likely to take you to either his cousin George's joint or the place that gives him drinks for bringing you.

Wherever you go, you're likely to face a cover charge of at least Dr3,500 ($10). Thereafter, each drink will cost—ouch!—between Dr3,500 and Dr7,000 ($10 to $20). Many clubs plop down a bottle on your table that's labeled as, but doesn't

Open in August

A great many popular after-dark spots close in August, when much of Athens flees the summer heat to the country. Some places that stay open include a number of bars, cafes, ouzeries, and tavernas on the pedestrian **Iraklion Walkway** near the Theseion. **Stavlos,** the restaurant, bar, and disco popular with all ages, remains open on August weekends. Nearby, **Berlin Booze,** which caters to a young crowd and specializes in rock-and-roll, is open most nights; **Ambibagio** has quite genuine Greek music. The sweet shop **Aistisis** has great views of the Acropolis and stays open as late as the nearby bars.

necessarily contain, Johnny Walker Red or Black, and then try very hard to charge you about Dr35,000 ($100) whether you drink it or not. It's best to go to these clubs with someone *trustworthy* who knows the scene.

Polis, Odos Pezmatzoglou 7 (☎ **01/324-9587-8**), a short ride from Syntagma Square, is usually open from mid-morning to well after midnight, offering up everything from recorded classical to live jazz and pop (both Greek and American). Since it's open most of the day, Polis draws regulars who hang out to read the newspaper, write letters—and, of course, talk on cell phones. Polis serves coffee, drinks, and snacks, but not full meals.

Be especially wary of heading out of the city to the places that spring up each summer on the airport road; these spots are usually overpriced and often unsavory. That said, the **Asteria Club** (☎ **01/894-4558**) and the **Bio-Bio Club** (☎ **01/894-1300**) in Glyfada were both popular during the summer of 2000, as was **Riba's** (☎ **01/965-5555**) in Varkiza. Expect to pay at least Dr6,000 ($17) per drink after paying a cover of perhaps Dr20,000 ($57) at all these live-music joints.

TRADITIONAL MUSIC

Walk the streets of the Plaka on any night and you'll find plenty of tavernas offering pseudo-traditional live music. As noted, many are serious clip joints, where if you sit down and ask for a glass of water, you'll be charged $100 for a bottle of scotch. At most of these places, there's a cover (usually at least Dr3,500/$10). We've had good reports on **Taverna Mostrou,** Odos Mnissikleos 22 (☎ **01/324-2441**), which is large, old, and best known for traditional Greek music and dancing. Shows begin around 11pm and usually last until 2am. The cover of Dr7,000 ($20) includes a fixed-menu supper. À la carte fare is available but expensive (as are drinks). Nearby, **Palia Taverna Kritikou,** Odos Mnissikleos 24 (☎ **01/322-2809**), is another lively open-air taverna with music and dancing.

Several tavernas that usually offer low-key music include fashionable **Daphne's,** Odos Lysikratous 4 (☎ **01/322-7971**); **Nefeli,** Odos Panos 24 (☎ **01/321-2475**); **Dioyenis,** Odos Sellei (Shelley) 4 (☎ **01/324-7933**); **Stamatopoulou,** Odos Lissiou 26 (☎ **01/322-8722**); and longtime favorite **Xinos,** Odos Agelou Geronta 4 (☎ **01/322-1065**).

POP MUSIC

For Greek pop music, try **Zoom,** Odos Kidathineon 37, in the heart of the Plaka (☎ **01/322-5920**). Performers, who are likely to have current hit albums, are showered with carnations here by adoring fans. The minimum order is Dr7,000 ($20). If you want to check out the local rock and blues scene along with small doses of metal, Athenian popsters play at **Memphis,** Odos Ventiri 5, near the Hilton east of Syntagma Square (☎ **01/722-4104**); open Tuesday through Friday from 10:30pm to 2:30am.

REMBETIKA & BOUZOUKIA

Those interested in authentic *rembetika* (music of the urban poor and dispossessed) and *bouzoukia* (traditional and pop music featuring the *bouzouki,* a kind of guitar, today almost always loudly amplified) should consult their hotel concierge, the listings in the weekly *Hellenic Times,* or the listings in *Kathimerini,* the daily insert in the *International Herald Tribune,* to find out what's going on. Another good place to ask is at the shop of the Museum of Greek Popular Musical Instruments. Rembetika performances usually don't start until nearly midnight, and though there's rarely a cover, drinks can cost as much as Dr6,000 ($20). Keep in mind that many clubs close during the summer.

One of the more central places for rembetika is the **Stoa Athanaton,** Sofokleous 19, in the Central Meat Market (☎ 01/321-4362), which serves good food and has live rembetika from 3 to 6pm and after midnight. It's closed Sunday; the minimum is Dr3,000 ($9). **Taximi,** Odos Isavron 29, Exarchia (☎ 01/363-9919), is consistently popular. Drinks cost Dr3,000 ($9); it's closed Sundays and the months of July and August. Open Wednesday through Monday, **Frangosyriani,** Odos Arachovis 57, Exarchia (☎ 01/360-0693), specializes in the music of rembetika legend Markos Vamvakaris. The downscale, smoke-filled **Rebetiki Istoria,** in a neoclassical building at Ippokratous 181 (☎ 01/642-4967), features old-style rembetika, played to a mixed crowd of older regulars and younger students and intellectuals. The music usually starts at 11pm, but arrive earlier to get a seat. The legendary Maryo I Thessaloniki (Maryo from Thessaloniki), sometimes described as the Bessie Smith of Greece, sometimes sings rembetika at **Perivoli t'Ouranou,** Lysikratous 19 (☎ 01/323-5517 or 01/322-2048), in Plaka; the cover is around Dr10,000 ($29).

JAZZ

A number of clubs and cafes specialize in jazz, but also offer everything from Indian sitar music to rock and punk. The **Café Asante,** Damareos 78 (☎ 01/756-0102), in Pangrati, has music most nights from 11pm; the cover varies, but count on spending at least Dr10,000 ($29) if you go and have a couple of drinks. The very popular **Half Note Jazz Club,** Trivonianou 17, Mets (☎ 01/921-3310), has everything from medieval music to jazz nightly; performance times vary from 8 to 11pm and later. The cover is usually between Dr4,000 and Dr8,500 ($11 and $24). At the **House of Art,** Sahtouri and Sari 4 (☎ 01/321-7678), and **Pinakothiki,** Ayias Theklas 5 (☎ 01/324-7741), both in newly fashionable Psirri, you can often hear jazz from 11pm; the cover of around Dr8,000 ($23) includes the first drink. The **Rodon Club,** Marni 24 (☎ 01/523-6293), west of Omonia Square, features live jazz and pop many nights from 10pm; the cover starts at Dr8,000 ($23).

DANCE CLUBS & DISCOS

In the newly trendy Psirri district, **Astron,** Odos Taki 3 (☎ 0977/469-356), describes itself as "freestyle" and has both canned and live music. The cover varies at this bar, which serves wicked shots of vodka and cointreau as well as a wide range of less lethal drinks. Astron practically bursts at the seams on Saturday nights. Hidden on the outskirts of the Plaka, **Booze,** Kolokotroni 57, second floor (☎ 01/324-0944), blasts danceable rock to a hip student crowd. There's art on every wall, stage lights, and two bars. The cover starts at Dr1,500 ($4.30), plus Dr1,500 ($4.30) per drink. If it's disco you're craving, head east to **Absolut,** Filellinon 23 (no phone), **Q Base,** Evripidou 49, Omonia (☎ 01/321-8256), or **R-Load,** Ermou 161 (☎ 01/345-6187). If you feel a bit too old there, head north to Panepistimiou, where the **Wild Rose,** in the arcade at Panepistimiou 10 (☎ 01/364-2160), and **Mercedes**

Rex, Panepistimiou 48 (☎ **01/361-4591**), usually have varied programs. If you go to a place that plays recorded music, keep an ear out for *I Learned to Live Free,* a medley sung by 12 monks from a monastery in Central Greece. It climbed to the top of the charts in the summer of 2000; the monks' second CD, *SOS,* is expected out in 2001.

GAY & LESBIAN BARS

The Athens gay scene is fairly low-key; get-togethers are sometimes advertised in the English-language press. Information is also available from the Greek national gay and lesbian organization **AKOE-AMPHI,** P.O. Box 26002, 10022 Athens; it's office is at Zalongou 6 (☎ **01/771-9221**). The friendliest bar is **Aleko's Island,** Tsakalof 42, Kolonaki (no phone), a fun place where you can actually have a conversation. **Granazi,** Lebesi 20 (☎ **01/325-3979**), attracts a loud and lively young crowd. The disco **Lambda,** Lembessi 15 and Syngrou 9 (☎ **01/922-4202**), is hip and trendy with the young locals. In Kolonaki, **Alexander's,** Anagnostopoulou 44 (☎ **01/ 364-6660**), is more sedate, with more variety. And **Porta,** Phalirou 10 (☎ **01/ 924-3858**), is the only true lesbian bar in town.

There's also a lively transvestite cruising scene along Leoforos Syngrou; **Koukles** (the name means "dolls"), at the corner of Zan. Moreas & Syngrou (no phone), has nightly drag shows.

See also "For Gay & Lesbian Travelers," in chapter 2.

MOVIES

Central Athens has lots of air-conditioned theaters showing new-release Greek, American, and European films. Listings appear in the *Athens News, Kathimerini* (the English language insert in the *International Herald Tribune*), and in the weekly *Hellenic Times.*

If you're in Athens in summer, keep an eye out for listings of neighborhood open-air cinemas, still a very pleasant way to pass an evening, although some old favorites have closed in recent years. Many of the open-air cinemas are family-owned and -run, and all are great places to watch Athenian families watching films—which is to say, talking to each other, pursuing toddlers who are trying to run away, munching snacks and sipping cold drinks, all the while keeping up a running commentary on the film. We're fond of the **Dexameni** (☎ **01/362-3942**), in Dexameni Square, Kolonaki, where there always seems to be a little breeze on a hot evening. The **Cine Paris** (☎ **01/322-2071**), on Kidathineon in the Plaka, is one of the oldest in town—and has great views of the Acropolis.

12 Piraeus: A Jumping-Off Point to the Islands

Piraeus has been the port of Athens since antiquity, and is still where you catch most island boats and cruise ships. What's confusing is that Piraeus has **three harbors:** the main harbor **(Megas Limani),** where you'll see everything from tankers to cruise ships; Zea Marina **(Zea Limani),** the port for most of the swift hydrofoils that dart to the islands; and **Mikrolimano** (Little Harbor, also called Turkolimano, or Turkish Harbor), with a yacht harbor and a number of fish restaurants. As if that weren't confusing enough, the absence of helpful signs at both the main harbor and Zea Limani and the constant hustle and bustle here mean that this is not an easy place to navigate. To be on the safe side, even if you have your tickets, try to get here an hour before your ship sails—and don't be surprised if it leaves late. And since schedules depend on the weather, and sailings are often delayed or canceled, it's not a good idea to plan to return to Athens by boat less than 24 hours before your flight home.

Insider Tips

From mid-July through the end of August, boats leaving Piraeus for the islands are heavily booked, and often overbooked. It is sometimes possible to get deck passage without a reservation, but even that can be difficult when as many as 100,000 passengers are leaving Piraeus on a summer weekend (as was common in July and August of 2000). Most ships will not allow passengers to board without a ticket. If possible, purchase your tickets in advance.

Note that Piraeus is not a good place for men or women to explore at night. We advise sticking to the harborfront.

As in antiquity, today's Piraeus has the seamier side of a sailors' port of call and the color and bustle of an active harbor—both aspects, somewhat sanitized, were portrayed in the film *Never on Sunday.* Piraeus also has a sprawling street market just off the main harbor, where you can buy produce brought each day on island boats, including bread baked that morning on distant islands. There are a number of fish restaurants here, but many are overpriced and serve fish that's less fresh than the bread. You're probably not going to fall in love with Piraeus, but if you have some time to kill, here are some suggestions.

ESSENTIALS

GETTING THERE　By Metro　The fastest and easiest way to Piraeus is to take the Metro from Omonia Square or Monastiraki to the last stop (Dr250/75¢), which will leave you a block from the domestic port. (This can feel like a very long block if you are carrying heavy luggage.)

By Bus　From Syntagma Square, take the (very slow) Green Depot bus no. 40 from the corner of Odos Filellinon; it will leave you a block from the international port, about a 10-minute walk along the water from the domestic port. From the airport, bus no. 19 goes to Piraeus; the fare is Dr300 (90¢).

By Taxi　A taxi from Syntagma Square will cost up to Dr2,000 ($6). A taxi from the airport to the port costs about Dr3,000 ($9).

RETURNING TO ATHENS　The easiest way is to take the Metro to central Athens, to either Monastiraki or Omonia squares. Most taxi drivers will try to overcharge tourists disembarking from the boats. They often offer a flat rate two or three times the legal fare. If you stand on the dock, you'll get no mercy. The only option is to pay up, try to get a policeman to help you, or walk to a nearby street, hail a cab, and hope for a fair rate.

VISITOR INFORMATION　For boat schedules, transit information, and other tourist information 24 hours a day, dial ☎ 171. The *Athens News* and the *Kathimerini* insert in the *International Herald Tribune* print major ferry schedules. The closest **Greek National Tourism Organization (EOT)** office (☎ 01/453-7107) is inconveniently located on the street above Zea Marina (the hydrofoil port) on the second floor of a shopping arcade stocked with yacht supplies. It's open Monday through Friday from 9am to 2:30pm, but its limited resources probably won't warrant the 20-minute walk from the ferry piers. You'd do better to try to get a ferry schedule from the **GNTO** office in central Athens at Odos Amerikis 2 (☎ 01/331-0437). The small **tourist office** (☎ 01/412-1181) in the Piraeus Metro station on Akti Poseidonos is usually open from 8am to 8pm.

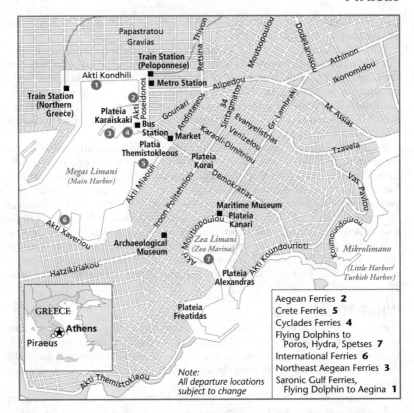

Papastratou
Gravias
Train Station
(Peloponnese)
Akti Kondhili ①
② Metro Station
Train Station
(Northern
Greece)
Plateia
Karaiskaki ③ ④
Bus
Station
Market
Platia
Themistokleous ⑤
Megas Limani
(Main Harbor)
⑥
Akti Xaveriou
Archaeological
Museum
Hatzikiriakou

Akti Poseidonos
Gounari
Andistaseos
Alipedou
34
Sintagmatatos
Karaoli-Dimitriou
Venizelou
Evanyelistrias
Gr. Lambraki
Retsina
Thivon
Moutsopoulou
Dodekanisou
Athinon
Ikonomidou
M. Assias
Tzavela
Vas. Pavlou
Plateia
Korai
Demokratias
Maritime Museum
Plateia
Kanari
Iroon Politehniou
Akti Miaouli
Akti Moutsopoulou
Zea Limani
(Zea Marina)
⑦
Plateia
Alexandras
Akti Koundourioti
Koumoundourou
Mikrolimano
(Little Harbor/
Turkish Harbor)

GREECE
★ Athens
Piraeus

Plateia
Freatidas

Akti Themistokleou

Note:
All departure locations
subject to change

Aegean Ferries **2**
Crete Ferries **5**
Cyclades Ferries **4**
Flying Dolphins to
  Poros, Hydra, Spetses **7**
International Ferries **6**
Northeast Aegean Ferries **3**
Saronic Gulf Ferries,
  Flying Dolphin to Aegina **1**

FAST FACTS   There are several **banks** along the waterfront. The **National Bank,** on Odos Ethniki Antistaseos, has extended hours in summer. A portable **post office** opposite the Aegina ferry pier also offers currency exchange; it's open Monday through Saturday from 8am to 8pm, Sunday from 8am to 6pm. The **main post office** is on Odos Tsamadoy; it's usually open from 8am to 4pm. There is also a sub-station in the Metro office on Akti Poseidonos. The **telephone office (OTE)** is a block away from the post office and is usually open 24 hours. There is another branch by the water, on Akti Miaouli at Odos Merarchias, open daily from 7am to 9:30pm. You'll find secure **luggage storage** in the Metro station at the **Central Travel Agency** (☎ **01/411-5611**); hours are usually from 6am to 8pm.

TICKETS TO THE ISLANDS   The quay of the main harbor is lined with **ticket agents,** many concentrated in Plateia Karaiskaki; some sell tickets for one or two lines or destinations only, some for more. Usually, there's a sign in the window telling you what the agent sells. Almost every agent will tell you that you're getting a good deal; almost no agent will give you one. Some readers have reported good luck dealing with **Explorations Unlimited,** Odos Kapodistriou 2 (☎ **01/411-6395** or 01/411-1243), just off Akti Poseidonos near the Metro; open Monday through Friday from 8am to 7pm and Saturday from 9am to 2pm.

FERRIES TO THE ISLANDS   You will be confused as to where to catch your boat; this is inevitable. Allow plenty of time. Even the person you buy your ticket from may give you a bum steer. Any information below may change at any moment. Sorry—but we thought you should know the truth!

Ferry tickets can be purchased at a ticket office up to 1 hour before departure; after that they can usually be bought on the boat. To book first-class cabins or buy advance-sale tickets, see one of the **harborside travel agents** (around Karaiskaki Square by the domestic ferries and along Akti Miaouli, opposite the Crete ferries). Most open at 6am and some will hold your baggage for the day (but without security). The **GNTO** publishes a list of weekly sailings, and the **tourist police** (☎ 171) or the **Port Authority** (☎ 01/451-1311) can provide you with schedule information.

Boats for the eastern Cyclades (including Mykonos and Santorini) usually leave in the morning from Akti Tzelepi across from Plateia Karaiskaki. Aegina boats usually leave from Akti Poseidonos. Boats for Rhodes usually sail in the afternoon from Akti Miaouli. Boats for the western Cyclades (including Sifnos) usually sail in the early evening from Akti Kalimassioti near Plateia Karaiskaki. Boats for Crete usually sail in the early evening from Akti Kondyli. Many additional island boats leave from the quay opposite the Metro station. Boats heading out of Greece leave from the quay on Akti Miaouli farthest away from the quays near the Metro and train stations. Boats for Aegina, Poros, Hydra, Spetses, Peloponnesian ports, and Kithira go from Zea Marina, across the Piraeus peninsula and opposite the great harbor, from which it is a good 30-minute walk.

WHAT TO SEE & DO

If you're stuck between boats, you may not want to do anything except pass the time as quietly as possible. If so, you might simply walk inland from the harbor on Odos Demosthenous to Plateia Korai and sit at a cafe. Or, if you want to be by the sea, take the no. 904 bus (Dr100/30¢) from the main harbor to Akti Themistokleous, where there are also cafes.

More energetic suggestions, if you're in Piraeus in the summer, include finding out if there's an **open-air theatrical performance** at the Kastella Theater, a few blocks inland from Mikrolimano. In 2000, the first **Poseidon Festival,** with a wide range of concerts, took place in Piraeus; it's supposed to become an annual event, and you might want to get details at the Piraeus Municipal Theater, Odos Ayiou Konstantinou (☎ 01/419-4550). In the winter, performances are staged indoors, at the Public Theater on the green at Leoforos King Constantine. The Sunday **flea market** on and around Odos Alipedou and Odos Skylitsi is an equally crowded variation on the Monastiraki flea market, with generally lower-quality goods. The daily **street market** just off the main harbor is a good place to get picnic supplies for your boat trip.

The **Maritime Museum,** Akti Themistokleous, near the pier for the hydrofoils (☎ 01/452-1598), has handsome models of ancient and modern ships. Don't miss the classical warship (*trireme*); scholars are still trying to figure out just how all those oarsmen rowed in unison. Open Tuesday through Saturday from 9am to 2pm; admission is Dr500 ($1.45). If you have time, stop by the **Archaeological Museum,** Odos Harilaou Trikoupi 32 (☎ 01/452-1598), to see three superb monumental bronzes depicting a youth (some say Apollo) and two goddesses (some say Athena and Artemis). Open Tuesday through Sunday from 8:30am to 3pm; admission is Dr500 ($1.45).

WHERE TO STAY

We don't recommend an overnight stay in Piraeus, but if it makes sense in your travel plans, try one of these decent, moderately priced choices: the 74-unit **Hotel Mistral,** Odos Vassileos Pavlou 105, Kastella (☎ 01/411-7150; fax 01/412-2096), with a nice roof garden; or the recently renovated 31-unit **Ideal Hotel,** Odos Notara 142 (☎ 01/429-4050; fax 01/429-3890). If you want something a bit nicer, try the 74-unit **Cavo D'Oro,** Odos Vasileos Pavlou 19 (☎ **01/411-3744;** fax 01/412-2210).

WHERE TO DINE

While there are some good restaurants in Piraeus, the places to eat along the harbor are generally mediocre at best. You'll do better if you walk in a few blocks along Odos Demosthenous to Plateia Korai, where there are a number of small cafes and restaurants actually patronized by Greeks. If you do decide to try one of the seafood restaurants in central Piraeus or Mikrolimani, make sure you know the price before ordering; some of these places prey on the unwary. If the final tab seems out of line, insist on a receipt, phone the tourist police, and sit tight.

For the best, freshest, most inventively prepared seafood you can imagine, see p. 127 for a review of ✿ **Varoulko,** Deligeorgi 14 (☎ **01/411-2043;** fax 01/422-1283).

Aschimopapo (The Ugly Duckling). Odos Ionon 61, Ano Petralona. ☎ **01/346-3282.** Reservations suggested. Meals Dr2,500–Dr4,000 ($7–$11). No credit cards. Mon–Sat 8:30pm–1am. GREEK.

Ano Petralona is the neighborhood between the western edge of the Filopappos Hill and the Athens-Piraeus train line, technically in Piraeus. It's not far from the center of town, but you'll need a cab driver who either knows this taverna or has the Athens street guide to get here. The Aschimopapo is on the last stretch of Ionon before the ring road around the Filopappos Hill, and the entrance is marked only by a light. This place offers much more than the regular taverna fare, and it's worth the trouble. The menu offers such specialties as lamb cooked in a clay pot, snails, and *eksohiko* (pork baked in aluminum foil in individual servings), plus many other good dishes, tasty mezedes, and wine from the barrel.

Dourambeis. Odos Dilaveri 29. ☎ **01/412-2092.** Reservations suggested. Fish prices (by the kilo) change daily, ranging from about Dr10,000–Dr15,000 ($29–$43). No credit cards. Mon–Sat noon–5pm and 8pm–1am. SEAFOOD.

This fish taverna near the Delphinario theater in Piraeus is where locals go when they want a good fish dinner. The decor is simple, the food excellent. The crayfish soup alone is worth the trip, but the whole point of going is for the excellent grilled fish.

Vassilenas. Etolikou 72, Ayia Sofia. ☎ **01/461-2457.** Reservations recommended Fri–Sat. Meals Dr6,000 ($17). No credit cards. Mon–Sat 8pm–midnight. Closed Aug. SEAFOOD/GREEK.

Vassilenas has been serving its flat-fee menu for decades. Come here hungry, and even then you probably won't be able to eat everything in the more than 15 courses set before you. There's plenty of seafood, plus good Greek dishes. This is a great place to come with friends, so you can compare notes on favorite dishes. Since Vassilenas is a fair hike from the waterfront, you may want to take a taxi.

13 Day Trips from Athens

Although there are a number of tempting excursions from Athens, simply getting in and out of the city is so unpleasant that we suggest you visit most of these places as you head off to the Peloponnese (Daphni and Eleusis are on the way) or visit Central or Northern Greece (you could take in Marathon, Brauron, or Rhamnous this way). Nonetheless, there are two excursions—the Monastery at Kaisariani and the Temple of Poseidon at Sounion—that can be easily done as day trips from Athens.

All these excursions take you into Attica, today, as in antiquity, the name of the countryside around Athens. According to legend, the hero Theseus unified the 12 towns of Attica under Athens. Although by no means one of the most fertile areas of Greece, the Attic countryside provided Athens with wine grapes, olives, honey, grains, fruits, marvelous marble from **Mount Pentelicus** (Pendeli) and **Mount Hymettus** (Imittos), and silver from the mines at Laurium, near Sounion. Today the Attic *Mesogeion* (the word means "the middle of the earth" and refers to the Attic plain) is still known for its fine grapes, most often used in making white retsina.

Sadly, serious fires have raged through much of Attica every summer since 1995. Some forests on Mounts Pentelicus and Hymettus have been totally destroyed. Much farmland has been wiped out, and the museum at Marathon was almost lost. Be prepared to see the signs of these terrible fires for some years when you visit Attica.

THE TEMPLE OF POSEIDON AT SOUNION

One of the easiest and most popular day trips from Athens is to the 5th-century B.C. Temple of Poseidon on the cliffs above Cape Sounion, 70 kilometers (43 miles) east of Athens (about 2 hrs. by bus). This is a very popular place at sunset for individuals, families, and tour groups—so popular that, if at all possible, you should not come on a weekend.

The easiest way to visit Sounion is on an **organized tour** run by CHAT, Key, or GO (see "Organized Tours," above). If you want to go on your own for far less money, take the Sounion **bus** leaving from Odos Mavromateon along the west side of the Pedion tou Areos park (off the eastern end of Leoforos Alexandras). Buses leave about every half hour, take 2 hours to reach Sounion, and cost under Dr1,200 ($3.45). To verify times, ask a Greek speaker to telephone the local **ticket office** (☎ 01/ 823-0179). Once you're in Sounion, you can catch a cab or walk the remaining kilometer to the temple. If you go to Sounion **by car,** heading out of Athens on Syngrou or Vouliagmenis boulevards, you'll probably fight your way through heavy traffic almost all the way, in both directions. Signs for Sounion appear around the Athens Airport.

The Temple of Poseidon. ☎ 0292/39-363. Admission Dr800 ($2.30). Daily 10am– sunset (sometimes in summer from 8am–sunset).

Cape Sounion is the southernmost point of Attica, and in antiquity, as today, sailors knew they were getting near Athens when they caught sight of the Temple of Poseidon's slender Doric columns. According to legend, it was at Sounion that the great Athenian hero Theseus's father, King Aegeus, awaited his son's return from his journey to Crete to slay the Minotaur. The king had told his son to have his ship return with white sails if he survived the encounter, with black sails if he met death in the Cretan labyrinth. In the excitement of his victory, Theseus forgot his father's words, and the ship returned with black sails. When Aegeus saw the black sails, he threw himself, heartbroken, into the sea—forever after known as the Aegean.

One of the things that makes Sounion so spectacular, other than its site, is that 15 of the temple's original 34 columns are still standing. A popular pastime here is trying to find the spot on one column where Lord Byron carved his name. After you find Byron's name, you may wish to sit in the shade of a column, enjoy the spectacular view over the sea, envy the solitude and quiet Byron found here, and recite these lines on Sounion from the poet's *Don Juan:*

> *Place me on Sunium's marbled steep,*
> *Where nothing, save the waves and I*
> *May hear our mutual murmurs sweep...*

It's easy to think that this sanctuary was purely a religious spot in antiquity. Nothing could be more wrong: The entire sanctuary (of which little remains other than the temple itself) was heavily fortified during the Peloponnesian War because of its strategic importance overlooking the sea routes. Much of the grain that fed Athens arrived from outside Attica in ships that had to sail past Cape Sounion. In fact, Sounion had something of an unsavory reputation as the haunt of pirates in antiquity; it would be uncharitable to think that their descendants run today's nearby souvenir shops, restaurants, and cafes. If you wish, you can take a swim in the sea below Sounion and grab a snack at one of the overpriced restaurants. Better yet, bring a picnic to enjoy on the beach.

THE MONASTERY OF KAISARIANI (KESSARIANI) & MOUNT HYMETTUS (IMITTOS)

The beautiful Kaisariani Monastery stands in a cool, bird-inhabited grove of pines and cypresses on the lower slopes of Mount Hymettus, famous for its beautiful marble and delicious honey. In fact, the 4th-century A.D. philosopher Synesius of Cyrene tells the story that the Sophists lured students to their lectures "not by the fame of their eloquence, but by pots of honey from Hymettus." This has long been a lovely place to escape the heat of Athens, especially after most of the bees left Hymettus and no longer vexed visitors. Alas, the forests were damaged in the fires of 1998, when four firemen died fighting the blazes. Keep in mind that the remaining pine groves here are a potential tinderbox. As always, be very careful if you smoke or use matches.

Kaisariani is 8 kilometers (5 miles) east of central Athens. The easiest way to visit is to take a **taxi** from Athens for about Dr4,500 ($13). Then, if you wish, you can return by bus, having spotted the bus stop on your way up to Kaisariani. If you want the cab to wait while you visit the monastery, negotiate a price in advance. Every 20 minutes, **bus no. 224** leaves from Panepistimiou and Vas. Sofias, northeast of Syntagma Square, to the suburb of Kaisariani. If it's not a hot day, it's a pleasant 2-kilometer walk (follow the signs) up the road to the wooded site, or you can take one of the cabs that waits for business by the bus stop.

We suggest that you do not drive unless you want to explore Mount Hymettus, which is no longer the woodsy place fabled in antiquity, but has become bleak after its recent fires. Kaisariani is poorly signposted, and you may have trouble finding it, even with a good map.

The Kaisariani Monastery. ☎ **01/723-6619.** Admission Dr800 ($2.30). Tues–Sun 8:30am–3pm.

When a spot is holy in Greece, it has usually been holy for a very long time indeed. Today's monastery occupies the site of an ancient temple to Aphrodite, probably built here because of the spring that still flows. You'll see the water pouring forth through the open mouth of the marble goat's head at the monastery's entrance. Incredibly, this spring once supplied much of Athens with drinking water. Now, Greek brides who wish to become pregnant often journey here to drink from the spring, whose waters are believed to speed conception.

This monastery was built in the 11th century over the ruins of a 5th-century Christian church, itself built over the temple. The monks supported themselves by bee-keeping and selling the honey, much as some religious orders today sell jams and liqueurs. The monastery's kitchen and refectory, which now house some sculptural fragments, are on the west side of a paved, flower-filled courtyard. To the south, the old monks' cells and a bathhouse are being restored (exploration at your own risk is usually permitted). The well-preserved church, built like so many in Greece in the shape of a Greek cross, has a dome supported by four ancient Roman columns. Most of the frescoes are relatively late, dating from the 17th and 18th centuries; the distinctive bell tower is from the 19th century.

THE SANCTUARY OF ARTEMIS AT BRAURON (VRAVRONA)

This little shrine to Artemis in the Attic hills is not much visited; more is the pity, since it's a lovely tranquil spot. It's located 38 kilometers (22 miles) east of central Athens between Porto Rafti and Loutsa, on the east coast of Attica.

Take **bus no. 304** for the Zappeion to the village of Loutsa, which is about 2 kilometers (about a mile) from the site. **By car,** drive through Peania and Markopoulo towards Porto Rafti, which the road signs also call Mesoyia. Go left at the first turn after Markopoulo. The sign indicates Mesoyia's Port (Porto Rafti) straight ahead 6 kilometers (3.7 miles) and has an arrow to the left toward Vravrona and Artemida, written only in Greek. The ancient sanctuary is just over 4 kilometers (2.5 miles) from this turn. On the left about 600 meters before the site are the remains of a 6th-century church. Traffic often backs up on the road between Stavrou and Markopoulo, particularly in Peania, so the trip probably will take the better part of an hour.

The Sanctuary of Artemis. ☎ 0294/71-020. Site admission Dr500 ($1.45); museum admission Dr500 ($1.45). Both open Tues–Sun 8:30am–3pm.

Just when you think that you're beginning to understand the ancient Greeks a little bit, you encounter something like the cult of Artemis at Brauron. According to legend, Agamemnon's ill-fated daughter Iphigenia served as a priestess here, and was buried here after her ritual sacrifice on the eve of the expedition to Troy. That's the easy part. The hard part is understanding why Iphigenia and Artemis were honored here with a quadrennial festival in which little girls were dressed as bear cubs. According to one story, the custom began when an epidemic broke out after a youth killed a bear that had attacked his sister. An oracle suggested that a purifying ceremony take place in which young girls dressed like bears, and this continued every four years throughout antiquity. As you sit on a shady slope, you may want to imagine the procession of little girls who came here in saffron-colored robes, and their bearlike antics. Just to confuse matters further, these ceremonies were believed to assist women in childbirth.

The most striking structure at Brauron is the **stoa,** restored in 1961. The stoa was built in the shape of an incomplete Greek letter "p" facing south toward the hill. Six rooms on the north of the stoa contained 11 small beds for the children, with stone tables by the beds. Four rooms on the west of the stoa may also have been used as bedrooms for the children. You can also see the foundations of the 5th-century **Temple of Artemis** here, as well as a cave, usually called the **Tomb of Iphigenia.** There's also a sacred spring and two chapels in this altogether delightful spot. The five-room **museum** is very charming, with a number of marble portrait heads of the little girls, plus some bear masks. We've enjoyed picnicking on the site, and there are also a number of tavernas nearby.

THE SANCTUARY OF NEMESIS AT RHAMNOUS

In antiquity, Rhamnous was a fortress town on the northern borders of Attica with an important sanctuary of Nemesis, the goddess of revenge. For the last several years, the Greek Archaeological Society has been carrying out extensive excavations in the area.

The ancient entrance road to the site has now been cleared, and several tombs at the beginning of this road have been reconstructed.

Rhamnous is 53 kilometers (33 miles) northeast of Athens and can be visited easily only **by car**. It can also be handily combined with a trip to **Marathon,** as it is only 12 kilometers (7.4 miles) beyond the site of the famous battle. From Athens, take the Neo Makri–Marathona road, turning right toward Kato Souli. The unmarked road to Rhamnous branches left 3 kilometers (1.9 miles) from Kato Souli and continues another 2.5 kilometers (1.6 miles) beside vineyards to the site. There's only the fence and the small ticket stand to indicate that you have reached the archaeological site.

The Sanctuary of Nemesis. ☎ **0294/69-477.** Admission Dr500 ($1.45). Daily 8:30am–3pm.

The Sanctuary of Nemesis has the remains of two temples, one built after Athens's victory over the Persians in 490 B.C. and one built in the mid–5th century B.C. Only the foundations of each remain, and this is another site to visit more for its pleasant location near the sea than for its ancient remains.

The smaller, older temple was dedicated to Themis (Justice), while the larger was dedicated to Nemesis (Revenge). The tireless 2nd-century A.D. traveler Pausanias tells a nice story about the temple of Nemesis. "The Persians," Pausanias wrote, "were so sure that nothing could stop them from taking Athens that they carried with them a block of Parian marble to raise a victory trophy after the battle." When the Athenians defeated the Persians in 480 B.C., the great sculptor Phidias used the Persians' block of Parian marble for a colossal figure of Nemesis for the temple here.

Nemesis, by the way, was one of many goddesses to catch the eye of Zeus. In her attempts to flee him, she changed herself into a goose, but Zeus was not fooled. According to one legend, the result of their union was an egg from which Helen, the wife of Menelaos and the cause of the Trojan War, eventually was born. Nemesis gave the egg to Leda, who raised Helen and is often considered Helen's mother. According to other legends, Leda herself was Helen's mother, impregnated by Zeus when the King of the Gods turned himself into a swan.

Because excavations are going on at Rhamnous, you may not be able to visit the fortress above the site, but you may get to see some recently excavated tombs.

MARATHON

In 490 B.C., the vastly outnumbered Athenians and their allies from the little Boeotian town of Plataea defeated the invading Persian army on the plain of Marathon, and saved Athens and much of Greece (and, some say, much of Europe) from Persian rule. In honor of their valor, the 192 Athenians who fell here were buried on the battlefield in an enormous burial mound. Beyond that, there's little to see at Marathon, as there is little to see at Gettysburg and Runnymede, but such sites are moving because of the battles that once tore up the ground and shaped the course of history. When Lord Byron came to Greece to fight in the War of Independence, he came to Marathon and wrote:

> The mountains look on Marathon,
> And Marathon looks on the sea.
> And musing there an hour alone,
> I dreamed that Greece might still be free…

Alas, before he could fight to free Greece, Byron succumbed to fever in the boggy, cholera-infested town of Mesolongi, where he died on April 19, 1824.

Marathon is 42 kilometers (26 miles) northeast of Athens between the villages of Nea Makri and Marathona. **Buses** leave Athens from Odos Mavromati along the east side of the Pedion tou Areos Park approximately every half hour in the morning and every hour in the afternoon. The trip costs about Dr700 ($2.00) and takes about 2½ hours. For departure times, call the **tourist police** (☎ 171) or ask a Greek speaker to call the local **ticket office** (☎ 01/821-0872). **By car,** drive north from Athens along Leoforos Kifissias, the more scenic route that rounds Mount Pendeli through Dionissos to the sea at Nea Makri, or along the National Highway toward Thessaloniki, from which signs will direct you to Marathon. Marathon is very close to the **Sanctuary of Nemesis** (see above); consider pairing the two sites on your day trip.

Marathon Battlefield & Burial Mound. ☎ **0294/55-155.** Admission of Dr500 ($1.45) includes both the mound and museum. Museum open Tues–Sun 8:30am–3pm.

By September of 490 B.C., the advancing force of Persia—then the most powerful empire in the world—reached Marathon, anchored its fleet in the bay, and made plans to attack Athens by land and by sea. The Athenians sent their swiftest runner, Pheidippides, to Sparta to ask for help, and marched their entire army of perhaps 9,000 men north to Marathon. When Pheidippides reached Sparta (most think it took him about a day and a half), the Spartans said they would be delighted to join the Athenians—as soon as an important Spartan religious festival observing the full moon was concluded. This was widely thought to be a delaying tactic, and Athens prepared to stand alone—and did, except for a small contingent of perhaps 1,000 soldiers from the little town of Plataea in Boeotia. The Persian force was at least 24,000 strong.

For some days, the two forces eyed each other, but neither attacked. Then, before dawn on September 12, the Athenians launched a surprise attack. As the Athenian right and left wings forged forward, the center gave way—but when the Persians pressed forward, the Athenian flanks surrounded them and the serious slaughter began. Many of the Persians tried to flee to the safety of their ships, anchored offshore, but were cut down in the marshy plain that lay between the battlefield and the sea. By nightfall, the victory was won, and Pheidippides was again dispatched, this time to run to Athens with news of the victory at Marathon. Pheidippides ran flat out, burst into the Athenian Agora, shouted "We have won"—and fell dead from exhaustion. Today's marathons commemorate Pheidippides's run.

Although the Athenians won the battle at Marathon, the Persian navy had not been harmed, and it set sail for Athens. The weary Athenian army marched post-haste back to Athens and prepared to do battle again, but the Persians, for whatever reason, after sailing up and down the coast of Attica, reversed course and returned to Asia Minor. Ten years later, they would be back—only to be defeated decisively in the Battle of Salamis.

The Athenian victory at Marathon, against such great odds, became the stuff of legend. Some said that the Athenian hero Theseus himself fought alongside his descendants. Others said that the god Pan had bewitched and confused the Persians, leading them to plunge to their deaths in the marshy swamp—leading them, in short, to panic, the word derived from the god's name. According to one legend, Pan also appeared to Pheidippides as he ran with news of the victory to Athens. Pointedly, Pan asked why the Athenians built so few shrines to him—a situation that was quickly rectified throughout Attica.

Although it was customary to bury war casualties in the Kerameikos cemetery in Athens, the 192 Athenian dead from this astonishing victory were cremated and buried together in the mound, which still stands on the battlefield. When the Athenian mound was excavated in the late 19th century, quantities of ashes and burnt bones were found.

Half a millennium after the battle, when the traveler Pausanias visited Marathon, he wrote, "Here every night you can hear the noise of whinnying horses and of men fighting." Indeed, there are those today who claim to have heard sounds of battle on moonlit nights at Marathon.

The mound where the Plataeans were buried, and the small archaeological museum with finds from the site and area, are both 2 kilometers (1.25 miles) from the battle-field in the village of Marathona. This area was one of many severely threatened in the fires that swept across Greece in the summer of 1998.

If you're not bothered by swimming near where so many Persians drowned in the marshy swamp, there are lots of opportunities to take a dip and enjoy a bite at a tav-erna along the coast here.

THE MONASTERY OF DAPHNI (DAFNI)

If you've never seen Byzantine mosaics and wonder what all the fuss is about, Daphni is the place to come. Daphni is one of the greatest masterpieces of the Byzantine empire, which was founded by the first Christian emperor, Constantine, in the 4th century A.D. and conquered by the Turks in 1453. The great art historian of Byzan-tine Greece, Sir David Talbot-Rice, has called Daphni "the most perfect monument" of the 11th century—and this sober scholar was not given to hyperbole.

Unfortunately, getting here is an ordeal. If possible, see Daphni on your way to or from the Peloponnese; if you're driving, you can easily stop here, or if you're traveling with a tour, most stop at Daphni. You could brave a taxi, but it's a very ugly ride—and the 9-kilometer (5.5-mile) trip west of Athens can take an hour.

By bus, take no. 860 from Odos Panepistimiou north of Sina (behind the univer-sity); nos. 853, 862, 873, or 880 from Eleftheria Square off Leoforos Pireos (north-west of Monastiraki); or nos. A15 or B16, marked Elefsina, from Odos Sachtouri, southeast of Eleftheria Square (this trip can be combined with a visit to **Eleusis,** reviewed below). The trip will take about an hour, and the bus stop at Daphni is about 150 meters from the monastery, which is behind the wall where you see trees.

If you're **driving,** follow the signs for Corinth out of Omonia Square. You will be on a very ugly and very crowded road for the entire journey of at least half an hour. After you cross an overpass over the National Road that runs north to Thessaloniki (Salonika), the road rises steadily for 5 kilometers (3 miles) to the gentle crest of a hill. There is a traffic light just over the crest and another traffic light approximately 500 yards further on. Turn left at the second light and then right along the parallel road some 300 yards to the monastery. *Warning:* Due to the heavy traffic, turning off the National Road is not always easy, so allow yourself plenty of time to get to the left to make the turn.

The Monastery of Daphni. ☎ 01/581-1558. Admission Dr800 ($2.30). Daily (except on major holidays) 8:30am–2:45pm.

When you reach Daphni, you may want to take a few minutes in the courtyard to look at the church's lovely brickwork and think about the long history of this sacred spot. There have been shrines here since antiquity, when there was a temple to Apollo. The temple is long since gone (except for one column near the entrance), but the name "Daphni" (Greek for "laurel," Apollo's favorite plant), still honors that god.

In the 6th century, a small monastery was built here, later greatly expanded in the 11th century. The monastic buildings have been almost entirely destroyed, but the domed church dedicated to the Virgin Mary remains. This is something of a miracle: Over the centuries, Daphni has been repeatedly damaged by invaders and earth-quakes, and repeatedly rebuilt. You'll see an example of that rebuilding in the twin gothic arches in front of the church's west entrance. These were added by the Cistercian monks who turned Daphni into a Catholic monastery after the Crusaders captured Constantinople in 1204. During the long period of the Turkish occupation, there was no functioning monastery here—indeed, for a while, the buildings were used as army barracks. After the Greek War of Independence, Daphni was reclaimed by the Greek Orthodox church and restored to its former glory.

A severe earthquake in the 1980s prompted another round of restoration in which the church was strengthened and its dazzling mosaic cycle repaired. When you step inside and let your eyes become accustomed to the dark, here's some of what you'll see. The **central dome** has the commanding mosaic of Christ Pantocrator (the Almighty). This image of Christ as an awesome judge is quite different from the Western tradition of Christ as a suffering mortal. If you're familiar with the Old and New Testament, you'll be able to pick out familiar stories in the mosaics throughout the rest of the church. As is traditional in Greek Orthodox churches, the Annunciation, Nativity, Baptism, and Transfiguration are in the squinches supporting the dome, and the 16 major prophets are displayed between the windows of the dome. The Adoration of the Magi and the Resurrection are in the **barrel vault** inside the main (southern) entrance of the church, and the Entry into Jerusalem and the Crucifixion are in the **northern barrel vault.** Mosaics showing scenes from the life of the Virgin are in the **south bay** of the narthex (passage between the entrance and nave). Even if you're not familiar with the stories, and even if you find the mosaic of Christ Pantocrator grim rather than awesome, you may well be enchanted by the charming details in scenes such as the Adoration of the Magi.

Daphni is also known for the **Wine Festival** which is usually held on the grounds every year from mid-August to mid-September. Unfortunately, you can't combine a visit to the monastery with a visit to the Wine Festival, which runs from 8pm to midnight. Admission is Dr1,000 ($2.90); for Dr2,500 ($7) you get a glass and can sample as many of the wines as you deem wise. Check with the **Athens Festival Office,** Odos Stadiou 4, near Syntagma Square (☎ 01/322-7944), for more information.

THE SANCTUARY OF ELEUSIS (ELEFSIS)

Although Eleusis was the site of the most famous and revered of all the ancient Mysteries, the present-day site is so grim (surrounded by the horrors, and horrible smells, of the industrial city of Elefsina), that you'll need a very keen interest in either archaeology, mystery cults, or oil refineries to enjoy a visit here. That said, we must admit that we have one friend who says that Eleusis is her favorite site near Athens. This makes absolutely no sense to us, but if you come here, you can see if she has a point.

Eleusis is 22.5 kilometers (14 miles) west of Athens. To get here **by bus,** take no. A16, 853, or 862 from Eleftherias Square off Leoforos Pireos near Omonia. (This trip can be combined with a visit to Daphni Monastery.) Ask the driver to let you off at the Sanctuary (Heron), which is off to the left of the main road, before the center of town. If you're **driving,** take the National Road and exit at Elefsina. At press time, the signs pointing to the site had been removed; you may have to ask repeatedly for directions. You'll know you're getting close when you go through a small, pleasantly wooded square with several restaurants and catch a glimpse of the site off to the side.

The Sanctuary of Eleusis. Elefsina. ☎ **01/554-6019.** Admission Dr500 ($1.45); free Sun. Tues–Sun 8:30am–3pm.

The unknown and the famous were initiated into the sacred rites here, yet we know almost nothing about the Eleusinian Mysteries. What we do know is that the Mysteries commemorated the abduction of Demeter's daughter Persephone by the god of the underworld, Hades (Pluto). Demeter was able to strike a bargain with the god, who allowed Persephone to leave the underworld and rejoin her mother for 6 months each year. The Mysteries celebrated this—and the cycle of growth, death, and rebirth of each year's crops.

Despite its substantial remains and glorious past—this was already a religious site in Mycenaean times—the sanctuary's present surroundings make it difficult to warm to the spot. Admittedly, there are the considerable remains of a **Temple of Artemis,** a 2nd-century A.D. **Roman Propylaea** (monumental entrance), and **triumphal arches** dedicated to the Great Goddesses and to the emperor Hadrian. Hadrian's arch here, by the way, inspired the Arc de Triomphe, on the Champs-Elysées in Paris. Nearby is the **Telesterion,** the Temple of Demeter, where only initiates of the cult knew what really happened—and they kept their silence.

One poignant spot at the Sanctuary is the **Kallichoron Well,** where the goddess Demeter wept over the loss of her daughter, whom Hades (Pluto) spirited away. The dark god may have dragged Persephone with him through the cave here known as **Ploutonion,** which was believed to be an entrance to the underworld. It seems ironic that modern Elefsina itself is so ghastly that it has become something of a hell on earth.

If you're in luck, the small **museum,** which has been closed since the 1999 earthquake, will have reopened. It has finds from the site, including several **figures of Demeter** and a lithe **statue of Antinous,** the beautiful boy who won the emperor Hadrian's heart.

6 The Saronic Gulf Islands

by Sherry Marker

The islands of the Saronic Gulf, which lies between Attica and the Peloponnese, are so close to Athens that each summer they are inundated with Athenians—all of whom, of course, are seeking to avoid the crowds of Athens. These islands are especially packed on summer weekends, as well as whenever there's a serious heat wave in Athens. In addition, the Saronic Gulf islands are popular destinations for travelers whose time is limited, but who are determined not to go home without seeing at least one Greek island.

The easiest island to visit is **Aegina,** a mere 30 kilometers (17 nautical miles) from Piraeus. The main attractions here are the graceful Doric temple of **Aphaia** (one of the best-preserved Greek temples), several good beaches, and some pleasant pine and pistachio groves. That's the good news. The bad news is that Aegina is so close to the metropolitan sprawl of Athens and Piraeus that you're unlikely to get any real sense of why the Greek islands are so beloved. It has become a bedroom suburb for Athens, with many of its 10,000 inhabitants commuting to the office by boat.

Poros is hardly an island at all: only a narrow (370m) inlet separates it from the Peloponnese. The landscape is wooded, gentle, and rolling, like the adjacent mainland, and there are several good beaches. Young Athenians and tour groups head here in profusion. On summer nights, the waterfront is either very lively or hideously crowded, depending on your point of view.

Hydra (Idra), with its bare hills, superb natural harbor, and elegant stone mansions, is the most strikingly beautiful of the Saronic Gulf islands. One of the first Greek islands to be "discovered" by artists, writers, and bon vivants, Hydra, like Mykonos, is not the place to go to experience traditional village life. The island has been declared a national monument and cars have been banished, which makes it blessedly quiet (although motorcycles are beginning to infiltrate the scene). One drawback: There's almost no decent beach, but lots of places to swim off the rocks. Despite the hydrofoils that link Hydra all too often with other islands and the mainland, this island manages to maintain a certain sense of resolute individuality.

Spetses has always been popular with wealthy Athenians, who built handsome villas here. There are several good beaches, but most are home to the large hotels that house tour groups. If you like your islands wooded, you'll love Spetses; if you think an island should be

The Saronic Gulf Islands

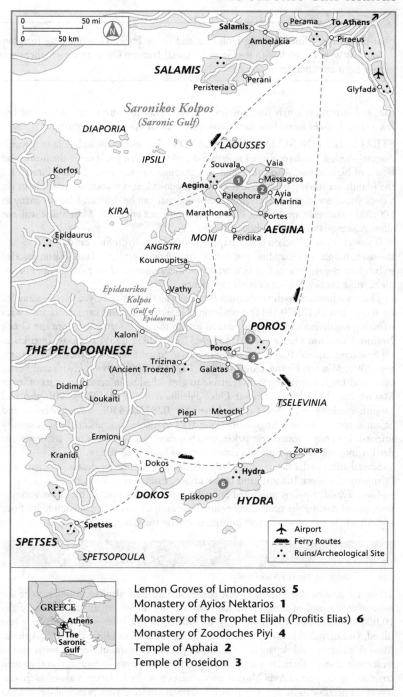

0   50 mi
0   50 km

Salamis   Perama   To Athens
Ambelakia   Piraeus

SALAMIS

Peristeria   Perani

Glyfada

Saronikos Kolpos
(Saronic Gulf)

DIAPORIA

IPSILI   **LAOUSSES**

Korfos   Souvala   Vaia
Messagros
Aegina ①
Paleohora ②   Ayia Marina

KIRA   Marathonas   Portes

Epidaurus   **MONI**   Perdika   **AEGINA**

ANGISTRI
Kounoupitsa

Epidaurikos
Kolpos
(Gulf of
Epidaurus)   Vathy

Kaloni   **POROS**

THE PELOPONNESE   Poros ③
④
Trizina
(Ancient Troezen)   Galatas ⑤

Didima
Loukaiti   **TSELEVINIA**

Piepi   Metochi

Ermioni   Zourvas

Kranidi   Dokos   Hydra

DOKOS   Episkopi ⑥   **HYDRA**

Spetses

SPETSES

SPETSOPOULA

✈ Airport
🚢 Ferry Routes
∴ Ruins/Archeological Site

GREECE
Athens
The Saronic Gulf

Lemon Groves of Limonodassos **5**
Monastery of Ayios Nektarios **1**
Monastery of the Prophet Elijah (Profitis Elias) **6**
Monastery of Zoodoches Piyi **4**
Temple of Aphaia **2**
Temple of Poseidon **3**

Insider Tip _____

At press time, Minoan Flying Dolphins and Ceres Flying Dolphin were merging. You may want to check with the Greek National Tourism Office to see whether there have been any changes in service.

---

bare and austere, you may find Spetses a bit too bland for your taste. Alas, in the last few years, summer forest fires have destroyed some of Spetses's pine groves.

STRATEGIES FOR SEEING THE ISLANDS   If possible, avoid late June through August—unless you have a hotel reservation and think that you'd enjoy the hustle and bustle of high season. Also, from mid-July through August, boats leaving Piraeus for the islands are heavily booked, and often overbooked. It is sometimes possible to get a deck passage without a reservation, but even that can be difficult when as many as 100,000 passengers are leaving Piraeus on a summer weekend. Most ships will not allow passengers to board without a ticket.

If you go to an island on a **day trip,** remember that hydrofoils cannot travel when the sea is rough. You may find yourself an unwilling overnight island visitor, grateful to be given the still-warm bed in a private home, surrendered by a family member to make some money. We speak from experience.

There are frequent **hydrofoils** from Piraeus to all these islands; you can visit any for no more than Dr12,000 ($34) round-trip. The schedules (and carriers) change with irritating regularity, so it's a good idea to get up-to-date information from the **Greek National Tourism Office** (☎ 01/331-9437 or 01/331-0561) at Odos Amerikis 2, off Syntagma Square. (Go to the office in person to get reliable information.) In summer 2000, **Minoan Flying Dolphins** (☎ 01/419-9200), serving Hydra and Poros, often had English-speaking staff available to give schedule information at its office at Marina Zea. Its Athens office, at Odos Filellinon 3 (☎ 01/324-4600), also had English-speaking staff. **Sea Falcon Line** (☎ 0297/26-430), serving Aegina and Salamis, sometimes had English-speaking staff available. Astonishingly, it is usually impossible to buy a round-trip ticket, which means that as soon as you arrive at your destination, you should rush to a ticket agent to book your return.

Several cruises offer day trips to Hydra, Poros, and Aegina; for details, see chapter 3, "Cruising the Greek Islands," and below under "Essentials" for Aegina.

Greek Island Hopping, published annually by Thomas Cook, is, by its own admission, out of date by the time it sees print. That said, it's a very useful volume for finding out where (if not when) you can travel among the Greek islands.

1 Aegina

30km (17 nautical miles) SW of Piraeus

Triangular Aegina (Egina), the largest of the Saronic Gulf islands, continues to be the most visited island of Greece, due to its proximity to Athens. In fact, many of the 10,000 who live here commute daily to Athens. If you have only one day for one island, you may decide on a day trip here to see the famous Doric temple of **Aphaia.** Most ships arrive and depart from the main port and capital of **Aegina town** on the west coast, though there are a few that stop at the resort town of **Souvala** on the north coast and at the port of **Ayia Marina** on the east coast. Ayia Marina is about as charmless as it's possible to be, but this port is your best choice if your principal destination here is the temple of Aphaia.

Despite massive tourism and the rapid development that is devouring much farm-land, there are still almond, olive, and, especially, pistachio orchards here. In fact, the island has an endemic water problem simply because of watering the pistachio groves. Wherever you buy pistachios in Greece, the vendor will often assure you that they are from Aegina to indicate their superior quality.

ESSENTIALS

GETTING THERE   **Car ferries** and **excursion boats** to Aegina usually leave from Piraeus's main harbor; confusingly, **hydrofoils** leave both from the main harbor and from Marina Zea harbor. Hydrofoil service is at least twice as fast as ferries and at least 40% more expensive (except to Aegina, for which the charge is only about 10% more expensive). The sleek little hydrofoils are outfitted like broad aircraft with airline seats, toilets, and a minimum of luggage facilities. (The fore sections offer better views, but they're also bumpier.) The newer Super Cats are bigger, faster, and more comfortable, with food and beverage service. Reservations are recommended on weekends.

By Organized Tour   A good way to see the Saronic Gulf is via a three-island day cruise, which can be booked through a travel agent, such as **Viking Star Cruises** (☎ **01/898-0729** or 01/898-0829), or at your hotel desk. **Epirotiki Lines** (☎ **01/429-1000**) provides transportation to and from your hotel in Athens to Flisvos Marina, where its *Hermes* departs daily around 8:30am for **Hydra** (swimming and shopping), **Poros** (lunch and sightseeing), and **Aegina** (the Temple of Aphaia or swimming), returning to Athens about 7:30pm. Lunch is served onboard. For about Dr30,000 ($86), you get a good tour and an introduction to travel aboard a cruise ship.

Ferry and excursion boat tickets can be purchased at the pier. Call the **Piraeus Port Authority** (☎ **01/451-1456**) for schedule and departure pier information. Hydrofoil tickets can be purchased in advance at **Ceres Hydrofoils,** Akti Themistokleous 8 (☎ **01/428-0001**), midway on the waterfront in Piraeus; at **Sea Falcon Line** (☎ **0297/26-430**), on the harbor at Ayia Marina and Souvala; or at the nearby departure pier.

VISITOR INFORMATION   There are several travel agencies on Aegina. **Pipins Tours,** Odos Kanari 2 (☎ **0297/24-456;** fax 0297/26-656), a block inland from the hydrofoil pier, is the Ceres Hydrofoil agent. **Aegina Island Holidays,** Demokratias 47 (☎ and fax **0297/25-860**), near the church, is also good. Both Pipins Tours and Aegina Island Holidays are good sources for rooms to let around the island. There's also a private **tourist office** at Lada 1 (☎ **0297/22-334**). For those wanting to pursue Aegina's history, look for Anne Yannoulis's *Aegina* (Lycabettus Press), usually on sale on the island.

GETTING AROUND   The **bus station** is on Plateia Ethneyersias, to the left from the ferry pier. There's good service to most of the island, with trips every hour in summer to the Temple of Aphaia and Ayia Marina (Dr350/$1.00); tickets must be

---

Insider Tip

If you visit the islands of the Saronic Gulf in July and August, keep an eye out for posters announcing exhibitions at local museums and galleries. Many Athens galleries close for parts of July and August, and some have shows on the islands. Also, the **Athens Center,** Odos Archimidous 48 (☎ **01/701-2268**), sometimes stages plays on Spetses and Hydra.

purchased at the small temporary office before boarding. **Taxis** are available nearby; fare to the temple should cost about Dr3,000 ($9). You can sometimes negotiate a decent rate for a round-trip with an hour's wait at the temple. **Bicycles** and **mopeds** can be rented at the opposite (south) end of the waterfront, near the beach. Careful: Prices can be exorbitant. An ordinary bike should cost no more than Dr1,500 ($4.30) a day, and mopeds should cost about Dr4,500 to Dr6,000 ($13 to $17) a day.

FAST FACTS The **National Bank of Greece** is one of four waterfront banks with currency-exchange service and ATMs; some travel agents, including **Aegina Island Holidays** (☎ **0297/23-333**), often exchange money both during and after normal bank hours, usually at less favorable rates. The island **clinic** (☎ **0297/22-251**) is on the northeast edge of town; for **first aid**, dial ☎ **0297/22-222**. The **police** (☎ **0297/22-391**) and the **tourist police** (☎ **0297/23-333**) share a building on Odos Leonardou Lada, about 200 meters inland from the port. The **port authority** (☎ **0297/22-328**) is on the waterfront. The **post office** is in Plateia Ethneyersias, around the corner from the hydrofoil pier. The **telephone office (OTE)** is 5 blocks inland from the port, on Odos Aiakou.

WHAT TO SEE & DO
EXPLORING AEGINA TOWN

Before you head out, try to pick up the useful pamphlet *Essential Aegina,* often available at travel agents, hotels, and the tourist police. Aegina town has a legacy of neoclassical buildings from its brief stint as the first capital of newly independent Greece (from 1826 to 1828), but your primary impression of this harbor town will be of fishing boats and the small cargo vessels that ply back and forth to the mainland. If you take a horse-drawn carriage (about Dr6,000/$17) or wander the streets back from the port, you'll easily see the neoclassical buildings, including the restored **Markelos Tower,** where the first Greek parliament met. Fans of Nikos Kazantzakis may want to take a cab to **Livadi,** just north of town, to see the house where he lived when he wrote *Zorba the Greek.*

North of the harbor, behind the town beach, and sometimes visible from boats entering the harbor, is the lone worn Doric column that marks the site of the **Temple of Apollo,** open Tuesday through Sunday from 8:30am to 3pm; admission is Dr500 ($1.45). The view here is nice, the ruins very ruined.

SEEING THE TEMPLE OF APHAIA

The **Temple of Aphaia,** set on a pine-covered hill 12 kilometers (7.5 miles) east of Aegina town (☎ **0297/32398**), is one of the best-preserved and most handsome Greek temples. No one really knows who Aphaia was, although it seems that she was a very old, even prehistoric, goddess who eventually became associated both with the huntress goddess Artemis and with Athena, the goddess of wisdom. According to some legends, Aphaia lived on Crete, where King Minos, usually preoccupied with his labyrinth and Minotaur, fell in love with her. When she fled Crete, he pursued her, and she finally threw herself into the sea off Aegina to escape him. At some point in the late 6th or early 5th centuries B.C., the temple was built (on the site of earlier shrines) to honor Aphaia.

Thanks to the work of restorers, 25 of the original 32 Doric columns still stand. The pedimental sculpture, showing scenes from the Trojan war, was carted off in 1812 by King Ludwig of Bavaria. Whatever you think about the removal of art treasures from their original homes, Ludwig probably did us a favor by taking it to the Glyptothek in Munich: when Ludwig had the sculpture removed, locals were busily burning much of the temple to make lime and hacking up other bits to use in building their homes. Admission to the site is Dr1,000 ($2.90); it's open Monday through Friday from 8:30am to 7pm, Saturday and Sunday from 8:30am to 3pm.

WHERE TO STAY

✪ **Eginitiko Archontiko (Traditional Hotel).** Odos Nikolaou and Thomaidou 1, 18010 Aegina. ☎ **0297/24-968.** Fax 0297/24-156. 12 units. High season Dr18,000 ($52) double. AE, MC, V. Closed Nov–Mar.

This mansion, near the cathedral, was built in 1820 and renovated in 1988 with some loss of original detail, although some lovely painted ceilings remain. The guest rooms are rather small, but are traditionally furnished, comfortable, and quiet. The pleasant downstairs lobby retains much 19th-century charm, while the garden is very appealing. The owners care about this handsome building (Greece's first president, Ioannis Kapodistrias, once stayed here) and try to make guests comfortable.

Eleni Rooms to Let. Odos Kappou, 18010 Aegina. ☎ **0297/26-450.** 7 units, 4 with bathroom. High season Dr12,000 ($34) single/double without bathroom; Dr15,000 ($43) single/double with bathroom. No credit cards. Closed Nov–Mar.

This excellent budget choice is in part of a house built in 1888. Rooms are cool, quiet, and exceptionally clean, with refinished pine floors and whitewashed walls. Each unit is different; the second-floor rooms with bathrooms are the best.

Hotel Apollo. Ayia Marina, 18010 Aegina. ☎ **0297/32-271.** Fax 0297/32-688. 107 units. TV TEL. High season Dr20,000 ($57) double. Breakfast buffet Dr1,500 ($4.30); lunch or dinner Dr3,500 ($10). AE, DC, MC, V. Closed Nov–Mar.

Ayia Marina, with lots of resort hotels, is not our cup of tea. That said, friends who stayed at this glitzy beach hotel were pleased with their large bathroom and bedroom (with balcony overlooking the sea). Amenities include fresh and saltwater swimming pools, minigolf, and tennis court.

House of Peace (Spiti tis Irinis). Plateia Ethneyersias, 18010 Aegina. ☎ **0297/28-726.** Fax 0297/24-742. E-mail: houseofpeacehotel@yahoo.com or houseofpeace@aig.forthnet.gr. 12 units, 6 with bathroom. High season Dr15,000 ($43) double. No credit cards. Closed Nov–Mar.

This place is popular with young travelers, who appreciate its e-mail facilities, travel information (the Scottish owner doubles as a travel agent), garden, and kitchen. The bedrooms have high ceilings, with some overlooking the garden.

Moondy Bay Bungalows. Profitis Elias, Perdika, 18010 Aegina. ☎ **0297/61-662.** Fax 0297/61-147. 90 units. A/C TEL. High season Dr28,000 ($80) double. Rates include breakfast. AE, V. Closed Nov–May.

This bungalow complex, 7 kilometers (4.5 miles) south of Aegina town in well-kept grounds overlooking the sea, is a good place for families. The bungalows have the usual pine furniture, and the bathrooms are decent sized. Facilities include a good seawater pool, tennis court, minigolf, and children's playground.

WHERE TO DINE

Estiatorion Economou. Odos Demokratias. ☎ **0297/25-113.** Main courses Dr1,200–Dr4,000 ($3.45–$11). AE, EC, MC, V. Daily 9am–1am. GREEK.

A reader suggested this excellent portside taverna with a dark-blue canopy about midway along the waterfront, and several visits have confirmed its high quality. We recommend the lemony fish soup and grilled fish; there are also meat dishes. Grilled local lobster is sometimes available; expect to pay at least Dr20,000 ($57) a kilo.

Maridaki. Odos Demokratias. ☎ **0297/25-869.** Main courses Dr1,500–Dr2,000 ($4.30–$6). No credit cards. Daily 8am–midnight. GREEK.

This lively portside spot has a wide selection of fish, grilled octopus, and the usual taverna fare of souvlaki and moussaka. The mezedes here are usually very good, and you can make an entire meal of them if you wish.

Taverna Vatsoulia. Odos Ayii Assomati. ☎ **0297/22-711.** Dr1,200–Dr3,000 ($3.45–$9). No credit cards. Wed and Sat–Sun 6pm–1am. GREEK.

This local favorite is about a 10-minute walk out of town on the road to the Temple of Aphaia, but call ahead before you go to make sure it's open. The menu is limited; rabbit is a specialty. There's sometimes live music.

AEGINA AFTER DARK

At sunset, the harbor scene gets livelier as everyone comes out for an evening **volta** (stroll). Kanella's **Piano Restaurant** usually has live pop music (heavy on the amplified bouzouki), while **N.O.A.,** a portside ouzeri, offers a more traditional scene. Dancers will want to find **Disco Elpianna** or the **Vareladiko** in Faros for Greek music, and the scene in Ayia Marina is sure to be lively, if a bit sordid (some holidaymakers attempt to set records for the amount of beer and retsina they consume). For more sedentary entertainment, there are two outdoor cinemas, the **Akroyiali** and **Olympia.**

2 Poros

55km (31 nautical miles) SW of Piraeus

Poros shares the gentle, rolling landscape of the adjacent Peloponnesian coastline, and has several good beaches, some decent tavernas, and a lively summer nightlife. If that sounds like lukewarm praise, we're afraid it is: Poros does not have enough of the atmosphere of an island to make us want to return often—and, in July and August, the island virtually sinks under the weight of package-tour groups.

As someone once said, "Geography is destiny": Poros (the word means "straits" or "ford") is separated from the Peloponnese by a narrow channel only 370 meters wide. This makes the island so easy to reach from the mainland that weekending Athenians and many tourists flock here each summer. In fact, there's a car ferry across the straits almost every 20 minutes in summer—which means there are a *lot* of cars here.

If you wish, you can use Poros as a base for visiting the nearby attractions on the mainland, including Epidaurus, ancient Troezen (modern Trizina), and the lemon groves of Limonodassos. In a long day trip, you can visit Nafplion (Nafplio), Mycenae, and Tiryns.

ESSENTIALS

GETTING THERE Hydrofoils to Poros, Hydra, and Spetses leave from Zea Marina in Piraeus. Most people take ferries or hydrofoils from Piraeus or the other Saronic Gulf Islands, but some cross the narrow (540m/1,150 ft.) strait from Galatas by ferry, which costs Dr200 (60¢) and takes only a few minutes. For information, call the **Piraeus Port Authority** (☎ **01/45-11-311**), **Ceres Hydrofoils** (☎ **01/ 42-80-001**) in Piraeus, or **Marinos Tours** (☎ **0298/23-423**) in Poros (the local agent for the hydrofoils). Reservations are recommended on weekends.

The other Saronic islands are all easy to reach from Poros. Marinos Tours runs a weekly **round-trip hydrofoil excursion** to Tinos (3½ hrs. each way) for Dr24,000

($69), and to Mykonos via Hydra (4 hrs. each way) for Dr35,000 ($101). (The one-way fare to Mykonos is Dr26,000/$74.)

VISITOR INFORMATION   The waterfront hotels are generally too noisy for all except heavy sleepers, so if you want to stay in town we suggest you check with **Marinos Tours** (☎ 0298/22-977; fax 0298/25-325), which handles several hundred rooms and apartments, as well as many island hotels. We've also had good reports of **Saronic Gulf Travel** (☎ 0298/24-555; fax 0298/24-802), which often has an excellent free map of the island available. To learn more about Poros, look for Niki Stavrolakes's enduring classic, *Poros* (Lycabettus Press), usually on sale on the island.

GETTING AROUND   You can walk anywhere in Poros town. The **island's bus** can take you to the beaches; the conductor will charge you according to your destination. The **taxi station** is near the hydrofoil dock, or you can call for one at ☎ 0298/23-003; the fare to or from the beach at Askeli should cost about Dr1,800 ($5.15). **Kostas Bikes** (☎ 0298/23-565), opposite the Galatas ferry pier, rents bicycles for about Dr1,800 ($5.15) a day and mopeds from about Dr3,500 ($10) a day. (Motorcycle and moped agents are supposed to, but do not always, ask for proof that you are licensed to drive such vehicles.)

FAST FACTS   The **National Bank of Greece** is one of a handful of waterfront banks with an ATM where you can also exchange money. The **police** (☎ 0298/22-256) and **tourist police** (☎ 0298/22-462) are on the paralia. The **port authority** (☎ 0298/22-274) is on the harborfront. For **first aid,** call ☎ 0298/22-600. The **post office** and **telephone office (OTE)** are also on the waterfront; their hours are Monday through Friday from 8am to 2pm. In summer, in addition to the normal weekday hours, the OTE is usually open Saturday and Sunday from 8am to 1pm and 5 to 10pm. Signs on the harborfront by the clock tower point to a place for **Internet access** (☎ 0298/24-404; e-mail: poros@compulink.gr) that charges Dr1,500 ($4.30) an hour.

WHAT TO SEE & DO
ATTRACTIONS IN POROS TOWN

As you cross over to the island, you'll see the streets of Poros town, the capital, climbing a hill topped with a clock tower. Poros town is itself an island, joined to the rest of Poros by a causeway. The narrow streets along the harbor are usually crowded with visitors inching their way up and down past the restaurants, cafes, and shops. At night, the adjacent hills are, indeed, alive to the sound of music; unfortunately, even the "Greek" music is usually heavily amplified pop.

Poros town has a **Naval Training School**—which means that there are usually a lot of young men looking for company here. Anyone wishing to avoid their attention might try to visit the small **Archaeological Museum** (☎ 0298/23-276), with finds from ancient Troezen. It's usually open Monday through Saturday from 9am to 3pm; admission is free.

EXPLORING THE ISLAND

By car or moped, it's easy to make a circuit of the island in half a day and see what there is to see here. What remains of the 6th century B.C. **Temple of Poseidon** lies scattered beneath pine trees on the low plateau of Palatia, east of Poros town. The remains are scant, largely because the inhabitants of the nearby island of Hydra plundered the temple and hauled away most of the marble to build their harborside Monastery of the Virgin. The Temple of Poseidon was the scene of a famous moment in Greek history in 322 B.C. when Demosthenes, the Athenian 4th-century orator and statesman, fled here for sanctuary from Athens's Macedonian enemies. When his enemies tracked him down, the great speech writer asked for time to write a last letter—and then bit off his pen nib, which contained poison. Even in his death agonies, Demosthenes had the presence of mind to leave the temple, lest his death defile the sanctuary. It seems a fitting that Demosthenes, who lived by his pen, died by same instrument.

Those who enjoy monasteries might want to continue on the road that winds through the interior to the 18th-century **Monastery of the Zoodhochou Pigis** (monastery of the lifegiving spring), south of Poros town. There are usually no monks in residence, but the caretaker should let you in, and there's a little taverna nearby.

Poros's beaches are not an enchantment. The beach northwest of town, at **Neorio,** is not always unpolluted; the better beaches are found southeast of town at **Askeli** and **Kanali.**

OFF THE ISLAND: A FESTIVAL, ANCIENT TROEZEN & LEMON GROVES

If you're in Poros in mid-June, you might want to catch the ferry across to Galatas and take in the annual **Flower Festival,** with floral displays and parades with floats and marching bands. (There are usually lots of posters up in Poros town advertising the festival.)

From Galatas you can catch a bus the 8 kilometers (5 miles) west to **Trizina** (ancient Troezen), birthplace of the great Athenian hero Theseus, and the scene of the tragedy of his wife, Phaedra, and son, Hippolytus. Phaedra, in one of the misogynistic fables beloved of the Greeks, fell in love with her stepson. When the dust settled, both she and Hippolytus were dead and Theseus was bereft. There's the remains of a temple to Asklepius here—but again, these ruins are very ruined.

About 4 kilometers (2.5 miles) south of Galatas near the beach of Aliki, you'll find the olfactory wonder of **Limonodassos** (Lemon Grove), where more than 25,000 lemon trees fill the air with their fragrance each spring. Alas, many were harmed in a harsh storm in March 1998, but it is hoped that most will survive and bloom again. There are several tavernas nearby where you can get freshly squeezed lemonade for about Dr600 ($1.75).

WHERE TO STAY

Hotel Latsi. Odos Papadopoulou 74, 18020 Poros, Trizinias. ☎ **0298/22-392.** 39 units, most with bathroom. TEL. High season Dr20,000 ($57) without bathroom; Dr25,000 ($72) with bathroom. No credit cards. Closed Nov–Mar.

The Latsi is on the quieter north end of the port near the Naval School, opposite the Galatas ferry, with balconies overlooking the port and the Peloponnese. Rooms are worn, but clean and comfortable. If you want an up-to-date bathroom, this hotel is not for you; otherwise, it may be just the spot.

Hotel Sirene. Monastiri, Askeli, 18020 Poros, Trizinias. ☎ **0298/22-741.** Fax 0298/22-744. 120 units. A/C TEL. High season Dr30,000 ($86) double. Half-board (Dr6,500/$19) optional. MC. Closed Nov–Mar.

If you're talking creature comforts, the Sirena, on the beach east of town beyond Askeli, is the best hotel on the island. Those creature comforts mean that the Sirena is very popular with tour groups; if you want to stay here, you must make a reservation in advance. Just about all the spacious rooms in this six-story building have excellent views. There's a saltwater pool near the private beach, and the restaurant is perfectly okay.

WHERE TO DINE

Caravella Restaurant. Paralia, Poros town. ☎ **0298/23-666.** Main courses Dr1,500–Dr5,000 ($4.30–$14). AE, MC, V. Daily 11am–1am. GREEK.

This portside taverna prides itself on serving organic home-grown vegetables and local (not frozen) fish. Specialties include traditional dishes such as veal stifado, moussaka, souvlaki, and stuffed eggplant, as well as seafood and lobster.

Lucas Restaurant. Paralia, Poros town. ☎ **0298/22-145.** Main courses Dr1,800–Dr5,000 ($5.15–$14). No credit cards. GREEK.

You'll find this small restaurant across from the private yacht marina. Fresh seafood and traditional dishes are well prepared and reasonably priced, especially for this upscale area.

Taverna Oasis. Paralia, Poros town. ☎ **0298/22-955.** Main courses Dr1,800–6,000 ($5.15–$17). No credit cards. GREEK.

Tables indoors and outdoors, excellent fresh fish, and the usually cheerful staff make this traditional taverna not far from the post office a pleasant spot for lunch or dinner.

POROS AFTER DARK

There's plenty of evening entertainment in Poros town, especially if you're in the mood to dance. **Korali**, in town, and **Scirocco,** about a kilometer south of town, are popular discos.

3 Hydra (Idra)

65km (35 nautical miles) S of Piraeus

Hydra is one of a handful of places in Greece that seemingly can't be spoiled. Even in summer, when the waterfront teems with day-trippers, many side streets remain quiet. If you can, arrive here in the evening, when most of the day-trippers have left.

With the exception of a handful of municipal vehicles, there are no cars on Hydra. You'll probably run into at least one example of a popular form of local transportation: the donkey. When you see Hydra's splendid 18th- and 19th-century stone **archontika** (mansions) along the waterfront and on the steep streets above, you won't be surprised to learn that the entire island has been declared a national treasure by both the Greek government and the Council of Europe. You'll probably find Hydra town so charming that you'll forgive its one serious flaw: no beach. Do as the Hydriotes do, and swim from the rocks at Spilia, just beyond the main harbor.

Whatever you do, be sure to go out on the deck of your ship as you arrive, so you can see Hydra's bleak mountain hills suddenly reveal a perfect horseshoe harbor. This truly is a place where arrival is half the fun.

ESSENTIALS

GETTING THERE   Several **ferries** and **excursion boats** make the 4-hour voyage between Piraeus and Hydra daily; there's also connecting service to several ports on the Peloponnese peninsula as well as with the other Saronic islands. Call the **Piraeus Port Authority** (☎ 01/451-1311) or **Hydra Port Authority** (☎ 0298/52-279) for schedules. **Ceres Hydrofoils** (☎ 01/428-0001) has several daily Flying Dolphins, some of them direct (1¼ hours), as well as Super Cat service between Piraeus's Zea Marina (the southwest corner) and Hydra. **Minoan Flying Dolphins** (☎ 01/419-9200) has service from Piraeus to Hydra and thence along the coast of the East Peloponnese and to the island of Kythera. Reservations are recommended on weekends.

VISITOR INFORMATION   The free publication *This Summer in Hydra* is widely available and contains much useful information, including a map and a list of rooms to rent; keep in mind that shops and restaurants pay to appear in it. **Saitis Tours** (☎ **0298/52-184**), in the middle of the harborfront, can exchange money, provide information on rooms and villas, book excursions, and help you make long-distance calls or send faxes. For those wanting to pursue Hydra's history, we recommend Catherine Vanderpool's *Hydra* (Lycabettus Press), usually on sale on the island.

GETTING AROUND   Walking is the only means of getting around on the island itself, unless you bring or rent a donkey or bicycle. **Caïques** provide water-taxi service to the island's beaches (Molos, Avlaki, Bitsi, and Limnioniza are the best) and the little offshore islands of Dokos, Kivotos, and Petasi, as well as to secluded restaurants in the evening; rates run from about Dr700 to Dr5,100 ($2 to $15) depending on destination, with an extra Dr600 ($1.75) charge if booked by phone.

FAST FACTS   The **National Bank of Greece** and the **Commercial Bank** are on the harbor; both have ATMs. Travel agents on the harbor will exchange money from about 9am to 8pm, usually at a less favorable rate. The small health **clinic** is signposted on the harbor; cases requiring complicated treatment are taken by boat or helicopter to the mainland. The **tourist police** (☎ **0298/52-205**) are on the second floor at Odos Votsi 9 (signposted in the harbor). The **port authority** (☎ **0298/52-184**) is on the harborside. The **post office** is just off the harborfront on Odos Ikonomou, the street between the two banks. The **telephone office (OTE),** across from the police station on Odos Votsi, is open Monday through Saturday from 7:30am to 10pm, Sunday from 8am to 1pm and 5 to 10pm. For **Internet access,** try HydraNet (☎ **0298/54-150;** fax 0294/54-123), signposted at the OTE.

WHAT TO SEE & DO
ATTRACTIONS IN HYDRA TOWN

In the 18th and 19th centuries, ships from Hydra transported cargo around the world and made Hydra very rich indeed. Just as on the American island of Nantucket, ships' captains demonstrated their wealth by building the fanciest houses money could buy. The captains' lasting legacy is the handsome stone mansions (*archontika*) that give Hydra town its distinctive character.

One archontiko that you can hardly miss is the **Tombazi house,** which dominates the hill that stands directly across the harbor from the main ferry quay. This is now a branch of the School of Fine Arts, with a hostel for students, and you can usually get a peek inside. Call the **mansion** (☎ **0298/52-291**) or the **Athens Polytechnic** (☎ **01/619-2119**) for information about the program or exhibits.

The nearby **Ikonomou-Miriklis mansion** (sometimes called the Voulgaris) is not open to the public, nor is the hilltop **Koundouriotis mansion,** built by an Albanian family that contributed generously to the cause of independence. If you wander the side streets on this side of the harbor, you will see many more handsome houses, some

On a mid-June weekend, Hydra celebrates the **Miaoulia,** honoring Hydriot Admiral Miaoulis, who set much of the Turkish fleet on fire by ramming them with explosives-filled fireboats. In early July, Hydra has an annual **puppet festival** which, in recent years, has drawn puppeteers from countries as far away as Togo and Brazil. As these two festivals are not on set dates, you should attempt to get additional information from the **Hydra tourist police** (☎ **0298/52-205**).

of which are being restored so that they can once again be private homes, while others are being converted into stylish hotels.

Some of Hydra's nicest boutiques and jewelry shops are concentrated on the waterfront, especially in the area below the Tombazi house. **Hermes Art Shop** (☎ **0298/52-689**) has a wide array of jewelry, some good antique reproductions, and a few interesting textiles. **Vangelis Rafalias's Pharmacy** is a lovely place to stop in, even if you don't need anything, just to see the jars of remedies from the 19th century.

Like many islands, Hydra boasts that it has 365 churches, one for every day of the year. The most impressive, the mid-18th-century **Monastery of the Assumption of the Virgin Mary,** is by the clock tower on the harborfront. This is the monastery built of the marble blocks that were hacked out of the (until then) well-preserved Temple of Poseidon on the nearby island of Poros. The buildings here no longer function as a monastery, and the cells are now municipal offices. The church itself has rather undistinguished 19th-century frescoes, but the elaborate 18th-century marble iconostasis (altar screen) is terrific. Like the marble from Poros, this altar screen was "borrowed" from another church and brought here. Seeing it is well worth the donation requested, Dr200 (60¢).

EXPLORING THE ISLAND: A MONASTERY, A CONVENT & BEACHES

If you want to take a vigorous uphill walk (with no shade), head up Odos Miaouli past Kala Pigadia (Good Wells), still the town's best local source of water. A walk of about an hour will bring you to the **Convent of Ayia Efpraxia** and the **Monastery of the Prophet Elijah** (Profitis Elias). Both have superb views, both are still active, and the nuns sell their hand-woven fabrics. (*Note:* Both the nuns and monks observe the midday siesta from 1 to 5pm. Dress appropriately—no shorts or tank tops.)

The only real **beach** on the island is at **Mandraki,** a 20-minute walk east of town, where a large hotel has been built. Just outside town, you can swim at the rocks at **Spilia** or **Kamini.** Farther west along a donkey trail is **Kastello,** with the small fort that gives it its name, and another rocky beach with less crowded swimming. Still farther west is the pretty pine-lined cove of **Molos.** The donkey path continues west to the cultivated plateau at **Episkopi,** from which a faint trail leads on west to **Bisti** and **Ayios Nikolaos** for more secluded swimming. (Most of these beaches are best reached by water taxi from the main harbor.)

One fairly good beach on the south coast, **Limioniza,** can be reached with strong legs, sturdy shoes, and a good map from Ayia Triada, though it's much easier to take a water taxi here and to Molos, Avlaki, and Bisti. The island of **Dokos,** northwest off the tip of Hydra, an hour's boat ride from town, has a good beach and excellent diving conditions—it was here that Jacques Cousteau found a sunken ship with cargo still aboard, believed to be 3,000 years old. You may want to take a picnic with you, as the taverna here keeps unpredictable hours.

WHERE TO STAY

Book well in advance; reservations in summer are almost invariably a necessity, especially on weekends. In addition to the following choices, you might also consider the 19-unit **Hotel Greco,** Odos Kouloura (☎ **0298/53-200;** fax 0298/53-511), a former fishing-net factory in a quiet neighborhood; or the **Hotel Leto** (☎ **0298/53-385**) just off the harbor.

Hotel Angelika. Odos Miaouli 42, 18040 Hydra. ☎ **0298/53-202.** Fax 0298/53-698. www.inn.gr/saronic/hydra/angelica/home.htm. E-mail: angelicahotel@hotmail.com. 15 units. TEL. High season Dr28,000 ($80) double. Rates include breakfast. MC, V. Closed Nov–Mar.

This pension, in a restored traditional Hydriot home, stands on a quiet street 10 minutes away from the port and out of the usual tourist hubbub. The rooms are simple, with touches of local decor in its prints and furnishings. Most overlook the quiet garden courtyard, where breakfast is served. You can request, but will not be guaranteed, one of the rooms with a rooftop terrace (rooms 6, 8, 9, and 10).

✪ **Hotel Bratsera.** Odos Tombazi, 18040 Hydra. ☎ **0298/53-971.** Fax 0298/53-626. 23 units. A/C TEL. High season Dr35,000–Dr48,000 ($101–$138) double; Dr45,000–Dr70,000 ($129–$201) suite. Rates include breakfast. AE, DC, EC, MC, V. Closed mid-Jan to mid-Feb.

The Bratsera keeps turning up on everyone's list of the best hotels in Greece, which says a lot about the state of hotels in Greece. True, this small hotel, in a lovingly restored 1860 sponge factory a short stroll from the harbor, is one of Hydra's nicest. The rooms are all different, distinctively decorated in Hydriot style. The small pool with wisteria-covered trellises is very welcoming; meals are sometimes served poolside in fair weather. The hotel restaurant offers such slightly off-beat treats as fisherman's linguine.

So, what's the problem? For one thing, we've had reports that room-service trays left in the hall after breakfast were still not collected by late afternoon, and we know that messages left for guests aren't always delivered. And surely a fisherman's linguine should be topped with more than a solitary shrimp and one forlorn crayfish. We're eager to hear more from readers on this hotel.

Hotel Hydra. Odos Voulgari 8, 18040 Hydra. ☎ **0298/52-102.** Fax 0298/53-330. 12 units, 8 with bathroom. TEL. High season Dr23,000 ($66) double without bathroom; Dr26,000 ($74) double with bathroom. Rates include breakfast. MC, V. Open year-round.

This is one of the best bargains in town if you don't mind the steep walk up to the beautifully restored two-story, gray-stone mansion on the western cliff, to the right as you get off the ferry. The rooms are carpeted, high ceilinged, and simply furnished, many with balconies overlooking the town and harbor.

✪ **Hotel Miranda.** 18040 Hydra. ☎ **0298/52-230.** Fax 0298/53-510. E-mail: mirhydra@ hol.gr. 14 units. A/C MINIBAR TV TEL. High season Dr25,000 ($72) double; Dr40,000 ($115) suite. Rates include breakfast. AE, V. Closed Nov–Mar.

Once, when we were trapped for the night on Hydra by bad weather, we were lucky enough to get the last room at the Miranda. The room was small, with a tiny bathroom and no real view—so it's a tribute to this hotel that we have wonderful memories of that visit. Most of the rooms here are good sized, with nice views of the lovely garden courtyard and town. Throughout, this handsome 1820 captain's mansion is decorated with oriental rugs, antique cabinets, worn wooden chests, marble tables, contemporary paintings, and period naval engravings. There's even a small art gallery—in short, this is a very classy place.

Hotel Mistral. 18040 Hydra. ☎ **0298/52-509.** Fax 0298/53-412. 20 units. A/C TEL. High season Dr28,000 ($80) double. Closed Nov–Mar.

The three-story Mistral (named for the strong northerly winds that cool the late summer) is another small hotel near the harbor in a nicely restored, traditional Hydriot house. The furnishings here are standard hotel contemporary, with some nice watercolors of local views. One plus here: the large courtyard, where the proprietor Sophia will, time permitting, serve dinner—but only to hotel guests.

Hotel Orloff. Odos Rafalia 9, 18040 Hydra. ☎ **0298/52-564.** Fax 0298/53-532. www.orloff.gr. E-mail: orloff@internet.gr. 10 units. A/C TEL. High season Dr35,000–Dr52,000 ($101–$150). Rates include breakfast. AE, MC, V. Closed Nov–Mar.

This recently restored mansion, just a short walk from the port, was built in the 18th century by a Russian philhellene, Count Orloff. Today it's a pleasant small hotel, distinctively decorated with antique furnishings. Each room is unique, quiet, and comfortable, and there's a very nice basement lounge with a bar. Breakfast is excellent.

Hydroussa. 18040 Hydra. ☎ **0298/52-217.** Fax 0298/52-161. 40 units. A/C TEL. High season Dr27,000–Dr35,000 ($77–$101) double. AE, V. Closed Nov–Mar.

If you don't need a swimming pool, the Hydroussa is almost as charming as the Bratsera, and less expensive; ask about the mid-week discounts here. Many of the spare but pleasant guest rooms have fine views over the town and harbor; some even have endurable reading lamps.

WHERE TO DINE

The harborside eateries are predictably expensive and not very good, although the view is so nice that you may not care. There are also a number of cafes along the waterfront, including **To Roloi** (The Clock), by the clock tower. Just off the harbor, the **Ambrosia Cafe** serves vegetarian fare and good breakfasts.

Bratsera. Odos Tombazi. ☎ **0298/52-794.** Reservations recommended in summer and on weekends. Main courses Dr2,000–Dr5,200 ($6–$15). AE, DC, EC, MC, V. Daily 8am–11pm. GREEK/INTERNATIONAL.

This restaurant in the Hotel Bratsera just off the harbor gets generally favorable reviews, although we've heard complaints of terribly slow service and small portions. The indoor dining area is charmingly rustic and decorated with antique maps, though sitting outdoors under the wisteria-covered trellis beside the pool may be more enjoyable. The menu includes pastas, fresh seafood, grilled meats, and even a few Chinese specialties. (See also the Hotel Bratsera under "Where to Stay," above.)

Marina's Taverna. Vlihos. ☎ **0298/52-496.** Main courses Dr1,800–Dr4,200 ($5.15–$12). No credit cards. Daily noon–11pm. GREEK.

Several readers report that they have enjoyed both the food and the spectacular sunset at this seaside taverna, appropriately nicknamed the Iliovasilema ("Sunset"). Perched on the rocks west of the swimming place at Kamini, it's a Dr3,000 ($9) water-taxi ride from town. The menu is basic, but the food is fresh and carefully prepared by the lovely Marina; her *kleftiko* (pork pie, an island specialty) is superb.

O Kipos (The Garden). Several blocks up from the quay side of the harbor. ☎ **0298/52-329.** Reservations recommended in the summer. Main courses Dr2,500–Dr5,300 ($7–$15). No credit cards. Daily 7pm–midnight. GREEK.

This very popular *psisteria* (grill) is in a tree-filled garden behind whitewashed walls. Grilled meat is, of course, the specialty, but there is also excellent swordfish souvlaki. The mezedes alone will be enough for many. The specialty is *eksohiko*—lamb wrapped in filo (thin leaves of pastry). We've always enjoyed eating here, except on one or two occasions when boisterous tour groups were in evidence.

To Steki. Odos Miaouli. ☎ **0298/53-517.** Main courses Dr1,400–Dr2,800 ($4–$8); daily specials Dr2,800–Dr5,300 ($8–$15). No credit cards. GREEK.

This small taverna, a few blocks up from the quay-side end of the harbor, has simple food at reasonable prices. The walls inside have framed murals showing a rather idealized traditional island life. The daily specials, such as moussaka and stuffed tomatoes, come with salad, vegetables, and dessert.

HYDRA AFTER DARK

The **Veranda** is up from the right (west) end of the harbor, near the Hotel Hydra; look for the sign SAVVAS ROOMS TO LET. It's an excellent place to sip a glass of retsina and watch the sunset. There are several discos, most of them fairly low-key and usually open from June to September. **Heaven** (☎ **0298/52-716**), which has grand views, is up the hill on the west side of town, while **Kavos** (☎ **0298/52-716**), west above the harbor, has a pleasant garden for a rest from the dancing. **Hydronetta** tends to play more western than Greek music—although the music at all these places is so loud that it's hard to be sure.

Portside, there are plenty of bars. **The Pirate** (☎ **0298/52-711**), near the clock tower, is the best known, although nearby **To Roloi** is probably a quieter place for a nightcap. Friends report enjoying a drink at the **Amalour,** just off the harbor, where they were surrounded by hip, black-clad 20- and 30-somethings. There are also a few local haunts left around the harbor; if you see them, you'll recognize them.

4 Spetses

98km (53 nautical miles) SW of Piraeus; 3km (2 nautical miles) from Ermioni

Despite a series of dreadful fires, Spetses's pine groves still make it the greenest of the Saronic Gulf islands. In fact, this island was called "Pityoussa" (pine-tree island) in antiquity. Although the architecture here is less impressive than on Hydra, there are some handsome **archontika** (mansions), built by wealthy 18th- and 19th-century sea captains, and the island has long been popular with wealthy Athenians.

Many Spetses homes have handsome pebble mosaic courtyards; if you're lucky, you'll catch a glimpse of some when garden gates are open. One real plus for visitors here: Cars are not allowed to circulate freely in Spetses town, which would make for a good deal of tranquility if motorcycles were not increasingly endemic.

In recent years, Spetses has become quite popular with foreign tourists, especially the British. Some are pilgrims to see the island where John Fowles set his novel *The Magus,* but more are with tour groups. Consequently, there are times when you can hear as much English as Greek spoken in cafes and restaurants. As always, if you come here off-season, you're bound to have a more relaxed experience and get a better sense of island life—even though some restaurants, shops, and small hotels will be closed.

ESSENTIALS

GETTING THERE   Several **ferries** and **excursion boats** make the 5-hour voyage from Piraeus daily, connecting with the other Saronic islands; contact the **Piraeus Port Authority** (☎ **01/451-1311**) for schedules. (*Note:* Cars are not allowed on the island without express permission.) Several **hydrofoils** (Flying Dolphins, Minoan Flying Dolphina, and Supercats) leave Piraeus's Zea Marina daily, most connecting with the other Saronic islands; express service takes 90 minutes. Contact **Ceres Hydrofoils** (☎ **01/42-80-001**) and **Minoan Flying Dolphins** (☎ **01/419-9200**) in Piraeus for schedules. Reservations are recommended on weekends.

There is less frequent service from Spetses to the island of Kithira and various ports on the Peloponnese; check with Minoan Flying Dolphins.

VISITOR INFORMATION   The island's main travel agencies are **Alasia Travel** (☎ **0298/74-098**), **Takis Travel** (☎ **0298/72-888**), and **Pine Island Travel** (☎ **0298/72-464**), all on the harbor. Pine Island sometimes handles rental of the villa John Fowles stayed in when he wrote *The Magus.* Andrew Thomas's *Spetses* (Lycabettus Press), usually on sale on the island, is recommended to those wanting to pursue Spetses's history.

GETTING AROUND   The island's limited public transportation consists of two municipal **buses** and three or four **taxis. Mopeds** can be rented everywhere, beginning at about Dr5,200 ($15) per day. **Bikes** are also widely available, and the terrain along the road around the island makes them sufficient means of transportation; three-speed bikes cost about Dr1,800 ($5.15) a day, while newer 21-speed models go for about Dr3,500 ($10). **Horse-drawn carriages** can take you from the busy port into the quieter backstreets, where most of the island's handsome old mansions are. (Take your time choosing a driver; some are friendly and informative, others are surly. Fares are highly negotiable.)

The best way to get to the various beaches around the island, as well as to the beach at Kosta, on the Peloponnese, is by **water taxi** (locally called a *venzina,* "gasoline"); these little boats hold about eight to 10 people. A tour around the island costs about Dr10,000 ($29); shorter trips, such as from Dapia to the Old Harbor, cost about Dr3,500 ($10). Schedules are posted on the pier. You can also hire a water taxi to take you anywhere on the island, to another island, or to the mainland. Again, prices are highly negotiable.

FAST FACTS The **National Bank of Greece** is one of several banks on the harbor with an ATM. Most travel agencies (usually open from 9am to 8pm) will also exchange money, usually at a less favorable rate than a bank. The **clinic** (☎ 0298/72-201) is signposted inland from the east side of the port. The **police** (☎ 0298/73-100) and **tourist police** (☎ 0298/73-744) are to the left off the Dapia pier, where the hydrofoils dock, on Odos Botassi. The **port authority** (☎ 0298/72-245) is on the harborfront. The **post office** is on Odos Botassi near the police station; it's open from 8am to 2pm. The **telephone office (OTE),** open daily from 7:30am to 3pm, is to the right off the Dapia pier, behind the Hotel Soleil. **Internet access** is available at Delphina Net-Café (☎ 0298/74-385) on the harborfront.

WHAT TO SEE & DO
EXPLORING SPETSES TOWN (KASTELLI)

Spetses town (also called Kastelli) meanders along the harbor and inland in a lazy fashion, with most of its neoclassical mansions partly hidden from envious eyes by high walls and greenery. Much of the town's street life takes place on the **Dapia,** the square where the ferries and hydrofoils now arrive; the old harbor, **Baltiza,** largely silted up, is just east of town, before the popular swimming spots at **Ayia Marina.**

If you sit at a cafe on the Dapia, you'll see pretty much everyone here coming and going. The handsome black-and-white pebble mosaic commemorates the moment during the War of Independence when the first flag with the motto "Freedom or Death" was raised. Thanks to its large fleet, Spetses played an important part in the War of Independence, routing the Turks in the Straits of Spetses on September 8, 1822. The victory is commemorated every year on the weekend closest to **September 8** with celebrations, church services, and the burning of a ship that symbolizes the defeated Turkish fleet.

As you stroll along the waterfront, you can't help noticing the monumental bronze statue of a woman, her left arm shielding her eyes as she looks out to sea. The statue commemorates one of the greatest heroes of the War of Independence, **Laskarina Bouboulina,** the daughter of a naval captain from Hydra. Bouboulina financed the warship *Agamemnon,* oversaw its construction, served as its captain, and was responsible for several naval victories. She was said to be able to drink any man under the table, and straitlaced citizens sniped that she was so ugly, the only way she could keep a lover was with a gun. You can see where Bouboulina lived when she was ashore by visiting the **Laskarina Bouboulina House** (☎ 0298/72-077) in Pefkakia, just off the port. It keeps somewhat flexible hours (which are usually posted at the house), but is usually open part of the morning and afternoon, with an English-speaking guide giving a half-hour tour; admission is Dr800 ($2.30). You can even see Bouboulina's bones, along with some archaeological finds and mementos of the War of Independence, at the **Spetses Mexis Museum,** in the handsome stone Mexis mansion (signposted on the waterfront). It's open daily from 9:30am to 2:30pm; admission is Dr500 ($1.45).

The **Hotel Possidonion** itself figures in Spetses's history. It was built in 1911 as one of Greece's first "European-style" hotels by the island's greatest benefactor, Sotiris Anaryiros. He also built Anaryiros College, just outside town, modeled on an English public school. The college is now most famous because John Fowles taught here, and is closed most of the year except during August, when it hosts the Anaryiria festival of art exhibits.

The harborfront has the usual tourist shops, but you might have a look by the OTE, behind the Hotel Soleil, at **Pityoussa** (no phone), which has a collection of decorative folk paintings, ceramics, and interesting gift items. The **Astrolavos-Spetses Gallery** (☎ **0298/75-228**) sometimes has special events for children in the summer, as well as exhibits by well-known Greek artists.

If you head east away from the Dapia, you'll come to the picturesque **Old Harbor** (the Baltiza, or Paleo Limani), where the wealthy moor their yachts. The **Cathedral of Ayios Nikolaos** (St. Nicholas) here is the oldest church in town; it has a lovely bell tower on which the Greek flag was first raised on the island. A pebble mosaic shows the event, as do a number of similar pebble mosaics in Spetses town. While you're at the old harbor, have a look at the boatyards where you can usually see caïques (*kaikia*) being made with tools little different from those used when Bouboulina's mighty *Agamemnon* was built here.

BEACHES

Ayia Marina, signposted and about a 30-minute walk east of Spetses town, is the best town beach. There are a number of tavernas, cafes, and discos here. On the south side of the island, **Ayii Anaryiri** has one of the best sandy beaches anywhere in the Saronic Gulf, a perfect C-shaped cove lined with trees, bars, and several tavernas (we prefer the Taverna Tassos). The best way to get here is by water taxi. Whichever beach you pick, go early, as both are usually seriously crowded by midday.

Some prefer the beach at **Ayia Paraskevi,** which is smaller and more private because it's more closely bordered by pine trees. There's a cantina and the **Villa Yasemia,** residence of the Magus himself, which can now sometimes be rented, usually through Pine Island Tours (See "Visitor Information," above). West over some rocks is the island's official nudist beach. **Zogeria** is on the northwest coast, with a few places to eat and some pretty rocky coves for swimming. West of Spetses town, **Paradise Beach** is usually crowded, littered, and to be avoided.

WHERE TO STAY

Finding a good, quiet, centrally located room in spread-out Spetses is not easy. Below are some suggestions.

Hotel Faros. Plateia Kentriki (Central Sq.), 18050 Spetses. ☎ **0298/72-613.** Fax 0298/4-728. 50 units. TEL. Dr14,000 ($40) double. No credit cards.

Though there's no *faros* (lighthouse) nearby, this older hotel shares the busy central square with a Taverna Faros, a Faros Pizzeria, and other establishments whose tables and chairs curb the flow of vehicular traffic. Try for the top floor, where the simple, comfortable, twin-bedded rooms are quietest, with balcony views of the island.

✪ **Hotel Possidonion.** Dapia, 18050 Spetses. ☎ **0298/72-208** or 0298/72-006. Fax 0298/72-208. 55 units. A/C TEL. Dr29,000 ($83) double; Dr35,000 ($101) double with sea view. Rates include breakfast. AE, DC, MC, V.

The landmark Poseidon (as we would call it) is a grand and gracious hotel that was built in 1911 and, under new management, was completely renovated in the early 1990s. This belle-époque classic boasts two grand pianos in its lobby and the statue of Bouboulina guarding the plaza in front. The spacious, high-ceilinged guest rooms are sparsely but elegantly furnished; the old-fashioned bathrooms have large tubs. The view over the harbor from the tall front windows is superb.

Spetses Hotel. 18050 Spetses. ☎ **0298/72-602.** Fax 0298/72-494. 77 units. A/C TEL. Dr38,500 ($111). MC, V.

The Spetses sits on its own beach and has its own restaurant, which makes it a good choice if you don't want to hassle with the summertime crowds in other restaurants. The rooms here are furnished with the standard Greek hotel twin beds and bedside tables. If you stay for more than a week, there is usually a discount of about $10 a night.

✪ **Star Hotel.** Plateia Dapia, 18050 Spetses. ☎ **0298/72-214** or 0298/72-728. Fax 0298/72-872. 37 units. A/C TEL. Dr19,000 ($54) double. No credit cards.

This blue-shuttered, five-story hotel—the best in its price range—is flanked by a pebble mosaic, making it off-limits to vehicles. All guest rooms have balconies, the front ones with views of the harbor. Each large bathroom contains a bathtub, shower, and bidet. Breakfast is available à la carte in the large lobby.

WHERE TO DINE

Spetses's restaurants can be packed with Athenians on weekend evenings, and you may want to eat unfashionably early (about 9pm) to avoid the Greek crush. The island's considerable popularity with tour groups seems to have led to a decline in the quality of restaurant fare. Let us know if you find someplace that you think is particularly good.

For standard Greek taverna food, usually including a number of vegetable dishes, try the rooftop taverna **Lirakis,** Dapia, over the Lirakis supermarket (☎ **0298/72-188**), with a nice view of the harbor. **To Kafeneion** (no phone), a long-established coffeehouse and ouzo joint on the harborfront, is a good place to sit and watch the passing scene. Spetses has some of the best **bakeries** in the Saronic Gulf; all serve an island specialty called *amygdalota,* small cone-shaped almond cakes flavored with rosewater and covered with powdered sugar.

The Bakery Restaurant. Dapia. No phone. Main courses Dr1,800–Dr5,200 ($5.15–$15). EC, MC, V. Daily 6:30pm–midnight. GREEK/CONTINENTAL.

This restaurant is on the deck above one of the island's more popular patisseries. The food is prepared fresh, with little oil, and served hot. The chef obviously understands foreign palates and offers smoked trout salad, grilled steak, roasted lamb with peas, and the usual Greek dishes.

Exedra Taverna. Paleo Limani. ☎ **0298/73-497.** Main courses Dr1,800–Dr5,200 ($5.15–$15). Fish priced by the kilo. No credit cards. Daily noon–3pm and 7pm–midnight. GREEK/SEAFOOD.

This traditional taverna on the Old Harbor, where yachts from all over Europe moor, is also known by locals as Siora's, after the proprietor. This is a good place to try fish Spetsiota (a broiled fish-and-tomato casserole). The freshly cooked zucchini, eggplant, and other seasonal vegetables are also excellent. If you can't find a table for supper, try the nearby **Taverna Liyeri,** also known for good seafood.

Lazaros Taverna. Dapia (inland and uphill about 400m from the water). No phone. Main courses Dr1,400–Dr4,200 ($4–$12). No credit cards. Daily 6:30pm–midnight. GREEK.

This traditional place is decorated with potted ivy, family photos, and big kegs of homemade retsina lining the walls. It's popular with locals who come here for the good, fresh, reasonably priced food. The small menu features grilled meats and daily specials, such as goat in lemon sauce.

SPETSES AFTER DARK

There's plenty of nightlife on Spetses, with bars, discos, and bouzouki clubs from the Dapia to the Old Harbor to Ayia Marina, and even the more remote beaches. For bars, try **Socrates,** in the heart of Dapia. The **Anchor** is more upscale, and there's the **Bracera Music Bar** on the yachting marina. For something a little more sedate, head to the **Halcyon** or the **Veranda,** with softer Greek music. To the west of town, in Kounoupitsa, near the popular Patralis Fish Taverna, **Zorba's** and **Kalia** are popular spots.

As for discos, there's **Figaro,** with a seaside patio and international funk until midnight, when the music switches to Greek and the dancing follows step—often till dawn. The **Delfina Disco** is opposite the Dapia town beach on the road to the Old Harbor. **Disco Fever,** with its flashing lights, draws the British crowd, while **Naos,** which looks more like a castle than a temple, features techno music. The **Fox** often has live Greek music and dancing; obvious tourists are usually encouraged to join in— information that may help you decide either to go here, or to stay away!

The Peloponnese

7

by Sherry Marker

What's special about the Peloponnese? It's tempting to answer, "Everything." With the exception of Athens and Delphi, just across the Gulf of Corinth, virtually every famous ancient site in Greece is in the Peloponnese—the awesome Mycenaean palaces of Kings Agamemnon and Nestor at Mycenae and Pylos (Pilos); the mysterious thick-walled Mycenaean fortress at Tiryns; the magnificent classical temples at Corinth, Nemea, Vassae, and Olympia; and the monumental theaters at Argos and Epidaurus, still used for performances today.

But the Peloponnese isn't just a grab bag of famous ancient sites. This peninsula, divided from the mainland by the Corinth Canal, is studded with medieval castles and monasteries, bounded by sand beaches, and dominated by two of Greece's most impressive mountain ranges: Taygetos and Parnon. Tucked away in the valleys and hanging precipitously from the mountainsides are hundreds of the villages that are among the Peloponnese's greatest treasures. An evening under the plane trees in tiny Andritsena, where the sheep bells are the loudest sound at night and oregano and flowering broom scent the hills, is every bit as memorable as a visit to one of the famous ancient sites. This is perhaps especially true in the mountains of Arcadia and deep in the Mani peninsula, where traditional Greek hospitality hasn't been eroded by too many busloads of visitors.

While many of the Aegean islands sag under the weight of tourists from May until September, the Peloponnese is still relatively uncrowded, even in midsummer. That doesn't mean that you're going to have Olympia all to yourself if you arrive at high noon in August, but it does mean that if you get to Olympia early in the morning, you may have a quiet hour under the pine trees. If you're traveling with a car and can set your own pace, you can avoid the crowds at the most popular tourist destinations of Corinth, Mycenae, Epidaurus, and Olympia by visiting early in the morning or late in the afternoon.

Still, even the most avid travelers do not live by culture alone, and one of the great delights of seeing the Peloponnese comes from the quiet hours spent in seaside cafes, watching fishermen mend their nets while Greek families settle down for a leisurely meal. *Leisurely* is the word to remember in the Peloponnese, an ideal place to make haste slowly. And what better place to watch shepherds on the hills or fishing boats on the horizon as you wait for dinner?

Peloponnesian culinary favorites include rabbit stew (*kouneli stifado*) with a surprising hint of cinnamon, or fish à la Spetsai (fish baked with

A Word on Forest Fires

In July 2000, more than 100 forest fires raged across Greece, devastating the island of Samos. Many of the most severe fires were in the Peloponnese. Fires along the north coast stopped only when they reached the sea, while deep in the Mani peninsula, fires ravaged the countryside around the port of Gerolimeni. From July 14 to 16, ashes and smoke from the fires blotted out the sun in Athens and much of the northern Peloponnese. More than 200 homes and 40,000 acres of crop and forest land were destroyed; the loss of farm animals and wildlife was a financial and ecological disaster. While some fires were set by arsonists, and some started in dry vegetation during a severe heat wave, others were thought to have been caused by travelers carelessly disposing of cigarettes. If you smoke, please dispose of all matches and butts *very* carefully.

tomato sauce). In summer—when it seems that every tree on the plain of Argos hangs with apricots and every vine is heavy with tomatoes—Peloponnesian food is at its freshest and best. If you're here in spring, look for delicious fresh artichokes and delicate little strawberries. The fresh lettuce grown here during the cool winter months is superb, Greek hothouses produce excellent tomatoes year-round, and there's less competition in restaurants to get the best and freshest fish.

A few suggestions for your trip to the Peloponnese: Don't forget sunscreen, a broad-brimmed hat, good walking shoes, and some books to read while you're sitting in that cafe. Bookstores with a good selection of English titles are few and far between here, although you will find excellent stores in Nafplion and Olympia. Most banks have ATMs, and all banks, most hotels, and many post offices change money at competitive rates.

Speaking of competitive rates, don't hesitate to ask if there's a cheaper rate for a room than the one first quoted at hotels. This is especially true for a long stay, or off-season, when many hotels are willing to be quite flexible in their prices.

You'll probably be pleasantly surprised at how very impressed locals are if you master the linguistic basics of hello (*yassas*) and thank you (*efcharisto*). If you have trouble pronouncing "efcharisto," here's a suggestion: It sounds a lot like the name "F. Harry Stowe." If you're still having trouble, try *merci* (French for "thank you"), which most Greeks use interchangeably with *efcharisto*.

And however relaxed you get on your Peloponnesian holiday, it's a good idea to remember that this is still one of the more conservative areas of Greece, and virtually the only area where there's strong sentiment to restore the monarchy and bring back the good old days. Most Peloponnesians are at best amused and at worst deeply offended by public drunkenness, elaborate displays of affection, and swimsuits or shorts and halters worn anywhere but on the beach. That said, *kalo taxidi* (bon voyage) on your trip to the Peloponnese, the most beautiful and historic part of Greece.

STRATEGIES FOR SEEING THE REGION   You can tour the region in either a clockwise or counterclockwise direction. Whichever approach you choose, at some point you'll probably head into the center of the Peloponnese, to see the Byzantine ghost town of Mistra outside ancient Sparta, or to take in some of the lovely mountain villages of Arcadia and the temple of Apollo at Vassae. Here's one suggested itinerary based on the assumption that you have your own car. If you're traveling by public transportation, you'd be wise to double the time allowed. Even if you do have a car, don't let yourself be deceived by the short distances between what you want to see in the Peloponnese. You'll be astonished at how long even a short drive on a winding

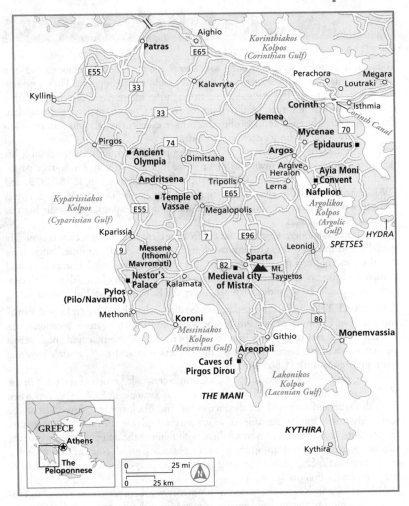

Peloponnese

mountain road can take—especially when you have to stop repeatedly to let flocks of goats cross that road!

In two days, you can see most of the important sites in the northern Peloponnese as well as the lovely harbor town of Nafplion. Head from Athens to **Corinth,** have a look at the canal, and visit the ancient site as well as **Acrocorinth,** the sugarloaf mountain that looms over the plain of Corinth. Head on to **Mycenae** before ending up for the night in **Nafplion,** where you can take a swim at the public bathing beach. In the morning, explore Nafplion and drive over to **Epidaurus,** to see the famous theater and site, before heading back along the coast to Athens.

If you have a couple of more days to spend here, you can head from Nafplion to **Tripolis** and **Olympia,** taking in some of the Arcadian mountain villages, and perhaps the **temple of Vassae,** en route. Then, you can head back to Athens along the **Gulf of Corinth,** which offers lots of chances for a swim. At this point, you still will have missed a great deal in the Peloponnese—so we hope you have at least a week to spend here.

1 Corinth

89km (55 miles) W of Athens

Today, as in antiquity, Corinth, along with Patras, is one of the two major gateways to the Peloponnese. Still, gates are there to pass through, not to linger in. There's no reason not to stop to see the ships slipping through the impressive Corinth Canal that cuts across the isthmus; then head straight for ancient Corinth, bypassing the modern city altogether. Mycenae and Nafplion both have excellent hotels and restaurants—and are only about an hour's drive from Corinth.

In fact, the entire modern town of Corinth (population 24,000) has remarkably little to recommend it. The town was moved here in 1834, after an earthquake devastated the settlement at ancient Corinth; successive earthquakes in 1858, 1928, and 1981 destroyed virtually every interesting building in the new town. As a result, Corinth is now a thicket of undistinguished, flat-roofed buildings, supposedly built to withstand future quakes.

All this makes modern Corinth a far cry from ancient Corinth, which was famously splendid and lively. As one Greek proverb had it, "See Corinth and die," suggesting that there was nothing to look forward to after visiting the splendid monuments (and fleshpots) of the city that dominated trade in Greece for much of the 7th and 8th centuries B.C. and had a second golden age under the Romans in the 2nd century A.D.

A LOOK AT THE PAST   Historians are fond of saying that "geography is destiny," and much of Corinth's power and prosperity came from its strategic location overlooking the sea and land routes into the Peloponnese. No enemy could sneak across the isthmus without being spotted by the soldiers stationed on Corinth's towering acropolis, Acrocorinth (1,863 feet).

During the 8th and 7th centuries B.C., Corinth controlled much of the trade in the Mediterranean and founded colonies as far away as Syracuse in Sicily. This was when Corinth made and exported the distinctive red-and-black figured pottery decorated with lively animal motifs, examples of which are on display in the excavation museum. Great sailors, the Corinthians were credited with refining the design of the *trireme*, the standard warship in Greek antiquity. The only obstacle Corinth couldn't overcome was the isthmus itself: Ships had to be dragged from the port of Kenchreai on the east to the port of Lechaion on the west.

Although Corinth's greatest period of prosperity was between the 8th and 5th centuries B.C., most of the ancient remains here are from the Roman period. Razed and destroyed when the Romans conquered Greece in 146 B.C., Corinth was refounded by Julius Caesar in 44 B.C. and began a second period of wealth and prosperity. When St. Paul visited here in A.D. 52, he found Corinth all too sophisticated and chastised the Corinthians for their wanton ways.

By the 2nd century A.D., with some 300,000 citizens and 500,000 slaves, Corinth was much larger and more powerful than Athens. During the next hundred years, a series of barbarian invasions and attacks undermined Corinth's prosperity. Thereafter, although the long series of invaders—Normans, Franks, Venetians, and Turks—fought for control of the strategic citadel of Acrocorinth, Corinth itself was a provincial backwater with a glorious past.

ESSENTIALS

GETTING THERE   **By Train**   There are several trains a day from Athens's Stathmos Peloponnisou (Train Station for the Peloponnese) to the Corinth station off Odos Demokratias (☎ **0741/22-522** or 0741/22-523). These trains are almost invariably

Tour Alternatives

If you don't want to travel through the Peloponnese on your own, but hate the thought of a conventional tour, you might want to contact one of the two English companies that run "green" tours to various sections of Greece, including the Peloponnese. ✪ **Filoxenia,** Sourdock Hill, Barkisland, Halifax, West Yorkshire HX4 OAG (☎ **0422/375-999** or 0422/371-796; fax 0422/310-340; www.filoxenia.co.uk; e-mail: travel@filoxenia.co.uk), offers fly-drive trips to the Peloponnese for small groups, as well as a wide range of rental villas and houses in appealing villages. **Zoe Holidays,** 34 Thornhill Rd., Surbiton, Surrey, KT6 7TL 9 (☎ **081/390-7623**), specializes in "alternative" Greece, arranging stays in monasteries, restored homes, and women's cooperatives in several villages.

---

late, often taking 3 hours or more. For information on schedules and fares, call ☎ **01/512-4913.**

By Bus   There are at least 15 buses a day, taking 2 to 2½ hours from the Stathmos Leoforia Peloponnisou (Bus Station for the Peloponnese) in Athens, Odos Kifissou 100 (☎ **01/51-34-110**), to the Corinth station at Odos Ermou and Odos Koliatsou (☎ **0741/24-481** or 0741/25-645), where you can catch a bus (15 to 20 minutes) to Archaia Korinthos. For information on Athens-Corinth-Athens schedules and fares, call ☎ **01/51-28-233.**

Buses for the Peloponnese leave Corinth from the station at the corner of Odos Konstantinou and Odos Aratou (☎ **0741/244-03**). For most destinations beyond Tripolis, you'll find yourself changing buses at Tripolis. At press time, there were rumors of new bus stations opening in Corinth. You may want to confirm the above information before setting out.

By Car   The National Highway runs from Athens to Corinth. The highway, which has been widened over the last decade, still contains some three-lane stretches that are particularly dangerous. The highway now sweeps over the Corinth Canal; if you want to stop here, look for the signs indicating the Canal Tourist Area. Shortly after the canal, you'll see signs for Corinth (the modern town and ancient site), Isthmia (site of the Isthmian Games), and Patras. Allow at least 1½ hours for the journey from Athens.

FAST FACTS   You can find **ATMs** and exchange currency at the **National Bank of Greece,** Odos Ethniki Antistaseos 7, and several banks on Leoforos Vas. Konstantinos. The **hospital** (☎ **0741/25-711**) is clearly signposted in town. The **police** (☎ **100** or 0741/22-143) and the **tourist police** (☎ **0741/23-282**) are both at Odos Ermou 51, near the Athens bus station. The **telephone office (OTE),** Odos Kolokotroni 33 (open from 6am to midnight), and the **post office,** by the park on Odos Adimantou (open Monday through Friday from 7:30am to 2pm), are both signposted.

WHAT TO SEE & DO

The new highway rushes you over the **Corinth Canal** very quickly, and unless you're vigilant you can miss the turnoff to the **Canal Tourist Area.** Before the new road was completed in 1997, almost everyone stopped here for a coffee, a souvlaki, and a look at the Corinth Canal that separates the Peloponnese from the mainland. Now, much traffic hurtles past, and the cafes, restaurants, and shops here are hurting. There's a small post office at the canal, along with a kiosk with postcards and English-language newspapers; most of the large souvlaki places have clean toilet facilities (and very tough souvlaki). One word of warning that is necessary here and almost nowhere else in Greece: Be sure to lock your car door. This is a popular spot for thieves to prey on unwary tourists.

The French engineers who built the Corinth Canal between 1881 and 1893 used lots of dynamite, blasting through 285 feet of sheer rock to make this 6.4-kilometer-long (4-mile), 30-yard-wide passageway. This utterly revolutionized shipping in the Mediterranean: Ships that previously had made their way laboriously around Cape Matapan at the southern tip of the Peloponnese could dart through the canal. The journey from Brindisi, Italy, to Athens was immediately shortened by more than 320 kilometers (200 miles).

Although it took modern technology to build the canal, the Roman emperors Caligula and Nero had tried, and failed, to dig a canal with slave labor. Nero was obsessed with the project, going so far as to lift the first shovelful of earth with a dainty golden trowel. That done, he headed back to Rome and left the real work to the 6,000 Jewish slaves he had brought here from Judea.

The Archaeological Museum. Old Corinth, on the site of ancient Corinth. ☎ **0741/31-207.** Admission Dr1,200 ($3.45), which includes admission to the site (see below). Summer daily 8am–8pm; winter daily 8am–3pm.

As you'd expect, this museum has a particularly fine collection of the famous Corinthian pottery that is often decorated with charming red-and-black figures of birds and animals. In addition, there are a number of statues of Roman worthies and several mosaics, including one in which Pan is shown piping away to a clutch of cows. The museum also has an extensive collection of finds from the shrine of Asklepios; as many of these are graphic representations of intimate body parts, they are kept in a room that is usually locked. If you express a scholarly interest, a guard may unlock the room. The museum courtyard is a shady spot to sit and read up on the ancient site. When you visit, check to see whether the handsome sculpture and vases stolen in 1990, and recently found in Miami, Florida, have been returned to the museum.

Ancient Corinth. Old Corinth. ☎ **0741/31-443.** Admission Dr1,200 ($3.45), which includes admission to the museum (see above). Summer daily 8am–8pm; winter daily 8am–3pm.

If you visit in summer, try to come here first thing in the morning or late in the afternoon: There will be fewer tourists, and the sun on this virtually shadeless site will be less fierce.

The most conspicuous—and the most handsome—surviving building at ancient Corinth is clearly the 6th-century B.C. **Temple of Apollo,** which stands on a low hill overlooking the extensive remains of the **Roman Agora** (marketplace). Only seven of the temple's 38 monolithic Doric columns are standing, the others having long since been toppled by earthquakes.

From the temple, ancient Corinth's main drag, a 40-foot-wide marble-paved road that ran from the port of Lechaion into the heart of the marketplace, is clearly visible. Pottery from Corinth was carried down this road to the ships that took it around the world; back along the same road came the goods Corinthian merchants bought in every corner of the Mediterranean. Everything made here and brought here was for sale in countless shops, many of whose foundations are still clearly visible in the agora.

Two spots in the agora are especially famous: the **Bema** and the **fountain of Peirene.** In the 2nd century A.D., the famous Roman traveler, philhellene, and benefactor Herodes Atticus rebuilt the original modest fountain house. Like most Romans, Herodes seemed to think that bigger was better: When he was done, the spring was encased in an elaborate two-storied building with arches and arcades and a

50-square-foot courtyard. Peirene, by the way, was a woman who wept so hard when she lost her son that she finally dissolved into the spring that still flows here. As for the Bema, this was the public platform where St. Paul had to plead his case when the Corinthians, irritated by his constant criticisms, hauled him up in front of the Roman governor Gallo in A.D. 52.

Acrocorinth. Old Corinth. ☎ **0741/319-66.** Free admission. Usually daily 8:30am–7pm.

A road twists from the ancient site to the summit of Acrocorinth, the rugged limestone sugarloaf mountain that looms 1,885 feet above the plain. On a clear day, the views from the summit are superb, although it's been a long time since the atmosphere was clear enough to spot the glistening columns of the Parthenon on the Athenian acropolis.

A superb natural acropolis, Acrocorinth was fortified first in antiquity. Everyone who came later—the Byzantines, Franks, Venetians, and Turks—simply added to the original walls. Today, there are three courses of outer walls, massive gates with towers, and a jumble of ruined houses, churches, and barracks. Before you head down, you can stop for a cold drink at the small cafe here and reflect on the fact that there was a Temple of Aphrodite on this summit in antiquity, staffed by an estimated 1,000 temple prostitutes—some of whom worked the streets in town, but others who worked here, awaiting those hardy customers who walked up from Corinth.

WHERE TO STAY

As noted, if at all possible, do not stay in Corinth, a noisy and unappealing town. If you must, try the 45-unit **Hotel Ephira,** Odos Ethniki Antistaseos 52 (☎ **0741/22-434;** fax 0741/24-514), near the park. The hotel is rather charmless, but the rooms are air-conditioned and have cable TV; a double goes for Dr16,000 ($46).

Kalamaki Beach Hotel. P.O. Box 22, 20100 Corinth. ☎ **0741/37-653,** or 01/323-5605 in Athens. Fax 0741/37-652, or 01/324-1092 in Athens. 82 units. TV TEL. Dr30,000 ($86) double. Compulsory breakfast Dr2,000 ($6). MC, V.

This sprawling beach resort, with its own restaurant, two pools, gardens, and tennis courts, is about 9.6 kilometers (6 miles) outside Corinth near Isthmia. The guest rooms are plainly furnished, with tile floors, decent beds, semi-comfortable reading chairs, and good-sized balconies and bathrooms. This is a popular place with tour groups and Greek families. If you're exploring the archaeological sites in the northern Peloponnese and want to stay on the water, you might consider the Kalamaki—but remember that independent travelers are in the minority here.

WHERE TO DINE

None of the cafes or restaurants along the Corinth Canal out of town or along the waterfront in town deserves to be singled out; most deserve to be avoided. Similarly, the restaurants near the ancient site tend to have high prices and mediocre food. That said, here are some suggestions if you find yourself hungry in Corinth (and can't wait until you get to Nafplion, where there are lots of good places to eat).

Locals speak well of the grandly named **Splendid** restaurant across from the site; a lunch or dinner of simple stews, chops, and salads costs around Dr2,400 ($8). The **Ancient Corinth** on the main square offers much the same food at similar prices.

In the modern town, a light meal goes for around Dr3,000 ($9) at any of the following three places. The **Pantheon Restaurant,** Odos Ethniki Antistaseos (☎ **0741/25-780**), serves standard Greek fare such as chops, salads, moussaka, and *pastitsio* (macaroni with cream sauce). If you're tired of struggling with Greek menus, try the **Neon** (☎ **0741/23-337**), one of a popular cafeteria-style chain, where much of the food is on display. If you like sardines, try **Theodorakis Taverna,** on the waterfront.

SIDE TRIPS FROM CORINTH
ISTHMIA

Isthmia was one of the four places in Greece where Panhellenic Games were held (the others being Delphi, Olympia, and Nemea). According to legend, the games here were founded in 582 B.C. in honor of a certain Meliertes, whose body was carried ashore by a dolphin at the very moment that the Delphic Oracle had revealed that a harsh famine would end only when the Corinthians honored someone who had died at sea. The Isthmian Games took place every two years at the Sanctuary of Poseidon, of which regrettably little remains. To get here from ancient Corinth, drive back toward the canal. Isthmia is signposted on your right just before you reach the canal.

The **Site and Museum of Isthmia** (☎ **0741/37-244**) are officially open Wednesday through Monday from 9am to 3pm. Admission is Dr500 ($1.45) for each. The principal **temple** in Isthmia was dedicated to Poseidon; foundations remain of the structure built in the 7th century B.C., first rebuilt after a fire in the 5th century B.C., and then rebuilt once again when the Romans refounded Corinth in 44 B.C. Speaking of the temple, even the excavator, Oscar Broneer, admitted that "the casual visitor will marvel chiefly, perhaps, at the thoroughness of its destruction." The **ancient stadium,** with its elaborate starting gate, which Broneer lovingly reconstructed, is better preserved.

Isthmia's interesting small **museum** seems to be closed unpredictably. If you do get in, you'll see exhibits on the Isthmian Games and some handsome **glass-mosaic panels** showing land- and townscapes and the figure of a philosopher, sometimes identified as Plato. These panels were found carefully packed in wooden crates, which preserved them for posterity after the ship they were on sank in the harbor of Kenchreai. Archaeologists speculate that the panels may have been intended to decorate the elegant home of one of the Roman officials who lived at Corinth.

LOUTRAKI & PERACHORA

To get to Loutraki from Corinth, cross the Corinth Canal. Once you're on the mainland, you'll see that Loutraki is signposted on your left. For Perachora, continue through Loutraki to Perachora, 32 kilometers (20 miles) or 30 minutes away by car.

Loutraki is the famous Greek spa whose springs churn out a good deal of the bottled water you'll see in restaurants. If possible, avoid visiting Loutraki or Perachora on summer weekends: It's slow going getting through Loutraki, which bursts at the seams with the Athenians who stream here to enjoy the beaches and "take the waters" at the **Hydrotherapy Thermal Spa,** Odos G. Lekka 26 (☎ **0744/22-215**); open Monday through Saturday from 8am to 1pm.

En route to Perachora from Loutraki, you'll see signs of the severe fires that raged here during the summer of 1998. You'll also pass **Lake Vouliagmeni,** a saltwater inlet from the Gulf of Corinth. There are a number of equally good fish restaurants along the lake; make your choice depending on what's on the menu.

After sprawling Corinth, **Perachora** will seem like a miniature model of an ancient site. The site was founded in the 8th century B.C. and had several temples to Zeus's wife, Hera, several stoas, and a number of useful water cisterns. Perched at the end of the peninsula, around a tiny cove, this is an idyllic spot; there's also a picturesque lighthouse chapel here. There would be more antiquities to see if the Romans hadn't dismantled the temples and stoas and ferried the stones across the gulf to rebuild Corinth.

The **Site of Perachora** is open daily, in summer from 8am to 7pm; in winter from 8am to 3pm. Admission is Dr500 ($1.45). The ancient Corinthians called this spot

Perachora, which means "the land beyond," meaning the land beyond the gulf. On a clear day, you can see the land beyond just about everything: There are superb views south across the Gulf to Acrocorinth and the mountains of the Peloponnese and along the north coast to the mountains of Central Greece.

This is an ideal spot to spend a few lazy hours swimming and picnicking (but not on weekends, when too many other people have the same idea). You may prefer simply to dangle your toes in the water and not swim in the cove: Sharks are not unknown just outside the harbor in the gulf.

2 Nafplion

145km (90 miles) SW of Athens

It's easy to overlook contemporary Greece as you travel from one ancient site to another in the Peloponnese. Nafplion (population 10,000) brings you face to face with the beginnings of modern Greece. For several years after the Greek War of Independence (from 1821 to 1828), this was Greece's first capital. Although the palace of Greece's young King Otto—a mail-order monarch from Bavaria—burned down in the 19th century, you can still see the former mosque off Plateia Syntagma (Constitution Square) where Greece's first parliament met. Another legacy of those years is the impressive number of handsome neoclassical civic buildings and private houses, as well as the generous number of commemorative statues of revolutionary heroes in Nafplion's squares and parks.

All this would be reason enough to visit this port on the east coast of the Gulf of Argos, but Nafplion also has two hilltop Venetian fortresses, a miniature castle on an island in the harbor, shady parks, an interesting assortment of small museums, and better-than-average hotels, restaurants, and shops.

In short, Nafplion is far and away the most charming town in the Peloponnese. You could spend several pleasant days here simply enjoying the port town itself, but you'll probably want to use Nafplion as your home base for day trips to the ancient sites at Argos, Nemea, Mycenae, Tiryns, Epidaurus, and—if you didn't see it on the way to Nafplion—Corinth. Keep in mind that *lots* of Athenians head here on weekends, when it's best not to arrive without a hotel reservation.

ESSENTIALS

GETTING THERE   By Car   From Athens, head south to the Corinth Canal. If you want to stop at Mycenae and/or Nemea en route, take the winding old road to Nafplion. If you want to stop at Epidaurus en route, turn left just after the canal at the sign for Epidaurus. If you want to get to Nafplion as quickly as possible, take the new Corinth-Tripolis road as far as the Argos exit. Follow the signs first into Argos itself, about 10 kilometers (6 miles) from the exit and thence on to Nafplion. You will almost certainly get lost at least once in Argos, which has an abysmal system of directional signs. Allow at least 3 hours for the drive from Athens to Nafplion, including a brief stop at the Corinth Canal and some time thrashing around in Argos. When you reach Nafplion, leave your car—and be sure to lock it—in the large municipal **parking lot** (no charge) by the harbor.

By Train   Unless you are a totally dedicated train buff, it makes no sense to come here by train. That said, there are several trains a day from Athens to Corinth and Argos, where you can catch a bus to Nafplion. Information on schedules and fares is available from the Stathmos Peloponnisou (Train Station for the Peloponnese) in Athens (☎ **01/513-1601**).

Insider Tip: Hairdressers

Women travelers might like to know that Dimitra Panagopoulou and Angeliki Skiada at **AD Hair Studio** (☎ **0752/24-861**), at the corner of Ypsilanti and Kotsonopoulou 5, both speak excellent English and do good work. There's another hairdresser nearby, so make sure that you get this one.

By Bus   There are at least a dozen buses a day to Nafplion from the Stathmos Leoforia Peloponnisou (Bus Station for the Peloponnese) in Athens, Odos Kifissou 100 (☎ **01/513-4110** or 01/513-4588). The trip is a slow one (about 4 hours) because the bus goes into both Corinth and Argos before reaching the Nafplion station on Plateia Kapodistrias (☎ **0752/28-555**).

By Boat   Monday through Saturday, there is Flying Dolphin hydrofoil service from Marina Zea, Piraeus, to Nafplion, weather permitting. The hydrofoil makes a number of stops and takes almost as long as the bus to reach Nafplion. It usually leaves Athens for Nafplion in the late afternoon and departs Nafplion for Athens in the early morning. For information on fares and schedules, call ☎ **752/27-950**, 01/324-2281, or 01/453-6107.

VISITOR INFORMATION   The **municipal tourist office** is at Odos 25 Martiou (☎ **0752/24-444**), catercorner from the bus station. It's usually open Monday through Friday from 9am to 1pm and 5 to 8pm. Ask for the useful brochure *Nafplion Day and Night.* Information and tickets for special events, such as the concerts in the **Nafplion Music Festival,** usually held during the first half of June, are sometimes available from the Town Hall (Demarkeion) in the old high-school building on Iatrou Square (☎ **0752/23-332**). There are a number of travel agencies in Nafplion, such as **Staikos Travel,** by the harbor (☎ **0752/27-950**), and **Yiannopoulos Travel,** on Plateia Syntagma (☎ **0752/28-054**), where you can get information on car rentals and day trips from Nafplion.

FAST FACTS   The **National Bank of Greece,** on Plateia Syntagma (Constitution Square), has an ATM and currency exchange, as do most other banks in town. The **hospital** (☎ **0752/27-309**) is at Kolokotroni and Asklepiou streets. The **police** are in National Assembly Square (☎ **0752/27-776**). The **tourist police** (☎ **0752/28-131**) are at Odos 25 Martiou, next to the municipal tourist information office. The **post office,** on Plateia Kapodistrias, and the **telephone office (OTE),** on Odos 25 Martiou flanking Plateia Kapodistrias, are both signposted from the bus station. **Internet access** is available at the Fillon cafe, by the post office.

WHAT TO SEE & DO

Nafplion is a stroller's delight; one of the great pleasures here is simply wandering along the harbor, through the parks (Kolokotronis and Kapodistrias parks run into each other), and up and down the stepped side streets, discovering unexpected Turkish fountains and small churches. Don't make the mistake of ending your harborside stroll when you come to the last of the large seaside cafes by the Hotel Agamemnon: If you continue on, you can watch fishing boats putting in at the pier, explore several cliffside chapels, and wind your way past the small beach on a cliffside path under the Acronafplia. If you walk from the center of town with the harbor on your left, you'll soon reach **Luna Park,** a summertime amusement park with tipsy-turvy rides. And don't ignore Nafplion's lush green parks at the foot of the Palamidi: You can usually find a cool spot to sit here even at midday. Nafplion is so small that you can't get seriously lost, so have fun exploring. Below are some suggestions on how to take in the official sights after you've had your initial stroll.

ACRONAFPLIA & PALAMIDI

Nafplion's two massive fortifications, the **Acronafplia** and the **Palamidi,** dominate the skyline. As you'll realize when you visit these fortresses, whoever held the heights here could keep a close watch on both the gulf and the plain of Argos. The Greeks began to fortify Acronafplia and Palamidi, and the Romans, Byzantines, Venetians, Franks, and Turks added a wall here and a turret there, with the results you see today. If you're here in the summer, try to visit the fortresses in the relative cool of either morning or evening; there's no charge to visit Acronafplia. If you're in Nafplion during the June **Music Festival,** check to see if any evening concerts are being held at the **Palamidi,** which is open in summer, Monday through Friday from 8am to 7pm, Saturday and Sunday from 8am to 3pm; in winter, daily from 8am to 3pm. Admission is Dr800 ($2.30).

If you want to walk up to the cliffs above Nafplion, known as the Acronafplia, follow signs in the lower town to the **church of St. Spyridon;** one of its walls has the mark left by one of the bullets that killed Ioannis Kapodistrias, the first governor of modern Greece. From St. Spyridon, follow signs further uphill to the Catholic **church of the Metamorphosis.** Note that this is not an easy walk, and you may prefer to take a taxi.

This church is as good a symbol as any for Nafplion's vexed history. Built by the Venetians, it was converted into a mosque by the Turks, and then reconsecrated as a church after the War of Independence. Inside, an ornamental doorway has an inscription listing philhellenes who died for Greece, including the nephews of both Lord Byron and George Washington. Greece's first king, young Otho of Bavaria, worshipped here wearing the Greek national costume, the short pleated skirt known as the *foustanella,* which he adopted to show solidarity with his new subjects. Ironically, while Otho wore his foustanella, the more fashion-conscious of his subjects here abandoned their Greek costumes and copied the Western clothes worn by the members of Otho's court.

As you continue to climb toward Acronafplia, you may see several **carvings of the winged lion** that was the symbol of St. Mark, the protector of Venice. The most important fortifications on Acronafplia were built during the first (1388 to 1540) and second (1686 to 1715) Venetian occupations. In the days before the Greek historical preservation movement dug in its tentacles, both the Xenia and the Xenia Palace Hotels were built over the fortifications, one reason that the original structures have been obscured. Unless you are a military historian, you may have to take it on faith that what you're looking at here is a Frankish castle and Venetian defense tower to the east and a Byzantine castle to the west. Nafplion retained its strategic importance well into this century: During World War II, the German occupying forces had gun emplacements here.

If you're not staying in the **Xenia Palace Hotel** (recently renamed the Nafplia Palace), whose bedrooms overlook the harbor, be sure to enjoy the view from

Take a Dip

The best place to swim is at the Arvanitia beach beneath the Palamidi. With the Bourtzi on your right, walk as far as you can along the quay until you come to the beach.

Acronafplia of the **Bourtzi fortress** in the harbor. The Venetians built the Bourtzi to guard the entrance to the harbor in the 15th century. Since then, it's had a checkered career, serving as a home for retired executioners in the 19th century and briefly as a small hotel in this century.

From Acronafplia, you can look down at the Bourtzi and up at the Palamidi. If you're not in the mood to climb the 800-plus steps to the **summit of Palamidi,** you can take a taxi up and then walk down. The Venetians spent three years building the Palamidi, only to be conquered the next year by the Turks in 1715. You'll enter the fortress the way the Turkish attackers did, through the main gate to the east. Once inside, you can trace the course of the massive wall that encircled the entire summit and wander through the considerable remains of the five defense fortresses that failed to stop the Turkish attack. Kolokotronis, the hero of the Greek war of Independence who later tried to subvert the new nation and seize power for himself, was held prisoner for 20 months in **Fort Miltiades,** the structure to your right as you enter the Palamidi.

MUSEUMS

○ **The Peloponnesian Folklore Foundation.** Odos V. Alexandros 1. ☎ **0752/28-947.** Fax 0752/27-960. www.pli.gr. E-mail: pff@otenet.gr. Admission Dr1,000 ($2.90). Wed–Mon museum 9am–3pm, shop 9am–2pm and 6–10pm. Closed Feb.

Shortly after it opened in 1981, this museum—with its astonishingly rich collection of traditional Greek costumes—won the European Museum of the Year Award. In September 1999, it reopened after several years of extensive renovations. The original museum emphasized the process from seed to costume (planting, harvesting, weaving, embroidering). Now, the museum highlights "The Best of the Peloponnesian Folk Foundation." Exhibits from the collection of more than 25,000 items include coins, ceramics, furniture, and farm implements—as well as all those costumes. The museum occupies three full floors in an elegant 18th-century house, with a shady courtyard and a welcome snack bar. Throughout, labels are in English as well as Greek; a number of dioramas (our favorite shows nine elegant matrons in a 19th-century parlor) help visitors imagine life in Greece. The excellent small gift shop offers pottery, weavings, Greek music CDs, and nice children's books and toys. The handsome museum catalogue (in English or Greek) is on sale for Dr21,000 ($60).

The Archaeological Museum. Plateia Syntagma (Constitution Square). ☎ **0752/27-502.** Admission Dr500 ($1.45). Year-round Tues–Sun 8:30am–1pm.

The Archaeological Museum is housed in the handsome 18th-century Venetian arsenal that dominates Plateia Syntagma. The thick walls make this a deliciously cool place to visit on even the hottest day. Displays are from sites in the area and include pottery, jewelry, and some quite horrific Mycenaean terra-cotta idols as well as a handsome bronze Mycenaean suit of armor.

The Military Museum. Leoforos Amalias. ☎ **0752/25-591.** Free admission. Year-round Tues–Sun 9am–2pm.

If you like old prints and old photographs, not to mention muskets, you'll enjoy strolling through the exhibits here, which cover Greek wars from the War of Independence to World War II.

The Museum of Childhood. Stathmos, Kolokotronis Park. Admission Dr400 ($1.15). Year-round Mon–Fri 4–8pm; Sat 9am–1pm. Frequent unscheduled closings.

An offshoot of the Folklore Museum, this museum has an eclectic collection of dolls, baby clothes, and toys. It seems to keep especially fluid hours; if you arrive and the door is locked, you can see a fair amount by peering through the windows.

SHOPPING

Nafplion has not escaped the invasion of mass-produced-souvenir shops that threatens to overwhelm Greece, but there are also some genuinely fine shops here, many on or just off **Odos Spiliadou,** the street immediately above Plateia Syntagma (Constitution Square). As in most Greek towns heavily dependent on tourism, many of these shops are closed in winter. On Saturdays, the weekly **market** occupies most of the road alongside Kolokotronis Park, from around 7am to 1pm. You can buy everything from handsaws to garlic here.

For a wide range of handsome jewelry, try **Preludio,** Vas. Constantinou 2, just off Plateia Syntagma (☎ 0752/25-277), with a very helpful staff. **Aelios,** Vas. Konstantinou 4 (☎ 0752/24-927), sometimes has unusually distinctive rings and bracelets. Virtually everything here is a pleasant departure from the mass-produced gold jewelry on sale elsewhere in Nafplion.

You can find lovely scarves and throws made from interesting hand-loomed fabrics and natural dyes at **Agnythes,** Ath. Siokou 10 and Vas. Alexandrou (☎ 0752/21-704). **The Corner,** Staikopoulou and Koletti, just off Plateia Syntagma (☎ 0752/21-359), has old prints, copper, and, sometimes, handsome old embroidered aprons and vests from traditional costumes.

Helene Papadopoulou, Odos Spiliadou 5, near the waterfront (☎ 0752/25-842), sells dolls made of brightly painted gourds and traditional weavings, priced from around Dr12,000 ($34). You'll know that you've found **To Enotion,** Odos Staikopoulou (no phone and no visible street number), when you see a window full of handsome museum-quality reproductions of characters from the Greek shadow theater, from country bumpkins to damsels in distress. The smallest of the colorful marionettes begin at about Dr12,000 ($34). A few doors along, **Nafplio tou Nafpliou,** Odos Staikopoulou 56A (no phone), paints and sells reproductions of icons showing virtually every saint in the Greek Orthodox church.

The fascinating **Komboloi Museum,** Odos Staikopoulou 25 (☎ and fax 0752/21-618; www.komboloi.gr), is on the second floor of a shop selling *komboloi,* usually referred to as "worry beads" (and priced from a few thousand to many thousands of drachmas); museum admission is Dr500 ($1.45). Owner Aris Evangelinos will lovingly explain the differences between the grades of amber and wood used to make the komboloi; his book *The Komboloi and Its History* is on sale for Dr3,000 ($9).

Konstantine Beselmes, Ath. Siokou 6 (☎ 0752/27-274), has magical paintings of village scenes, sailing ships, and idyllic landscapes. Although new, the paintings are done on weathered boards, which gives them a pleasantly aged look.

The **Odyssey,** Plateia Syntagma (☎ 0752/23-4300), has a wide selection of newspapers, magazines, and books in English, as well as a startling collection of pornographic drink coasters. This is also a good place to pick up a copy of Timothy Gregory's *Nafplion* (Lycabettus Press); although printed in 1980, this remains the best guide to the city's history and monuments.

The **Wine Shop,** Amalias 5 (☎ and fax 0752/24-446), is one of the best wine shops in the Peloponnese and an excellent place to head if you want to browse and learn about Greek wines.

WHERE TO STAY

Nafplion has enough hotels that you can usually find a room here, although you may end up on the outskirts of town in high season. Be sure to make a reservation if you want a view of the harbor, or if you are going to be here when there is a performance at Epidaurus, when tour groups reserve entire hotels.

EXPENSIVE

Hotel Nafsimedon. Odoa Sideras Merarhias 9 (on Kolokotronis Park), 21100 Nafplion. ☎ **0752/25-060.** Fax 0752/26-913. 13 units. A/C TV TEL. Dr30,000 ($86). No credit cards.

This new boutique hotel, in a handsome mid-19th-century neoclassical house painted a warm peach color, is a welcome addition to Nafplion's lodging choices. It's set back from the street, with two ornamental palms in the front garden, and overlooks relatively quiet Kolokotronis Park. We're eager to hear readers' reports on this new hotel, which was still experiencing some growing pains when we visited.

Nafplia Palace Hotel (formerly Xenia Palace Hotel). Acronafplia, 21000 Nafplion. ☎ **0752/28-981.** Fax 0752/28-783. 51 units, 54 bungalow units. A/C MINIBAR TV TEL. Dr58,200 ($168) double; Dr52,100 ($150) bungalow. Off-season reductions possible. Rates include breakfast. AE, DC, EC, MC, V.

When the Xenia Palace was built in the 1970s, its minibars, bathroom telephones, and disco made it relentlessly modern. For some years now, it has been sadly down at the heels (we're not just talking worn carpets here: a closet door came off in our hand a few years ago). One has to hope that Helios Hotels, which acquired the Xenia Palace and its less expensive sister hotel, the Xenia, in 1999, will undertake a thorough renovation. When we visited in summer 2000, the hotel was completely shut for renovations. (Information on the renovation schedule may be available from helios@ helioshotels.gr.) If the makeover is successful, this hotel, with its swimming pool and splendid views of the harbor and Bourtzi, may once again be the place to stay in Nafplion.

MODERATE

✪ **Byron Hotel.** Plateia Ayiou Spiridona, 21100 Nafplion. ☎ **0752/22-351.** Fax 0752/26-338. www.otenet.gr/byronhotel. E-mail: byronhotel@otenet.gr. 17 units. A/C TV TEL. Dr20,500 ($59) double. AE, MC, V.

This very pleasant small hotel, painted a distinctive pink with blue shutters, is in a quiet, breezy location overlooking the Church of Ayiou Spiridona, a short, steep hike up from the main plateia. The sitting rooms and bedrooms (some of which are quite small for two) contain a number of nice bits of Victoriana, including marble-topped tables. Word has gotten out about the Byron's charm, and it's almost impossible to stay here in July or August without a reservation.

Hotel Agamemnon. Akti Miaouli 3, 21100 Nafplion. ☎ **0752/28-021.** Fax 0752/28-022. 40 units. TV TEL. Dr16,500 ($47) double. Rates include breakfast, plus either lunch or dinner. AE, EC, MC, V.

The Agamemnon is on the harbor just past the string of cafes, which means that you're bound to hear voices if you have a front room with a balcony. Still, friends who have stayed here claim they were not bothered by noise and loved the view. The guest rooms are of the generic variety found in hotels throughout Greece. They're furnished with two single beds with pine bed frames and nightstands. This is a good deal, especially when you consider that the rates include lunch or dinner, as well as breakfast.

INEXPENSIVE

✪ **Epidaurus Hotel.** Odos Kokkinou 2 (beside the Commercial Bank), 21100 Nafplion. ☎ and fax **0752/27-541.** 15 units, all with shower only. Dr15,000 ($43) double. No credit cards.

The Epidaurus has an annex across the street as well as nearby pension quarters (Dr8,800/$25 double). The rooms here are small but very pleasant, with good, firm

iet street just off the main square, is excellent; the staff,
ng, is helpful, although messages tend to get misplaced.

'1100 Nafplion. ☎ **0752/27-585.** 12 units, 4 with shower
MC, V.

ho Hotel, in a pleasant neoclassical building with a
s still an excellent bargain. Don't expect frills here, but
and some overlook a nice small garden.

Sofroni 5, 21100 Nafplion. ☎ **0752/21-565.** www.
9 units, all with shower only. A/C TV TEL. Dr17,000
suite for up to five persons. Rates include breakfast.

nsion/hotel above the charming cafe by the same
ut: The restoration of the building gives guests the
'ion home—but with privacy. The beds are good,
lls are nice—there's nothing to fault here. This
ng the area. Families will like the rooms with
(Dr20,000 for three), as well as the breakfasts
cafe on the ground floor is also very charming.

... and just off Plateia Syntagma (Constitution Square)
.ourist traps you'd expect. Furthermore, you'll see a good number of Greeks
at the big harborside cafes on Akti Miaouli. In short, Nafplion has lots of good
restaurants—as well as one superb pastry shop and any number of ice-cream parlors
selling elaborate gooey confections.

Hellas Restaurant. Plateia Syntagma. ☎ **0752/27-278.** Main courses Dr1,800–Dr3,000
($5.15–$9). AE, MC, V. Daily 9am–midnight. GREEK.

Shady trees and awnings make this a cool spot to eat outdoors; there's also an indoor
dining room, where locals tend to congregate year-round. Excellent dolmades with egg
lemon sauce are usually on the menu, as well as stuffed tomatoes and peppers in season. Just about everyone in town passes through Plateia Syntagma, so this is a great
spot to watch the world go by.

Karamanlis. Bouboulinas 1. ☎ **0752/27-668.** Main courses Dr1,800–Dr3,000 ($5.15–$9);
fresh fish priced by the kilo. AE, EC, MC, V. Usually daily 11am to about midnight. GREEK.

This simple harborfront taverna several blocks east of the cluster of cafes tends to get
fewer tourists than most of the places in town. It serves up good grills and several kinds
of meatballs (keftedes, sousoutakia, and yiouvarlakia). If you like the food here, you'll
probably also enjoy the **Kanares Taverna** and the **Hundalos Taverna,** both also on
Bouboulinas.

✪ **Noufara.** Plateia Syntagma. ☎ **0752/23-648.** Fax 0752/23-945. Main courses
Dr1,500–Dr5,200 ($4.30–$15). EC, MC, V. Usually daily about 8am–1am. INTERNATIONAL/
GREEK.

If you're not sure that you can face another stuffed tomato, head for the Noufara,
which has a wide range of Italian dishes as well as the usual Greek favorites. You can
sit under the umbrellas here and have a cool drink or a full meal—or you can retreat
inside to the cool, air-conditioned dining room.

The **Noufara** also has a branch with the same menu (but a wider offering of fish)
just outside Nafplion, on the shore in Nea Chios (☎ **0752/52-314**).

Savouras Psarotaverna. Leoforos Bouboulinas 79. ☎ **0752/27-704.** Fish priced by the kilo according to availability. AE, EC, MC, V. Daily about noon–11pm. FISH.

This restaurant has been here for more than 20 years; its fresh fish attracts Greek day-trippers from Tripolis and even Athens. What you eat depends on what was caught that day. Expect to pay at least $60 for two fish dinners, a salad, and some house wine. On summer weekends, this restaurant can be terribly crowded.

Ta Phanaria. Staikopoulo 13. ☎ **0752/27-141.** Main courses Dr1,800–Dr3,500 ($5.15–$10). MC, V. Daily about noon–midnight. GREEK.

A shaded table under Ta Phanaria's enormous scarlet bougainvillea makes for one of the prettiest places in town for lunch or dinner. Ta Phanaria usually has several inventive vegetable dishes on the menu in addition to such standbys as moussaka. The stews and chops here are also good, and in winter there are usually hearty bean dishes available. Like the Hellas, Ta Phanaria continues to attract steady customers, despite doing much of its business with tourists.

OUZERIES, CAFES & SWEET SHOPS

The Pink Panther. Odos Staikopoulou. No phone. Ice-cream sundaes from Dr1,800 ($5.15). No credit cards. Daily about 10am–midnight. SWEETS/ICE CREAM.

There are those who swear that this place has the best ice cream in town. Anyone wanting to test the assertion might do a comparison taste test at the Fantasia, also on Odos Staikopoulou, and then try the mango sherbet at the Napoli di Romania cafe, on Akti Miaouli—although perhaps not all in 1 day!

Sokaki. Odos Ethniki Antistaseos 8. ☎ **0752/26-032.** Drinks and snacks Dr600–Dr2,500 ($1.75–$7). No credit cards. Daily about 8am–8pm (until midnight in summer). COFFEE/DRINKS/SNACKS/BREAKFAST.

In the morning, tourists tuck into the full American breakfast here, while locals toy with tiny cups of Greek coffee. In the evening, young men lounge here, some eyeing the women who pass by, others eyeing the men. A nice place to take a break and watch people watching people, over a yogurt and honey in the morning or a margarita in the evening.

✪ **Stathmos Cafe.** In the old Nafplion railroad station. No phone. Coca-Cola Dr600 ($1.75); bag of potato chips Dr500 ($1.45); mezedes from Dr1,000 ($2.90). No credit cards. Daily about 9am–midnight. DRINKS/SNACKS.

This is a nice spot to sit and take a break from tourist Nafplion, perhaps after visiting the Museum of Childhood next door. The old train station is decorated with a splendid painting of a steam engine, and has elaborate wooden gingerbread trim, comfortable chairs under shady trees, and a cozy inside room for cold weather.

SIDE TRIPS FROM NAFPLION
AYIA MONI CONVENT

Although this peaceful hillside convent is just minutes outside Nafplion—a 3-kilometer (1½-mile) drive—it seems a world away. To get here by car, head out of Nafplion on the Epidaurus road. Turn right at the sign for Ayia Moni and continue on a partly bumpy road to the convent. Avoid the afternoon siesta time, when the convent is usually closed.

Ayia Moni was founded in the 12th century, and the church is a fine example of Byzantine church architecture, with nice brickwork. Many of the other buildings here are modern and were built after a series of fires destroyed much of the original convent. The nuns sometimes have embroidery to sell and are usually more than willing to show you the church and garden.

The spring that feeds a small pond just outside the convent walls is one of a number of springs in Greece identified as the one in which Zeus's wife, Hera, took an annual bath to restore her virginity and renew Zeus's ardor. Today, the spring water is considered both holy and delicious; pilgrims here often fill bottles to take home.

TIRYNS

From the moment that you see Tiryns, you'll understand why Homer called this Mycenaean citadel "well-walled." The **Archaeological Site of Tiryns** (☎ 0752/ 22-657) is usually open in summer, daily from 8am to 7pm; in winter, Monday through Saturday from 8am to 5pm. Admission is Dr500 ($1.45). Tiryns is 5 kilometers (3 miles) outside Nafplion on the Argos road. If you have a car, this is an easy drive; if you don't, take one of the Argos-Nafplion-Argos buses and ask to be let off at Tiryns. Taxi drivers in both Argos and Nafplion will take you to Tiryns and wait while you visit; expect to pay around Dr10,500 ($30).

Tiryns stands on a rocky outcropping 87 feet high and about 330 yards long, and the entire citadel is encircled by the massive walls that so impressed Homer. Later Greeks thought that only the giants known as Cyclopes could have positioned the wall's 14-ton red limestone blocks, and archaeologists still call these walls "cyclopean." Even today, Tiryns's walls stand more than 30 feet high; originally, they were twice as tall—and as much as 57 feet thick.

According to Greek legend, the great hero Heracles (Hercules) was born at Tiryns after Zeus deceived and impregnated Alkmene, one of many maidens to catch his fancy. Zeus's wife, Hera, infuriated that her attempts to win back her husband's love had failed yet again, sent serpents to strangle the infant Heracles in his cradle. Instead, Heracles strangled the serpents. Hera, however, was nothing if not determined; years later she made Heracles kill his wife and children in a fit of temporary insanity.

As at Mycenae, people seem to have lived at Tiryns virtually forever. And, as at Mycenae, Tiryns seems to have increased its fortifications around 1,400 B.C. and been destroyed around 1,200 B.C. Most scholars assume that Tiryns was a friendly neighbor to the more powerful Mycenae, and some have suggested that Tiryns was Mycenae's port. Today, Tiryns is only a mile from the sea; in antiquity, before the plain silted up, it would have been virtually on the seashore.

Tiryns is a good deal better preserved than Mycenae. Once you climb the ramp and pass through the two gates, you'll find yourself in an impressive series of **storage galleries and chambers** on the east side of the citadel. Ahead, there are more galleries and chambers, including one long passageway with a corbelled arch whose walls have been rubbed smooth, probably by the generations of sheep that took shelter here after Tiryns fell.

The citadel is crowned by the **palace,** whose **megaron** (great hall) has a well-preserved circular hearth and the base of a putative throne. This room would have been gaily decorated with frescoed walls; you can see the surviving frescoes, some with scenes of elegant women riding in a chariot, in the National Archaeological Museum in Athens. These women, who would have lived in the royal apartments west of the megaron, probably freshened up in the bathroom, whose floor is a massive 20-ton limestone slab. Lesser folk would have lived below the citadel on the plain. Two tunnels led from the lower slopes of Tiryns out into the plain to the large **subterranean cisterns,** which held the secret water supply that allowed Tiryns to withstand even a lengthy siege.

As at Mycenae, there's no knowing why Tiryns finally fell into decline, with some scholars suggesting civil wars, others natural disasters, still others invasions by the mysterious "People of the Sea," sometimes credited with invading Greece about this time.

3 Mycenae

50km (31 miles) S of Corinth; 115km (71 miles) SW of Athens

According to Greek legend and the poet Homer, King Agamemnon of Mycenae was the most powerful leader in Greece at the time of the Trojan War. It was Agamemnon, Homer says, who led the Greeks from Mycenae, which he called "rich in gold," to Troy (around 1250 B.C.). There, the Greeks fought for 10 years to reclaim fair Helen, the wife of Agamemnon's brother Menelaus, from her seducer, the Trojan prince Paris.

The German archaeologist Heinrich Schliemann, who found and excavated Troy, began to excavate at Mycenae in 1874. Did Schliemann's excavations here prove that what Homer wrote was based on an actual event—and not myth or legend? Scholars are suspicious, although most admit that Mycenae could have been built to order from Homer's descriptions of Mycenaean palaces.

After you visit here, see if you agree with something that the English philhellene Robert Liddell once wrote: "Mycenae is one of the most ancient and fabulous places in Europe. I think it should be visited first for the fable, next for the lovely landscape, and thirdly for the excavations."

ESSENTIALS

GETTING THERE   By Car   From Corinth, take the old Corinth-Argos highway south from Corinth for about 48 kilometers (30 miles), and then take the left turn to Mycenae, which is about 8 kilometers (5 miles) down the road. **From Nafplion,** take the road out of town toward Argos. When you reach the Corinth-Argos highway, turn right and then, after about 16 kilometers (10 miles), right again at the sign for Mycenae. (If you are going to Nafplion when you leave Mycenae, try the very pleasant back road that runs through villages and rich farmland. You'll see the sign for Nafplion on your left shortly after you leave Mycenae.)

By Bus   There is frequent bus service from the Stathmos Leoforia Peloponnisou (Bus Station for the Peloponnese), at Odos Kifissou 100 in Athens (☎ 01/513-4100), to Corinth, Argos, and Nafplion (allow 3 to 4 hours). From any of these places you can travel on by bus to Mycenae (allow an hour). The Athens-Argos bus is usually willing to drop Mycenae-bound travelers at the turnoff at Fihtia—but don't count on finding a taxi to take you the rest of the way (about 2 kilometers, a bit more than a mile).

FAST FACTS   You can buy stamps and change money at the **mobile post office** at the ancient site, Monday through Friday from 8am to 2pm. This office is sometimes open on weekends and after 2pm, but don't count on it. There is a **pay phone** near the mobile post office.

WHAT TO SEE & DO

The Citadel and the Treasury of Atreus. Admission Dr1,500 ($4.30). Summer daily 8am–7:00pm; winter daily 8am–5pm.

As you walk uphill to Mycenae, you begin to get an idea of why people settled here as long ago as 3,000 B.C.: Mycenae straddles a low bluff between two protecting mountains and is a superb natural citadel. The site overlooks one of the richest plains in Greece, and whoever held Mycenae could control all the land between the narrow

---

Insider Tip
_____

If at all possible, visit Mycenae early in the morning, and wear a hat and sturdy shoes. There's no shade at the site (except in the cistern and the beehive tombs), and the rocks are very slippery. Bring a flashlight if you plan to explore the cistern.

_____

Dervenakia Pass to the north and the Gulf of Argos, some 16 kilometers (10 miles) to the south.

By about 1,400 B.C., Mycenae controlled not just the Plain of Argos, but also much of mainland Greece, as well as Crete, many of the Aegean islands, and outposts in distant Italy and Asia Minor. Then, some unknown disaster struck Mycenaean Greece; by about 1,100 B.C., the Mycenaeans were on the decline. By the time of the classical era, almost all memory of the Mycenaeans had been lost, and Greeks speculated that places like Mycenae and Tiryns had been built by the Cyclopes. Only those enormous giants, people reasoned, could have moved the enormous rocks used to build the ancient citadels' defense walls.

You'll enter Mycenae through just such a wall, passing under the massive **Lion Gate,** whose two lions probably symbolized Mycenae's strength. The door itself (missing, like the lions' heads) would have been of wood, probably covered with bronze for additional protection; cuttings for the door jambs and pivots are clearly visible in the lintel. Soldiers stationed in the **round tower** on your right would have shot arrows down at any attackers who tried to storm the citadel. Since soldiers carried their shields on their left arms, the tower's position made the attackers vulnerable to attack on their unprotected right side.

One of the most famous spots at Mycenae is immediately ahead of the Lion Gate: the so-called **Grave Circle A,** where Schliemann found the gold jewelry now on display at the National Archaeological Museum in Athens. When Schliemann opened the tombs and found some 14 kilos of gold here, including several solid-gold face masks, he concluded that he had found the grave of Agamemnon himself. At once, Schliemann fired off a telegram to the king of Greece, saying, "I have looked upon the face of Agamemnon bare." More sober scholars have concluded that Schliemann was wrong, and that the kings buried here died long before Agamemnon was born.

From the grave circle, head uphill past the low remains of a number of **houses.** Mycenae was not merely a palace, but a small village, with the palace at the crest of the hill and administrative buildings and homes on the slopes. The **palace** was considerably grander than these small houses and had several court rooms, bedrooms, a throne room, and a large megaron (ceremonial hall). You can see the imprint of the **four columns** that held up the roof in the megaron, as well as the outline of a **circular altar** on the floor.

If you're not claustrophobic, head to the northeast corner of the citadel and climb down the flight of stairs to have a look at Mycenae's enormous **cistern.** You may find someone here selling candles, but it's a good idea to bring your own flashlight. Along with Mycenae's great walls, this cistern, which held water channeled from a spring 500 meters away, helped to make Mycenae impregnable for several centuries.

If it's not too hot when you visit, try to give yourself some time to sit on the citadel and contemplate the sad history of the House of Atreus and enjoy the view of the farm fields below. On your way back down, take a look at the **little bathtub** in the palace, which Schliemann thought was the very bathtub where Agamemnon was stabbed to death by his wife, Clytemnestra.

There's one more thing to see before you leave Mycenae: the massive tomb known as the **Treasury of Atreus,** the largest of the tholos (beehive) tombs found here. You'll see signs for it on your right as you head down the modern road away from Mycenae. This treasury may have been built around 1300 B.C., at about the same time as the Lion Gate, in the last century of Mycenae's real greatness. The enormous tomb, with its 118-ton lintel, is 43 feet high and 47 feet wide. To build it, workers first cut the 115-foot-long passageway into the hill and faced it with stone blocks. Then the tholos chamber itself was built, by placing slightly overlapping courses of stone one on top of the other until a capstone could close the final course. As you look up toward the ceiling, you'll see why these are called beehive tombs. Once your eyes get accustomed to the poor light in the tomb, you can make out the bronze nails that once held hundreds of bronze rosettes in place in the ceiling. This tomb was robbed even in antiquity, so we'll never know what it contained, although the contents of Grave Circle A give an idea of what riches must have been here. If this was the family vault of Atreus, it's entirely possible that Agamemnon himself was buried here.

WHERE TO STAY & DINE

Most of the restaurants in Mycenae specialize in serving up set, fixed-price meals to groups. You won't starve if you eat at one of these big, impersonal roadside restaurants, but you're likely to be served a bland, lukewarm meal. You'll have better luck trying the smaller restaurants at one of the following hotels. It's also sometimes possible to avoid tour groups at the **Achilleus,** on the main street (☎ **0751/76-027**), where you can eat lunch or dinner from about Dr3,500 ($10).

La Belle Helene. Mycenae, Argolis, 21200. ☎ **0751/76-225.** Fax 0751/76-179. 5 units, none with bathroom. Dr12,500 ($36) double, sometimes lower in off-season. Rates include breakfast. DC, V.

The real reason to stay here is to add your name to that of Schliemann and other luminaries in the guest book. Sentiment aside, this small hotel, one of the most famous in Greece, is usually very quiet; the simple rooms are clean and comfortable. If you stay here, be sure to drive or walk up to the ancient site at night, especially if it's a full moon.

✪ **La Petite Planete.** Mycenae, Argolis, 21200. ☎ **0751/76-240.** 30 units. TEL. Dr22,600 ($65) double, sometimes lower in off-season. AE, V.

This would be a nice place to stay even without its swimming pool, which is irresistible after a hot day's trek around Mycenae. We've usually found it quieter here than at La Belle Helene, and friends who stayed here recently praised the restaurant and enjoyed the view over the hills from their window.

4 Epidaurus

32km (20 miles) E of Nafplion; 63km (39 miles) S of Corinth

The Theater of Epidaurus is one of the most impressive sights in Greece. Probably built in the 4th century, possibly by Polykleitos, the architect of the Tholos, this theater seated—and still seats—some 14,000 spectators. Unlike so many ancient buildings, including almost everything at the Sanctuary of Asklepios, the theater was not pillaged for building blocks in antiquity. As a result, it is astonishingly well preserved; restorations have been both minimal and tactful.

The village of Palea Epidaurus, a beach resort 10 kilometers (6 miles) from Epidaurus, is sometimes signposted ANCIENT EPIDAURUS; the theater and sanctuary are usually signposted ANCIENT THEATER.

To confuse things further, Palea Epidaurus has its own small theater and festival. If you want a swim, Palea Epidaurus is the nearest beach—but it is heavily developed.

ESSENTIALS

GETTING THERE   By Car   If you're coming from Athens or Corinth, turn left for Epidaurus immediately after the Corinth Canal and take the coast road to the Theatro (ancient theater), not to Nea Epidaurus or Palaia Epidaurus. From Nafplion, follow the signs for Epidaurus. If you drive to Epidaurus from Nafplion for a performance, be alert: The road will be clogged with tour buses and other travelers who are driving the road for the first time.

By Bus   Two buses a day run from the Stathmos Leoforia Peloponnisou (Bus Station for the Peloponnese), Odos Kifissou 100, Athens (☎ 01/513-4110), to Epidaurus. Buses take about 3 hours. There are three buses a day from the Nafplion bus station, off Plateia Kapodistrias (☎ 0752/27-323), to Epidaurus, as well as extra buses when there are performances at the Theater of Epidaurus. This bus takes about an hour.

FAST FACTS   The ancient site has both a **mobile post office** and a **pay phone.**

WHAT TO SEE & DO

✪ **The Sanctuary, Museum, and Theater at Epidaurus.** Combined admission Dr1,500 ($4.30). Hours for all 3: summer Mon–Fri 8am–7pm, Sat–Sun 8:30am–3:15pm; winter Mon–Fri 8am–5pm, Sat–Sun 8:30am–3:15pm.

Although it's pleasant to wander through the shady **Sanctuary of Asklepios,** it's not at all easy to decipher the scant remains here—visit the excavation museum first (see below). As at Olympia, the Asklepion had accommodations for visitors, several large bathhouses, civic buildings, a stadium, a gymnasium, and several temples and shrines. The remains here are so meager that you may have to take this on faith, but try to find the round **tholos** that you'll pass about halfway into the sanctuary. The famous 4th-century B.C. architect Polykleitos, who built similar round buildings at Olympia and Delphi, was the architect here. If you wonder why the inner foundations of the tholos are so convoluted and labyrinthine, you're in good company: Scholars still aren't sure what went on here, although some suspect that Asklepios's healing serpents lived in the labyrinth.

Next to the tholos are the remains of **two long stoas,** where patients slept in the hopes that Asklepios would reveal himself to them in a dream. Those who had dreams and cures dedicated the votive offerings and inscriptions now in the museum.

As you wander around the site, you'll probably notice signs of recent excavation and restoration work on the early 4th-century B.C. **altar of Apollo Maleatas.** Archaeologists think that the altar was destroyed in the 1st century B.C. by a band of Cilician pirates, irritated when they couldn't find any buried treasure here. The Greek Archaeological Service hopes to finish restoring the altar soon. So far, no hidden treasure has been found.

At the entrance to the site, the **excavation museum** helps to put some flesh on the bones of the confusing remains of the sanctuary. It has an extensive collection of architectural fragments from the sanctuary, including lovely acanthus flowers from the mysterious tholos. The terra-cotta body parts are votive offerings that show precisely what part of the anatomy was cured. The display of surgical implements will send you away grateful that you didn't have to go under the knife here, although hundreds of inscriptions record the gratitude of satisfied patients.

If you climb to the top of the **ancient theater,** you can look down over the 55 rows of seats, divided into a lower section of 34 rows and an upper section with 21 rows. The upper seats were added when the original theater was enlarged in the 2nd century B.C. The theater's acoustics are famous: You'll almost certainly see someone demonstrating how a whisper can be heard all the way from the round orchestra to the topmost row of seats. Just as the stadium at Olympia brings out the sprinter in many visitors, the theater at Epidaurus tempts many to step stage center and recite poetry, declaim the opening of the Gettysburg Address, or burst into song. Still, there's almost always a respectful silence here when a performance of a classical Greek play begins, as the sun sinks behind the orchestra and the first actor steps onto the stage (see "Epidaurus After Dark," below).

WHERE TO STAY & DINE

There are several kiosks selling snacks and cold drinks near the ticket booth at Epidaurus. In Nea and Palaia Epidaurus, you'll find a number of boring restaurants, most of which cater to large groups. In other words, you won't starve, but there's no place worth seeking out.

Epidaurus Xenia Hotel. Ligourio, Nafplias, 21059 Peloponnese. ☎ **0753/22-005.** 26 units, 12 with bathroom. TEL. Dr22,500 ($64) double, sometimes lower in off-season. Rates include breakfast. No credit cards.

The best place to stay overnight at Epidaurus is this hotel, at the site itself. Once everyone leaves, this is a lovely, quiet spot in a pine grove. The 26 bungalowlike units go quickly on the night of a performance, so book well in advance. The bungalows are, admittedly, absolutely undistinguished in terms of decor: Here, as so often, it's location, location, location that makes this the place to stay. The restaurant serves bland but acceptable food.

EPIDAURUS AFTER DARK

Classical performances at the **ancient theater** are usually given Saturday and Sunday at around 9pm from June through September. Many productions are staged by the **National Theater of Greece,** some by foreign companies. Ticket prices at press time ranged from Dr4,000 to Dr10,000 ($11 to $29). For the latest ticket prices and other information, contact the **Athens Festival Box Office,** Odos Stadiou 4 (☎ **01/ 322-1459**), or the **Epidaurus Festival Box Office** (☎ **0753/22-006**). It's also possible to buy tickets at most of the travel agencies in Nafplion and at the theater itself, starting at 5pm on the day of a performance. The ancient tragedies are usually performed either in classical or modern Greek; programs (Dr1,500/$4.30) usually have a full translation or synopsis of the play. The excellent Odyssey bookstore in Nafplion (see "Shopping" in section 2, above) usually has English translations of the plays being performed at Epidaurus.

Since 1995, the Society of the Friends of Music has sponsored the **"Little Epidaurus" Music Festival** in July. Performances take place at the recently restored 4th-century theater at Palea Epidaurus, 7 kilometers (4.5 miles) from Epidaurus. In 2000, a Bach festival and performances of traditional Greek folk music and dances were held during what is also known as **Musical July** at the Little Epidaurus theater. Also in 2000, a "mini-cruise" service was initiated from Neo Faliro to Palea Epidaurus; tickets cost Dr12,500 ($36) and included a meal en route. Information is available by calling ☎ **01/728-2333.**

Check with the **Greek National Tourism Organization** or the **Municipality of Palea Epidaurus** (☎ **0753/41-250**) for the schedule of performances and ticket prices. The **Athens Concert Hall,** the Megaron Musikis (☎ **01/728-2333**), also sometimes has information.

5 Nemea

25km (15 miles) SE of Corinth; 35km (21 miles) N of Argos

Panhellenic Games were held every four years at Olympia and Delphi and every two years at Isthmia, near Corinth, and at Nemea, in a gentle valley in the eastern foothills of the Arcadian mountains. The first Olympic Games were held in 776 B.C. and didn't begin at Nemea until 573 B.C. By about 100 B.C., Nemea's powerful neighbor Argos moved the festival from Nemea to Argos itself, putting an end to the games here. But, thanks to the Society for the Revival of the Nemean Games, games were held here for the first time in 2,000 years on June 1, 1996, when 1,000 contestants from around the world, ranging in age from 12 to 90, raced here. The 2000 games drew an even larger crowd, and the next games are planned for 2004. So, when you visit Nemea, you won't see just the stadium where athletes once contended, but also the site of the new Nemean Games. Contestants run barefoot, as in antiquity, but wear short tunics, rather than run naked. If you want to know more about the Nemean Games, contact the **Society for the Revival of the Nemean Games** (☎ **510/ 642-5924** in the U.S.; www.nemea.org).

Two excellent site guides are on sale at the museum: *Nemea* (Dr3,500/$10) and *The Ancient Stadium of Nemea* (Dr500/$1.45). You'll find shady spots to read them both at the site and at the stadium.

ESSENTIALS

GETTING THERE   By Car   From Athens, take the National Road to Corinth and then follow signs for Argos and Tripolis. The road divides just after the sign for Ancient Corinth. The speedy new Corinth-Tripolis toll road has green signposts with a drawing of a highway. Take the Nemea turnoff and follow signs to the site. If you take the old road, you'll see signs for Nemea just after the Nemea train station, where the main road bends sharply left; continue straight toward Nemea. Allow 30 minutes from Corinth to Nemea on the new road and an hour on the old road.

By Bus   There are about five buses a day from the Stathmos Leoforia Peloponnisou (Bus Station for the Peloponnese) in Athens, Odos Kifissou 100 (☎ **01/513-4110**), to Nemea. Allow about 2 hours for the trip and ask to be let off at the ancient site of Nemea (*Ta Archaia*) on the outskirts of the hamlet of Archaia Nemea, not in the village of Nea Nemea.

By Train   It's possible to take the train from Athens to the station several kilometers from the ancient site. The train, however, is very slow; it makes better sense to take the bus.

FAST FACTS   Nea Nemea has both a **post office** and a **telephone office,** but it's unlikely that you'll want to go there. There's a **pay phone** by the ancient site.

WHAT TO SEE & DO

The Museum and Ancient Site. ☎ **0746/22-739.** Admission Dr500 ($1.45). Year-round Tues–Sun 8:30am–3pm.

The Nemea Museum, set on an uncharacteristically Greek green lawn, is one of the most charming small museums in Greece. You'll get an excellent sense of the history of the excavation of Nemea and the Nemean Games, as well as the early Christian village here, much of which was built from material pillaged from ancient Nemea.

A display map just inside the museum's main gallery shows all the cities in the Greek world whose coins were found at Nemea and illustrates just how far people came to see these games. There are a number of excellent photographs of the excavations as well as enlarged photos of important finds, such as the small bronze figure of the infant Opheltes, in whose honor the Nemean Games may have been founded.

According to legend, the Seven Theban Champions founded the games in memory of the infant, who—not as agile as Heracles (Hercules)—was killed by a serpent. Because they were perceived as funeral games, the judges wore black mourning robes, just as they do today at the revived Nemean Games. Another legend says that the games were established not to honor Opheltes but to honor Heracles, who killed a fierce lion that had his lair in one of the caves in Evanyelistria hill, just behind the stadium. Fortunately, lions are unknown in today's Greece.

While you're in the museum, be sure to take a look out of one of the large picture windows that overlook the ancient site where the coins, vases, athletic gear, and architectural fragments on display were found. A raised stone path tactfully suggests the route from the museum to the site, passing a carefully preserved early Christian burial tomb and skirting a large Christian basilica and Roman bath before arriving at the Temple of Zeus.

This temple was built of local limestone around 330 B.C. on the site of an earlier temple, which may have burned down. Today, only three of the original 32 exterior Doric columns are still standing; the drums of the others are scattered on the ground. When Pausanias came by here in the 2nd century A.D., he felt that the temple was worth seeing but complained that "the roof has collapsed." Sometime later, the columns followed suit, perhaps when early Christian squatters pillaged the temple for building blocks, or after one of the many earthquakes that rocked the Peloponnese. In 1999, University of California archaeologist Stephen Miller initiated an ambitious plan to reerect a number of the fallen columns, starting with two columns at the temple's north end.

The Stadium. Admission Dr500 ($1.45). Year-round Tues–Sun 8:30am–3pm.

To reach the stadium, leave the site and head several hundred yards back along the road that brought you into Nemea. *The Ancient Stadium of Nemea,* on sale at the ticket booth, contains a self-guided tour of the stadium. The locker room just outside the stadium caused quite a stir when it was discovered in 1991, with few journalists able to resist cracks about what a locker room must smell like after 2,500 years.

Athletes would have stripped down in the locker room, oiled their bodies with olive oil, and then entered the stadium through the vaulted tunnel, just as football players today rush onto the playing field. Once you pass through the tunnel, you'll see where the judges sat while spectators sprawled on earthen benches carved out of the hillside itself. When they got thirsty, they could have a drink from the water carried around the racetrack in a stone channel. If you want, walk down onto the 178-meter race course and stand at the stone starting line where the athletes took their places for the footraces. Running naked and barefoot, the athletes kept their balance at the starting line by gripping the indentations in the stone with their toes.

WHERE TO STAY & DINE

There's no hotel here as yet. The **Pisina Restaurant,** in Nea Nemea next to the municipal swimming pool, keeps irregular hours.

6 Argos

48km (30 miles) S of Corinth

Argos was the most powerful city in the Peloponnese in the 7th century B.C. when it was ruled by its skillful tyrant, Pheidon, often credited with inventing coinage in Greece. There should be lots of impressive remains to visit here, but since modern Argos (population 20,000) is built precisely on top of the ancient city, there's little to see in town except the 4th-century theater and the excellent museum. Out of town is a different story: The fortifications on Argos's twin citadels, the Aspis and the Larissa, are very impressive.

As for the modern town itself, repeated earthquakes have left Argos with an undistinguished agglomeration of flat-roofed buildings, with only the occasional neoclassical house as a reminder of how nice this town once was. That said, the central plateia is very lively and the street market on Wednesday and Saturday mornings is one of the largest in the Peloponnese.

If your time in the Peloponnese is limited, you might consider saving Argos for a return trip. If you can spend a few hours here, give the theater a passing glance, concentrate on the museum, and try to drive up to the Larissa and Aspis citadels to take in the Venetian fortifications and the view over the plain.

ESSENTIALS

GETTING THERE   By Train   There are about five trains a day from Athens to Argos. Information on schedules and fares is available from the Stathmos Peloponnisou (Railroad Station for the Peloponnese) in Athens (☎ **01/513-1601**) or at the Corinth train station (☎ **0751/27-212**). Trains take at least 3 hours. The Argos train station, on Leoforos Vas. Sofias (☎ **0751/67-212**), is about a kilometer from the central square.

By Bus   There are five buses a day to Argos from the Stathmos Leoforia Peloponnisou (Bus Station for the Peloponnese) in Athens, Odos Kifissou 100 (☎ **01/513-4110**). Buses usually take just under 3 hours. Argos is also served by frequent buses from Nafplion (about 30 minutes). Argos has two bus stations: the Athinon Station (buses to and from Athens), on Leoforos Vas. Georgiou B. (☎ **0751/673-24**), and the Arcadia-Laconia Station (buses for Tripolis), at Odos Peithonos 24 (☎ **0751/67-324**).

By Car   From Athens, take the National Road to Corinth, and then follow signs for Argos and Tripolis. The road divides just after the sign for Ancient Corinth. The speedy new Corinth-Tripolis toll road has green signposts with drawings of highways. Take the Argos exit (the second exit) and follow the exit road until it reaches an obvious main road (the old Corinth-Argos road). Turn right, cross the bridge, and you'll soon enter Argos. If you take the old road to Argos, it runs straight into the town. It's never easy to park in Argos, but you'll probably find a place on one of the side streets off the central square or by the ancient theater.

A Word of Caution

Argos's confusing system of one-way streets and potentially lethal three-way intersections make driving here almost as chaotic as the night in 272 B.C. when Pyrrus of Epirus stormed the city with a large force—including two war elephants, one of which overturned and blocked the main gate into the city. In short, drive with particular care here.

FAST FACTS   The **National Bank of Greece,** along with several others, is on the main square, Plateia Ayios Petros; all have ATMs. The **hospital** (☎ **0751-24-455**) is signposted on the main road into town from Athens. The **police** are at Odos Agelou Bobou 10 (☎ **0751/67-222**). The **post office,** Odos Danaou 16, off the central square, is open Monday through Friday from 7am to 2pm. The **telephone office (OTE),** Odos Nikitara 8, is usually open Monday through Friday from 7am to midnight.

WHAT TO SEE & DO

The Theater at Argos. Admission Dr500 ($1.45). Summer Mon–Sat 9am–6pm; Sun 10am–3pm. Often open in winter as well. Sometimes closed unexpectedly (but clearly visible from the road).

If you've already seen the theater at Epidaurus, you'll find it hard to believe that Argos's 4th-century theater was not just larger, but probably the largest in classical Greece. Twenty thousand spectators could sit here, in 89 tiers of seats, many of which were carved from the hillside itself. The thronelike seats in the front rows were added by the Romans and reserved for visiting bigwigs, including the Roman emperor. The Romans remodeled the theater, so that the orchestra (stage) could be flooded and mock naval battles staged. Fortunately, they had a genius for building the aqueducts needed to channel enough water here to create a temporary inland sea. There was enough water left over to service the baths, whose remains are next to the theater.

The Museum at Argos. Admission Dr500 ($1.45). Tues–Sun 8:30am–3pm.

This small museum has a handful of superlative pieces that you'll want to take in, including the fragment of a 7th-century B.C. clay krater (vessel) showing a determined Ulysses blinding the one-eyed Cyclops Polyphemus. Nearby are a handsome lyre made from a tortoise shell and a stunning late geometric bronze helmet and suit of body armor. Downstairs, in the Lerna room, the tiny, stout Neolithic clay figure of a woman or goddess found at Lerna is one of the oldest known sculptural representations of the human body yet found in Europe. Nearby is a handsome pitcher in the shape of a bird with its head thrown back in song—and ornamental breasts on its chest.

Outside, in the museum's shady courtyard, are some terrific Roman mosaics showing the god Dionysos and the seasons. The figures in the seasons mosaics are bundled up in cloaks and heavy leggings in the cold months and casually dressed in light tunics and filmy cloaks in the summer months.

If you visit the museum (which has a welcome icy cold water fountain and very clean toilets) on Wednesday or Saturday morning, don't miss the **street market** that runs for several blocks to your left as you leave. This is the place to get anything from water glasses, baseball caps, and farm implements to live chickens and every possible seasonal fruit and flower. If you're here on a nonmarket day and need supplies, there's a large **supermarket** (Pharmatetras) just off the main square. To get to it, turn right as you leave the museum and then right again in the square.

The Larissa and the Aspis. Free admission. Usually open from sunrise to sunset.

You can climb up to the Larissa from the theater (allow at least an hour), and then hike across the ridge called the Deiras to the Aspis. If you drive, ask for directions to the Kastro, or castle, as the Larissa is called, at the museum or the police station, as roads in Argos are in a seemingly constant state of flux.

Argos was famous in antiquity for its two citadels; the 905-foot-high Larissa was well fortified by the 6th century B.C. When you reach the Larissa summit, you'll be able to spot the more elegant ancient blocks that were reused in the medieval battlements. There's an inner and outer system of walls, with several towers and the ruins of a church. The view's the thing here, and you get a bird's-eye view of the plain, Argos, the Gulf of Nafplion, and the lower citadel, the Aspis (328 ft. high).

The Greek word *Aspis* means "shield," which is what the Argives thought this hill looked like. This was the city's first acropolis, abandoned when the higher Larissa was fortified. With the exception of one tower, the summit here really is a confusing jumble of low walls and the indeterminate depressions in the earth that mark building foundations. Still, the views are tremendous.

You can wander around the Larissa or Aspis as you wish. Not many visitors come here, so be especially cautious about doing any dangerous climbing on the walls if you're alone.

WHERE TO STAY & DINE

With Nafplion just down the road, there's really no reason to stay overnight in Argos unless you prefer the bustle of this crowded Greek market town to Nafplion's more sybaritic pleasures. If you do stay here, the 24-unit **Hotel Mycenae,** Plateia Ayio Petrou (St. Peter's Square) 10 (☎ **0751/28-569**), is probably your best bet (although with no air-conditioning, this hotel can be very hot in summer); double rooms, many with balconies, start at around Dr25,000 ($72), including breakfast. Although the Hotel Mycenae is on Argos's energetic main square, the rooms are relatively quiet and you're certainly where the action is.

None of the small cafes and restaurants in Argos is worth seeking out, but the conveniently located **Aigle,** on the main square, has the usual chops, salads, and souvlaki, as well as pizza and veal in lemon sauce (*moskari lemonato*). Lunch or dinner costs from Dr3,000 ($9). If you want a sweet, try the place directly across from the Archaeological Museum; it offers snacks and drinks, including cappuccino.

SIDE TRIPS FROM ARGOS

The two sites of Argive Heraion and Lerna are easy to reach from Argos, and although neither has spectacular remains, each is worth visiting for its lovely locale, stirring legends, and great antiquity.

THE ARGIVE HERAION

The Argive Heraion is a lovely spot to come in the early evening, when the heat haze has diminished and the views over the plain are particularly fine. The earliest settlement here probably dates from the Neolithic era, but the remains you see are from an important sanctuary to Zeus's long-suffering wife, Hera; it was built between the 7th and 4th centuries B.C., although the Romans constructed the inevitable bath here in later years.

The Argive Heraion is about 13 kilometers (8 miles) outside Argos. To get here, head out of Argos on the inland road to Nafplion and take the left-hand turn toward Prosimna. At Nea Irea, the road divides; turn left for the Heraion. Admission is Dr500 ($1.45), and the site is open Tuesday through Sunday from 8am to 5pm.

As is often the case at the smaller ancient sites in the Peloponnese, you'll most likely enjoy the setting here more than the actual remains, which include several stoas, two temples, an altar, and the Roman baths. The sanctuary occupied three terraces, and the 7th-century B.C. temple on the highest terrace may have been the first building in the Peloponnese to be built with columns on all sides, rather than just in front. The

5th-century temple on the middle terrace contained a massive chryselephantine statue of Hera made by the sculptor Polykleitos that rivaled Phidias's similar statue of Zeus at Olympia. Nothing of these temples remains but low foundations, and you'll probably have more fun finding the nicely carved doves that ornament some building blocks than trying to decipher the ruins.

According to legend, Agamemnon was officially named leader of the Greek expedition against Troy at the Argive Heraion. And, according to the historian Herodotus, two of the happiest mortals ever to have lived died here: Cleobis and Biton. Herodotus tells us that when King Croesus of Lydia asked the Athenian statesman and sage Solon who was the happiest mortal in the world, Solon named Cleobis and Biton, whose mother was a priestess at the Argive Heraion. One day, when the oxen customarily yoked to the family chariot failed to turn up, the devoted Argive youths pulled their mother's chariot here from Argos so that she would arrive in time for a festival of Hera. Moments after they arrived, Herodotus says, "The two boys fell asleep in the temple and never awoke." As Solon pointed out to King Croesus, "Call no man happy until his death"—words Croesus would remember years later when he lost his great empire.

If you think this is only a pretty story, and that there never was a Cleobis or a Biton, consider this: Herodotus says that the Argives dedicated statues of the two boys at Delphi; the statues are lost, but their bases, inscribed in honor of Cleobis and Biton, were found in the excavations at Delphi and are now on display in the museum there.

LERNA

As you travel around the Peloponnese, you're often told that the sites you are visiting were occupied as long ago as the Neolithic era, but you very seldom see any actual building remains from that period. That's what makes Lerna's 4th-millennium B.C. palace, known as the House of the Tiles, so special. People lived at Lerna from the Neolithic period through the Mycenaean era, and pottery from as far away as Troy has been found here.

From Argos, take the old road to Tripolis, which passes through Myloi, shortly after leaving Argos. Lerna is just outside Myloi on the left-hand side of the road. The sign is very modest. Look for a straight path running through citrus groves to the site, which is protected by a metal roof.

The Archaeological Site at Lerna is open Tuesday through Sunday from 8am to 3pm; admission is Dr500 ($1.45). Although Lerna's remains are scant, the final fire that destroyed the House of the Tiles calcified its mud brick walls, leaving the remains you see today, including several enormous pottery-storage vessels. According to legend, Hercules killed the nine-headed Lernan Hydra in a nearby swamp. The swamp, long since drained, is now a fertile plain with citrus and fruit trees.

If you're hungry after your visit to Lerna, head back into Myloi, where there are any number of souvlaki places. Our favorite is across the street from the blue-and-white house that serves as the Nea Demokratia headquarters. You can dine outdoors under the trees, beside some very ruined ruins. About Dr2,000 ($6) will get you a couple of souvlaki, salad, fries, and an ice-cold beer.

If you'd rather have fish, try **To Mouragio** (☎ 0751/47-198), one of a string of fish tavernas on the water at Myloi (follow the signs for Nea Chios and Nafplion). Sit under the shady trees at this pleasant spot, and enjoy some grilled fish. As always, make sure you know how much the fish costs per kilo before you order; you could easily spend Dr17,500 ($50) for two for lunch here.

7 Sparta (Sparti)

248km (153 miles) SW of Athens; 58km (36 miles) S of Tripolis

Few sights in the Peloponnese are more imposing than the immense bulk of Mount Taygetos towering above Sparta. There's often snow on Taygetos until well into the summer, and when the sun sinks behind the mountain, the temperature seems to plummet instantly. The rich plain watered by the bottle-green Eurotas River that has made Sparta prosperous since antiquity stretches between the Taygetos and Parnon mountain ranges. Lush olive and citrus groves run for miles between the ranges, and there are even ornamental orange trees planted along Sparta's main avenues.

The Spartans earned their reputation for courage and military heroism in 580 B.C., when the Spartan general Leonidas and a band of only 300 soldiers faced down the invading Persian army at Thermopylae. From 431 to 404 B.C., Sparta and Athens fought the Peloponnesian War; Sparta finally won, but was exhausted by the effort. From then on, Sparta was a sleepy provincial town with a great future behind it. Greece's first king, young Otto of Bavaria, paid tribute to Sparta's past by redesigning the city with the wide boulevards and large central square that make it still charming today.

In a famously accurate prediction, the 5th-century B.C. Athenian historian Thucydides wrote that if Sparta were ever "to become desolate, and the temples and the foundations of the public buildings were left, no one in future times would believe that this had been one of the preeminent cities of Greece." The ancient remains here are so meager that only the truly dedicated will seek them out. Others will prefer to take in the small archaeological museum, enjoy the bustling town of Sparta itself, and head 8 kilometers (5 miles) down the road to the very impressive remains of the Byzantine city of Mistra (see "A Side Trip from Sparta: Mistra," below).

ESSENTIALS

GETTING THERE   By Bus   From Athens, seven buses a day depart from the Stathmos Leoforia Peloponnisou (Bus Station for the Peloponnese), Odos Kifissou 100 (☎ 01/512-4913), for the Sparta bus station at Odos Lykourgou, a street also known as Odos Metropolitou Dafnou and Odos Eurotas (☎ 0731/26-441). There are frequent buses from Sparta to Mistra.

By Car   From Athens, allow 5 hours; from Corinth, 3 hours; from Patras, 3 hours; from Tripolis, 2 hours. From Athens or Corinth, the new Corinth-Tripolis road is well worth taking.

VISITOR INFORMATION   It is usually possible to get visitor information in the Town Hall, on the main square (☎ 0731/26-517); hours are Monday through Friday from 8am to 3pm. Ask whether the English-language pamphlet *Laconia Traveller* is available. In recent years, there has been a **summer music and drama festival** in Sparta; inquire at the Town Hall.

FAST FACTS   The **National Bank of Greece,** on Odos Paleologou, exchanges currency and has an ATM. The **hospital** (☎ 0731/28-671) is signposted in town. The **police** and **tourist police** are at Odos Hilonos 8 (☎ 0731/26-229). Both the **post office,** on Odos Kleombrotou, and the **telephone office (OTE),** at Odos Kleombrotou 11, are signposted.

WHAT TO SEE & DO

A new service offers half- and full-day tours and hikes around Sparta. For information and prices, contact **Dimitra G. Colomvakou** (☎ and fax **0731/82-804;** mobile 0932/948-119; e-mail: spartanhiking@hotmail.com).

A Detour En Route to Sparta

If you reach or leave Sparta on the Sparta-Tripolis road, keep an eye out for the turn for Astros, 5 kilometers (3.1 miles) outside of Tripolis. In another 7 kilometers (4.3 miles), you'll reach **Ancient Tegea** (modern Alea), with the remains of the **Temple of Athena Alea** and the small site museum. A few miles away at the hamlet of **Palia Episkopi,** a shady park with cafes flanks an enormous church built with blocks pilfered from the temple and theater at Tegea. If you're here on a summer weekend, be sure to take in the excellent little **Folklore Museum of Tegea,** located in a handsome stone schoolhouse.

The Acropolis and Ancient Theater. Free admission. Usually open sunrise to sunset.

The ancient Spartans boasted that they didn't need fortifications because the Taygetos and Parnon mountains were their defense walls. In addition, as Thucydides reminds us, Spartans did not go in for much building. Consequently, there's not a lot to see on the Spartan acropolis.

The acropolis is at the north end of town, just beyond the monumental statue of Leonidas near the supposed site of his tomb. The grove of trees here makes this a pleasant place to sit and read at sunset, but you'll probably enjoy the view of Taygetos more than the scattered remains of the 2nd-century B.C. theater. Originally, this was one of the largest theaters in Greece, seating 16,000. The theater was dismantled and the blocks were carted off for reuse when the Franks built Mistra in the 13th century. A couple years ago, there were signs of restoration work here; perhaps by the time you visit, you'll be able to enjoy a play in this ancient theater.

The Temple of Artemis Orthia. Free admission. Usually open sunrise to sunset.

If you continue out of town on the Tripolis road, you'll see a small yellow sign for the Temple of Artemis Orthia, where little Spartan boys were whipped to learn courage and endurance. Today, the site, which dates from the 10th century B.C. but was extensively remodeled by the Romans, is often crowded with gypsy children, aggressively begging for money. This is not a pleasant place to visit, especially alone.

The Menelaion. Free admission. Usually open sunrise to sunset.

To visit the Menelaion, take the Tripolis road north out of town and turn right immediately after the bridge; the Menelaion is signposted about 5 kilometers (3 miles) down the road. The shrine, in honor of Helen of Troy's long-suffering husband, Menelaus, has three terraces of gray limestone blocks and is about a 10-minute walk uphill from the chapel, where you can park your car. Beside the shrine are the low remains of several Mycenaean houses, none of which seems remotely grand enough to have belonged to Menelaus. Again, as with the acropolis of ancient Sparta, the real reason to come here is for the view of the plain and Taygetos.

The Archaeological Museum. Admission Dr500 ($1.45). Tues–Sat 8:30am–3pm; Sun 8:30am–12:30pm. Entrance usually free in Jan.

The prize of this museum is a handsome 5th-century marble bust, believed to show Leonidas and to have stood on his tomb. The Spartans, however, were famous as soldiers, not as artists, and the museum's collection reflects Sparta's lack of a lively artistic tradition. Still, it's worth stopping here to see the statue of Leonidas, several fine Roman mosaics, and a small collection of objects found at Mycenaean sites in the countryside near Sparta. The museum's rose garden, peopled with decapitated Roman statues, is a nice spot to sit and read. *Be warned:* This museum has no rest rooms.

WHERE TO STAY

Hotel Byzantion. 23100 Mistra, Laconia. ☎ **0731/83-309.** Fax 0731/20-019. 22 units. A/C TV TEL. Dr20,000 ($57) double; lower in off-season. EC, MC, V. Usually closed Nov–Feb.

This is the place to stay if you want to be poised to visit Mistra first thing in the morning. There's very little traffic on the road through Mistra at night, but whatever there is passes by this hotel, so you may want to ask for a back room. Bedrooms and bathrooms are on the small side but are very clean, and the staff is helpful. There are several small tavernas in Mistra if you don't want to go to Sparta for dinner.

Hotel Maniatis. Odos Paleologou 72, 23100 Sparta, Laconia. ☎ **0731/22-665.** Fax 0731/29-994. 80 units. A/C TV TEL. Dr18,000 ($52) double. MC, V.

Despite its location at the corner of Paleologou and Lycourgou, Sparta's two main streets, the Maniatis is reasonably quiet (the rooms in back are smaller but quieter). The marble-and-glass lobby is considerably grander than the bedrooms, which, if not spartan, are simple, with functional bedside tables, straight chairs, and small bathrooms. The hotel restaurant, the Dias, is decorated in pastels that should be soothing but somehow aren't. The food is okay, but the place is often filled with noisy tour groups; it's worth walking a couple blocks to the excellent Diethnes restaurant (see below).

Hotel Melelaion. Odos Paleologou 91, 23100 Sparta, Laconia. ☎ **0731/22-161.** Fax 0731/26-332. 48 units. A/C MINIBAR TV TEL. Dr25,000 ($72) double. Rates include breakfast. EC, MC, V.

It's good to see the handsome neoclassical Menelaion, built in 1935, looking good again. For too many years, this once-elegant hotel, with high ceilings and stylish architectural detail, let itself go. Now redone, with a very nice swimming pool in the central courtyard, the Menelaion is an appealing place to stay (although the rooms fronting Paleologou get lots of traffic noise as well as noise from the main taxi stand). Friends who stayed here recently had no complaints, although those who like extra-firm mattresses might find the beds a bit soft.

Hotel Sparta Inn. Thermopilion 109, 23100 Sparta, Laconia. ☎ **0731/21-021,** or 416/ 362-4342 in Toronto. Fax 0731/24-855. 150 units. A/C TV TEL. Dr18,000 ($52) double. V.

This large hotel with a roof garden has a quiet location on a side street, but is often taken over by not-so-quiet tour groups. Guest rooms are air-conditioned, with firm beds, decent reading lights, and good-size bathrooms. There's nothing charming about this hotel, whose muted color scheme is rather gloomy, but its quiet location and two (small) pools are real pluses in Sparta, which tends to be noisy and hot in the summer. Ask for the hotel's handy English printout of area attractions.

WHERE TO DINE

✪ **Diethnes.** Odos Paleologou 105. ☎ **0731/28-636.** Main courses Dr1,800–Dr3,000 ($5.15–$9). No credit cards. Daily about 8am–midnight. GREEK.

On summer Saturdays, all of Sparta seems to eat lunch in the Diethnes's shady garden after shopping at the street market around the corner. If you're only going to eat one meal in Sparta, it should be here; in fact, unless you really don't like eating in the same

Shopping in Sparta

The weekly **market** in Sparta is on Saturday. **Lampropoulou,** on Odos Paleologou, stocks English-language guides, newspapers, magazines, and books.

place more than once, why go anywhere else? The grills (including local loukanika sausages) are excellent; the vegetables are drizzled, not drenched, in oil; and the waiters move with the speed of light through the crowds.

Elysse Restaurant. Odos Paleologou 113. ☎ **0731/29-896.** Main courses Dr1,800–Dr2,900 ($5.15–$8). No credit cards. Daily about 11am–11pm. GREEK.

If the Diethnes weren't just a few doors away, this would be a very tempting place to eat. The food is good, the staff is efficient, but in the summer, it's much more pleasant to sit in the garden at the Diethnes than in the Elysse's indoor dining room. If you're tired of Greek food by the time you reach Sparta, check to see whether any of the continental dishes listed on the Elysse's menu are actually being served: Chicken Madeira has been known to appear here.

The Stoa Cafeteria. Odos Lycourgou 140. ☎ **0731/23-237.** Coffee and loukoumades Dr900 ($2.60). Mon–Fri 8am–evening; Sat 8am–noon. LOUKOUMADES/SNACKS.

This little hole-in-the-wall next to a florist is the place to go for a Spartan favorite: *loukoumades,* airy deep-fried puffs of pastry drenched in honey syrup.

A SIDE TRIP FROM SPARTA: MISTRA

The deserted medieval city of ✪ **Mistra,** now Greece's most picturesque ghost town, sprawls down a distinctive conical hill on Taygetos's lower slopes. So much remains of Mistra and so little of ancient Sparta that it's not surprising that the early travelers here identified Mistra as ancient Sparta, lovingly describing the 13th-century A.D. Palace of the Despots, now undergoing restoration, as Menelaus's Mycenaean palace—a cautionary tale for all travelers trying to make sense of Greek ruins.

To reach Mistra, leave Sparta on Odos Lycourgou and follow the signs for Mistra 8 kilometers (5 miles). If you arrive here alone by car, you'll have to decide whether to park at the main gate and climb up to the castle (Kastro), or park at the castle entrance, work your way downhill to the main gate, and then climb back up to your car. If you're not traveling alone, try to persuade your companion to let you out at the castle entrance and meet you at the main gate. There are frequent buses from the main square in Sparta to Mistra.

If you visit Mistra in summer, try to go in the relative cool of the morning. There's little shade, and you'll find yourself climbing up and down a very steep hill for several hours. *Be warned:* There are no toilet facilities at Mistra. Vendors sometimes sell water and soft drinks outside the Kastro and main entrances to Mistra.

A LOOK AT THE PAST   In 1204, the Frankish leader William de Villehardouin chose this site as the headquarters for his Greek empire. De Villehardouin crowned Mistra with a fortress and defense walls, built himself a palace on the slopes below, and had 10 good years here, until the Byzantine Greeks defeated him at the Battle of Pelagonia in 1259. According to legend, de Villehardouin would have escaped capture if a Greek soldier had not identified him by his famously protruding buck teeth.

Mistra's real heyday came under the Byzantine Greeks, when most of its churches and more than 2,000 houses, as well as the enormous Palace of the Despots, were built. Some 25,000 people lived in Mistra—twice the population of Sparta today. Among them were the philosophers, writers, architects, and artists who made Mistra something of an international center of culture.

Mistra was such an important city that many Byzantine emperors sent their heirs here for some on-the-job training. After Constantinople and the Byzantine empire fell

The Volta, Spartan Style

Sit in the square almost any evening, and around 9pm you'll start to see the famous Spartan volta, or promenade. For years, this was a highly stylized affair, with men and women walking on separate sides of the square. Much courting went on under the watchful eye of parents; today, most young men and women stroll in pairs with no attending chaperones. Especially on weekends, this is a lively scene, as entire families saunter up and down and up and down again, sometimes taking a break to sit at one of the cafes for an ice cream.

to the Turks in 1453, Mistra held out; the last emperor of Byzantium was crowned in the Cathedral at Mistra, which finally fell to the Turks in 1460.

The Venetians captured Mistra from the Turks in 1687 and ruled here for a half century, during which time Mistra swelled to an enormous city of more than 40,000, largely supported by a flourishing silk industry. When the Turks regained power, Mistra began its long decline into what it is today: Greece's most picturesque ghost town.

THE ARCHAEOLOGICAL SITE OF MISTRA   The site is open from 8am to 3pm and sometimes later in summer. Admission is Dr1,500 ($4.30). If you start your tour of Mistra at the top, you can orient yourself by taking in the fine view over the entire site from de Villehardouin's **Castle** (the Kastro). The **Palace of the Despots,** which has been undergoing restoration for some years, stands out clearly, surrounded by the roofs of Mistra's magnificent **churches.** As you head down, you'll begin to pass some of the churches, most of which have elaborate brickwork decoration, a multiplicity of domes, and superb frescoes. Despite Mistra's "picturesque incoherence," the churches are signposted, and you should be able to find the most beautiful ones—the **Saint Sophia,** the **Pantannasa,** the **Panayia Hodegetria,** the **Peribleptos,** and the **Cathedral.**

Give your eyes time to adjust to the poor light inside the churches; once they do, you'll be able to pick out vivid scenes, such as the *Raising of Lazarus* and the *Ascension* in the 15th-century frescoes in the Pantannasa Monastery, the *Marriage of Cana* in the 14th-century Panayia Hodegetria, and the stunning *Birth of Christ* in the 14th-century Peribleptos Monastery. The frescoes that decorated Greek churches have been described as the "Books of the Illiterate"; any devout Byzantine Greek could have "read" these frescoes and identified every New and Old Testament scene, just as their descendants can today.

8 Vassae & Andritsena

45km (27 miles) from Megalopolis to Andritsena; 24km (15 miles) from Andritsena to Vassae

Vassae is one of the most impressive 5th-century Greek temples, its gray granite columns the perfect complement to its remote mountain setting. Unfortunately, the temple, badly damaged by time and earthquakes, is now hidden under a bizarre protective tent that looks rather like the Sydney opera house. When fires threatened to engulf Vassae in August 1998, the staff here hosed the tent all day and all night and successfully protected both tent and temple from the flames. Every year, the guard here says that he hopes Vassae will be mended and the tent removed "next year," a phrase that in Greek does not carry the specificity that its English translation suggests. Hearteningly, in the summer of 2000, the Committee for the Preservation of the Temple announced government-funded plans to begin a 20-year restoration. Initially, the foundation along the temple's north end, along with 10 columns, will be restored. Of course, while this vital work goes on, the entire temple itself will be even less visible to visitors.

Although it's perfectly possible to visit Vassae on a day trip from Olympia, ✪ **Andritsena,** with the scent of oregano and the sound of sheep bells everywhere, is one of the most charming of the Peloponnesian mountain villages. There's one decent hotel here and a number of small restaurants. The main street is punctuated by enormous plane trees, several of which have been fitted with pipes gushing forth the delicious local spring water. In the evening, villagers stroll the main street while sheep bells echo in the hills. In short, if you want to get away from it all and spend the night in a Greek mountain village, try to make it Andritsena.

ESSENTIALS
GETTING THERE **By Bus** There are several buses a day to Andritsena from Athens and from Argos, Tripolis, Olympia, and Megalopolis. The Greek National Tourism Organization office in Athens can provide information on these services.

By Car All the routes to Andritsena go through spectacular mountain countryside. The roads are excellent, but each winding mile takes about twice as long to drive as you might have anticipated.

FAST FACTS Everything you might need—the **bus station,** the **OTE,** the **post office,** the **bank,** the **police**—is clearly signposted on or just off Andritsena's main street.

WHAT TO SEE & DO
THE TEMPLE OF VASSAE
Coming around the last turn in the road and suddenly seeing the severe gray limestone columns of this 5th-century Doric temple to Apollo used to be one of the great sights in the Peloponnese. It seemed almost impossible that such a staggeringly impressive building should have been built in such a remote location—and designed by none other than Ictinus, the architect of the Parthenon. Evidently, the temple was built by the inhabitants of the tiny hamlet of Phigaleia, to thank Apollo for saving them from a severe plague.

If you saw the temple before it disappeared under its tent, cherish your memories and don't bother to visit now. The tent fits so snugly that the only way to get a sense of what the temple actually looks like is to buy a postcard.

If you haven't seen Vassae, you'll have to decide whether you want to see it this way, or hope that the guard will be right and that "next year" the tent will be gone. The temple is usually open daily from 8am to 7pm in summer, to 3pm in winter. Admission is Dr500 ($1.45).

THE VILLAGE OF ANDRITSENA
Tiny Andritsena has one of the finest libraries in Greece, the legacy of a 19th-century philhellene. If you like old books, check to see if the **library,** recently moved into a grand new building just off the main street, has opened.

The small **folk museum,** on the plateia below the main street, is usually locked, despite its posted hours. Admission is Dr200 (60¢); contributions are welcome. To see the endearing collection of local wedding costumes, rugs, farm tools, and family photographs, ask to be let in at the house nearest to the museum. If the people there don't have the keys, they'll phone Kyria Vasso at the Sigouri Restaurant (see below).

If you can, plan to be in Andritsena on Saturday, when the main street is taken over by the weekly **market,** an excellent place to buy every manner of sheep, goat, and cow bells, mountain tea, and herbs.

WHERE TO STAY

Theoxenia Hotel. 27061 Andritsena, Eleia. ☎ **0626/22-219.** 45 units. TEL. Dr12,000 ($34) double. MC, V.

This 1950s hotel is a casualty of the excellent Andritsena-Olympia road; now visitors who once spent the night here stop briefly to see Vassae and speed on to Olympia. Understandably (but not enjoyably), the hotel has let itself go; you can almost always show up and get a room here, but unless you're willing to drive on to Olympia, it's best to make a reservation in advance. The views from the front rooms overlooking the valley below Andritsena more than compensate for the basically shabby decor, and students of kitsch will appreciate the needlework pictures. The sometimes-less-expensive rooms in back have almost as good a view and are much quieter; trucks and buses tend to turn around in front of the hotel. The room rates are somewhat flexible, so you might bargain if you're quoted a high price. Avoid the restaurant, and hold onto your room key, as there's often no one at the front desk.

If the Theoxenia is full, consider the 6-unit **Pan Hotel** (☎ **0626/22-213**), and try to ignore its unfortunate location (next to the Shell station and its fumes and traffic). The Pan is usually closed from November through March.

WHERE TO DINE

Andritsena Kafezakeroplasteion (Coffee-Sweet Shop). On the main street, Andritsena. ☎ **0626/22-004.** Full breakfast Dr1,500 ($4.30). No credit cards. Daily about 7am–11pm. COFFEE/SWEETS.

Avoid your hotel breakfast by coming here for bread and honey, yogurt, or an omelet. In nice weather, you can sit outside under the umbrellas, looking at the elegant lace curtains in the cafe's six decorative fan windows.

Georgitsis. On the main street, Andritsena. No phone. Lunch or dinner Dr3,000 ($9). No credit cards. Usually open 11am–3pm and 7–10pm or so. GREEK.

Sit under the plane trees here and dine on simple grills and vegetable dishes. If you want some water, you can fill your glass from the spring water that gushes out of a pipe in one of the trees.

Sigouri. Odos Sofokleos (across from the metalworker's shop above the main plateia), Andritsena. No phone. Lunch or dinner Dr3,000 ($9). No credit cards. Open most days for lunch and dinner, usually closing by 10pm. GREEK HOME COOKING.

Kyria Vasso's *briam* (vegetable stew) is excellent, as are her stuffed tomatoes and barrel wine. A meal here consists of a salad, main course, and the local wine. If you like *kourouloudes* (rag rugs), ask to see the ones she makes and sells by the meter; for about Dr8,800 ($25), you can take home a colorful hand-loomed bedside rug. Kyria Vasso also usually has the keys to the Folk Museum.

The Trani Brisi. On the main street, Andritsena. No phone. Lunch or dinner Dr3,000 ($9). No credit cards. Open most days for lunch and dinner, usually closing by 10pm. GREEK.

This small restaurant has tables outside under extra-large beach umbrellas, in a widening of the road between the two upper plateias (squares). The menu varies from day to day, but often features some kind of lamb stew, fresh vegetables, and the local wine. If you like the wine, you can usually buy some to take away with you.

9 Monemvassia

97km (60 miles) S of Sparta; 340km (210 miles) S of Athens

Nicknamed "the Gibraltar of Greece" because of its strategic importance during the Middle Ages, Monemvassia was a virtual ghost town by the 20th century. Today, this rocky island just off the easternmost tip of the Peloponnese has a new lease on life: For some years, wealthy foreigners and Greeks have been buying and restoring old houses here. Furthermore, word is getting out that in addition to its medieval fortress, handsome churches, and drop-dead sunsets, Monemvassia has several of the most stylish small hotels in the Peloponnese. Monemvassia draws visitors year-round; when we stopped here for lunch on a late January weekend in 2000, the restaurants were full—and so were the hotels.

Unfortunately, an increasing number of round-the-Peloponnese bus tours make a brief stop here; try to arrive in the late afternoon or evening, have a swim, relax, and do your sightseeing in the early morning before the first tour bus arrives.

Although Monemvassia is an island, it's connected to the mainland by a causeway that you can drive or stroll across. Once you step through the massive Venetian Gate that is Monemvassia's only entrance (*mone emvasis* means "one entrance" in Greek), you're in a separate world. Cars are banned here—a wise decision, since the only approximation of a street on "the rock" is barely wide enough for two donkeys (which bring in supplies) to squeeze past each other.

ESSENTIALS

GETTING THERE   By Bus   There is one direct bus a day from the Stathmos Leoforia Peloponnisou (Bus Station for the Peloponnese), at Odos Kifissou 100 in Athens, to Gefyra (on the mainland directly across the causeway from Monemvassia), and six daily buses via Sparta. Call ☎ **01/24-913** for schedule information.

By Car   Take the National Road from Athens-Corinth-Tripolis. Head south to Monemvassia via Sparta. Allow at least 6 hours for the trip.

By Boat   The Minoan Flying Dolphin hydrofoil leaving from Marina Zea in Piraeus links Athens and Monemvassia for most of the year and is the fastest way to reach Monemvassia from Athens. For information, call ☎ **01/61-219** or 01/419-9200 in Athens, or the port authority in Monemvassia (☎ **0732/61-113**).

FAST FACTS   The **National Bank of Greece** in Gefyra (on the shore across the causeway from the old town) exchanges currency and has an ATM. You'll find the **post office** and the **OTE** in Gefyra. For **first aid,** call ☎ **0732/61-204.** The **Malvasia Travel Agency** (☎ **0732/61-752;** fax 0732/61-432) in Gefyra has several helpful English-speaking staff members.

WHAT TO SEE & DO
A STROLL THROUGH MONEMVASSIA

Monemvassia is a great place to wander. Sure, you'll get lost in the winding cobbled lanes, but how lost can you get on an island 1,600 feet long and half as wide? The answer (at least at night) is pretty lost: It's a good idea to wear decent walking shoes, bring along a flashlight, and save the 880-foot ascent of the citadel for daytime.

You might begin your visit at the lovely little **Monemvassia Archaeological Collection** (☎ **0732/61-403**), which finally opened in 1999 in the former mosque on the Plateia Dsami (Square of the Mosque). It's open daily from 8am to 7pm; admission is free. The exhibits of local architecture and artifacts include some old clay pipes; try to pick up the excellent guide *The Castle of Monemvasia* (Dr800/$2.30).

From the **citadel,** there are truly spectacular views down to the red-tile roofs of Monemvassia, out across the sea, and deep into the mountains of the Mani peninsula. While you're here, try to figure out just how the 13th-century **Church of Ayia Sophia** (Holy Wisdom) was built not just on, but virtually over, the edge of the cliffs.

After exploring the citadel, you'll probably want a swim, so head down to the **bathing jetty.** En route, you'll probably pass through the main square again, with the **Church of Christos Elkomenos** (Christ in Chains) across from a Venetian canon, as well as the **Venetian chapel of Panayia Chryssafiotissa.** The churches sometimes are and sometimes are not locked; if they're locked, content yourself with the thought that the **handsome stone houses** lining Monemvassia's winding lanes are the real treat to see here.

On the subject of treats, Monemvassia is one place in the Peloponnese where you don't have to contemplate yet another moussaka. Strung out along Monemvassia's main street are a number of restaurants: **Martina's** has a varied Greek menu, while **To Canoni** serves up pasta, including spaghetti Carbonara. No wonder knowledgeable travelers come back to Monemvassia every year: excellent food, marvelous sunsets, medieval ruins—and, as yet, relatively few tourists.

SHOPPING

There's no shop on "the rock" that's truly outstanding, but those along **Odos Ritsos** have thus far avoided the infestation of T-shirts and cheap museum reproductions so common elsewhere. Just inside Monemvassia's gate, **Costas Lekakis** has a good selection of books in English, including R. Klaus and U. Steinmuller's excellent guide *Monemvassia* ($6). **Bentouraki** has nice linen caps and straw boaters from around $40—a hat is a necessity to ward off the harsh sun here. **Ioanna Angelatou's shop,** next to the Byzantion hotel, often has a good selection of the deep-blue glassware made in Greece and well-done reproductions of antique wood carvings and copper. The **Kelari,** with a nice selection of wines and local souvenirs, often has information on renting rooms in Momemvasia.

WHERE TO STAY

Our preference is to stay on the rock, but there are a number of new hotels on the mainland in and around Gefyra, including the **Flower of Momemvassia** (Louloudi tes Monemvasias) (☎ **0732/61-395;** fax 0732/61-391), with views (over buildings) of the beach and the rock. As for Monemvassia itself, there are so few rooms here that this is one place where it's essential to try to make a reservation. We say "try" because records of reservations sometimes disappear mysteriously, even after several phone calls.

If the following recommendations are full, you might consider the **Kellia,** by the Panaiya Chrysafiotissa church (☎ **0732/61-520**). This former convent is run as a hotel by the GNTO, which, alas, does not seem to be keeping an eye on the place. The rooms are nicely furnished, but the service is haphazard.

Byzantion. Odos Ritsos, 23070 Monemvassia. ☎ **0732/61-351.** Fax 0732/61-331. 18 units. Dr18,000–Dr30,000 ($52–$86) double or suite. DC, EC, MC, V.

There's only one problem with staying in this small hotel in a beautifully restored and furnished house: A number of the rooms are built flush against a hillside, do not get cross-ventilation, and can be stuffy, with a strong odor of mildew. Ask for a bedroom with ventilation and a balcony (although you may hear street noise and sounds from the Byzantion's cafe). Some rooms are available with air-conditioning, TVs, and refrigerators.

Lazaretto. On the causeway, 23070 Monemvassia. ☎ **0732/61-991.** Fax 0732/61-992. 14 units. MINIBAR TV TEL. Dr25,000–35,000 ($72–$99) double; Dr65,000 ($186) suite. EC, MC, V.

The Lazaretto is very nice indeed, offering tastefully furnished guest rooms with beamed ceilings, hand-loomed rugs, and sea or garden views. The hotel restaurant is well above average. The only possible fly in the ointment: The Lazaretto is on the causeway, and on weekends, there's a lot of traffic to and from Monemvassia itself.

✪ **Malvasia.** Headquarters on Odos Ritsos, 23070 Monemvassia. ☎ **0732/61-323.** Fax 0732/61-722. 35 units. A/C MINIBAR TV TEL. Dr16,000–Dr26,000 ($46–$74) double; Dr26,000–Dr45,000 ($74–$129) suite. EC, MC, V.

This is far and away the finest hotel in Monemvassia and one of the most charming in Greece. Over the years, the owners have bought up a number of old houses, restored them, and furnished the rooms with old copper, hand-loomed rugs and bedspreads, and handsome wooden furniture. This would be a wonderful place to stay a week, or even a month (long-term reduced rates are available). If you can't do that, at least stay for a night and hope for a sea-view room in the Stellaki Mansion on the ramparts, or in the hotel's original building on Odos Ritsos. If you're here in winter, ask for a room with a fireplace. Some units have phones and refrigerators; some suites have full kitchens.

10 The Mani

Githio is 301km (186 miles) S of Athens and 45km (27 miles) S of Sparta; Areopoli is 32km (20 miles) W of Githio

The innermost of the Peloponnese's three tridentlike prongs, the Mani is still one of the least-visited areas in Greece. That's changing fast, as word gets out about the good beaches near Githio and Kardamili and the haunting landscape of the Inner Mani (the southernmost Mani). Good roads mean that you can now drive the circuit of the entire Mani in a day, but it's more fun to spend at least a night here, perhaps in one of the restored tower-house hotels.

The Inner Mani's barren mountains are dotted with tiny olive trees and enormous prickly pear cactuses. It's hard to believe that 100 years ago, this was a densely populated area, with almost every hillside cultivated. If you squint, you can still make out the stone walls and terraces that farmers built on the deserted hillsides.

Originally, the Maniotes chose to live in tower houses because they were easy to defend, an important consideration for these constantly feuding Peloponnesians who spent much of their time until the 20th century lobbing cannonballs at their neighbors. Fortunately, many tower houses survived, and the towers of the virtually deserted villages of Koita and Nomia look like miniature skyscrapers from a distance.

When the Maniotes weren't trying to destroy their neighbors' homes, they seem to have atoned by building churches: The area is dotted with tiny medieval chapels tucked in the folds of the hills. Keep an eye out for the stands of cypress trees that often mark the chapels, many of which have decorative brickwork and ornately carved marble doors. If you don't want to tramp around the countryside in search of chapels, at least take a look at the **Church of the Taxiarchoi (Archangels)** in Areopoli. Don't miss the droll figures of the saints and signs of the zodiac carved on the church's façade.

After World War II, when most Maniotes moved away, to Athens or abroad, entire villages of austere gray-stone tower houses were deserted. In recent years, many of these handsome houses are being restored as vacation or retirement houses by

A Worthwhile Shop

Kostas Brettos's business card reads "Sic Transit Gloria Mundi," which couldn't be more appropriate for his antiques shop, **Paliatzoures** (☎ **0733/22-944**), on Githio's harborfront. The shop is easy to spot: It's the one with the enormous bellows out front. Inside are old coins, crystal, chests, embroideries, flintlocks, swords—well, you get the idea. The proprietor keeps irregular hours, but you can try to make an appointment by phone. If the shop is open when you're here, it's well worth a visit.

Maniotes, other Greeks, and foreigners. Villages that were ghost towns 10 years ago are gaining a new lease on life.

ESSENTIALS
GETTING THERE   By Car   This is a long trip, but not as tedious as the bus, which makes many stops. Take the National Road Athens-Corinth-Tripolis, and then head south to Githio and Areopoli via Sparta.

By Bus   It's possible to travel from Athens to the Sparta bus station (☎ 0731/26-441) and from Sparta to the Githio bus station (☎ **0733/22-228**) or the Areopoli bus station (☎ **0733/51-229**), but this is a trip that takes a full day. For schedule information, call ☎ **01/24-913** or the numbers above for the bus stations in Sparta, Githio, and Areopoli.

GETTING AROUND   Longtime visitors to Greece wax nostalgic about the days when they had to hoof it around the Mani. You can get around today by local bus, but by far the most efficient method is by car.

FAST FACTS   There are **banks** with ATMs in both Githio and Areopoli. Don't count on finding banks elsewhere in the Mani. In Areopoli, most services are on or just off the main square: the **bank** (usually open Monday through Friday from 9am to noon), the **post office**, the **OTE**, the **bus station**, several **restaurants**, and an excellent small **bookstore, Mani** (☎ 0733/53-670), where you can pick up Patrick Leigh Fermor's enduring classic, *Mani*, and Bob Barrow's helpful *The Mani*. The **police** (☎ 0733/51-209) are signposted on the main square in Areopoli.

WHAT TO SEE & DO
❸ **The Caves of Dirou.** Pirgos Dirou. ☎ **0733/52-222.** Fax 0733/52-223. Admission Dr3,500 ($10). The visiting hours for the caves vary unpredictably; in general, the caves are open 9am–5pm in summer, with shorter hours off-season.

These caves, a very popular holiday destination for Greeks, are mobbed in summer, so try to arrive as soon as they open. If you get here later in the day, buy your ticket immediately; usually visitors are taken in some kind of order. Guided tours through the Glyfada cave take about 30 minutes and are not recommended for the claustrophobic: You ride in a small boat that your guide poles through the clammy caverns. The crystal-studded stalactites (the ones hanging from the ceilings like icicles) and stalagmites (the ones rising up from the cave's floor) are spectacular, in shades of rose, green, amber, black, blood red, and purple. It may be best not to trail your fingers in the cool water: Giant eels live just beneath the surface.

The Pirgos Dirou Caves were discovered in 1955 by a dog that crawled through a hole into the caves and returned several days later coated in red clay. Fortunately, his owner, spelunker Anna Petroclides, was curious about the red clay and followed her dog when he next set off on explorations. What she found was a vast network of caves, of which some 5,000 meters have now been explored. The caves themselves are impressive, but what has made them famous is the Paleolithic and Neolithic remains found here. In short, the Pirgos Dirou caves are one of the oldest inhabited spots in Greece, and the pottery, bone tools, and even garbage found here has shed light on Greece's earliest history.

Before you leave Pirgos Dirou, check to see if the small **Neolithic Museum** (☎ 0733/52-233), with displays of artifacts found in the caves, is open. Admission is Dr500 ($1.45).

The Demaglion Folklore Museum. Thalames. Admission Dr900 ($2.60). Usually open May 1–Sept 30, most days 9:30am–8pm; often closed at midday.

This small private collection in the village of Thalames, some 20 kilometers (12 miles) north of Areopoli, has old prints, costumes, olive presses, farm tools, ceramic plates commemorating various Greek monarchs—and just about anything else you'd expect to find if you cleaned out a number of Maniote attics. The owner, Mr. Demaglion, is a local schoolteacher who speaks a little English and a lot of German and enjoys lecturing visitors. From time to time, Mr. Demaglion sells duplicate items from his collection; you may be able to buy an inexpensive antique wood carving or piece of embroidery. Items for sale are usually on display in front of the museum.

WHERE TO STAY

Our recommendations below are in the Mani itself, but if you want to stay on the outskirts of the Mani, here are some suggestions. In Githio, harborfront choices offering doubles under Dr17,000 ($49) include the venerable (but recently restored) **Aktaion** (☎ 0733/23-500; fax 0733/22-294), our favorite with its seaside balconies; the **Pantheon** (☎ 0733/22-289; fax 0733/22-284); and **Leonidas** (☎ 0733/22-389; fax 0733/22-595). In Messenian Mani, at the seaside hamlet of Kardamili, the **Kalamitsi Hotel & Bungalows** (☎ 0721/73-131; fax 0721/73-135) has doubles in the main building for Dr23,500 ($67); suites and bungalows are also available.

Akroyiali Hotel. Gerolimenas, 23071 Lakonia, Mani. ☎ **0733/54-204.** Fax 0733/54-272. 6 units. Dr12,500 ($36). No credit cards.

The modest Akroyiali overlooks the harbor and contains an excellent restaurant. In summer 2000, the Akroyiali was busily expanding by adding 15 units in a handsome stone building built in traditional Maniote style. The new wing should be open by summer 2001; be sure to ask for a room there. The prices are bound to be a bit higher, but well worth it.

Hotel Itilo. Neo Itilo, 23062 Lakonia, Mani. ☎ **0733/59-222.** Fax 0733/29-234. 26 units. TEL. Dr22,500 ($64) double. Rates include breakfast. AE, MC, V.

This beachfront family-run hotel on the Gulf of Itilo, just north of Areopoli, attracts lots of families, whose children enjoy the little beachside playground. Many of the large guest rooms overlook the sea. If you show up here for just a night or two in high season, you may be relegated to the annex, just across the road from the beach. The hotel food, with lots of fresh fish, is excellent, but, as always with fish, expensive.

Kapetanakou Tower Hotel. Areopoli, 26062 Laconia, Mani. ☎ **0733/51-233.** 8 units (2 shared bathrooms on each floor). Dr15,000 ($43) double. AE, EC, MC, V.

One of the first of the traditional settlement hotels managed by the Greek National Tourism Organization, and now privately owned, the 180-year-old Kapetanakou

Tower stands in a walled garden just off the main street in Areopoli. Some of the rooms have sleeping lofts, and most have colorful rag rugs and locally handmade weavings. This is a wonderful place to stay to get an idea of what it was like to live in a Maniote tower. (Noisy, for one thing: When the wind blows, or other guests walk on the wooden staircase, you know it!) The hotel serves breakfast, and it's only a 5-minute stroll to Areopoli's restaurants.

Limeni Village Hotel. Limeni, Areopoli, 23062 Laconia, Mani. ☎ **0733/51-111.** Fax 0733/51-182. 32 units. MINIBAR TV TEL. Dr23,000 ($66) double; lower off-season. AE, EC, MC, V.

Before we stayed here, we regarded this hotel, built as a Maniote tower village, as a glaring example of bringing coals to Newcastle. But after enjoying the swimming pool each day before and after sightseeing, and taking in the sunset while sipping a gin and tonic on the balcony, we dropped our objections. The bedrooms (two units to most bungalows; some bungalows rented as suites) are outfitted with rag rugs, stone floors, and balconies overlooking the Bay of Itilo. The breakfast buffet is fine, if not inspired; the restaurant is desultory (but the superb Fish Taverna To Limeni is minutes away; see below). Most guests here seem to be Greek families visiting the Mani.

Tsimova Guesthouse. Areopoli, 26062 Laconia, Mani. ☎ **0733/51-301.** 10 units, 8 with bathroom. Dr15,000 ($43) double. Reductions possible off-season. No credit cards.

If you speak some Greek and want to find out about the Mani, this private home in a 300-year-old tower with gun slits is the place to stay. Owner George Bersakos has lived all his life in the Mani and turned much of his house into a small museum (which you can visit without staying here), stuffed with Maniote memorabilia. If you don't speak Greek, Mr. Bersakos will entertain you in his distinctive English, French, or German, or call in his daughter, who does speak English. You'll be beautifully taken care of, but you'll inevitably have less privacy than you would in a hotel. Two of the rooms have TVs.

Tsitsiris Castle. Stavri, 23071 Laconia, Mani. ☎ **0733/56-297** or 01/685-8960. Fax 0733/56-296. 20 units. TEL. Dr20,000 ($57) double. Rates include breakfast. MC, V. Usually closed Nov to mid-Apr, but open some weekends and holidays.

This tower-house hotel—10 kilometers (6.2 miles) south of Areopoli, in the virtually deserted hamlet of Stavri—has its lobby and dining room in a 200-year-old restored tower, with most of the bedrooms in two new wings flanking a lush rose garden. The lobby and dining room are handsome, with lots of exposed stone walls and interesting woven rugs. The bedrooms are more mundane, although when we stayed here, we had our own icon shrine and wonderful views across the hills. Not many independent travelers make their way here; you may either have the place to yourself, or be surrounded by tour groups and Greek families. The restaurant is excellent when there are a good number of guests; otherwise, choice is limited and the cooking is desultory.

WHERE TO DINE

In **Kardamili**, we've eaten well at **Lela's** (☎ **0721/73-541**) by the sea, reached by the twisting road from the main plateia. When Lela's is closed, there's usually a sign posted with directions to another family-run place.

We've eaten at most of the seaside seafood restaurants on the harbor in **Githio**— and still haven't found one that's good enough to make us come back again and again. You should get good, fresh fish at any one of these places, so you may want to make your choice based on other factors, such as atmosphere and noise level. En route from

Githio to Areopoli, in the narrow pass dominated by the castle of Passava, 10 kilometers (6 miles) out of Githio, the family-run **Kali Kardia** (☎ 0733/93250) serves good *spitiko* (homestyle) food.

The three basically interchangeable restaurants on **Areopoli's main square** serve equally good—or bad, depending on your point of view—food, featuring grilled meats and salads. Lunch or dinner at any one of these costs from about Dr2,700 ($9).

Barba-Petros. On the main street, Areopoli. ☎ 0733/51-205. Starters from Dr600 ($1.75); main courses Dr1,800–2,800 ($5.15–$8). No credit cards. Usually open for lunch and dinner.

This little taverna on Areopoli's sinuous main street, which runs from the main square to the cathedral, has a pleasant small garden and much better food than the restaurants on the square. If someone could only persuade the youths on motorcycles not to race up and down the street, this would be a totally gratifying place to sip the local wine and enjoy the tasty fried zucchini and eggplant, as well as chops and stews.

✪ **Fish Taverna To Limeni.** Limeni, Areopoli. ☎ 0733/51-327. Starters from Dr700 ($2); fish priced by the kilo. No credit cards. Usually open for lunch and dinner; sometimes closed in winter. SEAFOOD.

The superb fresh fish at this small restaurant in Limeni, the harbor of Areopoli, draws customers from as far away as Kalamata, so be sure to make a reservation if you want a seaside table. This is not the place to eat if you are squeamish about seeing fish cleaned a few feet away from where you are eating. On the other hand, the seafood here is so good that you may find yourself coming back meal after meal while you're in the Mani. The price per kilo for the seafood varies from day to day and is never cheap. The lobster diavalo (lobster with spaghetti in a tangy sauce with green peppers) is memorable, and costs around $55 for two.

11 Pylos (Pilo/Navarino)

50km (31 miles) W of Kalamata; 108km (67 miles) W of Sparta; 317km (196 miles) SW of Athens

We must admit that all too often in the Peloponnese, the modern village with a famous ancient name—Olympia or Corinth, for example—is a disappointment. That's not the case at Pylos (also known as Navarino), where the modern harbor town has considerable charm. Pylos is developing some sprawling suburbs, and a few of the nearby beaches are being developed with a vengeance, but the harbor and leafy main square are still very pleasant—so pleasant that it's hard to realize that Pylos's harbor has seen some very bloody battles. The Athenians trapped a Spartan force on the offshore island of Sfaktiria in 424 B.C., and in 1827, a combined French, Russian, and British armada defeated the massed Ottoman fleet here. More than 6,000 Ottoman sailors were butchered in what proved to be one of the critical battles of the Greek War of Independence. There's a monument to the three victorious admirals in Pylos's main square, which is understandably called the Square of the Three Admirals.

Ancient Pylos, site of the Mycenaean palace of King Nestor, is located about 17 kilometers (10 miles) north of the town. Homer described Pylos as "sandy Pylos, rich in cattle," and the hilltop palace still overlooks sandy beaches flanked by rich farmland. Ancient Pylos seems to be a site that people take to—or don't. For every visitor who complains about the protective plastic roof over the site, another raves about the palace's idyllic setting. Some call the remains here "scanty," while others find the low walls remarkably "evocative." You decide.

ESSENTIALS

GETTING THERE   By Bus   There are several buses a day from the Stathmos Leoforia Peloponnisou (Bus Station for the Peloponnese) in Athens, Odos Kifissou 100 (☎ **01/51-34-293**), to the Pylos station (☎ **0723/22-230**). There is also bus service to Pylos from Kalamata (☎ **0721/23-145** or 0721/22-851).

By Car   Pylos is a full day's drive from Athens and 3 to 4 hours from either Patras or Sparta. The drive from Sparta to Pylos is via the Langada pass to Kalamata, one of the most beautiful mountain roads in the Peloponnese.

FAST FACTS   Both **banks** in the main square offer currency exchange and have ATMs. The **hospital** (☎ **0723/22-315**) is signposted in town. The **post office,** the **telephone office (OTE),** the **police** (☎ **0723/22-316**), and the **tourist police** (☎ **0723/23-733**) are all signposted in the main square.

WHAT TO SEE & DO

Neokastro. Admission Dr800 ($2.30). Daily 8am–7pm.

The Turkish fortress known as Neokastro, to distinguish it from an earlier fortress, now contains a splendid small museum in a restored 19th-century barracks. The museum features the extensive collection of maps, prints, and watercolors of the French philhellene Rene Puaux, as well as a number of marvelously kitschy porcelain figurines of the English philhellene Lord Byron. Neokastro also contains a small church, clearly a former mosque, and some impressive fortification walls.

Ancient Pylos (Nestor's Palace) and Museum. ☎ **0763/31-358.** Admission to each Dr500 ($1.45). Tues–Sat 8:30am–3pm; Sun 9:30am–2:30pm. Head north out of Pylos on the main road and follow the signs for Hora.

The palace at Pylos belonged to Nestor, the garrulous old king who told stories and gave unsolicited advice while the younger warriors fought at Troy. The palace was rediscovered in 1939 by the American archaeologist Carl Blegen, who had the unbelievable good fortune of discovering the palace archives on his first day working here. Blegen uncovered some 600 clay tablets written in a mysterious language initially called Linear B, and later shown to be an early form of Greek.

Unlike Mycenae and Tiryns, Pylos was not heavily fortified: You'll see a sentry box, but no massive walls. The royal apartments are well preserved, and include a more-than-adequate bathroom with the tub still in place. The palace, with its central courtyard, was originally two stories high and richly decorated with frescoes, some of which are on display at the small archaeological museum a mile away in the village of Hora.

WHERE TO STAY

Hotel Miramare. Odos Paralia, 24001 Pylos, Messenia. ☎ **0723/22-751.** Fax 0723/22-226. 26 units, all with shower only. A/C TV TEL. Dr20,000 ($57) double. AE, EC, MC, V.

The Miramare is just above Pylos's public bathing beach and has its own small restaurant. The guest rooms are simply furnished, but most have balconies overlooking the harbor; some units have minibars. This hotel is usually considerably quieter than the Karalis Hotel, but not as quiet as seaside rooms at the Karalis Beach Hotel.

Hotel Zoe. Yalova Pylou 24001, Messenia. ☎ **0723/22-025.** Fax 0723/22-026. 35 units. Dr15,000 ($43). No credit cards.

This pleasant seaside hotel about 5 kilometers (3 miles) north of Pylos is very popular with German families. If you're traveling with children, the chance to begin and end a day of sightseeing with a swim here might be the salvation of a family holiday. The guest rooms are decent-sized, spare, and ferociously clean.

Karalis Beach Hotel. Paralia, 24001 Pylos, Messenia. ☎ **0723/23-021.** Fax 0723/22-970. 14 units, 4 with shower only. TEL. Dr17,500 ($50) double. Rates include breakfast. MC, V. Usually closed Nov–Apr.

With the best location in town, at the end of the harbor below the Turkish kastro, far from most traffic, this used to be the nicest place to stay in Pylos. But suddenly, the management has become dreadful: It takes forever to get a room cleaned and there's seldom anyone at the desk. The lobby is often filled with young friends of staff members. Speaking of the lobby, perhaps someone could persuade the owners that placing an enormous TV in front of the lobby picture window so that it blocks a good deal of the sea view is not the way to please guests. Nor is it clever to have TV brackets—but no TVs—in some bedrooms. In short, at press time, there's only one reason to stay here: If you can get one of the seaside rooms with a balcony. Otherwise, you'd probably be happier at the Hotel Miramare (see above).

The Karalis Beach Hotel often sends its overflow to the **Karalis Hotel,** Odos Kalamateas 26 (☎ **0723/22-980**), which is under the same management. Rooms here are pleasant, but suffer from traffic noise.

Navarone Hotel/Bungalows. Petrochori, 24001 Pilias, Messenia. ☎ **0723/41-571.** Fax 0723/41-575. E-mail: navaron1@otenet.gr. 17 units, 41 bungalows. TEL. Dr18,000–Dr22,000 ($52–$63). DC, MC, V.

Friends who stayed here report enjoying this new hotel and its pool, about 5 kilometers (3 miles) north of Pylos and a 5-minute walk from an excellent sand beach. Many of the rooms have seafront balconies, and most have good reading lights and handy desks. Keep in mind that the Navarone gets lots of tour groups.

WHERE TO DINE

Diethnes Taverna. Paralia. ☎ **0723/22-772.** Fish priced by the kilo. No credit cards. Mid-May to mid-Sept daily noon to at least 11pm. GREEK/SEAFOOD.

The Diethnes has been here forever, serving meals both indoors and at tables by the quay overlooking the harbor. As you'd expect from a restaurant on the sea and next to the government fish-inspection station, the seafood here is very fresh. Fish in Greece is never cheap, so be sure to ask how much your meal will cost before ordering. There are usually a number of chicken and meat dishes on the menu as well.

Philip Restaurant. On Pylos-Kalamata road. ☎ **0723/22-741.** Fax 0723-23-261. Main courses from Dr1,500 ($4.30). No credit cards. Daily about 11am–midnight. GREEK.

The Philip prides itself on "traditional home cooking," including fish soup, stews, and both octopus and eggplant salads. At press time, we learned that the Philip planned to rent studio apartments overlooking Pylos and its bay. If you plan a long stay in the area, you may want to inquire about these.

Restaurant 1930. On Pylos-Kalamata road by the Karalis Hotel. ☎ **0723/22-032.** Starters from Dr600 ($$1.75); main courses Dr1,800–3,000 ($5.15–$9); fish priced by the kilo. No credit cards. Most evenings in high season 8pm–midnight; sometimes open for lunch. GREEK.

As you might guess from the name, the decor here is emphasized, with the dining room aiming to recreate the ambience of 1930s Pylos. The menu offers good seafood as well as a wide range of other dishes. Let us know what you think of this place—serious foodie friends of ours adore it, but we've yet to be overwhelmed by the cuisine (although we admit the decor is very enjoyable).

SIDE TRIPS FROM PYLOS: METHONI AND KORONI

Methoni and Koroni are two of the most impressive medieval fortresses in Greece and would be worth seeing for that reason alone. But that's not the only appeal: Methoni has one of the best restaurants in Greece, and the drive through the lush Messenian countryside between Methoni and Koroni is ravishing. The route from Pylos to Koroni via Longa is especially blissful; by contrast, the southerly seaside route takes in the village of Finikounda, which is in the throes of overdevelopment. From Pylos, Methoni is 13 kilometers (8 miles) away, while Koroni is 30 kilometers (18 miles).

The long, sandy **Methoni beach** has won several awards for its ecosensitivity, including Greece's Golden Starfish and the Common Market's Blue Flag. Happily, ecosensitivity seems to include not only a clean beach, but also an absence of loud music at the children's playground and beachside cafes. Although it's perfectly possible to visit both Methoni and Koroni on a day trip from Pylos, the superb ☯ **Taverna Klimataria** (see below) makes it tempting to spend the night here.

The Venetians built Methoni on the Ionian Sea and Koroni on the Gulf of Messenia in the 13th century to safeguard their newly acquired Greek empire. In some of the bloodiest fighting on record, the fortresses, almost immediately nicknamed "the twin eyes of empire," passed back and forth between various powers for the next several centuries. In 1500, the Turks slaughtered all 5,000 Venetian defendants at Methoni; in 1685, the Venetians wiped out the 1,500-man garrison at Koroni.

Methoni stands at the end of a spit of land and covers enough ground to have contained a city of several thousand inhabitants during the Middle Ages. Ships filled with pilgrims bound for the Holy Land put in here for supplies; in 1571, Miguel de Cervantes was an unwilling visitor, one of many Spanish seamen captured and forced to work as galley slaves by the Turks after the Battle of Lepanto. Methoni's **exterior walls** are stupendous, although little remains inside the fortress itself. Don't worry about being locked in here when the gates close at 7pm: A very officious guard on a motorcycle rounds up any stragglers. The fortress is usually open from 8am to 7pm; admission is free.

Whereas Methoni's fortress is deserted except for visitors, the fortress at **Koroni** encloses a number of **village houses,** a flourishing **convent,** and several small **cemeteries.** Although the main road in town leads directly to the fortress gate, park before the road heads steeply uphill to the gate, unless you'd enjoy backing up over a sheer drop to the sea. The grounds inside the fortress walls are lovingly planted with roses and welcome shade trees; piles of cannonballs and the occasional cannon remind visitors of Koroni's bloody past. There's a string of seafood restaurants at the harbor below, but nothing here to compare with Methoni's Klimataria. This is a good place to avoid on summer weekends, when there's an influx of day-trippers from Kalamata.

WHERE TO STAY

Hotel Amalia. 24006 Methoni, Messenia. ☎ **0723/12-931.** Fax 0723/31-195. 36 units. TV TEL. Dr20,000 ($57) double. AE, DC, EC, MC, V.

This new hotel, with its large lobby and dining room, straddles a low hill outside Methoni, with fine views of the sea and fortress. The bedrooms here are larger than usual, as are the bathrooms. Each unit faces the sea and is entered through a pleasant rose garden. The only drawbacks: Although you can see the sea, you aren't *on* the sea—and the Amalia does a brisk tour-group business.

Hotel Korakakis Beach. 24006 Finikounda, Messenia. ☎ **0723/71-221.** Fax 0723/71-232. 25 units. TV TEL. Dr15,000 ($43) double. Reductions for stays of a week or more. No credit cards.

Finikounda, about halfway between Methoni and Koroni, is not our cup of tea: too developed, too many hotels, too many people. That said, Finikounda does have lots of fans of its lovely sand beach and small seaside hotels and restaurants. If this sounds appealing, try the Hotel Korakakis Beach, many of whose rooms boast seafront balconies. Beach-loving friends of ours who stayed here dream of a return visit, so this hotel must be doing something right!

WHERE TO DINE

The Akroyiali. Waterfront, Methoni. No phone. Snacks from Dr600 ($1.75); fish priced by the kilo. No credit cards. Open all day in summer. FISH/SNACKS.

This is a pleasant spot for a snack by the sea. Even though this place has good fresh fish, it's hard to resist the Klimataria (see below) at mealtime.

The Kaggelarios. Waterfront, Koroni. No phone. Snacks from Dr600 ($1.75); ouzo and octopus Dr1,800 ($5.15). No credit cards. OUZO/SNACKS/LIGHT MEALS.

This cafe seems to attract more locals than the other waterfront fish tavernas in Koroni. The octopus is certainly fresh—the day's catch can be seen hanging on a line at the restaurant.

✪ **Taverna Klimataria.** Methoni. ☎ **0723/31-544.** Fax 0723/31-320. Main courses from Dr1,800 ($5.15). DC, EC, MC, V. May 15 to about Oct 20 daily 1:30–6:30pm and 8pm–midnight. GREEK/ANATOLIAN/VEGETARIAN.

This restaurant, serving the best food we've eaten in the Peloponnese, is reason enough to visit Methoni. The chef somehow manages to take standard dishes familiar from any Greek menu (fried zucchini, eggplant salad, briam) and turn them into elegant delights. Then there are the delicately seasoned stews, the chicken breast in puff pastry, the stuffed zucchini flowers, and the fresh fish and lobster. The Klimataria is situated in a pleasant garden, and the service is fast and attentive. It's easy to be seduced by the wide variety of food: This is one of the few nonhotel restaurants in the Peloponnese where it's not difficult for a couple to spend more than $50 for dinner—and be eager to come back the next day and do it all over again. You'll hear lots of German, Italian, and French (and not much Greek) spoken here.

12 Messene (Ithomi/Mavromati)

25km (16 miles) N of Kalamata; 60km (39 miles) E of Pylos

Between 370 and 369 B.C., the great Theban general and statesman Epaminondas built the sprawling city of Messene and its almost 9.5 kilometers (6 miles) of walls below Mount Ithomi in the hopes of checking the power of Sparta. Today, the defense wall, with its two-story towers and turreted gates, is the best preserved classical fortification in the Peloponnese.

To get here by car from Pylos, Kalamata, or Tripolis, take the main Kalamata-Pylos road to the modern town of Messini, where the road to ancient Messene is signposted. The site of ancient Messene (also called Ithomi) is in the village of Mavromati, approximately 20 kilometers (13 miles) north of Messini.

WHAT TO SEE & DO

Ancient Messene. Admission Dr500 ($1.45). Tues–Sun 8am–3pm. (In reality, admission is seldom charged and the site is usually open.)

The most impressive stretches of the ancient wall are outside the site, north of the village of Mavromati. As you pass through Mavromati, try to pick up a copy of the excellent site guide at the postcard shop next to the village spring (Dr1,000/$2.90). Even at a distance, the sheer size of the wall, with its towers and gates, makes most visitors gasp. The **Arcadian Gate** is especially well preserved, with the grooves cut in the marble pavement by ancient chariot wheels still clearly visible. As you drive back toward Mavromati, you'll pass more of the defense wall and the site museum, which has been closed for some time and shows no signs of reopening.

The excavated ruins of Messene are clearly signposted past the museum. This is a vast, sprawling site, with a **Sanctuary of Asklepios** so large that it was originally thought to be the agora (marketplace). The partially excavated **Stadium,** with many of its marble benches well preserved, lies along the dirt road beyond the Asklepeion. To walk the entire site takes a minimum of several hours, but it's possible to see just the Asklepeion in an hour.

WHERE TO STAY & DINE

Ithome Restaurant. Mavromati-Ithome (across from the Klepsidra Spring). ☎ **0724/ 51-498.** Fax 0724/51-298. E-mail: ithome_2000@yahoo.com. Lunch or dinner with a beer from Dr3,000 ($9). V. GREEK.

This very simple restaurant has a terrific view over the ancient site and serves souvlaki, grills, salads, french fries, and the occasional vegetable dish.

Pension Zeus. Mavromati-Ithome, 24200 Messenia. ☎ **0724/51-025.** 5 units, 3 with bathroom. Dr12,000 ($34) double. Rates include breakfast. No credit cards.

This small family-run pension—which is about as far from the Greece of tour-group hotels as you can get—has several small bedrooms with balconies. The family is very helpful and pleasant, and the rooms perfectly acceptable. The only problem: You're on the one road through town, and will hear whatever traffic there is.

13 Olympia

311km (199 miles) W of Athens; 90km (55 miles) S of Patras; 21km (13 miles) E of Pirgos

With its shady groves of pine, olive, and oak trees, the considerable remains of two temples, and the stadium where the first Olympic races were run in 776 B.C., Olympia is the most beautiful major site in the Peloponnese—although the forest fires of 1998 badly damaged neighborhood groves and almost engulfed the site itself. When you realize that the archaeological museum is one of the finest in Greece, you'll see why you can easily spend a full day here.

A LOOK AT THE PAST   There's really no modern equivalent for ancient Olympia, which was both a religious sanctuary and an athletic complex, where the games took place every four years from 776 B.C. to A.D. 393. Thereafter, the sanctuary slipped into oblivion, and buildings were toppled by repeated earthquakes and covered by the flooding of the Alfios and Kladeos rivers. When the English antiquarian Richard Chandler rediscovered the site in 1766, most of Olympia lay under 10 feet of mud and silt. The Germans began to excavate here in 1852 and are still at it today.

Reports of the rediscovery of Olympia prompted the French Baron de Coubertin to work for the reestablishment of the Olympic Games in 1896. The first modern games were held in Athens in 1896, and Greece was very sorry to lose the 1996 100th-anniversary games to Atlanta. Greeks are hoping that at least one event in the 2004 Olympics in Athens can take place here, where it all began.

OLYMPIA TODAY   The straggling modern village of Olympia (confusingly known as Ancient Olympia) is bisected by its one main street, Leoforos Kondili. The town has the usual assortment of tourist shops selling jewelry, T-shirts, and reproductions of ancient pottery and statues, as well as more than a dozen hotels and restaurants. Two

The Ancient Olympic Games

The 5-day Olympic festival was held every 4 years between 776 B.C. and A.D. 393 at full moon in mid-August or September, after the summer harvest. Participants came from as far away as Asia Minor and Italy, and the entire Greek world observed a truce to allow athletes and spectators to make their way to Olympia safely. During all the years that the games took place, the truce was broken only a handful of times.

By the time the games opened, literally thousands of people had poured into Olympia; much of the surrounding countryside was a tent city. Women were barred from watching or participating in the games, although they had their own games in honor of Hera, Zeus's long-suffering wife, in non-Olympic years. Any woman caught sneaking into the Olympic Games was summarily thrown to her death from a nearby mountain.

No one knows precisely what the order of events was, but the five days included footraces, short and long jumps, wrestling and boxing contests, chariot races, the arduous pentathlon (discus, javelin, jumping, running, and wrestling), and the vicious pankration, which combined wrestling and boxing techniques.

The 3rd-century A.D. writer Philostratos recorded that participants in the pentathlon "must have skill in various methods of strangling." The most prestigious event was the *stade,* or short footrace, which gave its name to the stadium. Each Olympiad was named after the winner of the stade, and athletes like the 2nd-century B.C. Leonidas of Rhodes, who won at four successive Olympics, became international heroes. In addition to the glory, each victor won a crown made of olive branches and free meals for life in his hometown.

things worth visiting in town: the Museum of the Olympic Games and the excellent Galerie Orphee bookstore (see below).

The ancient site of Olympia is an easily walkable 15 minutes south of the modern village, but if you have a car, you might as well drive: The road teems with tour buses and the walk is less than relaxing.

ESSENTIALS

GETTING THERE   By Train   There are several trains a day from Athens to Pirgos, where you change to the train for Olympia. Information on schedules and fares is available from the Stathmos Peloponnisou (Railroad Station for the Peloponnese) in Athens (☎ 01/513-1601).

By Bus   There are three buses a day to Olympia from the Stathmos Leoforia Peloponnisou (Bus Station for the Peloponnese) in Athens, Odos Kifissou 100 (☎ 01/513-4110). There are also frequent buses from Patras to Pirgos, with connecting service to Olympia. In Patras, KTEL buses leave from the intersection of Odos Zaimi and Odos Othonos (☎ 061/273-694).

By Car   Olympia is at least a 6-hour drive from Athens, whether you take the coast road that links Athens-Corinth-Patras and Olympia or head inland to Tripolis and Olympia on the new Corinth-Tripolis road. Heavy traffic in Patras means that the drive from Patras to Olympia can easily take 2 hours.

VISITOR INFORMATION   Olympia is basically a one-street town; the few things you do not find on **Odos Praxitelous Kondili** will be just off it. The **tourist office,** on the way to the ancient site near the south end of the main street, is usually open daily, in summer from 9am to 10pm, and in winter from 11am to 6pm. Ask here for a map of the site and town and information on accommodations (☎ **0624/23-100** or 0624/23-125).

FAST FACTS   The **National Bank of Greece,** on Odos Praxitelous Kondili (the main drag), exchanges currency and has an ATM. The **health clinic** (☎ **0624/ 22-222**) is signposted in town. The **police** (☎ **0624/22-100**) are at Odos Eth-nossinelefseos 6. Both the **post office** (on the main street) and the **telephone office** (just off the main street) are signposted.

WHAT TO SEE & DO

The Archaeological Museum. Admission to museum and site Dr2,000 ($6). Summer Mon noon–6pm, Tues–Sat 8am–5pm. Winter Mon noon–6pm, Tues–Sat 11am–5pm.

If ever a building should not be judged by its façade, this is it. From outside, the museum has all the charm of a small factory. Inside, one of the finest collections in Greece is beautifully displayed in well-lit rooms, some of which look onto an interior courtyard. In August 1998, when forest fires were less than half a kilometer from both the site and museum, it was revealed that the museum owned, but had not installed, a fire-extinguishing system. Subsequent statements from the archaeological service suggested that the only thing unusual here was that a fire-extinguishing system had actually been purchased.

Even though you'll be eager to see the ancient site, it's a good idea to first visit the museum whose collection makes clear Olympia's astonishing wealth and importance in antiquity: Every victorious city and almost every victorious athlete dedicated a bronze or marble statue here. Nothing but the best was good enough for Olympia, and many of these superb works of art are on view. Most of the exhibits are displayed in rooms to the right and left of the main entrance and follow a chronological sequence from severe Neolithic vases to baroque Roman imperial statues, neither of which will probably tempt you from heading straight ahead to see the museum's superstars.

The monumental **sculpture from the Temple of Zeus** is probably the finest surviving example of archaic Greek sculpture. The sculpture from the west pediment shows the battle of the Lapiths and Centaurs raging around the magisterial figure of Apollo, the god of reason. On the east pediment, Zeus oversees the chariot race between Oinomaos, the king of Pisa, and Pelops, the legendary figure who wooed and won Oinomaos's daughter by the unsporting expedient of loosening his opponent's chariot pins. On either end of the room, sculptured metopes show scenes from the Labors of Hercules, including the one he performed at Olympia: cleansing the foul stables of King Augeus by diverting the Alfios River.

Just beyond the sculpture from the Temple of Zeus are the 5th-century B.C. **winged victory,** done by the artist Paionios, and the 4th-century B.C. figure of Hermes and the infant Dionysos, known as the **Hermes of Praxitelous.** The Hermes has a room to itself—or would, if tourists didn't make a beeline to admire Hermes smiling with amused tolerance at his chubby half-brother Dionysos. If you want to impress your companions, mention casually that many scholars think that this is not an original work by Praxitelous, but a Roman copy.

In addition to several cases of glorious bronze heads of snarling griffins and the lovely terra cotta of a resolute Zeus carrying off the youthful Ganymede, the museum has a good deal of **athletic paraphernalia** from the ancient games: stone and bronze weights that jumpers used, bronze and stone discuses, and even an enormous stone with a boastful inscription that a weight lifter had raised it over his head with only one hand.

Before you leave the museum, have a look at the two excellent **site models** just inside the main entrance. As the models make clear, ancient Olympia was quite literally divided by a low wall into two distinct parts: the Altis, or religious sanctuary, containing temples and shrines; and the civic area, with athletic and municipal buildings.

The Ancient Site. Admission Dr1,200 ($3.45). Usually open summer Mon–Fri 7:30am–7pm, Sat–Sun 8:30am–3pm; winter Mon–Fri 8am–5pm, Sat–Sun 8:30am–3pm.

In antiquity, every 4 years during the Olympic Games, so many people thronged here that it was said by the time the games began, not even one more spectator could have wedged himself into the stadium. So, if the site is very crowded when you visit, just remember that it would have been much worse in antiquity.

Olympia's setting is magical. Pine trees shade the little valley, dominated by the conical Hill of Kronos, that lies between the Alfios and Kladeos rivers. In July 2000, archaeologists excavating beside the Kladeos discovered a Mycenaean tholos (beehive) tomb with more than 100 amphorae, and expect to find more tombs as excavations continue. The discovery was a reminder of how much is yet to be discovered here.

The handsome temples and the famous stadium that you've come to Olympia to see are not immediately apparent as you enter the site. Immediately to the left are the unimpressive low walls that are all that remain of the **Roman baths,** where athletes and spectators could enjoy hot and cold plunges. The considerably more impressive remains with the slender columns on your right mark the **gymnasium** and **palestra,** where athletes practiced their footracing and boxing skills. The enormous gymnasium had a roofed track, precisely twice the length of the stadium, where athletes could practice in bad weather. Still ahead on the right are the fairly meager remains of a number of structures, including a **swimming pool** and the large square **Leonidaion,** which served as a hotel for visiting dignitaries until a Roman governor decided it would do nicely as his villa.

The **religious sanctuary** was, and is, dominated by two temples: the good-sized temple of Hera and the massive temple of Zeus. The **Temple of Hera,** with its three standing columns, is the older of the two, built around 600 B.C. If you look closely, you'll see that the temple's column capitals and drums are not uniform. That's because this temple was originally built with wooden columns, and as each column decayed, it was replaced; inevitably, the new columns had variations. The Hermes of Praxitelous was found here, buried under the mud that covered Olympia for so long due to the repeated flooding of the Alfios and Kladeos rivers.

The **Temple of Zeus,** which once had a veritable thicket of 34 stocky Doric columns, was built around 456 B.C. The entire temple—so austere and gray today—was anything but austere in antiquity: Gold, red, and blue paint decorated it, and inside stood the enormous gold-and-ivory statue of Zeus, seated on an ivory-and-ebony throne. The statue was so ornate that it was considered one of the Seven Wonders of the Ancient World—and so large that people joked that if Zeus stood up, his head would go through the temple's roof. In fact, the antiquarian Philo of Byzantium suggested that Zeus had created elephants simply so that the sculptor Phidias would have the ivory to make the statue of Zeus.

Not only do we know that Phidias made the 13-meter-tall statue, we know where he made it: The **Workshop of Phidias** was on the site of the well-preserved brick

A Worthwhile Shop

✪ **Galerie Orphee,** Antonios Kosmopoulos's bookstore on the main street in Ancient Olympia (☎ **0624/23-555**), carries an extensive range of cassettes and CDs of Greek music, plus frequent displays of contemporary art. It's a pleasant contrast to Olympia's other shops, which have all too many T-shirts, museum reproductions, and machine-made rugs and embroideries sold as genuine handmade crafts.

building clearly visible west of the temple, just outside the sanctuary. How do we know that this was Phidias's workshop? Because a cup with "I belong to Phidias" written on it and artists' tools were found here.

Between the temples of Zeus and Hera you can make out the low foundations of a round building. This is all that remains of the **shrine** that Philip of Macedon, never modest, built here to pat himself on the back after conquering Greece in 338 B.C.

Beyond the two temples, built up against the Hill of Kronos itself, are the curved remains of a once-elegant **Roman fountain** and the foundations of 11 **treasuries** where Greek cities stored votive offerings and money. In front of the treasuries are the low bases of a series of bronze **statues of Zeus,** dedicated not by victorious athletes but by those caught cheating in the stadium. These statues would have been the last thing that competitors saw before they ran through the vaulted tunnel into the stadium.

Ancient tradition clearly shows that the Olympic Games began here in 776 B.C. and ended in A.D. 395, but is less clear on just why they were held every 4 years. According to one legend, Herakles (Hercules) initiated the games to celebrate the completion of his 12 labors, one of which took place nearby when the hero diverted the Alfios River to wash out the fetid Augean stables that King Augeas had neglected for more than a decade. With the stables clean, Herakles paced off the stadium and then ran its entire length of 600 Olympic feet (192.27m) without having to take a single breath.

The Museum of the Olympic Games. Admission Dr500 ($1.45). Mon–Sat 8am–3:30pm, Sun and holidays 9am–2:30pm.

When you head back to town, try to set aside half an hour to visit the Museum of the Olympic Games. Not many tourists come here, and the guards are often glad to show visitors around. Displays include victors' medals, commemorative stamps, and photos of winning athletes, such as former King Constantine of Greece and the great African-American athlete Jesse Owens. There's also a photo of the bust of the founder of the modern Olympics, Baron de Coubertin. (The bust itself stands just off the main road east of the ancient site and marks the spot where de Coubertin's heart is buried.)

WHERE TO STAY

Olympia has more than 20 hotels, which means that you can almost always find a room—although if you arrive without a reservation in July or August, you may not get your first choice. As is often the case in major tourist centers, hotels here often raise and lower their rates depending on what kind of a season they're having. In winter, many hotels are closed.

Grecotel Lakopetra Beach. Kato Achaia, 25200 Achaia. ☎ **0693/51-713.** Fax 0693/51-045. 192 units. MINIBAR TV TEL. Dr35,000 ($99) double. Rates include breakfast. MC, V.

This resort hotel, with tennis courts, fresh- and saltwater pools, saunas, exercise facilities, restaurants, and boutiques, is set in extensive gardens a short walk from the beach. With a car, you can be at ancient Olympia in less than 30 minutes. The rooms here are large, with balconies or terraces, and the bathrooms are well appointed. In short, a comfortable place to come home to after a day's sightseeing.

Hotel Europa. 27065 Ancient Olympia. ☎ **800-528-1234** in the U.S., 0624/22-650, or 0624/22-700. Fax 0624/23-166. 80 units. A/C TV TEL. Dr35,000 ($99) double. Breakfast Dr2,000 ($6) extra. AE, DC, MC, V. Open year-round.

This member of the Best Western chain, a few minutes' drive out of town on a hill overlooking both the modern village and the ancient site, is clearly the best hotel in town—and one of the best in the entire Peloponnese. The only reason not to stay here is if you want to be able to walk out the door and be in the village of Ancient Olympia—or if you have trouble with stairs (there's no elevator, and the lobby, dining rooms, pool, and bedrooms are on different levels). The hotel lobby and restaurant gleam with marble and boast great views out the picture windows. Most of the guest rooms overlook the large pool and garden, and several overlook the ancient site itself. The spacious rooms are outfitted with colorful rugs, extra-firm mattresses, and generous balconies. Friends who travel through the Peloponnese every summer rave about the Hotel Europa's unusual tranquillity.

Hotel Neda. Odos Karamanli 1, 27065 Ancient Olympia. ☎ **0624/22-563.** Fax 0624/22-206. 43 units. TEL. Dr15,500 ($44) double. AE, V.

With a pleasant rooftop cafe, comfortable lobby, serviceable restaurant, and distinctive red-and-white façade, the Neda offers good value. The large double rooms, many decorated in shades of pink and rose, contain colorful shaggy flokati rugs and good bedside reading lamps. Some of the rooms have double beds, but most have twin beds, so specify which you want. All units have balconies, and are usually quieter than those at hotels on the main street.

✪ **Hotel Pelops.** Odos Varela 2, 27065 Ancient Olympia. ☎ **0624/22-543.** Fax 0624/22-213. E-mail: hotel_pelops@hotmail.com. 25 units. TEL. Dr17,500 ($50) double. MC, V. Closed Nov–Feb.

The English-speaking owner, Susanna Spiliopoulou, described by many visitors here as especially helpful, makes this one of the most welcoming hotels in Olympia. There are flokati rugs on the floors, good mattresses (and anti-allergy pillows) on the beds, and plants and vines shading the terrace.

Hotel Praxitelous. Odos Spiliopoulou 7, 27065 Ancient Olympia. ☎ **0624/225-92.** 10 units. Dr10,500 ($30) double. AE, EC, V.

This small, family-run hotel is the best bargain in town. It's just one street back from Olympia's main drag, and the neighborhood has a nice feel, with children often playing ball in front of the police station. The guest rooms are very small and spare, and some of the beds are showing signs of wear; the front rooms have balconies. If you want to avoid the murmurs of conversation from the Praxitelous's excellent restaurant on the sidewalk below the balconies, ask for a room at the back (and hope that the neighborhood dogs are quiet).

WHERE TO DINE

There are almost as many restaurants as hotels in Olympia. The ones on and just off the main street with large signs in English and German tend to have indifferent food and service, although it's possible to get good snacks of yogurt or *tiropites* (cheese pies) in most of the cafes.

Taverna Ambrosia. Behind the train station, Ancient Olympia. ☎ **0624/23-755.** Fax 0624/22-439. Main courses Dr1,800–Dr3,500 ($5.15–$10). AE, MC, V. Daily 8–11pm. Lunch served every weekend. GREEK.

This large restaurant (and threatening to get larger still with an expansion in the works) with a pleasant outside veranda continues to attract locals, although it does a brisk business with tour groups as well. You'll find the usual grilled chops and souvlaki, but the vegetable dishes are unusually good, as is the lamb stew with lots of garlic and oregano.

✪ **Taverna Kladeos.** Behind the train station, Ancient Olympia. ☎ **0624/23-322.** Main courses Dr1,800–Dr3,000 ($5.15–$9). MC, V. Daily 1:30–3pm and 6pm–1am. Sometimes closed Nov–Apr. GREEK.

The charming Kladeos, with the best food in town, is at the end of the little paved road that runs steeply downhill past the Ambrosia restaurant. You may not be the only foreigner, but you probably will find lots of locals here. In good weather, tables are set up under canvas awnings and roofs made of rushes. If you sit on the hillside, you'll be serenaded by the frogs that live beside the river. The menu varies according to what's in season, but often includes lamb flavored with oregano. In summer, the lightly grilled green peppers, zucchini, and eggplant are especially delicious. The house wine, a light rose, is heavenly. If you want to buy some to take with you, give your empty water bottle to your waiter and ask him to fill it with *krasi* (wine).

✪ **Taverna Praxitelous.** Odos Spiliopoulou 7, Ancient Olympia. ☎ **0624/23-570** or 0624/22-592. Main courses Dr1,000–Dr3,500 ($2.90–$10). AE, EC, V. Daily about 11am–3pm and about 7pm–midnight. GREEK.

The reputation of the Hotel Praxitelous's excellent and reasonably priced restaurant has spread rapidly—and it's packed almost every evening, first with foreigners, eating unfashionably early for Greece, and then with locals, who start showing up around 10pm. Although the main courses are very good, especially the rabbit stew with onions (*stifado*), you can make an entire meal out of the delicious and varied mezedes, which may include octopus, eggplant salad, taramosalata, fried cheese, and a handful of olives. In good weather, tables are set outside on the sidewalk; the rest of the time, meals are served in the pine-paneled dining room.

14 Patras (Patra)

207km (128 miles) SW of Athens

The third-largest city in Greece and far and away the largest in the Peloponnese, Patras's unappealing urban sprawl now extends for miles north and south of the city center. Although Patras does have sights worth seeing—the Cathedral of St. Andrew, the Archaeological Museum, a Roman Odeon (music hall) on the slopes of the ancient Acropolis, and a medieval castle on the summit—there's nothing here worth lingering over unless you have to mark time waiting for the ferry to Italy. In July and August, however, the **Patras International Festival of the Arts** (☎ **061/276-540** or 061/279-008) brings performances of everything from ancient drama to popular music to the Roman Odeon and the Patras Municipal Theater (☎ **061/623-730**). Or you may prefer to concentrate on the **Wine Festival,** featuring tastings at the Achaia Clauss winery (☎ **061/325-051**); check with the tourist office for schedule information. Patras also has a vigorous **carnival** that lasts nearly a month, with parades, costumes, and floats, ending the Monday before Lent.

ESSENTIALS

GETTING THERE   By Train   There are frequent trains from the Stathmos Peloponnisou (Railroad Station for the Peloponnese) in Athens (☎ 01/513-1601). The Patras train station, Odos Othonos Amalias 14 (☎ 061/273-694), is on the waterfront near the boat departure piers. If you're catching a ferryboat, keep in mind that Greek trains usually run late.

By Bus   There are some 15 buses to Patras daily from the Stathmos Leoforia Peloponnisou (Bus Station for the Peloponnese) in Athens, Odos Kifissou 100 (☎ 01/522-4914). The Patras bus station (☎ 061/623-886) is on Odos Amalias.

By Car   The drive on the National Highway from Athens to Patras takes about 6 hours. At press time, there was one gas station between Corinth and Patras. *Note:* In the Patras city center, the system of one-way streets, not always obviously marked, along with the profusion of foreign drivers who have just arrived from Europe by ferryboat, mean that you should drive with particular care.

If you're heading from Patras across the Gulf of Corinth into Central Greece, you'll take the Rio-AntiRio car ferry, which runs twice an hour from early morning until about 11pm. Keep an eye out for work on the ambitious new Rio-AntiRio bridge, scheduled to be up by the 2004 Olympics.

VISITOR INFORMATION   The **tourist office (EOT)** is at Odos Iroon Polytechniou 1, on the harbor near ferryboat gate no. 6 (☎ 061/650-353); it's usually open Monday through Friday from 7am to 9pm, Saturday and Sunday from 2 to 9pm. The **tourist police** (☎ 061/220-902) are in the same building.

FAST FACTS   A number of **banks** on the waterfront and on Plateia Georgiou exchange currency and have ATMs. The **post office** is signposted at the intersection of Mezonas and Zaimi. The **telephone office (OTE)** is on the waterfront by the customs sheds. Most of the **car-rental agencies** (Avis, Hertz, Kemwell) have clearly marked offices on the waterfront. The **hospital** (☎ 061/22-3812) is signposted in town. There is also an **emergency first-aid station** (☎ 061/277-386) at the corner of Karolou and Ayiou Dionysion.

WHAT TO SEE & DO

If you find yourself with a few hours in Patras, we suggest you head first for **Plateia Yioryiou** (George Square). Sit at a cafe and take in the façades of the handsome neoclassical theater and banks on the square. Patras has been hit repeatedly by earthquakes, and these buildings are among the few that remain from the 19th century, when the city was famous for its arcaded streets and neoclassical architecture.

Then, head down to the waterfront to the **Cathedral of St. Andrew.** Although the present rather hideous church was only built after World War II, the mosaics give a vivid picture of old Patras. Be sure to dress appropriately to visit the cathedral, a major pilgrimage shrine thanks to the presence of St. Andrew's skull in an ornate gold reliquary to the right of the altar. There are several pleasant cafes in the shaded park across from the cathedral.

If you have an attack of conscience, head for the **Archaeological Museum,** Mezonos 42 (☎ 061/275-070), open Tuesday through Sunday from 8:30am to 5pm; admission is Dr400 ($1.15). If you're here on the weekend and feel energetic, take in the **Patras Fortress,** a medieval castle on the ancient acropolis that's open Saturday and Sunday from about 8am to 7pm; admission is free. If you drive up, be pleasantly surprised if you don't get lost. If you're taking the Rio-AntiRio ferry from the Peloponnese across to Central Greece, you can take in another fortress, the 15th-century

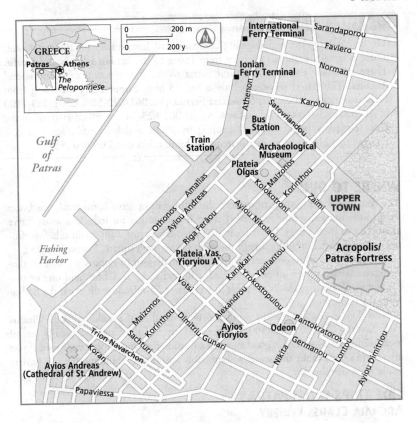

Fortress of Rio, while you wait for your boat. The fortress is open daily from 8am to 7pm; admission is free.

WHERE TO STAY

Astir Hotel. Ayiou Andreas 16, 26223 Patras. ☎ **061/277-502.** Fax 061/271-644. 120 units. A/C MINIBAR TV TEL. Dr35,000–Dr45,000 ($99–$129) double. MC, V.

If you arrive too late to continue your journey or have an early-morning boat to catch, this is a convenient hotel whose best feature is its roof garden with pool. The bedrooms are nothing special, and many seem to have been decorated by someone who couldn't decide on just which color to go with. Some units have harbor views, as does the rooftop terrace. For Patras, this is a quiet place to spend the night—which is to say that the street noise here is usually endurable.

Porto Rio Hotel. 26500 Rion. ☎ **061/992-102.** Fax 061/992-115. 269 units, 48 bungalows. A/C TV TEL. Dr24,000–Dr45,500 ($69–$130) double. AE, MC, V.

This sprawling hotel complex on the beach, a 20-minute drive north of Patras, does a brisk business with business conventions, tour groups, and European families on holiday. The Rio has several pools, a health club (with saunas and Jacuzzi), and two tennis courts. The guest rooms are large, and most have either a terrace or a balcony overlooking the extensive gardens. This is a good place to stay if you have a day to kill before catching a ferry in Patras. The only drawback is the unimaginative food.

The Ferry to the Ionian Islands & Italy

The major ferryboat and shipping companies all have offices on the waterfront. There is usually daily ferry service from Patras to the **Ionian islands** and **Corfu.** There are many daily services from Patras to the Italian towns of **Brindisi** and **Ancona.** The fastest service to Italy is the 18-hour **Super Ferry Crossing** from Patras to Ancona, offered by **Superfast Ferries** (☎ **061/622-500,** or 01/969-1100 in Athens, or 310/544-3551 in the U.S.; fax 061/623-547, or 301/541-0166 in the U.S.; e-mail: superfaxt@superfast.com). In 2000, a deluxe cabin for two cost Dr75,000 ($215); a bunk in a shared four-bunk cabin cost Dr8,400 ($24).

WHERE TO DINE

The restaurants along the harbor near the train station serve consistently mediocre food to the hordes of tourists arriving from and departing for Italy. You won't starve at any one of these places, but you can do better. If you just want an ouzo before dinner or a sweet after, head for any of the cafes in the main square, Plateia Yioryiou.

One place we can recommend is **Trikoyia,** Amalias 46 (no phone), a hole-in-the-wall taverna that serves up excellent fresh fish and octopus. Chops and one or two other meat dishes are usually available as well. It's a 15-minute walk along the harbor from the main port.

Next door at Amalias 48 (the number is not posted on the building) is the **Pharos Fish Taverna** (☎ **061/336-500**), with equally fresh fish. There are usually lots of locals eating here—always a good sign. Head inside first and choose your fish; if you arrive and sit at a table, the waiter will probably ignore you, thinking that you haven't made up your mind yet.

SIDE TRIPS FROM PATRAS
ARCHAIA CLAUSS WINERY

This winery is located above Patras in the hills, which are usually noticeably cooler than Patras itself, and can be reached by taking bus no. 7 from Odos Kolokotroni and Kanakari. Free tours of the winery, with its old barrels and grape presses, are given most weekdays (☎ **061/325-051** or 061/620-353 for information). The German vintner Clauss named his sweet dessert wine "Mavrodaphne" in memory of his beloved Greek wife, who died young. You may be offered a free sample of Mavrodaphne at the end of your tour. *Take note:* The wine is as sweet as molasses.

THE CASTLE AT CHLEMOUTSI

This is an astonishingly well-preserved 13th-century Frankish castle with crenelated walls, cavernous galleries, and an immense hexagonal keep. Like most castles in the Peloponnese, it passed back and forth among the Franks, Venetians, Turks, and Greeks. The gaps in the outer wall were caused by Ibrahim Pasha's cannon during the Greek War of Independence. The castle is open most days from sunrise to sunset; admission is free. The turnoff to the castle is signposted some 55 kilometers (34 miles) out of Patras on the main Patras-Olympia road.

Crete 8

by John S. Bowman

Few travelers need to be sold on the glories of the Minoan culture of Crete. But how many know that Crete also offers visitors cities with layers of at least 4,000 years of continuous inhabitation, including the vibrant heritage of centuries of Orthodox Christianity and the distinctive imprint left by almost 700 years of Venetian and Turkish rule? Not to mention endless beaches and magnificent mountains, intriguing caves and resonant gorges, and countless villages and sites that provide unexpected and unforgettable experiences. Per square mile, Crete must be one of the most "loaded" places in the world—loaded, that is, in the diversity of history, archaeological sites, natural attractions, tourist amenities, and more. In a world where increasing numbers of travelers have "been there, done that," Crete remains an endlessly fascinating and satisfying destination.

An elaborate service industry has grown up to please the thousands of foreigners who visit Crete each year. There are facilities now for everyone's taste, ranging from luxury resorts to guest rooms in villages that have hardly changed over several centuries. You can spend a delightful day in a remote mountain environment where you're treated to fresh goat cheese and olives; then be back at your hotel within an hour, lying on the beach and enjoying a cool drink.

Crete isn't always and everywhere a gentle Mediterranean idyll—its terrain can be raw, its sites austere, its tone brusque. But for those looking for a distinct destination, Crete will be rewarding.

STRATEGIES FOR SEEING THE ISLAND If possible, go in June or September, even late May or early October (unless you seek only a sun-drenched beach): Crete has become an island on overload in July and August (it's also very hot!). The overnight ferry from Piraeus is still the purists' way to go, but the hour-long flights give you more time for activities. There's enough to do to fill up a week, if not a lifetime of visits; by flying, you can actually see the major sites in two packed days. (By the way, you can fly into Iraklion and out of Chania, or vice versa.)

The following selection of destinations is designed to fill 5 to 7 days—allowing for a mix of activities and even time for collapsing on a beach at the end of the day. Iraklion is a must, what with its archaeological museum and nearby Knossos. An excursion to Phaestos and its associated sites could occupy most of a second day; if you don't need to see that second Minoan palace, we recommend you move on to Chania or Rethymnon. (The old road that winds through the mountains and villages has its charms, while the coastal expressway offers the extraordinary "tunnel" of flowering oleanders.) The walk through the famed Samaria Gorge requires one long day for the total excursion. Those seeking less strenuous activity might prefer a trip eastward to Ayios Nikolaos and its nearby attractions. None of these trips require a car, as public transportation or tour groups are so frequent. At some point, however, you might want to rent a car (although not in the cities or towns)—this allows you to leave the overdeveloped tourist trail and gives you access to countless villages, spectacular scenery, beaches at the end of the roads, and lesser known archaeological, historical, and cultural sites.

A LOOK AT THE PAST   Crete's diversity and distinction begin with its history, a past that has left far more remains than the Minoan sites many people first associate with the island. After being settled by humans around 6500 B.C., Crete passed through the late Neolithic and early Bronze ages, sharing the broader eastern Mediterranean culture.

Sometime around 3000 B.C., new immigrants arrived; by about 2500 B.C., there began to emerge a fairly distinctive culture that has been named Early Minoan. By about 2000 B.C., the Minoans were moving into a far more ambitious phase, the Middle Minoan—the civilization that gave rise to the palaces and superb works of art that now attract thousands of visitors to Crete every year.

Mycenaean Greeks appear to have taken over the palaces about 1500 B.C., and by about 1200 B.C., this Minoan-Mycenaean civilization had pretty much gone under. For several centuries, Crete was a relatively marginal player in the great era of Greek classical civilization.

When the Romans conquered the island in 67 B.C., they revived certain centers (including Knossos) as imperial colonies. Early converts to Christianity, the Cretans slipped into the shadows of the Byzantine world, but the island was pulled back into the light in 1204, when Venetians broke up the Byzantine Empire and took over Crete. The Venetians made the island a major colonial outpost, revived trade and agriculture, and eventually built quite elaborate structures.

By the late 1500s, the Turks were conquering the Venetians' eastern Mediterranean possessions, and in 1669 captured the last major holdout on Crete, the city of Candia—now Iraklion. Cretans suffered considerably under the Turks, and although some of Greece finally threw off the Turkish yoke in the late 1820s, Crete was left behind. A series of rebellions marked the rest of the 19th century, resulting in the Great Powers' sponsoring a sort of independent Crete in 1898.

Finally in 1913, Crete was for the first time formally joined to Greece. Crete had yet another cameo role in history when the Germans invaded it in 1941 with gliders and parachute troops; the ensuing occupation was another low point for the people of Crete. Since 1945, Crete has advanced amazingly in the economic sphere, powered by its agricultural products as well as by its tourist industry. Not all Cretans are pleased by the development, but all would agree that, for better or worse, Crete owes much to its history.

1 Iraklion (Iraklio)

Iraklion is home to the world's only comprehensive collection of Minoan artifacts, and is the gateway to Knossos, the major Minoan palace site. Beyond that, it has magnificent fortified walls and several other testimonies to the Venetians' time of power.

Iraklion is also big enough (Greece's sixth-largest city) and confident enough to have its own identity as a busy modern city. It often gets bad press simply because it's

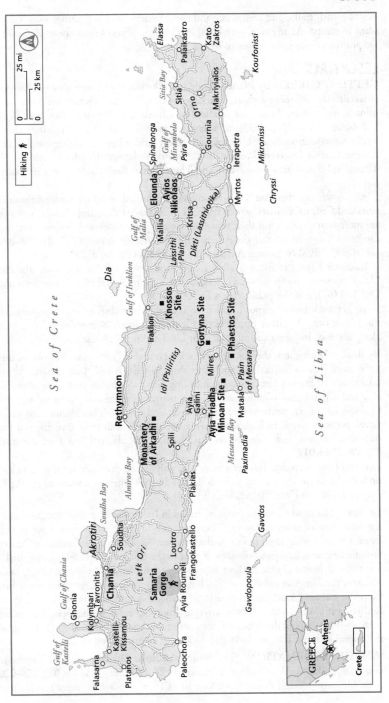

Hiking 🚶

25 mi

25 km

Sea of Crete

Sea of Libya

Elassa
Palaikastro
Kato Zakros
Koufonissi
Sitia Bay
Sitia
Ornó
Makriyialos
Spinalonga
Gulf of Mirambelo
Psira
Gournia
Ierapetra
Mikronissi
Elounda
Ayios Nikolaos
Kritsa
Myrtos
Chryssi
Gulf of Mália
Mália
Lassíthi Plain
Dikti (Lassithiotika)
Dia
Gulf of Iraklion
Knossos Site
Gortyna Site
Phaestos Site
Iraklion
Idi (Psiliritis)
Mires
Plain of Messara
Rethymnon
Ayia Galíni
Matala
Messara Bay
Ayia Triadha
Minoan Site
Paximadia
Monastery of Arkadhi
Spíli
Plakias
Gavdos
Almiros Bay
Soudha Bay
Akrotíri
Soudha
Lefka Ori
Loutro
Frangokastello
Gavdopoula
Gulf of Chania
Ghonia
Kolymbari
Tavronitis
Chania
Samaria Gorge
Ayia Roumeli
Paleochora
Gulf of Kastelli
Falasarna
Platanos
Kastelli Kissamou

GREECE
Athens
Crete

bustling with traffic and commerce and construction—the very things most travelers want to escape. At any rate, give Iraklion a chance. If you follow some of the advice we proffer, you just may come to like it.

ESSENTIALS

GETTING THERE   By Plane   Aside from the many who now fly from European cities directly to Crete on charter/package tour flights, most visitors will take the 40-minute flight from Athens to Iraklion or Chania on **Olympic Airways** (☎ 01/966-6666; fax 01/921-9933), at a cost of some Dr14,000 to Dr18,000 ($40 to $52) one-way. In summer, Olympic also offers service between Athens and Sitia (in eastern Crete); between Iraklion and Corfu, Mykonos, Rhodes, Santorini, and Thessaloniki; and between Chania and Thessaloniki. Reservations are a necessity in high season.

At this writing, there are two privately owned alternatives to Olympic, **Aegean Airlines** and **Cronus Airlines,** which fly from Athens to Iraklion and Chania. Their fares are somewhat cheaper, but their schedules are also rather spotty. Ask your travel agent for information, or contact the Athens offices of Aegean Airlines (☎ **01/998-8300;** fax 01/995-7598) or Cronus Airlines (☎ **01/994-4444;** fax 01/995-6405).

Iraklion's airport is about 5 kilometers (3 miles) east of the city, along the coast. Major car-rental companies have desks at the airport. A taxi to Iraklion costs about Dr2,500 ($7), and the public bus is Dr300 (90¢).

To get back to the airport, you have the same two choices—taxi or public bus no. 1. You can take either from Plateia Eleftheria (Liberty Square) or at other points along the way. Inquire in advance at your hotel about the closest possibility.

By Boat   Throughout the year, there is at least one ship (and as many as two or three) a day from Piraeus to Iraklion, and other ships to Chania and Rethymnon. (All trips take about 10 hours.) Less frequent ships link Crete to Rhodes (and Karpathos, Kassos, and Khalki, the islands between the two); Santorini and some of the other Cycladic islands en route to or from Piraeus; and even to Thessaloniki and various Greek ports en route. In high season, occasional ships from Italy, Cyprus, and Israel put into Iraklion. For information on all ships, call the Iraklion **Port Authority** (☎ **081/244-912**).

If you have arrived at Iraklion's harbor by ship, you'll probably want to take a taxi up into the town, as it's a steep climb. Depending on where you want to go, the fare may be Dr900 to Dr1,500 ($2.60 to $4.30).

By Bus   The third common mode of arrival in Iraklion is by public bus from one of the other Cretan cities or towns. Where you end up depends on where you've come from. Those arriving from points to the west, east, or southeast—Chania or Rethymnon, for instance, or Ayios Nikolaos or Sitia to the east—end up down along the harbor and will have a choice of three approaches to the center of town: walking, taking a taxi, or catching the public bus. The bus starts its route at the terminal where buses from the east and southeast stop; directly across the boulevard is the station for the Rethymnon-Chania buses. Those arriving from the south—Phaestos, Matala, and such—will end up at the Chania Gate on the southwest edge of town; walking will not appeal to most, but you have the choice of a public bus or a taxi.

VISITOR INFORMATION   The **National Tourist Office** is at Odos Xanthoudidou 1, opposite the Archaeological Museum (☎ **081/228-225;** fax 081/226-020); open Monday through Friday from 8am to 2:30pm. Among the most reliable travel

Iraklion

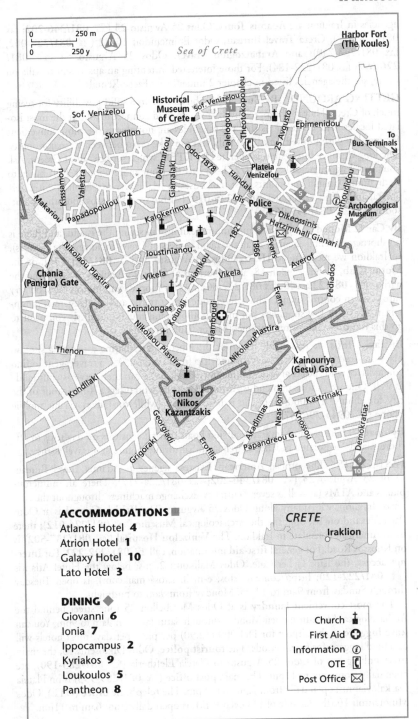

Sea of Crete

Harbor Fort
(The Koules)

Historical Museum
of Crete

Sof. Venizelou

Skordilon

Sof. Venizelou

Theotokopoulou

Palelogou

25 Avgusto

Epimenidou

To
Bus Terminals

Handaka

Plateia
Venizelou

Delimarkou

Giamalaki

Odos 1878

Idis

Police

Kissamou

Valestra

Makariou

Papadopoulou

Kalokerinou

Dikeossinis

Hatzimihali Gianari

Xanthoudidou

Archaeological
Museum

Ioustinianou

1821

1866

Evans

Averof

Pediados

Chania
(Panigra) Gate

Nikolaou Plastira

Vikela

Giamkou

Vikela

Spinalongas

Kounali

Giamboudi

Nikolaou Plastira

Evans

Thenon

Nikolaou Plastira

Kainouriya
(Gesu) Gate

Kondilaki

Tomb of
Nikos
Kazantzakis

Georgiadi

Grigoraki

Erofilis

Akadimias

Neas Ionias

Papandreou G.

Knossou

Kastrinaki

Demokratias

ACCOMMODATIONS ■
Atlantis Hotel **4**
Atrion Hotel **1**
Galaxy Hotel **10**
Lato Hotel **3**

DINING ◆
Giovanni **6**
Ionia **7**
Ippocampus **2**
Kyriakos **9**
Loukoulos **5**
Pantheon **8**

CRETE

Iraklion

Church ✝
First Aid ✚
Information ⓘ
OTE Ⓒ
Post Office ✉

251

agencies in Iraklion are **Adamis Tours,** Odos 25 Avgusto 23 (☎ **081/346-202;** fax 081/224-717); **Creta Travel Bureau,** Odos Epimenidou 20–22 (☎ **081/227-002;** fax 081/223-749); and **Arabatzoglou Travel,** Odos 25 Avgusto 54 (☎ **081/226-697;** fax 081/222-184). For those interested in renting an apartment or villa on Crete, see the agencies listed in chapter 2 under "Fast Facts: Rentals."

GETTING AROUND   By Bus   Public buses remain a solid possibility for seeing much of Crete. They're cheap, relatively frequent, and connect to all but the most isolated locales. The downside is that the schedules are not always the most convenient for travelers with limited time. Certainly you can take them between all major points. The long-distance bus system is operated by **KTEL,** which services all of Greece. Ask your travel agent or call ☎ **081/221-765** to find out more about KTEL buses to Rethymnon-Chania and points west. For buses to Mallia, Ayios Nikolaos, Sitia, Ierapetra, and points east, call ☎ **081/245-019.** For buses to Phaestos and other points south, call ☎ **081/255-965.**

By Car & Moped   A car gives maximum flexibility in seeing the island, and there is no shortage of rental agencies in all the main centers of Crete (including the airports). In Iraklion we recommend **Hertz,** Odos 25 Avgusto 34 (☎ **081/341-734**), or the **Motor Club,** Plateia Agglon 18, at the bottom of Odos 25 Avgusto, overlooking the harbor (☎ **081/222-408;** fax 081/222-862). As for mopeds and motorcycles, be *very* sure you can control such a vehicle in chaotic urban traffic and on dangerous mountain roads (with few shoulders but many potholes and much gravel). If you want to go this route, try the aforementioned Motor Club for rentals.

By Taxi   Taxis are reasonable if two or three people are sharing a trip to a site; no place on Crete is more than a day's round-trip from Iraklion. Ask a travel agent to find you a driver who speaks at least rudimentary English; he can then serve as your guide as well. One we can recommend is **Antonis Gratsas,** who offers a 4-hour tour of the city for about Dr30,000 ($86); he is best reached (while on Crete) via his mobile phone (☎ **0944-796237**).

By Boat   There are now several excursion boats that take visitors on day trips to offshore islands or isolated beaches as well as to Santorini; inquire at a travel agency.

FAST FACTS   The official **American Express** agency is Adamis Travel Bureau, Odos 25 Avgusto 23 (☎ **081/346-202;** fax 081/224-717). There are numerous **banks** and **ATMs** (as well as several currency-exchange machines) throughout the center of Iraklion, with many along Odos 25 Avgusto. The **British Consul** is at Odos Papa Alexandrou 16, opposite the Archaeological Museum (☎ **081/224-012**); there is no American consulate in Iraklion. The **Venizelou Hospital** (☎ **081/237-502**) is on Knossos Road. For general **first-aid** information, call ☎ **081/222-222.** For **Internet access,** the Istos Cyber Cafe, Odos Malikouti 2, just below the Hotel Atlantis (☎ **081/222-120;** http://come.to/istos; e-mail: istos@mail.com), is open Tuesday through Sunday from 9am to 12pm, Monday from 9am to midnight.

The most convenient **laundry** is at Odos Merebellou 25 (one street behind the Archaeological Museum); open Monday through Saturday from 9am to 9pm. You can leave **luggage** at the airport for Dr1,000 ($2.90) per piece per day; most hotels will also hold luggage for brief periods. The **tourist police,** Odos Dikiosenis 10, the main street linking top of Odos 25 Avgusto to Plateia Eleftheria (☎ **081/283-190**), are open daily from 7am to 11pm. The main **post office** (☎ **081/289-995**) is on Plateia Daskaloyiannis; open daily from 7:30am to 8pm. The **telephone office (OTE),** Odos Minotaurou 10 (the far side of El Greco Park), is open daily from 6am to 11pm.

WHAT TO SEE & DO
ATTRACTIONS

✪ **The Archaeological Museum.** Odos Xanthoudidou (far corner of Plateia Eleftheria), Iraklion. ☎ **081/226-092.** Admission Dr2,000 ($5.75) adults, Dr750 ($2.15) students with official ID and EU citizens 65 and over. Apr to mid-Oct Tues–Sun 8am–8pm; Mon 12:30–8pm. Mid-Oct to Mar, closes daily at 5pm.

This is the world's premier collection of art and artifacts from the Minoan civilization. Although many of its most spectacular objects are from Knossos, it does have finds from other sites. The variety of objects, styles, techniques, and materials will amaze all who have not previously focused on the Minoans. Among the most prized objects are the **snake goddesses** from Knossos, the **Phaestos Disc** (with its still undeciphered inscription), the **bee pendant** from Mallia, the **carved vases** from Ayia Triadha and Kato Zakros, and various objects testifying to the famous bull-leaping. Upstairs are the **original frescoes from Knossos** and other sites, their restored sections clearly visible (the frescoes now at Knossos are copies of these).

Tip: To avoid the tour groups in high season, plan to visit either very early or late in the day (allowing at least 1 hour for your visit); there are fewer groups on Sundays. Most displays have decent labels in English, but you may want to invest in one of the guidebooks for sale in the lobby.

✪ **The Palace of Knossos.** Knossos Rd., 5km (3 miles) south of Iraklion. ☎ **081/231-940.** Admission Dr2,000 ($5.75), Dr750 ($2.15) students. Apr to mid-Oct daily 8am–8pm. Mid-Oct to Mar Mon–Fri 8am–5pm; Sat–Sun 8:30am–3pm.

Until Arthur Evans began excavating here in 1900, little was known about this ancient people. Using every possible clue and remnant, he rebuilt large parts of the palace—walls, floors, stairs, windows, and columns. Visitors must now stay on a walkway, but you still get a good sense of the structure's labyrinthine nature. Realize that you are seeing the remains of two major palaces plus several restorations that were made from about 2000 B.C. to 1250 B.C. Understand, too, that this was not a palace in the modern sense of a royal residence, but a combination of that and the Minoans' chief religious-ceremonial center as well as their administrative headquarters and royal workshops.

Tip: The latter part of the day tends to be less crowded; Sunday is far less frequented by tour groups. Here is one place where a guided tour might be worth the expense; your hotel or a travel agency can arrange this.

Historical Museum of Crete. Odos Kalokorinou 7 (street behind Xenia Hotel on coast road), Iraklion. ☎ **081/283-219.** www.historical-museum.gr. Admission Dr1,000 ($2.90) adults, Dr750 ($2.15) students. Mar–Oct Mon–Fri 9am–5pm; Sat 9am–2pm. Reduced hours in winter.

This museum picks up where the Archaeological Museum leaves off, displaying artifacts and art from the early Christian era up to the present. You get some sense of the role the Cretans' long struggle for independence still plays in their identity. On display are traditional Cretan **folk arts;** the re-created study of **Nikos Kazantzakis,** Crete's great modern writer; and works attributed to the painter **El Greco,** another of the island's admired sons. Even if you take only an hour for this museum, it will reward you with some surprising insights on Crete.

Harbor Fort (The Koules). At mole on old harbor. ☎ **081/288-484.** Admission Dr500 ($1.45). Daily 9am–1pm and 4–7pm.

The harbor fort, built on the site of a series of earlier forts, went up between 1523 and 1540, and although greatly restored, is essentially the Venetian original. Both its exterior and interior are impressive in their dimensions, workmanship, and details: thick walls, spacious chambers, great ramparts, cannonballs, the Lion of St. Mark plaques—you may feel that you are walking through a Hollywood set! Young people will love it.

Venetian Walls and Tomb of Nikos Kazantzakis. The tomb is on the Martinengo Bastion, at the southern corner of the walls, along Odos Plastira. Free admission. Open sunrise to sunset.

These great walls and bastions were part of the fortress-city the Venetians called Candia. Two of the great city gates have survived fairly well: the Pantocrator or Panigra Gate, better known now as the Chania Gate (dating from about 1570), at the western edge; and the Gate of Gesu, or Kainouryia Gate (about 1587), at the southern edge. You can walk around the outer perimeter of the walls and get a feel for their sheer massiveness. They were built, of course, by the forced labor of Cretans.

But one non-Venetian presence has now come to rest on one of the bastions, the Martinengo Bastion at the southern corner. Here is the grave of Nikos Kazantzakis (1883–1947), a native of Iraklion and author of *Zorba the Greek* and *The Last Temptation of Christ*. From Kazantzakis's tomb is one of the best views to the south of Mount Iouktas, which appears in profile to be the head of a man. According to one ancient myth, this is the head of the buried god Zeus.

A STROLL AROUND IRAKLION

Start your stroll at **Fountain Square** (also known as Lions Square, officially Plateia Venizelou), perhaps fortified with a plate of *bougatsa* at one of the two cafes serving this distinctive filled pastry—it's not Cretan but was introduced by Greeks from Armenia. The fountain was installed here in 1628 by the Venetian governor of Crete, Francesco Morosini. Note the now fading but still elegant relief carvings around the basin. Across from the fountain is the **Basilica of St. Mark,** restored to its original 14th-century Italian style and used for exhibitions and concerts.

Proceeding south 50 meters to the crossroads, you'll see the **market street** (officially Odos 1866), now, alas, increasingly taken over by tourist shops but still a must-see with its purveyors of fresh fruits and vegetables, meats, and wines.

At the far end of the market street, you come out onto **Kornarou Square,** with its lovely Turkish fountain; beside it is the **Venetian Bembo Fountain** (1588). The modern statue at the far side of the square commemorates the hero and heroine of Vincenzo Kornarou's Renaissance epic poem *Erotokritos,* a Cretan-Greek classic.

Turning right onto Odos Vikela, proceed (always bearing right) until you come out at the imposing, if not artistically notable, 19th-century **Cathedral of Ayios Menas,** dedicated to the patron saint of Iraklion. Below and to the left is the medieval **Church of Ayios Menas,** which boasts some old wood carvings and icons.

At the far corner of the cathedral (to the northeast) is the 15th-century **Church of St. Katherine.** During the 16th and 17th centuries, this hosted the Mount Sinai Monastery School, where Domenico Theotokopoulou is alleged to have studied before moving on to Venice, Spain, and fame as **El Greco;** it now houses a small museum of icons, frescoes, and wood carvings. It's open Monday through Saturday from 10am to 1pm, with additional hours Tuesday, Thursday, and Friday from 4 to 6pm. Admission is Dr500 ($1.45).

Taking the narrow street that leads directly away from the facade of St. Katherine's—Odos Ayii Dheka—you'll come out onto **Leoforos Kalokerinou,** the main shopping street for locals. Turn right onto it and proceed up to the crossroads of the market and 25 Avgusto. Turn left and go back down past Fountain Square and, on the right, the (totally reconstructed) **Venetian Loggia,** originally dating from the early 1600s. The leading Venetians once met here to conduct affairs; it now houses offices of the city government.

A little farther down 25 Avgusto, also on the right, is the **Church of Ayios Titos,** dedicated to the patron saint of all Crete (the Titus of the Bible, who introduced Christianity to Crete). Head down to the **harbor** (with a side visit to the **Venetian fort,** or *Koules,* if you have the energy at this time; see description above), then pass, along the right, the two sets of great **Venetian arsenali**—where ships were built and repaired (the sea then came in this far). Climbing the stairs just past the arsenali, you turn left onto Odos Bofort and curve up under the **Archaeological Museum** to **Plateia Eleftheria (Liberty Square)**—where you can take a much deserved refreshing drink at any one of the numerous cafes at the far side.

SHOPPING

Costas Papadopoulos, the proprietor of **Daedalou Galerie,** Odos Daedalou 11, between Fountain Square and Plateia Eleftheria (☎ **081/346-353**), has been offering his tasteful selection of traditional Cretan-Greek arts and crafts for several decades—icons, jewelry, porcelain, silverware, pistols, and more. Some of it is truly old, and he'll tell you when it isn't.

Eleni Kastrinoyanni-Cretan Folk Art, Odos Ikarou 3, opposite the Archaeological Museum (☎ **081/226-186**), is the premier store in Iraklion for some of the finest in embroidery, weavings, ceramics, and jewelry; all new pieces but reflecting traditional Cretan folk methods and motifs. Get out your credit card and go for something you'll enjoy for years to come. It's closed October through February.

For one of Crete's finest selections of antique and old Cretan textiles (rugs, spreads, coverlets, and more) along with some unusual pieces of jewelry, try **Grimm's Handicrafts of Crete,** Odos 25 Avgusto 96, opposite the Venetian Loggia (☎ **081/ 282-547**). The finest objects are not cheap, but you get exactly what you pay for here, and even when not especially old, the textiles can be stunning.

A popular type of store that has sprung up all over Crete (and for that matter, all over Greece) is one that specializes in local agricultural products such as olive oil (Crete's is rated as among the finest in the world), honey, wines and spirits, raisins, olives, herbs, and spices. One of the best selections is at **To Kellari** ("The Pantry"), at Odos 1866 20 (Market Street).

WHERE TO STAY

In recent years, the trend has moved toward beach hotels, but there is still a good selection of accommodations in Iraklion—and you may still need reservations in high season.

Iraklion lies annoyingly close to the flight patterns of commercial airliners and occasional jet fighters of the Greek Air Force. Not to deny the nuisance element, but the total time of the overhead noise adds up to probably less than 30 minutes every 24 hours—and the sound of scooters and motorcycles outside your hotel at night will probably be more annoying. There are plans to add a runway out into the sea to eliminate the flights over Iraklion, but it will take some years for this to happen. All we can say is that we have made the search for quiet a major criterion in our selection of hotels; in any case, air-conditioning promises the best defense.

INSIDE THE CITY

✪ **Atlantis Hotel.** Odos Iyias 2 (behind the Archaeological Museum), 71202 Iraklion. ☎ **081/229-103.** Fax 081/226-265. E-mail: atlantis@atl.grecotel.gr. 160 units. A/C MINIBAR TV TEL. High season Dr39,000 ($112) double; low season Dr35,000 ($99) double. Buffet breakfast extra. Reduction possible for longer stays. Special rates for business travelers and half-board (breakfast and dinner). AE, DC, EC, MC, V. Private parking arranged.

The Atlantis is probably your best bet if you can afford it and want to be in the center of things. There are many more luxurious hotels in Greece, but few can beat the Atlantis's urban attractions: a central location, modern facilities, and views over a busy harbor. This superior Class A hotel is in the heart of Iraklion, yet just enough removed from the noise of the city (especially if you use the air-conditioning). The staff is friendly and helpful, and although the Atlantis is especially popular with conference groups, individuals will still get individual attention. Bedrooms are not plush, but are certainly comfortable. You can swim in the pool, work out in the fitness center, send e-mail via your laptop, and then within minutes be enjoying a fine meal or visiting a museum.

Amenities include a restaurant, two bars, rooftop garden, concierge, room service, laundry, massage, baby-sitting, pickup at airport by arrangement, video rentals, Jacuzzi, sundeck, fitness center, small pool, outdoor tennis court (across the street), bicycle rentals, children's playground (across the street), conference rooms, car-rental and tour arrangements, hairdresser, and boutiques.

Atrion Hotel. Odos Chronaki 9 (behind the Historical Museum), 71202 Iraklion. ☎ **081/229-225.** Fax 081/223-292. www.atrion.gr. 65 units, some with tub only, some with shower only. A/C MINIBAR TV TEL. High season Dr25,000 ($72) double; low season Dr23,000 ($66) double. Rates include buffet breakfast. Reductions for children. AE, EC, JCB, MC, V. Parking on street. Public bus within 200m.

This hotel has well-appointed public areas—a lounge, restaurant, cafeteria, bar, and refreshing patio garden—and pleasant, good-sized guest rooms. The front desk can arrange for such services as laundry, baby-sitting, and rentals. Best of all, the location offers quiet while still putting you within a 10-minute walk of the center of town and an even shorter walk to the coast road. The adjacent streets are not that attractive but are perfectly safe, and once inside you can enjoy your oasis of comfort and peace.

Galaxy Hotel. Leoforos Demokratias 67 (about half a mile out main road to Knossos), 71306 Iraklion. ☎ **081/238-812.** Fax 081/211-211. www.galaxy-hotels.com. E-mail: galaxyir@otenet.gr. 137 units, some with shower only, some with tub only. A/C MINIBAR TV TEL. High season Dr42,900 ($123) double; low season Dr35,000 ($100) double. AE, DC, EC, JCB, MC, V. Parking on street. Frequent bus to center within yards of entrance.

In recent years, this has gained the reputation as one of the finer hotels in Iraklion, and it *is* classy—once you get past its rather forbidding exterior. The public areas are striking, and the Galaxy boasts (for now at least) the largest indoor pool in Iraklion, as well as saunas. Guest rooms are stylish; ask for an interior unit, since you lose nothing in a view and gain in quietness.

The restaurant serves the standard Greek and international menu. The pastry shop and ice-cream parlor attract locals, who consider the fare delicious. Although one reader reported a less than gracious tone, we have always found the front desk courteous in handling all the usual requests for services.

Lato Hotel. Odos Epimenidou 15, 71202 Iraklion. ☎ **081/228-103.** Fax 081/240-350. www.lato.gr. E-mail: info@lato.gr. 50 units (some with shower only, some with tub only). A/C MINIBAR TV TEL. High season Dr32,000 ($92) double; low season Dr28,000 ($80) double. Rates include buffet breakfast. AE, DC, EC, MC, V. Parking on street.

One of several hotels on this street (east off the lower end of Odos 25 Avgusto), this one offers many rooms with an especially fine view of the harbor. Its buffet breakfast is among the best we've enjoyed in a hotel of this category. The Lato can host meetings of up to 60 (and will arrange to feed them). What earns this otherwise standard hotel its inclusion here is its harbor-view rooms, offering relatively more quiet at night—yet the hotel is still convenient to the center of town.

Poseidon. Odos Poseidonos 54, Poros (about 2.5km/1½ miles from Plateia Eleftheria, off the main road to the east), 71202 Iraklion. ☎ **081/222-545.** Fax 081/245-405. E-mail: poseidonhotel@hotmail.com. 26 units, all with shower only. TEL. High season Dr19,000 ($54) double; low season Dr17,000 ($49) double. Rates include continental breakfast. A/C available for Dr2,000 ($6) daily surcharge. Ask about a 10% reduction for Frommer's users who make reservations and pay cash. AE, V. Parking all around and frequent public buses 200m at top of street.

We include the Poseidon because it's a longtime favorite of Frommer's loyalists, and for good reason. Its owner/host, John Polychronides, and the desk staff (fluent in English) provide useful support and show genuine concern for your stay on Crete. Yes, it's on a not especially attractive street—but that's true of most of the city hotels, and few can match the fresh breezes and the view over the port. Yes, it gets the airplane noise—but so do virtually all the other hotels in Iraklion, and this one's new sound-insulating windows cut out most of the noise. It is a budget hotel—no elevator (but only three floors), small rooms, basic showers—but everything is clean and functional. Frequent buses and cheap taxi fares let you come and go into Iraklion center, a 20-minute walk away.

OUTSIDE THE CITY

One solution to avoiding the city noise is to stay on the coast. We're assuming that you want to be fairly close to Iraklion—if you just want a remote beach on Crete, such accommodations are described elsewhere. Although the hotels below can be reached by public bus, a car or taxi will save you some valuable time.

Candia Maris. Amoudara, Gazi (on beach about 3km/2 miles west of Iraklion center), 71303 Iraklion. ☎ **081/314-632.** Fax 081/250-669. www.maris.gr. E-mail: candia@maris.gr. 258 units. A/C TV TEL. High season Dr24,000–Dr28,000 ($69–$80) hotel room; Dr30,000–Dr36,000 ($86–$104) seafront bungalow. Low season Dr12,000–Dr15,000 ($34–$43) hotel room; Dr15,000–Dr19,000 ($43–$54) bungalow. All rates are per person per day, buffet breakfast included. Reductions for extra person in room and for children; half-board plan (including breakfast and dinner) available for additional Dr5,500 ($16). AE, DC, EC, JCB, MC, V. Public bus every half hour to Iraklion.

Although the beach on the west coast is not always as pleasant as that on the east, and you have to pass through a rather dreary edge of Iraklion to get here, this area has the advantage of being really close to town. The grandest and newest of the west coast hotels is the deluxe-class Candia Maris, which offers just about everything. It was also one of the first hotels in Greece to be handicapped accessible. The rooms are good sized and cheerful, but the exterior and layout are rather severe. If it looks like a brick-factory owner's idea of a hotel, it's because the owner is just that. Considering that you won't be spending much time looking at the outside of the building, this shouldn't deter you from trying this first-class resort hotel.

Amenities include three restaurants and four bars (with special Cretan nights of traditional music and dancing), concierge, room service, laundry, baby-sitting, airport transport arrangements, three pools, children's pool, health club, sundeck, tennis, squash court, volleyball, bowling, water-sports center, bicycle rentals, game room, children's program, conference facilities, car-rental and tour arrangements, hairdresser, and boutiques.

✪ **Minoa Palace.** Amnisos Beach (about 10km/6 miles east of Iraklion), 71110 Iraklion. ☎ **081/380-404.** Fax 081/380-422. E-mail: minoaplc@iraklio.hellasnet.gr. 127 units. A/C TV TEL. High season Dr29,000 ($83) double; low season Dr23,000 ($66) double. Rates include buffet breakfast. Half-board plan (including breakfast and dinner) may be arranged for Dr3,500 ($10) extra. AE, DC, EC, MC, V. Closed Nov–Mar. Public bus every half hour to Iraklion or points east.

Everything here is first class, but what makes the Minoa Palace truly special is its location: east of the airport yet only 10 kilometers (6 miles) from the center of Iraklion. The comfortable rooms have views of the sea, the beach is beautifully maintained, and there are as many activities as you care to engage in. With your own vehicle, you're only a couple of hours from any point of interest on the whole island. This is your chance to visit the Minoans while living in a palace of greater comfort than anything they ever knew.

Amenities include a restaurant and more informal taverna, weekly "Cretan Night" of traditional music and dancing, concierge, room service, laundry, baby-sitting, airport transport arrangements, children's playground and supervised activities, pool, children's pool, aerobics, sundeck, tennis court (lit at night), volleyball, water polo, water-sports equipment, bicycle rentals, table tennis, billiards, video games, conference rooms, car-rental and tour arrangements, hairdresser, gift shop, and mini-mart.

Xenia-Helios. Kokkini Hani (about 13km/8 miles east of Iraklion), 71500 Iraklion. ☎ **081/761-502.** Fax 081/418-363. 108 units. A/C TEL. High season Dr27,000 ($77) double; low season Dr25,000 ($72) double. Rates include half-board plan. EC. Closed Oct–May. Buses every half hour to Iraklion or points east.

We single out the Xenia-Helios because it's one of three such hotels run by the Greek Ministry of Tourism to train young people for careers in the hotel world (one is outside Athens, the other outside Thessaloniki). There's a pool as well as a beautiful beach, two tennis courts, a hairdresser, water-sports equipment, a fine restaurant, and a conference room for up to 200. The physical accommodations may not be quite as glitzy as some of the other beach resorts, but they're certainly first class and the service is especially friendly. You can pamper yourself, be convenient to any place on the island, help support the young Greeks in training for the future—and save a bit of money!

WHERE TO DINE

Avoid eating a meal on either Fountain Square or Liberty Square (Plateia Eleftheria) unless you simply want to have the experience—the food at those establishments is, to put it mildly, nothing special. Save these squares for a coffee or beer break.

EXPENSIVE

✪ **Kyriakos.** Leoforos Demokratias 53 (about half a mile from center on the road to Knossos). ☎ **081/224-649.** Reservations recommended for dinner in high season. Main courses Dr1,600–Dr4,900 ($4.60–$14). AE, DC, EC, MC, V. Daily noon–5pm and 7pm–1am. Closed Sun from June 20–July 10. Frequent public bus service to the restaurant. GREEK.

In recent years, this restaurant has gained the reputation of offering the most style as well some of the finest cooking in Iraklion. The menu is essentially traditional Greek, but it offers several specialties such as artichokes with potatoes and lettuce, lamb fricassee, and aubergines stuffed with feta. Snails are another specialty, and if that doesn't tempt you, come back at Christmas for the turkey. The wine choices are appropriately fine (and expensive). A couple should expect to drop Dr18,000 to Dr25,000 ($52 to $72) for the full works here, but think what you'd pay at home for such a meal.

Loukoulos. Odos Korai 5 (one street behind Daedalou). ☎ **081/224-435.** Reservations recommended for dinner in high season. Main courses Dr1,500–Dr5,000 ($4.30–$14); fixed-price lunch about Dr4,000 ($11). AE, DC, V. Mon–Sat noon–1am; Sun 6:30pm–midnight. ITALIAN/GREEK.

Another restaurant that has gained a stylish reputation, this is almost the opposite of the Kyriakos (see above) in that it's cramped into a tiny patio on a back street and features fanciful umbrellas over the tables. But the chairs are comfortable, the table settings lovely, and the selection of *mezedes* (appetizers) varied. The creative Italian menu features lots of pasta dishes, such as a delicious rigatoni with a broccoli-and-Roquefort-cream sauce. Treat yourself just once to Iraklion's "in" place.

MODERATE

Giovanni. Odos Korai 12 (one street behind Daedalou). ☎ **081/246-338.** Main courses Dr1,100–Dr3,200 ($3.70–$9); fixed-price meals Dr2,500–Dr3,800 ($7–$11). AE, EC, MC, V. Mon–Sat 12:30pm–2am; Sun 5pm–1:30am. GREEK.

A taverna with some pretensions to chic, this appeals to a slightly younger and more informal set than its neighbor, Loukoulos (described above). For some reason, it, instead of Loukoulos, has the Italian name while its fare is traditional Greek. House specialties include shrimp in tomato sauce with cheese, baked eggplant with tomato sauce, and *kokhoretsi* (a sort of oversize sausage made from the innards of lamb; much better than it may sound)—all quite tasty.

Pantheon. Odos Theodosaki 2 ("Dirty Alley," connecting the market street and Odos Evans). ☎ **081/241-652.** Main courses Dr1,300–Dr2,700 ($3.75–$8). No credit cards. Mon–Sat 11am–11pm. GREEK.

Anyone who spends more than a few days in Iraklion should take at least one meal in "Dirty Alley." The menus (all much the same at the several "Dirty Alley" locales) offer the taverna standards—stews of various meats, chunks of meat or chicken or fish in tasty sauces, vegetables such as okra or zucchini or stuffed tomatoes. These places are not especially cheap—you're paying for the atmosphere—but the food's all tasty. If you sit in the Pantheon, on the corner of the market street, you'll get a choice view of the passing scene.

INEXPENSIVE

Ionia. Odos Evans 3 (just to the left of the market street). ☎ **081/28-313.** Main courses Dr800–Dr2,300 ($2.30–$7). EC, MC, V. Mon–Fri 8am–10:30pm; Sat 8am–4pm. GREEK.

Founded in 1923, Ionia has served generations of Cretans as well as all the early archaeologists. Although it's greatly reduced in size, the food is as good as ever, and the staff encourages foreigners to step over to the kitchen area and select from the warming pans. You may find more refined food and fancier service elsewhere on Crete, but you won't taste heartier dishes than the Ionia's green beans or lamb joints in sauce. We recommend a visit to what is clearly a fading tradition.

Ippocampus. Odos Mitsotaki 3 (off to left of traffic circle as you come down Odos 25 Avgusto). ☎ **081/282-081.** Main courses Dr800–Dr2,000 ($2.30–$6). No credit cards. Mon–Fri 1–3:30pm and 7pm–midnight. SEAFOOD/GREEK.

This is something of an institution among locals, who line up for a typical Cretan meal of nothing but little appetizers. The zucchini slices, dipped in batter and deep-fried, are fabulous. A plate of tomatoes and cukes, another of sliced fried potatoes, some small fish, perhaps the fried squid—that's it. You can assemble a whole meal for as little as Dr4,000 ($11)—but go early.

IRAKLION AFTER DARK

To spend an evening the way most Iraklians themselves do, stroll about (the famous Mediterranean **volta**), then sit in a cafe and watch others stroll by. The prime locations for the latter have been Plateia Eleftheria (Liberty Square) or Fountain Square, but the packed-in atmosphere of these places—and the overly aggressive solicitation of your presence by some waiters—has considerably reduced their charm.

For far more atmosphere, go down to the old harbor and the **Marina Cafe** (directly across from the restored Venetian arsenals). For as little as Dr400 ($1.15) for a coffee or as much as Dr1,500 ($4.30) for an alcoholic drink, you can enjoy the breeze as you contemplate the illuminated Venetian fort, looking much like a stage set.

Another alternative is the **Four Lions Roof-Garden Cafe** (☎ 081/222-333), entered by an interior staircase in the shopping arcade on Fountain Square. It attracts a younger set of Iraklians, but adult foreigners are welcome. The background music is usually Greek. You get to sit above the crowded crossroads, and with no cover or minimum, enjoy anything from a coffee (Dr400/$1.15) or ice cream (from Dr900/$2.60) to an alcoholic drink (from Dr600/$1.75).

There is no end to the number of **bars** and **discos** featuring rock-and-roll and/or Greek popular music, although they come and go from year to year to reflect the latest fads. **Disco Athina,** Odos Ikarou 9, just outside the wall on the way to the airport, is an old favorite with the young set; newer favorites include the **Veneto Bar** and the **Club Itan,** both on Odos Epimenidou.

For those seeking **traditional Cretan music** and **dancing**—and by the way, almost every Class A hotel now has a **Cretan night,** when performers come to the hotel—there are a couple of clubs: **Aposperides,** out on the road toward Knossos, and **Sordina,** about 5 kilometers (3 miles) to the southwest of town, are well regarded; take a taxi to either.

For many years now, Iraklion has hosted an **arts festival** that, although hardly competitive with the major festivals of Europe, provides some interesting possibilities for those spending a few nights in town. The schedule usually begins in late June and ends about mid-September. Some of the performers have world-class reputations—ballet troupes, pianists, and such—but most come from the Greek realm and perform ancient and medieval-renaissance dramas, dances based on Greek themes, and Greek music both traditional and modern. Most performances take place outdoors in one of three venues: on the roof of the **Koules** (the Venetian fort in the harbor), the **Kazantzakis Garden Theater,** or the **Hadzidaksis Theater.** Ticket prices vary from year to year and for individual events, but are well below what you'd pay at such cultural events elsewhere. Maybe you didn't come to Crete expecting to hear Vivaldi, but why not enjoy it while you're here?

SIDE TRIPS FROM IRAKLION

Travel agencies arrange excursions setting out from Iraklion to virtually every point of interest on Crete, such as the **Samaria Gorge** in the far southwest (see p. 270). In that sense, Iraklion can be used as the home base for all your touring on Crete. If you have only one extra day on Crete, we recommend the following trip.

Gortyna, Phaestos, Ayia Triadha & Matala

If you have an interest in history and archaeology, this is probably the trip to make if you have only one other day after visiting Knossos and Iraklion's museum. The distance isn't that great—a round-trip of some 165 kilometers (100 miles)—but it would be a full day indeed to take it all in. If you don't have your own car, a taxi or guided

Films Alfresco

Another delight during the long summers is attending an outdoor movie. There are now three such theaters in Iraklion—the **Romantika,** the **Pallas,** and the **Galaxy**— and a fourth in nearby Halikarnassos, the **Studio.** The current film schedules are posted at several bulletin boards around the center of town. The movies start only as darkness settles. (As throughout Greece, most foreign films are shown in their original language, with Greek subtitles.)

---

tour is advisable as bus schedules won't allow you to fit in all the stops. (You can, of course, stay at one of the hotels down at the south coast, but they're usually booked up in high season.)

The road south takes you right up and across the **mountainous spine** of central Crete, and at about the 25th mile you get the experience of leaving the **Sea of Crete** (to the north) behind and seeing the **Libyan Sea** to the south. You then descend onto the **Messara,** the largest plain on Crete (some 32km/20 miles by 5km/3 miles), long a major agricultural center. At about 45 kilometers (28 miles), you'll see on your right the **remains of Gortyna;** many more lie scattered in the fields off to the left. Gortyna (or Gortyn or Gortys) first emerged as a center of the Dorian Greeks who moved to Crete after the end of the Minoan civilization. By 500 B.C., it was advanced enough to have a law code that was inscribed in stone. The inscribed stones were found in the late 19th century and reassembled here, where you can see this unique—and to scholars, invaluable—document testifying to the legal and social arrangements of this society.

Then, after the Romans took over Crete (after 67 B.C.), Gortyna enjoyed yet another period of glory: It was the capital of Roman Crete and Cyrenaica (Libya), and as such was endowed with the full selection of Roman structures—temples, a stadium, and so on. These are situated in the fields to the left. On the right, along with the **Code of Gortyna,** you'll see a small **Hellenistic odeon,** or theater, as well as the remains of the **Basilica of Ayios Titos**—dedicated to the Titus commissioned by Paul to head the first Christians on Crete; the church was begun in the 6th century but was later greatly enlarged.

Proceeding down the road another 15 kilometers (10 miles), turn left at the sign and ascend to the ridge where the **palace of Phaestos** sits in all its splendor. Regarded by scholars as the second most powerful Minoan center, it is also considered the most attractive by many visitors because of its setting—on a prow of land that seems to float between the plain and the sky. Italians began to excavate Phaestos soon after Evans began at Knossos, but they made the decision to leave the remains pretty much as they found them. The **ceremonial staircase** is as awesome as it must have been to the ancients, while the **great court** remains one of the most resonant public spaces anywhere.

Leaving Phaestos, continue down the main road 4 kilometers (2½ miles) and turn left onto a side road. Park here and make your way to at least pay your respects to another Minoan site, a mini-palace complex known as **Ayia Triadha.** To this day, scholars cannot be certain exactly what it was—something between a satellite of Phaestos and a semi-independent palace. Several of the most impressive artifacts now in the Iraklion Museum were found here, including the painted sarcophagus (on the second floor).

Back on the road, follow the signs to **Kamilari** and then **Pitsidia.** And now you've earned your rest and swim, and at no ordinary place: the nearby **beach at Matala.** It's a small cove enclosed by bluffs of age-old packed earth in which humans—possibly beginning under the Romans but most likely no earlier than A.D. 500—once dug **chambers,** some complete with bunk beds. Cretans long used them as summer homes, the German soldiers used them as storerooms during World War II, and hippies took them over in the late 1960s. They are now off limits except for looking at during the day. Matala has become one more overcrowded beach in peak season, so after a dip and a bit of refreshment, you'll be glad to depart and make your way back to Iraklion (going straight up via **Mires,** avoiding the turnoff back to Ayia Triadha and Phaestos).

2 Chania (Hania/Xania/Canea)

150km (95 miles) W of Iraklion

Until the 1980s, Chania was one of the best-kept secrets of the Mediterranean: a delightful town nestled between mountains and sea, a labyrinth of atmospheric streets and structures from its Venetian-Turkish era. Since then, tourists have flocked here, and there's hardly a square inch of the Old Town, which fans back from the harbor, that's not dedicated to satisfying them. Chania was heavily bombed during World War II; ironically, some of its atmosphere is due to still-unreconstructed buildings that are now used as shops and restaurants.

What's amazing is how much of Chania's charm has persisted since the Venetians and Turks effectively stamped the old town in their own image between 1210 and 1898. Try to visit any time except July and August, but whenever you come, dare to strike out on your own and see the old Chania.

ESSENTIALS

GETTING THERE   By Plane   Olympic Airways offers at least three flights daily to and from Athens in high season.(Flight time is about 40 minutes.) Olympic also has one flight weekly to and from Thessaloniki. **Aegean Airlines** and **Cronus Airlines** also offer a few flights weekly to and from Athens. See "Getting There" in the section on Iraklion, above, for contact information. The airport is located 15 kilometers (10 miles) out of town on the Akrotiri. Public buses meet all flights except for the last one at night, but almost everyone takes a taxi (about Dr3,000/$9).

By Boat   One ship sails daily between Piraeus and Chania, usually leaving early in the evening (10 hours). This ship arrives at and departs from Soudha, a 20-minute bus ride from the stop outside the Municipal Market. Many travel agents around town sell tickets. In high season, those with cars should make reservations in advance.

By Bus   There are frequent buses from early in the morning until about 10:30pm (depending on the season), connecting Chania to Rethymnon and Iraklion. There are less frequent (and often inconvenient) buses between destinations in western Crete. The main **bus station** (to points all over Crete) is at Odos Kidonias 25 (☎ **0821/93-306**).

VISITOR INFORMATION   The **National Tourism Office** is in the new town (off Plateia 1866) at Odos Kriari 40 (☎ **0821/92-943;** fax 0821/92-624). It's open Monday through Friday from 8am to 3pm. Of the many travel agencies, we recommend both **Lissos Travel,** Plateia 1866 (☎ **0821/93-917;** fax 0821/95-930), and **Zorbas Travel,** Halidon 14 (☎ **0821/70-078;** fax 0821/88-011; e-mail: zorbas@otenet.gr). A useful source of insider's information is **The Bazaar,** Odos Daskaloyiannis 46, the main street down to the new harbor (to the right of the Municipal Market). This shop sells used foreign-language books and assorted "stuff." Owned and staffed by non-Greeks, it maintains a listing of all kinds of helpful services.

A Taxi Tip

To get a taxi driver accustomed to dealing with English speakers, call **Andreas** at ☎ **0821/50-821,** or try him on his mobile phone at ☎ **0945-365-799.**

GETTING AROUND   Almost any place you will want to visit in Chania itself is best reached by foot. There are public buses to both nearby points and all the main destinations in western Crete. If you want to explore the countryside or more remote points in western Crete, we recommend renting a car to make the best use of your time.

FAST FACTS   **Banks** in the new city have ATMs. For the **tourist police,** dial ☎ **171.** The **hospital** (☎ **0821/27-231**) is on Odos Venizelou in the Halepa Quarter. **Internet cafes** include the Cafe Santé, on a second floor at the far (west) corner of the old harbor; Club Electric, Odos Apokoronou 16; and the one at Theotokopouli 53. The **Speedy Laundry,** Odos Kordiki 17, on the corner of Koroneou, a block west of Plateia 1866 (☎ **0821/88-411**), promises wash and dry in 90 minutes and will pick up and deliver for free. For **luggage storage,** try the KTEL bus station on Odos Kidonias. The **post office** is on Odos Tzanakaki (leading away from the Municipal Market); open Monday through Friday from 8am to 8pm, Saturday from 8am to noon. Beside it is the **telephone office (OTE),** open daily from 7:30am to 11:30pm.

WHAT TO SEE & DO

In summer, there are now several small **excursion ships** that offer 3- to 5-hour trips to the waters and islets off Chania. These trips depart from the old and new harbors and include stops for swimming at one or another of the islets; some provide free snorkeling gear. The glass-bottomed *Evangelos* features views of underwater life. The cost tends to run about Dr6,000 ($17), with children going along for free.

✪ **Archaeological Museum.** Odos Halidon 30. ☎ **0821/90-334.** www.culture.gr. E-mail: protocol@keepka.culture.gr. Admission Dr500 ($1.45). Mon 12:30–7pm, Tues–Sat 8am–7pm, Sun 8am–2:30pm.

Even short-term visitors should stop in here, if only for a brief walk-through. The museum is housed in the 16th-century Venetian Catholic Church of St. Francis (carefully restored in the early 1980s), and gives a fascinating glimpse of the different cultures that have played out on Crete, from the Neolithic through the Minoan, on to the Romans and early Christians. You'll come away with a sense of how typical people of these periods lived, as opposed to the various elites featured in so many museums.

A WALK AROUND OLD CHANIA

Start at **Plateia Santrivani,** the large clearing at the far curve of the old harbor. Head along the east side for the prominent domed **Mosque of Djamissis** (or of Hassan Pasha), erected soon after the Turks conquered Chania in 1645.

Proceeding around the **waterfront** toward the **new harbor,** you'll come to what remains of the great *arsenali,* where the Venetians made and repaired ships; exhibitions are sometimes held inside. Go to the far end of this inner harbor and walk out along the breakwater to the lighthouse, which is from the 19th century.

Turning inland at the near end of the arsenali onto Odos Arnoleon, and proceeding up Odos Daskaloyiannis, you'll come, on the left, to **Plateia 1821** and the present-day **Orthodox Church of St. Nicholas.** Begun as a Venetian Catholic monastery, it was converted by the Turks into a mosque—thus its campanile and minaret! The square is a pleasant place to sit and have a cool drink. Proceeding along, you come to Odos Tsouderon, where you turn right and (passing another minaret) come to the back steps of the great **Municipal Market** (1911)—definitely worth a walk-through. If you exit at the opposite end of where you entered, you'll come out on the edge of the **new town.** Go right along Hadzimikhali Giannari till you come to the top of **Odos Halidon,** the main tourist-shopping street. As you make your way down, you'll pass on the right the famous **Odos Skridlof,** with its leather workers; the **Orthodox Cathedral,** the Church of the Three Martyrs (from the 1860s); and then on the left the **Archaeological Museum** (see above).

As you come back to the edge of Plateia Santrivani, turn left one street before the harbor onto **Odos Zambeliou.** Proceeding along this street, you can then turn left onto any of the side streets and explore the **old quarter** (now, alas, somewhat overwhelmed by modern tourist enterprises). If you turn up Odos Kondilaki, then follow the signs at the right alley, you'll reach the **synagogue**; built in the 14th century and destroyed in World War II, it has now been beautifully restored. Continuing along Zambeliou (taking a slight diversion on Odos Moskhou to view the **Renieri Gate** of 1608), you'll ascend slightly until you come up to **Odos Theotokopouli**; turn right here to enjoy the structures and shops of this Venetian-style street as you make your way down to the sea.

At its end, on the right, is the recently restored **Church of San Salvatore,** converted into a fine little museum of Byzantine and post-Byzantine art (☎ 0821/96-046). After this, you're just outside the harbor; turn right and pass below the walls of the **Firkas,** the name given to the fort that was a focal point in Crete's struggle for independence at the turn of the century. If you're into naval history, the **Naval Museum** (☎ 0821/26-437) here has some interesting displays and artifacts (open daily from 10am to 4pm; admission Dr500/$1.45); or you can just sit at the **Cafe Meltemi,** on the slope just before the entrance to the museum, and join Chania's smart set in a much-deserved refreshment.

SHOPPING

Jewelers, leather-goods shops, and souvenir stores are everywhere—but it's hard to find that very special item that's both tasteful and distinctively Cretan. Our choices below offer authentic Cretan objects—or at least items you will not find anyplace else. Unless otherwise noted, the following shops are open daily.

Carmela, at Odos Anghelou 7, the narrow street across from the entrance to the Naval Museum (☎ 0821/90-487), has some of the finest ceramics, jewelry, and works of art in all of Crete—all original, but inspired by ancient works of art and even employing some of the old techniques.

To step into **Cretan Rugs and Blankets,** Odos Anghelou 5 (☎ 0821/98-571), is to enter a realm probably not to be experienced anywhere else on Crete. It's an old Venetian structure filled with gorgeously colored rugs, blankets, and kilims. Prices range from Dr30,000 to Dr500,000 ($86 to $1,440). Or visit **Roka Carpets,** Odos Zambeliou 61 (☎ 0821/74-736), even if only to see a traditional weaver at his trade. There are patterns and colors and sizes for every taste, with prices from Dr4,000 ($11) and up. These are not artsy textiles, but traditional Cretan weaving.

Although **Khalki,** Odos Zambeliou 75, near the far end of the street (☎ 0821/75-379), is one of many little shops that sell ceramics along with other trinkets and souvenirs, it's worth seeking out. It carries the work of several local and Greek ceramists who draw on traditional motifs and colors. For a varied selection by local amateur artisans, visit the **Local Artistic Handicrafts Association** (☎ 0821/41-885), located just where the new harbor turns the corner into the old harbor.

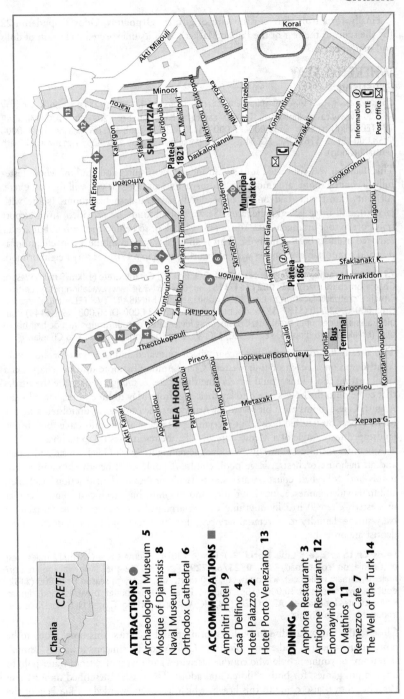

Chania

Korai

Akti Miaouli

Minoos

SPLANTZIA

Vourdouba

Plateia
1821

A. Melidoni

Daskaloyiannis

Nikiforou Episkopou

Nikiforou Foka

El. Venizelou

Konstantinou

Tzanakaki

Apokoronou

Grigoriou E.

Karaou

Kalergon

Sifaka

Arholeon

Daskaloyiannis

Karaoli - Dimitriou

Tsouderon

Municipal
Market

Skridlof

Hadzimikhali Giannari

Kriari

Plateia
1866

Sfakianaki K.

Zimivrakidon

Halidon

Skridlof

Kondilaki

Zambeliou

Atki Kountouriouto

Theotokopouli

NEA HORA

Pireos

Patriarhou Nikloui

Patriarhou Gerasimou

Metaxaki

Skalidi

Manousogianakidon

Bus
Terminal

Kidonias

Marigoniou

Konstantinoupoleos

Xepapa G.

Akti Enoseos

Akti Kanari

Apostolidou

| Information | OTE | Post Office |

CRETE

Chania

Finally, for a truly different souvenir or gift, try **Orphanos,** Odos Tsopuderon 22 (by the stairs at the rear of the Public Market), with its unexpected collection of dolls and marionettes.

WHERE TO STAY
EXPENSIVE

✪ **Casa Delfino.** Odos Theofanous 8, 73100 Chania, Crete. ☎ **0821/87-400.** Fax 0821/ 96-500. www.casadelfino.com. E-mail: casadel@cha.forthnet.gr. 20 units. A/C MINIBAR TV TEL. High season Dr53,000–77,000 ($153–$222) double. Low season Dr40,000– Dr58,000 ($115–$167). AE, EC, MC, V. Free parking in nearby area. Open year-round (with central heating).

This mansion was converted into stylish independent suites and studios, whose tastefully decorated rooms are among the most spacious and elegant you will find on Crete. All units (most with bed on an upper level) have modern bathrooms (some with Jacuzzi), and three have kitchenettes. Services of all kinds are provided, from airport transport to tour arrangements. You're only a block or so behind the harbor, but are far removed from its bustle and noise. This is an ideal way to combine a convenient location and comfortable amenities with old-world charm in a 17th-century neighborhood.

✪ **Creta Paradise Beach Resort Hotel.** P.O. Box 89, Gerani, Crete (14km/9 miles west of Chania on coast road). ☎ **0821/61-315.** Fax 0821/61-134. www.vacation.net.gr/cretpar. E-mail: cretpar@vacation.net.gr. 230 units. A/C MINIBAR TV TEL. High season Dr65,000–Dr82,000 ($187–$236) double. Low season Dr34,000–Dr50,000 ($98–$144) double. Rates include buffet breakfast. Considerably lower rates for tour groups include half-board plan (breakfast and dinner). AE, DC, EC, MC, V. Ample parking. Taxi or bus to Chania.

This already luxurious resort has recently been renovated and is perfect for those who want to sun on a beach or tour western Crete. Among its more unusual charms is a small petting zoo—kids would have a fine time here. A unique delight are the turtles that come onto the hotel's beach to lay their eggs from May to June; these hatch in late August. Guest rooms are a bit severe for Americans accustomed to upholstered luxury (don't expect overstuffed beds), but everything is tasteful and comfortable. Beautifully landscaped in the style of a Mediterranean villa, the resort lives up to its image.

Amenities include restaurants, weekly "theme nights" with Greek music and dance and an in-house orchestra, large pool, children's pool, small health club and sauna, tennis and volleyball courts, water sports (with professional instruction available), children's video games, salon, boutiques, and the most high-tech conference facilities in western Crete. Virtually anything can be arranged on request, from massage to baby-sitting, laundry to secretarial services, plus car rentals and tours. A doctor and a dentist are on call.

Louis Creta Princess Club Hotel. P.O. Box 9, 73014 Maleme Crete (18km/12 miles west of Chania on coast road). ☎ **0821/62-229.** Fax 0821/62-406. www.vacation.net.gr/ maleme. E-mail: maleme@vacation.net.gr. 420 units. A/C TEL. High season Dr46,000 ($132) double; low season Dr30,000 ($86) double. Rates include buffet breakfast and dinner. Reduced rates for children. AE, DC, EC, JCB, MC, V. Ample parking. Closed Oct–Mar. Taxis and frequent buses to Chania.

Close to the Creta Paradise in both its location and facilities, this hotel tends to be more family oriented and even a bit like a Club Med. This means it has an "animation team" of young people who conduct activities and diversions, from water polo to impromptu games, for both children and adults. The turtles (described under Creta Paradise, above) also come to this beach, which has been awarded a Blue Flag of the European Community for its fine condition. Guest rooms are not plush, but are comfortable and modern (units with TVs cost extra).

Amenities include a main restaurant, beach taverna, bars, disco, weekly "Greek night" with music and dancing, large pool and small children's pool, tennis courts, basketball and volleyball courts, minigolf course, table tennis, water sports (including waterskiing, windsurfing, water-parachuting, and canoeing), and conference room. The desk clerks can arrange laundry, baby-sitting, secretarial assistance, car rentals, and tours.

MODERATE

✪ **Doma.** Odos Venizelou 124 (3km/2 miles from town center along coastal road to airport), 73100 Chania, Crete. ☎ **0821/51-772.** Fax 0821/41-578. 25 units, all with private bathroom (22 with shower only). TEL. Dr32,000 ($92) double; Dr46,000–Dr57,000 ($132–$164) suite (with A/C and TV). Rates include buffet breakfast. Special rates for more than 2 persons in suite; reduced rates for longer stays. AE, EC, MC, V. Free parking on nearby streets. Closed Nov–Mar. Bus to Halepa or Chania center; can be reached by taxi or on foot.

The Doma has long been regarded as one of the most distinctive hotels on Crete, in part because it was one of the first in Greece to locate in a converted fine old building. In this case, it's a neoclassical mansion from the turn of the century that was once, among other things, the British consulate; its public areas are decorated with authentic Cretan heirlooms and historical pictures. Bedrooms and bathrooms are not especially large, but perfectly adequate. Front units have the great view of the sea but also the sound of passing traffic, although the hotel is far from the noise of the center of town. Amenities are there for the asking, including laundry on the premises, an elevator for those who can't take stairs, and a new ground-floor bar with a civilized ambiance (and a museum-quality display of headdresses from all over the world). The third-story dining room offers fresh breezes and a superb view of Old Chania; breakfast here includes several homemade delights, while evening dinner brings Cretan specialties. The Doma is not for those seeking luxury, but should appeal to travelers who appreciate a discreetly old-world atmosphere.

Halepa Hotel. Odos Eleftherios Venizelou 164 (on the street in Halepa just after the right turn to the airport), 73133 Chania, Crete. ☎ **0821/28-440.** Fax 0821/28-439. www.halepa. com. E-mail: hotel@halepa.com. 49 units (some with tub only, some with shower only). A/C MINIBAR TV TEL. High season Dr28,000 ($80) double; Dr34,000–Dr44,000 ($98–$126) suite for 2. Low season Dr25,000 ($72) double; Dr30,000–Dr44,000 ($86–$126) suite. Rates include buffet breakfast. AE, DC, EC, MC, V. Parking nearby. Open year-round with central heating. Frequent public buses to Chania (a 20-min. walk along the coast).

Like the better-known Doma, this hotel is in a converted neoclassical mansion. The Halepa is located in a quiet neighborhood, buffered from the street by its front garden. It's a restful oasis, with classical music often wafting through the air. Bedrooms are fair sized, bathrooms modern. The owners can take care of your every need, from laundry to car rentals. Facilities include a full bar and a sunroof that offers a spectacular view of Chania and the bay. *Tip:* Ask for a room in the main, or traditional, mansion— otherwise you must settle for a room (albeit quiet and comfortable) in the rather nondescript new wing.

Hotel Porto Veneziano. Enetikos Limin, 73122 Chania, Crete. ☎ **0821/27-100.** Fax 0821/27-105. http://agn.hol.gr/hotels/portoven. E-mail: portoven@otenet.gr. 57 units, all with private bathroom (51 with shower only). A/C MINIBAR TV TEL. High season Dr36,500 ($105) double; Dr56,000 ($161) suite for two. Low season Dr29,000 ($83) double; Dr44,000 ($126) suite. Rates include buffet breakfast. AE, DC, EC, MC, V. Free parking nearby. Within walking distance of everything.

This fine hotel (a member of the Best Western chain) is located at the far end of the so-called Old Harbor (follow the walkway from the main harbor all the way around to the east, or right) and offers proximity to the center with a minimum of noise. The tasteful bedrooms are relatively large, and many have a fine view of the harbor. Meals are served only to organized groups, but refreshments from the hotel's own Cafe Veneto may be enjoyed in the garden. The desk personnel are genuinely hospitable and can make any arrangements, from car rentals to laundry.

INEXPENSIVE

Amphitri Hotel. Odos Lithinon 31, 73100 Chania, Crete. ☎ **0821/56-470.** Fax 0821/52-980. 22 units. A/C MINIBAR TEL. High season Dr30,000 ($86) double. Low season Dr22,000 ($63) double. Rates include continental breakfast. EC. Parking on nearby streets.

This unpretentious hotel is an old favorite of regular visitors to Chania, who value the spectacular views over the harbor enjoyed by some rooms, the quiet street, the proximity to the very heart of Chania's action, and the comfortable rooms and homey atmosphere. Decidedly low-key, it should appeal to those who prize convenience above all. And you can enjoy your breakfast on a balcony with a view to die for.

Hotel Palazzo. Odos Theotokopouli 54 (around the corner of the far left/west arm of harbor), 73100 Chania, Crete. ☎ **0821/93-227.** Fax 0821/93-229. 11 units, some with shower only, some with tub only. High season Dr22,000 ($63) double; low season Dr16,000 ($46) double. Rates include breakfast. EC, MC, V. Ample parking 100m away. Closed Nov–Mar (but will open for special groups). Within easy walking distance of all of Chania.

This Venetian town house, now a handsome little hotel, gives the feel of old Crete, but various amenities make it a comfortable hotel—a fridge in every room, a TV in the bar, a roof garden with a spectacular view of the mountains and sea. Guest rooms are good sized; those on the front have balconies. It's generally quiet, and if occasionally the still night air is broken by rowdy youths (true of all Greek cities), that seems a small price to pay for staying on Odos Theotokopouli—the closest some will come to living on a Venetian canal. The owners speak English and will graciously help with all your needs—including laundry service, car rentals, and tours.

WHERE TO DINE
EXPENSIVE

✪ **Nykterida.** Korakies, Crete (about 6.4km/4 miles from town on road to airport, left turn opposite NAMFI Officers Club). ☎ **0821/64-215.** www.nykterida.com. E-mail: nykterida@otenet.gr. Reservations recommended for parties of seven or more. Main courses Dr1,200–Dr4,000 ($3.45–$11). MC, V. Mon–Sat 6pm–1am. Parking on site. Open year-round. Taxi required if you don't have a car. GREEK.

Many would nominate this as one of the finest restaurants in all Crete, especially for its setting, high on a point with spectacular nighttime views of Chania and Soudha Bay. The cuisine is traditional Cretan-Greek, but many of the dishes have an extra something. For an appetizer, try the *kalazounia* (cheese pies with specks of spinach) or the special *dolmades* (made with squash blossoms stuffed with spiced rice and served with yogurt). Any of the main courses will be well done, from the basic steak fillet to the chicken with okra. Complimentary *tsoukoudia* (a potent Cretan liquor) is served at the end of the meal. On Monday, Thursday, and Friday evenings through the high season (until the end of October), traditional Cretan music is performed.

MODERATE

Amphora Restaurant. Akti Koundouriotou 49 (near the far right/western curve of the harbor). ☎ **0821/93-224.** Fax 0821/93-226. Main courses Dr1,200–Dr3,800 ($3.45–$11); fixed-price meals Dr2,500–Dr6,500 ($7–$19); combination plates Dr1,800–Dr5,000 ($5.15–$14). AE, EC, MC, V. Daily 11:30am–midnight. Closed Oct–Apr. GREEK.

This is a favorite when it comes to balancing price with quality, choice with taste. As with any Greek restaurant, if you order the lobster or steak, you'll pay a hefty price.

But you can also assemble a delicious meal here at modest prices. To start, try the aubergine croquettes and the specialty of the house, a lemony fish soup. This restaurant belongs to the Amphora Hotel, a Category A, and although its tables and location suggest a basic harbor taverna, its food and friendly service make it first class.

Antigone Restaurant. Akti Enoseos (at farthest corner of new harbor). ☎ **0821/45-236.** Main courses Dr1,200–Dr4,000 ($3.45–$11). V. Daily 10am–2am. Parking at side of restaurant if you approach from behind; otherwise walk from the harbor. GREEK/SEAFOOD.

Start off here with an unusual appetizer such as a dip made of limpets and mussels, then move on to a specialty such as stuffed crab or whatever's the catch of the day, and you'll be eating fresh produce of the sea. Trust the staff to direct you to whatever is best that day. With its colorful interior, fresh flowers on the tables, and a view of the harbor, this can be a most pleasant dining experience.

The Well of the Turk. Kalinikou Sarpaki 1–3 (a small street off Odos Daskaloyiannis). ☎ **0821/54-547.** Reservations recommended for parties of seven or more. Main courses Dr1,700–Dr3,800 ($4.90–$11). No credit cards. Wed–Mon 7pm–midnight. MIDDLE EASTERN/ MEDITERRANEAN.

This restaurant, located in the heart of the old Turkish quarter (Splanzia), is in a historic old building with an interior well. Diners may choose to sit outside in a quiet street-court. The chef brings to the cuisine imaginative touches that make it more than standard Middle Eastern. In addition to tasty kebabs, there are such specialties as meatballs with eggplant mixed in, and *laxma bi azeen,* a pita-style bread with a spicy topping. Middle Eastern musicians sometimes play here, and you can settle for a quiet drink at the bar.

INEXPENSIVE

Enomayirio. In the Public Market, at the "arm" with the fish vendors. Main courses Dr1,500–Dr3,500 ($4.30–$10). A gigantic platter of mixed fish for two is Dr6,800 ($20). No credit cards. Monday–Saturday, 9am–3:30pm. SEAFOOD.

Here's a special treat for those who can handle eating in a cramped, unstylish restaurant smack in the center of the great public market of Chania. The fish and other seafood come from stalls barely 15 feet away. All the other ingredients also come straight from the nearby stands. Food doesn't get any fresher nor a dining experience more "immediate." Sit here and watch the world go by.

O Mathios. Akti Enoseos 3 (about midway along new harbor). ☎ **0821/54-291.** Main courses Dr900–Dr2,900 ($2.60–$8). No credit cards. Daily 11am–2:30am. GREEK.

At this traditional harborside taverna, you can enjoy a decent meal while watching the boats bobbing at the quay and the cats stalking beneath the tables. Traditionally, it is not patronized by that many foreigners, but this is no reflection on its service (prompt no-nonsense) or food (as good as any in its class). Try the basic tzatziki and Greek salad, moussaka, or stuffed tomatoes—you can't go wrong. Fish dishes are the specialty (and as elsewhere can cost considerably more than other choices).

Remezzo Cafe. Venizelou 16A (on corner of main square at old harbor). ☎ **0821/52-001.** Main courses Dr900–Dr2,400 ($2.60–$7). No credit cards. Daily 7am–2am. INTERNATIONAL.

Sooner or later, every tourist will say, "Enough of Greek salads!" and want to indulge in a club sandwich or tuna salad. Remezzo, at the very center of the action on the old harbor, is a great choice for breakfasts and light meals, and also offers a full range of coffee, alcoholic drinks, and ice-cream desserts. Sitting in one of the heavily cushioned chairs as you sip your drink and observe the lively scene, you'll feel like you have the best seat in the house.

CHANIA AFTER DARK

Chania's nightlife need not be limited to heading for a club/bar/disco packed with young people or walking around the harbor and Old Town—the ritual known in Greece as the **volta.** Instead, wander into the back alleys and see both the old Venetian and Turkish remains and the modern tourist enterprises. Sit in a quayside cafe and enjoy a coffee or drink, or treat yourself to a ride in a horse-drawn carriage down at the harbor. Or at the other extreme, stroll through the new town and be surprised at the modernity and diversity (and prices) of the stores patronized by typical Chaniots.

Clubs come and go from year to year, of course, so there's no use getting excited over last year's "in" place. Some popular spots include **El Mondo** and **Nota Bene,** both on Kondilaki (the street leading away from the center of old harbor); **Idaeon Andron,** Odos Halidon 26; and **Ariadne,** on Akti Enoseos (around the corner where the old harbor becomes the new). On Odos Anghelou (up from the Naval Museum) is **Fagotta,** a bar that sometimes offers jazz. **Meltemi,** at the far left (west) corner of the new harbor, is one of the more cosmopolitan cafes, attracting both locals and foreigners, some young, some old.

Two cafes stand out because of their special locations. One is the **Fortezza,** situated midway along the outer quay of the harbor; a little ferry carries you back and forth if you don't (or can't) walk here. Then there is **Pallas Roof Garden Cafe-Bar,** on Akti Tobazi (right at the corner where the new harbor meets the old harbor). You can sit high above the harbor, watch the blinking lights, listen to the murmur of the crowds below, and nurse a refreshing drink or ice cream. There has to be some drawback, and there is—you must climb 44 stairs to get here, but as the sign says, it's worth it.

A more unusual cafe is the **Tzamia-Krystalla,** at Odos Skalidi 35, the main street heading east out of the 1866 Square (☎ 0821/71-172; e-mail: tza-ury@otenet.gr). A welcome addition to the usual tourist scene, it's a combination art gallery/cafe/ performance space. The gallery hosts changing exhibits by Greek artists, as well as the award-winning ceramics of one of the owners. The cafe serves a standard selection of alcoholic and nonalcoholic drinks (no cover or minimum), and at times offers performances of live music. If you'd prefer to hear traditional Cretan music, try the **Café Lyriaka,** Odos Kalergon 22 (behind the arsenali along the harbor).

There has long been a gay community in Chania; one hangout is **Ta Padia Paizei,** on Odos Archoleon, at the far (east) end of the new harbor. The club has no street address but is distinguished by the wheelbarrows with flowers at the door.

There are several **movie houses** around town, too—both outdoor and indoor. They usually show foreign movies in the original language. (The one in the Public Gardens is especially enjoyable.) Watching a movie on a warm summer night in an outdoor cinema in Greece is one of life's simpler pleasures.

In recent years, there's been an effort to provide a **summer cultural festival** of sorts—occasional performances of dramas, symphonic music, jazz, dance, and traditional music. These performances take place from July into September at several venues: the **Firka** fortress at the far left of the harbor; the **Venetian arsenals** along the old harbor; the **East Moat Theater** along Odos Nikiforou Phokas; or in the **Peace and Friendship Park Theater** on Odos Demokratias, just beyond the Public Gardens. For details, inquire at one of the tourist information offices as soon as you arrive in town.

A SIDE TRIP FROM CHANIA: THE SAMARIA GORGE

Everyone with an extra day on Crete—and steady legs and solid walking shoes— should consider the descent through the Gorge of Samaria. This first involves getting to the top of the gorge, a trip of some 42 kilometers (26 miles) from Chania. Second comes the descent by foot and passage through the gorge itself, some 18 kilometers (11 miles). Third, a boat takes you from the village of Ayia Roumeli, at the end of the gorge, to Khora Sfakion; from there, it's a bus ride of about 75 kilometers (46 miles) back to Chania. (Some boats go westward to Paleochora, approximately the same distance by road from Chania.)

Most visitors do it all in a long day, but there are modest hotels and rooms at Ayia Roumeli, Khora Sfakion, Paleochora, and elsewhere along the south coast where you can put up for the night. We strongly advise most people to sign up with one of the many travel agencies in Chania that get people to and from the gorge. This way, you are assured of guaranteed seats on the bus and boat.

In recent years, the Gorge of Samaria has been so successfully promoted as one of the great natural splendors of Europe that on certain days, it seems that half of the continent is trekking through. It's only open from about April through October (depending on weather conditions), so your best chance for a bit of solitude is near those two extremes. On the most crowded days, you can find yourself walking single file with several thousand other people many of those 11 miles. As a hike or trek, it's only relatively taxing, but here and there you will scramble over some boulders. Bring your own water and snacks and wear those comfortable shoes.

After all this, is it worth it? We think so. The gorge offers enough opportunities to break away from the crowds in places. You'll be treated to the fun of crisscrossing the water, not to mention the sights of wildflowers and dramatic geological formations, the sheer height of the gorge's sides, and several chapels that you'll come across—it will all add up to a worthwhile experience, even a metaphor of your visit to Crete.

3 Rethymnon (Rethimno)

72km (45 miles) E of Chania; 78km (50 miles) W of Iraklion

Whether visited on a day trip from Chania or Iraklion or used as a base for a stay in western Crete, Rethymnon can be a most pleasant town—provided you pick the right Rethymnon.

The town's defining centuries came under the Venetians in the late Middle Ages and the Renaissance, then under the Turks from the late 17th century to the late 19th century. Its maze of streets and alleys are now lined with shops, its old beachfront is home to restaurants and bars, and its new beach-resort facilities (to the east of the old town) offer a prime (some might say appalling) example of how a small town's modest seacoast can be exploited. Assuming you have not come to see these "developments," however, we'll help you focus your time and attention on the old town—the side of Rethymnon that can still work its charm.

ESSENTIALS

GETTING THERE   Rethymnon lacks an airport but is only about 1 hour from Chania's and 1½ hours from Iraklion's.

By Boat   Rethymnon does have its own ship line, offering daily trips (about 10 hours) direct to and from Piraeus.

By Car   Many people now approach Rethymmnon by car, taking the highway from either Iraklion (some 79km/49 miles) or Chania (72km/45 miles). There is a public parking lot at Plateia Plastira, at the far (western) edge, just outside the old harbor; it is best approached via the coast road from the west.

By Bus   If you don't have your own vehicle, the bus offers frequent service to and from Iraklion and Chania—virtually every half hour from early in the morning until

For Wine Lovers

Rethymnon's annual wine festival takes place in the middle weeks of July. It's centered around the Public Gardens, with music and dancing to accompany the samplings of local wines. It's a modest affair, but we find it a welcome change from some of the more staged festivals.

---

midevening. (In high season, buses depart Rethymnon as late as 10pm.) The fare has been about Dr1,500 ($4.30) one-way. The **KTEL** bus line (☎ **0831/22-212**) that provides service to and from Chania and Iraklion is located at Akti Kefaloyianithon, at the west edge of the city (so allow an extra 10 minutes to get there).

By Taxi   One-way taxi fares are about Dr18,000 ($52) from Iraklion and Dr14,000 ($40) from Chania.

VISITOR INFORMATION   The **National Tourism Office** (☎ **0831/29-148**) is on Odos Venizelou, near the center of the town beach; it's open Monday through Friday from 8am to 2:30pm. Of the numerous private travel agencies in town, one of the oldest is **Creta Travel Bureau,** Odos Venizelou 3 (☎ **0831/22-915**), which can arrange trips to virtually anywhere on the island.

GETTING AROUND   Rethymnon is a walker's town—bringing a car into the maze of streets and alleys is more trouble than it's worth. The sites you'll want to see are never more than a 20-minute walk from wherever you are. Taxis, meanwhile, are there for anyone who can't endure a short walk—especially in the heat of the day.

To see the countryside of this part of Crete, unless you have unlimited time to use the buses, you'll need to rent a car. Among the many agencies with offices in Rethymnon are **Budget** (☎ **0831/56-910**), **Europeo** (☎ **0831/51-940**), **Hertz** (☎ **0831/26-286**), and **Reliable International** (☎ **0831/72-172**).

FAST FACTS   Several **banks** in both the old town and new city have ATMs and currency-exchange machines. The **hospital** is at Odos Trantallidou 7–9 in the new town (☎ **0831/27-491**). For **Internet access,** try the Caribbean Bar Café (behind the Rimondi Fountain) or the Alana Taverna (on Odos Salaminas near the Hotel Fortezza). The most convenient **laundry** is next to the Youth Hostel, Odos Tombazi 45; open Monday through Saturday from 8am to 8pm. The **tourist police** (☎ **0831/28-156**) share the same building with the tourist office, along the beach. The **post office** is east of the Public Gardens at Odos Moatsu 37 (☎ **0831/22-571**); open Monday through Friday from 8am to 8pm, Saturday from 8am to noon. The **telephone office (OTE)** is at Kountourioti 40; open daily from 7:30am to midnight.

WHAT TO SEE & DO
ATTRACTIONS
The Venetian Fortezza. ☎ **0831/28-101.** Admission Dr500 ($1.45). Daily 8:30am–7pm. On foot, climb Odos Katehaki, a fairly steep road opposite the Hotel Fortezza on Odos Melissinou; by car, ascend the adjacent Odos Kheimara.

Dominating the headland at the western edge of town, this massive fortress is the one site everyone should take time to visit. Built under the Venetians (but *by* Cretans) from about 1573 to 1580, its massive walls, some 1,130 meters in perimeter, were designed to deflect the worst cannon fire of the day. In the end, of course, the Turks simply went around it and took the town by avoiding the fort. There's a partially restored mosque inside as well as a Greek Orthodox chapel. It's in this vast area, by the way, that most

Rethymnon

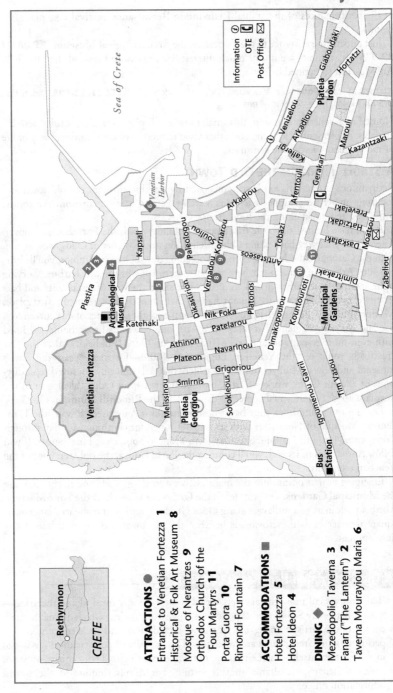

Sea of Crete

Venetian Harbor

Venetian Fortezza

Archaeological Museum

Municipal Gardens

Plateia Georgiou

Bus Station

Plateia Iroon

Information ⓘ
OTE ☎
Post Office ⊠

Streets: Plastira, Kapsali, Paleologou, Soutiou, Arkadiou, Venizelou, KalIergi, Afentouli, Gerakari, Arkadiou, Prevelaki, Hatzidaki, Moatsou, Daskalaki, Zabeliou, Kazantzaki, Marouli, Hortatzi, Giaboudaki, Vernadou, Kornarou, Antistaseos, Platonos, Dimakopoulou, Kountourioti, Dimitrakaki, Tim Yasou, Igoumenou Gavril, Sofokleous, Grigoriou, Navarinou, Patelarou, Nik Foka, Plateon, Athinon, Smirnis, Melissinou, Katehaki, Dikastirion, Tobazi

CRETE
Rethymnon

ATTRACTIONS ●
Entrance to Venetian Fortezza **1**
Historical & Folk Art Museum **8**
Mosque of Nerantzes **9**
Orthodox Church of the
Four Martyrs **11**
Porta Guora **10**
Rimondi Fountain **7**

ACCOMMODATIONS ■
Hotel Fortezza **5**
Hotel Ideon **4**

DINING ◆
Mezedopolio Taverna **3**
Fanari ("The Lantern") **2**
Taverna Mourayiou Maria **6**

273

of the performances of the annual **Rethymnon Renaissance Festival** take place (see below).

Just outside the entrance to the Fortezza is the **Archaeological Museum** (☎ 0831/ 29-975). Its exhibits are not of much interest; we recommend instead the little Folk Art Museum (described below).

Historical and Folk Art Museum. Odos Vernadou 30. ☎0831/23-398. Admission Dr500 ($1.45). Mon–Sat 9am–1pm.

Housed in a Venetian mansion, this small museum displays ceramics, textiles, jewelry, artifacts, implements, clothing, and other vivid reminders of the traditional way of life of most Cretans across the centuries.

A STROLL THROUGH THE OLD TOWN

Rethymnon's attractions are best appreciated by walking through the old town and focusing on whatever appeals to you. Start by getting a free map from the tourist office, located down along the beachfront.

If you have limited time, the first place you should visit is the **Fortezza** (see above). Then make your way back along Odos Melissinou to the corner of Odos Mesologiou, with the Catholic church at the corner. Proceeding down Odos Salaminos, you'll come to Odos Arkadiou; make a left here to the western edge of the **old harbor.** Curving right down to that harbor brings an unexpected sight: the wall of restaurants and bars that effectively obliterates the quaint harbor that drew them here in the first place. Making your way through that, you'll emerge at the southeast corner of this curved harbor and come to a square that faces the town's long beach, its broad boulevard lined with even more restaurants and cafes. Turn right up Odos Petikhaki, and at the first crossroads you'll see the **Venetian Loggia** (ca. 1600)—for many years the town's museum and now a Ministry of Culture gallery that sells officially approved reproductions of ancient Greek works of art. Continue up past it on Odos Paleologou to the next crossroads, where you'll come, on the right, to the **Rimondi Fountain** (1623).

Leaving the fountain at your back, head onto Odos Antistaseos toward the 17th-century **Mosque of Nerantzes** with its minaret (open for climbing Monday through Friday from 11am to 7:30pm, Saturday from 11am to 3pm; closed in August). If you follow Antistaseos to its end, you'll come to the **Porta Guora,** the only remnant of the Venetian city walls.

Emerging at that point onto the main east-west road, opposite and to the right are the **Municipal Gardens.** On your left is the **Orthodox Church of the Four Martyrs,** worth a peek in as you walk east along Odos Gerakari, until you come to a large open square that serves as the crossroads between the old town and the new beachfront development.

The Rethymnon Renaissance Festival

Rethymnon's cultural festival offers varied events—mostly musical and theatrical—from July to early September. Productions range from ancient Greek dramas to more contemporary artistic endeavors (and now include folk and rock concerts). Most performers are Greek; some are foreigners. The majority of performances are staged in the Fortezza itself—there's nothing quite like listening to 17th-century music or seeing a Renaissance drama in this setting. For details, inquire at the tourist information office.

Turning back into the old town on Odos Arkadiou, you'll see on your left the **Mosque of Kara Pasha,** now restored and used as a botanical museum (open daily from 9am to 6pm). As you continue along Arkadiou, in addition to the modern shops and their offerings, note the several remains of the Venetian era that survive—particularly the **façade of no. 154.** From this point on, you're on your own to explore the various narrow streets, to shop, or to simply head for the waterfront and enjoy some refreshment.

OUTDOOR PURSUITS

If you're interested in horseback riding, try the **Riding Center,** located southeast of town at Platanias, Odos N. Fokas 39 (☎ **0831/28-907**). Among the newer diversions offered in Rethymnon are the daily **excursion boats** that take people on a day trip for **swimming** on the beach either at **Bali** (to the east) or **Marathi** (on the Akrotiri to the west). The price, which has been about Dr8,000 ($23) for adults, includes a midday meal at a local taverna as well as all the wine you care to drink. **Nias Tours,** Odos Arkadiou 4 (☎ **0831/23-840**), also offers an **evening cruise** that provides a view of Rethymnon glittering in the night.

SHOPPING

Here, as in Chania and Iraklion, you may be overwhelmed by the sheer number of gift shops offering largely the same objects—mostly souvenirs. Those looking for something a bit different might try Nikolaos Papalasakis's **Palaiopoleiou,** Odos Souliou 40, which is crammed with some genuine antiques, old textiles, jewelry, and curiosities such as the stringed instruments made by the proprietor. At **Olive Tree Wood,** Odos Arambatzoglou 35, the name says it all—the store carries various bowls, containers, and implements carved from olive wood.

For a nice selection of Cretan embroidery, see **Haroula Spridaki,** Odos Souliou 36. Those interested in modern ceramics should stop into **Omodamos,** Odos Souliou 3, where the original works reflect imaginative variations on traditional Greek pottery. And **Talisman,** Odos Arabatzoglou 32, offers an interesting selection of blown glass, ceramics, plaques, paintings, and other handmade articles.

WHERE TO STAY

There is no shortage of accommodations in and around Rethymnon—but it has become increasingly harder to find a place in town that offers a convenient location, some authentic atmosphere, and a quiet night's sleep. Our choices try to satisfy the last-mentioned criterion first. Note that many places in Rethymnon shut down in winter.

✪ **Hotel Fortezza.** Odos Melissinou 16 (at western edge of town, just below the Venetian Fortezza, which is approached by this road), Rethymnon, Crete. ☎ **0831/55-551.** Fax 0831/54-073. 54 units. High season Dr24,000 ($69) double; low season Dr20,000 ($57) double. Rates include continental breakfast. Surcharge for third person sharing room; babies stay free. AE, DC, EC, MC, V. Parking nearby. Public bus service 100m.

The Fortezza is one of the more appealing hotels in Rethymnon, as its location isolates it from the noise of the inner town. This is especially true of its inside rooms, which overlook the modest but welcome pool. You're only a few blocks from the inner old town and then another couple of blocks to the town beach or the Venetian harbor. All guest rooms are good sized with modern bathrooms, and most have balconies. Half of the rooms have air-conditioning and phones. This relatively new hotel has become so popular that we recommend making reservations for the high season.

Hotel Ideon. Plateia Plastira 10 (on coast road just west of the Venetian harbor), Rethymnon, Crete. ☎ **0831/28-667.** Fax 0831/28-670. www.helsun.gr. 86 units, some with shower only, some with tub only. A/C TEL. High season Dr22,000 ($63) double; low season Dr16,000 ($46) double. Rates include buffet breakfast. Reduced rates for third person in room and children 2–12. AE, DC, EC, MC, V. Parking on adjacent street. Closed Nov to mid-Mar.

This old favorite now boasts a new pool and a sunbathing area as well as a conference room that can handle up to 80 persons. The friendly desk staff will arrange for everything from laundry service to car rentals. The guest rooms are the standard modern of Greek hotels. We like this place because it offers an increasingly rare combination in a Cretan hotel: It's near the active part of town and near the water (although it doesn't have a beach), yet it's relatively isolated from night noises. A solid choice for sheer convenience.

Kournas Village Hotel Bungalows. Kavros (20 min. west of Rethymnon, on the main road to Chania), Crete. ☎ and fax **0831/61-416.** 141 units. A/C TEL. High season Dr28,000 ($80) double; low season Dr20,000 ($57). No credit cards. Rates include breakfast and dinner. Parking on site. Closed Nov–Mar.

Here's an alternative for those who want to focus their Cretan stay on Rethymnon and Chania and western Crete, yet prefer to be based on a beach that's not an annex to a noisy town. Everything about this place is first class, yet you'll feel like you're living on a remote beach with the sea before you and the mountains behind. The village of Georgioupolis is close enough for an evening stroll. Guest rooms are of moderate size but have fully modern bathrooms; though it lacks the luxury of the grand resorts to the east of Rethymnon, the Kournas Village is more than adequate.

Amenities include a restaurant and cafeteria (and many other options within walking distance), bar, concierge, laundry arrangements, two pools, children's pool, health club, sauna, massage, sundeck, tennis court (with flood lights), table tennis, water-sports equipment, bicycle rentals, playground nursery, conference room, video games, car-rental and tour arrangements, and boutiques.

۞ Rethymna Beach Grecotel. P.O. Box 23, 74100 Rethymnon, Crete (7km/4 miles east of Rethymnon on the old road to Iraklion). ☎ **0831/71-002.** Fax 0831/71-668. E-mail: sales@crete.grecotel.gr. 568 units (including bungalows and villas, 7 with private pools). A/C TV TEL. High season Dr38,000–Dr40,000 ($109–$115) double; Dr44,000–Dr52,000 ($126–$150) bungalow. Low season Dr21,000 ($60) double; Dr25,000 ($72) bungalow. All rates are per person but include breakfast and one other meal. Reduction for third person sharing room; babies stay free. AE, DC, EC, MC, V. Parking on premises. Buses to and from Rethymnon (and Chania or Iraklion) about every half hour. Closed Nov–Mar.

This luxury beach hotel is one of the finest on the island, and offers an escape from the noise of the city. The bedrooms are modest in size and furnishings but do have fine bathrooms and views. This hotel's particular strength is the supervised activities for children. If you like to mix occasional sightseeing with luxurious facilities, pampered relaxation, and water-based activities, consider this rather glitzy choice.

Amenities include many restaurants, concierge, room service, laundry, newspaper delivery, massage, baby-sitting, secretarial services, courtesy car, children's activities, four pools, health club, aerobics, sauna, bridge room, video room, five tennis courts (two with lights), squash court at nearby Creta Palace, water-sports equipment (and instruction), bicycle rentals, nature trails, conference rooms, car-rental desk, tour desk, salon, and boutiques.

WHERE TO DINE

For standard but tasty Greek foods, you might consider the **Mezedopolio Taverna,** Plateia Plastira (☎ **0831/53-598**), behind the far western end of old harbor; or the

Ovelistirion, Odos Arambatzoglou, on the square overlooking the Church of the Annunciation.

Fanari ("The Lantern"). Odos Kefaloyianithon 16 (on coast road just west of Venetian harbor—past Ideon Hotel and Famagusta Restaurant). ☎ **0831/54-849.** Main courses Dr1,000–Dr2,600 ($2.90–$8); daily special combination plates about Dr1,500 ($4.30). No credit cards. Daily 11am–1:30am. Parking nearby. GREEK TAVERNA.

We list this place not because its menu or cooking are so exceptional, but because its location is so pleasant, overlooking the sea and well removed from the bustle of the center of Rethymnon. It offers prompt and pleasant service as well. The old harbor and the old beach strip have now become so geared to tourism that an unpretentious taverna like this comes as a relief and a retreat. Take a table at the railing, order a cool drink, and enjoy your meal: You can't go wrong with the standard fare, and fish here can be as tasty as at most of the more expensive locales.

Taverna Mourayiou Maria. Odos Nearchou 45 (Venetian harbor). ☎ **0831/26-475.** Main courses Dr1,200–Dr3,200 ($3.45–$9). AE, EC, MC, V. Daily 9am–midnight. Closed Nov–Mar. GREEK.

Like all of the restaurants on the Venetian harbor, this one specializes in lobster and fish in season, but it also offers a choice of traditional Greek dishes at the lower end of the price scale. The popularity of the area has somewhat overwhelmed the picturesque charm that originally attracted restaurants such as this one, but every visitor will want to try at least one meal on the harbor—and this is as good a choice as any.

A SIDE TRIP FROM RETHYMNON: MONASTERY OF ARKADHI

Anyone who wants some sense of modern Cretans should visit the **Monastery of Arkadhi.** It sits some 23 kilometers (15 miles) southeast of Rethymnon and can be reached by public bus. A taxi might be in order if you don't have a car, and you'll only need the driver to wait about an hour—it should total about Dr17,000 ($49). What you see when you arrive is a surprisingly Italianate-looking church façade, for although it belongs to the Orthodox priesthood, it was built under Venetian influence in 1587.

Like many monasteries on Crete, Arkadhi provided support for the rebels against Turkish rule. During a major uprising in 1866, many Cretan insurgents, along with their women and children, took refuge here. Realizing they were doomed to fall to the far larger besieging Turkish force, the abbot, it is claimed, gave the command to blow up the powder storeroom. Whether an accident or not, hundreds of Cretans and Turks died in the explosion. This occurred on November 9, 1866, and the event became known throughout the Western world, inspiring writers and revolutionaries and statesmen of several nations to protest at least with words. To Cretans it became and remains the archetypal incident of their long struggle for "freedom or death." (An ossuary outside the monastery contains the skulls of many who died in the explosion.) Even if you have never had occasion to think about Cretan history, a brief visit to Arkadhi should go a long way in explaining the Cretans you deal with.

4 Ayios Nikolaos

69km (43 miles) E of Iraklion

Ayios Nikolaos tends to inspire strong reactions, depending on what you're looking for. Until the 1970s, it was a lazy little coastal settlement, with no archaeological or historical structures of any interest. Then the town got "discovered," and the rest is the history of organized tourism in our time.

For about 5 months of the year, Ayios Nikolaos becomes one gigantic resort town, taken over by the package-tour groups who stay in beach hotels along the adjacent coast, but come into town to eat, shop, and stroll. During the day, Ayios Nikolaos vibrates with people. At night, it vibrates with music—the center down by the water is like one communal nightclub.

Yet somehow the town remains a pleasant place to visit, and serves as a fine base for excursions to the east of Crete. And if you're willing to stay outside the very center, you can take only as much of Ayios Nikolaos as you want—and then retreat to your beach or explore the east end of the island.

ESSENTIALS

GETTING THERE   By Plane   Ayios Nikolaos does not have its own airport but can be reached in 1½ hours by taxi or bus from the Iraklion airport. **Olympic Airways** also offers several flights weekly to Sitia, the town to the east of Ayios Nikolaos, but the drive from there to Ayios Nikolaos is a solid 2 hours.

By Boat   There are several ships a week each way that link Ayios Nikoloas to Piraeus (about 11 hrs.). There are also ships that link Ayios Nikolaos to Sitia (just east along the coast) and on, via the islands of Kassos, Karpathos, and Khalki, to Rhodes. In summer, there are several ships that link Ayios Nikolaos to Santorini (4 hrs.), and then via several other Cycladic islands to Piraeus. Schedules and even ship lines vary so much from year to year that you may want to wait until you get to Greece to make specific plans.

By Bus   Bus service almost every half hour of the day each way (in high season) links Ayios Nikolaos to Iraklion; almost as many buses go to and from Sitia. The **KTEL** bus line (☎ **0841/22-234**) has its terminal at Akti Atlantidos by the marina, around the headland.

VISITOR INFORMATION   The **Municipal Information Office** (☎ **0841/ 22-357**) is one of the most helpful in all of Greece, perhaps because it's staffed by eager young seasonal employees. It's open April 15 through October, daily from 8am to 10pm. In addition to providing maps and brochures, it can help arrange accommodations and excursions. Among the scores of travel agencies, we recommend **Creta Travel Bureau,** at the corner of Odos Paleologou and Odos Katehaki, just opposite Lake Voulismeni (☎ **0841/28-496;** fax 081/223-749).

GETTING AROUND   The town is so small that you can walk to all points, although there are taxis available. The KTEL buses (see above) service towns, hotels, and other points in eastern Crete. If you want to explore this end of the island on your own, it seems as though car and moped/motorcycle rentals are at every other doorway. We found some of the best rates at **Alfa Rent a Car,** Odos Kap. Nik. Fafouti 3, the small street between the lake and harbor road (☎ **0841/24-312;** fax 0841/25-639). Fotis Aretakis is the man to deal with.

FAST FACTS   There are several **ATMs** and currency-exchange machines along the streets leading away from the harbor. The **hospital** (☎ **0841/22-369**) is on the west edge of town, at the junction of Odos Lasithiou and Odos Paleologou. For **Internet access,** head to Peripou, Odos 28 Octobriou 25 (☎ **0841/24-876;** e-mail: peripou2@agn.forthnet.gr); open daily in high season from 9am to 9pm. The most convenient **laundry** is the Xionati Laundromat, Odos Chortatson 10 (a small street leading up from Akti Nearchou, down by the bus terminal and beach); open Monday through Friday from 8am to 2pm and 5 to 8pm, Saturday from 8am to 4pm.

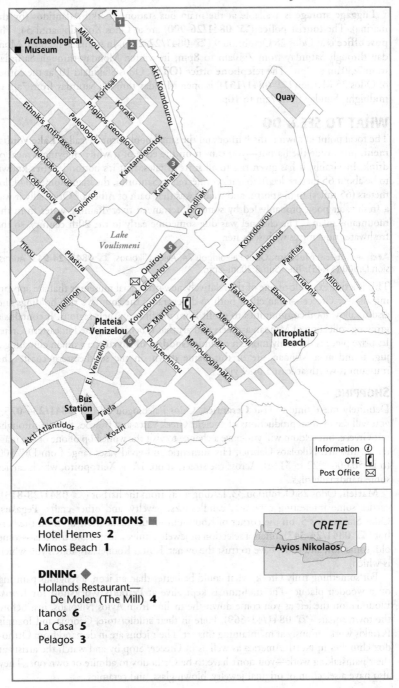

Milatou
Koritsas
Koraka
Prigipos Georgiou
Paleologou
Ethnikis Antistaseos
Theotokouloud
Kobnarouv
D. Solomos
Akti Koundourou
Kantanoleontos
Katehaki
Kondilaki
Titou
Plastira
Filellinon
Omirou
28 Octobriou
Koundourou
25 Martiou
Koundourou
Lasthenous
Pasifias
Ariadnis
Milou
M. Sfakianaki
Ebans
Alexomanoli
K. Sfakianaki
Manousogianakis
Polytechniou
El. Venizelou
Tavla
Koziri
Akti Atlantidos

Archaeological ■ Museum

Quay

Lake Voulismeni

Plateia Venizelou

Kitroplatia Beach

Bus Station ■

Information ⓘ
OTE Ⅽ
Post Office ✉

ACCOMMODATIONS ■
Hotel Hermes **2**
Minos Beach **1**

DINING ◆
Hollands Restaurant—
    De Molen (The Mill) **4**
Itanos **6**
La Casa **5**
Pelagos **3**

CRETE

Ayios Nikolaos

Luggage storage is available at the main bus station, at Akti Atlantidos (by the marina). The tourist police (☎ 0841/26-900) are at Odos Koundoyianni 34. The post office is at Odos 28 Octobriou 9 (☎ 0841/22-276). In summer, it's open Monday through Saturday from 7:30am to 8pm; in winter, Monday through Saturday from 7:30am to 2pm. The telephone office (OTE), Odos Sfakinaki 10, at the corner of Odos 25 Martiou (☎ 0841/131), is open Monday through Saturday from 7am to midnight, Sunday from 7am to 10pm.

WHAT TO SEE & DO

The focal point in town is the harbor and the small pool, formally called Lake Voulismeni, just inside the harbor—you can sit on the edge of it while enjoying a meal or drink. Inevitably, it has given rise to all sorts of tales: that it's bottomless (it's known to be about 65 meters deep); that it's connected to Santorini, the island some 104 kilometers (65 miles) to the north; and that it was the "bath of Athena." Originally it was a freshwater pool, probably fed by some subterranean river draining water from the mountains inland. The channel was dug sometime early in the 20th century, so the freshwater now mixes with seawater.

Archaeological Museum. Odos Paleologou 74, Ayios Nikolaos. ☎ 0841/24-943. Admission Dr500 ($1.45). Tues–Sun 8:30am–3pm.

This is a fine example of one of the relatively new provincial museums that are appearing all over Greece—in an effort both to decentralize the country's rich holdings and also to allow local communities to profit from the finds in their regions. It contains a growing collection of Minoan artifacts and art that is being excavated in eastern Crete. Its prize piece is the eerily modern ceramic Goddess of Myrtos, a woman clutching a jug, found at a Minoan site of this name down on the southeastern coast. The museum is worth at least a brief visit.

SHOPPING

Definitely make time to visit Ceramica, Odos Paleologou 28 (☎ 0841/234-075); you will see many reproductions of ancient Greek vases and frescoes for sale throughout Greece, but seldom will you have a chance to visit the workshop of one of the masters of this art, Nikolaos Gabriel. His authentic and vivid vases range from Dr7,500 to Dr50,000 ($22 to $144). Across the street, at no. 1A, is Xeiropoito, which carries some handmade rugs.

Marieli, Odos 28 Octobriou 33, leading away from the harbor (☎ 0841/28-813), carries some interesting ceramics, candlesticks, jewelry, and other crafts. Pegasus, Odos Sfakianakis 5, on the corner of Koundourou, the main street up from the harbor (☎ 0841/24-347), offers a selection of jewelry, knives, icons, and trinkets—some old, some not, and you'll have to trust the owner, Kostas Kounelakis, to tell you which is which.

For something truly Greek, what could be better than an icon, a religious painting on a wooden plaque? The tradition is kept alive at Petrakis Workshop for Icons, Elounda, on the left as you come down the incline from Ayios Nikolaos, just before the town square (☎ 0841/41-669). Here in their studio/store, Georgia and Ioannis Petrakis work seriously at maintaining this art. Their icons are in demand from Orthodox churches in North America as well as in Greece. Stop by and watch the artists at their painstaking work—you don't have to be Orthodox to admire or own one. They also have a selection of original jewelry, blown glass, and ceramics.

Lato Cultural Festival

Ayios Nikolaos's modest arts festival usually runs from late July to early September, with Cretan choral groups, Cretan traditional dance troupes, both classic and modern plays (usually in Greek), and concerts by Greek instrumentalists and vocalists. Admission is from Dr1,200 to Dr3,000 ($3.45 to $9). To show their appreciation for the foreigners who visit the town and support these and other events, the sponsors have also given parties about midway through the season and then at the end of September—a nice touch, suggesting that perhaps mass tourism need not totally wipe out local customs.

WHERE TO STAY
INSIDE TOWN

Hotel Hermes. Akti Koundourou (on the shore road around from the inner harbor), 72100 Ayios Nikolaos, Crete. ☎ **0841/28-253.** Fax 0841/22-058. www.hermes-hotels.gr. E-mail: ermis1@ath.forthnet.gr. 206 units. A/C TEL. High season Dr42,000 ($121) double; low season Dr32,000 ($92) double. Rates include half-board plan (breakfast and dinner); cheaper rate for breakfast only; special rate for longer stays. AE, DC, EC, MC, V. Parking on opposite seawall (but beware of seaspray!). Closed Nov–Mar.

This is perhaps the best you can do if you want to stay as close to the center of town as possible, yet be free from as much of the noise as possible. It's just far enough and around the corner from the inner harbor to escape the nightly din. This won't be in everyone's budget, but it's a compromise between the deluxe beach resorts and the cheaper in-town hotels. Guest rooms are done in the standard style, and most enjoy a view over the sea. All rooms have fridges, and suites have TVs. There's a private terrace (not a beach) on the shore, just across the boulevard. On the roof is a pool, with plenty of space to sunbathe. There's also a sauna and exercise room, as well as diversions such as video games and billiards. Other facilities include a restaurant and conference room.

If the Hermes is booked, you might try the **Hotel Coral,** Akti Koundourou next door to the Hermes on the shore road (☎ **0841/28-253**). It's under the same management, almost as classy, and somewhat cheaper.

Minos Beach. Amoudi (a 10-min. walk from center), 72100 Ayios Nikolaos, Crete. ☎ **0841/22-345.** Fax 0841/22-548. E-mail: mamhotel@otenet.gr. 12 units (in main building), 118 bungalows. A/C MINIBAR TEL. High season Dr38,600–Dr61,000 ($110–$174) double/bungalow; low season Dr34,200–Dr51,000 ($98–$146). All rates are per person and include buffet breakfast. Special rates for children. One meal a day for Dr6,000 ($17) extra. AE, DC, EC, MC, V. Closed late Oct to late Apr. Frequent public buses to Ayios Nikolaos center or Elounda.

This was the first of the luxury beach-bungalow resorts on Crete and remains a favorite among many loyal returnees. Its grounds now look a bit overgrown with greenery, and the common areas are not as glitzy as at newer resorts. As with almost all Greek deluxe hotels, the mattresses seem a bit thin—to Americans, at least. But the hotel does have a civilized air, enhanced by the original works by world-famous modern sculptors located around the grounds. It's a great place to enjoy complete peace and quiet and yet not be that far from Ayios Nikolaos.

Amenities include several fine restaurants and bars, concierge, room service, laundry, newspaper delivery, baby-sitting, secretarial services, valet parking, airport transport arrangements, TVs in VIP bungalows and large TV room, saltwater pool, sauna, sundecks, outdoor tennis court lit at night, water-sports equipment, bicycle rentals, table tennis, video games, conference center, car-rental desk, tour arrangements, hairdresser, and boutiques.

OUTSIDE TOWN

✪ **Elounda Beach.** 72053 Elounda (8km/5 miles from center of Ayios Nikolaos), Crete. ☎ **0841/41-412.** Fax 0841/41-373. www.eloundabeach.gr. E-mail: elohotel@ eloundabeach.gr. 258 units (including 21 suites and bungalows with private swimming pools). A/C MINIBAR TV TEL. High season Dr70,000–Dr120,000 ($201–$345) double; Dr91,000–Dr225,000 ($262–$648) bungalow suite. Low season Dr35,000–Dr63,000 ($99–$181) double; Dr45,000–Dr96,000 ($129–$276) bungalow suite. Rates are per person per day and include breakfast (1 meal supplement costs Dr10,000/$29 extra). AE, DC, EC, MC, V. Closed early Nov to early Apr. Public buses to Ayios Nikolaos or Elounda every hr.; Elounda is a 15-min. walk.

This is truly a world-class resort. It offers more extras than we can list, including a gala dinner every Sunday and open-air movies on Monday nights. There's not much more to say about such a place except that it's truly deluxe. From the prunes at the breakfast buffet to the mini-TV at your bathroom mirror, the management has thought of everything. And oh, in case you're concerned, the hotel does have its own heliport, so you can arrive that way if you please.

Restaurants and bars are located throughout the vast property. Amenities include concierge, room service, laundry, newspaper delivery, nightly turndown, baby-sitting, secretarial services, airport transport arrangements, VCRs and videos available from desk, pool, health and fitness center, Jacuzzi, sauna, sundecks, two lit tennis courts, water-sports equipment, bicycle rentals, table tennis, billiards, basketball, volleyball, minigolf, supervised children's activities during the day, business support by arrangement, conference center (at adjacent sister hotel, Elounda Bay), car-rental and tour arrangements, hairdresser, and boutiques.

✪ **Istron Bay.** 72100 Istro (12km/7 miles east of Ayios Nikolaos), Crete. ☎ **0841/61-347.** Fax 0841/61-383. www.istronbay.com. E-mail: istron@agn.forthnet.gr. 107 units (including bungalows). A/C MINIBAR TV TEL. High season Dr60,000 ($173) double; Dr90,000 ($259) suite or bungalow. Low season 35,000 ($101) double; Dr52,000 ($150) suite or bungalow. Rates include buffet breakfast. Special rates for extra beds in room, for children, for June, and for half-board plan. AE, DC, MC, V. Closed Nov–Mar. Public buses every hour to Ayios Nikolaos or Sitia.

Still another new and beautiful (and quiet!) beach resort, this one is nestled against the slope on its own bay. It's the resort's location, plus its own beach and the sense of being in some tropical paradise, that makes this such a special place. Plus, it's family owned and thus maintains a touch of the traditional Cretan hospitality—inviting newcomers to a cocktail party to meet others, for instance. The comfortable guest rooms have modern bathrooms and spectacular views. If you can tear yourself away from here, you're well situated to take in all the sights of eastern Crete.

The main dining room has a fabulous view to go with its award-winning cuisine; it takes special pride in offering choices based on the "Cretan diet," internationally recognized as especially healthy. Amenities include concierge, room service, laundry, baby-sitting, children's activities, pool, children's pool, aerobics, sundeck, outdoor tennis court (lit at night), water-sports equipment, table tennis, volleyball, video games, bicycle rentals, conference rooms, car-rental and tour arrangements, hairdresser, and boutique. It also operates a SCUBA diving school.

WHERE TO DINE

Ayios Nikolaos and nearby Elounda have so many restaurants that it's hard to know where to start or stop. When deciding, consider location and atmosphere; those factors have governed our recommendations below.

MODERATE

Hollands Restaurant—De Molen (The Mill). Odos Dionysos Solomos 10 (the road at the highest point above the lake). ☎ and fax **0841/25-582.** Main courses Dr1,100–Dr3,300 ($3.70–$10); combination plates offered. EC, V. Daily 10am–11:30pm. Closed Nov–Mar. A taxi is your only choice if you can't make it up the hill. DUTCH/INDONESIAN.

Who would go to Crete to eat Dutch cuisine? Aside from offering a new experience for your palate, this place commands the most dramatic nighttime view of Ayios Nikolaos. Specialties include pork fillet in a cream sauce. Vegetarian? Try the crêpe with eggplant, mushrooms, carrots, and cabbage, tied up with leeks. We tasted something even more exotic: one of the Indonesian dishes, Nasi Goreng—a heaping plate of rice with vegetables and pork, in a satay (peanut) sauce. Somehow it seemed to go with our perch overlooking exotic Ayios Nikolaos.

La Casa. Odos 28 Octobriou 31. ☎ **0841/26-362.** Main courses Dr1,300–Dr3,100 ($3.75–$9). AE, DC, DISC, EC, JCB, MC, V. Daily 9am–midnight. No parking in immediate area. GREEK/INTERNATIONAL.

With its lakeside location, tasty menu, and friendly Greek-American proprietress, this might be many travelers' first choice in Ayios Nikolaos. You'll enjoy any of the fine meals Marie Daskaloyiannis cooks up, including such specialties as fried rice with shrimp, lamb with artichokes, and rabbit stifado. Or try the "Greek sampling" plate—moussaka, dolmades, stuffed tomato, meatballs, and whatever other goodies Marie heaps on. There's always a slightly special twist to the food here.

Pelagos. Corner of Odos Koraka and Katehaki 10 (a block up from the waterfront). ☎ **0841/25-737.** E-mail: doxan45@hotmail.com. Reservations recommended in high season. Main courses Dr1,000–Dr4,000 ($2.90–$11.50). MC, V. Daily noon–1am. Parking on adjacent streets—but all but impossible in high season. Closed Nov–Feb. SEAFOOD.

Looking for a change from the usual touristy seafront restaurant—something a bit more cosmopolitan? Try Pelagos, in a handsome old house a block up from the hustle and bustle of the harbor. As its name suggests, it specializes in seafood, and from squid to lobster (expensive, as always in Greece), it's all done with flair. You can sit indoors in a subdued atmosphere or out in the secluded garden; either way you'll be served with style. This restaurant lets you get away from the crowd and share a more intimate meal.

Vritomartes. Elounda (on the breakwater). ☎ **0841/41-325.** Reservations recommended for dinner in high season. Main courses Dr1,000–Dr3,700 ($2.90–$11); fish platter special Dr3,300 ($10). EC, MC, V. Daily 10am–11pm. Closed Nov–Mar. SEAFOOD/GREEK.

It takes a slight amount of effort to get to this taverna out in Elounda, but there are buses every hour as well as taxis for the 12-kilometer (8-mile) trip, and anyone who's come as far as Ayios Nikolaos should get out to Elounda at least once. You can't beat dining at this old favorite—there's been at least a lowly taverna here long before the beautiful people discovered the area. (They're the reason you should either come early or make a reservation.) The specialty, no surprise, is the seafood. (You may find the proprietor literally "out to sea," catching that night's fish dinners.) If you settle for the red mullet and a bottle of Cretan white Xerolithia, you can't go wrong. The dining area itself is pretty plain, but this is still one experience you won't forget.

INEXPENSIVE

Itanos. Odos Kyprou 1 (just off Plateia Venizelos, at top of Koundourou). ☎ **0841/25-340.** Reservations not accepted, so come early in high season. Main courses Dr900–Dr2,700 ($2.60–$8). No credit cards. Daily 10am–midnight. GREEK.

A now familiar story on Crete: A simple local taverna where you go to experience "the authentic" gets taken up by the tourists, changing the scene somewhat. But the fact is, the food and prices haven't changed *that* much. It's still standard taverna oven dishes—no-nonsense chicken, lamb, and beef in tasty sauces with hearty vegetables—and grilled meats. The house wine comes out of barrels. During the day, you sit indoors, where you'll experience no-nonsense decor and service. But at night during the hot months, tables appear on the sidewalk, a roof garden opens up on the building across the narrow street, and your fellow travelers take over. Come here if you need a break from the harbor scene and want to feel you're in a place that still exists when all the visitors go home.

SIDE TRIPS FROM AYIOS NIKOLAOS

Almost everyone who comes to Ayios Nikolaos makes the two short excursions to Spinalonga and Kritsa. Each can easily be visited in a half day.

SPINALONGA

Spinalonga is the **fortified islet** in the bay off Elounda. The Venetians built another of their fortresses here in 1579, and it enjoyed the distinction of being their final outpost on Crete, not taken over by the Turks until 1715. When the Cretans took possession in 1903, it was turned into a leper colony, but this ended after World War II. Now Spinalonga is a major tourist attraction. In fact, there's not much to do here except walk around and soak in the atmosphere and ghosts of the past. Boats depart regularly from both Ayios Nikolaos harbor and Elounda as well as from certain hotels.

KRITSA

Although a walk through Spinalonga can resonate as a historical byway, if you have time to make only one of these short excursions, we advise taking the 12-kilometer (8-mile) trip up into the hills behind Ayios Nikolaos to the village of Kritsa and its 14th-century ✪ **Church of Panayia Kera.** Not only is the church of some interest architecturally, but its **frescoes,** dating from the 14th and 15th centuries, are also regarded as among the jewels of Cretan-Byzantine art. They have been restored, but the power emanates from the original work. Scenes depict the life of Jesus, the life of Mary, and the Second Coming. Guides can be arranged at any travel agency or the Municipal Information Office in Ayios Nikolaos. After seeing the church, go into the village of Kritsa itself and enjoy the view and the many fine handcrafted goods for sale.

The Cyclades 9

by Mark Meagher

From the summit of Mount Kinthos, the islands of the Cyclades lie close up and low to the horizon, sprawled across the windswept Aegean to a place where the sea turns a deeper blue with distance. The landscape is bare white rock and dust, poppies grow from crevices, and the air is redolent with the aroma of wild herbs. Immediately below lie the ruins of an ancient temple city; across the bay are beaches blazing white in the sun, and somewhat further off the brilliant form of Panayia Evanyelistria, a church that draws pilgrims from all of Greece.

This low hill on the tiny isle of **Delos** is the center of the Cyclades, in more ways than one. For the ancient Greeks, this island was the still point around which the chain of islands slowly turned (*kiklos* means "circle," thus the *Kiklades* are the circling islands). Geographically too, Delos is the near center of the Cyclades, and for this reason it's a great place to get your bearings.

The islands of **Mykonos, Paros,** and **Santorini** are rightfully acclaimed for their sunbathing, lively nightlife, abundant shops, and fine restaurants. You'll find that tourism on most of the Cyclades is concentrated in a few coastal villages and along the best beaches, while large areas (very often at the northern, windier extremities of the islands) remain unexplored by visitors—this is particularly true on **Sifnos, Folegandros,** and **Siros,** where the gently beautiful northern hills offer a taste of traditional island life. On islands like Folegandros, still reliant on small-scale agriculture, you'll even see donkeys returning from the fields laden with freshly reaped bales of barley. We recommend planning your island-hopping tour of the Cyclades so that you experience the appealingly hedonistic cosmopolitan scene without bypassing the world of the villages, which hasn't changed much in the past few centuries but may not be around much longer.

STRATEGIES FOR SEEING THE ISLANDS Although the Cyclades are bound by unmistakable family resemblance, each island is rigorously independent and unique, making this archipelago an island-hopper's paradise. Ease of travel is facilitated by frequent and reliable ferry service. Hydrofoils, however, are notoriously irregular, and service is often canceled at the whim of the *meltemi* (severe summer winds). A new fleet of catamarans has greatly facilitated travel between Piraeus and the Cycladic islands of Siros, Paros, Naxos, Mykonos, and Santorini. Keep in mind that service to most islands is highly seasonal, with frequency dropping off significantly between

October and April. Between May and September, you can go just about anywhere you want, whenever you want, although winds will often upset the most carefully arranged plans.

1 Santorini (Thira)

233km (126 nautical miles) SE of Piraeus

Santorini is that rare thing, a place where legend is matched by reality. One of the most spectacular islands in the world, Santorini's cliff-faced crescent isle graces tourist brochures and posters in Greek restaurants the world over. The real wonder is that the place itself meets and exceeds all glossy picture-postcard expectations. Like an enormous mandible, Santorini encloses the pure blue waters of its caldera, the core of an ancient volcano. Its two principal towns, **Fira** and **Ia,** perch at the summit of the caldera, their whitewashed houses resembling from an approaching ship a dusting of new snow on the mountaintop.

The eruption that blew out the center of this once circular island some 3,600 years ago buried the cosmopolitan city of **Akrotiri** under tons of ash, and sent tidal waves that may have inundated the Minoan cities of Crete and very nearly destroyed its civilization. Was Akrotiri the origin of the Atlantis legend? Don't miss the opportunity to visit the extensive excavations of this vast ancient city, and decide for yourself.

Ancient Thira is another of Santorini's archaeological wonders, spectacularly situated atop a high promontory. There is a paved road to the site, but the steep hike up from Kamari is rewarding. Arid Santorini isn't known for its agriculture, but the rocky island soil has long produced a plentiful grape harvest, and the local wines are among the finest in Greece; be sure to visit one of the island **wineries** for a tasting. Among the many other obligatory Santorini experiences are the **Ia sunset** (best seen from the ramparts of Lontza Castle or the footpath between Fira and Ia) and the **volta (stroll) in Fira,** whose nighttime streets seem steeped in the caldera's sublime stillness.

The best advice we can offer is to visit some time other than July or August. Santorini experiences an even greater transformation during the peak season than other Cycladic isles. With visitors far in the excess of the island's small capacity, trash collects in the squares and crowds make movement through the streets of Fira and Ia next to impossible. Accommodation rates will also be as much as 50% lower if you can travel in May, June, or September.

ESSENTIALS

GETTING THERE   By Plane   Olympic Airways (www.olympic-airways.gr) has daily flights between Athens and the Santorini airport at Monolithos (which also receives European charters). There is connection with Mykonos five times per week, service three or four times a week to and from Rhodes, and service two or three times a week with Iraklion, Crete. For information and reservations, check with the Olympic office in Fira on Odos Ayiou Athanassiou (☎ **0286/22-493**), just southeast of town on the road to Kamari, or in Athens at ☎ **0801/44-444** or 01/966-6666. **Aegean Airlines** (☎ **01/998-2888** in Athens), with an office at the Monolithos airport (☎ **0286/28-500**), also has several flights daily between Athens and Santorini. A bus to Fira (Dr500/$1.45) meets most flights; the schedule is posted at the bus stop, beside the airport entrance. A taxi to Fira costs about Dr2,000 ($6).

By Boat   There is ferry service to and from Piraeus at least twice daily; the trip takes 9 to 10 hours by car ferry on the Piraeus-Paros-Naxos-Ios-Santorini route, or 4 hours by catamaran on the Piraeus-Paros-Santorini route. In July and August, ferries connect

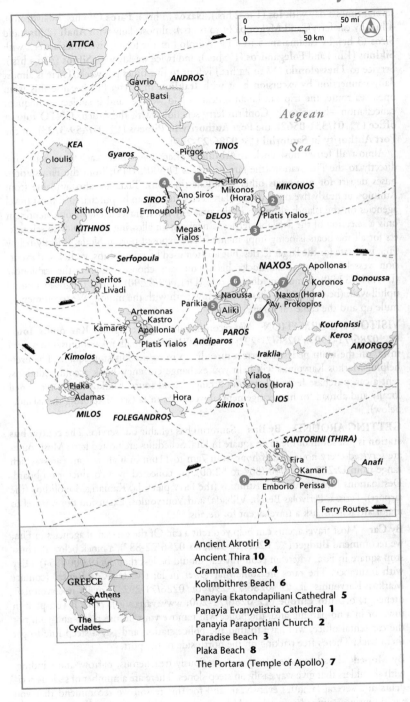

Ancient Akrotiri 9
Ancient Thira 10
Grammata Beach 4
Kolimbithres Beach 6
Panayia Ekatondapiliani Cathedral 5
Panayia Evanyelistria Cathedral 1
Panayia Paraportiani Church 2
Paradise Beach 3
Plaka Beach 8
The Portara (Temple of Apollo) 7

several times a day with **Ios** (1 to 2 hrs.), **Naxos** (3 hrs.), **Paros** (2½ hrs. by hydrofoil, 4 hrs. by car ferry), and **Mykonos** (4 to 6 hrs.); almost daily with **Anafi** (2 hrs.) and **Siros** (3 hrs. by catamaran, 5 to 6 by hydrofoil or car ferry); five times a week with **Sikinos** (1 hr.) and **Folegandros** (1½ hrs.); and twice weekly with **Sifnos** (3 to 4 hrs.). Service to **Thessaloniki** (17 to 24 hrs.) is four to five times per week. There is almost daily connection by excursion boat with **Iraklion** in Crete, but because this is an open sea route, the trip can be an ordeal in bad weather and is subject to frequent cancellation—better to fly. Confirm ferry schedules with the Athens **GNTO tourist office** (☎ **01/331-0562**), the **Port Authority in Piraeus** (☎ **01/459-3223**), or the **Port Authority in Santorini** (☎ **0286/22-239**).

Almost all ferries now dock at **Athinios,** where buses meet each boat, returning directly to the Fira station (the fare to Fira is Dr500/$1.45); from the Fira station, buses depart for numerous other island destinations. Taxis are also available from Athinios, at nearly five times the bus fare. Ferry tickets can be purchased at most travel agencies on the island; although in the past any given travel agency would represent only a selection of the available ferries, a new system allowing any agency to sell tickets for all the boats is being implemented. The exposed port at **Skala,** directly below Fira, is unsafe for the larger ferries, but is often used by cruise ships, yachts, and excursion vessels; if your boat docks here, you can choose between the cable car (Dr1,000/$2.90), a mule or donkey ride (Dr1,000/$2.90), and a tough 45-minute uphill walk (be prepared to share the narrow path with the mules). We recommend a mule up and the cable car down.

VISITOR INFORMATION   We recommend the travel agency **Karvounis Tours** (☎ **0286/71-290** or 0286/71-292; fax 0286/71-291; e-mail: mkarvounis@otenet.gr) in Ia, on the main pedestrian street directly up from the bus-stop square. The ever-helpful Markos Karvounis will help you exchange currency, book accommodations, rent a car, purchase ferry tickets, and arrange island tours. Markos is also renowned locally and abroad for his arrangement of weddings in Ia (see "Exploring the Island," below).

GETTING AROUND   **By Bus**   Santorini has reliable bus service. The **central bus station** is just south of the main square in Fira. Schedules are posted here: Most routes are serviced every hour or half hour from 7am to 11pm in high season. Fares, which range from Dr270 to Dr900 (80¢ to $2.60), are collected by a conductor on board. Destinations include Akrotiri, Athinios (the ferry pier), Ia, Kamari, Monolithos (the airport), Perissa, Perivolas Beach, Vlihada, and Vourvoulos. Excursion buses travel to major attractions; ask a travel agent for details.

By Car   Most travel agents can help you rent a car. Of the car-rental agencies in Fira, we recommend **Budget** (☎ **0286/22-900;** fax 0286/22-887), a block below the bus-stop square in Fira, where an economy car should be less than Dr19,000 ($54) a day with insurance. The rates are somewhat lower in Ia; try **Rea Car Rental** (contact Markos Karvounis at ☎ **0286/71-290** or 0286/71-292; e-mail: mkarvounis@ otenet.gr) or **Auto Europe** (☎ **0286/71-200;** www.vazeos.gr). *Note:* If you park in town or in a no-parking area, the police will remove your license plates and you, not the car-rental office, will have to find the police station and pay a steep fine to get them back. There's free parking on the north side of the port.

By Moped   Roads on the island are notoriously treacherous, narrow, and winding, with shoulders that give way easily on steep slopes. There are a number of serious accidents and several fatalities every year, and for this reason we recommend that you avoid renting a moped or motorcycle on Santorini unless you consider yourself to be

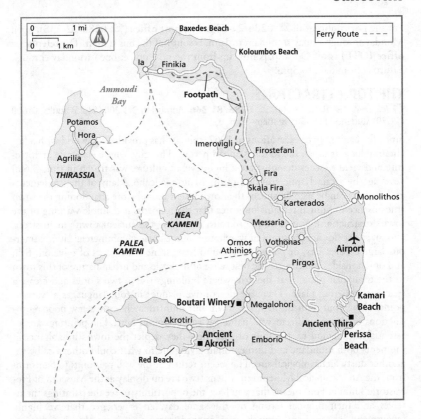

an experienced and cautious rider. Needless to say, there are numerous agencies renting bikes (assuming that you can show a valid motorcycle license); expect to pay Dr3,000 to Dr6,000 ($9 to $17) per day.

By Taxi The **taxi stand** (☎ 0286/22-555) is just south of the main square, though in high season you should book ahead by phone. Prices are (for the most part) standard from point to point. If you call for a taxi outside Fira, you'll be charged a pickup fee of at least Dr500 ($1.45). The maximum fare you should have to pay (from Ia to Akrotiri, for example) is Dr5,000 ($14), not including additional charges for luggage, pickup, or late-night travel.

FAST FACTS The **American Express** agent is X-Ray Kilo Travel Service (☎ 0286/22-624; fax 0286/23-600), at the head of the steps to the old port facing the caldera, above Franco's Bar; open daily from 8:30am to 9pm. The **National Bank** (open Monday through Friday from 8am to 2pm), with an ATM, is a block south from the main square on the right near the taxi station. The **health clinic** (☎ 0286/23-123) is on the southeast edge of town on Odos Ayiou Athanassiou, immediately below the bus station and the new archaeological museum.

For **Internet access,** try P.C. Club, on the main square in Fira, in the office of Markozannes Tours (☎ 0286/24-600). **Penguin Laundry** (☎ 0286/22-168) is at the edge of Fira on the road to Ia, 200 meters north of the main square. The **police** (☎ 0286/22-649) are several blocks south of the main square, near the post office.

For the **port police,** call ☎ **0286/22-239.** The **post office** (☎ **0286/22-238**), open Monday through Friday from 8am to 1pm, is south of the bus station. The **telephone office (OTE)** is off Odos Ipapantis, up from the post office; open Monday through Saturday from 8am to 3pm.

THE TOP ATTRACTIONS

✪ **Ancient Akrotiri.** Akrotiri. ☎ **0286/81-366.** Admission Dr1,200 ($3.45) adults, Dr600 ($1.70) students. Tues–Sun 8:30am–3pm.

Since the beginning of excavations in 1967, this site has provided the world with a fascinating look at urban life in the Minoan period. This city, whose elaborate architecture and vivid frescoes demonstrate a high level of culture, was frozen in time 3,600 years ago by a cataclysmic eruption of the island's volcano. Many of the implements and artifacts can be seen on site, as their owners left them before abandoning the town (the absence of human remains indicates that the residents had ample warning of the town's destruction). You enter the Akrotiri site along the ancient town's main street, and on either side are the stores or warehouses of the ancient commercial city: Numerous large earthen jars, or *pithoi,* were found here, some with traces of olive oil, fish, and onion inside. You can get the best sense of the scale and urban nature of this town in the triangular plaza, near the exit, where buildings rise to two stories and create a spacious gathering place. There are descriptive plaques in four languages at various points along your path through the town, but unfortunately only a few poor reproductions of the magnificent wall paintings can be found here. The paintings are an essential companion to any tour of this site—they depict the town's inhabitants in moments both mundane and immemorial, giving life to what could otherwise be yet another dusty archaeological site. The recent return of the wall paintings to Santorini from the Archaeological Museum in Athens (two are on display at the Museum of Pre-Historic Thira in Fira) means that you have the opportunity to see the paintings themselves and their original setting on the same day, an experience that we highly recommend. The roof enclosing the excavations is currently being replaced, with minimal disruption of visits to the site—the route through the site may, however, be different than that described above.

✪ **Ancient Thira.** Kamari. ☎ **0286/31-366.** Admission Dr1,200 ($3.45) adults, Dr600 ($1.75) students. Daily 8am–2:30pm. On a hilltop 3km (1.8 miles) south of Kamari by road.

The two popular beaches of Kamari and Perissa are separated by a high rocky headland called Mesa Vouna, on which stand the ruins of Ancient Thira. It's an incredible site, with cliffs dropping precipitously to the sea on three sides and dramatic views of Santorini and neighboring islands. The hilltop was first inhabited by the Dorians in the 9th century B.C., though most buildings date from the Hellenistic era when the site was occupied by Ptolemaic forces; there are also Roman and Byzantine remains. One main street runs the length of the site, passing first through two agoras. The arc of the theater embraces the town of Kamari, Fira beyond, and the open Aegean. It's an extensive group of ruins, and like all ruins it requires some imagination to bring it to life—in fact, a good tour guide wouldn't hurt. Tours leave from Kamari every

Insider Tip

Akrotiri is enclosed by a large metal shed that magnifies the afternoon heat. This, combined with the growing crowds, is a good argument for arriving as early in the day as possible.

hour in high season and cost Dr2,000 ($6) per person; contact **Kamari Tours** (☎ **0286/31-390**) for information. You can reach the site by taxi or, even better, on foot—passing on the way a cave that holds the only spring on the island (see "Walking" under "Outdoor Pursuits," below).

Boutari Winery. Megalohori. ☎ **0286/81-011.** Admission Dr1,500 ($4.30). Daily 9am–sunset. Located 1½ km (0.9 mile) south of Akrotiri village. Just outside Megalohori, on the main road to Perissa.

Boutari is the island's largest winery, and Greece's best known wine export. The admission cost includes a tasting of six wines, with *mezedes* or light snacks. There are three grape varieties grown on Santorini: Asirtiko, Aidani, and Athiri. From these are made the three whites for which the island is known: Nichteri, with its high alcohol content; Kalliste, a wine aged in smoked oak barrels; and Vin Santo, a sweet dessert wine traditionally used for communion in the local churches. Rounding out the tasting are reds and whites from Northern Greece.

Museum of Pre-Historic Thira. Fira. ☎ **0286/23-217.** Free admission. Tues–Sun 8:30am–3pm. Across the street from the bus stop in Fira; the entrance is behind the Orthodox Cathedral.

The most exciting holding of this new museum is the collection of wall paintings from Ancient Akrotiri, which were recently returned to Santorini from their previous home at the National Archaeological Museum in Athens. Two of these are currently on display, along with many finds from Akrotiri and objects imported from Crete and the Northeastern Aegean Islands. Also exceptional are the many items of pottery—cups, jugs and *pithoi*—which are delicately painted with motifs familiar from the wall paintings. We highly recommend visiting both the museum and the archaeological site at Ancient Akrotiri—in the same day, if possible. The large structure housing this collection was built in 1998 and opened to the public in 2000—at the moment the museum occupies only a small part of its building, and expansions are anticipated in the near future.

Thira Foundation: The Wall Paintings of Thira. Petros Nomikos Conference Center, Fira. ☎ **0286/23016.** Admission Dr1,000 ($2.90) adults, Dr500 ($1.45) students, free for youths under 18. Recorded tour Dr1,000 ($2.90). On the caldera, 5 minutes past the cable car on the way to Firostephani.

This exhibition presents copies of the wall paintings from ancient Akrotiri, created using a sophisticated technique of three-dimensional photographic reproduction that closely approximates the originals. Housed in a former wine storage cave, the exhibit presents some of the paintings in basic simulations of their original architectural context. The terrace in front of the foundation offers an astonishing view toward Fira and Imerovigli. For the moment, until the archaeological museum in Fira is expanded, this remains the only way to view all the extraordinary wall paintings of Akrotiri in a form approximating their original physical presence.

EXPLORING THE ISLAND
FIRA

Fira, the island's capital, is also its busiest and most commercial town. The abundance of **jewelry stores** on these streets is matched in the Cyclades only by Mykonos, as are the crowds in July and August. The town has a spectacular location on the rim of the caldera, a fact you can quickly verify by walking uphill from the main square. Odos M. Nomikou follows the edge of the caldera, and the evening **volta (stroll)** along this street is one of the most exquisite in the Cyclades—the chanted tones of evening prayer resound from the Orthodox Cathedral, and the streets are corridors of light and sound within the silent expanse of the dark sea. The town supports a wild bar scene that continues throughout the night, banishing all thought or hope of sleep in high season.

At the north end of Odos Ipapantis (also known as "Gold Street" for its abundance of jewelry stores), you'll find the **cable-car station.** The Austrian-built system, the gift of wealthy shipowner Evangelos Nomikos, can take you down to the port of Skala in 2 minutes. The cable car makes the trip every 15 minutes from 7:30am to 9pm for Dr1,000 ($2.90), and it's worth every drachma, especially on the way up.

Up and to the right from the cable-car station is a small **Archaeological Museum** (☎ 0286/22-217), which has some early Cycladic figurines, vases from Ancient Thira, some interesting Dionysiac figures, and finds from Ancient Thira. It's open Tuesday through Sunday from 8:30am to 3pm. Admission is Dr800 ($2.30) for adults, Dr600 ($1.75) for seniors, and Dr400 ($1.15) for students.

Ia

Ia is the most beautiful and pleasantly unconventional village on the island, if not in the whole Cyclades. It was severely damaged by the 1956 earthquake, and there aren't many buildings remaining from before that time. A few notable exceptions are the fine **19th-century mansions** at the top of the town near the castle—examples of restored neoclassical houses from this period include the **Restaurant-Bar 1800** and the **Naval Museum.** Much of the reconstruction continues the ancient Santorini tradition of dwellings excavated from the cliff face, and the island's most beautiful cliff dwellings can be found here. There are basically only two streets, one with traffic and the much more pleasant inland pedestrian lane, Odos Nikolaos Nomikou (the other end of the Nomikos street that began in Fira), paved with marble and lined with an increasing number of jewelry shops (as if there weren't enough in Fira), tavernas, and bars.

The battlements of the ruined **Lontza Castle** at the western end of town is the best place to catch the famous Ia sunset. Below the castle, a long flight of steps leads down to the pebble beach at **Ammoudi,** which is okay for swimming and sunning. To the west is the more spacious and sandy **Koloumbos Beach.** To the southeast below Ia is the fishing port of **Armeni,** where ferries sometimes dock and you can catch an excursion boat around the caldera.

The **Naval Museum** (☎ 0286/71-156) is a great introduction to this town, where, until the advent of tourism, most young people found themselves working at sea. The museum is housed in a restored neoclassical mansion; almost completely destroyed during the 1956 earthquake, the house was meticulously rebuilt using photographs of the original structure. The extensive collection includes ship models, figureheads, naval equipment, and some fascinating old photographs. The official hours are Wednesday through Monday from 12:30 to 4pm and 5 to 8:30pm, although these seem to vary considerably; admission is Dr800 ($2.30).

One thing English-speaking foreigners can do in Ia more easily than just about anywhere else in Greece is **get married.** Markos Karvounis, of **Karvounis Tours** (☎ 0286/71-290 or 0286/71-292; fax 0286/71-291; e-mail: mkarvounis@otenet.gr), has proven himself as good at arranging weddings (not marriages) as he is at making travel arrangements. If you're thinking of getting married in Ia, contact him as far in advance as possible and he'll take care of the live music, homemade food, photographs, donkeys, everything. You can call during office hours, from 10am to 2:30pm and 7 to 10pm, April through October.

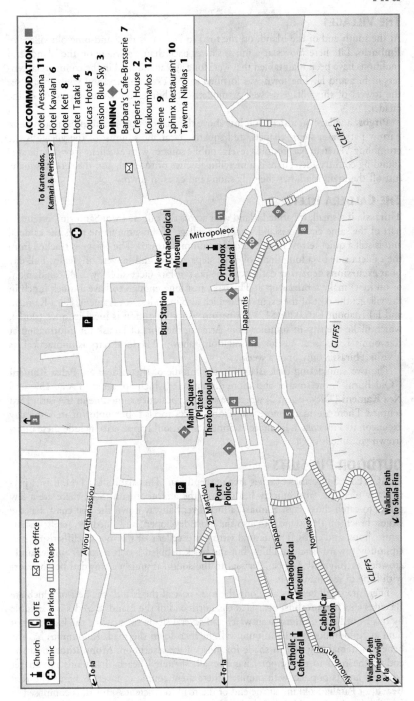

ACCOMMODATIONS
Hotel Aressana 11
Hotel Kavalari 6
Hotel Keti 8
Hotel Tataki 4
Loucas Hotel 5
Pension Blue Sky 3

DINING ◆
Barbara's Cafe-Brasserie 7
Crêperis House 2
Koukoumavlos 12
Selene 9
Sphinx Restaurant 10
Taverna Nikolas 1

To Karterados,
Kamari & Perissa →

† Church
✚ Clinic
📞 OTE
☒ Post Office
▥ Steps
P Parking

Ayiou Athanassiou

New
Archaeological
Museum

Mitropoleos

Bus Station

Orthodox
Cathedral

Main Square
(Plateia
Theotokopoulou)

Ipapantis

25 Martiou

Port
Police

Ipapantis

Archaeological
Museum

Nomikos

Catholic
Cathedral

Cable-Car
Station

Ayiou Ioannou

To Ia

To Ia

CLIFFS

CLIFFS

CLIFFS

Walking Path
← to Skala Fira

Walking Path
to Imerovigli
& Ia

THE VILLAGES

At the south end of the island, on the road to Perissa, is the handsome old village of **Emborio.** Life here moves at a much slower pace than elsewhere on the island, and traditions have been maintained that were long ago abandoned in the commercial centers of Fira and Ia. The town was fortified in the 17th century, and you can still see the towers of this village as well as modern-day homes built into the ruins of the citadel.

Pirgos, a village on a steep hill just above the island's port at Athinios, is a maze of narrow pathways, steps, chapels, and squares. Near the summit of the village is the crumbling Venetian Kastro, plus several public squares with excellent views of the surrounding countryside. There is a merciful absence of tourism, and the central square, just off the main road, has the only shops and cafes in town.

THE CALDERA ISLETS

Thirassia is a small, inhabited island west across the caldera from Santorini, originally part of the same circular island. A clifftop village of the same name faces the caldera, and is still a quiet retreat from Santorini's summer crowds. The village is reached from the caldera side by a long flight of steep steps, as Fira and Ia were originally. Full-day **boat excursions** departing daily from the port of Fira (accessible by cable car, donkey, or on foot) make a brief stop at Thirassia, just long enough to have a quick lunch in the village; the cost of the excursion (which also includes Nea Kameni, Palea Kameni, and Ia) is about Dr6,000 ($17) per person. Another option is **local caïques** (skiffs), which make the trip in summer from Armeni, the port of Ia; ask for information at Karvounis Tours (see "Visitor Information," above). The local ferry is impractical, as it visits Thirassia only once a week.

The two smoldering dark islands in the middle of the caldera are **Palea Kameni** ("Old Burnt"), the smaller and more distant one, which appeared in A.D. 157; and **Nea Kameni** ("New Burnt"), which began its appearance sometime in the early 18th century. There are many more interesting places to visit, but unfortunately the day excursion to Thirassia (a far more exciting destination) happens to include these litter-strewn volcanic isles.

OUTDOOR PURSUITS

BEACHES   Santorini's beaches aren't exceptional. The island's black sand isn't particularly plentiful, and quickly heats up in the afternoon sun. Still, there are a few places to catch those rays. **Kamari,** a little over halfway down the east coast, has the largest beach on the island. It's also the most developed, and lined by hotels, restaurants, shops, and clubs. The natural setting is excellent, at the foot of cliffs rising precipitously toward Ancient Thira, but the black pebbled beach becomes unpleasantly crowded in July and August. **Perissa,** to the south, is another crowded beach resort with little to recommend it.

There are small beaches all along the east coast of the island, the best of which are **Baxedes** and **Koloumbos,** near Ia at the north end of the island. Baxedes is accessible by bus from Ia, and offers clean water and several shade trees, while the kilometer of sand at Koloumbos is a 15-minute walk further down the road. Koloumbos has the benefit of remaining half in shade for most of the afternoon. **Monolithos,** near the end of the road to the airport, has a small, sheltered beach that tends not to get crowded and is popular with families; there are a couple of tavernas here. The **Red Beach,** or Paralia Kokkini, at the end of the road to Ancient Akrotiri, is composed of small red volcanic pebbles. There's a fine taverna just down from the parking for Ancient Akrotiri: **Melina's** (☎ **0286/82-764**), open from 9am to 11pm.

BICYCLING   Although Santorini's roads are in fairly good condition, it's the drivers you should be worried about. Unfortunately, not all visitors exercise appropriate caution in negotiating the island's roads, which present a potentially dangerous combination of tight curves and precipitous dropoffs. Off-road cycling is more appealing: **Lava Trails** (☎ **0286/31-165**) in Kamari runs guided mountain-bike tours of the island, with stops at sites of geologic and archaeological interest. The cost is Dr7,000 ($20) per person for the 6-hour, 10½-kilometer (6.6-mile) guided tour, including bike and helmet rental. High-quality suspension mountain bikes with toe clips, helmet, pump, and repair kit can be rented for Dr2,500 ($7) per day. Mountain bikes can also be rented at **Moto Chris** (☎ **0286/23-431**) in Fira for Dr2,000 ($6) a day, or at **Moto Piazza** (☎ **0286/71-055**) on the main road in Ia for the same price, but at both places the bikes are in sorry shape and receive almost no maintenance.

WALKING   The path from **Fira to Ia** follows the edge of the caldera, passing several churches and climbing two substantial hills along the way. Beginning from Fira, follow the pedestrian path on the caldera rim, climbing past the Catholic Cathedral to the villages of Firostephani and Imerovigli. In Imerovigli, there are signs on the path pointing the way to Ia—you'll be okay so long as you continue north, eventually reaching a dirt path along the caldera rim which parallels the vehicular road. The trail leaves the vicinity of the road with each of the next two ascents, returning to the road in the valleys. The descent into Ia eventually leads you to the main pedestrian street in town. The distance is 10 kilometers (6.2 miles); allow yourself at least 2 hours. This walk is especially beautiful around sunset.

In **Imerovigli,** there's a rocky promontory jutting into the sea, known locally as **Skaros.** From medieval times until the early 1800s, this was the site of an elaborate building complex which housed all the administrative offices of the island. There is nothing to be seen of the Skaros castle now, and it is thought that all was destroyed by a 19th-century earthquake. Skaros now offers a fantastic view of the caldera and a tranquil haven from the crowds and bustle of the adjacent towns. The trail begins from the terrace of a church just below the Blue Note Taverna in Imerovigli; from here it descends steeply to the isthmus connecting Skaros with the mainland. The path wraps around the promontory, reaching after a mile a small chapel with a unique panoramic view of the caldera. On the way, note the cliffs of glassy black volcanic rock, beautifully reflective in the brilliant sun—this is one of the materials with which so many of the older buildings on Santorini were built and decorated.

The trail from Kamari to the site of **Ancient Thira** is steep but worth the trouble, since it passes on the way the beautiful site of Santorini's only freshwater spring. To reach the trail from Kamari, follow the automobile road to Ancient Thira past the Kamari Beach parking, turning right into the driveway of a new hotel opposite the Hotel Annetta, just to the right of a minimarket. The trail begins just behind the hotel. Climbing quickly by means of sharp switchbacks, the trail soon reaches a small chapel with a terrace and olive trees at the mouth of a cave. You can walk back into the cave, which echoes with the purling water, a surprising and miraculous sound in this arid place. Continuing up, the trail rejoins the car road after a few more switchbacks, about 300 meters from Ancient Thira. The full ascent from Kamari takes about an hour.

SHOPPING

If you're interested in fine **jewelry,** the prices in Fira are just a little higher than they are in Athens, but the selection is fantastic. **Porphyra** (☎ **0286/22-981**), in the Fabrica Shopping Center near the cathedral, has some impressive work. Santorini's best known jeweler is probably **Kostas Antoniou** (☎ **0286/22-633**), on Odos Ayiou Ioannou north of the cable-car station. And there are plenty of shops between the two. Generally the further north you go, the higher the prices and the less certain the quality.

In Firostephani, **Cava Sigalas Argiris** (☎ **0286/22-802**) stocks all the local wines, including their own. Also for sale are locally grown and prepared foods, often served as *mezedes* (hors d'oeuvres or snacks): *fava,* a spread made with chickpeas; *tomatahia,* small pickled tomatoes; and *kapari,* or capers. The store is open from 8am to midnight.

The main street in Ia, facing the caldera, has many interesting stores in addition to the inevitable souvenir shops. **Replica** (☎ **0286/71-916**) is a source for contemporary statuary and pottery as well as museum replicas; it will ship purchases to your home at post-office rates. Further south on the main street is **Nakis** (☎ **0286/ 71-813**), which specializes in amber jewelry and has a collection of insects in amber.

WHERE TO STAY

Santorini is packed in July and August; try to make a reservation with deposit at least 2 months in advance or be prepared to accept pot luck. Don't accept lodging offered at the port unless you're exhausted and don't care how meager the room and how remote the village you wake up in the next morning.

The barrel-vaulted **cave houses,** built for earthquake resistance and economy, may at first strike you as rather cramped, dark, and stuffy, but like most visitors, you'll probably soon find them another aspect of the island's special charm. The best of them are designed with enough cross-ventilation that they always have fresh air, and since they are carved into the cliff face, these rooms have the welcome quality of remaining relatively cool throughout the summer.

Many apartments and villas have efficiency kitchens, but for the most part these are extremely minimal facilities. You'll probably find yourself frustrated if you try to prepare anything more elaborate than a coffee.

FIRA

In addition to the choices below, you might consider **Pension Blue Sky** (☎ **0286/24-351** or 0286/25-121; fax 0286/25-120), a humble but comfortable place on the edge of town, or **Hotel Tataki** (☎ **0286/22-389;** fax 0286/23-311; e-mail: hoteltataki@san.forthnet.gr), a simple hotel offering clean rooms, a central location, and air-conditioning, fridges, and TVs. *Note:* Due to the noise in Fira, light sleepers may want to consider one of the more remote villages.

Hotel Aressana. Fira, 84700 Santorini. ☎ **0286/23-900.** Fax 0286/23-902. www. aressana.gr. E-mail: aressana@otenet.gr. 48 units (1 with shower only). A/C TEL. Dr49,000 ($141) double; suites from Dr60,000 ($173). Rates include full breakfast. AE, DC, MC, V. Closed mid-Nov to Feb.

This newer hotel has abundant amenities in compensation for its one deficiency, the lack of a caldera view—though it's only a block away, just beyond the Orthodox Cathedral. Rooms are large, attractively furnished, and comfortable, with small balconies or shared terraces; some have the high, barrel-vaulted ceilings typical of this island. The suites boast generous private balconies, a rare benefit in this town where space is so precious. The breakfast room opens onto the pool terrace, as do most of the bedrooms; the elaborate buffet breakfast includes numerous Santorinian specialties. The Aressana also maintains seven nearby apartments facing the caldera, starting at Dr33,000 ($95), which includes use of the hotel pool.

Hotel Kavalari. Odos Ipapantis, Fira, 84700 Santorini. ☎ **0286/222-347** or 0286/22-455. Fax 0286/22-603. 20 units. A/C TEL. Dr36,000 ($104) standard double; Dr42,000 ($121) deluxe double; Dr46,000 ($132) triple. Rates include continental breakfast. AE, MC, V. Closed Feb.

Already into its second decade, the Kavalari is one of the more venerable hotels in Fira, and incorporates buildings which are older still: Parts of the hotel occupy a captain's house, and the breakfast room is a high vaulted stone hall carved from the cliffside. Eleven of the rooms are traditional cliff dwellings, while the rest look and feel like generic hotel rooms. All units face the caldera, and all have a shared terrace accessed by outdoor stairs that descend steeply from Odos Ipapantis; a few also have private balconies. The deluxe doubles are somewhat larger and include kitchenettes; most of these are traditional cave dwellings. Bathrooms are very compact.

Hotel Keti. Fira, 84700 Santorini. ☎ **0286/22-324** or 0286/22-380. Fax 0286/25171. 7 units. TEL. Dr16,000 ($46) double; Dr21,000 ($60) triple. No breakfast offered. No credit cards. Closed mid-Oct to mid-Apr.

This tiny hotel is very plain, but does offer one of the best bargains on the caldera. All of the small but clean rooms have the traditional vaulted ceilings, and open onto shared terraces overlooking the caldera; bathrooms are at the back of the rooms, carved into the rock of the cliff face. The furnishings are plain, even a bit flimsy. This place offers an experience more "authentic" than that of the slick hotels that surround it: Laundry hangs on the terrace, and local children play on the stairs.

✪ **Loucas Hotel.** Fira, 84700 Santorini. ☎ **0286/22-480** or 0286/22-680. Fax 0286/24-882. 22 units. A/C TV TEL. Dr32,300 ($92) double; Dr40,800 ($117) triple. MC, V. Closed mid-Oct to mid-Apr.

This is one of the oldest and best hotels on the caldera. Its terraces cascade down the side of the cliff, connected by a giddily steep flight of steps—definitely not for the acrophobic. The impeccably maintained bedrooms have barrel-vaulted ceilings; many of the bathrooms are carved into the rock of the cliff wall. Although many of the terraces overlooking the caldera are shared between rooms, thoughtful design provides a surprising degree of privacy. The Renaissance Bar is situated on a broad terrace above the rooms, and the unexceptional Aris Restaurant immediately below.

FIROSTEPHANI

This quieter and less-expensive neighborhood is just a 10-minute walk from Fira. The views of the caldera are just as good, if not better.

Dana Villas. Firostephani, 84700 Santorini. ☎ **0286/24-641** or 0286/24-643. Fax 0286/22-985. 30 units. A/C TV TEL. Dr43,600 ($125) double; Dr46,600 ($133) apt; Dr54,600 ($157) suite; Dr76,600 ($221) VIP suite. AE, DC, MC, V. Closed mid-Oct to mid-Apr.

These meticulously maintained terrace villas cling to the cliff face, perched vertiginously over the sea. They stand out from most of the other caldera villas by virtue of their tasteful furnishings and thoughtful design: Each villa has a small terrace, and more than a few villas have private terraces. The suites have two bedrooms and can sleep four adults comfortably; VIP suites are somewhat larger and come with added amenities like a king bed and Jacuzzi bath. The pool is quite large by local standards, and there's a poolside bar. Villas 20 and 22 are the studios to reserve well in advance, while 21 is the best apartment.

IMEROVIGLI

The next village north along the caldera rim is so named because it is the first place on the island from which one can see the rising sun: The name translates to "day vigil." By virtue of its height, Imerovigli also has the best views on this part of the caldera.

Altana Traditional Houses. Imerovigli, 84700 Santorini. ☎ **0286/23-240.** Fax 0286/ 23-204. In winter, call Athens: ☎ **01/277-4374;** fax 01/275-4636. 10 units. TEL. Dr43,000–Dr48,000 ($124–$138) studio; Dr58,000 ($167) 1-bedroom; Dr68,000 ($196) 2-bedroom. AE, MC, V. Closed mid-Oct to mid-Apr.

These traditional cave houses are located high on the cliff in Imerovigli, and have great views across the roofs of town toward Fira and the caldera. Each apartment is unique, with furniture built into the walls of the cave. All have incredible views, although the terrace for each apartment is either shared or serves as the path to another apartment as well. Units are on three levels; the apartments on the top level have the most privacy and the best views. On the street level is a cozy, bright breakfast room that serves as a bar in the evening. Although these apartments have a simple elegance that's very appealing, they are somewhat overpriced and the bathrooms a bit cramped.

✪ **Astra Apartments.** P.O. Box 45, Imerovigli, 84700 Santorini. ☎ **0286/23-641.** Fax 0286/24-765. www.astra.gr. E-mail: astra-ae@otenet.gr. 18 units (shower only). A/C MINI-BAR TV TEL. Dr42,000 ($121) studio; Dr63,000–Dr72,000 ($181–$207) 1-bedroom apartment (double occupancy); Dr90,000 ($259) 2-bedroom apartment (triple occupancy). Rates include breakfast. AE, V. Closed mid-Nov to Easter.

This is one of the nicest places to stay in all of Greece. The 18 units of the Astra Apartments look like a tiny, whitewashed village (flanking an elegant small pool) in still-sleepy Imerovigli. Every detail here is perfect: The floors are paved with handsome flagstones, the windows hung with hand-embroidered curtains, the bath towels luxuriously thick. Best of all, although each unit has its own kitchenette, breakfast is served on your private terrace or balcony, and you can order delicious salads and sandwiches from the bar day and night. Manager George Karayiannis is always at the ready to arrange car rentals, recommend a wonderful beach or restaurant—or even help you plan your wedding and honeymoon here. Our only problem when we stayed here: We didn't want to budge from our terrace, especially at sunset, when the view over the offshore islands is dazzling.

KARTERADOS

About 2 kilometers (1.2 miles) southeast of Fira, this small village is proliferating with new hotels and rooms to let. Buses stop at the top of Karterados's main street on their way to Kamari, Perissa, and Akrotiri. Nevertheless, it's a somewhat inconvenient location, not especially close either to Fira or to the beach. Karterados beach is a 3-kilometer (2-mile) walk from the center of town, and the longer beach of Monolithos is accessible by continuing south along the water's edge an additional half mile.

Pension George. Karterados, 84700 Santorini. ☎ and fax **0286/22-351.** www. pensiongeorge.com. 20 units. Dr16,000 ($46) double; Dr22,000 ($63) triple. No credit cards. Closed mid-Oct to mid-Apr.

The pension is surrounded by new hotels, and the views aren't great—what is exceptional here is the generosity of George Halaris and his wife, Helen, who are both great sources of information on the island. If given advance notice, George will meet you at the port or airport. Ten guest rooms are located on the upper two stories of their house; most have a small balcony, and the two rooms at the north side have large private terraces with an abundance of plants. The other 10 rooms are in a new building adjacent to the house, facing the pool. These spacious units have high vaulted ceilings and private balconies. All accommodations are simply and comfortably furnished, all have small fridges, and several units are equipped with air-conditioning.

Ia

Ia is quieter and somewhat less crowded than Fira, but also less convenient as a base if you're getting around the island by bus.

Canaves Ia Traditional Houses. Ia, 84702 Santorini. ☎ **0286/71-453.** Fax 0286/71-195. E-mail: canaves@otenet.gr. 32 units. A/C TV TEL. Dr81,000 ($233) double; Dr100,000 ($288) 2-bedroom suite. MC, V. Closed Nov–Apr.

These houses are fashioned in traditional island style, with curvaceous white walls carved into the cliffside; the two-bedroom apartments are especially spacious. All apartments have views of the caldera, and some also offer private terraces. In each a small bedroom (with double bed) opens onto a living room with barrel-vaulted ceiling. Bathrooms are extremely compact. There are two complexes within 200 meters of each other, each with its own pool and bar; the newer of the two is somewhat more luxurious (and more expensive), with marble floors and counters. Private parking is available nearby. Other amenities include safe-deposit boxes, room service, and fully equipped kitchens (which even have small ovens).

✪ **Chelidonia.** Ia, 84702 Santorini. ☎ **0286/71-287.** Fax 0286/71-649. www.chelidonia. com. 10 units. Weekly rates: Dr245,000 ($705) studio; Dr315,000 ($907) 1-bedroom; Dr385,000 ($1109) 2-bedroom. Daily rates also available—call for information. No credit cards. Closed mid-Oct to mid-Apr.

Many thoughtful details add up to make these the most appealing traditional apartments in Santorini. Most units have truly private terraces, many with small gardens of flowering plants and herbs for cooking. The rooms are spacious, the bathrooms luxuriously large, and the interiors simple and highly elegant: Slabs of white marble combine with extensions of the walls to form tables and shelves. These are all cave dwellings, each with its own unique geometry, and some with skylights illuminating rooms from above. All units enjoy the famous Ia view across the caldera toward Imerovigli, Fira, and the southern end of the island. Although there is little luxury here, there is clearly a great understanding of what makes guests feel at home.

Hotel Finikia. Finikia (about 1½km/1 mile south of the bus stop in Ia on the main road), 84702 Santorini. ☎ **0286/71-373,** or 01/654-7944 in winter. Fax 0286/71-118. E-mail: finikia@otenet.gr. 15 units. Dr20,500 ($59) double; Dr24,000 ($69) 2-person apartment; Dr29,000 ($83) 3-person apartment. Rates include breakfast. MC, V. Closed Nov–Mar.

This small, appealing hotel offers tastefully furnished rooms, several with traditional domed ceilings. Most units have semiprivate balconies or terraces with views toward the sea—the hotel is on the east-sloping side of the island, so the view is gentle rather than spectacular. The apartments are built in a group adjacent to the hotel. Facilities include a large pool and a restaurant/bar that remains open all day. Irene and Theodoris Andreadis are your very helpful and friendly hosts.

Perivolas Traditional Settlement. Ia, 84702 Santorini. ☎ **0286/71-308.** Fax 0286/71-309. www.perivolas.gr. E-mail: perivolas@san.forthnet.gr. 17 units. A/C TEL. Dr108,000 ($311) studio; Dr126,000 ($363) 1-bedroom suite. Rates include buffet breakfast. No credit cards. Closed mid-Oct to mid-Apr.

The interiors of these traditional cave dwellings are highly refined, with wall niches, skylights, and stonework providing a personal touch. Some of the suites are quite spacious, with a separate bedroom and sunken living room; the layout of each apartment is unique. All units have kitchenettes. A bar opens onto a terrace and incredible pool—the edge of which disappears into the bay, its horizon merging with that of the sea below. The only downside here is that just a couple of the units have terraces with a significant degree of privacy.

Youth Hostel Ia. Ia (near the bus stop), 84702 Santorini. ☎ and fax **0286/71-465**. 7 units (4-, 6- and 10-person dormitories). Dr3,500 ($10) per person. Rates include continental breakfast. No credit cards. Closed Nov–Apr.

This exceptional facility occupies the grounds of a former convent, although the only older building remaining is a beautiful long room (now divided into two women's dorms) with a high vaulted ceiling. Most of the buildings surrounding the hostel's bright courtyard were built 10 years ago; the dorms are large and well ventilated, and the bathrooms reliably clean. Breakfast is served on a large terrace with fine sea views, or in the hostel cafe, where light meals are available throughout the day. Laundry service is available.

MEGALOHORI

Vedema Hotel. Megalohori, 84700 Santorini. ☎ **0286/81-796** or 0286/81-797. In the U.S. and Canada 800/525-4800; in Australia 008-251-958; in Great Britain 0800-964-470. Fax 0286/81-798. 42 units. A/C MINIBAR TV TEL. Dr75,000–Dr95,000 ($216–$273) 1-bedroom apt; Dr106,000–Dr135,000 ($305–$389) 2-bedroom apt; Dr170,000 ($488) 3-bedroom apt. Minimum 3-night stay. AE, DC, EC, MC, V. Closed mid-Oct to mid-Apr.

The sleepy village of Megalohori is not where you'd expect to find a luxury hotel, but Santorini is full of surprises. The hotel is a self-contained world, surrounded by a wall like a fortified town. A member of "Small Luxury Hotels of the World," the Vedema is justly proud of its attentive but unobtrusive service. The residences are set around several irregular courtyards, much like those found in the village. Each apartment is unique, comfortable, and tastefully furnished, with marble bathroom, central heat, refrigerator, and bar. Amenities include a pool, the medieval chic **Vedema restaurant**, the charming **Canava Bar** in a 300-year-old wine cellar, laundry service, and an interesting gallery. The principal disadvantage of a stay here is the location: Megalohori is not a particularly convenient base for exploring the island.

KAMARI

Most of the hotels at Santorini's best and best-known beach resort are booked by tour groups in summer. In addition to the following choices, you might also try the 27-unit **Matina Hotel** (☎ **0286/31-491;** fax 0286/31-860), which has no views to speak of but is just a 2-minute walk from the beach; a double goes for Dr28,000 ($80). If you can't find a room, try the local office of **Kamari Tours** (☎ **0286/31-390** or 0286/31-455), which manages many of the hotels in Kamari and may be able to find you a vacancy.

Kamari Beach Hotel. Kamari, 84700 Santorini. ☎ **0286/31-216** or 0286/31-243, or 01/482-8826 in Athens. Fax 0286/32-120. 103 units. Dr40,000 ($115) double. Rates include breakfast. AE, DC, MC, V. Closed mid-Oct to mid-Apr.

This rather generic hotel has the best beachfront location, close to the small village of Kamari—if you plan to spend most of your time on the beach or by the pool, this may be the place for you. All of its spacious balconied rooms take advantage of the view over the Aegean and the large pool below. It looks like a resort, and it's run like one, too.

Rooms Hesperides. Kamari, 84700 Santorini. ☎ **0286/31-670**. Fax 0286/31-423. 20 units. TEL. Dr17,000 ($49) double. Rates include continental breakfast. AE, MC, V. Closed mid-Oct to mid-Apr. Located 50m from the beach, near the Kamari bus stop.

This neat, modern pension in the middle of the pistachio orchard (complete with excavated Byzantine ruins) is owned by Akis Giannakulias, a former ship's captain who also runs the Akis Hotel across the street; go to the Akis reception to book a room. Each of the simple guest rooms has a balcony with a view of the sea or of Mount

Profitis Elias. If you prefer a slightly larger room with fridge and air-conditioning, try the Akis, located across the street: The 20 rooms in this older building are clean, comfortable, and reasonable at Dr20,000 ($57) for a double. Breakfast for guests at both hotels is served at the Akis on a sunny terrace.

Venus and Aphroditi Hotels. Kamari, 84700 Santorini. ☎ **0286/31-183.** 124 units (60 with shower only). A/C TV TEL. Venus: Dr37,000 ($106) double; Dr48,600 ($140) triple. Aphroditi: Dr45,200 ($130) double; Dr58,200 ($168) suite. Rates include breakfast. DC, MC V. Closed mid-Oct to mid-Apr.

These two beach hotels recently merged, and now share the two pools found in the courtyard of the Aphroditi. The Venus rooms are plain and bright, while the Aphroditi rooms are somewhat more plush, with marble surfaces and a pastel color scheme. Bathrooms at the Aphroditi are slightly larger than those at the Venus, and all the Aphroditi bathrooms have shower and tub (Venus bathrooms have shower only). Breakfast at the Aphroditi is a buffet in the poolside restaurant, while the Venus offers a simple continental breakfast in a room facing the beach. In our opinion, the Venus is a better value, since the rates are considerably lower than those of the Aphrodite, and the Venus rooms are the only ones in the complex with a view of the beach.

WHERE TO DINE
FIRA

The closer you are to the cable car in Fira, the steeper the tabs at restaurants (someone has to pay the outrageous rents) and the smaller the incentive for quality (those tourists will never be back). The better restaurants on Odos Ipapantis are near the cathedral. *Note:* Some restaurants near the cable car have been known to present menus without prices, and then charge exorbitantly for food and wine. Refuse to order from any menu that doesn't have prices clearly displayed.

If all you want is breakfast or a light, cheap meal, try **Crêperis House,** Theotokopoulou Square (no phone), or **Barbara's Cafe-Brasserie,** in the Fabrica Shopping Center up from the bus station toward the cathedral (no phone). After 7pm, Barbara's becomes one of the least expensive bars in town.

✪ **Koukoumavlos.** Below the Hotel Atlantis, facing the caldera. ☎ **0286/23-807.** Reservations recommended for dinner. Main courses Dr4,000–Dr6,500 ($11–$19). AE, MC, V. Daily noon–3pm and 7:30pm–12:30am. GREEK.

The terrace at Koukoumavlos enjoys the famous caldera view, but unlike most caldera restaurants where a spectacular view has to compensate for mediocre food, here the view is a distraction from the delights of the kitchen. Most of the dishes offer creative variations on traditional Greek food, like the fava, which is served hot in olive oil with grilled zucchini, onions, tomato, olives, and toasted almonds. Many ingredients from Santorini and neighboring islands are used: Santorini wine, vinegar, and honey; pecorino cheese of Siros; Mykonian cheeses like *kopanisti* and *ladotiri*. Particularly good is the monkfish with grilled vegetables, sun-dried tomatoes, black olives, thyme, and feta. For dessert, try the yogurt pannacotta with pistachios, thyme honey, and sour cherry.

Selene. Just past the Hotel Aressana, facing the caldera. ☎ **0286/22-249.** Reservations recommended for dinner. Main courses Dr4,800–Dr6,100 ($14–$18). AE, MC, V. Daily noon–3pm and 7pm–midnight. GREEK.

This is one of the better restaurants on the island, and definitely merits a visit. Some establishments possess such a remarkable combination of outstanding qualities that it's difficult to assess any attribute individually. Take the setting: a coveted position along the caldera rim, on a terrace that wraps the hillside, with the heartbreaking beauty of island and bay. Or the dining room, with a lofty vaulted stone ceiling and massive walls—an unusually elegant space in this town. And the service? Excellent. As for the food, it's ultimately up to you to decide whether it lives up to expectations. Locally grown capers add a welcome pungency to several dishes, such as pork baked with fava and capers, or monkfish on caper leaves.

Sphinx Restaurant. Odos Mitropoleos, near the Atlantis Hotel. ☎ **0286/23-823.** Reservations recommended. Main courses Dr3,500–Dr8,500 ($10–$24). AE, DC, MC, V. Daily 11am–3pm and 7pm–1am. INTERNATIONAL.

This restored old mansion has been decorated with antiques, sculpture, and ceramics by local artists; there's also a large outdoor terrace with views of the caldera and the port at Skala Fira. The menu—a combination of continental dishes, taverna standards, and pasta—is overly eclectic and unremarkable, but the ingredients are reliably fresh and most dishes are well prepared.

Taverna Nikolas. Just up from the main square in Fira. No phone. Main courses Dr1,200–Dr3,000 ($3.45–$9). No credit cards. Daily noon–midnight. GREEK.

There are no menus in this taverna: The night's offerings are proclaimed (in Greek) on a blackboard over the kitchen, and the waiters gladly translate into the four or five languages they have at their disposal. This is one of the few restaurants in Fira where locals queue up alongside throngs of travelers for a table. There aren't any surprises here, just traditional Greek dishes prepared very well. There are some unfortunate concessions to economy—the baklava seems to be made with a sugar syrup rather than honey—but overall the food is hearty and delicious, well worth every drachma. The dining room is always busy, so arrive early or plan to wait.

Ia

The best place to eat in Ia is the port of **Ammoudi,** hundreds of feet below the village, huddled between the cliffs and the sea. Two of the five fish tavernas in Ammoudi are excellent. **Katina's** (☎ **0286/71-280**) is the first restaurant you reach when approaching from the automobile road, and ✪ **Sunset** (☎ **0286/71-614**), also known as Margarita's, is the third. Both have perfected the art of cooking fish on the charcoal grill, and at both restaurants the view is exceptional. Both are open from 10am to midnight, prices at both are Dr1,700 to Dr6,500 ($4.90 to $19) for a main course, and neither accepts credit cards. To get here, follow the stepped path down from the vicinity of Lontza Castle, hire a donkey (Dr1,200/$3.45 one-way), or call a taxi. We recommend the walk down (to build an appetite) and a taxi or donkey up.

Neptune Restaurant. Odos Nikolaos Nomikos. ☎ **0286/71-294.** Main courses Dr1,500–Dr4,500 ($4.30–$13). MC, V. Daily 6pm–midnight. GREEK.

One of the oldest restaurants in Ia, this very good choice is on the pedestrian lane near the church square. The rooftop garden has a partial view of the extraordinary Ia sunset. All the typical Greek dishes are well prepared, and the vegetable specials are made with the season's best produce.

Restaurant-Bar 1800. Odos Nikolaos Nomikos. ☎ **0286/71-485.** Main courses Dr5,000–Dr9,000 ($14–$26). AE, DC, EC, MC, V. Daily 6pm–midnight. CONTINENTAL.

For many years recognized as the best place in Ia for a formal dinner, the 1800 has a devoted following among visitors and locals. The restaurant, housed in a splendidly restored neoclassical captain's mansion, has an undeniable charm and an intimate dining room. This place creates an enticing atmosphere reminiscent of Ia's past grandeur, an accomplishment that compensates in part for the somewhat disappointing productions of the kitchen.

Skala. Odos Nikolaos Nomikos. ☎ **0286/71-362.** Main courses Dr1,800–Dr4,000 ($5.15–$11). Daily 1pm–midnight. MC. GREEK.

Skala represents, along with Neptune, the best of taverna food in Ia. All the staples of traditional Greek food are reliably good, and the management is helpful and friendly. The roasted meats are good here, as are the vegetable appetizers.

KAMARI

Camille Stephani. North end of Kamari Beach, 500m from the bus stop. ☎ **0286/31-716.** Reservations recommended July–Sept. Main courses Dr2,500–Dr6,000 ($7–$19). AE, DC, MC, V. Daily noon–midnight (Fri–Sun in winter). Open year-round. GREEK/ INTERNATIONAL.

Even if you're not staying at Kamari, it's worth a trip to this excellent, more formal restaurant. An old standard, the restaurant's kitchen continues to produce memorable fare (the house specialty is a tender beef fillet with green pepper in Madeira sauce). The outside tables face the water, and a moonlight stroll along the beach is the perfect end to a fine meal.

SANTORINI AFTER DARK

Fira has nightlife aplenty and in some variety. We suggest starting the evening with a drink on the caldera, taking in the spectacular sunset. **Franco's** (☎ **0286/22-881**) is still the most famous and best place for this magic hour, but be prepared to pay about Dr3,000 ($9) per drink. For more reasonable prices, a bit more seclusion, and the same fantastic view, continue through the Canava Cafe and below the Loucas Hotel to the **Renaissance Bar** (☎ **0286/22-880**). Underneath the square, the **Kirathira Bar** plays jazz at a level that permits conversation. Cross the main street and wander around the shopping area to find a number of smaller bars that come alive after 9pm. The **Town Club** appeals to clean-cut rockers, while the **Two Brothers** pulls in the biggest, chummiest, and most casual crowd on the island. A bit further north, the outdoor **Tropical Bar** attracts a louder, rowdier gang. For bouzouki, find **Bar 33.** Discos come and go, and you only need to follow your ears to find them. The **Koo Club** is the biggest, while the **Enigma** is still popular with those interested in good music. **Tithora** is popular with a young, heavy-drinking crowd. There's usually no cover, but drinks start at Dr2,500 ($7).

In Ia, **Zorba's** is a good cliffside pub. **1800** is a more sophisticated bar, without the view.

Kamari has its share of bars. The **Yellow Donkey Disco** (☎ **0286/31-462**) is popular with younger partyers, and the more sophisticated usually seek the chic **Valentino's,** near the bus stop.

Those visiting in August and September may be able to catch a performance of classical music at the 2-week **Santorini International Music Festival** (☎ **0286/23-166**), when international singers and musicians perform at the Nomikos Centre in Fira. Admission to most events is Dr5,000 ($14).

2 Folegandros

181km (98 nautical miles) SE of Piraeus

Most travelers who know of Folegandros have seen it only when passing its forbidding northern coast, where precipitous cliffs rise to a height of 250 meters. So far, relatively few have ventured up to experience the spare beauty of its capital, **Hora.** In this town huddled at cliff's edge, one square spills into the next, with green and blue paving slates outlined in brilliant white. On a steep slope overlooking the town is the looming form of **Panayia,** the church whose icon of the Virgin is paraded through Hora's streets with great ceremony and revelry each Easter Sunday.

The rugged northern slopes of Folegandros offer a contrast to the austere civility of Hora's streets and squares. Here the hills are ribboned with the terraced fields that allow local farmers to grow barley on the island's steep slopes. Rocky coves shelter pristine cobble beaches, and many trails weave their way through the hills, some of them ancient paths paved with marble or carved from the bedrock. If you want to explore Folegandros, you'll have to walk—there's simply no other way to see the many beautiful sites outside Hora.

ESSENTIALS

GETTING THERE **By Boat** Three ferries a week stop at Folegandros on the Santorini-Folegandros-Sikinos-Ios-Naxos-Paros-Piraeus route; travel times are about 2 to 3 hours to Naxos, 4 hours to Paros (or 1 hour by hydrofoil), and 10 hours to Piraeus. Two ferries per week stop on the Folegandros-Milos-Sifnos-Paros-Mykonos-Tinos-Siros hydrofoil run; it's 2 hours to Sifnos, 3 to 5 hours to Mykonos, 5 to 6 hours to Tinos, and 6 hours to Siros. Off-season, infrequent service and bad weather could easily keep you here longer than you'd intended. There is no local port authority; for ferry information, call **Maraki Travel Agency** (☎ 0286/41-273).

VISITOR INFORMATION The **Maraki Travel Agency** (☎ 0286/41-273), just around the southwest corner of the bus-stop square in Hora, exchanges money, helps with travel arrangements, and sells maps of the island. There's also a branch of Maraki Travel at the port (☎ 0286/41-198), where you can buy ferry tickets. **Diaplous** (☎ 0286/41-158; fax 0286/41-159; e-mail: diaplous@x-treme.gr), opposite Polikandia Hotel off the bus-stop square in Hora, offers tickets for excursion boats, hotel reservations, money exchange, and luggage storage. **Sottovento Travel** (☎ 0286/41-444; fax 0286/41-430) also serves as the local Italian consulate; it's located at the stop for the Angali and Ano Meria bus, at the opposite side of Hora from the bus stop to the port. Here you can book beach trips by caïque, arrange boat tours, book accommodations, and store luggage.

GETTING AROUND **By Bus** The bus to Hora meets all ferries in peak season, and most ferries during the rest of the year; it also makes eight or nine trips a day along the road which runs along the spine of the island between Hora and Ano Meria at the island's northern end. The fare is Dr300 (90¢).

By Moped There are two moped-rental outfits on Folegandros: **Jimmy's Motorcycle** (☎ 0286/41-448) in Karavostassis, and **Moto Rent** (☎ 0286/41-316) in Hora, near Sottovento Travel.

By Boat From mid-June through August, boat taxis or caïques provide transport to the island's southern beaches. From Karavostassis, boats depart for Katergo and Angali (Dr1,500/$4.30 round-trip); another boat departs from Angali for Ayios Nikolaos, Livadaki, and Ambeli (Dr1,500/$4.30 one-way). There is also a 7-hour tour of the island's beaches which departs from Karavostassis at least three times weekly in summer, and makes stops at five beaches; the cost is Dr6,500 ($19) per person, including lunch. Reservations can be made at Diaplous or Sottovento Travel (see above); note that tickets must be purchased a day in advance.

FAST FACTS Folegandros has neither bank nor ATM, but you can exchange money at **Maraki Travel** (☎ 0286/41-273), **Sottovento Travel** (☎ 0286/41-444), or **Diaplous** (☎ 0286/41-158). Note that commissions on money exchange are particularly high in Folegandros due to the absence of a local bank. The **post office**

and **telephone office (OTE)** are right off the central square in Hora, open Monday through Friday from 8am to 3pm. The **police station** (☎ **0286/41-249**) is behind the post office and OTE. There's one **taxi** (☎ **0286/41-048;** mobile 094/693-957) on the island, but with the frequency of bus service and dearth of places to drive to, you're unlikely to need it.

WHAT TO SEE & DO

Visitors arrive in the unimpressive port of **Karavostassis,** where there's a decent beach and a few hotels and rooms to let. Most will jump aboard the bus that's waiting to chug the 4 kilometers (2½ miles) up to Hora.

✪ **Hora** is one of the most beautiful capitals in the Cyclades. Above it, the Panayia Church beckons you to climb the hillside for a closer look and incredible views. Even from the bus-stop square, the sheer drop of the cliff offers an awesome sight. On the right in the next square, you'll find the **Kastro:** two narrow pedestrian streets connected by tunnel-like walkways, squeezed between the town and the sea cliffs. The town is centered around five closely connected squares, along and around which you'll find churches, restaurants, and shops.

Continue west from Hora by foot or bus to reach the village of **Ano Meria.** The small farms here are so widely dispersed that they're barely recognizable as a community, though Ano Meria is the island's second-largest town. There's an interesting **Folk Museum** here, open in the afternoons during July and August, with exhibits on local life.

BEACHES

Swimmers will want to get off the bus to Ano Meria at the first crossroad and walk down to **Angali,** the largest (and most crowded) fine-sand beach on the island. There are a few tavernas on the beach and rooms to let. **Ayios Nikolaos,** another popular beach where clothing is optional, is a couple of kilometers farther west—a well-used path follows the coast west from Angali, or you can take the boat (Dr1,500/$4.30 one-way from Angali). West from Ayios Nikolaos is a series of beaches, the best of which are **Livadaki** and **Ambeli**—both can be reached by boat from Angali (Dr1,500/$4.30 one-way) or on foot from the end of the road to Ano Maria (see "Walking," below). The best beach of the island, ✪ **Katergo,** is a stretch of fine pebbles at the base of a low cliff on the south side of the island, protected from the wind by rocky headlands. It is only accessible on foot (about 2 kilometers/1.25 miles from Livadi Beach, or 3 kilometers/1.9 miles from the port at Karavostassi) or by water: A boat departs from Karavostassi mid-June to August (Dr1,500/$4.30 round-trip). At the far northwest end of the island is **Ayios Yeoryios,** a pristine pebble beach in a rocky cove, accessible only on foot (the excursion boats don't often stop here). It's a great walk (see "Walking," below), but the beach is usually too windy for swimming, although on a still day it can be a good option for avoiding the crowds. For information on boat taxis to the beaches, inquire at Sottovento Travel or Diaplous (see above).

WALKING

The footpaths through the northern part of the island are for the most part well used and easy to follow. Numerous paths branch off to the southwest from the paved road through Ano Meria—the region of hills traversed by these trails, between the road and the sea, is particularly beautiful. One path that's easy to follow leads **from Ayios Andreas to the bay at Ayios Yeoryios.** Take the bus to the next-to-last stop, at the northern end of Ano Meria; it's next to the church of Ayios Andreas, and at the stop is a sign reading AG. GEORGIOS 1.5, and pointing to the right. Follow the sign, and continue along a road which quickly becomes a path and descends steeply toward the bay. Follow the main path at each of several intersections; you'll be able to see the bay for the last 20 minutes of the walk. The bay of Ayios Yeoryios holds a small pebble beach; there's no fresh water here, so be sure to bring plenty. Allow 2 hours round-trip.

The walk to **Livadaki Beach,** near the lighthouse of Aspropounta on Folegandros's sheltered southwestern coast, begins at the end of the paved portion of the road to Ano Meria. Take the bus to the last stop, in front of the Merovigli Taverna, and continue about 200 meters on the wide dirt road to a sign indicating the trail to Livadaki on the left. From here it's about 40 minutes down to the beach through terraced fields, passing on the way the remote hilltop church of Ayii Anaryiri. The beach itself is well worth the trouble: a stretch of fine pebbles in a glorious rocky cove, protected from the wind and with a gradually sloping bottom. Also beginning from the end of the bus line, you can continue a few meters past the turnoff for Livadaki to the signposted trail to **Ambeli Beach,** also a 40-minute walk. Ambeli is a lovely, small, intimate beach with some trees offering shade. Be sure to bring plenty of water.

WHERE TO STAY

We recommend that you stay in beautiful cliff-top Hora. Keep in mind that the island's limited facilities are fully booked in July and August, and advance reservations are essential.

✪ **Anemomilos Apartments.** Hora (just up from the central bus stop), 84011 Folegandros. ☎ **0286/41-309,** or 01/682-7777 in Athens. Fax 0286/41-407, or 01/682-3962 in Athens. 17 units. TEL. Dr26,000–Dr31,000 ($74–$89) studio (double occupancy); Dr40,000 ($11) suite (triple occupancy). Extra person Dr6,000–Dr7,000 ($17–$20). Continental breakfast Dr2,500 ($7) extra. V. Closed mid-Oct to Easter.

Hora's best luxury apartments are spectacularly situated at the edge of a cliff overlooking the sea. All but two have terraces facing the sea. One apartment is wheelchair-accessible. Every unit has a well-stocked kitchenette—you can actually do some cooking here. Cornelia Patelis, who manages the hotel with her husband, Dimitris, makes a delicious sweet breakfast pie with local cheese. Breakfast and snacks are served throughout the day on the pool terrace, where you can sunbathe, swim, and enjoy the fabulous view. Transport to and from the port is available for Dr1,500 ($4.30) per person one-way.

✪ **Castro Hotel.** Hora, 84011 Folegandros. ☎ **0286/41-230,** or 01/778-1658 in Athens. Fax 0286/41-230, or 01/778-1658 in Athens. 12 units. TEL. Dr19,000 ($54) double; Dr27,000 ($77) triple. Continental breakfast Dr3,000 ($9) extra. AE, V. Closed mid-Sept to June 10.

The Castro is a Venetian castle built in 1212; it's the oldest part of Hora, wedged against the cliffs and facing the Aegean 250 meters below. Guest rooms are small but comfortable, and seven are on the phenomenal cliff side of the hotel. The two most desirable units have balconies surveying the extraordinary view; these don't cost extra, and are a great bargain. (Try to reserve room 3, 4, 5, 13, 14, 15, or R1.) For those units without the view, a shared rooftop terrace offers the same magnificent prospect. The charming Despo Danassi, whose family has owned this house for five generations, will make you feel at home here—and her homemade fig jam is fabulous.

Kifines Apartments. Hora, 84011 Folegandros. ☎ **0286/41-274.** 4 units. Dr25,000 ($72) studio (double occupancy); Dr35,000 ($99) suite (double occupancy). Extra person Dr5,000 ($14); 2 extra persons Dr8,000 ($23). MC, V. Located 200m outside Hora on the road to Ano Maria.

New in 2000, the Kifines Apartments offer a quiet location outside Hora—the walk into town can be an inconvenience, but the view of town and sea is astonishing. Local building techniques and the drama of the site have been used to good advantage:

Floors throughout are blue-green slate outlined in white, and many of the exterior walls are exposed stone. Each apartment has a terrace with view, basic kitchen facilities, and beds for four people.

WHERE TO DINE

Main courses for all the restaurants listed here are Dr1,000 to Dr2,700 ($2.90 to $8); hours are generally from 9am to 3pm and 6pm to midnight.

The local specialty is a dish called *matsata,* made with fresh pasta and rabbit or chicken. The best place to sample it is **Mimi's,** in Ano Meria (☎ 0286/41-377), where the pasta is made on the premises. Also in Ano Meria are **Sinandisi** (☎ 0286/41-208), also known as Maria's, which has good *matsata* and swordfish (take the bus to the Ayios Andreas stop); and **Barbakosta** (☎ 0286/41-436), a tiny room that serves triple duty as bar, taverna, and minimarket; you buy a drink or sample the dish of the day here (the bus stop has no name, so ask the driver to let you know when to disembark).

Hora has a number of tavernas, whose tables spill into and partially fill the central squares. On the bus-stop square, **Pounda** (☎ 0286/421-063) serves a delicious breakfast of crêpes, omelets, yogurt, or coffee cakes; lunch and dinner, including a variety of vegetarian dishes, are also available. **Sik** (☎ 0286/41-515), on the Piatsa (third) Square, offers delicious variations on taverna fare, including numerous vegetarian options. **Piatsa** (☎ 0286/41-274), also on the third square, is a simple taverna operated by the friendly Yiannis Sideris and his wife, Kiriaki. **O Kritikos** (☎ 0286/41-219) is another local favorite, known for its grilled chicken.

3 Sifnos

172km (93 nautical miles) SE of Piraeus

Presenting an austere face to ferries arriving at the unexciting port of Kamares, Sifnos keeps its riches concealed within a hilly interior. Elegantly ornamented dovecotes rest in the cool green hollows, while ancient fortified monasteries and watchtowers occupy the arid summits of the island's hills. Beaches along the southern coast offer long stretches of fine amber sand; several smaller rocky coves are also excellent for swimming.

The island is sufficiently small that any town can be used as a base for touring; the most beautiful are the **seven settlements** spread across the central hills (notably Apollonia and Artemonas) and **Kastro,** a small medieval fortified town atop a rocky pinnacle on the eastern shore. A combination of bus rides and some short walks will allow you to visit the top attractions: the ancient acropolis at **Ayios Andreas,** the town of Kastro and its tiny but excellent **archaeological museum,** the southern **beaches,** and, for the ambitious, the **walled monastery of Profitis Elias** on the summit of the island's highest mountain. While you're on the island, don't miss the **pottery workshops:** Sifnos is renowned for its ceramics, and some of the island's best practitioners are in Kamares and Platis Yialos.

ESSENTIALS

GETTING THERE   By Boat   There's one ferry daily from Piraeus (3 hrs.); contact the Athens **tourist office** (☎ 01/331-0562) or the **Port Authority in Piraeus** (☎ 01/459-3223) for information. Ferries travel daily to nearby islands such as **Serifos** (30 to 60 mins.), **Kimolos** (30 to 40 mins.), **Milos** (45 mins.), and **Kithnos** (1½ hrs.). Hydrofoils travel two or three times a week on the route Santorini-Folegandros-Milos-Sifnos-Paros-Mykonos-Tinos-Siros (with variations); travel times are about

1 hour to Paros, 2 hours to Folegandros or Mykonos, 2½ hours to Tinos, and 3 hours to Santorini or Siros. Call the **Sifnos Port Authority** (☎ **0284/33-617**) for more information. *Note:* In the off-season, ferry connections to Sifnos are particularly sparse.

VISITOR INFORMATION   Your first stop should be the excellent **Aegean Thesaurus Travel and Tourism** (☎ **0284/33-527**), on the quay 100 meters from the pier, next to the Poseidon Restaurant. Here you can cash traveler's checks, book flights, buy ferry or hydrofoil tickets, book accommodations, or arrange a boat tour of the island. A packet of island information including bus schedule, hydrofoil and ferry schedule, and brief local history is offered for Dr200 (60¢). The main office of **Aegean Thesaurus Travel** is in Apollonia (☎ **0284/33-151;** fax 0284/32-190; www. travelling.gr/sifnos-aegean-thesaurus; e-mail: thesaurus@travelling.gr).

Note that Aegean Thesaurus currently provides tickets for most, but not all, of the hydrofoils and ferries. For complete representation of companies, inquire at **Ventouris Ferries,** next door to Aegean Thesaurus in Kamares (☎ **0284/31-700**), or at **Katsoulakis Travel,** with locations on the quay in Kamares and on the main pedestrian street in Apollonia (☎ **0284/31-004;** fax 0284/31-213).

GETTING AROUND   By Bus   Apollonia's central square, **Plateia Iroon,** is the main bus stop for the island. Buses run regularly to and from the port at Kamares, north to Artemonas, east to Kastro, and south to Faros, Platis Yialos, and Vathi. Pick up a schedule at Aegean Thesaurus Travel (see "Visitor Information," above).

By Car & Moped   Given the island's small size and the presence of a reliable bus system, renting a car or moped may not be necessary. Cars can be rented in Apollonia at **FS** (☎ **0284/31-795;** fax 0284/33-089) and **Aegean Thesaurus** (☎ **0284/33-151**). In Kamares, **Sifnos Car** (☎ and fax **0284/33-052**) is a good choice. The daily rate for an economy car with full insurance is about Dr18,000 ($52). Apollonia has a few moped dealers; try **Yannis** (☎ **0284/31-155**) on the main square.

By Taxi   Apollonia's main square is the island's primary taxi stand. There are about 10 taxis on the island, each privately owned, so you'll have to use the **mobile phone numbers** and hope someone's phone is turned on: Try ☎ **097/777-1742,** 094/444-904, 094/761-210, or 094/493-6111.

FAST FACTS   Visitor services are centered in Apollonia. The **National Bank** (☎ **0284/31-317**), with ATM, just past the Hotel Anthousa on the road to Artemonas, is open Monday through Thursday from 8am to 2pm, Friday from 8am to 1:30pm. The **post office** (☎ **0284/31-329**), on Plateia Iroon, the main square, is open in summer Monday through Friday from 8am to 3pm, Saturday and Sunday from 9am to 1:30pm. The **telephone office (OTE),** just down the vehicle road, is open daily from 8am to 3pm, and in summer from 5 to 10pm as well. There's a rudimentary **laundry** service in the courtyard of the Hotel Anthousa in Apollonia; inquire at Yerontopoulos patisserie, on the ground floor of the hotel. The **police** (☎ **0284/ 31-210**) are just east of the square, and a **first-aid station** is nearby; for **medical emergencies** call ☎ **0284/31-315.**

WHAT TO SEE & DO

The capital town of the island, **Apollonia,** is one of the **seven settlements,** which have grown together on these lovely interior hills. It's 5 kilometers (3 miles) inland from Kamares; a local bus makes the trip hourly in summer. The town's central square, **Plateia Iroon (Heroes' Square),** is the transportation hub of the island: All the vehicle roads converge here, and this is where you'll find the bus stop and taxi stand. Winding pedestrian paths of flagstone and marble slope up from the square and lead through this beautiful village. **Lakis Kafenion,** an open-air cafe on the square, is the island's principal hangout. Also on Plateia Iroon is the small **Popular and Folk Art Museum;** it's open July 1 to September 15 from 10am to 1pm and 6 to 10pm (admission is Dr500/$1.45).

○ **Kastro** is the finest medieval town on Sifnos, built on the dramatic site of an ancient acropolis. The 2-kilometer (1.2-mile) walk from Apollonia is easy, except under the midday sun: Start out on the footpath that passes under the main road in front of Hotel Anthousa, and continue through the tiny village of Kato Petali, finishing the walk into Kastro on a paved road. Whitewashed houses, some well preserved and others eroding, adjoin one another in a defensive ring abutting the sheer cliff. Venetian coats of arms are still visible above the doorways of the older houses. Within the maze of streets are a few tavernas, some beautiful rooms to let, and a gem of an **Archaeological Museum (☎ 0284/31-022)** housing pottery and sculpture found on the island; open Tuesday through Saturday from 9am to 3pm, Sunday and holidays from 10am to 2pm (admission is free).

About 2 kilometers (1.2 miles) south of Apollonia on the road to Vathi is a trail leading to the hilltop church of **Ayios Andreas** and the excavations of an **ancient acropolis.** It's hard to see the sign (in Greek only) for Ayios Andreas; it's across from a road sign reading KADES, at the top of a long uphill. Broad stone steps begin a long climb to the summit; count on about 20 minutes to ascend and 15 minutes to come back down. The ruins of the acropolis are at the top of the hill on your left. These ruins are made up of the outer walls and a block of houses from a Mycenaean fortified town. Excavations haven't been completed and there's no interpretive information at the site, but the location is stirring—it's worth a visit if only for the view.

BEACHES

The central part of **Kamares** cove harbors a sandy beach lined with tamarisk trees and dune grass, but due to the traffic of ferries and other boats in the harbor, the water here is not so clean.

The southern end of the island shelters a trio of coves with fine-sand beaches. The most popular of these is **Platis Yialos,** where a slew of hotels, tavernas, and shops have grown up around the beach. More upscale than Kamares, this town attracts the yachting crowd in summer. From here, it's a half-hour walk east through the olive groves and intoxicating oregano and thyme patches over the hill to **Panayia Chrissopiyi,** a double-vaulted whitewashed church on a tiny island. There's good swimming at **Apokofto,** a cove with a long sand beach and several shade trees just beyond the monastery, where rocky headlands protect swimmers from rough water. Nude bathing is permitted at nearby **Fasolou.**

Until 1997, the beach at **Vathi** was accessible only by foot or by boat, but a new automobile road has opened and permits regular bus service. There are a few tavernas here (but not yet the dense development of Kamares and Platis Yialos), plus one of the best beaches on the island.

WALKING

Like many of the Cyclades, the hills of Sifnos are traced with countless walking paths, many of them paved with slabs of limestone or schist. Sadly, the continuity of these fine paths has been interrupted in many places by the construction of new roads and houses.

Our favorite walk on the island leads **from Apollonia to Profitis Elias,** taking you through a valley of extraordinary beauty to the summit of the island's highest mountain, with a short detour to the church and ruined monastery at Skafis. From the center of Apollonia, walk south along the main pedestrian road, past Sifnos Taverna and the cathedral. About 1 kilometer (0.6 miles) from the center of Apollonia you'll reach the village of Katavati; look out for the small black arrow pointing to the right, painted with the words PR. ELIAS in Greek. From here the trail descends toward a paved road, makes a short jog to the right on the road, then turns left onto a footpath (with another PR. ELIAS arrow at the left turn). After about 1 kilometer (0.6 miles) of walking along the base of a valley, the path to the summit branches to the right. From here it's another hour or so of easy climbing to the summit. The 12th-century walled monastery is a formidable citadel, its interior courtyard lined with the monks' cells. The lovely chapel has a fine marble iconostasis. If you continue straight from the point where the summit path branches right and walk straight through the next intersection, you'll soon reach the church of Skafis, situated within the ruins of an old monastery and overlooking a small valley shaded by olive trees. Look for the remains of paintings on the walls of the ruined monastery, in what must have been a tiny chapel. Allow about 3 hours for the round-trip to Profitis Elias, with an additional half hour for the detour to Skafis.

SHOPPING

Sifnian ceramics are exported throughout Greece; they're in wide use because of their durability and charming folk designs. One of the most interesting shops is the ceramics workshop of **Antonis Kalogirou** (☎ 0284/31-651), on the main harborside lane in Kamares. Antonis sells folk paintings of island life and the typical pottery of Sifnos, which is manufactured in his showroom from the deep gray or red clay mined in the inland hill region. Another fine ceramics workshop is that of **Simos and John Apostolidis** (☎ 0284/71-258), on the main street in Platis Yialos.

In Apollonia, **Hersonissos** (☎ 0284/32-209) has a choice selection of contemporary jewelry and ceramics. There are several other contemporary ceramics galleries featuring the excellent work of Greek artisans in the town's winding back streets.

WHERE TO STAY

APOLLONIA

The island's capital and one of its most beautiful villages, Apollonia is our recommendation as a base on Sifnos. Buses depart from the central square to most island towns, and stone-paved paths lead to neighboring villages.

Numerous rooms in private houses (most are adjacent to the owner's house) can be booked through **Aegean Thesaurus Travel** (see "Visitor Information," above). A double costs about Dr14,000 ($40) in high season. We especially recommend the following two choices, both run by friendly proprietors (neither of whom speak English). Opposite Hotel Petali is the house of **Eirini Yeronti.** The view here is good, and the super-clean rooms open to a terrace shaded by a grape arbor. The rooms of **Margarita Kouki** are perched high above town, a 10-minute walk up from Plateia Iroon; the view is fantastic, but this isn't the place to go if you're traveling with heavy bags.

Hotel Anthousa. Apollonia, 84003 Sifnos. ☎ **0284/31-431** or 0284/32-200. 15 units. A/C TV TEL. Dr16,000 ($46) double; Dr20,000 ($57) triple. Continental breakfast Dr1,500 ($4.30) extra. MC, V. Open year-round.

The comfortable rooms of Hotel Anthousa are located in the center of Apollonia on the road to Artemonas, above the popular Yerontopoulos cafe. Abundant bougainvillea fills the small courtyard and covers the terrace of the cafe in front. All but two rooms have balconies facing the view east toward Kastro and the sea, or inland toward the slopes of Profitis Elias. Although the street-side units offer wonderful views over the hills, they're recommended only to night owls in high season, as they overlook a busy road and the late-night sweet-tooth crowd; the back rooms facing the mountain are much quieter.

Hotel Petali. Apollonia, 84003 Sifnos. ☎ and fax **0284/33-024.** E-mail: petali@par. forthnet.gr. 10 units. A/C TV TEL. Dr33,000 ($95) double; Dr37,000 ($106) triple; Dr44,000 ($124) suite. Continental breakfast Dr3,000 ($9) extra. AE, MC, V. Closed Nov–Mar.

The small, informal Petali was built recently in a style reminiscent of traditional island houses—though a new hotel, its bougainvillea terraces and whitewashed rooms fit in well with the older houses along the narrow pedestrian street between Apollonia and Artemonas. Each room opens onto a terrace facing the hills of Sifnos, the seven settlements, and the sea—from this high vantage you can see Paros, Andiparos, Serifos, and other Cycladic isles. This is a quiet location, far from the nearest road; the disadvantage is that the closest you can come by car is Plateia Iroon, a distance of about 200 meters (all uphill). Assistance with your bags is available on request. A restaurant on the main terrace serves continental breakfast and a full dinner menu.

✪ **Hotel Sifnos.** Apollonia, 84003 Sifnos. ☎ and fax **0284/31-624** or 0284/33-067. 7 units. A/C TV TEL. Dr18,000 ($52) double. AE, EC, MC, V. Open year-round.

This is our choice for best hotel in Apollonia—though the rooms are simple, the hospitality of the Diareme family is exceptional. Facing a small square on the town's pedestrian street, the hotel is a quiet retreat just a 3-minute walk from the trucks and buzzing mopeds of Plateia Iroon; to get here, walk uphill on the narrow street lined with restaurants and shops behind the Folklore Museum. The hotel restaurant (see "Where to Dine," below) offers good basic meals beneath a broad arbor, and it's just as popular with locals as it is with travelers and hotel guests.

ARTEMONAS

A small village overlooking terraced fields and the distant sea, Artemonas is a pleasant base, especially good if you have your own transport or don't mind the 15-minute walk to Apollonia.

Hotel Artemon. Artemonas, 84003 Sifnos. ☎ **0284/31-303** or 0284/33-158. Fax 0284/ 32-385. 23 units. MINIBAR TEL. Dr17,280 ($49) double. Continental breakfast Dr1,500 ($4.30) extra. AE, EC, MC, V. Closed Oct–Mar. Located on the road to Apollonia, just beyond the central plateia of Artemonas (where the bus from Apollonia turns around).

Built in 1968, this quiet, comfortable place is among the oldest hotels on Sifnos; the generic character of the building is offset by the friendly attentiveness of the owner, Voula Lembessis. Rooms on the ground floor have patios and views of the small hotel gardens; the units above have balconies and a view of wheat fields and olive groves sloping down to the sea. The Artemon has a large terrace shaded by a luxuriant grape arbor; breakfast is served here or in the adjoining dining room. The restaurant also serves lunch and dinner in July and August.

KASTRO

Aris Rafeletos Apartments. Kastro. ☎ and fax **0284/31-161.** 6 units. Dr13,000 ($37) room; Dr23,000 ($66) studio; Dr33,000 ($95) apt. No credit cards. The rental office is at the north end of the village, about 50m past the Archaeological Museum (the sign says TRADITIONAL ROOMS FOR RENT).

These traditional rooms and apartments are distributed throughout the medieval town of Kastro. Most have exposed ceiling beams, stone ceilings and floors, and the long narrow rooms typical of this fortified village. The two small units are somewhat dark and musty, but the three apartments are spacious and charming. All apartments have kitchenettes and terraces; three have splendid sea views. The largest apartment is on two levels and can comfortably sleep four. If the antiquity and charm of this hilltop medieval village appeals to you, then these accommodations may be the perfect base for your explorations of the island.

KAMARES

Kamares has the greatest concentration of hotels and pensions on the island, but unfortunately it has little of the beauty of Sifnos's traditional villages.

Hotel Boulis. Kamares, 84003 Sifnos. ☎ **0284/32-122.** Fax 0284/32-381. 45 units. TEL. Dr20,000 ($57) double; 24,000 ($69) triple. Rates include breakfast. AE. Closed Oct–Apr. Follow the main street 300m from the ferry pier, turning left opposite the Boulis Taverna (operated by the same family). The hotel is on your left.

This newer hotel, capably managed by Lyn and Antonis Kalogirou, is right on the port's beach. The large, carpeted rooms have balconies or patios, most with beach views; all have fridges and ceiling fans. The hotel has a spacious, cool, marble-floored reception area and a bright breakfast room.

PLATIS YIALOS

A busy beach resort on the island's south coast, Platis Yialos is a convenient base for visiting the southern beaches. The town exists for tourism during high season.

Hotel Philoxenia. Platis Yialos, 84003 Sifnos. ☎ **0284/71-221.** Fax 0284/71-222. E-mail: philoxenia@infixnet.gr. 9 units. A/C TV TEL. Dr23,000 ($66) double; Dr26,000 ($74) triple. Breakfast Dr1,500 ($4.30) extra. MC, V. Closed Nov–Mar.

A step above the town's average beachfront lodgings, this simple hotel on the main street facing the bay offers spacious, clean rooms, all with balconies. All units have refrigerators, and most have a view toward the beach. Bathrooms are small but efficient.

✪ **Hotel Platis Yialos.** Platis Yialos, 84003 Sifnos. ☎ **0284/31-324,** or 0831/22-626 in winter. Fax 0284/31-325, or 0831/55-042 in winter. 29 units. MINIBAR TV TEL. Dr45,000 ($129) double; Dr90,000 ($259) suite. Rates include breakfast. No credit cards. Closed Oct–Mar.

The island's best hotel is ideally situated overlooking the beach on the west side of the cove, set apart from the rest of the town's densely populated beach strip. Originally a government-owned Xenia hotel, its design is functional rather than beautiful. The ground-floor guest rooms, with patios facing the garden and water, are especially desirable; rooms on the upper stories have balconies. A new suite contains flagstone floors, beamed ceilings, beds for up to six people, and two bathrooms, one with Jacuzzi; it opens to a small terrace with views of the bay. Frescoes and small paintings by a local artist are displayed throughout the hotel. The Platis Yialos's flagstone sundeck extends from the beach to a dive platform at the end of the cove; a bar and restaurant share the same Aegean views.

WHERE TO DINE
APOLLONIA

Apostoli's Koutouki Taverna. Along the main pedestrian street. ☎ **0284/31-186.** Main courses Dr1,200–Dr4,500 ($3.45–$13). No credit cards. Daily noon–midnight. GREEK.

There are several tavernas in Apollonia, but this one with outdoor tables along the main pedestrian street is the best for simple Greek food. The vegetable dishes, most made from locally grown produce, are delicious. The service is slow, even by taverna standards.

Mama Mia. On the path between Apollonia and Artemonas. ☎ **0284/33-086.** Main courses Dr1,400–Dr6,000 ($4–$17). No credit cards. Daily 5pm–midnight. SPAGHETTERIA/ PIZZERIA.

When you need a break from taverna fare, try this trattoria—the food is simple and surprisingly good. House specialties include a variety of veal and lobster dishes, but we particularly recommend humbler fare like the pasta, risotto, or (best of all) excellent pizzas, which can also be ordered for takeout. The large outdoor terrace in back is a very pleasant spot to enjoy a leisurely dinner.

Sifnos Cafe-Restaurant. Along the main pedestrian street toward the cathedral. ☎ **0284/31-624.** Main courses Dr1,000–Dr3,000 ($2.90–$9). AE, EC, MC, V. Daily 8am–midnight. GREEK.

You'll find the best all-around place to eat in Apollonia under a grape arbor, between the Hotel Sifnos and a quiet plaza. The breakfast menu offers fresh fruit juice and a dozen coffees. Choose from a variety of snacks, light meals, and desserts during the day. At sunset, enjoy ouzo and mezedes. When you're ready for a big evening meal, go in and check out the refrigerator case displaying the catch of the day and other choices. Apostolos Diareme is a gracious host, as well as a great source of information about the island.

ARTEMONAS

To Liotrivi (Manganas). On central square of Artemonas. ☎ **0284/32-051.** Main courses Dr900–Dr3,300 ($2.60–$10). No credit cards. Daily noon–midnight. From Apollonia, follow the pedestrian street north from Plateia Iroon, past Mama Mia and the Hotel Petali; it's a pleasant 10- to 15-minute walk. GREEK.

Find out why the Sifnians, who pride themselves on their fine cooking, consider Yannis Yiorgoulis one of their best chefs. Try his delectable *kaparosalata* (minced caper leaves and onion salad), *revidokeftedes* (croquettes of ground chickpeas), or *ambelofasoula* (crisp local black-eyed peas in the pod)—or go for something ordinary like the beef fillet with potatoes baked in foil. The taverna is in a handsome new building, with dining inside or out on the square.

KAMARES

Boulis Taverna. At the top of the main street through town. ☎ **0284/31-648.** Main courses Dr900–Dr2,500 ($2.60–$7). No credit cards. Daily 11am–1am. GREEK.

With an unexceptional location at the top of the town's busy main street, this isn't the place to go for a romantic evening, but it does offer some of the best Greek food in town. Operated by Andonis Kalogirou of the Hotel Boulis, most of the vegetables, cheeses and meats are raised on the organic family farm. The walls of the vast interior room are lined with wooden wine casks. Outside, lamb, chicken, and steaks cook on the grill.

Captain Andreas. On the town beach. ☎ **0284/32-356.** Main courses Dr1,000–Dr2,100 ($2.90–$6); fish Dr3,000–Dr17,000 ($9–$49) per kilo. No credit cards. Daily 1–5pm and 7:30pm–12:30am. SEAFOOD.

Captain Andreas, a favorite place for seafood, has tables right on the town beach. Andreas, the proprietor and fisherman, serves the catch of the day. It's usually simply prepared and accompanied with terrific chips or a seasonal vegetable dish.

Pothotas Taverna O Simos. On the port. ☎ **0284/31-697.** Main courses Dr900–Dr2,100 ($2.60–$6). No credit cards. Daily 11am–midnight. GREEK.

This unobtrusive portside place has a basic Greek menu, and everything is done well. The bread brought to your table is sprinkled with sesame seeds, the *horiatiki* salad is

---

A Special Feast

The celebration in mid-July of **the Prophet Elijah's feast day** is a special tradition on Sifnos, which has had a monastery dedicated to this saint for at least 800 years. The celebration begins with a mass outing to the monastery of Profitis Elias on the summit of the island's highest mountain, and continues through the night with dancing and feasting.

---

made with locally aged *mizithra* cheese, the fish is fresh and not expensive, and the individually baked pots of moussaka are delicious.

PLATIS YIALOS

Sofia Restaurant. At the east end of the beach. ☎ **0284/71-202.** Main courses Dr900–Dr2,700 ($2.60–$8). No credit cards. Daily 9pm–1am. GREEK.

Platis Yialos's best restaurant for Greek taverna fare is popular for its outdoor terrace and large wine list. For many in Apollonia, the casual seaside ambience warrants an evening outing.

SIFNOS AFTER DARK

In Apollonia, the **Argo Bar** is one of the oldest establishments, and plays European and American pop music with some Greek tunes thrown in. **Botzi** and **Volto** on the main pedestrian street are good for the latest European and American pop music at very loud volumes. In summer, the large **Dolphin Pub** becomes a lively and elegant nightspot; it closes for the season in mid-September.

In Kamares at sunset, you can seek relative tranquility near the beach at the picturesque **Old Captain's Bar.** Or join the yacht set drinking Sifnos Sunrises at the rival **Collage Club.** Later, the **Mobilize Dance Club** and the more elegant **Follie-Follie,** right on the beach, start cranking up the volume for dancing.

In summer, the **Cultural Society of Sifnos** sometimes hosts concerts in Artemonas, and local festivals offer folk music and dance.

4 Paros

168km (91 nautical miles) SE of Piraeus

Every island-hopper in the Cyclades is likely to pass at some point through Paros, the transportation hub of the archipelago. With a few good beaches, as well as nightlife to rival Mykonos or Santorini, it's not surprising that Paros has become a tremendously popular destination in its own right. **Parikia,** its lively capital, offers an eclectic marketplace, the remains of a Venetian castle, a fine Byzantine cathedral, and some of the best culinary options of any town in the Cyclades.

On the north coast, the fishing village of **Naoussa** has grown into a full-scale resort, and is almost as crowded as Parikia in July and August; the most popular Paros beaches are within easy commuting distance of Naoussa's hotels. Charming **Lefkes,** set within the island's inland hills, has preserved many of its medieval buildings amidst a maze of steep narrow streets. The west coast of the island has long stretches of fine sand, plus wind conditions that have made this the site of the World Cup windsurfing championship every year since 1993.

We recommend taking a day or two to explore the island and visit its attractions before moving on. Rent a car or moped for an around-the-island tour that includes a morning visit to **Petaloudes,** enough time in Lefkes to get lost and find your way again, a stop for a good lunch in Naoussa, a swim at your beach of choice, and a night of shopping and barhopping in hectic Parikia.

ESSENTIALS

GETTING THERE   By Plane   Olympic Airways (www.olympic-airways.gr) has at least two flights daily between Paros and Athens. For schedules and reservations, call ☎ **0284/21-900** in Parikia, 0284/91-257 at the airport, or **0801/44444** or 01/966-6666 in Athens.

By Boat   Paros has more connections with more ports than any other island in the Cyclades. The main port, Parikia, has connections at least once daily with Piraeus by ferry (5 to 6 hrs.) and high-speed ferry (3 to 4 hrs.). Confirm schedules with the Athens **GNTO tourist office** (☎ 01/331-0562) or the **Port Authority in Piraeus** (☎ 01/459-3223). Daily ferry and hydrofoil service links Parikia with Ios, Mykonos (1½ hrs.), Naxos (30 mins.), Santorini (2½ hrs. by hydrofoil, 4 hrs. by car ferry), and Tinos (1½ to 3 hrs.). Several times a week, boats depart for Folegandros (2 hrs. by hydrofoil, 4 hrs. by car ferry), Sifnos (1 hr. by hydrofoil, 3 hrs. by car ferry), and Siros (1 to 4 hrs.). There are daily excursion tours from Parikia or Naoussa (the north coast port) to Mykonos. There's also overnight service to Ikaria and Samos (7 to 10 hrs.) four times a week. (From Samos you can arrange a next-day excursion to Ephesus, Turkey.) In high season, there's hourly caïque service to Andiparos from Parikia and Pounda, a small port 6 kilometers (3.7 miles) south of Parikia, with regular connection by bus. The east coast port of Piso Livadi is the point of departure for travelers heading to the "Little Cyclades": Ferries depart four times weekly for Heraklia, Schinoussa, Koufonissi and Katapola.

For general ferry information, call **Santorineos Travel** in Parikia (☎ **0284/ 24-245**) or try the **port authority** (☎ **0284/21-240**). Ferry tickets are sold by numerous agents around Mavroyenous Square and along the port; schedules are posted along the sidewalk.

VISITOR INFORMATION   There is a **visitor information office** on Mavroyenous Square, just behind and to the right of the windmill at the end of the pier. This office is often closed, but there are numerous travel agencies on the seafront, including the helpful **Santorineos Travel** (☎ **0284/24-245**; fax 0284/23-922; e-mail: santorinaios-travel@ticketcom.gr), 100 meters south of the pier (to the right as you get off the boat). Here you can store luggage, buy ferry and airline tickets, rent a car, and exchange money. The island has an excellent Web site, **www.parosweb.com**, with abundant information for visitors.

GETTING AROUND   By Bus   The **bus station** (☎ **0284/21-395**) in Parikia is on the waterfront, left from the windmill. There is hourly service between Parikia and Naoussa from 8am to midnight in high season. The other buses from Parikia run hourly from 8am to 9pm in two general directions: south to Aliki or Pounda, and southeast to the beaches at Piso Livadi, Chrissi Akti, and Drios, passing the Marathi Quarries and the town of Lefkes along the way. Schedules are posted at the stations.

By Car & Moped   Paros is large enough that renting a car makes sense; there are many agencies along the waterfront, and except in July and August you should be able to bargain. You can also try **Santorineos Travel** (☎ **0284/24-245**); Nikos Santorineos works with several agencies in town, and will call around to find the best price. Most of the town's moped dealers can be found along the waterfront, left from the windmill. Depending on size, mopeds cost Dr4,000 to Dr6,000 ($12 to $17) per day.

By Taxi   Taxis can be booked (☎ **0284/21-500**) or hailed at the windmill taxi stand. Taxi fare to Naoussa with luggage should be Dr2,500 to Dr3,000 ($7 to $9).

FAST FACTS The **American Express** agent is Santorineos Travel, on the seafront 100 meters south of the pier (☎ **0284/24-245;** fax 0284/23-922; e-mail santorinaios-travel@ticketcom.gr). There are five **banks** in Parikia on Mavroyenous Square, and one in Naoussa; open Monday through Thursday from 8am to 2pm, Friday from 8am to 1:30pm. The private **Medical Center of Paros** (☎ **0284/24-410**) is to the left (north) of the pier, across from the post office; the public **Parikia Health Clinic** (☎ **0284/22-500**) is on the central square, down the road from the Ekatondapiliani Cathedral. **Internet access** is available on the Wired Network (www.parosweb.com) at eight locations around the island; you can buy a "smart card" that stores your personal settings and provides access at any of these locations. The main office is in Parikia at the Wired Cafe on Market Street (☎ **0284/22-003**).

The **Laundry House** is on the paralia near the post office (☎ **0284/24-898**). For the **police,** call ☎ **0284/100** or 0284/23-333. In Marpissa, call ☎ **0284/41-202;** in Naoussa, ☎ **0284/51-202.** The **tourist police** (☎ **0284/21-673**) are in Parikia behind the windmill on the port. The **post office** in Parikia (☎ **0284/21-236**) is left from the windmill on the waterfront road, open Monday through Friday from 7:30am to 2pm, with extended hours in July and August. The **telephone office (OTE)** in Parikia (☎ **0284/22-135**) is just to the right from the windmill; open from 7:30am to 2pm. (If the front door is closed, go around to the back, as wind direction determines which door is open.) There's a branch in Naoussa with similar hours.

WHAT TO SEE & DO
THE TOP ATTRACTIONS

Panayia Ekatondapiliani Cathedral. Parikia. Museum ☎ **0284/21-243.** Admission Dr500 ($1.45). Daily 8am–1pm and 4–9pm. On the central square of Parikia, opposite and north of the ferry pier.

The town's most famous sight is the Byzantine cathedral of Panayia Ekatondapiliani (Our Lady of a Hundred Doors). The cathedral is surrounded by a high white wall built as protection from pirates; in the thickness of the wall are rows of monk's cells, now housing a small shop and ecclesiastical museum. After you step through the outer gate, the noise of the town vanishes, and you enter a garden with lemon trees and flowering shrubs. The cathedral contains several icons dating back as far as the 15th century, and a fine cruciform baptismal font from the 4th century. The museum contains many 16th- to 19th-century icons and beautiful objects used to celebrate the varied ceremonies of the Orthodox Church; although the museum is small, it's well worth the entrance fee.

Archaeological Museum. Parikia. ☎ **0284/21-231.** Admission Dr500 ($1.45) adults, Dr300 (90¢) students. Tues–Sun 8:30am–2:30pm. Behind the cathedral, opposite the playing fields of the local school.

The museum's most valued holding is a fragment of the famous Parian Chronicle; the Ashmolean Museum at Oxford University has a larger portion. The chronicle, carved on marble tablets, was found in the 17th century and contains valuable information from which many of the events of Greek history are dated. (Interestingly, it gives us information about artists, poets, and playwrights, but doesn't bother to mention political leaders or battles.) The museum also contains a Winged Victory from the 5th century B.C.; some objects found at the local temple of Apollo; and part of a marble monument with a frieze of Archilochus, the important 7th-century B.C. lyric poet known as the inventor of iambic meter and for his ironic detachment—"What breaks me, young friend, is tasteless desire, lifeless verse, boring dinners."

The Valley of Petaloudes. Petaloudes. Admission Dr400 ($1.15). Daily 9am–1pm and 4–8pm. Closed Oct–May. Head 4km (2½ miles) south of Parikia on the coast road, turn left at the sign for the nunnery of Christou sto Dassos, and continue another 2½km (1½ miles).

Another name for this oasis of plum, pear, fig, and pomegranate trees is *Psychopiani* ("soul softs"). The butterflies, actually tiger moths (*Panaxia quadripunctaria poda*), look like black-and-white–striped arrowheads until they fly up to reveal their bright red underwings. They have been coming here for at least 300 years because of the freshwater spring, flowering trees, dense foliage, and cool shade, and are most numerous in May and June. Kostas Gravaris, the custodian of this place, recommends that you come in the early morning or evening, when the butterflies are most active. There's a small snack bar. Donkey or mule rides from Parikia to the site along a back road cost about Dr2,500 ($7). You can take the Pounda and Aliki bus, which drops you off at the turnoff to the nunnery; you'll have to walk the remaining 2½ kilometers (1½ miles) in to Petaloudes.

Marathi Marble Quarries. Marathi. Open site.

The inland road to Lefkes and Marpissa will take you up the side of a mountain to the marble quarries at Marathi, source of the famous Parian marble. This marble was prized for its translucency and fine, soft texture, and was used by ancient sculptors for their best work, including the *Hermes* of Praxitelous and the *Venus de Milo.* The turnoff to the quarries is signposted, and a path paved with marble leads up the valley toward a group of deserted buildings. These once belonged to a French mining company, the last to operate here, which in 1844 quarried the marble for Napoleon's tomb. There isn't much to see now unless you're a spelunker at heart, in which case you'll find it irresistible to explore the deep caverns opened by the miners high above the valley (bring a flashlight).

BEACHES

The beaches of Paros are small and overcrowded in comparison with those of nearby Naxos, but there is an abundance of sea sand and a few truly exceptional beaches. One of the island's best and most famous, picturesque ✪ **Kolimbithres** ("Fonts"), is an hour's walk or a 10-minute moped ride west from Naoussa. It has smooth giant rocks, some reminiscent of baptismal fonts, that divide the gold-sand beach into several tiny coves. There are a few tavernas nearby; we recommend the **Dolphin Taverna,** to the south, open from 7am to 2am, for traditional Greek food. North of the beach at Kolimbithres, by the Ayios Ioannis Church, is **Monastery Beach,** with some nudism, and the **Monasteri Club,** a bar/restaurant with music and beach service.

About 2½ kilometers (1½ miles) north of Naoussa on an unimproved road is the popular **Langeri Beach.** A 10-minute walk further north will bring you to the nudist beach, with a gay and straight crowd. Before you reach Langeri, the road forks to the right and leads to ✪ **Santa Maria Beach,** one of the most beautiful on the island. It has particularly clear water and shallow dunes (rare in Greece) of fine sand along the irregular coastline. It also offers some of the best windsurfing on Paros. The nearby **Santa Maria Surf Club** (☎ 0284/52-490) provides windsurfing gear and lessons for about Dr5,000 ($14) per hour. There's bus service to Santa Maria beach from Naoussa twice a day; caïque day trips from Naoussa are Dr2,000 ($6) round-trip.

Southeast of Naoussa, connected by public bus, is the fishing village of **Ambelas,** which has a good beach and some inexpensive tavernas. About a half-hour's hike south of Ambelas along the east coast brings you to **Glyfades** and, just beyond it, **Tsoukalia,** which attract radical windsurfers. Both beaches have a few studios to rent and a restaurant. The main north-south road is almost 1 kilometer (0.6 miles) inland at this point.

The better beaches on the east coast can be reached by bus from Parikia and Naoussa. Unfortunately, the road is inland and you can't scope out the beaches from the bus window. Ask around about crowd conditions on the several beaches; once you've reached a beach, it's several miles to the next one.

Molos, at the tip of a small peninsula, is beautiful and convenient to the attractive inland villages of Marmara and Marpissa, where there are rooms to let, so it can sometimes get crowded.

The next major beach, ✪ **Chrissi Akti (Golden Beach),** a kilometer of fine golden sand, is generally considered the best beach on the island. It's also the windiest, although the wind is usually offshore. As a result, this has become the primary windsurfing center on the island and has hosted the World Cup championship every year since 1993. Many overnight visitors head south to nearby **Drios,** a pretty village that is fast becoming a resort town, with hotels, luxury villas, and waterside tavernas. Buses run from Drios to Parikia five times daily, hourly in summer.

The next beach south of Drios, **Loloantonis,** is about 200 meters long and protected from the *meltemi* winds by a rocky headland. The beach is usually uncrowded, and has a small taverna and a snack shop. If you take the bus, you'll have to walk in 1½ kilometers (1 mile) along a gravel road, signposted from the Drios-Parikia road.

Just south of Aliki, on the south shore of the island, is beautiful, sheltered **Faranga Beach,** a short walk in from the main road.

TOWNS & VILLAGES

Until recently, **Naoussa** was a fishing village with simple white houses in a labyrinth of narrow streets, but it's now a growing resort center with good restaurants, trendy bars, and sophisticated boutiques. Most of the new building has been concentrated along the nearby beaches, so the town itself still retains much charm. Colorful fishing boats fill the harbor and fishermen calmly go about their work on the docks, all in the shadow of a half-submerged ruined Venetian fortress. There are a number of good beaches within walking distance of town, or you can catch a caïque to the more distant ones.

The ruins of the Venetian fortress on the east end are most impressive when lighted at night. The most colorful local **festival** is held on August 23, when the battle against the pirate Barbarossa is reenacted by torch-lit boats converging on the harbor; this is followed by feasting, dancing, and general merriment.

The ever helpful **Nissiotissa Tours** (☎ **0284/51-480** or 0284/52-094; fax 0284/51-189) is off the left side of the main square near the bus station, across the lane from the Naoussa Sweet Shop. Cathy and Kostas Gavalas, Greek Americans who are experts on this area of the island, can help you find accommodations, change money, rent a car, book flights or ferries, and arrange excursion tickets, island tours, and outdoor activities.

Buses to Parikia leave the main square in Naoussa on the half hour from 8:30am to 8:30pm, more frequently in July and August. Service to other villages on narrow dirt roads is infrequent (check the schedule at the station). There are daily excursion tours from Naoussa to Mykonos; inquire with Nissiotissa Tours or any other local travel agent.

Hilltop **Lefkes** is the medieval capital of the island. Its whitewashed houses with red-tile roofs form a maze around the central square. Lefkes was built in such an inaccessible location and with an intentionally confusing pattern of streets to thwart pirates. Test your own powers of navigation by finding the **Ayia Triada** (Holy Trinity) **Church,** whose carved marble towers are visible above the town.

The Cave of Andiparos

To get away from all the crowds in Parikia, plan a visit to **Andiparos** ("Opposite Paros"). This islet, about a kilometer (0.6 miles) off the western coast of Paros, was once connected to it by a natural causeway. In recent years, Andiparos has begun to attract its own crowds—but even though you may not be able to completely escape civilization, this smaller, quieter island still has much to offer, including a huge cave full of fantastic stalactites. It was discovered on Andiparos during the time of Alexander the Great, and has been a compelling reason to visit ever since.

Excursion caïques leave the port of Parikia regularly (every 30 minutes in summer) beginning at 9:45am for the 45-minute ride to the busy little port of Andiparos (Dr600/$1.70 one-way). There is also a shuttle barge, for vehicles as well as passengers, that crosses the channel between the southern port of Pounda and Andiparos continuously from 9am; the fare is Dr170 (50¢), Dr1,700 ($4.90) with a car, and you can take along your bicycle for free. Bus fare from Parikia to Pounda is Dr230 (70¢). There are also caïque excursions that include a visit to the cave for about Dr3,000 ($9), departing from Parikia or Naoussa.

The impressive **cave** is a half-hour walk up from the boat landing or a 2-hour hike from the port of Andiparos; buses travel regularly between Andiparos and the cave (Dr1,200/$3.45 round-trip). From the church of Ayios Ioannis, you'll have an excellent view of Folegandros (farthest west), Sikinos, Ios, and part of Paros. Tourists once entered the cave by rope, but a concrete staircase now offers more convenient—if less adventuresome—access. The cave is about 90 meters (300 feet) deep, but the farthest reaches are now closed to visitors. Through the centuries, visitors have broken off parts of stalactites as souvenirs and left graffiti to commemorate their visit, but the cool, mysterious cavern is still worth exploring. An hour spent in the dark, echo-filled chamber trying to decipher some of the inscriptions offers a unique contrast to all your hours devoted to lying on a sun-drenched beach. You'll also be in the company of such distinguished guests as Lord Byron and King Otho of Greece, who each left behind evidence of his visit. The Marquis de Nointel celebrated Christmas mass here in 1673 with 500 paid attendants, plus explosions to add drama.

Andiparos town, with a permanent population of about 700, has several travel agents, a bank with limited hours, a post office, a telephone office (OTE), and an ATM. You'll find a plentiful selection of shops and tavernas along the harborfront, and inland a fine **Kastro,** the remains of the medieval fortified town.

If you're spending the night, we suggest the comfortable **Hotel Artemis,** at the end of the paralia (☎ **0284/61-460;** fax 0284/61-472); or the **Hotel Madalena** (☎ **0284/61-365;** fax 0284/61-206), which offers rooms with views of the sea and port.

OUTDOOR PURSUITS

WALKING Paros has numerous old stone-paved roads connecting the interior towns, many of which are still in good condition and perfect for walking. One of the best known trails is the **Byzantine Road** between Lefkes and Prodromos, a narrow path paved along much of its 4-kilometer (2½-mile) length with marble slabs. Begin in Lefkes, since from here the way is mostly downhill. There isn't an easy way to find the beginning of the Byzantine Road among the labyrinthine streets of Lefkes; we suggest starting at the church square, from which point you can see the flagstone-paved road in a valley at the edge of the town, to the west. Having fixed your bearings, plunge into the maze of streets and spiral your way down and to the right. After a 2-minute descent, you emerge into a ravine, with open fields beyond, and a sign indicates the beginning of the Byzantine Road. It's easy going through terraced fields, a leisurely hour's walk to the Marpissa Road, from which point you can catch the bus back to Parikia (check the schedule and exact pick-up point beforehand). This also makes a challenging mountain-bike outing.

WINDSURFING   The continuous winds on Paros's east coast have made it a favorite destination for windsurfers, and the **World Cup** has been held on Golden Beach for the past 7 years. The best months are July and August, but serious windsurfers may want to visit earlier or later in the season to avoid the crowds. The free *Paros Windsurfing Guide* is available at most tourist offices in Parikia or Naoussa. On Golden Beach, ✪ **Sunwind Surf Center** (☎ **0284/42-900;** fax 0284/42-901; www.sunwind.gr; e-mail: surf@sunwind.gr) charges about Dr5,000 ($14) for 1-hour rental of a board, sail, harness, and wet suit; instruction is an additional Dr1,500 ($4.30) per hour. Reasonable rates for daily or weekly rental are also available; Sunwind can assist in booking complete holiday packages as well. In Naoussa, you can rent equipment from **Club Mistral** (☎ **0284/52-010;** fax 0284/51-720), at the Porto Paros Hotel near Kolimbithres Beach.

SHOPPING

Market Street in Parikia is the shopping hub of the island, with many interesting alternatives to the ubiquitous souvenir stores. At **Geteki** (☎ **0284/21-855**), you'll find paintings and sculpture by French artist Jacques Fleureaux, now a full-time resident of Paros. He makes use of local materials (clay, driftwood) and motifs (Cycladic figurines) in his work. Also for sale here are Afghani rugs and local ceramics by other artists. Yvonne von der Decken's shop ✪ **Palaio Poleio** (☎ **0284/21-909**), opposite the Apollon Restaurant in the agora, has a fine selection of antique vernacular furniture from the islands and the Greek mainland. There are also many smaller items, such as finely decorated mirror frames, water jugs hollowed from solid wood, and handmade household utensils.

In Naoussa's old town, be sure to visit the **Metaxas Gallery** (☎ **0284/52-667**), which has exhibitions of paintings by local artists (sometimes for sale) and locally crafted jewelry. Also in Naoussa is the gallery **Ira,** opposite Nissiotissa Tours, just down the lane from the Naoussa Sweet Shop (☎ **0284/53-566**). It offers local pottery, jewelry, carpets from Greece and Turkey, and fine-arts books of local interest. Owner Hera Papamihail is a talented photographer, and her prints are also available for purchase.

Perched above the village of Kostos, on the road between Parikia and Lefkes, you'll find **Studio Yria** (☎ **0284/29-007**), where Stelio and Monika Ghikis produce functional earthenware that incorporates indigenous designs, including an abstract octopus motif. They also sell weavings and objects of cast bronze, forged iron, and Parian marble.

WHERE TO STAY
PARIKIA

The port town has three basic hotel zones: the **agora,** the **harbor,** and the **beach.** The agora is the heart of Parikia, and can get noisy; accommodations in the quiet back streets are most enticing. The harborside near the windmill is a convenient and lively place, but it's often too loud for a good night's rest. The strip of hotels along Livadi beach—north of the windmill, left coming from the ferry—have three common features: bland decor, proximity to the crowded town beach, and sea views.

We recommend ignoring the room hawkers at the port unless you're absolutely desperate—the rooms offered are usually a considerable distance from town, and many don't meet basic standards of comfort and cleanliness.

In addition to the choices below, you might also consider the small, simple, and inexpensive **Hotel Captain Manolis,** in the center of the agora (☎ **0284/21-244**).

⚫ **Hotel Argonauta.** Agora, Parikia, 84400 Paros. ☎ **0284/21-440.** Fax 0284/23-442. 15 units. A/C TV TEL. Dr20,000 ($57) double; Dr24,000 ($69) triple. MC, V. Closed mid-Oct to Easter. At the far end of Mavroyenous Square, opposite the Ethniki (National) Bank.

This charming and comfortable hotel is refreshingly quiet. The marble-floored bedrooms are reached through a flower-filled courtyard. All units have balconies overlooking the street, but double-paned window glass assures that you won't be disturbed by late-night revelry. One of the first hotels in Parikia, this place has been under the same ownership since 1977—Soula and Dimitri Ghikas make their spacious and attractive lobby feel like home.

Hotel Asterias. Parikia, 84400 Paros. ☎ **0284/21-797.** Fax 0284/22-172. 36 units. TEL. Dr18,000 ($52) double. Breakfast Dr1,800 ($5.15) extra. MC, V. Closed Nov–Mar.

A buffet breakfast is served in the breakfast room, the only room with some degree of character in this rather bland hotel. What the Asterias does offer is proximity to the town beach—the hotel is just across the street from the bay, and most units have balconies with a great view across the bay.

⚫ **Hotel Dina.** Market St., Parikia, 84400 Paros. ☎ **0284/21-325** or 0284/21-345. Fax 0284/23-525. 8 units. Dr11,500 ($33) double. No credit cards. The entrance is just off Market St., next to the Apollon Restaurant and across from the Pirate Bar.

More pension than hotel, these cozy rooms are reached through a narrow, plant-filled courtyard off one of the finest small plazas in Parikia. Dina Patelis has been the friendly proprietor for nearly three decades, and she offers a personal touch that keeps guests coming back year after year. Three bedrooms open to the square; room 2, with a private balcony, is especially desirable. The rest of the units face a small garden courtyard, and room 8 has the additional benefit of a view toward the hills and a private terrace. Air-conditioning will be installed in all rooms by the summer of 2001.

Pension Vangelistra. Parikia, 84400 Paros. ☎ **0284/21-482.** Fax 0284/22-464. 10 units. Dr12,000 ($34) double; Dr15,000 ($43) apt. No credit cards. Follow the central square to the cathedral, and continue back on a road just to the right of the town school, with the small Catholic church on your right. You'll reach an intersection in about 100m—turn right, and the pension will be on your left.

Call Yorgos and Voula Maounis, and one of their friendly English-speaking kids will help you find this cozy lodging in a quiet neighborhood, a 5-minute walk from the pier. All rooms have balconies, with views over the rooftops or toward the hills behind the town; most units have kitchenettes, and all have small fridges. The best option is the apartment in the back garden, a small cottage with kitchen and semiprivate terrace.

SOUTH OF PARIKIA

Hotel Yria. Parasporos, 84400 Paros. ☎ **0284/24-154.** Fax 0284/21-167. E-mail: yria1@otenet.gr. 68 units. A/C MINIBAR TV TEL. Dr45,000 ($129) double; Dr54,000 ($155) suite; Dr79,000 ($227) maisonette (for 4 people). Rates include full buffet breakfast. Lunch or dinner Dr6,000 ($17) extra. AE, DC, MC, V. Closed mid-Nov to Apr. Located 2½km (1½ miles) south of the port.

This new bungalow complex is just too good to be ignored. The architecture is traditional with a villagelike plan, and while not all units have a sea view, the grounds are so beautifully landscaped that you may not feel deprived if your room faces inward. Amenities include a freshwater pool, tennis and basketball courts, a children's playground, and a good dining room. The hotel offers currency exchange, car rental, travel arrangements, laundry, and fax and mail service. The staff is friendly and exceptionally helpful. There's a fair beach nearby.

NAOUSSA

If you're unable to find a room, try **Nissiotissa Tours** (☎ 0284/51-480), just off the east (left) side of the main square. In addition to the following choices, you might try the moderately priced **Captain Dounas Apartments** (☎ 0284/52-525 or 0284/52-585; in winter 01/894-4047; fax 0284/52-586; e-mail: dounas@par.forthnet.gr), which stand on a rocky promontory between Naoussa and Ayii Anaryiri Beach.

✪ **Astir of Paros.** Kolimbithres Beach (west of Naoussa, off the south end of the beach), 84401 Paros. ☎ **0284/51-976** or 0284/51-707. Fax 0284/51-985. http://agn.hol.gr/hotels/astir/astir.htm. E-mail: astir@mail.otenet.gr. 61 units. A/C MINIBAR TV TEL. Dr61,000 ($176) double; Dr69,000–Dr105,000 ($198–$302) suite. Rates include continental breakfast. AE, DC, MC, V. Closed Oct 20 to Easter.

The most extravagant hotel on the island is built like a self-contained Cycladic village within a luxurious garden. There's a small private beach, a 3-hole golf course, a good pool, a tennis court, and a gym. The staff is especially attentive. Double rooms are unexceptional, but the suites are spacious and elegantly furnished. Four units offer handicapped access. Produce for the two hotel restaurants is grown on a nearby farm, and meals are particularly sumptuous—the breakfast buffet (not included in the room rates) includes more than 70 items.

Hotel Fotilia. Naoussa, 84401 Paros. ☎ **0284/52-581** or 0284/52-582. Fax 0284/52-583. 14 units. A/C MINIBAR TEL. Dr22,000 ($63) double. Breakfast Dr1,500 ($4.30) extra. No credit cards.

Climb to the top of the steps at the end of town, and to the left of the hilltop church you'll see a restored windmill and pool terrace behind a stone archway. The companionable Michel Leondaris will probably meet you with a cup of coffee or glass of wine. The hotel bedrooms are spacious and furnished in an elegant country style, with crisp blue-and-white curtains that open to balconies overlooking the old harbor and bay. Studio apartments with kitchenette are available for the same price as a room.

Hotel Petres. Naoussa (1km/0.6 miles from town), 84401 Paros. ☎ **0284/52-467.** Fax 0284/52-759. www.petres.gr. E-mail: petres@otenet.gr. 16 units. A/C MINIBAR TV TEL. Dr30,000 ($86) double. Rates include breakfast. No credit cards. Closed Nov–Mar.

Clea Hatzinikolakis has decorated her charming reception area with antiques, and her guest rooms with loving care. The beds are made with handsome woven covers, the walls adorned with prints from the Benaki Museum. The "honeymoon suite" contains her grandmother's marriage bed. The breakfast buffet is unusually extensive, and dinner is available on request; most Saturdays in summer there's a barbeque at the poolside grill. Free transportation to and from the airport or port can be arranged. The location is very quiet but somewhat disconnected from the life of the town.

Kalypso Hotel. Ayii Anaryiri Beach, 84401 Paros. ☎ **0284/51-488.** Fax 0284/51-607. www.kalypso.gr. E-mail: kalypso@otenet.gr. 40 units. TV TEL. Dr19,000 ($54) double; Dr22,000 ($63) studio. Rates include buffet breakfast. AE, MC, V. Closed Nov to Easter.

A 10-minute walk along the coast from Naoussa brings you to this traditional-style hotel, built right on the sands of the pleasant beach. You enter the hotel through a cobblestone courtyard surmounted by a wooden mezzanine. Many rooms have balconies overlooking the sea; the remaining units face a narrow street behind the hotel. A row of shaded beachfront tables is a great place to have breakfast or just enjoy the view across the bay.

✪ **Papadakis Hotel.** Naoussa (a 5-min. walk uphill from the main square), 84401 Paros. ☎ **0284/51-643** or 0284/52-504. Fax 0284/51-269. 19 units. Dr22,000 ($63) double. Breakfast Dr2,500 ($7) extra. No credit cards.

The new Papadakis offers the best views in town—enjoyed from every room as well as from the new pool with Jacuzzi. The large guest rooms were renovated in 1998, with new wardrobes, beds, and desks in dark walnut; several units also have sofa beds. Ten rooms have satellite TV and minibars, five are air-conditioned, and several have kitchenettes. The excellent breakfast includes homemade baked goods prepared by owner Argyro Barbarigou, who happens to be an incredible chef—be sure to visit her new venture, the Papadakis fish taverna (see "Where to Dine," below).

WHERE TO DINE
PARIKIA

Walk along the bed of the dry river that cuts through Mavroyenous Square's north side to **Symposium** (☎ **0284/24-147**), an elegant coffeehouse perched on a bridge. Enjoy a slow cup of coffee or tea here, or try the dependable continental breakfast or crêpes.

Argonaut Restaurant. Mavroyenous Square. ☎ **0284/21-440.** Main courses Dr1,200–Dr3,000 ($3.45–$9). MC, V. Daily 8am–midnight. GREEK/INTERNATIONAL.

This unpretentious place on the upper end of Mavroyenous Square behind the Hotel Argonauta is dependable during all its long hours. Breakfasts are good and reasonably priced. Salads are fresh and generous. Grilled meats are well prepared, and the usual Greek standards are especially good.

Bountaraki. Paralia. ☎ **0284/22-297.** Main courses Dr1,200–Dr4,000 ($3.45–$12). No credit cards. Daily 1–5pm and 7pm–midnight. Walk all the way to the southern extremity of the paralia, where a bridge spans the dry streambed and the road curves up to the right toward the Xenia hotel; Bountaraki is on the left, just after the bridge. GREEK.

Many small details set this taverna apart from its neighbors: fresh brown bread that's refreshingly flavorful and simple main courses that aren't drowning in too much oil. There's a small porch in front, facing the quieter southern end of the paralia. As with all the local tavernas, don't bother with the desserts, which are clearly an afterthought.

Happy Green Cows. Agora. ☎ **0284/24-691.** Main courses Dr900–Dr2,500 ($2.60–$7). No credit cards. Daily noon–3pm and 6pm–2am. VEGETARIAN.

Four tables huddle in the tiny dining room of the Happy Green Cows, a funky place with simple vegetarian dishes thoughtfully prepared. Traditional Greek dishes are available, if you can call "souvlaki soya" traditional, and are joined by tacos, falafel, burritos, and curries; all the above are also available at the restaurant's take-out window, the only option if you feel like eating outside.

Porphyra. Paralia. ☎ **0284/22-693.** Main courses Dr1,500–Dr5,000 ($4.30–$14). AE, V. Daily 6:30pm–midnight. Closed Jan–Feb. Between the pier and the post office, just back from the waterfront. GREEK/FISH.

The small Porphyra serves the best fish in town. The nondescript, utilitarian service and decor are typical of your average taverna; the difference here is that the owner cultivates the shellfish himself, resulting in an exceptional Mussels Saganaki (mussels cooked with tomato, feta, and wine). The *tzatziki* and other traditional cold appetizers are also very good. The fish is predictably fresh, and offerings vary with the season.

✪ **Tamarisco.** Agora. ☎ **0284/24-689.** Reservations recommended July–Aug. Main courses Dr1,400–Dr4,000 ($4–$12). AE, V. Daily 7pm–midnight. Closed Jan–Feb. Follow the signs from Market St. to this quiet back plaza of busy Parikia. GREEK/VEGETARIAN.

Although most summer diners will sit outside in the garden courtyard, the indoor dining room here is particularly pleasant: Exposed ceiling beams, a flagstone floor, simple furniture, and tapestried walls combine to create a space of unusual comfort and warmth. Eleni, who runs the restaurant with her husband, Stavros, is a native of Paros and uses many local recipes that you won't find elsewhere. The menu features subtle and delightful use of fresh herbs, innovative vegetable dishes, fresh pasta, and a variety of fish. If you're looking for traditional Greek food that's full of surprises and refreshingly contemporary, this is the place.

NAOUSSA

Naoussa's main square has plenty of casual eateries. The **Naoussa Pâtisserie,** on the east side of the square, has delicious cheese pies, pastries, and espresso. The village's **bread bakery** is past the church near Christo's Taverna. The beautiful **Kavarnis Bar,** Odos Archilochus, around the corner from the post office (☎ **0284/51-038**), takes you back to Paris in the 1920s, serving up elaborate cocktails and delectable crêpes.

Barbarossa Ouzeri. Naoussa waterfront. ☎ **0284/51-391.** Appetizers Dr600–Dr2,000 ($1.75–$6). No credit cards. Daily 1pm–1am. Walk along the pier from the bus station, continuing past all the tavernas and cafes to the very end of the pier. GREEK.

This authentic ouzeri is right on the port. Old, wind-burned fishermen sit for hours nursing their milky ouzo in water and their miniportions of grilled octopus and olives. If you haven't partaken of this experience yet, this is the place to try it.

Christo's Taverna. Odos Archilochus. ☎ **0284/51-442.** Reservations recommended July–Aug. Main courses Dr1,600–Dr4,000 ($4.60–$11). No credit cards. Daily 7:30–11:30pm. EURO-GREEK.

Christo's is known for its eclectic menu and Euro-Greek style. Dinner is served in a beautiful garden filled with red and pink geraniums. The color of the dark purple grape clusters dripping through the trellised roof in late summer is unforgettable. Classical music soothes as you dine on elegantly prepared veal, lamb, or steak dishes.

✪ **Papadakis.** Naoussa waterfront. ☎ **0284/51047.** Reservations recommended. Main courses Dr1,800–Dr8,000 ($5.15–$23). AE, V. Daily 7:30pm–midnight. INNOVATIVE GREEK.

Papadakis is on our short list of the best restaurants in the Cyclades, a place where every item on the menu seems to have benefited from the same high level of thoughtfulness and culinary invention. Fresh fish grilled to perfection by Manolis Barbarigou is one of the specialties here, but be sure not to rush to the main course—the appetizers are meant to be savored slowly. Argyro Barbarigou is a truly imaginative chef, and her talent for invention is clear in the many subtle variations on traditional dishes. The *tzatziki* with dill is delicious and refreshingly different, the traditionally prepared *melitzanosalata* is redolent of wood-smoked eggplant, and fresh stuffed pies (fillings vary with the season) are delightful. Save room for one of the incredible desserts—we had the *kataifi ekmek,* a confection conjured from honey, walnuts, cinnamon, custard, and cream.

Beware the *Bomba*

Several places on the strip in Parikia offer very cheap drinks or "buy one, get one free"—this is usually locally brewed alcohol that the locals call *bomba*. It's illegal, and it makes one intoxicated quickly and very sick afterward.

Pervolaria. About 100m back from the port. ☎ **0284/51-598.** Main courses Dr1,900–Dr4,200 ($5.45–$12). AE, V. Daily 7pm–midnight. GREEK.

This good restaurant is set in a lush garden with geraniums and grapevines behind a white stucco house decorated with local ceramics. Favorite courses here include schnitzel à la chef (veal in cream sauce with tomatoes and basil) and tortellini Pervolaria (with pepperoni and bacon), but the Greek plate with souvlaki and varied appetizers is also recommended.

MARPISSA

Corina Taverna. Marpissa. ☎ **0284/41-049.** Main courses Dr1,300–Dr3,500 ($3.75–$10). No credit cards. Daily 9am–4pm and 7pm–midnight. GREEK.

A convivial atmosphere reigns at this small taverna, operated by French American Corina, who draws a loyal following. There's a variety of traditional Greek dishes, including the specialty of the house: a platter of 12 *mezedes* for two with wine. Several vegetable dishes are also offered. Corina, who has lived in Greece for more than 20 years, is a great source of information on the islands. Ask for her excellent photocopied map of attractions on Paros (in French).

PAROS AFTER DARK

Just behind the windmill in Parikia is a local landmark, the **Port Cafe,** a basic kafenio lit by bare incandescent bulbs and filled day and night with tourists waiting for a ferry, bus, taxi, or fellow traveler. The cafe serves coffee, pastry, and drinks; it's a good place for casual conversation.

The ✪ **Pebbles Bar** on the paralia plays classical music at sunset; it's a highly congenial place, as popular with locals as it is with visitors. Continue south from Parikia along the coast road, turn left at the bridge, and about 100 meters later you should have no difficulty finding **Dubliner** (☎ **0284/22-759**), a complex with several bars and a disco; the crowd here is very young.

If you're not in the mood to party, Parikia offers several more-elegant alternatives. The ✪ **Pirate Bar** (☎ **0284/21-114**), a few doors from the Hotel Dina in the agora, is a tastefully decorated nightspot with a stone interior and dark wooden beams; it plays mellow jazz, blues, and classical music. Back on the paralia, **Evinos Bar** has a great view of the harbor—it's above the retaining wall south of the OTE, high enough above the crowd that you can hear the music and enjoy the scenery. For partyers in Parikia, there's **Black Bart's** (☎ **0284/21-802**), midway on the paralia in Parikia, a good place for loud music and boisterous big drinkers. The outdoor **Ciné Rex** (☎ **0284/21-676**) in Parikia shows two features, often in English.

There seems to be little traditional Greek entertainment on Paros, but if you're interested, ask about the possibility of seeing a performance by the local community dance group in Naoussa—there are usually performances once in a fortnight. You can get information and purchase tickets at **Nissiotissa Tours** in Naoussa (☎ **0284/51-480**).

Bars in Naoussa tend to be more sophisticated and considerably less raucous than in Parikia. There's also an outdoor movie theater in Naoussa, **Makis Cinema** (☎ **0284/22-221**), with nightly features usually at 10pm and midnight; these are often action films in English.

5 Naxos

191km (103 nautical miles) SE of Piraeus

Fertile, self-sufficient Naxos is not yet as developed for tourism as neighboring Paros, but it's working hard to catch up. A wealthy agricultural island, Naxos exports an abundant harvest of olives, grapes, and potatoes throughout the Aegean, and until recently showed little interest in promoting itself as a tourist destination. That's all changed in the past 10 years—a new airport has increased the flow of visitors, and big new hotels keep sprouting up to either side of the port. The harborfront in Hora has undergone massive reconstruction, successfully erasing whatever individual character this part of the town once possessed.

Thankfully, the character of the island still isn't completely dominated by the recent development. The inland mountain villages, huddled on the lower slopes of imperious Mount Zas, still preserve the rhythms of agrarian life. In Apiranthos, you can taste bread redolent with the smoky aroma of a wood oven, and in Filoti sample local wines under the arms of a venerable plane tree. The locals still have an attitude of friendly indifference (which could be misconstrued as surliness) to the visitors who pass through.

The architecture of Naxos is distinct from that of any other Cycladic isle. You'll notice immediately the fortified Venetian towers, or *piryi*, punctuating the hillsides. Also specific to Naxos is the remarkable abundance of small Byzantine chapels, many of which contain exceptional frescoes dating from the 9th to the 13th centuries. The Kastro of Hora is one of the finest medieval fortified towns in the Cyclades, and a delight to explore.

Naxos is very well connected to other islands by ferry, so you shouldn't have any trouble getting here at most times of year. It's possible to catch a bus to a village that interests you, then explore it leisurely on foot; keep in mind that island buses are reliable but infrequent. A bike may be all the transport you need to the island's beaches, which happen to be among the best in the Cyclades.

ESSENTIALS

GETTING THERE   By Plane   Olympic Airways (www.olympic-airways.gr) has at least one flight daily between Naxos and Athens. For information and reservations, visit **Naxos Tours,** toward the south end of the paralia (☎ **0285/23-043**), the local representative for Olympic; or call Olympic's Athens office at ☎ **0801/44444** or 01/966-6666.

By Boat   From Piraeus, there is at least one daily ferry (6 hrs.) and one daily high-speed ferry (4 hrs.); schedules can be checked with the Athens **GNTO tourist office** (☎ **01/331-0562**), the **Port Authority in Piraeus** (☎ **01/459-3223**), or the **Naxos Port Authority** (☎ **0285/22-300**). There is at least once-daily ferry connection with Ios, Mykonos (1 to 2 hrs.), Paros (30 to 60 mins.), and Santorini (2 to 4 hrs.). There is ferry connection several times weekly with Siros (1½ to 2½ hrs. by high-speed ferry or hydrofoil), Tinos (2 to 4 hrs.), and Samos (7 hrs. to Vathi); and somewhat less frequently with Sifnos (1½ hrs. by hydrofoil), and Folegandros (3 hrs.). For ferry tickets, try **Zas Travel** (☎ **0285/23-330**), on the paralia opposite the ferry pier.

VISITOR INFORMATION   The privately operated **Naxos Tourist Information Center** (☎ **0285/22-993;** fax 0285/25-200), across the plaza from the ferry pier (not to be confused with the small office on the pier itself, which is often closed), is the most reliable source of information. Under the energetic direction of Despina Kittini, this office provides ferry information, books charter flights between various European airports and Athens, books accommodations, arranges excursions, sells maps, exchanges money, holds luggage, assists with phone calls, provides 2-hour laundry service, and offers a **24-hour emergency number** (☎ **0285/24-525**) for travelers on Naxos who need immediate assistance.

Naxos has an excellent Web site, **www.naxosnet.com**, with maps, bus schedules, hotel listings, and a photo tour of the island.

You will want to find a good map as soon as possible, as Hora (Naxos town) is old, large (with a permanent population of more than 3,000), and complex. The free *Summer Naxos* magazine has the best map of the city. The new *Harms-Verlag Naxos* is the best map of the island, but somewhat pricey at Dr2,500 ($7) a copy.

GETTING AROUND   By Bus   The bus station is right in the middle of the port plaza at the north end of the harbor. Ask at the nearby KTEL office, across the plaza to the left, for specific schedules. There's regular service throughout most of the island two or three times a day, more frequently to major destinations. In summer, there's service every 30 minutes to the nearby south coast beaches at Ayios Prokopios and Ayia Anna. A popular day trip is to Apollonas, near the northern tip. The competition for seats on this route can be fierce, so get to the station well ahead of time. In addition to the public buses, there are various excursion buses that can be booked through travel agents.

By Bicycle & Moped   Moto Naxos (☎ **0285/23-420**), on Protodikiou Square south of the paralia, has the best mountain bikes as well as mopeds for rent. A basic bike is Dr1,500 ($4.30) a day; aluminum-frame mountain bikes range from Dr2,000 to Dr5,000 ($6 to $14) a day. For a moped, expect to pay Dr4,000 to Dr6,000 ($11 to $17) a day. Naxos has some major inclines that require a strong motor and good brakes, so a larger bike (80cc or greater) is recommended.

By Car   This is the ideal mode of transport on Naxos, and most travel agents rent them. A basic four-door car is about Dr12,000 ($34) per day at **AutoTour** (☎ **0285/25-480**), off the north end of the port, up from the bus station across from the elementary school; or at **Auto Naxos** (☎ **0285/23-420**), on Protodikiou Square.

By Taxi   The taxi station (☎ **0285/22-444**) is on the port. A half-day round-the-island tour costs about Dr5,000 ($14) per hour. Find a compatible driver, then bargain and agree on a price before you depart. A taxi trip within Naxos shouldn't cost more than Dr1,000 ($2.90); the fare to Ayia Anna is about Dr2,000 ($6), and to Apiranthos, Dr5,000 ($14).

FAST FACTS   The **Commercial Bank,** on the paralia, has an ATM. It and other banks are open Monday through Thursday from 8am to 2pm, Friday from 8am to 1:30pm. Naxos has a good 24-hour **health center** (☎ **0285/23-333**) just outside Hora on the left off Odos Papavasiliou, the main street off the port. **Holiday Laundry,** on Periferiakos Road, Grotta area (☎ **0285/23-988**), offers drop-off service—you can leave your laundry with most hotels and some tourist offices. The **police** (☎ **0285/23-280**) are beyond Protodikiou Square, by the Galaxy Hotel. To find the **post office,** continue south on the paralia past the OTE to the basketball court; it's opposite the court on the left, on the second floor (open from 8am to 2pm). The **telephone office (OTE)** is at the south end of the port; summer hours are daily from 7:30am to 2pm.

WHAT TO SEE & DO
THE TOP ATTRACTIONS

The Portara. Hora. Open site.

Naxos harbor is dominated by the picturesque silhouette of the Portara ("Great Door"), all that remains of an ancient Temple of Apollo. The ruin stands on the islet of Palatia, accessible by a causeway off the northern tip of the harbor. The temple was once thought to honor Dionysos, the island's patron, and is associated in the popular imagination with his rescue of Ariadne after she was abandoned on Naxos by the ungrateful Theseus. The temple is now believed to be dedicated to Apollo, due to a brief reference in the Delian Hymns and because it directly faces Delos, Apollo's birthplace. Most of the temple was carted away to build the Kastro, but fortunately the massive posts and lintel of the Portara were too big for the Venetians to handle. **Palatia,** the small cafe/ouzeri at the end of the causeway, below the Portara, is a superb spot to watch the sunset.

Kastro/Archaeological Museum/Venetian Museum. Hora. Archaeological Museum ☎ **0285/22-725;** admission Dr500 ($1.45) adults, Dr300 (90¢) students; Tues–Sun 8am–2:30pm. Venetian Museum ☎ **0285/22-387;** admission Dr1,500 ($4.30) adults, Dr500 ($1.45) students; daily 10am–3pm and 6–10pm.

The archaeological museum is located in the heart of the exquisite Venetian Kastro, the medieval citadel that dominates the town. The Kastro (Castle) is Hora's greatest treasure, and you should allow yourself several hours to explore it. Built in the 13th century by Marco Sanudo, nephew of the doge of Venice, it was the domain of the Catholic aristocracy. By walking up from the seafront in Hora you'll soon reach the outer wall of the castle, which has three entryways. The most remarkable of these is the north entry, known as the **Trani Porta** or Strong Gate, a narrow marble arched threshold marking the transition to the Kastro's medieval world. Look for the incision on the right column of the arch, which marks the length of a Venetian yard, and was used to measure the cloth brought here for the ladies of the Venetian court. At the center of the Kastro is the 16th-century **Catholic cathedral,** with its brilliant marble façade; it contains an icon of the Virgin which is thought to be older than the church itself. To the right behind the cathedral is the French School of Commerce and the Ursuline Convent and School.

The French School has housed schools run by several religious orders, and among its more famous students was the Cretan writer Nikos Kazantzakis, who studied here in 1896. It now houses the ✪ **Archaeological Museum.** There have been many archaeological finds on Naxos, and this museum has a great diversity of objects from several different periods. Among the highlights are the early Cycladic figurines in white marble, the earliest example of sculpture in Greece. The other prize of this museum is its collection of late Mycenaean period (1400 to 1100 B.C.) artifacts found near Grotta, including vessels with the octopus motif that still appears in local art. The museum occupies long vaulted chambers in the walls of the Kastro, with a great view from its terrace and balconies to the hills of Naxos. There is little in the way of interpretive information, and almost all of it is in Greek; serious museum-goers will appreciate the descriptive booklet available at the ticket desk for Dr1,700 ($4.90).

The **Venetian Museum,** located at the north entry to the Kastro, is a typical Kastro house, home of the Della-Rocca family, recently opened to the public. The 40-minute tours, offered in English and Greek, include explanations of implements and objects belonging to the family, a tasting of local wines and liquors, and a brief history of the Kastro and the island's Catholic aristocracy.

Mitropolis Site Museum. Hora. ☎ **0285/24-151.** Free admission. Tues–Sun 8am–2:30pm. Turn in from the paralia at Zas Travel, and continue about 100m until you see the Mitropolis Cathedral Square on your right.

This innovative new museum, located in the square facing Naxos town's Mitropolis Cathedral, preserves the open space of the square while providing access to the excavated archaeological site below. Excavations undertaken from 1982 to 1985 revealed a history of continuous occupation from Mycenaean times to the present, with significant remains of a classical shrine to the founders of the city buried beneath the remains of the Roman city. The museum, a single subterranean room circled by a suspended walkway, is sited inconspicuously beneath the surface of the square.

Temple of Demeter. Ano Sangri. Open site. Depart from Hora on the road to Filoti, and turn off after about 10km (6.2 miles) on the signposted road to Ano Sangri and the Temple of Demeter. From here it's another 3½km (2.2 miles) to the temple, primarily on dirt roads (all the major turnings are signposted).

Until recently, the temple, built in the 6th century B.C., was in a state of complete ruin; it had been partially dismantled in the 6th century A.D. to build a chapel on the site, and what was left was plundered repeatedly over the years. A few years ago, it was discovered that virtually all the pieces of the original temple were on the site, either buried or integrated into the chapel. Then began a long process of reconstruction, which continues at present. Most of the work has been completed, and it's possible to see the basic form of the temple—one of the few known temples to be square in plan. Although work continues, the site is open to the public.

BYZANTINE CHURCHES

There is a remarkable number of small Byzantine chapels on Naxos, most dating from the 9th to the 15th centuries. The prosperity of Naxos during this period of Byzantine rule meant that sponsorship existed for elaborate frescoes, many of which can still be seen on the interior walls of the chapels. Restoration has revealed multiple layers of frescoes, and whenever possible the more recent ones have been removed intact during the process of revealing the initial paintings. Several frescoes removed in this way from the churches of Naxos can be seen at the Byzantine Museum in Athens.

Just south of Moni, near the middle of the island, is the important 6th-century monastery of ✪ **Panayia Drossiani** ("Our Lady of Refreshment"), which contains some of the finest frescoes on Naxos. Visits are allowed at all hours during the day; when the door is locked, ring the church bell to summon the caretaker (remember to dress appropriately). To get here, drive about 1 kilometer (0.6 miles) south from Moni and look for the low, gray rounded form of the church on your left.

About 8 kilometers (5 miles) from Hora along the road to Sangri, you'll see a sign on the left for the 8th-century Byzantine cathedral of **Ayios Mamas,** which fell into disrepair during the Venetian occupation but has recently been partly restored. South of the pretty little village of Ano ("Upper") Sangri is the small Byzantine chapel of **Ayios Ioannis Yiroulas.** It was built over an ancient temple of Demeter and is accessible on foot or by an unimproved road off the main road south from Sangri. About 1 kilometer (0.6 miles) west of Sangri on the road to Halki is the ✪ **Kaloritsa chapel,** a cave inside the hilltop ruins of a Byzantine chapel. The earliest of the frescoes seen here date from the 10th century. The chapel is accessible only on foot; for directions, see "Walking," below.

THE VILLAGES

There are many small villages within the folds of Naxos's hills. Each is unique, and you could easily spend several days exploring them. The bus between Hora and Apollonas makes stops at each of the villages mentioned below, but you'll have considerably more freedom if you rent a car.

Halki, 16 kilometers (9.9 miles) from Hora, has a lovely central square shaded by a magnificent plane tree. The 19th-century neoclassical homes of this town lend the streets a certain grandeur. The fine 11th-century white church with the red-tiled roof, **Panayia Protothronos** ("Our Lady Before the Throne"), is sometimes open in the morning. Turn right to reach the Frankopoulos (or Grazia) tower. The name says it's Frankish, but it was originally Byzantine; a marble crest gives the year of 1742, when it was renovated by the Venetians. Climb the steps for an excellent view of Filoti, one of the island's largest inland villages.

The brilliant white houses of **Filoti,** 2 kilometers (1.2 miles) up the road from Halki, are draped elegantly along the lower slopes of **Mount Zas,** the highest peak in the Cyclades. The center of town life is the main square, shaded by a massive plane tree; the kafenion at the center of the square and two tavernas within 50 meters are all authentic and welcoming. In the center of town is the church of **Kimisis tis Theotokou** ("Assumption of the Mother of God"), with a lovely marble iconostasis and a Venetian tower.

Apiranthos, 10 kilometers (6.2 miles) beyond Filoti, the most enchanting of the mountain villages, is remarkable in that its buildings, streets, and even domestic walls are built of the brilliant white Naxos marble. The people of Apiranthos were originally from Crete, and fled their home during a time of Turkish oppression. Be sure to visit **Taverna Lefteris,** the excellent cafe/restaurant just off the main square (see "Where to Dine," below).

Apollonas, at the northern tip of the island, is a small fishing village on the verge of becoming a rather depressing resort. It has a sand cove, a pebbled beach, plenty of places to eat, rooms to let, and a few hotels. From the town, a path leads about 1 kilometer (0.6 miles) south to the famous **kouros;** you can also drive, turning right on the road to Hora just south of town. The kouros is a colossal statue some 10 meters tall, begun in the 7th century B.C. and abandoned probably because of the fissures that time and the elements have exacerbated. Some archaeologists believe it was meant for the nearby temple of Apollo, but the beard suggests that it's probably the island's patron deity, Dionysos.

BEACHES

Naxos has the longest and some of the best beaches in the Cyclades, although you wouldn't know it looking at the crowded **Ayios Yioryios** beach just south of Hora. The next beach south is **Ayios Prokopios,** around the headland of Stellida. This fine-sand beach is less crowded at its northern end. **Ayia Anna,** the next cove south, is much smaller, with a small port for the colorful caïques that transport beachgoers from the main port. Both Ayios Prokopios and Ayia Anna are accessible by public bus in the summer.

South of Ayia Anna you'll find ✪ **Plaka Beach,** the best on the island, a 5-kilometer (3.1-mile) stretch of almost uninhabited shoreline where clothing is optional; you can reach it by walking south from Ayia Anna. Further south, 16 kilometers (9.9 miles) from Hora, are **Micri Vigla,** known for its windsurfing center, and **Kastraki Beach,** with waters recently rated the cleanest in the Aegean and a 7-kilometer (4½-mile) stretch of beach; both remain relatively uncrowded, even in peak season. Further still, 21 kilometers (13 miles) from Hora, **Pyrgaki,** the last stop on the coastal bus

Remember the Repellent

Note that both Ayios Prokopios and Ayia Anna have a mosquito problem in the summer due to several stagnant ponds behind the beach that serve as breeding grounds.

route, offers excellent swimming in the large protected bay. The 150 meters of sand and cobble beach in the sheltered cove of **Abrami**, about 6 kilometers (4 miles) past Apollonas at the north end of the island, is secluded and uncrowded. It's 500 meters in from the main road on a rough one-lane dirt track.

WALKING

If you're going to spend some time on the island, we recommend buying a copy of Christian Ucke's excellent guide *Walking Tours on Naxos*. Most of the start and finish points for the walks can be reached by island bus. It's available for Dr4,500 ($13) at **Naxos Tourist Information Center** on the paralia. As with all the Cyclades, you should also go equipped with a map and a good sense of direction.

One fascinating Naxos site that can only be reached on foot is the ✪ **Kaloritsa Chapel,** near the town of Ano Sangri. Inside the ruins of this Byzantine Church is a cave containing an iconostasis and some fine 13th-century frescoes—it's best seen in the late afternoon, when the low sun illuminates the cave's interior. You can take the bus to Ano Sangri and walk from there, or you can drive—200 meters past Ano Sangri on the road to Filoti, there's a fork to the right at a JetOil station, signposted for Kaloritsa. Another 200 meters brings you to the striking **Pirgos Timios Stavros;** park just past this medieval tower, where another sign for Kaloritsa points up the side of the hill. Look up the hill in the direction of the sign, and you'll see the ruined remains of the Kaloritsa Chapel about halfway up. There isn't a trail, but there are some goat paths that make the going easier. Make your way to a low stone wall that climbs in the direction of the chapel—there's a path along its base that goes most of the way. The cave itself is blocked off, but you can get a good view of the interior from above; binoculars are helpful for making out the details of the icons and frescoes inside.

SHOPPING

Hora is a fine place for shopping, both for value and variety. Toward the north end of the paralia, near the bus station, you'll find **O Kouros** (☎ **0285/25-565**), which has copies of Cycladic figurines in Naxian marble, other reproductions, and interesting modern ceramics. To the right and up from the entrance to the Old Market is ✪ **Techni** (☎ **0285/24-767**), which has two shops within 20 meters of each other. The first shop contains a good array of silver jewelry at fair prices; above it the second and more interesting of the two has textiles, many handwoven, and some by local women. Many are from earlier in the century, when the traditions of weaving and embroidery were still flourishing. There are also hand-painted copies of icons made at Mount Athos.

On the paralia next to Grotta Tours is tiny **Galini** (☎ **0285/24-785**), with a collection of local ceramics. Continue south along the paralia to the OTE, turn left on the main inland street, Odos Papavasiliou, and continue up the left side of the street until your nose leads you into the **Tirokomika Proïonda Naxou** (☎ **0285/22-230**). This delightful old store is filled with excellent local cheeses (*kephalotiri*, a superb sharp one, and milder *graviera*), barrels of olives, local wines, honey, spices, and other dried comestibles. It's also a good place to pick up a bottle of *kitron,* the island's famous sweet citron liqueur.

In the interior of Naxos, on the stretch of road between Sangri and Halki, you'll see a sign pointing toward the **Damalas Pottery Workshop** (☎ **0285/32-890**); 200 meters along this one-lane road brings you to the small workshop, operated by a father-and-son team. The father learned his trade on Sifnos, an island renowned for its pottery, and now father and son produce a variety of forms, some of them specific to Naxos. No English is spoken.

In Apiranthos, some local weaving and needlework is sold by the village women. **Stiasto** (☎ **0285/61-392**) has a good selection of popular art, including good ceramics.

WHERE TO STAY

Hora's broad paralia is too busy for quiet accommodations, so we recommend hotels in four nearby areas, all within a 10-minute walk of the port: Bourgo, the old section of town just above the harbor below the Kastro; Grotta, a development of newer houses left (north) and up from the port; behind the town; and Ayios Yioryios, a beach resort just south (right from the harbor) of town.

BOURGO

✪ **Chateau Zevgoli.** Bourgo, Hora, 84300 Naxos. ☎ **0285/22-993** or 0285/26-123. Fax 0285/25-200. www.greekhotel.net/cyclades/naxos/chora/zevgoli. 14 units. Dr25,000 ($72) double (hotel and Kastro); Dr30,000 ($86) honeymoon suite (Kastro). Hotel rates include breakfast. AE, MC, V. Closed Nov–Mar.

This small hotel, easily the most attractive in Naxos, is located at the foot of the Kastro walls. The lobby/dining area has been charmingly decorated with antiques and family heirlooms by the gracious owner, Despina Kitini. All guest rooms open onto a central atrium with a lush garden. The units are small but distinctively furnished; room 8 features a canopy bed and a private terrace, and several units have views of the harbor. For those interested in an experience of medieval grandeur, Despina Kitini also has four apartments in a 12th-century house in the Kastro, just 100 meters from the hotel. These share a magisterial sitting room, stone walls and floors, and appropriately antiquated and austere furnishings. The bedrooms here are simple and unremarkable, with the exception of the honeymoon suite, which has a balcony overlooking the town and the sea. (Inquire at the Naxos Tourist Information Center on the paralia.)

Hotel Anixis. Bourgo, Hora, 84300 Naxos. ☎ **0285/22-932,** or 0285/22-782 in winter. Fax 0285/22-112. 19 units. Dr14,000 ($40) double; Dr17,000 ($49) triple. Continental breakfast Dr1,000 ($2.90) extra. V. Closed Oct–Mar. From the bus station, take the nearest major street (with traffic) off the port and turn right through the lancet archway into the Old Market area; follow the stenciled blue arrows to the hotel.

This simple hotel near the Kastro's Venetian tower offers comfortable accommodations in a desirable old neighborhood of Hora. Located on a narrow pedestrian street, the entrance leads through a small walled garden to a terrace overlooking town and sea. The friendly manager, Dimitris Sideris, knows the island well, so be sure to ask him about excursions to uncrowded beaches, Byzantine chapels, and ancient sites. The rooms on the top floor have the best view of the sea, and six of them have their own small balcony. The breakfast terrace enjoys a splendid sea view. If you make advance arrangements, Dimitris will meet you at the port and drive you to the base of the hill—you'll still have to walk the last 100 meters up to the hotel.

GROTTA

Hotel Grotta. Grotta, Hora, 84300 Naxos. ☎ **0285/22-215** or 0285/22-201. Fax 0285/22-000. www.hotelgrotta.gr. E-mail: grotta@naxos-island.com. 20 units. TEL. Dr22,000 ($63) double, Dr28,000 ($80) triple. Rates include breakfast. MC, V. Closed Nov–Mar.

Follow the east coast road to the left after the school, and you'll find the friendly Lianos family's hotel off to the left. The spotless rooms have polished marble floors, large balconies, and fridges. Many also have excellent views across the harbor to the Portara and Naxos town. Rooms without sea views face a pleasant garden courtyard. You can call ahead and arrange to be picked up at the ferry or the airport.

AYIOS YIORYIOS

If the following choices are booked, you can try the unexciting but reliable **Galaxy Hotel,** 75 meters from the beach at Ayios Yioryios (☎ **0285/22-422** or 0285/22-423; fax 0285/22-889); some rooms have balconies or terraces facing the water.

Hotels Galini and Sofia. Ayios Yioryios, Hora, 84300 Naxos. ☎ **0285/22-516** or 0285/22-114. Fax 0285/22-677. www.naxos-island.com/hotels/galini. E-mail: h-galini@naxos-island.com or h-galini@nax.forthnet.gr. 30 units. MINIBAR TEL. Dr15,000 ($43) double. Breakfast Dr1,500 ($4.30) extra. AE, V. Closed Nov–Mar.

The hotels Galini and Sofia share the same building, the same friendly management, and the same sea views. In fact, they represent the curious phenomenon of one hotel with two names. There are some differences: The Sofia's bedrooms are decorated in bright pastels, while those in the Galini are a more conservative white. All but two unfortunate units on the interior courtyard have balconies with excellent sea views; the view from rooms 11 and 14 is especially good. The hotels are both run by the charming Sofia and her amiable son George. Guests are free to send and receive e-mail from the hotel computer. Transportation is provided to and from the port if you make arrangements in advance.

OUTSIDE HORA

Naxos Beach Two. Ayios Prokopios, 84300 Naxos. ☎ **0285/26-591.** Fax 0285/24-197. 50 units. A/C TV TEL. Dr39,000 ($112) double. MC, V. Closed Oct–Mar.

Built on a steep slope overlooking Hora, this is the most attractive complex of villas on the island. Constructed of tile, stone, and whitewashed plaster, the buildings evoke the traditional architecture of local villages. Each group of houses is built around a small flagstone courtyard, with one court connected to the next by steep steps curving through low archways. The rooms have been designed with many elements typical of vernacular buildings: wood ceiling beams, stone floors, and wood shutters, all effective in keeping the spaces cool in summer even without the aid of the air-conditioning. Units tend to be rather small, but all have a balcony or terrace. The downside of this place is that the immediately surrounding landscape is particularly desolate and packed with new development, making it necessary to rent a car to go to Hora, 3½ kilometers (2 miles) away; the nearest good beach, Ayios Prokopios, is about 2 kilometers (1.2 miles) by road or footpath.

WHERE TO DINE
HORA

The Bakery, on the paralia (☎ **0285/22-613**), has baked goods at fair prices. Further north, across from the bus station, **Bikini** (☎ **0285/24-701**) is a good place for breakfast and crêpes.

Boulamatsis. North end of paralia. ☎ **0285/24-227.** Main courses Dr900–Dr2,700 ($3–$9). No credit cards. Daily 7:30am–midnight. GREEK.

Toward the north end of the paralia, turn up a flight of stairs adjacent to Posto Travel Office to reach this unassuming establishment above the paralia shops. A TV in the dining room is turned to the Greek news or a soccer match, and the glass counter displays the day's fish and meats. At the back of the restaurant, a small terrace opens out to the port. The food is hearty and simple, prepared with fresh ingredients that are allowed to speak for themselves. The menu features several grilled meats (lamb, veal, pork, goat) and grilled fish (the mixed fish souvlaki is excellent). The *melitzanosalata* and other cold salads suffer from the addition of copious quantities of mayonnaise. The house retsina and rosé are palatable, local, and inexpensive.

Nikos. Paralia, above the Commercial Bank. ☎ **0285/23-153.** Main courses Dr1,500–Dr3,000 ($4.30–$9). MC, V. Daily 8am–1am. GREEK.

This is one of the most popular restaurants in town. The owner, Nikos Katsayannis, is himself a fisherman, and the range of seafood available will amaze you. It's all pretty good, and those not in the mood for fish can try the *eksohiko,* fresh lamb and vegetables with fragrant spices wrapped in crisp filo (pastry leaves). The wine list is quite long, with lots of local and Cyclades choices. The ice-cream desserts are also delightful.

The Old Inn. 100m in from the port. ☎ **0285/26-093.** Main courses Dr1,000–Dr3,500 ($2.90–$10). AE, DC, EC, MC, V. Daily 6pm–2am. INTERNATIONAL.

Dieter Ranizewski, who operated for many years the popular Faros Restaurant on the paralia, now runs this place. The courtyard offers a green haven from the noise and crowds of the paralia. The restaurant inhabits several buildings around the courtyard, once a small monastery, and the wine cellar is situated in a former chapel. Another vaulted room houses an eclectic collection of old objects from the island and from Dieter's native Berlin. The Germanic menu offers an alternative to standard taverna fare, and the food is simple, hearty, and abundant.

Taverna To Kastro. Braduna Sq. ☎ **0285/22-005.** Main courses Dr1,500–Dr3,000 ($4.30–$9). No credit cards. Daily 7pm–2am. GREEK.

Just outside the Kastro's south gate you'll find the small Braduna Square, which is packed with tables on summer evenings. There's an excellent view toward the bay and St. George's beach, and at dusk a pacifying calm pervades the place. The specialty here is rabbit stewed in red wine with onions, spiced with pepper and a suggestion of cinnamon. The local wines are surprisingly light and delicious.

APIRANTHOS

✪ **Taverna Lefteris.** Apiranthos. ☎ **0285/61-333.** Main courses Dr1,500–Dr3,000 ($4.30–$9). No credit cards. Daily 11am–11pm. GREEK.

Find your way to Apiranthos, the most beautiful town in Naxos, where you'll find one of the island's best restaurants. The small menu features the staples of Greek cooking, prepared in a way that reminds you how good this food can be. The dishes highlight the freshest of vegetables and meats, prepared with admirable subtlety; the hearty homemade bread is delicious. A cozy marble-floored room faces the street, and in back is a flagstone terrace shaded by two massive trees. The homemade sweets are an exception to the rule that you should avoid dessert in tavernas—it's worth making the trip for the sweets alone.

NAXOS AFTER DARK

Naxos certainly doesn't compare to Mykonos or Santorini for wild nightlife, but it has a lively and varied scene. **Portara,** just below its namesake at the far end of the harbor, is an excellent place to enjoy the sunset. Next, you can join the evening **volta** (stroll) along the paralia. **Fragile** (☎ 0285/25-336), through the arch in the entrance to the Old Town, is one of the older bars in town and worth a stop. Up in the Kastro, **Notos** offers a sedate evening with mellow jazz.

Day and Night, opposite the OTE, has a good blend of music which becomes more purely Greek in the early morning. At the end of the waterfront past the National Bank, you'll find **Vengera** (☎ 0285/23-567), which doesn't open until 9pm and doesn't get warmed up until much later; it plays mostly '70s and '80s rock. **Naxos By Night,** on the way to the beach from Protodikiou Square, has bouzouki music and dancing.

6 Mykonos (Mikonos)

177km (96 nautical miles) SE of Piraeus

Mykonos is an island that lives well with contradiction. Depending on the season, Mykonos, a place with multiple personalities, can be an island of partyers, of sophisticated travelers, of students, of "Greece for the Greeks"—what you experience depends largely on when you go. The most remarkable thing about Mykonos is that through all the transformations and responses to changing fashions, it has somehow managed to hold on to much of its charm and self-respect.

In July and August, the island is occupied by legions of young travelers attracted by Mykonos's reputation as *the* party destination in the Aegean, which it is during those months. In May and June, the nightlife is active on weekends, but you can walk through the streets at night without having to negotiate a sea of revelers. In September—perhaps the best month to visit—the sea is warm, the debris that fills the streets throughout the summer has mostly been cleared away, and you can actually eat in a decent restaurant without a reservation. Mykonos remains active year-round, and in winter hosts numerous cultural events, including a small film festival. Many who are scared off by the summer crowds find a different, tranquil Mykonos during this off-season, drawn by the deserved reputation of Hora as one of the most beautiful towns in the Cyclades. Mykonos is one of the only islands in the Aegean where scuba diving is permitted, and there are several dive centers that rent equipment and offer instruction.

During high season (July and August), the overcrowding is truly overwhelming. The best way to avoid the crowds is to get up early, visit the beaches before noon, and explore the streets of Hora in the late afternoon, when almost everyone in town wakes up and heads for the beach. We strongly recommend that you not plan a stay on Mykonos without reservations in high season, unless you enjoy sleeping out of doors.

ESSENTIALS

GETTING THERE   By Plane   Olympic Airways (www.olympic-airways.gr) has several flights daily (once daily in off-season) between Mykonos and Athens, and one flight daily from Mykonos to Iraklion (Crete) and Santorini. Book flights in advance and reconfirm at the Olympic office in Athens (☎ 0801/44-444 or 01/966-6666) or Mykonos (☎ 0289/22-490). The Mykonos office is near the south bus station; open Monday through Friday from 8am to 3:30pm. There are also several travel agencies on the port that sell Olympic tickets.

By Boat   From Piraeus, there are departures for Mykonos at least once daily by ferry (5 to 7 hrs.) and by high-speed ferry (3 hrs.). Check schedules in Piraeus with the **Port Authority** (☎ 01/459-3223), or with the Athens **GNTO tourist office** (☎ 01/331-0562). From Rafina, there's daily catamaran service to Mykonos (2 hrs.); check schedules with the local **Port Authority** (☎ 0294/22-300). There is daily ferry connection between Mykonos and Paros (40 mins. by catamaran, 1½ hrs. by car ferry), Naxos (1½ to 3 hrs.), Siros (30 mins. by high-speed ferry, 1 to 2 hrs. by ferry), Tinos

(15 to 30 mins.), and Santorini (3½ to 5½ hrs.); ferries travel less frequently to Folegandros (4 hrs.), Sifnos (2½ hrs.), and Thessaloniki (14 to 18 hrs.).

VISITOR INFORMATION Windmills Travel (☎ 0289/26-555; www. windmills-travel.com; e-mail: info@windmills-travel.com) has an office at the south bus station where you can get general information, book accommodations, arrange excursions, and rent a car or moped. Look for the free *Mykonos Summertime* magazine, available in cafes, shops, and hotels throughout the island.

GETTING AROUND   One of the best things to happen to Mykonos was the government decree that made Hora an architectural landmark and prohibited motorized traffic from its streets. You will see a few small delivery vehicles, but the only way to get around town is to walk. There is a busy peripheral road along which many of the town's large hotels are found, and much of the rest of the island is served by a good transportation system.

By Bus   Mykonos has a well organized bus system. Buses run frequently and cost Dr200 to Dr900 (60¢ to $2.60) one-way. There are two stations in Hora. The **north station** is near the middle of the harbor below the Leto Hotel. From here, buses leave for Tourlos, Ayios Stefanos, the northwest coast hotels, the inland village of Ano Mera, and the far east coast beaches of Elia, Kalo Livadi, and Kalafatis. Schedules are posted, though subject to change. The **south station** is a 10-minute walk inland from the harbor, near Plateia Laka. From this stop, buses leave for the airport, Ayios Ioannis, Ornos, Psarou, and Platis Yialos; from Ornos or Platis Yialos you can catch a caïque to one of the popular south coast beaches.

By Boat   Caïques to Super Paradise, Agrari, and Elia depart from Platis Yialos every morning, weather permitting; there is also service from Ornos in high season (July and August) only. Caïque service is highly seasonal, with almost continuous service in high season and no caïques from October through May. Excursion boats to Delos depart Tuesday through Sunday between 8:30am and 1pm, from the west side of the harbor near the tourist office. (For more information, see a travel agent; guided tours are available.)

By Car & Moped   Rental cars are available from about Dr17,500 ($50) per day, including insurance, in high season; most agencies are near one of the two bus stops in town. One reliable shop is **Apollon** (☎ 0289/24-136), with offices at the south bus station, the airport, and at Ornos Beach. The largest concentration of moped shops is just beyond the south bus station. Expect to pay about Dr3,500 to Dr11,000 ($10 to $32) a day, depending on engine size. Take great care when driving: The roads on the island can be treacherous.

By Taxi   There are two types of taxis in Mykonos: standard **car taxis** for destinations outside town, and tiny **scooters with a cart in tow** that buzz through the narrow streets of Hora. The latter are seen primarily at the port, where they wait to bring new arrivals to their lodgings in town—a good idea, since most in-town hotels are a challenge to find. Getting a car taxi in Hora is easy: Walk to Taxi (Mavro) Square, near the statue, and join the line. A notice board gives rates for various destinations. You can also call ☎ 0289/22-400. For late hours and out-of-town service, call ☎ 0289/23-700.

FAST FACTS   The **American Express** agent is at Delia Travel, on the harbor (☎ 0289/24-300); open daily from 8am to 9pm. The **Commercial Bank** and **National Bank of Greece** are on the harbor a couple blocks west of Taxi Square; both open Monday through Friday from 8am to 2pm. ATMs are available throughout

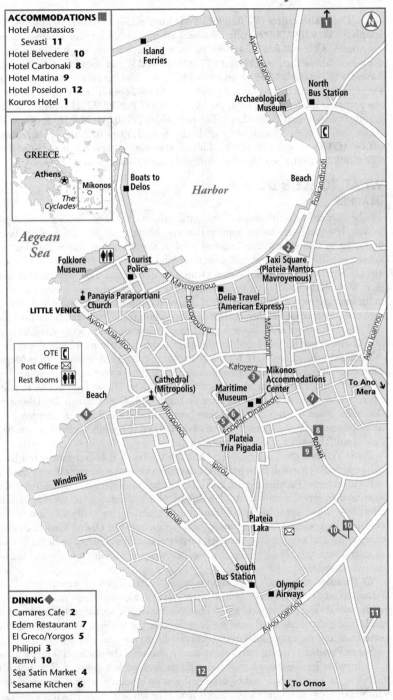

Mykonos Town

ACCOMMODATIONS ■

Hotel Anastassios
   Sevasti **11**
Hotel Belvedere **10**
Hotel Carbonaki **8**
Hotel Matina **9**
Hotel Poseidon **12**
Kouros Hotel **1**

GREECE

Athens ✪

Mikonos ○

The Cyclades

1

Island
Ferries

Archaeological
Museum

North
Bus Station

Αγίου Στεφανου

C

Πολικανδριοτι

Boats to
Delos

Harbor

Beach

*Aegean
Sea*

Folklore
Museum

🚻

Tourist
Police

Αλ Μαυρογενους

2

Taxi Square
(Plateia Mantos
Mavroyenous)

† Panayia Paraportiani
Church

LITTLE VENICE

Αγιον Αναργιρον

Δρακοπουλου

Delia Travel
(American Express)

Ματογιαννι

Αγίου Ιωαννου

OTE **C**
Post Office ✉
Rest Rooms 🚻

Cathedral
(Mitropolis)

Καλογερα

3

Mikonos
Accommodations
Center

To Ano
Mera

Beach

Maritime
Museum

7

4

Μιτροπολεως

5 **6**

Ενοπλαν Διναμεον

8

Plateia
Tria Pigadia

Ροχαρι

9

Ιπιρου

Windmills

Ξενιας

Plateia
Laka

✉

10 **10**

South
Bus Station

Olympic
Airways

11

DINING ◆

Camares Cafe **2**
Edem Restaurant **7**
El Greco/Yorgos **5**
Philippi **3**
Remvi **10**
Sea Satin Market **4**
Sesame Kitchen **6**

12

↓ To Ornos

↓ To Ornos

town. The **health center** (☎ **0289/23-944**) handles minor medical complaints. The **hospital** (☎ **0289/23-994**) offers 24-hour emergency service. For **Internet access,** try Angelo's Cafe (☎ **0289/24-106**), on the street between the south bus station and the windmills; or the Porto Market (☎ **0289/26-623**), just above the ferry pier. **Ace Laundry** (☎ **0289/28-389**) is on Ayios Efthimiou, 100 meters toward the port from the south bus station. The **tourist police** (☎ **0289/22-482**) are on the west side of the port near the ferries to Delos; the local **police** (☎ **0289/22-235**) are behind the grammar school, near Plateia Laka. The **post office** (☎ **0289/22-238**) is next to the police station; open Monday through Friday from 7:30am to 2pm. The **telephone office (OTE)** is on the north side of the harbor beyond the Hotel Leto (☎ **0289/22-499**), open Monday through Friday 7:30am to 3pm

WHAT TO SEE & DO
BEACHES

The beaches on the **south shore** of the island have the best sand, views, and wind protection, but these days are so popular that you'll have to negotiate a forest of beach umbrellas to find your square meter of sand. A few **(Paradise, Super Paradise)** are known as party beaches, and guarantee throbbing music and loud revelry until late at night. Others **(Platis Yialos, Psarou, Ornos)** are quieter and more popular with families. With all the south coast beaches, keep in mind that most people begin to arrive in the early afternoon, and you can avoid the worst of the crowds by going in the morning. The **north coast beaches** are less developed but just as beautiful. Since the buses and caïques don't yet make the trip, you'll have to rent a car or scooter; you'll be more than compensated for the trouble by the quiet and lack of commercial development.

For those who can't wait to hit the beach, the closest to Mykonos town is **Megali Ammos** ("Big Sand"), about a 10-minute walk south—it's very crowded and not particularly scenic. The nearest to the north is 2 kilometers (1.2 miles) away at **Tourlos,** where a new cruise-ship pier was recently completed. **Ornos,** about 2½ kilometers (1.6 miles) south of town, has a fine-sand beach in a sheltered bay with extensive hotel development along the shore; buses run hourly from the south station between 8am and 11pm. This beach is popular with families.

Platis Yialos is the best first stop: Although the beach is unexceptional and likely to be extremely crowded, from here you can catch a caïque to the more distant beaches of Paradise, Super Paradise, Agrari, and Elia. The bus runs every 15 minutes from 8am to 8pm, then every 30 minutes until midnight. Nearby **Psarou** is less overwhelmed by resort hotels and has a lovely pale-sand beach that remains reasonably uncrowded except in high season. Its water-sports facilities include the **Diving Center Psarou,** waterskiing, and windsurfing. **Paranga,** further east, can be reached easily on foot via an inland path from Platis Yialos; this small cove is popular with nudists, and usually isn't too crowded.

✪ **Paradise,** the island's most famous beach, is accessible by footpath from Platis Yialos (about 2km/1.2 miles), by bus, or by caïque. This was the original nude beach of the island, and still attracts many nudists. A stand of small trees provides some shade, and it's well protected from the predominant north winds. Several bars line the waterfront and pump out loud music throughout the day and night.

Super Paradise (Plindri) is in a rocky cove just around the headland from Paradise; it's somewhat less developed than its neighbor, but no less crowded. The beach is accessible on foot, by bus, and by caïque; if you go by car or moped, be very careful on the extremely steep and narrow access road. The left side of the beach is a nonstop party in summer, with loud music and dancing, while the right side is mostly nude and gay, with the exclusive Coco Club providing a relaxed ambience for its chic

Beach Notes

Activity on the beaches is highly seasonal, and all the information offered here per-tains only to the months of June through September. The prevailing winds on Mykonos (and throughout the Cyclades) blow from the north, which is why the southern beaches are the most protected and calm. The exception to this rule is a weather pattern with southern winds that occurs periodically during the summer months, making the northern beaches more desirable for sunning and swimming. In Mykonos town, this southern wind is heralded by particularly hot temperatures and perfect calm in the harbor. On such days, Mykonians will avoid Paradise, Super Paradise, and Elia, heading instead to the northern beaches of Ayios Sostis and Panormos.

---

clientele. Further east across the little peninsula is **Agrari,** a lovely cove sheltered by lush foliage, with all states of dress common and a good little taverna.

Elia, a 45-minute caïque ride from Platis Yialos and the last regular stop, is a sand-and-pebble beach with crowds nearly as overwhelming as at Paradise and minimal shade. Nevertheless, this is a beautiful beach, and one of the longest on the island. It's also accessible by bus. The next major beach is **Kalo Livadi** ("Good Pasture"). In a farming valley, this long, beautiful beach is accessible by a scramble over the peninsula east from Elia and by bus from the north station. There's a taverna and a few villas and hotels on the hills adjacent to the beach.

The last resort area on the southern coast accessible by bus from the north station is at ✪ **Kalafatis.** This fishing village was once the port of the ancient citadel of Mykonos, which dominated the little peninsula to the west. A line of trees separates the beach from the rows of buildings which have grown up along the road. This is one of the longest beaches on Mykonos, and less crowded than its neighbors to the west. Adjacent to Kalafatis in a tiny cove is lovely **Ayia Anna,** a short stretch of sand with a score of umbrellas. Several kilometers further east, accessible by a fairly good road from Kalafatis, is **Lia,** which has fine sand, clear water, bamboo wind breaks, and a small taverna.

Most of the north coast beaches are too windy to be of interest to anyone other than windsurfers—the long fine-sand beach at **Ftelia** would be one of the best on the island if it didn't receive the unbroken force of the north wind. There are, however, two well-sheltered northern beaches, and because you can only reach them by car or moped, they're much less crowded than the southern beaches. Head east from Mykonos town on the road to Ano Mera, turning left after 1½ kilometers (0.9 miles) on the road to Ayios Sostis and Panormos. At **Panormos,** you'll find a cove with 100 meters of fine sand backed by low dunes. Another 1.2 kilometers (0.75 miles) down the road is ✪ **Ayios Sostis,** a lovely small beach just below a village. There isn't any parking, so it's best to leave your vehicle along the main road and walk 200 meters down through the village. There's an excellent small taverna just up from the beach that operates without electricity, so it's open only during daylight hours. Both Panormos and Ayios Sostis have few amenities—no beach umbrellas, bars, or snack shops—but they do offer a break from the crowds.

DIVING

Mykonos is known throughout the Aegean as a place for diving—it's one of the few islands where this sport hasn't been forbidden to protect undersea archaeological trea-sures from plunder. The best month is September, when the water temperature is typically 24°C (75°F) and visibility is 30 meters. Certified divers can rent equipment and participate in guided dives; first-time divers can rent snorkeling gear or take an introductory beach dive. The best established dive center on the island is **Mykonos Diving Centre,** at Psarou Beach (☎ and fax **0289/24-808;** e-mail: prodive@otenet.gr). PADI certification courses (offered in English) are 5 days in duration and cost Dr130,000 to Dr160,000 ($374 to $461) with equipment rental; certified divers can join guided dives for Dr15,000 ($43) per dive; beginners can take a 2-hour class and beach dive for Dr18,000 ($52). There's a nearby wreck at a depth of 20 to 35 meters, and wreck dives are offered for Dr17,000 ($49). Another diving center offering lessons and equipment rental is **Dive Adventures,** on Paradise Beach (☎ and fax **0289/26-539**).

ATTRACTIONS

Getting lost in the labyrinthine alleys of Hora is an essential element of every Mykonian holiday. Searching for the right bar, a good place to eat, or your hotel is sure to be twice as difficult as you'd expected and twice as enjoyable. Despite its intense commercialism and seething crowds in high season, Hora is still the quintessential Cycladic town, and is worth a visit to the island in itself.

The best way to see the town is to simply venture inland from the port and wander. Just keep in mind that the town is bounded on two sides by the bay, and on the other two by the busy vehicular District Road, and that all paths funnel eventually into one of the few main squares: **Plateia Mantos Mavroyenous,** on the port (called **Taxi Square** because it's the main taxi stand); **Plateia Tria Pigadia;** and **Plateia Laka,** near the south bus station.

During your stay, be sure to experience the sunset from one of the bars in **Little Venice;** the evening **volta** (stroll), which is quietly civilized in the off-season and frenziedly hysterical in July and August; and a visit to some of the fine **art galleries** and **workshops** that populate the back streets of the town, and make this a cultural center as well as a party town.

The museums of Mykonos aren't among the island's main attractions, but as a rainy-day outing, consider the **Archaeological Museum** (☎ **0289/22-325**), on the north side of town beyond the OTE, across from the bus stop. It contains finds from the island of Rhenia, adjacent to Delos, and a few items from Mykonos. Among the objects on display are some exquisite painted ceramic vases, a large 7th-century B.C. storage jar with reliefs depicting scenes from the Trojan war, and a Parian marble statue of Hercules. It's open Wednesday through Saturday and Monday from 9am to 3:30pm, Sunday from 10am to 3pm; admission is Dr600 ($1.75).

The only other town on Mykonos is **Ano Mera,** 7 kilometers (4 miles) east of Hora near the center of the island, a quick bus ride from the north station. We especially recommend this trip to those interested in religious sites—the **Monastery of Panayia Tourliani** southeast of town dates from the 18th century and has a marble bell tower with intricate folk carvings. Inside the church are a huge Italian baroque iconostasis (altar screen) with icons of the Cretan school, an 18th-century marble baptismal font, and a small museum containing liturgical vestments, needlework, and wood carvings. One kilometer (0.6 miles) southeast is the 12th-century **Monastery of Paleokastro,** in one of the greenest spots on the island. Ano Mera also has the most traditional atmosphere on the island, with a fresh-produce market on the main square selling excellent local cheeses, and it's the island's place of choice for Sunday brunch.

SHOPPING

Mykonos has a large community of artists and several galleries. At ✪ **Apocalypse** (☎ **0289/24-267**), on Ayios Vlasis, just in from the port, you'll find the icon workshop of Maria Adama and Mercourios Dimopoulos. Their materials and techniques are drawn from the ancient tradition of icon painting. Much of their exquisite work is done on commission for churches and individuals. **Orama Art Gallery** (☎ **0289/26-339;** fax 0289/24-016) features the work of local painters Luis Orozco and Dorlies Schapitz. Many of the paintings depict local scenes, but this is not tourist art: The delightful use of color and joyous quality of the paintings is consistent, regardless of their subject.

The **Scala Gallery,** Odos Matoyianni 48 (☎ **0289/23-407;** fax 0289/26-993; www.scalagallery.gr), is one of the best galleries in town. All the artists represented are from Greece, many of them quite well known. There is a selection of jewelry, plus an interesting collection of recent works by Yorgos Kypris, an Athenian sculptor and ceramic artist. Nearby on Odos Panahrandou is **Scala II Gallery** (☎ **0289/26-993**), where the overflow from the Scala Gallery is sold at reduced prices.

Eleni Kontiza's tiny shop **Hand Made** (☎ **0289/27-512**), on a lane between Plateia Tria Pigadia and Plateia Laka, has a good selection of handwoven scarves, rugs, and tablecloths from around Greece.

The best bookstore on Mykonos is **To Vivlio** (☎ **0289/27-737**), on Odos Zouganeli, one street over from Odos Matoyianni. It carries a good selection of books in English, including many works of Greek writers in translation, plus some art and architecture books and a few travel guides.

Mykonos has an abundance of jewelry shops, most of them unexceptional and more expensive than their Athenian counterparts. However, the best known, **Elias Lalaounis,** Odos Polykandrioti 14, near the taxi station (☎ **0289/22-444**), has an international reputation for superb craftsmanship and design, especially in classical, Byzantine, and natural motifs. **Vildiridis,** Matoyianni 12 (☎ **0289/23-245**), has designs based on ancient jewelry as well as contemporary styles.

Works of culinary art can be found at **Skaropoulos** (☎ **0289/24-983**), 1½ kilometers (1 mile) out of Hora on the road to Ano Mera, featuring the Mykonian specialties of Nikos and Frantzeska Koukas (Nikos's grandfather started making confections here in 1921, winning prizes and earning a personal commendation from Winston Churchill). Try their famed *amygdalota* (an almond sweet) or the almond biscuits (Churchill's favorite). You can also find Skaropoulos sweets at **Pantopoleion,** Kaloyerou 24 (☎ **0289/22-078**), along with Greek organic foods and natural cosmetics. The shop is in a beautifully restored 300-year-old Mykonian house.

WHERE TO STAY

Greece's most popular resort destination seems to have developed every possible spot, yet there's still a shortage of desirable, affordable accommodations in high season. Needless to say, Mykonos is a much easier place to visit in spring or fall; the best month is September, when the water is warm and the crowds have departed. Those determined to visit the hottest spot during the hottest season should make reservations at least a month (if possible, 3 months) in advance.

The helpful staff of the **Mykonos Accommodations Center (MAC),** Odos Enoplon Dinameon 10 (☎ **0289/23-160** or 0289/23-408; fax 0289/24-137; http://mykonos-accommodation.com; e-mail: mac@mac.myk.forthnet.gr), will correspond, talk by phone, or meet with you to determine the best accommodation for your budget. The service is free when booking hotel stays of 3 nights or longer; shorter stays or bookings of budget accommodations will bring a fee of Dr7,000 ($20).

IN HORA

In addition to the options listed below, **Dimitris Roussounelos** (☎ and fax **0289/26-993;** e-mail: scala@otenet.gr) of the Scala Gallery manages a number of simple studios and apartments in Hora. All have TVs and kitchen facilities; most are equipped with phones and air-conditioning. The largest apartment ("Fratzeska's") has two bedrooms, two bathrooms, and a shaded terrace with views across the bay to Delos. Nightly rates are Dr32,000 ($92) for studios, Dr56,000 ($161) for "Fratzeska's apartment."

✪ **Hotel Belvedere.** Rohari, 84600 Mykonos. ☎ **0289/25-122.** Fax 0289/25-126. www.belvederehotel.com. E-mail: belvedere@myk.forthnet.gr. 41 units. A/C MINIBAR TV TEL. Dr75,000 ($216) double; Dr115,000 ($331) superior double; Dr94,000 ($270) triple; Dr115,000 ($331) suite; Dr135,000 ($389) VIP suite. Rates include buffet breakfast. AE, DC, MC, V. Just below the District Road and across from the School of Fine Arts.

The Belvedere is our choice for the finest hotel in Hora. Guest rooms have double-pane windows for extra quiet, large bathrooms with full tubs, balconies overlooking the town and sea, sound systems with CD players, and modem jacks. The courtyard contains a handsome pool, a bar, and a faithfully restored 1850 mansion where an extensive and delicious buffet breakfast is served; in the afternoon and evening, the mansion is the home of Remvi, one of the town's best restaurants (see "Where to Dine," below). A new exercise room offers top-of-the-line fitness machines, Jacuzzis, and a sauna. Check out the Web site, where you can find photos and off-season special offers available only with online booking.

Hotel Carbonaki. Odos Panahrandou 23, Hora, 84600 Mykonos. ☎ **0289/22-461** or 0289/24-124. Fax 0289/24-102. www.carbonaki.gr. E-mail: scala@otenet.gr. 21 units. A/C TV TEL. Dr32,000 ($92) double; Dr42,000 ($129) triple. Continental breakfast Dr1,500 ($4.30) extra. Closed Nov–Mar. Look for this hotel in a narrow lane, not far from Tria Pigadia and just toward the port from the Hotel Matina.

The Carbonaki's rooms are clustered around a bright courtyard, verdant with trees and potted plants. There's a small pool here, plus a terrace for sunning. A higher terrace has fine views across the rooftops of Mykonos and a glimpse of the sparkling bay. Bedrooms are small and tastefully outfitted with hardwood furniture; they don't have great views, opening to either the courtyard or the street. This is a primarily residential neighborhood, so it remains fairly quiet.

Hotel Matina. Odos Fournakion 3, Hora, 84600 Mykonos. ☎ **0289/22-387** or 0289/26-433. Fax 0289/24-501. 19 units. TEL. Dr30,000 ($86) double. Continental breakfast Dr1,900 ($5.45) extra. AE, V.

Guest rooms are small but clean, modern, and inside a walled garden that makes them especially quiet for their central location. Most units have balconies or small terraces. The hotel owner, Yannis Kontizas, was born on Mykonos, and is generous in offering information about the island.

ON THE EDGE OF TOWN

Most of the new hotel construction in town has been along the District Road (Odos Ayiou Ioannou), which circles the older Hora. There are also new hotels along two other roads: the one that leads south to Platis Yialos and the one leading north to Ayios Stefanos (the latter is particularly scenic and quiet, although it's a 10- to 15-minute walk to town). All three areas have good views of Hora and the sea, are easily accessible by car, and are an easy walk down to the nightlife spots.

In addition to the following listings, also consider the rather dull but reliable **Hotel Poseidon** (☎ **0289/24-441** or 0289/24-442; fax 0289/23-812), which has 58 units, some with fine sea views (avoid the rooms that face the busy District Road).

Hotel Anastassios Sevasti. Hora, 84600 Mykonos. ☎ **0289/23-545** or 0289/24-334. Fax 0289/24-336. 42 units. A/C TV TEL. Dr32,200 ($93) double; Dr41,750 ($120) triple. AE, EC, MC, V. Closed Nov–Mar.

This is the best of the many hotels on a steep hill overlooking town from above the District Road. Although it's only 100 meters from the edge of the old town, you'll want to have a car or the will to climb the 100 steps to the hotel's lofty perch. The pool has a fine view of the town and the bay. Guest rooms are plain and somewhat larger than the average hotel room in town; all have balconies or terraces with views of the sea or the hills. The bathrooms are small, but all have decent showers; six rooms have half-bathtubs.

Kouros Hotel. Tagou, 84600 Mykonos. ☎ **0289/25-381** or 0289/25-383. Fax 0289/ 25-379. E-mail: kouroshotelmykonos@hotmail.com. 29 units. A/C MINIBAR TV TEL. Dr59,000 ($170) double; Dr75,000 ($213) triple; Dr95,000 ($274) suite. Rates include buffet breakfast. Children under 12 stay for half price in parents' room; children under 2 stay free. AE, DC, EC, MC, V. Closed Nov–Mar. Located 300m from the port, a 10-minute walk from Mavroyenous (Taxi) Square.

This apartment hotel, just outside town on a steep hill above the Ayios Stefanos road, boasts superb sea views. All units have kitchenettes, modern bathrooms with tubs, and spacious balconies with views. The pool is filled with fresh water, the staff is friendly, and it's a good place for families. Transportation to and from the port or airport is provided.

AROUND THE ISLAND

There are hotels clustered around many of the more popular beaches on the island, but most people prefer to stay in town and commute to the beaches. Following each review is a short description of the beach the hotel serves.

Apollonia Bay Hotel. Ayios Ioannis, 84600 Mykonos. ☎ **0289/27-890** or 0289/27-895. Fax 0289/27-641. 30 units. A/C MINIBAR TV TEL. Dr55,000 ($158) double; Dr69,000 ($198) triple; Dr124,000 ($357) suite. Rates include breakfast. AE, DC, MC, V. Closed Nov–Mar.

Unlike many of the new hotels that are already crumbling at the edges, this fine small hotel feels like it was built to last. You'll notice many thoughtful details here—the trees planted in the midst of terraces for shade, the spacious bathrooms with tubs, the heavy rough-hewn ceiling timbers. There's a panoramic view of the bay from the large pool, itself just 100 meters from the edge of the sea. Guest rooms are simply furnished, most with balconies with sea views. The hotel restaurant serves a small menu of Greek dishes in addition to the substantial buffet breakfast.

Just 1½ kilometers (0.9 miles) past Ornos Beach, **Ayios Ioannis** feels more secluded and quiet than most of its neighbors. The beach here is small and pebbly, not satisfactory for true beach buffs. There are three fine tavernas on the beach, a small church, and a trail to larger Kapari Beach.

✪ **Hotel Petasos Beach.** Platis Yialos, 84600 Mykonos. ☎ **0289/23-437** or 0289/23-438. Fax 0289/24-101. www.petasos.gr. E-mail: info@petasos.gr. 82 units. A/C MINIBAR TV TEL. Dr53,500 ($154) double; Dr65,300 ($188) triple. Rates include buffet break-fast. AE, MC, V. Closed Nov–Mar.

Rooms here are large and comfortable, with balconies overlooking Psarou Bay. The hotel has a good-size pool and sundeck at the edge of a precipitous drop to the sea; a Jacuzzi, gym, and sauna are just below the pool terrace. The seaside restaurant has the best view in town as well as a large wine list. A trail leads from the hotel to the nearby Psarou Beach—in a small cove, this beach is the best-protected on the island from the predominant meltemi winds. Upon request you can take advantage of transportation from the harbor or airport, safe-deposit boxes, and laundry service. The gracious owners and their well-trained staff win a star.

The sandy, crescent-shaped beach at **Platis Yialos** is just a 15-minute bus ride from Hora. It's the caïque stop for shuttles to Paradise, Super Paradise, Agrari, and Elia beaches.

Hotel Yiannaki. Ornos Beach, 84600 Mykonos. ☎ **0289/23-393** or 0289/23-443. Fax 0289/24-628. 42 units. A/C TV TEL. Dr38,000 ($109) double. Rates include buffet breakfast. AE, DC, MC, V. Closed Nov–Mar.

This hotel is on a small rise, overlooking the town and the beach, surrounded by a stand of trees and a small garden. The beach is 200 meters away, and there's a short-cut path that starts from the pool. The restaurant is open throughout the day; an extensive breakfast buffet is served here each morning. Guest rooms are basic: All have a fridge, and most have balconies with sea views.

The beach on calm **Ornos Bay** is especially recommended for families because of its shallow, calm water, and because it isn't a party beach. There are water-sports facilities and some good tavernas.

WHERE TO DINE

Camares Cafe (☎ **0289/28-570**) on Mavroyenous (Taxi) Square is a slick place with good light meals and a fine view of the harbor from its terrace; it's open 24 hours.

Edem Restaurant. Above Panahrandou church, Hora. ☎ **0289/23-355.** Reservations recommended July–Aug. Main courses Dr2,500–Dr7,000 ($7–$20). AE, DC, EC, MC, V. Daily 6pm–1am. In off-season, sometimes open for lunch. Walk up Matoyianni, turn left on Kaloyera, and follow the signs up and to the left. GREEK/CONTINENTAL.

This is one of the oldest restaurants in Hora, with a reputation for good food built over 30 years. Tables are clustered around a courtyard pool—diners have been known to make a splash upon arrival with a pre-prandial swim—and the sunny courtyard is a pleasant place to enjoy a leisurely dinner even if you aren't dressed for the water. Edem is known especially for its grilled meat dishes, but the eclectic menu also includes steaks, pasta, and a variety of traditional Greek and continental dishes. The service is good, and the produce consistently fresh.

El Greco/Yorgos. Plateia Tria Pigadia, Hora. ☎ **0289/22-074.** Main courses Dr2,000–Dr7,000 ($6–$20). AE, DC, EC, MC, V. Daily 7pm–1am. GREEK/CONTINENTAL.

El Greco is a taverna with a difference, a place with cloth napkins and flowers on each table where you can find traditional recipes collected from various regions of Greece. This is one of the older restaurants in Hora, and unlike most Mykonian establishments is decidedly untrendy. The eclectic menu includes traditional dishes like the *bourdeto* from Kerkira, a monkfish-and-shellfish stew in tomato and wine sauce, and many concoctions featuring local produce, like the mushrooms with Mykonian cheese.

Philippi. Just off Matoyianni and Kaloyera behind the eponymous Hotel, Hora. ☎ **0289/22-294.** Reservations recommended July–Aug. Main courses Dr3,000–Dr7,000 ($9–$20). AE, MC, V. Daily 7pm–1am. GREEK/CONTINENTAL.

One of the island's most romantic dining experiences, Philippi inhabits a quiet garden. The food, which includes French classics, curries, and traditional Greek dishes, is good if not particularly memorable. What this restaurant does provide in abundance is *atmosphere*, and that's what has made this place a perennial favorite.

Remvi. Hotel Belvedere, Rohari. ☎ **0289/25-122.** Reservations recommended July–Aug. Main courses Dr3,400–Dr6,000 ($10–$17). AE, DC, MC, V. Daily 8am–midnight. GREEK/CONTINENTAL.

The intimate Remvi is a pleasantly surprising anomaly, a hotel restaurant that is quite exceptional. It inhabits a tastefully renovated mansion with two centuries of history;

the outside terrace enjoys a sweeping view of the town and harbor. The menu features a selection of traditional Greek *mezedes*—these are clearly a focus of attention here rather than the afterthought they often seem to be elsewhere. The dishes are uncomplicated and delicious, featuring the simple flavors of Greek cuisine: the smoky aroma of roasted eggplant, the succulence of grilled fish and lamb. The wine list is short and carefully composed, with some hard-to-find treasures.

✪ **Sea Satin Market.** Near the Mitropolis Cathedral, Hora. ☎ **0289/24-676.** Main courses Dr2,000–Dr10,000 ($6–$29). AE, V. Daily 6:30pm–12:30am. GREEK/SEAFOOD.

Below the windmills, beyond the small beach adjacent to Little Venice, the paralia ends in a rocky headland facing the open sea—this is the remarkable location for one of Hora's best new restaurants. Set apart from the clamor of the town, it's one of the quietest spots in town, and on a still summer night just after sunset, the atmosphere is simply intoxicating. In the front of the restaurant, the activities of the kitchen are on display along with the day's catch sizzling on the grill.

Sesame Kitchen. Plateia Tria Pigadia, Hora. ☎ **0289/24-710.** Main courses Dr1,500–Dr4,000 ($4.30–$11). AE, V. Daily 7pm–12:30am. GREEK/CONTINENTAL.

This small, health-conscious taverna, which serves some vegetarian specialties, is next to the Naval Museum. Fresh spinach, vegetable, cheese, and chicken pies are baked daily. There's a large variety of salads, brown rice, and soy dishes, including a vegetable moussaka, plus lightly grilled and seasoned meat dishes.

MYKONOS AFTER DARK

Mykonos has the liveliest, most abundant, and most varied nightlife in the Aegean. It's a barhopper's paradise, and you'll enjoy wandering through the maze of streets looking for the right spot—and looking at everyone else looking. Don't be too disappointed if some of the places we suggest are closed or have changed their name or image; such is the nature of nightlife on an island where everything is seasonal. And be warned: Drinks in Mykonos cost more than they do in London or New York.

A perfect beginning to a long night is the view of the sunset from one of the sophisticated bars in Little Venice. The **Kastro** (☎ **0289/23-070**), near the Paraportiani church, is famous for classical music and frozen daiquiris. The classic sunset scene is the **Caprice Bar,** up the block on Scarpa, which also has a seaside perch and plays soft rock in the early evening. The **Montparnasse** (☎ **0289/23-719**), on the same lane, is highly romantic and often plays classical music. The **Veranda** (☎ **0289/23-290**), in an old mansion overlooking the water with a good view of the windmills, is as relaxing as its name implies. **Galleraki** (☎ **0289/27-188**) also has tables near the water, and plays the latest pop music.

The "king of the scene" is **Pierro's** (☎ **0289/22-177**), very popular with gay visitors; it rocks all night to American and European music and draws crowds in sufficient quantity to impede your progress up the narrow Odos Matoyianni; the new upstairs **Pierro's Cafe Bar** is similar in character. At mostly gay and lesbian **Ikaros,** above Pierro's, the 2am drag show has become a popular attraction. If you'd like something a little more laidback, back up and check out the **Nine Muses,** on Taxi Square. Or squeeze past the throng to the **Lotus** (☎ **0289/22-181**), for good music, good food, and an interesting scene, or the **Anchor,** which plays blues, jazz, and classic rock for its 30-something clients. Further along Matoyianni at no. 42 is **Bar Uno** (☎ **0289/26-144**), playing mostly soft rock and populated by mostly middle-aged Europeans. **Astra,** on Tria Pigadia, is currently the place where visiting models and millionaires find each other.

Head right back toward the harbor for some wilder action. **Stavros Irish Bar** (☎ 0289/23-350), behind Town Hall, is still among the most unrestrained places for young heavy drinkers, and the nearby **Scandinavian Bar** rivals it in the anything-goes department. If you'd like to sample some Greek music and dancing, you're in the right neighborhood. **Thalami** (☎ 0289/23-291), a small club underneath Town Hall, may have room for you to experience something very nearly authentic. The **Mykonos Bar** is another good place for traditional Greek music and dancing.

The other end of the harbor also has some nightlife, especially at **Remezzo Disco**, near the OTE, where you can boogie into the morning under the stars (this is an Athenian chain, and caters almost exclusively to tourists). The music starts up around 2am.

It's well after midnight and you're still up for more. Don't worry: You haven't exhausted the possibilities. **MADD**, on Taxi Square, is only just coming alive at 1am, and its view of the port is sensational. The **Anchor Club**, on Odos Matoyianni, is transformed into a disco in these early morning hours.

If you're visiting between July and September, you may want to find out what's happening at the **Anemo Theatre** (☎ 0289/23-944), an outdoor venue for the performing arts in a garden in Rohari, just above town. It presents a variety of concerts and performances.

7 Delos

The small island of Delos, just 3 kilometers (1.9 miles) offshore from Mykonos, was considered by the ancient Greeks to be the holiest of sanctuaries, the sacred center around which the other Cyclades circled. Delos is known locally as the "brightest" island in the Cyclades, a tradition that seems to indicate both its continued significance as a sacred place and the simple fact that this is one place where you'll want to have sunglasses. It is unquestionably one of the most remarkable archaeological preserves in the world, displaying ample evidence of its former grandeur. Always a place set apart, with different rules than those of neighboring islands, in ancient times people were not allowed to die or be born on this sacred island. Today, they are not allowed to spend the night, and the site can be visited only between the hours of 8:30am and 3pm.

We recommend visiting Delos as early as possible in the day, especially in summer, when the crowds and heat become overwhelming by early afternoon. Sturdy shoes and water are necessary; a hat or cap and food are also advised. (There is a cafe near the museum, but the prices are high, the quality poor, and the service even worse.)

ESSENTIALS

GETTING THERE   Delos can be reached by sea only. Most people visit on excursion boats from neighboring Mykonos or Tinos. The island is also a prominent stop for cruise ships and yachts. From Mykonos, organized guided and unguided excursions leave Tuesday through Sunday from the west end of the harbor; the trip takes about 40 minutes and costs Dr1,900 ($5.45) round-trip for transportation alone. The ferries depart from Mykonos between 8:30 and 11am; the last boat returning from Delos is at 3pm. Most travel agents offer guided tours for about Dr8,500 ($24), including transportation and admission to the site; these depart at 9 or 10am and return at 12:30 or 2pm. From Tinos, there is an unguided excursion in summer only to Delos and Mykonos for Dr5,000 ($14) for adults and Dr2,500 ($7) or children under 11; the excursion departs Tuesday through Sunday at 10am, and

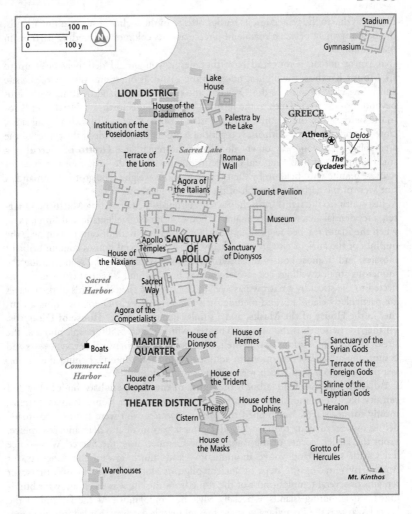

includes 3 hours on Delos and a short stop in Mykonos town, returning to Tinos at 7pm.

EXPLORING THE SITE

Entrance to the site costs Dr1,500 ($4.30); it's open Tuesday through Sunday from 8:30am to 3pm, and is **closed on Mondays.** At the ticket kiosk, you'll see a number of site plans and picture guides for sale; we recommend *Delos & Mykonos: A Guide to the History and Archaeology,* by Konstantinos Tsakos (Hesperos Editions), a reliable guide to the site and the museum. Because the excavations at Delos have been conducted by the French School, many signs are in French, and a thorough English map and guide are especially useful.

To the left (north) of the new jetty where your boat will dock is the **Sacred Harbor,** now too silted for use, where pilgrims, merchants, and sailors from throughout the Mediterranean used to land. The commercial importance of the island in ancient times was due to the protection its harbor offered in the shelter of surrounding islands, the best anywhere between mainland Greece and its colonies and trading partners in Asia Minor.

If you're not on a tour and have the energy, you should definitely head up to ✪ **Mount Kinthos,** the highest point on the island. It offers an overview of the site and a fine view of most of the Cyclades: the neighboring island of Rinia with Siros beyond it to the west, Tinos to the north, Mykonos to the northeast, Naxos and Paros to the south. From the summit, with the islands of the Cyclades sprawled on all sides, close up and low to the horizon, you get the sense that this is indeed the center of the archipelago. On your way down, don't miss the remarkable **Grotto of Hercules,** a small temple built into a natural crevice in the mountainside—the roof is formed of massive granite slabs held up by their own enormous weight. The grotto commands a fine view of the harbor and much of the archaeological site.

Just south (to the right) from the Sacred Harbor is the fascinating **Maritime Quarter,** a residential area with the remains of houses from the Hellenistic and Roman era, when the island reached its peak in wealth and prestige. Reminiscent of Pompeii, the outlines of the ancient city are remarkably preserved. Several houses contain brilliant mosaics, and in most houses the cistern and sewer systems can be seen. Among the numerous small dwellings are several palaces, built around a central court and connected to the street by a narrow passage. The mosaics in the courtyards of the palaces are particularly elaborate, and include such famous images as Dionysos riding a panther in the **House of the Masks,** and a similar depiction in the **House of Dionysos.** Further to the south is the massive **Theater,** which seated 5,500 people and was the site of choral competitions during the Delian Festivals, an event held every 4 years and comprising athletic competitions in addition to musical contests. Behind the theater is a fine arched **cistern,** which was the water supply for the city.

Adjacent to the Sacred Harbor is the **Agora of the Competialists,** built in the 2nd century B.C. when the island was a bustling free port under Rome. Roman citizens, mostly former slaves, worshipped the *lares competales,* who were minor "crossroad" deities associated with the Greek god Hermes, patron of travelers and commerce. From the far left corner of the Agora of the Competialists, the **Sacred Way**—once lined with statues and votive monuments—leads north toward the Sanctuary of Apollo. By retracing the steps of ancient pilgrims along it, you will pass the scant remains of several temples (most of the stone from the site was taken away for buildings on neighboring islands, especially Mykonos and Tinos). At the far end of the Sacred Way was the **Propylaea,** a monumental marble gateway that led into the sanctuary. In ancient times, the sanctuary was crowded with temples, altars, statues, and votive offerings.

The **museum** contains finds from the various excavations on the island. It displays some fine statuary, reliefs, masks, and jewelry, and is well worth a visit. Admission to the museum is included in the entrance fee to the site.

North of the Tourist Pavilion on the left is the **Sacred Lake,** where the oracular swans once swam. The lake is now little more than a dusty indentation most of the year, surrounded by a low wall. Beyond it is the famous guardian **Lions,** made of Naxian marble and erected in the 7th century B.C. (There were originally at least nine. One was taken away to Venice in the 17th century and now stands before the Arsenal there. The whereabouts of the others remain a mystery.) Beyond the lake to the northeast is the large square courtyard of the Gymnasium and the long narrow Stadium, where the athletic competitions of the Delian Games were held.

8 Tinos

161km (87 nautical miles) SE of Piraeus

Tinos is an important place of religious pilgrimage, yet it remains one of the least commercial islands of the Cyclades—and a joy to visit for that reason. **Panayia Evanyelistria** ("Our Lady of Good Tidings"), the "Lourdes of Greece," draws thousands of pilgrims seeking the aid of a miraculous icon enshrined there. Almost any day of the year you can see people, particularly elderly women, crawling from the port on hands and knees up the long, steep street leading to the hilltop cathedral. The market street of Tinos town is lined with stalls selling holy water vials, incense, candles (up to 2m long), and mass-produced icons. Don't even think about arriving without a reservation around August 15, when thousands of pilgrims travel here to celebrate the Feast of the Assumption of the Virgin.

The inland villages of Tinos are some of the most beautiful in the Cyclades. Many of the most picturesque are nestled into the slopes of **Exomvourgo,** the rocky pinnacle visible from the port, connected by a network of walking paths that make this island a hiker's paradise. In these villages and dotting the countryside, you'll see the ornately decorated medieval dovecotes for which the island is famous, and above the doors of village houses elaborately carved marble lintels. The island's beaches aren't worthy of superlatives, but they are plentiful and uncrowded throughout the summer.

ESSENTIALS

GETTING THERE   There are several ferries to Tinos daily from Piraeus (5 hrs.) and at least one catamaran daily from Rafina (1½ hrs.); schedules should be confirmed with the Athens **tourist office** (☎ 01/331-0562), the **Port Authority in Piraeus** (☎ 01/459-3223), or the **Rafina Port Authority** (☎ 0294/22-300). Several times a day, boats connect Tinos with nearby Mykonos (15 to 40 mins.). Boats to Siros (20 to 50 mins.) and hydrofoils to Santorini (4 to 6 hrs.), Paros (1½ hrs.), and Naxos (2 hrs.) are regular in summer and somewhat less frequent during the winter months (though Tinos has more winter connections than most Cycladic isles due to its religious tourism, which continues year-round). A summer day excursion to Delos and Mykonos departs from Tinos at 10am Tuesday through Sunday, returning to Tinos at 7pm; the fare is Dr5,000 ($14) for adults and Dr2,500 ($7) for children under 11.

There are three piers in Tinos harbor: Two of these receive ferries, and the third is reserved for hydrofoils, catamarans, and excursion boats. The original ferry pier is in the center of town, opposite the Posidonio Hotel and the bus station, while the newer one is 600 meters to the north just past the children's park in the direction of Kionia. The pier for hydrofoils, catamarans, and excursion boats is between the two, opposite the Lito Hotel. Be sure to find out from which pier your ship will depart; most ferries still dock at the old pier in the town center. It can happen that due to weather conditions, ferries will use a different pier than expected, in which case there will be an announcement by loudspeaker at the intended pier as little as 10 minutes prior to arrival—at this point you'll see a convoy of hotel buses and travelers mobilize themselves to get promptly to the other port. The **Tinos Port Authority** (not guaranteed to be helpful) can be reached at ☎ 0283/22-348.

VISITOR INFORMATION   For information on accommodations, car rentals, island tours, and Tinos in general, head to **Windmills Travel** (☎ and fax 0283/23-398; www.windmills-travel.com; e-mail: tinos@windmills-travel.com), near the new port, opposite the children's park. Sharon Turner is the friendly and outgoing manager.

GETTING AROUND **By Bus** The **bus station** (☎ 0283/22-440) is on the harbor, opposite the south (old) port. KTEL, the local bus company, sometimes posts its schedules here (you can also ask about bus times at Windmills Travel). The buses run infrequently, making travel by bus logistically difficult.

By Car & Moped The most reliable rental company in town is **Vidalis** (☎ 0283/23-400), just off the harbor on the main road out of town (turn inland at the supermarket). Car rentals start at Dr10,000 ($29) for a tiny two-door, including insurance. Mopeds are Dr3,000 to Dr5,000 ($9 to $14).

By Taxi The principal taxi stand is on the harbor, by the south (old) pier.

FAST FACTS There are several **banks** on the harbor, open Monday through Thursday from 8am to 2pm and Friday from 8am to 1:30pm; all have ATMs. The **first-aid center** can be reached at ☎ 0283/22-210. There's a drop-off **laundry** service (☎ 0283/32-765) opposite the Vidalis car-rental agency—but be forewarned that it can be slow, up to 3 days in peak season. For **luggage storage,** try Windmills Travel (☎ 0283/23-398), near the new port. The **police** (☎ 0283/22-255) are just after the new pier, past the children's park and the Asteria Hotel. The **post office** (☎ 0283/22-247), open Monday through Friday from 7:30am to 2pm, is at the south end of the harbor next to the Tinion Hotel. The **telephone office (OTE),** open Monday through Friday from 7:30am to 12:30pm, is on the main street leading to the church of Panayia Evanyelistria, about halfway up on the right (☎ 0283/22-399).

WHAT TO SEE & DO

✪ **Panayia Evanyelistria Cathedral and Museums.** Tinos. Free admission. Cathedral open daily 8am–8pm (off-season daily noon–6pm). Galleries open Sat–Sun (some weekdays during July and Aug) 8am–8pm (off-season noon–6pm).

The story of the cathedral began in 1822, during the War of Independence, when a nun at the Kerovouniou Convent had a vision that an icon was buried on a nearby farm. The present cathedral was built on the site of the ancient church, and today you can see the miraculous icon to the left of the central aisle where it's encased in gold, diamonds, and pearls. Below the church is the crypt where the icon was found, surrounded by smaller chapels; the crypt is often crowded with Greek parents and children in white, waiting to be baptized with water from the font. Particularly interesting are the hundreds of objects in silver and gold hanging from the roof—sometimes a hand or foot, a child's crib, a house, a car, and, to the right of the entrance, a gold lemon tree. Each one has a story to tell, a tale of thanks for a prayer answered.

Within the high walls that surround the church are various museums and galleries, most of which are interesting primarily as curiosities. The gallery of 19th-century religious art is to the left as you pass through the main gateway; another gallery houses Byzantine icons, and to the left of the foundation offices is a fascinating display of gifts offered to the cathedral. The sculpture museum, to the right and up a flight of stairs, is one of the best galleries; it contains gifts from sculptors, many quite renowned, who studied with the help of the cathedral charitable foundation. Just below the cathedral precinct on Leoforos Megaloharis is a small **Archaeological Museum,** open Tuesday through Sunday from 8:30am to 3pm; admission is Dr500 ($1.45). The collection includes finds from the ancient sanctuary of Thesmophorion near Exomvourgo, plus a sundial from the 2nd century A.D. found at the Sanctuary of Poseidon and Amphitrite at Kionia.

EXPLORING THE ISLAND

If it's a clear day, one of your first sights of Tinos from the ferry will be the pinnacle of rock towering over Tinos town, the site of the Venetian fortress of **Exomvourgo.** The fortress itself has long been in ruins, but you can still explore the remains and enjoy the superb view, one of the best in the Cyclades. The fortress is surrounded by sheer rock walls on three sides; the only path to the summit starts behind a Catholic church at the base of the rock, on the road between Mesi and Koumaros (you'll need to rent a car or walk from Tinos town, a distance of about 5km/3 miles). As you make the 15-minute ascent, you'll pass several lines of fortification—the whole hill is riddled with walls and hollow with chambers.

The towns circling Exomvourgo are some of the most picturesque on the island, and can be visited by car or on foot (see "Walking," below). **Dio Horia** has beautiful village houses and a spring in the main square, where some villagers still wash their clothes by hand. There's a town bus to the nearby **Convent of Kerovouniou,** one of the largest in Greece and dating to the 10th century. This was the home of Pelagia, the nun whose vision revealed the location of the island's famed icon; you can visit her cell and see a small museum of 18th- and 19th-century icons.

Loutra is an especially attractive village with a 17th-century Jesuit monastery that contains an excellent museum of village life—implements for making olive oil and wine are on display alongside old manuscripts and maps; it's open mid-June to mid-September daily from 10:30am to 3:30pm. **Volax** is situated in a remote valley known for a bizarre lunar landscape of rotund granite boulders—the villagers have recently constructed a stone amphitheater for theatrical productions, so be sure to ask at **Windmills Travel** (☎ and fax **0283/23-398**) for a schedule of performances (most occur in August). Volax is also known for its local basket weavers, whose baskets are remarkably durable and attractive; ask for directions to their workshops. Be sure to visit the town spring, down a short flight of steps at the bottom of the village: Channels direct the water to the fields, and the basket weavers' reeds soak in multiple stone basins.

Koumaros is a beautiful small village on the road between Volax and Mesi with many *stegasti,* streets occupying tunnels beneath the projecting second-floor rooms of village houses. At the tiny **self-service cafe,** visitors are invited to take what they want from an assortment of drinks, snacks, and ice creams, leaving payment in a box on the counter. You'll also find postcards, board games, and information about Koumaros. This small place in the center of town is open throughout the day.

Tinos is famous for its **dovecotes,** stout stone towers elaborately ornamented with slabs of the local shale. The doves were an important part of the local diet, and their droppings were used as fertilizer. Any excursion through the countryside of Tinos will reveal many of these curious structures; there are some 600 on the island, many more than 300 years old. The towns of **Tarambados** and **Smardakito** are known to have some of the most elaborate ones.

Pirgos, at the western end of the island, is one of Tinos's most beautiful villages. Renowned for its school of fine arts, the town is a center for marble sculpting, and many of the finest sculptors of Greece have trained here. A small **museum** houses mostly sculpture by local artists; it's open Tuesday through Sunday from 11am to 1:30pm and 5:30 to 6:30pm, and is located near the bus station, on the main lane leading toward the village.

BEACHES

There's a decent fine-sand beach 3 kilometers (1.9 miles) west of Tinos town at **Kionia,** and another 2 kilometers (1.2 miles) east of town at busy **Ayios Fokas.** From Tinos, there's bus service on the south beach road (usually four times a day) to the resort of **Porto,** 8 kilometers (5 miles) to the east. Porto offers several long stretches of uncrowded sand, a few hotel complexes, and numerous tavernas, several at or near the beach. The beach at Ayios Ioannis facing the town of Porto is okay, but you'd be better off walking west across the small headland to a longer, less populous beach, extending from this headland to the church or Ayios Sostis at its western extremity; you can also get here by driving or taking the bus to Ayios Sostis. There are two beaches at **Kolimbithres** on the north side of the island, easily accessed by car, although protection from the meltemi winds can be a problem—the second is the best, with fine sand in a small rocky cove and two tavernas. There are more beaches around the headland from here—longer, less populous, and more exposed to the wind; you can reach these by a short drive on a poor dirt road beyond the beach mentioned above. The pebble cove at **Livada** is accessible only by a long, rough dirt road, and the north-facing beach receives the worst of the meltemi winds. Several beaches on the southwest coast (**Ayios Romanos, Ayios Petros,** and **Isternion**) are accessible by paved road.

WALKING

Tinos is a walker's paradise, with a good network of paths and remote interior regions waiting to be explored. Some of the best walks are in the vicinity of **Exomvourgo**—paths connect the cluster of villages circling this craggy fortress, offering great views and many places to stop for refreshment along the way. There isn't currently an English-language guide to walks in Tinos, but you can ask for information at **Windmills Travel** (☎ and fax **0283/23-398**) in Tinos town; the office is planning to arrange walking tours in the future, and may be able to offer information about organized walks or about routes for you to explore on your own.

SHOPPING

The **flea market** on Odos Evanyelistria is a pleasant place for a ramble; Evanyelistria parallels Leoforos Megaloharis, the main street from the harbor up to the cathedral. The colorful stalls lining the street sell icons, incense, candles, medallions, and *tamata* (tin, silver, and gold votives). You'll also find local embroidery, weavings, and the delicious local nougat, as well as *loukoumia* (Turkish delight) from Siros.

Harris Prassas Ostria-Tinos, Odos Evanyelistria 20 (☎ **0283/23-893;** fax 0283/24-568), is particularly recommended for his fine collection of jewelry in contemporary, Byzantine, and classical styles; silver work; and beautiful religious objects, including reproductions of the miraculous icon. Harris is friendly, informative, and famous for the quality of his work. Near the top of the street on the left is the small **O Evangelismos Weaving School** (☎ **0283/22-894**) and a store selling reasonably priced tablecloths, bedcovers, and other woven items produced at the school.

Those interested in authentic hand-painted icons should find the small shop of **Maria Vryoni,** the first left from the port off Leoforos Megaloharis, the second shop on the left. Maria spends at least a week on each of her works of art; they start at around Dr50,000 ($144).

There are several sculptors working in **Pirgos,** the island's center for marble sculpture. Among the most accomplished is **Antonis Hondriannis** (☎ **0283/31-470**), whose studio is on the main road, downhill from the bus station. Uphill from the bus station on the main road is the studio of **Mihail Saltamanikas** (☎ **0283/31-554**), a recent graduate of the Fine Arts School who also does excellent work.

WHERE TO STAY

Unless you have reservations, avoid Tinos during important religious holidays, especially **March 25** (Feast of the Annunciation) and **August 15** (Feast of the Assumption). Summer weekends can also be busy, when Greeks travel here by the hundreds to make a short pilgrimage to the Panayia Evanyelistria.

For those planning to stay a week or longer, contact **Windmills Travel** (see "Visitor Information," above), which has houses for rent in several villages—a great way to see more of the island and get a taste for village life. The weekly cost is about Dr254,000 ($731) for a one-bedroom house, including car rental.

✪ **Akti Aegeou Apartments.** Ayios Panteleimon Beach, 84200 Tinos (5km east of Tinos town on the road to Porto). ☎ **0283/24-248** or 0283/25-523. Fax 0283/23-523. 11 units. TV TEL. Dr18,500 ($53) double; Dr22,000 ($63) triple. Units with A/C Dr2,000 ($6) extra. No credit cards. Closed Nov–Mar.

The Akti Aegeou is built right on the sand of Porto Beach, one of the island's finest, and maintains an atmosphere of friendly informality. The place was constructed with many traditional details, such as pebble designs on the terraces, flagstone floors, and beamed ceilings. Each roomy apartment has a kitchenette and a balcony facing the beach. Units on the upper floor are equipped with air-conditioning, but their balconies are unshaded; those on the lower floor make up for their lack of air-conditioning with a well-shaded terrace. Meals are served in a small restaurant on the pool terrace.

Avra Hotel. Tinos town, 84200 Tinos. ☎ **0283/22-242.** Fax 0283/22-176. 17 units. TEL. Dr15,000 ($43) double. Continental breakfast Dr1,000 ($2.90) extra. No credit cards.

A wooden spiral staircase leads to high-ceilinged rooms in this charming old hotel on the harbor, one of the first in Tinos when it was built in 1921. The hotel received a sharp new look when its façade was renovated in 1999; the interior is thankfully scheduled for a renovation in 2001. Several bedrooms have a view of the harbor, and three have balconies; unfortunately these front rooms also get the harbor noise. Other units face a rear courtyard and share a sunny terrace filled with palms and ferns.

Cavos Bungalows. Ayios Sostis, 84200 Tinos. ☎ **0283/24-224** or 0283/24-225. Fax 0283/22-580. 47 units. TEL. Dr19,000 ($54) studio (2 occupants), Dr22,800 ($65) studio (3 occupants); Dr33,000 ($95) apartment (2 occupants), Dr39,600 ($143) apartment (3 occupants). 3-night minimum stay. MC, V. Closed Nov–Mar.

On a steep promontory with sweeping views across the Aegean toward nearby Mykonos, the principal attraction of these simple bungalows is their superb location on Tinos's southern coast. The long, uncrowded fine-sand beach of Ayios Sostis is just a 2-minute walk away, and from there you can continue along the water to beautiful Porto Beach. Each apartment has a separate bedroom, a living room with two couches that can double as beds, basic kitchen facilities, and a balcony facing the extraordinary view.

✪ **Tinion Hotel.** Odos Alavanou 1, Tinos town, 84200 Tinos. ☎ **0283/22-261.** Fax 0283/24-754. E-mail: kchatzi@ath.forthnet.gr. 20 units. A/C TV TEL. Dr18,000 ($52) double. Continental breakfast Dr2,500 ($7) extra. MC, V. Closed Nov–Mar. From the old harbor, walk south (right) along the paralia; the hotel is just past the supermarket on the left.

This venerable hotel retains an old-world charm with marble floors, dark polished wood, and lace curtains. The guest rooms have high ceilings, tile floors, and handsome brass or carved walnut beds. The front rooms all have balconies with harbor views. Tinion is on a small square, just far enough from the harbor and its late-night activity to provide a quiet night's sleep.

Tinos Beach Hotel. Kionia (4km/2½ miles west of Tinos town on the coast road), 84200 Tinos. ☎ **0283/22-626** or 0283/22-627. Fax 0283/23-153. 180 units. TEL. Dr31,000 ($89) double; Dr43,300 ($124) triple; Dr47,000 ($135) suite. Rates include breakfast. Children 7 and under stay free in parents' room. AE, DC, MC, V. Closed Nov–Mar.

This is the best beachfront hotel on the island, despite its somewhat impersonal character and fading 1960s elegance. The spacious rooms all have balconies, most with views of sea and pool. Bathrooms all have half-tubs. The suites are especially pleasant— large sitting rooms open onto poolside balconies. Rooms located in a cluster of bungalows built to resemble a Cycladic village are similar in size and furnishings; all have shaded terraces, and most offer a view toward the sea. The pool is the longest on the island, and there's a separate children's pool as well. There are umbrellas on the stretch of sand and cobble beach fronting the hotel; paddleboats and canoes are available for rent.

WHERE TO DINE

As usual, avoid most harborfront joints, where food is generally inferior and service can be rushed. In addition to the places listed below, you'll find decent, simple fare at the following establishments: **Lefteris** (☎ 0283/23-013), a fish taverna on the harborfront, has a large and varied menu. There's plenty of room for dancing, and the waiters often demonstrate and urge diners to join in. **Palea Pallada** (☎ 0283/ 23-516), a venerable and popular place, is just in from the dolphin fountain on the harborfront, near the Seajet pier. **Peristerionas** (☎ 0283/23-425) is a friendly place where the food is filling and plentiful; to get here, turn in from the harborfront on Leoforos Megaloharis and take the first left.

Caffe Italia. New port, Tinos town. ☎ **0283/25-756.** Main courses Dr1,200–Dr3,500 ($3.45–$10). No credit cards. Daily 10am–3pm and 6pm–12:30am. Behind the children's park and just down the street from Windmills Travel. TRATTORIA.

Dora Coluccio and her husband, Yorgos Marazlis, are the friendly owners of this cozy spot near the new harbor. The stone-walled dining room decorated with old photos of Rome is a great place to linger over a cappuccino or a plate of pasta topped with one of Dora's delectable sauces—the *putanesca* is our favorite. The menu changes often, making use of seasonal local produce as well as cheese and wine imported from Italy. If you enjoy satisfying, simple fare and good company, you're likely to join the many locals and travelers who come back night after night.

Taverna Drosia. Ktikades, 5km (3 miles) from Tinos town. ☎ **0283/41-387.** Main courses Dr900–Dr3,000 ($2.60–$9). No credit cards. Daily 11am–midnight. GREEK.

This taverna, perched at the head of a steep valley overlooking the sea, seems a world away from the crowds and traffic of the harbor. From the shaded flagstone terrace, you can watch ships slowly approaching; Siros sits across the water, and in the valley are terraced fields, dovecotes, and an old windmill. The food is basic taverna fare, though considerably better than average—bread arrives at the table in thick wholesome slabs, salads are sprinkled with succulent capers, and everything is very fresh.

To Koutouki tis Eleni. Paralia, Tinos town. ☎ **0283/24-857.** Main courses Dr900–Dr3,000 ($2.60–$9). No credit cards. Daily noon–midnight. From the harbor turn onto Odos Evanyelistria, the market street; take the first right up a narrow lane with 3 tavernas; Koutouki is the first on the left. GREEK.

There's usually no menu at this excellent small taverna, known in town simply as Koutouki. Basic ingredients are cooked up into simple meals that remind you how delightful Greek food can be. Local cheese and wine, fresh fish and meats, delicious vegetables—these are the staples that come together so delightfully in this taverna, which demonstrates that you don't have to pay a fortune to experience cooking as a fine art.

9 Siros (Syros)

144km (78 nautical miles) SE of Piraeus

Having lost most of its foreign tourism to other, more glamorous Cycladic isles, Siros offers a rare opportunity to vacation as the Greeks do. Excellent food, a long tradition of popular music (known as *rembetika*), glorious little-known beaches, and the most vivacious island capital in the Cyclades are among the benefits of a visit to Siros.

Anything but a backwater, **Ermoupolis** is the administrative capital of the Cyclades, a thriving port that was the busiest in Greece in the 19th century. Signs of this former affluence are concentrated in the vicinity of the harbor, where neoclassical mansions abut the rocky waterfront and grandiose public buildings line spacious squares. Although Ermoupolis has seen several decades of decline, recent restoration efforts have brought back much of the glory of the city's heyday, and several of the most elaborate mansions have been converted to hotels and guest houses. Other signs of urban revival are a busy calendar of lively public events and some of the best food in the Cyclades.

The north end of the island is a starkly beautiful region of widely dispersed farms, terraced fields, and plentiful walking paths. The best beaches of the island are here, accessible only on foot or by boat, and the spectacularly situated archaeological site at Kastri can be reached by trail. The San Mihali and kopanisti cheeses are made here, as well as a delicious thyme honey; all of these can be found in the Ermoupolis open-air market.

The best months to visit Siros are May, June, and September; the worst month is August, when vacationing Greeks fill every hotel room on the island. Getting around this small island by bus is so easy and convenient that you may not need to rent a car or moped.

ESSENTIALS

GETTING THERE By Plane In summer, there's at least one flight daily from Athens. Contact the **Olympic Airways** (www.olympic-airways.gr) office in Ermoupolis, 100 meters from the port in the direction of Hotel Hermes (☎ **0281/88-018** or 0281/82-634), or in Athens (☎ **0801/44-444** or 01/966-6666). **Hellenic Star,** a new airline with daily flights between Athens and Siros, is represented in Ermoupolis by Teamwork Holidays, to the left of the Casino at the ferry pier (☎ **0281/83-400;** fax 0281/83-508).

By Boat Ferries connect Siros at least once daily with Piraeus (2½ hrs. by high-speed ferry, 4½ hrs. by ferry), Naxos (1½ hrs. by high-speed ferry or hydrofoil, 2½ hrs. by ferry), Mykonos (30 mins. by high-speed ferry, 1½ hrs. by ferry), Paros (45 mins. by high-speed ferry, 1½ hrs. by ferry), Tinos (1 hr.), and Santorini (4 to 7 hrs.); and once or twice weekly with Folegandros (5 to 6 hrs.), Sifnos (3 hrs.), Iraklion (5 to 10 hrs.), Samos (7 to 9 hrs. to Vathi), and Thessaloniki (12 to 15 hrs.). There are also daily catamarans from Rafina (2 hrs.). You'll find numerous ferry-ticket offices at the pier; **Alpha Syros** (☎ **0281/81-185**), opposite the ferry pier, and its sister company, **Teamwork Holidays** (☎ **0281/83-400**), sell tickets for all the ferries. Ferry information can be verified with the local **Port Authority** (☎ **0281/88-888** or 0281/82-690); Piraeus ferry schedules can be confirmed with the Athens **tourist**

office (☎ 01/331-0562) or the **Port Authority in Piraeus** (☎ 01/459-3223); for Rafina schedules, call the **Port Authority in Rafina** (☎ 0294/28-888).

VISITOR INFORMATION   The **Hoteliers Association of Siros** operates an information booth at the pier in summer; it's open daily from 9am to 10pm. Note that the list of hotels offered here is not complete. The **GNTO** office, Odos Dodekanisou 10, a side street just to the left of the pier (☎ 0281/86-725; fax 0281/82-375), is open Monday through Friday from 7:30am to 2:30pm. **Teamwork Holidays** (☎ 0281/83-400; fax 0281/83-508), opposite the ferry dock to the left of the Casino, is open daily from 9am to 9pm. Its staff can book rooms; change money; sell Olympic Airways, Hellenic Star, and charter airline tickets; sell ferry tickets; and arrange rental cars. It also offers a round-the-island full-day beach tour by yacht (Dr7,000/$20) and a full-day excursion to Mykonos and Delos (Dr10,000/$29).

GETTING AROUND   By Bus   The **bus stop** in Ermoupolis is at the pier; the schedule is posted here. Buses circle the southern half of Siros hourly in summer between 8am and midnight. There are no buses to the northern part of the island. The off-season schedule is irregular due to the fact that the buses also bring children to and from school. The fare is Dr220 to Dr500 (66¢ to $1.45).

By Car & Moped   Of the several car-rental places along the harbor in the vicinity of the pier, a reliable choice is **Siros Rent A Car** (☎ 0281/80-409), next to the GNTO office on Odos Dodekanisou, a side street just to the left of the pier. A small car will cost about Dr16,000 ($46) per day in summer, including insurance. A 50cc scooter is Dr6,000 ($17) a day.

By Taxi   The taxi stand is on the main square, Plateia Miaoulis (☎ 0281/86-222).

FAST FACTS   Several **banks** on the harbor have ATMs. The Ermoupolis **hospital** (☎ 0281/86-666) is the largest in the Cyclades; it's just outside town to the west near Plateia Iroon. There's a friendly drop-off **laundry/dry-cleaning** service opposite the post office on Odos Protopapadaki. For free **luggage storage,** ask at Teamwork Holidays (☎ 0281/83-400). The **police** (☎ 0281/82-610) are on the south side of Miaoulis Square. The **port authority** (☎ 0281/88-888 or 0281/82-690) is on the long pier at the far end of the harbor, beyond Hotel Hermes. The **post office** (☎ 0281/82-596) is between Miaoulis Square and the harbor on Odos Protopapadaki; open Monday through Friday from 7:30am to 2pm. The **telephone office** (OTE) is on the east side of Miaoulis Square (☎ 0281/87-399), open Monday through Saturday from 7:30am to 3pm.

WHAT TO SEE & DO
MUSEUMS

Ermoupolis Industrial Museum. Just off Plateia Iroon and opposite the hospital, Ermoupolis. ☎ **0281/86-900.** Admission Dr1,000 ($2.90) adults, Dr500 ($1.45) students; free on Wed. Tues–Sun 10am–2pm and 6–9pm.

Behind the copious cranes and warehouses of the Neorion Shipyard at the southern end of the port, you'll find the new Industrial Museum of Ermoupolis, which opened in 2000. It's worth the 20-minute walk from the ferry pier to check out this extensive collection of artifacts from the town's industrial past: weaving machines, metalworking tools, and, of course, a collection relating to the town's famed shipyards. Also check out the fine collection of original drawings by the architects of Ermoupolis's neoclassical heyday, the interesting photographs and engravings depicting various aspects of island life, and the old maps of Siros and the Cyclades.

Archaeological Museum. On the west side of the town hall below the clock tower, Ermoupolis. ☎ **0281/86-900.** Free admission. Tues–Sun 8:30am–3pm.

The highlight of this museum's small collection is a room containing finds from the excavations at Halandriani, a prehistoric cemetery in the northern hills of Siros, including several fine Cycladic figurines; there is also a temporary exhibition documenting the 19th-century excavation of this site. (You can visit the Bronze Age fortified settlement at Kastri, near Halandriani, where many of the museum's artifacts were found—see "Hiking in Northern Siros," below.) The collection also includes two beautiful miniature Hellenistic marble heads, a Roman-era sculpture from Amorgos, and a black granite statue from Egypt which dates back to 730 B.C.

EXPLORING ERMOUPOLIS

Ermoupolis is a flourishing city, a city with a life of its own that clearly doesn't rely on tourism. In the 19th century, Ermoupolis was the busiest port in Greece, and the sophisticated neoclassical architecture of this period dominates the low-lying areas of the city in the vicinity of the harbor. The central square, **Plateia Miaoulis**, and the elaborately elegant **Town Hall** seem more typical of a wealthy French provincial town than a Greek island capital, and it is this cosmopolitan quality that sets Ermoupolis apart from the relative insularity of most island towns. To reach Plateia Miaoulis from the port, turn inland on Odos Venizelou, near the bus station. Ringed by high palm trees and facing the Town Hall, Plateia Miaoulis is the center of civic life in Ermoupolis. Outdoor theatrical and musical events are often put on here, and every night the square is filled with promenading Ermoupolites.

A couple of blocks northeast of the Town Hall is the 19th-century **Apollon Theater,** a smaller version of Milan's La Scala. It's being restored, thanks to funding from the European Union. (Contact the **GNTO** at ☎ **0281/86-725** for information and tickets.) Northeast behind it is the lovely church of **Ayios Nikolaos,** with a green marble iconostasis carved by Vitalis, a famed 19th-century marble carver from Tinos. (Vitalis also sculpted the monument to an unknown soldier in the garden near the entrance.) A short stroll beyond the church will bring you to the neighborhood called **Vaporia,** named after the steamships that brought it great prosperity.

Ano Siros, the taller hill seen to the left of Ermoupolis as you enter the harbor, can be visited by local bus or on foot, a half-hour hike up Odos Omirou from the main square. This medieval quarter with an intricate maze of streets was built by the Venetians in the 13th century. Ano Siros originally spread across the summit of both hills, where its inhabitants were protected from pirate raids. Several Roman Catholic churches stand here; the most important is the **Church of Ayios Yioryios.** The large buff-colored building on the hilltop is the medieval **Monastery of the Capuchins.** Remnants of castle walls, stone archways, and narrow lanes make this area a delight to explore.

Shopping in Ermoupolis

The shops here tend to be functional rather than funky, and there aren't any that stand out. However, just about anything you need can be found somewhere in town. The best street for shopping is **Odos Protopapadaki,** two streets from the port, which is open to car traffic and full of shops; the post office is also on this street. The town **produce market** is on **Odos Hios,** west of the main square; it's open daily, but is particularly lively on Saturdays. Don't leave the market without trying the local specialties *loukoumia,* better known as Turkish delight, and *halvodopita,* a sort of nougat.

The other hill, **Vrondado,** with its blue-domed Greek Orthodox Church of the Resurrection, was built up after the Greek immigration of 1821. Its narrow streets, marble-paved squares, and dignified mansions lend a certain old-world charm to the bustling inner city. There's a great view of Ermoupolis and the neighboring islands from the terrace outside the Church of the Resurrection.

BEACHES

Megas Yialos, as its name states, is the largest beach on the island and the prettiest on the south coast. Its sandy beach is shaded by tamarisk trees and is especially good for families because it's gently shelved. **Agathopes,** a 10-minute walk south of Possidonia in the island's southwest corner, has a sandy beach and a little offshore islet; the beach here is not yet overdeveloped.

A few kilometers to the north, **Galissas** has one of the best beaches on the island, a crescent of sand bordered by tamarisks, but it's a bit too popular in high season. **Armeos beach,** a short walk south of town, is less crowded and mostly nude.

Kini is a small fishing village on the west coast with two beaches on sheltered Delfini Bay, valued for its sunsets and a local family of bouzouki musicians. The best of the two beaches at Kini is the primarily nudist **Delfini beach,** 2 kilometers (1.2 miles) north of town over the headland; there's a small taverna here that operates in summer. The bus from Ermoupolis makes the trip to Kini hourly in summer.

Lia and **Grammata,** two of the finest beaches on the island, can be reached only by boat or on foot. There is no regular boat taxi service to these beaches, although there are numerous boat owners who may be willing to take you there. For information, contact **Teamwork Holidays** (☎ 0281/83-400). To get here on foot, see "Hiking in Northern Siros," below.

HIKING IN NORTHERN SIROS

The northern part of Siros is hilly and wild, with poor roads, no bus service, and widely dispersed houses. It's a beautiful part of the island to explore on foot, and has several marked hiking trails. The region is home to dairies that produce the popular San Mihali cheese, milk, and butter that visiting Greeks love to take home.

✪ **Kastri,** north of Halandriani, is thought to be one of the oldest archaeological sites in the Cyclades, and its remote cliff-rimmed perch high above the Aegean makes a great destination for a hike. It's a long walk from Ermoupolis, about 7 kilometers (4.3 miles) each way, but you can shorten the hike considerably by taking a taxi to the tiny village of Halandriani, about 4½ kilometers (2.8 miles) north of Ermoupolis, off the Kampos road. The marked trail to Kastri is signposted from the village—follow the signs and painted arrows through terraced fields to the bottom of a dry streambed near a remote beach. From here, the trail climbs steeply to the top of a long, narrow ridge with the remains of the settlement at its summit, surrounded by craggy slopes on three sides. There isn't much to see—the ruins of a defensive outer wall and the outlines of the individual houses—but the view is spectacular and the setting satisfyingly remote. A great way to end the day is with dinner at Mitakas (see "Where to Dine," below), one of the island's best tavernas, located about 3 kilometers (1.9 miles) from Ermoupolis on the main northern (Kampos) road.

The best **beaches** on Siros are at the north end of the island, and all are accessible only on foot or by boat. Sheltered in sandy coves, these quiet and idyllic beaches are shaded by tamarisk and palm trees. There isn't reliable fresh water, so be sure to bring your own. The beach trails begin at Kastri, about 8 kilometers (5 miles) north of Ermoupolis; the best way to get there is by rental car or moped, since the public buses don't travel this far north and there are no public phones you can use to call a return taxi. Just before the road turns to dirt, you'll see a sign for **Lia,** the longest of the northern beaches; the walk is about an hour round-trip. ✪ **Grammata,** the most beautiful small beach on the island, is situated in a palm oasis at the outlet of a natural spring. The walk in from Kampos is 2 hours round-trip; there's no shade on the trail, so try to avoid walking during the hottest midafternoon hours.

WHERE TO STAY

The kiosk of the **Hoteliers Association of Siros,** right as you come off the ferry in Ermoupolis, provides a list of island hotels. Note that hotels pay to become members of this association, so not all of the island's best lodgings are represented. In August, when vacationing Greeks pack the island, don't even think of arriving without a reservation.

Hotel Apollonos. Odos Apollonos 8, Ermoupolis, 84100 Siros. ☎ **0281/81-387** or 0281/80-842. Fax 0281/81-681. 3 units. A/C MINIBAR TV TEL. Dr55,000 ($158) double. Rates include breakfast. No credit cards.

This mansion on the water in Vaporia has been meticulously restored and decorated; it's one of the best of the town's period hotels. Those looking for a fully authentic restoration might be disappointed—the furnishings and lighting are contemporary in style—but the overall effect is one of complete harmony between new and old, creating an atmosphere of understated elegance. The best bedrooms are the two facing the water at the back of the house: Both are quite spacious, and one has a loft sleeping area with sitting room below. Bathrooms are large, with tile and wood floors. A large common sitting room faces the bay, while a breakfast room faces the street.

Hotel Hermes. Plateia Kanari, Ermoupolis, 84100 Siros. ☎ **0281/83-011** or 0281/83-012. Fax 0281/87-412. 51 units. A/C TV TEL. Dr20,000–Dr26,000 ($57–$74) double; Dr24,000–Dr31,200 ($69–$90) triple. Continental breakfast Dr1,500 ($4.30) extra. AE, DC, MC, V.

The Hermes presents a bright, modern façade to busy Plateia Kanari at the east end of the harbor; what you can't see from the street is that many of the rooms face directly onto a quiet stretch of rocky coast at the back of the building. The functional, rather dull standard rooms have shower-only bathrooms and views of the street or a back garden. The deluxe rooms in the new wing are worth the extra money—every unit has a sofa bed, minibar, bathtub, and even an extra phone in the bathroom. Many also have balconies perched over the bay—the view of the sunrise is superb. The hotel restaurant serves three meals a day and offers quality Greek food at reasonable prices.

Hotel Omiros. Odos Omirou 43, Ermoupolis, 84100 Siros. ☎ **0281/84-910** or 0281/88-756. Fax 0281/86-266. 13 units. A/C TEL. Dr27,500 ($79) double; Dr33,000 ($95) suite. Continental breakfast Dr2,500 ($7) extra. MC, V.

In 1988, when the work of restoration was begun, this building was in a state of near ruin; now the transformation is complete, and the Omiros has become one of the most appealing of the neoclassical mansion hotels in Ermoupolis. Rooms are furnished with simple antiques; some details from the original building have been retained, such as marble hand basins and massive fireplaces. The architectural highlight of the building is the spiral stair that climbs through a shaft of light to the glass roof. Breakfast, drinks, and light meals are served in a small walled garden. The hotel is on a hill above Miaoulis Square—it's a steep climb from the port, so it's best to take a taxi. There is parking, although the route from the port is complex and difficult to follow; call ahead for directions.

✪ **Hotel Vourlis.** Odos Mavrokordatou 5, Ermoupolis, 84100 Siros. ☎ and fax **0281/88-440** or 0281/81-682. 8 units. A/C TEL. Dr30,000–Dr50,000 ($86–$144) double; Dr55,000 ($158) suite. Continental breakfast Dr2,700 ($8) extra. MC, V. Open year-round.

On a hill overlooking the fashionable Vaporia district, the elegant Hotel Vourlis occupies one of the finest of the city's mansions. Built in 1888, the house has retained all its grandeur and charm. The fine details which have sadly been lost in many other restored mansions are here in all their glory: The plaster ceilings in the front rooms are especially resplendent. Most furniture also dates to the 19th century, creating a period setting which incorporates all the comforts you expect from a fine hotel. Bathrooms are spacious, and all have tubs. The two front rooms on the second floor have great sea views. Winter guests will be glad to know that the house is centrally heated.

WHERE TO DINE

There are numerous excellent tavernas in and around Ermoupolis. The **Boubas Ouzeri** and the **Yacht Club of Siros** are both excellent for ouzo and mezedes. In addition to the tavernas mentioned below, try the excellent **Petrino Taverna** (☎ **0281/84-427**), around the corner from To Arhontariki; and **Fragosiriani** (☎ **0281/84-888**), with a great view from its high terrace in Ano Siros (just down the street from Taverna Lilis).

Taverna Lilis. Ano Siros. ☎ **0281/88-087.** Reservations recommended. Main courses Dr1,500–Dr3,500 ($4.30–$10). No credit cards. Daily 7pm–midnight. Follow Odos Omirou from the center of Ermoupolis, past the Hotel Omiros, and continue straight up the long flight of steps that leads to Lilis's brightly lit terrace. If all those steps don't appeal, call a taxi. GREEK/SEAFOOD.

Lilis is the best of the tavernas in Ano Siros, the town cresting a high conical hill behind Ermoupolis. From the outdoor terrace, there's a stellar view of Ermoupolis, the bay, distant Tinos, and, even farther out, the shores of Mykonos. It's highly calming to sit here as the sun sets and watch the ships moving silently into port. The food is better-than-average taverna fare—meats and fish are grilled on a wood fire, and the ingredients are reliably fresh.

Taverna Mitakas. Mitakas. ☎ **0281/82-752.** Main courses Dr900–Dr2,500 ($2.60–$7). No credit cards. Daily 11am–midnight. About 3km (1.9 miles) from Ermoupolis on the Kampos road. GREEK.

You will have go out of your way to find this small taverna in the hills north of Ermoupolis, but this is one detour you won't regret. Much of the farming in Siros takes place on the slopes of these northern hills, so the food on your plate is mostly local and consistently fresh. The cheeses from nearby San Mihali are especially delicious, and the lamb is from local farms. The *melitzanosalata* is near perfection—redolent of wood smoke and lemon and just the right amount of garlic. The view from the terrace is great, but if the wind is blowing at all you'll want to a table indoors or behind the sheltering hedgerow.

To Arhontariki. Ermoupolis. ☎ **0281/81-744.** Main courses Dr900–Dr3,000 ($2.60–$9). No credit cards. Daily noon–midnight. GREEK.

This is the best of the tavernas in Ermoupolis center, a small place that fills the narrow street with tables precariously perched on the cobblestones. It's easy to find—just plunge into the maze of streets at the corner of Miaoulis Square between Pyramid Pizzeria and Loukas Restaurant, and weave your way left—it's 2 blocks or so in, between Miaoulis and the harbor. The menu is largely composed of specials that change nightly. It always includes a few vegetable main courses, which are subtly spiced and delicious.

✪ **To Koutouki Tou Liberi.** Kaminia (2km/1.2 miles from Ermoupolis center). ☎ **0281/ 85-580.** Reservations recommended several days in advance in high season. Main courses Dr800–Dr3,000 ($2.30–$9). No credit cards. Fri–Sat 9pm–1am. GREEK.

This place has become legendary in Siros. You'll have to hire a taxi to get here—it's not easy to find, and your driver may have some difficulty if he hasn't been here before. It may seem like a lot of trouble, but this place is definitely worth it. There is no menu—the night's offerings are brought out to you on a massive tray, and each dish is explained in turn. The food is often innovative, making slight but significant departures from traditional recipes. The spicing is subtle, and the dishes make use of the best of what's in season. The owner is also renowned locally for his bouzouki playing—late at night, after the last diners have finished their meals, there are sometimes impromptu traditional music sessions. And did we mention the view? It's exquisite.

SIROS AFTER DARK

In Ermoupolis, the waterfront is the best place to be at sunset. **Kimbara** (☎ **0281/ 80-878**) maintains a calm mood with soft rock, while the music at **Highway** is loud and gets louder as the evening continues. You can also join in the evening **volta (stroll)** around Plateia Miaoulis, or take a seat to watch it. For information and tickets to a performance at the **Apollon Theater,** contact the **Greek National Tourism Organization** (☎ **0281/86-725;** fax 0281/82-375) or look out for the posters that always abound throughout the town before a big performance. There's also the outdoor **Pallas Cinema,** east of the main square, which has one nightly showing, often in English.

Be sure to pick up a list of events scheduled as part of **Ermoupoleia,** a summer-long arts festival featuring prominent visiting artists; all events are free. The principal venues include the Apollon Theater, Miaoulis Square, and Pallas Cinema, with several theatrical, musical, or cinematic events each week. Programs are available at the GNTO office, most hotels, and travel agencies throughout town.

Ermoupolis has the only **Casino** (☎ **0281/84-400**) in the Cyclades, and it's quite an elegant establishment, worth a look even if you aren't interested in gambling. The main entrance is directly opposite the bus station and ferry pier; there's another entrance on the street immediately behind the harbor. The management is British, and most of the staff speak perfect English. The entrance fee is Dr3,000 ($9); the minimum bet ranges from Dr1,000 to Dr2,000 ($2.90 to $6). There are also slot machines that take Dr100 (30¢) coins. There's no cover charge for the restaurant and bar, on the back street. The casino is open daily from 8pm to 6am in summer; slot machines are open from 2pm.

Siros was among the most fertile grounds for *rembetika,* and you will find this special music played more authentically in several venues outside town, such as **Rahanos** and **Lilis** (☎ **0281/28-087**) in Ano Siros, which sometimes have late-night performances on the weekends; reservations are a must.

10 The Dodecanese

by Robert E. Meagher

The first thing to notice about this far-eastern Greek archipelago is that the Dodecanese—"the 12"—is in fact comprised of 32 islands: 14 inhabited and 18 uninhabited. They have been known collectively as "the Dodecanese" since 1908, when 12 of them joined forces to resist the recent revocation of the special status which they had long enjoyed under the sultans.

The Dodecanese are far-flung from the Greek mainland and mostly hug the coast of Asia Minor. As frontier or borderline territories, their struggles to remain free and Greek have been intense and prolonged. Although they have been recognizably Greek for millennia, only in 1948 were the Dodecanese reunited with the Greek nation.

Long accustomed to watching the seas for invaders, these islands now spend their time awaiting tourists—who, like migrating birds, show up each spring and stay until October. The coming of the tourist season awakens a pattern of activity largely created and contrived for the sake of drawing and entertaining outsiders. Such is the reality of island life today. As in the past, however, the islanders proudly retain their own character even as they accommodate the onslaught of foreigners.

The islands we feature represent a considered selection from "the 12." In high season, you can travel easily from one to the other. The principal islands, south to north, are **Rhodes, Kos,** and **Patmos.** North of Rhodes lies the lesser yet exquisite island of **Simi.** Patmos and Simi are quite barren in summer, while the interiors of Rhodes and Kos remain fertile and forested. The spectacular historical sights, from ancient ruins to medieval fortresses, are concentrated on Patmos, Kos, and Rhodes; so are the tourists. Simi is the not-quite-secret getaway you will not soon forget.

STRATEGIES FOR SEEING THE ISLANDS In planning your excursion to the Dodecanese, keep in mind that the longest tourist season is on Rhodes. So, if you're pushing the season in April, begin in Rhodes, or, if you're stretching the season into October, end up in Rhodes. In general, avoid the Dodecanese from late July through August, when they are so glutted with tourists that they nearly sink.

The three islands most worth visiting—both for their own sake and as bases to explore other nearby islands—are **Rhodes, Kos,** and **Patmos.** From the mainland, all are best reached by air. Rhodes and Kos have airports; Patmos is a short jaunt by hydrofoil from Samos, which

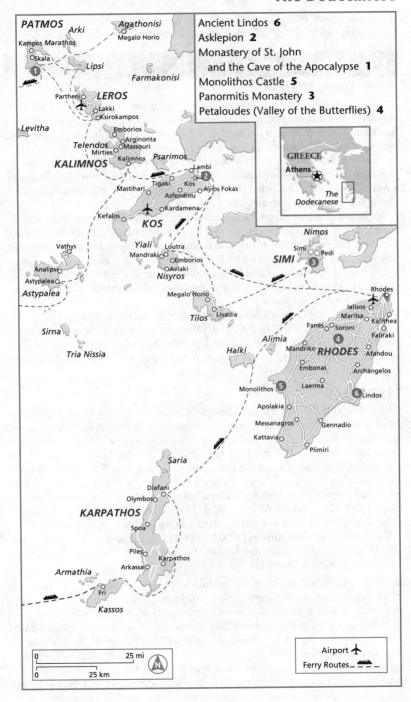

The Dodecanese

Ancient Lindos **6**
Asklepion **2**
Monastery of St. John
  and the Cave of the Apocalypse **1**
Monolithos Castle **5**
Panormitis Monastery **3**
Petaloudes (Valley of the Butterflies) **4**

GREECE
Athens
The
Dodecanese

PATMOS
Arki
Agathonisi
Kampos *Marathos*
Megalo Horio
Skala
①
Lipsi
Farmakonisi
Partheni
LEROS
Levitha
Lakki
Ksirokampos
Emborios
Telendos
Arginonta
Massouri
Mirties
KALIMNOS
Kalimnos
Psarimos
Lambi
②
Mastihari
Tigaki
Kos
Ayios Fokas
Asfendiou
Kefalos
Kardamena
KOS
Nimos
Vathys
Yiali
Loutra
Simi
Pedi
Mandraki
Emborios
SIMI
③
Analipsi
Avlaki
Astypalea
Nisyros
Astypalea
Megalo Horio
Rhodes
Sirna
Tilos
Livadia
Ialisos
Maritsa
Kalithea
Fanes
Soroni
Faliraki
Alimia
④
Tria Nissia
Halki
Mandriko
RHODES
Afandou
Embonas
Archangelos
Monolithos
⑤
Laerma
⑥ Lindos
Apolakia
Messanagros
Gennadio
Kattavia
Plimiri
Saria
Diafani
Olymbos
KARPATHOS
Spoa
Piles
Karpathos
Armathia
Arkassa
Fri
Kassos

0   25 mi
0   25 km

Airport ✈
Ferry Routes ▬▬▬

also has an airport. From Kos and Rhodes, you can get just about anywhere in the eastern Aegean, including nearby **Turkey,** which is worth at least a day's excursion.

1 Rhodes (Rodos)

250km (155 miles) E of Piraeus

Selecting a divine patron was serious business for an ancient city. Most Greek cities played it safe and chose a mainline god or goddess, a ranking Olympian, someone like Athena or Apollo or Artemis or Zeus himself. It's revealing that the people of Rhodes, even then, chose **Helios,** the Sun, as their signature god.

Indeed, millennia later, the cult of the Sun is alive and well on Rhodes, and, in return for its solar piety, the island receives on average more than 300 days of sunshine a year. What's more, Rhodes is a place of pilgrimage for sun-worshippers from colder, darker, wetter lands around the globe.

But Rhodes has more to offer its visitors than a tan. Rhodes's unique location at the intersection of east and west ensured that it would be in the thick of commerce and conflicts. The scars left by its rich and turbulent history have become its treasures. Knights, Turks, Italians—all the island's invaders—left behind objects of great beauty in the trail of devastation. Through it all, Rhodes remains beautiful. Its beaches are among the cleanest in the Aegean, and its interior is still home to unspoiled mountain villages and rich fertile plains.

Several days in Rhodes will allow you to gaze at its marvels as well as to bake a bit, adding, perhaps, a day trip to the idyllic island of Simi or to the luring shoreline of Turkey. If Rhodes is your last port of call, it will make a grand finale; if it is your point of departure, you can launch out happily from here to just about anywhere in the Aegean or Mediterranean.

ESSENTIALS

GETTING THERE   By Plane   Olympic Airways offers domestic service between Rhodes and the following Greek airports: Athens, Crete (Iraklion), Karpathos (Kasos), Kastellorizo, Mykonos, Santorini, and Thessaloniki. The local Olympic office is at Odos Ierou Lohou 9 (☎ **0241/24-571** or 0241/24-555). Flights fill quickly, so reserve in advance. **Air Greece** flies four times daily to Athens. The new **Cretan Airlines** also offers service to Rhodes. Tickets for any flight in or out of Rhodes can be purchased directly from **Triton Holidays,** near Mandraki Harbor, Odos Plastira 9, Rhodes city (☎ **0241/21-690;** fax 0241/31-625; www.tritondmc.gr). Triton will either send your tickets to you or have them waiting for you at the airport.

The Rhodes **Paradissi Airport** (☎ **0241/83-214**) is 13 kilometers (8 miles) southwest of the city and is served from 6am to 10:30pm by bus. The bus to the city center (Plateia Rimini) is Dr450 ($1.30). A taxi costs Dr3,000 ($9).

By Boat   Rhodes is a major port with sea links not only to Athens, Crete, and the islands of the Aegean, but also to Cyprus, Turkey, and Israel. Service and schedules are always changing; check with the tourist office or a travel agency for the latest information.

In late spring and summer, there's daily hydrofoil or catamaran service from Mandraki Harbor to Kos, Tilos, Nissiros and Simi, and less predictable service to many destinations, including Kalimnos, Leros, Patmos, Kastellorizo, and Samos. The advantage of hydrofoils and catamarans is that they make the voyage in half the time. But when the wind blows up the waves, the sailings are canceled. Air quality is also poor, especially compared to the air on larger open-deck excursion boats or ferries.

Rhodes Attractions

Rhodes

0   330 m
0   330 y

RHODES

GREECE
Athens ✱
Rhodes
Crete

Acropolis of Rhodes **8**
Archeological Museum
   of Rhodes **2**
Church of Our Lady
   of the Castle **4**
Clock Tower **5**
Hospice of St. Catherine **9**
Mosque of Suleiman **6**
Municipal Art Gallery **3**
Municipal Baths **7**
Square of the Jewish
   Martyrs **10**
Street of the Knights **1**

■Aquarium

100 PALMS

Vas. Konstantinou

Orthonos
Kritis
Dragoumi
Amalias

Akti Miaouli
28 Octobriou
Amerikis
Vas. Marias

Ioannou Kazouli
Martiou
Vas. Marias
Amerikis
Sofias

■ Government
  Buildings

Fort St. Nicholas
Lighthouse

Mandraki
Harbor

NEW
TOWN

Ioannou Metaxa
Alexandrou
Diakou

Papalouka

Market

Plateia
Rimini

Palace
of the
Knights

Eleftheria
(Liberty)
Gate

■ Windmills *Akandia*
              Harbor

Mill
Tower ■

Commercial
Harbor

Customs
House

President
Enoplon Dynameon
Chimairas

Kennedy
Them. Sofouli

Pindou

Riga Fereou
Pavlou Mela
Ioannou

Diagondon

Mount Smith
8

Ayiou
Komninon

Democratias

City Walls

Ippodamou
Fanouriou

①Ippoton
⑤
⑥ Sokratous
⑦
Omirou

③②
④

OLD
TOWN

Pythagora

Perikleous

⑨
⑩

City Walls

Fitellinon Vyrono

Lighthouse ⚓

Wherever it is you want to go, whether by ferry, hydrofoil, catamaran, or excursion boat, schedules and tickets are available from **Triton Holidays,** Odos Plastira 25 (☎ **0241/21-690;** fax 0241/31-625; www.tritondmc.gr). Although travel agents throughout Rhodes city and island can issue air and sea tickets, we recommend Triton Holidays because the staff focuses on catering to independent travelers.

VISITOR INFORMATION The staff at the **Greek National Tourism Office (EOT),** at the intersection of Odos Makariou and Odos Papagou (☎ **0241/23-655;** fax 0241/26-955), give exact and congenial advice about the whole island, will check on the availability of accommodations, and provide free maps, bus timetables, and copies of *Rodos News*. Hours are Monday through Friday from 7:30am to 3pm. There's also a helpful **Rhodes Municipal Tourist Office** down the hill at Plateia Rimini near the port taxi stand (☎ **0241/35-945**). It has information and advice on local excursions, buses, ferries, and accommodations, and offers currency exchange as well. It's open June to mid-July, Monday through Saturday from 8am to 9pm and Sunday from 8am to 3pm; and mid-July through October, Monday through Saturday from 8am to 10pm and Sunday from 8am to 3pm. The oft-recommended **Triton Holidays** (see above), whose office is a stone's throw from the Mandraki Harbor and several doors down from the Hotel Hermes (see "Where to Stay," below), is also ready, willing, and able to answer any traveler's question, free of obligation. Triton Holidays is often open when the tourist offices are closed.

GETTING AROUND   Rhodes is not an island you can exhaust on foot. You need wheels of some sort: public buses, group-shared taxis, a rental car, or an organized bus tour for around-the-island excursions. The city is a different story. Walking is the best and most pleasurable mode of transport; you'll need a taxi only if you're going to treat yourself to a meal at one of the farther-out restaurants or if you're decked out for the casino and don't want to walk. Note that wheeled vehicles, except those driven by permanent Old Town residents, are not allowed within the walls. This goes for all taxis, unless you have luggage.

By Bus   There's a good public bus system throughout the island; the tourist office publishes a schedule of routes and times. Buses to points **east** (except for the eastern coastal road as far as Falilraki) leave from the East Side Bus Station on Plateia Rimini, while buses to points **west,** including the airport, leave from the nearby West Side Bus Station on Odos Averof. Buses for the eastern coastal road as far as Falilraki also leave from the West Side Bus Station. Island fares range from Dr230 (70¢) within the city to Dr1,800 ($5.15) for the most remote destinations. The city bus system also offers six different tours, details of which are available from the tourist office.

By Bicycle, Moped & Motorcycle   Petitions have been filed to reserve a strip of the newly widened major island roadways for bicycles, but until that is approved, cyclists are up against very uneven odds. Remember that you need a proper license to rent anything motorized. The **Bicycle Center,** Odos Griva 39 (☎ **0241/28-315**), rents bikes, mopeds, and motorcycles. The best-looking mountain bikes we've seen are at **Moto Pilot,** Odos Kritis 12 (☎ **0241/32-285**). Starting prices per day are roughly Dr1,500 ($4.30) for a 21-speed; Dr2,500 ($7) for an aluminum mountain bike; from Dr3,000 ($9) for a moped; and Dr6,500 to Dr10,000 ($19 to $29) for a motorcycle. **Rent A Harley Rhodes,** Odos 28 Octobriou 80 (☎ **0241/74-925**), has Harleys for Dr22,000 to Dr38,000 ($63 to $109) a day.

By Taxi   In Rhodes city, the largest of many taxi stands is in front of the Old Town, on the harborfront in Plateia Rimini (☎ **0241/27-666**). There, posted for all to see and agree upon, are the set fares for sightseeing throughout the island. Since many of the cab drivers speak sightseer English, a few friends can be chauffeured and lectured at a very reasonable cost. Taxis are metered, but fares should not exceed the minimum on short round-the-city jaunts. For longer trips, negotiate directly with the drivers. Or better yet, **Triton Holidays,** at no extra charge, can arrange for a private full- or half-day taxi with a driver who will not only speak English fluently but will also respect your wishes regarding smoking or nonsmoking en route. For **radio taxis,** call ☎ **0241/64-712.** There is a slight additional pickup charge when you call for a taxi.

By Car   Apart from the array of international companies—among them **Alamo/National** (☎ **0241/73-570**), **Avis** (☎ **0241/82-896**), **Europcar** (☎ **0241/21-958**), and **Hertz** (☎ **0241/21-819**)—there are a large number of local companies. The latter often offer the lowest rates, but the concern here is whether, with possibly only a handful of cars, they have the resources to back you up in the event of an accident. Be very certain that you are fully covered before signing anything. An established Greek company with roughly 200 cars—reputedly the newest fleet on

---

A Helping Hand

The **Dodecanese Association for People with Special Needs** (☎ **0241/73-109;** mobile 094/463810) provides free minibus door-to-door service from the port, airport, and hotels—or even if you just want to go out for coffee or a swim.

Rhodes—is **DRIVE Rent-a-Car** (☎ **0241/68-243**), with an excellent reputation for personal service, as well as low prices (from about Dr14,500/$42 per day).

By Organized Tour & Cruise   Several operators feature nature, archaeology, shopping, and beach tours. In Rhodes city, **Triton Holidays** (see above) is one of the largest and most reliable agencies and the only one offering excursions designed for the independent client. Triton offers day and evening cruises, hiking tours, and excursions in Rhodes, as well as to the other Dodecanese islands and to Mamaris in Turkey. We recommend the full-day guided tours, either the tour to Lindos (Dr8,000/$23) or the "Island Tour" (Dr8,000/$23), which takes you to small villages, churches, and monasteries, including lunch in the village of **Embonas,** known for its local wines and fresh-grilled meat. There is also a fascinating half-day guided tour to the Filerimos Monastery, the Valley of the Butterflies, and to the ancient city of Kamiros (Dr8,000/$23). Along Mandraki Harbor, you can find excursion boats that leave for **Lindos** at 9am and return around 6pm (Dr5,000/$14); and daily excursions to **Simi** also for (Dr5,000/$14). For an in-depth island experience, Triton Holidays also offers a combination package of car rental and hotel accommodation in four small villages around the island (Kalavarda, Monolithos, Prassonisi, and Asklepion), ranging from 4 to 10 nights.

CITY LAYOUT   Rhodes is not the worst offender in the Dodecanese, but it does share the widespread aversion to street signs. This means that you need a map with every lane on it, so that you can count your way from one place to another. We recommend the two maps drawn and published by Mario Camerini in 1995, of which the mini-atlas entitled *Map of Rhodes Town* is the best. You'll wind up buying it eventually, so you might as well start out with it.

Rhodes city (population 42,400) is divided into two sections, the ✪ **Old Town,** dating from medieval days, and the New Town. Overlooking the harbor, the Old Town is surrounded by massive walls—4 kilometers (2½ miles) around and in certain places nearly 40 feet thick—built by the Knights of St. John. The **New Town** embraces the old one and extends south to meet the **Rhodian Riviera,** a strip of luxury resort hotels. At its north tip is the city beach, in the area called 100 Palms, and famed **Mandraki Harbor,** now used as a mooring for private yachts and tour boats.

Walking away from Mandraki Harbor on Odos Plastira, you'll come to **Cyprus Square,** where many of the New Town hotels are clustered. Veer left and continue to the park where the mighty fortress begins. Opposite it is the EOT office, and nearby, down the hill at Plateia Rimini, is the Municipal Tourist Office (see "Visitor Information," above, for information on both).

FAST FACTS   The local **American Express** agent is Rhodos Tours, Odos Ammochostou 29 (☎ **0241/21-010**), in the New Town; open Monday through Saturday from 8:30am to 1:30pm and 5 to 8:30pm. The **National Bank of Greece,** on Cyprus Square, exchanges currency Monday through Thursday from 8am to 2pm, Friday from 8am to 1:30pm, Saturday from 9am to 1pm. There are other currency-exchange offices throughout the Old Town and New Town, often with rates better than those of the banks. For emergency care, call the **hospital** (☎ **0241/80-000**) or, if necessary, an **ambulance** (☎ **166**).

For **Internet access,** try the Rock Style Internet Café, Odos Dimokratous 7, opposite the Agora Stadium (☎ **0241/70-041;** www.rockstyle.gr), open daily from 10am to 1am; or, closer to the tourist core of the new city, the Rodos Internet Club, Odos Iroon Politehniou (☎ **0241/22-100**), open from 10am to 11:30pm daily. **Express Laundry,** Odos Kosti Palama 5, behind Plateia Rimini (☎ **0241/22-514**), is open daily from 8am to 11pm. The **International Pharmacy,** Odos A. Kiakou 22

(☎ 0241/75-331), is near the Thermai Hotel. The **police** (☎ 0241/23-849) in the Old Town are available from 10am to midnight to handle any complaints of over-charging, theft, or other price-related problems. The **tourist police** (☎ 0241/27-423), on the edge of the Old Town near the port, address tourists' queries, con-cerns, and grievances. The main **post office** on Mandraki Harbor is open Monday through Friday from 7am to 8pm. A smaller office is on Odos Orfeon in the Old Town, open daily with shorter hours.

WHAT TO SEE & DO IN RHODES CITY

Rhodes is awash in first-rate sights and entertainment. As an international playground and a museum of both antiquity and the medieval era, Rhodes has no serious com-petitors in the Dodecanese and few peers in the eastern Mediterranean. Consequently, in singling out its highlights, we necessarily pass over sights that on lesser islands would be main attractions.

EXPLORING THE OLD TOWN

Best to know one thing from the start about Old Town: It's not laid out on a grid—not even close. There are roughly 200 streets or lanes that simply have no name. Get-ting lost here is not a defeat; it's an opportunity. Whenever you feel the need to find your bearings, you can ask for **Odos Sokratous,** which is the closest Old Town comes to having a main street.

When you approach the walls of Old Town, you are about to enter the oldest inhab-ited medieval town in Europe. It's a thrill to behold. Although there are many gates, we suggest that you first enter through **Eleftheria (Liberty) Gate,** where you'll come to **Plateia Simi,** containing ruins of the **Temple of Venus,** identified by the votive offerings found here, which may date from the 3rd century B.C. The remains of the temple are next to a parking lot (driving is restricted in the Old Town), which rather diminishes the impact of the few stones and columns still standing. Nevertheless, the ruins are a reminder that a great Hellenistic city once stood here and encompassed the entire area now occupied by the city, including the old and new towns. The popula-tion of the Hellenistic city of Rhodes is thought to have equaled the current popula-tion of the whole island (roughly 100,000).

Plateia Simi is also home to the **Municipal Art Gallery of Rhodes,** above the Ion-ian and Popular Bank (hours vary but are generally Monday through Saturday from 8am to 2pm; admission is Dr500/$1.45), whose impressive collection is comprised mostly of works by eminent modern Greek artists. The gallery now has a second beau-tifully restored venue in the Old Town (across from the Mosque of Suleiman) to house its collection of antique and rare maps and engravings (open Monday through Friday from 8am to 2pm); and, within the next several years, it will expand into a new and third site located in the New Town. One block farther on is the **Museum of Decora-tive Arts,** which contains finely made objects and crafts from Rhodes and other islands, most notably Simi (open Tuesday through Sunday from 8:30am to 3pm; admission is Dr600/$1.75). Continue through the gate until you reach the **Museum Reproduction Shop** (with a precious painted tile of the Madonna above its door), then turn right on Odos Ippoton toward the Palace of the Knights.

The **Street of the Knights** (you'll see the name Ippoton on maps) is one of the best preserved and most delightful medieval relics in the world. The 600-meter-long, cobble-paved street was constructed over an ancient pathway that led in a straight line from the Acropolis of Rhodes to the port. In the early 16th century, it became the address for most of the inns of each nation, which housed Knights who belonged to the Order of St. John. The inns were used as eating clubs and temporary residences

From the Outside Looking In

Of all the inns on the Street of the Knights, only the **Inn of France** is open to the public (Monday through Friday from 8am to noon). The ground floor houses the Institut Français, but you can see its garden and an occasional art show held in the second-floor gallery. The other inns are now offices or private residences and are closed to the public.

for visiting dignitaries, and their façades reflect the various architectural details of their respective countries.

Begin at the lowest point on the hill (next to the Museum Reproduction Shop) at the **Spanish House,** now used by a bank. Next door is the **Inn of the Order of the Tongue of Italy,** built in 1519 (as can be seen on the shield of the order above the door). Then comes the **Palace of the Villiers of the Isle of Adam,** built in 1521, housing the Archaeological Service of the Dodecanese. The **Inn of France** now hosts the French Language Institute, constructed in 1492. It's one of the most ornate of the inns, with the shield of three lilies (fleur-de-lis), royal crown, and that of the Magister d'Aubusson (the cardinal's hat above four crosses) off center, over the middle door. Typical of the late Gothic period, the architectural and decorative elements are all somewhat asymmetrical, lending grace to the squat building. Opposite these inns is the side of the **Hospital of the Knights,** now the **Archaeological Museum,** whose entrance is on Museum Square. It's a grand and fascinating structure and well worth a visit. (Like so many public buildings in Rhodes, its hours are subject to change without much notice, but in summer it's generally open Tuesday through Friday from 8am to 7pm and Saturday and Sunday from 8:30am to 3pm. Admission is Dr800/$2.30.) Across from the Archaeological Museum is the **Byzantine Museum,** housed in the ✪ **Church of Our Lady of the Castle,** the Cathedral of the Knights, and often hosting superior rotating exhibits of Christian art. Its hours vary but are generally Tuesday through Sunday from 8am to 7pm or later; admission is Dr500 ($1.45).

The church farther on the right is **Ayia Triada** (open when it's open), next to the Italian consulate. Above its door are three coats-of-arms: those of France, England, and the pope. Past the arch that spans the street, still on the right, is the **Inn of the Tongue of Provence,** which was partially destroyed in 1856 and is now shorter than it once was. Opposite it on the left is the traditionally Gothic **Inn of the Tongue of Spain,** with vertical columns elongating its façade and a lovely garden in the back.

The culmination of this impressive procession should be the **Palace of the Knights** (also known as the Palace of the Grand Masters), but it was destroyed in a catastrophic accidental explosion in 1856. What you see before you now is a grandiose palace built in the 1930s to accommodate Mussolini's visits and fantasies. Its scale and grandeur are more reflective of a future that failed to materialize than of a past that has disappeared. Today it houses mosaics stolen from Kos by the Italian military as well as a collection of antique furniture. Hours vary, but in summer are Monday from 12:30 to 7pm, Tuesday through Sunday from 8am to 7pm. Admission is Dr1,200 ($3.45).

The **Mosque of Suleiman** and the public baths are two reminders of the Turkish presence in Old Rhodes. Follow Odos Sokratous west away from the harbor or walk a couple of blocks south from the Palace of the Knights, and you can't miss the mosque with its slender, though incomplete, minaret and pink-striped Venetian exterior.

The **Municipal Baths** (what the Greeks call the "Turkish baths") are housed in a 7th-century Byzantine structure. They merit a visit by anyone interested in the vestiges of Turkish culture that still remain in the Old Town, and are a better deal than the charge for showers in most pensions. The *hamam* (most locals use the Turkish word for "bath") is in Plateia Arionos, between a large old mosque and the Folk Dance Theater. Throughout the day, men and women go in via their separate entrances and disrobe in the private shuttered cubicles. A walk across the cool marble floors leads you to the bath area—many domed, round chambers sunlit by tiny glass panes in the roof. Through the steam you'll see people seated around large marble basins, chatting while ladling bowls of water over their heads. It's open Tuesday through Saturday from 11am to 7pm; the baths cost Dr500 ($1.45) on Tuesday, Thursday, and Friday, but only Dr300 (90¢) on Wednesday and Saturday. Note that Saturday is extremely crowded with locals. In the summer of 2000, the baths were closed for restoration, so they are likely to emerge quite enhanced.

The Old Town was also home to the Jewish community, whose origins go back to the days of the ancient Greeks. Little survives in the northeast or Jewish Quarter of the Old Town other than a few homes with Hebrew inscriptions, the Jewish cemetery, and the **Square of the Jewish Martyrs** (Plateia ton Martiron Evreon, also known as Seahorse Square because of the seahorse fountain). There is a lovely **synagogue,** where services are held on Friday night; a small black sign in the square shows the way. The synagogue is on Odos Dosiadou, off the square, and is usually open daily from 10am to 1pm. This square is dedicated to the thousands of Jews who were rounded up here and sent to their deaths at Auschwitz. If you walk around the residential streets, you'll still see abandoned homes and burned buildings.

While you are at the Square of the Jewish Martyrs, be sure to visit the ✪ **Hospice of St. Catherine** (open Monday through Friday from 8am to 2pm; free admission), a prize winner in 1997 for its restoration and interpretive presentation. Built in the late 14th century by the Order of the Knights of St. John (the Knights Hospitaller) to house and entertain esteemed guests, it apparently lived up to its mission; one such guest, Niccole de Martoni, described it in the 1390s as "beautiful and splendid, with many handsome rooms, containing many and good beds." The description, in fact, still fits, though only one "good bed" can be seen today. The restored Hospice has exceptionally beautiful sea-pebble and mosaic floors, carved and intricately painted wooden ceilings, a grand hall and lavish bedchamber, and engaging exhibits. There's a lot here to excite the eyes and the imagination.

After touring the sites of the Old Town, you might want to walk around the **walls.** (The museum operates a 1-hour tour on Tuesday and Saturday at 3pm, beginning at the Palace of the Knights.) The fortification has a series of magnificent gates and towers, and is remarkable as an example of a fully intact medieval structure. Admission is Dr1,200 ($3.45) for adults, Dr600 ($1.75) for students, and free for children.

EXPLORING THE NEW TOWN

The New Town is best explored after dark, since it houses most of the bars, discos, and nightclubs, as well as innumerable tavernas. In the heat of the day, its beaches—**Elli Beach** and the **municipal beach**—are also popular. What few people make a point of seeking out but also can't miss are landmarks such as **Mandraki Harbor** and the wannabe imperial architecture (culminating in the Nomarhia or Prefecture) along the harbor, all of which date from the Italian occupation. Other draws are the lovely park and ancient burial site at **Rodini** (2km/1.2 miles south of the city) and the impressive ancient **Acropolis of Rhodes** on Mount Smith.

The Acropolis of Rhodes. Open site.

High atop the north end of the island above the modern city, with the sea visible on two sides, stand the remains of the ancient Rhodian acropolis. This is a pleasant site to explore leisurely and enjoy a picnic, with plenty of shade available. The restored stadium and small theater are particularly impressive, as are the remains of the Temple of Pythian Apollo. Even though only several pillars and a portion of the architrave stand in place, they are provocative and pleasing, giving loft to the imagination.

SHOPPING

In Rhodes city, it's the Old Town that is of special interest to shoppers. Here you'll find classic and contemporary **gold and silver jewelry** almost everywhere. The top-of-the-line Greek designer **Ilias LaLaounis** has a boutique on Museum Square. **Alexandra Gold,** on Odos Sokratous next to the Alexis Restaurant, offers stylish European work, elegant gold and platinum link bracelets, and beautifully set precious gems. For a dazzling collection of authentic antique and reproduction jewelry, as well as ceramics, silver, glass, and everything you'd expect to find in a bazaar, drop into **Royal Silver,** Odos Apellou 15 (off Odos Sokratous).

For imported **leather goods** and **furs** (the former often from nearby Turkey and the latter from northern Greece), stroll the length of Odos Sokratous. Antiquity buffs should drop into the **Ministry of Culture Museum Reproduction Shop** on Odos Ippitou, which sells excellent reproductions of ancient sculptures, friezes, and tiles. True **antiques**—furniture, carpets, porcelain, and paintings—can be found at **Kalogirou Art,** Odos Panetiou 30, in a wonderful old building with a pebble-mosaic floor and an exotic banana-tree garden near the Knights Palace.

Although most of what you find on Rhodes can be found throughout Greece, several products bear a special Rhodian mark. **Rhodian wine** has a fine reputation, and on weekdays you can visit two distinguished island wineries: **C.A.I.R.,** at its new factory 2 kilometers (1.2 miles) outside of Rhodes city on the way to Lindos; and **Emery,** in the village of Embonas. Another distinctive product of Rhodes is a rare form of **honey** made from bees committed to Thimati (very like oregano). To get this you may have to drive to the villages of Siana or Vati and ask who has some extra. It's mostly sold out of private homes, as locals are in no hurry to give it up. **Olive oil** is also a local art, and the best is sold out of private homes, meaning that you simply have to make discreet inquiries regarding the best current sources.

Rhodes is also famed for handmade **carpets** and **kilims,** an enduring legacy from centuries of Ottoman occupation. There are currently some 40 women around the island who make carpets in their homes; some monasteries are also in on the act. There's a local carpet factory known as **Kleopatra** at Ayios Anthonias, on the main road to Lindos near Afandou; and, in the Old Town, these and other Rhodian handmade carpet and kilims are sold at **Elafos,** Odos Sokratous 25, and **Royal Carpet,** Odos Apellou 15. Finally, there is "Rhodian" **lace** and **embroidery,** much of which comes from Hong Kong. Ask for help to learn the difference between what's local and what's imported.

SPORTS & OUTDOOR PURSUITS

Most outdoor activities on Rhodes are beach- and sea-related. For everything from **parasailing** to **jet skis** to **canoes,** you'll find what you need at **Faliraki,** if you can tolerate everything and everyone else that you'll have to wade through to get to it.

No license is required for **fishing,** with the best grounds reputed to be off Kamiros Skala, Kalithea, and Lindos. Try hitching a ride with the fishing boats that moor opposite Ayia Katerina's Gate. For sailing and yachting information, call the **Rodos Yacht Club** (☎ 0241/23-287) or the **Yacht Agency Rhodes** (☎ 0241/22-927; fax 0241/23-393), which is the center for all yachting needs.

If you've always wanted to try scuba diving, both **Waterhoppers Diving Schools** (☎ and fax **0241/38-146**) and **Dive Med** (☎ **0241/61-115;** fax 0241/66-584; www. rodos.com/dive-med/index.html) offer 1-day introductory dives for beginners, diving expeditions for experienced divers, and 4- to 5-day courses leading to various certifications.

Other sports are available at the **Rhodes Tennis Club** (☎ **0241/25-705**) in the resort of Elli, or the **Rhodes-Afandu Golf Club** (☎ **0241/51-225**), 19 kilometers (11.8 miles) south of the port. A centrally located, fully equipped fitness center can be found at the **Fitness Factory** (☎ **0241/37-667**), at Odos Akti Kanari 17.

If you want to get some culture as you get in shape, information on taking traditional **Greek folk-dance lessons** can be obtained from the **Old Town Theater** (☎ **0241/29-085**), where Nelly Dimoglou and her entertaining troupe perform, or by contacting the **Traditional Dance Center,** Odos Dekelias 87, Athens (☎ **01/ 25-1080**). Classes run from June to early August, 30 hours per week; each week, dances from a different region are studied. There are also shorter courses available.

WHERE TO STAY IN RHODES CITY
IN THE OLD TOWN

Accommodations in the Old Town have the aura of ages past, but character does not always equal charm. There are few really attractive options here, and they are in considerable demand, with all of the attending complications. One is that some hosts, regardless of the ethics and legalities involved, will hold you to the letter of your intent—so if you need or wish to cancel a day or more of your stay, they will do their best to extract the last drachma. And there is some hedging of bets, which means that the exact room agreed upon may at the end of the day be "unavailable." You should also try to be explicit and keep a paper trail.

Expensive

✪ **S. Nikolis Hotel.** Odos Ippodamou 61, 85100 Rhodes. ☎ **0241/34-561.** Fax 0241/ 32-034. www.greekhotel.com. E-mail: nikoliss@hol.gr. 12 units. A/C TV TEL. Dr30,000– Dr50,000 double ($86–$144); Dr70,000 ($201) Jacuzzi suite. Rates include breakfast. AE, MC, V. Open year-round (call ahead to confirm from Nov–Mar).

This hotel is one of a kind. Within the ancient walls, it is quite simply the only place with real finesse and class. Don't confuse this with five-star luxury: What you pay for and get here is neither grand nor sumptuous, but it is unique, and in its own way exquisite. Host Sotiris Nikolis is a true artisan with a fine eye. Here, on the site of an ancient Hellenistic agora, he has restored several medieval structures using the original stones and remaining as faithful as possible to the original style. The result is immensely pleasing (though not plush). In addition to the hotel rooms, there are four simply stunning honeymoon suites (Dr45,000 to Dr65,000/$129 to $187), as well as eight appealing though less extraordinary apartments. All units contain fridges, firm beds, and often handcrafted furniture; two new suites have Jacuzzis and sleep from two to four people comfortably using traditional loft areas. In the hotel's enclosed garden are a small fitness center and computer nook with Internet access. Plans are underway for a deluxe business suite complete with fax and computer. If you are resolved to stay within the walls of the Old Town—an unforgettable experience—and if you are willing and able to pay a premium for aesthetic taste, this is the place. (Note that smoking is not permitted here.)

Be sure to check out the adjacent **Ancient Agora Bar and Restaurant,** where, in 1990, a 10-ton marble pediment dating from the 2nd century was found beneath the medieval foundations.

Rhodes Accommodations & Dining

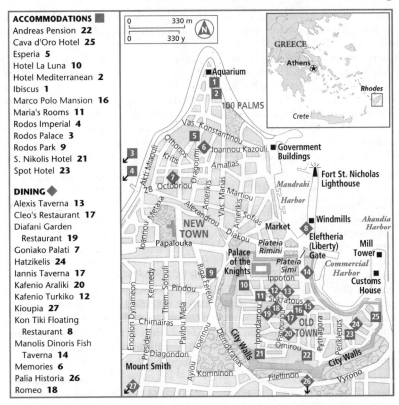

ACCOMMODATIONS
Andreas Pension **22**
Cava d'Oro Hotel **25**
Esperia **5**
Hotel La Luna **10**
Hotel Mediterranean **2**
Ibiscus **1**
Marco Polo Mansion **16**
Maria's Rooms **11**
Rodos Imperial **4**
Rodos Palace **3**
Rodos Park **9**
S. Nikolis Hotel **21**
Spot Hotel **23**

DINING
Alexis Taverna **13**
Cleo's Restaurant **17**
Diafani Garden
  Restaurant **19**
Goniako Palati **7**
Hatzikelis **24**
Iannis Taverna **17**
Kafenio Araliki **20**
Kafenio Turkiko **12**
Kioupia **27**
Kon Tiki Floating
  Restaurant **8**
Manolis Dinoris Fish
  Taverna **14**
Memories **6**
Palia Historia **26**
Romeo **18**

Moderate

Marco Polo Mansion. Odos Fanouriou 42, 85100 Rhodes. ☎ and fax **0241/25-562.** www.marcopolomansion.web.com. E-mail: marcopolomansion@hotmail.com. 7 units. Dr20,000–Dr36,000 ($57–$104) double with bathroom. Rates include breakfast. V. Closed Nov–Mar.

Already, in its first year, featured in several glossy fashion and travel magazines, the Marco Polo Mansion has captured the attention of anyone with a nose for timeless style and good taste. As if squeezed from tubes of ancient pigments and weathered in the bleaching sun, the color palate here is all deep blues, mustard, wine, and pitch, the colors of boats as much as temples. Each guest room is unique, steeped in a history of its own and furnished with antiques and folk art. One was a harem, another a *hamam* (Turkish bath). The "Imperial Room" has six windows, while the "Antika 2" room, lined with kilims, has a view of minarets. The smaller garden rooms, nestled in fragrant greenery, reflect the house's Italian period. Ceiling fans and cross breezes stand between you and the heat of the day. If you want a history lesson as well as a room, plus a bit of exotic fantasy with your morning coffee, you'll find it and more here.

Inexpensive

Andreas Pension. Odos Omirou 28D (located between Omirou 23 and 20, *not* just before 29), 85100 Rhodes. ☎ **0241/34-156.** Fax 0241/74-285. E-mail: andreasch@otenet.gr. 12 units, 6 with private bathroom. Dr8,000–Dr12,050 ($23–$34) double with bathroom. Breakfast Dr2,000 ($6) per person extra. AE, V. Closed Nov–Feb.

This exceptionally well-run pension offers relief from the cardboard walls and linoleum floors that haunt many of the town's budget choices. Housed in a restored 400-year-old Turkish sultan's house, it also offers attractive rooms, some of which have panoramic views of the town. Other units have wooden lofts, which can comfortably sleep a family of four. The bedrooms (with commendably firm beds) were once occupied by the sultan's harem, while the sultan held forth in room 11, a spacious corner unit with three windows and extra privacy, perfect for a guy for whom every day was a honeymoon! Hosts Dmitri and Josette serve breakfast on a shaded terrace that boasts gorgeous vistas of the town and the harbor, the best views in Old Town. A full bar with wide-screen TV is also at hand, patrolled by a pet tortoise. Laundry service is provided. Rooms 10 and 11 have the best views; rooms 8 and 9 have private terraces.

✪ Cava d'Oro Hotel. Odos Kistiniou 15, 85100 Rhodes. ☎ **0241/36-980.** 13 units. A/C TV TEL. Dr10,000–Dr15,000 ($29–$43) double. MC, V. Closed Dec–Feb.

This 800-year-old structure, nearly flush against the eastern defensive wall of the Old Town, was at the time of the Knights a home within the Jewish quarter. The immediate neighborhood is today neither quaint nor scenic, but that translates into quiet, which is what you want at the end of the day. This is where Michael Palin stayed while filming the Rhodes section of his *Pole to Pole* series. In 1999 and 2000, all of the guestrooms were restored and refurnished with true artistry. Ancient stone walls were exposed, bathrooms were redesigned with lovely tiles and mosaics, and a tasteful blend of antique and modern furnishings were introduced. The result is both simple and elegant. Each room is uniquely charming. Five have balconies; two have lofts ideal for families; and half are no-smoking. There is a pleasant garden and private steps up onto the town's fortification wall. In sum, this is a remarkably interesting, appealing, and affordable haven.

Hotel La Luna. Odos Ierokleous 21, 85100 Rhodes. ☎ and fax **0241/25-856.** www.helios.gr/exr. 7 rooms, none with bathroom. Dr14,500 ($42) double. Rates include breakfast. No credit cards. Closed Nov–Mar. Turn off Odos Orfeos between the two halves of the Don Kichotis taverna.

This small, delightful hotel is a block in from the taverna-lined, touristy Odos Orfeos, nestled between two churches in a calm residential neighborhood. It features a large, shaded garden with bar and breakfast tables. Looking at the clean, modest rooms, all without toilet or bathtub, you may wonder why this is a prime spot in Old Town, sought after by diplomats, barons, and movie stars like Ben Kingsley and Helen Mirren. The answer is charm, which the ancient Greek poets knew to be capricious and inscrutable. It also has a lot to do with the private 300-year-old Turkish bath, which more than makes up for the one you don't have in your room. This is a place for visitors who want and respect quiet; blast your radio or make a ruckus, and you'll be asked to leave. Our favorite double is room 2 (Ben stayed in room 1). Currently, just beyond the encircling walls of La Luna, there is a fascinating archaeological project underway, involving two ancient churches, a traditional Turkish residence and garden, a Byzantine monastery, and much more, making this an even more intriguing corner of Old Town in which to ensconce yourself.

Maria's Rooms. Odos Menekleous 147-Z, 85100 Rhodes. ☎ **0241/22-169.** E-mail: vasilpyrgos@hotmail.com. 8 units, 3 with bathroom. Dr7,000–Dr10,000 ($20–$29) double with private bath. No credit cards. Open Easter–Oct.

This pristine little pension near the Archontiko Restaurant merits very high marks for both price and quality. The accommodations are sparkling white and squeaky clean, and Maria is a warm and welcoming hostess. Even without air-conditioning, the rooms are cool and enjoy enough seclusion from the bustle of the Old Town to be surprisingly quiet.

Spot Hotel. Odos Perikleous 21, 85100 Rhodes. ☎ **0241/34-737.** www.islandsinblue.gr. E-mail: spothot@otenet.gr. 9 units. Dr10,000–Dr11,000 ($29–$32) double. No credit cards.

Spotless would be a more suitable name for this small hotel. By Old Town standards, this building is an infant, only 25 years old, which means there's no issue here with the damp and mold that plague many of the centuries-old structures. The rooms are simple and tasteful; over the next several years, gradual and substantial enhancements that are underway will add such architectural touches as exposed stone, stucco arches, wooden shutters, enlarged garden and terrace sitting areas, and air-conditioning in five units. The aim is to give Spot more of an island and medieval atmosphere in keeping with its location. Guests enjoy a large communal fridge, access to a phone for free local calls, free limited use of a PC for e-mail, and free luggage storage. Spot is located near the harbor right off Plateia Martiron Hevreon.

IN THE NEW TOWN & ENVIRONS

Unlike the Old Town, the New Town doesn't prohibit new construction. You'll find a wild array of options, from boardinghouses to package-tour hotels to luxury resorts. Most are dull and some are dazzling, but the vast majority are so undistinguished that you may forget which one you're in. Cleanliness, a little comfort, and proximity to beaches and bars are what most travelers expect, so this is what you'll find.

Very Expensive

Rodos Imperial. Leoforos Ialisou, Iksia (4 km/2½ miles out of the New Town), 85100 Rhodes. ☎ **0241/75-000.** Fax 0241/76-690. 404 units. A/C MINIBAR TV TEL. Dr90,800 ($261) double with sea view; Dr239,000 ($680) one-bedroom suite with sea view; Dr390,000 ($1,123) presidential suite. Rates include buffet breakfast. AE, DC, MC, V. Closed Nov–Mar.

This luxurious Aegean-style hotel, across the road from the beach, has every possible facility you might desire, plus a beach with windsurfing, sailing, jet-skiing, paragliding, and swimming. You can stash your kids in the supervised miniclub while you're working out in the gym or taking your *sirtaki* (dancing) or aerobic lessons, and use an in-house baby-sitter while attending one of the hotel's evening shows. The guestrooms are spacious and comfortable, each with a large balcony—but on their own they don't have much over a top-of-the-line Holiday Inn. What you pay for here is proximity to the beach and extensive private resort facilities.

You can dine at the Marco Polo (adventurous cuisine with an Asian touch), the Castellania (fine traditional and international fare poolside), or the more informal Pergola. The high season brings live entertainment and fish festivals. The Imperial's amenities are too numerous to list, but include a water-sports school, tennis club, full-service health club, several freshwater pools (indoor and outdoor), and an ample shopping arcade.

Note that from January 2001, the Imperial will be operated by Hilton and is likely to undergo significant changes. No glimpse, however, into the future Hilton Rhodes was available to us at press time.

✪ Rodos Palace. Leoforos Trianton, Iksia, 85100 Rhodes. ☎ **0241/25-222.** Fax 0241/25-350. www.rodos-palace.gr. E-mail: info@rodos-palace.gr. 785 units, 2 presidential villas. A/C MINIBAR TV TEL. Dr61,600–Dr78,500 ($177–$226) executive double with sea view; Dr53,700–Dr68,600 ($155–$197) executive double with garden view. Rates include breakfast. AE, MC, V. Closed Dec–Mar.

"Palace" is indeed the word for the largest five-star hotel in Greece, set amid 30 acres of gardens and facing the sea just outside Rhodes city. It was decorated by the famed designer Maurice Bailey, who cut his teeth designing the sets for *Quo Vadis* and *Ben Hur.* Needless to say, this has been the uncontested king of the mountain on Rhodes for the past 25 years. It has never rested on its laurels, but is always adding to and improving what it offers, which is just about everything. The latest addition is a new family center, a resort within a resort designed to provide the ultimate holiday for families with children. The largest of the several pools lies beneath a massive dome constructed by Boeing—and while you're swimming, you can have a suit custom cut for you, from the finest English wool, by the hotel tailor. As for the guestrooms, we recommend the executive doubles for couples, the corner suites for families.

It is simply not possible to recount the full array of dining options, entertainment, shopping, and so on offered within this world-class resort. The emphasis is admittedly on sun and water, with everything from water polo to scuba diving. There's also a full health center with a *hamam* (bath) and much more. And for the less aerobically inclined, you can shop yourself into a modest Greek fury here.

Expensive

✪ **Rodos Park.** Odos Riga Fereou 12, 85100 Rhodes. ☎ **800/525-4800** in the U.S., or 0241/89-700. Fax 0241/24-613. www.rodospark.gr. E-mail: info@rodospark.gr. 60 units. A/C MINIBAR TV TEL. Dr43,000–Dr53,500 ($124–$154) double; Dr64,500–Dr84,500 ($186–$252) suite. Breakfast buffet Dr5,250 ($15) per person. AE, MC, V. Open year-round. The hotel is only a few minutes from the Old Town and Mandraki Harbor as well as the New Town shopping and dining areas.

This superb New Town luxury hotel, with gleaming marble and polished wood interiors, enjoys a uniquely convenient yet secluded location just outside the Old Town. If you want a Jacuzzi in your room, opt for a suite, preferably one with a superb view of the Old Town walls. If you need to work off surplus calories from the 24-hour room service or the in-house gourmet restaurant, head down to the fitness center, then pamper yourself with a Swedish massage, sauna, or steam bath. A dip in the outdoor pool will offer the perfect finish to your regime.

Several excellent dining choices include Le Café (with appetizing views of the hotel's gardens and pool), the Park Side (a cafe-brasserie), and Le Jardin, where the art of Greek dining takes a timely French turn. For those who won't come in out of the air for love or money, there's an open-air grill bar. In addition to all the amenities you would expect from a first-class international hotel, there's a fully equipped gym and an inviting outdoor pool. The biggest fringe benefit of all is the Park's location on the perimeter of the old walls, placing its guests within a short stroll to the heart of the old city.

Moderate

Hotel Mediterranean. Kos Beach, 85100 Rhodes. ☎ **0241/24-661.** Fax 0241/22-828. www.mediterranean.gr. E-mail: info@mediterranean.gr. 241 units. A/C MINIBAR TV TEL. Dr23,550–Dr46,000 ($67–$132) double; Dr32,750–Dr57,500 ($94–$166) suite. Rates include breakfast. AE, DC, MC, V. Open year-round.

This hotel has undergone a transformation so dramatic and successful that its former self drops from memory. Directly across from Kos Beach and next to the new Playboy Casino, its location speaks for itself. The interior of the hotel, from the common to the private rooms, is grand and elegant. The Mediterranean calls itself "Rhodes's newest boutique hotel," which suggests stylish sophistication, and rightfully so. The double rooms have adjoining twin beds, pull-out sofas, and spacious tiled baths. Of the three views offered, the spectacular sea view far outshines the garden (pool and veranda) or side (city) view. (Rates vary according to the view.) The suites all have sea views, sitting areas, and king-sized beds. All units have balconies. Facilities include a modest pool, a snazzy cafe and bar with a string of attractive lounges for drinks and conversation, and an elegant, exclusive restaurant for fine dining in both Greek and international style. Handicapped-accessible rooms are available upon request.

⭘ **Ibiscus.** Kos Beach, 85100 Rhodes. ☎ **0241/24-421.** Fax 0241/27-283. 205 units. A/C TV TEL. Dr23,900–Dr33,900 ($68–$98) double; Dr30,900–Dr40,900 ($89–$118) suite. Rates include breakfast. AE, DC, MC, V. Closed Nov–Mar.

The Ibiscus was already an attractive and well-situated beachfront hotel before it underwent a makeover in 2000. But "makeover" doesn't really suffice—this qualifies as sheer metamorphosis, taking the Ibiscus from attractive to striking. The spacious marble entrance hall opens into a stylish cafe bar, from which you can take your drinks out front to face the beach or back into the garden veranda, poolside. The tasteful, spacious, and fully carpeted double rooms have king-sized orthopedic beds, large wardrobes, ample desk areas, tile and marble baths, and hair dryers. The suites are especially appealing, with rich wood paneling, parquet floors, and two bedrooms (one with a king bed and one with twin beds). Every unit has a balcony, many of which face the sea. Also on site are a large dining room, a small arcade of shops, and a small "dipping" pool, all you need when the sea is only a stone's throw away.

Inexpensive

Esperia. Othos Griva 7, 85100 Rhodes. ☎ **0241/23-941.** Fax 0241/77-501. 171 units. A/C TEL. Dr13,000–Dr22,000 ($37–$63) double. Rates include breakfast. AE, DC, MC, V. Open year-round.

This hotel is a class above its cost. It is rare in Rhodes to find this kind of quality at such reasonable rates. Newly renovated in 1999 and 2000, the guestrooms are tasteful and exceptionally clean, each with fridge, hair dryer, and large balcony with pleasant views. New double-glazed sliding balcony doors effectively seal the rooms off from most of the town's noise. TVs are available on request at a small additional cost. The bar, lounge, and breakfast room are inviting, and the walled outdoor pool and poolside bar are well above average for a modest hotel. The buffet breakfast is extensive and tasty. The hotel is located near the restaurant district and only a short walk from the beach. It also has 19 apartments for rent, but only in the winter.

WHERE TO DINE IN RHODES CITY
IN THE OLD TOWN

The Old Town is thick with tavernas, restaurants, and fast-food nooks, all doing their best to lure you into their lair, which in some cases is just where you want to be. The more brazen their overtures, the more bold you must be in holding to your course. Don't imagine, however, that all Old Town restaurants are tourist traps. Many Rhodians consider this area to have some of the best food on the island, particularly for fish.

Expensive

⭘ **Alexis Taverna.** Odos Sokratous 18. ☎ **0241/29-347.** Reservations recommended. Individually designed dinners without wine average Dr15,000 ($43). AE, V. Mon–Sat 10am–4pm and 7–11pm. SEAFOOD.

For more than 40 years, this fine restaurant has been the one to beat in Old Town, setting the standard by which all the other seafood restaurants are measured. Two brothers, Iannis and Constantine, today preserve the tradition established by their grandfather Alexis. The list of appreciative diners over the years includes Winston Churchill, Jackie Kennedy, presidents, royalty, and innumerable tourists in the know. This is one place, if you can afford it, to abandon restraint and invite Iannis to conceive a seafood feast for you, selecting a perfect wine from his cellar (which represents vineyards all over Greece). Iannis goes down to the harbor himself each day and chooses the best of the catch. Insisting on quality and freshness, he and Constantine have built their own greenhouse on the outskirts of town to cultivate organic vegetables. We started with a bounteous seafood platter, with delicately flavored sea urchins, fresh clams, and a tender octopus carpaccio. The sargos, a sea-bream–type fish, was charcoal-grilled to perfection. The creamy Greek yogurt with homemade greenwalnut jam was a perfect ending for a superb culinary experience. Every meal here begins with a chef's consultation and should end with applause.

Manolis Dinoris Fish Taverna. Museum Sq. 14A. ☎ **0241/25-824.** Appetizers Dr1,600–Dr3,500 ($4.60–$10); main courses Dr8,500–Dr14,000 ($24–$40); fixed-price dinners Dr10,000–Dr15,000 ($29–$43). AE, MC, V. Year-round daily noon–midnight. SEAFOOD.

This restaurant, housed in the former stables of the 13th-century Knights of St. John's Inn, provides a unique setting to enjoy delicious and fresh seafood delights. Either choose à la carte or the set menu, which includes coquille St. Jacques, Greek salad, grilled prawns, swordfish, baklava, coffee, and brandy. In warm weather, the quiet side garden is delightful; in winter, a fire roars in the old stone hearth indoors.

Moderate

Cleo's Restaurant. Odos St. Fanouriou 17. ☎ **0241/28-415.** Appetizers Dr1,000–Dr4,300 ($2.90–$12); main courses Dr1,850–Dr4,950 ($5.30–$14). AE, MC, V. Year-round Mon–Sat 7pm–midnight. ITALIAN.

This tranquil place, with its whitewashed courtyard and elegantly furnished two-story interior, is found down a narrow lane off noisy Odos Sokratous. Owner Romildo Fistolera, from Como, Italy, prepares the best Italian and nouvelle European cuisine in Rhodes. He also has a superb wine selection from lesser-known boutique wineries. We savored the homemade tagliatelle with salmon sauce, and found the beef fillet with white mushroom sauce superb. The fixed-price three-course dinners are especially good buys. For dessert, the creamy tiramisu is sinfully exquisite.

Hatzikelis. Odos Alhadeff 9. ☎ **0241/27-215.** Appetizers Dr800–Dr2,500 ($2.30–$7); main courses Dr1,800–Dr3,500 ($5.15–$10); Fisherman's Plate (for two) Dr15,000 ($43); traditional plates (for two) Dr8,400 and Dr9,500 ($24 and $27). No credit cards. Year-round daily 11am–2am. GREEK/SEAFOOD.

This delightful fish taverna enjoys a peaceful and pleasant setting, in the midst of a small neighborhood park just behind the Church of Our Lady of the Burgh in the Square of the Jewish Martyrs. Although there is an extensive à la carte menu, the various special dinners for two are all but irresistible, even if you must loosen your belt and consume it all on your own. The Fisherman's Plate offers lobster, shrimp, mussels, octopus, squid, and a liter of wine, while the plates of traditional Rhodian dishes include such specialties as pumpkin balls and shrimp saganaki. The portions are challenging, but the quality of the cuisine and the fact that you have until 2am to do your duty practically assure congenial closure to your meal. To find Hatzikelis easily without winding your way through the Old Town, just enter the walls at the Pili Panagias (St. Mary's Gate).

Romeo. Odos Menekleous 7–9 (off Odos Sokratous). ☎ **0241/25-186.** Appetizers Dr900–Dr3,000 ($2.60–$9); main courses Dr1,400–Dr4,800 ($4–$14). AE, MC, V. Mid-Mar to mid-Nov daily 10am–1am. GREEK/SEAFOOD.

Though under siege from tourists, many locals gladly frequent the Romeo, as there is a good deal that's authentic within its walls. For one thing, there are the walls themselves, roughly 500 years old. More important, besides the predictable taverna fare, are the number of local dishes on offer. The gracious and helpful waiters will happily explain and discuss the menu with you and accommodate special preferences whenever possible. Two of the specialties of the house are the mixed fish grill and the stuffed souvlaki. The fish grill is comprised of whatever you select from a generous array of fresh deep-sea options. The tender marinated octopus is an especially gripping surprise. The finely cut grilled souvlaki stuffed with melted cheese and tomatoes, a regional specialty from the north end of the island, is also a sit-up-and-take-notice selection. With each, the very reasonably priced dry house wines are quite suitable. Set back in a quiet enclave, just off and out of the crush of Odos Sokratous, Romeo offers both courtyard and roof garden seating, as well as tasteful live traditional Greek music and song. If you're keen on a smoke-free environment, the roof garden is usually quite breezy and the air particularly fresh.

Inexpensive

Diafani Garden Restaurant. Plateia Arionos 3 (opposite the Turkish bath). ☎ **0241/ 26-053.** Appetizers Dr500–Dr1,000 ($1.45–$2.90); main courses Dr800–Dr3,500 ($2.30–$10). No credit cards. Year-round daily noon–midnight. GREEK.

Several locals recommended this family-operated taverna, which cooks up fine traditional Greek fare at bargain prices. Sitting under the spreading walnut tree in the vine-shaded courtyard, we enjoyed the potpourri of the Greek plate and the splendid *papoutsaki*, braised eggplant slices layered with chopped meat and a thick, cheesy béchamel sauce, delicately flavored with nutmeg and coriander. You won't find better authentic Greek home cooking than this anywhere in Rhodes, especially at lunch.

Iannis Taverna. Odos Platonos 41. ☎ **0241/36-535.** Appetizers Dr300–Dr900 (90¢–$2.60); main courses Dr500–Dr2,900 ($1.45–$8). No credit cards. Year-round daily 9am–midnight. GREEK.

For a budget Greek meal, visit chef Iannis's small place on a quiet back lane. The moussaka, stuffed vegetables, and meat dishes are flavorful and well prepared by a man who spent 14 years as a chef in the Greek diners of New York. His Greek plate is the best we found in Rhodes, with an unbelievably large variety of tasty foods. Portions are hearty and cheap, and the friendly service is a welcome relief from nearby establishments. The breakfast omelets are a great deal, too.

Kafenio Araliki. Odos Aristofanous 45. ☎ **0241/73-708.** Appetizers/snacks Dr1,000–Dr1,800 ($2.90–$5.15). No credit cards. Year-round Mon–Sat 11am–3pm and 7pm–1am. GREEK.

A *kafenio* is a place to eat small plates of savory dishes while sipping retsina or ouzo. Off the tourist circuit, this picturesque hideaway, run by two super-friendly Italian women, Valeria and Miriam, is our favorite place to sit among locals and expatriates, munching on the delightful vegetarian, fish, and meat mezedes. The upstairs gallery is especially charming.

Kafenio Turkiko. Odos Sokratous. No phone. Drinks/snacks Dr200–Dr600 (60¢–$1.75). No credit cards. Year-round daily 11am–midnight. SNACKS.

Located in a Crusader structure, this is the only authentic place left on touristy Odos Sokratous, otherwise replete with Swatch, the Body Shop, Van Cleef, and a multitude of souvenir shops. Each rickety wooden table comes with a backgammon board for idling away the hours while you sip on Greek coffee or juice. The old pictures, mirrors, and bric-a-brac on the walls enhanced our feeling of bygone times. Closed for restoration in 2000, the once and future Kafenio Turkiko is likely to emerge refreshed and ready for a new millennium.

IN THE NEW TOWN & ENVIRONS
Expensive

✪ **Kioupia.** Tris village. ☎ **0241/91-824.** Reservations required. Fixed-price meals Dr6,500 ($19) and Dr12,000 ($34) per person, wines and service extra. À la carte also available. MC, V. Year-round Mon–Sat 8pm–midnight. GREEK.

Rated by the *London Guardian* as one of the world's 10 best restaurants, this unique place offers an exquisite gourmet experience that you will long treasure. Kioupia was founded in 1972 by the creative and artistic Michael Koumbiadis, called by Athenian society "the Colossus of Rhodes," who has discovered the true harmony in the taste of Greek traditional cuisine, using the best of local ingredients and village recipes. In this elegantly decorated, rustic old house, the meal begins with a rinsing of hands in rose-water, and then perhaps a choice from three soups, including the unusual *trahanas,* a Greek wheat-and-cheese soup. And then, another difficult choice from an amazing array of appetizers: sautéed wild mushrooms, pumpkin *beignee* (dumplings), savory braised red peppers in olive oil, accompanied by home-baked carrot bread and pastrami bread. The main dishes are equally superb—broiled veal stuffed with cheese and sprinkled with pistachio nuts with yogurt sauce, or delectable pork souvlaki with yogurt and paprika sauce on the side. For dessert, go all the way with light crêpes filled with sour cherries and covered with chocolate sauce and vanilla crème. Many of the foods are prepared in a traditional wood-burning oven in clay pots, the faint smell of wood permeating the restaurant. The grand fixed-price meal, like the Orthodox liturgy, requires fasting, devotion, and time (roughly 3 hrs.), and involves no small share of mystery.

Moderate

Goniako Palati (Corner Palace). Odos Griva 110 (corner of Griva and 28 Oktobriou). ☎ **0241/33-167.** Appetizers Dr300–Dr2,350 (90¢–$7); main courses Dr1,450–Dr5,650 ($4.15–$16). AE, MC, V. Year-round daily 9am–midnight. GREEK.

The new Goniako Palati may not be a palace, but it is on the corner—a busy corner, something you overlook once the food arrives. Great canvas awnings spread out to cover the seating area, raised well above street level. The extensive taverna menu is basic Greek, fresh and skillfully prepared in a slightly upscale environment at reasonable prices. This is one place local New Towners go for reliable, and then some, taverna fare. The grilled swordfish souvlaki, served with a medley of steamed vegetables, is quite tasty. The saganaki here is a performance art, and delicious to boot.

Kon Tiki Floating Restaurant. Mandraki Harbor. ☎ **0241/22-477.** Appetizers Dr900–Dr1,500 ($2.60–$4.30); main courses Dr1,500–Dr6,000 ($4.30–$17). AE, MC, V. Year-round daily 8am–midnight. GREEK/INTERNATIONAL.

Still floating after 36 years of serving good food, this was one of Rhodes's first decent restaurants, and it's still a great place to watch the yachts bobbing alongside while enjoying well-prepared, creative dishes, such as the sole *valevska* (fillet of sole with shrimps, crabs, and mushrooms gratinéed in a béchamel sauce). The *saganaki* shrimp are exceptionally tasty, served with feta cheese, local herbs, and tomato sauce. The new owner is implementing tasteful incremental enhancements in the decor and unleashing the chef's imagination, with immediate and enticing results like the Royal Greenland shrimps. The restaurant is also open for breakfast and for coffee or a drink at the bar, if that's all you want.

Memories. Iannis Dragoumi 24. ☎ **0241/23-003.** Appetizers Dr950–Dr2,500 ($2.75–$7); main courses Dr1,350–Dr4,500 ($3.90–$13). V. Apr–Oct daily 9:30am–1am. GREEK.

This restaurant just down from the Esperia Hotel was only three days old when we first ate here in 1998, and we wondered whether the excellent taverna cuisine and gracious service were merely a burst of beginners' fervor. On that night, the party next to us had eaten here on opening night and had come back the following two nights as well. Their record, however, has since been broken, as one of our readers has now eaten here 10 nights in a row. While we never intended to inaugurate a new Guinness competition, we stand by our initial recommendation. The ambience and decor here are exceptionally tasteful and warm. The designer has a gifted eye, and the chef a discerning palate. For traditional taverna fare as well as an array of chef's specialties, this remains a cut above the eateries that line the nearby streets.

✪ **Palia Historia (The Old Story).** Odos Mitropoleos 108. ☎ **0241/32-421.** Reservations recommended. Appetizers Dr950–Dr2,000 ($2.75–$6); main courses Dr2,600–Dr5,300 ($8–$15). AE, MC, V. Year-round daily 7pm–midnight. GREEK.

Actually, this restaurant is not an old story, as it is only 10 years old—but it is well on its way to becoming a legend. It's worth a taxi ride from wherever you're staying. Most of the clientele is Greek, drawn by the subtle cuisine and lack of tourists. If you've maxed out on run-of-the-mill Greek taverna fare, this is one place to come. The marinated salmon and capers are worthy of the finest Dublin restaurant, and the broccoli with oil, mustard, and roasted almonds is inspired. As a main course, the shrimps saganaki leave nothing to the imagination. With fish, the dry white Spiropoulos from Mantinia is perfect. For a great finish, go for the banana flambé.

RHODES CITY AFTER DARK

Rhodes by night is brimming with energy. Outside of Athens, Rhodes claims one of the most active nighttime scenes in Greece. Granted, some of that energy is grounded in the resort complexes north of the city, but there is enough to go around.

Your own good sense is as good a guide as any in this ever-changing scene. In a city as compact as Rhodes, it's best to follow the lights and noise, not worrying about getting a little lost. When you decide to call it quits, shout down a taxi to bring you back, if you can remember where you're staying.

As a rule of thumb, the **New Town** is more lively than the Old Town. In the New Town, several **cafe scenes** are on the harbor, behind Academy Square, or on Odos Galias, near New Market. The **bar scene** tends to line up along Odos Diakonou. There are at least 100 **nightclubs** on Rhodes, so you're sure to find one to your liking. Complicating matters is a recent announcement that the police, after countless complaints of noise and mayhem until all hours, have decided to designate one area of the city for discos and bars, enabling them to stay open until whenever. When this area will be designated and where it will be is anyone's guess.

Gambling is a popular nighttime activity in Greece. Rhodes has had for many years one of only three legal casinos in Greece, a government-operated roulette and blackjack house adjoining the Grand Hotel. In January 1999, however, this was replaced by a much more extensive casino and hotel operated by Playboy International. The home of this new complex is the once-grand **Hotel Rodon** facing Elli Beach.

The **Sound-and-Light** (*Son et Lumière*) presentation dramatizes the life of a youth admitted into the monastery in 1522, the year before Rhodes fell to invading Turks. In contrast to Athens's Acropolis show, the dialogue here is more illuminating, though the lighting is unimaginative. Nevertheless, sitting in the lush gardens below the palace on a warm evening can be pleasant, and we heartily recommend it to those smitten by the medieval Old Town. Check the posted schedule for English-language performances; they take place at Odos Papagou, south of Plateia Rimini (☎ **0241/21-922**). Admission is Dr1,500 ($4.30) for adults, Dr1,000 ($2.90) for youths, and free for children under 11.

We thoroughly recommend the **Traditional Folk Dance Theater,** presented by the Nelly Dimoglou Dance Company, Odos Adronikou, off Plateia Arionos, Old Town (☎ **0241/20-157**). It is always lively, filled with color, and totally entertaining. Twenty spirited men and women perform dances from many areas of Greece in colorful, often embroidered, flouncy costumes. The five-man band plays an inspired and varied repertoire. Performances take place from May through early October, Monday, Wednesday, and Friday at 9:15pm. Admission is Dr3,500 ($10) for adults.

EXPLORING THE ISLAND

Sun, sand, and the rest is history. That's nowhere more true than on Rhodes. Ruins and beaches—that nearly sums up what lures visitors out of Rhodes city. First things first: For the best **beaches,** head to the east coast of the island. Visitors also flock to archaeological sites identical to the three original Dorian city-states, all nearly 3,000 years old: **Lindos, Kamiros,** and **Ialisos.** Of these, Lindos was and is preeminent; it is by far the top tourist destination outside of Old Town. So we begin here with Lindos, and then explore the island counterclockwise.

LINDOS

Lindos is without question the most picturesque town on the island of Rhodes. Since Lindos has been designated a historic settlement, the Archaeological Society has control over all development in the village (God bless 'em!), and the traditional white stucco homes, shops, and restaurants form the most unified, classically Greek expression in the Dodecanese. Be warned, however, that Lindos is often deluged with tourists, and your first visit may be unforgettable for the wrong reasons. Avoid the crush of mid-July to August, if at all possible.

There are two entrances to the town. The first and northernmost leads down a steep hill to the bus stop and taxi stand, then veers downhill to the beach. If you're driving, park above the town in the lot. At this square you'll find the friendly, extremely informative **Tourist Information Kiosk** (☎ **0244/31-900;** fax 0241/31-288), where Michalis will help you from April through October, daily from 9am to 10pm. Here, too, is the commercial heart of the village with the Acropolis above. The rural **medical clinic** (☎ **0241/31-224**), **post office,** and **telephone office (OTE)** are nearby. The second road leads beyond the town and into the upper village, blessedly removed from the hordes. This is the better route for people more aesthetically minded. Just follow signs to the Acropolis. For Dr1,000 ($2.90) you can ride a donkey (also known as a Lindian taxi) all the way to the top; you'll pass their stand.

All along the way, your path will be strewn with embroidery and lace, which may or may not be the handiwork of local women. Embroidery from Rhodes was highly coveted in the ancient world. In fact, it is claimed that Alexander the Great wore a grand Rhodian robe into battle at Gaugemila, and in Renaissance Europe, the French ladies used to yearn for a bit of Lindos lace. Much of what is for sale in Lindos today, however, is from Hong Kong.

At the top, from the fortress ramparts, there are glorious views of medieval Lindos below, where most homes date from the 15th century. To the south you can see the lovely beach at St. Paul's Bay—named from the tradition that St. Paul put ashore here—along with Rhodes's less-developed eastern coastline. Across to the southwest rises Mount Krana, where caves, dug out to serve as ancient tombs, are thought to have been cult places to Athena well into the Christian period.

The ✪ **Acropolis** (☎ **0241/27-674**) is open Tuesday through Sunday from 8am to 7pm, Monday from 12:30 to 7pm. Admission is Dr1,200 ($3.45) for adults and Dr600 ($1.75) for students and children. This is one of three original Dorian acropoleis in Rhodes. Ensconced within the much later medieval walls stand the impressive remains of the Sanctuary of Athena Lindos, with its large Doric portico from the 4th century B.C. St. John's Knights refortified the Acropolis with monumental turreted walls and built a small church to St. John inside. Today, stones and columns are strewn everywhere as the site undergoes extensive restoration.

On your descent, as you explore the labyrinthine lanes of medieval Lindos, you will come to the exquisite late 14th- or early 15th-century ✪ **Byzantine Church of the Panayia,** still the local parish church. More than 200 iconic frescoes (dating from the 18th century) cover every inch of the walls and arched ceilings. Quite recently, all of the frescoes were painstakingly restored at great expense and with stunning results. Be sure to spend time with these icons, many of them sequentially narrative, depicting the Creation, the Nativity, the Christian Passover, and the Last Judgement. And after you've given yourself a stiff neck looking up, be sure to look down at the extraordinary floor, made of sea pebbles.

Adjoining the Church of the Panayia is the **Church Museum** (☎ **0244/32-020**), open April through October daily from 9am to 3pm; a donation of Dr500 ($1.45) is requested for admission. The historical and architectural exhibits and collected ecclesiastical items, including frescoes, icons, texts, chalices, and liturgical embroidery, comprise a surprisingly significant collection. A visit here will prove helpful in guiding you through the medieval town.

Then, of course, there's the inviting **beach** below, lined with cafes and tavernas.

Where to Stay & Dine in Lindos & Environs

In high season, Lindos marks the spot where up to 10,000 day-trippers from Rhodes city converge with 4,000 resident tourists. Since no hotel construction is permitted, almost all of the old homes have been converted into pensions (called "villas" in the brochures) by English charter companies. **Triton Holidays** (☎ **0241/21-690;** fax 0241/31-625; www.tritondmc.gr; e-mail: info@tritondmc.gr) books six-person villas, including kitchen facilities (reservations are often made a year in advance). In peak season, Michalis at the local **Tourist Information Kiosk** (☎ **0244/31-900;** fax 0244/31-288) has a list of homes that rent rooms. Plan to pay Dr8,000 ($23) for a double and Dr10,000 to Dr15,000 ($29 to $43) for a studio apartment. The big news, however, is that Michalis Melenos's own hotel may be completed as early as May or June of 2001. The new **Melenos Hotel** promises to be the most elegant and exclusive small hotel in Lindos. The aim is to recreate an authentically Lindian-style villa, with hand-painted tiles, local antiques, hand-crafted lamps—in short, traditional splendor combined with every contemporary comfort and convenience. To reach Michalis, send a fax to 0244/32-060 or e-mail mime@astronet.gr.

You'll have a paralyzing array of restaurants and tavernas to choose from in tiny Lindos. On the beach, the expansive **Triton Restaurant** gets a nod because you can easily change into your swimsuit in its bathroom, essential for nonresidents who want to splash in the gorgeous water across the way. It's also not as pricey as all the others.

Argo Fish Taverna. Haraki Beach (10km/6.2 miles north of Lindos). ☎ **0244/51-410.** Reservations recommended. Appetizers Dr750–Dr3,900 ($2.15–$11); main courses Dr3,800–Dr16,900 ($11–$48); two-person seafood platter Dr25,900 ($74). AE, MC, V. Daily noon–1am. Open Easter–Oct. GREEK/SEAFOOD.

Haraki Bay is a quiet fishing hamlet with a gorgeous, crescent-shaped pebbly beach and this excellent seafood taverna. Consider stopping here for a swim and lunch on a day trip to Lindos. We appreciated the freshness of the food, as well as the creative variation on a Greek salad: an addition of mint and dandelion leaves with fresh herbs, served with whole-wheat bread. The lightly battered fried calamari was tasty and a welcome relief from the standard over-battered fare. The mussels, baked with fresh tomatoes and feta cheese, were also right on.

✪ **Atrium Palace.** Kalathos Beach, 85100 Rhodes. ☎ **0244/31-601.** Fax 0244/ 31-600. 256 units. A/C MINIBAR TV TEL. Dr26,000–Dr48,000 ($74–$138) double; Dr32,000–Dr96,000 ($92–$276) suite for two. Rates include breakfast. AE, DC, MC, V. Closed Nov–Mar.

Located just over 4 miles out of Lindos on the long beach of crystal-clear Kalathos Bay, this luxurious resort hotel features an eclectic architectural design—a neo-Greek, Roman, Crusader, and Italian pastel extravaganza. The inner atrium is an exotic, tropical garden of pools and waterfalls. The beautifully landscaped outside pool complex is a nice alternative to the nearby beach, and the indoor pool, sauna, and fitness club will keep you busy. To keep the whole family fully entertained on the rainy days that never occur, there are game rooms, a mini-club for young children, and an arcade of shops. Despite its five-star status, the atmosphere here is relaxed, without pretense, and quite friendly, all perhaps due to the Atrium Palace's excellent staff.

Ladiko Bungalows Hotel. Faliraki, P.O. Box 236, 85100 Rhodes. ☎ **0241/85-560.** Fax 0241/80-241. 42 units. A/C TEL. Dr15,000–Dr24,000 ($43–$69) double. Rates include breakfast. MC, V. Closed Nov–Mar.

Anthony Quinn obtained permission to build a retirement home for actors on this pretty little bay on the road to Lindos, 2 miles south of the swinging beach resort of Faliraki; he never realized his plans, but the bay retains his name. We especially enjoyed the quiet and the convenient location of this friendly family-operated lodge, with nature-lover activities such as swimming, fishing, and hiking to nearby ruins and less-frequented beaches, and its proximity (a 20-minute walk) to noisy and bustling Faliraki. The new (in 2000) outside terrace bar and dining area with a splendid view of the Ladiko Bay provides a lovely tranquil spot for a drink or a meal. The guest rooms are not exceptional, but are quite comfortable and have new mattresses. Fourteen rooms come with fridges.

✪ **Lindos Mare.** Lindos Bay, 85100 Rhodes. ☎ **0244/31-130.** Fax 0244/31-131. E-mail: lindmare@otenet.gr. 138 units. TV TEL. Dr28,000–Dr50,000 ($80–$144) junior suite for two with half-board plan (breakfast and dinner). AE, DC, MC, V. Closed Nov–Mar.

This relatively small and classy cliffside resort hotel is a prime site to drop anchor on the east shore. The rooms are a grade up from most of the otherwise comparable luxury hotels on the coast, and the views of the bay below are heart-stopping. A tram descends from the upper lobby, restaurant, and pool area to the lower levels of attractive Aegean-style bungalows, and continues onward down to the beach area, where there are umbrellas and water sports. It's only a 2-kilometer (1.2-mile) walk or ride into Lindos, although you just might want to stay put in the evenings to enjoy the in-house social activities, such as barbecue, folklore evenings, or dancing.

✪ **Mavrikos.** Main Sq., Lindos. ☎ **0244/31-232.** Reservations recommended. Appetizers Dr1,200–Dr2,500 ($3.45–$7); main courses Dr1,300–Dr4,500 ($3.75–$13). V. Year-round daily noon–midnight. GREEK/FRENCH.

Brothers Michalis and Dimitri continue a family tradition of fine Greek and French cuisine, such as their oven-baked lamb and fine beef fillets, or the perfectly grilled and seasoned fresh red snapper. The venerable restaurant and expansive shaded terrace have retained their special rustic charm—David Gilmore of Pink Floyd fame was so furious when they brought in new, modern chairs that Michalis quickly restored and returned the originals. Other notable fans have included Nelson Rockefeller and Jackie Kennedy. Most recently, in July 2000, King Abdullah of Jordan, when visiting Rhodes, had his private yacht sail to Lindos just to eat his supper here at Mavrikos. Clearly, this is not just our first choice for a memorable meal in Lindos or, for that matter, on Rhodes.

The Mavrikos also run a great ice-cream parlor, **Geloblu,** serving homemade frozen concoctions and cakes. It's located within the labyrinth of the old town near the church.

SIGHTS & BEACHES ELSEWHERE ON THE ISLAND

An around-the-island tour provides a chance to view some of the wonderful variations of Rhodes's scenery. The sights described below, with the exception of Ialisos and Kamiros, are not of significant historical or cultural importance, but if you get bored with relaxing, these places provide a pleasant diversion. The route traces the island counterclockwise from Rhodes city, with a number of suggested sorties into the interior. Even a cursory glance at a map of Rhodes will explain the many zigs and zags in this itinerary. Keep in mind that not all roads are equal and that all-terrain vehicles are required for some of the detours suggested below. Rhodian rental-car companies usually stipulate that their standard vehicles be driven only on fully paved roads.

Ialisos was the staging ground for the four major powers that were to control the island. The ancient ruins and monastery on Mount Filerimos reflect the presence of two of these groups. The Dorians ousted the Phoenicians from Rhodes in the 10th century B.C. (An oracle had predicted that white ravens and fish swimming in wine would be the final signs before the Phoenicians were annihilated. The Dorians, quick to spot opportunity, painted enough birds and threw enough fish into wine jugs so that the Phoenicians left without raising their arms.) Most of the Dorians left Ialisos for other parts of the island; many settled in the new city of Rhodes. During the 3rd to 2nd centuries B.C., the Dorians constructed a temple to Athena and Zeus Polios, whose ruins are still visible, below the monastery. Walking south of the site will lead you to a well-preserved 4th-century B.C. fountain.

When the Knights of St. John invaded the island, they too started from Ialisos, a minor town in Byzantine times. They built a small, subterranean chapel decorated with frescoes of Jesus and heroic knights. Their little whitewashed church is built right into the hillside above the Doric temple. Over it, the Italians constructed the **Monastery of Filerimos,** which remains a lovely spot to visit. Finally, Süleyman the Magnificent moved into Ialisos (1522) with his army of 100,000 and used it as a base for his eventual takeover of the island.

The site of Ialisos is open in summer, Monday through Saturday from 8am to 7pm; the rest of the year, irregular hours. Proper dress is required. Admission is Dr800 ($2.30). Ancient Ialisos is 6 kilometers (3.7 miles) inland from Trianda on the island's northwest coast; buses leave from Rhodes frequently for the 14-kilometer (8.7-mile) ride.

Petaloudes is a popular attraction because of the millions of black-and-white–striped **"butterflies"** (actually a species of moth) that overtake this verdant valley in July and August. When resting quietly on plants or leaves, the moths are well camouflaged. Only the wailing of infants and the Greek rock blaring from portable radios disturbs them. Then the sky is filled with a flurry of red, their underbellies exposed as they try to hide from the summer crush. The setting, with its many ponds, bamboo bridges, and rock displays, is admittedly a bit too precious. Petaloudes is 25 kilometers (15½ miles) south of Rhodes and inland; it can be reached by bus, but is most easily seen on a guided tour. It's open daily from 8:30am to 6:30pm; admission is Dr750 ($2.15) from mid-June to late September and Dr300 (90¢) the rest of the year.

The ruins at **Kamiros** are much more extensive than those at nearby Ialisos, perhaps because this city remained an important outpost after the new Rhodes was completed in 408 B.C. The site is divided into two segments: the upper porch and the lower valley. The porch served as a place of religious practice and provided the height needed for the city's water supply. Climb up to the top and you'll see two aqueducts, which assured the Dorians a year-round supply of water. The small valley contains ruins of homes and streets, as well as the foundations of a large temple. The site is in a good enough state of preservation to imagine what life in this ancient Doric city was like more than 2,000 years ago. (Think about wearing a swimsuit under your clothes: There's a good stretch of **beach** across from the site, where there are some rooms to let, a few tavernas, and the bus stop.) The site is open Tuesday through Sunday from 8:30am to 3pm. Admission is Dr800 ($2.30). Kamiros is 34 kilometers (21 miles) southwest of Rhodes city, with regular bus service.

Driving south along the western coast from Kamiros, you'll come to the late 15th-century Knights castle of **Kastellos** (Kritinias Castle), dominating the sea below. From here, heading south and then cutting up to the northeast, make your way inland to **Embonas,** the wine capital of the island and home to several tavernas famed for their fresh meat barbecues. This village is on the tour-group circuit, and numerous tavernas offer feasts accompanied by live music and folklore performances. If you then circle around the island's highest mountain, **Attaviros** (3,986 feet), you come to the village of **Ayios Issidoros,** where devoted trekkers can ask directions to the summit. (It's a 5-hr. round-trip hike from Ayios Issidoros to the top of Mount Attaviros.) Otherwise, proceed to the picturesque village of **Siana,** nestled on the mountainside. From here, head to **Monolithos,** with its spectacularly sited crusader castle perched on the pinnacle of a coastal mountain.

If, to reach the eastern coast, you now decide to retrace your path back through Siana and Ayios Issidoros, you will eventually reach **Laerma,** where you might consider taking a 5-kilometer (3-mile) seasonal road to the **Thami Monastery,** the oldest functioning monastery on the island, with beautiful though weather-damaged frescoes. From Laerma, it's another 10 kilometers (6.2 miles) to Lardos and the eastern coastal road, where you can either head straight to **Lindos** (see above) or take another detour to **Asklipio,** with its ruined castle and impressive Byzantine church. The church has a mosaic-pebbled floor and gorgeous cartoon-style frescoes, which depict the seven days of Creation (check out the octopus) and the life of Jesus.

The **beaches** south of Lindos, from Lardos Bay to Plimmiri (26km/16 miles in all), are among the best on Rhodes, especially the short stretch between Lahania and Plimmiri. At the southernmost tip of the island, for those who seek off-the-beaten-track places, is **Prasonisi** (Green Island), connected to the main island by a narrow sandy isthmus, with waves and world-class windsurfing on one side and calm waters on the other.

From Lindos to Faliraki, there are a number of sandy, sheltered beaches with relatively little development. **Faliraki Beach** is the island's most developed beach resort, offering every possible vacation distraction imaginable—from bungee jumping to laser clay shooting. The southern end of the beach is less crowded and frequented by nude bathers.

North of Faliraki, the once-healing thermal waters of **Kalithea,** praised for their therapeutic qualities by Hippokrates, have long since dried up—but this small bay, only 10 kilometers (6.2 miles) from Rhodes city, is still a great place to swim and snorkel. Mussolini built a fabulous art-deco spa here; its derelict abandonment retains an odd grandeur evoking an era thankfully long gone.

2 Simi

11km (7 miles) N of Rhodes

Tiny, rugged Simi is often called "the jewel of the Dodecanese." Arriving by boat affords a view of pastel-colored neoclassical mansions climbing the steep hills above the broad, horseshoe-shaped harbor. Yialos is Simi's port, and Horio its old capital. The welcome absence of nontraditional buildings is due to an archaeological decree that severely regulates the style and methods of construction and restoration for all old and new buildings. Simi's long and prosperous tradition of shipbuilding, trading, and sponge diving is evident in its gracious mansions and richly ornamented churches. Islanders proudly boast that there are so many churches and monasteries that one could worship in a different sanctuary every day of the year.

During the first half of this century, Simi's economy gradually deteriorated as the shipbuilding industry declined, the maritime business soured, and somebody went and invented a synthetic sponge. Simiots fled their homes to find work on nearby Rhodes or in the North America and Australia, though they have also had a startling 70 percent return rate later in life. Today, the island's picture-perfect traditional-style houses have become a magnet for moneyed Athenians in search of real-estate investments, and Simi is a highly touted "off-the-beaten-path" resort for European tour groups trying to avoid other tour groups. The onslaught of tourists for the most part arrives at 10:30am and departs by 4pm.

In recent years, the **Simi Festival,** running from June through September, has put Simi on the cultural map as a serious seasonal contender, offering an exciting menu of international music, theater, and cinema. In July, August, and September, there's something happening virtually every night.

ESSENTIALS

GETTING THERE   By Boat   Several **excursion boats** arrive daily from Rhodes; two of them (the *Simi I* and *Simi II*) are owned cooperatively and are booked locally in Rhodes through **Triton Holidays** (☎ **0241/21-690**). Round-trip tickets are Dr5,000 ($14). The schedules and itineraries for the boats vary, but all leave from Mandraki Harbor and stop at the main port of Simi, Yialos, with an additional stop at Panormitis Monastery or the beach at Pedi, before returning to Rhodes. Currently, there are daily **car ferries** from Piraeus, and two **local ferries** weekly via Tilos, Nissiros, Kos, and Kalimnos. From late spring to summer, **hydrofoils** skim daily from Rhodes to Simi, usually making both morning and afternoon runs. In summer 2001, plans call for a new high-speed ferry, owned by the citizens of Simi.

VISITOR INFORMATION   Check out the wonderfully helpful Web site launched by Simi's delightful and informative independent monthly, *The Symi Visitor:* **www.symi-island.com**. Through the site's e-mail option, you can request information on accommodations, buses, weather, and more. Webmaster Wendy Wilcox says you can ordinarily expect a response within an hour. Or you can address your queries to *The Symi Visitor,* P.O. Box 64, Simi, 85600 Dodecanese. Don't ask them, however, to recommend one hotel over another; just say exactly what you're looking for and they'll provide suggestions. *The Symi Visitor* can also be reached at ☎ and fax **241/72-755** or via its own Web site, **www.symivisitor.com**. Once you're on Simi, you'll find free copies of the latest *Symi Visitor* at tourist spots.

The immensely resourceful George Kalodoukas of **Kalodoukas Holidays** (☎ **0241/71-077**; fax 0241/71-491), just off the harbor up the steps from the Cafe Helena, can help with everything from booking accommodations (often at reduced rates) to chartering a boat. Once you've arrived on Simi, drop into the office, open Monday through Saturday from 9am to 1pm and 5 to 9pm. In summer, George plans a special outing for every day of the week, from cruises to explorations of the island. Most outings involve a swim and a healthy meal, and sometimes champagne.

A **tourist information kiosk** is on the harbor, but its hours remain an enduring mystery. Information and a free pamphlet may also be obtained at the **Town Hall,** located on the Town Square behind the bridge.

GETTING AROUND   Ferries and excursion boats dock first at hilly **Yialos** on the barren, rocky northern half of the island. Yialos is the liveliest village on the island and the venue for most overnighters. The clock tower, on the right as you enter the port, is used as a landmark when negotiating the maze of car-free lanes and stairs. Another landmark used in giving directions is the bridge in the center of the harbor.

Simi's main road leads to **Pedi,** a developing beach resort one cove east of Yialos, and a new road rises up to **Horio,** the old capital. The island's 4,000 daily visitors most often take an excursion boat that stops at the Panormitis Monastery or at the beach at Pedi. **Buses** leave every hour from 8am until 11pm to Pedi via Horio (Dr200/60¢). There are a grand total of four **taxis** on the island—leaving from the taxi stand at the center of the harbor and charging a set fee of Dr600 ($1.75) to Horio and Dr700 ($2) to Pedi. **Mopeds** are also available, but due to the limited network of roads, you'd do better on public transportation and your own two feet. **Caïques** shuttle people to various beaches: Nimborios, Ayia Marina, Ayios Nikolaos, and Nanou; prices range from Dr1,500 to Dr2,000 ($4.30 to $6) depending on distance.

FAST FACTS   For a **doctor,** call ☎ **0241/71-316;** for a dentist, ☎ **0241/71-272,** for the **police,** ☎ **0241/71-11.** The **post office** (☎ **0241/71-315**) and **telephone office (OTE)** (☎ **0241/71-212**) are located about 100 meters behind the waterfront; both open Monday through Friday from 7:30am to 3pm. For **Internet access,** try the Vapori Bar (e-mail: vapori@otenet.gr), just in from the harbor at the taxi stand and next to the Bella Napoli Restaurant, open most evenings.

WHAT TO SEE & DO

Simi's southwestern portion is hilly and green. Located here is the medieval **Panormitis Monastery,** dedicated to St. Michael, the patron saint of seafaring Greeks. The monastery is popular with Greeks as a place of pilgrimage and of refuge from modern life; young Athenian businessmen speak lovingly of the monk cells and small apartments that can be rented for rest and renewal. There is also an "alms house" that provides a home for the elderly. Call the **guest office** (☎ **0241/72-414**) to book accommodations, ranging from Dr3,000 to Dr10,000 ($9 to $29) for an apartment or house. All units are self-contained, with their own stove and fridge. The least expensive units have shared outdoor toilets. Most sleep at least four people.

The whitewashed compound has a verdant, shaded setting and a 16th-century gem of a church inside. The **Taxiarchis Mishail of Panormitis** boast icons of St. Michael and St. Gabriel adorned in silver and jewels. The combined folk and ecclesiastical museums are well worth the Dr400 ($1.15) entrance fee, which all goes to support the "alms house" mentioned above.

The town of **Panormitis Mihailis** is most lively and interesting during its annual festival on November 8, but can be explored year-round via local boats or bus tours from Yialos. The hardy can hike here—it's 10 kilometers (6.2 miles), about 3 hours from town—and then enjoy a refreshing dip in the sheltered harbor and a meal in the taverna.

A Pair of Local Crafts

One local craft still practiced on Simi is **shipbuilding.** If you walk along the water toward Nos beach, you'll probably see boats under construction or repair. It's a treat to watch the men fashion planed boards into a graceful boat. Simi was a boat-building center in the days of the Peloponnesian War, when spirited sea battles were waged off its shores.

Sponge fishing is almost a dead industry in Greece. Only a generation ago, 2,000 divers worked waters around the island; today only a handful undertake this dangerous work, and most do so in the waters around Italy and Africa. Working at depths of 50 to 60 meters (in the old days often without any apparatus), many divers were crippled or killed by the turbulent sea and too-rapid depressurization. The few sponges that are still harvested around Simi—and many more imported from Asia or Florida—are sold at shops along the port. Even if they're not from Simi's waters, they make inexpensive and lightweight gifts. For guaranteed-quality merchandise and an informative explanation and demonstration of sponge treatment, we recommend the **Aegean Sponge Center** (☎ 0241/71-620), operated by Kyprios and his British wife, Leslie.

In Yialos, by all means hike the gnarled, chipped stone steps of the **Kali Strate** ("the good steps"). This wide stairway ascends to Horio, a picturesque community filled with images of a Greece in many ways long departed. Old women sweep the white-washed stone paths outside their homes, and occasionally a young boy or very old man can be seen retouching the neon-blue trim over doorways and shutters. Nestled between the immaculately kept homes, dating back to the 18th century, are abandoned villas, their faded trim and flaking paint lending a wistful air to the village. Renovated villas are now rented to an increasing number of tourists. And where tourists roam, tavernas, souvenir shops, and bouzouki bars soon follow. Commercialization has hit once-pristine Simi, but it remains at a bearable level despite constant pressure to transform the island for the worse.

There's an excellent small **Archaeological Museum** in Horio, housing archaeological and folklore artifacts that the islanders consider important enough for public exhibition. You can't miss the blue arrows that point the way; it's open Tuesday through Saturday from 9am to 2pm. Admission is Dr350 ($1.05). The **Maritime Museum** in the port also costs Dr350 ($1.05) and is open daily from 11am to 2:30pm.

Crowning Horio is the **Church of the Panayia.** The church is surrounded by a fortified wall and is therefore called the *kastro* (castle). It's adorned with the most glorious frescoes on the island, which can be viewed only when services are held (Monday through Friday from 7 to 8am, all morning Sunday).

Simi is blessed with many, but not wide or sandy, beaches. Close to Yialos are two beaches: **Nos,** a 50-foot-long rocky stretch, and **Nimborios,** a pebble beach.

A bus to **Pedi** followed by a short walk takes you to either **St. Nikolaos beach,** with shady trees and a good taverna, or **St. Marina,** a small beach with little shade but stunning turquoise waters and views of the islet St. Marina and its cute church.

The summertime cornucopia of outings provided by Kalodoukas Holidays has already been mentioned; but if you want to set out on your own, be sure to pick up a copy of *Walking on Symi: A Pocket Guide,* a private publication of (guess who?) George Kalodoukas (Dr2,000/$6). It outlines 25 walks to help you discover and enjoy Simi's historic sites, interior forests, and mountain vistas.

WHERE TO STAY

Many travelers bypass hotels for private apartments or houses. Between April and October, rooms for two with shower and kitchen access go for Dr7,000 to Dr12,000 ($20 to $34). More luxurious villa-style houses with daily maid service rent for Dr15,000 to Dr30,000 ($43 to $86). To explore this alternative, contact Kalodoukas Holidays or the Simi Web site (see "Visitor Information," above).

Aliki Hotel. Akti Gennimata, Yialos, 85600 Simi. ☎ **0241/71-665.** Fax 0241/71-655. 15 units. A/C TEL. Dr28,000–Dr32,000 ($80–$93) standard double; Dr36,000–Dr40,000 ($104–$115) suite. Rates include breakfast. MC, V. Closed mid-Nov to Mar.

This grand Italianate sea captain's mansion, dating from 1895, is the most elegant and exclusive tourist address on Simi. Restored and redecorated with fine Italian taste in 2000, it has the atmosphere of a boutique guest house, intimate and charming. It offers tastefully styled accommodations furnished with Italian antiques. Four rooms have balconies. Several units enjoy dramatic waterfront views, and the roof garden provides a spectacular 360-degree vista of the sea, town, and mountains. The Aliki has become a chic overnight getaway from bustling Rhodes; reservations are absolutely required.

Dorian Studios. Yialos, 85600 Simi. ☎ **0241/71-181.** 10 units. TEL. Dr11,000–Dr16,000 ($32–$46) double. MC, V. Just up from the Akti Gennimata at the Aliki Hotel. Closed Nov to mid-Apr.

Located in a beautiful part of town, only 10 meters from the sea, this rustically furnished hotel offers comfortable lodging (orthopedic beds!) and a kitchenette in every room. Some of the studios have bedrooms with vaulted beamed ceilings as well as balconies or terraces overlooking the harbor, where you can enjoy your morning coffee or evening ouzo. Five units have air-conditioning.

✪ **Hotel Nireus.** Akti Gennimata, Yialos, 85600 Simi. ☎ **0241/72-400.** Fax 0241/72-404. 37 units. A/C TV TEL. Dr18,000–Dr25,000 ($52–$72) double; Dr21,000–Dr29,000 ($60–$83) suite. Rates include breakfast buffet. MC, V. Open Easter–Oct.

This beautifully maintained, new (in 1994) hotel right on the waterfront has become a popular venue for vacationing Greeks. The traditional Simiot-style façade has been preserved, while the spacious guest rooms are contemporary and comfortable. All have fridges, and the beds are perhaps the best we've found in Greece. Ask for one of the 18 units that face the sea and offer stunning views; if you're fortunate, you might get one with a balcony. All four suites face the sea. This is a most gracious and inviting hotel, with its own shaded seafront cafe and restaurant, sunning dock, and swimming area. For its location, amenities and price, this is our personal favorite on Simi.

Hotel Nirides. Nimborios Bay, 85600 Simi. ☎/fax **0241/71-784.** 11 units. A/C TEL. Dr16,000–Dr24,000 ($46–$69) double. Rates include breakfast. MC, V. Closed Nov–Mar.

If you crave tranquil seclusion, this small cluster of studio apartments, on a rise overlooking Nimborios Bay and only minutes on foot from the one-taverna-town of Nimborios, may be exactly what you're looking for. It's about 35 minutes from Yialos on foot and appreciably less by land or sea taxi. Each attractive and spotless apartment sleeps four (two in beds and two on couches) and has a bedroom, bathroom, salon, and kitchenette. Seven apartments have balconies, three have terraces, and all face the sea. The Nirides has its own small bar and rents bicycles for excursions to town or beyond. There's a small beach with pristine water just several minutes down the hill.

WHERE TO DINE

For traditional home cooking and a respite from the crowds, you might try the tiny **Family Taverna Meraklis,** hidden on a back lane behind the Alpha Credit Bank and the National Bank (☎ **0241/71-003**).

○ **Hellenikon ("The Wine Restaurant of Simi").** Yialos. ☎ **0241/72-455.** E-mail: psarrosn@otenet.gr. Appetizers Dr1,500–Dr2,500 ($4.30–$7); main courses Dr2,900–Dr3,900 ($8–$11). MC, V. May–Oct daily 8pm–midnight. GREEK/MEDITERRANEAN.

If you have the impression that the Greek culinary imagination spins on a predictable wheel, you need a night at the Hellenikon. In addition to spectacular fare, this diminutive open-air restaurant on the Yialos town square often provides, by virtue of its location, free evening concerts, compliments of the Simi Festival. The menu is a real page-turner. The chef's fish soup, which starts with the head of a grouper and finishes with saffron and yogurt, is spectacular, as are the grilled vegetables. In additional to a stimulating array of other entrees, you can select one of seven homemade pastas and combine it with any of 19 sauces. The black pasta with shrimp, tomatoes, saffron, and feta is magnificent. Best of all, your host, Nikos Psarros, is a wine master who has over 140 Greek wines in his cellar, all organic and all from small independent wineries. Every meal here begins with a personal consultation with Nikos in his cellar, where he will help you select an exquisitely wine for your meal. Short of Dionysos himself, Nikos is your man of the Greek vine, so here's your chance for an education and a feast all in one night.

Milo Petra ("The Mill Stone"). Yialos. ☎ **0241/72-333.** Fax 0241/72-194. Appetizers Dr2,900–Dr4,400 ($8–$13); main courses Dr4,300–Dr9,000 ($12–$26). V. May–Oct daily 7pm–midnight. MEDITERRANEAN.

Owners Eva and Hans converted this 200-year-old flour mill into an exquisite setting for a gourmet dining experience. Their collection of antique Greek furniture and fabrics graces this most unusual space in simple yet elegant style. (Note the 2,000-year-old grave visible through a glass window in the floor; it's made of pebble mosaic and rose marble.) Find an excuse to ascend to the toilet on the upper veranda to get an overall view of the wonderful interior. Guests dine outdoors on the patio or inside by the open kitchen, enjoying a different menu every day. We were especially impressed by the lamb and fish dishes, using wonderful Simiot hill spices, and the homemade pastas, such as ravioli Larissa, filled with potatoes and homemade cheese and served in sage butter.

Muragio Restaurant. Yialos. ☎ **0241/72-133.** Appetizers Dr600–Dr1,800 ($1.75–$5.15); main courses Dr1,500–Dr7,000 ($4.30–$20). V. Year-round daily 11am–midnight. GREEK/SEAFOOD.

This restaurant, which opened in 1995, has become a big hit among locals, who praise the generous main courses and the quality of the food. Try the *bourekakia,* skinned eggplant stuffed with a special cheese sauce and then fried in a batter of eggs and bread crumbs. We were told to try the extremely popular lemon lamb, but instead we chose the saganaki shrimp in tomato sauce and feta cheese, and were delighted.

Nireus Restaurant. Yialos. ☎ **0241/72-400.** Appetizers Dr700–Dr1,800 ($2–$5.15); main courses Dr1,200–Dr3,500 ($3.45–$10). MC, V. Daily 11am–11pm. Open Easter–Oct. GREEK.

We met people in Rhodes who extolled the fine cooking of Michalis, the chef of this superior restaurant located in the Nireus Hotel on the waterfront. Kudos goes to his *frito misto,* a mixed seafood plate with tiny, naturally sweet Simi shrimp and other local delicacies. We also recommend the savory fillet of beef served with a Madeira sauce. They say you can't eat the scenery, but the view from here is delicious all the same.

Taverna Neraida. Yialos. ☎ **0241/71-841.** Appetizers Dr400–Dr2,500 ($1.15–$7); main courses Dr900–Dr3,500 ($2.60–$10). No credit cards. Year-round daily 11am–midnight. SEAFOOD.

Following our time-proven rule that fish is cheaper far from the port, this homey taverna on the town square has among the best fresh-fish prices on the island, as well as a wonderful range of mezedes. Try the black-eyed-pea salad and *skordalia* (garlic sauce). The grilled daily fish is delicious, while the very typical ambiance is a treat.

3 Kos

370km (230 miles) E of Piraeus

Kos has been inhabited for roughly 10,000 years, and has for a significant portion of that time been both an important center of commerce and a line of defense. Its population in ancient times may have reached 100,000, but today is less than a third of that number. Across the millennia, the unchallenged favorite son of the island has been Hippokrates, the father of Western medicine, who has left his mark not only on Kos but also on the world.

Today, Kos is identified with and at times nearly consumed by tourism, in which perhaps three-quarters of the island's working people are directly engaged. The scale of demand tells you something about Kos's beauty and attractions, which some visitors have done their best to diminish. But the island and its people have endured greater threats, and so will you, with a little determination and good advice.

The principal attractions of Kos are its **antiquities**—most notably the Asklepion—and its **beaches.** You can guess which are more swamped in summer. But the taste of most tour groups is thankfully predictable and limited. The congestion can be eluded, if that's your preference.

You'll get the most out of Kos by learning to follow the locals. If you're in a village and see no schools or churches, and no old people, chances are you're not in a village at all, but in a resort. Kos has many, especially along its coasts. In Kos town, the same is true of neighborhoods and, by extension, restaurants. Greek food is what Greeks eat, not necessarily what they sell.

Kos town is still quite vital. Since the island is small, you can base yourself in Kos, in an authentic neighborhood if possible, and venture out from there.

GETTING THERE   By Plane   The only scheduled flights into and out of the Kos airport are via **Olympic Airways,** whose Kos town office is at Odos Vas. Pavlou 22 (☎ **0242/28-331**). Although Olympic has experimented with expanded service and may do so again, at present the only direct flights to Kos are from Athens and Rhodes. Currently, there are three flights daily from Athens, and several each week from Rhodes. From **Hippokrates Airport** (☎ **0242/51-229**), a bus will take you the 26 kilometers (16 miles) to the town center for Dr1,000 ($2.90), or you can take a taxi for Dr4,000 ($11). If you're flying out of Kos, Olympic will provide bus service to the airport, provided you arrive at its town center office 2 hours prior to departure.

By Boat   As the transportation hub of the Dodecanese, Kos offers, weather permitting, a full menu of options: car ferries, passenger ferries, hydrofoils (Flying Dolphins), excursion boats, and caïques (converted fishing boats). Though most schedules and routes are always in flux, the good news is that you can, with more or less patience, make your way to Kos from virtually anywhere in the Aegean. Currently, the only ports linked to Kos with year-round nonstop and at least daily ferry service are Piraeus, Rhodes, Kalimnos, and Bodrum. Leros and Patmos enjoy the same frequency but with a stop or two along the way. The Kos harbor is strewn with travel agents who can assist you, or check current schedules with the Municipal Tourism Office (see below).

VISITOR INFORMATION   The **Municipal Tourism Office** (☎ **0242/24-460;** fax 0242/21-111; e-mail: dotkos@hol.gr), on Odos Vas. Yioryiou, facing the harbor near the hydrofoil pier, is your one-stop source of information in Kos. It's open May through October, Monday to Friday from 8am to 8:30pm and Saturday and Sunday from 8am to 3pm; and November through April, Monday to Friday from 8am to 3pm. Hotel and pension owners keep the office informed of what rooms are available in the town and environs; you must, however, book your room directly with the hotel. Be sure to pick up a free map of Kos. For a more extensive and detailed guide to Kos— beaches, archaeological sites, birds, wildflowers, tavernas, and much more—pick up a copy of *Where and How in Kos,* available at most news kiosks for Dr900 ($2.60).

GETTING AROUND   By Bus   The **Kos town (DEAS) buses** offer service within roughly 7 kilometers (4.3 miles) of the town center, while the **Kos island (KTEL) buses** will get you nearly everywhere else. For the latest schedules, consult the **town bus office,** on the harbor at Akti Kountourioti 7 (☎ **0242/26-276**), or the **island bus station,** at Odos Kleopatras 7 (☎ **0242/22-292**), around the corner from the Olympic Airways office. The majority of DEAS town buses leave from the central bus stop on the south side of the harbor.

By Bicycle   This is a congenial island for cyclists. Most of Kos is quite flat, and the one main road from Kos town to Kefalos has all but emptied the older competing routes of traffic. Since bike trails are provided until well beyond Kos town, you can also avoid the congested east-end beach roads. But don't expect to pedal one-way and then hoist your bike onto a bus, because that won't work here. Rentals are available throughout Kos town and can be arranged through your hotel. Prices range from Dr1,000 to Dr3,000 ($2.90 to $9) per day.

By Moped & Motorcycle   It's easy to rent a moped through your hotel or a travel agent, or, as with bicycles, to walk toward the harbor and look for an agency. Rentals range from Dr5,000 to Dr7,000 ($14 to $20) per day. Or call **Motoway,** Odos Vas. Yioryiou 9 (☎ **0242/20-031**), for mopeds and motorcycles.

By Car   It's unlikely that you'd need to rent a car for more than a day or two on Kos, even if you wanted to see all its sights and never lift a foot. Numerous companies, including **Avis** (☎ **0242/24-272**), **Europcar** (☎ **0242/24-070**), and **Hertz** (☎ **0242/28-002**), rent cars and all-terrain vehicles. Expect to pay at least Dr30,000 ($86) per day including insurance and fuel. Gas stations are open Monday through Saturday from 7am to 7pm; there are also several stations open (in rotation) in Kos town on Sunday; ask your hotelier or the tourist office for directions.

By Taxi   For a taxi, drop by or call the **harbor taxi stand** beneath the minaret and across from the castle (☎ **0242/23-333** or 0242/27-777). All Kos drivers are required to know English, but then again we were once required to know trigonometry.

ORIENTATION   Kos town is built around the harbor from which the town fans out. In the center is an **ancient city** (*polis*) consisting of ruins, an old city limited mostly to pedestrians, and the new city with wide, tree-lined streets. Most of the town's hotels are near the water, either on the road north to Lambi or on the road south and east to Psalidi. If you stand facing the harbor, with the castle on your right, **Lambi** is to your left and **Psalidi** on your right. In general, the neighborhoods to your right are less overrun with and defined by tourists. This area, although quite central, is overall more residential and pleasant. The relatively uncontrolled area to your left

From the Kos Museum, you might want to walk directly across to the **Municipal Fruit Market,** then have a picnic at the foot of the oldest tree in Europe, only a short walk toward the harbor at the entrance bridge to the castle. Standing with extensive support, this is said to be the **Tree of Hippokrates,** where he once instructed his students in the arts of empirical medicine and its attending moral responsibilities.

(except for the occasional calm oasis, like that occupied by the Pension Alexis) has been largely given over to tourism. Knowing this will help you find most of the tourist-oriented services by day and action by night, as well as where to find a bit of calm when you want to call it quits. Most recommended places to stay lie to your left, east of the castle.

FAST FACTS Of the three banks offering currency exchange, the **Ionian Bank of Greece,** Odos El. Venizelou, has the most extensive hours: Monday through Friday from 8am to 2pm and 6 to 8pm. For a **dentist,** contact Dr. Yioryos Karounis (☎ 0242/29-686). (The local dentist whom we had recommended for years is now the mayor of Kos, presumably still pulling teeth!) The **hospital** is at Odos Hippokratous 32 (☎ 0242/22-300). The **Del Mare Internet Cafe,** Odos M. Alexandrou 4a (☎ 0242/24-244; www.cybercafe.gr; e-mail: sotiris@zeus.cybercafe.gr), is open daily from 9am to 2am. **Happy Wash,** Odos Mitropoleos 20, across from Ayios Nikolaos (☎ 0242/23-424), is open May through October, daily from 8am to 9pm, and November through April, daily from 9am to 1:30pm and 4 to 9pm. The **post office** on Odos Vas. Pavlou (at Odos El. Venizelou) is open Monday through Friday from 7:30am to 2:30pm. Across from the castle, the **tourist police** (☎ 0242/22-444) are available 24 hours to address any outstanding need or emergency, even roomlessness.

WHAT TO SEE & DO
ATTRACTIONS IN KOS TOWN

Dominating the harbor, the **Castle of the Knights** stands in and atop a long line of fortresses defending Kos since ancient times. What you see today was constructed by the Knights of St. John in the 15th century and fell to the Turks in 1522. Satisfying your curiosity is perhaps the only compelling reason to pay the minimal admission of Dr800 ($2.30). The castle is a hollow shell, with nothing of interest inside that you can't imagine from the outside, except when it serves as a venue for concerts. Best to stand back and admire from a distance this massive reminder of the vigilance that has been a part of life in Kos from prehistory to the present.

At the intersection of Odos Vas. Pavlou and E. Grigoriou stands the **Casa Romana** (☎ 0242/23-234), a restored 3rd-century Roman villa that straddles what appears to have been an earlier Hellenistic residence. It's open Tuesday through Sunday from 8:30am to 3pm and costs Dr500 ($1.45) for adults. If you have no fire in your belly for ruins, this won't ignite one. Nearby, however, to the east and west of the Casa Romana, are a number of interesting open sites, comprising what is in effect a small archaeological park. To the east lie the remains of a **Hellenistic temple** and the **Altar of Dionysos,** and to the west and south a number of impressive excavations and remains, the jewel of which is the **Roman Odeon,** with 18 intact levels of seats. The other extensive area of ruins is in the agora of the **ancient town** just in from Akti Miaouli. Kos town is strewn with archaeological sites opening like fissures and interrupting the flow of pedestrian traffic. Rarely is anything identified for passersby, so they seem like mere barriers or building sites, which is precisely what they were. The rich architectural tradition of Kos did not cease with the eclipse of antiquity—Kos is adorned with a surprising number of striking and significant structures, sacred and secular, enfolded unselfconsciously into the modern town.

✪ **Asklepion.** Located 4km (2½ miles) southwest of Kos town. ☎ **0242/28-763.** Admission Dr800 ($2.30) adults, Dr400 ($1.15) seniors and students, free for children under 17. Oct to mid-June Tues–Sun 8:30am–3pm; mid-June to Sept Tues–Fri 8:30am–7pm and Sat 8:30am–3pm.

Unless you have beaches on the brain, this is reason enough to come to Kos. On an elevated site with grand views of Kos town, the sea, and the Turkish coastline, this is the Mecca of modern Western medicine, where Hippokrates—said to have lived to the age of 104—founded the first medical school in the late 5th century B.C. For nearly a thousand years after his death, this was a place of healing where physicians were consulted and gods invoked in equal measure. The ruins date from the 4th century B.C. to the 2nd century A.D. Systematic excavation of the site was not begun until 1902.

Kos Museum. Plateia Eleftherias (across from the Municipal Market). ☎ **0242/28-326.** Admission Dr800 ($2.30) adults, Dr400 ($1.15) seniors and students, free for children under 17. Year-round Tues–Sun 8:30am–3pm.

For a town the size of Kos, this is an impressive archaeological museum, built by the Italians in the 1930s to display mostly Hellenistic and Roman sculptures and mosaics uncovered on the island. Although there is nothing startling or enduringly memorable in the collection, a visit reminds visitors of the former greatness of this now quite modest port town. Look in the museum's atrium for the lovely 3rd-century mosaic showing how Hippokrates and Pan once welcomed Asklepios, the god of healing, to this, the birthplace of Western medicine.

SHOPPING

Kos town is compact and the central shopping area all but fits in the palm of your hand, so you can explore every lane and see what strikes you. If you've grown attached to the traditional music you've been hearing since your arrival in Greece and want some help in making the right selection, stop by either of the **Ti Amo Music Stores,** Odos El. Venizelou 11 and Odos Ipsilandou 4, where Giorgos Hatzidimitris will help you find the traditional or modern Greek music that suits you best. At either shop you may sit and listen before making a purchase.

If you're unwilling to pack another thing, you won't notice the weight of the unique handmade gold medallions at the jewelry shop of **N. Reissi,** opposite the museum at Plateia Kazouli 1 (☎ **0242/28-229**). Especially striking are the Kos medallions designed and crafted by Ms. Reissi's father (Dr20,000 to Dr35,000/$57 to $101). Handcrafted rings, charms, and earrings are also on display.

Visit the mountaintop studio of Kos's most eminent artist, **Alexandros Alwyn,** in Evanyelistria (see "Exploring the Hinterlands," below). Alwyn is a painter and sculptor of international stature; his work is simply stunning and can be purchased here for a fraction of what it would cost in galleries in New York or London. Although there is as yet no plaque celebrating this fact, he is the artist who created the exquisite monumental sculptures in the Garden of Hippokrates opposite the Dolphins Square. Another sort of treasure to bring home is a hand-painted Greek icon. **Panajiotis Katapodis** has been painting icons for over 40 years, both for churches and for individuals. His studio and home are on a lovely hillside little more than a mile west of Kos center at Ayios Nektarios, and visitors are welcome from April through October, Monday through Saturday from 9am to 1pm and 4 to 9pm. The way is signposted from just east of the Casa Romana.

BEACHES & OUTDOOR PURSUITS

The beaches of Kos are no secret. Every foot of the 180 miles of mostly sandy coastline has been discovered. Even so, for some reason, people pack themselves together in tight spaces. You can spot the package-tour sites from afar by their umbrellas, dividing the beach into plots measured in centimeters. **Tingaki** and **Kardamena** epitomize this avoidable phenomenon. Following are a few guidelines to help you in your quest for uncolonized sand.

The beaches just 3 to 5 kilometers (2 to 3 miles) east of Kos town are among the least congested on the island, probably because they're pebbled rather than sandy. Even so, the view is splendid and the nearby hot springs worth a good soak. In summer, the water on the northern coast of the island is warmer and shallower than that on the south, though less clear due to stronger winds. If you walk down from the resorts and umbrellas, you'll find some relatively open stretches between **Tingaki** and **Mastihari.** The north side of the island is also best for **windsurfing;** try Tingaki and Marmara, where everything you need can be rented on the beach. A perfect day exploring the northwestern tip of the island would consist of a swim at **Limnionas Bay** followed by grilled red mullets at Taverna Miltos.

Opposite, on the southern coast, **Kamel Beach** and **Magic Beach** are less congested than **Paradise Beach,** which lies between them. Either can be reached on foot from Paradise Beach, a stop for the Kefalos bus. The southwestern waters are cooler yet calmer than those along the northern shore; and, apart from Kardamena and Kefalos Bay, the beaches on this side of the island are less dominated by package tourists. Note that practically every sort of water sport, including jet-skiing, can be found at **Kardamena.** Finally, for **surfing,** the extreme southwestern tip of the island, on the **Kefalos peninsula** near Ayios Theologos, offers an ideal stretch of remote shoreline. You can end the day watching the sunset at **Sunset Wave Beach,** where you can also enjoy a not-soon-forgotten family-cooked feast at the **Agios Theologos Restaurant,** which rents molded plastic surfboards as well.

For yachting and sailing, call the **Yachting Club of Kos** (☎ 0242/20-055) or **Istion Sailing Holidays** (☎ 0242/22-195; fax 0242/26-777). For diving, contact the **Kos Diving Centre,** Plateia Koritsas 5 (☎ 0242/20-269 or 0242/22-782), **Dolphin Divers** (☎ 094/548-149), or **Waterhoppers** (☎ 0242/27-815; mobile 0944/130533).

As already outlined (see "Getting Around," above), the island is especially good for **bicycling,** and rentals are widely available. Guided horseback excursions are also available through the **Marmari Riding Centre** (☎ 0242/41-783), which offers 1-hour beach rides and 4-hour mountain trail rides. For **bird-watchers,** there are at least two unique offerings: Wild peacocks inhabit the forests at Skala, and migrating flamingos frequent the salt-lake preserve just west of Tingaki.

EXPLORING THE HINTERLANDS

The most remote and authentic region of the island is comprised of the forests and mountains stretching roughly from just beyond Platani all the way to Plaka in the south. The highest point is Mount Dikeos, reaching nearly 3,000 feet. The mountain villages of this region were once the true center of the island. Only in the last 30 years or so have they been all but abandoned for the lure of more level, fertile land and, since the 1970s, the cash crop of tourism.

There are many ways to explore this region, which begins little more than a mile beyond the center of Kos town. Trekkers will not find this daunting, by car or motorbike it's a cinch, but by mountain bike the ups and downs may be a challenge. Regardless of which way you go, the point is to take your time. You could take a bus from

Venturing Offshore

Two very nearby explorations offer unique opportunities. Hop one of the daily ferries from Kardamena and Kefalos to the small island of **Nissiros.** Nissiros is not quite attractive, but has at its center an active volcano, which blew the top off the island in 600 B.C. and last erupted in 1873. There are also daily ferries from Kos harbor to **Bodrum, Turkey** (ancient Halikarnassos). Note that you must bring your passport to the boat an hour before sailing so that the captain can draw up the necessary documents for the Turkish port police.

Kos to Zia and walk from Zia to Pili, returning then from Pili to Kos town by bus. The 5-kilometer (3-mile) walk from Zia to Pili will take you through a number of traditional island villages. Sights along the way include the studio of painter-sculptor **Alexandros Alwyn** (a don't miss—see "Shopping," above); the ruins of **old Pili,** a mountaintop castle growing so organically out of the rock that you might miss it; and, as your reward at day's end, a **dinner in Zia** at the **Sunset Taverna,** where at dusk the view of Kos island and the sea is magnificent. Zia also has a ceramics shop and a Greek art shop to occupy you as you wait for your taxi.

WHERE TO STAY

Kos is not a safe drop-in location in either high or low season, as most places are booked solid in summer and closed tight in winter. Plan ahead and make a reservation well in advance.

MODERATE

Hotel Astron. Akti Kountourioti 31, 85300 Kos. ☎ **0242/23-703.** Fax 0242/22-814. 80 units. A/C TEL. Dr23,000–Dr28,500 ($66–$82) double; D26,000–Dr33,500 ($74–$96) suite. Rates include breakfast. AE, MC, V. Open year-round.

This is the most attractive hotel directly on the harbor. The entrance and lobby—a mélange of glass, marble, and Minoan columns—are quite striking and suggest an elegance that does not in fact extend to the rooms and suites. All units are tasteful and very clean, with firm beds, fridges, and balconies. The pricier units include extras such as harbor views and Jacuzzis. In the larger and more expensive suites, the extra space is designed to accommodate a third person and is wasted if you intend to use it as a sitting area. The only extra worth the money, in our opinion, is a harbor view, but remember that by night you are facing the action—Kos is no retirement community. In summer, about 65 percent of the rooms here are allotted to package tours. The 14-meter pool, 12-person Jacuzzi, children's wading pool, and patio behind the hotel are pleasant, although diminished by the adjoining vacant lot.

Hotel Kipriotis Village. P.O. Box 206, Psalidi Beach, 85200 Kos. ☎ **0242/27-640.** Fax 0242/23-590. 1,900 beds. A/C TV TEL. Dr28,400 ($81) double; Dr37,050 ($107) apt for two (including breakfast). Dr3,700 ($11) extra per person for half-board plan. AE, MC, V. Closed mid-Oct to mid-Apr.

If you wish to spend part of your vacation amid loads of fun-seeking Europeans with all the possible holiday facilities, try this luxurious new resort, only 4 kilometers (2½ miles) from Kos and right on the beach. Constructed as a village of sorts, the two-story bungalows and apartments surround an attractively designed activity area, which includes five pools; tennis, volleyball, and basketball courts; and a state-of-the-art fitness room, sauna, hydromassage, Turkish bath, and solarium. There's a full day of supervised activities for children. With three restaurants and two bars, you never have to leave the premises, but there is public transportation every 15 minutes into Kos town.

INEXPENSIVE

☼ **Hotel Afendoulis.** Odos Evrepilou 1, 85300 Kos. ☎ **0242/25-321.** Fax 0242/25-797. 17 units. TEL. Dr9,000–Dr12,000 ($26–$34) double. No credit cards. Closed mid-Oct to mid-Apr.

Nowhere in Kos do you receive so much for so little. Nestled in a gracious residential neighborhood a few hundred yards from the water and less than 10 minutes on foot from the very center of Kos, Afendoulis offers the magical combination of convenience and calm. The rooms are clean and altogether welcoming, with firm beds. Nearly all units have private balconies, and most have views of the sea. Whatever room you have, you can't go wrong here. This is a long-established family place, and the Zikas family—Alexis, Hippokrates, Dionisia and Kiriaki—spare nothing to create a very special holiday community in which guests enjoy and respect one another. If you are coming to Kos to raise hell, do it elsewhere. Note that the hotel has an elevator.

Although this is likely to be many people's nonnegotiable first choice in Kos, don't despair if you haven't made a reservation. Alexis Zikas holds several extra rooms, including a two-room apartment, open and unreserved in order to accommodate such emergencies.

Hotel Yiorgos. Odos Harmilou 9, 85300 Kos. ☎ **0242/23-297.** Fax 0242/27-710. E-mail: yiorgos@kos.forthnet.gr. 35 units. TEL. Dr6,000–Dr10,000 ($17–$29) double. Rates include breakfast. No credit cards. Open year-round.

This is an inviting, family-run hotel a block from the sea and no more than a 15-minute walk from the center of Kos town. Although the immediate neighborhood is not residential, the hotel enjoys a relatively quiet location. Guest rooms are modest and very clean. All units have balconies, most with pleasant but not spectacular views of either sea or mountains. Each room contains a fridge, radio, and coffee maker—and individually controlled central heating makes this an exceptionally cozy small hotel at the chilly edges of the tourist season. Convenience, hospitality, and affordability have made this a place to which guests happily return.

Pension Alexis. Odos Irodotou 9, 85300 Kos. ☎ **0242/28-798** or 0242/25-594. Fax 0242/25-797. 14 units. Dr7,000–Dr9,000 ($20–$26) double. No credit cards. Closed mid-Oct to mid-Apr.

Ensconced in a quiet residential neighborhood only a stone's throw from the harbor, Pension Alexis feels like a home because it is one, or was until it opened as a guest house. The expansive rooms have high ceilings and open onto shared balconies. Most have sweeping views of the harbor and the Castle of the Knights. This is a gracious dwelling, with parquet floors and many tasteful architectural touches. Individual rooms are separated off from the halls by sliding doors, and share three large bathrooms. Room 4 is a truly grand corner space with knock-out views. What was a great location is now even better with the new Hippokrates Gardens located just across from the pension, closing the one street to cars. In summer, the heart of the pension is the covered veranda facing private gardens, where guests can enjoy breakfast and share their stories late into the night.

WHERE TO DINE

In Kos, as anywhere else, there's a lot of fast food, fast consumed and fast forgotten. But there's no need to make eating on Kos a Greek tragedy; the key is to follow the locals, who know where not to be disappointed. Along with your meals, you may want to try some of the local wines: the dry **Glafkos,** the red **Appelis,** or the crisp **Theokritos** retsina.

EXPENSIVE

⭘ **Petrino.** Plateia Theologou 1 (abutting the east extremity of the ancient agora). ☎ **0242/27-251.** Reservations recommended. Appetizers Dr900–Dr3,200 ($2.60–$9); main courses Dr1,800–Dr12,000 ($5.15–$34). AE, DC, MC, V. Mid-Dec to Nov 5 daily 5pm–midnight. GREEK.

When royalty come to Kos, this is where they dine—so why not live the fantasy yourself? Housed in an exquisitely restored, century-old, two-story stone (*petrino*) private residence, this is hands-down the most elegant taverna in Kos, with cuisine to match. In summer, sit outside on the spacious three-level terrace looking out over the ancient agora; but be sure to take a look inside (especially upstairs), because this is an architectural glory.

Although the menu focuses on Greek specialties, it is vast enough to include lobster, filet mignon, and other Western staples. But don't waste this opportunity to experience Greek traditional cuisine at its best. The stuffed peppers, grilled octopus, and *beki meze* (marinated pork) are perfection. More than 50 carefully selected wines, all Greek, line the cellar—this is your chance to learn why Greece was once synonymous with wine. The dry red kalliga from Kefalonia is exceptional.

MODERATE

Platanos Restaurant. Plateia Platanos. ☎ **0242/28-991.** Appetizers Dr1,600–Dr4,000 ($4.60–$11); main courses Dr2,800–Dr6,300 ($8–$18). AE, MC, V. Apr–Oct daily noon–11:30pm. GREEK/INTERNATIONAL.

Situated in the best location in Kos overlooking the Hippokrates Tree, this restaurant is in a gorgeous building that was a former Italian officers' club, replete with arches and the original tile floor. Try reserving a place on the upstairs balcony with its impressive vista. The creatively prepared Greek specialties include snapper rolled in prosciutto with sauce of wine and wild mountain tea; shrimp in tomato sauce with feta; octopus stifado; and the unusual Hippokrates escalope, prepared with pork, cheese, mushrooms, and asparagus in a béarnaise sauce. For a change of palate, try the Indonesian fillet with pineapple and curry sauce, then an Irish coffee flambé for dessert. Live music and gracious service make for a splendid evening.

⭘ **Taverna Mavromatis.** Psalidi Beach. ☎ **0242/22-433.** Appetizers Dr700–Dr2,500 ($2–$7); main courses Dr950–Dr3,300 ($2.75–$10). AE, MC, V. Year-round Wed–Sun 11am–11pm. A 20-min. walk southeast of the ferry port, or accessible by the local Psalidi Beach bus. GREEK.

One of the best choices in town is this 30-year-old vine- and geranium-covered beachside taverna run by the Mavromati brothers. Their food is what you came to Greece for: melt-in-your-mouth saganaki, mint- and garlic-spiced sousoutakia, tender grilled lamb chops, moist beef souvlaki, and perfectly grilled fresh fish. In summer, the taverna spills out along the beach; you'll find yourself sitting only feet from the water watching the sunset and gazing at the nearby Turkish coast. A dinner here can be quite magical, something locals know very well; so arrive early to assure a spot by the water.

INEXPENSIVE

Arap (Platanio) Taverna. Platinos-Kermetes. ☎ **0242/28-442.** Appetizers Dr400–Dr2,000 ($1.15–$6); main courses Dr1,100–Dr2,800 ($3.70–$8). No credit cards. Apr–Oct daily 10am–midnight. Located 2km (1¼ miles) south of town on the road to the Asklepion. GREEK/TURKISH.

Like the population of Platinos, the food here is a splendid mix of Greek and Turkish. The pride and spirit of this unpretentious family restaurant are contagious. The menu is extensive, and we know no way of going wrong no matter which direction you take. Although there are many meat dishes, vegetarians will have a feast. The roasted red peppers stuffed with feta and the zucchini flowers stuffed with rice are splendid, as are the *bourekakia* (a kind of fried pastry roll stuffed with cheese). If you want to be sure to experience the "best of show," just put yourself in the hands of the Memis brothers and let them design your meal. Afterwards, you can walk across the street for the best homemade ice cream on Kos, an island legend since 1955. This combination is well worth the walk or taxi ride.

Olimpiada. Odos Kleopatras 2. ☎ **0242/23-031.** ☎ **0242/22-433.** Appetizers Dr600–Dr1,000 ($1.75–$2.90); main courses Dr1,000–Dr2,300 ($2.90–$7). EC, MC, V. Year-round daily 11am–11pm. GREEK.

Located around the corner from the Olympic Airways office, this is one of the best values for simple Greek fare. The food is fresh, flavorful, and inexpensive, and the staff is remarkably courteous and friendly. The okra in tomato sauce and the several vegetable dishes are a treat.

Taverna Ampavris. Odos Ampavris, Ampavris. ☎ **0242/25-696.** Appetizers Dr500–Dr800 ($1.45–$2.30); main courses Dr700–Dr2,500 ($2–$7). No credit cards. Apr–Oct daily 5:30pm–1am. GREEK.

This is undoubtedly one of the best tavernas on Kos. It's outside the bustling town center on the way to the Asklepion, down a quiet village lane. In the courtyard of this 130-year-old house, you can feast on local dishes from Kos island. The *salamura* from Kefalos is mouth-watering pork stewed with onions and coriander; the *lahano dolmades* (stuffed cabbage with rice, minced meat, and herbs) is delicate, light, and not at all oily. The *faskebab* (veal stew on rice) is tender and lean, while the vegetable dishes, such as the broad string beans cooked and served cold in garlic and olive-oil dressing, are out of this world. Hats off to Emanuel Scoumbourdis and his family, who operate this fine place.

✪ **Taverna Ampeli.** Tzitzifies, Zipari. ☎ **0242/69-682.** Appetizers Dr800–Dr3,000 ($2.30–$9); main courses Dr500–Dr1,300 ($1.45–$3.75). MC, V. Apr–Oct daily 10am–midnight; Nov–Mar daily 6–11pm. Closed Easter week and 10 days in early Nov. Just off the beach road 1km (0.6 mile) east of Tingaki. Take a bus to Tingaki and walk, or take a taxi. GREEK.

This may be as close as you can come in Kos to authentic Greek home cooking, due in no small part to the fact that Mom is in the kitchen here. Facing the sea and ensconced in its own vineyard, Ampeli is delightful even before you taste the food. The interior is unusually tasteful, with high beamed ceilings, and the outside setting is even better. The dolmades are the best we've had in Greece. Other excellent specialties are the *pliogouri* (gruel), *giouvetsi* (casserole), and *revithokefteves* (meatballs); if you're less venturesome, the fried potatoes set a new standard. The house retsina is unusually sweet, almost like a sherry. The house white wine, made from the grapes before your eyes, is dry and light and quite pleasing, while Ampeli's own red is less memorable. If you're here on Saturday or midday on Sunday, the Easter-style goat, baked overnight in a low oven, is not to be missed.

Taverna Nikolas. Odos G. Averof 21. ☎ **0242/23-098.** Appetizers Dr700–Dr1,300 ($2–$3.75); main courses Dr850–Dr2,500 ($2.45–$7); fixed-price dinners Dr1,850–Dr2,600 ($5.30–$8), with a seafood dinner for two Dr6,000 ($17). No credit cards. Year-round daily noon–midnight. GREEK/SEAFOOD.

Known on the street as Nick the Fisherman's, this is one taverna in Kos that wasn't created for tourists. Year-round, it's a favorite haunt for locals, with whom you'll have to compete for one of its eight tables—until summer, when seating spills freely out onto the street. Although you can ask for and get everything from filet mignon to goulash, the point of coming here is seafood. If the Aegean has it, you'll find it here: grilled octopus, shrimp in vinegar and lemon, calamari stuffed with cheese, and mussels souvlaki, for a start. The menu is extensive, so come with an appetite.

KOS AFTER DARK

Kos nightlife is no more difficult to find than your own nose. Just go down to the harbor and follow the noise. The **port-side cafes** opposite the daily excursion boats to Kalimnos are best in the early morning. **Platanos,** across from the Hippokrates Tree, has live music, often jazz; and just across from Platanos is the beginning of **Bar Street,** which needs no further introduction. The lively **Fashion Club,** Kanari 2, Dolphins Square, has the most impressive light-and-laser show. On Zouroudi there are two popular discos, **Heaven** and **Calua,** with its swimming pool. If you want to hit the bar scene, try the **Hamam** on Akti Kountourioti, **Beach Boys** at Kanari 57, or **The Blues Brothers** on Dolphins Square. Another option is an old-fashioned outdoor movie, Kos style, at the **Open Cine Orfeas,** Odos Vas. Yioryiou 10, showing relatively recent films, often in English, and costing Dr1,700 ($4.90).

4 Patmos

302km (187 miles) E of Piraeus

Architects sometimes speak of "charged sites," places where something so powerful happened that its memory must always be preserved. Patmos is one such place. It is where **St. John the Divine,** traditionally identified with the Apostle John, spent several years in exile, dwelling in a cave and composing the Apocalypse, or the Book of Revelation. From that time on, the island has been regarded as hallowed ground, reconsecrated through the centuries by the erection of more than 300 churches, one for every nine residents. This is not to say that either the people of Patmos or their visitors are expected to spend their days in prayer, but it does show that the Patmians demand and deserve a heavy dose of respect for their traditions.

If we were to compose and dedicate a piece to Patmos, it might be a suite for rooster, moped, and bells (church and goat), for these are the sounds that fill the air. Although it's a remarkably sophisticated island, it is not uncommon to see a farmer guiding his plow behind two donkeys. Patmos is wonderfully unspoiled without being remote. Many other guidebooks highlight the island's prohibitions on nude bathing and how to get around them—but if this is a priority for you, then you've stumbled on the wrong island.

ESSENTIALS

GETTING THERE   By Plane   Patmos has no airport, but it is quite convenient (especially by hydrofoil and catamaran in spring and summer) to three islands which do: Leros, Kos, and Samos. Rather than endure an all but interminable ferry ride from Piraeus, fly from Athens to one of these, then hop a boat or hydrofoil the rest of the way to Patmos.

By Boat   Patmos, the northernmost of the Dodecanese Islands, is on the daily ferry line from Piraeus to Rhodes—confirm schedules with the **Piraeus Port Authority** (☎ 01/417-2657 or 01/451-1310) or the **Rhodes Port Authority** (☎ 0241/23-693 or 0241/27-695). It has numerous sea links with the larger islands of the Dodecanese, as well as with the islands of the northeast Aegean. Options are limited from late fall to early spring, but from Easter through September, sea connections with most of the islands of the eastern Aegean are numerous and convenient.

VISITOR INFORMATION   The **tourism office** (☎ 0247/31-666) in the port town of Skala is directly in front of you as you disembark from your ship; it's open

June through August daily from 9am to 10pm. It shares the Italianate "municipal palace" with the post office and the **tourist police** (☎ 0247/31-303), who take over when the tourism office is closed. The **port police** (☎ 0247/31-231), in the first building on your left on the main ferry pier, are very helpful for boat schedules and whatever else ails or concerns you; it's open year-round, 24 hours a day. There is also a host of helpful information about Patmos at **www.travelpoint.gr**.

Apollon Tourist and Shipping Agency, on the harbor near the central square (☎ 0247/31-724; fax 0247/31-819), can book excursion boats and hydrofoils and arrange lodging in hotels, rental houses, and apartments throughout the island. It's open year-round from 8am to noon and 4 to 6pm, with extended summer hours. **Astoria Tourist and Shipping Agency** (☎ 0247/31-205; fax 0247/31-975) is also quite helpful. For the "do-it-yourselfer" in you, pick up a free copy of *Patmos Summertime*. It should be noted, however, that the map of the island provided in that publication is grossly inaccurate, as are many other tourist maps of Patmos. Figure that out!

GETTING AROUND   By Bus   The entire island has only one bus, whose current schedule is available at the tourist office and is posted at various locations on the island. Needless to say, it provides very limited service—to Skala, Hora, Grikos, and Kambos—so it's probably best to think of other ways to get around.

By Moped & Bicycle   Mopeds are definitely the vehicle of choice on the island, provided you have a proper license. At the shops that line the harbor, 1-day rentals start around Dr2,000 ($6) and go up to Dr7,000 ($20). Michael Michalis at **Australis Motor Rent** (☎ 0247/32-284), in Scala's new port, operates a first-rate shop and is quite conscientious. Unlike at most dealers, you can rent for less than a full day at a discounted rate. You can also contact **Billis** (☎ 0247/32-218) or **Theo & Georgio's** (☎ 0247/32-066), both on the harbor in Skala. Bicycles are hard to come by on the island, but Theo & Georgio's has 18-speed mountain bikes for Dr1,200 ($3.45) per day.

By Car   Two convenient car-rental offices, both in Skala, are **Patmos Rent-a-Car,** just behind the police station (☎ 0247/32-203); and **Avis,** on the new port (☎ 0247/33-095). Daily rentals in high season start at Dr6,500 ($19). The island has only two gas stations, the **Argo** station at the east side of the harbor in Skala, and the **Elin** station just out of Scala on the road to Kambos.

By Taxi   The island's main taxi stand is on the pier in Skala Harbor, right before your eyes as you get off the boat. From anywhere on the island, you can request a taxi by calling ☎ 0247/31-225. As the island is quite small, it's much cheaper to hire a taxi than to rent a car.

ORIENTATION   Patmos lies along a north-south axis; were it not for a narrow central isthmus, it would be two islands, north and south. **Skala,** the island's only town of any size, is situated near that isthmus joining the north island to the south. Above Skala looms the hilltop capital of **Hora,** comprising a mazelike medieval village and the fortified monastery of St. John the Divine. There are really only two other towns on Patmos: **Kambos** to the north and **Grikou** to the south. While Kambos is a real village of roughly 500 inhabitants, Grikou is mostly a resort, a creation of the tourist industry.

Most independent visitors to Patmos, especially first-timers, will choose to stay in Skala (Hora has no hotels) and explore the north and south from there. Patmos is genuinely infectious, an island to which visitors, Greek and foreign, return year after year. Consequently, on your first visit to Patmos, it makes sense to be centrally located. From then on, when you return, you will have no need for our advice.

For Your Health

One essential you need to know about Patmos from the outset is that tap water is not for drinking. *Drink only bottled water.*

FAST FACTS   The **Commercial Bank of Greece** on the harbor and the **National Bank of Greece** on the central square offer exchange services and ATMs. Both are open Monday through Thursday from 8am to 2pm and Friday from 8am to 1:30pm. You will also find an ATM where ferries and cruises dock at the main pier. For **dental or medical emergencies,** call ☎ 0247/31-211; for special **pharmaceutical needs,** call ☎ 0247/31-500. The **hospital** (☎ 0247/31-211) is on the road to Hora. The **post office** on the harbor is open Monday through Friday from 8am to 1:30pm. The **tourist police** (☎ 0247/31-303) are directly across from the port.

For **Internet access,** the Internet Cafe at Blue Bay (Blue Bay Hotel) is open April through October, daily from 8am to 8pm, and the Millennium Internet Cafe (on the lane to Horio, near the OTE office) is open year-round, daily from 9am to 10pm. A short walk down toward the new port will bring you to **Just Like Home** (☎ 0247/33-170), where a load of laundry costs Dr3,000 ($9). It's open daily until 9pm year-round, and until 10pm in July and August. Cold-water wash and rinse are available, as are hand washing and dry cleaning.

WHAT TO SEE & DO
THE TOP ATTRACTIONS

What Patmos lacks in quantity it makes up in quality. Apart from its natural beauty and its 300-plus churches, to which we can't possibly provide a detailed guide here, there are several extraordinary sights: the **Monastery of St. John,** the **Cave of the Apocalypse,** and the medieval town of ✪ **Hora.** The latter is simply there to be explored, a labyrinthine maze of whitewashed stone homes, shops, and churches, in which getting lost is the whole point.

Off season, the days and times of opening for the **cave** and the **monastery** are unpredictable, as they are designed to accommodate groups of pilgrims and cruise-ship tours rather than individual visitors. Neither is a public place. The cave is enclosed within a convent, and the monastery is just that. It's best to consult the tourist office or one of the travel agents listed above for the open hours on the day of your visit (the times given below are for the peak season from May through August). To visit both places, appropriate attire is required, which means that women must wear long skirts or dresses, and men must wear long pants.

The road to Hora is well marked from Skala; but if you're walking, take the narrow lane to the left just past the central square. Once outside the town, you can mostly avoid the main road by following the uneven stone-paved donkey path, which is the traditional pilgrims' route to the sanctuaries above.

✪ **Cave of the Apocalypse.** On the road to Hora. ☎ 0247/31-234. Free admission. May–Aug Sun 8am–1pm and 2–6pm, Mon 8am–1:30pm, Tues–Wed 8am–1:30pm and 2–6pm, Thurs–Sat 8am–1:30pm. Otherwise, hours vary (see above).

Exiled to Patmos by the Roman Emperor Domitian in A.D. 95, St. John the Divine is said to have made his home in this cave, though Patmians insist quite reasonably that he walked every inch of the small island, talking with its people. The cave is said to be the epicenter of his earth-shaking revelation, which he dictated to his disciple and which has come down as the Book of the Apocalypse, or Revelation, the last book of the Christian Bible. The cave is now encased within a sanctuary, which is in turn encircled by a convent. A stirring brochure written by Archimandrite Koutsanellos, Superior of the Cave, provides an excellent description of the religious significance of each niche in the rocks, as well as the many icons in the cave. Other guides are also available in local tourist shops. The best preparation, of course, is to bone up on the Book of Revelation.

✪ **Monastery of St. John.** Hora. ☎ **0247/31-234.** Admission free to monastery; Dr1,200 ($3.45) to treasury. May–Aug Sun 8am–1pm and 2–6pm, Mon 8am–1:30pm, Tues–Wed 8am–1:30pm and 2–6pm, Thurs–Sat 8am–1:30pm. Otherwise, hours vary (see above).

Towering over Skala and, for that matter, over the south island, is the medieval Monastery of St. John, which looks far more like a fortress than a house of prayer. Built to withstand pirates, it is certainly up to the task of deterring runaway tourism. The monastery virtually controls the south island, where the mayor wears a hat but the monastic authority wears a miter. In 1088, with a hand-signed document from the Byzantine Emperor Alexis I Comnenus ceding the entire island to the future monastery, Blessed Christodoulos arrived on Patmos to establish here what was to become an independent monastic state. The monastery chapel is stunning, as is the adjoining **Chapel of the Theotokos,** whose frescoes date from the 12th century. On display in the treasury are but a fraction of the monastery's exquisite Byzantine treasures, second only to those of the monastic state of Mount Athos.

OUTDOOR PURSUITS

The principal outdoor activities on Patmos are walking and swimming. The best **beaches** are highlighted below (see "Exploring the Island") and the best **walking trails** are the unmarked donkey paths, which crisscross the island. You won't find jet-skis or surfboards on Patmos, although limited **water sports** are available. Paddleboats and canoes can be rented and water-skiing arranged on Agriolivada Beach at Hellen's Place, as well as on the beach at Grikos. Also at Grikos is a **summer club** where you can join in a volleyball game or play tennis (rackets and balls provided). For **snorkeling** and **skin diving,** accompanied if you wish by your own underwater photographer and cameraman, call ☎ 0247/33-059.

SHOPPING

Patmians are quick to lament and apologize for the fact that just about everything, from gas to toothpaste, is a bit more expensive here. Patmos doesn't even have its own drinking water, and import costs inevitably get passed along to the customer. That said, the price differences are much more evident to the locals than to tourists.

There are several excellent jewelry shops, like **Iphigenia** (☎ 0247/31-814) and **Midas** (☎ 0247/31-800) on the harbor, though **Filoxenia** (☎ 0247/31-667) and the **Art Spot** (☎ 0247/32-243), both just behind the main square in the direction of Hora, have more interesting contemporary designs, often influenced by ancient motifs. The Art Spot also sells ceramics and small sculptures, and is well worth seeking out. Farther down the same lane is **Parousia** (☎ 0247/32-549), the best single stop for hand-painted icons and a wide range of books on Byzantine subjects. The proprietor, Mr. A. Alafakis, is quite learned in the history and craft of icon painting and can tell you a great deal about the icons in his shop and the diverse traditions they represent.

The most fascinating shop on Patmos may be **Selene** (☎ 0247/31-742), directly across from the Port Authority office. The highly selective array of Greek handmade art and crafts here is extraordinary, from ceramics to hand-painted Russian and Greek icons to marionettes, some as tall as 4 feet. And be sure to notice Selene's structure, also a work of art. Built in 1835, it was once a storage space for sails and later a boat-building workshop. Look down at the shop's extraordinary floor made of handmade stamped and scored bricks, quite unique and traditional to Patmos.

WHERE TO STAY IN SKALA

There are no hotels or pensions in Hora, although Skala makes up for it. Unless you're planning to visit Patmos during Greek or Christian Easter or from late July through August, you should not have difficulty finding a room upon arrival, though it's always safer to book ahead. You will probably be met at the harbor by residents offering private accommodations. If you're interested in renting a kitchenette apartment or villa, contact the **Apollon Agency** (☎ 0247/31-724; fax 0247/31-819).

EXPENSIVE

✪ **Porto Scoutari.** Scoutari, 85500 Patmos. ☎ **0247/33-123.** Fax 0247/33-175. www.12net.gr/scoutari. 30 units. A/C MINIBAR TV TEL. Dr32,000–Dr49,000 ($92–$141) double; Dr34,000–Dr78,000 ($98–$225) studio or suite. Rates include full breakfast buffet. MC, V. Open Easter–Oct. Note that this hotel overlooks, but is not in, Meloï Bay—so follow the signs to Kambos, not to Meloï Bay. It's less than 2 miles from the center of Skala.

High on a bluff overlooking Meloï Bay, this new luxury hotel is seductively gracious, with the largest rooms and the largest pool on the island. Ground-level suites are designed with families in mind, while upper-level suites, with four-poster beds and bathtubs, have honeymoon written all over them. The decor, a blend of reproduction antiques and contemporary design, offers elegance and comfort. Each bungalow-style studio has a kitchenette, year-round climate control, and private balcony. The common areas—breakfast room, lounge, piano bar, and pool—are simultaneously informal and refined.

MODERATE

Romeos Hotel. Skala (in the back streets behind the OTE), 85500 Patmos. ☎ **0247/31-962.** Fax 0247/31-070. E-mail: romeosh@12net.gr. 60 units. A/C MINIBAR TEL. Dr26,000 ($74) double; Dr35,000 ($101) suite. Rates include breakfast. MC, V. Closed Nov–Mar.

Of all Skala's newer lodgings, this one, run by a Greek-American family from Virginia, is especially commodious, with its large pool and quiet garden. The simply decorated, spotless rooms come with countryside-view balconies, and are built like semi-attached bungalows on a series of tiers, with views across to Mount Kastelli. Large honeymoon suites, with double beds, full bathtubs, and a small lounge, are also available. One slight downside is the undeveloped lot in front of the property, though it's hardly a factor once you're inside the hotel compound.

Skala Hotel. Skala, 85500 Patmos. ☎ **0247/31-343.** Fax 0247/31-747. E-mail: skalahtl@12net.gr. 78 units. A/C TV TEL. Dr16,000–Dr30,000 ($46–$86) double. Rates include breakfast. MC, V. Closed Nov–Mar.

Tranquilly but conveniently situated well off the main harbor road behind a lush garden overflowing with arresting pink bougainvillea, this comfortable hotel has aged like a fine wine to become an established Skala favorite. Attractive features include the beautifully landscaped garden, a large pool with an inviting sundeck and bar, a large breakfast buffet, climate control and fridges in all rooms, and personalized service. The three views to choose from are the sea, the western mountains, and the Monastery of St. John—and all are striking. At Easter or in late July and August, you're likely to be out of luck without an advance reservation, but at other times, you'll probably be able to find a room here.

INEXPENSIVE

Australis Hotel and Apartments. Skala (a 5-minute walk from the center), 85500 Patmos. ☎ **0247/31-576.** Fax 0247/32-284. 29 units. Dr11,000–Dr15,000 ($32–$43) double room; Dr20,000–Dr50,000 ($57–$144) apartment, depending on size and season. Room rates include breakfast. No credit cards. Closed Nov–Mar.

On approach, you may have misgivings regarding the location of this hotel, down a less than charming lane off the new port area. But all your doubts will vanish when you enter the startlingly lovely hotel compound, a veritable blooming hillside oasis. Once featured in *Garden Design* magazine, the grounds are covered with bougainvillea, fuchsias, dahlias, and roses. The pleasant communal porch, where breakfast is served, offers delightful views of the open harbor. The guest rooms are bright, tasteful, and impeccably clean, with some of the best (firmest) beds we've found in Greece; some units have fridges as well. Within the same compound and enjoying the same floral and sea vistas, Fokas Michellis's four new luxury apartments offer spacious homes away from home for families or groups of four to six people. They are fully equipped with kitchenettes, TVs, and heat for the winter months. (The five-bed apartment price goes down to a bargain rate of Dr10,000/$29 in winter.) In addition to these apartments, Fokas's oldest son, Michael Michellis, has three handsome new studios over his house on the old road to Hora. Each has a well-stocked kitchen and goes for Dr10,000 to 16,000 ($29 to $46) per day.

⭕ **Blue Bay Hotel.** Skala, 85500 Patmos. ☎ **0247/31-165.** Fax 0247/32-303. E-mail: bluebayhotel@yahoo.com. 26 units. A/C TEL. Dr11,000–Dr18,000 ($32–$52) double; Dr15,000–Dr21,000 ($43–$60) suite. Breakfast buffet Dr1,500 ($4.30) extra. MC, V. Closed Nov–Mar.

Two unique features distinguish this hotel, our favorite on Patmos. First, its stellar location on the southwest side of the harbor offers a rare fusion of convenience and quiet. Second, guests are requested not to smoke anywhere in the hotel except on their private balconies. The bedrooms are spacious, immaculate, and comfortable. Rooms 114 and 115 share a terrace the size of a tennis court overlooking the sea. There is a special emphasis here on service and gracious hospitality; at breakfast, for instance, we were offered fresh figs picked only minutes before by Kyria (Mrs.) Karantanis. In addition to the breakfast room, there is a private bar and the new Blue Bay Internet Cafe, offering Internet access for Dr600 ($1.75) per 20 minutes.

Castelli Hotel. Skala, 85500 Patmos. ☎ **0247/31-361.** Fax 0247/31-656. 45 units. A/C TEL. Dr13,900–Dr18,900 ($40–$54) double. Rates include breakfast. No credit cards. Open year-round.

Guests are accommodated here in two white-stucco blocks framed with brown shutters. The rooms, with white walls and beige tile floors, are large and spotless and have their own fridges and covered balconies, while the common lounge and lobby areas are filled with photographs, flower-print sofas, seashells, fresh-cut flowers from the surrounding gardens, and other knickknacks of seaside life. The hotel's striking sea vista can be enjoyed from cushioned wrought-iron chairs on each room's balcony or from a pleasant covered guests' terrace/bar. The price you pay for the view is a mildly challenging 5-minute climb from the harbor.

Villa Knossos. Skala, 85500 Patmos. ☎ **0247/32-189.** Fax 0247/32-284. 7 units. Dr10,000–Dr14,000 ($29–$40) double. No credit cards. Closed Nov–Mar.

This small white villa just off the new port is set within an abundant garden of palms, purple and pink bougainvillea, potted geraniums, and hibiscus. The tasteful bedrooms are spacious with high ceilings (making them cool even in the summer's heat), and all but one have private balconies. The two units facing the back garden are the most quiet, while room 7 in front has its own private veranda. There's a comfortable guests' sitting room, and all rooms have their own fridge.

WHERE TO DINE IN SKALA & HORA

The culinary scene in Skala and Hora is at present surprisingly unpredictable. In the summer of 2000, the two stellar restaurants in Hora, whose reputations have for many years extended well beyond the island—the **Patmian House** (☎ 0247/31-180) and the **Arhonitko** (☎ 0247/31-668)—were closed and may not reopen in 2001. If they do, be sure to seek them out. Otherwise, there are no true standout restaurants in Skala and Hora, though there are many that will not disappoint. In Hora, on the path to the Monastery of St. John, you'll find the **Pirgos** and the **Balcony View** facing Skala Harbor and (following signs from the monastery) **Vagelis** in Plateia Theofakosta (Central Square). Vagelis enjoys lovely views of the south island. In Skala, you will want to browse for yourself, though we suggest below our favorite local haunts. Your alternative is to venture out to the north and south islands, which offer some of Patmos's most enticing dining opportunities (see "Exploring the Island," below).

Grigoris Grill. Opposite Skala car ferry pier. ☎ 0247/31-515. Appetizers Dr300–Dr1,300 (90¢–$3.75); main courses Dr1,300–Dr2,200 ($3.75–$6). No credit cards. Easter–June and Sept–Oct 6pm–midnight; July–Aug 11am–midnight. GREEK.

One of Skala's better-known eateries, this place was formerly the center of Patmian chic. We recommend any of the grilled fish or meat dishes, particularly in the off-season, when more care and attention are paid to preparation. Well-cooked veal cutlets, tender lamb chops, and the swordfish souvlaki are favorites. Grigoris also offers several vegetarian specials. Both curbside seating and a more removed and quiet roof garden are available.

○ **Pantelis Restaurant.** Skala (one lane back from the port). ☎ 0247/31-922. Appetizers Dr600–Dr1,500 ($1.75–$4.30); main courses Dr1,000–Dr3,300 ($2.90–$10). No credit cards. Year-round daily 11am–11pm. GREEK.

Pantelis is a proven local favorite for no-frills Greek home cooking. The food here is consistently fresh and wholesome—the basics prepared so well that they surprise you. Daily specials augment the standard menu. Portions are generous, so pace yourself, and if you're not yet a convert to the Greek cult of olive oil, speak up or order something grilled. The lightly fried calamari, chickpea soup, swordfish kebab, and roasted lamb were all up to expectation. In winter, the spacious dining hall with very high ceilings makes this a relatively benign environment for nonsmokers.

PATMOS AFTER DARK

Going to Patmos for nightlife is a little like going to Indiana to ski. The scene here, while not ecclesiastical, doesn't swing. Clubs tend to open for a few weeks in season, then close, like flowers. In Hora at Plateia Agia Lesvias, within earshot of the monastery, there's Kafe 1673, locally known as **Astivi,** where you can dance to whatever the DJ offers. In Scala, a sturdy standby—never fully "in" and never fully "out"—that survives each year's fads is the **Consolato Music Club,** to the left of the quay. At press time, Skala also has the **Kahlua Club,** at the far end of the new port, and **Sui Generis,** behind the police station. Although their posters abound and their T-shirts are worn with pride, these newcomers may not survive the test of time. In a lesser but more reliable key, both Hora and Skala have a number of **bars,** which you can't miss; and, on a more traditional note, the **Aloni Restaurant** in Hora offers Greek music and dance performances in traditional costume a few nights each week in summer.

EXPLORING THE ISLAND

Apart from the seductive contours of the Patmian landscape, the myriad seascapes, and the seemingly countless churches, it's the **beaches** of Patmos that draw most visitors beyond the island's core. Don't be tempted to think of the strand between the old and new ports in Skala as a beach. Better and safer to take a shower in your room. Most beaches have tavernas on or very near the beach, as well as rooms to rent by the day or week. They're too numerous and similar to list here.

THE NORTH ISLAND

The most desirable beaches in the north lie along the northeastern coastline from Lambi Bay to Meloï Bay. The northwestern coastline from Merika Bay to Lambi is too rocky, inaccessible, and exposed to warrant recommendation. The most desirable northern beaches are located in the following bays (proceeding up the coast from south to north): **Meloï, Agriolivada,** and **Lambi.** Meloï offers some shade and good snorkeling. **Kambos Bay** is particularly suitable for children and families, offering calm, shallow waters, rental umbrellas, and some tree cover, as well as a lively seaside scene with opportunities for windsurfing, paragliding, sailing, and canoeing. Its waterside taverna also happens to serve the best lobster on the island. East of Kambos Bay at Livada, it's possible to swim or sometimes to walk across to **Ayiou Yioryiou Isle;** be sure to bring shoes or sandals, or the rocks will do a number on your feet. The stretch of shoreline from **Thermia to Lambi** is gorgeous, with crystalline waters and some rocks from which you can safely dive. The drawback here is that access is only by caïque from Skala. Also, avoid the north coast when the *meltemi* (severe north summer winds) are blowing.

Where to Stay & Dine

Aspri. Geranos Cape. ☎ **0247/32-240.** Appetizers Dr700–Dr3,000 ($2–$9); main courses Dr1,300–Dr4,500 ($3.75–$13). MC, V. June–Sept 7pm–midnight. GREEK.

Poised on a north island headland just minutes by taxi from Skala, this dramatically situated restaurant enjoys splendid views of Meloï Bay, Aspris Bay, and Skala and Hora from its multiple terraces. While you're feasting your eyes, it can be easy to neglect the feast on your plate, which would be a serious mistake. Apart from the standard taverna fare offered throughout the islands, which Aspris prepares with great skill, there are some more unusual and enticing items on this menu, such as cuttlefish with Patmian rice. The portions are very generous (something for which you will be glad!) and extra attention is paid to presentation in this quite stylish and widely recommended spot.

Patmos Paradise. Kambos Bay, 85500 Patmos. ☎ **0247/32-590.** Fax 0247/32-740. 37 units. A/C MINIBAR TEL. Dr20,000–Dr43,000 ($57–$124) double. Rates include breakfast. MC, V. Open Easter–Oct.

Perched high above Kambos Bay, this is one of several upscale hotels on the island. The rooms are spacious and inviting, with private balconies that enjoy spectacular sea vistas, in some cases broken by a power line. Amenities include a large terrace pool, sauna, and outdoor tennis and indoor squash courts. This place is exceptionally pleasant and quite chic, while avoiding any major pretense. Down below, in Kambos Bay, there's a modest strand, a handful of shops and tavernas, and the opportunity to rent windsurfing boards, paddleboats, and canoes. A hotel minibus will bring you to and from Skala Harbor when you arrive and depart Patmos.

✪ **Taverna Leonida.** Lambi Bay. ☎ **0247/31-490.** Appetizers Dr500–Dr900 ($1.45–$2.60); main courses Dr1,200–Dr1,900 ($3.45–$5.45). No credit cards. Easter–Oct daily noon–11pm. GREEK.

Ancient Leonidas was, you could say, the Greek General Custer, except that he died defending his land rather than taking someone else's. Today's more benign invaders are tourists, and Leonidas of Lambi is winning his eternal fame preparing for them "the best saganaki in the world" according to Anna, a Patmian in the know. Our taxi driver added his two cents, saying "number-one taverna" as he dropped us off on Leonida's pebble beach. The drama of this restaurant begins with its location, only several yards in high tide from the pounding waters of Lambi Bay, and continues with the arrival of your flaming saganaki. Next comes a visit to the day's catch, soon to appear on your plate. The rest is history. Icons of the chef are available in shops around the island.

Taverna Panagos. Kambos. ☎ **0247/31-570.** Appetizers Dr500–Dr1,000 ($1.45–$2.90); main courses Dr1,200–Dr6,500 ($3.45–$19). No credit cards. Year-round daily noon–midnight. GREEK.

Just above Kambos Bay sits the sleepy village of Kambos; and squarely on its pulse, directly across from the village church, sits the Cafe-estiatorion-taverna (covering every base) Panagos. There are no sea vistas, only myriad glimpses into Patmian village life as it touches base here in what is clearly the local hangout for everyone from children and cats to timeless, bent figures in black. The food is what the village eats at home, only here they don't have to cook it for themselves. The menu is eclipsed by the recital of the day's specials, whose origins are visible on the nearby hillsides. Capons in wine, kid in tomato sauce, lamb in lemon sauce, Patmian goat cheese—all are succulent. It's the total experience you want and receive here, and you can take it with you.

THE SOUTH ISLAND

There are two principal beaches in the south of the island, one at **Grikou Bay** and the other at **Psili Ammos.** Grikou Bay, only 4 kilometers (2½ miles) from Skala, is the most developed resort on Patmos and home to most of the package-tour groups on the island. Psili Ammos is another story, an extraordinary isolated fine-sand cove bordered by cliffs. Most people arrive by one of the caïques leaving Skala Harbor at 10am, and on arrival (at 10:45am) proceed to do battle for the very limited shade offered by some obliging tamarisks. The only way to assure yourself of a place in the shade is to arrive before 10:30am; the best way to do that is to take a taxi to Diakofti for Dr2,000 ($6) and ask the driver to point the way to Psili Ammos, which is from here about a 30-minute trek on goat paths (wear real shoes). The caïques returning to Skala leave Psili Ammos around 5pm. At any given time, there are a range of caïques providing this service; the shapeliest of these is appropriately named the *Afroditi* and charges Dr2,500 ($7) round-trip and Dr1,500 ($4.30) one-way.

Another reason for heading south is to dine at Benetos (only a short taxi ride from Skala), currently touted as the finest restaurant on the island.

Where to Stay & Dine

✪ **Benetos Restaurant.** Sapsila. ☎ **0247/33-089.** Reservations necessary in high season. Appetizers Dr900–Dr2,300 ($2.60–$7); main courses Dr1,200–Dr3,900 ($3.45–$11). No credit cards. June–Sept Tues–Sun 7:30pm–1am. MEDITERRANEAN.

A Tuscan villa at sea's edge, light jazz filling the air, a fresh arugula salad with shaved parmesan, shrimp baked in filo, filet mignon, a finale of Bailey's chocolate-chip cheesecake, all accompanied by an exclusively Greek wine list—where could this all be happening? The only answer is Benetos, named by the Greek *Alpha Guide* in 2000 as the best restaurant on Patmos and one of the 30 finest restaurants in Greece. Benetos and Susan Matthaiou have made it their goal to give Greeks and their visitors "a night out"—way out—from what they will find anywhere else on these islands. Their winning recipe begins with the freshest and finest local ingredients, mostly from their own organic garden and from nearby waters, and adds to them an element of surprise. The regular menu is quite focused—striking primarily Greek notes with its appetizers and a more Italian theme with its entrees—while offering a handful of daily specials inspired by the day's best crop or catch. For fashionable and fine dining on Patmos, without pretense, this is currently the place; and, with only 12 tables on offer, you would do well to reserve yours several days in advance.

Joanna Hotel-Apartments. Grikos, 85500 Patmos. ☎ **0247/31-031.** Fax 0247/32-031, or 01/981-2246 in Athens. 17 units. A/C TEL. Dr14,000–Dr18,000 ($40–$52) apt for two persons. Full hot breakfast Dr1,300 ($3.75) extra. V. Open Easter to mid-Oct.

These comfortable, relatively spacious and fully equipped apartments are situated only a few minutes on foot from the beach. Each has a fridge, kitchenette, balcony, and fan. Rooms with air-conditioning cost an extra Dr1000 ($2.90) per day. The layout and feel of the one-bedroom apartments is better than that of the two-bedroom apartments, in which the kitchen area is very limited. Room 15 has a large private deck enjoying a sea view, but is usually reserved for friends, clients, and guests staying 2 to 3 weeks—still, there's no harm in asking. A special feature is the attractive air-conditioned lounge with satellite TV and a bar.

Petra Apartments. Grikos, 85500 Patmos. ☎ **0247/31-035.** ☎/fax 0247/34-020. Off-season ☎/fax in Athens 01/806-2697. 25 units. A/C TV TEL. Dr24,970–Dr29,590 ($71–$85) apt for two persons. Breakfast Dr1,800–Dr2,500 ($5.15–$7) extra. MC. Closed Oct–May.

The Stergiou family takes loving care of our favorite lodging in Grikos. Petra, true to its name, is a rock-solid sure thing. If the folks aren't home, Christos and his sheep-dog, Lumpi, will happily show you around these stylish, spacious apartments—either one- or two-bedroom—with small kitchenettes, compact bathrooms, and verandas enjoying splendorous views of Grikos Bay. Each is simply and handsomely decorated, with the necessities of home plus some local touches. It's a perfect family place, just a 5-minute walk from the beach, but with an elegant outdoor bar for the adults. It's popular with Europeans in August, so advance reservations are advised.

Stamatis Restaurant. Grikos Beach. ☎ **0247/31-302.** Appetizers Dr500–Dr1,300 ($1.45–$3.75); main courses Dr800–Dr3,000 ($2.30–$9). No credit cards. Daily 10am–11pm. Open Easter–Oct. GREEK.

Stamatis, offering consistently reliable taverna fare since 1965, is a landmark by now in Grikou. On its covered terrace practically at water's edge, diners enjoy drinks and consume prodigious amounts of fresh mullet while watching yachts and windsurfers. This is a very pleasant spot to let the evening unravel while enjoying delicious island dishes.

Central Greece 11

by Sherry Marker

Central Greece (Sterea Ellada) is the least well-defined area of the country. Unlike, for example, the Peloponnese, which is clearly set off from the rest of Greece by the Corinth Canal, or Macedonia, which has a distinct identity, Central Greece is harder to define. In fact, the name Central Greece dates only from 1821, when it was used as a shorthand term for the area of mainland Greece that had been liberated from the Turks. Today, most Greeks would agree that Central Greece stretches from Boetia and Phocis in the south to as far north as Thessaly. Some Greeks hold that Mount Olympus is the southernmost point in Northern Greece, while others consider Olympus to be the northernmost point in Central Greece.

When you set off for Central Greece, keep in mind that you will be traveling through one of Greece's most varied landscapes. There's the shore that runs along the Gulf of Corinth and the heights of Mount Parnassus. This is where Greece's most famous ancient oracle and most beautiful ancient site, Delphi, is located. There's the city of Thebes, famed for its magnificence in Mycenaean days, today an undistinguished modern town. There's the dusty plain of Thessaly and the extraordinary cliffs and promontories of the monasteries of the Meteora. And there's the lush, wooded mountain range of Mount Pelion, studded with small traditional villages. As if that weren't enough, there are famous ancient battle sites—Thermopylae and Chaironeia—and one of the legendary beauty spots of Greece, the Vale of Tempe.

STRATEGIES FOR SEEING THE REGION   If you're setting out from Athens, head via Thebes to Osios Loukas and Delphi and try to spend two nights in Delphi. Then head up to the Meteora for another night or two. From here, cross over to Volos and Mount Pelion, where you could easily spend a week relaxing in the mountain villages and taking in some of the best beaches. If you feel like making extra excursions en route, you'll find plenty of suggestions in what follows.

1 Delphi

178km (110 miles) NW of Athens

Delphi is the big enchilada of Greek sites. More than even Olympia, this place has everything: a long and glorious history, spectacular ancient remains, a superb museum, and a heartbreakingly beautiful location on the slopes of Mount Parnassus. Look up and you see the cliffs and crags of Parnassus; look down and you see Greece's most

Insider Tip

Mount Parnassos is a *very* popular winter ski destination for Greeks, who come here from Athens, the Peloponnese, and all of Central Greece. Don't expect to turn up in Delphi or Arachova on a winter weekend and find a place to stay: This is one area where it's usually more difficult to find lodgings in the winter than in the summer. Most people head home after lunch on Sunday—something to keep in mind if you're coming here on a Sunday, when traffic in Delphi and Arachova backs up for miles.

---

beautiful plain of olive trees stretching as far as the eye can see toward the town of Itea on the Gulf of Corinth.

Delphi is especially magical in the spring, when there's both snow and wildflowers on Parnassus—and relatively few tourists tramping around the site. But whenever you visit, you'll understand why the ancient Greeks believed that Delphi was the center of the world, the spot Apollo chose as the home of his most famous oracle.

A LOOK AT THE PAST Pilgrims came to Delphi from all of the Greek world and much of the non-Greek world to ask Apollo's advice on affairs of state as well as small, personal matters. Unfortunately, the god's words were famously hard to interpret. "Invade and you will destroy a great empire," the oracle told Lydian King Croesus when he asked whether he should go to war with his Persian neighbors. Croesus invaded and destroyed a great empire: his own.

Delphi was also the site of the Pythian Games, the most famous festival in Greece after the Olympics. The games commemorated Apollo's triumph over his oracular predecessor here, the snaky Python. Because Apollo was the god of music, the Pythian games had more artistic contests than the Olympic Games. When you sit in the theater here, you can imagine the flute and lyre contests and the dances and plays staged every 4 years throughout antiquity to honor Apollo.

Like so many ancient sites, Apollo's sanctuary at Delphi was first neglected, then virtually forgotten, during the Christian era. Kings and generals looted Delphi of its treasures; later, locals hacked up the buildings to build their houses. The modern village of Delphi sat atop the ancient site until this century, when it was relocated just down the road so that archaeologists could help Delphi reclaim its past.

ESSENTIALS

GETTING THERE **By Bus** There are five daily buses to Delphi from the Athens bus station at Odos Liossion 260 (Athens ☎ **01/831-7096;** Delphi ☎ **0265/82-317**).

By Car Take the Athens-Corinth National Highway 74 kilometers (46 miles) west of Athens to the Thebes turnoff. Continue west to Levadia. If you wish to stop at the monastery of Osios Loukas, take the Distomo turnoff and continue 9 kilometers (5½ miles) to Osios Loukas (be prepared to meet tour buses thundering along this road). Return to Distomo and continue via Arachova 26 kilometers (16 miles) or the seaside town of Itea 65 kilometers (40 miles) to Delphi. The approach from Itea is well worth the time, if you are not in a hurry.

By Organized Tour Athens-based companies such as **GO,** Odos Voulis 31–33 (☎ **01/322-5951**), and **CHAT,** Odos Stadiou 4 (☎ **01/322-3137**), offer 1- and 2-day trips to Delphi. If possible, take the 2-day trip, which lets you enjoy a less frantic visit. Most tours leave Athens by 8am and arrive at Delphi by 3pm after a stop at Osios Loukas. On the second day, you leave Delphi around 3pm, arriving back in Athens about 7pm. The price (including transportation, site and museum admissions,

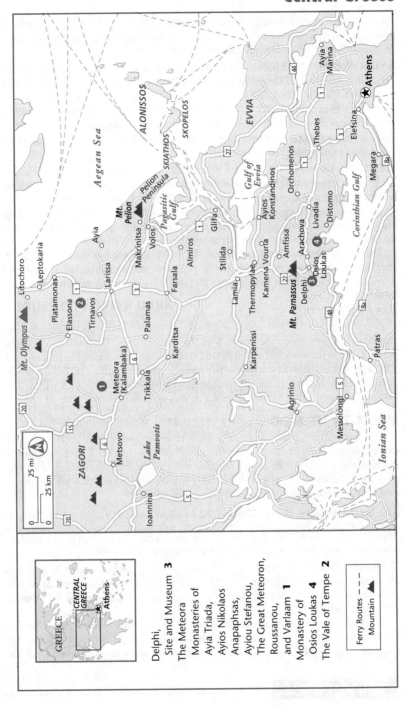

Aegean Sea

ALONISSOS

SKOPELOS

SKIATHOS

Pelion Peninsula

Mt. Pelion

Pagasitic Gulf

EVVIA

Gulf of Evvia

Corinthian Gulf

Mt. Olympus

Litochoro
Leptokaria
Platamonas
Elassona
Tirnavos
Larissa
Ayia
Makrinitsa
Volos
Almiros
Stilida
Glifa
Farsala
Palamas
Karditsa
Lamia
Thermopylae
Kamena Vouria
Amfissa
Arachova
Livadia
Distomo
Ayios Konstandinos
Orchomenos
Thebes
Elefsina
Megara
Athens
Ayia Marina

Meteora (Kalambaka)
Trikkala
Metsovo
ZAGORI
Ioannina
Karpenissi
Agrinio
Messolongi
Patras

Mt. Parnassus
Delphi
Osios Loukas

Lake Pamvotis

Ionian Sea

25 mi
25 km
0

20
15
20
6
5
1
2
3
6
5
48
27
27
1
3
8a
8a
1
44

Ferry Routes - - -
Mountain ▲

GREECE
CENTRAL GREECE
Athens

guide, hotel, and most meals) is about Dr35,000 ($101) for one person in a private room. An exceptionally well-traveled friend who was leery of a group tour had nothing but praise for her 2-day excursion in May 2000.

VISITOR INFORMATION Most services, such as the post office and banks, are located in the village of Delphi (population 2,500) on the obvious main street, which is named after King Paul and Queen Frederika, although no one seems to use the name. The **tourist office** (☎ 0265/82-900), in the town hall on the main street, is open Monday through Friday from 8am to 2:30pm and sometimes reopens from 6 to 8pm in summer. The ancient site (signposted) is about 1 kilometer (0.6 miles) out of town, on the Arachova Road.

GETTING AROUND If you can, you should walk everywhere in Delphi. Parking spots are at a premium both in the village and at the site. If you have to drive to the site rather than making the 5- to 10-minute walk from town, be sure to set off early to get one of the few parking places. Whether you walk or drive, keep an eye out for the enormous tour buses that barrel down the center of the road—and for the not terribly well marked one-way streets in the village.

Delphi taxi driver **Elias Karatzogles** (☎ 0265/82-741; mobile 093/202-3659) speaks English, drives an air-conditioned taxi, and will whisk you off to see Osios Loukas, Arachova, Mount Parnassos, or just about anywhere you want to go at competitive prices.

FAST FACTS There are several banks on the main street where you can exchange currency or use the ATM; the **National Bank of Greece,** in addition to normal weekday hours, is sometimes open from 6 to 7pm in summer. The **police** (☎ 0265/82-222) are in the town hall (☎ 0265/82-310) on the main street. For **first aid,** call (☎ 0265/82-307). Both the **post office** and the **telephone office (OTE)** are on the main street. In addition to normal weekday hours (Monday through Friday from 8am to 2pm), the post office and OTE are sometimes open Sunday from 9am to 1pm.

WHAT TO SEE & DO

As at Olympia, the most important thing is to begin your visit as early as possible. Note that starting your day at the museum will give you an overall understanding of the site, and you'll then be able to visualize many of the important works of art that decorated the sanctuary on your visit. *Tip:* Both the site and museum are sometimes relatively uncrowded during the hour before closing time.

The Delphi Museum. Delphi. ☎ **0265/82-312-3.** Admission Dr1,200 ($3.50). Summer Mon 11am–7pm; Tues–Fri 8am–7pm; Sat–Sun and holidays 8am–3pm. Winter Mon 11am–5:30pm; Tues–Fri 8am–5:30pm; Sat–Sun and holidays 8am–5pm. (Be sure to check these hours when you arrive in Delphi, as they can change without warning.)

With luck, the museum's new wing will have opened by the time you visit. This may mean that you'll pay a bit more for admission and that some things will be in new locations—more than worth it to see treasures that have languished for years in museum storehouses.

At present, the first thing you see in the museum (once you climb the stairs beyond the inevitable shop) is a 4th-century B.C. **marble egg,** a copy of the yet older egg (or *omphalos*) that symbolized Delphi's unique position as the center (or naval) of the

---

Outdoor Pursuits

If you're interested in hiking or skiing, see the side trip to Parnassus, below.

Ancient Delphi

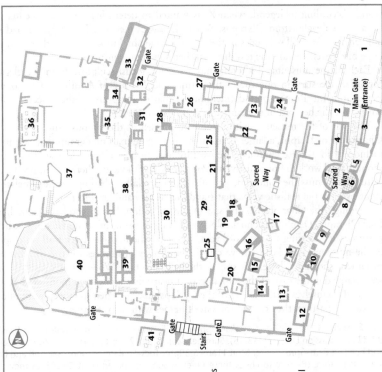

1 Roman Agora (Marketplace)
2 Votive offering of Corfu ("Bull")
3 Votive offering of Athens
   ("Victory at Marathon")
4 Votive offering of
   Lacedaemonians
5 Votive offering of Argos
   ("Seven Against Thebes")
6 Votive offering of Argos
   ("Descendants")
7 Votive offering of Argos
   ("The King of Argos")
8 Votive offering of Taras
9 Treasure House of Sikyon
10 Treasure House of Siphnos
11 Treasure House of Megara
12 Treasure House of Thebes
13 Treasure House of Boeotia
14 Treasure House of Potidaea
15 Treasure House of Athens
16 Bouleuterion (Council House)
17 Treasure House of Cnidus (Knidos)
18 Rock of Sibylla
19 Naxian Column

20 Asklepion
21 Portico of the Athenians
22 Treasure House of Corinth
23 Prytaneion
   (Magistrates' Building)
24 Treasure House of Cyrene
25 Supporting Polygonal Wall
26 Tripod of Plateae
27 Votive offering of Rhodes
28 Grand Altar
29 Spring
30 Temple of Apollo
31 Votive Tripods
32 Treasure House of Acanthus
33 Portico of Attalus
34 Shrine of Neoptolemos
35 Votive offering of Daochos
36 Club of the Cnidians
37 Kassotis Spring
38 Ischegaon–Supporting Wall
39 Votive offering of Krateros
40 Theater
41 Western Portico

415

world. According to legend, when Zeus wanted to determine the earth's center, he released two eagles from Olympus. When the eagles met over Delphi, Zeus had his answer. You may still see eagles in the sky above Delphi, but more often than not, the large birds overhead are the less distinguished Egyptian vultures.

Each of the museum's 13 rooms has a specific focus: sculpture from the elegant **Siphnian treasury** in one room, finds from the **Temple of Apollo** in two rooms, items from the Roman period (including a marble sculpture of the epicene youth **Antinous,** the beloved of the emperor Hadrian) in another.

The star of the museum, with a room to himself, is the famous 5th-century B.C. **Charioteer of Delphi,** a larger-than-life bronze figure (part of a group that originally included a four-horse chariot). The wealthy Sicilian city of Gela dedicated this near monumental work to honor its tyrant Polyzalos's chariot victory here. It's an irresistible statue: Don't miss the handsome youth's delicate eyelashes shading wide enamel-and-stone eyes, or the realistic veins that stand out in his hands and feet.

Although the Charioteer is the star of the collection, he's in good company here. Like Olympia, Delphi was chockablock with superb works of art donated by wealthy patrons, such as King Croesus of Lydia, who gave the massive **silver bull** on display in the museum. And keep an eye out in the display of bronzes for the tiny **bronze ornament** showing Ulysses clinging to the belly of a ram. When Ulysses and his men were trapped in the cave of the ferocious (but nearsighted) one-eyed monster Cyclops, they tied themselves to the bellies of the Cyclops's sheep. When the sheep went out of the cave to pasture, they carried the Greek heroes with them to safety.

The Sanctuary of Apollo. Castalian Spring and Sanctuary of Athena Pronaia. ☎ **0265/ 82-313.** Admission Dr1,200 ($3.45). Summer Mon 11am–7pm; Tues–Fri 8am–7pm; Sat–Sun and holidays 8am–3pm. Winter Mon 11am–5:30pm; Tues–Fri 8am–5:30pm; Sat–Sun and holidays 8am–3pm. (Be sure to check these times as soon as you arrive at Delphi, as they can change without warning.)

The Sanctuary of Apollo is immediately beyond and just above the museum. The less well-known Sanctuary of Athena on the lower slopes of Parnassus is a 10-minute walk past the museum. The Castalian Spring is between the two sanctuaries. If you can't visit everything here, spend your time at the Sanctuary of Apollo, stroll to the Castalian Spring, and then cross the Delphi-Arachova Road to take a peek down at the Sanctuary of Athena. You may want to buy a site map when you get your ticket to help you orient yourself at this sprawling site, many of whose monuments are unlabeled.

As you enter the Sanctuary of Apollo, you'll be on the marble **Sacred Way,** the road that visitors here have walked for thousands of years. The road runs uphill past the remains of **Roman stoas** and a number of **Greek treasuries** (including the Sifnian and Athenian treasuries, whose sculpture is in the museum). Cities built these small templelike buildings at Delphi for several reasons: to impress their neighbors and to store riches and works of art dedicated to Apollo. Take a close look at the **treasury walls.** You'll see not only beautiful dry-wall masonry but also countless inscriptions. The Greeks were never shy about using the walls of their buildings as bulletin boards.

Alas, so many recent visitors were bent on adding their names to the ancient inscriptions that the Greek archaeological service no longer allows visitors inside the massive 4th-century B.C. **Temple of Apollo,** which was built after the 7th- and 6th-centuries B.C. temples were destroyed. In antiquity, one of the three Pythian priestesses on duty gave voice to Apollo's oracles from a room deep within the temple. That much is known, although the details of what precisely happened here are obscure. Did the priestess sit on a tripod balanced over a chasm, breathing in hallucinatory fumes? Did she chew various herbs, including the laurel leaf sacred to Apollo, until she spoke in tongues, while priests interpreted her sayings? Perhaps wisely, the oracle has kept its secrets.

The Festival of Delphi

Each June, the European Cultural Center of Delphi sponsors a festival featuring ancient Greek drama and works inspired by ancient drama. Tickets and schedules are usually available at the center's Athens office at Frynihou 9, Plaka (☎ 01/ 331-2798), and at the center's Delphi office (☎ 0265/82-733), just out of town on the Itea road (set back from the road in a grove of trees).

From the temple, it's a fairly steep uphill climb to the remarkably well-preserved 4th-century B.C. **theater** and the **stadium,** which was extensively remodeled by the Romans. Events in the Pythian festival took place in both the stadium and the theater. In 1927, the Greek poet and eccentric Angelos Sikelianos and his equally eccentric wife attempted to revive the ancient contests here (see the Sikelianos Museum, below). Today, the theater and stadium are used most summers for the **Festival of Delphi,** which, on occasion, has featured exceptionally unclassical pop music.

Keep your ticket as you leave the Sanctuary of Apollo and head along the Arakova-Delphi Road toward the Sanctuary of Athena (also called the Marmaria, which simply refers to all the marble found here). En route, you'll pass the famous **Castalian Spring,** where Apollo planted a laurel he brought here from the Vale of Tempe. Drinking from the spring inspired legions of poets in antiquity; now, poets have to find their inspiration elsewhere, as the spring is off limits, purportedly to allow repairs to the Roman fountain facade. (Once an antiquity is closed in Greece, it often stays closed quite a while.) Above are the rose-colored cliffs known as the **Phaedriades** (the Bright Ones), famous for the way that they reflect the sun's rays.

North of the Castalian Spring, a path descends from the main road to the **Sanctuary of Athena,** the goddess of wisdom who shared the honors at Delphi with Apollo. As the remains here are quite fragmentary, except for the 4th-century B.C. **gymnasium,** you can simply wander about and enjoy the site without trying too hard to figure out what's what. The round 4th-century **tholos** with its three graceful Doric columns is easy to spot, though no one knows why this building was built, why it was so lavishly decorated, or what went on inside. Again, the oracle keeps its secrets.

The Angelos and Eva Sikelianos Museum. ☎ 0265/82-173. Fax 0265/82-722. E-mail: epkdelfi@otenet.gr. Admission Dr200 (60¢). Wed–Mon 8:30am–3pm.

The road that leads steeply uphill through the village of Delphi ends at the handsome stone-and-brick Sikelianos home, now a museum commemorating the work of the Greek poet Sikelianos and his American wife, Eva Palmer. An artist, writer, and, ultimately, costume designer, Eva helped her husband stage Greek tragedies in Delphi's theater in the 1920s and 1930s. The couple's attempts to revive the Pythian games was not long-lived, but their desire to make use of Greece's ancient theaters had lasting effects, as all who have seen plays performed here or at the theater at Epidaurus know. This museum is a pleasant place to spend an hour and see Sikelianos's manuscripts and the beautiful costumes Eva designed. Few tourists visit this elegant home, which has spectacular views from most windows, cozy fireplaces, and the best bathroom in town.

WHERE TO STAY

There's no shortage of hotels in Delphi; you can usually find lodging even in July or August. Still, if you want a room in a specific price category (or with a view), it's best to make a reservation. Finally, consider staying in nearby Arachova, where the hotels are usually less crowded and the restaurants are better (see "Side Trips from Delphi," below).

In addition to the following options, we've also had good reports of the **Olympic Hotel,** Vasileos Pavlou 53a and Frederikis (☎ **0265/82-793;** fax 0265/82-780), and the **Hermes Hotel,** Vasileos Pavlou 29 and Frederikis (☎ **0265/82-318;** fax 0265/82-639). Both are owned by the Droseros family.

Amalia Hotel. Signposted on the Delphi-Itea Rd., 33054 Delphi. ☎ **0265/82-101.** Fax 0265/82-290. 185 units. TEL. Dr49,000 ($141) double. Rates include breakfast. AE, MC, V.

Like all the Amalia Hotels, the Delphi Amalia has all the creature comforts: a swimming pool, several shops, restaurants, and a vast lobby. The Amalia is outside town, above the Delphi-Itea Road, so you may not want to stay here unless you have a car. Most of the bedrooms face each other across a generous garden; when several tour groups are in residence, you'll be aware that you are not alone here.

Castalia Hotel. Vasileos Pavlou and Frederikis 13, 33054 Delphi. ☎ **0265/82-205.** Fax 0265/82-208. 26 units. TEL. Dr32,000 ($92) double. Rates include breakfast. AE, DC, MC, V. Usually open Fri–Sun only from Jan–Feb.

The Castalia, on Delphi's main street, has been here since 1938, but was completely remodeled in 1986. Actually, it looks more "traditional" now than it did originally, with attractive projecting balconies, a white stucco facade, and some nice touches (embroideries, hand-loomed rugs) in the guest rooms. The back bedrooms have fine views over the olive plain. If the Castalia is full, the Maniatis family may suggest that you try their other hotel, the Frederikis, at Pavlou 38 and Frederikis.

✪ **Hotel Varonos.** Pavlou 25 and Frederikis, 33054 Delphi. ☎/Fax **0265/82-345.** 9 units (8 with tub/shower, 1 with shower only). A/C TV TEL. Dr22,000 ($63). Rates include breakfast. Inquire about the 20% discount often available. Room without breakfast often possible. MC, V.

This small, family-owned hotel has very clean, spare bedrooms with fine views out over the olive plain. If you can, take in the rooftop view. This is a very welcoming place: We once arrived with an ailing gardenia plant, and the entire family pitched in to make sure it was well taken care of during our stay. The breakfast room is pleasant; if you plan to have an early breakfast, tell the desk the night before. Be sure to check out the owners' shop next door, with local produce and crafts.

✪ **Hotel Vouzas.** Pavlou and Frederikis 1, 33054 Delphi. ☎ **0265/82-232.** Fax 0232/82-033. 59 units. TV TEL. Dr43,000 ($123). Rates include breakfast. AE, DC, MC, V.

If you don't mind sacrificing the swimming pool at the Amalia, this is the place to stay—cozy fireplace in the lobby, spectacular views, and a short walk to everything you've come to see. That said, perhaps you could persuade the owners that running a wide band at eye level through the dining-room picture window is not very clever. The bedrooms and bathrooms here are quite comfortable (and were partly renovated in 1999); balconies have not only a table and chairs, but also, in season, a welcoming pot of basil.

WHERE TO DINE

Frankly, we weren't enchanted with any of our meals here; the restaurants seemed desultory at best. Let's hope things improve in the future. We suggest that you consider eating in Arachova, 10 kilometers (6.2 miles) east of Delphi.

Taverna Vakchos. Odos Apollonos 31. ☎ **0265/82-448.** Main courses Dr1,400–Dr4,300 ($4–$12). No credit cards. GREEK.

This small taverna gets many of its customers from the youth hostel next door. This means that the prices are very reasonable, the clientele casual, and the food basic. The back room has good views.

Topiki Gefsi. Odos Pavlou and Frederikis 19. ☎ **0265/82-480.** Main courses Dr2,000–Dr5,200 ($6–$15). AE, DC, MC, V. GREEK.

This large restaurant on the main street has a nice view and reasonably good food. Unfortunately, as with most establishments here, the staff is pretty sure that they'll never see you again and the service is consequently haphazard. That said, the stuffed vine leaves and stews are usually reliable, and there's sometimes live music in the evening.

SIDE TRIPS FROM DELPHI
ARACHOVA

The mountain village of Arachova, 10 kilometers (6.2 miles) east of Delphi, clings to Mount Parnassus some 950 meters above sea level. Arachova is famous for its hand-loomed rugs, including fluffy flokati, tagari bags, and blankets. When several tour buses stop here during the daytime, this tiny village can be seriously crowded. Don't despair: Try to come back in the evening, when the shops are still open and the cafes and restaurants give you a chance to escape from the tourist world of Delphi to the village world of Greece. There's usually an energetic evening **volta** (stroll) on the main street, and if you climb the steep stairs to the upper town, you'll find yourself on quiet neighborhood streets, where children play and families sit out in front of their homes.

On the main street, have a look at the weavings in Georgia Charitou's shop **Anemi** (☎ 0267/31-701), which also has some nice reproductions of antiques. **Katina Panagakou** (☎ 0267/31-743) has examples of local crafts as well.

For lunch or dinner here, try the simple family fare at the **Taverna Karathanassi,** by the coffee shops in the main street square with the lovely freshwater springs. The nearby **Taverna Dasargyri,** which specializes in delicious *kokoretsi* (stuffed entrails), *loukanika* (sausages), and grills, often has an almost entirely local crowd. Expect to pay about $12 for dinner at both places.

If you want to stay in Arachova, the **Xenia Hotel** (☎ 0267/31-230; fax 0267/ 32-175), with 42 rooms, each with a balcony (but charmless decor), has doubles at Dr21,000 ($70). The very pleasant **Best Western Anemolia** (☎ 800/528-1234 in the U.S., or 0267/31-640; e-mail: bwgreece@travelling.gr), on a hill just outside Arachova above the Delphi Road, has 52 rooms and charges Dr15,000 to Dr33,000 ($43 to $95) for a double, depending on the day of the week; the dining room is desultory. The **Arachova Inn,** with 40 rooms and a cozy fireplace in the lobby, is just outside town; it charges Dr15,000 ($43) double. All these hotels are usually full on winter weekends, when Greeks flock here to ski Parnassus.

PARNASSUS (PARNASSOS)

Parnassus is an odd mountain: It's difficult to see its peaks from either Delphi or Arachova, although if you approach from the north, you'll have fine views of the twin summits.

The good news is that you can drive the 27 kilometers (16.7 miles) from Arachova to the **ski resort at Fterolaki,** 2,253 meters up Mount Parnassus, in about an hour. The bad news is that the road and several incipient hamlets of ski lodges built by Greeks who vacation here are spoiling the mountain's isolation and much of its beauty. If you drive to Fterolaki in summer, don't expect to find any of the cafes and restaurants open. In winter, of course, things are livelier, with a dozen ski runs, several small shops, and a **cafeteria** (☎ 0234/22-689). If you do come in winter, you can rent ski equipment either in Arachova or at the ski resort at Fterolaki. Keep in mind that fog can sweep in here suddenly; the road down is often closed, standing day-trippers until it reopens.

If you want to hike Parnassus, there are two possibilities. You can head uphill in Delphi past the Sikelianos house and keep going. Four hours will bring you to the upland meadows known as the **Plateau of Livadi,** where shepherds traditionally pasture their flocks. As always in the mountains, it's not a good idea to make such an excursion alone. If you plan to continue on past the meadows to the **Corcyrian Cave** (known locally as Sarantavli, or "Forty Rooms"), where Pan and the Nymphs once were thought to live, or to the summits, you should check on conditions locally or with the **Hellenic Mountaineering Club** in Athens (☎ **01/323-4555**). It's also possible to begin your ascent from Arachova, where you can get directions locally.

The excellent Road Edition map of Parnassos (No. 42 in the series of mountain maps) is an excellent investment (Dr2,000/$6), as is Tim Salmon's *The Mountains of Greece* (Cicerone Press), but nothing substitutes for a companion, especially one who knows the terrain.

THE MONASTERY OF OSIOS LOUKAS

You'll probably want to see Osios Loukas en route to or from Delphi, although you could do the 96-kilometer (60-mile) round-trip via Arachova as a day excursion. If you go to Osios Loukas via Levadia, pause at **Schiste (Triodos),** where three roads cross. This is the spot where the ancients believed that Oedipus unknowingly slew his father. Things got worse: Still unknowingly, he married his mother and brought tragedy on himself and his descendants.

Osios Loukas (the Monastery of Saint Luke) is a spectacular church and monastery founded in the 10th century, with much of what you see dating from at least the 11th century. This is not just a tourist destination: Devout Greek Orthodox visitors consider it a holy spot, something to keep in mind during your visit. This is not the place for sleeveless shirts, shorts, or a casual attitude toward the icons or the tomb of Saint Luke.

Osios Loukas is a lavishly decorated complex—not just brick but a wide variety of different jewel-like polychrome marbles were used in the buildings. Along with the mosaics at Daphne, outside Athens, and the splendid churches of Thessaloniki, Osios Loukas's **mosaics** are among the finest in Greece. If you are lucky enough to be here when the **Katholikon (Main Church)** isn't too crowded, let yourself enjoy the changing light and shadow they play on the marbles and mosaics. You may see visitors handing their family icons to a monk, who takes it into the church for a special blessing. Then head over to the smaller **church of the Theotokos (Mother of God),** with its lovely mosaic floor. If you have time, visit the crypt, with its frescoes, and then sit in the courtyard and imagine what Osios Loukas would have been like when hundreds, not today's handful, of monks lived and worshipped here.

Admission to Osios Loukas costs Dr800 ($2.30). Hours are daily from 8am to 2pm and 4 to 7pm from early May to mid-September, 8am to 5pm the rest of the year. (Note that these are the posted times; they are not always observed.)

2 Thebes

87km (53 miles) W of Athens off the Athens-Corinth National Hwy.

Thebes was one of the most important Mycenaean settlements in Greece. The Athenian dramatist Agamemnon commemorated Thebes in his play *Seven Against Thebes,* and the poet Pindar was born here. When Alexander the Great captured Thebes in 336 B.C., he leveled the town, sparing only Pindar's birthplace.

Unfortunately, several 20th-century earthquakes have also leveled a good deal of Thebes, and the new city, though energetic, is not charming. If you're pressed for time, you might give Thebes a miss altogether, unless you're heading for the Archaeological Museum (see below). There's no good hotel here, but several really down-at-the-heels ones, so we don't recommend spending the night. As for food, you won't starve, but if you find a superior restaurant, please let us know. We haven't, despite many attempts.

If you're driving, the turnoff for Thebes, just after Eleusis, is signposted on the National Highway. Allow 2 hours from Athens. Frequent buses depart from the Athens station, Odos Liossion 260 (☎ **01/831-7096**), arriving at the Thebes bus station (☎ **0262/275-11**) in the center of town.

The Archaeological Museum. Odos Pindararou. ☎ **0262/27-913.** Admission Dr600 ($1.75). Mon and Wed–Sat 8:30am–3pm; Sun 9am–2pm. Parking on side streets nearby.

There's only one thing to detain you in Thebes: the Archaeological Museum, which has a Frankish tower in its garden. Although the collection includes a wide range of pottery, inscriptions, and sculpture, the Mycenaean objects are the highlight. There are several painted Mycenaean sarcophagi, some fine gold jewelry, and handsome body armor. The scant remains of ancient Thebes—the unexcavated ancient city lies under the modern one—are signposted at the museum.

3 Two Famous Battlefields: Thermopylae & Chaironeia

THERMOPYLAE
194km (120 miles) N of Athens on the Athens-Thessaloniki National Hwy.

If you find yourself on the Athens-Thessaloniki Highway, keep an eye out for the larger-than-life-size **statue of the Spartan king Leonidas,** about halfway through the 6.4-kilometer-long (4-mile-long) Pass of Thermopylae that snakes between the mountains and the sea. One of the most famous battles in history was fought here in 480 B.C. during the Persian King Xerxes's attempt to conquer Greece. To this day, historians speculate on just how different the world might have been if Xerxes had succeeded, and Greece had become part of the Persian Empire.

When Xerxes invaded Greece in 480 B.C. with perhaps 100,000 men, soldiers from almost every city-state in south and central Greece rushed to Thermopylae to try to stop the Persian king's advance. The Greeks might have succeeded in holding the narrow pass of Thermopylae had not a traitor told the Persians of a secret mountain path

A Break En Route

If you're driving from Central Greece into Northern Greece along the Athens-Thessaloniki National Highway, you may want to take a break from the road. The seaside town of **Kamena Vourla** is just off the highway and has several hotels and restaurants (most separated from the sea by a road). The **Astir Hotel Galini** (☎ **0235/22-245,** or 01/324-3961 in Athens; fax 0253/22-307) has 100 units with balconies facing either wooded hills (Dr24,000/$69) or the sea (Dr29,000/$83). In summer, the hotel's pool and thermal baths are open. About a block from the Astir, the excellent **Thronio** cafe/restaurant/pizzeria (☎ **0235/22-354**) is open daily from 11am to midnight and serves delicious spaghetti carbonara and cannelloni. Although you'll be welcomed with open arms here out of season (except on weekends, when city dwellers from as far away as Athens come here), it's risky to count on getting a room in the summer unless you have a reservation.

that allowed them to turn the pass. As Leonidas and his 300-man royal guard stood and fought at Thermopylae, the main Greek force retreated south to regroup and fight another day. When the fighting at Thermopylae was over, Leonidas and his men lay dead, but the Spartan king had earned immortal fame for his heroism.

The name Thermopylae (Hot Gates) refers to the warm springs that bubbled here in antiquity, when the pass was considerably narrower than it is now that centuries of silt have built up the seashore. Many of Thermopylae's springs have been partly diverted to spas, such as Kamena Vourla, but unfortunately, overdevelopment has seriously undercut the former charm of the seaside towns nearby. If you want to take a fast look at some of the springs, keep an eye out for plumes of smoke when you park near the statue of Leonidas. If you don't see the plumes, follow your nose: The smell of sulfur is strong.

CHAIRONEIA
132km (81 miles) NW of Athens on the Athens-Levadhia-Lamia Hwy.

Just north of Levadhia, the Athens-Lamia Highway passes an enormous **stone lion** that marks the site of the common grave of the Theban Sacred Band of warriors, who died here in the Battle of Chaironeia in 338 B.C. It was at Chaironeia that Philip of Macedon, with some 30,000 soldiers, defeated the combined forces of Athens and Thebes and became the most powerful leader in Greece. It was also at Chaironeia that Philip's 18-year-old son Alexander first distinguished himself on the battlefield, when he led the attack against the superbly trained Theban Sacred Band, which fought to the last man. Philip's admiration for the Thebans' courage was such that he allowed them to be buried where they fell on the battlefield.

The lion itself, sitting on its haunches with a surprisingly benign expression on its face, was probably erected by Thebes sometime after the battle. With the passing of time, the winds blew soil from the plain almost entirely over the lion. In 1818, two English antiquarians stumbled upon the lion's head; excavations in 1904 and 1905 led to the lion's restoration and re-erection here on the dusty plain of Chaironeia.

4 The Vale of Tempe & Ambelakia
326km (202 miles) N of Athens; 27km (16 miles) N of Larissa

This steep-sided 8-kilometer (5-mile) gorge between Mounts Olympus and Ossa has been famous since antiquity as a beauty spot. According to legend, this is where Apollo caught a glimpse of the lovely maiden Daphne, bathing in the Peneios River. When Apollo pursued Daphne, she cried out to the gods on nearby Olympus to save her— which they did, by turning her into a laurel tree (*daphne* in Greek). Apollo, who didn't give up easily, then plucked a branch from the tree and planted it at his shrine at Delphi. Thereafter, messengers came to Tempe from Delphi every 9 years to collect laurel for Apollo's temple.

To this day, there are laurel, chestnut, and plane trees growing in the Vale of Tempe. Unfortunately, since virtually all north-south traffic in Greece now passes through the Vale, this is no longer the sylvan spot that was once the haunt of nightingales. Still, if you're lucky enough to be here off-season, the sound of the gurgling river may be louder than that of tourists' footsteps on the suspension bridge over the gorge. The car toll is Dr500 ($1.45).

Keep an eye out for the remains of the **Kastro tis Oreas** ("Castle of the Beautiful Maiden") on the cliffs above Tempe and the little chapel deep in the gorge. Unfortunately, you won't have any trouble spotting the souvenir stands throughout the Vale, or the signs advertising a "Love Boat" cruise on the river.

The Wildflowers of Greece

Every spring, the arid Greek countryside is carpeted with a staggering variety of wildflowers. Small wonder that one of the oldest Greek poems, *The Homeric Hymn to Demeter*, celebrates meadows blooming with "roses, crocuses, lovely violets, irises and hyacinth and narcissus." Shrub roses bloom high on the Pindus Mountains of Northern Greece, there are poppies as far as the eye can see on the dusty plain of Thessaly, and the wild iris flourishes on seashores deep in the Peloponnese. Even more astonishingly, poppies and oleanders continue to bloom on hillsides and even grow from tiny cracks in the marble blocks of fallen temples during the hottest summer months.

Greeks call almost all wildflowers just that—*agria louloudia*—and don't usually bother with specific names, although they do call the wild carnation *agriogarifalo.* The ancient Greeks thought that this little pink, red, or white flower was Zeus's particular favorite, just as the laurel was beloved of Apollo.

Like many Greek flowers, the more humble broom plant, whose vibrant yellow blossoms scent much of Greece each spring, is both beautiful and useful: After the broom blooms, its stalks are gathered and made into the brooms that you see in use throughout Greece. After the orchidlike caper flowers, the capers are gathered, pickled, and used in salads, along with the dried flowers of the richly scented herb oregano, whose distinctive taste makes Greek salads so unmistakably Greek.

There are lots of books on Greek wildflowers. Two of the best are *Flowers of Greece and the Aegean,* by Anthony Huxley and William Taylor (Chatto and Windus), and *Flowers of Athens,* by Elias Cainadas and Marios Theodorakakis (Patakis Publications). Both are usually available at Eleftheroudakis Bookstore in Athens (see "Shopping" in chapter 5).

If you can, take an hour or two to visit the mountaintop village of **Ambelakia,** some 6.4 kilometers (4 miles) southeast of the Vale of Tempe, with spectacular views of Mount Olympus. The village is one of six in Greece to have formed the **National Network of Tradition, Culture, and Community Life** to attempt to preserve their traditions and base economic development on local crafts. (The other villages are Ia on Santorini, Panormus in Tinos, Makrinitsa on Mount Pelion, Pappingo in Zagori, and Nympheon in Florina.) There's also a branch here of the **Women's Agrotourism Cooperative** (☎ 0495/93-401), which runs To Rhodi café and is often able to help visitors find places to stay.

Ambelakia, whose name means "vineyards" in Greek, is perched amidst old oak trees on Mount Kissavos. Astonishingly, this tiny village was an important center of cotton and silk production in the 17th century, with offices in far-off London. Today, little remains of Ambelakia's earlier wealth, but what does remain is well worth a visit: the handsome 19th-century **Schwartz House.** (It's open somewhat unpredictably, but is usually closed Mondays and open Tuesday through Sunday from 9am to 2pm; admission is Dr800/$2.30.) The Schwartz brothers were two of Ambelakia's wealthiest merchants, and their handsome wooden house, with its overhanging balconies and elaborately frescoed interiors, is an absolute delight.

If you want to stay here, it's a good idea to call ahead to the charming little **Nine Muses Hotel** (☎ 0495/93-405 or 041/550-774), which has 12 rooms at Dr15,500 ($44) double. If the Nine Muses is full, ask for help finding a room in one of the local "rent rooms" bed-and-breakfasts. There are several small restaurants on the main square serving simple grills and salads. If you want a break from tourist Greece, spend a night or two here, and experience village Greece—and spectacular views of Mount Olympus.

5 Mount Olympus

390km (241 miles) N of Athens; 70km (43 miles) N of Larissa

Greece's most famous mountain range, home of the Olympian gods, towers 2,919 meters (9,751 feet) above the plains of Thessaly and Macedonia. From a distance, it's almost impossible to pick out Olympus's summit, Mytikas—nicknamed the "needle," or **Stafani,** and called the "throne of Zeus"—although the massive, gnarled, snow-capped range is often visible from Thessaloniki (albeit less and less so, given the area's increasing pollution).

The first recorded successful ascent of the summit was in 1913, when two Swiss mountaineers with a local guide made it to the top. For such an imposing mountain, Olympus is surprisingly easy to climb, in large part because so many people since 1913 have climbed it. Consequently, there are a number of well-marked paths to the summit as well as shelters at Stavros (944 meters) and Spilios Agapitos (2,100 meters), where climbers can rest or even spend the night. In summer, these paths can be very heavily trafficked, with some elegant Greek women making the ascent in high heels.

Still, Olympus is a serious mountain, and no one should attempt it alone. As always in the mountains, weather conditions can change for the worse without warning. Well into May, severe snowstorms are not uncommon on the heights of Olympus—which helps to explain why the area has been developed in recent years as a ski resort. The main town on the slopes, and the base camp, as it were, for climbers, is Litochoro.

ESSENTIALS

GETTING THERE   By Bus   Four buses that stop at the Litochoro station (☎ 0352/81-271) run daily from Athens to Katerini; seven buses per day run from Athens to Larissa, from which there is frequent service to Litochoro. All buses leave Athens from the station at Odos Liossion 260 (☎ 01/831-7059). There are at least eight buses a day from Thessaloniki to Litochoro.

By Train   There are frequent daily trains from Athens to Larissa, and from Thessaloniki to Larissa; from Larissa, you can continue to Litochoro by bus. You can also take a train from Athens or Thessaloniki to the Litochoro station (☎ 0352/22-522)—but the station is on the coast 9 kilometers (5.6 miles) from town, and you'll have to continue on by bus or taxi. Only train lovers will want to come here this way.

By Car   Take the Litochoro exit on the Athens-Salonika Highway.

VISITOR INFORMATION   The **tourist office** (☎ 0352/83-100) faces the bus stop. The **Greek Mountaineering Club (GMC)** can be reached at ☎ 01/323-4555 in Athens, 031/278-288 in Thessaloniki, or 0352/81-944 in Litochoro. The GMC can give you information on conditions on Olympus, which is usually climbable from June 1 to October 1, and will let you know whether you can just show up at, or need a reservation for, one of its overnight shelters. The **Spilios Agapitos** refuge can be reached at ☎ 0352/81-800; rates are rather flexible, but usually less than Dr3,000 ($9). Climbing information and conditions can be obtained from the **SEO (Association of Greek Climbers)** at ☎ 0352/82-300, or the **EOS (Hellenic Alpine Association)** at ☎ 0352/81-944. Both offices are signposted in Litochoro, and both keep irregular hours.

FAST FACTS   The **National Bank of Greece,** on Plateia Kentriki, offers currency exchange and has an ATM. The **clinic** (☎ 0352/22-222), 5 kilometers (3 miles) outside Litochoro, is signposted; in the event of a nonemergency try to get to Thessaloniki for medical care. The **police station** (☎ 0352/81-111) is signposted just off the central square (Plateia Kentriki) on the road up Olympus to Priona. The **post office** is on Plateia Kentriki. The **telephone office (OTE)** is just off Plateia Kentriki on the road up Olympus to Priona.

CLIMBING MOUNT OLYMPUS

If you plan to climb Olympus, you will want to check with the EOS and SEO (see above) and probably get a copy of Marc Dubin's *Trekking in Greece* and the excellent Road Edition map of Olympus (no. 31; Dr1,836/$5.30). You should not attempt the climb alone; weather here can change in an instant from pleasant to life-threatening. In July and August of 1998, high winds whipped the flames of a serious fire that burnt portions of Olympus's magnificent forests.

Purists will want to begin the ascent at the rapidly developing **ski resort of Litochoro,** while others may prefer to drive from Litochoro as far as **Prionia** (18km/ 11 miles) and begin the climb there. On foot, it takes about 4 hours from Litochoro to Prionia; by car, it's about an hour, but seems longer on the twisting road. Fortunately, there's a small **cafe** at Priona, where you can reward yourself with a decent meal, or even a stiff drink.

From Priona, it's at least a 3-hour climb, much of it over slippery schist slopes and knobby limestone outcroppings, to the **shelter at Spilios Agapitos.** If you don't mind communal quarters, this is the place to spend the night, especially since both bedding and meals are available. Most climbers begin the final 3-hour ascent at dawn and then do the entire descent, arriving back in Litochoro before dusk. The **Monastery of Ayios Dionysos,** not far from Spilios Agapitos, is a good place to break your downward trek and enjoy the views. The monastery was destroyed by the Germans during World War II, but is now being rebuilt.

WHERE TO STAY & DINE

You can get information on the **refuges** on Mount Olympus from the EOS and SEO (see "Visitor Information," above). As far as the dining scene is concerned, one has to conclude that climbers are not foodies. There are a number of small restaurants in Litochoro, none worth seeking out. If you find one that is, we'd love to hear about it.

Dion Palace Resort Hotel. Litochoro Beach, Pierias, 60200 Macedonia. ☎ **0352/22-731.** Fax 0352/22-735. 182 units. MINIBAR TV TEL. Dr25,600 ($73) double. AE, MC, V. Sometimes closed in winter.

This enormous beachfront resort has a main hotel building, two restaurants, a disco, shops, a fitness center, and lots of cabanas. There are two swimming pools, one saltwater, one fresh, and all the creature comforts in the guest rooms. In summer, this is a popular family destination, and anyone with children will see why.

Markissia Hotel. Litochoro, Pierias, 60200 Macedonia. ☎ **0352/81-831.** Fax 0352/61-862. 19 units. TEL. Dr10,000 ($29). MC, V.

We're had good reports of this hotel in the center of Litochoro. All units have minifridges, some have kitchenettes, and the rooms are light, bright, and more cheerful than at most Greek hotels in this price range.

Mirto Hotel. Litochoro, Pierias, 60200 Macedonia. ☎ **0352/81-398.** Fax 0352/82-298. 20 units. TV TEL. Dr14,000 ($40). No credit cards.

Like many of the newer hotels in Litochoro, the Mirto is built in a sort of pseudo–Swiss chalet style, with lots of wood. The guest rooms have nice balconies, firm beds, and adequate bathrooms.

Villa Drossos. Litochoro, 60200 Macedonia. ☎ **0352/84-561.** Fax 0352/84-563. 13 units. TEL. Dr18,000 ($$52). MC, V.

The big plus here (which makes reservations in summer a necessity) is the swimming pool in the garden (which makes the hotel popular with families traveling with children). The guest rooms have balconies, and many are furnished in bright pastels and floral prints.

6 The Meteora

Kalambaka is 356km (220 miles) NW of Athens; the circuit of the Meteora monasteries is approximately 25km (15 miles)

As you drive across the plain of Thessaly, which can seem endless on a hot summer's day, you'll suddenly see a cluster of gnarled black rocks. Some travelers have compared these crags to the mountains of the moon, but the fact is that the rock formations of the Meteora (the word means "in midair") are unique. Many geographers speculate that some 30 million years ago, all Thessaly was a vast inland sea; when the sea receded, sweeping the topsoil along, only rock formations were left behind. Over the millennia, the Peneios River and the wind carved the rock into the weird, twisted shapes that now rise some 300 meters (984 feet) above the plain. The Meteora is especially stunning in winter, when the Pindos range is capped with snow and mists swirl around the monasteries.

When you get closer to the Meteora and see that these sheer, slippery, seemingly unscalable rocks are topped with large monasteries, you'll probably find yourself asking two questions: Why did monks settle here, and how did they build anything larger than a hut on the rocks? Small wonder that many monks believe that St. Athanasios, founder of the first monastery here, the Great Meteoron (Monastery of the Transfiguration), did not scale the rock, but was carried there by an eagle.

The first monks who came here were probably 10th-century ascetics who scaled the rocks, lived as hermits in caves, and spent their days in prayer and meditation. In fact, the word monk comes from the Greek for "alone." Over the centuries, more and more hermits and monks seeking to lead the solitary life made their way to the Meteora until, by the 14th century, there were enough monks here for St. Athanasios to found the Great Meteoron. While some monks continued to live alone and pursue the solitary religious life called idiorrhythmic, others chose to live together and follow the cenobitic, or communal, life.

Important Reminders

Although many of the monasteries are officially open from 9am to 6pm, many close from about 1 to 3pm, and others keep abbreviated hours. It's best to start your visit as early in the day as possible, so that you're not left cooling your heels while the monks and nuns have their afternoon siestas. Try to allow at least a full day here—the last thing you want to do is to rush experiencing the contemplative life! Don't forget modest attire: long-sleeved shirts and skirts for women, slacks and shirts for men. If you come in winter, dress warmly, as many of the monasteries have little or no heat. Also note that in winter, many small restaurants and hotels may be closed. In compensation, you might get to see the Meteora at its most beautiful: covered in snow and shrouded in mists.

By 1500, there were 24 monasteries here, of which six—the Great Meteoron, Varlaam, Rousanou, Ayia Triada, Ayios Nikolaos Anapaphsas, and Ayiou Stefanou—are still inhabited and welcome visitors.

Visiting the Meteora is not recommended for those suffering from acrophobia, or any who might find it difficult to climb steep flights of stairs cut in the rock face. Still, even these vertiginous stepped paths are an improvement over what earlier travelers had to endure. When the English traveler Leake visited here in the 19th century, he was ferried up to the Great Meteoron in a net attached by a slender rope to a winch. Leake later wrote, "Visitors' morale was not helped by persistent rumors that the monks only replaced the homemade ropes which held the nets when they broke—usually in midair!"

ESSENTIALS

GETTING THERE   By Train   At press time, the Larissa-Kalambaka branch line was not in operation while new tracks were being laid. Once service has resumed, there will probably be about seven daily trains from Athens's Larissa station (☎ **01/821-3882**) to Larissa and thence to the Kalambaka station (☎ **0432/22-451**). Allow at least 8 hours for the Athens-Kalambaka trip.

By Bus   There are seven daily buses to Trikkala from the Athens terminal at Odos Liossion 260 (☎ **01/831-1434**). Allow at least 8 hours for the Athens-Kalambaka trip. There are frequent buses from Trikkala (☎ **0431/73-130**) to Kalambaka (☎ **0432/22-432**). Several buses a day connect Kalambaka and the Meteora monasteries.

By Car   From Athens, take the Athens-Thessaloniki National Highway north to Lamia; from Lamia, take the highway northwest to Kalambaka. From Delphi, take the Lamia-Karditsa-Trikkala-Kalambaka Highway north. Allow at least 6 hours for the Athens-Kalambaka trip.

GETTING AROUND   If you don't have a car, you may want to hire a taxi to visit the Meteora monasteries. Expect to pay between Dr15,000 and Dr35,000 ($43 and $100) to visit the six monasteries usually open to the public. Your fee will vary depending on whether you simply want a drive-by tour with a stop at one or two monasteries or a more thorough visit with stops at each. Be sure you are in agreement as to how long you will have at each monastery; most drivers are content to wait 30 minutes at each one, while some drivers will accompany you into the monastery and act as guide.

FAST FACTS   The **National Bank** and the **Ionian Bank** on Plateia Riga Fereou, the main square, exchange currency and have ATMs. The **clinic** in Kalambaka (☎ **0432/24-111**), the **police** (☎ **0432/22-109**), and the **tourist police** (☎ **0432/76-100**) are about 1 kilometer outside town on the road to Ioannina. The **post office** and **telephone office (OTE)** are signposted off Plateia Riga Fereou. For **Internet access,** try the Café Hollywood, Trikalon 67 (☎ **0432/24-964;** e-mail: hollynet@ hotmail.com).

WHAT TO SEE & DO
THE METEORA MONASTERIES

The road from Kalambaka through the Meteora takes you past Ayios Nikolaos, Roussanou, the Great Meteron, Varlaam, Ayia Triada, and Ayios Stephanos. If you only have time to visit one monastery, it should be the **Great Meteoron.** Try to allow time for a leisurely visit, so that you can chat with the monks and enjoy the stunning views through the forest of rocks from monastery to monastery. You'll find souvenir stands and places to buy bottled water or soft drinks (but usually no food) outside each monastery.

We've listed the individual phone number for each monastery below, but don't be surprised if no one answers: Telephones and the monastic life are not really compatible. There's also a central number for the monasteries (☎ **0432/22-649**). And don't be surprised if you find one or more of the monasteries closed—usually the one you've just climbed up a long series of rock-cut steps to reach.

Ayios Nikolaos Anapaphsas. ☎ **0432/22-375.** Admission Dr500 ($1.45). Daily 9am–6pm. Often closed in winter.

This little 14th-century monastery, approached by a relatively gentle path, has splendid **frescoes** by the 16th-century Cretan painter Theophanes the Monk. Don't miss the delightful fresco of the garden of Eden, with elephants, fantastic beasts, and all manner of fruits and flowers. There's also a nice painting of the death of St. Ephraim the Syrian, which shows scenes from the saint's life, including the pillar that he lived atop for many years in the Syrian desert.

At the time of our visit, there were no monks in residence at Ayios Nikolaos, and because tour buses often rush past to get to the Great Meteoron, you may find that you have this spot all to yourself.

Roussanou. No phone. Admission Dr500 ($1.45). Daily 9am–1pm and 3–6pm.

Roussanou is relatively accessible, thanks to its new bridge. This 13th-century monastery is now a nunnery, whose inhabitants are usually much more jolly than the monks. If the nuns offer you sweets while you sit in the courtyard between the refectory and the octagonal-domed church, be sure to leave a contribution in the church collection box.

✪ **The Great Meteoron.** ☎ **0432/22-278.** Admission Dr500 ($1.45). Wed–Mon 9am–1pm and 3:20–6pm.

Although the Great Meteoron was founded in the 14th century, most of what you see here was built in the 16th century by monks from the Holy Mountain of Mount Athos. The **church** here is especially splendid, in the form of a Greek cross inscribed on a square, topped by a **12-sided dome.** Once your eyes get accustomed to the darkness, you'll be able to enjoy the elaborate **frescoes.** If you look up to the dome, you'll see Christ, with the four evangelists, apostles, and prophets ranged below, the church fathers by the altar, and the liturgical feasts of the church year along the walls of the nave. There's also a rather bloodcurdling *Last Judgment* and *Punishment of the Damned* in the narthex. After visiting the church, you may wish to sit awhile in the shady courtyard before visiting the small **museum,** which has a collection of icons and illustrated religious texts. Don't miss the **wine cellar,** whose enormous wooden barrels suggest that monastic life is not all prayer and meditation.

Varlaam. ☎ **0432/22-277.** Admission Dr500 ($1.45). Sat–Thurs 9am–1pm and 3:30–6pm.

A narrow bridge from the main road runs to this 16th-century monastery, which was named for a hermit who lived here in the 14th century and built a tiny chapel on this promontory. The **chapel,** considerably enlarged and decorated with **frescoes,** is now a side chapel of the main church. Varlaam's founders were two brothers from Ioannina, who found the monastery and gentle lakeside scenery there too sybaritic for their tastes. Presumably the brothers found the Meteora's harsh landscape more to their liking: According to legend, they had to drive away the monster who lived in a cave on the summit before they could settle here. The nicest thing about Varlaam is its **garden,** and the monk who sometimes sits here and is willing to chat with visitors.

Ayia Triada. ☎ **0432/22-220.** Admission Dr500 ($1.45). Daily 8am–1pm and 3–6pm.

It's not easy to say which of the monasteries has the most spectacular position, but Ayia Triada would be near the top of most lists. Perched on a slender pinnacle, reached only by laboring up 140 steps, Ayia Triada really does seem to belong to another world. The one monk who lives here is usually glad to see visitors and show them around the **church, refectory,** and **courtyard.** Don't miss the **winch,** for years used to bring up supplies and visitors. If this monastery looks more familiar to you than the others, perhaps you remember it from the James Bond movie *For Your Eyes Only,* which was filmed here.

Ayiou Stefanou. No phone. Admission Dr500 ($1.45). Usually open Tues–Sun 9am–1pm and 3:20–6pm.

Founded in the 14th century, Ayiou Stefanou, now a nunnery, is almost on the outskirts of Kalambaka. A bridge from the main road makes it easy to get here, and the nuns usually make you feel glad that you've come. The nuns sometimes sell very reasonably priced embroideries.

Ayiou Stefanou was badly damaged in both World War II and the Civil War that followed. Many priceless frescoes were defaced and others were totally destroyed, but the monastery's most famous relic was saved: the **head of St. Charalambos,** whose powers include warding off illness. There's also a small **museum** here, with ecclesiastical robes and paraphernalia. Recently, the nuns have been attempting to restore sections of the monastery that had been allowed to decline. Donations are welcomed.

THE CATHEDRAL OF THE DORMITION OF THE VIRGIN

After visiting the monasteries of the Meteora, you may find it a relief to know that there's only one church to see back in Kalambaka: the 12th-century Cathedral of the Dormition of the Virgin, which is often locked. If it's open, take a look at the frescoes, which date from the 12th to the 16th centuries. You might also keep an eye out for the ancient marble blocks and column drums that the builders of this church pilfered from the earlier Temple of Apollo that once stood here.

SHOPPING

There are a lot of tourist shops in Kalambaka (most of which close for the winter) that sell the usual carved wooden canes and spoons, ceramics, and rugs. One shop that opened a couple years ago is worth a look: **Kava Nikos,** on the main drag, Odos Trikalon 114 (☎ and fax **0432/77-881**). This small wine-and-liquor shop has a good selection of wines both in the bottle and from the barrel, and also stocks local Macedonian and Thessalian *tsipouro,* a firewater that makes ouzo seem like a delicate aperitif. If you're lucky enough to be in Kalambaka on a Friday, you can't help but notice the **farmers' market** that spills out into the streets off Odos Kondyli.

WHERE TO STAY

For now, we're only suggesting hotels in Kalambaka, and not in the hamlet of Kastraki, just outside Kalambaka. This village has become very noisy, due to the coaches that rumble to and from the Meteora, the proliferating campgrounds, and the discos. Let us know if you find a tranquil place to stay.

Amalia. Outside Kalambaka on the Meteora Rd., 42200 Kalambaka. ☎ **0432/72-216.** Fax 0432/72-457. 173 units. A/C TV TEL. Dr50,000 ($144) double. Rates include breakfast buffet. Often significantly cheaper off-season. AE, DC, MC, V.

This rather handsome, large new hotel—with two restaurants, a souvenir shop, and a pool—looks almost like a small village from the road. Like most other Amalia hotels, this one is located just too far out of Kalambaka to make the walk into town appealing. The large bedrooms (most with balconies) are tastefully decorated, and bathrooms have actual shower stalls. This is a very comfortable place to stay, although you may find yourself feeling like the odd man out if all the other rooms are occupied by tour groups. On the other hand, this is a popular spot for local wedding receptions and baptisms, so you may get to spy on Kalambaka society.

Divani Motel. Outside Kalambaka on the Meteora Rd., 42200 Kalambaka. ☎ **0432/ 23-330.** Fax 0432/23-638. 165 units. A/C TV TEL. Dr35,000 ($99). Often cheaper off-season. AE, DC, MC, V.

Like the Amalia, the slightly cheaper and less fancy Divani has a pool—although it doesn't hold a candle to the Amalia's. One thing that may sway you toward the Divani: Rooms at the back have very nice balconies and especially fine views toward the Meteora. The restaurant is perfectly decent but bland—as you'd expect, since it turns out masses of meals for tour groups, many of which are Greek in the summer, Japanese in the winter.

Edelweiss. El. Venizelou 3, 42200 Kalambaka. ☎ **0432/23-884.** Fax 0432/24-733. 48 units. A/C TV TEL. Dr15,000 ($43) double. Rates include breakfast. MC, V.

The Edelweiss is low-key and attractive, and—a real plus—has a small swimming pool. Some guest rooms have views of the Meteora.

✪ **Hotel Meteora.** Ploutarchou 13, 42200 Kalambaka. ☎ **0432/22-367.** Fax 0432/ 75-550. E-mail: gekask@otenet.gr. 20 units. TV TEL. Dr10,000 ($29). No credit cards.

The price is right, some of the rooms have balconies with Meteora views, and there's Internet access for about Dr500 ($1.45) per hour. All that and the very helpful manager, Costa Gekas, make this an excellent budget choice.

WHERE TO DINE

We have to admit that we've never had a (pleasantly) memorable meal in Meteora. The places we suggest are perfectly fine, but do let us know if you find something out of the ordinary.

Gertzos. Economou 4. ☎ **0432/22-316.** Main courses Dr1,800–3,500 ($5.15–$10). No credit cards. Usually closed November 1 to Easter. GREEK.

This simple taverna has been in Kalambaka for more than 50 years, serving up the standard Greek fare but also offering a number of dishes reflecting the owners' Greek heritage in Asia Minor. Unless it's so hot—as it can be in the summer here—that you feel you must order a cold drink, try one of the local wines.

Vachos. Plateia Riga Fereou. ☎ **0432/24-678.** Main courses Dr1,800–Dr3,500 ($5.15–$10). No credit cards. Usually closed Nov–Feb. GREEK.

If you want to eat outdoors, head for Vachos's small garden with views toward Meteora. As at Gertzos, the food here is so well prepared that even standard dishes like zucchini and eggplant stuffed with rice and ground meat taste new and different. One plus here: There are usually several tasty sweets on the menu, so you don't have to finish your meal and then search out a *zacheroplasteion* (sweet shop) for dessert.

Panellino. Plateia Riga Fereou. ☎ **0432/24-735.** Main courses Dr1,000–3,200 ($2.90–$9). GREEK.

On our last visit to the Meteora, in February, the Panellino was resolutely open when many other places were closed. The menu consisted of the usual chops and stews, as well as some tasty vegetable dishes.

7 Pelion

Volos is 324km (200 miles) NE of Athens

There comes a time on almost every trip when you need to take a brief vacation from your vacation. That's the time to head for the Mount Pelion peninsula, whose chestnut, apple, and fruit trees make this one of Greece's few year-round lush and verdant havens (although forest fires in the summer of 2000 caused some damage to Pelion's groves). It's possible to drive the circuit of Pelion's most handsome villages in a day, but it seems a shame to rush through an area that preserves a sense of yesterday's leisurely pace at today's breakneck speed. If you can, spend a week here, staying in both mountain and seaside villages. If you can't, spend at least a night at one of the traditional settlement inns. For dinner, try one of the local specialties, such as bean soup (*fasolada*) or the spicy pepper and sausage stew (*spetzofai*).

In antiquity, Mount Pelion was thought to be the home of the centaurs, the legendary half-man, half-horse creatures who roamed the hills and dales here. Although most centaurs had a reputation for brutish behavior, the wise old centaur Chiron helped to raise Achilles, the great hero of the Trojan war; Jason, who spent so many years searching for the Golden Fleece; and Asclepius, who became the god of medicine.

Presumably the centaurs found Pelion's lush green hills a pleasant change from the dusty plain of Thessaly. Certainly, generations of visitors have come to Pelion in search of cool breezes in summer and a glimpse, if not of centaurs, of traditional village life. Pelion's villages are among the most beautiful in Greece, shaded by enormous plane trees and watered by gushing springs. The architecture here is special, too: Most of Pelion's churches are low, three-aisled basilicas, often with large porches, rather than the more familiar cross-in-square design. Pelion's stone houses, many with elaborately frescoed walls, slate roofs, and overhanging wooden balconies, are among the most handsome in all Greece. In part, this is because the Pelion peninsula has been just isolated enough over the centuries to have escaped the ravages of civil war that destroyed so many villages, as well as the horrors of recent development that have spoiled so many others.

In recent years, the Greek government has begun to worry that pell-mell development might threaten the beauty of Pelion's mountain and seaside villages. Consequently, the entire area now has a strict building code, and some villages, such as Vizitsa, have been declared national landmark settlements. Another, Makrinitsa, has banded together with six villages from throughout Greece to preserve local traditions and base development on local crafts and occupations. With luck these steps will help Pelion preserve its unique architecture and character.

In addition, the GNTO has established a number of "traditional settlement guest houses" by renovating abandoned village houses. These small inns give visitors a glimpse of traditional village life—and the visitors provide much-needed income for locals, who otherwise might have had to leave their beloved villages in search of work.

ESSENTIALS

GETTING THERE   By Air   Olympic Airways (☎ **01/966-6666** in Athens; 0421/20-910 in Volos) serves Volos on a daily basis. The **Volos Airport** information number is ☎ **0428/76-886.**

By Train　There are seven daily trains from Athens's Stathmos Larissa (☎ 01/ 362-4402) to the Volos station (☎ 0421/24-056). The trip takes at least 6 hours.

By Bus　There are frequent daily buses to Volos from two Athens terminals: Odos Liossion 260 (☎ 01/22-527), and the corner of Grigoriou Lambraki and Lachana streets (☎ 01/831-7186). Allow 6 hours for the trip. There are frequent daily buses from Volos to the Pelion villages. For schedules, check with the Volos bus station on Grigoriou Lambraki (☎ 0421/25-527) or the GNTO office at Plateia Riga Fereou (☎ 0421/23-500 or 0421/24-915).

By Car　Volos is the jumping-off point for touring Pelion, and it's 324 kilometers (200 miles) northeast of Athens. To get to Volos from Athens, take the Athens-Thessaloniki National Highway; allow at least 4 hours. To reach Pelion from Volos, take Eleftheriou Venizelou Boulevard, which runs from the Volos harbor northeast out of town 5 kilometers (3 miles) to Ano Volos, the suburb of Volos that is the first town on Mount Pelion.

VISITOR INFORMATION　Volos (a port that could hardly be more different than the Pelion villages) is, nonetheless, the main town (the only city, actually) on Pelion. You'll probably begin your visit to Pelion in Volos—and try to get out of Volos as quickly as possible. (This isn't easy: Despite its grid plan, Volos is a very confusing city to drive in.) The **National Tourism Office (EOT)** is on Plateia Riga Fereou in Volos, usually open Monday through Friday from 9am to 2pm (☎ 0421/23-500 or 0421/24-915).

GETTING AROUND　The easiest way to visit Mount Pelion is by private car, although village buses do make their way (on a leisurely schedule) around. If you rent a car, keep in mind that the roads are narrow, and a tour bus may be heading toward you from around the next corner. Car rentals are available in Volos at **Avis,** Odos Argonafton 41 (☎ 0421/20-849; fax 0421/22-849), and **European,** Odos Iasonos 79–83 (☎ 0421/36-238; fax 0421/24-192). If you like old-fashioned narrow-gauge trains, take the 90-minute ride on the *trenaki* from Ano Lehonia, just outside Volos, to the village of Milies. It usually leaves Ano Lehonia around 9am, returns around 5pm, and costs Dr4,000 ($11) one-way. Information is available from the tourist office on Plateia Riga Fereou.

FAST FACTS　The **area code** for Volos is 0421. The Pelion villages have several area codes: For Portaria and Makrinitsa, it's 0428; for Milies and Vizitsa, 0423; and for Zagora, 0426. There are a number of **banks** with ATMs on Plateia Riga Fereou, the main square in Volos. The **hospital** (☎ 0421/30-126 or 0421/27-531) is signposted on Odos Plastira at the east end of the harbor. The **police** (☎ 0421/23-652) and **tourist police** (☎ 0421/72-421) are at Odos 28 Octobriou 179. The **post office** is at Pavlou Mela 63. The **telephone office (OTE)** is at Eleftheriou Venizelou 22; as in many port towns, the OTE keeps extended hours from 6am to midnight. For **Internet access,** go to **Magic Café,** Argonafton 56 (☎ 0421/20-992), or **Diavlos Café,** Topali 14 (☎ 0421/25-363; fax 0421/33-692).

WHAT TO SEE & DO

The thing to do on Pelion is make haste slowly and enjoy the beauty of this unique region. From Volos, you can head around the peninsula in either a basically clockwise or counterclockwise fashion. Clockwise, this takes you from Volos through Ano Volos, Portaria, Makrinitsa, Hania, Zagora, Horefto, Tsangarada, Milopotamos, Miles, Vitizsa, Kato Lehonia, Agria, and back to Volos. Along the way, you can make lots of stops to see the villages and to take in the spectacular views of the Pagassitikos Gulf and Aegean. Following are suggestions of what to watch for on your visit.

Volos, Briefly

This bustling port town seems to be bursting at the seams. Almost every evening (especially on weekends), the harborside cafes and restaurants are packed and the street life is lively indeed. Volos has excellent *ouzo* and *tsipouro,* both served in many harborside ouzeries. Volos also has Greece's best collection of very rare—and very lovely—painted Hellenistic grave stelai, with haunting pastel images of the deceased. The stelai are at the **Volos Archaeological Museum,** on Odos Plastira at the east end of the harbor (☎ **0421/25-285**); hours are Tuesday through Sunday from 8:30am to 3pm, and admission is Dr500 ($1.45). The **Damtsas Museum,** Odos Metamorfoseos 3 (☎ **0421/31-701**), has a permanent collection of Greek art of the 19th and 20th centuries. It keeps flexible hours and charges Dr500 ($1.45) admission.

If you're very lucky, you may find someone in the cheek-by-jowl villages of **Anakassia** and **Ano Volos** who will show you the **Archontiko Kondos,** the 18th-century house with wall paintings by the primitive painter **Theophilos** (1873–1934), who was something of an eccentric. (The Theophilos House is officially open daily; admission is free.) Long after anyone else, Theophilos dressed in a *foustanella,* the old Greek national costume of a short pleated skirt, long woolen hose, and heavy wooden shoes with turned-up toes—the same costume that the guards outside the Greek Parliament in Athens still wear. If you don't find the vital villager with the key to the house Theophilos decorated, don't despair: You can see examples of his frescoes showing figures from myth and history at the Museum of Greek Folk Art in Athens (on Odos Kidathineon 17 in Plaka) and at the Theophilos Museum on Mytilene.

The village of **Portaria,** although only 14 kilometers (8.7 miles) out of seaside Volos, is 600 meters up on the mountainside. The central square has the fountains and plane trees that make Pelion villages so charming, as well as several cafes where you can sample the local wine and cheese. As you might expect, since this is the easiest Pelion village to reach from Volos, people stream here for dinner in the summer.

Still, Portaria usually has fewer visitors than nearby **Makrinitsa,** sometimes called the "balcony of Pelion." Handsome three-story houses flank the main square, which has fantastic sunset views back toward Volos. The **Diamantis cafe** in the main square and the **Church of Ayia Triada** on the hill above the square both have examples of Theophilos's work; the church of **Ayios Ioannis** on the main square is a typical, but especially handsome, Pelion church. There are several nice traditional settlement hotels in Makrinitsa (see "Where to Stay," below). The **Topalis Mansion Folklore and Folk Art Museum** (☎ **0428/99-505**) keeps irregular hours.

If you're here in summer, there's no reason to stop at **Hania,** which is currently being developed as a ski center for the slopes at **Agriolefkes.** In winter, information on ski conditions is available from the **Ski Center** (☎ **0421/96-417**).

Zagora, Pelion's largest village (population 3,000), has a splendid 18th-century church with a bell tower that looks almost Alpine, along with several buildings with exterior porches that were built to protect people not from the summer sun, but from the winter snow. If you're here in spring, you'll smell the apple blossoms; Zagora is Greece's largest producer of apples. Alas, the orchards were damaged by the severe forest fires in the summer of 2000. If you're here in summer, you might want to head south from Zagora to the fine **beaches** at **Ayios Ioannis** or **Milopotamos,** before continuing on to the villages of Milies and Vizitsa.

Milies has a splendid history. During the long years of the Turkish occupation, the school here (which you can still see today) helped to preserve Greek learning and culture. That tradition is continued today at Milies's small **folk museum,** on the second floor of the Town Hall (☎ 0423/86-204; fax 01/362-4118 in Athens). Photographs, tools, household objects, and mementos from the Greek War of Independence give a glimpse of life in old Milies. Several books on Milies and Pelion in both English and Greek, as well as posters and postcards, are usually for sale. The museum is generally open Tuesday through Sunday from 10am to 2pm, is sometimes open other days in the afternoon, and is often closed from the 10th to the 20th of March, June, and September; admission is free. While you're here, check to see if the narrow gauge steam railroad from Volos to Milies is back in service, as promised in 1998. If you want to spend the night, Milies has several traditional settlement inns.

Vizitsa, like Vathia in the distant Mani peninsula in the Peloponnese, was well on its way to becoming a ghost town when the GNTO declared the entire village (population 400) a national treasure and began to restore eight houses as ✪ **small inns** (see "Where to Stay," below). There's also one luxury hotel, the modestly named **Glorious Peleys Luxury Castle** (see below). The village offers several simple tavernas as well as the inevitable souvenir stands. The GNTO office has a small display of local items and sometimes has local weavings for sale.

It's hard not to have mixed feelings about what the GNTO has done in Vizitsa, which includes organizing **folk festivals** where traditional crafts are demonstrated. On the one hand, it's very pleasant to stay here and know that you are helping to revitalize a lovely area. On the other hand, it's hard to not worry that Vizitsa—and other Pelion villages—may end up being a kind of Greek Colonial Williamsburg: an outdoor museum of living history rather than true living communities.

BEACHES

Whereas the inland villages are striving to maintain their character, tourist-oriented hamlets are springing up along Pelion's coastline. The best beaches on Pelion are at the resort of **Platanias** and the smaller seaside hamlet of **Mylopotamos,** which shows signs of becoming a serious resort town. If you have a car and are driving around Pelion, you will also see dirt roads leading down to a number of secluded and pleasant beaches.

WHERE TO STAY
MAKRINITSA

If you want to stay in one of Makrinitsa's traditional settlement guest houses, it's a good idea to make a reservation well in advance through one of the hotels or the main office (☎ 0421/99-250). Reservations are particularly necessary at Easter and in early May, popular times here. Doubles go for about Dr18,000 to Dr35,000 ($52 to $100). All of these inns are decorated with local weavings and some old furnishings. The Sisilianou overlooks the main square, while the others are off the square. It should be said that friends who visit Pelion every year think that the service at these guest houses has fallen off sharply in the last few years. You should also keep in mind that Greek families and friends often take over virtually all the rooms in an inn. This usually makes for a very merry (and not very quiet) scene.

You'll probably have to take potluck with which inn you are assigned to, but if you arrive early and case the possibilities, you can lodge a specific request at the local GNTO office (☎ 0423/86-373). The guest houses in Makrinitsa are: the 12-unit **Archontiko Diomidi** (☎ 0428/99-430; fax 0428/99-114), the nine-unit **Archontiko Karamarli** (☎ 0428/99-570; fax 0428/99-779), the seven-unit **Archontiko**

Mousli (☎ **0428/99-228** or 0428/99-250; fax 0428/99-228), the five-unit **Archon-tiko Pandora** (☎ **0428/99-404;** fax 0428/90-113), the seven-unit **Archontiko Repana** (☎ **0428/99-548;** fax 0428/99-548), the seven-unit **Archontiko Sisilianou** (☎ **0428/99-556**), the five-unit **Archontiko Theofilos** (☎ **0428/99-435**), and the **Archontiko Xiradaki** (☎ **0428/99-250**).

MILIES

The traditional guest house here is the **Archontiko Filippidi** (☎ 0423/86-714), which has eight units. There are also two other small hotels in Milies in nicely restored traditional buildings: the former train station, which is now the eight-unit **Palios Stathmos** (☎ **0423/86-425**), reached by a stone path; and the seven-unit **Spiti Evangelinaki** (☎ **0423/86-714**).

VIZITSA

The Greek National Tourist Office has restored eight houses as traditional guest houses in Vizitsa. You can get information (and make reservations) through the **GNTO** at ☎ **0423/86-373.** You can also inquire about reservations at the GNTO offices in Athens and Thessaloniki, or try to make reservations directly with the one of the hotels. They include the **Archontiko Mihopoulou** (☎ **0423/86-860**), which has nine units, and the **Archontiko Blana** (☎ **0423/86-840;** fax 0421/43-614), which has four units.

In addition to the GNTO guest houses in Vizitsa, there are several other small hotels. The **Archontiko Karagianopoulou** (☎ **0423/86-717**) has six units, the **Archontiko Vafeladi** (☎ **0423/86-765;** fax 0423/86-045) has eight units, and the **Archontiko Kontou** (☎ **0423/86-793;** fax 01/806-5341) has 10 especially appealing units.

The 11-unit **Glorious Peleys Luxury Castle** (☎ **0423/88-671;** fax 0423/86-661) is a serious (some would say pretentious) boutique hotel, charging around Dr52,000 ($150), with breakfast compulsory at Dr4,000 ($11). The restored 18th-century kastro (castle) is furnished with antiques, and has both a library and sauna.

WHERE TO DINE

Although Pelion attracts a lot of Greek tourists who come back year after year, restaurants here, although perfectly pleasant, are not adventurous. Some popular local dishes include *kouneli stifado* (rabbit stew with little onions and cinnamon), various bean dishes, and *tirosomi* (cheesebread). In every village, you'll find the local restaurants on the main square; in our experience, there's no real point in searching down side streets for other places. What you see is what you get here—and it's very pleasant to sit under the plane trees on the main plateia in one of the Pelion villages.

We've had good meals at or heard good things about the **Galini,** on the main square in Makrinitsa; the **Palios Stathmos** (old railroad station), in Milies; and the **Georgaras** and **Balkonaki,** in Vizitsa. Expect to pay about Dr3,500 to Dr7,000 ($10 to $20) for wine and a simple meal.

12 The Sporades

by John S. Bowman

Looking to experience some Greek islands that no one else in your crowd knows about? Try the Sporades ("Scattered" Islands), verdant islands with fragrant pine trees growing down to the edge of golden sand beaches. The Sporades would seem to have always been natural magnets for tourists, but lacking major archaeological remains and historical associations, for a long time did not compete with other parts of Greece.

The Sporades are no longer quite the natural retreats they once were. Skiathos and Skopelos are the most popular islands, with excellent beaches, fine restaurants, fancy hotels, and an international (heavily British) following. **Skiathos** is among the most expensive islands in Greece and becomes horrendously crowded in high season, but in spring and fall remains a lovely and pleasant place. It's still worth a visit, especially by those interested in a beach vacation, good food, and active nightlife. **Skopelos** is nearly as expensive as Skiathos in the high season, but isn't quite as sophisticated. Its beaches are fewer and less impressive, but Skopelos town is among the most beautiful ports in Greece, and the island offers some pleasant excursions. More remote **Skyros** seems hardly a part of the group, especially as its landscape and architecture are more Cycladic. But it has a few excellent beaches, as well as a colorful local culture, and it remains a good destination for those who want to get away from the crowds.

STRATEGIES FOR SEEING THE ISLANDS If you have only 1 to 3 days, you had better settle on just one of the Sporades. If you have a bit more time, you will be able to get a ship directly (from various ports, identified below for each island) to any of them—and a plane in the case of Skiathos and Skyros; if time is a factor, we strongly advise flying to Skiathos or Skyros. If you have more time, you can continue around the islands via hydrofoils (known as "Flying Dolphins") or ferryboats. (Note, however, that the frequency of all connections is cut back considerably from September through May.)

1 Skiathos

108km (58 nautical miles) from Ayios Konstandinos, which is 166km (103 miles) from Athens

Skiathos remained isolated and agrarian until the early 1970s. Today it's one of the most cosmopolitan and attractive islands in Greece, and this rapid change has created a few disturbing ripples. Although the island's inhabitants are eager to please, in high season they can be overextended, inevitably relying on imported help, many from Athens, who often don't care much about providing any local flavor. Meanwhile, the sheer numbers of foreigners means that some show little concern for the island's indigenous character. This is a "package tour" island, and Skiathos town at high season can have the atmosphere of a shopping mall. Yet Skiathos town, sometimes called Hora, does have attractive elements, and at its best seems fairly sophisticated, with the handsome Bourtzi fortress on its harbor, elegant shops, excellent restaurants, and a flashy nightlife. And if you want a break from all this, take one of the horse-drawn carriages around town.

The rest of the island retains much of its natural allure. For most visitors, in fact, the main attractions are the purity of the water and the lovely fine-sand beaches. The island boasts more than 60 beaches, the most famous of which, **Koukounaries,** is considered one of the very best in Greece. If you relish sun, sand, sea, and crowds, you'll love it.

If possible, visit Skiathos before or after July 10 to September 10, when the tourist crush is at its worst and the island's population of under 5,000 swells to over 50,000. If you must visit during high season, reserve a room well ahead of time and be prepared for the crush.

ESSENTIALS

GETTING THERE   **By Plane**   **Olympic Airways** has service daily (twice daily in April and May, five times daily June through September) from Athens; contact the Athens office (☎ **01/966-6666**) for information and reservations. At this time, Olympic does not maintain an office in Skiathos town, but can be reached at the nearby airport (☎ **0427/22-200**). Public bus service to the airport is so infrequent that everyone takes a taxi; expect to pay about Dr1,500 ($4.30), depending on your destination.

By Boat   Skiathos can be reached by either ferryboat (3 hrs.) or hydrofoil (1½ hrs.) from Volos or Ayios Konstandinos. (Ayios Konstandinos is a 3-hour bus ride from Athens.) From Kimi on Evvia, there is also hydrofoil service (50 mins.) and ferryboat service (4 hrs.). In high season, there are frequent hydrofoils daily from Volos and from Ayios Konstandinos, as well as service from Thessaloniki (3 hrs.). There are also the hydrofoils linking Skiathos to Skopelos (30 to 45 mins.), Alonissos (60 to 75 mins.), and Skyros (2⅓ hrs.).

In Athens, **Alkyon Travel,** Odos Akademias 97, near Kanigos Square (☎ **01/ 384-3220**), can arrange bus transportation from Athens to Ayios Konstandinos as well as hydrofoil or ferry tickets. The 3-hour bus ride costs about Dr3,500 ($10) one-way.

For hydrofoil schedules and information, contact the **Minoan Flying Dolphins** in Athens (☎ **01/428-0001;** fax 01/428-0001; e-mail: sales@mfd.gr). For ferryboat information, contact the **Minoan Lines** in Athens (☎ **01/428-0001**). Ferry tickets can be purchased at travel agents in Athens or on the islands.

VISITOR INFORMATION   The town maintains an **information booth** at the western corner of the harbor; in summer at least, it's open daily from about 9am to 8pm. Meanwhile, private travel agencies abound and can help with most all of your requests. We highly recommend **Mare Nostrum Holidays,** Odos Papadiamandis 21 (☎ **0427/21-463;** fax 0427/21-793). It books villas, hotels, and rooms; sells tickets to many around-the-island, hydrofoil, and beach caïque (skiff) trips; books Olympic flights; exchanges currency; and changes traveler's checks without commission. Katerina Michail-Craig, the charming managing director, and her staff speak excellent English, are exceedingly well informed, and have lots of tips on everything from beaches to restaurants. The office is open daily from 8am to 10pm.

GETTING AROUND   By Bus   Skiathos has public bus service along the south coast of the island from the bus station on the harbor to Koukounaries Dr300 (90¢), with stops at the beaches in between. A conductor will ask for your destination and assess the fare after the bus is in progress. Buses run at least six times daily April through November; every hour from 9am to 9pm May through October; every half hour from 8:30am to 10pm June through September; and every 20 minutes from 8:30am to 2:30pm and 3:30pm to midnight July through August.

By Car & Moped   Reliable car and moped agencies, all located on the paralia, include **Avis** (☎ **0427/21-458;** fax 0427/23-289; e-mail: avis.skiathos@skiathosinfo. com), run by the friendly Yannis Theofanidis; **Aivalioti's Rent-A-Car** (☎ **0427/ 21-246**); and **Creator** (☎ **0427/22-385**). In high season, expect to pay Dr20,000 to Dr25,000 ($58 to $72) for a car. Mopeds start at about Dr5,000 ($14) per day.

By Boat   The north coast beaches, adjacent islands, and historic Kastro are most easily reached by caïque; these smaller vessels, which post their beach and island tour schedules on signs, sail frequently from the fishing harbor west of the Bourtzi fortress. An around-the-island tour that includes stops at Lalaria Beach and Kastro will cost about Dr6,000 ($17).

The Minoan Flying Dolphins agent, **Skiathos Holidays,** on the paralia, is open from 7am to 9:30pm; in high season there are as many as eight high-speed hydrofoils daily to Skopelos and Alonissos. There are also daily excursions to Skyros in high season. Call ☎ **0427/22-018** for up-to-date schedules. Note that even if you have a ticket, you must appear at the agent's ticket office at least 30 minutes before the scheduled sailing to get your ticket confirmed and seat assigned. **Vasilis Nikolaou** (☎ **0427/22-209**), the travel agent at the corner of the paralia and Odos Papadiamandis, sells tickets for the ferryboats to the other islands.

FAST FACTS   The official **American Express** agent is Mare Nostrum Holidays, Odos Papadiamandis 21 (☎ **0427/21-463;** fax 0427/21-793); open daily from 8am to 10pm. There are many banks in town, such as the **National Bank of Greece,** Odos Papadiamandis, open Monday through Friday from 8am to 2pm and 7 to 9pm, Sunday from 9am to noon. The **hospital** (☎ **0427/22-040**) is on the coast road at the far west edge of town. For **Internet access,** try Internet Zone Café, Odos Evangelistrias 28 (e-mail: zonecafe@hotmail.com), or Internet Center, Odos Miauli 13 (off Odos Evangelistrias). Hopefully, at least one will still be in operation at the time of your visit.

A self-service **laundry** is at Odos Georgios Panora 14, 85 meters up Odos Papadiamandis, opposite the National Bank (☎ **0427/22-341**); or you can drop off a load at the Snow White Laundry one street up from the paralia, behind the Credit Bank (☎ **0427/24-256**); both are open daily from about 8am to 2pm and 5 to 11pm. The **police station** (☎ **0427/21-111**) is about 250 meters from the harbor on Odos Papadiamandis, on the left. The **tourist police** booth is about 15 meters further along on the right. The **post office** (☎ **0427/22-011**) is on Odos Papadiamandis, away from the harbor about 160 meters and on the right; open Monday through Friday from 7:30am to 2pm. The **telephone office (OTE)** is on Odos Papadiamandis, on the right, some 30 meters beyond the post office; open Monday through Friday from 7:30am to 10pm, Saturday and Sunday from 9am to 2pm and 5 to 10pm (☎ **0427/ 22-135**).

WHAT TO SEE & DO

Skiathos is a relatively modern town, built in 1930 on two low-lying hills, then reconstructed after heavy German bombardment during World War II. The handsome

The Sporades

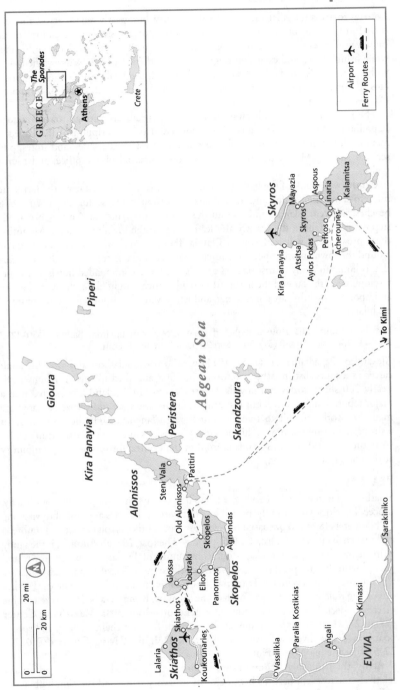

Airport ✈
Ferry Routes ----

GREECE
The Sporades
Athens
Crete

Skyros
Mayazia
Aspous
Kalamitsa
Skyros
Linaria
Pefkos
Acherounes
Atsitsa
Ayios Fokas
Kira Panayia

Piperi

Aegean Sea

Gioura

Skandzoura

To Kimi

Peristera
Kira Panayia
Steni Vala
Patitiri
Alonissos
Old Alonissos

Sarakiniko

Skopelos
Agnondas
Glossa
Loutraki
Elios
Panormos
Skopelos

Skiathos
Lalaria
Koukounaries

Vassilikia
Paralia Kostikias
Angali
Kimassi
EVVIA

20 mi
20 km

439

Bourtzi fortress (originally from the 13th century, but greatly rebuilt across the centuries) jutting out into the middle of the harbor is on an islet connected by a broad causeway. Ferries and hydrofoils stop at the port on the right (east) of the fortress, while fishing boats and excursion caïques dock on the left (west). Whitewashed villas with red-tile roofs line both sides of the harbor, with the small church of **Ayios Nikolaos** dominating the hill on the east side and the larger church of **Trion Ierarchon** ("Three Archbishops") on the west side.

The main street that leads away from the harbor and up through town is named **Papadiamandis,** after the island's best-known son (see description of the Papadiamandis House, below). Here you'll find numerous restaurants, cafes, and stores, plus services such as Mare Nostrum Holidays, post office, telephone office, and tourist police.

On the west flank of the harbor (the left side as you disembark from the ferry) are numerous outdoor cafes and restaurants, excursion caïques (for the north coast beaches, adjacent islands, and around-the-island tours), and, at the far corner, the stepped ramp (above the Oasis Café) leading up to the town's next level. Mounting these broad steps will lead you to **Plateia Trion Ierarchon,** a stone-paved square around the town's most important church. The eastern flank, technically the New Paralia, is home to many tourist services as well as a few recommended hotels and many restaurants; at the far end the harborfront road branches right along the yacht harbor, an important nightlife area in summer, and left toward the airport and points of interest inland.

The Papadiamandis House. Right off main street, 50m up from harbor. ☎ **0427/ 23-843.** Admission Dr350 ($1). Tues–Sun 9:30am–1pm and 5–8pm.

Alexandros Papadiamandis (1851–1911) was born on Skiathos, and after his adult career as a journalist in Athens, returned in 1908 and died in this very house. His nearly 200 short stories and novellas, mostly about Greek island life, assured him a major reputation in Greece, but his rather idiosyncratic style and vernacular language made his work difficult to translate into foreign languages. His house is more of a shrine than a museum, with his personal possessions and tools of his writing trade. (A statue of Papadiamandis stands in front of the Bourtzi fortress on the promontory at the corner of the harbor.)

BEACHES

Skiathos is famous for its beaches, and we'll cover the most important ones briefly, proceeding clockwise from the port. The most popular beaches are west of town along 12 kilometers (8 miles) of coastal highway. At most of them, you can rent an umbrella and two chairs for about Dr2,000 ($6) per day. The first, **Megali Ammos,** is the sandy strip below the popular package-tour community of Ftelia; so close to town and packed with the groups, it probably won't appeal to most. **Vassilias** and **Achladias** are also crowded and developed; **Tzanerias** and **Nostos** are slight improvements. Further out on the Kalamaki peninsula, south of the highway, **Kanapitsa** begins to excite some interest, especially among those fond of water sports; **Kanapitsa Water-Sport Center** (☎ **0427/21-298**) has water and jet skis, windsurfing, air chairs, sailing, and speedboat hire. Scuba divers will want to stop at the **Dolphin Diving Center** (☎ **0427/ 22-520**) at the big Nostos Hotel.

Across the peninsula, **Vromolimnos** ("Dirty Lake") is fairly attractive and usually relatively uncrowded, perhaps because of its unsavory name and the cloudy (but not polluted) water from which it comes; it offers water-skiing and windsurfing. **Koulos** and **Ayia Paraskevi** are fairly well regarded. **Platanias,** the next major beach, is usually uncrowded, perhaps because the big resort hotels here have their own pools and sundecks. Past the next headland, **Troulos** is one of the prettiest because of its relative isolation, crescent shape, and the islets that guard the small bay. Nearby, too, is the **Victoria Leisure Center** (☎ 0427/49-467), which has rooms to rent, a pool, shops, and two tennis courts.

The last bus stop is at the much ballyhooed **Koukounaries** (16km/10 miles from Skiathos town). The bus chugs uphill past the Pallas Hotel luxury resort, then descends and winds alongside the inland waterway, Lake Strofilias, stopping at the edge of a fragrant pine forest. *Koukounaries* means "pine cones" in Greek, and behind this grove of trees is a half-mile-long stretch of fine gold sand in a half-moon–shaped cove. Tucked into the evergreen fold are some changing rooms, a small snack bar, and the concessionaires for beach chairs, umbrellas, and windsurfers. The beach can be extremely crowded but with an easy mix of families, singles, and topless sunbathers. On the far west side of the cove is the former Xenia Hotel; out of commission in 2000, it is supposed to reopen under new ownership. (There are many lodgings in the area, but because of the intense mosquito activity and ticky-tacky construction, we prefer to stay back in town or along the coast road.)

Ayia Eleni, a short but scenic walk from the Koukounaries bus stop (the end of the line) west across the tip of the island, is a broad cove popular for windsurfing, as the wind is a bit rougher than at the south coast beaches but not nearly as gusty as at the north. Across the peninsula behind the former Xenia Hotel, 15 to 20 minutes of fairly steep grade from the Koukounaries bus stop, is **Banana Beach** (sometimes called Krassa). It's slightly less crowded than Koukounaries, but with the same sand and pine trees. There's a snack bar or two, plus chairs, umbrellas, windsurfers, and jet skis for rent. One stretch of Banana Beach is the island's most fashionable nude beach.

Limonki Xerxes, also called Mandraki, north across the tip of the island, a 20-minute walk up the path opposite the Lake Strofilias bus stop, is a cove where Xerxes brought in 10 *triremes* (galleys) to conquer the Hellenic fleet moored at Skiathos during the Persian Wars. It's a pristine and relatively secluded beach for those who crave a quiet spot. **Elia,** east across the little peninsula, is also quite nice. Both beaches have small refreshment kiosks.

Proceeding along the northeast coast from Mandraki, you arrive at **Megalos Aselinos,** a windy beach where free camping has taken root. It is linked to the southern coastal highway via the road that leads to the Kounistria monastery (see below); you must continue north when the main road forks off to the right toward the monastery. There's also an official campsite and a fairly good taverna. **Mikros Aselinos,** further east, is smaller and quieter, and you can reach it via a dirt road that leads off to the left just before the monastery.

Skiathos's north coast is much more rugged and scenically pure, with steep cliffs, pine forests, rocky hills, and caves. Most of these beaches are accessible only by boat, but one definitely rewards those willing to make the trip: ✪ **Lalaria,** on the island's northern tip, is regarded as one of the most picturesque beaches in Greece. One of its unique qualities is the **Tripia Petra,** perforated rock cliffs that jut out into the sea on both sides of the cove. These have been worn through by the wind and the waves to form perfect archways. You can lie on the gleaming white pebbles and admire the neon-blue Aegean and cloudless sky through their rounded openings. The water at Lalaria is an especially vivid shade of aquamarine because of the highly reflective white pebbles and marble and limestone slabs, which coat the sea bottom. The swimming here is excellent, but the undertow can be quite strong; inexperienced swimmers should not venture very far. There are several naturally carved caves in the cliff wall that lines the beach, providing privacy or shade for those who have had too much sun exposure. Lalaria is reached by caïque excursions from the port; the fare is about

Dr6,000 ($17) for an around-the-island trip, which usually includes a stop for lunch (not included in the fare) at one of the other beaches along the northwest coast.

Three of the island's most spectacular grottoes—**Skotini, Glazia,** and **Halkini**—are just east of Lalaria. Spilia Skotini is particularly impressive, a fantastic 20-foot-tall sea cave reached through a narrow crevice, just wide enough for caïques to squeeze through, in the cliff wall. Seagulls drift above you in the cave's cool darkness, while below, fish swim down in the 30-foot subsurface portion. Erosion has created spectacular scenery and many sandy coves along the north and east coasts, though none are as beautiful or well sheltered from the meltemi as Lalaria beach.

THE KASTRO & THE MONASTERIES

For those preferring other pursuits, there is at least one excursion that should appeal: the **Kastro,** the old fortress capital, located on the northernmost point of the island, east of Lalaria beach. Kastro was built in a remote and spectacular site in the 16th century, when the island was overrun by the Turks. It was abandoned shortly after the War of Independence, when such fortifications were no longer necessary. Once joined to firm ground by a drawbridge, it can now be reached by cement stairs. The remains of more than 300 houses and 22 churches have mostly fallen to the sea, but three of the churches, with porcelain plates imbedded in their worn stucco facades, still stand, and the original frescoes of one are still visible. From this citadel prospect there are excellent views to the **Kastronisia** islet below and the sparkling Aegean. Kastro can be reached by excursion caïque, by mule or donkey tour (available through most travel agencies), or by car via the road that leads northeast out of town, passing the turnoff to the Moni Evangelistrias (see below), and continuing on to the end near the church of Panayia Kardasi; from here it is a mildly demanding 2-kilometer (1.2-mile) walk.

The **Moni Evangelistrias** is probably the more rewarding of the two monasteries that draw many visitors. There are occasional public buses, but with your own vehicle it can be easily visited in not much more than an hour from Skiathos town; this will also allow you to stop and admire the views. Take the road out of the northeast end and pass by the turnoff to the airport; after less than a kilometer take the sharp right turnoff (signed) and climb about 3 kilometers (1.9 miles) to the monastery. Dating from the late 18th century, it has been completely (but authentically) restored; its architecture, icons, and wood carvings reward even those who do not know of its intimate involvement with the history of the island.

The other monastery, **Panayia Kounistria,** is approached from the coastal highway along the beaches (described above); just before Troulos Beach, take the right branch of the road (signed ASELINOS) and climb about 4 kilometers (2.5 miles) to the monastery, a pretty 17th-century structure containing some fine icons (although its most important icon is now displayed in the Tris Ierarches Church in Skiathos town). Nothing spectacular, but a satisfying excursion. Horseback enthusiasts should note that the **Pinewood Horse Riding Club** is also located on the road to this monastery.

SHOPPING

Skiathos town has no shortage of shops, many offering the standard wares but some offering distinctive items. The highlight for Greek crafts and folk art is **Archipelago** (☎ 0427/22-163), adjacent to the Papadiamandis House; it offers a world-class assemblage of exquisite objects of art and folklore, both old and new, including textiles, jewelry, and sculpture. **Galerie Varsakis** (☎ 0427/22-255), on Trion Ierarchon Square above the fishing port, also has a virtually museum-quality collection of folk antiques, embroidered bags and linens, rugs from around the world, and other collectibles. Less stylish but full of curiosities is the **Gallery Seraina** (☎ 0427/22-0390), at the first junction of Odos Papadiamandis (opposite the alleyway to the Papadia-mandis House); it has a goodly selection of ceramic plates, jewelry, some textiles, and unusual glass lampshades.

WHERE TO STAY

Between July 1 and September 15, it can be literally impossible to find accommoda-tions. Try calling ahead from Athens to book a room or, better still, book your accom-modations before you leave home. Note that most of the "luxury" hotels were thrown up quickly some years ago, and some have since been managed and maintained poorly—so if you plan an extended stay at a beach resort, we recommend you first check into one of the hotels in town and then look over the possibilities before you commit to an extended rental.

If you crave the restaurant/shopping/nightlife scene, or you've arrived without reser-vations at one of the resort communities, try setting up base in **Skiathos town.** From here, you can take public buses to the beaches on the south coast or go on caïque excursions to the spectacular north coast or other islands. Then again, many families prefer to stay in two- to four-bedroom villas outside of town or at hotels overlooking a beach, with only an occasional foray into town.

One of the most pleasant parts of Skiathos town is the quiet neighborhood on the hill above the bay at the western end of the port. Numerous **private rooms** to let can be found on and above the winding stairs/street. Take a walk and look for the signs, or ask a passerby or neighborhood merchant. All over the hillside above the eastern harbor are several unlicensed "hotels," basically rooms to rent. Ask passersby, and you'll be surprised at which buildings turn out to be lodgings.

By the way, the in-town hotels (Alkyon excepted) cannot provide adjacent parking, but there are possibilities at the far eastern edge of the harbor.

IN & AROUND SKIATHOS TOWN

In addition to the following options, consider the moderately priced **Hotel Athos,** on the "ring road" that skirts above Skiathos town (☎ and fax **0427/22-4777**), which offers ready access to town without the bustle; and the **Hotel Meltemi,** on the paralia (☎ **0427/22-493;** fax 0427/21-294), a comfortable, modern place on the east side of the harbor (but avoid the front units, which can be noisy). An inexpensive choice is the 30-unit **Hotel Bourtzi,** Odos Moraitou 8 (☎ **0427/22-694;** fax 0427/23-242), where doubles go for Dr16,000 ($46). Ask for a unit that faces the back garden.

✪ **Hotel Alkyon.** At far eastern end of paralia, 37002 Skiathos. ☎ **0427/22-981.** Fax 0427/21-643. 85 units. A/C MINIBAR TEL. Dr23,000 ($66) double. Rates include buffet breakfast. AE, EC, MC, V. Parking in adjacent area.

This is probably the favored place for those who want it all—to be near the harbor of Skiathos town, to enjoy some quiet seclusion, and to return to a hotel with some crea-ture comforts. It's not glitzy or luxurious, but modern and subdued; its rooms are of medium size (and offer taped music) and bathrooms are modern. On site is a small swimming pool with an adjacent bar. Best of all, it's a great place for those who look forward to a shady retreat after time in the sun or at the town's activities.

Hotel Australia. Parados Evangelistrias, 37002 Skiathos. ☎ **0427/22-488.** 16 units. Dr14,000 ($40) double; Dr16,000 ($46) studio with kitchen. No credit cards. Turn right off Odos Papadiamandis at the post office, then take the first left.

If you've come to Skiathos expecting some style, this plain, clean, quiet hotel is not for you. Run by a couple who lived in Australia and speak English quite well, the rooms are sparsely furnished but comfortable, with small balconies; bathrooms are small but functional, and guests can share a fridge in the hallway. Definitely for budget travelers.

Hotel Morfo. Odos Anainiou 23, 37002 Skiathos. ☎ **0427/21-737.** Fax 0427/23-222. 17 units. TEL. Dr17,000 ($49) double. AE, EC, MC, V.

Looking for a slightly "atmospheric" offbeat hotel? Turn right off the main street opposite the National Bank, then left at the plane tree (signed), and find this attractive hotel on your left on a quiet back street in the center of town. You enter through a small garden into a festively decorated lobby. The rooms are comfortable and tastefully decorated.

✪ **Hotel Orsa.** Plakes, 37002 Skiathos. ☎ **0427/22-430.** Fax 0427/21-952. E-mail: helio@n-skiathos.gr. 17 units. TEL. Dr25,000 ($72) double. Rates include breakfast. No credit cards.

One of the most charming small hotels in town is on the western promontory beyond the fishing harbor. To get here, walk down the port west past the fish stalls and Jimmy's Bar, proceed up two flights of steps, and watch for a recessed courtyard on the left, with handsome wrought-iron details. Rooms are standard in size but tastefully decorated; most have windows or balconies overlooking the harbor and the islands beyond. A lovely garden terrace is a perfect place for a tranquil breakfast. Contact Heliotropio Travel on the east end of the harbor (☎ **0427/22-430;** fax 0427/21-952; e-mail: helio@n.skiathos.gr) for booking.

ON THE BEACH

Atrium Hotel. Platanias (some 8km/5 miles along the coast road southeast of Skiathos town), 37002 Skiathos. ☎ **0427/49-345.** Fax 0427/49-444. 75 units. A/C TEL. Dr40,000 ($115) double. Dr54,000 ($155) for family of four. Rates include buffet breakfast. EC, MC, V. Parking on grounds.

This is probably the class act of Skiathos when it comes to hotels. Its location (on a pine-clad slope overlooking the sea) plus its various amenities (billiard room, fitness room, water-sports gear) make it a most pleasant place to vacation. A sandy beach is some 100 meters below; a beautiful Olympic-size pool sits on a plaza high above the Aegean. The rooms are only fair-sized, but compensate with balconies or terraces that offer views over the sea; bathrooms are fully appointed. The hotel has a bar and a restaurant that serves up decent meals, outdoors if you like. We have always found the desk personnel and staff most courteous and helpful, but yes, it is expected that guests observe a certain level of style.

✪ **Troulos Bay Hotel.** Troulos (9km/6 miles along the coast road southeast of Skiathos, down from the Alpha Supermarket), 37002 Skiathos. ☎ **0427/49-390.** Fax 0427/49-218. E-mail: troulosbay@skt.forthnet.gr. 43 units. TEL. Dr25,000 ($72) double. MC, V. Parking on grounds.

Though it's not exactly luxurious, this is our first choice among beach hotels. It's set on handsomely landscaped grounds on one of the south coast's prettiest little beaches. Like most of Skiathos's hotels, it's used mostly by groups, but individual rooms are often available. The restaurant serves good food at reasonable prices, and the staff is refreshingly attentive and truly helpful. The bedrooms are large, attractive, and comfortably furnished; most have a balcony overlooking the beach with the lovely wooded islets beyond.

WHERE TO DINE

As is the case with most of Greece's overdeveloped tourist resorts, there's a plethora of cafes, fast-food stands, and overpriced restaurants, but there are also plenty of good and even excellent eateries in Skiathos town. Some of the more well-regarded restaurants are above the west end of the harbor, approaching and beyond Trion Ierarchon church.

EXPENSIVE

✪ **Asprolithos.** Odos Mavroyiali and Odos Korai (up Odos Papadiamandis a block past the high school, then turn right). ☎ **0427/21-016.** Reservations recommended. Main courses Dr1,600–Dr5,500 ($4.60–$16). EC, MC, V. Daily 6pm–midnight. Closed late Oct to mid-Mar. GREEK/INTERNATIONAL.

An elegant ambiance and friendly, attentive service combined with superb meals of light, updated taverna fare make this one of our favorites on Skiathos. You can get a classic moussaka here if you want to play it safe, or try specialties like artichokes and prawns smothered in cheese. The excellent snapper baked in wine with wild greens is served with thick french fries that have obviously never seen a freezer. The main dining room is dominated by a handsome stone fireplace, and there are also tables outside where you can catch the breeze.

Le Bistrot. Odos Martinou (high above western end of harbor). ☎ **0427/21-627.** Reservations recommended. Main courses Dr2,000–Dr4,500 ($6–$13). EC, MC, V. Daily 7pm–1am. CONTINENTAL/CHINESE.

This intimate restaurant and its twin (which functions as a bar), across the street, are lovely spaces overlooking the water. The full-course meals are beautifully prepared from their own stocks and sauces and should be savored slowly, so as to leave room for the delicious desserts. And at least during the year 2000, Le Bistrot also offered a Chinese menu prepared by a special Asian chef.

✪ **The Windmill Restaurant.** Located on peak east of Ayios Nikolaos church. ☎ **0427/24-550.** www.skiathosinfo.com. Reservations strongly recommended. Dr2,600–Dr5,000 ($8–$14). EC, MC, V. Daily 7–11pm. INTERNATIONAL.

The town's most special dining experience is at what is literally an old windmill, visible from the paralia. (There are several ways to approach it, but the signed one begins on the street between the back of the Akti and the San Remo hotels at the eastern end of the harbor.) It is quite a climb, but well worth it. You couldn't ask for a more romantic setting than one of the terraces, where you can enjoy the sunset with your meal. From year to year the menu changes, but many of the main courses are distinctive, even exotic. The desserts, too, are unusual, and there are nearly two dozen wines to choose from, including the best from Greece.

MODERATE

Carnayio Taverna. Paralia. ☎ **0427/22-868.** Main courses Dr1,400–Dr3,900 ($4–$11). AE, V. Daily 8pm–1am. TAVERNA/SEAFOOD.

One of the better waterfront tavernas is next to the Hotel Alkyon. Favorites over the years have been the fish soup, lamb *youvetsi,* and grilled fish. The garden setting is still special, and if you're here late enough, you might be lucky to see a real round of dancing waiters and diners.

Taverna Limanakia. Paralia (at far eastern end, past Hotel Alkyon). ☎ **0427/22-835.** Main courses Dr1,400–Dr5,800 ($4–$17). MC. Daily 6pm–midnight. TAVERNA/SEAFOOD.

In the style of its next-door neighbor Carnayio, the Limanakia serves some of the best taverna and seafood dishes on the waterfront. We vacillate about which of the two we prefer, but we've always come away feeling satisfied after a meal at this reliable eatery.

Taverna Mesoyia. Odos Grigoriou (follow the signs behind Trion Ierarchon, high above western end of the harbor). ☎ **0427/21-440.** Main courses Dr1,600–Dr3,200 ($4.60–$9). No credit cards. Daily 7pm–midnight. TAVERNA.

You'll have to exert yourself a bit to find some of the best authentic traditional food in town, as this little taverna is in the midst of the town's most labyrinthine neighborhood, above the western end of the harbor, but there are signs once you approach it. Try an appetizer such as the fried zucchini balls, enjoy the evening specials, or go for fresh fish in season. (As all Greek restaurants are supposed to, this one discloses when something is frozen—as some fish must be at certain times of the year, when it's illegal to catch.) You'll feel like you're at an old-fashioned neighborhood bistro, not a large tourist attraction.

INEXPENSIVE

Kabourelia Ouzeri. Paralia (on western stretch of harbor). ☎ **0427/21-112.** Main courses Dr1,000–Dr3,200 ($2.90–$9). AE, EC, MC, V. Daily 10am–1am. GREEK.

Although it bills itself as an ouzeri—for drinks and snacks—this is really your standard taverna, and one of the most authentic eateries in town. You can have the ouzo and octopus (which you can see drying on the front line!) combo for Dr1,600 ($4.60), or even make a meal of the rich supply of cheese pies, fried feta, olives, and other piquant mezedes.

SKIATHOS AFTER DARK

The **Aegean Festival** presents nightly performances of ancient Greek tragedies and comedies, traditional music and dance, modern dance and theater, and visiting international troupes. Festival events take place from late June to early October in the outdoor theater at the **Bourtzi Cultural Center,** on the promontory on the harbor. (The center itself, open daily from 10am to 2pm and 5:30 to 10pm, hosts art exhibits in its interior.) Performances begin at 9:30pm and usually cost Dr5,000 ($14); call ☎ **0427/23-717** for information.

Skiathos town has a lively nightlife scene, more concentrated on each end of the port, but many prefer to pass the evening with a **volta** (stroll) along the harbor or around and above the Plateia Trion Ierarchon. In fact, we feel the best-kept secret of Skiathos town is the **little outdoor cafe** at the tip of the promontory with the Bourtzi fortress, a 3-minute stroll from the harbor. Removed from the glitter of the town, you can sit and enjoy a (cheap) drink in the cool of the evening and watch the ships come and go—this is the Aegean lifestyle at its best.

The main concentration of **nightclubs** is in the warren of streets west of Papadiamandis (left as you come up from the harbor). On the street opposite the post office is the **Blue Chips Club.** Further along Papadiamandis, another turn to the left leads to the **Borzoi,** which claims to be the oldest club on the island; you may want to check it out several times during the evening, as it generally gets livelier toward midnight. Continue past it to find the **Banana Bar,** for "surprising dance music," on the right; then the **Admiral Benbow Club,** which offers something more soulful. Across from the Benbow Club is the flashy **Spartacus.** At the next intersection south you'll find **Kirki,** which offers jazz and blues.

Back across Odos Papadiamandis, just before the post office, along Parados Evangelistrias you can find **Adagio,** a gay establishment that plays classical music and Greek ballads at volumes low enough for conversation. Wander back down the main street to find **Kentavros Bar,** on the left beyond the Papadiamandis House, which plays classic rock and jazz.

On the far west end of the harbor, if you want videos with your drinks, try the **Oasis Cafe,** where the draft beer is only Dr500 ($1.45); if there's a game of any sort going on, it'll be on the tube. Meanwhile, at the far eastern end of the harbor are three clubs popular with the younger set—the **Kavos, Remezzo,** and **B.B.C.**

Movie fans might enjoy the **Cinema Paradiso,** up along the "ring road," which shows recent films in English nightly at 8:30 and 11pm; tickets are Dr1,500 ($4.30).

2 Skopelos

121km (65 nautical miles) from Ayios Konstandinos, which is 166km (103 miles) from Athens

It was inevitable that handsomely rugged Skopelos would follow Skiathos in its development, but it has done so a bit more wisely and at a slower pace. Its beaches are not so numerous or as pretty, but Skopelos town is one of the most beautiful ports in Greece, and the island is richer in vegetation, with windswept pines growing down to secluded coves, wide beaches, and terraced cliffs of angled rock slabs. The interior is densely planted with fruit and nut orchards. The famous plums and almonds from Skopelos are liberally used in the island's unique cuisine. The coastline, like that of Skiathos, is punctuated by impressive grottoes and bays, and you'll find frequent need for a camera.

ESSENTIALS

GETTING THERE By Plane   Skopleos cannot be reached directly by plane, but you can fly to nearby Skiathos and take a hydrofoil or ferry to the northern port of Loutraki (below Glossa) or the more popular Skopelos town.

By Boat   If you're in Athens, take a boat or hydrofoil from Ayios Konstandinos to Skopelos (75 mins.). **Alkyon Travel,** Odos Akademias 97, near Kanigos Square (☎ 01/383-2545), can arrange the 3-hour bus ride from Athens to Ayios Konstandinos (about Dr3,500/$10 one-way) and hydrofoil or ferry tickets. Coming from Central or Northern Greece, depart for Skopelos from Volos (about 2 hrs.).

From Skiathos, the ferry to Skopelos takes 90 minutes if you call at Skopelos town, or 45 minutes if you get off at Glossa/Loutraki; the one-way fare to both is about Dr1,500 ($4.30). Ferry tickets can be purchased at **Vasilis Nikolaou** (☎ 0427/22-209), the travel agent at the corner of the Paralia and Odos Papadiamandis. The Flying Dolphin hydrofoil takes 15 minutes to Glossa/Loutraki (four to five times daily; Dr2,500/$7), and 45 minutes to Skopelos (six to eight times daily, Dr2,800/$8). From Skiathos, you can also take one of the many daily excursion boats to Skopelos.

It's possible to catch a regular ferry or hydrofoil from Alonissos to Skopelos (seven times daily; Dr2,500/$7) or ride on one of the excursion boats. Expect to pay a little more on the excursion boats—but if they're not full, you can sometimes negotiate the price.

There are infrequent ferryboat connections from Kimi (on Evvia) to Skopelos. Check with the **Skopelos Port Authority** (☎ 0424/22-180) for current schedules, as they change frequently. We think hydrofoils are worth the extra expense for hopping around the Sporades.

In the port of Skopelos town, hydrofoil tickets can be purchased at the Flying Dolphin agent, **Madro Travel,** immediately opposite the dock (☎ 0424/22-300); it's open all year, also operates as the local Olympic Airways representative, and can generally make any arrangements you need.

VISITOR INFORMATION   The **Municipal Tourist Office** of Skopelos is on the waterfront, to the left of the pier as you disembark (☎ 0424/323-231); open daily from 9:30am to 10pm in high season. It offers information, changes money, and reserves rooms. If you want to call ahead to book a room, the **Association of Owners of Rental Accommodation** maintains a small office on the harbor (☎ 0424/24-567).

At the travel agency **Skopelorama,** about 100 meters beyond the Hotel Eleni on the left (east) end of the port (☎ 0424/23-250; fax 0424/23-243), the friendly staff can help you find a room, exchange money, rent a car, or take an excursion; they know the island inside-out and can provide information on just about anything. It's open daily from 8am to 10pm.

GETTING AROUND   By Bus   Skopelos is reasonably well served by public bus; the bus stop in Skopelos town is on the east end of the port. There are four routes. Buses run the main route every half hour in the high season beginning in Skopelos and making stops at Stafilos, Agnondas, Panormos, the Adrina Beach Hotel, Milia, Elios, Klima, Glossa, and Loutraki. The fare from Skopelos to Glossa is Dr600 ($1.75).

By Car & Moped   The most convenient way to see the island is to rent a car or moped at one of the many shops on the port. A four-wheel-drive vehicle at **Motor Tours** (☎ 0424/22-986; fax 0424/22-602) runs around Dr30,000 ($86), including insurance; expect to pay a few thousand drachmas less for a Fiat Panda. A moped should cost about Dr5,000 ($14) per day.

By Taxi   The taxi stand is at the far end of the waterfront, and taxis will provide service to almost any place on the island. Taxis are not metered—negotiate the fare before accepting a ride. A typical fare, from Skopelos to Glossa, runs Dr7,500 ($22).

By Boat   To visit the more isolated beaches, take one of the large excursion boats; these cost about Dr15,000 ($43) including lunch, and should be booked a day in advance in high season. Excursion boats to Glisteri, Gliphoneri, and Sares beaches operate only in peak season (about Dr2,500/$7). From the port of Agnondas, on the south coast, there are fishing boats to Limnonari, one of the island's better beaches.

FAST FACTS   There are several **ATMs** at banks around the harbor. The **health center** is on the road leading out of the east end of town (☎ 0424/22-222). Plynthria, a self-service **laundry,** is located (in a basement) just past the Adonis Hotel on the upper road at the east end of the harbor (☎ 0424/22-123); open Monday through Saturday from 9:30am to 1:30pm and 6 to 8pm. The **police station** (☎ 0424/ 22-235) is up the narrow road (Parados 1) to the right of the National Bank, along the harbor. For **Internet access,** try Click & Surf (e-mail: ermis777@hotmail.com), just up from the police station. The **post office,** on the far east end of the port (take the stepped road leading away from the last kiosk, opposite the bus/taxi station), is open Monday through Friday from 8am to 2:30pm. The **telephone office (OTE)** is at the top of a narrow road leading away from the center of the harbor; open Monday through Saturday from 8am to 5pm.

WHAT TO SEE & DO

The ferries from Alonissos, Skyros, and Kimi and most of the hydrofoils and other boats from Skiathos dock at both Glossa/Loutraki and Skopelos town. Most boats stop first at **Loutraki,** a homely little port near the northern end of the west coast, with the more attractive town of ✪ **Glossa** high above it. We suggest you stay onboard for the trip around the northern tip of the island and along the east coast—getting a better sense of why the island's name means "cliff" in Greek—to the island's main harbor, especially if this is your first visit. You'll understand why when your boat pulls around the last headland into that huge and nearly perfect C-shaped harbor, and you get your first glimpse of Skopelos town rising like a steep amphitheater around the port.

Skopelos town (also called Hora) is one of Greece's most treasured towns, on a par with Hydra and Simi. It scales the steep, low hills around the harbor and has the same winding, narrow paths that characterize the more famous Cycladic islands to the south. Scattered on the slopes of the town are just a few of the island's 123 churches, which must be something of a record for such a small locale. The oldest of these is **Ayios Michali,** up past the police station. The waterfront is lined with banks, cafes, travel agencies, and the like. Interspersed among these prosaic offerings are some truly regal-looking shade trees. Many of the shops and services are up the main street leading away from the center of the paralia. The back streets are amazingly convoluted (and unnamed); the best plan is to wander around and get to know a few familiar landmarks.

The **Venetian Kastro,** which overlooks the town from a rise on the western corner, has been whitewashed and looks too new to have been built over an archaic temple of Athena, and too serene to have been deemed too formidable for attack by the Turks during the War of Independence in the early 19th century.

At the far eastern end of town is the **Photographic Center of Skopelos** (☎ 0424/ 24-121), which during the high season sponsors quite classy photography exhibitions in several locales around town.

SHOPPING
Skopelos has a variety of shops selling Greek and local ceramics, weavings, and jewelry. One of the most stylish is **Armoloi,** in the center of the shops along the harbor (☎ 0424/22-707). It sells only Greek jewelry, ceramics, weavings, and silver; some of the objects are old, and most of the handsome ceramics are made by the owners. **Nick Rodios** (☎ 0424/22-924), whose gallery is located between the Hotel Eleni and the Skopelorama agency, is from a Skopelos family who have made ceramics for three generations. His elegant black vessels, at once both classical and modern, are a change from the usual pottery found around Greece.

EXPLORING THE ISLAND
The whole island is sprinkled with monasteries and churches, but five **monasteries** south of town can be visited by following a pleasant path that continues south from the beach hotels. The first, **Evangelistria,** was founded by monks from Mount Athos, but it now serves as a nunnery, and the weavings of its present occupants can be bought at a small shop; it's open daily from 8am to 1pm and 4 to 7pm. The fortified monastery of **Ayia Barbara,** now abandoned, contains 15th-century frescoes. **Metamorphosis,** very nearly abandoned, is very much alive on the 6th of August, when the feast of the Metamorphosis is celebrated here. **Ayios Prodromos** is a 30-minute hike further, but it's the handsomest and contains a particularly beautiful iconostasis. **Taxiarchon,** abandoned and overgrown, is at the summit of Mount Polouki to the southeast, a hike recommended only to the hardiest and most dedicated.

There is basically only one highway on the island, with short spurs at each significant settlement. It runs south from Skopelos town, then cuts north and skirts the west coast northwest, eventually coming to Glossa, then down to Loutraki. The first spur leads off to the left to **Stafilos,** a popular family beach recommended by locals for a good seafood dinner, which you must order in the morning. About half a kilometer across the headland is **Velanio,** where nude bathing is common.

The next settlement west is **Agnondas,** named for a local athlete who brought home the gold from the 569 B.C. Olympics. This small fishing village has became a tourist resort thanks to nearby beaches. **Limnonari,** a 15-minute walk further west and accessible by caïque in summer, has a good fine-sand beach in a rather homely and shadeless setting.

The road then turns inland again, through a pine forest, coming out at the coast at **Panormos.** With its sheltered pebble beach, this has become the island's best resort with a number of taverns, hotels, and rooms to let, as well as water-sports facilities.

The road then climbs again toward ✪ **Milia,** which is considered **the island's best beach.** You will have to walk down about half a kilometer from the bus stop, but you'll find a lovely light-gray sand-and-pebble beach with the island of Dassia opposite and water-sports facilities at the **Beach Boys Club** (☎ **0424/23-995**).

The next stop, **Elios,** is a town that was thrown up to shelter the people displaced by the 1965 earthquake. It's become the home of many of the locals who operate the resort facilities on the west coast, as well as something of a resort itself.

The main road proceeds on to ✪ **Glossa,** which means "tongue," and that's what the hill on which the town was built looks like from the sea. It was mostly spared during the earthquake, and remains one of the most Greek and charming towns in the Sporades. Those who are tempted to stay overnight will find a number of rooms for rent, a good hotel, and a very good taverna. Most of the coastline here is craggy, with just a few hard-to-reach beaches. Among the best places to catch some rays and do a bit of swimming is the small beach below the picturesque monastery of **Ayios Ioannis,** on the coast east from town, which reminds many of Meteora. (Bring food and water.) As for the port of **Loutraki,** it's a winding 3 kilometers (2 miles) down; we don't recommend a stay there.

That ends the road tour of Skopelos, but other sites can be reached from Skopleos town by caïque. Along the east coast north of Skopelos is **Glisteri,** a small pebbled beach with a nearby olive grove offering some respite from the sun. It's a good bet when the other beaches are overrun in summer. You can also go by caïque to the grotto at **Tripiti,** for the island's best fishing, or to the little island of **Ayios Yioryios,** which has an abandoned monastery.

The whole of Skopelos's 95 square kilometers (38 square miles) is prime for **biking,** and the interior is still waiting to be explored. There's also **horseback riding, sailing** (ask at the Skopelos travel agencies), and a number of interesting **excursions** to be taken from and around the island. Skopelorama (see "Visitor Information," above) operates a fine series of excursions, such as monasteries by coach, a walking tour of the town, and several cruises. One boat excursion that might appeal to some is to the waters around Skopelos that are part of the **National Marine Park;** if you're lucky, you will see some of the Mediterranean monk seals, an endangered species that is protected within the park.

WHERE TO STAY

In high season, Skopelos is nearly as popular as Skiathos. If you need advice, talk to the Skopelorama agency (see "Visitor Information," above) or the officials at the town hall. Be sure to look at a room and agree on a price before accepting anything, or you may be unpleasantly surprised. To make matters confusing, there are few street names in the main, older section of Skopelos town, so you'll have to ask for directions in order to find your lodging.

IN SKOPELOS TOWN

The handsome, traditional-style **Hotel Amalia,** along the coast, 500 meters from the center of the port (☎ **0424/22-688;** fax 0424/23-217), is largely occupied by groups, but should have some spare rooms in spring and fall.

Hotel Denise. 37003 Skopelos. ☎ **0424/22-678.** Fax 0424/22-769. www.denise.gr. 25 units. A/C MINIBAR TEL. Dr20,000 ($57) double. Rates include continental breakfast. EC, MC, V.

One of the best hotels in Skopelos thanks to its premier location, clean facilities, and pool, the Hotel Denise stands atop the hill overlooking the town and commands spectacular vistas of the harbor and Aegean. Each of the hotel's four stories is ringed by a wide balcony. The guest rooms have hardwood floors and furniture, and most boast a view that is among the best in town. The Denise is popular and open only in high season; before hiking up the steep road, call for a pickup and to check for room availability—or better yet, reserve in advance.

Hotel Drossia. 37003 Skopelos. ☎ **0424/22-490.** 10 units. Dr12,000 ($34) double. No credit cards. Open July–Aug only.

This small hotel next to the Hotel Denise (see above), atop the hill overlooking the town, is for bargain-hunters. The Drossia is of the same vintage as the Denise, with exceptional views but slightly less expensive and less well-equipped rooms. All in all, it represents good value.

Hotel Eleni. 37003 Skopelos. ☎ **0424/22-393.** Fax 0424/22-936. 37 units. TEL. Dr15,000 ($43) double. EC, MC, V.

The Hotel Eleni is a modern hotel, set back from the coast and 300 meters from the center of the harbor. After many years spent operating several pizzerias in New York, Charlie Hatzidrosos returned from the Bronx to build this establishment. His daughter now operates the hotel and provides gracious service. All guest rooms have balconies.

✪ **Hotel Prince Stafilos.** 37003 Skopelos. ☎ **0424/22-775.** Fax 0424/22-825. 65 units. TEL. Dr36,000 ($104) double. Rates include large buffet breakfast. AE, EC, MC, V.

Although it charges a bit more than other Skopelos hotels, this one is well worth it. The most handsome and traditional hotel on the island is about a half mile south of town. (It provides rides from the ferry dock.) The friendly owner, Pelopidas Tsitsirgos, is also the architect responsible for the establishment's special charm. The lobby is spacious and attractively decorated with local artifacts. Facilities include a pool, restaurant, and bars.

Hotel Rania. 37003 Skopelos. ☎ **0424/22-486.** 11 units. TEL. Dr11,000 ($32) single or double. No credit cards.

Another bargain-hunter's hotel, the Rania is back from the coast, to the left of the Hotel Amalia. The simply furnished rooms have balconies and are reasonably well maintained.

Skopelos Village. About a half mile southeast of town center, 37003 Skopelos. ☎ **0424/ 22-517.** Fax 0424/22-958. 36 units. AC MINIBAR TEL TV. Bungalow for two persons, high season Dr50,000 ($144), low season Dr40,000 ($115) EC, V.

Visitors intending to settle in for a while can take advantage of this mini-resort's pool, nearby tennis court, children's playground, and room service. The buildings are tastefully constructed as "traditional island houses." Each bungalow is equipped with kitchen, private bathroom, and one or two bedrooms, and can sleep from two to six persons. Facilities include a breakfast room and snack bar. In the evening, the restaurant offers Greek meals accompanied by Greek music and dance. The hotel provides free transport to various beaches.

IN PANORMOS

This pleasant little resort is on a horseshoe-shaped cove along the west coast, about halfway between Skopelos town and Glossa. Here you'll find several cafeteria-style snack bars and minimarkets. We recommend it as a base, especially since one of the best hotels on the island—the Adrina Beach Hotel—is just above it.

The **Panormos Travel Office** (☎ 0424/23-380; fax 0424/23-748) has some decent rooms to let, offers phone and fax services, exchanges money, arranges tours (including night squid fishing), and rents cars, motorbikes, and speedboats.

✪ **Adrina Beach Hotel.** Panormos, 37003 Skopelos. ☎ **0424/23-373**, or 01/682-6886 in Athens. Fax 0424/23-372. 55 units. A/C TEL. Dr38,000 ($109) double. Rates include breakfast. AE, DC, MC, V.

This traditional-style hotel, 500 meters on the beach beyond Panormos, rates as one of the better ones on the island. The guest rooms are large and tastefully furnished in pastels, each with its own balcony or veranda. In addition to the main building's rooms, eight handsome "maisonettes" are ranked down the steep slope toward the hotel's private beach; these have air-conditioning and cost Dr40,000 ($114). The complex has a big saltwater pool with its own bar, a restaurant, a bar, a buffet room, spacious sitting areas indoors and out, a playground, and a minimarket.

If you can't get a room at the Adrina, try the 38-unit **Afroditi Hotel** (☎ **0424/ 23-150;** fax 0424/23-152), a more modern choice about 100 meters across the road from the beach at Panormos.

IN GLOSSA

There are approximately 100 rooms to rent in the small town of Glossa. Expect to pay about Dr10,000 ($29) for single or double occupancy. The best way to find a room is to visit one of the tavernas or shops and inquire about a vacancy. You can ask George Antoniou at the **Pythari Souvenir Shop** (☎ **0424/33-077**) for advice. If you can't find a room in Glossa, you can always take a bus or taxi down to Loutraki and check into a pension by the water or head back to Panormos.

WHERE TO DINE
IN SKOPELOS TOWN

Anatoli Ouzeri. On a hill south of town. ☎ **0424/22-851.** Main courses Dr1,200–Dr2,500 ($3.45–$7). No credit cards. Summer daily 8:30pm–1am. Closed in winter. GREEK.

It's quite a climb (or else take a taxi) to reach this diminutive ouzeri high above town, but many feel the whole experience justifies the effort. A usual meal features several delicious mezedes, including lightly fried green peppers and an exceptional octopus salad. Specialties include *bourekakia* (fried eggplant) and fried cheese pie. *Note:* No wine is served—only *tsipouro,* a strong ouzo-like drink. If you're in luck, Yiorgios Xindaris, the rail-thin proprietor/chef, will play his bouzouki and sing classic rembetika songs, sometimes with accompanists. If you come early or late in the season, bring a sweater.

✪ **Finikas Taverna and Ouzeri.** Upper backstreet of Skopelos town. ☎ **0424/23-247.** Main courses Dr1,300–Dr1,800 ($3.75–$5.15). No credit cards. Daily 7:30pm–2am. GREEK.

Tucked away in the upper backstreets of Skopelos is a picturesque garden taverna/ouzeri dominated by a broadleaf palm. The Finikas offers what might be Skopelos's most romantic setting, thanks to its isolated and its lovely garden seating. Among the many fine courses are an excellent ratatouille and pork cooked with prunes and apples, a traditional island specialty.

Good Will Garden. At far eastern end of harbor, first left at corner of Amalia Hotel. ☎ **0424/22-349.** Reservations recommended in high season. Main courses Dr1,000–Dr4,000 ($2.90–$11). V. Daily 11am–midnight. Closed Oct to mid-June. GREEK.

Some locals claim this is the best restaurant in town, at least for a complete dining experience. Two young brothers operate what most people call simply "The Garden," with a garden-like setting and a casual atmosphere. The food is tasty and often a bit different: appetizers such as mushrooms with garlic, and main courses such as kalamares with cheese.

Platanos Jazz Bar. Beneath the enormous plane tree just to the left of the ferry dock. ☎ **0424/23-661.** Main courses Dr800–Dr1,900 ($2.30–$5.45). No credit cards. Daily 5am–3am. SNACK/BAR FOOD.

For everything from breakfast to a late-night drink, try this pub. Breakfast in the summer starts as early as 5 or 6am for ferry passengers, who can enjoy coffee, fruit salad with nuts and yogurt, and fresh-squeezed orange juice, all for about Dr2,000 ($6). Platanos is equally pleasant for evening and late-night drinks. Accompanying your meal will be music from the proprietors' phenomenal collection of jazz records.

You might also consider a local favorite, **Molos Taverna and Ouzeri,** near the ferry stop on the paralia (☎ **0424/22-551**). **Spiros' Taverna,** to the left as you leave the ferry dock (☎ **0424/23-146**), is a simple outdoor cafe popular for its spit-roasted chicken. A bit farther along is the **Selene Taverna** (☎ **0424/22-393**), offering tasty favorites at moderate prices.

IN GLOSSA

✪ **Taverna T'agnanti.** Glossa. ☎ **0424/33-076.** E-mail: agnanti@hotmail.com. Main courses Dr1,000–Dr3,200 ($2.90–$9). No credit cards. Daily 11am–midnight. About 200m up from the bus stop. GREEK/TRADITIONAL SKOPELITIAN.

This is the place to meet, greet, and eat in Glossa. The food is inexpensive, the staff friendly, and the view spectacular. The menu is standard taverna style, but the proprietors make a point of using the finest fresh products and wines. Specialties include herb fritters, fish stifado with prunes, pork with prunes, and almond pie. There's occasionally traditional music. The Stamataki and Antoniou families run this and the nearby souvenir shop Pythari.

SKOPELOS AFTER DARK

The nightlife scene on Skopelos isn't nearly as active as on neighboring Skiathos, but there are still plenty of bars, late-night cafes, and discos. Most of the coolest bars are on the far (east) side of town, but you can wander around checking out the scene around Platanos Square, beyond and along the paralia. Above the Hotel Amalia is the indoor **Cocos Club;** continue on along the beachfront to find the outdoor **Karyatis.** The best place for bouzouki music is the **Metro.** And don't forget the possibility of live music at the **Anatoli Ouzeri,** above the town and offering a spectacular view.

3 Skyros (Skiros)

47km (25 nautical miles) from Kimi, which is 182km (113 miles) from Athens

Skyros is an island with good beaches, attractive whitewashed pillbox architecture, picturesque surroundings, low prices—and relatively few tourists. Why? First, it's difficult to get to. In summer, there are occasional ferries and hydrofoils linking Skyros to the other Sporades as well as to ports on the mainland, but these links are either fairly infrequent or involve land transportation to ports that are not on most tourists' itineraries. Second, most visitors to the Sporades seem to prefer the other, more thickly forested (and thickly touristed) islands. Some of us find that Skyros's more meager tourist facilities and the stark contrast between sea, sky, and rugged terrain make it all the more inviting.

Also, many Skyriots themselves are ambivalent, at best, about developing this very traditional island for tourism. Until about 1990, there were only a handful of hotels on the entire island. Since then, Skyros has seen a miniboom in the tourist business, and with the completion of a giant marina, it's setting itself up to become yet another tourist Mecca. Don't let this deter you, however; at least for now, Skyros remains an ideal place for a getaway vacation.

ESSENTIALS

GETTING THERE   By Plane In summer, **Olympic Airways** has about two flights a week between Athens and Skyros. Call the Olympic office in Athens (☎ **01/ 966-6666**) for information and reservations; the local Olympic representative is **Skyros Travel and Tourism** (☎ **0222/91-123**). A bus meets most flights and goes to Skyros town, Magazia, and sometimes Molos; the fare is Dr500 ($1.45). A taxi from the airport is about Dr1,500 ($4.30), but expect to share a cab.

By Boat   The **Lykomides Company** offers the only ferry service to Skyros; it's operated by a company whose stockholders are all citizens of the island. In summer, it runs twice daily (usually early afternoon and early evening) from Kimi (on the east coast of Evvia) to Skyros and twice daily (usually early morning and mid-afternoon) from Skyros to Kimi; the trip takes a little over 2 hours. Off-season, there's one ferry each way, leaving Skyros early in the morning and Kimi in late afternoon. The fare is Dr2,500 ($7). For information, call the Lykomides office either in Kimi (☎ **0222/22-020**) or Skyros (☎ **0222/91-790**). The Lykomides offices also sell connecting bus tickets to Athens; the fare for the 3½-hour ride is about Dr3,500 ($10). In Athens, **Alkyon Travel,** Odos Akademias 97, near Kanigos Square (☎ **01/383-2545**), arranges bus transportation to Kimi and sells hydrofoil and ferry tickets.

In summer, Skyros can also be reached from several ports by the hydrofoils known as Flying Dolphins; this is the most convenient way to go, though a little more expensive than the ferry. (For example, the hydrofoil between Kimi and Skyros costs about Dr4,000/$11.) Hydrofoil schedules both ways are: about once a week from and to Kimi; about twice a week from and to Ayios Konstandinos; about once a week from and to Volos (4½ hrs.); and about twice a week from and to Thessaloniki (a 6-hr. ride, or 5 hrs. if you get on at Moudiana, south of Thessaloniki). From other Sporades, in summer there are several trips per week between Skyros and Skiathos, Skopelos, and Alonissos (about five times a week, starting in mid-May, daily in July and August). For hydrofoil information, contact the **Minoan Flying Dolphins** in Athens (☎ **01/428-0001; e-mail: sales@mfd.gr**).

If you're trying to "do" the Sporades and want to make connections at Kimi, the tricky part can be the connection with ferries or hydrofoils from the other Sporades islands. When they don't hold to schedule, it's not uncommon to see the Skyros ferry disappearing on the horizon as your ship pulls into Kimi. You might have to make the best of the 24-hour layover and get a room in Paralia Kimi. (We recommend the **Hotel Kimi,** at ☎ **0222/22-408,** or the older **Hotel Krineion,** at ☎ **0222/22-287.**)

From Athens, buses to Kimi and Ayios Konstandinos leave the Terminal B (Odos Lission 260) six times a day, though you should depart no later than 1:30pm; the fare for the 3½-hour trip is about Dr3,500 ($10). From Kimi, you must take a local bus to Paralia Kimi. Ask the bus driver if you're uncertain of the connection.

On Skyros, the ferries and hydrofoils dock at **Linaria,** on the opposite side of the island from Skyros town. The island's only public bus will meet the boat and take you over winding, curvy roads to Skyros town for Dr250 (75¢). On request, the bus will also stop at Magazia beach, immediately north below the town, next to the Xenia Hotel.

VISITOR INFORMATION   The largest tourist office is **Skyros Travel and Tourism** (☎ **0222/91-123;** fax 0222/92-123), next to Skyros Pizza Restaurant in the main market. It's open daily from 8am to 2:30pm and 6:30 to 10:30pm. English-speaking Lefteris Trakos offers assistance with accommodations, currency exchange, Olympic Airways flights (he's the local ticket agent), phone calls, some interesting bus and boat tours, and Flying Dolphin tickets.

GETTING AROUND **By Bus** The only scheduled service is the Skyros-Linaria shuttle that runs four to five times daily and costs Dr300 (90¢). Skyros Travel (see above) offers a twice-daily beach-excursion bus in high season. It now also offers day-long excursions around the island in a small bus with an English-speaking guide (Dr10,000/$29); for many this may be the best way to get an overview of the island.

By Car & Moped A small car rents for about Dr20,000 ($57) per day, including insurance. Mopeds and motorcycles are available near the police station or the taxi station for about Dr6,000 ($17) per day. The island has a relatively well developed network of roads.

By Taxi Taxis can be hired to go about any place on the island at the standard Greek rates, but discuss the price before setting off; service between Linaria and Skyros costs about Dr3,000 ($9).

On Foot Skyros is a fine place to hike. The island map, published by Skyros Travel and Tourism, will show you a number of good routes, and it seems to be pretty accurate.

FAST FACTS As of this writing, there is only one ATM on Skyros, at the **National Bank of Greece** in the main square of Skyros town. Because of its limited hours (Monday through Friday from 8am to 2pm), and in case its ATM is out of service, we recommend bringing cash and/or traveler's checks. The **clinic** is near the main square (☎ 0222/92-222). The **police station** (☎ 0222/91-274) is on the street behind the Skyros Travel Center. The **post office** is near the bus square in Skyros town; open Monday through Friday from 8am to 2pm. The **telephone office (OTE)** is opposite the police station. It's open Friday only, from 7:30am to 3pm, but there are card phones in town.

WHAT TO SEE & DO

The Faltaits Historical and Folklore Museum. Plateia Rupert Brooke. ☎ 0222/91-232. Dr500 ($1.45). Summer daily 10am–1pm and 6–9pm; in off-season, ring the bell and someone will let you in.

Located in a large, old house of the Faltaits family, this is the private collection of Manos Faltaits, and it's one of the best island folk-art museums in Greece. It contains a large and varied collection of plates, embroidery, weaving, woodworking, and clothing, as well as many rare books and photographs, including some of the local men in traditional costumes for Carnival. Attached to the museum is a workshop where young artisans make lovely objects using traditional patterns and materials. The proceeds from the sale of workshop items go to the upkeep of the museum. The museum also has a shop, **Argo,** on the main street of town (☎ 0222/92-158), open daily from 10am to 1pm and 6:30 to 11pm.

EXPLORING THE ISLAND

All boats dock at **Linaria,** a plain, mostly modern fishing village on the west coast, pleasant enough but not recommended for a stay. Catch the bus waiting on the quay to take you across the narrow middle of the island to the west coast capital, Skyros town, which is built on a rocky bluff overlooking the sea. (The airport is near the northern tip of the island.) **Skyros town,** which is known on the island as Horio or Hora, looks much like a typical Cycladic hill town, with whitewashed houses built on top of one another. The winding streets and paths are too narrow for cars and mopeds, so most of the traffic is by foot and hoof. As you alight from the bus at the bus stop square, continue on up toward the center of town and the main tourist services.

Near the market, signs point up to the town's **Kastro.** It's a 15-minute climb, but worth it for the view, and on the way you'll pass the church of **Ayia Triada,** which

contains some interesting frescoes, and the monastery of **Ayios Yioryios Skyrianos.**
The monastery was founded in 962 and contains a famous black-faced icon of
St. George that was brought from Constantinople during the Iconoclastic controversy.
From one side of the citadel, the view is over the rooftops of the town, and from the
other the cliff drops precipitously to the sea. According to one myth, King Lykomides
pushed Theseus to his death from here.

The terrace at the far (northern) end of the island is **Plateia Rupert Brooke,** where
the English poet, who is buried on the southern tip of the island, is honored by a nude
statue of Immortal Poetry. (Brooke died on a hospital ship off Skyros in 1915 while
en route to the Dardanellese as an army officer.) The statue is said to have greatly
offended the local people when it was installed; you're more likely to be amused when
you see how pranksters have chosen to deface the hapless bronze figure. (The Faltaits
Folklore Museum, described above, is located near this site, as is the not especially
distinguished archaeological museum.)

Local customs and dress are currently better preserved on Skyros than in all but a
few locales in Greece. Older men can still be seen in baggy blue pants, black caps, and
leather sandals constructed with numerous straps, and older women still wear long
head scarves. The **embroidery** you will often see women busily working at is famous
for its vibrant colors and interesting motifs—such as people dancing hand-in-hand
with flowers twining around their limbs and hoopoes with fanciful crests.

Peek into the doorway of any Skyrian home and you're likely to see what looks like
a room from a dollhouse with a miniature table and chairs, and **colorful plates**—loads
of plates hanging on the wall. The story behind these displays is said to have begun
during the Byzantine era, when the head clerics from Epirus sent 10 families to Skyros to serve as governors. They were given control of all the land not owned by Mount
Athos and the Monastery of St. George. For hundreds of years, these 10 families dominated the affairs of Skyros. With Kalamitsa as a safe harbor, the island prospered, and
consulates opened from countries near and far. The merchant ships were soon followed by pirates, and the ruling families went into business with them; the families
knew what boats were expected and what they were carrying, and the pirates had the
ships and bravado to steal the cargo. The pirates, of course, soon took to plundering
the islanders as well, but the aristocrats managed to hold on to much of their wealth.

Greek independence reduced the influence of these ruling families, and during the
hard times brought by World War I, they were reduced to trading their possessions to
the peasant farmers for food. Chief among these bartered items were sets of dinner-
ware. Plates from China, Italy, Turkey, Egypt, and other exotic places became a sign of
wealth, and Skyrian families made elaborate displays of their newly acquired trophies.
Whole walls were covered, and by the 1920s local Skyrian craftsmen began making
their own plates for the poorer families who couldn't afford the originals. This, at least,
is the story they tell.

Skyros is also the home of a unique breed of **wild pygmy ponies,** often compared
to the horses depicted on the frieze of the Parthenon and thought to be at least similar to Shetland ponies. Most of these rare animals have been moved to the nearby
island of Skyropoula, though tame ones can still be seen grazing near town. Ask
around and you might be able to find a local who will let you ride one.

BEACHES & OUTDOOR PURSUITS

To get to the beach at **Magazia,** continue down from Plateia Rupert Brooke. (If your
load is heavy, take a taxi to Magazia, as it is a hike.) From Magazia, once the site of
the town's storehouses (magazines), it's about a half mile to **Molos,** a fishing village,

The Famous Carnival of Skyros

The 21-day Carnival celebration is highlighted by a 4-day period leading up to Lent and the day known throughout Greece as *Kathari Deftera* (Clean Monday). On this day, Skyros residents don traditional costumes and perform dances on the town square. Unleavened bread (*lagana*) is served with *taramosalata* and other meatless specialties. (Traditionally, vegetarian food is eaten for 40 days leading up to Easter.) Much of this is traditional throughout Greece, but Skyros adds its own distinctive element. Culminating on midafternoon of the Sunday before Clean Monday are a series of ritual dances and events performed by a group of weirdly costumed men. Some dress as old shepherds in animal skins with a belt of sheep bells and a mask made of goatskin. Other men dress as women and flirt outrageously. (Skyros seems to have an age-old association with cross-dressing: It was here that Achilles successfully beat the draft during the Trojan war by dressing as a woman, until shrewd Odysseus tricked him into revealing his true gender.) Other celebrants caricature Europeans, and all behave outlandishly, reciting ribald poetry and poking fun at bystanders. This ritual is generally thought to be pagan in origin and causes some people to reflect on the antics of ancient Greek comedy and even tragedy ("goat song"), with men playing all the roles, and catharsis as the goal.

though the two villages are quickly becoming indistinguishable because of development. There's windsurfing along this beach, and there are some fair isolated beaches beyond Molos, with some nudist activity.

South of town, the beaches are less enticing until you reach **Aspous,** which has a couple of tavernas and some rooms to let. **Ahili,** a bit further south, is where you'll find the big new **marina,** so it's no longer much of a place for swimming. Further south, the coast gets increasingly rugged and there is no roadway.

If you head back across the narrow waist of the island to **Kalamitsa,** the old safe harbor, 3 kilometers (1.9 miles) south of Linaria, you'll find a good clean beach. It's served by buses in summer.

The island is divided almost evenly by its narrow waist; the northern half is fertile and covered with pine forest, while the southern half is barren and quite rugged. Both halves have their attractions, though the most scenic area of the island is probably to the south toward **Tris Boukes,** where Rupert Brooke is buried. The better beaches, however, are in the north.

North of Linaria, **Acherounes** is a very pretty beach. Beyond it, **Pefkos,** where marble was once quarried, is better sheltered and has a taverna that's open in summer. The next beach north, **Ayios Fokas,** is probably the best on the island, with a lovely white pebble beach and a taverna open in summer. Locals call it paradise, and like all such places it's very difficult to reach. Most Skyrians will suggest walking, but it's a long hilly hike. To get here from Skyros town, take the bus back to Linaria, tell the driver where you're going, get off at the crossroads with Pefkos, and begin your hike west from there.

North of Ayios Fokas is **Atsitsa,** another beach with pine trees along it, but it's a bit too rocky. It can be reached by road across the Olymbos mountains in the center of the island, and it has a few rooms to let. It is also the location of a **holistic health-and-fitness holiday community;** for information on its activities, contact Skyros Holistic Vacations, 92 Prince of Wales Rd., London NW5 3NE (☎ 020/7284-3065 in England; www.skyros.com; e-mail: rochelle@skyros.com). (This same British outfit runs the **Skyros Centre** at the edge of Skyros Town; it differs from the one at

Atsitsa in that it offers courses and a somewhat more conventional touristic experi-ence.) There's a sandy beach a 15-minute walk further north at **Kira Panayia** that's a bit better.

The northwest of the island is covered in dense pine forests, spreading down to the Aegean. The rocky shore opens onto gentle bays and coves. This area provides won-derful **hiking** for the fit. Take a taxi (Dr6,000/$17) to **Atsitsa,** and arrange for it to return in 5 or 6 hours. Explore the ruins of the ancient mining operation at Atsitsa, then head south for about 7 kilometers (4½ miles) to **Ayios Fokas,** a small bay with a tiny taverna perched right on the water. Kali Orfanou, the gracious hostess, will pro-vide you with the meal of your trip: fresh fish caught that morning in the waters before you, vegetables plucked from the garden for your salad, and her own feta cheese and wine. Relax, swim in the bay, and then hike back to your taxi. The ambitious may con-tinue south for 11 or 12 kilometers (7 or 8 miles) to the main road and catch the bus or hail a taxi. Note that this part of the road is mainly uphill. In case you tire or can't pry yourself away from the secluded paradise of Ayios Fokas, Kali offers two extremely primitive rooms with the view of your dreams, but without electricity or toilets.

SHOPPING

Skyros is a good place for buying local crafts, especially ceramics. **Ergastiri,** on the main street, has interesting ceramics, Greek shadow puppets, and a great selection of postcards. Popular for his handmade plates is **Yiannis Nicholau,** whose studio is next to the Xenia Hotel. You can find good hand-carved wooden chests and chairs made from beech (in the old days it was blackberry wood) from **Lefteris Avgoklouris,** for-mer student of the recently departed master, Baboussis, in Skyros town; his studio is on Odos Konthili, around the corner from the post office (☎ **0222/91-106**). Another fine carver is **Manolios,** in the main market.

WHERE TO STAY

The whole island has only a few hotels, so most visitors to Skyros take private rooms. The best are in the upper part of Skyros town, away from the bus stop, where women in black dresses accost you with cries of "Room! Room!" A more efficient procedure is to stop in at Skyros Travel and Tourism (see "Visitor Information," above). The island of Skyros is somewhat more primitive in its facilities than the other Sporades, so before agreeing to anything, check out the room to ensure that it's what you want.

IN SKYROS TOWN

✪ **Hotel Nefeli.** Skyros town, 34007 Skyros. ☎ **0222/91-964.** Fax 0222/92-061. 19 units. TEL. Dr23,000 ($66) double. Breakfast Dr1,400 ($4) extra. AE, MC, V.

One of the best in-town options is built in the modern Skyrian style. The bedrooms and bathrooms are decent sized and well appointed; many units have fine views, and the large, downstairs lobby is a welcoming space. As the Nefeli is one of the favorite choices on Skyros, you'd do well to reserve in advance.

IN MAGAZIA BEACH & MOLOS

Hotel Angela. Molos, 34007 Skyros. ☎ **0222/91-764.** Fax 0222/92-030. E-mail: anghotel@ otenet.gr. 14 units. TEL. Dr22,000 ($63) double.

This is among the most attractive and well-kept abodes in the Molos/Magazia beach area, located near the sprawling Paradise Hotel complex. All rooms are clean and tidy with balconies, but because the hotel is set back about 100 meters from the beach, there are only partial sea views. Nevertheless, the facilities and hospitality of the young couple who run the Angela make up for its just-off-the-beach location, and it's the best bet for the money.

Paradise Hotel. Molos, 34007 Skyros. ☎ **0222/91-220.** Fax 0222/91-443. 60 units. TEL. Dr18,000 ($52) double in the new building. Breakfast Dr1,200 ($3.50) extra.

This pleasant lodging is at the north end of Magazia beach, in the town of Molos. The older part of the hotel has 40 rooms; these more basic units run about 50% less. We recommend one of the newer section's 20 rooms, which are better kept and have much better light. The hotel is somewhat removed from the main town, but there is a taverna on the premises and another down the street.

Pension Galeni. Magazia Beach, 34007 Skyros. ☎ **0222/91-379.** 13 units. Dr11,000 ($32) double.

The small but delightful Pension Galeni offers modest rooms, all with private bathroom. We like the front, sea-facing rooms on the top floor for their (currently) unobstructed views. The Galeni overlooks one of the cleanest parts of Magazia beach.

Xenia. Magazia Beach, 34007 Skyros. ☎ **0222/92-063.** Fax 0222/92-062. 22 units. TEL. Dr30,000 ($86) double. Rates include buffet breakfast. V.

With the best location on the beach at Magazia, the Xenia offers some of the best (if not cheapest) accommodations on Skyros. The guest rooms have handsome 1950s-style furniture and big bathrooms with tubs, as well as wonderful balconies and sea views. You can get all your meals here if you so desire. Perhaps the hotel's greatest drawback is the unsightly concrete breakwater that's supposed to protect the beach from erosion.

IN ACHEROUNES BEACH

Pegasus Apartments. Acherounes Beach, 34007 Skyros. ☎ **0222/91-552.** 8 units. MINI-BAR. Dr12,800 ($37) studio for two persons; Dr25,800 ($74) apt for three to five persons. EC, MC, V.

These fully equipped studios and apartments were built by the resourceful Lefteris Trakos (owner of Skyros Travel). They are located at Acherounes, the beach just south of the port of Linaria, on the east coast. One of the pluses of staying here is the chance to see (and ride, if you're under 15) Katerina, a Skyriot pony.

IN YIRISMATA

✪ **Skyros Palace Hotel.** Yirismata, 34007 Skyros. ☎ **0222/91-994.** Fax 0222/92-070. 80 units. TEL. Dr24,000 ($69) double. Rates include breakfast. AE, DC, EC, MC, V.

This out-of-the-way resort—about a mile north of Molos, thus 2 miles north of Skyros town—offers the most luxurious accommodations on the island. The guest rooms are plainly furnished but comfortable, with large balconies. The beach across the road is an especially windy, rocky stretch of coastline, with somewhat treacherous water. Facilities include a lovely pool and adjacent bar, tennis courts, some air-conditioned rooms, and a well-planted garden—not to mention a soundproofed disco, the most sophisticated on the island. A minibus heads into town twice a day. If you want to get away from it all and enjoy some upscale amenities to boot, this might be the place for you.

WHERE TO DINE

The food in Skyros town is generally pretty good and reasonably priced. **Anemos,** on the main drag (☎ **0222/92-155**), is a good place for breakfast, with filtered coffee, omelets, and freshly squeezed juice. The nearby **Skyros Pizza Restaurant** (☎ **0222/91-684**) serves tasty pies as well as other Greek specialties. For dessert, there's the **Zaccharoplasteio,** the Greek name for sweet shop/bakery, in the center of town.

In Linaria, there are three decent tavernas to choose from—**Almyria, Filippeos,** and **Psariotos.**

✪ **Kristina's/Pegasus Restaurant.** Skyros town. ☎ **0222/91-123.** Reservations recommended in summer. Main courses Dr1,400–Dr3,600 ($4–$10). No credit cards. Mon–Sat 7am–4pm and 7pm–1am. INTERNATIONAL.

Kristina's has been an institution in Skyros town for some years, but in 2000 it moved to the locale of the former Pegasus Restaurant, a neoclassical building (ca.1890) in the center of town. The Australian proprietor/chef, Kristina, brings a light touch to everything she cooks. Her fricasseed chicken is excellent, her herb bread is tasty, and her desserts, such as cheesecake, are exceptional. Definitely the place if you need a break from standard Greek fare.

Maryetes Grill. Skyros town. ☎ **0222/91-311.** Main courses Dr1,100–Dr2,200 ($3.70–$6). No credit cards. Daily 1–3pm and 6pm–midnight. GRILL.

One of the oldest and best places in town, the Maryetes is a second-generation-run grill that's equally popular with locals and travelers. The dining room is as simple as simple gets, so what you go for is the food. We recommend the grilled chicken and meat. There's a small sampling of salads as well.

Restaurant Kabanero. Skyros town. ☎ **0222/91-240.** Main courses Dr1,000–Dr1,600 ($2.90–$4.60). No credit cards. Daily 1–3pm and 6pm–midnight. GREEK.

One of the best dining values in town, this perpetually busy eatery serves the usual Greek menu: moussaka, stuffed peppers and tomatoes, fava, various stewed vegetables, and several kinds of meat. The dishes are tasty and prices somewhat lower than at most other places in town.

SKYROS AFTER DARK

If you've gotta dance, try the **Kastro Club,** in Linaria, or **Stone,** on the road to Magazia. Linaria's **O Kavos** is another popular hangout. Aside from these, there are few evening diversions other than barhopping on the main street of Skyros town. **Apocalypsis** draws a younger crowd. **Kalypso** attracts a more refined set of drinkers who appreciate their better-made but pricier cocktails. **Renaissance** is loud and lively. **Rodon** is best for actually listening to music, while **Kata Lathos** ("By Mistake") has also gained a following.

Highlights of Western Greece: Epirus & Ioannina

by John S. Bowman

Evergreen slopes, deep-set rivers and lush valleys, villages of timbered houses with slate or tile roofs—this can't be Greece. But it is. It's the northwestern corner the Greeks know as **Epirus.** Plentiful rainfall, the rugged Pindos mountains, and a generally more temperate climate seem to remove this region from familiar Mediterranean Greece—at times, it almost seems Alpine. It's one of the few places in Greece where you'll spend time away from the sea.

Epirus and its capital city, **Ioannina,** seem immune to the throngs who crowd the beaches and restaurants, the ferries and ancient sites, of so many parts of Greece these days. It isn't the travel-poster Greece many have come to expect, and it certainly hasn't organized itself around tourism and foreigners. Although there are plenty of hotels and restaurants, the pace of life in Ioannina and other cities, not to mention in the villages, is governed by local customs. During the off-season, for instance, places such as the post office and information offices may be closed all weekend. Museum hours are cut back, as are the hours of gift shops and many restaurants. And except for some staff in the hotels, better restaurants, and visitor information and car-rental offices, few people speak English, although they may speak Italian, French, or German. You may find yourself sharing a hotel with Greek commercial travelers, and it will probably be harder to find your English-language newspaper or fresh-squeezed orange juice. In other words, it's for those who enjoy traveling in an authentic foreign land.

A STRATEGY FOR SEEING THE REGION   Visitors to this corner of Greece will come by ship from Italy or Corfu (via Igoumenitsa), by plane from Athens or Thessaloniki, or by car or bus from other parts of Greece. We recommend basing yourself in Ioannina, a city that offers a fine mix of natural attractions, historical associations, and modern amenities. It's easy to fill the better part of two days by walking around Ioannina, and you could visit Epirus's other main destination, **Metsovo,** by bus. But you really should rent a car to see most of the other attractions of Epirus—**Dodona,** the **Zagori** villages, and the cave at **Perama.** We recommend a minimum of 4 days for Epirus—2 days for Ioannina and Dodona, 1 day for Metsovo, and 1 day for Zagori and Perama Cave.

A LOOK AT THE PAST   In its history, Western Greece and Epirus in particular have often gone in different directions from the rest of the country. It was settled by Greek-speaking peoples about the same time as other parts of Greece (ca. 2000 B.C.), and over the centuries they worshipped many of the same gods and carried on much the same culture. But there were many non-Greek peoples in this area, and this plus a natural remoteness meant that the region did not participate in the grand classical civilization. Social organization remained more tribal, led by small-time kings. The greatest of the Epirote kings, **Pyrrhus** (318–272 B.C.), was constantly making war, and his victories over the Romans outside Rome have given us the term Pyrrhic victory—because won at great cost, they came to nothing. Epirus itself was reduced to a Roman province after 168 B.C.

During the **Middle Ages,** Greece's whole western region was constantly prey to invaders, and with the conquest of Constantinople by the Crusaders in 1204, some Greeks decided to set up a new state with Ioannina as the capital, the so-called Despotate of Epirus. It never amounted to much and soon fell under outside control. Finally it was taken over by the Turks in 1431, and soon they controlled virtually all of Greece, although the Venetians and various other Western Europeans would gain possession of parts of Western Greece.

It was near the end of this long phase that Epirus experienced its most dramatic moment in the spotlight of history, under the "Lion of Ioannina," **Ali Pasha** (1741–1822). He was born in Albania and rose to prominence fighting on behalf of the Ottoman Sultan in Constantinople. But in 1788, Ali Pasha decided to set up a virtually independent domain with his capital in Ioannina. An international celebrity in his day, visited by Byron among others, he was a cruel despot who boasted of killing 30,000 people, often in the most brutal fashion. The Ottomans tolerated Ali Pasha as long as they could, but in 1822 sent a large force to capture him; he hid in a monastery on the islet off Ioannina but was tracked down, killed, and beheaded.

When the Greeks rose up against the Turks in the 1820s, the southern part of Western Greece, centered around Messolonghi, took an active role, but the bulk of Epirus did not join in. The southwestern district of Arta was freed from Turkish rule in 1881, but Epirus was not formally joined to Greece until after the Second Balkan War of 1913.

Epirus became a battleground twice more, against the invading Italians and Germans in World War II, and then in the Greek civil war. Since then it has enjoyed peace and quiet prosperity.

GETTING TO & AROUND EPIRUS

GETTING THERE   By Plane   Olympic Airways (☎ 01/966-6666; www.olympic-airways.gr) offers flights to Ioannina from Athens—usually two a day. At least once a day there are Olympic flights between Ioannina and Thessaloniki. **Aegean Airlines** (☎ 0801/20-000) offers daily flights between Athens and Ioannina; call ahead or contact a travel agent. Olympic also flies about once a day from Athens to Aktion, just outside Preveza on the southernmost coast of Epirus; from here you can get a bus to Igoumenitsou and Ioannina or even to the island of Lefkada, which is connected by a viaduct to the mainland.

By Boat   Igoumenitsou, on the coast opposite Corfu, is the point of entry to northwestern Greece for many people. In summer, ferries connect hourly to Corfu (a trip varying from 1 to 2 hours, depending on the ship) and less frequently to Kefalonia, Ithaka, and Paxi. There is also hydrofoil service, twice daily at least during high season, between Corfu and Igoumenitsou (a trip of about half an hour). Numerous ferries and ships that put into Igoumenitsou go to and from ports in Italy—Ancona, Bari, Brindisi, Venice; some of these connect to Patras or Piraeus in Greece or even more distant ports such as Iraklion in Crete, or Cesme in Turkey.

Travel Tip

Epirus is one part of Greece best visited between early June and late September, unless you don't mind cooler weather. In the winter, you can come up here to ski.

In high season, there is also a ferry connecting **Astakos**—on the Ionian coast south of Preveza and north of Messolonghi—and the offshore islands of Ithaka and Kefalonia.

There are so many changes in scheduling of all these ships that it's useless to provide specific details, but if you want information in advance, contact **Thalassa Travel** in Igoumenitsou, located at Odos Ethniki Antistasseos 20 (☎ **0665/22-001;** fax 0665/22-506).

By Bus   The **KTEL** line (☎ **01/512-5954** in Athens; **0651/26-211** in Ioannina) enters northwestern Greece from distant points such as Athens (7½ hours) or Thessaloniki (8 hours).

By Car   There are several approaches to Western Greece from distant points. **From Athens,** there are two main routes. One is the inland route north via Livadia, Lamia, Karditsa, Trikkala, Kalambaka, and Ioannina. The second is via Corinth and then along the southern coast of the Gulf of Corinth to Rion, the ferry to Antirion, and then via Messolonghi, Agrinio, Arta, and Ioannina. Alternatively, you can head to the Ionian coast after Messolonghi, and go up to Igoumenitsou via Astakos, Preveza, and Parga.

The preferred route **from Thessaloniki** is via Veria west to Kozani and Konitsa and then south to Ioannina. If the former Yugoslavia has settled down enough to allow for transit, it might be possible to take the once well-traveled route from western Europe via Skopje (now capital of the Former Yugoslavia Republic of Macedonia) down into Northern Greece at Florina, and from there south to Kastoria and Ioannina.

GETTING AROUND   By Bus   With enough time, you can see most of Western Greece by bus, but as always, you'll need extra hours for the little side trips. But given the many mountainous roads and curves, you might prefer to let others do the driving. **KTEL** provides bus links between virtually all points in Western Greece. Points to **Athens** and the **north, northwest,** and **northeast** (Igoumenitsou, Metsovo, Konitsa, Kastoria, and Thessaloniki) are serviced from Ioannina's **main bus terminal** at Odos Zosimadon 4 (☎ **0651/26-211**). Points to the **south** (Parga, Arta, Preveza, Astakos, Messolonghi, and Patras) are serviced from a smaller **bus terminal** in Ioannina at Odos Vizaniou 19 (☎ **0651/25-014**).

By Car   Having a car is probably the best way to experience the full variety of Western Greece. Distances are not all that great, although trips do take much longer than a map might suggest due to the many mountainous and curving roads. (Mopeds or motorcycles are not advised except for the most experienced.) Western Greece doesn't offer the choice in car rentals as in more touristy parts of Greece. We think **Budget Rent-A-Car** in Ioannina, at Odos Dodonis 109 (☎ **0651/43-901;** fax 0651/45-382), is the best to deal with; it's a family affair, run by owner Angela Tsamatos, her son Stelios, and the genial manager, Paul Angelis. But don't expect to haggle during high season—there are a limited number of vehicles for the influx of tourists.

By Taxi   There are so many switchbacks and hairpin roads here that you might prefer to take a taxi. Agree on a fee before you set out. Each hour's drive should cost about Dr9,000 ($26); each hour's waiting, about Dr2,500 ($7). Try to get a driver who speaks at least basic English, or a foreign language you understand—and you'll get a guide in the bargain. He in turn should get a generous tip.

1 Ioannina

106km (65 miles) E of Igoumenitsou; 452km (277 miles) N of Athens

Ioannina had long been a sleepy medieval town when Greeks fleeing Constantinople after its capture by the Crusaders in 1204 arrived to make it the capital of the Despotate of Epirus. The first Despot, Michael I, started building the walls that over the next centuries would be enlarged and strengthened by various conquerors—Greeks, Italians, Serbs, and Turks—to become the quite magnificent walled old town that still exists.

ESSENTIALS

GETTING THERE   **Ioannina** is a good 7 hours from Athens by car. **Olympic Airlines** flies to Ioannina from Athens, usually twice a day. At least once a day there are Olympic flights between Ioannina and Thessaloniki. Aegean Airlines also has been offering daily flights from and to Athens.

Olympic's office in downtown Ioannina is in a building at the far side of the triangle of greenery at the top of the Central Square (☎ **0651/26-518** or 0651/23-120). Hours are Monday through Friday from 8am to 3pm; outside of those hours, try the airport office at ☎ **0651/39-131.** The **airport** is about 4 kilometers (2½ miles) from the center of town; it's well serviced by public buses (nos. 2 and 7) from the main square, but you will probably find it more convenient to take a taxi.

VISITOR INFORMATION   Ioannina's **National Tourism Information Office** is located at Leoforos Dodonis 39, up past the Xenia Hotel (☎ **0651/41-142;** fax 0651/49-139). Summer hours are Monday through Friday from 7:30am to 2:30pm and 5:30 to 8:30pm, Saturday from 9am to 1pm; winter hours are Monday through Friday from 7:30am to 2:30pm.

In summer, the city also maintains an information booth down on the lake, to the left of the fortress and by the quay where you get the boats to the islet Nissi; it's open Monday through Saturday from 10am to 8pm.

Also helpful are the many travel agencies, including **Dascalopoulos Harris,** in the Orphea Gallery off Odos 28 Octobriou 9 (☎ and fax **0651/64-661**), and **Daskalopoulos Yiannis Tour World,** Odos 28 Octobriou 13 (☎ **0651/29-667;** fax 0651/21-222).

FAST FACTS   There are numerous **ATMs** in the center of Ioannina (and also a couple in Metsovo); branches of the big national **banks** can handle all money exchanges. There is an internationally known medical school and **hospital** at Dourouti, some 7 kilometers (4 miles) south of Ioannina. There is another hospital at Hatzikosta (2km/1 mile). For **Internet access,** try the **Webcafe** (☎ **0651/83-215**), well back on the left in the Sarka Stoa, opposite Odos Pirsinella 16 (leading off the main square); it's open daily from 11am to 3am.

The **Self Service Laundry,** Odos Tsirigoti 3, around the corner from the KTEL bus station (☎ **0651/25-542**), is open Monday through Saturday from 8am to 2pm, and also Tuesday, Thursday, and Friday from 5 to 8:30pm. The **tourist police** are located at **Police Headquarters,** Odos 28 Octobriou 11 (☎ **0651/25-673**); open daily from 7am to 2am. The main **post office** is on Odos 28 Octobriou 3 (☎ **0651/26-437**). It's open Monday through Saturday from 7:30am to 8pm; in the off-season, it's closed on Saturdays. The **telephone office (OTE)** is at the rear (right) on Odos 28 Octobriou 4; open daily from 7am to 10pm.

WHAT TO SEE & DO

Ioannina Museum. Plateia 25 Martiou (behind clock tower and the Greek Army base on Central Sq.). ☎ **0651/25-490.** Fax 0651/22-595. Admission Dr500 ($1.45) adults, Dr300 (90¢) for seniors over 65. Tues–Sun 8:30am–3pm.

Housed in a modern building, this fine little provincial museum has just enough to engage anyone who has come this far. Most displays are from graves and burial sites in Epirus, but the range of items extends from Paleolithic implements (including one of the oldest stone tools in all Greece) through the Bronze Age to Roman times. Various bronze works are especially interesting, as is the superb Attic-style sarcophagus dating from the 2nd to 3rd centuries A.D., with carved scenes from the *Iliad.*

But undoubtedly, the display case that will entrance most people holds some of the little lead tablets found at the **Oracle of Dodona** (see "Side Trips from Ioannina," below). People from all stations of life came to Dodona and had some desire or query inscribed on a strip of lead that was then submitted to the oracle. Today we can read these actual pleas. Some are quite practical: "Should I buy a certain property?" "Should I engage in shipping?" Others have a religious tinge: "To which god should we pray or sacrifice to get certain results?" But the most intriguing are the personals: "Is it better to marry?" "Shall I take another wife?" "Am I the father of her children?" These tablets speak to us as do few remains from the ancient world.

A STROLL AROUND THE *FROURIO*: THE WALLED OLD TOWN & CITADEL

For many of the centuries that Ioannina fell under the occupation of foreign conquerors, city walls enclosed all the most important structures. There's virtually nothing of historic or architectural importance outside the citadel except on the islet of Nissi. Originally the fortress was separated from the mainland by a moat, which was crossed by three bridges. The moat has since been filled in. An esplanade now circles the lakeside below the walls, and there are several openings in the wall, but most people will enter the walls from the **Plateia Yioryio,** which is lined by tavernas and gift shops.

A left turn inside the Plateia Giorgio gate onto Odos Ioustinianou leads (in about 2 blocks) to the **Synagogue.** Dating from 1790, this white-walled synagogue, with a Hebrew inscription above its locked door, will be interesting to those willing to track down someone who can let you in—try asking at the shop of Mrs. Allegra Matsa, Odos Anexartisias 18 (☎ **0651/27-008**). The Jewish community of Ioannina traces its origins to Jews who came here at least by the 13th century. The Germans removed all 5,000 or so in 1941 and took them to labor and extermination camps. After the war, about 150 survivors came back, but today only some 100 Jews still live in Ioannina. A small **Holocaust Memorial** is just outside the citadel, on the corner of Odos Karamanlis and Odos Soutsou.

If you continue on around the inside perimeter of the walls, you will come to a large clearing. From here, ascend a cobblestoned slope to the **Aslan Pasha Cami,** a 17th-century school with cells for Islamic scholars. Its **mosque** now houses the **Municipal Popular Art Museum.** In summer, it's open daily from 8am to 8pm; in winter, Monday through Friday from 8am to 3pm, Saturday and Sunday from 9am to 3pm. Admission is Dr600 ($1.75). The mosque was erected in 1618 on the site of an Orthodox church, razed by Aslan Pasha to punish the Christian Greeks for a failed revolt. Entering the mosque, observe in the vestibule the recesses for shoes. The exhibits, which include traditional costumes, jewelry, weapons, documents, and household wares, are grouped around the three major religious-ethnic communities of Ioannina: the Orthodox Greeks, the Muslims, and the Jews. There's an adjacent minaret, and when it and the mosque are illuminated each night, the scene from the lake is captivating.

Ioannina

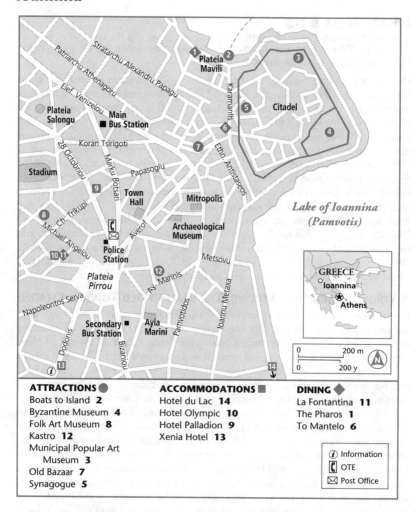

ATTRACTIONS ●
Boats to Island **2**
Byzantine Museum **4**
Folk Art Museum **8**
Kastro **12**
Municipal Popular Art
    Museum **3**
Old Bazaar **7**
Synagogue **5**

ACCOMMODATIONS ■
Hotel du Lac **14**
Hotel Olympic **10**
Hotel Palladion **9**
Xenia Hotel **13**

DINING ◆
La Fontantina **11**
The Pharos **1**
To Mantelo **6**

ⓘ Information
🄲 OTE
✉ Post Office

In the opposite and far corner of the walled town is the innermost citadel, known
by its Turkish name, **Itz Kale.** Within it are the Victory Mosque (**Fethiye Cami**); the
base of a circular tower; the remains of the palace of Ali Pasha, the cruel Albanian who
dominated Epirus from 1788 until 1822; and the alleged **tombs** of Ali Pasha and his
wife. The Greek army long occupied this part of the citadel, but its structures have
now been restored and there is an interesting **Byzantine Museum** here, located in two
buildings, the virtually rebuilt **palace** and the **harem.** The former houses the icons and
other church-related objects, the latter concentrates on silver work. Hours are daily
from 9am to 3pm; admission is Dr500 ($1.45).

A STROLL AROUND IOANNINA

Ioannina has become a busy commercial center for all of northwestern Greece (its
population is some 100,000), and its streets can be filled with vehicles of all kinds gen-
erating noise and fumes, but there are some interesting retreats from all this. One is
the old **Turkish Bazaar,** down near the walled town and just off the main street, Odos
Averoff. Although gradually vanishing, in its tiny shops you will still see a few men

practicing the old crafts—metalsmiths, jewelry makers, cobblers, tailors, and the like. Proceeding up Odos Averoff, you come to the edge of the Central Square with the **clock tower** (on the left). Up behind this is the city's **archaeological museum** (see above). When you leave the museum, stroll across the broad terraced gardens built over the site of what was once the **walled Kastro,** where the Christians lived during the Turkish era. There was a cafe/restaurant on the far corner, but as of our last visit it was closed; hopefully new owners will revive it, as the location's outdoor tables provide a fine view of the lake and distant mountains. Returning to the main street, you are now on the **Central Square** (officially Plateia Pyrros), also with its share of cafes and restaurants.

A Boat Trip to the Islet of Nissi (Nissaki)

If you have only a day in Ioannina, try to spend at least 2 to 3 hours (including an hour for a meal) on a visit to **Nissi,** the islet in Lake Pamvotis. Small boats leave from the quay below the fortress every half hour in summer, from 6:30am to 11pm. In the off-season, service is every hour—but note that the last boat leaves the island around 10pm. The fare is Dr200 (60¢). The lake has unfortunately become overgrown with algae and is so polluted that local restaurants do not serve the fish taken from it (or so we've been assured).

The boat ride is barely 10 minutes and, day and night, provides a fine view of Ioannina. You get off in what is virtually the lobby of three restaurants—each displaying a tank filled with seafood. Resist all until you are truly ready to eat. The specialties of these restaurants include eel, frogs' legs, carp, crayfish, trout, and other imported fish.

The small village here is said to have been founded only in the 16th century by refugees from the Mani region of the Peloponnese, but its five monasteries predate this, and they are your destination. Take the narrow passage between the two restaurants; signs are posted to your left and right. Following the signs to the left (east), you will come to the **Monastery of Panteleimon.** Although founded in the 16th century, it has been so heavily restored that little of the original remains.

The monastery houses a **small museum** devoted to the infamous **Ali Pasha,** with numerous pictures and personal items including his clothing and water pipe. It's open daily, and an attendant will come if it's closed. Admission is Dr200 (60¢). Pasha took refuge here in 1820 and was eventually killed here in 1822 by Turks. You may even be shown holes in the floor where it is alleged he was shot from below.

Directly beside this monastery is the **Monastery of the Prodromos (St. John the Baptist),** but most people will want to move on to the western edge of the islet, following the signs to the **Moni Filanthropinon** (also known as the **Monastery of Ayios Nikolaos Spanos**). It's sometimes referred to as the "Secret School" because of claims that Orthodox priests maintained a secret school here during the Turkish occupation. Founded in the 13th century, it was rebuilt in the 16th century, when magnificent frescoes were painted on its walls. (There's no admission, but it's customary to leave a gratuity with the caretaker.) Seldom does the public get to view such an ensemble of Byzantine frescoes so close up. Although the dim light can be a problem (bring a flashlight), you should be able to recognize such subjects as the life of Christ on the walls of the apse, God and the Apostles in the central dome, and the many saints. Most unexpected, however, are the portrayals of ancient Greek sages on the wall of the narthex as you enter—Apollonius, Aristotle, Cheilon, Plato, Plutarch, Solon, and Thucydides.

About 100 meters farther along the trail is **Ayios Nikolaos Dilios** (or **Moni Stratgopoulou**), the oldest monastery (dating from the 11th century) on Nissi. Its 16th-century frescoes are also of some interest but are in poor condition. (A small tip to the caretaker is also called for.) The fifth monastery, **Ayios Eleouses,** is closed to the public.

By now you have earned your meal on Nissi. Choose one of the restaurants (see "Where to Dine," below). And as you sip your wine, you can contemplate what such a locale means while enjoying the view.

SHOPPING

If you get the impression that every third store in old Ioannina sells jewelry, silverware, hammered copper, and embossed brass work, you're right—these are the traditional crafts here. Many of the jewelry stores really sell nothing but modern work in gold and silver and/or precious and semiprecious jewels. Prices are probably lower than in more cosmopolitan cities, but be wary of "antiques" that may be offered in some shops—they may not be all that old, and if they are older than 1830, you need an export license!

There's a cluster of jewelry and gift shops opposite the walled citadel. Typical selections of metal work (and also water pipes) may be found at **Politis Douvflis,** Plateia Yioryio 12, or at **Nikos Gogonis,** Odos Karamanlis 13. At two shops on Odos Averoff, 56 and 65, **George Minos Moschos** offers a somewhat more unusual selection of silver, jewelry, and older secondhand objects ("antiques"). Here and there you may see embroidered clothing or woven socks, but this is not a region known for delicate needlework.

WHERE TO STAY

Ioannina and its immediate environs don't offer luxury resorts, but that's not why travelers come here. There are, however, several quite special hotels and plenty of more-than-adequate accommodations.

In addition to the following options, the **Hotel Galaxy,** Plateia Pyrros (Central Square), 45221 Ioannina (☎ **0651/25-432;** fax 0651/30-724), offers convenient, clean, and cheap rooms.

✪ **Hotel du Lac.** Leoforos Andrea Miaouli and Odos Ikkou (along the lake, half a mile right of walled citadel), 45221 Ioannina. ☎ **0651/59-100.** Fax 0651/59-200. 130 units. A/C MINIBAR TV TEL. All year Dr40,000 ($115) double. Rates include buffet breakfast. AE, DC, EC, JCB, MC, V. Open year-round. Parking on grounds. Taxis can be ordered from desk.

This hotel opened in the summer of 1998 and immediately became Ioannina's prime showplace. With its marble and woodwork and carpets, it exudes luxury; more important, its service lives up to its image. The rooms are a bit larger than in many Greek hotels and most enjoy a view across the lake; bathrooms are state-of-the-art. In addition to all the expected amenities of a first-class hotel (room service, laundry service, secretaries or babysitters on request, and more), it offers data/fax lines for computer modems, a swimming pool, and a children's pool and playground. The buffet breakfast is almost excessive; the regular meals are what you'd expect from a fine hotel. Some might find its distance from the center (a 15-min. walk) a downside, but in return you get a quiet lakeside locale.

Hotel Olympic. Odos Melanidi 2 (1 block off Central Sq.), 45220 Ioannina. ☎ **0651/ 25-888.** Fax 0651/22-041. 54 units. A/C TV TEL. High season Dr24,000 ($69) double; low season Dr19,000 ($54) double. No credit cards. Open year-round. Parking in lot across from hotel.

For those who like to be at the center of the action, such as it is in Ioannina, the Olympic is the hotel. It has long attracted members of the foreign diplomatic corps, government dignitaries, and such. All that means nothing, of course, if you aren't made to feel welcome and comfortable, and you can be assured of both. The lobby is modest, but the desk service and 24-hour room service are what count. All the corridors, bedrooms, and bathrooms have recently been renovated. The upper-story front rooms enjoy a view of the distant lake, and all units have small fridges and safes.

Hotel Palladion. Odos Botsari 1 (off 28 Octobriou), 45444 Ioannina. ☎ **0651/25-856.** Fax 0651/74-034. E-mail: palladion@otenet.gr. 128 units. A/C TV TEL. High season Dr21,000 ($60) double; low season Dr19,000 ($54) double. Rates include buffet breakfast. AE, DC, EC, MC, V. Open year-round. Private parking lot.

We like this place for its combination of features: convenient yet quiet, a professional and helpful desk staff, no frills but good value. Rooms are of decent size and decor, bathrooms are standard issue, and everything works. (And when we asked to move from one because of lingering cigarette odor, this happened instantly and with no further questions. Since then, the hotel has set aside floors for non-smokers.) The Palladion often hosts groups, but this won't interfere with your stay. A final advantage: The hotel has its own parking lot.

✪ **Xenia Hotel.** Odos Dodonis 33 (up past the Central Sq.), 45221 Ioannina. ☎ **0651/47-301.** Fax 0651/47-189. 60 units. TV TEL. Dr27,000 ($77) double. Rates include buffet breakfast. AE, DC, EC, MC, V. Open year-round. Parking on grounds. An easy walk from the Central Sq., or take one of the many public buses that pass by.

This was long Ioannina's finest, and although the rooms are not exceptional (but certainly tasteful and comfortable), what you get for your money is a sense of seclusion in a park at the very heart of town. The hotel is set well back from the street, and the bedrooms at the rear enjoy fine views. There's an outdoor cafe that allows you to relax in a garden atmosphere; the indoor restaurant is highly regarded and certainly convenient if you don't care to explore Ioannina's many others. The front desk will see to basic needs (laundry, car rental, excursions), and room service is available.

WHERE TO DINE
MODERATE

The Gastra Restaurant. Eleousa, along the Airport-Igoumenitsou Hwy. (7km/4.3 miles outside Ioannina; 3km/1.9 miles past the airport, just before turnoff to Igoumenitsou). ☎ **0651/61-530.** Reservations recommended in high season on weekend evenings; on Sunday, you are advised to leave it to the citizens of Ioannina. Main courses Dr1,200–Dr3,700 ($3.45–$11). No credit cards. Tues–Sun 1–5pm and 8pm–1am. Open year-round. Public bus 2. GREEK REGIONAL.

This is a must for all those willing to try a special type of regional cooking that involves heaping red-hot embers over a *gastra*—the conical cast-iron lid that's lowered onto the baking dish holding the food (lamb, goat, pork, or chicken), which then roasts slowly to appear on your table as an especially succulent meal. It's delicious. The restaurant also has other specialties; for an appetizer, try the *skordalia karithia* (walnut-garlic dip), and for dessert, the special crème caramel.

In pleasant weather, you can eat out front in the shaded garden and watch your meal cooking in the open fireplace. On cooler evenings, you can sit inside the handsome restaurant. When the spirit moves, diners are encouraged to dance to the music. Come here for a leisurely experience, not just for the food. (And if it's too crowded and you need your gastra, proceed less than a mile after taking the left turn signed to Igoumenitsou to another such restaurant, the **Diogenes.**)

La Fontantina. Odos Melanidi 2 (on ground floor of Olympic Hotel, 1 block off Central Sq.). ☎ **0651/25-147.** Fax 0651/22-041. Reservations recommended on holidays and weekends in high season. Main courses Dr1,100–Dr4,500 ($3.70–$13). No credit cards. Daily 10am–midnight. GREEK/ITALIAN.

This is the house restaurant of the Olympic Hotel and has become a favorite gathering spot for foreigners and Greeks who like to feel they're at Ioannina's crossroads. The decor is hotel classy, service is a bit casual, and the menu ranges from Greek to Italian standards. But go for a change from the usual Greek foods, to enjoy the risotto or spaghetti carbonara or a steak fillet with one of the fine red wines from Northern Greece—a Naoussa, an Amyntaion, or a Carras. Florence it's not, but La Fontantina offers a taste of upscale Ioannina.

INEXPENSIVE

Pamvotis. Nissi Ioannina (the offshore islet). ☎ **0651/81-081.** Fax 0651/81-631. Main courses Dr1,000–Dr2,600 ($2.90–$8). EC, MC, V. High season daily 11am–midnight; low season daily 11am–10pm. Ferry from Ioannina's lakefront. GREEK.

If you have only one meal to eat in Ioannina, it has to be at one of the restaurants on the islet out in the lake. And if you ask around as to which is the best, you'll get a different answer from everyone. In fact, they're all about the same quality, so choose one with a location that appeals. We like this one—located near the dock where the little ferries put in, so you get a lively scene along with the local specialties. (If you prefer a more natural setting, go to the **Propodes Restaurant** at the side of the Ayios Panteleimon Monastery, which you'll want to visit. See "A Boat Trip to the Islet of Nissi (Nissaki)," above.) You can pick your lobster, *karavides* (a cross between crayfish and shrimp), trout, or other fish of the day right out of holding tanks. If you're game, try one of the two local specialties: frogs' legs or eel. The white Zitsa Primus, a slightly sparkling white wine from the region, is a perfect accompaniment.

The Pharos. Plateia Mavili 13 (down along lakefront). ☎ **0651/26-506.** Main courses Dr1,200–Dr3,000 ($3.45–$9). No credit cards. Daily 9am–10pm. Closed mid-Oct to Mar. Bus from Central Sq. or a 10-min. walk. GREEK.

One of several restaurants set back from the lakefront, the Pharos should appeal to those who just want a good meal in a pleasant setting. In warm weather, you can sit under the awning in the square opposite. The menu is traditional but with some variants. For an appetizer, try the fried peppers in a garlic sauce. For your main course, order whatever's being grilled that day, and get the pilaf instead of potatoes. If you're feeling flush, try the crab or trout; if you're just there for the location, try the fresh fruit salad plate.

To Mantelo. Plateia Georgio 15 (opposite the main entrance to citadel). ☎ **0651/25-452.** Main courses Dr900–Dr1,800 ($2.60–$5.15). No credit cards. Daily 10am–2am. GREEK.

Here's one for those who prefer their Greek tavernas to look traditional and to attract Greeks. It's a no-frills place that gives you a front-row seat on the square outside the old walled town, where all kinds of characters congregate. For an appetizer, try one of the fried-marinated dishes—peppers, squash, or eggplant. Go for any of the grilled dishes—veal, chicken, lamb—or the calves' liver. In all cases, ask for the pilaf. The taverna can feel cramped when it's crowded, but that's what makes it Greek.

2 Side Trips from Ioannina

DODONA (DODONI)

Even if you aren't the kind who chases after every classical ruin, this one offers a real reward: a spectacular theater at one of the major oracles of the ancient world. In August there are performances of the classical Greek dramas; ask at travel agencies if you wish to plan your visit around them.

✪ **Dodona** is located only 22 kilometers (14 miles) from Ioannina, so it can easily be visited in about 2 hours if you have a car. The bus service is inconvenient—basically only one bus very early in the morning, and then you're stuck here for many hours; it's better to spring for a **taxi**—about Dr10,000 ($29) for the round-trip, including an hour's wait. The first 7 kilometers (4.3 miles) are on a main highway due south (signed to Arta); the turn to the left becomes (after an additional 3km/2 miles) an ascending and curving road. You'll arrive on a plateau ringed by mountains. The trip becomes part of the experience—you get the sense that you're on a pilgrimage to a remote shrine. Admission to the sacred precincts is Dr500 ($1.45). In high season, it's open daily from 8am to 8pm; off-season, Monday through Saturday from 10am to 3pm.

The **Oracle of Zeus** at Dodona traces its roots back to the early Hellenistic peoples who had arrived in northwestern Greece by about 2000 B.C. They themselves probably worshipped Zeus, but it now appears that at Dodona there was already some cult of the earth goddess, possibly with an oracle that based its interpretations on the flights of pigeons. In any case, by about 1400 B.C., it appears that the Zeus-worshipping Greeks had imposed their god on the site and turned the goddess into his consort, Dione.

By this time, too, the priests were linking Zeus's presence to the rustling leaves of an oak tree at Dodona and were interpreting these sounds as oracular messages. The Greeks set up a shrine around this tree, at first nothing more than a protective fence. Over the centuries they built more and more elaborate structures on the site, but the first temple to Zeus was not erected here until the 4th century B.C.

Eventually the oracle spoke through the bronze statue of a youth with a whip that was stirred by the wind to strike adjacent metal cauldrons, and the reverberating sound was interpreted. Many ambitious structures, both religious and secular, were erected at Dodona, but the oracle effectively ceased functioning in the 4th century A.D.—about the time when, it is claimed by some, the original oak died. The oak now on the site of the shrine is, of course, a recent planting.

Only traces of walls are left of other structures, but the magnificent **theater** survives, albeit thanks to what was virtually a reassembling in the 19th century. The first theater was built in the 3rd century B.C. and was said to have seated 17,000. It was destroyed, but another as large replaced it in the 2nd century B.C. Later, the Romans converted it into an arena for gladiatorial contests. The theater was one of the largest on the Greek mainland and has almost the same marvelous acoustics as the famous (but smaller) one at Epidaurus. Even if you do not explore the other remains, just to sit in this theater for a while is an evocative experience.

PERAMA CAVE

Only some 5 kilometers (3 miles) north of Ioannina (the turnoff is past the airport), this cave—actually more a series of caverns—was discovered in 1941, during World War II, when people were seeking hiding places. It has since been thoroughly developed, with electric lights, steps, and handrails that allow for a perfectly safe walk through. In high season, it's open daily from 8am to 8pm; in winter, from 9am to sunset (☎ 0651/81-521). Guided tours set out about every 15 minutes from the well-signed entrance in Perama village; the fee is Dr1,000 ($2.90). The guides often don't speak much more English than to repeat the names assigned to unusually shaped stalagmites or stalactites, and they have an annoying habit of making everyone rush through—but you can in fact linger behind and join the next group.

Whether or not Perama lives up to its boast as one of the most spectacular caves in the world, it's worth a visit if you haven't been in many such caves. *Warning:* At the very end, you must climb what seems like an endless number of steps to come out of the cave—but at least you finish at a cafe!

METSOVO

This is a traditional mountain village that has become so popular that at times the original appeal is in danger of being overwhelmed by tourism at its worst. Still, most visitors find it satisfying—some even find it magical. It's about a 1½-hour bus ride east of Ioannina. Although there are a couple of buses to Metsovo in the morning, there's really only one back from Metsovo in the late afternoon that allows for a day in the village—so either pay close attention to the always-changing bus schedule or, better still, rent a car. (It can also be approached by buses coming from Athens or Thessaloniki.)

The village sits at about 1,000 meters (3,300 ft.) above sea level, nestled among peaks of the Pindos mountains, so in addition to attracting day-trippers, it draws serious nature lovers and hikers from all over Greece and Europe. Overnight accommodations are often strained, especially during Greek holidays. And because there are ski slopes nearby, Metsovo is a popular destination even during the winter.

Assuming that you'll come here on a day's excursion, what you will experience is a village that has maintained a certain style of architecture; traditional customs such as clothing and dances; crafts such as weaving, embroidery, and woodwork; and several food specialties. The buildings, of course, can be seen at all times just by strolling around. They're what most of us think of as Alpine style—stone, with wooden balconies and slate roofs. A declining few of the older people wear traditional clothing all the time, but the fancier costumes are worn only on Sundays and holidays.

If you want to see the **dances,** July 26 is the village's feast day, but also one of its most overcrowded days. **Crafts** are always on display and for sale in dozens of shops up and down the main street. Some is touristy kitsch, but some is authentically local and handsome. The best of the latter is at the **Metsovo Folk Art Cooperative,** about 50 meters from the Egnatia Hotel on the slope above it. The traditional **Epirote foods** can be sampled in several restaurants (see "Where to Dine," below). Disneyland it ain't, but don't go to Metsovo thinking you're discovering a quaint native village. There's even a fairly ambitious conference center in town.

There remains yet another reason to go to Metsovo. It's the center (in Greece, at least) of the **Vlach people,** who claim descent from Latin-speaking Wallachians of what is now Romania. The Vlachs were originally shepherds who followed their flocks, and some still do just that; but over the centuries, many other Vlachs settled down in northern Greece and prospered in crafts, commerce, and trade. Some of the wealthier Vlachs have made their money from dealing in wool and other products from the flocks, and now many in Metsovo prosper from the tourist trade. Because the Vlachs wrote little of their distinctive Latin-based language down and because it's not taught in the schools, it's in danger of being lost as the new generation marry and move out of their relatively small circles. You'll find the Vlachs of Metsovo extremely congenial—and patient as foreigners constantly ask them to "say something in Vlach." (Don't expect your Latin to help much!)

In addition to walking about the village, there are several special attractions that may appeal. The **Museum of Folk Art** is in the Arhondiko Tositsa, a 17th-century mansion that's been completely restored by Baron Michalis Tositsa, a wealthy Vlach living in Switzerland. With its paneled rooms, furniture, rugs, clothing, crafts, and domestic furnishings of all kinds, it's a superb example of how a prosperous family might once have lived in Epirus. The museum, located on a road above the main street, is open in summer, Monday through Wednesday and Friday through Saturday from 8:30am to 1pm and 4 to 6pm; in winter, it's open the same days but from 3 to 5pm only. Admission is Dr500 ($1.45).

Much more typical of Metsovo is the little **church of Ayia Paraskevi** on the main square, with its carved-wood altar screen, silver chandeliers, and copies of Ravenna mosaics.

And if you can handle the half-hour walk down and an hour walk (including frequent stops for air!) back up, you can visit the restored 14th-century **Moni Ayios**

Nikolaos. A signed trail for this monastery leads off from the main square; take the second left, head for the clock tower, then follow the signs. You can drive closer to it by taking the road out of the town square (signed Ioannina); at about 1 kilometer (0.6 mile) turn left onto the asphalt road where it is signed Anilio, and wind downward for another 3½ kilometers (2 miles); the monastery sits up on the slope and you have to scramble up through the vineyard. The resident caretaker (a lovely lady who has some of her own handsome weavings for sale) will allow entry during all reasonable hours (until 7:30pm in high season). The church has some quite spectacular 18th-century frescoes (long lost until the 1950s), a fine iconostasis, and several icons.

WHERE TO STAY

If you want to overnight in Metsovo, there are about a dozen hotels to choose from, all quite acceptable and all to some degree decorated in the traditional style of the region.

Galaxias. On a terrace above the main square. ☎ **0656/41-202.** Fax 0656/41-124. 10 units, some with shower, some with tub. TV TEL. High season Dr24,000 ($69) double; low season Dr16,500 ($47) double. Rates include continental breakfast. EC, MC, V.

If you want to be at the center of things, then this should be your choice—but it's for travelers who appreciate staying in a country inn. It's by no means a fancy hotel—the rooms are modest in size and decor, the bathrooms just adequate. Ask for a room in the front with a view of the distant mountains. The homey atmosphere emanates from the Barbayanni family, who run this hotel and the restaurant reviewed below.

✪ **The Hotel Victoria.** About 1km (half a mile) from the main square. ☎ **0656/41-771.** Fax 0656/41-454. 37 units, some with shower, some with tub. TV TEL. Regular season Dr24,000 ($69) double; Christmas and Easter seasons Dr28,000 ($80). Rates include continental breakfast. EC, MC, V.

If you want a more natural setting and a bit more luxury, try the Victoria, out on the edge of town. As you approach the hotel down a steep road, the traditional Epirote style of architecture will remind you somewhat of an Alpine inn. The interior, with its generous use of natural materials and large fireplaces (functioning in winter), plus its hearty furnishings, confirm this impression. The rooms are not especially large, but feel quite cozy; all have balconies and/or views. And because the Victoria is relatively new (from the late 1980s), its bathrooms are modern. The hotel maintains its own fine restaurant, but what you really come here for is the isolation and the views. In winter, it becomes a ski lodge, but it's highly popular year-round with Greeks and Europeans, so reservations are advised.

Kassaros Hotel. About 100 yds. along road leading from main square back to Ioannina. ☎ **0656/41-800.** Fax 0656/41-262. 31 units, some with shower, some with tub. TV TEL. High season Dr20,000 ($57) double; low season Dr16,000 ($46) double. Rates include continental breakfast. AE, DC, EC, MC, V.

For a location away from the square, but not as far as the Victoria, and as a favor to your budget, try the Kassaros Hotel. This is the perfect place for those who intend an extended or active stay in Metsovo—the proprietor also runs a travel agency, Kassaros Travel, which has ski equipment and a snowmobile for rent as well as its own buses for excursions throughout Epirus.

WHERE TO DINE

Even if you spend only a few hours in Metsovo, you should try a meal at a restaurant that offers traditional Epirote fare. There are a couple decent ones along the main street, Odos Tositsa—Taverna Panormiko, Restaurant Toxotis, and Cafe Chroni Roof Garden—but the following is our favorite.

✪ **Galaxias.** In the Galaxias hotel, just above the main square. ☎ **0656/41-202.** Main courses Dr1,000–Dr2,800 ($2.90–$8). EC, MC, V. Daily noon–11pm. GREEK.

In warm weather, you can sit outdoors; in cooler weather, eat in the handsome dining room warmed by a cheerful fire. Begin a meal of the local specialties with the bean soup (*trachana*) or a cheese pie with leek. Move on to the spicy sausage or beef patties with leeks and celery baked in a pot. For dessert, try the baklava or yogurt, but be sure to save room for one of the local cheeses, of the smoked variety (*metsovonay*), or the mild *vlachotiri*. To accompany your meal, ask for the local red wine, Katoyi, or if that's in short supply, just the house wine.

ZAGORI (ZAGORIA/ZAGOROHORIA) & THE VIKOS GORGE

For some, this might be a more appealing way to spend an extra day in northwest Greece than at Metsovo or Dodona or Perama Cave. The Zagori is the mountainous area just north of Ioannina, a region of perhaps 400 square miles. The whole region is now part of the **Greek National Park System** and has about 45 villages. These have remained virtually unchanged through the centuries. Note that the mountainous roads can make for slow going even to visit a few sites.

Becoming a part of the national park system has put a stop to the unrestricted development that has spoiled so many locales in Greece; it has also required any new structures to be built in the traditional manner, with stone buildings and slate roofs. But it has also so cramped life that young people leave and many of the villages are now all but abandoned. The villages you'll visit tend to be interesting rather than quaint, and much of the appeal of the excursion is in the scenery and such elements as the old bridges. Some disagreement exists as to which are villages, which are hamlets, and which are mere settlements.

The region's most spectacular sight is the **Vikos Gorge,** and for those who are up to it, this can be an excursion of its own. (See "Trekking into the Vikos Gorge," below.)

Getting around the Zagori without your own vehicle is all but impossible. The few buses simply don't allow you to get to more than one destination and back to Ioannina in a day. With a car, you can visit several villages, view the Vikos Gorge from above, experience the scenery, and be back in Ioannina within 6 to 8 hours.

Take the main road north out of Ioannina toward Konitsa; turnoffs are clearly marked. Your first destination should be **Monodendri;** after taking the highway north for 19.4 kilometers (13 miles), just past Metamorfosi, take the right turn signed VIKOS GORGE. At about 5 kilometers (3 miles), a sign to the right indicates **Kipi;** it is well worth the brief diversion (8km/5 miles) to see the famous high-arched bridges. Usually thought of as old Turkish, they were most likely built in the 19th century for the convenience of packhorse caravans. The first, single-span one is the Kokkoros; beyond that is the three-arched Plakida Bridge. (If you have the time and inclination, another 11km/7 miles on through Kipi village leads to **Nigades,** with its strikingly handsome **Church of Ayios Yioryios,** built in 1795.) Returning to the main route, proceed about 39 kilometers (25 miles), where a sign indicates a turn right into the lower square of Monodendri.

Driving to the small parking lot on the edge of the village square, you will proceed on foot (following the sign) about 10 minutes to the lovely little 15th-century **Monastery of Ayia Paraskevi,** perched on the edge of the Vikos Gorge. The viewing areas here are well protected and this will be spectacular enough for most; only the most sure-footed will want to get back on the trail above the monastery and proceed on for several hundred meters to enjoy even more spectacular views of the gorge—but also more dramatic drops from the totally unprotected and narrow path.

Trekking into the Vikos Gorge

For those who want to go into the Vikos Gorge, the lower square of Monodendri offers one of the most accessible approaches. The path down into the gorge is signed here. But even to get to where the gorge begins to open out ahead of you is a rugged 4½- to 5-hour walk—and then it would be still longer to come back up. So no one should attempt this without proper gear, supplies, and experience. The walk through the entire gorge—some 16 kilometers (10 miles)—is even more demanding. If you would like to go on a more ambitious expedition, our advice is to join one of the groups organized by **Robinson Travel Agency,** at the edge of Ioannina on the main road to the airport, Odos 8 Merarchias 10 (☎ **0651/29-402;** fax 0651/25-071). More experienced trekkers might prefer to contact the **Mountain Climbing Association of Papingo** (☎ **0653/41-138**), based in one of the Zagori villages.

Back at the parking lot, if you continue on the main road for about another half mile, you'll come to the upper square of **Monodendri.** (There's a short cobblestone path that leads from the lower square to this upper square.) The upper square is home to several modest hotels and decent restaurants, but unless you are seeking such amenities, you need not go up there. If you want to have a meal while here, we recommend either **Katerina's Restaurant** (try her tasty chicken or meat pies!), at the top of the square, or **To Petrino Dasos,** the little taverna on the right as you come up to the square. The **Oxio,** a hotel and restaurant opposite To Petrino Dasos, is another possibility.

If you want another view of the gorge, you can drive up through the upper square and on for another 7 kilometers (4½ miles), signed to Osia; you again leave your car and walk down a stone path to what is known as the **Vikos Balcony,** offering a truly spectacular view. Local signs claim that the Vikos Gorge, at 900 meters (2,950 ft.), is "the world's deepest," but several places around the world might dispute that.

Our next stop is at **Papingo.** Drivers are usually advised to retrace their entire route back to the main Ioannina-Konitsa highway and then proceed north to the turnoff to Papingo. This is a 1½-hour drive (because you are first heading south again). If you're a bit adventurous—and more important, able to ask basic directions in Greek—you can take a perfectly fine asphalt road that cuts off half that time by going more directly to that highway. You start down from Monodendri, but at about 5 kilometers (3 miles), take the (signed) right turn and head across the flatland for Elafatopos; do not go on up to Elafatopos, however, but continue and take the left turn signed Kato Pedina; you will then come out onto the main highway; turn right and proceed some 4 kilometers (2½ miles) until a sign to the right indicates Papingo. The drive from this point on offers the kind of scenery best described by a young English traveler we fell in with, Simon, who said, "It makes you want to stop the car and get out and applaud."

There are two villages, **Megalo Papingo** and **Micro Papingo**—"Big" and "Little" Papingo—and we recommend visiting at least the first. Many regard this as the archetypal Zagori village, with its terrain, streets, homes, roofs, public buildings, and everything else seemingly all made of the same stone. Megalo Papingo has several cafes and restaurants as well as modest hotels; you can always be sure of a meal in Papingo, but rooms may be booked up at various times of the year—such is the reputation of the Zagori in Greece and elsewhere in Europe.

We recommend the **Hotel Koulis** (☎ **0653/41-115**), where a double costs Dr13,000 ($37); rates include private bathroom and breakfast. If you want something more elegant, try the **Saxonis Houses** (☎ **0653/41-615**), where a double runs Dr23,000 ($66). Rates include private bathroom and breakfast.

If you drive on another mile from Megalo Papingo, you'll come to Micro Papingo, which offers another vista. If you really want to get away from it all, stay at the little **Hotel Dias** here, with its "restaurant" (☎ **0653/41-257** or 0653/41-892); a double runs Dr14,000 ($40), but that's probably negotiable.

After all this, you are now only some 60 kilometers (38 miles) from Ioannina. You can return feeling you have at least had a taste of the true Epirus.

The Ionian Islands

14

by John S. Bowman

"The isles of Greece, the isles of Greece"—when Lord Besyron tossed his bouquet, he was not under the spell of today's popular Cycladic islands but of the Ionian Islands. Located off Greece's northwest coast, the Ionians offer some of the loveliest natural settings (and beaches) in the country, a fine selection of hotels and restaurants, a distinctive history and lore, and some unusual architectural and archaeological sites.

The Ionians are rainier, greener, and more temperate than other Greek islands, with a high season lasting from late June to early September. The roads are generally in good condition, even if unavoidably steep and twisting. Accommodations range from luxury resorts to quiet little rooms on remote beaches. The local cuisine and wines offer numerous special treats. Among the best are *sofrito,* a spicy veal dish; *bourdetto,* a spicy fish dish; and the Theotaki and Liapaditiko wines.

The Ionian Islands include **Corfu** (Kerkira), **Paxos** (Paxoi), **Levkas** (Lefkas, Lefkada), **Ithaka** (Ithaki), **Kefalonia** (Kefallinia, Cephalonia), and **Zakinthos** (Zakynthos, Zante); the seventh, **Kithira** (Cythera, Cerigo), is linked only as a government administrative unit. There are many more islands in the archipelago along Greece's northwest coast, including several that are inhabited.

STRATEGIES FOR SEEING THE ISLANDS In this chapter, we single out **Corfu** and **Kefalonia,** with a side trip to **Ithaka.** With a couple of weeks to spare, you can take a ship or plane to either Corfu at the north or Zakinthos in the south and then make your way by ship to several of the others (although outside high season, you will have to do some backtracking). If you have only a week, you should fly to one and then use ships to get to a couple of the others. In either case, rent a car to get around the larger islands. If it comes down to visiting only one, Corfu is a prime candidate, but if you want to get off the beaten track, consider Kefalonia or Ithaka. All the Ionians—especially Corfu—are overrun in July and August; aim for June or September.

A LOOK AT THE PAST In the fabric of their history, the Ionian Islands can trace certain threads that both tie and distinguish them from the rest of Greece. During the late Bronze Age (1500 to 1200 B.C.), there was a Mycenaean culture on at least several of these islands. Although certain names of islands and cities were the same as those used today—Ithaka, for instance—scholars have never been able to agree on exactly which were the sites described in the *Odyssey.*

The islands were recolonized by people from the city-states on the Greek mainland, starting in the 8th century B.C. The Peloponnesian War, in fact, can be traced back to a quarrel between Corinth and its colony at Corcyra (Corfu) that led to Athens's interference and eventually the full-scale war. The islands later fell under the rule of the Romans, then the Byzantine empire, and remained prey to warring powers and pirates in this part of the Mediterranean for centuries. By the end of the 14th century, Corfu fell under Venice's control, and the Italian language and culture—including the Roman Catholic church—came to predominate.

With the fall of Venice to Napoleon's France in 1797, the French took over and held sway until 1815. The Ionian Islands then became a protectorate of the British; although the islands did experience peace and prosperity, they were in fact a colony. When parts of Greece gained true independence from the Turks by 1830—due in part to leadership from Ionians such as Ioannis Capodistrias—many Ionians became restless under the British. Attempts at gaining union with Greece culminated with Prime Minister Gladstone's granting this in 1864.

During World War II, the islands were at first occupied by the Italians, but when the Germans took over from them, the islands, especially Corfu, suffered greatly. Since 1945, the Ionian Islands have enjoyed considerable prosperity, due mainly to the waves of tourists.

1 Corfu (Kerkira)

32km (20 nautical miles) W of mainland; another 558km (342 miles) NW of Athens

There's Corfu the coast, Corfu the town, and Corfu the island, and they don't necessarily appeal to the same vacationers. Corfu the coast lures those who want to escape civilization and head for the water—whether an undeveloped little beach, with a simple taverna and some rooms to rent, or a spectacular resort. Then there's the more cosmopolitan **Corfu town,** with its distinctive layers of Greek, Italian, French, and British elements. Finally, there's a third and little-known Corfu, the interior with its lush vegetation and gentle slopes, modest villages and farms, and countless olive and fruit trees. (It should also be admitted that there's now a fourth Corfu—rather tacky beach resorts crowded with "package tourists" from Western Europe who sometimes can be a bit raucous. We prefer to think that our readers will know enough to avoid this Corfu.)

Whichever Corfu you choose, it should prove pleasing. It was, after all, this island's ancient inhabitants, the Phaeacians, who made Odysseus so comfortable. Visitors today will find Corfu similarly hospitable.

ESSENTIALS

GETTING THERE **By Plane** **Olympic Airways** provides at least three flights daily from and to Athens and three flights weekly from and to Thessaloniki. One-way fare for each route is about Dr15,700 to Dr20,000 ($45 to $57). The Olympic Airways office in Corfu town is at Odos Polila 11, the street opposite the office of the Greek National Tourism Organization (☎ 0661/38-694), but many agents all over town sell tickets. **Aegean Airlines** also offers occasional but slightly cheaper flights; in Corfu, call ☎ 0661/27-070.

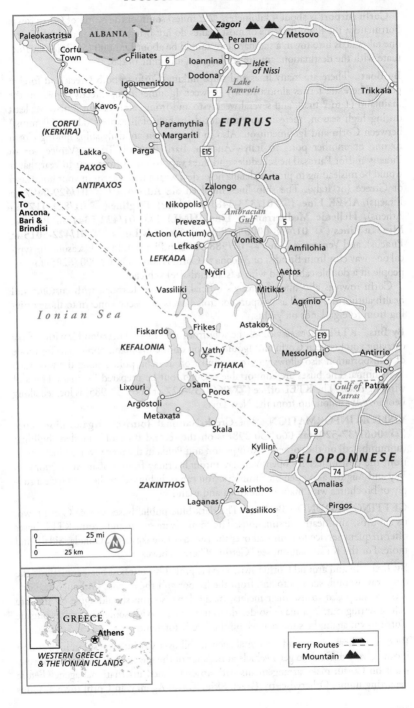

Paleokastritsa
ALBANIA
Corfu Town
Benitses
Kavos
Filiates
6
Igoumenitsou
Zagori
Perama
Metsovo
Ioannina
Islet of Nissi
Dodona
Lake Pamvotis
Trikkala
5

CORFU (KERKIRA)

Paramythia
Margariti
Parga
E15
EPIRUS
Arta
Zalongo
Nikopolis
Ambracian Gulf
Preveza
Action (Actium)
Lefkas
Vonitsa
Amfilohia
5
LEFKADA
Nydri
Aetos
Mitikas
Vassiliki
Agrinio

Lakka
PAXOS
ANTIPAXOS

To Ancona, Bari & Brindisi

Ionian Sea

Fiskardo
Frikes
Astakos
KEFALONIA
Vathy
Messolongi
Antirrio
ITHAKA
Rio
Lixouri
Sami
Gulf of Patras
Argostoli
Poros
Patras
Metaxata
Skala
9
Kyllini
PELOPONNESE
ZAKINTHOS
74
Zakinthos
Amalias
Laganas
Vassilikos
Pirgos

0   25 mi
0   25 km

GREECE
Athens
WESTERN GREECE
& THE IONIAN ISLANDS

Ferry Routes
Mountain

Corfu Airport is about 4 kilometers (2½ miles) south of the center of Corfu town. Fortunately, the flight patterns of most planes do not bring them over the city. Everyone takes taxis into town; a standard fare should be about Dr2,000 ($6) but may fluctuate with the destination, amount of luggage, and time of day.

By Boat There are many lines and ships linking Corfu to both Greek and foreign ports. There are ferries almost hourly between Igoumenitsou, directly across on the mainland (1 to 2 hrs.), and several weekly to and from Patras (about 7 hrs.). At least during high season, there is now a twice-daily hydrofoil express (about 30 mins.) between Corfu and Igoumenitsou. Also in high season are daily ships linking Corfu to one or another ports in Italy—Ancona, Bari, Brindisi, Trieste, Venice—or to Piraeus and/or Patras. The schedules and fares vary so much from year to year that it would be misleading to provide details here; deal with a travel agent in your homeland or Greece (or Italy). The ship lines involved are **Adriatica** (☎ **01/429-0487** in Piraeus), **ANEK Lines** (☎ **01/323-3481** in Athens), **Fragline** (☎ **01/821-4171** in Athens), **Hellenic Mediterranean Line (HML)** (☎ **01/422-5341** in Piraeus), **Minoan Lines** (☎ **01/408-0006** in Piraeus), **Strintzis Lines** (☎ **01/422-5015** in Piraeus), and **Ventouris Line** (☎ **01/988-9280** in Piraeus). In high season, the typical one-way cost from Brindisi or Ancona to Corfu is about Dr100,000 ($285) for two people in a double cabin and with a (standard-size) vehicle.

Corfu town is also one of Greece's official entry/exit harbors, with customs and health authorities as well as passport control. This is of special concern to those arriving from foreign lands on yachts.

By Bus KTEL offers service all the way from Athens or Thessaloniki, with a ferry carrying you between Corfu and Igoumenitsou on the mainland opposite. This mode of transportation also allows you to get on or off at main points along the way, such as Ioannina. The buses are comfortable enough, but be prepared for many hours of winding roads. The **KTEL office** (☎ **0661/39-627** or 0661/39-985) is located along Leoforos Avramiou, up from the New Port.

VISITOR INFORMATION The **Greek National Tourism Organization** office (☎ **0661/37-520;** fax 0661/30-298) is on the second floor of a modern building (unnumbered) on the corner of Rizospaston and Polila in the new town, a block across from the post office. It's open Monday through Friday from 8:30am to 1:00pm; in July and August, also open on Saturdays. You can only hope that they will have a supply of brochures with maps of the town and island.

GETTING AROUND **By Bus** The dark-blue public buses service Corfu town, its suburbs, and nearby destinations. The semiprivate green-and-cream KTEL buses offer frequent service to points all over the island—Paleokastritsa, Glifada, Sidari, and more. For the KTEL station, see "Getting There," above.

By Taxi In and around Corfu town, a taxi is probably your best bet—sometimes the only way around, such as to and from the harbor and the airport. Although taxi drivers are supposed to use their meters, many don't, so you should agree on the fare before setting out. You may also decide to use a taxi to visit some of the sites outside Corfu town; again, be sure to agree on the fare beforehand.

By Car There are myriad car-rental agencies all over Corfu; even so, in high season it can be very difficult to get a vehicle at the spur of the moment. If you're sure of your plans on Corfu, make arrangements with an established international agency before departing home. Otherwise, try **Greek Skies Travel Agency,** in Corfu town at Odos

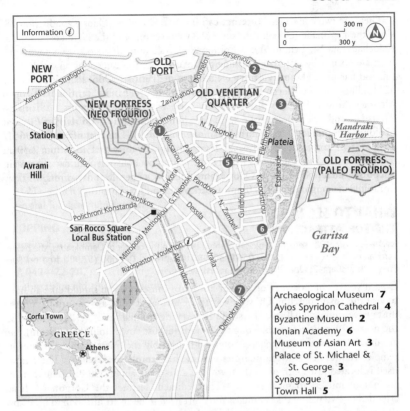

Information (i)

0   300 m
0   300 y

NEW
PORT

OLD
PORT

Arseniou

Donzelot

②

Xenofondos Stratigou

Zavitsianou

OLD VENETIAN
QUARTER

③

Mandraki
Harbor

NEW FORTRESS
(NEO FROURIO)

Solomou

N. Theotoki

④

Eleftherias

Bus
Station ■

Velisariou

Paleologo

Plateia

OLD FORTRESS
(PALEO FROURIO)

Avrami
Hill

Avramiou

Voulgareos

⑤

Kapodistriou

Esplanade

I. Theotikos

G. Markora

G.Theotok

Pandova

N. Zambeli

Guildford

Polichroni Konstanda

San Rocco Square
Local Bus Station (i)

Mitropoliti Methodiou

Dessila

⑥

Garitsa
Bay

Rizospaston Voulefton (i)

Alexandros

Vraila

Corfu Town

GREECE

Athens

Demokratias

⑦

Archaeological Museum **7**
Ayios Spyridon Cathedral **4**
Byzantine Museum **2**
Ionian Academy **6**
Museum of Asian Art **3**
Palace of St. Michael &
   St. George **3**
Synagogue **1**
Town Hall **5**

Kapodistriou 20A (☎ **0661/33-410;** fax 0661/36-161), or **Avanti Rent A Car,** Ethnikis Antistasseos 12A, along the new port (☎ **0661/42-028**).

By Moped   It's easy to rent all kinds of mopeds and scooters and motorcycles, but the roads are so curvy, narrow, and steep that you should be very experienced before taking on such a vehicle.

CITY LAYOUT   The **new town** of Corfu town is relatively modern and even a bit cosmopolitan. You probably won't be spending much time in this new town, except for visits to the post office or the GNTO office.

It's easy to spend several days wandering through the **old town,** with its *cantouni,* Greece's largest complex of picturesque streets and buildings, effectively unchanged for many centuries. The crown jewel of the old town is the **Liston,** the arcaded row of cafes where you can spend a lazy afternoon watching a cricket match on the great green of the adjacent Esplanade (Spianada).

FAST FACTS   The official **American Express** agent for Corfu is Greek Skies Travel Agency, Odos Kapodistriou 20A (☎ **0661/33-410;** fax 0661/36-161). There are numerous **banks** in both the Old Town and New Town; you'll find ATMs on most of their exteriors. The **British Consul** is at Odos Menekrates 1 (☎ **0661/30-055**), at the south end of the town, near the Menekrates monument; it will take care of all British Commonwealth citizens. There is no U.S. consulate in Corfu. The **hospital** is on Odos Julius Andreatti, and is signed from around town.

There are two convenient **Internet cafes:** the Café Online, Odos Kapodistriou 28, along the Esplanade (e-mail: cafe_online1@yahoo.com), and the Netoikos, on Odos Kalochairetou 14, behind Ayios Spiridon Church (e-mail: netoikos@netoikos.gr); both are open daily from late morning to late evening. You can count on quick, careful, and fair-priced **laundry** or **dry cleaning** at the Peristeri, Odos Ioannis Theotikos 42 (leading from San Rocco Square on the way to the KTEL Bus Terminal). It's open Monday through Saturday from 8am to 2pm, with additional hours on Tuesday, Thursday, and Friday from 6 to 8pm. The **police station** (☎ **0661/39-575**) is at Leoforos Alexandros 19 (catercorner from the post office). The **post office** (☎ **0661/ 25-544**) is at Leoforos Alexandros 26. It's open Monday through Friday from 7:30am to 8pm; in July and August, it's usually open for a few hours on Saturday. The main **telephone office (OTE)** is at Odos Mantzarou 9; it's open Monday through Friday from 7:00am to midnight, to 10pm on Saturdays and holidays.

WHAT TO SEE & DO
THE TOP ATTRACTIONS

Archaeological Museum. Odos P. Armeni-Vraila 1 (on the corner of Demokratias, the boulevard along the waterfront). ☎ **0661/30-680.** Admission Dr1,000 ($2.90); free on Sun. Tues–Sun 8:30am–2:30pm. Wheelchair accessible.

Even if you're not a devotee of ancient history or museums, you should take an hour to visit this small museum. On your way to see its masterwork, as you turn left off the upstairs vestibule, you'll pass the **stone lion** dating from around 575 B.C. (found in the nearby Menekrates tomb, along the waterfront just down from the museum). Go around and behind it to the large room with arguably the finest example of Archaic temple sculpture extant, the **pediment from the Temple of Artemis.** (The temple itself is located just south of Corfu town and dates from about 590 B.C. The remains are not of interest to most people.) The pediment features the **Gorgon Medusa,** attended by two pantherlike animals. You don't need to be an art historian to note how this predates the great classical works such as the Elgin marbles—not only in the naiveté of its sculpture but also in the emphasis on the monstrous, with the humans so much smaller.

Interesting for comparison is the fragment from another Archaic pediment found at Figare, Corfu. Displayed in an adjoining room, it shows Dionysos and a youth reclining on a couch. In this work, only a century younger than the Gorgon pediment, the humans have reduced the animal in size and placed it under the couch.

Museum of Asian Art. The Palace of St. Michael and St. George, north end of Esplanade. ☎ **0661/38-124.** E-mail: protocol@hepka.culture.gr. Admission Dr1,000 ($2.90). Tues–Sun 8am–2:30pm.

The museum's building itself is an impressive example of neoclassical architecture. It was constructed between 1819 and 1824 to serve as the residence of the Lord High Commissioner, the British ruler of the Ionian islands; to house the headquarters of the Order of St. Michael and St. George; and to provide the assembly room for the Ionian senate. When the British turned the Ionians over to Greece, this building was given to the king of Greece. As the king seldom spent much time here, it fell into disrepair, until after World War II when it was restored and turned into a museum.

The centerpiece of the museum is the collection of Chinese porcelains, bronzes, and other works from the Shang Dynasty (1500 B.C.) to the Ching Dynasty (19th century). There are also strong holdings of Japanese works—woodblock prints, ceramics, sculpture, watercolors, and *netsuke* (carved sash fasteners). You may not have come to Greece to appreciate Asian art, but this is one of several unexpected delights in Corfu.

Old Fort (Paleo Frourio). The Esplanade (opposite the Liston). Admission Dr1,000 ($2.90) adults, Dr500 ($1.45) students and seniors over 60. Tues–Fri 8am–8pm; Sat–Sun and holidays 8:30am–3pm.

Originally a promontory attached to the mainland, its two peaks—*koryphi* in Greek—gave the modern name to the town and island; the promontory itself was for a long time the main town (and appears as such in many old engravings). The Venetians dug the moat in the 16th century, enabling them to hold off several attempts by the Turks to conquer this outpost of Christianity; the apparent Greek temple at the south side is in fact a British church (1830). Each peak is crowned by a castle; you can get fine views of Albania to the east and Corfu, town and island, to the west.

In summer, a **Sound-and-Light** show is held several nights a week (in different foreign languages, so be sure to check the schedule).

The *Kalypso Star.* Old Port, Corfu town. ☎ **0671/46-525.** Fax 0671/23-506. Fee Dr3000 ($9) adults, Dr1,500 ($4.30) children. In high season, trips leave daily, hourly from 10am–6pm, plus a 10pm night trip; off-season, call for schedule.

The *Kalypso Star* is a glass-bottomed boat that takes small groups on trips offshore and provides a fascinating view of the marine life and undersea formations.

The Petrakis Line. Odos Venizelou 9, New Port, Corfu town. ☎ **0661/31-649.** Fax 0661/ 38-787. E-mail: petrakis@hol.gr.

During high season, this line offers several 1-day excursions a week to destinations including Albania, Kefalonia, and Paxoi. Be aware, though, that in Albania, you do not get to the capital, Tirana; and on Kefalonia, you visit the Melissani Grotto and the Drogarati Cave (see below) but not Argostoli.

A STROLL AROUND CORFU TOWN

This is definitely a browser's town, where as you're strolling around in search of a snack or souvenir, you'll serendipitously discover an old church or monument. To orient yourself, start with the **Esplanade area** bounded by the Old Fort (see above) and the sea on one side; the small haven below and to the north of the Old Fort is known as **Mandraki Harbor,** while the shore to the south is home port to the **Corfu Yacht Club.**

The Esplanade is bisected by Odos Dousmani; at the far side is the circular monument to the union of the Ionian Islands with Greece in 1864. The north part has the field known as the **Plateia,** where cricket games are played on lazy afternoons. At the far north side of the Esplanade is the Palace of St. Michael and St. George, now housing the **Museum of Asian Art** (see above). If you proceed along the left (northwest) corner of the palace, you'll come out above the coast and can make your way around Odos Arseniou above the medieval sea walls (known as the *mourayia*).

On your way you will pass (on the left, up a flight of stairs) the **Byzantine Museum** in the **Church of Antivouniotissa.** Even those who have never been especially taken by Byzantine art should enjoy its small but elegant selection of icons from around Corfu; of particular interest are works by Cretan artists who came to Corfu, some of whom went on to Venice. It's open Monday from 12:30 to 7pm, Tuesday through Saturday from 8am to 7pm, and Sunday and holidays from 8:30am to 3pm. Admission is Dr800 ($2.30).

Proceed along the coast road and come down to the square at the Old Port; above its far side rises the **New Fortress,** and beyond this is the New Port. Off to the left of the square is a large gateway, what remains of the 16th-century Porta Spilia; proceeding through this leads you into the Plateia Solomou.

If you go left from Plateia Solomou along Odos Velissariou, you'll see on the right (with the green doors) the 300-year-old **Synagogue,** with its collection of torah crowns. It's open on Saturday from 9am until early evening. To gain entry during the week, call the Jewish Community Center at ☎ **0661/38-802.**

This is now a good way to continue into the section of Old Corfu known as **Campiello,** with its stepped streets and narrow alleys. You may often feel lost in a labyrinth—and you will be—but sooner or later you'll emerge onto one or another busy commercial street that will bring you down to the Esplanade.

Heading south on the Esplanade, you'll see a bandstand and at its far end the **Maitland Rotunda,** commemorating Sir Thomas Maitland, the first British lord high commissioner of the Ionian Islands. Past this is the statue of Count Ioannis Kapodistrias (1776–1836), the first president of independent Greece. On the edge of the south end of the Esplanade is a newly renovated building that once housed the Ionian Academy and is now used by the Ionian University.

If you head south along the shore road from this end of the Esplanade, you'll pass the Corfu Palace Hotel (see below) on your right; then the **Archaeological Museum** (see above), up Odos Vraila on the right. After two more blocks, off to the right on the corner of Odos Marasli, you'll see the **Tomb of Menekrates,** a circular tomb of a notable who drowned about 600 B.C. Proceeding to the right here onto Leoforos Alexandros will bring you into the heart of new Corfu town.

Back at the Esplanade, the western side of the north half is lined by a wide tree-shaded strip filled with cafe tables and chairs, then a street reserved for pedestrians, and then arcaded buildings patterned after Paris's Rue de Rivoli. These arcaded buildings, known as the **Liston,** were begun by the French and finished by the British. Sit here with a cup of coffee (or a glass of ginger beer!) and enjoy the passing scene.

At the back of the Liston is **Odos Kapadistriou,** and perpendicular from this extend several streets that lead into the heart of Old Corfu—a mélange of fine shops, old churches, souvenir stands, and other stores in a maze of streets, alleys, and squares that seem like Venice without the water. The broadest and most stylish is **Odos Nikiforio Theotoki.** At the northern end of Kapadistriou, you turn left onto Odos Ayios Spiridon and come to the corner of Odos Filellinon and the **Ayios Spiridon Cathedral,** dedicated to Spiridon, the patron saint of Corfu. A 4th-century bishop of Cyprus, Spiridon is credited with saving Corfu from famine, plagues, and a Turkish siege. The church hosts the saint's embalmed body in a silver casket, as well as precious gold and silver votive offerings and many fine old icons. Four times a year the faithful parade the remains of St. Spiridon through the streets of old Corfu: on Palm Sunday, Holy Saturday, August 1, and the first Sunday in November.

Proceeding up Odos Voulgareos behind the southern end of the Liston, you'll come up along the back of the **Town Hall,** built in 1663 as a Venetian loggia; it later served as a theater. Turn into the square it faces and enter into what seems like a Roman piazza, with steps and terraces, the Roman Catholic cathedral on the left, and, reigning over the top, the restored Catholic archbishop's residence (now housing the Bank of Greece).

From here, finish your walk by wandering up and down and in and out the various streets of Old Corfu.

SHOPPING

Corfu town has so many shops selling jewelry, leather goods, olive wood objects, and handmade needlework that it is impossible to single out one or another. All we can advise is to look around—especially along Odos Filarmonikis (off Odos N. Teotoki), if needlework's your thing—and select something that pleases; prices are generally fair and uniform.

Standing out from the many standard souvenir-gift shops, **Antica,** Odos Ayios Spiridon 25, leading away from the north end of Liston (☎ **0661/32-401**), offers unusual older jewelry, plates, textiles, brass, and icons. **Gravures,** Odos Ev. Voulgareos 64, where the street emerges from the old town to join the new town (☎ **0661/41-721**), has a fine selection of engravings and prints of scenes from Corfu, all nicely matted. Originals (taken from old books or magazines) can cost Dr40,000 ($115), reproductions as little as Dr2,500 ($7). The elegant **Terracotta,** Odos Filarmonikis 2, just off Odos N. Theotoki, the main shopping street (☎ and fax **0661/45-260**), sells only contemporary Greek work: jewelry, one-of-a-kind pieces, ceramics, and small sculptures, some by well-known Greek artists and artisans. Nothing is cheap, but everything is classy.

There is no end of ceramics to be found in Corfu, but we like the **Pottery Workshop,** 15 kilometers (10 miles) north of Corfu on the right of the road to Paleokastritsa (☎ **0661/90-704**), where you get to observe Sofoklis Ikonomides and Sissy Moskidou making and decorating all the pottery on sale here. Whether decorative or functional, something here will certainly appeal to your taste. Two kilometers further along the road, on the left, is the **Wood's Nest,** offering a large selection of olive wood objects just slightly cheaper than in town.

WHERE TO STAY

The island of Corfu has an apparently inexhaustible choice of accommodations, but in high season (July and August) many will be taken by package groups from Europe. Reservations are recommended if you have specific preferences for that period, especially for Corfu town.

IN TOWN
Very Expensive
✪ **Corfu Palace Hotel.** Leoforos Demokratias 2 (along Garitsa Bay, just south of center), 49100 Corfu. ☎ **0661/39-485** to 487. Fax 0661/31-749. www.corfupalace.com. E-mail: info@corfupalace.com. 115 units. A/C MINIBAR TV TEL. High season Dr60,000–Dr80,000 ($173–$230) double; low season Dr45,000–Dr61,000 ($129–$177) double. Children up to age 12 stay free in parents' room (without meals). Rates include buffet breakfast; half-board available. AE, DC, ER, MC, V. Free parking. A 5-min. walk from Esplanade.

This is a grand hotel with every creature comfort, modern business and conference services, and elegant service that lives up to its decor. It combines the most up-to-date features of a Swiss enterprise (which it is) with Greek hospitality. The landscaping creates a tropical ambiance; the lobby and public areas bespeak luxury. Neither bedrooms nor bathrooms are exceptionally large, but they are highly comfortable and well appointed. All units enjoy balconies and views of the sea. Aside from the splendid surroundings, superb service, and grand meals, the main appeal of this hotel is probably its combination of restful isolation above the bay with its proximity to the city center.

The hotel's two restaurants, the Scheria (a grill room on the poolside terrace) and the Panorama (with a view of the bay), serve both Greek and international menus; both vie to claim the finest cuisine on Corfu. Amenities include concierge, room service, laundry, newspaper delivery, baby-sitting, three pools (one for children), sundeck, tennis nearby (outdoors, lit in evening), bicycle rentals, game room, conference and banquet rooms, car rentals, tour arrangements, hairdresser, jewelry store, and foreign-language books. Guests can use the facilities of the nearby Corfu Tennis Club and Yacht Club and the Corfu Golf Club, 14 kilometers (9 miles) away.

Moderate

If you prefer old-fashioned period hotels to shiny new accommodations, consider the **Astron Hotel,** Odos Donzelot 15 (waterfront road down to old harbor), 49100 Corfu (☎ **0661/39-505;** fax 0661/33-708).

Arcadion Hotel. Odos Kapodistriou 44 (catercorner from south end of Liston, facing the Esplanade), 49100 Corfu. ☎ **0661/30-104.** Fax 661/45-087. 33 units. A/C MINIBAR TV TEL. High season Dr34,000 ($98) double; low season Dr28,000 ($80) double. Rates include buffet breakfast. AE, JCB, MC, V. Open year-round. Public parking lot (fee) nearby.

This hotel's total renovation, completed in late 2000, now makes it as pleasurable as it is convenient. We haven't been able to inspect the new rooms and bathrooms but assume they will be up to the highest standards for this class, along with all the other amenities. If you like to be at the center of a city, you can't get much closer than this: When you step out the door, the Esplanade and the Liston are 50 feet away. Admittedly, this also means that on pleasant evenings there will be crowds in front of the hotel, but just ask for a room off the front. (All windows are double-glazed for sound control.) Hard to beat for location and comfort.

✪ **Bella Venezia.** Odos N. Zambeli 4 (approached from far south end of Esplanade), 49100 Corfu. ☎ **0661/46-500.** Fax 0661/20-708. E-mail: belvenht@hol.gr. 32 units. A/C TV TEL. High season Dr24,000 ($69) double; low season Dr21,000 ($60) double. Rates include buffet breakfast. AE, DC, EC, MC, V. Open year-round. Parking on adjacent streets. Within walking distance of old and new town.

Like the gold-medal winner of the decathlon, this hotel may not win in any single category, but its combined virtues make it the first choice of many. The building is a restored neoclassical mansion, with character if not major distinction. The location is just a bit off center and lacks fine views, but it's quiet and close enough to any place you'd want to walk to; a decent beach is 150 meters away. The common areas are not especially stylish, but do have a certain atmosphere. Although not luxurious or large, the guest rooms have some old-world touches; the showers, however, are undeniably cramped. There is no restaurant, but there's a colorful patio-garden for breakfast and an enclosed kiosk for light snacks. Finally, its rates are below what similar hotels charge.

Cavalieri. Odos Kapodistriou 4 (at far south end of Esplanade), 49100 Corfu. ☎ **0661/39-041.** Fax 0661/39-283. 50 units. A/C TV TEL. High season Dr30,000 ($86); low season Dr23,000 ($66). Rates include buffet breakfast. AE, DC, MC, V. Open year-round. Parking on adjacent streets. Within easy walking distance of old and new town.

If you like your hotels in the discreet old European style, this place is for you; those who prefer glitz should look elsewhere. The Cavalieri is in an old building with a small elevator. The main lounge is Italian-velvet, its restaurant is nothing special, service is low-key, rooms are spare, and bathrooms standard. But the hotel must be doing something right, as advance reservations are usually required. Location answers for much of the appeal: Ask for one of the front rooms on the upper floors, which boast great views of the Old Fort. Another draw is the rooftop garden, which after 6:30pm offers drinks, sweets, and light meals along with a spectacular view; even if you don't stay here, it's a grand place to pass an hour in the evening.

OUTSIDE TOWN
Expensive

Corfu Holiday Palace (formerly Hilton). P.O. Box 124, Odos Nausicaa, Kanoni (some 5km/3 miles south of Corfu town), 49100 Corfu. ☎ **0661/36-540.** Fax 0661/36-551. 266 units. A/C MINIBAR TV TEL. High season Dr40,000–Dr46,000 ($115–$132) double; low season Dr24,000–Dr30,000 ($69–$86) double. Rates include buffet breakfast. Ask travel agents about special packages for extended stays. AE, DC, EC, MC, V. Open year-round. Free parking on grounds. Hotel offers a shuttle bus; public bus no. 2 stops 200m away; a taxi is easily summoned.

This is a grand hotel in the contemporary manner—more like a resort in the range of its facilities and amenities. Its lobby sets the tone—spacious and relaxed—while the staff is professional yet friendly. The grounds create a semitropical ambiance. In addition to the pools, there's a lovely private beach down below. The famous locale known as Kanoni is a couple hundred yards from the hotel. The island's airport is off in the middle distance—not a major problem, but we suggest you ask for a room facing the sea and not the airport.

The main restaurant serves a fixed menu for those paying for the half-board plan. There's also a bar, a casino, and a grill restaurant. Amenities include concierge, room service, laundry, baby-sitting, two pools, health club, sundeck, two tennis courts (lit at night), water-sports equipment, jogging track, bowling, billiards, table tennis, 50% discount at Corfu Golf Club (18km/12 miles away), conference rooms, car-rental desk, tour arrangements, beauty salon, and boutiques.

Inexpensive
Hotel Royal. Odos Figareto 110, Kanoni (3km/2 miles from Corfu center, a few hundred yards before Corfu Holiday Palace, above), 49100 Corfu. ☎ **0661/37-512.** Fax 0661/38-786. 125 units. TEL. High season Dr14,000 ($40) double; low season Dr12,000 ($34) double. Rates include continental breakfast. No credit cards. Closed Nov–Mar. Parking on grounds. Public bus no. 2 stops 100m away, but a taxi may be easier.

This might be considered an alternative to the nearby Corfu Holiday Palace if your desire is to stay outside Corfu town but you can't afford the Palace. It's a kind of funky place: The architecture is neo-baroque, the interior decor is folksy, and the lobby is filled with traditional works of art. Bedrooms and bathrooms are standard. The most spectacular features are the three tiered pools—it's a great place to come back to (in high season only) with the kids after a day spent sightseeing. As with the Palace, the airport is off in the middle distance, but the noise problem exists only during a relatively small portion of a day. It's a big hotel with a family atmosphere, and you can't beat the rates.

WHERE TO DINE
IN TOWN
Expensive
If you're in a celebratory mood, you might also consider **Chambor,** Odos Guilford 71 (☎ 0661/39-031); much of what you pay, though, goes for the elaborate settings and presentation.

۞ Venetian Well. Plateia Kremasti (small square up from Old Harbor, behind Greek Orthodox cathedral). ☎ **0661/44-761.** Reservations recommended in high season. Main courses Dr2,500–Dr5,000 ($7–$14). No credit cards. Mon–Sat noon–midnight. Open year-round. MIDDLE EASTERN/INTERNATIONAL/GREEK.

This remains our top pick in Corfu town. Diners sit at a candlelit table in a rather austere little square with a Venetian wellhead (1699) and a church opposite. (When the weather changes, guests sit in a stately room with a mural.) The atmosphere is as discreet as the food is inventive. There is no printed menu—you learn what's available from a chalkboard or from your waiter—and there's no predicting what the kitchen will offer on any given evening. Since the chef uses seasonal vegetables, salads vary from month to month. Main courses may range from standard Greek dishes such as beef *giouvetsi* (cooked in a pot) to chicken prepared with exotic ingredients. The wine list is more extensive than in most Greek restaurants.

Moderate

If you want to dine along the coast, consider **Antranik,** Arseniou 19 (☎ 0661/
22-301), located under the awnings on the seaside of the road leading from north of
the Esplanade down to the New Port. **Faliraki,** at the corner of Kapodistrias and Arseniou, below the wall (☎ 0661/30-392), also has a wonderful location, right on the
water (although the food is standard Greek fare).

○ **Aegli Garden Restaurant.** Odos Kapodistriou 23 (within Liston). ☎ 0661/31-949.
Fax 0661/45-488. Main courses Dr1,500–Dr4,000 ($4.30–$11). AE, DC, EC, MC, V. Year-
round daily 9am–1am. GREEK/CONTINENTAL.

The tasty and varied menu of this old favorite attracts both residents and transients to
its several dining areas—indoors, under the arcade, along the pedestrian mall of
Kapodistriou, or under awnings across from the arcade. Try the selection of *orektika*
with some of the wine or beer on tap. The staff take special pride in their Corfiote specialties, several of which are traditional Greek foods with rather spicy sauces: fillet of
fish, octopus, *pastitsada* (baked veal), *baccala* (salted cod fish), and *sofrito* (veal). If
spiciness isn't your thing, try the swordfish or prawns. Everything is done with great
care, including a delicious fresh-fruit salad that you can order by itself.

Bellissimo. Plateia Lemonia (just off Odos N. Theotoki). ☎ 0661/41-112. Main courses
Dr1,000–Dr3,500 ($2.90–$10). No credit cards. Daily 10:30am–11pm. GREEK/
INTERNATIONAL.

This restaurant has lived up to its promise of being a welcome addition to the Corfu
scene—unpretentious but tasty. Located on a central and lovely town square, it's run
by the hospitable Stergiou family. They offer a standard Greek menu with some
"exotics," including hamburgers and chicken curry. Especially welcome is their modestly priced "Greek sampling plate"—tzatziki, tomatoes-and-cucumber salad, keftedes
(meatballs), fried potatoes, grilled lamb, and pork souvlaki.

Gloglas Taverna. Odos Guilford 16. ☎ 0661/37-147. Main courses Dr1,000–Dr3,000
($2.90–$9). No credit cards. Daily 11:30am–midnight. GREEK.

You want authenticity? This is it, right on a corner in the heart of the old town, a block
back from the Esplanade. You sit under a grape arbor among your fellow diners, a mixture of locals and tourists, united in their desire for a no-nonsense taverna meal. The
specialties of the house tend to be off the spit or grill. Winners include souvlaki
(kebab), chicken, pork, and kokoretsia (lambs' intestines roasted on the spit). The
cooked vegetables—green beans, eggplant, and whatever is in season—are also tasty.
Add a glass of the house red and you'll wonder why anyone would want to go to a
fancier place.

CORFU TOWN AFTER DARK

Corfu town definitely has a nightlife scene, though many people are content to linger
over dinner and then, after a promenade, repair to one of the cafes at the Liston, such
as the **Capri, Liston, Europa,** or **Aegli**—all of which have a similar selection of light
refreshments and drinks. (Treat yourself to the fresh-fruit salad at the Aegli!) Others
are drawn to the cafes at the north end of the Esplanade, just outside the Liston—**Cafe
Bar 92,** the **Magnet,** or **Cool Down.** For a special treat, ascend to the rooftop cafe/bar
at the **Cavalieri Hotel** (see "Where to Stay," above). Another change of scene is the
Lindos Cafe, overlooking the beach and facilities of the Nautical Club of Corfu; it
is approached by a flight of steps leading off Leoforos Demokratias, just south and
outside the Esplanade. And one of the best-kept secrets of Corfu town is the little

Art Cafe, to the right and behind the Palace that now houses the Museum of Asian Art; its garden provides a wonderful cool and quiet retreat from the hustle and bustle of the rest of the town.

If you enjoy a bit more action, there are several nightspots along the coast to the north, between Corfu town and the beach resort of Gouvia; they include **Ekati,** a typical Greek nightclub; **Esperides,** featuring Greek music; and **Corfu by Night,** definitely touristy. Be prepared to drop some money at these places.

As for the younger crowd, there are any number of places that go in and out of favor (and business) from year to year. Among the more enduring up around the Esplanade are the relatively sedate **Aktaion,** just to the right of the Old Fort, and the **Café Classico,** in an old mansion at Odos Kapodistriou 10, featuring the latest music. Young people seeking more excitement go down past the New Port to a strip of flashy discos—**Apokalypsis, Hippodrome,** and **DNA.** Be aware that these clubs charge a cover (usually Dr3,000/$9, including one drink).

In summer, there are frequent **concerts** by the town's orchestras and bands, mostly free, on the Esplanade. Corfu town boasts the oldest band in Greece. The **Sound-and-Light** performances are described in the listing for the Old Fort (see "What to See & Do," above). September brings the **Corfu Festival,** with concerts, ballet, opera, and theater performances by a mix of Greek and international companies. **Carnival** is celebrated on the last Sunday before Lent with a parade and a burning of an effigy representing the spirit of Carnival.

For those who like to gamble, there's a well-known **casino** at the **Corfu Holiday Palace** (see "Where to Stay," above), a few miles outside of town. Bets are a Dr1,000 ($2.90) minimum and a Dr250,000 ($715) maximum. Open nightly, it may not have the glamour of Monte Carlo, but it attracts quite an international set during the high season.

SIDE TRIPS FROM CORFU TOWN
KANONI, PONDIKONISI & ACHILLEION

Although these sites and destinations are not literally next door to one another and have little in common, they are grouped here because they do, in fact, all lie south of Corfu town and can easily be visited in half a day's outing. And they are all places that everyone who comes to Corfu town will want to visit, even if they go nowhere else on the island. History buffs will revel in their many associations, and even beach people cannot help but be moved by their scenic charms.

Kanoni is approached south of Corfu town via the village Analepsis; it's well signed. Ascending most of the way, you come at about 4 kilometers (2½ miles) to the circular terrace (on the right), the locale known as Kanoni (after the cannon once sited here). Make your way to the edge and enjoy a wonderful view. Directly below in the inlet are two islets. If you want to visit one or both, you can take a 10-minute walk down a not-that-difficult path from Kanoni; with a vehicle you must retrace the road back from Kanoni a few hundred yards to a signed turnoff (on the left coming back).

One islet is linked to the land by a causeway; here you'll find the **Monastery of Vlakherna.** To get to the other islet, **Pondikonisi ("Mouse Island"),** you must be ferried by a small boat, which is always available (Dr500/$1.45). Legend has it that this rocky islet is a Phaeacian ship that was turned to stone after taking Odysseus back to Ithaka. The chapel here dates from the 13th century, and its setting among the cypress trees makes it most picturesque. Many Corfiotes make a pilgrimage here in small boats on August 6. It's also the inspiration for the Swiss painter Arnold Boecklin's well-known work *Isle of the Dead,* which in turn inspired Rachmaninoff's music of the same name.

| Taking a Dive |

All of the bays and coves that make up Paleokastritsa boast sparkling-clear turquoise waters. There is a professional diving school here, run by a German, called **Korfu Diving.** If you're interested in its weeklong courses for beginners or day excursions for advanced divers, call or fax ☎ **0663/41-604** for details.

There is a causeway across the little inlet to Perama over on the main body of the island (the Kanoni road is on a peninsula), but it is only for pedestrians. So to continue on to your next destination, the villa known as the **Achilleion,** you must drive back to the edge of Corfu town and then take another road about 8 kilometers (5 miles) to the south, signed to Gastouri and the villa of Achilleion. It's open daily from 9am to 4pm. Admission is Dr1,000 ($2.90). Bus no. 10, from Plateia San Rocco, runs directly to the Achilleion several times daily.

This villa was built between 1890 and 1891 by Empress Elizabeth of Austria, whose beloved son Rudolf and his lover died mysteriously (most likely a double suicide) at Mayerling in 1889. The empress identified him with Achilles, and so the villa is really a memorial to Rudolf (and her grief)—thus the many statues and motifs associated with Achilles (including the dolphins, for Achilles' mother was the water nymph Thetis). As you approach the villa from the entrance gate, you will see a slightly Teutonic version of a neoclassical summer palace. Take a walk through at least some of the eclectic rooms. Among the curiosities is the small saddle-seat that Kaiser Wilhelm II of Germany sat on while performing his imperial chores. (He bought the villa in 1907, after Elizabeth was assassinated in 1898.)

The terraced gardens that surround the villa are now lush and tropical. Be sure to go all the way around and out to the back terraces. Here will you see the most famous of the statues Elizabeth commissioned, *The Dying Achilles,* by the German sculptor Herter; also you cannot miss the 15-foot-tall Achilles that the Kaiser had inscribed, "To the greatest Greek from the greatest German," a sentiment removed after World War II. But for a truly impressive sight, step to the edge of the terrace and enjoy a spectacular view of Corfu town and much of the eastern coast to the south.

If you have your own car, you can continue on past the Achilleion and descend to the coast between **Benitses** and **Perama;** the first, to the south, has become a popular beach resort. Proceeding north along the coast from Benitses, you come to Perama (another popular beach resort), where a turnoff onto a promontory brings you to the pedestrian causeway opposite Pondikonisi (see above). The main road brings you back to the edge of Corfu town.

PALEOKASTRITSA

If you can make only one excursion on the island, this is certainly a top competitor with Kanoni and the Achilleion. Go to those places for their fascinating histories, to Paleokastritsa for its natural beauty.

The drive here is northwest out of Corfu town via well-marked roads. Follow the coast for about 8 kilometers (5½ miles) to Gouvia, then turn inland. (It is on this next stretch that you pass the **Pottery Workshop** and the **Wood's Nest;** see "Shopping," above.) The road eventually narrows but is asphalt all the way as you gradually descend to the west coast and **Paleokastritsa** (25km/16 miles). There's no missing it: It's been taken over by hotels and restaurants, although some of the bays and coves that make up Paleokastritsa are less developed than others. Tradition claims it as the site of **Scheria,** the capital of the Phaeacians—and thus one of these beaches is where Nausicaa found Odysseus, though no remains have been found to substantiate this.

You can continue on past the beaches and climb a narrow winding road to the **Monastery of the Panayia** at the edge of a promontory (it's about a mile from the beach, and many prefer to go by foot). Although founded in the 13th century, nothing that old has survived, but having come this far, it's worth a brief visit, especially at sunset. It's open April through October, daily from 7am to 1pm and 3 to 8pm.

More interesting in some ways, and certainly more challenging, is a visit to the **Angelokastro,** the medieval castle that sits high on a pinnacle overlooking all of Paleokastritsa. Only the most hardy will choose to walk all the way up from the shore, a taxing hour at least. The rest of us will drive back out of Paleokastritsa (about 2.5km/1½ miles) to a turnoff to the left, signed LAKONES. There commences an endless winding and ascending road that eventually levels out and provides spectacular views of the coast as it passes through the villages of Lakones and Krini. (*A word of warning:* Don't attempt to drive this road unless you are comfortable pulling over to the very edge of narrow roads—with sheer drops—to let trucks and buses by, something you will have to do on your way down.) Keep going until the road takes a sharp turn to the right and down, and you'll come to the end of the line and a little parking area. From here you walk up to the castle, only 200 meters away but seemingly further because of the condition of the trail. What you are rewarded with, though, is one of the most spectacularly sited medieval castles you'll ever visit, some 1,000 feet above sea level.

If you've come this far, reward yourself with a meal and the spectacular view at one of the restaurant/cafes on the road outside Lakones—the **Bella Vista, Colombo,** or **Casteltron.** *Be forewarned:* At mealtimes in high season, these places are taken over by busloads of tour groups. If you have your own transport, try to eat a bit earlier or later.

On your way back to Corfu town from Paleokastritsa, you can vary your route by heading south through the **Ropa Valley,** the agricultural heartland of Corfu. Follow the signs indicating Liapades and Tembloni (but don't bother going into either of these towns). If you have time for a beach stop, consider going over to **Ermones Beach** (the island's only golf club is located above it) or **Glifada Beach.**

WHERE TO STAY & DINE If you want to spend some time at Paleokastritsa, it's good to get away from the main beach. We like the 70-unit **Hotel Odysseus** (☎ **0663/41-209;** fax 0663-41342), high above the largely undeveloped cove before the main beach. A double in high season goes for Dr18,000 ($52), in low season Dr15,000 ($43); both rates include breakfast. It's open May to mid-October, and there's a pool.

On its own peninsula and both fancier and pricier is the 127-unit **Akrotiri Beach Hotel** (☎ **0663/41-237**), where an air-conditioned double in high season goes for Dr36,000 ($104), in low season Dr21,000 ($60), including buffet breakfast. All rooms have balconies and sea views. In addition to the adjacent natural beaches, there are two pools. It's open May through October.

The restaurants on the main beach in Paleokastritsa strike us as over-touristy. However, if you like to eat where the action is, the best value and most fun at the main beach can be had at the **Apollon Restaurant** in the Hotel Apollon-Ermis (☎ **0663/ 41-211**). Main courses are Dr1,100 to Dr3,500 ($3.70 to $10). It's open mid-April to late October, daily from 11am to 3pm and 7 to 11pm.

We prefer someplace a bit removed, such as the **Belvedere Restaurant** (☎ **0663/ 41-583**), just below the Hotel Odysseus and serving solid Greek dishes at reasonable prices. Main courses range from Dr1,000 to Dr3,000 ($2.90 to $9). It's open mid-April to late October from 9am to midnight.

2 Kefalonia (Cephalonia)

Don't come to Kefalonia for glamour. Come to spend time in a relaxing environment, to enjoy handsome vistas and a lovely countryside. This is a Greek island the way they used to be—it pretty much goes its own way while you travel around and through it. It does boast several natural wonders, a few historical buildings and archaeological sites, and many fine beaches. Kefalonia also has a full-service tourist industry, with some fine hotels, restaurants, travel agencies, car-rental agencies, the whole show. Since Kefalonia was virtually demolished by the earthquake of 1953, most structures on this island are fairly new. It has long been one of the more prosperous and cosmopolitan parts of Greece, thanks to its islanders' tradition of sailing and trading in the world at large.

ESSENTIALS

GETTING THERE **By Plane** From Athens, there are at least three flights daily on **Olympic Airways** (with some flights via Zakinthos). The Argostoli office is at Odos Rokkou Vergoti 1, the street between the harbor and the square of the Archaeological Museum (☎ **0671/28-808**). The **Kefalonia airport** is 8 kilometers (5 miles) outside Argostoli. As there is no public bus, everyone takes a taxi, which costs about Dr2,500 ($7) to Argostoli and about Dr2,000 ($6) from Argostoli.

By Boat As with most Greek islands, it's easier to get to Kefalonia in summer than in the off-season, when weather and reduced tourism eliminate the smaller boats. Throughout the year there is one car-passenger ferry that leaves daily from Patras to Sami (about 2½ hours); for details, call the **Patras Port Authority** (☎ **061/341-002**) or **Sami Port Authority** (☎ **0674/22-031**). There is also at least one car-passenger ferry daily (1½ hours) from Killini (out on the northwest tip of the Peloponnese) to Argostoli and Poros (on the southeastern coast of Kefalonia) via the **Strintzis Line** (☎ **01/823-6011** in Athens); if you haven't made arrangements with a travel agent, you can buy tickets dockside.

Beyond these more or less dependable services, during the high-season months of July and August there are usually other possibilities—ships to and from Corfu, Ithaka, Levkas, or other islands and ports—but they do not necessarily hold to the same schedules every year.

VISITOR INFORMATION The **Greek National Tourism Organization (EOT)** information office in Argostoli is on Odos Ioannis Metaxa, on the harbor by the Port Authority office (☎ **0671/22-248**). It's open in high season, daily from 7:30am to 2:30pm and 5 to 10pm; low season, Monday through Friday from 8am to 3pm.

GETTING AROUND **By Bus** You can get to almost any point on Kefalonia—even remote beaches, villages, and monasteries—by **KTEL bus** (☎ **0671/22-276** in Argostoli). Schedules, however, are restrictive and may cut deeply into your preferred arrival at any given destination. KTEL also operates special tours to several of the major destinations around the island. The new **KTEL station** is on Leoforos A. Tritsi, at the far end of the harbor road, 200 meters past the Trapano Bridge.

By Taxi For those who don't enjoy driving twisting mountain roads, taxis are the best alternative. If you're based in Argostoli, go up to Central (Vallianou) Square and work out an acceptable fare. A trip to Fiskardo, with the driver waiting a couple of hours, might run to Dr35,000 ($99)—with several passengers splitting the fare, this isn't unreasonable. Aside from such ambitious excursions, taxis are used by everyone on Kefalonia. Although drivers are supposed to use their meters, many don't, so agree on the fare before you set off.

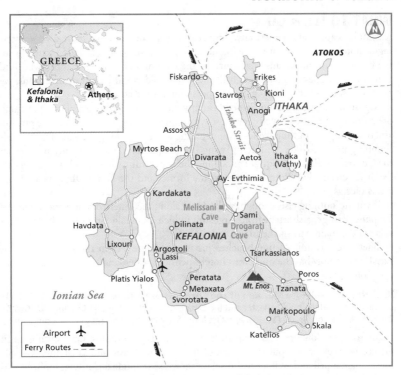

By Car   There are literally dozens of car-rental firms, from the well-known international companies to hole-in-the-wall outfits. In Argostoli, we found both **Auto Europe,** Odos Lassis 3 (☎ **0671/24-078**), and **Euro Dollar,** R. Vergoti 3a (☎ **0671/23-613**), to be reliable. In high season, you'll find rental cars scarce, so don't expect to haggle. A compact will come to at least Dr16,000 ($46) a day (gas extra); better rates are usually offered for rentals of three or more days.

By Moped & Motorcycle   The roads on Kefalonia are asphalt and in decent condition, but are often very narrow, lack shoulders, and twist around mountain ravines or wind along the edges of sheer drops to the sea. That said, many choose to get around Kefalonia this way. Every city and town has places that will rent mopeds and motorcycles for about Dr6,000 to Dr8,000 ($17 to $23) per day for a two-seater.

FAST FACTS   There are several **banks** in the center of Argostoli with ATMs. The **hospital** (☎ **0671/22-434**) is on Odos Souidias (the upper road, above the Trapano Bridge). **Internet access** is available at Excelixis Computers, Odos Minoos 3 (☎ **0671/25-530**; e-mail: xlixis@otenet.gr). **Express Laundry,** Odos Lassi 46B, the upper road that leads to the airport, is open Monday through Saturday from 9:30am to 9pm. A load costs Dr700 ($2). Argostoli's **tourist police** (☎ **0671/22-200**) are on Odos Ioannis Metaxa, on the waterfront across from the Port Authority. The **post office** is in Argostoli on Odos Lithostrato, opposite no. 18 (☎ **0671/22-124**); open Monday through Saturday from 7:30am to 2pm. The main **telephone office (OTE)** is at Odos G. Vergoti 8. It's open daily, April through September from 7am to midnight and October through March from 7am to 10pm.

WHAT TO SEE & DO

Kefalonia's capital and largest city, **Argostoli** has far and away its most diverse offering of hotels and restaurants. Staying here allows you to go off on daily excursions to the beaches and mountains, yet return to the comforts of a city. For those who find that Argostoli doesn't offer enough in the way of old-world charm or diversions, we point out some of the other "getaway" possibilities on Kefalonia.

Argostoli's appeal does not depend on any archaeological, historical, architectural, or artistic particulars. It's a city for those who enjoy strolling or sitting in a foreign land and observing the passing scene—ships coming and going along the waterfront, locals shopping in the market, children playing in the squares. There are plenty of cafes on the **Central (Vallianou) Square** and along the **waterfront** where you can nurse a coffee or ice cream. The **Premier Cafe** on the former and the **Hotel Olga** on the latter are as nice as any.

If you do nothing else, though, walk down along the waterfront and check out the **Trapano Bridge,** a shortcut from Argostoli (which is actually on its own little peninsula) to the main part of the island.

There are a couple of fine **beaches** just south of the city in the locale known as **Lassi,** which now has the numerous hotels, pensions, cafes, and restaurants that package groups love.

Historical and Folklore Museum of the Corgialenos Library. Odos Ilia Zervou (2 blocks up the hill behind the public theater and the square with Archaeological Museum). ☎ **0671/ 28-835.** Admission Dr500 ($1.45). Apr–Oct Mon–Sat 9am–2pm; off-season, by arrangement.

Many so-called folklore museums, little more than typical rooms, have sprung up in Greece in recent years, but this is one of the most authentic and satisfying. Meticulously maintained and well-labeled displays showcase traditional clothing, tools, handicrafts, and objects used in daily life across the centuries. Somewhat unexpected are the various displays revealing a stylish upper-middle-class life. Most engaging is a large collection of photographs of pre- and post-1953 earthquake Kefalonia. The gift shop has an especially fine selection of items, including handmade lace.

SHOPPING

Interesting ceramics are for sale at **Hephaestus,** on the waterfront at Odos 21 May; **Alexander's,** on the corner of Plateia Museio (the square one block back from the waterfront); and **The Mistral,** Odos Vironis 6, up the hill opposite the post office, offering the work of the potter/owner.

For a taste of the local cuisine, consider Kefalonia's prized Golden Honey, tart quince preserve, or almond pralines. Another possibility is a bottle of one of Kefalonia's wines. You can visit the **Calliga Vineyard** (selling white Robola and red Calliga Cava) or the **Gentilini Vineyard** (with more expensive wines), both near Argostoli, or the **Metaxas Wine Estate,** well south of Argostoli. The tourist office (see "Visitor Information," above) on the waterfront will tell you how to arrange a tour.

WHERE TO STAY

Accommodations on Kefalonia range from luxury hotels to basic rooms. During peak times, we recommend making reservations; **Filoxenos Travel** (☎ **0671/23-055;** fax 0671/28-114) can help.

EXPENSIVE

✪ **White Rocks Hotel & Bungalows.** Platys Yialos (the beach at Lassi, outside Argostoli), 28100 Argostoli. ☎ **0671/28-332** or 0671/28-335. Fax 0671/28-755. 102 units, 60 bungalows. A/C TEL. High season Dr42,000 ($121) double; low season Dr32,000 ($92) double. Rates are for either rooms or bungalows and include breakfast and dinner. AE, DC, EC, V. Open

May–Oct. Private parking. Occasional public buses go from the center of town to and from Yialos, but most people take taxis.

The White Rocks is the kind of low-key place where people catch up on the reading they've meant to do all year. It is probably the most elegant hotel on Kefalonia, located a couple of miles south of Argostoli just above two beaches, one small and for hotel guests, the other larger and public. The hotel also has a new pool. On arriving, you descend a few steps from the main road to enter an almost tropical setting. The lobby is subdued and stylish, a decor that extends to the hotel's guest rooms, which are modest in size but have first-rate bathrooms. Amenities include a fine restaurant with views, a bar, a TV lounge, and conference facilities. The desk will take care of all your needs.

MODERATE

In addition to the following options, you might consider the 60-unit **Hotel Miramare,** Odos Metaxa 2, at the far end of the paralia (☎ **0671/25-511;** fax 0671/ 25-512); it's slightly removed from the town's hustle yet within walking distance of any place you'd want to go.

Cephalonia Star. Odos I. Metaxa 50 (along waterfront, across from the Port Authority), 28100 Argostoli. ☎ **0671/23-181.** Fax 0671/23-180. 40 units, some with shower, some with tub. A/C TV TEL. High season Dr17,000 ($49) double; low season Dr12,000 ($34) double. Rates include breakfast. MC, V. Open year-round. Street parking.

A location along the bay and balconied front rooms with fine views earn this Class C hotel more appeal than many. Rooms are standard size, bathrooms standard issue, but all are clean and well serviced. There's a cafeteria-restaurant on the premises, but except for breakfast, you'll probably want to patronize Argostoli's many fine eateries, all within a few minutes' walk. In August, a mobile amusement park has been known to set up on the quay just opposite, but then August all over Greece is a carnival.

✪ **Hotel Ionian Plaza.** Vallianou Sq. (the central square), 28100 Argostoli. ☎ **0671/ 25-581.** Fax 0671/25-585. 43 units. A/C TV TEL. High season Dr22,000 ($63) double; low season Dr16,000 ($46) double. Rates include buffet breakfast. AE, MC, V. Open year-round. Street parking.

Although it isn't quite a grand hotel, this is the class act of Argostoli and a fine deal. The lobby, public areas, and rooms share a tasteful, comfortable, and natural tone. Bedrooms are larger than most, while bathrooms are modern if not mammoth. Breakfast takes place under the awning, the evening meal at the hotel's own **Il Palazzino** restaurant, indoors and outdoors; the menu has a strong Italian flavor and prices are surprisingly modest. Stay here if you like to be in the heart of a city; the front rooms look out over the central square, but as no vehicles are allowed there, it's not noisy.

Mouikis Hotel. Odos Vironis 3, 28100 Argostoli. ☎ **0671/23-281.** Fax 0671/28-010. www.mouikis.com. E-mail: reservations@mouikis.com. 39 units. TEL. High season Dr25,000 ($72) double; low season Dr17,000 ($49) double. Rates include buffet breakfast. AE, MC, V. Open year-round. Street parking.

This is your basic Class C hotel, popular with groups but usually with a few rooms available for individual travelers. Although its rooms don't provide air-conditioning or TVs, its common areas do. Bedroom and bath amenities are standard for the class. Definitely for those on a limited budget.

WHERE TO DINE

Try to taste at least one of the two local specialties: *kreatopita* (meat pie with rice and a tomato sauce under a crust) and *crasato* (pork cooked in wine). The island's prized white wines include the modest Robola and the somewhat overpriced Gentilini.

EXPENSIVE

Captain's Table. Leoforos Rizopaston (just around corner from Central Sq.; identifiable by its boat-model display case). ☎ **0671/23-896.** Main courses Dr1,200–Dr4,500 ($3.45–$13). EC, JCB, MC, V. Daily 6pm–midnight. GREEK/INTERNATIONAL.

This slightly upscale choice offers specialties such as the Captain's Soup (fish, lobster, mussels, shrimp, and vegetables), fillets of beef, delicate squid, and fried *courgette* (small eggplants). You could get out cheap by ordering the low end of the menu, but then why eat here? Most guests dress up a bit, and there's definitely a touch of celebration to meals here. It can also get crowded in high season. Go early, order a bottle of wine, and enjoy!

MODERATE

Also consider the **Old Plaka Taverna,** Odos I. Metaxa 1, at the far end of the waterfront (☎ **0671/24-849**), for modest prices and tasty Greek dishes.

La Gondola. Central Sq. ☎ **0671/23-658.** Main courses Dr1,000–Dr3,100 ($2.90–$9). AE, EC, MC, V. Daily 6pm–2am. GREEK/ITALIAN.

Everyone will want to eat at least one meal on the main square to experience the sense of attending a "dinner theater," with Argostoli's citizens providing the action. Frankly, all of the restaurants on the square are about the same in quality and menu, but we've enjoyed some special treats at this one. It offers a house wine literally made by the house, and serves a special pizza-dough garlic bread, a zesty chicken with lemon sauce, and a cannelloni that stands out with its rich texture and distinctive flavor. Both the staff and your fellow diners always seem to be enjoying themselves, so we think you will, too.

✪ **Patsouras.** Odos I. Metaxa 32 (along waterfront). ☎ **0671/22-779.** Main courses Dr1,100–Dr3,200 ($3.70–$9). V. Daily noon–midnight. A 5-min. walk from Central Sq. GREEK.

Patsouras continues to live up to its reputation as the favorite for those seeking authentic Greek taverna food and ambiance. Dine under the awnings on the terrace across from the waterfront, and try either of the local specialties, *kreatopita* (meat pie) or *crasto* (pork in wine). We found a special zest to even such standards as the tzatziki and moussaka. Greeks love these unpretentious tavernas, and you'll see why if you eat at Patsouras.

INEXPENSIVE

Portside Restaurant. Odos I. Metaxa 58 (along the waterfront, opposite Port Authority). ☎ **0671/24-130.** Main courses Dr1,000–Dr2,500 ($2.90–$7). EC, MC, V. Apr–Oct daily 10am–midnight. GREEK.

This unpretentious taverna is what the Greeks call a *phisteria*, a restaurant specializing in meats and fish cooked on the grill or spit. Run by a native of Argostoli and his Greek-American wife, it offers hearty breakfasts, regular plates with side portions of salads and potatoes, and a full selection of Greek favorites. On special nights outside the high season, the restaurant roasts a suckling pig. It's popular with Greeks as well as foreigners, and you've got a front-row seat for the harborside activities.

ARGOSTOLI AFTER DARK

Free outdoor concerts are occasionally given in the Central Square. At the end of August, there's a **Choral Music Festival,** with choirs from all over Greece and Europe participating. There's a quite new and grand **public theater** where plays are performed, almost always in Greek and seldom in high season. Popular cafes include

Mythos and **Politiko.** Young people looking for a bit more action can find a number of cafes, bars, and discos in the streets leading away from the Central Square; they change names from year to year, but **Da Capo, Polo, Antico,** and **Metropolis** have been fairly steady. At the beach resort of Lassi, the **So Simple Bar** has become popular. If your style runs more to British-style pub-crawling, try the **Pub Old House,** Odos St. Metaxas 57, on a corner of tiny streets between the Central Square and the waterfront.

SIDE TRIPS FROM ARGOSTOLI
FISKARDO, ASSOS & MYRTOS BEACH

This is probably the preferred excursion for those who have only one day for a trip outside Argostoli. The end destination is **Fiskardo,** a picturesque port-village, which owes its appeal to the fact that it's the only locale on Kefalonia to have survived the 1953 earthquake. Its charm comes from its many surviving 18th-century structures and its intimate harbor.

You can make a round-trip from Argostoli to Fiskardo in one day on **KTEL** bus line (Dr1,800/$5.15). But with a rental car, you can also detour to the even more picturesque port-village of **Assos** (another 10km/7 miles up the upper coast road) and then reward yourself with a stop at **Myrtos Beach,** a strong candidate for one of the great beaches of Greece.

There are plenty of restaurants around Fiskardo's harbor. We recommend **Tassia's, Vassos, Nicholas Taverna,** and the **Panormos**. The latter two offer rooms as well. For advance arrangements, contact **Fiskardo Travel** (☎ **0674/41-315;** fax 0671/41-026) or **Aquarius Travel** (☎ and fax **0674/41-306**). Britons may prefer to deal with the **Greek Islands Club,** which specializes in waterfront apartments and houses; its main office is at 66 High St., Walton-on-Thames, Surrey KT12 1BBU (☎ **0932/220-477;** fax 0932/229-346).

SAMI, MELISSANI GROTTO & DROGARATI CAVE

Many who come to Kefalonia arrive at Sami, the town on the east coast. The island's principal point of entry before tourism put Argostoli in the lead, Sami is still a busy port. Sami itself is nothing special, although its harbor is framed by unusual white cliffs. Of more interest to travelers are the **two caves** to the north of Sami, both of which can easily be visited on a half-day excursion from Argostoli.

The first is **Spili Melissani,** about 5 kilometers (3 miles) north of Sami and well signed. Proceeding through the entryway, you get into a small boat and are rowed around a relatively small, partially exposed, partially enclosed lake, whose most spectacular feature is due to the sun's rays striking the water and creating a kaleidoscope of colors. It's open daily from 9am to 6pm. Admission is Dr1,500 ($4.30). It was once believed that this water flowed underground westward to a locale outside Argostoli, Katavothres; it's now known that the flow is from Katavothres into Melissani.

On the road that leads away from the east coast and west to Argostoli (4km/2 miles from Sami), there's a well-signed turnoff to the **Drogarati Cave.** Known for its unusual stalagmites, its large chamber has been used for concerts (once by Maria Callas). You walk through it on your own; it's well illuminated but can be slippery. It's open daily from 9am to 6pm, with an admission of Dr1,000 ($2.90).

ITHAKA

Because of its association with Odysseus, Ithaka might seem to rate the treatment of a major destination. But it is small, not easily approached, and does not in fact offer that many touristy or historical attractions. Given its "sites" linked to the Homeric epic, however, it will appeal to certain travelers, and its rugged terrain and laid-back villages reward those who enjoy driving through the unspoiled Greek countryside.

We strongly recommend that you rent a car in Argostoli first. The boat connecting to Ithaka sails not from Argostoli but from Sami, the port on the east coast of Kefalonia; to make a bus connection with that boat, and then to take a taxi from the tiny isolated port where you disembark on Ithaka, costs far too much time. Rather, in your rented car, drive in 40 minutes from Argostoli to Sami; the boat fare for the car is Dr3,000 ($9), for each individual Dr500 ($1.45). Once on Ithaka, you can drive to **Vathy,** the main town, in about 10 minutes, and you'll have wheels to explore Ithaka in a day if you desire.

Vathy itself is a little port, a mini version of bigger Greek ports with their bustling tourist-oriented facilities. For help in making any arrangements, try **Polyctor Tours** on the main square (☎ **0674/33-120**). You might enjoy a cold drink or coffee and admire the bay stretching before you, but otherwise there's not much to do or see here. Instead, drive 16 kilometers (10 miles) north to **Moni Katheron;** the 17th-century monastery itself is nothing special, but the bell tower offers a spectacular view over much of Ithaka. For a more ambitious drive, head north via the village of **Anogi,** stopping to view the little church in its town square, with centuries-old frescoes, and the Venetian bell tower opposite it; proceed on via Stavros and then down to the northeast coast to **Frikes,** a small fishing village; then take a winding road along the coast to **Kioni,** arranged like an amphitheater around its harbor.

As for the sites associated with the *Odyssey,* what little is to be seen is questioned by many scholars, but that should not stop you; after all, it's your imagination that makes the Homeric world come alive. There are four principal sites (all signed from the outskirts of Vathy). Three kilometers (1½ miles) northwest of Vathy is the so-called **Cave of the Nymphs,** where Odysseus is said to have hidden the Phaeacians' gifts after he had been brought back (supposedly to the little **Bay of Dexia,** north of the cave); known locally as Marmarospilia, the small cave is about a half-hour's climb up a slope.

The **Fountain of Arethusa,** where Eumaios is said to have watered his swine, is some 7 kilometers (4 miles) south of Vathy; it is known today as the spring of Perapigadi. The **Bay of Ayios Andreas,** below, is claimed as the spot where Odysseus landed in order to evade the suitors of Penelope. To get to the fountain, drive the first 3 kilometers (2 miles) by following the sign-posted road to south of Vathy as far as it goes; then continue on foot another 2 miles along the path.

About 8 kilometers (5 miles) west of Vathy is the site of **Alalkomenai,** claimed by Schliemann among others as the site of Odysseus's capital; in fact, the remains date from several centuries later than the accepted time of the Trojan War. And finally, a road out of Stavros leads down to the **Bay of Polis,** again claimed by some as the port of Odysseus's capital; in the nearby cave of Louizou was found an ancient pottery shard inscribed "my vow to Odysseus," but its age suggests only that this was the site of some hero-cult.

For lunch, we recommend **Gregory's Taverna,** on the far northeast corner of Vathy's bay (keep driving, with the bay on your left, even after you think the road may be giving out). Ideally you will find a table right on the water, where you can look back at Vathy while you enjoy your fresh fish dinner.

Most visitors will be able to see what they want of Ithaka in a day before setting off back to the little port, where the last ferryboat to Kefalonia leaves, usually at 5pm—but ask!

15

Highlights of Northern Greece: Thessaloniki, Mount Athos, & the Philip & Alexander Sites

by Sherry Marker

Northern Greece, with its lofty mountain ranges, deep rivers, wide plains, and profusion of little-known archaeological and historic monuments, is rapidly losing its status as one of Greece's few remaining "undiscovered" regions. Although the monasteries of the Holy Mountain of Mount Athos are still off-limits to women, improved roads mean that Athos is no longer a difficult trek from Northern Greece's largest city, Thessaloniki (Salonika). In addition, the formerly difficult-to-reach sites connected with the mighty warrior Philip II of Macedon and his famous son, Alexander the Great, are now linked by good, new roads. Furthermore, the National Road from Athens to Thessaloniki makes it possible to drive between Greece's two most important cities in just 8 hours. Thessaloniki is the best place to begin your explorations of Northern Greece—and you'll find plenty to explore both in and around Greece's "Second City."

1 Thessaloniki (Salonika)

516km (320 miles) N of Athens

When a Greek tells you he's from Athens, he always sounds a bit apologetic, or regretful; Greeks from Thessaloniki, on the other hand, sound, if not smug, very pleased to be from Greece's "Second City." Thessaloniki may be second to Athens in political importance and population, but in popular songs, Thessaloniki is celebrated as "the mother of Macedonia," "the most blessed of cities," and "the city whose praises are sung."

You, too, may be tempted to sing this city's praises when you take in its wonderful situation along the broad expanse of the Thermaic Gulf. You're never far from the sea here; when you least expect it, you'll catch a glimpse of waves and boats in the distance. Alas, especially in the summer, you'll almost certainly get less pleasant whiffs of the harbor's ripe, polluted odor. If you're very lucky, you'll see Mount Olympus while you're here: Pollution has increasingly obscured even that imposing landmark.

Greeks are fond of reminding foreigners that when their ancestors were painting themselves blue, or living in rude huts, Greeks were sitting in the shade of the Parthenon, reading the plays of Sophocles. Similarly, Thessalonians like to remind Athenians that when Athens languished in the long twilight of its occupation by the Romans and Ottomans, Thessaloniki flourished. It's true: Thessaloniki's strategic location on the main land route from Europe into Asia made it a powerful city during the Roman Empire—you'll see many monuments built here by the 4th-century A.D. emperor Galerius.

During the Byzantine Empire (the 4th to 15th centuries A.D.), Thessaloniki boasted that it was second only to the capital, Constantinople. That's when Thessaloniki's greatest pride, its superb and endearing churches, were built. After the Turks conquered the Byzantine Empire, Thessaloniki continued to flourish as an important commercial center and port. In the 18th and early 19th centuries, the city's Jewish community was so strong and so prosperous that some called Thessaloniki the "second Jerusalem."

Then, in August 1917, a devastating fire destroyed 80% of the city. Phoenix-like, Thessaloniki rose from the ashes. Unfortunately, only part of the city was rebuilt according to the grand plan of the French architect Ernest Hébrard—between 1922 and 1923, 130,000 Greek refugees from Asia Minor flooded into Thessaloniki, almost doubling the city's population and leading to enormous unregulated development. Still, Thessaloniki has the broad tree-lined boulevards and parks that Athens so sadly lacks.

After World War II, and again in the 1960s, two more growth spurts left much of the city's outskirts crowded and ugly—and all too much of the city center lined with bland apartment buildings. You'll notice, however, that Thessaloniki has none of the horizon-blocking skyscrapers that have proliferated in Athens—earthquake regulations forbid this. The last major earthquake was in 1978.

Glimpses of the sea, tree-lined streets, magnificent Byzantine churches—all these make visiting Thessaloniki delightful. And there's something else here that's quite wonderful: the food. In part, this is because of the long tradition of Macedonian cuisine; in part, because this is still a city whose establishments are supported by local customers. There are no restaurants here—as yet—that make their living off visitors.

If you're a visitor to Thessaloniki, you'll appreciate all this. You'll also enjoy the fact that Thessaloniki's location in the virtual center of Macedonia makes it the perfect place from which to set off to the sites associated with **Philip II of Macedon** and his son **Alexander the Great.**

If you are a man, you can also take in the monasteries of **Mount Athos,** the Holy Mountain. If you are a woman, you'll have that much more time to enjoy Thessaloniki—or to sit patiently in the little port of Ouranopolis, the jumping-off point for Mount Athos, and envy those lucky enough to travel on to the Holy Mountain.

STRATEGIES FOR SEEING THESSALONIKI   Our suggestions on exploring Thessaloniki (see "Suggested Itineraries," below) are really just that: suggestions. Unlike Athens, which few visitors would be bold enough to visit without seeing the Acropolis, Thessaloniki has no one "must-see" monument. Some might argue that the splendid **Archaeological Museum** fits the bill, but others would plead the case of the **Upper City (Ano Poli),** the old Turkish Quarter. Still others would recommend a loop through both the Upper City and the **city center** to take in as many Byzantine churches and Roman monuments as possible. In short, you're here to enjoy the city itself: a city filled with Byzantine churches and chapels, a city with squares built around Roman palaces, whose markets pulse with life, and whose harborside cafes and promenade refresh the weary.

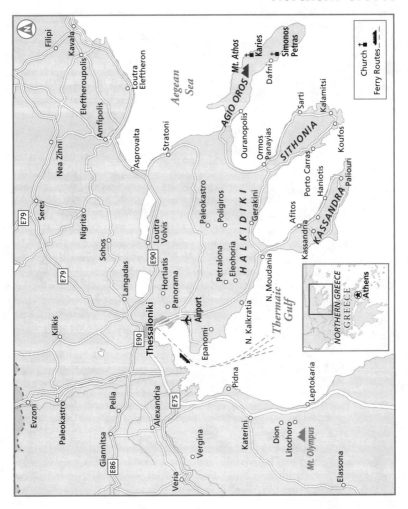

ESSENTIALS

GETTING THERE **By Plane** Thessaloniki is served from Athens by **Olympic Airways** (☎ 031/230-240), **EasyJet** (☎ 031/236-1111), and **AirGreece** (☎ 031/236-946). From the U.S., there are no direct flights to Thessaloniki. Connections can be made at a number of European cities, including London, Amsterdam, Brussels, Frankfort, Stuttgart, Munich, Zurich, and Vienna. From London, there are direct flights on **Olympic** and **EasyJet**. Thessaloniki's airport (☎ 031/411-997) is 13 kilometers (8 miles) southeast of the city at Mikras, a 20-minute drive from the city center. Bus no. 78 runs into the city (usually stopping in Aristotelous Square and at the train station) from about 6am to 11pm and costs Dr150 (45¢). A taxi ride is about Dr1,500 ($4.30).

By Train Five daily express trains make the trip from Athens to Thessaloniki in about 6 hours, but most are extremely crowded, without air-conditioning, and subject to various unexplained delays. If you must take a train, then let it be the overnight sleeper, which has first-class compartments for four to six passengers and sleeper

Thessaloniki

compartments for four to six passengers. Nothing, however, can be done about the noisy and sometimes bumpy ride on antiquated tracks. Reservations for sleeping compartments should be made many days in advance at the Larissa train station in Athens (☎ 01/323-6747). First-class tickets are Dr15,000 ($43); second-class, Dr10,300 ($30); sleeper supplement, Dr12,000 ($34).

In Thessaloniki, the **train station** (☎ 031/517-517) is on Odos Monastiriou, which is the extension of Odos Egnatia west of Vadari Square, site of numerous shady bars. A taxi ride to Aristotelous Square takes about 10 minutes and costs about Dr1,200 ($3.45). To avoid the trek to the train station to get information and buy tickets, use the OSE (train) office at Aristotelous Square 18 (☎ 031/518-113).

By Bus Ten daily buses from Athens make the trip to Thessaloniki in about 7 hours, including a 20-minute stop at a roadside restaurant with toilet facilities. Buses are air-conditioned, much less expensive than the trains, and usually arrive on time. Reservations should be made in advance at the Athens bus terminal, Odos Kifissou 100

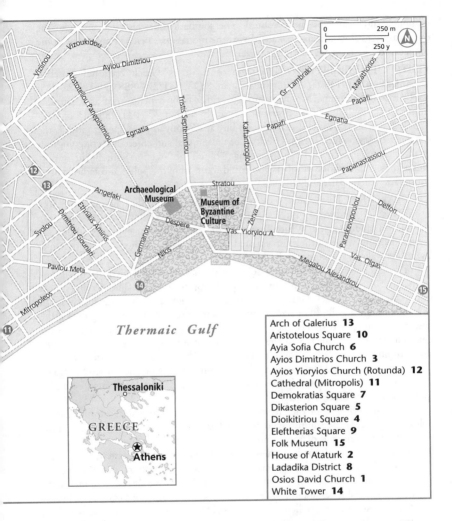

Thermaic Gulf

Arch of Galerius	**13**
Aristotelous Square	**10**
Ayia Sofia Church	**6**
Ayios Dimitrios Church	**3**
Ayios Yioryios Church (Rotunda)	**12**
Cathedral (Mitropolis)	**11**
Demokratias Square	**7**
Dikasterion Square	**5**
Dioikitiriou Square	**4**
Eleftherias Square	**9**
Folk Museum	**15**
House of Ataturk	**2**
Ladadika District	**8**
Osios David Church	**1**
White Tower	**14**

(☎ **01/514-8856**). A one-way fare costs Dr9,000 ($26). The buses arrive in Thessaloniki at the station on Monastiriou opposite the train station, where there are always taxis.

By Car From Athens, take the 516-kilometer (320-mile) National Road, a four-lane highway that's the best in Greece, although stretches are always being repaired or widened, which leads to frequent slow-downs. The trip from Athens takes 6 to 8 hours. Much of the drive is extremely scenic. Although there are gas stations at frequent intervals along the National Road, you often must exit to reach them.

If you're coming from other parts of **Europe,** you must take the ferry from the Italian ports of Bari, Ancona, or Brindisi to Igoumenitsou on the northwest coast of Greece, and then drive across the Pindus Mountains to Thessaloniki. The trip takes 7 to 8 hours and is scenically spectacular. The southern route via Ioannina and Kalambaka to Larissa and the National Road is much less treacherous than the northern alternative through Kozani—particularly in winter—and is thus recommended (although snow can close both routes). The southern route also will give you the opportunity to stop at Kalambaka and visit the monasteries perched on the awesome pinnacles of the Meteora (see chapter 11).

VISITOR INFORMATION   The main office of the **Greek National Tourism Organization (EOT)** is at Aristotelous Square 8 (☎ **031/271-888** or 031/222-935; fax 031/265-507); open Monday through Friday from 8am to 8pm and Saturday from 8:30am to 2pm. There's also a branch at the airport (☎ **031/985-215** or 031/ 473-212, ext. 215). A useful magazine to buy at virtually any newspaper kiosk is the quarterly *Pillotos,* which lists in Greek all of the cultural and entertainment goings-on in the city. *Pillotos* has an English-language "Blue Pages" section with all the important addresses and phone numbers you could want, from the police and radio taxis to consulates, banks, bars, and cinemas.

CITY LAYOUT   Thessaloniki rests on the northern coast of the Thermaic Gulf like a somewhat lopsided turban tilted slightly to the northwest. In its center sits the city's best-known landmark, the **White Tower.** To the east sprawl the ever-expanding residential districts, while to the west, situated in the area once defined by its fortresslike Byzantine walls, is the **commercial heart** of the city.

In this latter area, bounded on the south by the harbor and on the north by the rising heights of what is called the **Ano Poli** or the **Upper City,** are Thessaloniki's most important shops, banks, hotels, restaurants, archaeological remains, and churches. On its western edge are the train station, most bus terminals, many shipping docks, the customs building, and streets lined with warehouses—many now converted into the chic restaurants and galleries of the **Ladadika district.** On the city center's eastern side, just north of the White Tower and outside of what was once the eastern gate, are the grounds of Aristotle University, the International Trade Fair, and the **Archaeological** and **Byzantine museums.** Between the latter and the White Tower are the **Municipal Park** and the **State Theater.**

The commercial area of the city is traversed by four main streets running on an oblique angle from the southwest to the northeast. The largest, **Odos Egnatia,** runs across the northern side of the commercial district. On its western end at **Vardari Square,** it connects with roads to the west, north, and east; on its eastern end (under the name of New Egnatia), it connects with highways to the airport and to the peninsulas of Halkidiki. Along its route in the heart of the city are discount shops, cheap hotels, and affordable restaurants. The city's second most important commercial route is **Odos Tsimiski,** which parallels Egnatia 2 blocks to the south and runs one-way from east to west. Along its tree-shaded length are the city's most prestigious shops and department stores. One block south of Tsimiski and running one-way from west to east is **Odos Mitropoleos,** so named because the Metropolitan Cathedral is situated near its center. Like Tsimiski, it has a number of fine shops and boutiques. Finally, another block to the south and running along the seaside promenade is **Leoforos Nikis.** Also one-way from west to east, it begins at the shipping docks and ends at the White Tower. Along its length is a virtually uninterrupted line of outdoor cafes and bars.

The heart of downtown Thessaloniki is the spacious expanse of **Aristotelous Square,** which borders the sea. Ringed with outdoor cafes and restaurants, it's also the site of the city's major political rallies. Running north and south and connecting Aristotelous with the city's other major square, Dikasterion, is **Odos Aristotelous.** Along its arcaded sidewalks are a number of book and record stores. **Dikasterion Square** overlooks the partially excavated Roman marketplace and has welcome trees, the lovely Byzantine church called Our Lady of the Copper Smiths (the Panayia Chalkeon), and a restored Turkish bathhouse. Increasingly, Greek and other refugees from eastern Europe hold an informal market here. This is also where most local buses begin and end their runs to and from the heart of the city.

To the south of Dikasterion Square, across Egnatia and on either side of Odos Aristotelous, are the city's main **market areas,** where you can find flowers, fish, sandals, and just about anything else you can think of. To the east of Odos Aristotelous is the city's second main north-south route, **Odos Ayias Sofias.** In its center, between Egnatia and Tsimiski, is the major Byzantine church of St. Sofia. Along Odos Ayias Sofias are a number of excellent clothing stores. Running diagonally southeast from the rear of the church directly to the White Tower is **Odos Pavlou Mela,** with a number of fine bars and cafes; leading directly south to Tsimiski from virtually the same point are the tree-lined pedestrian walkways of **Odos Iktinou** and **Odos Zevksidos,** site of several outdoor cafes and restaurants. Two blocks east of the rear of Ayias Sofias Square is Thessaloniki's major pedestrian walkway, **Odos Dimitriou Gounari.** Its shop-lined length covers a major Roman thoroughfare leading down from the arch to the imperial palace. The area containing the palace is now partially excavated and opens into the tree-shaded park of **Navarino Square,** crowded with outdoor cafes, bars, and tavernas, and second only to Aristotelous as the city's major gathering place—although many of the artists and intellectuals who gather here would place it first.

Another 2 blocks east is **Odos Ethnikis Aminis.** While it runs one-way south from Egnatia down to the State Theater and the White Tower, it becomes a two-way street above Egnatia at **Sintrivaniou (Fountain) Square** (the former eastern gate of the city) and leads into winding roadways that run outside the ancient walls to the Upper City.

On the hillside leading down to Thessaloniki proper from the Upper City is the old **Turkish Quarter**—called, variously, **Ano Poli** (the **Upper City**), Eptapirgou (the Seven Gates), and Kastro (Fortress)—where some of the finest Byzantine churches are located. This is easily the most pleasant part of Thessaloniki to explore, especially the winding streets around Kalitheas Square, Odos Irodotou, Romfei Square in the district known as Koule Kafe, Tsinari Square, at the juncture of Odos Kleious and Odos Alexandras Papadopoulou, and the Seih Sou, the pine forest on the upper hills. Unfortunately, severe fires in 1997 and 1998 greatly damaged the pines of Seih Sou. A reforestation project has begun, but it will be years before new growth brings back Thessaloniki's "green lungs."

Just to the north of the Upper City is the **Ring Road,** which goes around Thessaloniki from the southwest to the southeast and connects the National Road from Athens with highways to Thrace and Halkidiki and the airport at Mikras along the sea to the east.

FINDING AN ADDRESS   Because of the orderly east-west, north-south arrangement of streets, finding an address in the city center is not difficult. Numbers begin at the eastern and southern ends of streets and go upwards, with even numbers on the right and odd numbers on the left. However, most Thessalonians think of addresses in terms of the cross streets or various well-known structures near them, and buildings seldom have visible numbers; ask for what you want by name, not number.

Outside of the city center, particularly north of Odos Egnatia, finding what you want is difficult, as the streets begin to meander. Even with a good map, you'll probably have trouble, but take it, as the Greeks say, *"Siga, Siga"* ("Slowly, Slowly"), and you'll find your way.

MAPS   The GNTO office on Aristotelous Square often has maps and the free booklet *Thessaloniki and Halkidiki.* Two excellent guides to the city are *The Thessaloniki Handbook* (with section-by-section maps), by Christos Zafiris, and *Thessaloniki* (with an excellent city-center map), by Apostolos Papagiannopoulos. Both are usually available at **Molhos's Bookstore,** Odos Tsimiski 10. The most detailed map, but very cumbersome, is the one published by **Welcome Tourist Guides,** available at most bookstores.

GETTING AROUND　　In the city center, most of the attractions, restaurants, and shops are easily reachable on foot in no more than 20 minutes. Otherwise, taxis are your best bet, unless you're going to the Upper City, which is a steep uphill walk, but served by bus nos. 22 and 23, which leave from Eleftherias Square. Taxis are reluctant to take this trip because there is little guarantee of a return fare down, and they may—unlawfully—refuse. But if you're in the cab before you state your destination, there's little the driver can do but take you there.

By Bus　　Buses with double cars are boarded in the rear, where there is a conductor to make change and give you a ticket. Single-car buses are boarded in the front. On these, exact fare is required in the form of Dr50, Dr20, Dr10, and Dr5 pieces, which are deposited in a ticket-issuing machine situated behind the driver's seat. You should keep your ticket in case a conductor boards the bus to check. Fares vary according to the distance traveled; a journey within Thessaloniki usually costs Dr100 (30¢).

By Taxi　　This is your best bet except, as noted, when you want to go to the Upper City. Take along a map or have someone write out your destination in Greek, so that you can show the driver where you want to go. Rates are moderate when compared to those in the U.S.; tips are not expected. Make sure, however, that the driver turns on his meter and that, within the city limits, the rate that it uses is number 1. Rate number 2 is for outside the city limits. There's an extra Dr500 ($1.45) charge for trips from the airport. After midnight, all fares on the meter are doubled.

By Car　　There is little reason to use a car within Thessaloniki. Traffic is terrible and legal parking spots are almost impossible to find. But having a car for excursions into Northern Greece will allow you to see and enjoy a lot more than you would either with a bus or on a guided tour. Keep in mind that if you take a day trip, you'll spend at least an hour getting out, and another hour getting back into the city. It makes better sense to see what you want to see outside of town on your way in, or out, of Thessaloniki.

　　Budget Rent-a-Car has offices at the airport (☎ 031/471-491) and in the city at Odos Angelaki 15 (☎ **031/274-272** or 031/229-519), opposite the International Fairgrounds. Other options are **Avis,** Leoforos Nikis 3 (☎ **031/227-126** or 031/683-300), at the western end of the harbor, opposite the docks; **Europcar,** Odos Papandreou 5 (☎ **031/836-333**); and **Hertz,** Odos El. Venizelou 4 on Eleftherias Square (☎ **031/224-906**). Booking in advance (especially from abroad) usually gets you a cheaper rate. A car with unlimited mileage costs around Dr20,500 ($59) per day in high season. Remember to ask if the price quoted includes all taxes and insurance—and be sure to take full insurance if your credit card does not provide it.

　　If you need to park within Thessaloniki, try the free **Municipal Parking Lot** just south of the Museum of Byzantine Culture at the eastern end of Odos Vas. Olgas. It's about a 20-minute walk from the city center, but very near the White Tower and Archaeological Museum. Unfortunately, late at night this is not a very savory spot.

By Boat　　It's possible to take ferries and boats from Thessaloniki to a number of Aegean islands, including Crete, Santorini, Mykonos, and to the Sporades (Skiathos, Skopelos, and Alonissos). There are lots of travel agents around Aristotelous Square, many of which sell ferry tickets. Centrally located agencies include: **Karaharissis,** at the corner of Odos Nikis and Odos Kountouriotou, near Eleftherias Square (☎ **031/513-005** or 031/524-444); **Polaris Travel,** Odos Pavlou Mela 22, between Odos

Tsimiski and Ayia Sofia church (☎ **031/278-613** or 031/232-078); and **Zorpidis Travel,** Odos Egnatia 76, at Odos Aristotelous, second floor (☎ **031/286-812** or 031/286-825).

Fast Facts: Thessaloniki

American Express   The office is at Odos Tsimiski 19 (☎ **031/239-797**); open Monday through Thursday from 8am to 2pm and Friday from 8am to 1:30pm.

Currency Exchange/ATMs   All banks exchange currency, as do most hotels and the central post office. The major banks along Odos Tsimiski and Aristoteleos Square have ATMs.

Dentists   The Thessaloniki dentists most preferred by foreigners are Dr. Dimitris Sirris, at Odos Ayios Theodoras 10 (☎ **031/275-868**), off Odos Ayias Sofias between Tsimiski and Ermou, and Dr. Dimitra Konstantinidou, at Vas. Olgas 39 (☎ **031/815-526**), east of the Municipal Park. Both are excellent and speak fluent English.

Doctors   In Greece, almost all doctors specialize and few fit the American concept of a general practitioner. An excellent English-speaking physician who happens to be a pediatrician but can also provide general assistance is Dr. Christos Chrysanthopoulos, Odos Ayias Sofias 43A (☎ **031/267-292**). In addition, the U.S. Consulate (☎ **031/266-121** or 031/260-716) has a continually updated list of recommended doctors.

Drugstores   See "Pharmacies," below.

Embassies/Consulates   The **U.S. Consulate** (☎ **031/266-121** or 031/260-716) is at Leoforos Nikis 59, 2 blocks west of the White Tower. It offers a bare minimum of services. The **UK/Commonwealth Honorary Consul** is at Odos Venizelou 8 (☎ **031/278-006** or 031/269-984), by appointment only.

Emergencies   The **police hotline** is ☎ **100.** For **first aid,** call ☎ **166.** For **car breakdowns,** call ☎ **104** (the Greek Automobile Touring Club, or ELPA). Also try the **tourist police,** Dodekanisou 4, near the eastern end of Odos Tsimiski (☎ **031/254-870** or 031/254-871).

Hospitals/Clinics   At Greek hospitals, you may not find anyone who speaks good enough English for your purposes. Two private clinics, **Ahepa Hospital,** Kiriaki 1 (☎ **031/993-111**), and **Ayios Loukas** (St. Luke's), on the road to Panorama village northeast of the city (☎ **031/342-102** to 031/342-104), both have English-speaking doctors.

Internet Access   Thessaloniki has lots of Internet cafes, including **Globus Internet Cafe,** Aminta 12 (☎ **031/232-901**), **Ground Floor,** Pavlo Melas 82 (☎ **031/282-450**), and **Indigo Internet Cafe,** Meg. Alexandrou 53 (☎ **031/851-581**).

Lost Property   Call the tourist police at ☎ **031/522-656.**

Newspapers & Magazines   English-language publications are available at several kiosks in Aristotelous Square, on Odos Tsimiski, and at the excellent **Molhos Bookstore,** Odos Tsimiski 10, at the corner of Odos El. Venizelou.

Pharmacies   Pharmacies alternate late-night hours. Lists and addresses of the ones open on a particular night can be found in the local newspapers and the windows of all pharmacies.

Police   The 24-hour emergency number is ☎ **100.** The tourist police number is ☎ **031/522-656.**

Post Office   The main post office is at Odos Tsimiski 45, just east of Odos Aristotelous (☎ **031/278-924**). Hours are Monday through Friday from 7:30am to 8pm, Saturday from 7:30am to 2pm, and Sunday from 9am to 1:30pm.

Rest Rooms   All but the smallest eateries and bars have rest rooms that you can request to use without embarrassment.

Safety   Thessaloniki is still an extremely safe city, although the influx of a rough element in recent years means that anyone walking around alone late at night should exercise caution. The only area absolutely to avoid is around Vardaris Square, which attracts some shady characters.

Taxis   Radio taxis in the city center can be called at ☎ **031/517-417.** See also "Getting Around," above.

Suggested Itineraries

If you've already been to Athens, you probably arrived there with a pretty clear idea of what you wanted to see first: The Acropolis, the National Archaeological Museum, and Plaka head most lists. Thessaloniki also has its top attractions—the **Archaeological** and **Byzantine museums** and its superb **Byzantine churches**—but one of the great delights of visiting here is getting to know the city itself. Thessaloniki—rather than any monument or museum—is its own greatest attraction. There are lots of pleasant squares here, often near the churches and monuments you want to see, often with the shady trees that make this city so much more pleasant to visit than Athens.

Be sure to give yourself time to stroll along the waterfront (especially if the much-delayed harbor cleanup has reduced the ripe summer smell of the polluted water), time to sit in cafes across from the marvelous Byzantine churches, and time to wander the streets high above the city in the old Turkish quarter, the **Upper City (Ano Poli).** You may find that you agree with those who think that whereas Athens is a great place to visit, but not live, Thessaloniki is both a wonderful place to visit and an appealing spot to live.

If You Have 1 Day

The city's two major museums—the **Archaeological Museum** and the **Museum of Byzantine Culture**—are handily located side by side near the fairgrounds. Decide whether you'd rather see the gold from the tomb of Philip of Macedon or images of life in Byzantine Thessaloniki, and be the first one through the door at the museum you choose. Then, head next door to the other museum, perhaps treating yourself en route to a coffee at a nearby cafe. After visiting the museums, stroll back along the harbor past the White Tower to the center of town for lunch. If you feel more energetic, hop a bus or taxi up to the **Upper City (Ano Poli),** have lunch and stroll downhill—but remember: Most of the churches you want to see here are closed in midafternoon.

After a nap, you might visit the churches of **Ayia Sofia** and **Ayios Dimitrios** in the city center and see some of the Roman monuments, keeping in mind that there are cafes handily located near most of what you'll want to see. When you're ready for dinner, head to one of the restaurants in the restored warehouse district, **Ladadika,** or the always lively **Thanasis,** in the Modiano Market.

Note: This makes for a very full day, and you'll certainly enjoy Thessaloniki a lot more if you have more than a day here. Byzantine churches take time to find, to see, and to enjoy. Many of the frescoes and mosaics are high up on walls, or faded by time (be sure to bring a strong flashlight). If you possibly can, see some one day, some another day.

If You Have 2 Days

Abbreviate your first day, so that you are not trying to wipe out the city in one fell swoop. You might begin your second day with the **Upper City** and work your way downhill. Start at the **Vlatadon Monastery** and then stroll downhill, stopping at the enchanting little churches of **Osios David, Nikolaos Orphanos,** and **Profitias Elias.** Even if church architecture, mosaics, and frescoes are not your passion, you'll be walking through the narrow streets of very charming old neighborhoods. If you didn't see them on your first day, take in the churches of Ayia Sofia and Ayios Dimitrios when you get back down to the city center.

Then, for a change of pace, take in the **Modiano Market,** the **Outdoor Market,** and the **Flea Market.** If you visit all three, you can buy anything from a copper bucket—to milk a sheep into—to the sheep itself. Along the way, you can nibble souvlaki, pastry, or whatever seasonal fruit catches your fancy. In the cool of evening, you may want to have a look at the **arch of Galerius,** the **Rotunda,** and the **Roman agora**—in the way you can take in so much here—while relaxing at a nearby cafe.

If You Have 3 Days or More

Thessaloniki is a very lively town; it's pleasant to spend a day here simply wandering and browsing through the shops and galleries along **Odos Tsimiski, Odos Aristotelous, Odos Ayias Sofias,** and pedestrianized **Odos Dimitriou Gounari.** Like all Greeks, the Salonikans are serious shoe-shoppers—don't miss the enormous neon high heel at Karidas Shoe Store on the Via Egnatia across from the ruined Turkish bath. Even if you think you can't face one more museum, stop in at the wonderful **Museum of Musical Instruments** and enjoy the reproductions of classical and Byzantine wind and string instruments.

Or you may want to head out of Thessaloniki to see some of the sites associated with Philip and Alexander, such as **Vergina, Dion,** or **Pella.** The easiest way to do this is to sign up for one of the efficient day trips that take in these sites (See "Organized Tours" and "Side Trips from Thessaloniki," later in this chapter). If you plan to do this by car, try exploring on your way out of town rather than as a day trip to avoid fighting your way in and out of city traffic.

THE TOP ATTRACTIONS

The Archaeological Museum. Odos Manoli Andronikou 6 (opposite the south side of the International Fairgrounds). ☎ **031/830-538.** Fax 031/861-306. E-mail: istepka@culture.gr. Admission Dr1,500 ($4.30); combined admission to both the Archaeological and Byzantine museums Dr2,000 ($6). Mon noon–7pm; Tues–Sun 8am–7pm. Hours subject to unannounced changes. Bus no. 58 from Dikasterion Sq. or bus no. 11 heading east from anywhere on Odos Egnatia.

The stars of the museum are the finds displayed in Room 9 from the tombs at Derveni and the Royal Tombs at Vergina. Most Greek (and fewer non-Greek) archaeologists think that the gold *larnax* (box) with the 16-pointed star held the bones of Philip II of Macedon, the father of Alexander the Great, that the small ivory head is his portrait, and that the bronze greaves were part of his armor. The spoilsport foreign scholars think these finds belonged to another royal Macedonian—but just try telling that to any Greek, especially since the Former Yugoslav Republic of Macedonia began to lay claim to a Macedonian heritage, and tried to put the 16-point star on its flag. The 4th-century bronze crater from Derveni, with wild scenes of a Dionysiac revel, is less

An Important Warning

Strikes that close museums and archaeological sites can occur without warning. Decide what you most want to see in Thessaloniki and go there as soon as possible after your arrival. The fact that something is open today says nothing about tomorrow. One thing to check as soon as you arrive: In January 2000, plans were announced to keep all major attractions open in summer until 7pm. If you're here off-season, check with the **Greek National Tourism Organization (☎ 031/ 271-888)** for the abbreviated winter hours of sites and museums. Keep in mind that the opening hours posted at sites and listed at the tourist office often vary considerably. Alas, no information is utterly reliable.

controversial, and absolutely superb. Once you've seen it, you'll know that the Hellenistic Greeks did not go in for understatement. While you're at the museum, check to see if the 3rd-century B.C. Derveni papyrus, which was exhibited here in 1998, is still on view. The papyrus, found in one of the Derveni tombs, seems to be a philosophical tract, and is the only substantial papyrus found in Greece. Virtually all known ancient papyrus manuscripts have been found in Egypt, whose dry climate preserved them for posterity.

Don't let these treasures, however famous and wonderful, keep you from the rest of the museum, whose exhibits are nicely displayed to suggest the history of Thessaloniki from prehistoric days through the Roman period. These rooms are usually uncrowded, and the delicate Hellenistic glass—how could these paper-thin vessels have survived?— and Roman mosaics from private houses are quite wonderful. There's also a portrait bust of the 4th-century A.D. Emperor Galerius, whose arch is one of Thessaloniki's landmarks. Galerius looks like what he was: a brawler who entered the army as a recruit and ended as emperor.

This severe, low museum was built in 1962, and is considered to be the best example of "architectural modernism" in Thessaloniki—a sad commentary on that genre. The museum shop has postcards, guidebooks, and a number of souvenirs with the 16-point star of Macedon. The museum toilet facilities are good.

Museum of Byzantine Culture. Leoforos Stratou 2 (just west of the Archaeological Museum). ☎ **031/868-570.** Fax 031/838-597. Admission Dr1,000 ($2.90); combined admission to both the Byzantine and Archaeological museums Dr2,000 ($6). Mon 12:30–7pm; Tues–Sun 8am–7pm. Hours subject to unannounced changes. Bus no. 58 from Dikasterion Sq. or bus no. 11 heading east from anywhere on Odos Egnatia.

At present, this is the only museum in the world entirely devoted to Byzantine art and civilization. When all the exhibits here are in place, the museum will cover the 1,100-year development of Byzantine culture from its early beginnings in the Roman world through the fall of Constantinople in 1453; it will also explore the lasting influence of Byzantine culture on Greek art. At present, exhibits on three topics have been installed: Early Christian Churches, the Early Christian City and Private Homes, and Burials and Cemeteries in the Early Christian World. As at the Archaeological Museum, the exhibits here attempt to tell the story of Thessaloniki and look at its social history through art and artifacts.

The most impressive exhibits are the 4th- to 6th-century barrel-vaulted tombs found in Thessaloniki, with frescoes showing Old and New Testament scenes as well as scenes in Paradise. You'll see Daniel in the Lions' Den, Christ as the Fisher of Men, and blissful scenes in Paradise, where fruit, fowl, and wine are shown in abundance.

The text accompanying the exhibit looks at the transition from the ancient image of the Afterworld as the Elysian Fields to the Christian images of Paradise. There are also some bright mosaics and elaborately carved marble panels salvaged from the church of Ayios Dimitrios after the great fire of 1917.

This museum took as long to build as some of Thessaloniki's Byzantine monuments—work began in 1989 and was finished in 1993, and the museum opened in 1997. The bricks in the severe façade are meant to remind visitors of the Byzantine use of bricks—and do, although the comparison works to the detriment of this bland building. The museum shop usually has a range of books on Byzantine culture (sometimes including the superb catalogue of the Treasures of Mount Athos exhibit), as well as museum reproductions and postcards. The toilet facilities are good.

The White Tower. Odos Nikis and Odos Pavlou Mela on the seaside promenade just south of the Archaeological Museum. ☎ **031/267-832.** Free admission. Tues–Fri 8am–7pm; Sat–Sun 8:30am–3pm. Bus no. 58 from Dikasterion Sq. or bus no. 11 heading east from anywhere on Odos Egnatia.

What Big Ben is to London, or the Eiffel Tower to Paris, the 16th-century White Tower is to Thessaloniki: the city's most famous landmark. The tower was built as part of the city's defense walls, and then used as an Ottoman prison and place of execution. In 1985, the tower was restored and fitted out as a museum as part of the celebrations of the 2,300th anniversary of Thessaloniki's founding. At present, it houses a number of icons not yet on display at the Museum of Byzantine Culture, as well as exhibits on Thessaloniki's history. After the icons go back to the Byzantine Museum, there will be more exhibits here on Thessaloniki.

Right now, the most fun is the building itself, with its steep winding staircase that goes up six floors and offers terrific views of the city and harbor. Each floor has a round room with alcoves, some of which were once prison cells. At the very end, a rooftop cafe rewards you for the climb. If you're here in winter, you'll get an idea of just how dank and forbidding a prison this thick-walled stone tower must have been.

The Rotunda (also known as Ayios Yioryos, after the adjacent church). Ayios Yioryos Sq. at Odos Filipou (1 block north of the juncture of Odos Egnatia and Odos Dimitriou Gounari, just above the Arch of Galerius). ☎ **031/213-627.** Free admission except for special events. Daily 8:30am–3pm. Bus nos. 10 or 11 heading east from anywhere on Odos Egnatia.

Some say that Galerius built this massive brick-and-stone structure as his modest mausoleum, while others think that he intended it to be a temple, perhaps of Zeus. Later in the 4th century, the Byzantine emperor Theodosius the Great converted the rotunda into a church of St. George, and began the ornamentation of its 6-meter-thick walls with mosaics. When the Turks conquered Thessaloniki in the 15th century,

---

History 101: The Galerian Monuments

In the 4th century, the Roman empire was briefly ruled by a complicated system of two primary emperors, each of whom had an assistant—an emperor in training, as it were. The idea was that this system (known as the tetrarchy) would make it easier to administer the vast Roman empire. In the early 4th century A.D., Galerius, one of the tetrarchs, moved his capital from Asia Minor to Thessaloniki. Then he did what no Roman, emperor or not, could ever resist—he began to build. As a good Roman, he built on a nice, neat, north-south axis flanking the Via Egnatia. The **Rotunda,** the **Arch of Galerius,** the **Palace** at Navarino Square, the **Hippodrome,** and the **Greek Agora** and **Roman Forum** are some of what survive from his ambitious building program.

they converted it into a mosque (you'll see one minaret left from this period), and destroyed many of the exquisite mosaics.

The Rotunda reopened in 1999 after more than a decade of restoration to repair the damage done in the horrific earthquake of 1978. Artisans and archaeologists worked with literally millions of tesserae to restore these dazzling mosaics. Now you can see (especially if you bring binoculars) the indigo peacocks, garlands of flowers and fruit, and blond, curly-haired saints and martyrs (and martyred saints) in the mosaics that cover the walls. If possible, try to visit on a Wednesday, when the neighborhood street market stretches for blocks around the Rotunda.

The Arch of Galerius. Just below the Rotunda on Odos Egnatia and Odos Dimitriou Gounari.

If you need directions here, try asking for *ee kamara* ("the arch"), which is what Thessalonians call this hefty monument that Galerius built around A.D. 305 to celebrate a victory over the Persians a few years earlier. Originally, the arch was even larger: Almost half—another entire arch—is missing. You'll see the Persians, some in the peaked caps and trousers that the Greeks and Romans found so effeminate and absurd, in the carved panels that tell the story of Galerius's battles. Until 1953, the tram line ran right under this arch, which still sits in the middle of the traffic whose fumes are steadily eroding many sculptural details.

The Palace. Navarino Sq.

Of course, Galerius built himself a palace in Thessaloniki. After all, his co-emperor Diocletian was building himself a perfectly splendid palace at Split, on the Dalmatian coast. Little remains of Galerius's palace, but even these low remains give an idea of how large this two-story palace with a large, central courtyard must have been—fit, in short, for an emperor. The best-preserved part of the complex is the **Octagon,** the mysterious building that some archaeologists think may have been Galerius's throne room. Why do they think this? First, the Octagon was exceptionally richly decorated with a multicolored marble floor and interior recesses, of which one is a good deal larger than the others—the ideal place for a throne. That said, it should be noted that a very similar structure built by Diocletian in Spoleto, Italy, was not a throne room, but a mausoleum.

The Hippodrome. Ippodromou Sq.

We know that the ancient hippodrome, where chariot races took place, lies under the square of the same name, because of finds made when today's apartment blocks were built here. There's virtually nothing above ground to see of this ancient racetrack where, in A.D. 390, the Emperor Theodosius the Great ordered the slaughter of some 7,000 spectators. The reason: Theodosius's favorite charioteer had been lynched by a mob that supported one of his opponents. After that terrible day, the Hippodrome was abandoned and gradually covered by layers of buildings from successive eras; some say that they can still make out the oval shape of the Hippodrome in the shape of today's square.

Ippodromou Square is generally a place of evil associations: In 1566, St. Cyril was executed here by the Turks for not converting to Islam. The charming little church of St. Anthony here was, during the Turkish Occupation, a lunatic asylum. You can still see some of the manacles with which "patients" were imprisoned on view in the church.

The Greek Agora and Roman Forum. Dikasterion Sq., bounded by Filipou, Agnostou Stratiotou, Olimbou, and Makedonikis Amnis sts.

In the 1960s, workmen digging to lay the foundations of new law courts for Thessaloniki came across the remains of the city's ancient Greek agora, later the Roman forum. Archaeologists took over and excavated the large complex you see today, bounded by one of the city bus terminals. As in Athens, this agora/forum was the heart of the ancient city: its commercial, governmental, social, and artistic center.

When the Romans came here, they inevitably expanded the Greek agora, creating a forum that was on two levels. You can see the arched remains of the **cryptoporticus,** a retaining wall that supported part of the upper forum. The best-preserved remain here is the large **Odeum,** or Odeon, a theater where Romans enjoyed watching both musical performances and fights to the death between gladiators and wild beasts. The Odeum is sometimes used today for summer concerts.

In modern times, the most famous monument here was the stoa with a series of statues facing the Via Egnatia, known as the *Colonnade of the Enchanted Idols,* or *Incantadas,* the name given them by Thessaloniki's then-flourishing community of Sephardic Jews. By the 19th century, much of the colonnade was lost, but a segment remained, incorporated into the courtyard of a Jewish home. When the French scholar Emmanuel Miller saw the colonnade, he knew he had to have it—and got permission to cart the remaining "incantadas" off to the Louvre, where they are to this day. If you browse in book and print shops in Thessaloniki, you'll probably see reproductions of a charming engraving of the colonnade by the 18th-century English antiquarians Stuart and Revett.

CHURCHES

Thessaloniki's churches are a clear case of the whole being greater than the sum of its parts. Although Ayia Sofia and Ayios Dimitrios are the two best-known churches, your greatest pleasure may come from seeing the smaller churches. As you visit, try to identify those that were built in the **basilica form** (usually a rectangular church with side aisles) and those in the **cross-in-square form,** which is just what its name says.

Keep in mind that many of these churches keep irregular hours, often closing from about 1 to 5pm. In short, the best way to see them is probably on one or more morning excursions.

IN DOWNTOWN THESSALONIKI

Church of Ayia Sofia. Ayia Sofia Sq., between Odos Tsimiski and Odos Egnatia. ☎ **031/270-253.** Free admission. Daily 8am–9pm (but often closed about 1–5pm).

It's a pity that Thessaloniki's two most important churches—Ayia Sofia (Holy Wisdom) and Ayios Dimitrios (St. Demetrios)—are both heavily restored. Still, each is worth visiting for its importance in the city's history and for its fine mosaics, although both lack the pleasantly dusty ambiance of Thessaloniki's less heavily restored churches.

Thessaloniki's 7th-century Ayia Sofia was inspired by the emperor Justinian's famous 6th-century church of Ayia Sofia in Constantinople. Like that earlier Ayia Sofia, Salonika's namesake has an impressively large dome—in fact, this was the first church built in Thessaloniki by builders skillful enough to engineer such a large dome. The ornately carved marble columns supporting the dome were, as so often in antiquity and throughout the Byzantine era, pillaged from earlier monuments.

Fortunately, many of Ayia Sofia's original mosaics have survived. The Ascension, with an oddly foreshortened Christ (supported by young angels), and the Virgin Mary with the infant Jesus are especially fine. If you look carefully at the mosaics, you'll notice that some show only crosses and stars and have no human representations. These date from the 8th-century Iconoclastic period, when there was a ban on showing the human figure in religious art. The iconoclasts destroyed many earlier works of

Dress Appropriately!

All these churches are places of worship where casual attire (short skirts for women, shorts or sleeveless shirts for men or women) is considered highly disrespectful. Remember to wear clothing that covers your arms and legs.

art, including many sacred icons—and left us with the word "iconoclast" to describe someone who destroys the past or challenges tradition.

Ayia Sofia Square is one of Thessaloniki's nicest, and most important, squares—this is where the service of Thanksgiving was held when the city was liberated from the Germans on November 2, 1944. Keep an eye out for the "red house," at Ayias Sofias 36, built in 1925 for a wealthy industrialist, and one of few fine old houses here to have survived the fire of 1917 that gutted Thessaloniki—and, of course, severely damaged Ayia Sofia church. Across the way at Ayias Sofias 33, now with the Terkenlis and Byzantium pastry shop on the ground floor, is another handsome mansion built in the 1920s. The pastry shop is an excellent spot to rest and refresh after seeing the church.

Church and Crypt of Ayios Dimitrios (sometimes given as Ayios Demetrios). Corner of Odos Ayiou Dimitriou and Odos Ayiou Nikolaou, 1 block north of the Roman market, at the base of the Upper City. ☎ **032/213-627.** Free admission. Church and crypt usually open Mon 12:30–7pm; Tues–Sat 8am–8pm; Sun 10:30am–8pm. Bus nos. 22 and 23, which leave about every 10 min. from the southeast side of Eleftherias Sq., stop near the church.

Like Ayia Sofia, Ayios Dimitrios was heavily restored—in fact, almost entirely rebuilt—after the fire of 1917. Consequently, this is a church with an imposing history, some fine mosaics, but very little soul. In the 4th century A.D., a small church was built here on the site of a former Roman bath to commemorate Dimitrios, the patron saint of Thessaloniki who refused to renounce his Christian faith and was promptly put to death in A.D. 303 by the emperor Galerius. About 100 years later, the church was considerably enlarged into its present five-aisled basilical form. After the 1917 fire, the church was rebuilt on and off from 1926 to 1949, and you can still see scorch marks from the 1917 conflagration on some of the interior walls.

Almost all the mosaics here are restorations of what was lost in 1917, but keep an eye out for the lovely original portrait of the boyish saint with two young children. (You can see other mosaics salvaged after the fire on display in the Museum of Byzantine Culture.) The crypt, which you enter down a narrow, twisting staircase, is pleasantly mysterious, with several small anterooms and remains of the Roman baths. Particularly venerated are the spot where Dimitrios is believed to have been martyred and the spot with a holy water font. For centuries, the faithful noted a sweet scent here, and believed that a myrrh, or perfumed fluid, from the saint himself flowed from the font.

As you leave the church, have a look at the delightful chapel of St. Euthymius, built into the wall of Ayios Dimitrios. The 14th-century frescoes in the little chapel have all the verve that the heavily restored mosaics in Ayios Dimitrios lack.

The Panayia Acheiropoietos (The Church of the Virgin Made Without Hands). Odos Ayias Sofia, north of Odos Egnatia. No phone.

This charming 5th-century basilica is the only church from Thessaloniki's early Christian days to have survived virtually intact, without the restorations and renovations that have changed the character of Ayia Sofia and Ayios Dimitrios. The marble columns, with their elaborate "perforated" acanthus leaf decorations, give you a good idea of the Byzantine love of the elaborate—which was achieved here by vigorous drill work. What a contrast to the mosaics, with the simple gold cross and the delicate floral and vine motifs interspersed with birds. The 13th-century frescoes showing some of the 40 Martyrs are equally appealing; those that are missing were destroyed when this church was converted to a mosque. Due to the inexorable rise in the street level over the centuries, the church now sits below the level of today's streets and roads.

The Panayia Chalkeon (The Virgin of the Copper Workers). Dikasterion Sq. No phone.

This tiny church with its three domes looks as if it would fit nicely into a miniature village. It has some fine frescoes, but its real glory is its façade, with windows piled above windows, domes above domes. Like the Panayia Acheiropoietos, the 11th-century Panayia Chalkeon now sits considerably below Thessaloniki's modern street level. Several nearby streets still have the copper workers' shops from which, centuries ago, this church took its name. Locals call this the "red church" for its rosy bricks.

Ayios Panteleimon. Corner of Odos Egnatia and Odos Iassonidou.

This church, dedicated to one of the physician saints, is a popular place to light a candle and say a prayer for good health. The church, all that remains of a large monastery on this spot, is usually closed, but its elaborate brick and stone work makes it a delight even to glimpse from the street. If you do get inside, note how the central dome is supported by four barrel vaults, a distinctive characteristic of Macedonian churches.

IN THE UPPER CITY (ANO POLI)

One of the great pleasures of visiting these churches is exploring the narrow streets of the Upper City, with the considerable remains of the massive Byzantine Eptapirigion Walls ("Seven-Gated Walls"). The Upper City is a maze of cobbled streets, wooden houses with the second floor built overhanging the first, street-side fountains, corner groceries, and cafes. In the 1960s, this area was practically falling down; now, as young Thessalonians reclaim the old quarter, an address here is considered very chic. When you come here, be prepared to get lost at least once—and probably to find a wonderful little church, or courtyard, or schoolyard, while you try to find your way back to your original destination. *Remember:* All these churches are closed from about 1 to 5pm.

It's very pleasant to ride up to the Upper City on bus nos. 22 or 23 from Eleftherias Square, then walk back downhill. When you get out of the bus in the Upper City, have a look at the Byzantine walls around the Acropolis and the Byzantine defense tower called the Tower of Trigoniou.

Vlatodon Monastery (also known as Vlatades). By the Gate to the Acropolis.

As you toil uphill, you'll keep seeing the overhanging walls of the substantial Vlatodon Monastery, founded in the 14th century. In the last few years, it has been substantially renovated and expanded, but the inner courtyard is still charming—and a cool spot to rest for a moment or two. If the main church is locked, don't feel too bad; the frescoes were badly damaged by the Turks, and have not been restored. By tradition, the little chapel of saints Peter and Paul was built on the spot where St. Paul preached when he visited Thessaloniki in A.D. 50.

✪ Osios David (The Latomou Monastery). Odos Timotheou, off Odos Ayias Sofia.

We manage to get lost almost every time we come here, but always eventually find this absolutely charming 5th- or 6th-century church, with its pleasant shaded courtyard. Indeed, what a tempting fantasy to think of taking over the caretaker's job, sitting with a book in the little shelter in the courtyard, tending the flowers, and unlocking the church for visitors—who are bound to be impressed, because nothing about Osios David's simple exterior can prepare you for the glorious mosaic of the vision of Ezekiel inside. The vision shows Christ surrounded by the symbols of the four apostles (the angel, eagle, lion, and bull). If there's a finer mosaic in the city, we can't imagine what it could be. According to local lore, the mosaic spent several centuries hidden beneath a calf's skin, which prevented the Turks from finding and destroying it.

Ayios Nikolaos Orfanos. Odos Apostolou Pavlou.

Like Osios David, this seemingly unprepossessing brick-and-stone church holds an astonishing treasure: well-preserved frescoes from the 14th century, the zenith of Thessaloniki's artistic excellence. You can pick out St. Nikolaos himself, with his halo, standing at the helm of the little boat that he's guiding across stormy waters. The other frescoes, as usual in such cycles, show scenes from the Old and New Testaments, as well as depicting saints and prophets. Next to the church, part of its once-flourishing monastery, with an attractive veranda, has just been restored, and makes the traveler envy those lucky enough to live here.

Ayia Katerini. Corner of Odos Sachini and Odos Tsamadou, near the Byzantine walls.

This is another of Thessaloniki's fine 14th-century churches, built with a central dome flanked by four cupolas, and elegant brick and stone work. Now surrounded by new apartment buildings and old homes, it is a dignified reminder of one of the city's finest artistic periods. If you get inside, look for the wall painting showing the healing of the blind.

Profitias Elias. Odos Olympiados.

This substantial 14th-century church, whose elaborate brick exterior has recently been restored, is nice in and of itself, and is a fine vantage point to look out over the city. Women, who cannot visit Mount Athos, will get an idea from Profitias Elias of the cross-in-square with central dome style of many of the churches on Mount Athos.

MARKETS

The Modiano Market. The block bounded by Aristotelous, Ermou, Vasileos Irakleiou, and Komninon sts. Mon–Sat about 7am–5pm.

It's been a while since we've seen gypsies with dancing bears in the Modiano Market, although there are still gypsies aplenty, as well as other street musicians, here most days. You could easily spend a morning in the glass-roofed market that covers an entire square block, happily wandering from stall to stall and eyeing the fish, meat, fruit, vegetables, flowers, spices, and baked goods on sale. Whenever you get hungry, sit down in any one of a number of cafes or ouzo joints (including the delicious **Thanasis**).

The roofed market was built in 1922 by the wealthy Jewish merchant Eli Modiano, whose handsome family mansion at Odos Megalou Alexandrou (Alexander the Great) 65 is now the home of the **Folklore and Ethnography Museum of Macedonia.** If you wish, take a bus or drive along both Odos Megalou Alexandrou and Odos Vas. Olgas and have a look at Thessaloniki's surviving 19th-century mansions.

The Kapani (Vlali) Market. Bounded by Komninon, Egnatia, Aristotelous, and Menexe sts. Mon–Sat about 8am–5pm.

This market sells foods, dry goods, fabrics, and just about everything else you can think of, in a hodgepodge of ramshackle shops crowded one next to the other for as far as the eye can see. There's been a market here at least since Turkish times, and probably long before that.

The Flea Market. Odos Tositsa. Usually Mon–Sat 8am–7pm.

Just what its name implies, this market, which sprawls along Odos Tositsa, sells everything from genuine junk to genuine antiques (much more of the former than the latter). Of late, many Eastern Europeans sell their wares here, usually leather jackets, fake Leica cameras and designer watches, and an odd assortment of alarm clocks, mirrors, and socks.

The Bezesteni. Odos Venizelou and Odos Solomou. Usually Mon–Sat 9am–7pm.

It would be wonderful to have a bird's-eye view of the Bezesteni's six domes and four entrances, one on each side. This covered market, today specializing in textiles and jewelry, was built in the late 15th century by Sultan Bayezid II, and is one of the best preserved Turkish monuments in Thessaloniki. It's also a terrific place to browse and feel transported into an Oriental bazaar.

MORE ATTRACTIONS

The Alatza Imaret. Dimitrion Sq., just off Odos Ayiou Nikolaou, half a block north of Odos Kassandrou, 1½ blocks north of the church of Ayios Dimitrios. ☎ **031/278-587.** Free admission. Open intermittently for exhibitions.

Along with the Bezesteni, the Alatza Imaret, a former 15th-century mosque with a poorhouse, or almshouse, is one of the best-preserved Turkish buildings in Thessaloniki. "Alatza" means "many-colored," and refers to the tiles and stones that covered the mosque in its days of glory. If you're lucky, it may be open when you visit, as exhibitions are sometimes held here.

Atatürk's Birthplace. Odos Apostolou Pavlou 17 (8 short blocks east of the church of Ayios Dimitrios). ☎ **031/248-452.** Free admission. Daily 10am–5pm. Bus no. 22 or 23 from Eleftherias Sq. or stops along Odos El. Venizelou north to Odos Ayiou Dimitriou. Entrance through the front gate of the Turkish consulate, passport or identity card necessary.

Just behind the consulate, this modest wood-framed house was the birthplace in 1881 of Mustafa Kemal (Atatürk), the man who created the modern Turkish state and was its first president. Given to Turkey as a present by the Greek government in 1933, the house has been restored and furnished to reflect the way it must have been at Atatürk's birth. It contains numerous photos of the man, young and old; various letters and papers; and cases containing the clothes and uniforms he wore. There is an excellent English-language booklet available with all the relevant information as well as photos.

Folk and Ethnological Museum. Vas. Olgas 68. ☎ **031/850-591.** Hours and admission not available.

Be sure to call before you visit this museum, which hopes to reopen in 2001—but had similar aspirations for 1999 and 2000. That said, if it is open, the collection of costumes and items of Macedonian daily life is superb. The elegant 19th-century town house that houses the museum once belonged to the prominent Greek-Jewish Modiano family, after whom the Modiano Market takes its name.

International Fairgrounds. Entrances at the corners of Odos Angelaki and Odos Tsimiski and Odos Angelaki and Odos Egnatia. Free admission except during special exhibitions. Open irregular hours.

If you're in Thessaloniki during the September Trade Fair, you may want to take in some of the exhibits here. Usually any special exhibitions or events taking place are posted conspicuously throughout Thessaloniki. This is also the home of the **Macedonian Museum of Contemporary Art** (☎ 031/240-002), open Tuesday through Sunday from 9am to 5pm, June through September, and Tuesday through Sunday from 10am to 2pm and 5 to 9pm, October through May. Admission is Dr500 ($1.45).

Jewish History Museum (also known as the Museum of the Jewish Presence in Thessaloniki). Odos Agios Mina 13. ☎ **031/250-406.** Fax 031/229-063. E-mail: jct@ compulink.gr. Free admission. Call for hours.

This small museum in the heart of the Modiano Market uses photographs and artifacts to portray Jewish life in Thessaloniki. Thessaloniki Jews established the city's first printing press in the early 1500s, and founded the city's first newspaper, *El Lunar,* in 1865. The community thrived under the Ottoman Empire, and in 1900, 80,000 of Thessaloniki's 173,000 inhabitants were Jews. Just before World War II, there were 60,000 Jews here; 2,000 survived the death camps. Today there are almost none.

To visit or attend services at one of Thessaloniki's remaining synagogues, phone the **Jewish Community Office,** Odos Tsimiski 24 ☎ **031/272-840.** If you're interested in learning more about the Jewish community in Greece, ask at the GNTO office for the excellent pamphlet *Jewish Heritage in Greece* and keep an eye out for the locally published *Jewish Community of Thessaloniki* and Niko Stavroloulakis's books *The Jews of Greece* and *Jewish Sites and Synagogues of Greece.*

Lambrakis Monument. Intersection of Odos Venizelou, Odos Ermou, and Odos Spandoni.

On May 22, 1963, a leftist member of the parliament, Grigoris Lambrakis, who had been speaking at a peace meeting, was run down and killed on this spot. Vassilis Vassilikos based his novel *Z* on Lambrakis's death; the novel was later adapted for a film by Costas-Gavras and starred Yves Montand. Lambrakis's assassination by right-wing forces and the protests that followed were part of a long series of events culminating in the dictatorship of the colonels in the late 1960s. The monument shows a bronze figure, arms upraised in supplication, flanked by a dove of peace.

✪ **The Museum of Ancient Greek, Byzantine, and Post Byzantine Musical Instruments.** Odos Katouni 12–14, Ladadika. ☎ **031/555-263/4.** Admission Dr1,500 ($4.30). Tues–Sun 9am–3pm and 5–10pm.

What is it about music museums? The one in Athens is one of that city's finest small museums, and Thessaloniki has its own appealing music museum. The three floors here house beautifully displayed reproductions of stringed and wind instruments, along with marvelous photographs of depictions of the instruments from ancient vase paintings or Byzantine manuscripts. Purists may object to the absence of period instruments here, but the reproductions do their best to give viewers a sense of what the actual instruments looked like. Music sometimes softly plays in the background, and there's a cafe that is sometimes open.

Museum of the Macedonian Struggle. Proxenou Koromila 23. ☎ **031/229-778.** Fax 031/233-108. E-mail: mma.the.forthnet.gr@nefeli. forthnet.gr. Free admission. Tues, Thurs, and Fri 9am–2pm; Wed 9am–2pm and 6–8pm; Sat–Sun 11am–2:30pm.

As its name suggests, this museum (in a handsome neoclassical building) contains artifacts, uniforms, and weapons from the struggle that raged on and off from 1870 to 1919 to liberate Macedonia. The exhibits are stirring, and several new English-language brochures help explain this long and bloody conflict.

ART GALLERIES

Thessaloniki has a number of excellent galleries that often have exhibitions well worth taking in. You can find out about them from posters in town, from the Greek National Tourism Organization office in Aristotelous Square, and from the "Thessakibuju Report" listing, usually published on Tuesdays in *Kathimerini,* the English-language supplement to the *International Herald Tribune.* Galleries worth checking out include **Apothiki,** Odos Nikis on the waterfront (☎ **031/240-877**); **Foka,** Odos Foka 17 (☎ **031/240-362**); and **Metamorfosis,** Odos Tsimiski 128 (☎ **031/285-071**).

Hitting the Beach

Any beaches within the bay of Thessaloniki are too polluted to be safe, although people do swim here. Those in the communities of Perea and Ayia Triada, 16 to 24 kilometers (10 to 15 miles) along the bay east of the city, are considered reasonably safe. Just past Ayia Triada, on the headland of the bay, is the Greek National Tourism Organization facility of **Akti Thermaikou,** which also has a children's playground, changing cabins, snack bars, and tennis courts.

In addition to these, several museums and galleries emphasize the art and life of Thessaloniki and Macedonia, with particular reference to the lively pre– and post–World War II art scene here. These include the **Gallery of Fine Arts,** Odos Nic. Germanou 1, inside the National Theater Building (☎ 031/238-601); the **Municipal Gallery,** Odos Vas. Olas 162 (☎ 031/425-531); the **Macedonian Museum of Contemporary Art,** in the International Fairgrounds (☎ 031/240-002); the **National Museum of Contemporary Art in Thessaloniki,** Kolokotroni 21, in the Lazariston Monastery (☎ 031/589-140); and the **National Bank Cultural Foundation,** Vas. Olgas 108 (☎ 031/295-170). Most of these places keep irregular hours; we advise checking with the GNTO office in Aristotelous Square for information.

ORGANIZED TOURS

Reputable companies offering tours of Thessaloniki and of the Philip and Alexander sites include **Zorpidis Travel,** Odos Egnatia 76, at the corner of Odos Aristotelous, second floor (☎ 031/286-812; fax 031/242-364), and **Kinissi Tour Agency,** Odos Venizelou 2 (☎ 031/241-080; fax 031/286-824). Try the respected British agency **Filoxenia,** Odos Tsimiski 17, fourth floor (☎ 031/280-560; fax 031/285-170; www.filoxenia.co.uk), for "green" ecological tours to the countryside as well as mountaineering excursions.

SPECTATOR SPORTS

Like most Greeks, Thessalonians are keen soccer and basketball fans, rooting for the home teams (confusingly, the Aris and PAOK stadiums are home to both basketball *and* soccer teams). Your best bet if you don't speak or read Greek and want to catch a game is to check with the concierge at your hotel, or at the GNTO tourist office in Aristotelous Square (don't attempt this by phone). In general, soccer games are in the spring and fall, basketball year-round. The **Aris stadium** is in the suburb of Harilaou (☎ 031/305-402), while the much-easier-to-reach **PAOK stadium** is on Ayios Dimitrios, 2 blocks northeast of the International Fairgrounds (☎ 031/238-560).

SHOPPING

As you'd expect from Greece's second-largest city, Thessaloniki has a wide variety of shops, and since the city center is quite compact, it's easy to explore the major shopping districts. As in Athens—indeed, throughout Greece—most chic boutiques stock imported goods from Europe and the States, with a hefty import duty. If you shop the winter (January) and summer (late July and August) sales, you may find some bargains.

If you want to see where Thessalonians shop, take a stroll along **Tsimiski, Mitropoleos,** and **Proxenou Koromila** streets between **Odos Pavlou Mela** (the diagonal street connecting the church of Ayia Sofia with the White Tower) and the north-south vertical of **Odos Venizelou.** In this area are the city's few department stores, many boutiques selling the latest in expensive haute couture, shops selling jeans and casual clothing, *lots* of shoe stores, jewelry and antiques stores, record shops selling both Greek and foreign items, the best English- and French-language book and magazine store in town, and a number of confectioneries.

Thessaloniki also still has a number of shops selling the handiwork of local craftspeople, such as coppersmiths and jewelers. This is where you're likely to find something tempting, sometimes at what constitutes a bargain price for a foreigner. Not surprisingly, most of the shops are near the church of the Panayia Chalkeon (The Virgin of the Copper Makers) in **Dikasterion Square.**

What you won't find in Thessaloniki is anything remotely equivalent to the streets of shops packed with souvenirs—many made in the Far East—that have proliferated in Athens and on many islands. If you get a souvenir here, it's likely to be just that: something you find that will remind you of your visit, rather than a mass-produced memento.

ANTIQUES

Relics, Odos Yioryio Lassani 3 (☎ 031/226-506), offers the best variety of high-quality antiques in the city, from silver- and glassware to jewelry, ceramics, prints, art-nouveau lamps, and Victorian-era dolls. This is a serious shop with serious prices. It's located a block east of the Mitropoleos Cathedral off Odos Mitropoleos; closed Sundays.

ART

Probably the best gallery in Thessaloniki for paintings, engravings, and sculpture, **Terracotta,** Odos Chrys. Smirnis 13 and Mitropoleos 76 (☎ **031/235-689;** fax 031/220-191; www.terracotta.gr; e-mail: info@terracotta.gr), features works from all of the most famous contemporary Greek artists, such as Fasianos, as well as those of the emerging generation. It's located 1½ blocks north of the U.S. Consulate between Leoforos Nikis and Odos Mitropoleos; closed August 1 to 20. You can also try **Art Forum,** Odos Nikiforo Foka 29 (☎ **031/224-060**), a gallery focusing on contemporary Greek art. It's off Odos Tsimiski, a block east of Navarino Square. Hours are Monday, Tuesday, Thursday, and Friday from 10am to 2:30pm and 6 to 9pm; closed July through August.

BOOKS, NEWSPAPERS & MAGAZINES

Apostolic Diakonta Bookstore. Ethnikis Aminis 9A, near the Archaeological and Byzantine museums. ☎ **031/275-126.**

Although this handsome bookstore specializes in books on religious matters, it also carries a wide selection (in English and French, as well as in Greek) on Greece. This is a wonderful place to browse, and even if you can't afford one of the superb books of photos of Greece, you can find wonderful cards, as well as nice reproductions of icons.

✪ **Molhos.** Odos Tsimiski 10 (between Odos El. Venizelou and Odos Dragoumi). ☎ **031/ 275-271.** Fax 031/229-738. E-mail: molho@imagine.gr.

Molhos has the best selection of foreign-language books, magazines, and newspapers in the city, and this wonderful family-run, multiple-level bookstore is a Thessaloniki institution. These people love books, and the staff can assist you in English, French, and German—and probably a great many other languages. Many of the most tempting books (including some dazzling books on Greece) are on the second floor.

Rentzis. Odos Tsimiski 24. ☎ **031/236-175.** Fax 031/271-477.

This small bookstore in an arcade between Mitropoleos and Tsimiski has a helpful staff and a good selection of English-language books on Thessaloniki and Greece.

Details, Details

In Thessaloniki, old-style, pre–European Community **shopping hours,** unfathomable to foreigners, are still in force. Stores open at about 9am and close around 1:30 or 2pm for the afternoon siesta. On Tuesday, Thursday, and Friday evenings, some (but not all) reopen from about 5:30 to 8:30pm. In July, however, virtually all shops are closed in the evening. The safest course is to shop in the morning. Note that many of these stores will take major credit cards, but almost all, especially the smaller ones, prefer not to.

COPPER

At the family-run **Adelphi Kazanzidi,** Odos Klissouras 12 off the western side of Dikasterion Square, a block north of Odos Egnatia (☎ **031/262-741**), the copper-working skills have been passed down from generation to generation. It sells numerous finely crafted copperware items such as wine carafes, skillets, water heaters, and trays, all handmade on the premises.

CRAFTS

Skitso, Odos Grigori Palama 11 (☎ **031/269-822**), sells a delightful variety of handmade objects, mostly in wood, including puppets, ships, crosses, and children's toys. It's a block west of the intersection of Odos Pavlou Mela and Odos Tsimiski.

DEPARTMENT STORES

Fokas, with three centrally located branches at Odos Tsimiski 48–50 (☎ **031/241-954**), Odos Tsiniski 64 (☎ **031/268-031**), and Odos Ermou 14 (☎ **031/279-876**), has got it all, including men's and women's clothing and shoes. If you want to check out the offerings before you visit, go to www.fokas.gr. Meanwhile, **Lambropoulos,** Odos Tsimiski 18 (☎ **031/269-971**), is the best in the city with five floors full of everything and anything you might want, from cosmetics to basketballs. It's located a block west of Odos Aristotelous, at the corner of Odos Komninon.

FASHION

For both men's and women's fashions, try the department stores such as **Lambropoulos** (see above) or the chic—and expensive—boutiques on pedestrian **Odos Dimitriou Gounari.** One centrally located men's shop (with staff speaking some English) is the long-established **Oxford Company,** Palaion Patron Germanou 4 (☎ **031/273-087**), with nice photos on the walls of the family's old cotton mills in Volos.

GIFTS & SOUVENIRS

At **Tanagrea,** Odos Vogatsikou (a block east of the Metropolitan Cathedral between Odos Mitropoleos and Odos Proxenou Koromila), you'll find a wide selection of handcrafted items by a stable of artisans employed by this well-known chain of stores, which also has outlets in Athens, Crete, and Spetsai. Offerings include ceramics, pewter, silver, leather goods, paintings, glassware, and jewelry.

Pronounced *zeeta mee,* **ZM,** Proxenou Koromila 1, a block east of Aristotelous Square (☎ **031/240-591**), offers three floors of expensive but well-crafted Greek souvenir items such as worry beads, pottery, folk art, rugs, toys, handcrafted caïques, prints, and a few antique silver place settings and jewelry. An extremely tempting place to browse.

Pack 'n' Send

Office supplies may sound like just what you *don't* want to think about on vacation, but if you need stationery, packing tape, scissors, or large envelopes to mail purchases home, **Spondilides,** Odos Tsimiski 24, in the stoa (☎ 031/269-825), is your place. Remember, don't seal up your packages until you get to the post office. All parcels must be inspected before they are shipped.

JEWELRY

Specializing in gold, but not exclusively, the eponymous owner of **Marina,** Odos Mitropoleos 62, a block east of the Metropolitan Cathedral (☎ 031/238-361), offers her own designs as well as copies of the works of famous Greek jewelers such as Lalaounis, with whom she apprenticed.

LEATHER

The best of several leather-goods shops in the area is **Falli,** Odos Askitou 11 (☎ 031/229-197). Located on the southwest corner of the outdoor market, near Odos Ermou and Odos El. Venizelou, Falli makes and sells shoulder bags, backpacks, attaché cases, and sandals. Some of these items are of very high quality and very reasonably priced. You should try to bargain. (If you want good quality leather, you should also resist the Eastern European leather vendors who set up stalls on many street corners.)

MARKETS

See "Markets" (p. 516) for the Modiano, Kapani, Bezesteni, and Flea markets.

MUSIC

Both **Blow Up: The Music Stores,** Odos Aristotelous 8, on the east side of the street a block north of Odos Tsimiski (☎ 031/233-255; fax 031/237-101; www.blowup.gr; e-mail: blowup@the.forthnet.gr), and **Patsis,** Odos Tsimiski 39, at the corner of Odos Aristotelous (☎ 031/231-805), have excellent selections of Greek music well displayed in their windows and on their shelves. **En Chordes,** Ipodromiou 3 (☎ 031/282-248), has a wide selection of musical instruments and CDs, including Byzantine music.

PERFUME

The little shop **Aroma,** Odos Mitropoleos 62, a block east of the Mitropoleos Cathedral (☎ 031/286-010), with its enticing rows of colored perfume jars, offers a multitude of scents, copying famous perfumes or mixing ones of your own choosing at extremely reasonable prices. If you don't find what you want here, most Greek pharmacies have a wide range of scents.

SHOES

Pak, Ayias Sofias Square 3, opposite the north side of the church (☎ 031/274-863), carries a wide selection of high-quality Greek shoes—from hiking boots to high heels—at very acceptable prices. It also carries foreign brands, but these are much more expensive.

SWEETS

In a city where sweetness is next to godliness, the venerable **Agapitos,** Odos Tsimiski 53, between Odos Ayias Sofias and Odos Karolou Dil (☎ 031/279-107), is heaven's best. There are a wide variety of items to choose from, all made with great, mouth-watering, high-caloric care. Closed Sundays.

WHERE TO STAY

Because of Thessaloniki's long history as a center for national and international trade, its hotels have traditionally focused on serving the needs of commercial rather than leisure travelers. Most are blandly functional, and the few that aspire to elegance are almost entirely lacking in charm—the one notable exception being the Mediterranean Palace Hotel (see below).

Reserve in advance during both summer and winter to avoid difficulties during the numerous trade fairs and associated cultural events. Bookings peak in September and October, when the grand International Trade Fair is quickly followed by the month-long Demetria cultural festival. During Demetria, there is often a surcharge on the regular rates. If you have trouble finding accommodations, check with the **Greek National Tourism Organization (EOT),** with offices at the airport (☎ **031/471-170** or 031/473-212, ext. 215) and in the city center at Aristotelous Square 8 (☎ **031/271-888** or 031/222-935).

VERY EXPENSIVE

Macedonia Palace. Leoforos Megalou Alexandrou 2 (on the seafront promenade half a mile east of the White Tower), 54640 Thessaloniki. ☎ **031/897-197.** Fax 031/867210. 284 units. A/C MINIBAR TV TEL. Year-round Dr52,500–Dr71,800 ($151–$206). AE, DC, MC, V. Parking Dr3,500 ($10) a day.

The Macedonia Palace is now managed by the Grecotel Group, and seems to be back on track as a five-star luxury resort hotel. All the large rooms have been redone, but only in the usual Greek hotel decor, which seems to concentrate the glitz in the lobby and leave the bedrooms rather bland. All units have balconies, but if you stay here, insist on a seaside room. (Why pay all that money and not have the view?)

The Macedonia's own restaurants (one Greek, one international) are perfectly good and, as you'd expect, expensive. There are fresh- and saltwater pools in addition to the sea itself. If you can foot the bill, this is a great place to stay with kids—as many Greek families do.

✪ **Mediterranean Palace Hotel.** Odos Salaminos 3 and Odos Karatassou, 54626 Thessaloniki. ☎ **031/552-554.** Fax 031/552-622. www.mediterranean-palace.gr. E-mail: mphotel@otenet.gr. 118 units. A/C MINIBAR TV TEL. Dr66,500 ($192) double. American-style breakfast Dr3,000 ($9). AE, DC, MC, V.

The Mediterranean Palace opened in the Ladadika district, with its tempting restaurants and cafes, in 1997, and is clearly Thessaloniki's best hotel. Front rooms have balconies overlooking the harbor, and virtually every unit in the house is large and furnished with comfortable beds, spiffy wall-to-wall carpeting, and cozy chairs, including some relaxing leather recliners. Many of the guest rooms have especially nice touches, such as decorative moldings and large walk-in closets—and if you want to make a phone call from your bathroom, this is the place to do it. As for the suites, with their large living rooms, kitchenettes, and bedrooms, we could happily live in one for months. Small wonder that the Greek magazine *Odyssey* voted this the best hotel in Thessaloniki, mentioning that it "calms the souls of frazzled executives and travelers." Everyone we know who has stayed here agrees that this is *the* place to stay in Thessaloniki.

EXPENSIVE

Capsis Hotel. Odos Monastiriou 18, 54629 Thessaloniki. ☎ **031/521-321.** Fax 031/510-555 or 031/510-556. 428 units. A/C MINIBAR TV TEL. Dr45,500 ($131) double. Compulsory breakfast Dr3,700 ($11). AE, DC, MC, V.

The best feature of this large 17-year-old hotel on busy Odos Monastiriou, which becomes Egnatia as it gets closer to the center of town (about 15 minutes by foot), is its rooftop pool. The Capsis does a lot of convention business, so you can't expect much in the way of a personal touch, but you will get the comforts (including free parking, in-house laundry service, and a hairdresser) of a hotel that caters to business travelers. The guest rooms are furnished in pale pastels and have decent reading lights, small desks, and good-sized bathrooms with hair dryers. The in-house restaurant is nothing special; the breakfast buffet is good (and should be at $11!).

Electra Palace Hotel. Aristotelous Sq. 9A, 54624 Thessaloniki. ☎ **031/232-221** to 229. Fax 031/235-947. E-mail: electrapalace@the.forthnet.gr. 70 units. A/C MINIBAR TV TEL. Dr35,000–Dr50,750 ($99–$147). Rates include American-style buffet breakfast. AE, DC, MC, V.

Overlooking Thessaloniki's main square, the Electra Palace, with its handsome, curved, arcaded façade, has the nicest location in town—except when there are noisy demonstrations in Aristotle Square. For years, this was the city's only really good hotel; sad to say, when we stayed here most recently, our small interior double bedroom had scruffy carpeting and dingy furniture, and needed serious renovations. If you do stay here, insist on one of the fourth- or fifth-floor rooms with balcony overlooking the square.

Hotel Astoria. Odos Salaminos 9 (at the corner of Odos Tsimiski), 54626 Thessaloniki. ☎ **031/500-910** or 031/500-914. Fax 031/531-564. E-mail: paphotels@the.forthnet.gr or astoria@papcorp.gr. 90 units, 30 with shower only. A/C MINIBAR TV TEL. Dr50,000 ($144) double. AE, MC, V.

The Astoria is still one of the best hotels in town, although the Mediterranean Palace, just around the corner, aces it for luxury, and the Electra on Aristotelous Square has a better location. That said, the Astoria offers all the creature comforts of a business traveler's hotel: spacious bedrooms (admittedly, with resolutely anonymous decor) and bathrooms, soundproofed windows, and an in-house restaurant and bar. The location just off the harbor in the Ladadika district, with its restaurants, cafes, and galleries, is only a 10-minute walk from the center of town.

Hotel Capitol. Odos Monastiriou 8, 54629 Thessaloniki. ☎ **031/516-221.** Fax 031/517-453. E-mail: capitol@hol.gr. 178 units. A/C TV TEL. Dr38,500 ($111). Compulsory breakfast Dr3,700 ($11). AE, MC, V.

Friends who have stayed at this 30-year-old hotel find it less impersonal than the nearby Capsis Hotel—but missed the rooftop pool at the Capsis. There's an on-site restaurant and bar, some of the bedrooms have quite comfortable floral-print sofas and chairs, and almost all units come with a small desk. As at the Capsis, you're a good 15-minute walk along a busy commercial street from anything you've come to see in Thessaloniki.

Hotel Olympia. Odos Olympou 65, 54631 Thessaloniki. ☎ **031/235-421.** Fax 031/276-133. 111 units. A/C TV TEL. Dr36,000 ($104). Compulsory breakfast Dr3,000 ($9). AE, DC, MC, V. Free parking.

Like most hotels in Thessaloniki, the Olympia caters to businesspeople, but Greek families also stay here. The bathrooms are somewhat archaic and the bedrooms are rather bland, with carpets and chairs that have seen better days (the last overhaul here was in 1980). In short, your heart won't leap up at the sight of your room here, but the Olympia's location, at the northern end of the Roman market, is convenient for visiting the city, and traffic here is less thunderous than on some of the main avenues. As always, units on the top floors tend to be quieter than those closer to the street—and, in this case, the flea market.

A Note About Rates

The rates given in this section are for high season in summer—they should be lower in winter, and higher during trade fairs and the Demetria. As always, ask about discounts if you plan a long-term or off-season visit. Note that many hotels require that you pay for an expensive breakfast.

MODERATE

Hotel ABC. Odos Angelaki 41, 54621 Thessaloniki. ☎ **031/265-421.** Fax 031/276-542. E-mail: hotelabc@spark.net.gr. 102 units. A/C TV TEL. Dr35,000 ($99). Compulsory breakfast Dr3,000 ($9). AE, MC, V.

The ABC juts out into busy Sindrivaniou Square, across from the International Fairgrounds and a short walk from Aristotle University and the Archaeological Museum. Staff members claim that the windows are soundproofed, but we'd say that you'll still be well aware of traffic noises from the lower floors of this eight-story hotel. The bedrooms, many decorated in bland browns and beiges, are perfectly functional and perfectly charmless. Why stay here? The price isn't bad, and you're very close to the Archaeological Museum and the inexpensive restaurants that cater to the area's university students. The hotel's own restaurant is not worth trying for lunch or dinner.

✪ **Hotel Queen Olga.** Vas. Olgas 44, 54641 Thessaloniki. ☎ **031/824-621.** Fax 031/868-581. 148 units. A/C MINIBAR TV TEL. Dr25,000 ($72) double. DC, MC, V.

Most of the Olga's good-size rooms have balconies and fully modern bathrooms. The decor is the usual pastel walls and pine beds—standard hotel stuff—but the balconies are a very nice feature. One of the pleasures of staying here is walking along the street that Thessalonians call the "Avenue of the Mansions" and looking at the elegant 19th-century buildings. This hotel is in the eastern part of town, but buses run frequently along Vas. Olgas into the center (about a 20-min. walk).

Hotel Tourist. Odos Mitropoleos 21, 54624 Thessaloniki. ☎ **031/270-501.** Fax 031/226-865. 37 units. TV TEL. Dr23,000 ($66). Inquire about reduced rates. No credit cards.

A friend of ours has stayed here every time she has visited Thessaloniki in the last 30 years. What she likes is that the hotel has changed imperceptibly over that time. True, there are now TVs in the rooms, but many guests prefer to gather and watch television in the communal sitting rooms, with their ornate hanging chandeliers and amazingly uncomfortable chairs. When we stayed here, we loved our old-fashioned, high-ceilinged bedroom and tolerated the archaic bathroom (a little closet shoehorned into the room). We were less fond of the constant noise of traffic and the middle-of-the-night comings and goings to the rooms of some young, female Russian guests who described themselves as "entertainers."

Palace Hotel. Odos Tsimiski 12, 54624 Thessaloniki. ☎ **031/257-400.** Fax 031/256-589. 58 units. TV TEL. Dr 25,000 ($72). MC, V.

We're including the Palace because several readers mentioned liking its central location and good-sized rooms. When we visited, we found the desk staff curt and the rooms in need of some freshening up. Let us know what you think.

Philippion. Odos Antheon (in the forest of Sheih-Sou to the north of the Upper City), 56610 Thessaloniki. ☎ **031/203-320,** 031/203-321, or 031/203-322. Fax 031/218-528. 89 units. A/C MINIBAR TV TEL. Dr35,000 ($99) double. Rates include continental breakfast. AE, MC, V. Free parking. Take the Ring Rd. north around Thessaloniki and exit at the sign labeled PHILIPION. Shortly afterwards, another sign to the left will lead you to the hotel.

For those who cannot abide staying in any city in the summer, but still want to spend time in one, this sprawling, modern four-story hotel complex, renovated in 1992, is a good choice—although the fires of 1998, 1999, and 2000 harmed the lovely surrounding forests. The Philippion overlooks Thessaloniki from a hilltop and is a 10-minute drive from the city center (hotel shuttle buses go into town frequently). The guest rooms are large and sunny, the best being on the third floor to the rear, with a view of the city.

Facilities include a pool, outdoor cafeteria, barbecue, and children's playground. The hotel restaurant is good, with local specialties such as mussels in hot pepper sauce; there's sometimes live entertainment in the evening. The clientele are mostly vacationing Greek families, who can be rather boisterous. The hotel's proximity to the Ring Road makes it extremely easy to reach the airport (15 mins. away) and the main highways to Athens, Halkidiki, and Thrace.

INEXPENSIVE

Hotel Orestias Castorias. Agnostou Stratiotou 14, 54631 Thessaloniki. ☎ **031/536-280.** Fax 031/276-572. 28 units. Dr12,000 ($34). No credit cards.

We were seriously tempted to stay at this small, very cheap, modest hotel across from the Roman Forum. Room 27, overlooking a quiet garden, was especially tempting. What made us hesitate was that almost every guest here seemed to be part of a large group of eastern Europeans, and we had the feeling that we might be crashing a quite lively private party. We'd be eager to have an update on this hotel, whose manager assured us that we would be "comfortable and safe" at his establishment.

WHERE TO DINE

The cuisine of Thessaloniki has long been renowned throughout Greece for its delicate, aromatic character (a heritage of its historically close contact with the Levant) and the splendid variety of its game and hors d'oeuvres (*mezedes* or *mezedakia*). Recently, due to the efforts of a number of enterprising young Thessalonians, it has now become better than ever before, perhaps the finest in all of Greece.

Even in the most expensive establishments, the dress code is very casual for men, with ties and jackets rarely worn. Women, on the other hand, are usually resolutely chic, in little black dresses or more conservative trouser suits. Reservations can be made, but the only guarantee that a table will be available when you arrive is if you get there before most Greeks come out to dine. If you don't want to risk waiting, try to arrive for lunch before 1pm and dinner no later than 8:30pm.

Restaurants and tavernas offer cuisine of a distinctly Thessalonian character, including game, while ouzeries specialize almost exclusively in mezedes. The former usually have an excellent selection of mezedes as well (you may be tempted to make a meal of starters alone), while the ouzeries may also offer more-substantial main courses. Sadly, the increased pollution in the bay has reached a point that we no longer recommend that visitors head off to one of the fish tavernas on the outskirts of town.

Note: Most Thessaloniki restaurants do not accept credit cards.

RESTAURANTS & TAVERNAS
Expensive

Aigli. Odos Kassandrou and Odos Ayiou Nikolaou (near the church of Ayios Dimitrios). ☎ **031/270-061.** Reservations recommended. Main courses Dr2,800–Dr5,300 ($8–$15). Surcharge of Dr3,000 ($9) when there is entertainment. No credit cards. Thurs–Sun 10pm–2:30am. Mon–Wed open only for private parties. GREEK/CONTINENTAL.

Established in 1992 in an exquisitely restored Turkish hamam (bathhouse), this is certainly the most beautiful restaurant in Thessaloniki. Indoors, one dines beneath the

The Food of Thessaloniki

Without examining the vexed question of the extent to which Thessaloniki's cuisine has been heavily influenced by Turkish cuisine, let us just observe that the use of spices, the delicate hand with fish, the wide variety of vegetable dishes, and the extravagantly rich pastries so popular in Thessaloniki are not unknown in Turkey. As any Greek will tell you, this is because the Turks, during their long occupation of Greece, absorbed—stole, actually—the secrets of Greek cuisine. Some might argue that when the Turks withdrew from Greece, they took many of those secrets with them. Others would simply say that in some parts of Greece—such as Thessaloniki—a love of cuisine and a devotion to spices lives on.

In fact, it's the spices that set Thessaloniki's cuisine apart from that of the rest of Greece. Take the peppers. The most famous Macedonian peppers are the red *florines,* originally grown in the town of Florina, but now raised throughout Macedonia. These can be sweet, or so hot that they lift off the top of your head. We like both varieties, but we'd be a lot more relaxed when taking that first bite if we knew whether any individual *florina* were going to be sweet or pyrotechnic.

In addition to the florines, there are some *really* hot peppers traditionally grown in the Macedonian town of Piperia ("pepper"). These peppers are dried, then flaked, and the result, called *boukovo,* is sprinkled liberally into just about anything you'd care to cook. In some Thessaloniki restaurants, in addition to the salt and black pepper on your table, you'll find another shaker, of red pepper. Treat it with respect.

high double domes of the former bathhouse; outdoors, in the gardened grounds of an old, open-air cinema that sometimes shows films in summer at 9 and 11pm. The Aigli used to boast the best haute cuisine in Thessaloniki, but the management has recently decided to shift its emphasis from cooking to entertainment and to booking the entire establishment for private parties. That said, the food is still very good; specialties include chicken kebab, Turkish dolmades, and grilled fillet of chicken breast. There's often live music in the evening.

Moderate

Draft. Lycourgous 3, Ladadika. ☎ **031/555-518.** www.draft.gr. Main courses Dr2,500–Dr4,200 ($7–$12). DC, V. Mon–Sat 9pm–1am. GREEK/INTERNATIONAL.

Draft is yet another new Ladadika spot capitalizing on the seemingly endless local love of beer and *mezedes.* After all, what could be more pleasant than to sit in Draft's garden nibbling on salmon rolls with caviar, a selection of vegetable dips and fritters, and some shrimp in hot sauce? That may be why we've never managed to order an entrée here, but chosen instead to make a very tasty meal out of the mezedes. Non–beer loving friends report that there's also a wide variety of ouzo and wine available.

Kioupia. Morihovou Sq. 3–5, Ladadika. ☎ **031/553-239.** Fax 031/553-579. www.kioupia.gr. E-mail: kioupia@metor.gr. Reservations recommended after 9pm. Main courses Dr3,000– Dr3,500 ($9–$10). AE, V, M. Mon–Sat 1pm–1am. GREEK.

There are more than 65 items on the menu at this taverna with brick walls and a wood floor in the old warehouse district. There's excellent *stifada* (stews), *keftadakia* (meat balls), and spicy *gardoubitsa* (liver and garlic). A number of dishes including eggplant, zucchini, lamb and cheese, and minced beef and cheese are wrapped in crisp layers of filo (pastry). Dessert brings a range of Greek and Turkish sweets, the house retsina is excellent, and there's an extensive wine list. The same management has recently taken over the nearby **Amorgos,** Panaiou 4 and Doxis, Ladadika (☎ **031/557-161**), which specializes in fresh fish.

✪ **Krikelas.** Eth. Antistaseos 32 (☎ **031/451-289;** fax 031/451-690), and Salaminos 6, Ladadika (☎ and fax **031/501-600**). Reservations necessary. Main courses Dr3,500– Dr5,300 ($10–$15). No credit cards. Mon–Sat 11:30am–2am. Usually closed July–Aug (but the Ladadika branch is possibly open then). GREEK.

In 1999, Krikelas, a Thessaloniki institution since the 1940s, opened a branch in the Ladadika district, just across from the Mediterannean Palace Hotel. For visitors to Thessaloniki, the new Krikelas is very conveniently located, and all the reports are that the food here is just as good as ever. The specialties are the mouthwatering variety of *mezedes* and whatever game is in season (including quail, pheasant, rabbit, boar, and partridge). For starters, try the special feta cheese, creamed with butter and hot green peppers, or the smoked Gruyère from Metsovo. An interesting regional specialty is *spetzofai,* a mixture of seasonal vegetables and pungent country sausage. For dessert, try the homemade halva with almonds. The wine list at both branches is serious, although you can get a perfectly fine bottle for less under Dr3,500 ($10).

Le Café. Odos Tsimiski 12 (corner of Tsimiski and Venizelou). ☎ **031/275-625.** Fax 031/ 221-270. Main courses Dr2,000–Dr3,500 ($6–$10). No credit cards. Mon–Sat about 9am–1am. GREEK/CONTINENTAL.

You can get a salad, spaghetti, a sandwich, or just a coffee at this cafe, which has a curved balcony and large windows on the ground floor. Some people seem to show up to read their morning paper and are still here by midafternoon. This is a nice spot to sit and read, people-watch, and eavesdrop on cell phone conversations.

Tiffany's. Iktinous 3 (on the walkway between Odos Tsimiski and the church of Ayia Sofia). ☎ **031/274-022.** Reservations recommended after 10pm. Main courses Dr2,200–Dr5,200 ($6–$15). No credit cards. Daily 11:30am–2am. GREEK/CONTINENTAL.

This popular place, with wood paneling and pictures of old Salonika on the walls, seats about 100 and attracts an interesting mix of people—those who seem to drop in every night for a quick bite, and then the gaggles of 20-somethings who sit in the window tables and wait to be watched. We're in the distinct minority in that we find the two house specialties, *bifsteki* Tiffany's (stuffed with cheese and tomatoes) and *hanoym borek* (casserole of roasted chicken, ham, veal, and cheese) both rather bland. On the other hand, we've had fun trying to figure out the principle behind the music here, which sometimes alternates Harry Belafonte and Greek golden oldies.

Wolves. Vas. Olgas 6 (1 block in and 2 blocks east of the Macedonia Palace Hotel). ☎ **031/ 812-855.** Main courses Dr2,500–Dr3,500 ($7–$10). No credit cards. Mon–Sat 12:30pm–1am; Sun 12:30–5pm. Usually closed Dec 12–March 1 and Aug 5–15. GREEK.

This warm, dark-wood, old-fashioned restaurant, established in 1977, has a cook reputed among locals to be one of the best in Thessaloniki when it comes to making a delicacy out of such basic Greek fare as pastitsio and moussaka. Try the roasted red peppers from Florina as one of your starters. For the main course, sample the moussaka Wolves, the oregano-flavored stewed pork or lamb, or the batter-fried codfish in garlic sauce—or take a look in the display counter in the kitchen at whatever specialty might be available that particular day.

✪ **Zythos.** Katouni 5, Ladadika. ☎ **031/540-284.** Main courses Dr2,500–Dr4,500 ($7–$13). No credit cards. Daily 11am–1am. GREEK/CONTINENTAL.

This was one of the first restaurants to open in the restored warehouse district, and it's still very popular with ladies who lunch, young lovers, harried businessmen, and groups of golden youths. The decor is lots of wood and brick, as you'd expect in a former warehouse—although the slim young waiters in their chic black slacks or skirts hardly suggest warehouse workers. We can vouch for the croquettes of vegetables, *saganaki* (fried cheese), and veggie pasta. There are usually two daily specials, including one vegetarian choice, on the menu.

Inexpensive

If you're around Aristotelous Square, **Lokanda,** at the corner of Mitropoleos and Venizelou (☎ 031/288-432), is a good spot for a coffee, stuffed croissant, or sandwich—at prices much lower than similar places in the square. **Tsarouhas,** Odos Olymbou 78, near Dikastirion Square, seems to be open all hours (although it closes in July and August), and serves up *patsatzidhika:* the tripe soup that's supposed to cure all that ails you. In the Upper City, head to **To Yedi,** Odos Ioannis Papareska 13, outside the gates of the Eptapirgiou prison (☎ 031/246-495), to sit under the trees, relax, and try the keftedes and other mezedes.

Corner. Odos Ayias Sofias 12 and Odos Ethnikis Aminis 6, a block north of the White Tower, behind the State Theater. ☎ **031/426-531.** Main courses Dr1,800–Dr4,500 ($5.15–$13). No credit cards. Daily about 11am–1am. PIZZA.

Locals and visiting pizza fans agree that this place serves the best pizza in town, perhaps because a wood-burning oven is used. Not surprisingly, it's a popular hangout for young Salonikans. There's another branch at Ayias Sofias 28.

Kentrike Stoa. Vas. Hrakleiou 32. ☎ **031/278-242.** Snacks Dr1,000–Dr2,200 ($2.90–$6). No credit cards. Mon–Sat noon–1am. GREEK/CONTINENTAL.

This snacks-and-drinks place in the Central Market is up a winding metal staircase from the market itself. The ceiling is covered with parachute cloth, jazz contends with the shouts from the market below, and the languid 20-something crowd tolerates outsiders gracefully—and are fun to spy on as they vie to impress one another.

Loutros. M. Kountoura 5. ☎ **031/228-895.** Main courses Dr1,800–Dr3,500 ($5.15–$10). No credit cards. Mon–Sat 11am–midnight. GREEK.

For years, Loutros occupied part of an old Turkish bath; now it's in new quarters, but still serves up fried minnows (which you eat whole) and delicious mussels, as well as tasty *horta* (greens) and *florines* (spicy red peppers). The music here is usually very Levantine-sounding—which, in Greece, is a polite way of saying that it sounds absolutely Turkish.

✪ **Thanasis (Mypobolos Smyrnh).** Odos Ermou and Odos Komninon 32 (just inside the Modiano Market). ☎ **031/274-170.** Fax 031/347-062. Reservations necessary after 10pm. Main courses Dr1,800–Dr2,900 ($5.15–$8). No credit cards. Daily about 8am–3am. GREEK.

For 47 years, Thessalonians have been beating a path to this small taverna that serves home-style cooking—including stuffed squid and mussels, both fried and steamed—with zest. In fact, the first customer through the door here in the new millennium was Greek Prime Minister Simitis. The sign over the door reads H MYPOBOLOS SMYRNH (ee-me-*ro*-volos *smear*-ni) and translates as "Miraculous Smyrna," but everyone knows it equally well by the name of its marvelously genial owner, Thanasis. He, his wife, and relatives labor incessantly during market hours to satisfy the cravings of a seemingly endless number of workers, businesspeople, artists, prostitutes, actors, and various other characters from the high and low walks of Thessaloniki. The potato salad, cheese croquettes, spicy peppers with cheese, squid stuffed with cheese and rice, grilled fish and meats, and excellent batter-fried cod (*bakaliaro*) are all wonderful, as is the mood in this tiny restaurant with photos and old prints on the walls. The music is usually very loud here, but if we could eat at only one place in Thessaloniki, this would be it.

To Makedoniko. Odos Yioryiou Papadopoulou 32 (in the Upper City, inside the arch at the western end of the walls). ☎ **031/627-438.** Main courses Dr1,400–Dr2,800 ($4–$8). No credit cards. Mon–Sat 9am–2am. Sometimes closed in Jan. Bus no. 23. GREEK.

You couldn't get more basically Greek than this. Rugged, rudimentary, and full of local color, To Makedoniko is a watering hole and eatery equally popular among the neighborhood working class and the downtown intellectuals, artists, and university students. If you have the constitution to handle it, you must drink the local schnapps—*tsipouro,* a delicately perfumed but powerful variety of ouzo—with your mezedes. While the limited menu can vary from day (or even from hour to hour), the pork *riganato* and mussels in a hot-pepper broth (*midia saganaki*) are usually available.

OUZERIES

As can be gathered from the name, ouzeries are places specializing in ouzo and the mezedes that go with them. One need not, however, drink ouzo—or any kind of alcoholic beverage—to enjoy the marvelous variety of foods they offer: octopus, meatballs, shrimp, squid, taramosalata (fish roe puréed with oil and bread), tzatziki (cucumber, yogurt, and garlic), melitzanosalata (eggplant purée), cheeses, and potato, beet, and bean salads. Go with your waiter to look at the offerings and point out what you want.

Aproopto Light. Odos Zevksidos 6 (a pedestrian walkway off the eastern end of the church of Ayia Sofia). ☎ **031/241-141.** Main courses Dr1,800–Dr4,200 ($5.15–$12). No credit cards. Daily noon–1:30am. GREEK.

Highly popular with professionals of the nearby State Theatre and other artistic types, this place serves excellent mezedes as well as some main-course dishes. Its relatively small, well-decorated sidewalk and interior dining areas are usually packed and rife with conviviality. Try the mussels with spinach and the leeks à la Parisienne as well as the *taganaki,* a cheese-and-potato dish.

Aristotelous. Odos Aristotleous 8 (in a cul-de-sac between office buildings on the east side of Odos Aristotelous, just north of Odos Tsimiski). ☎ **031/230-762.** Reservations not accepted. Dr3,000–Dr5,200 ($9–$15) for a variety of mezedes. No credit cards. Mon–Sat 10am–2am; Sun 11am–6pm. GREEK.

First on the list and the best. Highly popular with writers, artists, and everyone else in the know, Aristotelous is constantly packed during the peak lunch and dinner hours, so you should come either early or late, or you'll end up waiting at least 20 minutes. Indoor and outdoor seating areas in between high-rise office buildings contribute to the crush and somehow the charm. You can and should linger for hours, which is why it's often so hard to get a table. The variety of mezedes is sumptuous. Try the fried zucchini and eggplant; the feta cheese mashed with hot peppers and olive oil (*ktipiti*); and, for something more substantial, the stuffed cuttlefish (*soupia*). Also delicious is the homemade halva for dessert.

Totti's. Aristotelous Sq. 3 (southwest corner fronting the sea). ☎ **031/237-715.** Main courses Dr3,200–Dr4,200 ($9–$12). No credit cards. Daily 7am–2am. GREEK.

Facing the broad east-to-west expanse of Thessaloniki harbor, Totti's is a place to linger, particularly in the evenings when the sun sets into the sea in front of you—and especially since the service here is very slow. The food is typical ouzeri fare, but the tableware and other accoutrements exhibit considerably more elegance, which is reflected in the price. This is also a great place for breakfast. There are a number of Totti's in Thessalonika; you'll bump into others in your explorations.

THESSALONIKI AFTER DARK

Thessaloniki does not really awaken until after dark, and when it does, it seems at times as if the entire populace has come out to amuse itself. In addition to the cultural festivals held in the fall, numerous theatrical events and pop and classical concerts take place year-round. Meanwhile, the city seems festooned with enough bars and clubs to serve a population twice its size, yet all of them are crowded to the bursting point— and more open every year.

While there a number of publications listing the various events, and posters splattered everywhere announcing them, they will all be Greek to you, so the best thing to do is ask for information at your hotel or stop by the office of the **Greek National Tourism Organization (EOT),** Aristotelous Square 8 (☎ **031/271-888** or 031/ 222-935).

ONLY IN THESSALONIKI

Taking what the Greeks call a *volta* (stroll) along the seaside promenade, particularly at sunset or under a full moon, is one of the great pleasures of being in Thessaloniki. Start at **Aristotelous Square,** perhaps with a coffee, a drink, or sweets at one of its many cafes, and walk east past the White Tower and toward the bright lights of the city's amusement park at the other end of the promenade, about 3 kilometers (2 miles) distant. Along **Leoforos Nikis,** which borders the promenade in the city center, are a number of cafes and bars. At the **White Tower,** there are usually peanut vendors and, occasionally, the city's only horse-drawn carriage for rent.

You might also decide to take an hour-long **cruise** around the harbor on the various small boats that dock just east of the tower. Several companies make the trip, including **Ampari Lines** (☎ **094/359-330**), which has cruises scheduled every 2 or 3 hours from 12:30pm to 3am. The cost is Dr1,800 ($5.15). You can buy coffee, fruit juices, and beer on board.

THE PERFORMING ARTS

The **State Theatre of Northern Greece (Kratiko Theatro)** has two venues. In winter, it stages plays in the **State Theatre,** which is opposite the White Tower (☎ **031/ 223-785**); in summer, at the **Forest Theatre (Theatro Dasous),** an open-air amphitheater located in the forested hilltop area east of the Upper City (☎ **031/ 245-307**). The company presents both ancient and modern Greek plays, as well as Greek translations of old and new foreign plays, including those by such well-known playwrights as Christopher Marlowe and Arthur Miller.

In summer, the Forest Theatre, which has a marvelous view of the city, also hosts lively, well-attended concerts by popular Greek singers and composers, as well as performances by visiting ballet companies.

Thessaloniki's new **Concert Hall** is slated to open its doors in 2001. When it does, Thessaloniki hopes to attract the kind of world-class orchestras and performers that perform at Athens's Megaron Mousikis Concert Hall. Until then, concerts are held at the **Aristotle University concert hall** on Odos Nea Egnatia, opposite the northern entrance of the International Trade Fairgrounds, from September through May (☎ **031/283-343**). You can find out whether the new Concert Hall is open at the GNTO in Aristotle Square.

FESTIVALS

THE DEMETRIA FESTIVAL   In honor of the patron saint of Thessaloniki, St. Dimitrios, whose nameday is October 26, this prestigious cultural festival runs every October and includes the Greek Film Festival as well as many theatrical and musical events, all of them performed by major and minor artists from all over the country.

Late Night Bites

Virtually all cafes and many restaurants stay open almost all night in summer, but in case you're in town in winter, when things tend to close down much earlier, try one of the two branches of **Corner,** Odos Ayias Sofias 28, between the church of Ayia Sofia and Odos Egnatia (☎ **031/273-310**), and Odos Ethnikis Aminis 6, a block north of the White Tower, behind the State Theater (☎ **031/426-531**). They serve alcoholic drinks, the best pizza in town, and other delicacies until 1am (see also "Where to Dine," above). Another option is **Xatzi,** Odos Eleftheriou Venizelou 50, just north of Odos Egnatia (☎ **031/279-058;** www.chatzis.gr; e-mail: xatzia@ spark.net.gr), established in 1908 and now run by the fourth generation of the same family. It's the perfect place to go for a midnight sweet—or breakfast coffee, since it opens before 7am. There's a superb selection of Levantine pastries and desserts whose recipes have not changed an iota since its opening. Xatzi also now has a shop at Them. Sofouli and Argonafton streets (☎ **031/415-474**), where you can get the same rich treats to eat in or take away.

THE FEAST OF SAINTS CONSTANTINE & ELENI (MAY 21)   On or around the feast of the first Christian emperor and his mother, villagers in the village of **Ayia Eleni** (80km/50 miles northeast of Thessaloniki) and at **Langadas** (12km/7.4 miles northeast of Thessaloniki) engage in *pirovassia* (fire dancing). Crowds come from all over Macedonia to see the faithful dance over a bed of hot coals. When they're done, they feast on the roasted black bull that has been sacrificed earlier in the day. Just in case you're wondering—yes, much of what's done here preserves pre-Christian rites.

THE INTERNATIONAL TRADE FAIR FESTIVAL   This takes place every year during the first 2 weeks in September and draws businesspeople from around the world. There are lots of exhibits at the international fairgrounds—and hotel rooms are very hard to find.

THE BAR, CLUB & MUSIC SCENE

In the summer, virtually all of Thessaloniki's best bars and clubs shut down. Some immediately reopen branches along a section of the road leading east along the coast, about a mile before the airport. This, plus the fact that new or newly decorated and renamed venues are constantly opening while others go out of fashion and close, makes it virtually impossible to recommend any with certainty.

There is one place, however, that we can recommend without hesitation. Not only is it a permanent fixture of Thessaloniki nightlife year-round, but it also incorporates by far the best of the bar, music, and club scenes in the city.

✪ **Milos.** Odos Andreadou Yioryiou 56. ☎ **031/551-838** or 031/525-968. Cover varies depending on entertainment, usually no more than Dr10,000 ($29); drinks around Dr 1,800 ($5.15). The ouzeri, cafe, and galleries open from about 11am on. The clubs open at 10pm. Go west on Odos Tsimiski to its end and turn left onto Odos Octobriou 28. At the first traffic light, turn right onto Andreadou Yioryiou and continue to the end of the street. This is quite a hike from the center, and you may want to take a cab.

Within the grounds of an old, wonderfully restored flour-mill complex, the Milos (*mee*-los) complex contains a club for blues, folk, jazz, and pop groups; a nightclub featuring Greek singers and comedians; a bar/disco; an outdoor concert stage and movie theater; several exhitition rooms and art galleries; a cafe; and an ouzeri serving more than 30 kinds of *mezedes*. Almost as soon as it opened in 1990, Milos became one of the top musical venues in the country. During July and August of 2000, performers from the Caribbean, Portugal, Cuba, Zimbabwe, Japan, and Louisiana (as well as from throughout Greece) appeared here. It you want to be sure of a seat, it's a good idea to arrive before the clubs open at 10pm.

2 In the Footsteps of Philip of Macedon & Alexander the Great

Every year, more people head north to Macedonia to see the cluster of ancient sites associated with **Philip II of Macedon** (382–336 B.C.) and his famous son, **Alexander the Great** (356–323 B.C.); these include **Pella, Vergina,** and **Dion.** Many of those visiting Northern Greece these days are Greeks, whose interest in things Macedonian was enormously intensified a few years ago when, just across the border, the former Yugoslavian district of Macedonia proclaimed itself a republic. How dare these non-Greeks take the name of Macedonia, Greeks asked—forgetting that their own ancestors had not considered Philip of Macedon a Greek! Most of all, Greeks were furious that Philip's best-known royal symbol—a star with 16 rays—appeared on the new Macedonia's flag. Throughout Greece, debates raged over whether the new self-styled Macedonia had imperialistic aims. For once, Greece's longstanding enmity with Turkey was virtually ignored, as Greeks painted MACEDONIA IS GREECE on virtually every road and wall in the country. Things have calmed down a bit now that the new Republic of Macedonia has changed its flag, but Greeks are still rediscovering their ancestral links with Philip, the northern king who conquered Greece in 338 B.C.

The renewed interest in Philip, Alexander, and Macedonia itself has led the Greek Archaeological Service to redouble its efforts to excavate the Macedonian royal sites and build site museums. And that, of course, means that there's much more to see above ground than there was even a few years ago.

ESSENTIALS

GETTING THERE   The only enjoyable and efficient way to see the places where Philip of Macedon and Alexander the Great lived and reigned is by car or with a tour. **Budget Rent-A-Car** has offices at the airport (☎ 031/471-491) and in the city at Odos Angelaki 15 (☎ 031/274-272 or 031/229-519), opposite the International Fairgrounds. Other rental offices are **Avis,** Leoforos Nikis 3 (☎ 031/227-126 or 031/ 683-300), at the western end of the harbor, opposite the docks; **Europcar,** Odos Papandreou 5 (☎ 031/836-333); and **Hertz,** Odos El. Venizelou 4 (☎ 031/ 224-906), on Eleftherias Square. (See "Getting Around" in the Thessaloniki section, p. 506, for more car-rental information).

Several Athens-based companies, such as **CHAT** and **American Express,** offer tours of Central and Northern Greece that take in the most important Macedonian sites. Reputable Thessaloniki companies offering tours of the Philip and Alexander sites include **Zorpidis Travel,** Odos Egnatia 76 (at Odos Aristotelous), second floor (☎ 031/286-812; fax 031/242-364), and **Kinissi Tour Agency,** Odos Venizelou 2 (☎ 031/241-080; fax 031/286-824). A day trip to Pella, Edessa, Veria, and Vergina or to Philippa, Kavala, and Amphipolis costs about Dr35,000 ($99). It is vital to make an advance reservation. If possible, avoid visiting on a summer weekend, when crowds of Greeks flock to these sites.

By Bus   If you try to visit these sites by local bus, you may feel that it is taking you longer to see them than it took Alexander to conquer the world. Still, if you have lots of time and love buses, you can visit the following sites by bus from Thessaloniki. For

Seeing the Sights

Once you reach these sites, each is clearly marked and easy to visit. Nonetheless, we recommend wearing sturdy shoes and, in summer, a hat and sunscreen.

Pella, there are sometimes direct buses; failing that, take a bus to Edessa and ask to be let off at Pella. For **Vergina,** take a bus to Veria, and then a local bus to the site of Vergina. If you wish to go to Pella and continue to Vergina, you can do so by taking the Thessaloniki bus from Pella to the town of Halkidona, where you can get a bus to Veria. This may involve a substantial wait. For **Dion,** take a bus to Katerini and then a local bus to Dion. For up-to-date information on bus schedules and departure points, check with the **Greek National Tourism Organization** in Thessaloniki (☎ **031/271-888**); the bus information line (☎ **031/924-444**) is unlikely to have English speakers answering the phone. If you read Greek, the Thessaloniki daily newspaper *Macedonia* also lists bus schedules.

VISITOR INFORMATION If you're stopping in Athens or Thessaloniki before visiting these sites, drop by the **Greek National Tourism Organization (EOT)** in Athens at Odos Amerikis 2 (☎ **01/331-0561**), or in Thessaloniki at Aristotelous Square (☎ **031/271-888**), and get a copy of the brochure *Greece/Macedonia* and any other brochures available for individual sites. At each site, ask whether there is a free Culture Ministry brochure available.

PELLA

Pella, once the capital of the Macedonian kingdom and the birthplace of Philip II of Macedon in 382 B.C. and his famous son, Alexander the Great, in 356 B.C., is easy to spot: The **archaeological site** and **museum** (☎ **0382/31-160**) are right beside the highway (a 40km/24-mile drive west of Thessaloniki on the E86 highway to Edessa). Museum admission is Dr1,000 ($2.90); site admission is Dr1,000 ($2.90). Hours are Monday from noon to 7pm, Tuesday through Friday from 8am to 7pm, and Saturday, Sunday, and holidays from 8:30am to 3pm.

In antiquity, Pella's situation was more appealing—a navigable inlet connected it to the broad Thermaic Gulf that borders Thessaloniki. Over the centuries, the inlet silted up, leaving Pella landlocked, but in Philip and Alexander's day, ships would have sailed here and docked at what is now a dusty plain. The city itself is thought to have covered at least 5 square miles, of which only a fraction has been excavated.

Nonetheless, there's more than enough of Pella above ground to give you an idea of this stylish city, with its large, square agora (market and civic center) bordered by colonnaded stoas and flanked by streets lined with shrines, sanctuaries, temples, and private homes. The lovely frescoes that once adorned the house walls are gone, but a number of the handsome **pebble mosaic floors** remain, both on the site and in the museum. These houses must have been exceptionally pleasant, with their gaily painted walls, handsome mosaic floors, and sheltered inner courtyards. There families could have passed an evening, perhaps discussing the Athenian playwright Euripides's *The Bacchae*, which had its premiere around 408 B.C. in the as yet undiscovered theater here.

Unfortunately, the dwelling you'd probably most like to see—the **palace** where both Philip and his son Alexander were born—is not yet open to the public. Not to worry: You can drive or walk to the hilltop north of the site, peer over the wire fence, and get an idea of how large this royal home was. In fact, the palace covered 60,000 square meters—only 10,000 less than the agora itself! Somewhere in this vast complex, Aristotle tutored the young Alexander. The view from the hill is still tremendous, but must have been truly breathtaking in antiquity, when the palace overlooked both the plain and the channel down which ships sailed, bringing supplies here from around the Mediterranean.

Pella's small **museum** is superb, especially its glorious pebble mosaics found in some of the 4th-century B.C. homes excavated here. The two best-known mosaics show a lion hunt and the god of wine, Dionysos, riding a leopard. The lion hunt is worth looking at not only for its powerful depiction of two youths and a lion, but also because this mosaic may show Alexander himself. Some scholars have suggested that the mosaic records the incident when the young Alexander was saved by a friend from a lunging lion. Others suspect that it's too good to be true that the mosaic actually shows that famous incident and suggest that this is simply a genre scene of a hunt. You can compare the marble bust of Alexander in the museum with the youth under attack in the lion hunt and decide for yourself.

WHERE TO STAY & DINE

After you visit the site, you may want to take in **Edessa,** 45 kilometers (27 miles) west of Pella, a scenic clifftop town with bubbling waterfalls and several pleasant small cafes and restaurants beside them. We've eaten at several, and can't say that we find one better than another—the real point of dining here is enjoying the rushing waterfall. Note that this is not the best place to visit on summer weekends, when many Thessalonians come here to escape the summer heat.

If it's the weekend, or if you're rushed after visiting Pella, you can grab a bite at one of the small roadside restaurants by the fountain beside the (signposted) remains of "Baths of Alexander," a Hellenistic fountain incorporated into a Roman bath about a kilometer from Pella on the Edessa road.

As far as overnighting here, keep in mind that Edessa is a very popular year-round destination for Thessalonians, that it has only about 125 hotel rooms, and that you may have trouble finding a vacancy if you simply appear on the weekend. That said, we suggest the 44-unit **Katarraktes,** Odos Karanou 18, Edessa (☎ **0381/22-300;** fax 0381/27-237), which has a nice location near a waterfall. Its guest rooms, which go for Dr20,000 ($57) double, are furnished in the usual bland Greek-hotel style: pine beds, pale walls—acceptable, but in no way memorable. If the Katarraktes is full, you might try the 36-room **Alfa,** Egnatia 28 (☎ **0381/22-221;** fax 0381/24-777); friends of ours found it just fine for a night.

VERGINA & ENVIRONS: THE TOMBS AT LEUKADIA, THE TOWN OF VERIA & NEARBY VINEYARDS

Vergina is 20 kilometers (12 miles) south of Pella, and 62 kilometers (38 miles) west of Thessaloniki; located just outside the hamlet of Palatitsa, it's very well signposted. If you only have time to visit either the site or the museum, there's no choice here—head for the museum. If you have time for both, here's what you'll see at the **Vergina site** and **Royal Tombs Museum** (☎ **0331/92-347**). Museum admission is Dr1,200 ($3.45); site admission is Dr500 ($1.45). Summer hours for both are Monday from noon to 7pm and Tuesday through Sunday from 8:30am to 7pm; the site and museum close at 5pm in the off-season.

Vergina (anciently known as Aigai) was where Philip lived when not at Pella and where he died in 336 B.C., and is the most important of the royal Macedonian sites. Preliminary excavations suggest that the palace was enormous, with an inner courtyard some 147 feet square. Around the courtyard ran a Doric colonnade; the bases of some of the 60 columns of the colonnade are still in place and give a sense of the courtyard's size. The palace also had a long airy colonnaded veranda running the length of its

Philip & Alexander

When Philip was born in 382 B.C., most Greeks thought of Macedonians—if they thought of them at all—as one of the rude northern tribes of barbarians who lived in the back of beyond. Macedonians, after all, were not even allowed to participate in the Panhellenic Games at Delphi. Clearly, this irritated Philip. By 346 B.C., after conquering a number of Athenian colonies and allied cities, Philip had won a place on Delphi's governing board. A few years later, in 338 B.C., despite Demosthenes's best oratorical efforts to alert the Athenians to Philip's intentions, the Macedonian king had conquered all Greece. Two years later, Philip was dead, cut down as he strolled to see a performance in the theater at his capital city of Vergina. Some said that his young son Alexander was behind the assassination, while others wondered how the unproven youth could rule Macedonia, let alone Greece.

No one, except perhaps Alexander himself, could have imagined that by the time he died at 33, he would have conquered much of the known world as far east as India. Alexander's early death makes it impossible to know what he would have done with the rest of his life, once he had no new worlds to conquer. Some scholars think that Alexander was a visionary bent not just on conquering, but also uniting the world into a "brotherhood of man." This, they suggest, is why Alexander contracted so many foreign marriages and accepted conquered princes into his retinue. Other scholars, more cynical, think that both Alexander's marriages and his use of former enemies were simply shrewd political moves. The truth probably lies somewhere in between the two theories.

In any event, after Alexander's death, his former comrades turned on one another and destroyed his empire. Within a few generations, Macedon was once more a northern kingdom in the back of beyond, living on memories of its brief period of international importance.

north side, overlooking the theater. It's quite possible that the royal family watched some spectacles in the theater from the comfort of the palace veranda.

Unfortunately for Philip, that's not what he did on the fatal day in 336 B.C. when he was assassinated en route from the palace to take in a performance at the theater. Some said Alexander himself was behind the assassination, others simply said that the young prince was not notably grief-stricken by the death of his father. You can sit in the **theater**—the only really impressive remains—and contemplate the moment when Philip realized that he was about to be struck down.

As you drive from the site to the Royal Tombs Museum, you'll notice hundreds of low mounds on the gentle hills of the Macedonian plain. These are some of the more than 300 **burial mounds** found here, some dating from as long ago as the Iron Age, but many from the time of Philip himself. Virtually all of these graves were robbed in antiquity, but fortunately—and almost miraculously—the tomb identified as that of Philip himself was undisturbed for almost 2,000 years. How it was found is one of the great stories of archaeology, deserving a place beside accounts of how Schliemann found Troy and excavated the "Tomb of Agamemnon" at Mycenae.

Vergina's first excavator, the French archaeologist Leon Heuzey, prophesied in 1876 that when Vergina was fully excavated, "the importance of its ruins for Macedonia will be comparable to Pompeii." The Greek Archaeological Service began to work here in the 1930s, and uncovered several tombs that looked like small temples. For years, the excavators nibbled away at the largest burial mound of all, the **Great Tumulus,** measuring 110 meters across and 12 meters high, containing a number of burials. One tomb they found was almost totally destroyed, another well preserved but robbed. Still, head excavator Manolis Andronikos remained convinced that he was excavating ancient Aigai, Philip's capital city, and might yet find Philip's own tomb.

Finally, in 1977—on the last day of the excavation season—Andronikos and his workers opened the massive marble gates of the last remaining tomb. As Andronikos later wrote in *Vergina: The Royal Tombs:*

> We saw a sight which it was not possible for me to have imagined, because until then such an ossuary [container for bones] had never been found . . . all-gold . . . with an impressive relief star on its lid. We lifted it from the sarcophagus, placed it on the floor, and opened it. Our eyes nearly popped out of our sockets and our breathing stopped; there unmistakably were charred bones placed in a carefully formed pile and still retaining the colour of the purple cloth in which they had once been wrapped . . . If those were royal remains . . . then . . . had I held the bones of Philip in my hands?

Andronikos—and virtually all of Greece—answered his question with a resounding "Yes," in large part because of the other objects found in the tomb. The gold wreaths, Andronikos felt, were too fine to belong to anyone but a king. And surely the little ivory portrait heads were the spitting images of Philip and Alexander themselves. And, most persuasive of all, what about the bronze greaves (shin guards) found in the tomb? Were they not of unequal size? And was not Philip known to have legs of different length, due to an early injury?

It is difficult to overestimate the Philip-fever that swept through Greece when Andronikos announced that he had found Philip's tomb and identified Vergina as Ancient Aigai, Philip's capital city. Although some scholars have questioned whether this is, in fact, Philip's tomb, those scholars are not Greek. Greeks regard with horror any suggestion that this splendid tomb may have belonged to Arrhidaeos, the son of Philip known only for his lack of distinction.

The arched roof of the **Royal Tombs Museum** re-creates a sense of the Great Tumulus itself, as does the passageway leading into the tomb area. Each of the five tombs is protected by a glass wall, but seeing the tombs this way is the next-best thing to being able to stand inside them. Give your eyes time to get accustomed to the darkness, then enjoy the lovely decorative paintings on the façades of the templelike tombs. And, of course, be sure to see the treasures from these tombs now on display in the Archaeological Museum in Thessaloniki.

A DETOUR TO LEUKADIA

If Vergina has whetted your appetite for royal tombs, you might consider heading north to Leukadia, 20 kilometers (12 miles) south of Edessa in the beautiful foothills of Mount Vermion. Be forewarned: This is one of those excursions based on suggestions such as "ask for directions in the village" and "ask if the custodian will accompany you and open the tombs." If you're lucky and find the custodian and the tombs (ask in cafes and the main square in Leukadia), you'll get to see three spectacular tombs. The 3rd-century B.C. **Great Tomb** is decorated with paintings of battles of Lapiths and Centaurs and Greeks and Persians. The **Kinch Tomb** (named after its discoverer) and the **Tomb of Lyson and Kallikles** are decorated with paintings of funeral swags of pomegranates and snakes, symbol both of the underworld (since snakes often live underground) and rebirth (because snakes shed old skins for new ones). The claustrophobic may find the descent down a dank shaft into the Tomb of Lyson and Kallikles unappealing. If the custodian does take you to see these tombs, you should slip him at least Dr1,000 to Dr2,000 ($2.90 to $6) along with your thanks.

VERIA (VEROIA) & ITS TURKISH REMAINS

If an excursion to Leukadia seems too much like work, try the nearby hill town of Veria (Veroia), 15 kilometers (9 miles) northwest of Vergina. Veria is in the throes of development, but still has a number of old streets, wood houses with overhanging bay windows, small Byzantine churches (usually locked), a 15th-century cathedral, and a good number of buildings from the Ottoman period, including a former mosque and *hamam* (bath). The truly devoted will wish to visit the small **Archaeological Museum** on Odos Anixeos, with finds from local sites (admission is Dr500/$1.45; open Tuesday through Sunday from 8:30am to 3pm). Don't feel bad if it's closed; you'll have much more fun just wandering the streets of this old town, with its considerable Turkish remains.

THE NAOUSSA VINEYARDS

About halfway between Veria and Edessa, on the slopes of Mount Vermion, several vineyards are open to the public; you'll see their roadside signs. At Naoussa, a region famous for its wine, the **Stenimachos Winery,** run by the well-known Boutari vintners, is open to the public. Tours of the winery are given most work days and are sometimes offered in English. For information, call ☎ **0332/42-687,** or check with the **GNTO** in Thessaloniki (☎ **031/271-888**).

WHERE TO STAY & DINE

The 37-unit **Hotel Makedonia,** Odos Kontogeorgaki 50, Veria (☎ and fax **0331/ 66-902** or 0331/66-946), is the best hotel in town, which is to say that it is not a fleabag like some of the others, and has a quiet location. It basically has the bland ambience of a businessman's, rather than a traveler's, hotel; rooms come with air-conditioning and TVs. The new **Veria,** kilometer 6.5 on the Veria-Naousa Highway (☎ **0331/93-112;** fax 0331/93-556), gets a fair amount of tour business. Although staying here makes exploring Veria itself a mini-excursion, you may find the pool so welcoming that you never leave. The rooms are standard Greek-hotel quality, but most have pleasant balconies as well as air-conditioning and TVs; the hotel is set back from the highway just enough to make the traffic noise manageable.

Near the Vergina site, there are a number of small cafes and restaurants, including the pleasant **Filippion,** as well as several overnight possibilities at "rent rooms" establishments. Veria's restaurants serve food that is almost guaranteed to be better than that dished out around the site of Vergina. Try **Sarafopoulos,** on Odos Kentrikis, or **Kostalar,** on Afroditis; Kostalar has the more pleasant location on a shady square.

DION

The **Dion archaeological site** and **museum** (☎ **0351/53-206**) are outside the village of Dio, about 8 kilometers (5 miles) west of the Dion sign on the E75, the main Athens-Thessaloniki highway (and 78km/48 miles south of Thessaloniki). *Warning:* This is a dangerous turn off the highway; reentry is also difficult. Admission to site is Dr800 ($2.30); museum admission is Dr800 ($2.30). Hours are Monday from 10:30am to 7pm and Tuesday through Sunday from 8:30am to 7pm; the site and museum close at 3pm in the off-season.

If you haven't been to Dion in a few years, you may want to know that there's good news and bad news. The good news is that excavations are continuing, unearthing more of ancient Dion. New pathways have been constructed to help visitors tour the site, and helpful signs have gone up. In mid-August, the **Olympos Festival** (☎ **0351/ 76-401**) presents concerts at the ancient site.

The bad news is that this site, until recently one of the few left in Greece that you could wander around at will, imagining that you had just stumbled upon an ancient city, has been fenced in and tidied up with a vengeance.

Nonetheless, Dion still has a beautiful location, just outside the Vale of Tempe, in the foothills of Mount Olympus. This is an unusually green spot, with pine groves and farm fields watered by springs fed by the melting snow that clings to Olympus's peaks year-round. If you can, bring a picnic; after you visit the excavations and museum, you can linger a while at the picnic tables at the site.

Dion was founded as a religious sanctuary, and for some time was Macedonia's most important sanctuary, something of a sacred city. Later, its constant water supply led both Philip and Alexander to establish military training camps here. Philip bivouacked here before he marched south to conquer Greece, while Alexander drilled his men here before heading east to conquer Asia.

According to a story preserved by the 2nd-century A.D. biographer Plutarch, it was at Dion that Alexander, then only 8 years old, first saw Bucephalos, the handsome black stallion soon to be his favorite mount. Philip himself had bought the horse, but found that neither he nor any of his men could ride it. Alexander asked his father if he could have a go at taming the creature. Muttering that if *he* could not tame the horse, an 8-year-old hardly could, Philip nonetheless agreed to give Alexander a chance. Immediately, Alexander turned Bucephalos so that he could not see his shadow, leapt up, and galloped away. When the young prince returned from his ride, Philip said, "My son, look for a kingdom equal to you. Macedonia is too small."

Although Dion—which sits by a narrow pass between Thessaly and Macedonia—was an important military camp for first the Macedonians and then the Romans, it was not merely the Fort Bragg of antiquity. The Romans adorned Dion with a **theater** (bigger and better than the Hellenistic one, as was the Roman habit), and built **sanctuaries** to the healing god Asclepius, the nurturing goddess Demeter, and the popular Egyptian goddess Isis. In addition, of course, the Romans built **baths**—and baths being the large structures that they are, a good deal remains for you to explore. Copies of some of the statues found in the sanctuaries have been erected at the site, while the originals are tucked away safely in the museum.

There's a great deal to see at Dion, but we have to confess that some of our happiest visits here have been spent in the shade of the trees with a picnic. From here, you can make excursions onto the site, following the course of a stoa, admiring the statue of Isis seemingly admiring her reflection in a pool, and imagining the day that Alexander, all of 22 years old, mounted Bucephalos and set off to conquer the world.

The Dion **museum** is a heartening example of what a provincial museum can be when it is well funded and well cared for. An English-language video and the English-language museum labels help foreign visitors understand the importance of what they are seeing, while models of the ancient site make the Dion of Philip and Alexander easy to visualize. Exhibits include statues of the children of Asclepius (lined up as though posing for a family photo), grave monuments, votive offerings, mosaics, and, best of all, a wonderful copper water organ, probably made in the 2nd century A.D., that would be the hit of any music hall today.

WHERE TO STAY & DINE

There's a string of cafes and restaurants directly across from the Dion museum; an archaeologist friend reports consistently eating well at the **Dionysos,** which serves good roast goat, *loukanika* (sausages), and the usual chops and salads. Expect to pay about Dr1,800 ($5.15) for lunch or dinner unless you go overboard on the roast goat, which is priced by the kilo and may bring your tab to Dr3,500 ($10).

Dion Palace Resort Hotel. Litochoro Beach, Gritsa, 60200 Macedonia. ☎ **0352/22-731.** Fax 0352/22-735. 182 units. A/C MINIBAR TV TEL. Dr35,000 ($99) double. Compulsory breakfast Dr2,000 ($6). AE, MC, V. Sometimes closed in winter.

This enormous beachfront resort has a main hotel building, two restaurants, a disco, shops, a fitness center, and lots of cabanas. There are two swimming pools—one salt-water, one fresh—and all the creature comforts. In summer, this is a popular family destination, and anyone with children will see why. Others may prefer the little Hotel Dion, described below.

✪ **Hotel Dion.** Dion, 60200 Macedonia. ☎ **0351/53-336.** 20 units. Dr19,000 ($54) double. Rates include breakfast. MC, V. Considerable reductions often possible off-season.

The rooms here are good sized, economically furnished, and pleasant; most have balconies. When we stayed here, the town was deliciously quiet all night—except for a few late-night motorcycles and some early-morning roosters. One problem: The owners are not always around, so if you stop here without a reservation, it may take a bit of time to find them.

3 Mount Athos (The Holy Mountain)

130km (80 miles) SE of Thessaloniki

The most important thing to know about Mount Athos is that you can't just come here. And if you're a woman, you can't come here at all (see "Permits," below). Recently, there have been mutterings that antidiscrimination regulations of the European Common Market may force Athos to open its doors to women; to avoid any potential complications, Mount Athos has refused any Common Market funds for restoration of monasteries. It is highly unlikely that the bureaucrats of the Common Market will prove a match for the monks of Athos and their centuries of tradition.

Many destinations are hyped as being a "step back in time" or a "glimpse of an unknown world," but both statements really are true of Mount Athos. Most monasteries here still follow the Julian calendar, which puts Athos 13 days behind the Gregorian calendar. The day is divided not into 24 equal hours, but organized according to an elaborate Byzantine scheme based on the times of sunset and sunrise; midnight, in this system, is at sunset. The flag that flies outside most monasteries is the double-headed eagle of Byzantium—symbol of the empire that fell in 1453.

Athos is very much a place of prayer and contemplation, and while some monks welcome visitors, most simply tolerate them, unless a visitor has a sincere interest in the Greek Orthodox faith and the monastic life. The monks' life focuses on prayer—usually 8 hours a day—and meditation. A local saying sums up the monks' life: "Write, read, sing, sigh, pray, keep silent."

No one is sure when monks and hermits first began to live on this rugged promontory. Some say that the place became holy when a storm blew the Virgin Mary's ship ashore here, as she was traveling from Jerusalem to Cyprus. As she stepped ashore, all the pagan idols crashed to the ground and were destroyed, a sure sign that this was a holy place.

Certainly, there were enough men of God here by A.D. 885 for the Byzantine Emperor Basil I to formally declare all Athos a "place of Quietism." The first, and still most important monastery, the **Great Lavra** or **Meyistis Lavras** ("Lavra" simply means a community of monks), was founded around 960, and others quickly followed. In 1060, an imperial decree barred "every woman, every child, eunuch, smooth faced person and female animal" from Athos, which suggests that there had been incidents of inventive nonchastity over the years. In recent years, hens have been allowed onto Athos to produce eggs, and cats to catch vermin.

What to Pack for Mount Athos

Bring sturdy shoes, long-sleeved shirts and long slacks (the monks are offended by short-sleeved shirts and shorts), a hat, insect repellent, a flashlight, reading material, any prescription or nonprescription medication you might need, a map, and the best lightweight (you will have to carry it everywhere) guide you can find. If you own the archaeologically oriented *Blue Guide* to Greece, you can photocopy the excellent section on Athos to bring along. One book you may enjoy reading is Robert Byron's *The Station,* an account of his visit here in 1931.

Until the fall of Constantinople in 1453, successive Byzantine emperors gave the monasteries rich donations of icons and manuscripts. After the fall of Byzantium, and during the Turkish occupation of Greece, the monasteries struggled to survive; many treasures were neglected, some sold. When the traveler Robert Curzon visited Athos in 1849, he inquired about purchasing a manuscript. To his horror, Curzon later recorded in his *Visits to the Monasteries of the Levant,* a monk pulled out his knife and "cut out an inch thickness of the leaves before I could stop him."

In 1917, the execution of the Russian royal family put an end to Athos's last major source of royal patronage. In 1926, Athos was declared a Theocratic Republic. Although it is part of Greece, it is self-governing—hence, the need for an entry permit. Today, there are 20 active monasteries, with at least that many again having closed over the centuries. There are still solitary hermits on Athos, but most monks follow a communal (cenobitic) rather than an isolated (idiorrhythmic) life. In fact, of late, monastic life has had something of a revival; Father Gabriel, gardener at the Iviron Monastery, was quoted in the July 28, 1988, Athenian newspaper *Kathimerini* as saying that "More are interested in becoming monks than we are ready to accept." According to the same story, Father Gabriel has added to his gardening duties the preparation of a computer catalog of manuscripts and icons. When asked if this would not take a very long time, he replied, "We've got all eternity."

ESSENTIALS

PERMITS   Unless you have proof that you are a Greek national or Greek Orthodox, you must be at least 21 and male, as well as have an entry permit (Dr8,000/$23), to visit Mount Athos. To get a permit, you must have your **passport** and a **letter of recommendation** from your embassy or consulate in Athens or Thessaloniki. The United States does not charge for this; the United Kingdom and most other embassies charge about £10 (Dr5,500/$16). Getting the letter of recommendation is usually pro forma, but it's a good idea to have yourself described as a student or scholar.

Once you have the letter, take it to the **Ministry of Foreign Affairs,** in Athens at Akadamias 3, fifth floor (open Monday, Wednesday, and Friday from 11am to 1pm), or to the **Pilgrims' Office for Mount Athos** (*Grafeo Pfoskyniton Ayiou Oros*), in Thessaloniki at Konstantinou Karamanli 14 (☎ **031/861-611;** fax 031/861-811), open Monday through Friday from 8:30am to 1:30pm and Monday, Tuesday, Thursday, and Friday from 6 to 8pm. It may help expedite matters if you fax all your documents in advance to the latter office, telling them when you will arrive. After a wait, which may be minutes or even days, you will be issued a permit for a 4-day visit to Mount Athos.

When you reach Ouranopolis, the jumping-off point for Athos, you must take your permit to the **Grafio Proskyniton** (Visitors Bureau), open daily from 8:30am to 2pm, and pay Dr8,000 ($23) for a *diamonitirion*—your passport, as it were, to Mount Athos. *Important note:* The names and phone numbers of the monasteries are posted in this office; it is advisable to phone ahead to make a reservation at the monasteries where you want to stay the night. Increasingly, monasteries are requiring visitors to make reservations in advance.

When you reach Mount Athos, you must present your diamonitirion at the monastery/hamlet of Khilandariou, where you will be registered. Thereafter, you may be asked for your diamonitirion from time to time as you visit the monasteries.

GETTING THERE   By Car   If you drive to Mount Athos from Thessaloniki, check with the **Greek National Tourism Organization** in Aristotelous Square to see if there is road work on any of the major roads you might take, as this may help you plan the best route. You can take the E90 across the top of Chalkidiki east as far as Stavros, and then head south along the coast to Ouranopolis, or you can head south from Thessaloniki along the airport road and then continue across the southern coast of Chalkidiki to Ouranopolis. Allow 4 to 8 hours, depending on how many stops you want to make en route.

By Bus   From Thessaloniki, take the bus to Ouranopolis from the Halkidiki terminal at Karakassi 68. Allow 6 hours.

By Boat   However you reach Ouranopolis, you will continue from there to Mount Athos by boat. There is almost always at least one boat a day at 9:45am from Ouranopolis to Mount Athos. In summer, there are usually additional departures scheduled, as well as excursion boats that circle Mount Athos, so that those who do not wish—or are not allowed—to go ashore can see Mount Athos.

GETTING AROUND   Be prepared to do a lot of walking on Mount Athos. Feet are the preferred method of transportation. There are many footpaths on the island, and you would do well to get as good a map as you can find either in Thessaloniki or in Ouranopolis (compare maps and dates to see which is most detailed and up-to-date).

FAST FACTS   Ouranopolis, the jumping-off point for Mount Athos, has a **post office** and **telephone office (OTE);** it was rumored to be getting a bank in 2001. **Karyes,** the main town on Athos, also has both a **telephone office (OTE)** and **post office.** It, too, is awaiting the opening of a bank—but do not count on this having happened before you visit. At present, a **mobile bank van** appears on an irregular schedule in Ouranopolis, so be sure to take adequate funds with you.

WHAT TO SEE & DO

Ouranopolis is the jumping-off point for Mount Athos, but unfortunately, it has become a nasty little town filled with tacky souvenir shops in recent years. However, the handsome tower immortalized in Joyce Nankivell Loch's *A Fringe of Blue* still stands (and is rumored to open someday as a museum of Byzantine art). Joyce Loch and her husband, Sydney, both Quakers, lived in Ouranopolis on and off from the 1920s to the 1960s and worked with villagers and refugees from Asia Minor. For some years, the tower was both the Lochs' home and a weaving school.

If you can't go to Athos itself, try to take one of the **excursion boats** from Ouranopolis that cruises around the peninsula (when Prince Charles visited Athos in 1999, his companion, Camilla Parker Bowles, circled the Holy Mount on the Royal Yacht). The views of the rugged, pine-clad mountain promontory are superb, and you'll be able to see a number of the monasteries. Most look like little villages from the outside, perched on astonishingly high and sturdy stone foundations and surrounded by massive walls. Virtually all of the monasteries are built according to a similar plan, in which a **central church** (the katholikon) fronts an arcaded courtyard, often with a bell tower. Around the courtyard are the monastic buildings, including the dining quarters (refectory or trapeza), kitchens, laundry rooms, and bedrooms (the cells).

A Worthy Stop

On Mount Athos, you will be walking almost everywhere you go, and staying and eating at the monasteries you have come to visit, which certainly simplifies things. "Simple" is a key word here—both your accommodations and food (Athos is a vegetarian's paradise) will be very basic. Look out for some of the wine made on Athos and sold throughout Greece; the Tsantali white (not all of which is made here, despite its labels) is particularly refreshing, while the Metochi Mylopotamou made at the Great Lavra Monastery is well regarded. Keep in mind that although most monasteries will not accept cash offered in direct payment for food and lodgings, you can always make a donation in the church.

As always when walking in Greece, keep the danger of fires in mind, and be sure to dispose of any matches or cigarettes with care—although Athos escaped the fierce fires of the summer of 2000, in 1998 fires raged through the pine forests here for several days.

Finally, remember that many monasteries close (and lock) their gates during the midday siesta, and virtually all close (and lock) their gates at sunset.

If you do take a boat trip around Athos, and encounter rough seas, you'll understand why the Persian King Xerxes tried to cut a channel through Athos at just about the point where Ouranopolis sits today: He wanted to spare his fleet the rough seas here as he sailed north to attack Athens in 480 B.C. For centuries, scholars thought that Herodotus's story of Xerxes's canal was one of the historian's flights of fancy. The technology, the scholars said, simply didn't exist so long ago for such a massive project. In 1998, archaeologists and geologists announced that they had discovered at Ouranopolis—just where Herodotus placed it—signs of Xerxes's canal. Soundings revealed a massive channel some 65 feet wide at its base, 114 feet broad at the top, hidden beneath the 22 feet of earth that slowly filled in the canal over the centuries.

At present, there are 20 functioning monasteries on Mount Athos. Given the rough terrain, there's no way you can visit them all during a 4-day visit—thus we mention here just the five most important monasteries. Keep in mind that if you can't visit Athos, you can see most of these monasteries from the sea. Almost all were built close enough to the water to be able to get supplies ashore with ease.

THE GREAT LAVRA   The first (about A.D. 960) monastery founded on Athos and hence the foremost, the Great Lavra has the red-painted *katholikon* characteristic of Athos's monasteries. Its 15th-century frescoes, especially those showing exuberant singers and dancers in the Chapel of Koukouzelissa, are delightful. Try ☎ **0337/ 23-758** to make a reservation to spend the night here.

THE MONASTERY OF VATOPEDI   Founded only a decade after the Great Lavra, Vatopedi's long outline with red-and-white tile-roofed buildings is clearly visible from the sea. Try ☎ **0337/23-219** for overnight reservations.

THE MONASTERY OF IVERON   Iveron, founded in the 10th century, looks from the sea like a medieval hilltown—only the hill is actually the monastery's solid foundation. Try ☎ **0337/23-643** for overnight reservations.

THE MONASTERY OF CHELANDARIOU   This monastery was founded in the 12th century by St. Sabbas of Serbia. Fortunately, Sabbas's father was the King of Serbia, which guaranteed a handsome endowment. Some scholars think that the lovely frescoes in the church here were done by the same painter who decorated the walls of

Ayios Nikolaos Orfanos in Thessaloniki (see p. 516). You can try to make a reservation here by calling ☎ **0337/23-797.**

THE MONASTERY OF DIONYSIOU   This 14th-century monastery seems to grow right out of a rock above the sea, and has dizzily overhanging balconies, braced by rather precarious-looking wood supports. Favored by the emperor Alexios III Komnenos, Dionysiou has a superb collection of manuscripts, as well as an icon said to be the oldest on Athos. You can try to make a reservation here by calling ☎ **0337/ 23-687** or faxing 0337/23-686.

WHERE TO STAY IN OURANOPOLIS

Xenia. Ouranopolis, 63075 Macedonia. ☎ **0377/71-412.** Fax 0377/71-362. 120 units. MINIBAR TV TEL. Dr50,000 ($144). Compulsory breakfast Dr3,500 ($10). AE, DC, MC, V.

This sprawling beachside resort hotel with two-story stone-and-concrete bungalowlike units by the sea is less than 5 minutes outside Ouranopolis. The large, tile-floored rooms have balconies (ask for a room facing the sea), most have desks and good reading lamps, and all have excellent bathroom facilities. The Xenia offers all the creature comforts you may have missed visiting Athos, including several restaurants and fresh- and saltwater pools.

If the Xenia is full, try the 167-unit **Eagle's Palace** (☎ **0377-31-047;** fax 0377/ 31-383), which sprawls across a sandy beach. Doubles go for Dr55,000 ($168); discounts of 15% are sometimes available for stays of more than 3 nights.

16

The Northeastern Aegean Islands

by Mark Meagher

The four islands covered in this chapter—Samos, Hios, Lesvos, and Limnos—are dispersed along the coast of Turkey, and far removed from the mainland and the other Aegean islands. Their remoteness is definitely a benefit. Unlike other areas of Greece, parts of these islands remain relatively undiscovered. The crowds here tend to be concentrated in a few overpopulated resorts, leaving the vast interior (and much of the coast) open to exploration. Along the coastline you'll find some of the finest beaches in the Aegean, and within the interior richly forested valleys, precipitous mountain slopes, and exquisite mountain villages. Since these are agricultural islands, olives, grapes, and honey are grown in abundance, providing the basis for excellent food and wine.

The influence of Asia Minor is not as evident as you might expect, given the proximity of the **Turkish coast.** What you will notice immediately is the sizable Greek military presence—large areas of each island are occupied by the military and are strictly off-limits (a particular annoyance to hikers and mountain bikers). Even though this military presence is a sore point with the Turks, who regularly demand the demilitarization of Limnos and stage regular flyovers in defiance of Greek airspace, travel between Greece and Turkey remains unrestricted and relations between Greeks and Turks on a personal level seem to be mostly amicable. Many travelers use the Northeastern Aegean islands as jumping-off points to Turkey: **Samos** is the closest island to Turkey (only 3km/1.9 miles at the closest point) with easy access to Ephesus; **Lesvos** is the closest to Ancient Troy; and **Limnos** to Istanbul.

STRATEGIES FOR SEEING THE ISLANDS Since the distances between islands are substantial, island-hopping by boat can be costly and time-consuming. Add the fact that each island is quite large, and it becomes clear that you're best off choosing one or two islands to explore in depth rather than attempting a grand tour. **Olympic Airlines'** flights between the islands are inexpensive, frequent, and fast; **Aegean Airlines** offers daily flights between Mitilini and Athens; and several other smaller airlines may be initiating service to these islands in the near future. If you travel by **ferry,** you'll find that departure times are more reasonable for travel from north to south, whereas traveling in the opposite direction usually involves departures in the middle of the night. The islands are too large and the roads too rough for mopeds to be a safe option; since the bus routes and schedules are highly restricting, you'll find that if you want to get around it's necessary to rent a car.

1 Samos

322km (174 nautical miles) NE of Piraeus

The most mountainous and densely forested of the Northeastern Aegean isles, Samos appears wild and mysterious as you approach its north coast by plane or ferry. The abrupt slopes of hills plunging to the sea are jagged with cypresses, and craggy peaks hide among the clouds. Samos experienced a series of wildfires during the summer of 2000, which briefly brought the island to the attention of the international press—the signs of these recent events are unmistakable, and it will be some time before the interior forests fully recover.

Unfortunately, Samos has given itself over in recent years to a highly impersonal form of mass tourism. This is mostly confined to the eastern coastal resorts—Vathi, Pithagorio, and Kokkari—which have all developed a generic waterfront of cafes, souvenir shops, and big hotels. The most interesting and beautiful villages are found in the rugged splendor of the island's interior. Difficult terrain and a remote location made these villages an apt refuge from pirates in medieval times; in this age, the same qualities have spared them from tourism's worst excesses.

Although Samos has several fine archaeological sites, the island is most notable for its excellent beaches and abundant opportunities for hiking, cycling, and windsurfing. Also, Samos is the best crossover point for those who want to visit **Ephesus,** one of the most important archaeological sites in Asia Minor.

GETTING THERE   Although ferries connect Piraeus to Samos, it's a long trip and the boats serving this route are slow. The best way to get here is to fly.

By Plane   Olympic Airways has three flights daily (five daily in summer) between Athens and Samos. The **Olympic office** (☎ **0473/25-065**) in Vathi is at the corner of Kanari and Smirnis streets, 1 block from the bus station. Contact Olympic Airways in Athens at ☎ **0801/44444** or 01/966-6666, or check out **www.olympic-airways.gr**. **Avionic Airways** flies five times weekly between Athens and Samos; for ticket information in Samos contact the Pithagorio Municipal Tourist Office (☎ **0273/61-389**). The Samos airport is 3 kilometers (1.9 miles) from Pithagorio, on the road to Ireon; from the airport you can take a taxi to Vathi (Dr3,500/$10) or Pithagorio (Dr1,500/$4.30).

By Boat   The principal port of Samos is at **Vathi,** also called Samos; the other two ports are **Karlovassi** and **Pithagorio.** Ferries from the Cyclades usually stop at both Vathi and Karlovassi: Take care not to get off at the wrong port! There are daily boats (sometimes two) from Piraeus via Paros and Naxos to Karlovassi (9 to 12 hrs.) and Vathi (10 to 14 hrs.); in the opposite direction ferries travel daily or nearly daily from Samos to Mykonos (5½ hrs.). Boats to Hios from Vathi via Karlovassi (5 hrs.) travel three times per week; there is also a once-weekly Rhodes-Vathi-Lesvos-Alexandroupoli run. Boats (mostly hydrofoils) to the Dodecanese islands depart regularly from Vathi and Pithagorio. If you want to travel one-way to Turkey, there are daily Turkish ferries; a visa is required for all American, British, and Irish citizens who intend to stay for more than 1 day—be sure to inquire in advance about current visa regulations with a local travel agency. For more information on visas, see "A Side Trip to Turkey: Kusadasi & Ephesus," below. Contact **I.T.S.A. Travel** (☎ **0273/23-605;** fax 0273/27-955; e-mail: itsa@otenet.gr) for current schedules, or visit **www.gtpnet.com**. Otherwise, try the **port authority** in Piraeus (☎ **01/459-3223**), Vathi (☎ **0273/27-318**), Pithagorio (☎ **0273/61-225**), or Karlovassi (☎ **0273/30-888**).

The Northeastern Aegean Islands

BULGARIA

0 _____ 25 mi
0 _____ 25 km

TURKEY

Kavala

Alexandroupolis

Sea of
Marmara

Limenas (Thassos)
Makriammos
Limenaria
Panayia

THASSOS

Gallipoli

Hora *SAMOTHRAKI*

Kamariotissa ▲ *Mt. Fengari*

Aegean

Canakkale

Sea

GÖKÇEADA

TURKEY

Kornos
Mirina
Skandali

LIMNOS

Ayvalik

Pergamon

Molivos
(Mithimna)

LESVOS (Mitilini)

Eressos   Petra   Mandamados

Sigri

Ayiassos

Skala
Eressos

Mitilini

Plomari

SKYROS

PSARA   Kardamila   *INOUSSES*

Hios Town

Izmir

HIOS

Çesme

Mesta
Piryi

Ephesus

Kokkari   Kusadasi

Karlovassi   Vathi

SAMOS Mitilini

Pithagorio

Psili
Ammos

IKARIA

BULGARIA

GREECE

Athens ⊛

TURKEY

*THE NORTHEASTERN
AEGEAN ISLANDS*

547

VATHI, KARLOVASSI & THE NORTHERN COAST

Vathi on the northeast coast and Karlovassi to the northwest are the two principal ports of Samos, and the island's largest towns. Neither is particularly exciting, and we recommend both as convenient bases rather than as destinations in themselves.

Vathi is a tired resort town, beautifully situated in a fine natural harbor. An extensive development project in Pithagora Square and along the paralia was mostly completed in 2000, resulting in a widened pedestrian walkway along the water and a large bandstand for open-air concerts. The old town, **Ano Vathi,** rises to the hilltops in steep narrow streets that hide a few small tavernas and cafes. Karlovassi is somewhat less interesting as a town—although it's adjacent to several of the best beaches on the island, the town is spread out and offers fewer amenities than Vathi. Most tourist facilities are clustered along the water at the west end of town, forming a tiny beach resort with several hotels, restaurants, grocery stores, and souvenir shops. The old town hovers above the lower town on the slopes of a near-vertical pillar of rock; there's a cafe and a taverna here, and the lovely small chapel of **Ayia Triada** at the summit of the rock. Along the seafront to the east is the former industrial quarter, with rows of abandoned stone warehouses once used by a flourishing leather industry.

The **north coast** of the island is wild and steep, with mountains rising abruptly from the water's edge. One of the most interesting areas to explore is the **Platanakia** region, known for its rushing streams, lush valleys, and picturesque mountain villages. There is also a sequence of excellent **beaches** between Kokkari and Karlovassi, with the two finest beaches on the island—✪ **Micro Seitani** and ✪ **Megalo Seitani**— a short boat excursion or somewhat long hike to the west of Karlovassi.

ESSENTIALS

VISITOR INFORMATION   The **Greek National Tourism Organization (EOT)** has an office in Vathi (☎ **0273/28-582**), a half block in from the port, one lane toward the ferry pier from the main square; open Monday through Friday from 8am to 3pm, with weekend hours in high season. The EOT staff won't make room reservations by phone, but will help you find accommodations if you're at their office.

I.T.S.A. Travel (☎ **0273/23-605;** fax 0273/27-955; e-mail: itsa@otenet.gr), the agency nearest the port in Vathi, is the best and friendliest; here you can make travel arrangements (including excursions to Turkey, Patmos, and Fourni, as well as tours of Samos), find accommodations, change money at good rates, and store your luggage for free. The Diavlos Web site (**www.diavlos.gr**) has information on ferries, attractions, and accommodations.

GETTING AROUND   By Bus   There's good public bus service on Samos throughout the year, with significantly expanded summer schedules. The **Vathi bus terminal** (☎ **0273/27-262**) is a block inland from the south end of the port on Odos Kanari. The bus makes the 20-minute trip between Vathi and Pithagorio frequently. Buses also travel to Kokkari, the inland village of Mitilini, Pirgos, Marathokambos, Votsalakia beach, and Karlovassi. Schedules are posted in English at the bus terminal.

By Boat   From Karlovassi there are daily excursion boats to **Megalo Seitani,** the best fine-sand beach on the island. A once-weekly around-the-island tour aboard the *Samos Star* is a great way to see the island's remarkable coastline, much of it inaccessible by car. The excursion boat departs from Pithagorio at 8:30am (a bus from Vathi departs at 7:30am), currently on Tuesdays, and returns to Pithagorio at 5:30pm; the fare is Dr12,000 ($34). Most excursions depart from Pithagorio, although many offer bus service from Vathi an hour prior to departure; for descriptions see "Pithagorio & the Southern Coast," below.

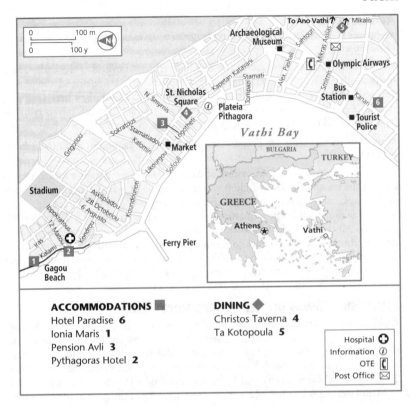

Map of Vathi showing streets and landmarks including Archaeological Museum, St. Nicholas Square, Plateia Pithagora, Vathi Bay, Olympic Airways, Bus Station, Tourist Police, Stadium, Ferry Pier, and Gagou Beach. Inset map shows Greece with Athens and Vathi, Bulgaria, and Turkey.

Scale: 0–100 m / 0–100 y

To Ano Vathi ↑   Mikalis
Archaeological Museum
Sahtouri
Alex. Pashali
Mikras Assias
Kapetan Katavani
Stamati
Iompari
Smyrnis
N. Smyrnis
St. Nicholas Square
Plateia Pithagora
(i)
Logotheti
Sokratous
Stamatiadou
Kalomiri
Grigoriou
Likourgou
Sofouli
Market
Vathi Bay
Olympic Airways
Bus Station
Kanari
Tourist Police
Stadium
Asklipiadou
28 Oktobriou
6 Avgusto
Koundourioti
Ipookratous
12 Matou
Iras
Kalami
Kondrou
Gagou Beach
Ferry Pier

BULGARIA
TURKEY
GREECE
Athens ★
Vathi

ACCOMMODATIONS ■
Hotel Paradise **6**
Ionia Maris **1**
Pension Avli **3**
Pythagoras Hotel **2**

DINING ◆
Christos Taverna **4**
Ta Kotopoula **5**

Hospital ✚
Information *(i)*
OTE **C**
Post Office ✉

By Car & Moped   Aramis Rent a Motorbike-Car at the pier in Vathi (☎ 0273/ 23-253) offers the best prices and selection. The least expensive car is about Dr11,000 ($32), including insurance and 100 free kilometers. Mopeds go for Dr3,000 to Dr6,000 ($9 to $17) a day. There are plenty of other agencies, so shop around.

By Taxi   The principal taxi stand in Vathi is on Plateia Pithagora, facing the paralia. The fare from Vathi to Pithagorio is Dr2,500 ($7). To book by phone, call ☎ 0273/ 28-404 in Vathi, 0273/33-300 in Karlovassi.

FAST FACTS   The **banks** in Vathi are on the paralia in the vicinity of Plateia Pithagora, and are open Monday through Thursday from 8am to 2pm, Friday from 8am to 1:30pm; most have ATMs. Most travel agents change money, sometimes at bank rates, and they're open later. The island's **hospital** (☎ 0273/27-407 or 0273/27-426) is in Vathi. **Internet access** is available at Diavlos (www.diavlos.gr) on the paralia next to the police station, just around the corner from the bus stop. Diavlos is open daily from 9:30am to 11pm, and it's a bargain at Dr600 ($1.75) for 30 minutes. There's a **self-service laundry** (☎ 0273/28-833) behind the Aeolis Hotel on the town's market street, open daily from 8am to 11pm. The **post office** (☎ 0273/27-304) is on the same street as the Olympic Airways office, 1 block further in from the paralia and 2 blocks from the bus station. The **telephone office (OTE)** is just down the street from the Olympic Airways office in the direction of the archaeological museum (☎ 0273/28-499). The **tourist police** (☎ 0273/81-000) are on the paralia, by the turn in to the bus station.

Attractions

Archaeological Museum. Vathi. ☎ **0273/27-469.** Admission Dr800 ($2.30). Tues–Sun 8am–2:30pm.

This fine museum is comprised of two buildings at the south end of the harbor, near the post office. The newest building houses sculpture—much in demand, the island's best sculptors traveled all over the Hellenistic world to create their art. The most remarkable work is a massive *kouros* (statue of a boy), which stands 5 meters tall. The large and varied collection of bronze votives found at the Heraion is also impressive.

Moni Vronta. Vourliotes. No phone. Free admission. Daily 8am–5pm. 23km (14½ miles) west of Vathi.

The 15th-century fortified monastery of Moni Vronta is on a high mountain overlooking the sea and the lovely hilltop village of Vourliotes. *Vrontiani* means "thunder on Mount Lazarus," a name resonant with the majesty of this mountain setting. There is only one monk left in the monastery, and 10 soldiers who operate a nearby surveillance post. If the gate is locked when you arrive, try knocking and one of the soldiers may be around to let you in. Ask to see the *speleo,* or cave, an old chapel in the thickness of the outer wall containing a collection of ancient objects, some from the time of the monastery's founding. To get there, continue driving uphill about 2 kilometers (1.2 miles) past Vourliotes.

Three Hill Towns on the Rugged North Coast

Amidst the densely wooded valleys, cascading streams, and terraced slopes of Samos's *Platanakia* Region, many hidden villages were settled as an attempt to evade the pirates who repeatedly ravaged all settlements visible from the sea. Three of the most picturesque of the surviving hill towns in this region are Manolates; Vourliotes, about 20 kilometers (12½ miles) west of Vathi; and Stavrinides (not far from Manolates).

Manolates is a 4-kilometer (2½-mile) drive uphill from the coast road. The village was until recently inaccessible by car, but once the paved road was built, many more visitors have come here to explore the steep, narrow cobblestone streets. There are several tavernas, numerous shops, and two kafenions (where the locals go).

Vourliotes was settled largely by repatriated Greeks from the town of Vourla in Turkey. It's the largest producer of wine in the region, and the local wine is among the best on the island. Walk from the parking lot at the Moni Vronta turnoff to the charming central square. Try **Manolis Taverna** (☎ **0273/93-290**), on the left as you enter the square, which has good *revidokeftedes,* a delicious local dish made with chickpea flour and cheese. The proprietress, Elena Glavara, is originally from Mexico and makes a fine chili con carne. Also on the square, across from Manolis, is a small market whose displays seem not to have changed in the past 50 years. Be sure to visit the monastery of **Moni Vronta** (also known as Vrontiani), just 2 kilometers (1.2 miles) above the town (see "Attractions," above).

Stavrinides, perched on the mountainside high above Ayios Konstantinos, is the least touristic of the Platanakia villages. Here the tavernas and the few shops cater primarily to the villagers. **Taverna Irida** in the first square of the village offers good simple food. A walking path between Stavrinides and Manolates makes an exceptional outing; the route out from Stavrinides is signposted.

The easiest way to visit these towns is by car; the island buses are also an option if you don't mind the steep 4- to 6-kilometer (2½- to 3.7-mile) walk from the coast road to the villages. There are abundant footpaths connecting these villages—ask locally for particular routes. **Ambelos Tours** (☎ **0273/94-136;** fax 0273/94-114; e-mail: ambelos@sam.forthnet.gr) in Ayios Konstantinos, operated by the friendly and extremely knowledgeable Mihailis Folas, is a useful resource. Also ask Mihailis about traditional houses for rent in the hilltop village of Ano Ayios Konstandinos: Each apartment sleeps three, and costs about Dr7,000 ($20) per night.

A SIDE TRIP TO TURKEY: KUSADASI & EPHESUS

In high season there are two boats a day between Vathi and Kusadasi, Turkey, a popular, well-developed resort 20 minutes from the magnificent archaeological site at Ephesus; there's one excursion each week from Pithagorio to Turkey, currently on Thursdays. A round-trip ticket to Kusadasi runs Dr11,000 ($32); the guided tour with entrance fee and transport from the port is an additional Dr7,000 ($20). If you're not returning the same day, you'll need to investigate visa requirements. Visas are granted without difficulty, and cost $45 for Americans, £5 for Irish citizens, £10 for U.K. citizens, $45 for Canadians, and $20 for Australians; New Zealanders don't need a visa. The most helpful and knowledgeable travel agency is **I.T.S.A. Travel** (☎ 0273/23-605), operator of the *Samos Star,* a boat traveling between Vathi and Kusadasi.

BEACHES

The closest decent beach to Vathi is **Gagou,** 2 kilometers (1.2 miles) north of the pier. But the best beaches on Samos are found along the north coast, the most beautiful and rugged part of the island. The busy seaside resort of **Kokkari,** 10 kilometers (6.2 miles) west of Vathi, has several beaches in rock coves as well as the crowded stretch of sand running parallel to the town's main road; to find the smaller cove beaches, head seaward from the main square. Just west of Kokkari is **Tsamadou,** a short walk down from the coast road, which offers sufficient seclusion for nudism at one end. Continue west past Karlovassi to find **Potami,** an excellent long pebble-and-sand beach with road access.

The two best beaches on the island, ✪ **Micro Seitani** and ✪ **Megalo Seitani,** are accessible only on foot or by boat; boat excursions depart daily from the pier in Karlovassi. To get here on foot, continue past the parking lot for the beach at Potami on a dirt road; the walking time to the first beach is 45 minutes. After about 5 minutes of uphill walking, the road splits—turn right, continuing to follow the coast. After another 5 minutes of walking, there are three obvious paths turning off to the right in close succession. Take the third, marked by a cairn, and follow the well-worn path another half hour to Micro Seitani, a glorious pebble-and-cobble beach in a rocky cove. On the far side of the beach a ladder scales the cliff, leading to the continuation of the trail which will take you after an additional 30 minutes of walking to Megalo Seitani, as incredible a stretch of sea sand as any in the Aegean. At the far end of Megalo Seitani are a few houses and a taverna; the near end, at the outlet of a magnificent cliff-walled gorge, is completely undeveloped.

OUTDOOR PURSUITS

BICYCLING   Samos has many dirt roads and trails that are perfect for mountain biking. The only obstacles are the size of the island, which limits the number of routes available for day trips, and the fact that much of the backcountry is off-limits due to Greek military operations. Bike rentals, information about trails, and guided mountain-bike tours are available at **Bike** (☎ 0273/24-404), managed by the friendly and knowledgeable Yiannis Sofoulis. The shop is open daily from 8:30am to 2pm and 5 to 9pm; it's behind the old church opposite the port, on the market street. The bikes are very high quality—aluminum frames with front or full suspension and good components—and the rental includes helmet, pump, and repair kit; clipless pedals and shoes are also available for an extra charge. The basic aluminum-frame bike is Dr2,000 ($6) per day; the full-suspension bike is Dr4,000 ($11).

WALKING   Some of the best walking on the island is in and around the Platanakia region of Samos's north coast, where well-marked trails connect several lovely hilltop villages—Manolates and Vourliotes (see above) are among the villages on this network of trails. There is also a trail from Manolates to the summit of Mount Ambelos, the second-highest peak on Samos at 1,153 meters (3,780 ft.); the round-trip time for this demanding walk is about 5 hours. For information on walking in the Platanakia region, contact Mihailis Folas of **Ambelos Tours** (☎ **0273/94-136;** fax 0273/ 94-114; e-mail: ambelos@sam.forthnet.gr) in Ayios Konstandinos.

WHERE TO STAY
Vathi
Hotel Paradise. Odos Kanari 21, Vathi, 83100 Samos. ☎ **0273/23-911.** Fax 0273/28-754. 47 units. A/C TEL. Dr20,000 ($57) double. Rates include continental breakfast. MC, V.

Despite a central location just off the paralia and a block away from the bus station, the walled garden and pool terrace here seem a world away from the traffic and dust of Vathi. Drinks and simple Greek food are served all day at the poolside bar—the pool invites lingering, with lounge chairs and umbrellas for sunning and shaded tables for a meal or drinks. All guest rooms have balconies, although the views aren't great; bathrooms are small, but they do have full tubs. You should note that although there is airconditioning in every room, it isn't turned on until sometime in July (unlike the majority of hotels, which will turn on the A/C in June if it's needed—and it usually is).

Ionia Maris. Gagou Beach, Vathi, 83100 Samos. ☎ **0273/28-428** or 0273/28-429. Fax 0273/23-108. 56 units. A/C TV TEL. Dr25,000 ($72) double; Dr33,750 ($97) triple. Rates include breakfast. EC, MC.

The Ionia Maris is the best beachfront hotel in Vathi. It has a good location and facilities but somewhat plain rooms. Gagou is a pleasant pebble beach 2 kilometers (1.2 miles) north of Vathi, with a small taverna; the hotel is 50 meters back from the water. There is a large pool terrace with two pools (one for children), a snack bar, and abundant umbrellas. A buffet breakfast and dinner are served daily, and full-board rates are available. The rooms are moderate in size, with tile floors and small balconies—units on the pool side of the hotel have an oblique view toward the sea. Two rooms are wheelchair accessible.

Pension Avli. Odos Likourgou, Vathi, 83100 Samos. ☎ **0273/22-939.** 10 units. Dr8,000 ($23) double. No credit cards. Turn in from the paralia at the Agrotiki Trapeza (just down from the Aeolis Hotel), turn left on the town's market street, and you'll see the Avli's unassuming sign directly ahead.

Although you won't find any luxuries here, you will discover the most charming and romantic pension on the island. Abundant bougainvillea fills the arcaded courtyard of this former 18th-century convent. The 10 rooms open to guests occupy half the building; 10 more units are due for renovation and may be available soon. The rooms are spartan, with minimal furnishings and bare walls; bathrooms are tiny and encased completely in a shell of bright orange plastic, making a shower a surreal experience.

Pythagoras Hotel. Odos Kalami, Vathi, 83100 Samos. ☎ **0273/28-422.** Fax 0273/ 28-893. E-mail: smicha@otenet.gr. 19 units. Dr9,000 ($26) double. MC, V. On the coast road, 600m north of the pier.

This plain but comfortable family hotel on a hill overlooking Vathi Bay offers the best views in town from its nine seaside units and from the restaurant terrace. Guest rooms on the side of the road can be very noisy—book ahead to assure a seaside unit. Rooms and bathrooms are small, clean, and minimally furnished. The neighborhood cafe downstairs serves a good, inexpensive breakfast, light meals, and snacks from 6:45am to midnight. Stelios Michalakis, the friendly manager, will meet you at the port at any time, a generous offer given the frequency of early-morning ferry arrivals.

Ayios Konstandinos

This coastal town in the heart of the Platanakia region is a great base for touring the north coast of Samos. Ask Mihailis Folas of **Ambelos Tours** (☎ **0273/94-136;** fax 0273/94-114; e-mail: ambelos@sam.forthnet.gr) about several traditional houses for rent: Each apartment sleeps three, and costs only Dr7,000 ($20) per night.

✪ **Daphne Hotel.** Ayios Konstandinos, 83200 Samos. ☎ **0273/94-003** or 0273/94-493. Fax 0273/94-594. www.daphne-hotel.gr. E-mail: info@daphne-hotel.gr. 35 units. A/C TEL. Dr15,000 ($43) double. Rates include breakfast. V. Take the first right after turning onto the Manolates road, 19km (12 miles) from Vathi.

The Daphne is the finest small hotel on the island. Artfully incised into the steep hillside in a series of terraces, the hotel commands a fine view of the stream valley leading to Manolates and a wide sweep of sea. The dining room has a large picture window and an outdoor terrace that steps down to the pool and an exquisite view. All rooms are moderate in size and have balconies with the same great view; bathrooms have both shower and tub. This is a good location for walkers, with many trails nearby to Manolates and other hill towns. Make your reservations well in advance, as this hotel is filled through much of the summer by European tour groups. There is free transportation to and from the airport or the port; due to the somewhat remote location, you'll probably want a car during your stay here.

WHERE TO DINE

Vathi

The food along the paralia in Vathi is mostly tourist-quality and mediocre; the best restaurants are to be found in the small towns. The local wines on Samos can be excellent. (As Byron exclaimed, "Fill high the bowl with Samian wine!") A preferred wine is the dry white called Samaina. There's also a delicious relatively dry rose called Fokianos. The Greeks here also like sweet wines, with names like Nectar, Dux, and Anthemis. Almost any restaurant on the island will serve one or all of these wines.

Christos Taverna. Plateia Ayiou Nikolaou. ☎ **0273/24-792.** Main courses Dr700–Dr2,200 ($2–$6). No credit cards. Daily 11am–11pm. GREEK.

This simple little taverna, under a covered alleyway decorated with odd antiques, is left off Plateia Pithagora as you come up from the port. The food is simply prepared and presented; it comes in generous portions and is remarkably good. Try the *revidokeftedes*, a Samian specialty made with cheese fried in a chickpea batter.

Ta Kotopoula. Vathi. ☎ **0273/28-415.** Main courses Dr800–Dr2,100 ($2.30–$6). No credit cards. Daily 11am–11pm. GREEK.

Ta Kotopoula is on the outskirts of Vathi, somewhat hard to find but worth the trouble. From the south end of the harbor, walk inland past the Olympic Airways office and the post office, bearing right with the road as it climbs toward Ano Vathi. Where the road splits around a large tree, about 700 meters from the harbor, you'll see the vine-sheltered terrace of this taverna on the left. The food is basic Greek fare, but the ingredients are exceptionally fresh. Local wine is available by the carafe.

Ayios Nikolaos

✪ **Psarades.** Ayios Nikolaos. ☎ **0273/32-489.** Main courses Dr800–Dr4,000 ($2.30–$11). No credit cards. Daily 8am–midnight. Drive 6km (3.7 miles) east from Karlovassi, turning left at the sign for Ayios Nikolaos, and descend the treacherously narrow road to the sea. SEAFOOD.

This restaurant is on the water, and the outside terrace overlooks tide pools and a long stretch of coast to the west—it's a highly romantic setting, and a fabulous place to watch the sunset. The fish, simply prepared and cooked on a wood fire, is consistently excellent. The tastes are strong and straightforward, like the *tzatziki* pungent with garlic, or the *melitzanosalata* redolent with the smoky aroma of roasted eggplant.

Ayios Konstandinos

Platanakia Paradisos. Ayios Konstandinos. ☎ **0273/94-208.** Main courses Dr800–Dr3,000 ($2.30–$9). No credit cards. Daily 3–11pm. GREEK.

Paradisos is a large garden taverna located at the Manolates turnoff from the coast highway; it has been in the Folas family for nearly 30 years, and has been operating as a taverna for more than 100. Mr. Folas, the owner, makes his own wine from the excellent Samian grapes. Mrs. Folas's *tiropita* (freshly baked after 7pm) is made from local goat cheese and butter; it's wrapped in a flaky pastry. Live traditional music is performed Wednesday and Saturday nights in the summer.

VATHI AFTER DARK

The hottest disco in Vathi is **Metropolis,** behind the Paradise Hotel. For bouzouki, there's **Zorba's,** out of town on the road to Mitilini. There are several bars of various kinds on the lanes just off the port. **Number Nine,** at Kephalopoulou 9, beyond the jetty on the right, is one of the oldest and best known.

PITHAGORIO & THE SOUTHERN COAST

Pithagorio, south across the island from Vathi, is a charming but overcrowded seaside resort built on the site of an ancient village and harbor. Although this is a convenient base for touring the southern half of Samos, the town exists primarily for the tour groups that pack its streets in the summer. We recommend staying here for a day or two to explore the nearby historic sites, then moving on to the more interesting and authentic villages of the north coast.

ESSENTIALS

GETTING THERE **By Plane** The Samos airport is 3 kilometers (1.9 miles) from Pithagorio; from the airport, you can take a taxi into town for Dr1,500 ($4.30).

By Boat Ferries from the Cyclades typically don't stop at Pithagorio, so you'll need to take a taxi or bus from Vathi. There is near-daily hydrofoil service between Pithagorio and Patmos (60 to 90 mins.), Lipsi (1½ to 3 hrs.), Leros (1½ to 3 hrs.), Kalymnos (3 to 6 hrs.) and Kos (3 to 4 hrs.); there are also excursion boats to Patmos four times weekly. Check the most current ferry schedules at the **Pithagorio Municipal Tourist Office** (☎ **0273/61-389** or 0273/61-022), **www.gtpnet.com**, or the **Pithagorio Port Authority** (☎ **0273/61-225**).

By Bus The trip between Vathi and Pithagorio takes 20 minutes, and buses depart frequently. Contact the **Vathi bus terminal** (☎ **0273/27-262**) for current schedules.

VISITOR INFORMATION The **Pithagorio Municipal Tourist Office** (☎ **0273/61-389** or 0273/61-022) is on the main street, Odos Likourgou Logotheti, 1 block up from the paralia; open daily from 8am to 10pm. Here you can get information on ferries, buses, island excursions, accommodations, car rental, and just about anything else. Pick up the handy *Map of Pithagorion,* which lists accommodations, attractions, and other helpful information.

GETTING AROUND **By Bus** The Pithagorio **bus terminal** is in the center of town, at the corner of Odos Polykrates (the road to Vathi) and Likourgou Logotheti.

The bus makes the 20-minute trip between Vathi and Pithagorio frequently. There are also four buses daily from Pithagorio to Ireon (near the Heraion archaeological site).

By Boat   Summertime **excursion boats** from the Pithagorio harbor go to **Psili Ammos beach** (on the east end of the island) daily, and to the island of **Ikaria** three times weekly. There is a popular day cruise to **Samiopoula,** a small island with a single taverna and a long sandy beach; boats leave daily at 9:15am and return to Pithagorio at 5pm; the fare of Dr5,500 ($16) includes lunch. Four times each week the *Samos Star* sails to **Patmos,** departing from Pithagorio at 8am and returning the same day at 4pm; travel time to Patmos is 2 hours, and the fare is Dr8,000 ($23). A Sunday excursion to the tiny isle of **Fourni,** also aboard the *Samos Star,* leaves you with 6 hours to check out the beaches and sample the island's renowned fish tavernas; the boat leaves Pithagorio at 8:30am and the cost is Dr7,000 ($20) per person. A once-weekly **around-the-island tour** aboard the *Samos Star* offers a great way to see this island's remarkable coastline, much of it inaccessible by road. The excursion boat departs from Pithagorio at 8:30am (a bus from Vathi departs at 7:30am), currently on Tuesdays, and returns to Pithagorio at 5:30pm; the fare is Dr12,000 ($34).

By Car & Moped   **Aramis Rent a Motorbike-Car** has a branch near the bus station in Pithagorio (☎ 0273/62-267); it often has the best prices, but shop around.

By Taxi   The taxi stand is on the main street, Likourgou Logotheti, where it meets the harbor. The fare from Vathi to Pithagorio is Dr2,500 ($7). To book by phone, call ☎ 0273/61-450.

FAST FACTS   The **National Bank** (☎ 0273/61-234), opposite the bus stop, has an ATM. A small **clinic** is on Plateia Irinis, next to the town hall, 1 block in from the beach near the port police (☎ 0273/61-111). There's **Internet access** at **Nefeli** (☎ 0273/61-719), a cafe on the north side of the paralia (left if you're facing the harbor), open from 11am to 2am daily. There are currently two computers, and the rate is Dr1,500 ($4.30) per hour. Alex Stavrides runs a self-service **laundry** off the main street on the road to the old basilica, Metamorphosis Sotiros; open daily from 9am to 9pm, in summer until 11pm. The **post office** is several blocks up from the paralia on the main street, past the bus stop. The **telephone office (OTE)** is on the paralia near the pier (☎ 0273/61-399). The **police** (☎ 0273/61-100) are a short distance up Odos Polikrates, the main road to Vathi.

ATTRACTIONS

Efpalinion Tunnel. Pithagorio. ☎ 0273/61-400. Admission Dr500 ($1.45) adults, Dr300 (90¢) students and seniors, free for youths under 18. Tues–Sun 8:45am–2:45pm. Located 3km (1.9 miles) northwest of Pithagorio, sign posted off the main road to Vathi.

One of the most impressive engineering accomplishments of the ancient world, this 1,000-meter tunnel through the mountain above Pithagorio was excavated to transport water from mountain streams to ancient Vathi. The great architect Efpalinos directed two teams of workers digging from each side, and after nearly 15 years they met within a few meters of each other. If you can muster the courage to squeeze through the first 20 meters—the tunnel is a mere sliver in the rock for this distance— you'll see that it soon widens considerably, and you can comfortably walk another 100 meters into the mountain. Even though there is a generator that supposedly starts up in the event of a power outage, you might be more comfortable carrying a flashlight.

Heraion. Ireon. ☎ 0273/95-277 or 0273/27-469 (the Archaeological Museum in Vathi). Admission Dr800 ($2.30) adults, Dr400 ($1.15) students and seniors, free for youths under 18. Tues–Sun 8am–2:30pm. Located 9km (5.6 miles) southwest of Pithagorio, signposted off the road to Ireon.

All that survives of the largest of all Greek temples is its massive foundation, a lone reconstructed column, and some copies of the original statuary. The temple was originally surrounded by a forest of columns, one of its most distinctive and original features. In fact, rival Ionian cities were so impressed that they rebuilt many of their ancient temples in similar style. The Temple of Artemis in nearby Ephesus is a direct imitation of the great Samian Structure. The Heraion was rebuilt and greatly expanded under Polycrates; it was damaged during numerous invasions and finally destroyed by a series of earthquakes.

BEACHES

In Pithagorio, the local beach stretches from Logotheti Castle at the west side of town several kilometers to Potokaki and the airport. Expect this beach to be packed throughout the summer. Excursion boats depart daily in the summer for **Psili Ammos,** 5 kilometers (3.1 miles) to the east. Boat excursions leave daily from Pithagorio for **Samiopoula,** an island off the south coast with two good beaches.

On the south coast of the island, the most popular beaches are on Marathokambos Bay. The once-tiny village of **Ormos Marathokambos** has several tavernas and a growing number of hotels and pensions; its rock-and-pebble beach is long and narrow, with windsurfing an option. A couple of kilometers further west of Ormos Marathokambos is **Votsalakia,** a somewhat nicer beach.

WHERE TO STAY

Rooms in Pithagorio are quickly filled by tour groups, so don't count on finding a place here if you haven't booked well in advance.

George Sandalis Hotel. Pithagorio, 83103 Samos. ☎ **0273/61-691.** Fax 0273/61-251. 13 units. Dr13,000 ($37) double. No credit cards. Head north on Odos Polykrates (the road to Vathi), and you'll see the hotel on your left, about 100 meters from the bus station.

Above Pithagorio, this homey establishment has a front garden bursting with colorful blossoms. The tastefully decorated rooms all have balconies with French doors. In back, the rooms face quiet hills and another flower garden, while the front units face a busy street and can be noisy. The friendly Sandalises are gracious hosts; they spent many years in Chicago and speak perfect English.

Hotel Zorba. Odos Damos, Pithagorio, 83103 Samos. ☎ **0273/61-009.** Fax 0273/61-012. 12 units. TEL. Dr12,000 ($34) double; Dr16,000 ($46) triple. Breakfast Dr1,500 ($4.30). No credit cards.

This homely place is more pension than hotel, but the rooms are comfortable; seven units have great views of Pithagorio Harbor. The atmosphere is decidedly casual and friendly—the hotel lobby doubles as the Mathios family's living room. The hotel is on a steep hill on the north side of town, a steep climb up from the paralia at the port police station. Rooms facing the sea all have spacious balconies with a view over the rooftops to fishing boats docked in the harbor, while street-side rooms are a bit noisier and have no view. Breakfast is served on a terrace facing the sea.

WHERE TO DINE

Esperides Restaurant. Pithagorio. ☎ **0273/61-767.** Reservations recommended in summer. Main courses Dr1,200–Dr4,000 ($3.45–$11). No credit cards. Daily 6pm–midnight. INTERNATIONAL.

This pleasant restaurant with a walled garden is a few blocks inland from the port, and west of the main street. There are uniformed waiters and a dressier crowd here. The continental and Greek dishes are well presented and will appeal to a wide variety of palates. We resented the frozen french fries served with the tasty baked chicken, but the meats and vegetables were fresh.

I Varka. Paralia, Pithagorio. ☎ **0273/61-088.** Main courses Dr1,500–Dr3,500 ($5–$14). EC, MC. V. Daily noon–midnight. Closed Nov–Apr. SEAFOOD.

This ouzeri/taverna is in a stand of salt pines at the south end of the port. Delicious fresh fish, grilled meats, and a surprising variety of *mezedes* (appetizers) are produced in the small kitchen. The grilled octopus, strung up on a line to dry, and the pink *barbounia* or clear gray mullet, all cooked to perfection over a charcoal grill, are the true standouts of a meal here. The new cafe pavilion by the water is a cool, breezy location for a drink or dessert.

2 Hios (Chios)

283km (153 nautical miles) NE of Piraeus

"Craggy Hios," as Homer dubbed it, remains very much unspoiled—and that's why we recommend it. The black-pebble beaches on the southeast coast of the island are famous and not neglected, but there are white-sand beaches on the west coast that see only a few hundred people in a year. The majestic mountain setting of **Nea Moni,** an 11th-century Byzantine monastery in the center of the island, and the extraordinary mosaics of its chapel make for a unforgettable visit. The mastic villages in the south of the island are among the finest medieval towns in Greece, and the crop for which they are named (a tree resin used in chewing gum, paints, and perfumes) is grown nowhere else in the world.

The paralia of **Hios town** is likely to be your first glimpse of the island, and it isn't a pretty sight—unappealing modern buildings and generic cafes have taken over what must once have been a fine harbor. Thankfully, there are a few pockets of the original town further inland which have survived earthquakes, wars, and neglect. The Kastro, the mosque on the main square, the mansions of Kampos, and the occasional grand gateway (often leading nowhere) are among the only signs of a more prosperous and architecturally harmonious past.

ESSENTIALS

GETTING THERE   By Plane   Olympic Airways (☎ 0801/44444 or 01/ 966-6666; www.olympic-airways.gr) has flights four times a day between Athens and Hios. There is a connection once or twice a week with Lesvos (Mitilini) and Thessaloniki. The **Olympic office** in Hios town is in the middle of the harborfront (☎ **0271/24-515**). To contact the **airport,** call ☎ **0271/23-998.** If you arrive by plane, count on taking a cab into town at about Dr1,800 ($5.15) for the 7-kilometer (4.3-mile) ride.

By Boat   From Piraeus, one car ferry leaves daily bound for Hios (8 to 9 hrs.); there's also daily connection with Lesvos (3 hrs.). There are three ferries weekly to Limnos (9 hrs.) and Thessaloniki (16 to 19 hrs.), two ferries weekly to Samos (5 hrs.), and one weekly to Siros (5 hrs.). Check with the **Hios Port Authority** (☎ 0271/44-434) or **www.gtpnet.com** for current schedules.

VISITOR INFORMATION   The **Tourist Information Office** on Odos Kanari 18 (☎ 0271/44-389) stocks a remarkable amount of useful free brochures, including many maps; it's located on the second street from the north end of the harbor, between the harbor and the Central (Plastira) Square. It's open Monday to Friday from 7am to 2:30pm and 7 to 10pm, Saturday from 10am to 1pm, and Sunday from 7 to 10pm.

An Important Note on Car Rentals

Currently, anyone who is not carrying a driver's license from a country in the European Union will need an international driver's license to rent a car anywhere on Hios. If you expect to rent a car during your stay on Hios, plan to acquire an international driver's license before leaving your home country.

Another mine of information is **Hios Tours** (☎ **0271/29-444;** fax 0271/21-333), at the southern end of the paralia. The office is open Monday through Saturday from 8:30am to 1:30pm and 5:30 to 8:30pm; the staff will assist you with a room search, often at a discount. Hios Tours or the tourist office will change money after the portside banks' normal hours. The free *Hios Summertime* magazine has a lot of useful information, as well as maps. The site **www.chios.com** is also helpful.

GETTING AROUND   By Bus   All buses depart from one of the two bus stations in Hios town. The **blue buses** (☎ **0271/22-079**), which leave from the blue bus station on the north side of the public garden by Plateia Plastira, serve local destinations like Karfas to the south and Daskalopetra to the north. The **green long-distance KTEL buses** (☎ **0271/27-507**) leave from the green bus station, a block south of the park near the main taxi stand. There are six buses a day to Mesta, eight a day to Piryi, five to Kardamila, and four to Emborio, but only two buses a week to Volissos and to Nea Moni. Fares are Dr100 to Dr900 (30¢ to $2.60).

By Car   Hios is a large island and fun to explore, so a car is highly recommended. We suggest **John Vassilakis Rent-A-Car** (☎ and fax **0271/29-300**), at Odos Evgenias Handri 3 (the same street as the Hotel Kyma) in Hios, or at the branch office in **Megas Limionas** (☎ **0271/31-728**), about 10 kilometers (6.2 miles) south of Hios town. There's no extra charge for airport pickup.

By Taxi   Taxis are easily found at the port, though the taxi station is beyond the OTE, on the northeast corner of the central square. You can call ☎ **0271/41-111** or 0271/26-379 for a cab. Fares from Hios town run about Dr4,500 ($13) to Piryi, Dr5,500 ($16) to Mesta, and Dr5,000 ($14) round-trip to Nea Moni.

By Moped   Hios is too large, and the hills too big, for mopeds—if you don't have the license to rent a genuine motorbike, you would be better off with a car.

FAST FACTS   The **Commercial Bank** (Emboriki Trapeza) and **Ergo Bank,** both at the north end of the harbor near the corner of Odos Kanari, have ATMs; both are open Monday through Thursday from 8am to 2pm, Friday from 8am to 1:30pm. The English-speaking **dentist** Dr. Freeke (☎ **0271/27-266**) is highly recommended. The **hospital** is 7 kilometers (4.3 miles) from the center of Hios town (☎ **0271/44-301**). **Internet access** is available at **Enter Internet Café** (☎ **0271/41-058**), on the south end of the paralia next to the Metropolis Café. It's open daily from 9am to midnight; 1 hour online costs Dr1,000 ($2.90). There's a full-service **laundry** just around the corner from the post office on Odos Psichari (☎ **0271/44-801**); one load costs Dr3,000 ($9), and the turnaround time is about 24 hours. The **post office** is at the corner of Odos Omirou and Odos Rodokanaki (☎ **0271/44-350**). The **telephone office (OTE)** is across the street from the tourist office on Odos Kanari (☎ **131**). The **tourist police** are headquartered at the northernmost tip of the harbor, at Odos Neorion 35 (☎ **0271/44-427**).

ATTRACTIONS

Argenti Museum and Koraï Library. Odos Koraï, Hios town. ☎ **0271/44-246.** Museum admission Dr400 ($1.15); free admission to library. Both open Mon–Thurs 8am–2pm; Fri 8am–2pm and 5–7:30pm; Sat 8am–12:30pm.

Philip Argenti is the great historian of Hios, a local aristocrat who devoted his life and savings to the recording of island history, costumes, customs, and architecture. The museum consists largely of his personal collection of folk art, costumes, and implements, supplemented with a gallery of family portraits and copies of Eugene Delacroix's *Massacre of Hios,* a masterpiece depicting the Turkish massacre of the local population in 1822. The entrance lobby has numerous old maps of the island on display. The library is excellent, with much of its collection in English and French. Those who have any interest in local architecture and village life should ask to see the collection of drawings made by Dimitris Pikionis (a renowned 20th-century Greek architect) of the Kampos mansions and village houses—the drawings are beautiful, and have yet to be published.

✪ **Nea Moni.** Hios. No phone. Free admission to monastery grounds and katholikon; museum admission Dr500 ($1.45) adults, Dr300 (90¢) students and seniors. Monastery grounds and katholikon, daily 8am–1pm and 4–8pm; museum, Tues–Sun 8am–1pm. Located 17km (10½ miles) west of Hios town.

The 11th-century monastery of Nea Moni is one of the great architectural and artistic treasures of Greece. The monastery is in a spectacular setting high in the mountains overlooking Hios town. Its grounds are extensive—this monastery was once home to 1,000 monks—but the present population has dwindled to two monks and a single elderly nun (the monks often give tours of the monastery in Greek or French). The focus of the rambling complex is the **katholikon,** or principal church, whose nave is square in plan with eight niches supporting the dome. Within these niches are a sequence of extraordinary **mosaics,** among the finest examples of Byzantine art— sadly, a seemingly interminable process of restoration continues to conceal the most beautiful of these behind scaffolding. You can still see the portrayals of the saints in the narthex, and a representation of Christ washing the disciples' feet. The museum contains a collection of gifts to the monastery, including several fine 17th-century icons. Also of interest is the **cistern,** a cavernous vaulted room with columns (bring a flashlight), and the small **Chapel of the Holy Cross** at the entrance to the monastery, dedicated to the martyrs of the 1822 massacre by the Turks (the skulls and bones displayed are those of the victims themselves). The long barrel-vaulted refectory is currently being restored—it's a beautiful space, and its curved apse dates from the 11th century.

The bus to Nea Moni is part of an island excursion operated by KTEL, departing from the Hios town bus station Tuesday and Friday at 9am and returning at 4:30pm. The route is Hios town to Nea Moni to Anavatos to Lithi beach to Armolia and back to Hios town; it costs Dr4,000 ($11) per person. A taxi will cost about Dr5,000 ($14) round-trip from Hios town, including a half hour at the monastery.

A DAY TRIP TO THE MASTIC VILLAGES: PIRYI, MESTA & OLIMBI

The most interesting day trip on Hios is the excursion to the mastic villages in the southern part of the island, which offer one of the best examples of medieval town architecture in all of Greece. Mastic is a gum derived from the resin of the mastic tree, used in candies, paints, perfumes, and medicines. It was a source of great wealth for these towns in the Middle Ages, and is still produced in small quantities. All the towns were originally fortified, with an outer wall formed by an unbroken line of houses with no doors and few windows facing out. You can still see this distinctive plan at all three towns, although in Piryi and Olimbi the original medieval village has been engulfed by more recent construction.

Piryi is known for a rare technique of geometric decoration, known as *Ksisti*. In the main square this technique reaches a level of extraordinary virtuosity. The beautiful **Ayioi Apostoli** church and every available surface of every building are covered with horizontal banded decorations in a remarkable variety of motifs. At the town center is the tower for which the village was named, now mostly in ruins. It was originally the heart of the city's defenses, and a place of last refuge in time of siege.

Mesta is the best preserved medieval village in Hios, a maze of narrow streets and dark covered passages. The town has two fine churches, each unique on the island. **Megas Taxiarchis,** built in the 19th century, is one of the largest churches in Greece, and it was clearly built to impress. The arcaded porch with its fine pebble terrace and bell tower create a solemn and harmonious transition to the cathedral precinct. The other church in town, **Paleos Taxiarchis,** is located a few blocks below the main square. As the name suggests, this is the older of the two, built in the 14th century. The most notable feature here is the carved wooden iconostasis, whose surface is incised with miniature designs of unbelievable intricacy. If either church is closed, you can ask for the gatekeeper in the central square; Despina Flores of the **Messaionas Taverna** (☎ 0271/76-050) will probably know where he can be found.

Olimbi is the least well known of the three, not so spectacular as Piryi nor as intact as Mesta, but many of its medieval buildings still exist. There is a central tower similar to that of Piryi, and stone vaults connecting the houses.

Piryi is the closest of the three villages to Hios town, at 26 kilometers (16.1 miles); Olimbi and Mesta are both within 10 kilometers (6.2 miles) of Piryi. The easiest way to see all three villages is by car. Taxis from Hios to Piryi cost about Dr4,500 ($13). KTEL buses travel from Hios to Piryi eight times a day, and to Mesta five times a day. The bus to Piryi is Dr650 ($1.90), and to Mesta Dr850 ($2.45).

BEACHES

There's no question that Hios has the best beaches in the Northeastern Aegean. They're cleaner, less crowded, and more plentiful than those of Samos or Lesvos, and would be the envy of any Cycladic isle.

The fine-sand beach of **Karfas,** 7 kilometers (4.3 miles) south of Hios town, is the closest decent beach to the town center; it can be reached by a local (blue) bus. The rapid development of tourism in this town assures, however, that the beach will be crowded.

The most popular beach on the south coast is **Mavra Volia** ("black pebbles") in the town of Emborio. Continue over the rocks to the right from the man-made town beach to find the main beach. Walking on the smooth black rocks feels and sounds like marching through a room filled with marbles. The panorama of the beach, slightly curving coastline, and distant headland is a memorable sight. There are regular buses from Hios town or from Piryi (8km/5 miles away) to Emborio. A short distance south is the best beach of the south coast, ✪ **Vroulidia,** a 5-kilometer (3-mile) drive in from the Emborio road. This white-pebble-and-sand beach in a rocky cove offers great views of the craggy coastline.

The west coast of the island has a number of stunning beaches. **Elinda Cove** shelters a long cobble beach, a 600-meter drive in from the main road between Lithi and Volissos. Another excellent beach on this road is **Tigani–Makria Ammos,** about

4 kilometers (2½ miles) north of Elinda; turn at a sign for the beach and drive in 1½ kilometers (0.9 mile) to this long white-pebble beach (there's also a small cove-sheltered cobble beach about 300 meters before you reach the main beach). There are three beaches below Volissos, the best of which is Lefkathia, just north of the harbor of Volissos (Limnia).

South of Elinda, the long safe beach at **Lithi Bay** is popular with families. There are several tavernas, of which **Ta Tria Adelphia,** The Three Brothers (☎ 0271/73-208), is recommended—it's the last taverna you come to as you're walking along the beach.

The beaches of the north coast are less remarkable. **Nagos** (4km/2½ miles north of Kardamila) is a charming town in a small spring-fed oasis, with a cobble beach and two tavernas on the water. This beach can get very crowded—the secret is to hike to the two small beaches a little to the east. To find them, take the small road behind the white house near the windmill.

WHERE TO STAY
HIOS TOWN

✪ Hotel Kyma. Odos Evyenias Handri 1, 82100 Hios. ☎ **0271/44-500.** Fax 0271/44-600. E-mail: kyma@chi.forthnet.gr. 59 units. A/C TV TEL. Dr21,000 ($60) double. Rates include breakfast. No credit cards.

Our favorite in-town lodging was built in 1917 as a private villa for John Livanos. (You'll notice the portraits of the lovely Mrs. Livanos on the ceiling in the ground-floor breakfast room.) Though the hotel is of historic interest (the treaty with Turkey was signed in the Kyma in 1922), most of the original architectural details are gone, and the rooms have been renovated in a modern style. Many units have views of the sea, and a few have big whirlpool baths. The management, under the amiable direction of Theo Spordilis, is friendly, capable, and helpful—Theo is also a bountiful source of information on the island, and he serves an excellent breakfast as well. Ask about his self-guided island tour packages, which include car rental and accommodation options to several of the island's most beautiful villages.

KARFAS

Karfas, 7 kilometers (4½ miles) south of Hios town around Cape Ayia Eleni, is an exploding tourist resort with a fine-sand beach lined with resort hotels. The area is packed with tour groups throughout the summer months.

Hotel Erytha. Karfas, 82100 Hios. ☎ **0271/32-060** or 0271/32-064. Fax 0271/32-182. E-mail: erytha@compulink.gr. 102 units. A/C MINIBAR TV TEL. Dr34,500 ($99) double; Dr41,500 ($118) triple. Rates include breakfast. AE, DC, MC, V.

Built in 1990, the Erytha currently offers the most luxurious accommodations in the vicinity of Hios town. The spacious double rooms of this sprawling resort are distributed among five beachfront buildings connected by plant-filled terraces. The outdoor breakfast area steps down to the pool terrace, which is just above a tiny cove and private beach. Guest rooms are simply furnished: All have balconies and most face the sea, although a few open onto the terraces between buildings. Bathrooms are moderate in size, and include a bathtub with shower. There are 21 studios and apartments in a separate building, but these aren't as well maintained as the main hotel, and the kitchen facilities are very minimal: You're better off avoiding them entirely. The air-conditioning operates only in July and August.

KARDAMILA

Kardamila, on the northeastern coast, is our choice among the resort towns because it's prosperous, self-sufficient, and not at all touristy.

Hotel Kardamila. Kardamila, 82300 Hios. ☎ **0272/23-353.** Fax 0271/23-354. (Contact Hotel Kyma for reservations.) 32 units. A/C TEL. Dr28,000 ($80) double. Rates include breakfast. No credit cards.

This modern resort hotel was built for the guests and business associates of the town's ship owners and officers, and it has its own small cobble beach. The guest rooms are large and plain, with modern bathrooms and balconies overlooking the beach. The gracious Theo Spordilis of the Hotel Kyma has taken over its management, so you can be sure the service will be good.

VOLISSOS

This small hilltop village is one of the most beautiful on the island. A fine Byzantine castle overlooks the steep streets of the town, which contains numerous cafes and tavernas. It's too far north to be a convenient base for touring the whole island, but if you want to get to know a small part of the island, you couldn't choose a better focus for your explorations.

✪ **Volissos Traditional Houses.** Volissos, Hios. ☎ **0274/21-421** or 0274/21-413. Fax 0274/21-521. E-mail: volissos@otenet.gr. 16 units. Dr12,000–Dr25,000 ($34–$72) per night. No credit cards.

The care with which these village houses have been restored is unique on this island, if not in the whole Northeastern Aegean. Stella Tsakiri is a trained visual artist, and the influence of her discerning eye is evident in every detail of the reconstruction. The beamed ceilings, often supported by a forked tree limb—a method of construction described in the *Odyssey*—are finely crafted and quite beautiful. Built into the stone walls are niches, fireplaces, cupboards, and couches. This spirit of inventiveness is also seen in imaginative recycling: A cattle yoke serves as a beam, while salvaged doors and shutters from the village become a mirror or piece of furniture. The houses and apartments are distributed throughout the village of Volissos, so your neighbors are likely to be locals rather than fellow tourists. All apartments and houses have a small kitchen, a spacious bathroom, and one or two bedrooms; the largest places (on two floors of a house) have two bedrooms, a sitting room, a kitchen, and a large terrace.

MESTA

The best-preserved medieval fortified village on Hios, Mesta is a good base for touring the mastic villages (see above) and the island's south coast.

Pipidis Traditional Houses. Mesta, Hios. ☎ **0271/76-029.** 4 units. Dr12,000 ($34) double; Dr13,200 ($38) triple; Dr14,400 ($41) for 4 persons. No credit cards.

These four homes, built more than 500 years ago, have been restored and opened by the Greek National Tourism Organization as part of its traditional settlements program. The apartments have a medieval character, with vaulted ceilings and irregularly sculpted stone walls (covered in plaster and whitewash). One unfortunate aspect of these authentic dwellings is the dearth of natural light: If a room has any windows at all, they're usually small and placed high in the wall. Each house comes equipped with a kitchen, bathroom, and enough sleeping space for two to six people. They're managed by the admirable Pipidis family.

WHERE TO DINE
HIOS TOWN

Hios Marine Club. Odos Nenitousi 1. ☎ **0271/23-184.** Main courses Dr800–Dr3,500 ($2.30–$10) EC, MC, V. Daily noon–2am. GREEK.

This good, simple taverna serves the usual Greek dishes, pasta, grilled meats, and fish. Don't be put off by the ugly yellow-and-white concrete façade—the sign in front reads simply RESTAURANT-FRESCA PSARIA. It's on the bay at the edge of town, just south of the port, 50 meters beyond the Hotel Chandris.

Hotzas Taverna. Yioryiou Kondili 3. ☎ **0271/23-117.** Main courses Dr700–Dr3,500 ($2–$10). No credit cards. Mon–Sat 6–11pm. GREEK.

Hotzas is a small taverna that offers simple, well-prepared food. It's the best option in a town not known for its restaurants. The summer dining area is a luxuriant garden with lemon trees and abundant flowers. There's no menu, just a few unsurprising but delicious offerings each night. You won't find much fish, as most of the dishes are meat-based. This place isn't easy to find—take Odos Kountouriotou in from the harbor, and look for the first right turn after a major road merges at an oblique angle from the right; after this it's another 50 meters before the taverna appears on your left.

Theodosiou Ouzeri. Paralia, Hios. No phone. Appetizers Dr400–Dr3,500 ($1.15–$10). No credit cards. Daily 7pm–midnight. GREEK.

In the evening, many residents pull up a streetside chair at a cafe along the waterfront and eat *mezedes* with *ouzo.* Of the many ouzeries on the paralia, we like Theodosiou, located on the far right (north) side of the port, for both the scene and its menu.

LANGADA

Yiorgo Passa's Taverna. Langada. ☎ **0271/74-218.** Fish from Dr10,000 ($29) per kilo. No credit cards. Daily 11am–2am. Located 20km (12.4 miles) north of Hios town on the Kardamila road. SEAFOOD.

Langada is a fishing village with a strip of five or six outdoor fish taverns lining the harbor. Our favorite of these is **Yiorgo Passa's Taverna,** the first on the left as you approach the waterfront. Prices are low, portions are generous, and the ambiance is warm and friendly. *Note:* There are evening dinner cruises to Langada from Hios; check with **Hios Tours** (see "Visitor Information," above) for details.

MESTA

Messaiones Taverna. Mesta. ☎ **0271/76-050.** Main courses Dr1,000–Dr2,000 ($2.90–$6). No credit cards. Daily 11am–midnight. GREEK.

You'll find Despina Sirimi's taverna on the main square in Mesta. The menu features a great variety of *mezedes,* many with interesting variations on traditional dishes. The stuffed tomatoes with pine nuts and raisins are delicious, as are the fried dishes like *domatokeftedes* (fried tomatoes with herbs) or *tiropitakia* (fried cheese balls). Despina knows the village well, and can direct you to its most distinctive features, like Paleos Taxiarchis church and its remarkable carved wooden iconostasis.

3 Lesvos (Mitilini)

348km (188 nautical miles) NE of Piraeus

Roughly triangular Lesvos, often called Mitilini, is the third-largest island in Greece, with a population of nearly 120,000. At the tips of the triangle are the three principal towns: **Mitilini, Molivos,** and **Eressos.** Due to its remote location, Eressos is a good destination for a day trip, but not a recommended base for touring the island.

Mitilini and Molivos are about as different as two towns on the same island could possibly be. Loud and obnoxious, Mitilini is a tough cousin to Thessaloniki, a port town low on sophistication or pretense, with little organized tourism and lots of local character. Molivos is a picture-postcard seaside village, a truly beautiful place, but in the summer existing only for tourism.

Not to be missed are the Archaeological and Theophilos museums in Mitilini; the town of **Mandamados** and its celebrated icon (the east coast road, between Mandamados and Mitilini, is the most scenic on the island); the remarkable, mile-long beach of Eressos; and the labyrinthine streets of Molivos's castle-crowned hill.

Getting around on Lesvos is greatly complicated by the presence of two huge tear-shaped bays in the south coast, which divide the island down its center. East-west distances are great, and since bus service is infrequent, this is one island where you'll definitely need a car.

GETTING THERE   By Plane   The **airport** (☎ **0251/61-490** or 0251/61-590) is 3 kilometers (1.9 miles) south of Mitilini; there's no bus to the town, and a taxi will cost about Dr1,200 ($3.45). **Olympic Airways** (☎ **0801/44444** or 01/966-6666; www.olympic-airways.gr) has several flights daily to Mitilini from Athens. There are connections with Thessaloniki daily; with Limnos three times weekly; and with Hios twice weekly. The **Olympic office** in Mitilini (☎ **0251/28-660**) is at Odos Kavetsou 44, about 200 meters south of Ayia Irinis park. To find it, walk 300 meters south from the harbor; turn right at a large park, just before the World War II monument (a statue of a woman with sword); take the first right; and the office will be immediately on your left. **Aegean Airlines** (☎ **01/998-2888** in Athens), with an office at the Mitilini airport (☎ **0251/61-120**), also has three flights daily between Athens and Mitilini, and two flights daily between Thessaloniki and Mitilini.

By Boat   The principal port of Lesvos is Mitilini, and almost all the ferries arrive and depart from here, although there is some ferry traffic through the west coast port of Sigri. There's one ferry daily to Mitilini from Piraeus, stopping at Hios (10 to 12 hrs.); there are also several ferries weekly from Rafina to Sigri (9 hrs.). There are daily boats in both directions between Mitilini and Hios (3 hrs.), and four ferries weekly from Mitilini to Limnos (6 to 7 hrs.); there are also two ferries weekly between Sigri and Limnos (4½ hrs.). Two boats call weekly to Mitilini from Kavala (10 hrs.) and Thessaloniki (10 to 13 hrs.), stopping at Limnos on the way; there's also one ferry a week from Siros (9 hrs.). Check schedules with a local travel agent, **www.gtpnet.com**, the **Mitilini Port Authority** (☎ **0251/28-827**), or the **Sigri Port Authority** (☎ **0253/ 54-433**).

Once you get to Lesvos double-check the boat schedule for your departure, as the harbor is extremely busy in the summer and service is often inexplicably irregular.

MITILINI & SOUTHEAST LESVOS

With a big-city ambiance more like a mainland city than an island capital, Mitilini isn't to everyone's taste. Your first impression is likely to be one of noise, car exhaust, and crazy taxi drivers. Sadly, recent development has resulted in a generic paralia; the only signs of a more auspicious past are the cathedral dome and the considerable remains of a hilltop castle. Still, once you leave the paralia there's little or nothing in the way of amenities for tourists, a quality that can be remarkably refreshing. In the vicinity of Ermou (the market street), Mitilini's crumbling ochre alleys contain a mix of traditional coffeehouses, the studios of artisans, ouzeries, stylish jewelry shops, and stores selling antiques and clothing. Although good restaurants are notably absent in the town center, there are a few authentic tavernas on the outskirts of town.

ESSENTIALS

VISITOR INFORMATION   The **Greek National Tourism Organization (EOT)** office is in Mitilini at Odos Aristarhou 6 (☎ **0251/42-511;** fax 0251/42-512), 20 meters back from the building housing the Customs office and the tourist police, to the left (east) from the ferry quay, in what may appear at first to be a private house. This is primarily an administrative center, and the office is not very well equipped. It's open daily from 8am to 2:30pm, with extended hours in the high season. The **tourist police** (☎ **0251/22-276**) may also be helpful.

GETTING AROUND   By Bus   There are two bus stations in Mitilini, one for local and the other for round-the-island routes. The **local bus station** (☎ **0251/ 28-725**) is near the north end of the harbor, by the (closed) Folklife Museum and across from the Commercial Bank (Emporiki Trapeza). Local buses on Lesvos are frequent, running every hour from 6am to 9pm most of the year. The destinations covered are all within 12 kilometers (7½ miles) of Mitilini, and include Thermi, Moria, and Pamfilla to the north and Varia, Ayia Marina, and Loutra to the south. The most expensive local fare is Dr350 ($1). The posted schedule is hard to read, but there's usually someone selling tickets who can decipher it. You can catch the **round-the-island KTEL buses** (☎ **0251/28-873**) in Mitilini at the south end of the port behind the Argo Hotel. There's daily service in summer to Kaloni and Molivos (four times), Mandamados (once), Plomari (four times), and to Eressos and Sigri (once).

By Car   Rental prices in Mitilini tend to be high, so be sure to shop around. A good place to start is **Payless Car Rental** (e-mail: automoto@otenet.gr), with offices at the airport (☎ **0251/61-665**) and on the port in Mitilini (☎ **0251/43-555**), near the local (north) bus station. Summer daily rates start at around Dr14,000 ($40) with 100 free kilometers; each kilometer over 100 is an additional Dr50 (15¢). Assuming an average day's drive is 150 kilometers (94 miles), count on paying about $7.50 a day.

By Taxi   Lesvos is a big island. The one-way taxi fare from Mitilini to Molivos is about Dr9,000 ($26); from Mitilini to Eressos or Sigri, about Dr14,000 ($40). The main taxi stand in Mitilini is on Plateia Kyprion Patrioton, a long block inland from the southern end of the port; there's a smaller taxi stand at the north end of the port, near the local bus station and the (closed) Folklife Museum.

FAST FACTS   The **area code** for Mitilini is 0251, for Molivos (Mithimna) and Eressos 0253, and for Plomari 0252. There are **ATMs** at several banks on the port, including the Ioniki Trapeza and Agrotiki Trapeza (both south of the local bus station). The **Vostani Hospital** (☎ **0251/43-777**) on Odos P. Vostani, just southeast of town, will take care of emergencies. **Glaros Laundry** (☎ **0251/27-065**), opposite the tourist police near the ferry pier, is open from 9am to 2pm and 6 to 8pm; the turnaround time is usually 24 hours. The **post office** and the **telephone office (OTE)** are on Plateia Kyprion Patrioton, 1 block inland from the town hall at the south end of the port. The principal **taxi stand** is also on Plateia Kyprion Patrioton. The **tourist police** (☎ **0251/22-776**) are located near the EOT, left (east) from the ferry quay.

ATTRACTIONS

Archaeological Museums of Mitilini. Odos Eftaliou 7, Myrina. ☎ **0251/28-032.** Admission Dr500 ($1.45) adults, Dr300 (90¢) students and seniors. Tues–Sun 8:30am–3pm. A block north of the tourist police station, just inland from the ferry pier.

The excellent Mitilini Archaeological Museum was augmented recently by the construction of a large new museum a short distance up the hill toward the Kastro. The museums have the same hours, and the price of admission includes both locations. The new museum presents extensive Roman antiquities of Lesvos and some finds from the early Christian basilica of Ayios Andreas in Eressos. The highlight of its collection is a reconstructed Roman house from the 3rd century B.C., whose elaborate mosaic floors depict scenes from comedies of the poet Menander and from Classical mythology. All the exhibits are thoughtfully presented, with plentiful explanatory notes in

English. Entering the yard of the original archaeological museum, you're greeted by massive marble lions rearing menacingly on their hind legs, perhaps representing the bronze lion sculpted by Hephaestus, which is said to roam the island of Lesvos and serve as its guardian. A rear building houses more marble sculpture and inscribed tablets, while the main museum contains figurines, pottery, gold jewelry, and other finds from Thermi, the Mitilini Kastro, and other ancient sites of Lesvos.

✪ **Theophilos Museum.** Varia. ☎ **0251/41-644.** Admission Dr500 ($1.45). Tues–Sun 9am–1pm and 4:30–8pm. Located 3km (1.9 miles) south of Mitilini, on the road to the airport, next to the Theriade Museum.

One of the most interesting sights near Mitilini is this small museum in the former house of folk artist Hatzimichalis Theophilos (1868–1934). Most of Theophilos's works adorned the walls of tavernas and ouzeries, often painted in exchange for food. Theophilos died in poverty, and none of his work would have survived if it weren't for the efforts of art critic Theriade (see below), who commissioned the paintings on display here during the last years of the painter's life. These primitive watercolors depicting ordinary people, daily life, and local landscapes are now widely celebrated, and are also exhibited at the Museum of Folk Art in Athens. Be sure to take in the curious photographs showing the artist dressed as Alexander the Great.

Theriade Library and Museum of Modern Art. Varia. ☎ **0251/23-372.** Admission Dr600 ($1.75). Tues–Sun 9am–1pm and 5–8pm. Located 3km (1.9 miles) south of Mitilini, on the road to the airport, next to the Theophilos Museum.

The Theriade Library and Museum of Modern Art is in the home of Stratis Eleftheriadis, a native of Lesvos who emigrated to Paris and became a prominent art critic and publisher (Theriade is the Gallicized version of his surname). On display are copies of his published works, including the *Minotaure* and *Verve* magazines, as well as his personal collection of works by Picasso, Matisse, Miro, Chagall, and other modern artists.

Kastro. Odos 8 Noemvriou, Mitilini. ☎ **0251/27-297.** Admission Dr500 ($1.45) adults; Dr300 (90¢) students and seniors. Tues–Sun 8am–2:30pm. Just past the new Archaeological Museum, turn right on the path to the Kastro.

Perched on a steep hill just north of the city, the extensive ruins of Mitilini's castle are fun to explore and offer fine views of city and sea from the ramparts. The Kastro was founded by Justinian in the 6th century A.D., and was restored and enlarged in 1737 by the Genoese; the Turks also renovated and built extensively during their occupation of the castle. In several places you can see fragments of marble columns embedded in the castle walls—these are blocks taken from a 7th-century B.C. temple of Apollo by the Genoese during their rebuilding of the walls. Look for the underground cistern at the north end of the castle precinct: This echoing chamber is a beautiful place, with domed vaults reflected in the pool below. In summer, the castle is sometimes used as a performing-arts center.

A SIDE TRIP TO TURKEY: AYVALIK, PERGAMUM & ANCIENT TROY

From Mitilini, there's a direct connection to Turkey via the port of Ayvalik; about 3,000 tourists make the crossing annually. Ayvalik, a densely wooded fishing village, makes a refreshing base camp from which to tour Pergamum or ancient Troy. The acropolis of Pergamum is sited on a dramatic hilltop, with substantial remains of the town on the surrounding slopes. The complex dates back to at least the 4th century B.C., and there are significant remains from this period through to Roman and Byzantine times. It is one of Turkey's most important archaeological sites. All-inclusive tours to Pergamum with lunch, bus, and round-trip boat fare are available; inquire at Mitilini travel agencies. Ships to Turkey sail Wednesday, Friday, and Saturday. Tickets

Excursion to a Mountain Village

An enjoyable destination for a day trip is the rural hamlet of **Ayiassos,** 23 kilometers (14 miles) west of Mitilini. The town, built up on the foothills of Mount Olymbos, consists of traditional gray stone houses (with their wooden "Turkish" balconies, often covered in flowering vines), narrow cobblestone lanes, and fine small churches. Here local craftsmen still turn out their ceramic wares by hand. There are excursion buses from Mitilini, or you can share a taxi (about Dr7,500/$22) for the 1-hour ride.

for the Turkish boats are sold by **Aeolic Cruises Travel Agency** (☎ 0251/23-960), on the port in Mitilini. The round-trip excursion fare (returning the same day) is about Dr20,000 ($57), and a visa is not required; the fare on the Turkish boat is Dr15,000 ($43) round-trip, with an additional visa fee upon arrival in Turkey ($45 for Americans, £5 for Irish citizens, £10 for U.K. citizens, $45 for Canadians, and $20 for Australians; New Zealanders don't currently need a visa).

WHERE TO STAY

Hotel Erato. Odos P. Vostani, Mitilini, 81000 Lesvos. ☎ **0251/41-160.** Fax 0251/47-656. 22 units. A/C TV TEL. Dr16,800 ($48) double; Dr18,000 ($52) triple. EC, MC, V. Open year-round.

On a busy street just south of the port, this hotel offers convenience, cleanliness, a friendly and helpful staff, and a noise level marginally below that experienced in the many portside hotels. Most of the small bright rooms have balconies facing the street, with a view over the traffic to Mitilini Bay. The four-story hotel was converted from a medical clinic, and does retain an atmosphere of institutional anonymity; on the positive side, it's very well maintained, and the high-pressure showers and fluffy towels are a bonus. *An important note:* Although credit cards are accepted, the hotel staff doesn't seem accustomed to dealing with them, and there can be long delays. If you pay by credit card, do so well in advance of your planned departure.

Hotel Sappho. Odos Kountourioti, Mitilini, 81000 Lesvos. ☎ **0251/22-888.** Fax 0251/ 24-522. 29 units. A/C TV TEL. Dr16,000 ($46) double. Continental breakfast Dr1,500 ($4.30). AE, V.

The Sappho is one of the better hotels on the port, offering simple accommodations in a recently renovated building. Nine rooms have balconies facing the port; the rest have no balcony and face a sunny rear courtyard. All units have wall-to-wall carpets, white walls, minimal furnishings, and tiny bathrooms with showers. A breakfast room on the second floor has an outdoor terrace with a fine port view.

Villa 1900. Odos P. Vostani, Mitilini, 81000 Lesvos. ☎ **0251/23-448.** Fax 0251/28-034. 7 units. Dr9,500–Dr15,000 ($27–$43) double. No credit cards. Located 150m south of the Olympic Airways office, opposite the stadium.

The Villa 1900 is a somewhat upscale pension in a fine old house on the edge of town, about 700 meters south of the Mitilini port. The best rooms (nos. 3 and 7) are quite spacious, with ornate painted ceilings. However, the smaller ones (nos. 6, 8, and 9) are claustrophobic and overpriced. The remaining two units are plain but adequate, and offer reasonable value for your money. The house is buffered from the noise of the street by a small garden in front; a larger garden with abundant fruit trees begins at the back terrace and offers a pleasant shaded retreat. The amiable owners speak no English, but there is usually someone on hand to translate.

WHERE TO DINE

Mitilini has more portside cafes than your average bustling harbor town. A cluster of chairs around the small lighthouse at the point heralds the most scenic (as well as the windiest) of the many small ouzeries, specializing in grilled octopus, squid, shrimp, and local fish. We found the best restaurants to be a short taxi ride outside the city.

Averof 1841 Grill. Port, Mitilini. ☎ **0251/22-180.** Main courses Dr1,000–Dr3,200 ($2.90–$9). No credit cards. Daily 7am–5pm and 7–11pm. GREEK.

This taverna, located midport near the Sappho Hotel, is one of the better grills around, and one of the only restaurants in Mitilini center worth trying. It has particularly good beef dishes. Try any of the tender souvlaki dishes or the lamb with potatoes.

O Rembetis. Kato Halikas, Mitilini. ☎ **0251/27-150.** Main courses Dr900–Dr3,600 ($2.60–$10). No credit cards. Daily 8pm–12am. GREEK.

Kato Halikas is a hilltop village on the outskirts of Mitilini, and although this simple taverna might be hard to find, it's well worth the effort. At the south end of the ter-race you can sit beneath the branches of a high sycamore and enjoy a panoramic view of the port. The food isn't sophisticated or surprising, but it's very Greek, and the clientele is primarily local. There's no menu, so listen to the waiter's descriptions or take a look in the kitchen—there's usually some fresh fish in addition to the taverna standards. The wind can be brisk on this hilly site, so bring a jacket if the night is cool. The best way to get here is by taxi; the fare is about Dr500 ($1.45) each way.

Salavos. Mitilini. ☎ **0251/22-237.** Main courses Dr1,000–Dr3,000 ($2.90–$9). No credit cards. Daily noon–1am. GREEK.

Despite an unfortunate location on the busy airport road, this small taverna is one of the best in Mitilini. A garden terrace in back offers partial shelter from the road noise. The seafood is fresh and delicious; try the kalamari stuffed with feta, vegetables, and herbs. The restaurant is very popular with locals, who fill the place on summer nights. Traveling south from Mitilini toward the airport, it's about 3 kilometers (1.9 miles) south of town on the right. Taxi fare is about Dr600 ($1.75) each way.

MITILINI AFTER DARK

In Mitilini, there's plenty of nightlife action on both ends of the harbor. The east side tends to be younger, cheaper, and more informal. The more sophisticated places are off the south end of the harbor. There's also the outdoor **Park Cinema,** on the road immediately below the stadium, open May through September. There might also be entertainment at the Kastro.

MOLIVOS & NORTHEAST LESVOS

Molivos, also known by the more specifically Hellenic name "Mithimna," is at the northern tip of the island's triangle. It's a highly picturesque castle-crowned village with stone and pink-pastel stucco mansions capped by red-tile roofs, balconies, and windowsills decorated with geraniums and roses.

The town has long been popular with package-tour groups, especially during the summer months. Souvenir shops, car-rental agencies, and travel agents outnumber local merchants, and the restaurants are geared toward tourists. Despite this, it is a beautiful place to visit and a convenient base for touring the island.

ESSENTIALS

GETTING THERE   By Bus   KTEL buses (☎ 0251/28-873) connect Molivos with Mitilini four times daily in the high season. The Molivos bus stop is just past the Municipal Tourist Office on the road to Mitilini.

By Taxi   The one-way taxi fare from Mitilini to Molivos is about Dr9,000 ($26).

VISITOR INFORMATION   The **Municipal Tourist Office** (☎ 0253/71-347), housed in a tiny building next to the National Bank on the Mitilini Road, is open Monday through Friday. **Tsalis Tours,** on the road heading down to the sea from the National Bank (☎ **0253/71389;** fax 0253/71-345; e-mail: tsalis@otenet.gr), can book car rentals, accommodations, and excursions; open daily in summer from 8:30am to 9:30pm.

GETTING AROUND   By Car   There are numerous rental agencies in Molivos, and rates are comparable to those in Mitilini.

By Boat   Boat taxis to neighboring beaches can be arranged at the port or in a travel agency (see Tsalis Tours, above).

By Bus   Tickets for day excursions by bus can be bought in any of the local travel agencies. The destinations include Thermi/Ayiassos (Dr9,000/$26), Mitilini (Dr4,000/$11), Sigri/Eressos (Dr9,000/$26), and Plomari (Dr10,000/$29); the excursions are offered once or twice each week in the summer.

FAST FACTS   There's an ATM at the **National Bank,** next to the Municipal Tourist Office on the Mitilini Road. There's **Internet access** at Communication and Travel (☎ **0253/71-900**) on the main road to the port. The **police** (☎ **0253/71-222**) are up from the port, on the road to the town cemetery; the **port police** (☎ **0253/ 71-307**) are (predictably) on the port. The **post office** (☎ **0253/71-246**) is on the path circling up to the castle—turn right (up) just past the National Bank.

ATTRACTIONS

Kastro. Molivos. No phone. Admission Dr500 ($1.45) adults, Dr300 ($90¢) students and seniors. Tues–Sun 8:30am–3pm.

The hilltop Genoese castle is in a better state of preservation than that of Mitilini, but it's much less extensive and not as interesting to explore. There is, however, a great view from the walls, worth the price of admission in itself. There's a stage in the southwest corner of the courtyard, often used for theatrical performances in the summer. To get here by car, turn uphill at the bus stop and follow signs to the castle parking lot; on foot, the castle is most easily approached from the town, a steep climb no matter which of the many labyrinthine streets you choose.

Mandamados Monastery. Mandamados. Free admission. Daily 6am–10pm. Located 24km (15 miles) east of Molivos, 36km (22½ miles) northwest of Mitilini.

Mandamados is a lovely village on a high inland plateau, renowned primarily for the remarkable icon of the Archangel Michael housed in the local monastery. A powerful story is associated with the creation of the icon: It is said that during a certain pirate raid (these raids were tragically common during the later middle ages), all but one of the monks were slaughtered. This one survivor, emerging from hiding to find the bloody corpses of his dead companions, responded to the horror of the moment with an extraordinary act. Gathering the blood-soaked earth, he fashioned in it the face of man, an icon in relief of the Archangel Michael. This simple icon, its lips worn away by the kisses of pilgrims, can be found at the center of the iconostasis at the back of the main chapel.

AN EXCURSION TO WESTERN LESVOS: ERESSOS & SKALA

Western Lesvos is hilly and barren, with many fine-sand beaches concealed among rocky promontories. Admirers of Sappho's poems and avid beachgoers should be sure to travel the steep and winding 65 kilometers (41 miles) between Molivos and Eressos, on the island's westernmost shore. Excursion buses (Dr7,000/$20) make this trip daily from Mitilini; inquire at **Samiotis Tours,** Odos Kountourioti 43 (☎ 0251/ 42-574).

Eressos is an attractive small village overlooking the coastal plain. Its port, Skala Eressou, 4 kilometers (2½ miles) to the south, has become a full-blown resort popular with Greek families as well as with gay women. This isn't surprising, since the beach here is the best in Lesvos, a wide, dark sandy stretch over a mile long and lined with tamarisks; a stretch of sandy beaches and coves extends from here to Sigri, the next town to the north. Skala Eressou has a small **archaeological museum** (☎ 0253/ 53-332), near the 5th-century basilica of Ayios Andreas, with local finds from the Archaic, Classical, and Roman periods. It's open Tuesday through Sunday from 7:30am to 3:30pm; admission is free.

BEACHES

The long, narrow town beach in Molivos is rocky and crowded near the town, but becomes sandier and less populous as you continue south. The beach in **Petra,** 6 kilometers (3.7 miles) south of Molivos, is considerably more pleasant. The beach at **Tsonia,** 30 kilometers (19 miles) east of Molivos, is only accessible via a difficult rutted road, and isn't particularly attractive. The best beach on the island is 70 kilometers (44 miles) west of Molivos in **Skala Eressos** (see "An Excursion to Western Lesvos," above).

SHOPPING

Molivos is unfortunately dominated by tacky souvenir shops. To find more authentic local wares you'll have to explore neighboring towns. **Mandamados** is known as a center for pottery, and there are numerous ceramics studios here. **Eleni Lioliou** (☎ 0253/61-170), on the road to the monastery, has brightly painted bowls, plates, and mugs. **Anna Fonti** (☎ 0253/61-433), on a pedestrian street in the village, produces plates with intricate designs in brilliant turquoise and blue. Also in Mandamados is the diminutive studio of icon painter **Dimitris Hatzanagnostou** (☎ 0253/ 61-318), who produces large-scale icons for churches and portable icons for purchase.

WHERE TO STAY

Hotel-Bungalows Delphinia. Molivos, 81108 Lesvos. ☎ **0253/71-315** or 0253/71-580. Fax 0253/71-524. http://users.otenet.gr/d/delfinia. E-mail: delfinia@otenet.gr. 125 units. A/C MINIBAR TV TEL. Dr20,000–Dr21,700 ($57–$62) double; Dr30,800–Dr36,900 ($88–$106) 2-person bungalow; Dr37,800–Dr45,000 ($109–$129) 3-person bungalow. Rates include breakfast. AE, DC, V.

The best thing about this white-stucco and gray-stone resort is its panoramic setting above the Aegean. A path leads 200 meters from the hotel to a fine-sand beach and a recreation complex with saltwater swimming pool, snack bar, and tennis courts (the latter illuminated for night games). The hotel rooms are simple, with small shower-only bathrooms. The 57 bungalows are more spacious: The living room has a couch that pulls out to provide an extra bed, most bathrooms include a bathtub, and all units have a large terrace or balcony. Breakfast at the hotel is served in a large dining room, while the bungalows include free room service for breakfast only. The second-floor rooms in the bungalows are the most spacious, have the best views, and cost a bit more.

Hotel Olive Press. Molivos, 81108 Lesvos. ☎ **0253/71-205** or 0253/71-646. Fax 0253/ 71-647. 50 units. TEL. Dr25,000 ($72) double (includes breakfast); Dr36,000 ($104) studio. AE, DC, V.

The most charming hotel in town is built down on the water in the traditional style. The rooms are on the small side, but they're quiet and very comfortable, with terrazzo floors, handsome furnishings, and bathtubs. Some of the units have windows opening onto great sea views, with waves lapping just beneath. There is a nice inner courtyard with several gardens. The staff is gracious and friendly.

Sea Horse Pension (Thalassio Alogo). Molivos, 81108 Lesvos. ☎ **0253/71-630** or 0253/71-320. Fax 0253/71-374. 16 units. A/C TV TEL. 14,000 ($40) double. Continental breakfast Dr2,100 ($6). No credit cards.

A cluster of recently built Class C hotels is set below the old town, near the beach—among them is this smaller, homier pension. The friendly manager, Stergios, keeps the rooms (which have good views) tidy. All rooms come with refrigerator, hair dryer, and balcony facing the sea; four also have minimal kitchen facilities. On site are a restaurant and an in-house travel agency.

WHERE TO DINE

Captain's Table. Molivos. ☎ **0253/71-241.** Main courses Dr1,000–Dr3,000 ($2.90–$9). V. Daily 11am–1am. SEAFOOD/VEGETARIAN.

Melinda McRostie, the talented chef behind the enduringly popular Melinda's Restaurant, recently moved to the harbor in Molivos to start this new venture. Although the emphasis is now on fresh fish, the menu still offers some of the excellent vegetable dishes which were the trademark of her former establishment—try the Imam Bayeldi, a dish made with eggplant, onions, tomato, and garlic. There's live bouzouki music three nights a week.

Tropicana. Molivos. ☎ **0251/71-869.** Snacks/desserts Dr500–Dr3,000 ($1.45–$9). No credit cards. Daily 8am–1am. CAFE FARE.

Stroll up into the old town to sip a cappuccino or have a dish of ice cream at this outdoor cafe, which offers soothing classical music and a relaxed ambiance. The owner, Hari Procoplou, learned the secrets of ice creamery in Los Angeles.

MOLIVOS AFTER DARK

Vangelis Bouzouki (no phone) is Molivos's top acoustic bouzouki club. It's located west from Molivos on the road to Efthalou, past the Sappho Tours office. After about a 10-minute walk outside of town, you'll see a sign that points to an olive grove. Follow it for another 500 meters through the orchard until you reach a clearing with gnarled olive trees and a few stray sheep. When you see the circular cement dance floor, surrounded by clumps of cafe tables, you've found it. Have some ouzo and late-night *mezedes,* and sit back to enjoy the show. Inquire at the tourist offices about summer theatrical performances in the Kastro.

4 Limnos (Lemnos)

344km (186 nautical miles) NE of Piraeus

Limnos is decidedly tame in comparison with its Northeastern Aegean neighbors. Here low hills break up the cultivated plains, circled by a rocky but gently sloping coastline. The towns are more functional than beautiful, and the beaches pleasant but not spectacular. This absence of superlatives, combined with a remote location at the edge of Asia Minor, explains the small scale of local tourism and the refreshing simplicity of village life in the principal port of Mirina.

Low on picture-postcard sights but full of small-town charm, **Mirina** is the best base for exploring the island. Several of the town's restaurants and hotels cluster around a small square at the port, in the shadow of the fine Ottoman castle on its lofty promontory. Connecting port and beach is the market street, Odos P. Kida, where you can find preserves made from the local black plums, Limnian honey (a favorite of the gods), and the famous Limnian wines—Kalavaki, a dry white (Aristotle's favorite), and the sweet Moschato. The two town **beaches**—Romeïkos Yialos and Riha Nera—are slivers of sand extending north as far as the renowned Akti Marina luxury resort, now a private club. Don't miss the excellent **archaeological museum** on Romeïkos Yialos; it's a good introduction to the rest of the island's archaeological sites.

Due to its remote location, Limnos is one island you'll want to reach by plane—ferry journeys can be painfully long. Once on the island, you'll find that public bus schedules are scarce, and that a rented car or moped is the best option.

ESSENTIALS

GETTING THERE   By Plane   Olympic Airways (☎ **0801/44444** or 01/ 966-6666; www.olympic-airways.gr) has three flights daily between Limnos and Athens, one connection daily with Thessaloniki, and daily flights to Lesvos. The office (☎ **0254/22-214**) is on Odos Garoufalidou, in Mirina. The **airport bus** meets all flights, and costs a reasonable Dr1,000 ($2.90); it departs from the Olympic office to the airport about 90 minutes before flight time.

By Boat   The principal port of Mirina has frequent connections with Northeast Aegean destinations: Ferries depart four times weekly for the port of Kavala in Macedonia (4 to 5 hrs.), and five times weekly for Mitilini in Lesvos (5 to 6 hrs.). There is twice-weekly service to and from Hios (11 hrs.) and Samothrace (1½ hrs.). There is also a connection three or four times weekly with Rafina (10 to 15 hrs.) and Thessaloniki (8 hrs.). We recommend avoiding the 21-hour journey from Mirina to Piraeus via Lesvos and Hios—instead, catch a ferry on the Mirina-Ayios Efstratios-Piraeus route (10 hrs.), or opt to fly (1 hr.). For current ferry information, contact **Vayiakos Travel** (☎ **0254/22-460**) on the port in Mirina, **www.gtpnet.com**, or the **Mirina Port Authority** (☎ **0254/22-225**).

VISITOR INFORMATION   Mirina has several helpful travel agencies. **Petrides Travel** (☎ **0254/22-039;** fax 0254/22-219; e-mail: mapet@lim.forthnet.gr), 50 meters beyond the main square on the town's market street (Odos P. Kida), offers car rentals, accommodations booking, luggage storage, island excursions, and a very strange mural painting. **Pravlis Travel** (☎ and fax **0254/22-471**), on the port square, specializes in air tickets and will also book accommodations. There is an **EOT (Greek National Tourism Organization)** office in the *Eparhion*, a municipal building on the road to the airport, a 3-minute walk from the central square. The office is staffed by two very helpful women, and is worth seeking out. You can call the **Eparhion** (☎ **0254/22-996**) for more information.

GETTING AROUND   By Bus   In Mirina, the **central bus station** (☎ **0254/ 22-464**) is 3 blocks up from the main (taxi) square on the right. A schedule is posted, but you're not likely to find much on it. Except for Moudros and Kondias, most places on the island get service only once a day, usually in the afternoon. Excursion bus tours can be booked through Petrides Travel, and include various combinations of island villages and archaeological sites. The frequency depends upon demand; tours depart at least weekly in the summer. The cost is Dr2,500 ($7) for the half-day and Dr4,500 ($13) for the full-day tour.

By Boat   There are caïques on the north side of the harbor in Mirina; they offer service to the island's beaches and the grottos at Skala. You can buy tickets at most of the town's travel agencies.

By Car   Car-rental prices on Limnos tend to be high compared with its Northeastern Aegean neighbors. We recommend **Myrina Rent a Car** (☎ **0254/24-476**), where a basic car costs about Dr15,000 ($43) in the peak season, with insurance.

FAST FACTS   Both the **National Bank** and the **Agrotiki Trapeza,** 100 meters past the square in the direction of Romeïkos Yialos, have **ATMs.** There's a drop-off **laundry** (☎ **0254/24-392**) on Odos Garoufalidou across from the Olympic Airline office, next to the Hotel Astro; if it's closed, ask for help at the hotel. Continue a couple of blocks past the laundry and turn left to find the **hospital** (☎ **0254/22-222**). The **post office** is on Odos Garoufalidou, 1 block toward Romeïkos Yialos from the square and to the right, just down the street from the Olympic Airlines office. The **taxi station** (☎ **0254/23-033** or 0254/22-348) marks what might conveniently be called a main square, midway along the market street. The **telephone office (OTE)** is on this square, as is the National Bank. The **tourist police** (☎ **0254/22-200**) are on the port, just down from the port police.

ATTRACTIONS

✪ **Archaeological Museum.** Mirina. ☎ **0254/22-990.** Admission Dr500 ($1.45) adults, Dr300 (90¢) students and seniors. Tues–Sun 8am–2:30pm. On Romeïkos Yialos Beach, next to the Castro Hotel.

This unassuming building, originally a Turkish Commandery during the Ottoman occupation, was thoroughly renovated and now houses one of the finest archaeological museums in the Aegean. The artifacts are very well presented, and the descriptive plaques offer fascinating insights concerning the exhibits. If your appetite for exploration is whetted by the exhibits, it is possible to visit three of the island's archaeological sites by bus excursion: Poliochni, the Ifestia (sanctuary of Hephaestus), and the sanctuary of the Kaviri (see "Getting Around," above).

Kastro. Mirina. Open site. The best access path is reached via a steeply climbing road from the port, between the port police and the police station.

The Ottoman fortress that dominates Mirina from its craggy perch is easily accessible from the town, and the extensive ruins are a delight to explore. The climb from the port is long and exposed, so go in the early morning or wait for the relative cool of late afternoon. The foundations of the walls date to Byzantine times, and rock-carved inscriptions indicate that the site was once occupied by a temple to Artemis. There are numerous subterranean vaults and caves within the castle walls, so bring a flashlight. The shores of the castle's rocky promontory offer several secluded coves for bathing.

EXPLORING THE ARCHAEOLOGICAL SITES

There isn't much to see at the archaeological sites on Limnos's northern and eastern shores, but they do offer a great follow-up to the fascinating exhibits of Mirina's archaeological museum. **Kavirio,** dramatically situated on a rocky coastal promontory 10 kilometers (6.2 miles) north of the Hephaistia, is the most spectacularly placed of the three sites; only the floor plan remains of the once extensive temple. The **Hephaistia** on the island's northern shore, about 40 kilometers (25 miles) from Mirina, is the ruins of an ancient city dedicated to Hephaestus, the god of metallurgy who is said to have inhabited a volcano. Born ugly, Hephaestus was rejected by his father, Zeus, and as Milton wrote, "Dropt from the zenith like a falling star, on Limnos, the Aegean isle." At the site is a Greek theater, a temple of Hephaestus, and the excavation site of a pre-Hellenic necropolis which provided many of the items now housed in the archaeological museum in Mirina. Of less interest is **Poliochni,** about 5 kilometers (3.1 miles) east of Moudros, which is still being excavated and offers little for the imagination. All three sites are open from 9:30am to 3:30pm, and admission is free.

Some travel agencies include one or two of these sites as part of a **bus tour** of Limnos (see "Getting Around," above); the only alternative is to rent a car.

WHERE TO STAY

Castro Hotel. Romeïkos Yialos, Mirina, 81400 Limnos. ☎ **0254/22-772** or 0254/22-748. Fax 0254/22-784. 76 units. A/C MINIBAR TV TEL. Dr20,000 ($57) double; Dr22,000 ($63) double with sea view. Rates include breakfast. AE, MC, V. Located 1km (0.6 miles) north of the port.

The Castro is the best seafront hotel in Mirina, its neoclassical façade facing the water and the narrow strip of sand called Romeïkos Yialos. The marble reception room is built on a large scale and offers a suggestion of elegance, which is, unfortunately, not continued in the rest of the hotel. The rooms are plain, with wall-to-wall carpeting and more amenities than any of the neighboring hotels along the paralia. All units have balconies, although only a few actually face the sea.

Hotel Ifestos. Riha Nera, Mirina, 81400 Limnos. ☎ **0254/24-960.** Fax 0254/23-623. 41 units. TEL. Dr21,000 ($60) double. Rates include breakfast. MC, V. Located 2km (1.2 miles) north of the port.

The Ifestos is in a quiet neighborhood of Mirina, surrounded by greenery. Built in 1991, the hotel facade imitates the wide arcaded porches of the town's older houses. The rooms are plain and clean; all have a small balcony or terrace and views over the neighboring gardens. The beach is a 2-minute walk, and the port a leisurely 15-minute walk.

Hotel Lemnos. Odos Arvanitaki, Mirina, 81400 Limnos. ☎ **0254/22-153.** Fax 0254/23-329. 29 units. TV TEL. Dr16,000 ($46) double; Dr21,000 triple ($60). No credit cards.

This hotel on the harbor is attractive, clean, comfortable, and quiet. Less than 100 meters from the ferry pier, it's the most convenient option if you're arriving by boat. The owners, Harry Geanopoulos and Bill Stamboulis, spent many years in New Jersey and speak excellent English. They've also patterned their hotel on an American standard: a good night's sleep at a fair price. Breakfast (not included in the room rate) is available à la carte in the hotel cafe.

WHERE TO DINE

Mirina is not known for its restaurants. A host of fast-food places inhabit the paralia along Romeïkos Yialos Beach, but the most attractive options are on the market street or at the port.

Taverna Avra. Mirina. ☎ **0254/22-523.** Main courses Dr1,000–Dr2,500 ($2.90–$7). No credit cards. Daily 11:30am–12:30am. Next to the Port Authority, near the pier. GREEK.

Sheltered from the bustle of the port by a luxuriant grape arbor, the Avra is a good basic taverna with fair prices. There isn't a menu, so go inside and choose from the dishes displayed on the steam table. There's nothing surprising about the offerings, except perhaps the scarcity of fish in a taverna meters from the sea.

Taverna O Platanos. Mirina. ☎ **0254/22-070.** Main courses Dr1,000–Dr2,500 ($2.90–$8). No credit cards. Daily 11am–11pm. On the market street, 100m from the central square toward Romeïkos Yialos. GREEK.

O Platanos is a good, reliable taverna. The "platanos" in question is a handsome mammoth of a tree arching above this small square on Mirina's market street, offering abundant shade in the afternoon. The limited menu changes daily; and the standard taverna fare is complemented by a variety of vegetables.

Appendix A:
Greece in Depth

by Robert E. Meagher

In Greece, you will inevitably lose track of time—and not just what day it is. The timelessness of Greece's mountaintops and beaches, its natural and constructed temples, its glistening waters and slow sunsets bring a cleansing confusion of past and present, a delightful disorientation, even before your first glass of *ouzo*. Greece—defined by seas and mountains and a translucent sky—is a land of vistas, a place of spectacle.

That said, it is easy to overlook something you are not prepared to see. One of the oldest and greatest of the Greek philosophers, Heraclitus, known even in his own day as "the obscure," once pointed out that "Reality likes to hide." So does much of Greece. And so the aim of what follows in this chapter is both to excite the imagination and to guide the eyes. Think of it as a collection of trail notes—things to keep in mind and to look for as you make your own way around Greece.

1 History 101

Before asking *who* the Greeks were, it is important to notice *where* they were. Geography, after all, is often destiny. It has certainly been so for the Greeks. By situation and disposition, Greece faces both east and west, both north and south. Its roots and branches reach into three continents. In the ancient world, Greece was in the right place at the right time. It was, indeed, a "corner store," the inevitable meeting place of ancient European, African, and Asian cultures. Temporally, the coming of age and flowering of ancient Greece coincided with arguably the most decisive turning point in human history.

The Greeks, however, have also been at the mercy of their strategic location, finding themselves over and over again in the wrong place at the wrong time. Trapped at the crossroads between east and west, they became a prize everyone else wanted, the battleground where foreigners from several continents fought their wars, wars in which Greeks not infrequently fought on both sides.

THE FIRST GREEK CIVILIZATION At around 3000 B.C., the first real flare of Greek civilization began when a wave of Anatolians brought to the islands and mainland a new skill (the working of bronze), a new language (a forefather to Greek), and with them the Aegean age. Their principal areas of settlement were the Cycladic Islands, the eastern shores of Central Greece and the Peloponnese, and

Dateline

- **40000 B.C.** The first traceable human incursions into Greece appear in several caves in the Louros Valley.

- **3000 B.C.** Waves of Anatolians introduce bronze-working and an early form of Greek to Crete, the Cyclades, and the mainland, beginning the Bronze Age.

- **1700 B.C.** A massive earthquake on Crete destroys the great Minoan palaces at Knossos and Phaestos. Undeterred, Minoans rebuild even more luxurious digs.

- **1500 B.C.** A volcanic eruption on Santorini (Thira)—one of the most violent on record—buries ancient Akrotiri and helps speed Minoan decline.

- **1400–1100 B.C.** The Mycenaean civilization rises and abruptly collapses, sending Greece into centuries of strife and cultural isolation.

- **800–600 B.C.** Glints of Greece's resurrection appear in the form of city-states. Homer and Hesiod initiate the first great age of Greek poetry.

- **525–485 B.C.** Aeschylus, Sophocles, and Euripides are born; Athens theater scene markedly improves.

- **490–480 B.C.** Xerxes, emperor of Persia, invades Greece, burning Athens to the ground. Greeks get revenge on land at Marathon and Plataea, and at sea near Salamis and Mycale.

- **431–404 B.C.** Peloponnesian War leads to the fall of Athens and its empire.

- **399 B.C.** Socrates is tried for heresy and sentenced to death. Given the chance to escape, he declines and drinks hemlock potion. Plato immortalizes him in *The Apology* and other philosophical dialogues.

continues

Crete. Farmers surrounded by ocean, they became equally at home behind the plow and at the helm. The island civilizations' enchanting art and buried cities easily captivate the imagination. The rich palace culture of Crete, prosperous and unfortified, suggests that for a time the early Aegean farmers and seafarers had little to fear from their neighbors. Mother Nature, however, was another matter. Greece has always been prey to great seismic events, few more dramatic than the earthquake triggered near Santorini around 1450 B.C., sinking part of the island, leveling Akrotiri, and giving birth to the myth of Atlantis.

But it took more than earthquakes to eclipse the **Minoans.** Newcomers from the north—the Achaeans or "blow-ins"—were already on their way, full of bold aggression and a few bright ideas. The tongue they spoke and wrote, linear B, was an early form of the Greek spoken today. Within 300 or 400 years, they had developed an extensive and powerful civilization named in retrospect after its supposed capital city, Mycenae, in the Argolis. The **Mycenaean** civilization—a loose confederation of warlords and clan chiefs—combined a form of early feudalism, commerce, and piracy to amass considerable wealth and clout in the eastern Mediterranean. By the mid–second millennium, the Mycenaeans had colonized the Aegean coast of Anatolia and controlled Crete, whose culture they in part absorbed. Their trade connections, whether direct or indirect, extended as far as Britain and Scandinavia. Empire arguably entered the Greek imagination with the Mycenaeans and, like most acquired tastes, was very slow to leave.

After making its mark and wreaking more than its share of havoc in the world, the Mycenaean civilization suffered a mysterious dissolution. By 1100 B.C., most of its great centers had burned to the ground and been all but abandoned. Fortunately, beyond the ruins and artifacts it left behind, the Mycenaean world managed to inspire Greece's greatest poet, Homer, who preserved forever this lost world in his *Iliad* and *Odyssey.*

By the late 12th century B.C., the **Dorians** brought fresh and fierce blood, making the Peloponnese their stronghold. What followed, for several centuries, was a period of cultural isolation and hardship. By the 8th century, however, the Greeks were back on their feet and in their boats. Once again they reached out to the wider Mediterranean and Near Eastern world, founding new colonies and re-establishing old trade connections. Meanwhile, at home, without great upheaval, a revolution was taking place. Increasingly, the freeborn, landholding farmer was calling the shots. Village clusters grew into independent city-states, united in a common cult to their presiding deity, who replaced the ancient king. The polis, or city-state, which became the standard of Greek social organization, was comprised of a small mass of land with a governmental, cultic, cultural, and commercial center. The polis was not a Greek invention. Like so many other ideas, it was something they borrowed, adapted, and brought to full fruition.

The **preclassical** or **archaic** period (800 to 500 B.C.) saw the emergence of hundreds of such city-states, each with its own face. The one common denominator of all Greeks, irrespective of city, was their language, which made them more or less comprehensible to one another. Even so, there was as yet no sense of a unifying government, religion, or race. Greece was a patchwork waiting to be sewn together.

THE CLASSICAL AGE The classical age is synonymous with the emergence of **Athens** as the preeminent city-state in the Greek world. Peaking in the 5th century, the vision and achievements of this one insanely ambitious city conceived Western civilization. Whether in art or science, athletics or architecture, poetry or philosophy, Athens presided over the splendor that was classical Greece.

Athenian splendor, to be sure, had its dark side. The opportunities it offered were narrowly funneled to a minority of its population. Its radical democracy gave surprising power to the people, but "the people" meant only pure-blooded Athenian men—excluding women, slaves, and landed immigrants. Still more troubling was its foreign policy. After twice playing the crucial hand against Persian invaders, Athens created a permanent military alliance called the **Delian League,** whose members were eventually reduced to subject states. Its founding aim was to deter future Persian aggression, but it also served the convenient purpose of marginalizing Athens's greatest rivals, Corinth and Sparta. This play for power provoked Greece's first civil war, the so-called **Peloponnesian War,** whose scale and duration (431 to 404 B.C.) led to the complete collapse of Athens

- **338 B.C.** Battle of Chaironeia unifies Greece under Macedon rule.
- **336–323 B.C.** Alexander the Great establishes reign over a kingdom that stretches as far as Egypt and India.
- **323 B.C.** Worn out by a host of dissipations, Alexander dies in Babylon. His successors squabble amongst themselves, squandering great parts of his empire.
- **146 B.C.** After a series of wars, Rome crushes Greece, renaming the northern parts Macedonia, the southern and central parts Achaea.
- **1st & 2nd centuries A.D.** New Testament is written in Greek dialect, the *koine.* Local author John of Patmos gets the last word, in Revelation.
- **A.D. 328** Constantine the Great moves his capital to Byzantium.
- **476** Rome falls to the Goths; Greece is left to fester for 700 years.
- **1204** Fourth Crusade sacks Constantinople and divides up the empire.
- **1453** Constantinople falls to Sultan Mehmet II, initiating more than 350 years of Turkish domination.
- **1571** Turkish fleet destroyed at Lepanto, undermining aura of invincibility.
- **1821–1829** Greeks fight War of Independence, enlisting Britain, Russia, and France as allies.
- **1833** Lacking royal blood of their own, Greeks crown Prince Otho of Bavaria as their first king.
- **1863–1913** Reign of George I sees Greece regain much of its lost territory.
- **1913** King George I is assassinated at Thessaloniki.
- **1917** Greece enters World War I aligned with Britain and France.

continues

- **1919** Greece occupies Izmir; Mustafa Kemal (Atatürk) rises from ranks of military to stir Turkish nationalism.
- **1923** The Greco-Turkish War ends in disaster for Greece.
- **1924–1928** Greece declares itself a republic, but political upheaval leads to 11 military coups.
- **1936–1944** Dictator George Metaxas takes over, modeling his Greece on the examples of Mussolini and Hitler.
- **1940–1941** Italy invades Greece, followed by more determined German forces.
- **1944** Greece is liberated; civil war soon breaks out in Athens and the north.
- **1949** Civil war ends.
- **1952** Greek women win the right to vote.
- **1967** Operation Prometheus establishes military junta; long hair, miniskirts, and Euripides are banned.
- **1974** Turkey invades Cyprus; the junta collapses and a democratic republic is established.
- **1981** Greece joins EC; PASOK victory brings Andreas Papandreou to power.
- **1989** Papandreou government collapses under corruption charges.
- **1993** After a 3-year hiatus, PASOK and Papandreou are victorious at the polls.
- **1996** Papandreou resigns and is succeeded by Costas Simitis.
- **1997** Athens is selected as the site for the 2004 Olympic Games.
- **1998** The European Council begins entry negotiations with Cyprus with a view towards its inclusion in the European Union.
- **1999** The growth rate of the Greek economy remains strong for a fourth consecutive year, surpassing most of

continues

and its empire, something Greece's most formidable enemies had never come close to accomplishing.

One legacy of the Peloponnesian War was the revival of empire as a Greek aspiration. Sparta, Corinth, Thebes, and a resuscitated Athens were powerhouses in the scramble for domination, but neither one nor all of them proved a match for the armies of **Philip II of Macedon,** who at Chaironeia in 338 B.C. left no doubt who was king. The independent Greek city-state was at this point history. Bound by a common oath to the Macedonian royal house, the Greek people were of one mind and one will for the first time—and both belonged to Philip, who promised to pay back an ancient debt with the conquest of Persia.

THE HELLENISTIC EPOCH Philip's promise was kept by his son **Alexander,** who ascended to his assassinated father's throne in 336 B.C. Alexander—king at 20, conqueror of the Persian empire at 27, and dead at 33—is one of the world's barely believable legends. Like Achilles, he was to live gloriously and die young. But that is where the likeness ends, for the siege of Troy was a turkey shoot compared to the Asian campaigns of Alexander, which brought him south to Egypt and east to India, where his army convinced him to call it a day.

After Alexander drank himself to death at Babylon in 323 B.C., 20 years of chaos ensued as his generals fought over his empire. The Greek world was now stretched across the east Mediterranean and was neither confined to nor centered in territorial Greece. Alexandria in Egypt and Pergamon in Asia Minor far outshone any city in Greece as centers of learning and the arts. In these new centers, the language was Greek but the culture was international.

ROMAN CONQUEST Without a center, the empire of Alexander unraveled. By the close of the 3rd century B.C., Rome had emerged as the power to be reckoned with. Philip V of Macedon made his first crucial error in allying himself with Carthage, an enemy Rome had resolved to eliminate. Predictably, the Roman army, after defeating Carthage in 201 B.C., moved on to Macedonia. Unpredictably, the Roman commander Flamininus celebrated his victory over Philip by granting independence to the cities of Greece. The Greek cities, in turn, celebrated their new freedom by fighting among themselves and resisting Roman "protection," which they resented as an intrusion. Eventually, after a number of limited military engagements, Roman patience wore thin and Rome crushed Greece, annexing it to the ever-expanding empire. Under Roman occupation, Northern Greece became the province of Macedonia, and Central and Southern Greece the province of Achaea.

Everyone knows that Rome fell, but not until it had been divided. Diocletian began the process of partition in the late 3rd century. Hoping to shore up an unwieldy and threatened empire, he divided it in two, north and south. The imperial power was, in turn, divided four ways, between two emperors (*Augusti*), each with a designated successor (*Caesar*). Diocletian appointed himself the southern *Augustus* and remained in Rome, while his *Caesar*, Galerius, established his own court in Thessaloniki. Each of these decisions bore implications for the future, underlining the pre-eminence of the southern empire and suggesting that its capital might well move east. As it happened, Diocletian's fragile tetrarchy fell apart amidst civil war, from which Constantine eventually emerged in A.D. 324 as Diocletian's sole successor. Recently crowned and well-disposed to Christianity, Constantine moved his capital in A.D. 328 from Rome to the banks of the Bosporos, to the Greek city of Byzantium, which soon became known as Constantinopolis, "the city of Constantine." The reign of Byzantium had begun and would survive for over a millennium.

- its European partners, and the Minister of Finance speaks of a "new Greece."
- **2000** The Panhellenic Socialist Movement, led by Costas Simitis, wins a third term. Greece applies to become the 12th member of the Eurozone, exchanging the millennia-old drachma for the toddling euro. The Olympic flame is lit at Olympia for the 2000 Summer Games in Sydney, as Athens awaits its turn in 2004.

RULE BYZANTIUM   **Constantinople** sat atop Byzantium like a crown on a commoner's head. The emperor sacked his own empire to adorn his "Nova Roma," built like the old Rome on seven hills, a city of indescribable splendor dedicated in A.D. 330. Seven years later, Constantine lay on his deathbed, his conversion to Christianity complete. When Rome took the sword from the Goths in A.D. 476, its fall was presumably all but inaudible within the secure walls of Constantinople.

Less than a century later, Muhammad was born in the Arabian desert city of Mecca. His birth was barely noted in Mecca much less in Constantinople, but in his name the walls of Constantinople would a thousand years later come down. In the meantime, Constantinople was the shining center of the Christian world, a unique fusion of the secular and the ecclesiastical.

For reasons more parochial than perceptive, the Byzantine chapter is at best abridged in most Western histories. The story of the Byzantine Empire is far too vast to be encapsulated here. What is essential to note, however, is that from its Greco-Roman origins it became profoundly multiethnic, interacting with the Islamic Near East as well as the Latin West and becoming entangled with regions as far-flung as Sicily, Cyprus, Egypt, Georgia, Bulgaria, Syria, and the Holy Land. The identification of "Greece" with Byzantium—the city and the empire—is complex and problematic. The tightest knot here is religion, not race. Byzantium, after all, was not only a political state but also the center of Christian Orthodoxy, whose baptismal waters ran thicker than blood.

THE ECLIPSE OF GREEK CIVILIZATION   The strategic position of Constantinople, as well as its power and wealth, made it a pole of attraction for foreign invaders. The most profound threat came from the **Turks,** who by the end of the 11th century were the controlling power in the east. This provoked the Latin West to intervene with a series of crusades, whose unproclaimed purpose was revealed by the crusaders' plundering of the Byzantine empire while en route to the Holy Land. Finally, in 1204, the Fourth Crusade besieged Constantinople. The Roman Catholic pope and the Orthodox Patriarch of Constantinople had excommunicated each other exactly 50 years earlier, creating a schism which made the sacking of Constantinople and the slaughter of its people a little less unthinkable.

Despite a Byzantine revival in the 13th and 14th centuries, the Turks' conquest of Greece was imminent. In 1452, a new sultan, **Mehmet II,** began construction of a massive fortress on the European side of the Bosporos. In less than two months, the walls of Constantinople, perhaps the most formidable in the world, were breached and their defenders overwhelmed. Within 8 years of the fall of Constantinople, Mehmet was in complete control of the Greek world, a yoke that would not lighten for another 3½ centuries, during which time the tenacity of Hellenic memory was put to its ultimate test.

Meanwhile, the Greek people once again found themselves in the wrong place at the wrong time. Caught between the two greatest powers in the eastern Mediterranean—the **Ottoman Empire** and the **Republic of Venice**—the Greeks hosted one conflict after another. In one such engagement, a Venetian cannonball struck a Turkish store of gunpowder on the Acropolis, blowing the roof off the Parthenon. Mercifully, the majority of Greeks now lived in Asia Minor and in Central and Northern Greece, which rarely saw combat. It fell to them, instead, to finance the sultan's wars with their taxes and to feed them with fresh recruits.

While only Muslims could hold public office or positions of power in the empire, everyone else was free to practice the religion of their birth. Everyday Greek life fell under the jurisdiction of Orthodox priests and primates, who conducted the schools, seminaries, and monasteries. This daily fact of life preserved the Byzantine fusion of the sacred and the secular, and meant that "Greek" remained all but synonymous with "Orthodox Christian." Measured against the atrocities and brutalities of European regimes during the same period, the subjects of the sultan fared no worse and perhaps better than their European counterparts. This is not to say that Greeks were content with their lot, nor that they had forgotten Constantine, still waiting for resurrection.

A GREEK RESURGENCE The revolutionary period may be traced to the close of the 17th century, when the Ottoman Empire began losing more battles than it won, and succession became a bloody, unpredictable affair. Soon the central Ottoman authority faced myriad regional and local rivals. And, as the 18th century dawned, revolution was in the air in America and Europe.

The Greeks knew that on their own, they would be no match for the Ottomans, and so they looked around for powerful friends—Russians, British, French. In addition, a formidable Greek diaspora stretched from Moscow to Calcutta. In 1814, a band of Greek expatriates in Odessa founded the *Etairia Filike,* the **"Friendly Society."** This revolutionary society resolved, under the leadership of Alexander Ypsilantis, to strike at the Ottomans simultaneously in the Peloponnese and in the Balkans.

Not at all according to plan, the Friendly Society was upstaged by **Ali Pasha,** a Turkish governor who provoked the sultan to war. Hoping that a distracted sultan would be a vulnerable sultan, Ypsilantis and his would-be army crossed the River Prut, dividing the Russian and the Ottoman empires. Only weeks later, in March 1821, Bishop Germanos of Patras, himself a member of the *Etairia Filike*, raised the standard of revolt over the monastery of Ayia Lavra, near Kalavrita (southeast of Patras), which still lays claim to being the first town liberated in the War of Independence. Meanwhile, the army of liberation made its way across what is now Hungary to face the sultan's elite corps of Janissaries. The outcome, in June 1821 at Dragasani (northwest of Bucharest), was simple slaughter, which is not to say that the Greeks lost.

The sacrifice at Dragasani provided the needed spark for revolution. One by one the Turkish strongholds in the Peloponnese—all but Nafplion—fell to the Greek rebels. Turks, who had for generations made their homes in the Peloponnese, ran for their lives. Thousands of Turks were tortuously executed, while many Jews were crucified. When the sultan, after dealing with Ali Pasha, dispatched his armies into the Peloponnese, a betting man would have put his money on the Turks—and would have lost. Momentum is a mysterious force, and for now, it was on the Greeks' side.

Despite some setbacks, by 1826 the Turks had taken most of the Peloponnese and were laying siege to the Acropolis. Without European assistance, the Greek cause was clearly lost. The reluctant powers of the West proclaimed an independent Greek principality at the Treaty of London in 1827. After the allies arrived in force, they annihilated the combined Turkish and Egyptian fleets in Navarino Bay. Meanwhile, the Greeks were learning that with friends like Britain, France, and Russia, they barely needed enemies at all. For the next hundred years, they would be a pawn moved around a board whose edges they could barely envision.

After the allies had helped themselves to some of its choice portions, the lines of the new Greek free state were drawn to include the Peloponnese, Central Greece, and the Cyclades. Its 800,000 inhabitants represented less than a third of the ethnically Greek population, and its first appointed leader was **Ioannis Kapodistrias,** a former minister of the Tsar. One measure of his popularity was his assassination in 1831. In the 1832 Treaty of Constantinople, the signatory powers decided that Greece would not be a republic, but rather a protectorate with a hereditary monarchy. However, Greeks, who had discarded monarchy more than 2,000 years earlier, were without royal blood of their own. The King of Bavaria offered his 17-year-old son Otho, a Catholic. Greek gratitude was not overflowing.

All of **King Otho's** instincts ran in the direction of autocracy, and he tried to rule by decree without a constitution. When the army joined antigovernment demonstrators in 1843, Otho reluctantly gave his people a conservative constitution, which he followed some of the time. Under the new constitution, **Ioannis Kolettis** rose to significance as prime minister and gave voice to an idea, a "Great Idea," which Otho was incapable of realizing. For this and a host of other reasons, Otho was persuaded to abdicate his throne in 1862.

THE GREAT IDEA   Impoverished and humiliated, the Greek people had lost most everything of any magnitude, except their imaginations. The "Great Idea" (Megali Idea) was quite simply to reunite the Greek people, not by bringing them to Greece but by bringing Greece to them. It was—though disguised and diminished—the old idea of empire, a third Greek civilization "spanning two continents and five seas." Within the imaginary boundaries drawn by the Great Idea, there lived, of course, not just Greeks. In fact, in some regions, Greeks were in the minority. But so it had been in the two previous Greek empires of Alexander and Constantine.

As its contribution to the Great Idea, Britain gave back the Ionian Islands in 1864. In the same year, Greece received a new constitution, in theory further limiting the powers of the king and extending franchise to a wider spectrum of Greeks. A major voice across the next two decades was that of **Kharilaos Trikoupis,** who served seven terms as prime minister and implemented major economic and social reforms aimed at both modernizing and Westernizing Greece. By 1897, Greece—overextended and watching its major export (currants) plummet in price—fell into national bankruptcy. Its brief period of reform, out of gas, was stopped in its tracks. The failure of a revolution in Crete represented a disheartening setback to Greek aspirations, but the ceding of Thessaly and Arta to Greece, after the Russian-Turkish War of 1877, was an unexpected boon. Macedonia, an essential yet elusive element of the Great Idea, remained an obsession and frustration, as it does today.

GREECE IN THE 20TH CENTURY   The new century was marked from the beginning by upheaval. In 1909, the Athenian garrison established a Military League, which exiled the political parties and placed in power a fresh new voice from Crete, **Eleftherios Venizelos,** who dominated Greek politics for the next quarter of a century. Like Trikoupis, Venizelos was a reformer. He was also a charismatic expansionist, who soon led the Greeks into war against the Turks, this time with astounding success. Greece emerged from the Balkan Wars (1912 to 1913) with its territory increased by two-thirds. Modern Greece now included southern Epirus, Macedonia, part of western Thrace, and the islands of Samos, Hios, and Crete. These were great gains, but not as great as the idea implanted in the people's imaginations to liberate the millions of Greeks still unredeemed in the Ottoman Empire.

Before long, Europe was at war and Greece's new king, crowned Constantine XII, favored neutrality, while Venizelos argued for a military alliance with Britain, France, and Russia. The result was a national schism, in which Venizelos established his own government in Thessaloniki to rival that of the king's in Athens. Once again the protectors intervened, this time to remove Constantine; Venizelos returned to Athens as prime minister alongside a new and slightly more congenial king, Alexander. Venizelos soon realized his intention to bring Greece into the war on the side of the Entente, and Greece was amply rewarded for its loyalty. As a result of the postwar negotiations of 1919 and 1920, Greece not only added western and eastern Thrace (except for Constantinople) and the islands of Imbros and Tenedos, but was also authorized to occupy the coastal city of Smyrna (Izmir) and a large swathe of Ottoman Asia Minor. And so Greece—itself a protectorate—became a protector. Greece again occupied two continents and touched five seas.

Venizelos failed to anticipate, however, the Turkish nationalism that the Greek occupation of Aegean Turkey would ignite. As the Greeks began to secure their military grip on coastal Turkey, Mustafa Kemal, **Atatürk** ("Father of the Turks"), was rallying a new nation to its feet. In 1920, the Turks announced their own state in defiance of Greece and its protectors. The Greek dream was about to become a nightmare. Venizelos was swept out of office, and in the winter of 1921, the Greeks decided to confront Atatürk and to invade Anatolia. Early victories lured Greek forces deeper into central Turkey, where they far exceeded their own resources. The Turks drove the Greeks back to the sea, seized Smyrna, and massacred some 30,000 people.

At the 1923 Treaty of Lausanne, the Greek nation state lost eastern Thrace, all territory in Asia Minor, and Imbros and Tenedos. More painful was the exchange of refugees called for by the redrawing of boundaries—roughly

1.3 million spilled into Greece. The boundaries of mainland Greece were now more or less fixed and its population rendered remarkably homogeneous, at least in terms of religion—the decisive factor in determining who belonged in Greece and who did not.

Not surprisingly, Greece entered a period of profound turmoil after the Greco-Turkish War. Punctuated by a series of dictatorships and military coups, Greece lurched towards the republican constitution of 1927, under which an old legend, Eleftherios Venizelos, returned to power and accomplished a number of important reforms. The world economic crisis of the early 1930s meant more political chaos for Greece; General **George Metaxas** was called on to restore order, which he did in his own way with the notorious "Regime of the Fourth of August 1936," modeled after those of his mentors, Mussolini and Hitler. The Greek parliament, to say the least, was out of session and would not reconvene until 1944.

The only good thing to be said of the 1930s was that they were nowhere near as hideous as the 1940s. Ironically, it was Metaxas's famous *"Ochi!"* ("No!") to Mussolini, whom he admired, that helped plunge Greece into World War II, a war Metaxas was trying desperately to sit out. The dramatic Greek victory over Italy's Alpine Division and the ensuing Greek offensive brought a moment of elation followed by years of horror. Provoked by the arrival of a British expeditionary force in Greece, Hitler invaded Greece on a massive scale in the spring of 1941. The fall of Greece was rapidly followed by that of Crete, where the Germans would continue to pay a high price for their victory.

There is no describing the sufferings of the Greek people under the wartime occupational forces of Germany, Italy, and Bulgaria. The winter famine of 1941 and 1942, which killed 100,000 people, the massacre of more than 1,400 Greeks at Kalavrita, and the relocation of over 50,000 Jews from Thessaloniki to Auschwitz provided a bitter taste of what the occupation meant. Regrettably, the Greek resistance was deeply divided against itself. Its two main bodies—ELAS (the National Popular Liberation Army) and EAM (the National Liberation Front)—were both leftist and to a degree communist in their politics, while their right-wing rival, the far less significant EDES (National Greek Democratic League), spent its time undermining both the Germans and ELAS/EAM. Clearly it would take more than the removal of the Germans and their allies to bring peace to Greece.

After the liberation of Greece in 1944, Greece had a new set of protectors and a fresh set of problems. Churchill and Stalin had already agreed that postwar Greece would fall under Britain's sphere of influence, which among other things meant that by December 1944, British troops and ELAS resistance fighters were warring against each other, leaving 11,000 dead in the Battle of Athens alone. And the ensuing civil war would be allowed to end only when it reached an acceptably anticommunist outcome. When Britain's ability to interfere was exhausted, the United States took its turn, testing the Truman Doctrine and its latest experimental weapon, napalm. There is no easy map through the Greek terror and chaos of the 5 years following World War II.

POSTWAR GREECE   In the shambles that was Greece in 1950, a general election was held, with 44 parties vying for power. As postwar reconstruction got underway, some of the same foreign fists that had helped destroy the country were now opening wide and extending aid. The Dodecanese were ceded to Greece in 1948, comprising the final revision to today's national boundaries. Greece became a charter member of the United Nations in 1946, joined

NATO in 1952, and secured associate status in the EC (European Community) in 1962, with the promise of full membership in 1984.

The 1960s brought radical change. After the political right, with considerable support from the United States, had more or less held the Greek stage for a decade (from 1952 to 1963), **Georgios Papandreou's** Center Union Party rose to power and undertook, with the release of all political prisoners, to close wounds still open since the civil war. Together with his son Andreas (formerly chair of the economics department at the University of California at Berkeley), whom he named minister of the economy, Papandreou also launched a program of ambitious reforms. Furthermore, Greece's new 23-year-old king, Constantine II, seemed congenial to Papandreou's government and its direction. Civil harmony and social progress appeared within reach, until Cyprus—an independent republic since 1959—erupted into violence. Papandreou, already doubtful whether Greece's alliance with the West was in its best interests, was provoked by the Cyprus problem to explore other options. It was when Papandreou attempted to confront and control the Greek military that Greece's demons were again released. The king backed the military, Papandreou resigned, and the king canceled elections. Greek politics were being conducted once more in the streets. In fact, the next regime would come rolling down those streets, in tanks.

The junta of April 21, 1967—code-named "Operation Prometheus"—brought Greece to new depths of repression and despair. **"The Colonels,"** as they were known—Papadoulos, Pattakos, and Makarevzos, by name—were little else than self-serving nonentities, who ruled with a great deal of violence and with very few ideas. They banned any imagined challenge to their political and moral fundamentalism—from long hair to miniskirts to Euripides—and purged the country of every conceivable opponent, including the king. In fact, early on in the regime, one of the three colonels, Georgios Papadoulos, eclipsed the others, appropriating one ministry after another until he became a political one-man band. He in turn was removed by Dimitrios Ioannides, the former head of the secret police, who made the regime still more repressive. Sensing that he stood for nothing but fear, Ioannides hoped to rally the Greek people behind him by confronting the Turks in Cyprus. The result was still another Greek disaster and one more sign that the junta was a savage farce.

Four days after the Turkish invasion of Cyprus in 1974, former prime minister Constantine Karamanlis was summoned from exile in Paris to Athens to pick up the pieces of a shredded democracy. Within a year, the monarchy was abolished and Greece had a new constitution, establishing a democratic republic modeled after that of France. Since that time, Greece has solidified its democratic institutions and realized a new prosperity both as a sovereign state and as a member of the European Union.

2 A Legacy of Art & Architecture

Whether we dig or dive (being restless mariners, the Greeks lost many of their treasures to the sea) into the Greek past, what we find is mostly things and not words, a rubble of stones and pots. Even after vases are reconstructed and walls are rebuilt, they don't speak to us or tell us their stories. At best, they mumble. Like the Oracle at Dodona, whose voice spoke through the sacred oaks, the past speaks through the ruins of cities and wrecks of ships, but not without professional assistance, in our time via the increasingly accurate stories of archaeologists.

Another bridge to the prehistoric past is offered by ancient authors who wrote about what for them was already the remote past. Until recently, Homer's stories of Helen, Achilles, and Odysseus were assumed to be as much works of fantasy as the stories of Tolkien. Troy was assumed to be no more historical than Mirkwood. Likewise, Euripides's stories of human sacrifice, and Plato's accounts of lost Atlantis. Modern archaeology, however, has illuminated and certified the accounts of these and other ancient writers.

THE DIGGERS   The most notorious instance of modern shovel being led by ancient book is surely that of **Heinrich Schliemann's** discovery of **Troy.** He wasn't entirely alone in thinking that Homer wrote about real times and real places, but he went further than anyone else to prove it. Schliemann was a man with a single obsession: to unearth Homer's Troy. At age 7 he swore to find Troy, and at 48 he stuck his shovel into the mound at **Hissarlik** in northwestern Turkey, where he eventually unearthed Homer's ancient city. To get there he had used the *Iliad* as a divining rod, leading him from text to stone, from poetry to prehistory.

From Troy, Schliemann went on to other Bronze Age sites straight from the pages of Homer. His excavations at **Mycenae, Tiryns,** and **Orchomenos**—the three cities called "golden" by Homer—were characterized by the same bold and impetuous enthusiasm, genius, and miscalculation. By the time of his death in 1890, the shape and stature of the Mycenaean world had risen from the pages of Homer to open sight.

What Schliemann was to the Mycenaean world, **Arthur Evans** became to the still earlier and more fantastic world of the Minoans. Evans's initial interest in **Crete** was linguistic, and he went there to test a theory of hieroglyphic interpretation. What he found astounded him and the rest of the world. At **Knossos,** Evans unearthed the all but unknown Minoan civilization, the legendary and splendorous kingdom of Minos. Homer had once again proved to be a man of his word. Indeed, the world of the late Bronze Age—the geographical and cultural context of the *Iliad* and the *Odyssey*—as it continues to emerge from excavations in the Peloponnese, on Crete, and throughout the East Mediterranean, looks more and more as Homer described it.

THE SITES   The ancient Greeks were convinced that there are, here and there, portals or openings into the next world, the world beyond this one. They even found a few to their satisfaction, like **Eleusis, Dodona,** and **Delphi.** Entrances to the old world, the world before this one, are still easier to find, especially in Greece. Nowhere is the archaeological "water table" any higher. A little digging, almost anywhere, and the past, the ancient past, is uncovered.

There is evidence of human habitation in mainland Greece as early as 40000 B.C. Several caves in the **Louros River Valley** in Epirus have yielded deposits from the middle and late Paleolithic period. Hunters and gatherers, however, traveling light, left only faint traces behind. By contrast, the settled communities of the Neolithic period, though 6,000 to 8,000 years old, left enough evidence behind to be read like a book. This is where the story of ancient Greece begins, with the first agricultural settlements. The site at **Sesklo,** in Thessaly, has given its name to a thriving, 6th to 5th millennium agricultural civilization, which found no need for fortifications, produced fine pottery, and engaged in trade with nearby islands. Mostly what we find here are private spaces, modest homes of mud brick on stone foundations.

Only a thousand years later, at the nearby site of **Dimini,** we find signs that life had changed, dramatically. Fortification walls, arranged in concentric rings, tell of social division and turbulence. On the hill, a great house, whose plan points towards the later *megara* or palaces of the Mycenaeans, indicates that already there was a human heap, with a few on the top and most at the bottom. Here, in these stones, the focusing of power, the accumulation of wealth, and the organization of society are recognizably underway. From here it is only a matter of time and development to the feudal hilltop citadels and palaces of the Bronze Age—**Mycenae, Athens,** and **Tiryns,** to mention a few—and from there to the city-states and empires of the archaic and classical periods.

The first question to ask of any site is "why here?" Before any people build, they look around for a place to build—and their choice of site is revealing. Is the construction to be open or closed to its surroundings? Porous or defensible? What will it reach for or look to, and on what will it turn its back? Before we concern ourselves with whether a temple is of the Doric, Ionic, or Corinthian order, we need to remember, for instance, that the word temple (*templum* in Latin, *hiera* in Greek) does not refer to a building but to something sacred, a sacred place or object, to which the building is a secondary response. Buildings only mark or point to temples. Nowhere is this more clear than at **Delphi.** Delphi is first of all itself a *templum,* a sanctuary, which accounts for all of the constructions located there. While the latter lie in ruins, the power of the place endures. Thus the absence of temple buildings on **Minoan Crete** does not mean that the Minoans were without temples. Their temples, their sacred places or environs, were instead the surrounding mountaintops and caves—notably **Mount Ida** and the **Dicteon Cave,** by which and in whose embrace they laid their palaces, such as **Knossos** and **Phaestos.** The Mycenaeans, in contrast, occupied and fortified the peaks, building mountaintop citadels like **Mycenae** and **Tiryns** for their royalty. Still later, in the city-states of archaic and classical Greece, the mountaintops were returned to the gods and goddesses, where they were housed in royal fashion.

The next thing we notice at most every ancient site is the absence of private or domestic structures. We find stones—not brick or wood, but stones. After the Neolithic period, cut stones were mostly reserved for palaces, temples, public buildings, and fortifications. Private homes were made mostly of wood beams and sunbaked brick. For the most part, these vanished quickly, without a trace, like their inhabitants. What endured were the structures, the pillars, as it were, of society.

THE GODS & GODDESSES   The ancient Greeks were neither the first nor the last of peoples to acknowledge the existence and activity of forces, personal and impersonal, beyond their grasp and control. Wisdom and piety began, then as always, with knowing where to draw the line between what lay within human control and what lay beyond human control. No line, however, could be in more constant flux and dispute. Birth, death, agriculture, war, travel, commerce, weather, health, beauty, art, love—all of the ingredients of life as we know it—were realms where humans and gods had their hands in the same pot. One minute everything seemed to depend on human initiative and energy; the next minute human effort appeared to count for nothing. The controversial 5th-century philosopher Protagoras, a friend of the playwright Euripides, began his famous theological treatise with the confession that everything about the gods—whether or not they exist and what they may be like—outstrips human understanding, both because the subject is so obscure and because life is so short.

In the Greek imagination, then, the world was full of divine forces. Death, sleep, love, fate, memory, laughter, panic, rage, day, night, justice, victory—all

Principal Olympian Gods & Goddesses

Greek Name	Latin Name	Description
Zeus	Jupiter	Son of Kronos and Rhea, high god, ruler of Olympus. Thunderous sky god, wielding bolts of lightning. Patron-enforcer of the rites and laws of hospitality.
Hera	Juno	Daughter of Kronos and Rhea, queen of the sky. Sister and wife of Zeus. Patroness of marriage.
Demeter	Ceres	Daughter of Kronos and Rhea, sister of Hera and Zeus. Giver of grain and fecundity. Goddess of the mysteries of Eleusis.
Poseidon	Neptune	Son of Kronos and Rhea, brother of Zeus and Hera. Ruler of the seas. Earth-shaking god of earthquakes.
Hestia	Vesta	Daughter of Kronos and Rhea, sister of Hera and Zeus. Guardian of the hearth fire and of the home.
Hephaestos	Vulcan	Son of Hera, produced by her parthenogenetically. Lord of volcanoes and of fire. Himself a smith, the patron of crafts employing fire (metalworking and pottery).
Ares	Mars	Son of Zeus and Hera. The most hated of the gods. God of war and strife.
Hermes	Mercury	Son of Zeus and an Arcadian mountain nymph. Protector of thresholds and crossroads. Messenger-god, patron of commerce and eloquence. Companion-guide of souls en route to the underworld.
Apollo	Phoebus	Son of Zeus and Leto. Patron-god of the light of day, and of the creative genius of poetry and music. The god of divination and prophecy.
Artemis	Diana	Daughter of Zeus and Leto. Mistress of animals and of the hunt. Chaste guardian of young girls.
Athena	Minerva	Daughter of Zeus and Metis, born in full-armor from the head of Zeus. Patroness of wisdom and of war. Patron-goddess of the city-state of Athens.
Dionysos	Dionysus	Son of Zeus and Semele, born from the thigh of his father. God of revel, revelation, wine, and drama.
Aphrodite	Venus	Born from the bright sea foam off the coast of Cyprus. Fusion of Minoan tree goddess and Near Eastern goddess of love and war. Daughter of Zeus. Patroness of love.

of the timeless, elusive forces confronted by humans—were named and numbered among the gods and goddesses with whom the Greeks shared their universe. Understandably, in such a world, the cities, homes, roads, gardens, mountains, caves, forests, and countrysides of ancient Greece were thick with temples, altars, shrines, and consecrated precincts, where people left their offerings and petitions, hoping to be blessed with or spared the gods' interventions. To make these forces more familiar and approachable, the Greeks (like every other ancient people) imagined their gods to be somehow like themselves. They were male and female, young and old, beautiful and deformed, gracious and withholding, lustful and virginal, sweet and fierce.

Most of the myriad divine forces, named and nameless, familiar and faceless, in the Greek tradition can be found in the pages of the two great poets of archaic Greece, **Hesiod** and **Homer**—but the "plotlines" driving the poets' stories are dominated by one particular family of divinities, the **Olympians,** the household of Zeus and Hera ensconced on a great mountain in the northeast corner of Thessaly. Thanks, in part, to the stature and notoriety bestowed on them by their poets, these gods and goddesses were not only cast in leading roles in the theaters of Greece but were also made the focal point for the civic cults of most Greek states and, in sum, became household words.

As told by the ancient poets, the "Lives of the Olympians" is nothing less than a Greek soap opera. They are notoriously petty, quarrelsome, spiteful, vain, frivolous, and insensitive. They resemble nothing so much as a dysfunctional brood of spoiled children, children who have never been taught or made to experience the cost, the consequences, of their own choices and actions. And how could it be otherwise with the Olympians? Not made to pay the ultimate price of death, they cannot know the cost of anything. With *ichor,* not blood, in their veins, their wounds—however deep—heal overnight. Fed on *ambrosia* ("not mortal") and *nektar* ("overcoming death"), they cannot go hungry, much less perish. When life is endless, everything is reversible.

THE GREEK THEATER   Ancient Greek **tragedy,** a unique art form developed in Athens in the 6th and 5th centuries B.C., was essentially musical. Greek music, the "realm of the Muses," encompassed what we know as poetry, dance, and music. Tragedy represented the fusion of all three—dramatic poetry, music, and dance—in a single art form.

The **Greek theater** was quite literally a "seeing-place," a place of shared spectacle and insight, where—during two annual festivals—the citizens of Athens and their guests assembled in the Theater of Dionysos to see the latest original work of their master playwrights. Here, before the eyes of thousands, the great figures of myth and legend—Agamemnon, Helen, Herakles, and others—appeared in open sight and reenacted the stories that had shaped the Greek imagination. The ultimate spectacle of the Greek theater was and is humanity: humanity denied, deified, bestialized, defiled, and restored, which is why the works of Aeschylus, Sophocles, and Euripides play today with undiminished power and poignancy.

In ancient Greece, every city deserving the name had its theater, many of which even today host **festival productions** of the ancient masterworks. The most eminent of these is held every summer in the stunning theater at **Epidaurus.** There are also performances in the ancient theaters of Dodona, Thasos, and Phillipi, as well as the archaeological site at Eleusis, which has an annual "Aeschylia" in honor of the founder of Greek tragedy. Other summer arts festivals include theatrical performances, notably the Athens Festival, held in the striking Odeum of Herodes Atticus on the southwest slope of the Acropolis. The Lycabettus Theater also stages a variety of performances, with a recent emphasis on contemporary and ethnic music. Additionally, the International Festival at Patras, the Epirotika Festival in Ioannina, the Hippokrateia Festival on Kos, the Demetria Festival in Thessaloniki, the Aegean Festival on Skiathos, the Molyvos Festival on Lesvos, and the Lefkada Festival include theatrical performances. In September, the Ithaki Theater Festival recognizes the work of the new generation of playwrights.

3 The Greek People

If you were truly to beware of Greeks bearing gifts, a visit to Greece would call for sleepless vigilance, for the Greeks are among the most spontaneously generous people you are likely ever to meet, provided you do not offend them. And they can be easily offended, for their pride matches their generosity. In a recent poll, it was shown, to no one's surprise, that the Greeks' pride in being Greek surpasses the ethnic satisfaction of any other European nation. More specifically, 97% of the Greek population are proud as punch to be Greek; only the Irish come close to this level, at 96%.

Although Greek politics sometimes resembles the sheer chaos of a circus fire, the social fabric remains intact: 99% of the Greek people speak Greek as their first language, and 98% belong to the Greek Orthodox Church. Elsewhere in the world, one might have to look in a Benedictine monastery to find the same level of homogeneity. The core of Greek society, however, remains the family; and this is unlikely to change anytime soon. In a 1997 poll, 9 out of 10 Greek youth (ages 15 to 29), when asked to identify the one most important thing in their lives, said the family. One begins to wonder whether the Cleavers might not have been Greek.

4 A Taste of Greece

Greek food and drink tell a long story. The ancient Athenians are said to have invented the first hors d'oeuvre trolley, and most Greek dinners still start off with *mezedes,* a selection of hot and cold dishes served on small plates and shared from the center of the table. Spit-roasted mutton, goat, and pork were what Patroclus prepared for Achilles's late-night dinner party in the *Iliad,* and you'll still find them featured on Greek menus (though pork, much less boar, has declined in popularity across the millennia and been upstaged by chicken). You'll also find the freshly netted catch of the day, reminiscent of ancient Aegean murals from Santorini or Minoan Crete. Other ancient staples were olives, figs, barley, and almonds—crops still draping the Greek countryside. Take away olive oil from Greek cooks and you might as well cut off their hands.

The distinctive flavor of Greek cuisine may be traced to oregano and lemons: oregano from the hillsides of Greece and lemons first hauled from South Asia at the urging of Empress Theodora. As the first lady of Byzantium, she used her imperial clout to encourage the importing of rice, lemons, and eggplant from India, all of which have helped condition the Greek palate. The soups and stews employing various pastas and tomato-based sauces are a Venetian contribution welcomed by Greek households, which until recently had no ovens. The Italians also brought with them a spree of Eastern spices—cinnamon, aniseed, pepper, cloves, and allspice—now well ensconced in the Greek diet. The Turks too left their mark with yogurt, the omnipresent kabob, and an inky sweet syrup imagined to be coffee. Finally, a Greek meal is likely to end with a flaky *filo* pastry—first brought from Persia in Byzantine times—soaked in honey, of which the ancient poets sang. There it is: the history of Greece on a plate.

A DINING PRIMER You probably already know about the common **taverna,** where you can usually find a number of grilled meats, including *souvlaki* (shish kebab to the Turks), commonly available in lamb, pork, and chicken, and *keftedes* (meatballs), usually fried (though on Hios they may turn out to be made of ground chickpeas and equally delicious). You may also be familiar with many of the other dishes, like the dependable Greek salad with feta cheese, the usually reliable *moussaka* (eggplant casserole, with lots of regional variation, often with minced meat) and *yemista* (tomatoes or green peppers filled with rice and sometimes minced meat), and the often bland but filling *pastitsio* (baked pasta).

Many tavernas still don't serve desserts, which are often very sweet. Examples include *baklava* (filo soaked in honey, which some Greeks insist is actually Turkish) and *halva* (a sort of nougat, sweeter yet and undeniably Turkish). Those with a serious sweet tooth may want to stop at a **zaharoplastion** (confectioner) or **patisserie,** as French bakeries are fairly common.

In some places, you'll find that the tavernas don't open for lunch and you may have to settle for a simpler **estiatorio,** where the menu may be not just limited, but nonexistent. Your few choices may all be on display in the kitchen or under steamed-over glass. Yes, it was made earlier and it's probably tepid—hot food is thought to be bad for the stomach—but it's likely to be tasty and even healthful. The oil it's swimming in is olive oil—no cholesterol there.

Another venue is the **ouzeri**—usually informal though not necessarily inexpensive—which serves ouzo, the clear anise-flavored national aperitif. Ouzo is especially intoxicating on an empty stomach—which is why ouzeries serve food, usually an assortment of *mezedes,* hearty appetizers eaten with bread: the common *tzatziki* (yogurt with cucumber and garlic), *taramosalata* (fish-roe dip), *skordalia* (hot garlic and beet dip), *melitzanosalata* (eggplant salad), *yigantes* (giant beans in tomato sauce), *dolmades* (stuffed grape leaves), grilled *kalamarakia* (squid), *oktapodi* (octopus), and *loukanika* (sausage).

There is also the **psarotaverna,** which specializes in fish and seafood. Fish is no longer abundant in Greek waters and trawling with nets is prohibited from mid-May to mid-October, so prices can sometimes be exorbitant. Often you'll have to settle for the smaller fish, such as *barbounia,* which are delicious if not overcooked. Ask locals to recommend a place for a fish dinner, always choose your own fish—in reputable places you shouldn't have to insist—and try to make sure it isn't switched on you.

Fast food is fast becoming common, especially pizza, which can be okay but rarely good. Many young Greeks seem to subsist on *gyros* (thin slices of meat slowly roasted on a vertical spit, sliced off, and served in pita bread). Here's a tip: if the spindle of meat is "skinny" in the morning, you should guess it isn't fresh and pass it by.

A few other warnings: Much of the squid served in Greece is frozen and many restaurants serve dreadful *keftedes, taramosalata,* and *melitzanasalata* made with more bread than any other ingredient. That's the bad news. The good news is that the bad news leaves you free to order things you may not have had before—grilled green or red peppers or a tasty snack of *kokoretsia* (grilled entrails)—or something you probably have had, such as Greek olives, but never with such variety and pizzazz.

To avoid the ubiquitous favorites-for-foreigners, you may prefer to indicate to your waiter that you'd like to have a look at the food display case, often

Insider Tip

Most restaurants, even very good restaurants, have no objection to meals comprised of multiple appetizers or mezedes, which is both the most interesting and the most economical way of putting a meal together.

The rules for tipping continue to perplex many visitors to Greece. Until the early 1990s, menus in restaurants and cafes usually had two columns—one for the price of the item, the other for its price with the mandatory service/ tip included. This practice has been abolished, and all you see now is one price, which includes a service charge (as well as the VAT tax and the local city tax). Although some menus clearly disclose the service charge, many neglect to make it clear. Effectively a tip, the charge is usually 13%. In addition, it remains a tradition to round off, by either telling the waiter to keep the change or giving him or her some reasonable extra. (A total tip of 15% is a generally acceptable compromise.)

It also used to be the practice in Greek restaurants that a "water boy" serviced your table separately from the main waiter, usually setting and clearing the table as well as providing fresh water. This practice has also pretty much disappeared—you're lucky if anyone brings water!—but if there is an assistant waiter, it is still the custom to leave a couple of hundred drachmas on the table.

positioned just outside the kitchen, and then point to what you'd like to order. Many restaurants are perfectly happy to have you take a look in the kitchen itself, but it's not a good idea to do this without checking first. Not surprisingly, you'll get the best value for your money, and the tastiest food, at establishments serving a predominantly Greek, rather than a tourist, clientele.

When it's not being used as filler, fresh Greek bread is generally tasty, substantial, nutritious, and inexpensive. If you're buying bread at a bakery, ask for *mavro somi* (black bread). It's almost always better than the more bland white stuff. An exception is the white bread in the *koulouria* (pretzel-like rolls covered with sesame seeds); you'll see Greeks buying them from street vendors on their way to work in the morning.

One of the most reliable of snacks is the ubiquitous *tiropita* (cheese pie), usually made with feta, though there are endless variations. On Naxos, the tiropita may look like the usual flaky round pastry but contain the excellent local cheese, *graviera*. In Metsovo, it may resemble cornbread and contain leeks and *metsovella,* a mild local cheese made from sheep milk. On Alonissos, the tiropita may contain the usual feta but be rolled in a big spiral and deep-fried. A close relative to the tiropita is *spanokopita* (spinach pie), which is also prepared in a variety of ways.

MEALS **Breakfast** is not an important meal to the Greeks. In the cities, you'll see people grabbing a *koulouri* (pretzel-like roll) as they hurry to work. Most hotels will serve a continental breakfast of bread or rolls with butter and jam, coffee and usually juice (often fresh), and occasionally yogurt. Better hotels may serve an American buffet with eggs, bacon, cheese, yogurt, and fresh fruit.

Lunch is typically a heavier meal in Greece than it is in most English-speaking countries, and most Greeks still take a siesta afterwards. Keep siesta hours, about 2 to 5pm, in mind when planning your own day, especially in more provincial destinations. (Even in Athens you should be considerate about contacting friends or acquaintances at home during these hours.)

Dinner is often an all-evening affair for Greeks, starting with mezedes at 7 or 8pm, and the main meal itself as late as 11pm. (You might consider a snack before joining Greek friends in their long evening meal.)

IN THE GLASS There's also history in the glass. Until classical times, most Greeks drank water at their meals and broke out the wine only for special occasions. Today you'll find both, side by side. The wines for which ancient Greeks were most famous—the wines of Hios and Lesvos—were sweet and thick, almost a sticky paste, requiring serious dilution of up to 20 parts water to 1 part wine, though Alexander the Great is said to have taken his wine "neat" until it killed him. A fine or not so fine Tokay might today come closest to the legendary wines of the Aegean Islands.

Today, the most characteristic Greek wine is *retsina,* or resinated wine. It is definitely an acquired taste and possibly an addictive one, as you will find yourself years later longing for Greece and a glass of retsina, all in the same breath. At first gulp, however, it's a bit like drinking your Christmas tree. The ancient Greeks were big on adding herbs and spices to their wine, but they threw in pine pitch mostly to wines they considered otherwise undrinkable. Draw your own conclusions. Most every village makes its own home-brewed retsina of which they are fiercely proud. If you prefer a more canonized blend, we recommend Kourtaki, available throughout Greece as well as overseas, in case you learn to crave the resinated cask. Otherwise, ask for *krasi*—Greek wine without the resin—of which there are many.

All of the controlled appellations of origin in Greece (identified by a blue banderole), however, are liqueur wines, such as the Mavrodaphne of Kefalonia or the Muscat of Limnos. Beyond these, 20 areas throughout Greece boast appellations of origin of superior quality (identified by a red banderole), including dry reds from western Macedonia and Crete, and dry whites from Attica, Patras, Crete, and several islands. Local table wines can be full of surprises. Finally, what might be called the Greek national drink is *ouzo,* an 80- to 100-proof anise-flavored aperitif, served with water or ice, for which you can always substitute a glass of Metaxa, which calls itself "the Greek spirit."

5 Recommended Books & Films

BOOKS Let's begin in the beginning, with the man himself. **Homer,** though reputedly blind, will open your eyes to a Greece that is timeless. The *Iliad* and the *Odyssey* remain *the* imaginative gateways to Greece; and lest you have any doubts that Homer was describing the same landscape you'll be seeing, be sure to read, as a companion to the epics, John V. Luce's *Celebrating Homer's Landscapes,* winner of the prestigious Steven Runciman Prize in 2000.

For a glimpse into **ancient Greek history,** the men on the ground at the time are still the most exciting. *The History* of Herodotus and Thucydides's *Peloponnesian War* hold their own as consummate storytelling and will place you firmly in classical Greece. If you plan on attending any of the country's dramatic festivals, you will want to become familiar in advance with the play(s) you will be seeing and even bring along your favorite translation. And to see Greek temples as you've never seen them before, you might consult Vincent Scully's classic, *The Earth, the Temple and the Gods.*

For the **Byzantine period,** dive into the historical works of Steven Runciman, as well as the writings of Ernst Kitzinger on Byzantine art. And, if you want an insider's account of scandal and splendor in the court of Justinian, pick up *The Secret History* of Procopius, a Byzantine soap opera and then some. To put all this in some quick perspective, as well as to follow the full sweep of Greek history down to the present decade, *A Traveller's History of Greece,* by Boatswain and Nicolson, is pocket-sized and quite helpful.

Once into the **modern period,** Nikos Kazantzakis is the name to remember. His *Zorba the Greek* is a must, with *The Odyssey: A Modern Sequel* a close second. They are guaranteed to deliver you to Greece before your plane lands. After that, it's something of a free-for-all, with everyone shouting their own favorites. For sheer enchantment, we still smile every time we think of Gerald Durrell's *My Family and Other Animals,* about childhood on Corfu; and for beach reading, John Fowles's *The Magus* is spellbinding. In a far more serious vein, you will begin to grasp the pain still haunting the eyes of Greece's oldest citizens if you make your way through Nicholas Gage's *Eleni* or the much more recent *Corelli's Mandolin,* by Louis de Bernières. Each in its own way is stunning.

FILMS   Of the countless films made in and about Greece, several come to mind, all more or less readily available on video. The films of Michael Cacoyannis—from his Euripides trilogy, including *Trojan Women* and *Iphigenia,* to his famed *Zorba the Greek*—are essential viewing. So too is Costa-Gavras's *Z,* a gripping political thriller inspired by the assassination of Grigorios Lambrakis in 1963. The film version of Gage's *Eleni* manages to be nearly as disturbing as the book. Finally, in the interest of self-knowledge as a traveler, and for a good laugh, you will want to find Irene Papas and Jacqueline Bisset teaming up to confront *High Season* on the island of Rhodes. And don't forget, 007 has "done" Greece (*For Your Eyes Only*), as did Gregory Peck in *The Guns of Navaronne.*

Appendix B:
The Greek Language

1 Making Your Way in Greek

The first bit of wisdom here is to admit defeat from the outset. The most we can hope for in confronting the Greek language and its complexities is to negotiate a workable surrender. In fact, there are many different kinds of Greek—the Greek of conversation in the street, the Greek used at a fashionable dinner party, the Greek used in newspapers, the Greek of a government notice, the Greek used by a novelist or a poet, and more—and they can differ from one another in grammar and in vocabulary much more than the English of, for example, a conversation at the water cooler and that of an editorial in the *New York Times*. Why that should be so is a long—and we mean *long*—story. (Much of the difficulty has arisen because Greek, like English, has a long written history in which it has been molded by influential works of literature, works that continue to be read and studied for centuries—in Greek even for millennia—so that, as in English, older words and styles of expression remain available for use even while the spoken language goes on happily evolving on its own. Also like English, Greek has kept the spelling of its words largely unchanged even though their pronunciation has changed in fundamental ways; in English this spelling lag has extended for some 5 centuries, but in Greek it is 25 centuries old. This makes it easier for us to read Shakespeare and for Greeks to read Herodotus than it would otherwise be, but it also means that Greek children, like English speakers, have a long, long row to hoe in school as they learn to spell the words they already know how to speak and to use.)

Our dilemma is further complicated by the fact that many Greek words and names have entered our language not directly but by way of Latin or French, and so have become familiar to English speakers in forms that owe something to those languages. When these words are directly transliterated from modern Greek (and that means from Greek in its modern pronunciation, not the ancient one that Romans heard as they borrowed them into Latin), they almost always appear in a form other than the one you may have read about in school. "Perikles" for Pericles or "Delfi" for Delphi are relatively innocent examples; "Thivi" for Thebes or "Omiros" for Homer can give you an idea of the traps often in store for the innocent traveler. The bottom line is that the names of towns, streets, hotels, items on menus, historical figures, archaeological sites—you name it—are likely to have more than one spelling as you come across them in books, on maps, or before your very eyes.

Sometimes, the name of a place has simply changed over the centuries. If you think you've just arrived in Santorini but you see a sign welcoming you to Thira, smile, remember you're in Greece, and take heart. (Santorini is the name the Venetians used, and it became common in Europe for that reason; Thira is the original Greek name.) You're where you wanted to be. Besides, you will acquire more compassion for first-time visitors to the United States who land at JFK and find themselves welcomed to "The Big Apple."

What we offer here are a few aids to making your way in Greek. The table below will help you move from Greek signs or directions to a sense of how they should sound. This scheme for transliterating modern Greek is the one we have used throughout this book, except when referring to names which have become household words in English, like Athens, Socrates, Olympus, and so on. The good news here is that you won't be confused as long as you have your nose in your book; the bad news is that some confusion is probably inevitable as soon as your eyes leave the page. But all you have to do is to say what you are looking for, as closely as you can to the way it should sound, raising your voice at the end of the word to let your listener know it's a question, and bingo!—you'll find you're right on the mark. Just remember that *óhi*, although it can sound a bit like "okay," in fact means "no," and that *ne*, which can sound like a twangy "nay," means "yes." To complicate matters, some everyday gestures will be different from what you are used to: Greeks nod their heads upward to express an unspoken *óhi* and downward (or downward and to one side) for an unspoken *ne*. When a Greek turns his or her head from side to side at you—and you will sometimes, despite your best efforts, have this happen—it is a polite way of signaling "I can't make out what you're saying."

One additional tip on finding your way in Greek: When you're confronting a word or name which doesn't exactly correspond to what's on your map or in your book, you can go straight to the "root" of the word, which is likely to be more or less in its middle. Greek nouns and verbs are inflected, which means that they change their forms in order to express different meanings. These changes take the form of extra letters at the beginning or the end of the word, or both, while the core or root of the word usually remains more or less unchanged at the center. And that's the thing to look for. If, for instance, the middle of the word on your map looks like the middle of the word on the sign you're looking at, then you're probably not lost.

ALPHABET	TRANSLITERATED AS		PRONOUNCED AS IN
A α	álfa	a	f*a*ther
B β	víta	v	*v*iper
Γ γ	gámma	g before α, o, ω, and consonants	*g*et
		y before αι, ε, ει, η, ι, οι, υ	*y*es
		ng before κ, γ, χ, or ξ	si*ng*er
Δ δ	thélta	th	*th*e (not as the *th*- in "thin")
E ε	épsilon	e	s*e*t
Z ζ	zíta	z	la*z*y
H η	íta	i	magaz*i*ne

ALPHABET		TRANSLITERATED AS	PRONOUNCED AS IN
Θ θ	thíta	th	*th*in (not as the *th*- in "the")
Ι ι	ióta	i	maga*zi*ne
		y before a, o	*y*ard, *y*ore
Κ κ	káppa	k	*k*eep
Λ λ	lámtha	l	*l*eap
Μ μ	mi	m	*m*arry
Ν ν	ni	n	*n*ever
Ξ ξ	ksi	ks	ta*x*i
Ο ο	ómicron	o	b*ou*ght
Π π	pi	p	*p*et
Ρ ρ	ro	r	*r*ound
Σ σ/ς	sígma	s before vowels or θ, κ, π, τ, φ, χ, ψ	*s*ay
		z before β, γ, δ, ζ, λ, μ, ν, ρ	la*z*y
Τ τ	taf	t	*t*ake
Υ υ	ípsilon	i	maga*zi*ne
Φ φ	fi	f	*f*ee
Χ χ	chi	h	*h*ero (before e and i sounds; like the *ch*- in Scottish "loch" otherwise)
Ψ ψ	psi	ps	colla*ps*e
Ω ω	ómega	o	b*ou*ght

COMBINATIONS	TRANSLITERATED AS	PRONOUNCED AS IN
αι	e	g*e*t
αϊ	ai	*ai*sle
αυ before vowels or β, γ, δ, ζ, λ, μ, ν, ρ	av	*Av*e Maria
αυ before θ, κ, ξ, π, σ τ, φ, χ, ψ	af	pil*af*
ει	i	maga*zi*ne
ευ before vowels or β, γ, δ, ζ, λ, μ, ν, ρ	ev	*ev*er
ευ before θ, κ, ξ, π, σ, τ, φ, χ, ψ	ef	l*ef*t
μπ at beginning of word	b	*b*ane
μπ in middle of word	mb	lu*mb*er
ντ at beginning of word	d	*d*umb
ντ in middle of word	nd	sle*nd*er
οι	i	maga*zi*ne
οϊ	oi	o*i*l
ου	ou	s*ou*p
τζ	dz	roa*ds*
τσ	ts	ge*ts*
υι	i	maga*zi*ne

The Greek Language

2 Useful Words & Phrases

When you're asking for or about something and have to rely on single words or short phrases, it's an excellent idea to use "sas parakaló" to introduce or conclude almost anything you say.

Airport	Aerothrómio
Automobile	Aftokínito
Avenue	Leofóros
Bad	Kakós, -kí, -kó*
Bank	Trápeza
The bill, please.	Tón logaryazmó(n), parakaló.
Breakfast	Proinó
Bus	Leoforío
Can you tell me?	Boríte ná moú píte?
Car	Amáxi
Cheap	Ft(h)inó
Church	Ekklissía
Closed	Klistós, stí, stó*
Coast	Aktí
Coffeehouse	Kafenío
Cold	Kríos, -a, -o*
Dinner	Vrathinó
Do you speak English?	Miláte Angliká?
Excuse me.	Signómi(n).
Expensive	Akrivós, -í, -ó*
Farewell!	Stó ka-ló! (to person leaving)
Glad to meet you.	Chéro polí.**
Good	Kalós, lí, ló*
Good-bye.	Adío or chérete.**
Good health (cheers)!	Stín (i)yá sas or Yá-mas!
Good morning or Good day	Kaliméra.
Good evening.	Kalispéra.
Good night.	Kaliníchta.**
Hello!	Yássas or chérete!**
Here	Ethó
Hot	Zestós, -stí, -stó*
Hotel	Xenothochío**
How are you?	Tí kánete or Pós íst(h)e?
How far?	Pósso makriá?
How long?	Póssi óra or Pósso(n) keró?
How much does it cost?	Póso káni?
I am a vegetarian.	Íme hortophágos.
I am from New York.	Íme apó tí(n) Néa(n) Iórki.
I am lost or I have lost the way.	Écho chathí or Écho chási tón drómo(n).**
I'm sorry.	Singnómi.
I'm sorry, but I don't speak Greek (well).	Lipoúme, allá dén miláo elliniká (kalá).
I don't understand.	Thén katalavéno.
I don't understand, please repeat it.	Thén katalavéno, péste to páli, sás parakaló.
I want to go to the airport.	Thélo ná páo stó aerothrómio.
I want a glass of beer.	Thélo éna potíri bíra.
I would like a room.	Tha íthela ena thomátio.

It's (not) all right.	(Dén) íne en dáxi.
Left (direction)	Aristerá
Ladies' room	Ghinekón
Lunch	Messimerianó
Map	Chártis**
Market (place)	Agorá
Men's room	Andrón
Mr.	Kírios
Mrs.	Kiría
Miss	Despinís
My name is…	Onomázome…
New	Kenoúryos, -ya, -yo*
No	Óchi**
Old	Paleós, -leá, -leó* (*pronounce* palyós, -lyá, -lyó)
Open	Anichtós, -chtí, -chtó*
Pâtisserie	Zacharoplastío**
Pharmacy	Pharmakío
Please *or* You're welcome.	Parakaló.
Please call a taxi (for me).	Parakaló, fonáxte éna taxi (yá ména).
Point out to me, please…	Thíkste mou, sas parakaló…
Post office	Tachidromío**
Restaurant	Estiatório
Rest room	Tó méros *or* I toualétta
Right (direction)	Dexiá
Saint	Áyios, ayía, (*plural*) áyi-i (*abbreviated* ay.)
Shore	Paralía
Square	Plateía
Street	Odós
Show me on the map.	Díxte mou stó(n) chárti.**
Station (bus, train)	Stathmos (leoforíou, trénou)
Stop (bus)	Stási(s) (leoforíou)
Telephone	Tiléfono
Temple (of Athena, Zeus)	Naós (Athinás, Diós)
Thank you (very much).	Efcharistó (polí).**
Today	Símera
Tomorrow	Ávrio
Very nice	Polí oréos, -a, -o*
Very well	Polí kalá *or* En dáxi
What?	Tí?
What time is it?	Tí ôra íne?
What's your name?	Pós onomázest(h)e?
Where is…?	Poú íne…?
Where am I?	Pou íme?
Why?	Yatí?

The Greek Language

* Masculine ending -os, feminine ending -a or -i, neuter ending -o.

** Remember that *ch* should be pronounced as in Scottish *loch* or German *ich*, not as in the word *church*.

NUMBERS

0	Midén	3	Tría	6	Éxi
1	Éna	4	Téssera	7	Eftá
2	Dío	5	Pénde	8	Októ

9	Enyá	40	Saránda	200	Diakóssya
10	Déka	50	Penínda	300	Triakóssya
11	Éndeka	60	Exínda	400	Tetrakóssya
12	Dódeka	70	Evdomínda	500	Pendakóssya
13	Dekatría	80	Ogdónda	600	Exakóssya
14	Dekatéssera	90	Enenínda	700	Eftakóssya
15	Dekapénde	100	Ekató(n)	800	Oktakóssya
16	Dekaéxi	101	Ekatón éna	900	Enyakóssya
17	Dekaeftá	102	Ekatón dío	1,000	Chílya*
18	Dekaoktó	150	Ekatón penínda	2,000	Dío chilyádes*
19	Dekaenyá	151	Ekatón penínda	3,000	Trís chilyádes*
20	Íkossi		éna	4,000	Tésseris chilyádes*
21	Íkossi éna	152	Ekatón penínda	5,000	Pénde chilyádes*
22	Íkossi dío		dío		
30	Triánda				

DAYS OF THE WEEK

Monday	Deftéra
Tuesday	Tríti
Wednesday	Tetárti
Thursday	Pémpti
Friday	Paraskeví
Saturday	Sávvato
Sunday	Kiriakí

THE CALENDAR

January	Ianouários
February	Fevrouários
March	Mártios
April	Aprílios
May	Máios
June	Ioúnios
July	Ioúlios
August	Ávgoustos
September	Septémvrios
October	Októvrios
November	Noémvrios
December	Dekémvrios

The Greek Language

MENU TERMS

arní avgolémono	lamb with lemon sauce
arní soúvlas	spit-roasted lamb
arní yiouvétsi	baked lamb with orzo
astakós (ladolémono)	lobster (with oil-and-lemon sauce)
bakaliáro (skordaliá)	cod (with garlic)
barboúnia (skáras)	red mullet (grilled)
briám	vegetable stew
brizóla chiriní	pork steak or chop
brizóla moscharísia	beef or veal steak
choriátiki saláta	"village" salad ("Greek" salad to Americans)
chórta	dandelion salad
dolmádes	stuffed vine leaves
domátes yemistés mé rízi	tomatoes stuffed with rice

eksóhiko	lamb and vegetables wrapped in filo
garídes	shrimp
glóssa (tiganití)	sole (fried)
kalamarákia (tiganitá)	squid (fried)
kalamarákia (yemistá)	squid (stuffed)
kaparosaláta	salad of minced caper leaves and onion
karavídes	crayfish
keftédes	fried meatballs
kokorétsia	grilled entrails
kotópoulo soúvlas	spit-roasted chicken
kotópoulo yemistó	stuffed chicken
kouloúri	pretzel-like roll covered with sesame seeds
loukánika	spiced sausages
loukoumádes	round donut center–like pastries that are deep-fried, then drenched with honey and topped with powdered sugar and cinnamon
melitzanosaláta	eggplant salad
moussaká	meat-and-eggplant casserole
oktapódi	octopus
païdákia	lamb chops
paradisiakó	traditional Greek cooking
pastítsio	baked pasta with meat
piláfi rízi	rice pilaf
piperiá yemistá	stuffed green peppers
revídia	chickpeas
revidokeftédes	croquettes of ground chickpeas
saganáki	grilled cheese
skordaliá	hot-garlic-and-beet dip
soupiés yemistés	stuffed cuttlefish
souvláki	lamb (sometimes veal) on the skewer
spanokópita	spinach pie
stifádo	stew, often of rabbit or veal
taramosaláta	fish roe with mayonnaise
tirópita	cheese pie
tsípoura	dorado
tzatzíki	yogurt-cucumber-garlic dip
youvarlákia	boiled meatballs with rice

* Remember that *ch* should be pronounced as in Scottish *loch* or German *ich*, not as in the word *church*.

Index

Index

Index

NOTES

FROMMER'S® COMPLETE TRAVEL GUIDES

Alaska
Amsterdam
Arizona
Atlanta
Australia
Austria
Bahamas
Barcelona, Madrid &
  Seville
Beijing
Belgium, Holland &
  Luxembourg
Bermuda
Boston
British Columbia & the
  Canadian Rockies
Budapest & the Best of
  Hungary
California
Canada
Cancún, Cozumel &
  the Yucatán
Cape Cod, Nantucket &
  Martha's Vineyard
Caribbean
Caribbean Cruises & Ports
  of Call
Caribbean Ports of Call
Carolinas & Georgia
Chicago
China
Colorado
Costa Rica
Denmark
Denver, Boulder & Colorado
  Springs
England
Europe

European Cruises & Ports
  of Call
Florida
France
Germany
Greece
Greek Islands
Hawaii
Hong Kong
Honolulu, Waikiki & Oahu
Ireland
Israel
Italy
Jamaica
Japan
Las Vegas
London
Los Angeles
Maryland & Delaware
Maui
Mexico
Montana & Wyoming
Montréal & Québec City
Munich & the Bavarian
  Alps
Nashville & Memphis
Nepal
New England
New Mexico
New Orleans
New York City
New Zealand
Nova Scotia, New Brunswick
  & Prince Edward Island
Oregon
Paris
Philadelphia & the
  Amish Country

Portugal
Prague & the Best of the
  Czech Republic
Provence & the Riviera
Puerto Rico
Rome
San Antonio & Austin
San Diego
San Francisco
Santa Fe, Taos & Albuquerque
Scandinavia
Scotland
Seattle & Portland
Shanghai
Singapore & Malaysia
South Africa
Southeast Asia
South Florida
South Pacific
Spain
Sweden
Switzerland
Thailand
Tokyo
Toronto
Tuscany & Umbria
USA
Utah
Vancouver & Victoria
Vermont, New Hampshire
  & Maine
Vienna & the Danube Valley
Virgin Islands
Virginia
Walt Disney World &
  Orlando
Washington, D.C.
Washington State

FROMMER'S® DOLLAR-A-DAY GUIDES

Australia from $50 a Day
California from $60 a Day
Caribbean from $70 a Day
England from $70 a Day
Europe from $70 a Day

Florida from $70 a Day
Hawaii from $70 a Day
Ireland from $60 a Day
Italy from $70 a Day
London from $85 a Day

New York from $80 a Day
Paris from $80 a Day
San Francisco from $60 a Day
Washington, D.C.,
  from $70 a Day

FROMMER'S® PORTABLE GUIDES

Acapulco, Ixtapa &
  Zihuatanejo
Alaska Cruises & Ports of Call
Bahamas
Baja & Los Cabos
Berlin
California Wine Country
Charleston & Savannah
Chicago
Dublin

Hawaii: The Big Island
Las Vegas
London
Los Angeles
Maine Coast
Maui
Miami
New Orleans
New York City
Paris

Puerto Vallarta, Manzanillo
  & Guadalajara
San Diego
San Francisco
Sydney
Tampa & St. Petersburg
Venice
Washington, D.C.

FROMMER'S® NATIONAL PARK GUIDES

Family Vacations in the
  National Parks
Grand Canyon

National Parks of the
  American West
Rocky Mountain

Yellowstone & Grand Teton
Yosemite & Sequoia/
  Kings Canyon
Zion & Bryce Canyon

FROMMER'S® MEMORABLE WALKS

Chicago
London

New York
Paris

San Francisco
Washington, D.C.

FROMMER'S® GREAT OUTDOOR GUIDES

New England
Northern California

Southern California & Baja
Southern New England

Washington & Oregon

FROMMER'S® BORN TO SHOP GUIDES

Born to Shop: France
Born to Shop: Italy

Born to Shop: London
Born to Shop: New York

Born to Shop: Paris

FROMMER'S® IRREVERENT GUIDES

Amsterdam
Boston
Chicago
Las Vegas

London
Los Angeles
Manhattan
New Orleans

Paris
San Francisco
Seattle & Portland
Vancouver

Walt Disney World
Washington, D.C.

FROMMER'S® BEST-LOVED DRIVING TOURS

America
Britain
California

Florida
France
Germany

Ireland
Italy
New England

Scotland
Spain
Western Europe

THE UNOFFICIAL GUIDES®

Bed & Breakfasts in
  California
Bed & Breakfasts in
  New England
Bed & Breakfasts in
  the Northwest
Bed & Breakfasts in
  Southeast
Beyond Disney
Branson, Missouri

California with Kids
Chicago
Cruises
Disneyland
Florida with Kids
Golf Vacations in the
  Eastern U.S.
The Great Smoky &
  Blue Ridge
  Mountains

Inside Disney
Hawaii
Las Vegas
London
Miami & the Keys
Mini Las Vegas
Mini-Mickey
New Orleans
New York City
Paris

San Francisco
Skiing in the West
Southeast with Kids
Walt Disney World
Walt Disney World
  for Grown-ups
Walt Disney World
  for Kids
Washington, D.C.

SPECIAL-INTEREST TITLES

Frommer's Britain's Best Bed & Breakfasts and
  Country Inns
Frommer's Britain's Best Bike Rides
The Civil War Trust's Official Guide
  to the Civil War Discovery Trail
Frommer's Caribbean Hideaways
Frommer's Adventure Guide to Central America
Frommer's Adventure Guide to South America
Frommer's Adventure Guide to Southeast Asia
Frommer's Food Lover's Companion to France
Frommer's Gay & Lesbian Europe
Frommer's Exploring America by RV
Hanging Out in Europe

Israel Past & Present
Mad Monks' Guide to California
Mad Monks' Guide to New York City
Frommer's The Moon
Frommer's New York City with Kids
The New York Times' Unforgettable
  Weekends
Places Rated Almanac
Retirement Places Rated
Frommer's Road Atlas Britain
Frommer's Road Atlas Europe
Frommer's Washington, D.C., with Kids
Frommer's What the Airlines Never Tell You